# FAIRCHILD'S DICTIONARY OF FASHION

# FAIRCHILD'S Dictionary of Fashion

## Charlotte Mankey Calasibetta, Ph.D.

## 2nd EDITION

**Fairchild Publications**
New York

# ABOUT THE ILLUSTRATIONS

Except in the cases she has mentioned in her *Preface*, the drawings in this book are by Charlotte Mankey Calasibetta. Many of those depicting the 19th and early 20th c. were adapted from her own collection of old prints and periodicals, including *Godey's Lady's book*, *Peterson's Magazine*, and *Demorest's Magazine*. Fashions from earlier periods were drawn, whenever possible, from the art of the time.

The color illustrations were obtained from the following sources (number refers to the number of the illustration: **1.** The Metropolitan Museum of Art, Rogers Fund, 1930. **2, 3, 4.** *Costume and Fashion: The Evolution of European Dress through the Earlier Ages*, Herbert Norris; London: J. M. Dent & Sons, Ltd., 1925. **5, 8, 15.** *The History of Fashion in France: The Dress of Women from the Gallo-Roman Period to the Present Time*, C. Hoey and J. Lillie; New York: Scribner and Welford, 1882. **6.** *English Costume of the Early Middle Ages: The 10th–13th Centuries*, Iris Brooke; A. & C. Black, Ltd., 1936. **7.** *Costume du Moyen Age*, Bruxelles: Librairie Historique-Artistique, 1847. **9.** *English Costume of the Later Middle Ages; The 14th–15th Centuries*, Iris Brooke; London: A. & C. Black, Ltd., 1935. **10.** *Les Arts Somptaires: Histoire du Costume et d' L'Ameublement*; Paris: Chez Hangard-Mauge, 1858. **11.** The Metropolitan Museum of Art, Gift of J. Pierpont Morgan, 1911. **12.** *English Costume of the Age of Elizabeth: The 16th Century*, Iris Brooke; London: A. & C. Black, Ltd., 1933. **13, 14.** *Costume*, Herbé. **16.** *English Costume of the 18th Century*, Iris Brooke; London: A. & C. Black, Ltd., 1931. **17.** The Metropolitan Museum of Art, Gift of Collis P. Huntington, 1896. **18.** The Metropolitan Museum of Art, Purchase, Irene Lewisohn Bequest, 1961. **19.** The Metropolitan Museum of Art, The Henry L. Phillips Collection, Bequest of Henry L. Phillips, 1940. **20.** *English Costume of the 19th Century*, Iris Brooke; London: A. & C. Black, Ltd., 1929. **21, 22.** *La Mode Pendant Quarante Ans de 1830 à 1870*. Paris: Publication des Grand Magazins du Louvre. **23, 25.** *Les Modes de Paris de 1797 à 1897*, Octave Uzanne; Paris: Sociétè Française d'Éditions d'Art, 1898. **24.** The Metropolitan Museum of Art, Gift of The New York Historical Society, 1979. **26.** *English Children's Costume Since 1775*, Iris Brooke; London: A. & C. Black, Ltd., 1930. **27.** *English Costume of the 19th Century*, Iris Brooke; London: A. & C. Black, Ltd., 1929. **28.** The Metropolitan Museum of Art, Purchase,

Irene Lewisohn Trust Gift, 1983. **29.** The Metropolitan Museum of Art, Purchase, Isabel Shults Gift, 1981. **30.** *The Delineator,* 1910. **31.** *Ladies Home Journal,* 1912. **32, 33, 34, 35.** *Très Parisien.* **36.** The Metropolitan Museum of Art, Gift of Toni Frissell Bacon, 1974. **37.** The Metropolitan Museum of Art, Costume Institute, Gift of the Estate of Lady Mendl, 1955. **38.** The Metropolitan Museum of Art, Gift of Baroness Philippe de Rothschild, 1973. **39, 44.** *All-American: A Sportswear Tradition.* New York: Fairchild Visuals, 1987. **40.** The Metropolitan Museum of Art, Gift of Paco Rabanne, 1967 (*left*): gift of Mrs. Charles Wrightsman, 1970 (*center*); gift of Mrs. Robert A. Fowler, 1978 (*right*). **41, 42, 43, 45-50.** *Women's Wear Daily.*

# PREFACE

The history of fashion involves the whole sweep of world history and the people who made it. Fashion is part of the sociology, culture, and art of every era. The study of fashion is not a frivolous pursuit, but a complicated reflection on how people live, and how they project their personalities through the clothes they wear. Where people have lived, what their occupations and avocations were, these have affected their clothes. So strong is fashion's influence that even the powers of religion and the law have been overruled by the dictates of fashion. People have worn whatever was in style, even when they were faced by state fines or chastisement by the Church.

Fashion is thought by some people to be a superficial kind of knowledge, but, when investigated thoroughly, it can be found to intersect many different fields of learning. Understanding man-made textiles requires a knowledge of chemistry; the various aspects of color take one into the realm of physics; information on gems involves the field of mineralogy; to understand mink mutations, it is necessary to grasp something about genetics.

*Fairchild's Dictionary of Fashion* presents clothing terminology from both historical and contemporary viewpoints. This dictionary evolved from a college course in fashion. In an attempt to teach students a vocabulary of fashion terms that would not become outdated, lists were assembled of collars, necklines, sleeves, skirts, and so on, and each considered in the light of the existing fashion trends—which were "in"; and which were "out." The basic categories for this dictionary grew from these lists. The addition of historical terms and some of the vocabulary of clothing manufacturers rounded out the entries.

It is hoped that this volume will prove helpful to students who are pursuing a career in fashion and wish to acquire a larger vocabulary. This dictionary should also aid fashion designers seeking inspiration; to individuals involved in productions for theater, films, opera, or television; to newspaper, magazine, and advertising writers and editors; to retailers, buyers, and salespeople—all of them should find it a useful reference. This volume should prove interesting, too, to the person who cares about fashion for fashion's sake.

*Fairchild's Dictionary of Fashion*, Second Edition, represents a complete revision of the former work. The new edition includes approximately 1,700 additional entries. Eleven more categories have been added to make a total of 98. Also, 400 more line drawings have been added to give a total of approximately 1,000 pen and ink illustrations. The new entries were selected from approximately 5,000 newly published books and periodicals—mainly newspapers, magazines, and catalogues that deal with fashion.

Much thanks is due Edward Gold, Manager of the Book Division of Fairchild Publications, for his idea to update the dictionary and for his patient persistence and helpful support during the five years it took to complete the revision.

Also thanks to Olga T. Kontzias, my very talented and enthusiastic editor, whose suggestions for additional items, ingenuity in solving problems during the process of the manuscript, discriminating attention to details, and keen sense of fashion made her an inspiration to work with.

Many thanks to Merle Thomason, head of the Fairchild Library, for her endless research of some of the more difficult facts. Thanks are also extended to all the staff of Fairchild's Book Division for their part in transferring the manuscript and drawings into print. Particular thanks to the book designer, Janet Solgaard.

Thanks to Judith Straeten who conscientiously read the manuscript and offered suggestions.

Thanks are extended to Betty Garrabrant, Kathleen Brady, Linda and Ray Church for their help in determining the list of designers used in the Appendix.

Many others helped during the revision of this book. I would like to thank particularly Helen Mankey Ware for her help in finding new entries; Kay Monks for help in researching some of the items; Sherry Schodt, Ellen Rishel, Elizabeth Mazzullo, Karen Wagner, and Dorothy Russell for their help in filing and typing the entries; Sarah D. Brady for the final typing of the manuscript; Lisa Hartman for collating the pictures; and Kathleen Houser for help in proofreading the galleys.

Thanks also to Doctors John W. and Isabel B. Wingate and to Eugene and Jane Landon for their encouragement during the writing of the manuscript. And lastly, thanks to my husband, Dr. Charles J. Calasibetta, for his continuing patience and support during the process of revision.

Williamsport, Pennsylvania                    Charlotte Mankey Calasibetta
1988

# PUBLISHER'S NOTES

Just about every 13 years we get to update our notes on the *Dictionary of Fashion*, the second edition of which we now launch proudly since it represents the best we do at Fairchild Books.

Once again, Dr. Calisabetta, who seems to have begun this major revision in 1975, authored this major effort, and will detail trials and triumphs from her perspective in her *Preface*.

From the publisher's point of view, it is fair to say this is our most complex and important Fairchild book. Once more, the vital link between our division and the noted Fairchild fashion newspapers, *Women's Wear Daily* and *W*, has been exploited to maximum effect. For example, a large number of the designer photos in this new edition come from the *WWD International Collection*, an odyssey of the great fashion shows here and abroad which has become part of our visuals division.

Even more pertinent has been the contribution from Fairchild's Costume Library, run by one of the most tenacious of researchers, Merle Thomason, who assists us on many projects.

In a dictionary of this scope and reputation, clarity, accuracy, completeness and currency are all vital to success. So finding a consultant with the right set of credentials became a top priority. Judith Straeten fulfilled our best hopes. Formerly Assistant Curator of the Costume Institute at the New York Metropolitan Museum of Art, she is now Archivist at Brunschwig & Fils, Inc., specializing in its collection of period textiles and wallpaper documents. In addition, she has been a guest curator and lecturer in preparing exhibits and speaking on a wide range of subjects relating to costume history.

The project was further enhanced by the continuing understanding and rapport that exists between Dr. Calasibetta and our Fashion Editor, Olga Kontzias.

We wish to thank Deanna Cross and the staff of the Photograph Library at The Metropolitan Museum of Art and Raeanne Rubenstein and John Parnell, photographers, for their assistance and cooperation in the preparation of the color illustrations.

Other contributors of note on the "home front" include Janet Solgaard, book designer; Walter Lindell, Production Manager; and Cathy Saladino, manuscript typist.

A 13-year run is pretty good in any cultural field. We're confident this second edition will solidify our reputation in fashion dictionary publishing.

As usual, you'll make the final decision.

New York City
January, 1988

E. B. Gold
Manager, Fairchild Books

# HOW TO USE THIS BOOK

In order that this book may be more useful, it is arranged in alphabetical order—interrupted by CATEGORIES. When the reader comes to the word **blouse, coat, dress,** etc., a group of these items is inserted as a **category.** These words represent different contemporary styles in current usage. This listing may help the reader to find new words. For example, a person may have found a style of dress for which he wants to find a name. In looking through the dresses category, he may easily spot the dress he is trying to identify. Words in each category are also listed in the alphabetical sections, but no definition is given as the reader is referred to the category where the word is defined.

Terms which are historical in nature are arranged strictly in alphabetical order. Pronunciation is provided for words which are difficult to pronounce. No pronunciation is provided for those words easily pronounced. Many of the terms have their origin in foreign language. In these cases, a *derivation* has been added. The abbreviation *der.* is used to conserve space.

*SMALL CAPS* refer to other entries which may further explain the term. *Italics* have been used within the entry to indicate that these terms may also be found in the book in alphabetical order.

When used in writing a novel or magazine article, many terms (frequently French or other foreign language) are written in *italics*. This is not indicated here as the reader must determine whether to italicize the word according to the use in his writing. For example, the words kimono, chesterfield, and fez are not italicized as they are commonly used in English, while words like *chang-ot, heko-obi,* and *saya,* are not in common use in English and are usually written in *italics*.

Initial capital letters are used to indicate trademarked items and other words which are capitalized. Words such as cardigan and catogan, although named for people, are not capitalized; while Cheviot, Harris Tweed, and Jacquard are still capitalized.

Biographical sketches of important fashion designers around the world, both living and dead, are brought together in an appendix and are listed alphabetically. The designer's name is followed, whenever available, by important dates. The name of the country where they work or worked is listed below the designer's name. Designer's names are also listed alphabetically in the dictionary and cross-referenced to the appendix. Portraits of the designers and photographs of their most noted styles are also included in the appendix.

# INDEX TO CATEGORIES

# A

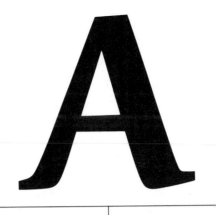

**A 1. Shoe size:** Letter indicating a width; widths run from AAAA to EEEEE with AAAA's being the narrowest and EEEEE's the widest. **2. Pajama Size:** Men's regular height (5′8″ to 5′11″) size corresponding to 32″ to 36″ chest measurement. For other sizes, see BIG, REGULAR, EXTRA-TALL, and TALL. **3. Shirt Size:** For men's extra-tall with 15–15½ collar measurement. **4. Bra Cup Size:** Sizes run AAA, AA, A, B, C, D, DD; AAA is the smallest size and DD the largest.

**ABA**

**aba 1.** Coarse wool and camel's hair fabric used in the Middle East. **2.** Rectangular plain, sometimes striped, tunic or robe of this fabric, worn by Arabian and North African men; also made of silk for upper classes. Embroidery and silk cords ornament the slit neckline, shoulder seam, and front seams. Fastened with tasseled cords at the neckline. Also spelled *abba, abayeh, haba*. **3.** A more primitive garment similarly shaped and made of pounded felted wool. Worn as protection from wind and rain by shepherds in rural Turkey.

**abaca** (ah-bak-kah) Natural durable fiber from a banana-like plant, native to Philippines and Central America, used for "Manila" hats. Also called *Manila hemp* (though unlike true hemp), *Cebu hemp, Davao hemp,* and *Tagal hat braid.* Also spelled *abaka.*

**abalone** See MOTHER-OF-PEARL and BUTTONS.

**abayeh/abba** See ABA.

**abilements/abillements** See BILLIMENTS.

**abito** Italian word for clothes, suit, dress.

**abraded yarn** A continuous filament rayon, acetate, or other man-made yarn which has been rubbed at intervals raising fuzzy projections which increase bulk. Yarn is then twisted and usually made two-ply.

**abstract** Term meaning opposed to naturalistic or not related to reality. May emphasize line, color, or geometric forms. See HAIRSTYLES and PRINTS.

**academic costume** Caps, gowns, and hoods, usually black with color trim on hood, worn at commencement exercises. Designed by Gardner Cotrell Leonard of Albany, N.Y., in 1887 and adopted by the American Intercollegiate Code of 1894, revised in 1932. Code states style of cap, gown, and hood to be worn by persons with Bachelor's, Master's and Doctor's degrees along with the colors to be used on the hood. Originated at the Universities of Oxford and Cambridge over 600 years ago. Also called *academic regalia.* Also see BACHELOR's, DOCTOR's and MASTER's GOWN and HOOD, ACADEMIC HOOD and HOOD COLORS, MORTARBOARD, and LABEL #2.

**academic hood** Decorative drape which comes close to neck in front and hangs down the back of academic gowns in various lengths and shapes according to degree held, usually in black with colored facing indicating degree granted. Lining colors represent school colors of

**ACADEMIC HOOD**

institution conferring degree, the outer band of velvet shows field of study. *Der.* From the cowl cape attached to gowns of undergraduates since end of 15th c. Also see BACHELOR'S, MASTER'S, and DOCTOR'S HOODS, and ACADEMIC HOOD COLORS.

**academic hood colors** The lining colors at the back of the ACADEMIC HOOD representing the school colors of the college or institution conferring the degree. The outer band of velvet which extends around the front of the neck indicates the different faculties, or fields of study, as follows: Agriculture, maize; Arts and Letters, white; Chiropody, nile green; Commerce and Accounting, drab; Dentistry, lilac; Economics, copper; Engineering, orange; Fine Arts, brown; Forestry, russet; Humanities, crimson; Law, purple; Library Science, lemon; Medicine, green; Music, pink; Nursing, apricot; Optometry, seafoam; Oratory, silver gray; Pedagogy, light blue; Pharmacy, olive green; Philanthropy, rose; Philosophy, blue; Physical Education, sage green; Public Administration, drab; Public Health, salmon pink; Science, golden yellow; Social Science, citron; Theology, scarlet; and Veterinary Science, gray.

**acala** See COTTON.

**acca** A richly brocaded silk fabric using gold threads made with animal or pastoral designs. Used in Great Britain for formal, regal, and conventional cloth. Also used by church digni-taries for vestments since 14th c. *Der.* First made in Acre, Syria.

**accordion pleats** Named for resemblance to the folds of the musical instrument, accordion. See HANDBAGS, PLEATS, PANTS, and SKIRTS.

**acetate** **1.** Generic term for fiber man-made from cellulose acetate. **2.** Yarn or thread made from this fiber. **3.** Knitted or woven fabrics made from this yarn. Acetate drapes well, has a silklike appearance, resists wrinkles and fading, and is low cost. Used for dress and coat linings, blouses, lingerie, shoe linings, and backing on *bonded fabric.* Taffeta acetates are used for linings in coats and suits. Originally acetate *fume-faded* and turned a purplish color, but *solution-dyed* acetates retain the color better. Acetate fabrics will melt, or fuse, when pressed with a hot iron. Also see TRIACETATE and ARNEL.

**achkan** (atch-kan) Full-skirted, knee-length, white cotton coat buttoned down front with a high neckline worn by men in India.

**Acrilan®** Trademark of Monsanto Textiles for wide variety of acrylic staple and filament fibers manufactured for different end use, each designated by number; type 16 is a basic fiber for apparel.

**acrobatic slipper** See SLIPPERS.

**acrylic** **1.** Generic name for fibers and yarns man-made from acrylic resins. **2.** Knit or woven goods made from acrylic yarns. Acrylics have warm hand, are easy to wash, dry quickly; are wrinkle, moth and mildew resistance; retain pleats. Used for sweaters and hosiery and in bonded fabrics for dresses.

**action back** Term used to describe the extra fullness worked into back of a jacket, coat or dress from shoulder blades to waist usually in form of pleats, to permit freedom of movement. See BI-SWING.

**action gloves** See GLOVES.

**acton** (ak-tun) **1.** Padded jacket worn under armor in 12th and 13th c. **2.** Later, steel-plated jacket worn as armor. Also spelled *aketon, auqueton, hacketon, haqueton*. Also see GAMBE-SON.

**adaptation** **1.** Dress designing term for an interpretation of an expensive designer dress reproduced in a less expensive model. Not a direct copy but made with modification of design and fabric. Most dresses sold today are adaptations of designer dresses or couture originals. Compare with KNOCK-OFF and LINE-FOR-LINE. **2.** Historical-type dress made for a play or film made in the same period style, *e.g., Shakespearean*, but with modifications of design and fabric.

**Adelaide boot** Woman's ankle-high side-laced boot with patent-leather toe and heel, sometimes with fur or fringed trimming at top. Worn in U.S. from about 1830s to 1860s.

**Adelaide wool** High quality merino wool from southern Australia, used for worsted fabrics. *Der.* Named after Adelaide, the port from which it is shipped.

**adjustable** See RINGS and VESTS.

**admiral coat** See COATS.

**admiralty cloth** Melton-type fabric used by the British Naval forces for officer's uniforms and coats. U.S. Navy uses a heavier weight of the same fabric for *pea jackets* and *overcoats*.

**Adolfo** See APPENDIX/DESIGNERS.

**Adri** See APPENDIX/DESIGNERS.

**Adrian, Gilbert** See APPENDIX/DESIGNERS.

**Adrienne gown** See SACK #2.

**aegis** **1.** Shield carried by Zeus, king of the gods, or his daughter Athena, goddess of wisdom. **2.** Later, a type of breastplate made of metal scales with head of Gorgon, Medusa, and fringe of serpents, worn as a part of armor by Athena.

**Aeolian®mink** See MUTATION MINK under FURS.

**aerobics** Type of exercise to music for which special clothing and accessories are worn. See AEROBIC ENSEMBLE under SPORT SUITS and SHOES.

**aesthetic dress** Style of dress advocated by small group of cultured class in England at end of 19th c., who adopted a modified form of 14th-c. costume called a SMOCK in protest against tightly corseted contemporary fashion. Also called *rational dress*. Also called *Greenery-yallery, Grosvenor gallery costume* by W. S. Gilbert in an operetta and satirized in *Punch*.

**Afghanistan clothes** Native clothing adapted from clothing worn in Afghanistan as part of ethnic influence of late 1960s. See SPORT JACKETS, VESTS, and AFGHANISTAN WEDDING TUNIC under SHIRTS.

**afghan stitch** See STITCHES.

**Afro styles** African-inspired hairstyles, clothes and accessories introduced in late 1960s. See AFRICAN, BUBA, DASHIKI, and SELOSO under DRESSES. Also see AFRO PUFFS under HAIRSTYLES, NECKLACES, and LOOKS.

**afternoon dress** **1.** Term used during the 19th c. to indicate a type of dress suitable for visiting in the afternoons. **2.** In the early 20th c. indicated a dressy dress, frequently full-length in the 1920s and 1930s, suitable for a garden party or formal tea. Usually worn with a large picture hat.

**after-ski boot** See APRÈS-SKI.

**after-ski slipper** See SLIPPER SOCKS under SLIPPERS.

**KAFFIYEH-AGAL**

**agal** (ah-gaul) Thick cord of wool used by Arabians, Bedouins, and desert dwellers to secure the *kaffiyeh*, or headscarf. Also see KAFFIYEH-AGAL.

**agate** See GEMS.

**agave** Natural fiber from the *henequen* with the biological name *Agave fourcroydes*. Grown principally in Mexico, fiber comes from the leaf tissue and measures from three to five feet in length. It is straw-colored, hard, wiry and elastic. Also fiber from sisal with botanical name *Agave sisalana* from Java, Indonesia, east and west Africa. Uses: binder twine and lariats. Also called *aloe*.

**age** See EDGE #2.

**aggravators** Term used for semi-curls near the eye or temple, worn by men from 1830s to 1850s.

**Agilon®** Trademark of Deering Milliken Research Corp. for licensed textured processed monofilament yarn, usually nylon. Used for women's hosiery and pantyhose because of great elasticity. Also used for woven goods, sweaters, tricot knits, and men's hose.

**aglet** Ornamental metal tag, frequently of gold or silver, similar to modern shoelace tip at end of lacing. Called a POINT in the 15th c. for joining men's DOUBLET and HOSE; later used in bunches for a decorative effect. Also spelled *aiglet*.

**Agnès** See APPENDIX/DESIGNERS.

**Agnès Sorel** See SOREL, AGNÈS.

**Agnès Sorel bodice** Woman's dress bodice of 1861 with square neckline front and back, and full bishop sleeves.

**Agnès Sorel coiffure** Woman's hairstyle with ribbon bands in front and a knot in back; worn from 1830s to 1850s.

**Agnès Sorel corsage** Woman's loose-fitting bodice of a *pelisse robe* similar to a jacket, fastened high at neck or worn open revealing waistcoat. Worn in 1851 and named after Agnès Sorel. Also see SOREL, AGNÈS.

**Agnès Sorel style** Princess-style dress worn in early 1860s. See PRINCESS STYLE.

**agraffe** **1.** Circular, square, or diamond-shaped clasp, used in pairs to fasten the mantle at neck in Middle Ages; and made of bronze, gold, or silver embossed in elaborate patterns, set with jewels. **2.** Pin used to fasten slashes in garments in 16th c. Also spelled *agraf, agrafe*. Compare with FERMAILS. *Der.* Norman, *aggrape*, "clasp on medieval armor."

**aida cloth** Loosely constructed fabric available with 8 to 22 holes per running inch used for counted cross-stitch embroidery and other fancy work. Also called *aida canvas*. See COUNTED CROSS-STITCH EMBROIDERY and LINEN CANVAS.

**aiglet** See AGLET.

**aigrette** (ai-gret) See FEATHERS.

**AIGUILLETTE**

**aiguillette** (ah-gwel-yet) Shoulder decoration made of gilt cord, frequently braided, used on military dress uniforms. Also called *aiguille*. The cord (aiguillette) has AGLETS at the end.

**aigulet** See AGLET.

**aile de pigeon** See PIGEON-WINGED TOPEE. *Der.* French, "*pigeon-wing*".

**Ainu kimono** (i-new) Short *kimono* with narrow *obi* sash, wide sleeves tapered to wrist. Made of elm bark fabric decorated with bold scroll-like embroidered appliqué designs. Worn by the Ainu on the island of Yezo, now Hokkaido, north of Japan.

**airplane fabric** Strong fabric made of two-ply cotton yarns in warp and filling which have been tightly twisted, combed, and mercerized. When treated with *dope* it is used for airplane and glider wings, elevators, and rudders. Untreated lightweight fabrics used for shirtings and children's garments.

**ajiji**   Cotton fabric from India, similar to muslin, with silk or rayon stripes.

**ajour**   French term for openwork making the design in lace.

**aketon**   See ACTON.

**alarm watch**   See WATCHES.

**Alaska**   **1.** In early 20th c., an overshoe or storm rubber with a high tongue over the instep. **2.** A British yarn mixture of one-third long staple cotton and two-thirds carded wool. Used for hand-knitting and weaving. **3.** British fabric woven of these yarns in twill or plain weave, finished by napping.

**Alaskan fur seal**   See FURS.

**ALB**

**alb**   Full-length long-sleeved *liturgical robe* with drawstring neckline or cowl hood worn by priests at Mass. Originally of white linen, now often of blended cotton and man-made fibers. *Der.* Latin, "white."

**albatross**   **1.** Fine, lightweight, soft woolen or worsted fabric with a lightly napped, pebbly surface made in an open plain weave. Surface effect is made by twisted, or creped, yarns. Frequently piece-dyed in plain pale colors or black. Used for infants' wear, negligees, and nuns' habits. **2.** Cotton fabric made in imitation of above which may have a slight nap.

**albernous/albernoz**   See BURNOOSE.

**Albert**   See ITALIAN CLOTH.

**Albert boots**   Man's side-laced boot with fabric top and *patent-leather* toe, frequently decorated down front with *mother-of-pearl* buttons; worn from 1840s on. *Der.* From fashion popularized by *Prince Albert*, the consort of England's Queen Victoria.

**Albert driving cape**   Single- or double-breasted, loose, Chesterfield coat of 1860 with no back seam, or no underarm seam—thus requiring a back seam. Also called *driving sac*.

**Albert jacket**   Man's single-breasted jacket with or without waistline seam and side pleats, and no breast pocket; worn in 1848.

**Albert overcoat**   Man's loose-fitting mid-calf overcoat with fly front, small shoulder cape, flapped hip pockets, long back vent, and vertical slit breast pockets; worn in 1877. Also called *Albert driving sac* or *cape*.

**Albert riding coat**   High-buttoned single-breasted man's coat of 1841 with front cut away in slanted style. Made with broad collar, narrow lapels, and hip pockets.

**Albert sac**   See ALBERT DRIVING CAPE.

**Albert top frock**   Men's heavy overcoat styled like a FROCK COAT, made with wide velvet collar, flap pockets, wide cuffs, and lapels; worn from 1860s to 1900.

**Alençon lace**   See LACES.

**alexandrite**   See GEMS.

**Alice blue**   Medium-light blue with slight gray-green cast, said to have been the favorite color of Alice Roosevelt Longworth, daughter of President Theodore Roosevelt. Color was popularized by the song "Alice Blue Gown."

**Alice in Wonderland dress**   See PINAFORE DRESS under DRESSES.

**A-line**   Term introduced in 1955 by Paris couturier Christian Dior to describe apparel styled close and narrow at the shoulders and flaring gently away from the body from under arms to hem—resembling letter A. One of the most popular silhouettes used for coats, dresses and jumpers during the 1960s. See COATS, DRESSES, JUMPERS, SKIRTS, and SILHOUETTES. Also see SHIFT and SKIMMER under DRESSES.

**alkalouk** (al-ka-luke)   Native ancient Persian undergarment with pockets, worn by men. Outer tunic KAMARCHIN, worn over it, has vertical slits in order to reach pockets.

**alligator**   See LEATHERS.

**alligator-grained**   Term for alligator-skin pattern embossed or printed on cowhide, calfskin leather, plastic, or imitation leather.

**all-in-one**   See FOUNDATIONS and SLEEVES.

**allover**   See LACES and PRINTS.

**all rounder**   See DOG COLLAR.

**all sheer pantyhose**   See PANTYHOSE.

**all-weather**   Adjective used for clothing and accessories worn on rainy or sunny days, or for variations in temperature. See BOOTS, COATS, and RAINCOATS.

**alma**   Obsolete silk fabric characterized by a distinct diagonal twill weave. Originally made in black or purple and worn for mourning. *Der.* From Egyptian word, "a mourner or singer at a funeral."

**almain coat jacket**   Jacket worn by men over doublet in second half of 15th and early 16th c. Made close fitting with short, flared skirt and long HANGING SLEEVES, and slashed at front seams.

**almain hose**   Full, slashed TRUNK HOSE, with undergarment pulled through the slashes, worn by men in late 16th c. Also called *German hose*. Also see PLUDERHOSE.

**almandine garnet/spinel**   See GEMS.

**almoner**   See AULMONIÈRE.

**almuce**   **1.** A cowl-like hood, frequently of fur or fur-lined, introduced in the 13th c., worn by the clergy in inclement weather for church services. **2.** Medieval TIPPET, or small cape with attached hood and fur lining, tied under the chin. Also spelled *amuce, almusse, aunice, aumusse.*

**aloe**   **1.** Textile term used loosely for *Agave, Ceylon hemp,* and *Piteiria fibers.* **2.** See EMBROIDERY. **3.** See LACE. **4.** Liquid contained in the large leaves of the aloe plant is also used for cosmetics.

**aloha shirt**   See HAWAIIAN under SHIRTS.

**alpaca**   **1.** A sheeplike animal of the camel family, related to the llama, native to the Andes in South America. Yarn spun from fleece is lustrous and shiny. **2.** Springy shiny fabric made originally with silk warp, later with cotton warp and alpaca filling in a plain weave. Usually dyed black and used for dresses. Originated in Bradford, England, and called *alpaca Orleans.* Appearance similar to *mohair* and *brilliantine* and sometimes called by these names. **3.** Yarns of alpaca, alpaca and cotton, wool or rayon used in a plain woven fabric.

**alpaca crepe**   Rayon and acetate fabric made to look like genuine wool alpaca fabric. Made in plain weave, with a combination two-ply creped yarns of acetate and rayon. When used for dresses should be labeled *rayon and acetate alpaca.*

**alpargata** (ahl-par-gah-ta)   See SANDALS.

**Alpine boot**   Ankle-high shoe of early 1900s designed with bent nails on a sturdy sole to give mountain climbers a secure footing. See HIKING BOOT under BOOTS.

**ALPINE HAT, 1898**

**Alpine hat 1.** Woman's straight-brimmed hat with peaked crown decorated with wide ribbon band with bow and feather at side worn in 1890s. **2.** Man's felt hat with crease in center of low crown introduced in 1890s. **3.** See HATS.

**Alpine jacket 1.** Waist-length jacket worn with *Lederhosen* as part of a Tyrolean mountain climber's costume. **2.** Englishman's jacket similar to a NORFOLK JACKET, made double-breasted with vertical flap pockets and pleat down center back. Worn buttoned to neck, often without a vest, in 1876.

**Alsatian bow** Women's native headdress of Alsace-Lorraine consisting of an enormous bow of taffeta ribbon placed with the knot on top of head, the loops rising like two wings and then falling almost to shoulders with longer ends falling down back. Originally a small bow, later in colors to indicate religious faith of wearer—Protestants, black; Catholics, bright colors, especially red and plaids; and Hebrews, lavender. Also called *bow headdress*.

**Alsatian system** Yarn-making method. See FRENCH SYSTEM.

**alum tanning** Process used to produce soft, pliable, white leathers. Mainly used for gloves. Primary disadvantage is that leather is not washable.

**amadis sleeve** Sleeve with tight cuff, buttoned at the wrist, worn in 1830s. Revived in 1850s, sleeve was buttoned to elbow with upper sleeve full and pleated into armhole. *Der.* Said to have originated by an opera singer to cover her unattractive arms.

**amárah** Large white turban worn by Moorish men in Morocco.

**AMAZON COLLAR, 1863**

**Amazon collar** Standing collar, similar to a CHINESE COLLAR, with gap in center front. Used on women's blouses in early 1860s and worn with a black ribbon necktie.

**Amazon corsage** Plain bodice buttoned up front to high neckline and trimmed with small white cambric collar and cuffs; tailored style for women in 1842.

**Amazon corset** English corset worn for riding in mid-19th c. made with elastic lacings that shortened the garment by three inches when hidden cord was pulled.

**Amazone** Woman's scarlet riding habit with high waistline and full-length skirt worn in early part of 19th c. in U.S., France, and England. *Der.* From legendary Greek women warriors called *Amazons*.

**Amazon plume** See FEATHERS.

**ambari hemp** See DECCAN HEMP.

**amber** See GEMS.

**amens** See AMIENS.

**American buskins** Shoes with stout leather soles and knee-high cloth uppers, or leggings, fastened with lacings, worn by American Colonists. Similar to STARTUPS.

**American coat** British term for man's single-breasted full-length coat, usually black, made with narrow lapels, wide collar, and full skirt; worn in 1829.

**American Fashion Critics' Award** Original name for the COTY AWARD.

**American Indian** Late 1960s fashion influence, borrowed by young people from American Indians, for clothing and accessories. For items see: BEADS, BELTS, DRESSES, HAIRSTYLES, LOOKS, NECKLACES, PRINTS, SHOES (INDIAN MOCCASIN); see SQUAW under BLOUSES, BOOTS, HANDBAGS, and DRESSES; see APACHE under SCARFS and SHIRTS.

**American Indian beadwork** Tiny glass beads in various colors woven to make headbands, necklaces, and used for trimmings—sometimes in shape of medallions—by various American Indian tribes. Popular as part of the ethnic fashions of the 1960s. Also see BEADS, BELTS, and NECKLACES.

**American Indian blanket** Originally handwoven blankets made by North American Indians in western U.S.—usually all wool, in tribal motifs. Similar designs copied in machine-made items.

**American Indian headband** Narrow band of leather, fabric, or beadwork placed low on the forehead and tied at side or back, sometimes with a feather in back, worn by American Indians. Adopted by young people in the late 1960s for AMERICAN INDIAN LOOK.

**American Marten** See FURS.

**American neckcloth** British term for a STOCK—plain in center front with vertical pleating on each side, narrow ends brought around to front and tied at base of neck in a *Gordian knot*; worn by men in 1820s. Also called *Yankee neckcloth*.

**American shoulders** British term for padded shoulders popular in U.S. at end of 19th c.

**American trousers** British term for men's trousers worn without suspenders, pants gathered or pleated into waistband with adjustable strap and buckle in back. Worn from late 1850s on.

**American vest** British term for man's single-breasted vest, usually with V-neck and no collar, buttoned up center front; worn with a suit from 1860s on.

**amethyst** See GEMS.

**Amiens** Hard-twisted worsted yarns woven into twilled fabric made in solid colors, stripes, or novelty patterns similar to LASTING, but of better quality. Also spelled *amens*. *Der.* Named for Amiens, France, where it was first woven.

**Amies, Hardy** See APPENDIX/DESIGNERS.

**amorphous** A property of gems meaning without a crystalline structure. Semi-precious or ornamental gems such as the opal and turquoise are amorphous, as opposed to the diamond, ruby, and amethyst which are CRYSTALLINE. See individual GEMS or this property.

**amout** Sealskin tunic with hood attached at back to carry an infant; worn by Greenland Eskimo women.

**amuce** See ALMUCE.

**amulet** Small object believed to possess magical powers—a good-luck charm worn as protection against evil by primitive people and surviving to present time in various forms of jewelry.

**anadem** Wreath or garland of leaves or flowers, worn on hair by women in late 16th and early 17th c. Also spelled *anademe*.

**ancient madder** Fabric of *madder* colors with small foulard-type or paisley designs, printed in England in dull red, dull green, dull medium blue, dark brown, and pale yellow outlined with black, and napped to give a suedelike hand.

**Andalouse cape** (an-da-looz) Cape worn outdoors by women in 1846, made of silk and trimmed with fringe.

**Andalusian casaque** (an-da-loozian cask) Woman's evening tunic fastened down center with series of ribbons with front of skirt cut away, sloping to knee-length in the back. Worn over another skirt in 1809.

**Andean shift** See DRESSES.

**andradite garnet** See GEMS.

**androgynous** (an-drodg-e-nus) Possessing both male and female characteristics. James Laver, fashion historian, says ideal fashion figure of 1920s and late 1960s and 1970s is the androgynous female who resembles a boy. *Der.* From Greek words *andros,* "man" and *gynacea,* "woman." Also see LOOKS.

**anelace** Man's long two-edged dagger worn hanging from the belt in 13th and 16th c. Also spelled *anlace.*

**anga** White or colored long cotton coat with wide sleeves, fastened with loops above waist, worn by Mohammedans in India. Also see ANGHARKA.

**angel overskirt** Woman's short overskirt having two long points on either side used as part of daytime dress in 1894.

**angel sleeves** Long square panels from shoulders reaching nearly to floor. Used on women's mantles of 1889. Also see SLEEVES.

**angharka** (an-gar-ka) Short coat reaching to waist and opening on left side worn by Mohammedan men in India. Also see ANGA and CHAPKAN.

**angiya** (an-gee-a) Short-sleeved bodice just covering the bust, worn by Moslem women in southern India. Also see KURTA.

**angled pocket** See HACKING POCKET under POCKETS.

**angled shawl collar** See COLLARS.

**angle-fronted coat** Variation of man's MORNING COAT, cut away diagonally on each side to reveal triangles of waistcoat; worn from 1870 to 1880. Also called *university coat.*

**anglesea hat** (angle-see) Man's hat with flat brim and high cylindrical-shaped crown, worn about 1830.

**Angleterre, point d' lace** See POINT D'ANGLETERRE under LACES.

**Anglo-Greek bodice** Woman's bodice with wide lapels edged with lace, placed far apart. Worn in 1820s with FICHU-ROBINGS.

**Anglo-Saxon embroidery** See EMBROIDERIES.

**angola** **1.** British term for a wool and cotton yarn made with 75% to 80% wool. **2.** Overcoating fabric in a low count twill weave and a thick nap. **3.** British shirting fabric made in plain or twill weave with cotton warp and cotton angola yarn filling. **4.** Twilled red cotton fabric. **5.** Cream-colored rough cotton fabric used for embroidery.

**angora** Soft fuzzy yarn made from underhair of angora rabbit; popular for sweaters in late 1930s, and for sweaters and knit dresses in 1970s and 1980s.

**Angoulême bonnet** (ahn-goo-lem) Straw bonnet of 1814 made with high pleated crown, broad front brim narrowed at sides, and tied with bow at side. Worn by women in French Empire period, and named for Duchesse d'Angoulême, daughter of Marie Antoinette.

**Anguilla cotton** (ang-gwi-a) Cotton first produced in West Indies on island of Anguilla; may have been the source of SEA ISLAND COTTON.

ANKH

**ankh** Egyptian symbol for eternal life, somewhat like a *cross* with vertical bar forming a loop at top. Popular as jewelry motif, especially as necklaces and rings, in late 1960s and 1970s. Also called *ansate cross.* Also see NECKLACES and RINGS.

**ankle boots**  See DEMI-BOOT, GEORGE and PANTS BOOTS under BOOTS.

**ankle bracelet**  See BRACELETS and KHAL-KHAL.

**ankle-jacks**  Man's ankle-high boot, laced up front with five pairs of eyelets. Popular in East End of London in 1840s.

**ankle length**  See LENGTHS.

**ankle-length hose**  See HOSE.

**ankle socks**  See SOCKS.

**ankle-strap**  Strap that fastens around the ankle usually used on shoes. Also see SANDALS and SHOES.

**anklet  1.** See BRACELETS and KHALKHAL. **2.** See ANKLE SOCKS under SOCKS.

**ankle watch**  See WATCHES.

**anlace**  See ANELACE.

**Annamese band turban**  Open-crowned wrapped cotton turban with folds sewn into place, wide at sides. Native headdress worn by upper class women of the country of Annam, present day Vietnam, who originally believed good spirits entered body through open crown.

**Annette Kellerman**  One-piece knit bathing suit with short sleeves, knee-length pants, and high round neck. Originally worn under bathing suits by women from late 19th c. to 1920s. Named for Annette Kellerman, the swimmer who first wore it without the bathing dress on top in early 20th c. Similar suits were worn for everyday sportswear during the summer of 1987. See KELLERMAN, ANNETTE.

**Annie Hall**  Clothes worn in uncoordinated manner as exemplified by movie *Annie Hall* written and directed by Woody Allen, starring Diane Keaton. Also see LOOKS.

**annular brooch**  See PENANNULAR BROOCH.

**anorak** (an-no-rack)  See SPORT JACKETS.

**ansate cross**  See ANKH and NECKLACES.

**anslet**  See HANSELINE.

**antelope**  See FURS and LEATHERS.

**antelope-finished lambskin**  Soft finish applied to lambskin, calfskin, or goatskin in imitation of genuine antelope skin. Also see LEATHERS.

**antery** (an-tery)  Waist- or below-the-knee-length vest worn by Egyptian and Turkish men over linen shirts. Also spelled *antree*.

**Anthony, John**  See APPENDIX/DESIGNERS.

**antigropolis** (an-te-grah-po-lis)  Man's long *gaiter*, usually leather; coming over thigh in front, but cut away to knee in back; worn in mid-19th c. for walking or riding.

**antique bodice**  Long-waisted tight bodice with low décolletage and deep point at front waistline; worn for evening by women in 1830s and 1840s.

**antique finish**  Finish applied to leather giving a shaded effect by dyeing, buffing, wrinkling, waxing, and oiling the surface to resemble old leather.

**antique lace**  See LACES.

**antique satin**  Reversible fabric with a dull face and a satin back, characterized by *nubs* or *slubs* of yarn at intervals in the filling. Usually woven in a combination of rayon and acetate yarns. Uses: evening gowns, shoes, handbags, cocktail dresses, and dressy suits.

**antique taffeta**  Crisp taffeta which may have irregular slubs throughout in imitation of 18th-c. fabrics. May be made of DOUPIONI silk or man-made fibers. Also made in iridescent effects with warp and filling yarns of different colors.

**Antoinette fichu**  Woman's long scarf of 1850s draped around the neck and crossed at the waistline to form two long cords which fall to the hips. Also called *Marie Antoinette fichu*.

**Antron®**  Trademark of E. I. du Pont de Nemours & Company for several types of nylon used for silky-looking sweaters and lingerie.

**Antwerp lace**   See LACES.

**ao dai**   Pantsuit consisting of a long-sleeved mid-calf tunic, slashed on side seams (or one side), and full-length pants; worn by men and women in Vietnam. Also see CAI-AO and CAIGUAN.

**AO DAI**

**Apache** (a-patch-e)  **1.** Styles similar to clothes worn by American Southwest Indian tribe from Arizona and New Mexico. **2.** In France, *apache* (a-pash) is slang for gangster or thug, especially as depicted by French night-club dancers. The French word taken from the American Indian tribe, thought to be very fierce. Also see HANDBAGS, SCARFS, and SHIRTS.

**ape drape**   See SHAG under HAIRSTYLES.

**apex**  **1.** Originally the spike of olive wood on the peak of cap worn by Roman *flamen*, a priest of some particular deity. Later the entire cap was known by this name. **2.** The point at which a dart tapers to an end.

**Apollo corset**   Waist cincher stiffened with whalebone, worn by both men and women about 1810. Compare with BRUMMELL BODICE and CUMBERLAND CORSET.

**Apollo knot**   Woman's elaborate evening hairstyle, worn from 1824 to 1832, made with wired loops of false hair, projecting up from crown of head, and finished with decorative comb, flowers, or feathers.

**apparel**  **1.** Any type of clothing worn by men, women, and children. Synonyms: ATTIRE, CLOTHES, COSTUME, DRESS, GARB, GARMENT, HABIT, UNIFORM, ROBE, RAIMENT, and VESTMENTS, the latter used particularly for clerical dress. **2.** Term used since early 14th c. to denote clothing, particularly a suit of clothes. **3.** Late 14th-c. term for embroidered borders of ecclesiastical garments. **4.** Late 14th-c. term for embellishment of armor.

**apparel industry**   The manufacturers, jobbers, and contractors engaged in the manufacture of ready-to-wear clothing for men, women, and children. Also called *cutting-up trade, garment trade, needle trade,* and *rag business.*

**Appenzell**   See EMBROIDERIES.

**applejack cap**   See NEWSBOY CAP under CAPS.

**appliqué** (ap-plee-kay)  **1.** Surface pattern made by cutting out fabric or lace designs and attaching them to another fabric or lace by means of embroidery or stitching. **2.** See LACES. **3.** Applied leather designs on shoes and handbags.

**appurn**   See NAPERON.

**après-ski**   Clothing and accessories featured at ski resorts after skiing. *Der.* French, "after-ski." See APRÈS-SKI BOOTS under BOOTS, SLIPPER SOCKS under SLIPPERS, and LOOKS.

**apron**  **1.** Item of apparel designed to protect regular clothing or used as a decorative accessory. **2.** Dress with a free-hanging panel attached to the front of a skirt, which resembles an apron. Historically, aprons were worn from the 13th c. on by men and women. Originated in Middle Ages from an extra piece of cloth tied over skirt by women before sitting down at the table. See BARMECLOTH. This style was later adopted by servants and worn with a bib top. Also see BELLE-CHETE **3.** In the 16th to 18th c. color of the apron denoted the trade of workman or artisan. See CHECKERED APRON MAN, BLUE-APRONED MAN, and GREEN-APPRONED MAN. **4.** Decorative aprons of lace and embroidery were worn over dresses in the first half of the 17th c., throughout the 18th c., and in the 1870s. *Der.* Old French, *napperon*, the diminutive *nappe* meaning "cloth." During the Middle Ages a *napperon*, or napkin, became apron. (Older spelling *appurn*.) See CHECKS, DRESSES, and SWIMSUITS.

## APRONS

**barber's a.** Long circular cape, fastening at the neckline in back, originally made of cotton fabric and now sometimes of plastic, worn to protect clothes while hair is being cut.

**bib a.** Apron which extends high on chest held by straps over the shoulders crossing in center back and attached at the waistline. First worn in the 17th c.

**butcher's a.** Apron made of heavy fabric—usually white. Styled all-in-one piece coming to the chest in front, having a strap going around the back of the neck, curved under the arms, and tied at center back. *Der.* From apron worn by butchers when cutting meat. Also see CHEF'S APRON.

**carpenter's a.** Large pocket made of fabric or leather divided into sections and mounted on a belt. Worn to carry nails, small tools, etc.

**cartoon a.** Usually a butcher's type apron printed with humorous pictures or slogans.

**chef's a.** Apron of canvas, terry cloth, or other type of fabric styled like a BUTCHER'S

**CHEF'S APRON**

**COCKTAIL APRON**

**WORK APRON, 1892**

**COBBLER'S APRON**

**Front View**

**HALF APRON**

**Back View**

APRON and worn by cooks for outdoor barbeques as well as in the kitchen. May have a *kangaroo pocket* across the center front and screen printed with name, or message.

**cobbler's a.** Hip-length, large-pocketed apron originally worn by shoemakers, carpenters, and other workmen to hold nails. Popular as woman's fashion in late 1960s, and usually made of fabric. Also see CARPENTER'S APRON.

**cocktail a.** Tiny half apron made of net, lace, or fabric.

**half-a.** Bibless apron coming only to waist.

**Hoover a.** Utility *wraparound dress* with two half-fronts and attached sash that goes through slot at each side seam to tie in back. *Der.* Originated during World War I when Herbert Hoover was food administrator in U.S.

**pinafore a.** Apron worn by young girls made with a gathered skirt, bib-top, and suspender straps. Sometimes made with ruffles over the shoulders extending to waistline. Also see alphabetical listing.

**trucker's a.** Shaped similar to a *butcher's apron* with large pockets in front. Has a slit in center front and ties around each leg.

**work a.** Any apron designed to cover the clothes amply while the wearer is working at a job that might soil or harm garments.

---

**apron tongue** Extra long leather tongue, often fringed at end, used on shoe. It fits behind lacing, then flops over covering laces completely.

**aquamarine** See GEMS.

**Arabian Nights look** See HAREM under LOOKS.

**araneum lace** See LACES.

**Aran Isle sweater** See SWEATERS.

**ARBA KANFOTH, 18th c.**

**arba kanfoth** Undergarment worn by Orthodox Jewish men, consisting of a rectangle of cloth with hole or slit in center for head and tassels or fringe at the corners.

**Arcot diamond** See DIAMONDS.

**Arctics** See BOOTS.

**Arcturus® mink** See MUTATION MINK under FURS.

**Argenta® mink** See MUTATION MINK under FURS.

**argentan lace** See LACES.

**Argentina borregos lamb** See LAMB under FURS.

**argentine cloth** Open-weave fabric similar to glazed tarlatan, made in plain weave and glazed to make it dustproof. Finish is nonpermanent and comes out when washed.

**Argyle** Diamond-shaped plaid pattern with narrow overplaid superimposed in several colors. Popular for hand- or machine-knitted socks and sweaters in 1920s and 1930s, and again in late 1960s and 1980s. *Der.* Tartan of Duke of Argyle and Clan Campbell of Argyll, a county in West Scotland. Also spelled *argyll, Argyl*. See PLAIDS, SOCKS, and SWEATERS.

**arasaid** Long dress worn by women of Scotland during the early 17th c. Possible white with few small stripes of black, blue, and red forming a plaid. Skirt of dress was pleated around waist and secured by a belt of leather and silver. A pin of silver or brass was worn at the chest.

**Arizona ruby** See RUBY under GEMS.

**Arlesienne coif** Headdress native to Arles, France, consisting of white cap worn on crown of head, almost covered by black velvet cap with long broad ribbon extending down back. With this coif a lacey or ruffled fichu was worn around the neck—then called *Arlesienne coif and fichu.* Headdress can be seen in French Post-Impressionist Vincent van Gogh's painting, *L'Arlesienne.*

**Armani, Giorgio** See APPENDIX/DESIGNERS.

**armband bracelet** See BRACELETS.

**Armenian lace** See LACES.

**Armenian mantle** Loose-fitting *pelisse* without a cape, enriched with passementerie made of braid, worn by women in 1847.

**armhole** Section of garment through which arm passes or into which sleeve is fitted. Usually round but may be squared underneath the arm. Originally called ARMSCYE or ARMSEYE.

**armlet** See BRACELET.

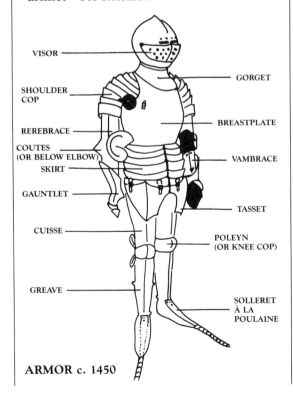

VISOR

SHOULDER COP

REREBRACE

COUTES (OR BELOW ELBOW)

SKIRT

GAUNTLET

CUISSE

GREAVE

GORGET

BREASTPLATE

VAMBRACE

TASSET

POLEYN (OR KNEE COP)

SOLLERET À LA POULAINE

**ARMOR c. 1450**

**armor** Protective garments worn by soldiers and knights from early times, especially those made of chain mail and cast metal from Middle Ages through 17th c. For individual items see: ACTON, CAMAIL, CANNON #2, COIF DE MAILLES, COINTISE #2, COUTES, CUISSE, DEMI BRASSARD, ÉPAULIÈRE, GAUNTLET, GORGET #2, GREAVE, HAUBERK, JACK, MAIL, MORION, PAULDRON, POLEYN, REREBRACE, SHOULDER COP, SOLLERET, TABARD #2, TASSET, VAMBRACE, VISOR.

**armozine** Heavy French corded silk or taffeta fabric, generally black, used from 17th to 19th c. for waistcoats, dresses, mourning, etc. Also spelled *armazine, armozeen, armoise, armoisin, armozin.*

**armscye** Variant for ARMSEYE.

**armseye/arm's eye** Term which refers to the ARMHOLE of an item of apparel. Formerly spelled *armscye.*

**armure** Classification of fabrics with a pebbly surface sometimes using small motifs in a repeat design. Woven in a variation of the rib weave called *armure weave.* Originally made of silk, now made of various fibers and blends. Used for dresses and ties. *Der.* French, *armure,* "armor," as the original fabrics had a linked effect similar to chain mail.

**Army/Navy clothes** Surplus items of clothing worn by the U.S. Army and Navy sold in special stores, usually located in larger cities throughout the country. Includes such items as BLOUSES, BOMBER JACKETS, BOOTS, CAPS, FATIGUES, FIELD JACKETS and PEA COATS.

**army-type duck** Plain woven fabric, lighter in weight than *numbered duck,* with medium or heavy piled yarns. Used for utility clothing. *Der.* Originally used for sails in the 19th c., imported from Holland or Scotland; lightweight fabrics were stenciled with a picture of a raven, heavier weight with a duck.

**Arnel®** 1. Trademark of Celanese Corp. for a triacetate filament and staple fiber produced in the U.S. and Canada. It is texturized; has a higher melting point than other synthetics; garments may be made with heat-set pleats. **2.** A licensed merchandising term used by Celanese Corp. on fabrics which are made with the fiber and come up to performance standards set by the manufacturer of the yarn. Washes well, needs little pressing, packs well, and has good dimensional stability.

**Arrasene** See EMBROIDERIES.

**Arrow collar®** See DETACHABLE COLLAR.

**arrowhead** See EMBROIDERIES and STITCHES.

**Art Deco** Geometric non-representational style of jewelry and fabric design popular in late 1920s. Inspired by Exposition International des Arts Décoratifs et Industriels Modernes in Paris, 1925. Revived in late 1968-69, continuing into the 1980s as inspiration for fabric and jewelry design. Also see ART MODERNE. *Der.* French, *art decoratif,* "decorative art." Also see EARRINGS, HOSE, LOOKS, and PRINTS.

**artichoke** See HAIRSTYLES.

**artificial crinoline** See CAGE PETTICOAT.

**artificial silk** Term used before 1925 to describe rayon and acetate. Also called *art silk.*

**artillery twill** Another name for WHIPCORD.

**ARTIST'S SMOCK**

**artist's smock** **1.** Traditionally a smock used by artists. Usually three-quarter length with full sleeves gathered into band at wrist and a large round collar with black tie. **2.** Any smock worn when painting.

**art linen** 100% linen fabric which is usually hand-blocked printed or screen-printed. Used bleached, unbleached, or dyed a solid color. Originally used for towels and tablecloths and now used for dresses, blouses, and sportswear. Also used for embroidery work. Also called *embroidery crash* and *embroidery linen.*

**Art Moderne** (art mod-airn) French design style for jewelry and fabrics that followed the Exposition International des Arts Décoratifs et Industriels Modernes in Paris, 1925 featuring straight lines and angles. Also see ART DECO.

**Art Nouveau** (ar noo-vo) Decorative style popular for jewelry and fashions from late 19th to early 20th c. Characterized by use of natural forms in curving, stylized designs of climbing vines, leaves, flowers, and women's long hair. Revived in late 1960s, continuing into 1980s. *Der.* French, "new art." Also see HOSE and LOOKS.

**artois** (ahr-twah) Long loose cloak with lapels and several capes, the longest ending near the waistline; worn by men and women in late 18th c.

**Artois buckle** See BUCKLES D'ARTOIS.

**art silk** See ARTIFICIAL SILK.

**art to wear** Craftsmanship in fabric artistry to design clothes with originality and individuality which follow a specific fashion trend and make no claim to fashion. Resulting designs are looked upon as "art" while wearability is of secondary importance. Clothing is of the more exotic type—not worn for business. American fiber artists use resist dyeing and painting techniques; "sculpt" with pre-pleated heat-set fabrics; develop unusual crocheted effects; use hand-knitting machines to produce distinctive fabrics; and use several layers of varicolored fabric which is quilted, slashed, and frayed in a process called "reverse appliqué."

**Ascot** Fashionable horse-racing spot, Ascot Heath, in England, for which a number of fashions have been named. See COLLARS, NECK-LINES, SCARFS, and TIES.

**ascot jacket** Loose-fitting man's jacket with rounded hems in front and matching fabric belt pulling in the waistline worn in 1876.

**ashes-of-roses** Grayed-pink color. Also called *bois de rose*.

**A-shirt** Short for ATHLETIC SHIRT. See KNIT SHIRTS.

**Ashmouni** See EGYPTIAN COTTON.

**asooch** 17th-c. term meaning "sash-wise" or "scarf-wise"; draped diagonally from shoulder to hip. Also spelled *aswash*.

**assasins** See PATCHES #3.

**asterism** Ability of a gemstone to project a star-shaped pattern as in rubies and sapphires. Produced synthetically in trademarked LINDE STAR® and Hope® sapphires.

**astrakhan** **1.** Woven fabric in a pile weave with curly surface in imitation of Persian lamb or broadtail fur. Originally made from curly wool of sheep raised in Astrakhan, U.S.S.R. Today yarns are curled prior to weaving and may be woven either as a filling pile or a warp pile, either cut or uncut, or of luster wool, worsted, or mohair warp with wool or cotton in the filling. Usually bleached or dyed gray or black in imitation of fur. Used for collars, cuffs, hats, and jackets. **2.** A knitted fabric made with yarns that have been curled before they are knitted. **3.** Name for wool fibers obtained from KARAKUL LAMBS. Also spelled *astrachan*. **4.** See FURS.

**astrolegs hose** See HOSE.

**astronaut's cap** See CAPS.

**aswash** See ASOOCH.

**asymmetric** The principle of informal balance, rather than formal balance, with each side of the garment offering a different silhouette. Garments may be draped to one side, have uneven hemlines, side closings, or cover only one shoulder. See CLOSINGS, COLLARS, DRESSES, HEMS, NECKLINES, SILHOUETTES, SKIRTS, and SWIMSUITS.

**Ata** See TALLITH.

**atef** Headdress consisting of tall white cap with two plumes, or feathers, arranged at the sides. Symbolic headdress of certain Egyptian gods, particularly Osiris, also depicted as worn by Egyptian kings.

**athletic clothes** Apparel worn originally for active sports, now worn as everyday wear. See PANTS, SHORTS, SOCKS, and SPORT SUITS.

**athletic shirt** Man's undershirt also worn for gym and sports. Also called *A-shirt*. See KNIT SHIRTS.

**at-home wear** Informal clothing more acceptable to wear at home particularly when entertaining. See CAFTAN and HOSTESS ROBE under ROBES.

**atours** (a-toor) Padded, horned headdress worn by women in 14th and 15th c.

**attache case** See BRIEFCASE under HANDBAGS.

**attached collar** See COLLARS.

**attic look** Term introduced in early 1970s for old clothes and accessories found in the attics of old houses. Also see LOOKS.

**attifet** Woman's headdress of 16th c. arched on either side of forehead to form a "widow's peak" and draped completely with a veil as seen in paintings of Mary Stuart, Queen of Scots. Also see MARIE STUART BONNET, or CAP.

**attire** **1.** Synonym for APPAREL. **2.** Term used since the 15th c. for woman's headdress of gold and gems worn on state occasions, later shortened to *tire*.

**aubergine** (o-ber-jheen) Dark purple color. *Der.* French, "eggplant."

**Aubusson stitch**   See STITCHES.

**Audubon Plumage Law**   Law passed early in 20th c. prohibiting use and importation of feathers from rare birds, such as the *egret* which were used as fashionable trim on women's hats from late 19th to early 20th c. *Der.* Named for John James Audubon, American ornithologist who died in 1851.

**Augustabernard**   See APPENDIX/DESIGNERS.

**aulmoniere** (all-mon-y-air) Medieval pouch of silk or leather suspended from girdle worn by nobles from the 13th c. until the Reformation to carry alms. Also used by women in 14th c. to carry mirrors and tweezers for their hair. Also spelled *aumoniere, aulmonier, almoner.* Compare with GIPSER.

**aumusse/aunice**   See ALMUCE.

**auqueton** (aw-ke-tawn)   See ACTON.

**aureole** (or-e-ole) A white cap tied under chin, with a starched, five-inch lace frill of 64 flutes framing the face. The flutes are in imitation of the rays of the solar corona. Native headdress worn by women of Boulogne, France.

**aurora borealis crystal**   See BEADS.

**Australian opossum**   See FURS.

**Austrian cloth**   Fine woolen or worsted fabric woven from highest grade merino wool. Originally made in Austria, today it is used for men's formal wear.

**Austrian crystal**   See BEADS.

**Austrian seal**   Term used in early 20th c. for rabbit fur. Used prior to the Fur Labeling Act, it is no longer correct.

**automobile cap**   Cap and hood of waterproof fabric worn by women for automobile riding in early 1900s. Flat-topped cap with brim

**AUTOMOBILE CAP, 1907**

rolled down in front and up in back, worn over a tight-fitting hood exposing only the face. Also called *havelock cap.*

**AUTOMOBILE COAT, 1904**

**automobile coat**   Pongee-colored lightweight full-length coat worn when riding in an automobile in early 20th c. to protect clothing from dust. Worn with AUTOMOBILE VEIL. Also called a DUSTER.

**automobile veil**   Wide, sheer, long veil placed over wide-brimmed hat and tied under chin with ends flowing over front of duster;

worn for motoring in early 1900s. Also called MOTORING VEIL.

**Autumn Haze®** See MUTATION MINK under FURS.

**avant-garde** (a-vahnt guard) Forward thinking or advanced. When referring to art or costume, sometimes implies erotic or startling. *Der.* French, "advance guard."

**aviator** Adjective used for clothing and accessories used by pilots and adopted for general use. See GLASSES, HELMETS, and FLIGHT JACKET under SPORT JACKETS.

**Avignon** Lightweight silk taffeta lining fabric made in France.

**award sweater** See LETTER SWEATER under SWEATERS.

**awning stripe** **1.** Heavy durable fabric similar to canvas but lighter in weight. Made of heavy coarse cotton yarns, it may be left natural, bleached, dyed, printed, or woven in stripes. Introduced for sport clothes, jackets, and shorts in 1960s. Also used for handbags. **2.** Type of stripe consisting of one-inch bands of color alternating with white. See STRIPES.

**Ayrshire embroidery** See MADEIRA EMBROIDERY under EMBROIDERIES.

**azoic dyes** Group of colors formed directly in the fiber by a chemical reaction which produce vibrant colors. Inexpensive; used on cotton and viscose rayon fabrics. Also called *naphthol dyes* and *ice dyes*.

**Aztec print** See PRINTS and SWEATERS.

**Azurene® mink** See MUTATION MINK under FURS.

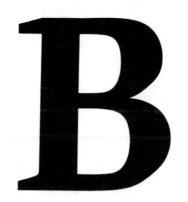

**B 1. Shoe Size:** Letter indicating a width; widths run from AAAA to EEEEE with AAAA's being the narrowest and EEEEE's the widest. **2. Pajama Size:** Men's regular height (5′8″–5′11″) size corresponding to 37″–40″ chest measurement. For other sizes, see BIG, EXTRA-TALL, REGULAR, and TALL. **3. Shirt Size:** For men's extra-tall size with 16–16½ collar measurement. **4. Bra Cup Size:** Sizes run AAA, AA, A, B, C, D, DD: AAA is the smallest size and DD the largest.

**babet bonnet** Small cap for evening worn by women in 1838. Usually made with wide side frills and flattened top, sometimes of tulle.

**babet cap** Woman's morning cap of muslin with ribbon trimming, covering ears and part of cheeks; worn from 1836 to 1840s.

**babouche/baboosh** (bah-boosh) Heelless slipper of Moroccan leather with pointed toe; worn in Northern Africa, Turkey, and Armenia. Also spelled *babooch, babouch, babush.* Also called *paboudi.*

**babushka** (bah-boosh-ka) See SCARFS.

**baby beads** See BEADS.

**baby blue** Delicate pale-blue color, traditionally worn by boy babies since 1920; earlier worn by girls.

**baby bodice** Daytime bodice introduced in 1878 with lingerie features similar to baby's dress such as vertical pleats down front, a wide sash, *basques* below waistline, and a square neck. Later in 1897, worn with a high drawstring neckline fastened with ribbon and a wide sash.

**baby bonnet** See BONNETS.

**baby boot** Term used for an infant's *bootee,* in second half of 19th c. usually made of fabric or felt, and elaborately trimmed with embroidery. Also see BOOTIE #1.

**baby bunting** Infant's outdoor combination blanket-sack with zipper up front and separate or attached hood, frequently made of blanket cloth and bound with satin. Also called *bunting* and *grow bag.*

**baby combing wool** Fine wool fiber from 2″ to 2½″ long.

**baby doll** Term used to refer to clothing and accessories used for children's dolls and infants' clothes, in the early 20th c. (popularity somewhat enhanced by movie *Baby Doll* produced in 1956 in which Carroll Baker played the lead). For individual items see: DRESSES, LOOKS, NIGHTGOWNS, PAJAMAS, SHOES, SILHOUETTES, and SLEEVES.

**baby dress** Dresses popular until mid-20th c. for infants, regardless of sex, usually made of fine white cotton in shift style and trimmed with tucks, embroidery, and lace. Also see CHRISTENING DRESS and DRESSES

**baby Irish/baby lace** See LACES.

**baby Louis heel** See LOUIS under HEELS.

**baby pink** Pale tint of pink. Traditionally worn by girls babies since 1920, earlier worn by boys.

**baby ribbon** Narrow ribbon ⅛″ to ¼″ in width, sometimes made of reversible satin. Originally used for baby clothes and also to thread through insertion, lace, and beading in late 19th and early 20th c.

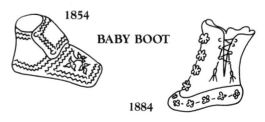

1854

**BABY BOOT**

1884

**baby sash** Woman's sash of ribbon tied in bow at back; popular at end of 19th c.

**baby skirt** Short flared or pleated skirt worn over bathing suit or playsuit during 1930s and 1940s.

**Baby Stuart cap** Classic type of infant's close-fitting cap with narrow chin band, illustrated in portrait of Charles II painted by Van Dyck in 1634.

**BACHELOR'S GOWN**

**Bachelor's gown** Black academic gown, formerly of worsted or similar fabric, opening in front with two wide box pleats extending to the hem; large flowing sleeves ending in points; back and sleeves set into square yoke with CARTRIDGE PLEATS. Worn with the BACHELOR'S HOOD and MORTARBOARD at graduation by candidates, or former recipients, of Bachelor's degree. Since 1970s colors sometimes worn instead of black.

**Bachelor's hood** Black decorative drape, three feet long in back with a two-inch colored

**BACHELOR'S HOOD**

velveteen band around the neck in front and a pendant tail in the back which is turned over to reveal colors of institution granting the degree. Worn with the BACHELOR'S GOWN and MORTARBOARD at graduation by candidates, or former recipients, of Bachelor's degree. Also see ACADEMIC HOOD COLORS.

**bachlick** Woman's *fichu* of cashmere edged with swansdown, with a hoodlike point finished with tassel in back. Worn over daytime dresses in late 1860s.

**bacinet** See BASINET.

**back** **1.** Underside or reverse side of fabric as differentiated from the FACE or right side. **2.** 14th-c. term sometimes used to describe any outer garment.

**back-combing** Hair-dressing technique of lifting each strand of hair and combing or brushing lightly toward the scalp to increase bulk; used widely in 1950s and 1960s for *bouffant* and *beehive* hairdos. Also called *teasing*. See HAIRSTYLES.

**backed cloth** Any fabric which is woven with an extra warp or an extra filling, making three yarns in all. Frequently made with two-toned effect with a different color on each side. Differs from DOUBLE CLOTH in that double cloth has five yarns—two warps, two fillings and a binder. If the binder yarn is cut, two fabrics will result. In backed cloth removing any of the yarns destroys the fabric.

**backed weave** Weave made with three interlacing yarns. The extra yarn may be in the warp or filling. Fabrics are usually made of two colors with a different color showing on each side; sometimes one side is printed. Makes a thick fabric which cannot be cut apart; used particularly for *bathrobe cloth*. Compare with DOUBLE CLOTH.

**backing** Term for extra piece of fabric laminated to flesh side of leather or shoe fabric to give added strength, making it appear plumper.

**backless dress** See DRESSES.

**back pack** See HANDBAGS.

**backs** Term used in the 14th c. to refer to clothing in general.

**backstitch** **1.** Sewing term for reversing stitch on sewing machine. Used to secure threads at the beginning and ending of seams. Also called *staying a seam* or *stay.* **2.** See STITCHES. **3.** See EMBROIDERIES.

**back strings** Term used in the 18th c. for ribbons attached to the shoulders of children's dresses. Also see LEADING STRINGS.

**back-wrap dress** See DRESSES.

**badger** See FURS.

**bäffchen/beffchen** German name for a clerical collar of two white linen tabs hanging over minister's robe at front of neck and tied in back with strings. Same as English SHORT BANDS and GENEVA BANDS.

**bag** **1.** Shortened form of word HANDBAG; an accessory used to carry small possessions. See HANDBAGS. **2.** An 18th-c. wig. See BAGWIG.

**bag bodice** Woman's bodice with plastron cut to blouse over belt or waistband, worn in daytime in 1883.

**bag bonnet** Woman's bonnet with soft crown which fitted loosely over back of head worn in early 19th c.

**bag cap** Man's cloth cap, sometimes made of velvet, shaped like a turban, trimmed with fur or ornamental band; worn in 14th and 15th c.

**baggies** See BAGGY JEANS under PANTS.

**bagging shoe** See STARTUP.

**baggy pants** See PANTS.

**bagheera** (ba-gee-ra) Fine uncut velvet with short, closely set loops which make it crush-resistant.

**bag-irons** Iron, bronze, or silver frames with suspension units made of a crossbar and swivel. Lower section of concentric semi-circular rings act as stiffeners for opening and closing. Used for medieval pouches worn hanging from belt in 15th and 16th c. Also called *bag-rings*.

**bagnolette** (ban-yo-let) Woman's wired hood standing away from face, covering shoulders; worn in 18th c.

**bagpipe sleeve** Full sleeve gathered like a pouch on outer side of arm ending in wide band at wrist. Worn in 15th c. by men and women primarily in the HOUPPELANDE. *Der.* From shape of Scottish bagpipe.

**bag-rings** See BAG-IRONS.

**bags** Slang term for men's trousers in 19th c. Also see OXFORD BAGS under PANTS.

**baguette** See GEM CUTS.

**bag-waistcoat** Man's vest, full in front and bloused to form a pouch, worn in 1883.

**BAGWIG**

**bagwig** Man's 18th-c. wig, styled with hair pulled back and stuffed into a square black silk bag tied with bow at nape of neck. Also called *coiffure en bourse*, *crapaud*, or *bag*. Also see BOURSE #2.

**baju** Short-sleeved loose Malaysian jacket cut short and open in front; usually made with simple collar and patch pockets on chest.

**Bakst, Leon Nikolaevich** Russian artist who, after leaving Russia for Paris in 1909, won international fame designing sets and costumes for the Ballets Russes produced by Diaghilev. Helped to start a wave of Orientalism in women's dresses in pre-World War I era.

**baku** **1.** Fine, lightweight dull-finished inexpensive straw from Baku, China. Obtained from Buri palm in the Philippines, along Ceylon and Malabar coast. It is woven in China, also sold as *Buntal* fiber. **2.** A hat body of buntal fibers woven in China. *Shantung Baku* is fine, close, even, and given a glazed finish. **3.** A Philippine fiber obtained from the stalk of the *buri palm*.

**balaclava** Hood covering the head and shoulders exposing the face, made of knitted wool. Worn mainly by soldiers in 1890s and in World War I and II in cold weather. Also worn by mountain climbers and skiers. *Der.* Named for Crimean War, Battle of Balaklava, fought October 25, 1854.

**balas ruby** See SPINEL under GEMS.

**balayeuse** (bah-lah-yuz) See DUST RUFFLE.

**balbriggan** Soft, lightweight tubular knit fabric made of cotton, man-made, or blended yarns in a plain stitch. It may be slightly napped on the reverse side. Used for *pajamas* and *snuggies*. *Der.* Named for Balbriggan, Ireland, where name was first used for type of unbleached hosiery.

**baldachin/baldaquin** (bal-da-kin) Medieval fabric of silk interwoven with gold, like modern brocade. Sometimes studded with precious stones. Also spelled *baldac*, *baldchine*,

baudekin, bodlan. *Der.* Italian, *Baldacco*, meaning Baghdad where the fabric was first manufactured.

**baldric/baldrick** Wide decorative belt used to hold dagger worn at hip level. Worn diagonally from right shoulder to left hip, where sword was placed from 13th to 17th c. Also see BELTS.

**Balenciaga, Cristobal** (bal-lawn-see-áh-gah) See APPENDIX/DESIGNERS.

**Bali dancer's costume** Woman's costume consisting of sarong skirt and long strip of elaborate fabric wrapped tightly around the bust. Worn with GALUNGAN and without shoes by temple dancers on the island of Bali, a part of Indonesia.

**ballantine** Same as RETICULE.

**ball earring** See EARRINGS.

**ballerina length** See LENGTHS.

**ballerina-length skirt** Calf-length full skirt of 1940s and 1950s in gored, gathered, or flared style, used mainly for evening dresses. *Der.* Adapted from the skirts worn by ballet dancers.

**ballerina shoe** See SHOES.

**ballet laces** Wide satin ribbons used as lacings for ballet slippers, crisscrossing at intervals around ankle and calf and tied in bow. Worn in 1870s on bathing slippers and during World War I with high-heeled pumps. Reintroduced in 1980s.

**ballet skirt** Tiered skirt of evening dress worn in 1880s, made with three or four layers of tulle in a variety of lengths attached to a silk foundation. Top layer was sprinkled with stars, pearls, or beetle wings.

**ballet slipper** Delicate shoe of leather pulled around and attached to very small sole usually worn with BALLET LACES crisscrossing the ankle and leg. Shoes were originally made by Capezio, trademark of Capezio Ballet Makers, a division of U.S. Shoe Corp. Also see SLIPPERS. Also see BALLERINA SHOE under SHOES.

**ball fringe**  Type of braid with little fuzzy balls suspended at regular intervals. Used on beach ponchos and robes, and fashionable in late 1870s and 1880s for dress trimming.

**ball gown**   See FORMAL GOWN under DRESSES.

**ball heel**   See HEELS.

**ballibuntl**  **1.** Fine, lightweight glossy straw, similar to BAKU, woven of *buntal* fibers from the leaves of the *buri palm* from the Philippines. Also spelled *balibuntal.* **2.** Smooth lightweight dull straw. Also called *Bangkok straw.*

**balloon cloth**  Strong, lightweight, plain-woven fabric with high luster and high count, made of fine combed yarns. Originally coated and used for airplanes and balloons. Used uncoated for ski wear, shirts, and sportswear.

**balloon hat**  Woman's hat with wide brim and large puffed-out crown, of gauze over a wire or straw foundation. Fashionable from 1783 to 1785. Inspired by balloon flight of Lunardi. Also called *Lunardi hat* and *parachute hat.*

**balloon links**   See CHAIN.

**balloon shorts**   See SHORTS.

**balloon skirt**  Full puffed skirt, narrower at hem than at hips, similar to BUBBLE SKIRT and TULIP SKIRT. See SKIRTS.

**balloon sleeve**   See SLEEVES.

**ballpoint embroidery**   See LIQUID EMBROI-DERY under EMBROIDERIES.

**ballroom neckcloth**  Man's pleated, starched evening neckcloth crossed over in front with ends secured to suspenders on either side. Fastened with an elaborate brooch in center front; worn in 1830s.

**balmacaan coat** (bal-má-can)   See COATS.

**Balmain, Pierre**   See APPENDIX/DESIGNERS.

**bal/Balmoral**   See OXFORDS.

**Balmoral**  Castle near Braemar, Aberdeenshire, Scotland, purchased by Queen Victoria

in 1852 who built another granite castle on this site using it as a fashionable retreat.

**Balmoral bodice**  Woman's dress bodice with pleated back peplum worn in the 1860s. Later called *postillion corsage.*

**Balmoral boot**  Short black boot worn by women from 1850s to 1870s with a walking dress. Made with front lacings, sometimes colored.

**Balmoral cap / bonnet**  Flat Scottish beret somewhat similar to a TAM-O-SHANTER with wide checked band around head. Usually dark blue with a red or blue pompon on top, with feather and badge of the clan on one side. Worn with *kilts* in Scotland.

**Balmoral jacket**  **1.** Woman's jacket, buttoned to neck with front and back points below waist in 1867. **2.** Woman's belted double-breasted semi-fitted jacket with lapels and small gauntlet cuffed sleeves, similar to coat of riding habit, worn c. 1870.

**Balmoral mantle**  Cloak of velvet, cashmere, or wool styled like an *Inverness cape* and popular for outdoor wear in the 1860s.

**BALMORAL PETTICOAT**

**Balmoral petticoat**  Colored petticoat, originally red with wide decorative black band mitered to form squared half frames, which projected below a looped-up outer skirt, worn in mid-1860s.

**Balmoral tartan**   See TARTANS.

**Baltic seal**  Term used in early 20th c. for rabbit fur; considered incorrect terminology since Fur Labeling Act of 1938.

**Baltic tiger**  Term used in early 20th c. for rabbit fur; considered incorrect terminology since Fur Labeling Act of 1938.

**balzo**  Woman's headdress composed of a high, stuffed turban-shaped roll of gilded leather or copper foil worn in 16th c. in Italy.

**bamberges**  Shin guards worn during Carolingian Period, mid-8th to 11th c.

**bambin/bambino hat** (bam-been)  Woman's hat with a halo-shaped brim rolling away from the face worn in the 1930s.

**band**  1. Wide, flat collar, usually linen, lace, or cambric worn by men and women in 16th and 17th c. Also called a FALLING BAND. 2. For BANDS see GENEVA BANDS. Also see NECKLINES.

**bandanna**  1. Cotton calico fabric usually *resist-printed* on red or navy-blue with black and white designs. 2. See SCARFS. 3. Silk printed square from India used as neckcloth or snuff handerchief in 18th and 19th c. 4. See PRINTS. *Der.* From Hindu *bandhnu*, a "method of tie dyeing cloth."

**bandbox**  1. 16th- and 17th-c. term for box in which collars, called BANDS were kept. In U.S. used for storage and transportation of clothing, hats, etc., during the 19th c. Bandboxes developed for use in Europe from mid-18th c. on. After Civil War declined in popularity, and by late 19th c. replaced by more utilitarian trunks, portmanteaux, and HATBOXES. 2. Hatbox, usually round, of cardboard or thin wood covered with stiff paper which in U.S. by 1820s was printed with pictorial panoramas. In Europe boxes were plainer. Both were used to carry small items as well as hats. Also see HATBOX.

**band briefs**  See PANTIES.

**bandeau**  1. Narrow piece of ribbon or fabric, sometimes decorated, worn around head as substitute for a hat. 2. Synonym for BRA. 3. See SWIMSUITS. *Der.* French, "bandage."

**bandeau d'amour**  Woman's hairstyle or wig with high slanting and hanging curls worn in 1770s and 1780s.

**bandeau slip**  Slip with top cut like a bra, similar to bra-slip *Der.* French, "bandage."

**banded agate**  See AGATE under GEMS.

**banded collar**  See COLLARS.

**banded cuff**  See CUFFS.

**banded neckline**  See NECKLINES.

**bandelet**  1. Glove term for wide hem at wrist. Also called *bord*. Also spelled *bandelette*. 2. 16th-c. term for any type of scarf.

**band-leg panties**  See BAND BRIEFS under PANTIES.

**bandle linen**  Coarse plain weave linen about 2' wide. Woven in homes in southern Ireland since 1760. Named for an Irish measure called a *bandle* which is about 2' wide.

**bandoleer**  1. Wide belt having loops to hold cartridges with one or two straps extending over shoulders. Also spelled *bandolier*. 2. Cotton sheeting woven to U.S. Army specifications for bandoleers.

**bandolier**  1. Shoulder bag carried by women of Great Plains Indian tribes. Made in pouch style and used to carry small items, *e.g.*, combs, needle and thread. 2. See BANDOLEER #1.

**bandore and peak**  Widow's black headdress with heart-shaped brim and black veil, draped in back; worn from 1700 to about 1830.

**banging chignon** (sheen-yon)  Women's hairstyle of 1770s with wide flat loop of ribbon-tied hair, hanging from crown of head to nape of neck.

**Bangkok straw**  Type of Siamese straw with smooth lightweight body similar to BAKU. Woven of buntal fibers in the Philippines. *Der.* Named for the capital of Siam. Also see BALLIBUNTL.

**bangle bracelet**  Round rigid bracelet of

metal, plastic or wood worn on the arm. See BRACELETS and WATCHES.

**bangs**   See HAIRSTYLES.

**banian/banjan**   See BANYAN.

**Banlon®**   Trademark of Joseph Bancroft & Sons Inc. for fabrics and apparel made from quality controlled man-made bulky yarns. Used for socks, sweaters, knit shirts, and dresses.

**bannockburn**   Napped twilled wool fabric, similar to cheviot, woven with a ply-yarn in warp and single yarns in filling. Used for coats and suits. Originally a tweed fabric made with two-ply yarn of different colors alternating with single yarns. *Der.* Named for Bannockburn, a village in Scotland, where the Scots, led by Robert Bruce, defeated the English in 1314.

**Banton, Travis**   See APPENDIX/DESIGNERS.

**BANYAN #1**

**banyan   1.** Loose, knee-length coat, sometimes produced in costly fabric, worn for informal occasions indoors and outdoors by 17th-c. Englishmen. **2.** Ankle-length dressing gown with pleat in center back worn by men and women in 18th and 19th c. Also spelled *banian, banjan. Der.* Named for shirt worn by "banians," a caste of Hindu merchants.

**barathea** (bar-a-thee-a)   **1.** Fabric with a pebbly texture originally a registered trademark for a silk tie fabric. Now made of silk, rayon or synthetic fabrics in broken rib weave. Used for ties. **2.** Dress fabric with silk warp and worsted filling made in rib weave. **3.** Worsted uniform fabric made with twilled effect of fine two-ply yarns.

**Bara, Theda**   American silent-film star from 1915 to 1920s, known for exotic harem costumes and jeweled headdresses. Her 1915 film *The Vampire* was the inspiration for *vampire look* and introduced of slang term "vamp" to describe a seductive woman.

**baracan   1.** Heavy warp-ribbed silk or wool waterproof fabric with a moiré appearance. **2.** A weatherproof coat or mantle of thick fabric worn in Asia, U.S.S.R., and Balkans. Made of heavy fulled wool or mixtures. Originally of camel's hair. Also spelled *barracan, berkan, bouracan, perkan, percan.*

**BARBE**

**barbe**   Long piece of white linen fabric, pleated vertically, worn encircling the chin with a black hood and long black veil by widows and mourners from 14th to 16th c.

**barber's apron**   See APRONS.

**barbette** (bar-bet)   Term used in the 13th and first half of 14th c. for the linen chin band worn pinned on the top, or sides, of the head, and worn with a small white FILLET or COVERCHIEF. Also spelled *barbet*. The BARBETTE and COVERCHIEF formed the WIMPLE in France.

**barbula** See PIQUÉ DEVANT.

**Barcelona handkerchief** Colored or black silk handkerchief made in checks or fancy designs in twill weave. Worn around neck or head, or carried in hand, in 18th and 19th c. *Der.* From Barcelona, Spain, where first made.

**Bardot, Brigitte** French movie actress who became the sex symbol of the 1950s and 1960s after the movie *And God Created Woman* (1956). Responsible for a wave of interest in tousled hairstyles, tight jeans, body sweaters, and blue and pink checked gingham little-girl dresses. Also see HAIRSTYLES.

**bar drop pin** See PINS.

**bare bra** See BRAS.

**barège** (ba-rezh) **1.** Open weave fabric used for veiling or dresses. Made in a *leno weave*, with a worsted filling and a warp of silk, cotton, or other fibers. Named for French valley of Barrèges where it was first manufactured. **2.** See BARÈGE SHAWL.

**barège shawl** (ba-rezh) A printed shawl made in France in the 1850s from fabric with worsted filling and organzine warp.

**bare look** Fashions gradually revealing more of the body popular through 1970s and 1980s. Also see TOPS and TOPLESS LOOK, under LOOKS.

**bare-midriff** Exposing the body from under the bust, baring the rib cage to the waist or hips. Also see DRESSES, LOOKS, PAJAMAS, and TOPS.

**bare top** See TOPS.

**barette** See BARRETTE #1.

**bargello stitch** See STITCHES.

**bark cloth** Category for different types of fabrics native to many countries made from fibers of the inner barks of various trees, *e.g.,* the paper mulberry tree. See TAPA CLOTH.

**bark crepe** Classification of rough-textured crepe fabrics usually made with man-made or silk fibers in the warp and wool or rayon in the filling. Used for dresses and coats.

**bark tanning** See VEGETABLE TANNAGE.

**barmecloth** Early medieval term for an apron. Gradually replaced by the word APRON after the end of the 14th c. Also called BARMHATRE.

**barmfell** Term for a leather apron from 14th to 17th c. Also called *barmskin*.

**barmhatre** See BARMECLOTH.

**barmskin** See BARMFELL.

**baronet satin** Lustrous fabric made in satin weave. Fabric popular before 1930 made with rayon warp and cotton filling which washed and draped well. Used for blouses and sportswear. Also spelled *baronette*.

**barong** Fiber obtained from the plant, *Eugenia apiculata*, in the Philippines. Used locally for twine and cordage.

**barong tagalog** See SHIRTS.

**baroque** (bar-roak) Art and decorative style in the 17th and first half of 18th c., characterized by heavy ornate curves and excessive ornamentation. Term is applied to certain jewelry and embroidery designs.

**baroque pearl** See PEARLS under BEADS and GEMS.

**barouche coat** (bar-roosh) Woman's tight-fitting three-quarter-length outdoor coat with full sleeves, fastened in front with gold barrel-shaped snaps and an elastic-type belt with buckle worn in 1809.

**bar pin** See PINS.

**barracan** See BARACAN.

**barré** (ba-ray) **1.** Defect in woven fabric consisting of differences in warps or filling as to color or texture. Also spelled *barry*. **2.** French adjective for fabrics or knits with horizontal stripes in two or more colors. Used for neckwear.

**barred buttonhole**   See BUTTONHOLES.

**barrel**   Cylindrical-shaped object. See CUFFS, CURLS, HANDBAGS, and SLEEVES.

**barrel hose**   BOMBASTED TRUNK HOSE, cut very full and stuffed with horsehair, worn from 1570 to 1620. Compare with BOMBAST and GALLIGASKINS.

**barrel knot tie**   See OSBALDISTON TIE.

**barrel-shaped muff**   Large muff made of or trimmed in fur, sometimes concealing arms to elbows. Illustrated in paintings such as *Madame Moie Raymond* by Lebrun and *Mrs. Siddons* by Gainsborough.

**barrel sleeve**   See SLEEVES.

**barrel-snaps**   Tubular-shaped gilded-metal fasteners, used for cloaks and pelisses from 1800 to 1830. Also see BAROUCHE COAT.

**barrette** (ba-ret)   **1.** Clip worn in the hair. May be small and worn one on either side of head, or larger and worn in back or at nape of the neck. Made of plastic or metal in various shapes, *e.g.*, bar or bow knot. *Der.* French, diminutive of *barre*, "bar." Also spelled *barret, barette*. **2.** Brimless hat with round flat top worn by Jewish men and boys. Clement VII on June 13, 1525, ordered all Jews to wear a yellow *barrette*. Later revoked, but Pope Paul IV in 1555 ordered all Jews to wear a green *barrette*. Same style worn for synagogue dress until early 19th c. by Jewish men. Also spelled *beret*. **3.** See BIRETTA #2.

**barrister's wig**   White wig with smooth top and sausage curls over ears, a small pigtail tied with ribbon in back, worn by British trial lawyers.

**barrow**   **1.** A small piece of flannel wrapped around a baby's body which covered the feet in the 19th c. **2.** Layette item of early 1900s used

**BARROW COAT #2, 1916**

to describe a long wraparound petticoat with wide band under infant's arms. Worn with hem pinned up with big safety pins. Also called PINNING BLANKET or BARROW COAT.

**barry**   See BARRÉ.

**Barrymore collar**   See COLLARS.

**bascinet**   See BASINET.

**bas de chausses**   Term used about 1550 for lower part of *chausses* when they were made in two pieces. *Der.* French, "bottom of hose." Also see LOWER STOCKS.

**base**   **1.** Lower portion of a *brilliant-cut* stone. Also see GIRDLE #3, gem cuts, and PAVILION. **2.** See TONLET.

**baseball**   Clothes adopted for general wear by the public influenced by American sport of baseball. See CAPS, KNIT SHIRTS, and SPORT JACKETS.

**baselard**   See BASLARD.

**base coat**   Man's jacket or *jerkin* with short sleeves, square neckline, with skirts, or BASES, hanging in tubular unpressed pleats to just above the knees; worn from 1490 to 1540.

**bases**   **1.** Man's separate skirt which hung in unpressed tubular pleats worn with the padded doublet or armor from about 1490 to 1540. When worn as armor sometimes made of steel. **2.** Skirt of a jacket or *jerkin*, hanging in unpressed pleats. Also see BASE COAT.

**basic dress** See DRESSES.

**basinet** Pointed steel helmet worn as armor from 1350 to 1450. Also spelled *bascinet, bacinet, basnet.*

**basket** Woman's hat resembling a wicker basket, 1½′ high; worn in second half of 16th c.

**basket bag** See HANDBAGS.

**basketball shoe** See SHOES.

**basket button** Fashionable metal button in embossed basket weave pattern, used on men's coats in 18th and 19th c.

**basket stitch** See STITCHES.

**basket weave** Variation of plain weave, made by weaving two or more fillings over and under same number of warps to produce checkerboard effect. Used for OXFORD CLOTH. Also see STITCHES.

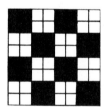

**BASKET WEAVE**

**baslard** A saber, large sword, or ornamental dagger of the Middle Ages. Also spelled *baselard.*

**basnet** See BASINET.

**basque** (bask) **1.** In the 17th c. term originally referred to part of a man's doublet extending below the waist made with a series of vertical slashes forming tabs. **2.** By mid-19th c. term was extended to mean any woman's bodice that extended below the waistline. **3.** In the early 20th c. term referred to a woman's waist-length jacket or dress that fits tightly through waist and rib cage.

**basque beret** (bask be-ray) Round, flat, soft woolen cap worn by Basque peasants who in-habit the western Pyrenees region of France and Spain. The forerunner of the BERET.

**basque-habit** Bodice with square-cut tabs below the waistline worn from 1860s on.

**basque waistband** Belt or waistband decorated with five pointed tabs worn on afternoon dresses by women in latter half of 19th c.

**basquina** (bas-keen-a) See BASQUINE #3.

**basquin body** Woman's daytime bodice of 1850s extending below the waistline with no waistline seam.

**basquine** (bas-keen) **1.** Woman's coat with PAGODA SLEEVES, fringed trimming and long BASQUE worn in 1857. **2.** Outdoor jacket worn in 1860s. Also spelled *basquin, vasquine.* **3.** Wide underskirt of rich fabric held out by hoops worn in 16th c. Also called *basquina* in Spain.

**Bass Weejuns®** See SHOES.

**bast** Woody vegetable fibers including FLAX, RAMIE, HEMP, and JUTE, processed by retting from inner bark of *dicotyledonous* plants.

**baste** To stitch fabrics together either by hand or with large machine stitches to hold in place prior to sewing final seams. After stitching, bastings are removed.

**basting stitch** See STITCHES.

**bateau neckline** (ba-toe) See NECKLINES.

**bathing cap** See CAPS.

**bathing slipper** Woman's flat fabric shoe, sometimes laced up leg similar to ballet slipper, worn while swimming and popular in late 19th c. After 1920s similar shoes without lacing, frequently of rubber, were worn on beach and in water.

**bathing suit** **Women:** Innovation of about 1865 consisting of knee-length dress and ankle-length pants in woven fabric. By 1880 combination suits made in one piece with top, pants, and skirt. By mid 1920s ANNETTE KELLERMAN SUIT accepted for beach. From then until about

1940 all bathing suits were made of knitted fabrics, preferably wool jersey. By 1920s TANK-TOP suits were introduced. By late 1930s two-piece suits and rubber bathing suits were worn. In 1940s DRESSMAKER-TYPE suits of woven fabric were worn. The BIKINI was first worn at Mediterranean resorts in the 1940s. **Men:** At turn of century one-piece striped jersey suit with knee-length legs, sometimes short-sleeved, worn for swimming. By 1920s men wore navy-blue wool shorts or trunks and white wool knitted tank tops with CRAB BACK. By 1930s men did not wear tops, just trunks. For individual styles see SWIMSUITS.

**bathrobe**    See DRESSES and ROBES.

**bathrobe cloth**    Heavyweight fabric which has been heavily napped to give it a soft fuzzy hand. Constructed with the *backed cloth method*, it has two lightly twisted cotton filling yarns and one warp which is highly twisted. Usually printed in different colors on each side so that it appears to be a woven *double cloth fabric*. Used for bathrobes for men, women, and children. Also called *blanket cloth*.

**batik** (bah-teek)    **1.** Method of dyeing fabric by drawing the design on silk or cotton, then covering with hot wax all areas which are to remain white, dyeing, and removing wax—resulting in a pattern with a crackled effect; process originated in Indonesia. **2.** See PRINTS.

**bating**    Term for processing of skins and hides to reveal grain of leather after hair has been removed.

**batiste** (bah-teest)    **1.** Fine, soft, lightweight cotton fabric of high quality, combed mercerized yarns in plain weave. May be bleached or printed; used for dresses and men's shirts. **2.** A similar fabric made of cotton and man-made blends which resists wrinkles and requires little ironing. Used for dresses and men's shirts. **3.** A smooth sheer wool fabric similar to NUN'S VEILING and lighter in weight than CHALLIS. **4.** Plain or figured sheer silk fabric similar to MULL. **5.** Spun rayon fabric used for dresses and blouses. *Der.* First made by Jean Baptiste, a weaver in Cambrai, France, in 1300. Also see CORSET BATISTE.

**batswing tie**    Man's bow tie cut with wide flaring ends, worn in late 1896.

**batt**    Heavy laced low shoe used for country wear in England in 17th c., sent to New England Colonists in 1630s.

**battant l'oeil** (bah-tan loy)    Woman's cap, worn in 1770s, with sides projecting forward over temples, eyes, and cheeks in exaggerated fashion.

**Battenberg jacket**    Woman's loose-fitting outdoor jacket with large buttons and a turned-down collar worn in 1880s.

**Battenberg lace**    See LACES.

**battening**    Weaving term for the pushing of each filling yarn, shot through by the shuttle, tight against the finished cloth on the loom.

**batter**    Baseball term for the player "up at bat." See CAPS and HELMETS.

**batting**    Matted sheets of fibers used in quilting or stuffing, may be cotton, wool, kapok, spun rayon, or fiberfill.

**battle jacket**    See SPORT JACKETS.

**battlements**    Trimming consisting of square-cut tabs used in same manner as scallops on dresses, skirts, jackets, and basques in the 19th c.

**batwing sleeve**    See SLEEVES.

**baudekin/baudekyn**    See BALDACHIN.

**baum marten**    See FURS.

**bautte/bautta** (bah-oot)    Black cloth wrap of 18th c. with hood that could be drawn down over face to form a half mask.

**Bavarian dress**    Woman's carriage dress trimmed with bands of fabric down the front worn in 1820s.

**Bavarian lace**    See LACES.

**bave** See RAW SILK.

**bavolet** (ba-vo-lay) **1.** A veil, or *curtain*, at back of woman's bonnet to shade the neck worn from 1830 on. **2.** Plain cap worn by French peasant women.

**bayadère** (by-yah-deer) Long narrow scarf of silk or lace worn in early 19th c. *Der.* Costume of Indian *bayadère* or "dancing girl."

**bayadère stripe** **1.** Term used in 1850s for flat velvet trimming used either woven in or applied to dresses. **2.** Name of fabric which has brilliant contrasting horizontal stripes. **3.** See STRIPES. *Der.* Costume of Indian *bayadère* or "dancing girl."

**bayeta** Scarlet-colored American Indian blanket, made of Spanish baize fabric, in which Navajo Indians of New Mexico buried their dead.

**Beach cloth®** Trademark of Burlington Industries, G.S. Division, for men's, women's, and children's outergarments. Also a summer suiting fabric made of wool, mohair, or man-made fibers in variety of patterns. Trademark is registered in thirty foreign countries.

**beach coat** See ROBES.

**beach pajamas** Full-length culottes often made of printed fabric worn sometimes with matching bolero as sportswear in 1920s and 1930s, revived in 1970s.

**beach toga** See ROBES.

**beachwear** Items of apparel or accessories specifically for use at the beach. See DRESSES, HATS, PONCHOS, ROBES, SWIMSUITS, and WIGS.

**beach wrapup** See ROBES.

**bead** **1.** A piece of glass, plastic, wood, crystal, gem, or other material bored through the center and strung on leather, cord, thread or chain to wear as necklace, bracelet, anklet, headband, or used for embroidery. Usually round but may be cylindrical, square, disc-shaped, pendant-shaped, oblong, etc. **2.** A string of beads, synonym for necklace, made and worn since earliest recorded history. Egyptians used carved beads of lapis lazuli, amethyst, feldspar, and agate. Romans wore ropes of pearls. Manufacture of glass beads started in Venice in 14th c. Also see NECKLACES BEADED BAG under HANDBAGS, and BEADED SWEATER under SWEATERS.

## BEADS

**American Indian b.** **1.** Tiny opaque beads of various colors used to make necklaces and belts. Also used for embroidery on moccasins, headbands, belts, and other American Indian clothes. **2.** Shell beads used by Native American Indians in 16th c. as money and called *wampum*. The amount of trimming on garments indicated wealth of individual. Also see NECKLACES.

**aurora borealis crystal** (aw-ror-a bore-e-al-is) Glass beads coated with solution causing them to reflect rainbow colors.

**Austrian crystal** Lead crystal made with 32% lead oxide, faceted and polished to give full spectrum light reflection in sunlight or artificial light. Usually colorless but may be coated on back to reflect a color, *e.g.*, red or blue (or both colors if coated on both sides). Made in village of Innsbruck, Austria.

**baby b.** Tiny beads with letters on them. Originally used in hospitals to spell out the name of the newborn child on a bracelet. Now used for personalized bracelets, barrettes, and necklaces.

**baroque pearls** (ba-rok) Pearls of an irregular shape, as opposed to round smooth pearls—

may be *simulated,* *cultured,* or *genuine Oriental*—prized for shape, color, and luster. Color often blue-gray or off-white. Also see GEMS.

**beggerbeads**   Hand-carved ornamental gemstones in elongated shape strung on necklace between gold beads. Stones include *moss agates, green jaspers, bloodstones, brown* or *orange carnelians,* and other non-precious stones. Originally worn in India for good luck.

**bubble b.**   Oversized spherical beads, often hollow, popular for choker necklaces in 1950s and revived in mid-1960s.

**bugle b.**   Long tubular-shaped glass beads, often black, white, or silver, popular for trimming dresses from last half of 19th c. to present.

**crystal b.**   Beads carved out of genuine transparent quartz. Popular from late 19th c. to about 1930s. Not used today because of the expense of making them. Glass is usually substituted for genuine crystal.

**cultured pearls**   Pearls produced by oysters artificially implanted with tiny pieces of mother-of-pearl—first sold in 1921. Also see PEARL under GEMS.

**cut-steel b.**   Tiny faceted steel or other metal beads, similar in appearance to marcasite, popular in last half of the 19th and early 20th c.

**freshwater pearls**   Natural pearls from mussels whose habitat is rivers of the U.S. Chalk white in color and not as lustrous as Oriental pearls.

**genuine pearls**   **1.** Pearls secured from saltwater oysters which have made a deposit over a grain of sand. Very expensive and rare as they must be matched in color and size. **2.** Used by Romans in ropes and extensively from late 16th to 17th c. by both Queen Elizabeth I of England and Marie de Medici, Queen of France. See FRESHWATER, ORIENTAL, and SEED PEARLS.

**gold b.**   **1.** 14K gold beads sometimes purchased one at a time and added to chain for

necklace. **2.** Beads plated with gold. **3.** Costume jewelry with different bases and gilt finishes.

**hippie b.**   Beads adopted by *hippies,* an avant-garde group of young people in the U.S. in the mid-1960s. Usually small beads worn chest length by both sexes. Influenced conventional men to adopt the fashion of wearing chains or medallion necklaces.

**imitation pearls**   See SIMULATED PEARLS.

**jet b.**   Genuine beads made from a very hard coal which takes a high polish. Most black beads sold are not genuine but plastic or glass. Also see JET under GEMS.

**LAMPSHADE BEADS**

**lampshade b.**   Short lengths of tiny strung beads, hung in a fringe from a ribbon tied close to neck, worn in early 1970s. *Der.* Beaded fringe on lampshades popular in late Victorian era and 1920s.

**love b.**   Carryover of the *hippie beads* by another avant-garde 1960s group known as the "flower children." Some love beads were made of wood.

**Oriental pearls**   Highly prized natural pearls from Japan, the Pacific Islands, the Persian Gulf, Australia, Venezuela, and Panama. The most beautiful and expensive of all pearls. Also see GEMS category.

**pearl b.** See CULTURED, FRESHWATER, SEED, ORIENTAL, SIMULATED, and GENUINE PEARLS. Also see PEARLS under GEMS.

**rosary** String of beads arranged on a chain with a pendant cross. Used by Roman Catholics for counting the prayers of the Rosary.

**seed-pearls** Tiny genuine or simulated pearls of irregular shapes. Formerly used in necklaces, now used primarily for embroidery on sweaters or wedding dresses.

**simulated-pearls** Beads made with plastic or glass base and coated with solution called *pearl essence*. Made from an adhesive combined with fish scales giving an iridescent luster similar to natural pearls.

**worry b.** Short string of beads, often made of semiprecious stones. Originally carried in hand to fidget with by men in Middle Eastern countries, Greece, and Turkey. Popular in America in late 1960s. *Der.* From string of 33 beads used to count the 99 names of Allah during prayers in Moslem countries.

---

**beaded velvet** See CUT VELVET.

**beading** **1.** Term used for embroidery in which beads of various kinds are sewn onto blouses, dresses, handbags, wedding dresses, sweaters, or blouses. **2.** Term used in late 19th and early 20th c. for narrow slotted lace, or embroidered bands, through which ribbon was pulled.

**beanie** See CAPS.

**beard** Hair on man's face permitted to grow, sometimes trimmed and shaped around the jaw and chin, fashionable throughout 19th c., and late 1960s on. By 1980 some very full beards with moustaches and sideburns worn by men of all ages. Also see BODKIN BEARD, VANDYKE #5, PIQUÉ DEVANT, and GOATEE.

**beard box** Early American device made of pasteboard, worn at night over beard to keep its shape.

**beard brush** Term used for small brush used in public to comb the beard; popular during the first half of 17th c.

**bearer** A padded roll, similar to a BUSTLE, worn under back of skirt by women from second half of 17th and early 18th c.

**bear paw** See SABATON.

**bearskin** **1.** See CAPS. **2.** Pelt of the bear.

**Beatles** Avant-garde rock-music group from Liverpool, England, who became very popular in early 1960s: George Harrison, John Lennon, Paul McCartney, and Ringo Starr. They appeared in MOD clothing, and long hairstyles that started a trend for young people in England, U.S., and throughout the world. Also see BOOTS, HAIRSTYLES, and LENNON SPECS under GLASSES.

**Beaton, Sir Cecil** (1904–1980) Beaton was born in England. He began as an illustrator for *Vogue* magazine in 1928 creating drawings of clothes worn at society parties as well as caricatures of well-known English actresses. As a photographer did both fashion and portraiture photos, becoming favorite of the British royal family. During World War II photographed in North Africa, Burma and China for Ministry of Information. He designed scenery and costumes for ballet, opera, and theater productions in both London and New York. Beaton designed the costumes for stage productions of *My Fair Lady* and the film *Gigi*. Queen Elizabeth II knighted him in 1972.

**beau** (pl. beaux) Term used from 1680s to mid-19th c. for a gentleman who was fastidious about his clothes and accessories, similar to but not as effeminate as a *fop*. Also see DANDY.

**Beau Brummell** See BRUMMELL, BEAU.

**Beaufort coat** Man's suit jacket of 1880s

with single-breasted, four-button closing, narrow straight sleeves, and seams often double-stitched. Also called *jumper coat*.

**Beaulard**   See APPENDIX/DESIGNERS.

**beau monde** (bow mond) French term meaning the "world of fashion"; literally, "the beautiful world."

**Beautiful People**   Term coined by writer Rebecca Warfield in *Vogue* magazine in 1962 to describe rich and fashionable people.

**beauty spot**   Mark on the face either natural, such as small mole, or artificial drawing attention to a good feature. Also see PATCH #3.

**Beauvais embroidery**   See EMBROIDERIES.

**beaux**   Plural of BEAU.

**beaver**   See FURS.

**beaver cloth**   See IMITATION BEAVER CLOTH.

**beaverette**   Term used in the early 20th c. for rabbit fur; considered incorrect since Fur Labeling Act of 1938.

**beaver hat**   **1.** Hat worn from 14th c. by men and women. Originally made of beaver skins, later with beaver-hair nap felted over wool and rabbit hair base. Also called a *castor*. Also see CODOVEC. **2.** Man's tall hat made of silk in imitation of beaver fur, fashionable in 17th and 18th c. In the 19th c. called SILK HAT, OPERA HAT, and TOP HAT.

**bebe bonnet**   Tiny outdoor bonnet of 1877 trimmed with ribbons, flowers, and tulle worn with brim turned up showing a cap underneath.

**bebop cap**   See NEWSBOY CAP under CAPS.

**becca**   Long strip of fabric hanging forward from the BERRETINO, sometimes worn slung over the shoulders. Very popular in the reign of Henry VI of England.

**Bedford cord**   Heavyweight cotton fabric characterized by heavy warpwise cords or stripes. The heavy ribs are made by heavy yarns

used as backing or stuffer yarns. Carded single- or two-ply yarns are used in face of fabric. Popular for women's and men's summer suits where word is shortened to *cord*. Also made in a variety of a man-made fibers or knitted, called *cord knit*. Lighter weights called *warp piqué*.

**bedgown**   Dressing gown with loose sleeves worn only in bedrooms by men and women in 18th c.

**bed'iya**   North African vest worn over the shirt, and under the GHLILA.

**bed jacket**   See ROBES.

**bedroom slipper**   See SLIPPERS.

**bed socks**   See SOCKS.

**BEEFEATER'S UNIFORM**

**beefeater's uniform**   Tudor-period uniform consisting of knee-length red doublet, elaborately trimmed with gold and black with white ruff at neck, red trunk hose; red stockings with garters below knees; black hat with soft, high crown flared slightly at top, pleated into headband with narrow brim; and black shoes trimmed with rosettes. Worn since 1485 by Yeoman of the Guard of the royal household in England, appointed by Henry VII. Same costume worn today by Yeoman Extraordinary of the Guard, appointed Wardens of the Tower of London by Edward VI. *Der.* From about the middle of the 17th c. alluding to British fondness for roast beef. Also see HATS.

**beehive hairstyle** See HAIRSTYLES.

**beehive hat** **1.** Woman's hat with large bubble-shaped crown and narrow brim trimmed with ribbon tied under chin; worn in 1770s and 1780s. Also called *hive bonnet.* **2.** Same style decorated to look like a beehive and fashionable about 1910.

**Beene, Geoffrey** See APPENDIX/DESIGNERS.

**beer jacket** Short, boxy cotton jacket with patch pockets and brass buttons originally worn by upper classmen at Princeton University in 1930s, and copied by other students.

**beetling** Pounding or hammering of fabrics made of round linen or cotton yarns to make yarns flatter and increase luster.

**beggarbeads** See BEADS.

**beggar's lace** See TORCHON LACE under LACES.

**beguin** Early 16th c. headdress made from stiffened rectangle of white linen creased in center over the forehead and draped to form a heart-shaped opening for the face. The back was caught together at nape of neck and remainder was folded symmetrically to form a wide streamer which hung from top of head down the back. *Der.* French, *beguine,* "nun." Also called a *Flemish hood.*

**beige** **1.** Tan or natural color. **2.** Term for cloth as it comes from the loom in the undyed or greige (gray) state. **3.** Serge fabric of natural, black, brown, or gray wool made in Poitou, France. **4.** Wool vicuna cloth used in England in the late 19th c. *Der.* French, *beige,* "natural colored."

**Belcher handkerchief** Blue neckerchief with large white polka dots, each centered with a dark blue eye; worn by men in first half of 19th c. *Der.* Named for Jim Belcher, a fighter during English Regency Period who originated style—other neckwear of the era was very formal.

**belette** Term used for an ornament or jewel from the 13th to 16th c. Also spelled *bilett.*

**Belgian lace** See LACES.

**BELGRAVE SHOE**

**Belgrave shoe** Woman's evening shoe cut like a PUMP, but coming up high in the back, fastened in front with gillie lacings; worn in 1870s.

**bell** Circular cape used as traveling cloak, sometimes hooded, sometimes with side and back vents; worn by men and women from late 13th to early 15th c.

**bell-bottom heel** See HEELS.

**bell-bottom trousers** Also called *bell-bottoms.* See PANTS.

**bellboy** Term used for a hotel employee who wears distinctive uniform consisting of waist-length red jacket with high Chinese collar closing diagonally, trimmed with gold braid and buttons, and small red pillbox hat. Also called *bellhop.* See CAPS and JACKETS.

**bell hoop** Dome-shaped hoop-skirt petticoat popular in England from about 1710 to 1780. Also called *cupola coat.*

**bellied-doublet** See PEASCOD-BELLIED DOUBLET.

**bellows pocket** See POCKETS.

**bellows sleeve** Full sleeve, gathered into cuff at wrist, with vertical slit from upper arm to below elbow; could be worn as short hanging sleeve in 14th and 15th c.

**bellows tongue**  Shoe tongue stitched to sides of vamp of shoe and pleated so it expands across instep.

**bell skirt**  **1.** Woman's full skirt with front fitted by darts rather than gores. Sometimes with two buttoned openings rather than back placket, the hem stiffened with muslin. Popular in 1891. **2.** See SKIRTS.

**bell sleeve**  See SLEEVES.

**bell umbrella**  Dome-shaped umbrella of transparent plastic, or of fabric with a plastic window, deeper than most umbrellas to protect the face. Also called a *bell-shaped umbrella* or a *dome umbrella*.

**belly-chete**  16th-c. slang term for apron.

**belly piece**  Stiffened triangular ridge down front of man's doublet lined with buckram, pasteboard, or whalebone; worn from 1620 to 1660s.

**belt**  **1.** Decorative or functional item worn circling above, below, or at the natural waistline. Also worn over the shoulder in military fashion. May be made of fabric, leather, chain, etc. Also called a *girdle*. **2.** Early belts of Greeks and Romans were mostly of sash type. **3.** In Middle Ages with fitted garments, belts became important and a woman's wealth could be determined by the richness of her linked, elaborately jeweled belt. Also see BELT BAG under HANDBAGS. In alphabetical listing see DIP BELT, MARGUERITE GIRDLE, and SWISS BELT.

## BELTS

**American Indian b.**  Leather belt decorated with woven American Indian beadwork in bright colors and motifs.

**bikini chain b.**  Fine gold chain worn with bikini or hip-hugger pants. Introduced in late 1960s.

**black b.**  See JUDO BELT.

**braided b.**  Belt made by plaiting narrow strips of leather, vinyl, elastic, thong, or fabric that may buckle or tie.

**brown b.**  See JUDO BELT.

**cartridge belt**  **1.** Webbed or leather belt worn by armed forces and law enforcement officers with individual spaces for ammunition, usually has an attached holster for gun. **2.** Fashion fad with no holster which holds a row of fake bullet cartridges.

**chain b.**  Belt made of various sizes of chain. May be a single chain or a series of chains looped to medallions or imitation jewels at intervals.

**cinch b.**  Wide belt worn pulled tight, usually of elastic or fabric, either laced or clasped in front, popular in 1940s and 1950s.

**cincture**  (sink-cher)  **1.** Twisted rayon, silk, or rope belt—approximately eight feet in length—worn by clergy with the *alb*. It is worn doubled, with one end pulled through the loop and the long ends hanging free. When it has tassels on the end, called *traditional* when knotted at end, called *contemporary*. **2.** Synonym for belt. *Der.* Latin, *cinctur*, "a girdle."

**contour b.**  Curving belt shaped to the body, wider in front or back; first popularized in 1890s. See DIP BELT in alphabetical listing.

**corselet b.**  Wide belt, sometimes enclosing the rib cage, frequently laced up front in manner similar to peasant's bodice. See SWISS BELT in alphabetical listing.

**cowboy b.**  Wide leather belt, sometimes with tooled designs, worn at top of hipbone by frontier cowboy to hold gun holster. Adapted for women's and men's sportswear.

**cummerbund** Wide fabric belt, sometimes pleated lengthwise and fastened in back. Worn with men's semiformal dinner suit, also worn by women. Copied from wrapped cloth belts worn in Eastern countries. *Der. kamarband,* "loinband." Also see alphabetical listing.

**D-ring b.** A narrow belt closed by pulling the end through two D-shaped rings.

**gaucho b.** (gow-cho) Belt made of medallions of leather and metal joined with chain; introduced in late 1960s. *Der.* Spanish, "cowboy of South America."

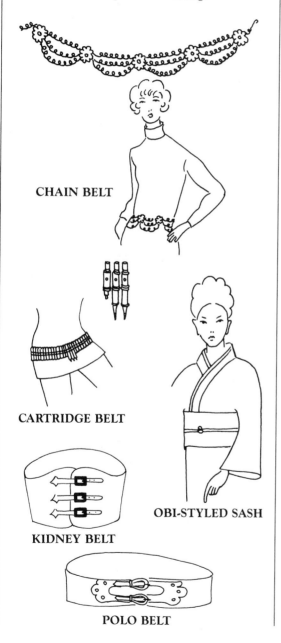

**CHAIN BELT**

**CARTRIDGE BELT**

**KIDNEY BELT**

**OBI-STYLED SASH**

**POLO BELT**

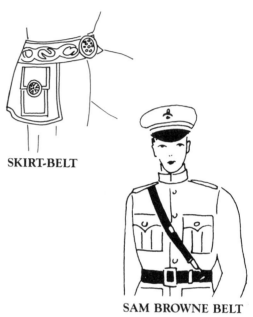

**SKIRT-BELT**

**SAM BROWNE BELT**

**PELT-BELT®**

**Greek b.**   Long narrow sash that crosses over chest and winds around waist, a fashion innovation of the 1960s copied from sash worn in ancient Greece. Also called *cross-girdling*.

**half b.**   Belt which does not extend around the entire waistline. It may be used in the back only. Also see MARTINGALE BELT.

**judo b.**   Belt worn with *judo clothes*; *black* denoting highest achievement in the sport, *brown* indicating intermediary, and *white* worn by novices.

**kidney b.**   Extremely wide belt similar to a POLO BELT worn when motorcycling to prevent injury.

**martingale b.**   Half belt worn on back of garment above or below normal waistline. *Der.* Part of horse's harness designed to hold head down. Also see HALF BELT.

**mesh b.**   Belt made of extremely small metal links fastened together to form a flexible fabric-like band.

**money b.**   Belt worn under or over clothing when traveling with hidden zippered compartment for money.

**monk's b.**   **1.** Same as CINCTURE. **2.** Fashion belt of cincture-type made of rope, braided rayon, or nylon with tassels on the ends.

**obi-styled sash**   Sash that is approximately 4 to 5 inches wide at the center and tapers to 1 to 1½ inch at the ends. It is worn wrapped around the waist twice and tied with the ends hanging down the front. The tapered ends may be of contrasting colors or fabrics. Although it is a single piece of fabric, it gives the appearance of a double sash. Adapted in 1980s from the original *obi* worn by Japanese women. Also see OBI in alphabetical listing.

**Pelt-Belt®**   Featherweight jacket which folds to three inch-wide belt and can be fastened around waist as emergency protection against weather. Introduced in 1968.

**polo b.**   Wide leather belt covering rib cage fastening in front with three small buckles on narrow leather straps. Originally worn by polo players for protection. Also see KIDNEY BELT.

**safari b.**   Wide belt with attached flap pockets in front.

**Sam Browne b.**   Belt worn around waist with extension strap over right shoulder worn by U.S. Army officers, guards, and some policemen. *Der.* From British general, Sir Samuel Browne, who having lost his left arm, couldn't support his sword without this special belt.

**sash**   Any belt of soft material that loops over and ties in a knot or bow rather than buckling.

**self-covered b.**   Any belt cut out of the same fabric as garment usually stiffened with a liner. Available in kits for the home sewer. If tied, it is called a *self sash*.

**serpentine b.**   Belt made in wavy design, zigzagging around the body.

**shoulder b.**   **1.** Sword belt worn diagonally from right shoulder to left hip by men in 17th c., formerly called BALDRICK. **2.** Belt which is worn diagonally over the shoulder rather than around the waist, *e.g.* SAM BROWNE belt.

**skirt-b.**   Belt with attached peplum forming a short skirt. Introduced in late 1960s to wear over jumpsuits, body stockings, and pants.

**spaghetti sash**   A sash made of a long narrow piece of fabric, with cording inserted as filler to give a rounded effect, sometimes knotted at the ends.

**surcingle b.**   A webbed belt woven in plain or striped fabric fastened with a metal buckle through which a harness leather tab is pulled. Sometimes has a zippered pocket for money. *Der.* From the girth that fastens a horse's saddle or blanket.

**thong b.**   **1.** Wide leather belt with eyelets at each end through which a piece of rawhide is laced. **2.** Belt made of braided rawhide.

**tooled leather b.** **1.** Handmade leather belt of various widths embossed with various motifs. May be purchased in kits. **2.** Belts imitating the above, stamped out by machine, sometimes imported from Mexico and Central America. **3.** Belts from India in intricate designs that are inked in various colors.

**webbed b.** Belt of heavy canvas webbing, usually wide and fastened with a clip buckle, worn by military. Used in a narrower width on bathing suits in the 1920s. Adapted for casual wear by men and women in various widths and colors from 1960 on.

**weight b.** **1.** Belt of nylon webbing fitted with approximately twelve pound weights. Used for scuba diving and underwater swimming, extra weights may be added. **2.** Wide leather-textured vinyl or fabric belt with eight to ten pound weights worn under or over clothing as a reducing aid or figure improver.

**white b.** See JUDO BELT.

---

**belt buckle** Any ornamental or functional device, usually plastic or metal, used to fasten a belt. See BUCKLE.

**beluque** Woman's cape or mantle worn in the 15th c.

**Ben Casey** Television series of the 1950s portraying a physician. As a result of its popularity, the *Ben Casey collar* and the *Ben Casey shirt* were copied for general use. See MEDIC SHIRT and MEDIC COLLAR.

**bench coat** See BENCHWARMER under SPORT JACKETS.

**benchwarmer** See SPORT JACKETS.

**bench wig** Tightly curled wig with flaps that hang down over the ears. Worn by British judges when they sit on the "bench."

**bend** **1.** Leather term for the best section of leather cut from a whole hide. **2.** Term used from 11th to end of 15th c. for band of fabric on a dress, fillet for hair, or a hat band. **3.** Synonym for stripe in Middle Ages.

**Ben Franklin glasses** See GLASSES.

**bengaline** Heavyweight lustrous fabric characterized by corded effect in the filling. Cord yarns or several filling yarns are used to give rib effect. Warp yarns are finer and cover the filling completely. Made in many combinations of fibers, *e.g.*, wool warp with cotton filling, rayon or silk warp with cotton filling, etc. Frequently dyed black and used for dressy suits, coats, millinery, and ribbons.

**benjamin** Overcoat worn by working men in the 19th c. Also called *benny*. Also see LILY BENJAMIN.

**benjy** **1.** British slang term used in the 19th c. for a man's waistcoat or vest. **2.** British slang term for straw hat with a wide brim.

**benny** See BENJAMIN.

**BENOITON COIFFURE**

**Benoiton coiffure** Women's elaborate coiffure of 1866 with hair parted in center, smooth on top, chignon and curls in back. Three gold chains were worn over the top of the head and hung in dangling loops under the chin; sometimes garlands of flowers were used instead of chains. *Der.* Named after *La Famille Benoiton*, a play by Victorien Sardou, 1865.

**berdash** See BURDASH.

**beret** **1.** A flat tam made of wool. See CAPS. **2.** A cap with a large flat halo crown with elaborate trim, worn from the 1820s to the 1840s. Also see BASQUE BERET. **3.** See BARRETTE #2.

**beret sleeve** See SLEEVES.

**bergère hat** Woman's straw hat with low crown and a wide floppy-type brim tied under chin. Worn from 1730 to 1800, and revived in 1860s. Popularized by Marie Antoinette (1755–1793), wife of Louis XVI of France, when she played at farming on the grounds of the palace at Versailles. Also called *milkmaid hat* or *shepherdess hat. Der.* French, "shepherdess."

**berkan** See BARACAN.

**Berlin gloves** Sturdy cotton glove worn by English middleclass men from 1830 on.

**Berlin work** See EMBROIDERIES.

**Berlin yarn** Worsted knitting or embroidery yarn from Germany. Also called *Berlin wool* or *German wool.*

**Bermuda collar** See COLLARS.

**Bermuda shorts** See SHORTS.

**Bernhardt mantle** Woman's short outdoor cape with loose front and DOLMAN or SLING SLEEVES: worn in 1886. *Der.* Named after SARAH BERNHARDT.

**Bernhardt, Sarah** (burn-hart) Famous French actress (1845–1923) known as the "Divine Sarah," whose elaborate costumes, hairstyles, and jewels influenced fashion in Europe and U.S. in late 19th c.; credited with FRENCH GIGOT SLEEVE, MOUSQUETAIRE GLOVE, BERNHARDT SLEEVE and MANTLE.

**Bernhardt sleeve** Long, fitted sleeve made with a point extending over the hand; worn in the latter part of 19th c. *Der.* Named for SARAH BERNHARDT.

**bernos** See BURNOOSE.

**berretino** See ROUNDLET #1.

**berretta/berrette** See BIRETTA.

**bertha** Large capelike collar falling over shoulders and bodice of dress, introduced about 1839 as a lace ruffle encircling the décolleté neckline of evening dress. Fashionable in 1930s as a large cape collar, revived in 1980s. Spelled *berthe*, when first introduced.

**bertha pelerine** Lace ruffle or *bertha* worn in 1840s on low-necked dress with ends carried down center front to waist.

**Bertin, Rose** See APPENDIX/DESIGNERS.

**berundjuk** Chemise of silk worn by Turkish women for at-home wear with full trousers called SHALWAR, and a coat or jacket called a YELEK.

**beryl** See GEMS.

**besom pocket** See POCKETS.

**Bessarabian lamb** See LAMB under FURS.

**Bethlehem headdress** Truncated cone-shaped hat covered with a veil, decorated with rows of dangling coins or jewels across forehead; worn by Moslem women in ancient times, copied in 1930s. Also see SHATWEH.

**betrothal ring** 16th-c. ring, broken in half after wedding ceremony and halves given to bride and groom.

**Betsie ruff** Small ruff worn around the neck with high or low neckline in late Empire period.

**beutanol** (bew-ta-not) Vinyl plastic-coated fabric made of lawn. Dyed, then treated with five coats of vinyl plastic which makes it waterproof, flameproof, and dustproof. Used for raincoats.

**bevel** Slanted cut on gemstone, to give light reflection, especially on square-cut gemstones.

**Bewdley cap** MONMOUTH CAP made at Bewdley, Worcester, England. Worn by country folk from 1570 to 19th c.

**bezel** (behz-el) Upper faceted portion of a brilliant-cut gem such as diamond. Same as *crown*.

**biarritz gloves** See GLOVES.

**bias** (by-as) A line diagonally across grain of fabric. See BIAS CUT, DRESSES, PLEATS, SKIRTS, and SLIPS. *Der.* Term used since medieval times. Also spelled *byesse*.

**BIAS BINDING**

**bias binding** Narrow strips of fabric cut on the bias, thus pliable for use in covering raw edges of curved necklines and armholes, or used as trimming. May be either hand-cut or sold in packages.

**bias cut** Manner of cutting diagonally across grain of fabric, resulting in a garment that clings and follows body curves closely. French couturiere VIONNET, was famous for bias cut dresses in 1920s and 1930s. *Der.* Term used since medieval times, when used for hose to obtain a close fit. Also spelled *byesse*.

**biaz** Lightweight, white, glossy cotton fabric in plain weave. Beetled, starched, and glazed in imitation of linen. Available in three grades varying from coarse to fine in narrow widths from Russia and Central Asia.

**bib** 1. Piece of fabric, square or rounded, worn under chin and tied around neck, used to protect clothing while eating, first worn in 16th c. 2. Extra piece of cloth attached to waist of apron, pants, or skirt extending upward over chest. See APRONS, BLOUSES, JUMPERS, PANTS, SHORTS, and TOPS. 3. See COLLARS and NECKLACES.

**bib cravat** Man's wide neck piece, in shape of a bib, usually lace-edged and held on by colored cravat string at end of 17th c.

**bibi bonnet** (bee-bee bun-neh) Small woman's bonnet worn in 1830s with sides flaring upward and forward around the face and tied with lace-trimmed ribbons. Also called *English cottage bonnet*.

**bicorne hat** Man's hat of the Napoleonic era in shape of a crescent, with front and back brims pressed against each other making points on either side. Frequently trimmed with a COCKADE. *Der.* Latin, *bicornis*, "two-horned." Also spelled *bicorn*.

**bicycle** Two-wheeled device used for transportation. Also used for recreation since latter part of 19th c. Accent on "fitness sports" in 1980s increased popularity and special clothing was designed. Sometimes abbreviated to *bike*. See GLOVES, HATS, HELMETS, SPORT JACKETS, SHORTS, and BIKE SUIT under SPORT SUITS. ALSO SEE CYCLING COSTUME.

**bicycle bal** Shoe with protective toe cap and a circle stitched over ankle joint. Closed with laces extending toward the toes. Designed for bicycling in latter part of 19th c. and later adopted for other sports.

**bifocals** See GLASSES.

**big coat** See COATS.

**big easy sweater** See SWEATERS.

**biggin/biggonet** (big-in/big-on-net) 1. 16th- and 17th-c. term for woman's or child's cap similar to COIF. 2. Man's nightcap, worn from second half of 16th through 17th c. 3. Large mob cap made without chin ties, worn in early 19th c. Also spelled *biggon*. *Der.* French *beguine*, "nun."

**big look** See V-SHAPE LOOK under LOOKS.

**big regular** Men's size for pajamas, corresponding to a chest measurement of 48″ or more, and a height of 5′7″ to 5′11″.

**big shirt** See OVERSIZED SHIRT under SHIRTS. Also see BIG TEE SHIRT under KNIT SHIRTS.

**bikini** Very tiny two-piece swimsuit introduced in 1946 about the same time as the atomic bomb was tested at Bikini atoll. So called because of its "shock" effect. See PANTIES, PANTYHOSE, SWIMSUITS, and TOPS.

**bikini brief** Men's brief low-rise underwear made in all colors and styles of knit cotton or man-made yarns.

**bikini chain** See BELTS.

**bilett** See BELETTE.

**billfold** Leather folding case designed to hold paper money, sometimes also credit cards and photos, usually folding in center. Also called a WALLET.

**billicock** See BILLYCOCK.

**billim** Knotted string carry-all with a string handle, used by women of New Guinea as an all-purpose substitute for purse, pocket, and infant cradle. Suspended from the head when used.

**billiment** **1.** 16th-c. term for the decorative jeweled border on French hoods, sometimes made by goldsmiths. **2.** Head ornament worn by brides in 16th c. Also spelled *billment*. Also called *habillement (habiliment)*, *abillements*, or *borders*.

**billycock** 19th-c. colloquial term for man's soft, wide, curved-brimmed hat with low crown. Also spelled *billicock*. *Der.* From either *1)* bully-cocked hat of 18th c. or *2)* from hat first worn by Mr. William (Billy) Coke for shooting parties at Holkham, England.

**binche** (bansh) See LACES.

**binding** **1.** Sewing term for narrow fabric strips used to cover seams or raw edges of clothing, *e.g.*, BIAS BINDING and SEAM BINDING.

**2.** Glove term for reinforcement or piping of leather or fabric around wrist and placket.

**binding off** Knitting term for removing stitches from the needles on a hand-knitted article in such a way that the piece of knitting will not ravel.

**binette** Wig of late-17th c. worn by Louis XIV of the *full-bottomed* type with three hanging locks of hair designed by sieur Binet, wigmaker.

**bingle** See HAIRSTYLES.

**binoculars** See FIELD GLASSES under GLASSES.

**bird cage** See VEILS.

**bird-of-paradise feathers** See FEATHERS.

**bird's-eye** **1.** Fabric woven in linen or cotton on a *dobby loom* in small diamond design with dot in center. Filling yarns are heavier and loosely twisted to make fabric more absorbent to use for diapers. Also called *diaper cloth*. **2.** Clear-finished worsted suiting woven with a geometrical design in diamond effect with small dot in center. Used for men's and women's suits.

**BIRETTA**

**biretta** (bi-ret-ah) **1.** Stiff square clerical cap with three or four upright projections on top radiating from center, sometimes finished with a pompon. **2.** 16th-c. term for a round cap which later became square on top when hatters learned to use a rigid frame. Worn by clergy today, *e.g.*, cardinals and bishops. Also called *barrette*. Also spelled *birretta, berrette*.

**birlet**   See BOURRELET.

**birrus**   **1.** Hooded cape of rough cloth, worn in bad weather by Romans of all classes under the last emperors. **2.** Coarse brown woolen cloth used for outer garments by lower classes in Middle Ages. Also spelled *byrrus, buros*.

**birthday suit**   **1.** Man's court suit worn in 18th c. for a royal birthday. **2.** (slang) Naked, as when born.

**birthstone**   Precious or semiprecious stone assigned to the month of birth, often worn in a ring. Although the breastplate of Jewish high priests (worn first by Aaron) contained 12 stones, and there were in ancient times 12 stones for the signs of the Zodiac, the custom of a birthstone for each month is comparatively recent. Became popular among the Hebrews in Poland in the 18th c., reaching its greatest popularity in the 20th c. Also see NECKLACES and RINGS. POPULAR BIRTHSTONES ARE:

> January—*garnet*
> February—*amethyst*
> March—*aquamarine, bloodstone*
> April—*diamond, white sapphire*
> May—*emerald*
> June—*alexandrite, moonstone, pearl*
> July—*ruby*
> August—*peridot, sardonyx*
> September—*sapphire*
> October—*opal, tourmaline*
> November—*citrine (yellow quartz), topaz*
> December—*lapis lazuli, turquoise, zircon*

**bisette**   (bee-set)   **1.** Term used in Lyons, France, in the mid-16th c. to describe the silver thread trim on apparel. **2.** See LACES.

**bishop collar**   See COLLARS.

**bishop sleeve**   **1.** Full large sleeve to wrist where it is gathered into a cuff, worn in the 1850s and called *full bishop*. **2.** In the 1890s same style but much smaller and called *small bishop*. **3.** See SLEEVES.

**bister/bistre**   Dark yellowish-brown color.

**bi-swing**   Suit or sport jacket with set-in belt in back and deep pleats extending upward to each shoulder to give freedom of movement. Has single-breasted closing and conventional notched collar with lapels. Popular in the 1930s for men and women.

**bivouac mantle**   (bi-wak)   Full-length loose cape of scarlet cloth, styled with high collar, padded and lined with ermine. Worn by women in 1814.

**black belt**   See JUDO BELT under BELTS.

**black fox**   See FURS.

**Blackglama®**   See MUTATION MINK under FURS.

**black lenos**   See GRENADINE #1.

**black opal**   See OPAL under GEMS.

**black tie**   Abbreviated term designating a man's semiformal evening attire. Compare with WHITE TIE. Also see TIES and TUXEDO under SUITS.

**Black Watch tartan**   See TARTANS.

**black work**   See EMBROIDERIES.

**blade jacket**   Man's business jacket of the 1930s made with extra fullness at upper arm and back, or shoulder blades, giving broad-shouldered look and freedom of movement.

**Blake**   Term used for a shoe utilizing a sole-stitching method invented by Lyman Blake in 1861; same as *McKay method*.

**blanchet**   **1.** Originally long white cotton camisole with sleeves, collar, and fur lining; worn over the shirt in the 15th c. **2.** Term used from 12th to 14th c. for white paint or powder used as a cosmetic.

**Blanchot, Jane**   See APPENDIX/DESIGNERS.

**blanket**   **1.** Fur-industry term for small pieces of fur sewn to form a pattern, making a piece large enough for a fur coat, *e.g.*, mink in brown and white, used to form herringbone, windowpane or checkerboard patterns. Usually imported from Greece. **2.** Fur-industry term for extra large beaver skins. Also see BATHROBE CLOTH, PLAIDS, STITCHES, and BLANKET SLEEPER under PAJAMAS.

**Blass, Bill** See APPENDIX/DESIGNERS.

**blazer** Single-breasted sport jacket first introduced in Great Britain in 1890. Originally crimson-colored, later stripes alternating with white. Also see SOCKS, SPORT JACKETS, STRIPES, and SWEATERS.

**blazer cloth** Woolen or worsted fabrics made in sateen weave with woven or printed stripes, or in plain colors. Poorer quality uses cotton filling. Used for sportswear and blazer jackets.

**BLAZER COSTUME, 1895**

**blazer costume** Tailored suit with matching jacket and skirt; worn with a shirtwaist by girls and women in mid-1890s. Jacket usually had wide lapels and did not fasten in front.

**bleached jeans** See BLUE JEANS under PANTS.

**bleaching** Chemicals applied to fabric to whiten them. Some fabrics are woven "in the *gray*" or natural color of the yarns and are *bleached* when cloth is finished. Sometimes the yarn is bleached before the fabric is woven.

**blé d'or** (blay-dor) Golden-grain color. *Der.* French, "golden corn" or "wheat."

**bleeding** Tendency of dyed fabric to lose color or run when wet.

**bleeding madras** See MADRAS.

**blehand/blehant** See BLIAUD.

**blended yarn** Yarns which are composed of two or more fibers mixed together then spun to form one yarn, *e.g.*, cotton fibers and polyester staple. When this yarn is used to make a fabric, the fabric possesses the qualities of both yarns.

**blending** Fur-industry term for lightly applying dye to tips of hairs of furs, such as mink and sable, to improve the coloring.

**bleu drapeau** (blur dra-po) French term for flag-blue color.

**bliaut** (blee-o) **1.** Long overgown worn by men and women, from 12th to early 14th c. **2.** First fitted garment for women made with tight-fitting bodice fastened up sides or back; full skirt attached at low waistline; long wide, sometimes double embroidered sleeves, laced into armholes; embroidered neckline; and belt of twisted metal. **3.** Narrow-sleeved garment for men, slit from hem to knee, worn under coat of chain mail. Loose-fitting version worn by workmen and soldiers was ancestor of farmers' work *smock.* **4.** Costly fabric of Middle Ages. Also spelled *bliaud, bliaunt, blehant, blehand.*

**blind eyelet** Shoe-industry term for metal eyelet concealed in the inner surface of leather while outside layer has punched hole through which shoestring is pulled.

**blind stitch** See SLIP STITCH under STITCHES.

**blistered** Late 16th- and early 17th-c. term for fashion of cutting or slashing sleeves or

TRUNK HOSE so that fabric underneath appeared through holes in puffed effect. Also see SLASHED.

**block heel**   See HEELS.

**blocking**   **1.** Process of shaping knitted clothing after completion or washing by drawing outline on paper and shaping article to conform. **2.** Millinery term for placing a felt or straw *hood* over a block of wood, then using heat or steam for desired shape.

**block pattern**   See SLOPER.

**block printing**   Method of hand-printing fabric by cutting separate wood or linoleum blocks for each color in relief, then inking and printing individual colored blocks. See HAND-BLOCKED PRINT under PRINTS.

**blonde**   See LACES.

**blonde de fil**   See MIGNONETTE LACE under LACES.

**bloodstone**   See GEMS.

**AMELIA BLOOMER, 1850**

**Bloomer, Amelia Jenks** (1818–1894) Advocate of dress reform for women who lec-

tured on temperance and woman's suffrage in America and abroad in 1851 wearing a Turkish costume, consisting of a knee-length dress over full pants gathered at the ankle. A costume originally designed for outdoor work by women. Horace Greeley, editor of the *New York Tribune*, publicized the costume. The trousers were later called BLOOMERS.

1927                    1919

**BLOOMER DRESS**

**bloomer dress**   **1.** Dress popularized for children after World War I worn with matching bloomers underneath. See OLIVER TWIST DRESS. **2.** Pantdress introduced for women in late 1960s.

**bloomer girl**   Slang term used in U.S. and England in late 19th and early 20th c. for daring girl who wore *bloomers*.

**bloomers**   Women's and girls' underpants or gym pants, with loose legs gathered into elastic, with length varying from knee to hip. Very popular in 1920s. *Der.* See AMELIA BLOOMER. Also see PANTIES, PANTS, and SWIMSUITS.

**blouse**   **1.** Clothing for the upper part of the body, usually softer and less tailored than a *shirt*, worn with matching or contrasting skirt, pants, suit or jumper. Formerly called a *waist*. **2.** Top of dress attached to skirt. **3.** A type of shirt worn by a member of the armed forces of the U.S., *e.g.*, an Army blouse, or Navy *middy blouse*. Term *blouse* first used when the middy blouse was adopted for boys in 1860s. (Prior to this called a *bodice*.) Used in reference to women's fashion when the *shirtwaist* was introduced in the 1890s. When more sportswear and suits were worn in 1920s and 1930s, became an essential part of a woman's wardrobe. *Der.* French, *blouson*, "to blouse." Also see SHIRTS and TOPS. In alphabetical listing see GIBSON WAIST.

### ■ BLOUSES ■

**bib b.** Back-buttoned blouse with high band collar and *plastron* in front.

**blouson b.** (blue sohn) Type of overblouse with fullness at the waist usually gathered into a band.

**bluey** Shirt worn by an Australian bushman usually in a blue color.

**bodyshirt** See BODYSUIT in SHIRT category.

**bow b.** Blouse with band around neck having two long ends in front that tie in a bow.

**capelet b.** Blouse with a double-tiered collar in the shape of a cape which is sometimes made in bow-tie style with *bishop sleeves*.

**choli** Blouse worn with Indian *sari*, reaching just to the ribs, made with short tight sleeves and scooped neckline. Frequently made of fine silk and sometimes trimmed with gold braid or embroidery. Worn by Hindu women and popular in the U.S. since 1968 when bare-midriff styles became popular. Also spelled *cholee, coli*. See SARI in alphabetical listing. *Der.* Hindu, *coli*.

**Cossack b.** Long overblouse made with a high standing collar, full sleeves, fastened asymmetrically in front, and secured with a belt or sash. Embroidery is frequently used for trim on collar, down front, and on cuffs. Same as ZHIVAGO BLOUSE and *Russian blouse*.

**dandy b.** Ruffle-trimmed blouse reminiscent of *dandy* styles of early 19th c.

**dashiki** Contemporary blouse made with caftan neckline styled with full kimono sleeves having long points at wrist. Made of cotton fabric with wide borders of multicolored geometrical print at neckline, sleeves, and hem. Popular in U.S. in late 1960s and early 1970s.

**drawstring b.** Blouse that fastens at neckline with drawstring, *e.g.*, GYPSY, or PEASANT BLOUSE.

**dueling/fencing b.** Blouse borrowed from European man's shirt of the 17th c. worn by men and women generally in white cotton, crepe or jersey. Tailored with notched collar, dropped shoulder, and long full sleeves gathered into tight cuffs.

**flip-tie b.** See STOCK-TIE BLOUSE and STOCK-TIE SHIRT under SHIRTS.

**granny b.** Prim style of blouse copied from the Victorian era with high neckline, long sleeves, and a yoke. Sometimes trimmed with tucks and ruffles.

**gypsy b.** Full blouse with drawstring neckline and either short puffed or long full sleeves. Popular in late 1960s. *Der.* Originally worn by gypsies, a nomadic people of Europe, Asia, and North America. Similar to PEASANT BLOUSE.

**Indian wedding b.** Blouse with caftan neckline, long set-in sleeves flaring at wrist, and rounded shirttails. Elaborately embroidered (currently by machine chain stitch) around neckline, down front, around hems of sleeves, and hem. Usually imported from India in a cotton fabric.

**jabot b.** (zha-bo) **1.** Back-buttoned blouse having standing band collar with attached ruffle or jabot in center front. **2.** Front-buttoned blouse with jabot-like ruffles on either side of opening.

**maternity b.** Overblouse worn by expectant mothers with maternity skirt or pants. Origi-

TUXEDO BLOUSE

CHOLI

COSSACK BLOUSE

JABOT BLOUSE

BOW BLOUSE

PEASANT BLOUSE

STOCK-TIE BLOUSE

DRAWSTRING BLOUSE

MIDDY BLOUSE, 1927

TUNIC BLOUSE

nally designed with yoke to hang straight without belt. Introduced in 1940s, in 1980s styled similar to any type blouse, shirt, t-shirt, or top.

**middy b.   1.** Slip-on blouse made with a braid-trimmed *sailor collar* and cuffs worn with a *sailor tie* slipped through loop on blouse. Sometimes has an insignia on left sleeve. Worn in blue serge and white duck by members of the U.S. Navy and by boys since the 1860s. By 1890s it was adopted for women for lawn tennis, canoeing, boating, and yachting. In 1906 worn with black sateen or serge-pleated *bloomers* as a *gymnasium suit*. From World War I period on worn with *knickers* for hiking and sportswear. In 1920s worn for gym classes and camping. Also see PETER THOMPSON DRESS and GYMNASIUM COSTUME in alphabetical listing. **2.** Any slip-on blouse made with a *sailor collar*. Also called a *nautical blouse*.

**nautical b.**   See MIDDY BLOUSE.

**overblouse**   Worn over the skirt or pants rather than tucked inside, *e.g.*, TUNIC BLOUSE, COSSACK BLOUSE, or MATERNITY BLOUSE.

**peasant b.**   Folkloric woman's blouse called by national names, *e.g.* Rumanian, Polish, or Swedish. Usually white with puffed or long raglan sleeves made with embroidered borders. Neckline is sometimes square and trimmed with embroidery or round and made with elastic or drawstring. Also see GYPSY BLOUSE.

**peplum b.**   Overblouse made two ways: *(a)* with separate seam at waist to which ruffle or bias-cut circular piece is added for fullness, or *(b)* long and full with elasticized waistline thus making a ruffle below waistline.

**pullover/pull-on b.**   Any blouse which has no fasteners and pulls on over the head. Also called a *slip-on blouse*.

**Russian b.**   See COSSACK BLOUSE.

**see-through b.**   Blouse of transparent fabric worn by women with or without a bra or body

stocking underneath. Widely accepted by 1969. Also see SHIRTS.

**shell**   Sleeveless slip-on blouse often buttoned in back, made in woven or knitted fabric. Very popular in early 1960s and frequently made to match or contrast with skirt and jacket.

**sleeveless b.**   Any style of blouse that has no sleeves, *e.g.*, SHELL.

**slip-b.**   Combination slip and blouse with top cut like a blouse and lower part serving as a slip under skirt. Also called *blouse-slip*.

**slip-on b.**   See PULLOVER BLOUSE.

**squaw b.**   Heavily embroidered blouse resembling *peasant blouse*, inspired by American Indian styles. *Der.* Name for a North American Indian woman.

**stock-tie b.**   Plain blouse with an ASCOT NECKLINE. Also called *flip-tie blouse* and *stock-tie shirt*.

**sweater b.**   Sweater made of fine yarn and worn as blouse, sometimes having ruffled details or dressmaker styling and worn tucked inside skirt. Worn intermittently since 1930 and particularly popular in 1980s.

**tailored b.**   Any style of blouse with little or no ornamentation or trimming. Similar in style to a man's shirt.

**torso b.**   Overblouse that fits snugly and extends to hips.

**tunic b.**   Thigh-length, sleeved or sleeveless overblouse, usually slightly fitted and beltless worn over skirt, slacks or alone as short dress. Popular in 1940s and revived in 1960s. Also see DRESSES.

**tuxedo b.**   Woman's blouse styled like a man's *formal shirt*. There are many variations of this blouse: *(a)* a bib style with contrasting collar; *(b)* a blouse with tucked front; and *(c)* a blouse trimmed with vertical ruffles. A black bow tie and black coat styled like a *tuxedo jacket* are sometimes worn to complete the costume.

**twinset** A matched set of blouses designed to be worn together which may be made of the same fabric or contrasting fabric. The over-blouse is usually long-sleeved with a buttoned front the other blouse is styled like a SHELL or with a CAMISOLE TOP.

**Victorian b. 1.** Back-buttoned romantic-type blouse, usually white, made with *choker collar*, long sleeves, and trimmed with lace, ruffles, or *insertion*. Introduced in late 1960s as a version of the *shirtwaist* of late Victorian era. **2.** Front-buttoned blouse with lace-edged high standing collar, lace-edged yoke, and *leg-of-mutton* sleeves. Usually made of plaid or printed fabric.

**wrap b.** Blouse with two bias-cut front sections extended into long sash ends which are crossed and wrapped around waist. Worn in mid-1960s and revived in 1980s.

**Zhivago b.** Blouse popularized for men and women by the film, *Dr. Zhivago* in 1965. Same as COSSACK or RUSSIAN BLOUSE.

---

**blouse coat** Coat with V-shaped neckline, *dolman* or *kimono* sleeves, and single-button closing at waistline; frequently made with slightly flounced skirt and lavish, high fur collar; popular in the 1920s.

**1884**    **1887**

**BLOUSE-DRESS**

**blouse dress** Boy's or girl's dress of 1870s and 1880s made with *blouson* top and low waistline. Usually the short skirt was pleated. Also called a *blouse costume*. For later versions see FRENCH DRESS.

**blouse slip** See SLIPS.

**blousette** Sleeveless blouse for wear under cardigans or suits. Popular from 1930s to 1940s. Also see DICKEY.

**blouson** (blue-sohn) French, "blouse." See BLOUSES, DRESSES, JACKETS, SILHOUETTES, and SWIMSUITS.

**blouson-noir** (blue-sohn nwar) French, "black shirt," name for a young delinquent.

**blucher** (bloocher or bloo-ker) **1.** See OXFORDS. **2.** Man's ankle-length riding boot that laces up center front through six pairs of eyelets worn from 1820 to 1850. *Der.* After Field-Marshal von Blücher, Prussian commander at battle of Waterloo, 1815. Also see BLUCHER and BLUCHER BAL under OXFORDS.

**blue-aproned men** English tradesmen of 16th to 18th c. who were recognized by their aprons of blue fabric—a color not worn by the upper classes. Also see BLUE COAT.

**blue billy** Neckcloth made of blue fabric with white polka dots; introduced by the fighter William Mace and worn from about 1800 to 1820.

**BLUEBONNET**

**bluebonnet** Small-sized Scotch TAM, of blue wool with narrow *tartan* band fitting around head, long black streamers in back, and colored pompon on top. Originally made in leather for protection when fighting. Also called *bonaid, Der.* Scottish, "bonnet."

**blue coat** **1.** Coat worn by apprentices and servants from end of 16th c. to end of 17th c., a color avoided by gentlemen as an indication of lower class. Also see BLUE-APRONED MEN and GREEN-APRONED MEN. **2.** Currently worn by undergraduate students of Christu Hospital in rural West Sussex, England. Coat is belted low on the hips and skirt reaches to ankles. **3.** Bluecoat: a policeman.

**blue fox** See FURS.

**blue jeans** See PANTS.

**blue pelt** Fur pelt taken in early fall, too soon to be PRIME PELT.

**bluey** See BLOUSES.

**boa** Round long scarf worn from 1829 on. Very fashionable in 1890s. Made of feathers, fur, or swansdown. See SCARFS. Also see FRENCH BOA.

**boarded finish** Leather finish that makes the grain of the leather more pronounced. Hand-processed by folding the leather with grain sides together and rolling it back and forth while pressing it with a cork board.

**boater** British term for man's flat-topped flat-brimmed hat worn from 1880s to 1930s. Introduced about 1865 for children, later adopted by women. The *Henley boater*, popular since 1894, was a blue or gray felt hat of similar shape, named for Henley-on-Thames, England, site of boat races. See HATS.

**boater tie** See TIES.

**boating shoe** Also called *deck shoes*. See SHOES.

**boat neckline** See BATEAU under NECKLINES.

**bob** See HAIRSTYLES.

**bobbin** **1.** Small spool such as the one on which lower thread in sewing machine is wound. **2.** In textile production the spool or core on which yarn is wound, which has a hole to fit on the spindle. See QUILL #2. **3.** Small spindle on which thread is wound when making lace, tatting, or knitting. **4.** See QUILL #2.

**bobbinet** Lacy netlike fabric knitted on a special machine called a *bobbinet machine*. Yarns are twisted so they form hexagonal-shaped holes. Cotton, silk, nylon, or rayon yarns are used. When nylon is used, fabric is stiff, wiry, and crush-resistant. Used for evening gowns, petticoats, and stiffening. Generally shortened to *net*.

**bobbin lace** See LACES.

**bobby pin** Small flexible piece of metal bent in half with prongs held together by the spring of the metal; worn to keep hair in place or to set hair in *pin curls*.

**bobby's hat** See HATS.

**bobby socks** See SOCKS.

**bobby soxer** Slang for teenager of the 1940s who followed current fashion fads such as BOBBY SOCKS and SADDLE SHOES.

**bobtailed coat** Short-tailed man's coat with narrow *revers* worn at end of 18th and early 19th c.

**bob-wig** 18th-c. man's informal wig without queue; *long bob* covered back of neck, *short bob* ended at nape of neck.

**bocskor** Heelless leather shoes, similar to American Indian moccasins, worn by shepherds in Hungary.

**bodice** (bod-iss) Since 19th c. term for close-fitting upper part of woman's dress, sometimes cross-laced in peasant dresses. See BODY #2.

**bodice en coeur** See MARQUISE BODICE.

**bodkin** **1.** Long flat needle with blunt end used to string elastic and ribbon through *eyelet insertion, headings,* or *waistbands.* **2.** 16th to 19th c. term for long hairpin used by women.

**3.** Instrument for punching holes in leather or fabric. **4.** See BALDACHIN.

**bodkin beard** Beard with long point in center of chin; worn by men from early 1520 to early 17th c.

**BODY #2**

**body** **1.** Quality of a fabric that drapes well, hangs well, and stands up under use. **2.** Term used from 15th to 17th c. to denote woman's *bodice.*

**body boot** See BOOTS.

**body briefer** See FOUNDATIONS.

**body clothes** Tightly fitted clothes with built-in comfort, *e.g., stretch jeans, leotards, body stockings, bodysuits,* and *body briefers,* made of basic yarns combined with *spandex* to give stretch.

**body coat** 19th-c. men's tailoring term used to distinguish a suit coat from an outdoor coat or overcoat.

**body hose** See BODY STOCKING.

**body jewelry** Highly decorative accessories designed to be worn on all parts of the body, face and head, over body stockings or clothing. Includes items which may be pasted on as well as elaborate pieces of metal jewelry and decorative chains; or a cape, dress, cap, pants, coat, or

**BODY JEWELRY**

**BODY STOCKING**

scarf made of loose strands of pearls. Popular in late 1960s. Designed by Bill Smith, Kenneth J. Lane, Quasar Khanh, and Paco Rabanne. Also see CADORO BRA under BRAS.

**body painting** Fad of late 1960s for painting face and body with fantasy flowers, geometrics and other designs. See TATTOO and CASTE MARK.

**body shirt** See BODYSUIT and SHIRT #3.

**body shorts** See SHORTS.

**body stocking** Introduced in early 1960s as a one-piece knitted body garment with legs and feet, with or without sleeves. In 1964 Warners won a Coty Fashion Award for a filmy nude-colored stretch garment designed with shoulder straps and no legs made of Lycra tricot-knit. Legless variety also known as BODYSUIT, BODY SHIRT, or *body sweater.* When designed as a control undergarment, called BODY BRIEFER.

**bodysuit** **1.** One-piece fitted garment without legs having a snap crotch. Made in a variety of plain, patterned, or ribbed knits. Made sleeveless or with long or short sleeves, and with many styles of collars and necklines. Sometimes substitutes as a blouse or sweater. Also called a BODY SHIRT or *body sweater.* **2.** See FOUNDATIONS. **3.** In 1986, Donna Karan changed the concept of the bodysuit silhouette somewhat to include a variety of "blouse" or "shirt" styles in a variety of fabrics, suede, or leather.

**body wave** See PERMANENT WAVE.

**Bohan, Marc** See APPENDIX/DESIGNERS.

**Bohemian lace** See LACES.

**boiled shirt** Slang term for man's formal white shirt with stiffly starched front, formerly worn with *tuxedo* or *tails.*

**bois de rose** (bwa-de-roz) Soft rosy-brown color similar to rosewood. *Der.* French, "rosewood."

**Bokhara shawl** (bo-kar-a) Shawls made in Bokhara, Turkestan (now U.S.S.R.), of camel's hair spun into yarn. Dyed with vegetable dyes and woven into eight-inch strips of patterned fabric joined invisibly to form shawls.

**Boldini hairstyle** See POMPADOUR under HAIRSTYLES.

**bolero** (bo-lehr-o) **1.** Woman's waist or rib-length jacket, open in front, with or without sleeves, often embroidered; popular at end of 19th c., and again in 1950s and 1960s. Also see JACKETS. **2.** Matador's jacket, elaborately embroidered in gold braid and beads, with large epaulets on shoulders; worn by bullfighters in Spain and Mexico. See SUIT OF LIGHTS under SPORT SUITS. **3.** Classic garment in variety of colors and embroideries worn as part of peasant or national costume in many European and Balkan countries. *e.g.,* Albania and Czechoslovakia. **4.** See SWEATERS. *Der.* A lively Spanish dance; also the music for this dance.

**bolero blouse.** Long-waisted blouse with attached pieces of fabric forming a false bolero, popular for women during 1920s and 1930s.

**bolero cape** Elbow-length cape, worn by women at end of 19th c., cut like a bolero in front and tapered to waistline in back. Also called *bolero mantle.*

**bolero costume** Dress with matching bolero, reaching nearly to the waist, or separate jacket and skirt worn with a shirtwaist. Worn from early 1900s to 1920. Some boleros were fitted, some had elaborate full caped sleeves.

**bolero mantle** See BOLERO CAPE.

**bolero toque** Woman's small draped hat of fabric or fur, with black trimming extending up over the crown, worn in 1887.

**bolivia** Velvety, light- to heavyweight, coating fabric made in a pile weave with tuffs running diagonally or vertically. Usually made in wool sometimes with the addition of mohair and alpaca fibers. Used for coats and suits.

**bollinger** Man's hat, worn from 1858 to late 1860s, having bowl-shaped crown with knob in center and narrow circular brim. First worn by

British cab drivers, later adopted by gentlemen for country wear. Also called *hemispherical hat*.

**bolo tie** See TIES.

**bolster collar** See COLLARS.

**bolt** See CUT #3.

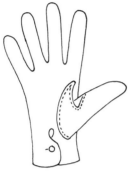

**BOLTON THUMB**

**Bolton thumb** Thumb of glove with extra point protruding from base of thumb, allowing more flexibility. Also called *English thumb*.

**bombachas** Baggy trousers usually pleated at the waistline, worn by the South American gaucho. Very full at the hem, and worn tucked into boots.

**bombanas** Fibers obtained from leaves of *bombanassa* palm used for straw hats.

**bombast** Term used in 16th and 17th c. for garments, especially *trunk hose* and sleeves, stuffed or padded with horsehair, wool, rags, flax, or cotton. Also called *bombasted*.

**bombazine** **1.** Lightweight fabric woven in a twill weave with a silk warp and worsted filling. Originally made at Norwich, England, in 1572, in a natural color. From 19th c. on was usually dyed black and used for mourning. Also spelled *bombasin, bombasine, bombazin*. **2.** In rainwear it refers to a rubberized cloth dyed solid colors or printed.

**bomber jacket** See FLIGHT JACKET under SPORT JACKETS.

**bonaid** See BLUEBONNET.

**Bonaparte, Napoleon** (1769–1821) Emperor of France, 1804–1815. Encouraged use of French textiles, influenced EMPIRE STYLES, as depicted by court painter, J. L. David; cashmere shawls; and military fashions for men *e.g.*, tight cream-colored breeches, *bicorne* hat, high rolled-collared jackets. Also see NAPOLEONIC COLLAR under COLLARS.

**bonbon pink** Pastel pink color. *Der.*, French, "candy." Also called *candy pink*.

**bonding** Textile process involving joining of two fabrics into one by backing with adhesive or foam. Acetate tricot is usually used for backing. Also see BACKED CLOTH and NONWOVEN FABRICS.

**bone lace** See LACES.

**bones** STAYS, used lightly in a corset bra, swimsuit bodice, or strapless dress for shaping and stiffening. May be made of whalebone, plastic, or steel. Also see FEATHER BONING, FOUNDATIONS, and STAYS.

**bongrace** **1.** Stiffened oblong woman's head-covering with drapery in back; worn in 16th and early 17th c. over a coif. **2.** Pendant flap in back of French hood, which was brought up over crown and fastened so as to project forward over forehead. Also called *burn grace*.

**bonnaz embroidery** See EMBROIDERIES.

**bonnet** **1.** Headcovering for women, children, and infants usually fitting over back and top of head and tying with strings under chin. **2.** Scotchman's cap, *e.g.*, BLUEBONNET. Bonnets were first worn in the Middle Ages. Worn primarily outdoors from 1800 to 1830. More popular than hats until about 1870. Rarely worn since 1920s except by babies and young girls. In alphabetical listing see: BABET BONNET, BONNET À BEC, CABRIOLET BONNET, CHIP BONNET, cottage bonnet, Marie Stuart bonnet, and POKE BONNET.

## BONNETS

**baby b.**  Infant's cap, sometimes lace-trimmed, fitted to shape of head and tied under chin.

**Easter b.**  Another name for an Easter hat. May be any type of hat, not necessarily tied under the chin, worn by ladies to announce the arrival of spring season. Worn on Easter Sunday and in Easter Parades which take place in New York and in various other cities. Also see EASTER PARADE in alphabetical listing.

**rain b.**  Accordion-pleated plastic covering for head that ties under chin. Folds up to fit in purse when not in use.

**sleep b.**  Any net, snood, or cap worn to bed to protect hairstyle.

**sun b.**  Wide-brimmed fabric bonnet tied under chin especially worn by infants and children for protection against the sun. Worn originally by early pioneers on western treks across the U.S. for protection against the sun. Revived for Centennial celebrations throughout the U.S.

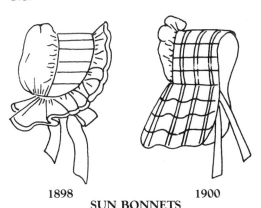

**1898                        1900**
**SUN BONNETS**

**wind b.**  Lightweight fold-up covering for head made of net, point d'esprit, or chiffon to protect hair.

**bonnet à bec** (bon-neh)  Woman's early 18th c. bonnet that covered top of head and had a peak over the forehead. Lower edge touching the hair was called the *papillon*. Also called *bonnet en papillon*.

**bonnet babet**  See BABET BONNET.

**bonnet en papillon** (bon-neh pah-pe-yon) See BONNET À BEC.

**bonnet rouge** (bon-neh rooje)  Red wool peaked-top cap, symbol of liberty, worn by patriots in French Revolution of late 18th c. *Der.* French, "red bonnet." Also called LIBERTY CAP.

**Bonnie and Clyde look**  Styles inspired by the film *Bonnie and Clyde* in 1967. Also see LOOKS.

**book bag**  See HANDBAGS.

**bookbinder print**  See PRINTS.

**boots**  **1.** Shoe which extends to the ankle or above. Classified as utility boots and used for various purposes, *e.g.*, skiing, skating, hunting, mountain climbing, etc., and fashion boots, intended to be worn indoors and out in place of shoes. Made as a fashion item and not intended to be waterproof, they became very fashionable in the mid and late 1960s in all lengths and in many fabrics as well as leather. **2.** Boots have been worn since Anglo-Saxon times in various lengths. More popular during some eras such as Louis XIII period and Regency period. From 1820s to 1880s ankle-high dainty boots were worn outdoors by women. In 1890s calf-high boots, either buttoned or laced, with medium heel were worn. In mid-19th c. very fashionable for children. In alphabetical listing see CONGRESS GAITER, FRENCH-FALL, HESSIAN, JACK BOOT, and OXONIAN.

### BOOTS

**after-ski b.** See APRÈS-SKI BOOT.

**all-weather b.** Calf-high boot made with fleece-lined upper attached to molded waterproof rubber sole with low heel.

**ankle b.** See DEMI-BOOT, GEORGE, and PANTS BOOT.

**après-ski b.** (app-reh skee) Bulky insulated boot often calf-length and made of long-haired shaggy fur worn for warmth after skiing. *Der.* French, "after ski." Also called *after-ski boots.* Also see SLIPPERS.

**Arctics** **1.** Waterproof rubber boot worn over regular shoes usually with zipper closing, popular in 1940s, revived in 1970s. **2.** Over-the-shoe boots introduced in late 19th c. made of fabric lined with rubber and made with molded rubber soles. Fastened in front with series of metal hooks and slotted fasteners; still worn by children and sportsmen. Also called GALOSH.

**Beatle b.** Ankle-high boot with pointed toe and side gores of elastic styled for men. Probably the first fashionable ankle-high shoe to be worn by men for general wear in place of oxfords since World War I period. *Der.* Introduced in the 1960s by the Beatles, an avantgarde rock-music group from Liverpool, England. Also called *Chelsea boot.*

**body b.** Women's long, tight-fitting boot, reaching to the thigh introduced in late 1960s. Also see STOCKING BOOT.

**Chelsea b.** See BEATLE BOOT.

**chest-high b.** See WADERS.

**chukka b.** Men's and boys' ankle-high boot laced through two sets of eyelets, made of splits of unlined sueded cowhide with thick crepe-rubber sole. Originally worn by polo players and adopted for general wear in 1950s. *Der.* From *chukka,* a period in polo games.

**combat b.** Ankle-high laced boot worn by U.S. armed forces made of special retanned leather designed to be waterproof.

**Courrèges b.** White calf-length low-heeled fashion boot introduced by French designer, André Courrèges, in fall of 1963 for wear with miniskirts.

**cowboy b.** High-heeled dip-top calf-high boot of highly ornate tooled or appliquéd leather, often two tone. First worn by cowboys of Western U.S. now adapted for women and children. Also called *dip-top boot* and *western boot.*

**demi-b.** Short boot reaching just to the ankle. Also called *half-boot.*

ARCTICS

COWBOY BOOT

CHUKKA BOOT

DEMI-BOOT

DESERT BOOT

**desert b.** Type of *chukka boot* made primarily of sueded cowhide or calfskin with two sets of eyelets. Introduced in 1960s, it differs from a *chukka boot* in that it is usually lined and has a rubber sole. Also similar to FLOATS.

**dip-top b.** See COWBOY BOOT.

**engineer's b.** Man's 12-inch high, straight-sided boot with low heel and leather strap buckled across the instep. Also has buckle and strap over elastic gore set in the top.

**fashion b.** Women's boot designed to be worn instead of shoes. Made as a fashion item—style is stressed rather than utility. Types include BODY BOOT, COURRÈGES BOOT, MOUSERS, PANTS BOOT, AND STOCKING BOOT.

**figure skate** Fancy skating boot with reinforced instep and counter, laces to above the ankle with speed lacing to the top. Color is usually white for women, black for men.

**fishing b.** See HIP BOOT and WADERS.

**floats** Similar to CHUKKA BOOT and DESERT BOOT, but with thick crepe soles and a thick pile lining, introduced in early 1960s.

**Frye® b.** Boots of Wellington type, first manufactured by Frye, registered trademark of John A. Frye Co., a subsidiary of Alberto-Culver

Co., in 1863 for Union soldiers and still produced as a quality boot.

**galosh** **1.** Waterproof ankle-high boot worn over the shoe which fastens with a snap, buckle, or zipper. Also spelled *golosh*. **2.** See ARCTICS. **3.** A wooden platform elevating the foot from the street, worn from 14th to 17th c. Also called a *patten*. See alphabetical listing.

**George b.** Ankle-high boot made with one-buckle fastening similar to JODHPUR BOOT. Widely accepted for general wear by men in late 1960s.

**go-go b.** Calf-length white boot, similar to Courrèges boot. *Der.* Named because worn by go-go dancers.

**granny b.** Women's boots laced up the front in imitation of high-topped shoes of 19th c.

**half-b.** See DEMI-BOOT.

**hiking b.** Above-the-ankle boot with sueded leather upper, padded collar, and soft leather lining. Laced up front through riveted D-rings with speed lacing at top. Usually has a cushioned insole and padded quarter and tongue. Heel and lug-type outsole are made of Vibram® (a durable synthetic rubber blend) welded to

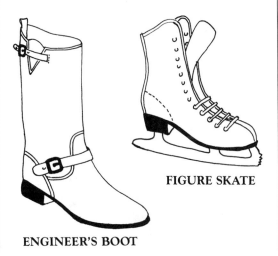

**ENGINEER'S BOOT**

**FIGURE SKATE**

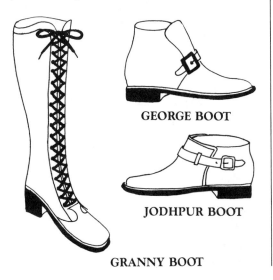

**GEORGE BOOT**

**JODHPUR BOOT**

**GRANNY BOOT**

upper. Also called *hikers* and MOUNTAIN CLIMB-ING BOOT.

**hip b.** Rubber fishing boot, thigh-length with straps at sides to fasten to belt at waist. Usually insulated and made with a cushioned innersole, steel shank, semi-hard toe cap, and cleated sole. Also see WADERS.

**hockey skate** Skate rounded in front attached to boot with reinforced toe. Sometimes has a strap across the instep, worn for ice hockey.

**insulated b.** Any boot with a lining for protection against cold, rain, snow, and bad weather. May be lined with fur, acrylic pile, wool, or foam-bonded fabric.

**jockey b.** High leather boot similar to *riding boot*, worn by jockeys in horse races. Also see HALF JACK BOOT in alphabetical listing.

**jodhpur b.** Ankle-high boot fastened with one buckle on the side, worn for horseback riding and for general wear. Similar to GEORGE BOOT. *Der.* Named for Jodhpur, a city in India.

**jungle b.** Combat boot used for U.S. Army in Vietnam. Made with heavy steel shank and tiny drainage holes in sides and heel.

**kamik** Boot made of fine leather trimmed with embroidery, usually handmade, and worn by Greenland Eskimos.

**lineman's b.** High-top or above-the-ankle leather boot, usually black with laces up the center front, made of retanned leather. May have eyelets at the bottom and hooks for speed lacing near the top.

**lounger** Pull-on boot for cold weather with full grain cowhide upper stitched to rubber shoe. Made with cushioned innersole vulcanized to chain-tread crepe outer sole. Sometimes lined and insulated with wool pile and sheepskin innersole.

**majorette b.** Calf-high white boot worn by majorette or cheerleader at athletic events since the 1940s. Some have long white tassel attached to front.

**Mexican wedding b.** Soft white leather above-the-calf boot made in moccasin style fastened down the outside with four large buttons. Colorful embroidery extends from vamp up to top of boot.

**mod b.** Various types of boots worn by boys and girls in mid-1960s in imitation of English mod fashions, *e.g.*, BEATLE BOOT.

**molded b.** A ski boot, sometimes of fiberglas®, closed with buckles, made with entire sole and part of shoe molded in one piece. Introduced for skiwear in the late 1960s.

**mountain climbing b.** See HIKING BOOT.

**mousers** Women's leather stocking-pants reaching to the waist with attached chunky-type shoes made of shiny wet-look leather. Introduced by Mary Quant, British designer, in 1969.

**mukluk** **1.** Boot reaching to lower calf worn by Alaskan Eskimos made of walrus hide or sealskin in moccasin construction, tanned with the hair left on. Copied for winter wear for men, women and children in same style since 1960s. **2.** See SLIPPERS.

**pac b.** Laced boot coming to the lower calf of the leg, sometimes made with traction-tread for sole and heel. Insulated and pile-lined, sometimes made in rubber. Basic type boot originally made in moccasin-type construction worn by sportsmen, hunters, and workmen.

**pants b.** Ankle-high shoe-boot designed to wear with pants.

**police b.** Black leather boot reaching to below the knee made in shiny, stiff leather. Similar to a RIDING BOOT. Worn by motorcycle police, some state police, and by mounted police in U.S. and Canada.

**rain b.** **1.** Lightweight plastic or rubber stretch galoshes that may be folded and carried in the purse. Same as TOTES®. **2.** Clear fold-up plastic coverings extending to ankle with zip front. Made with hole at heel through which high-heeled shoe can be worn.

**riding b.** High boot coming to below the knee made of high-quality leather, usually custom-ordered to fit leg. Worn with breeches for horseback riding. May have boot straps at top for ease in dressing.

**roller skate** Above-the-ankle boot made with polyurethane wheels, rubber toe stop, closed with eyelets and speed lacing. Worn for roller skating.

**rubber b.** Molded rubber waterproof boot with or without insulated lining but usually fabric-lined, worn over the shoe (especially by children) or in place of the shoe as protection against rain or snow. In mid-1980s made in many colors, *e.g.*, red, yellow or purple.

**skating b.** See FIGURE SKATE, HOCKEY SKATE, and ROLLER SKATE.

**ski b.** Waterproof, thick-soled ankle-high boot of leather or molded plastic, closed with laces or buckles. Sometimes has an inner boot, or foam-lining. Attaches to ski by clamp that grips the sole. Also see MOLDED BOOT.

**snowmobile b.** Waterproof boot with an attached nylon top tightened with drawstring around calf of leg. Sometimes has a strap and buckle at ankle, tread soles, and removable felt liners of 80% wool and 20% rayon for warmth. Worn for snowmobiling and in winter by children.

**squaw b.** Below-the-knee boot made of buckskin with fringed turned-down cuff at top, soft sole, and no heel. Originally worn by North American Indian women, it became a fashion item in late 1960s.

**squaw bootie** Ankle-high American Indian boot made of buckskin. Styled like a moccasin trimmed with beads on front and with long fringe around collar.

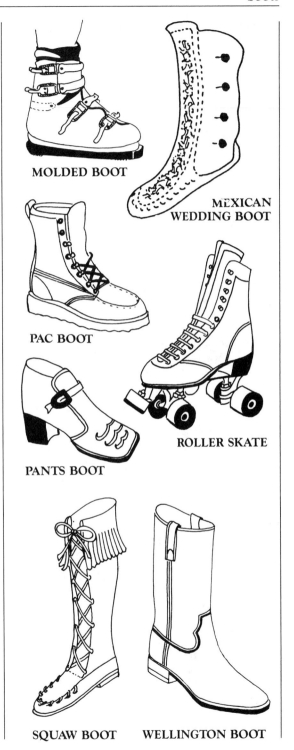

MOLDED BOOT

MEXICAN WEDDING BOOT

PAC BOOT

ROLLER SKATE

PANTS BOOT

SQUAW BOOT          WELLINGTON BOOT

**stadium b.** Calf-high sheepskin-lined boot popular to wear to football games in the 1950s. One of the first boots designed to be worn by women on the foot, not over the shoe.

**stocking b.** Fashion boot made of stretch vinyl, leather, or fabric with no zipper fitting the leg closely like a stocking. Sometimes reaches to thigh with attached panties in late 1960s. Also called BODY BOOT.

**storm b.** Any type of boot worn in inclement weather. Also see ALL-WEATHER, RAIN, and RUBBER BOOTS.

**stretch b.** See TOTES.®

**Totes®** Trademark name for lightweight, fold-up unlined rubber boot, worn over shoes. Also called *stretch boot* or RAIN BOOT.

**waders** Pants and boot in one piece reaching to above waist with suspenders over shoulders. Made of lightweight, flexible vinyl pressed to cotton jersey or rubber, welted to seamless boots with felt liners and cleated non-skid soles. Also called *fishing boot.* Also see HIP BOOTS.

**Wellington b.** Calf-length or below-the-knee boot with a seam below ankle making it look like a top has been joined to a man's low shoe with a long tongue-like projection at vamp. Seams also extend down the sides of the boot to the ankle with boot loops at top. Usually made of water-repellent leather with oak-tanned soles and rubber heels, sometimes leather-lined. *Der.* Named for Duke of Wellington, British military hero who defeated Napoleon in the battle of Waterloo in 1815. Also see WELLINGTON STYLES in alphabetical listing.

**western b.** See COWBOY BOOT.

**wilderness b.** Ankle-high laced boot with reinforced rubber toe, reinforced counter, and strap stitched diagonally from arch over ankle to aid in arch support. Made with lug sole and upper of olive-drab cotton duck backed with cotton drill for quick drying. Worn for mild weather hiking, wading streams, canoeing, or in African bush country.

**boot blow-up** Plastic or rubber boot form inserted to retain shape when boots are not being worn.

**boot bracelet** See BRACELETS.

**boot cuff** Large turned back cuff, reaching nearly to elbow. Popular for men's coats from 1727 to about 1740, used on a BOOT SLEEVE.

**boot-cut pants** See PANTS.

**bootee/bootie** 1. Infants' soft knitted, fabric, or leather shoe worn until replaced by walking shoe. Also see BABY BOOT. 2. Type of sock worn by astronauts in flight. 3. See SLIPPERS.

**boot garters** 18th-c. term for straps attached to back of man's boot, which wound around the leg above knee over top of the breeches.

**boot hook** 1. 19th-c. term for leather loop attached to back or sides of boot at top, used to aid in pulling on boots. Also called *boot strap.* 2. Long L-shaped piece of metal with a handle used to pull boots on.

**boot hose** Long stockings of coarse linen with flared tops. Worn by men from mid-15th to 18th c. to protect silk stockings under heavy boots. Also called *boot stocking.*

**boot hose tops** Decorated borders at tops of boot hose made of gold or silver lace, ruffled linen, or fringed silk.

**boot jack** Implement used to aid the wearer in removing his boots, introduced in the 18th c.

**bootlace tie** See STRING TIE under TIES.

**boot sleeve** Man's coat sleeve with BOOT CUFF; popular from 1727 to about 1740.

**boot stocking** See BOOT HOSE.

**boot strap** See BOOT HOOK #1.

**Borazon® diamond** See DIAMONDS.

**bord** See BANDELET.

**border** **1.** Trimming at edge, or just above edge, on an item of apparel or an accessory. **2.** Decorative woven cords or stripes in handkerchiefs. **3.** Decorative edge on fabric or one used for identification purposes.

**border prints**    See PRINTS.

**borders**    See BILLIMENT.

**borel**    14th-c. term for clothing.

**bosom bottles**    Term used in latter half of 18th c. for tiny bottles holding water, worn by ladies to keep bouquets of flowers fresh. Bottle was formed like a small vial which could be fastened to shoulder or tucked into the neckline of dress.

**bosom flowers**    Artificial flowers worn by men and women in the 18th c., usually with full evening dress. Also worn by the MACARONI or DANDIES in daytime. Also see BOUTONNIERE and CORSAGE.

**bosom friends**    Chest protectors which were also bust improvers, made of wool, flannel, or fur worn by fashionable ladies in late 18th and early 19th c. Also see BUST IMPROVERS.

**bosom knot**    See BREASTKNOT.

**BOSOM SHIRT**

**bosom shirt** **1.** Man's formal white shirt with starched bib front. **2.** Shirt worn in late 19th and early 20th c., made with collar and bib front of shirt fabric and rest of shirt of an inferior fabric, sometimes knitted.

**bosses**    Decorative snoods of gold or linen covering thick coils of braided hair arranged at each side of face with a coverchief, or veil, over entire headdress. Worn from late 13th to end of 14th c. Also see TEMPLERS.

**botews** (bot-toos)    15th-c. term for BUSKINS.

**bottine**    Woman's knee-high riding boot of 16th c.

**boubou**    An oblong piece of material cut like a *poncho*, loose-fitting and full. Worn by the natives of Guinea in Africa.

**bouché** (boo-she)    French fabric of fine wool woven in plain weave. Left undyed and used by Italian and Spanish clergy for shirts.

**bouchette** (boo-shet)    Large buckle used in medieval times to fasten breast plate of armor.

**bouclé** (boo-clay)    Fabric characterized by a looped or nubbed surface caused by using *bouclé yarn* in the filling. Yarn may be a different color, texture, or fiber from the warp making an interesting two-toned effect. Made in wool, cotton, or combinations of fibers, either knitted or woven. Used for sportswear, suits, and dresses. *Der.* French, "buckle" or "curl."

**bouclé yarn**    Two-ply yarn made by relaxing one yarn at regular intervals when spinning to give a looped or curled effect. Used in the filling, bouclé yarn gives a looped effect over the entire fabric. *Der.* French, "buckle" or "curl."

**boudoir cap** (boo-dwar)    Soft lace-trimmed cap with gathered crown and ruffled edge worn over woman's hair in bedroom in 19th and early 20th c.

**boudoir slippers**    See SLIPPERS.

**bouffant** (boo-fawn)    French, "full" or "puffed." See DRESSES, HAIRSTYLES, PETTICOATS, SILHOUETTES, and SKIRTS.

**bouffant mécanique** (boo-fawn mek-can-eek)    Sleeve created by hidden spring attached to corset neckline and projected into sleeve to extend it, worn in 1828.

**bouffant neckwear** (boo-fawn) Lace, linen, or gauze worn around woman's neck, shoulders, and over chest in the form of a puffed FICHU. Worn in late 18th and early 19th c. Also see BUFFON.

**bouillonné** (bwee-yon-nay) Crinkled or blistered texture. *Der.* French, "bubbled," "puffed."

**boulevard heel** See HEELS.

**Boulogne hose** English term for round or oval *trunk hose* worn from 1550 to 1610. Frequently paned and worn with CANIONS, after 1570. Also called *bullion-hose* or *French hose.*

**bound** A sewing term used for finishing the raw edges of a garment, either with band of machine stitching, bias binding, or tape. See BUTTONHOLES, HEMS, POCKETS, SEAMS, and BIAS BINDING.

**bouracan** See BARACAN.

**Bourbon hat** (boor-bon) Blue satin hat decorated with pearls in a fleur-de-lis pattern. Popular in 1815 to celebrate Napoleon's defeat at Waterloo and return of Bourbon, Louis XVIII, to the throne.

**Bourbon lock** See LOVE LOCK.

**bourdon lace** See LACES.

**bourette** (bur-et) Lightweight, rough-textured silk woven in a twill or plain weave of *bourette yarn.* Used for suiting and dresses.

**bourette yarn** A ply yarn made of various colored fibers of spun silk, worsted, or mohair which has nubs or knots of a different color throughout.

**bourka** Man's winter overcoat of thick black cloth woven from goat's hair or horsehair. Worn in Georgia in the Russian Caucasus. Also see CZERKESKA.

**bourkha** See BURKA.

**bournouse** See BURNOOSE.

**bourrelet** (boor-lay) **1.** 15th-c. term for padded sausage-shaped roll worn by men and women for headdress, or as base of headdress. Also spelled *birlet, burlet.* **2.** Another name for bustle called BUM ROLL, worn by women in 16th and 17th c. **3.** Term used for stuffed, rolled trimming.

**bourse** (boorce) **1.** Large purse or bag worn from 1440 until mid-18th c. Later spelled *burse.* **2.** 18th-c., rarely used, French term for the black silk bag of a BAGWIG. *Der.* French, "bag." Also see COIFFURE EN BOURSE.

**Boussac, Marcel** See APPENDIX/DESIGNERS.

**boutique** (boo-teak) Small shop selling a variety of merchandise including dresses, jewelry, accessories, antique bibelots, or objects d'art. *Boutique de la Maison Couture* originated in Paris in 1929 by *Lucien Lelong,* in his *Edition* department. *Elsa Schiaparelli* was the first couturiere to open a separate boutique on Place Vendome. Term applied to small shops everywhere since 1950; now such shops are often contained within large department stores.

**boutonnière** (boo-ton-yair) **1.** Flower worn in lapel buttonhole, initiated by wealthy boulevardiers and popular for formal functions since the 19th c. **2.** Small bouquet, or flower, worn by women on left shoulder or lapel. See BOSOM FLOWERS and CORSAGE #1. *Der.* French, "buttonhole."

**bow** **1.** Knot usually having two loops and two ends—often a narrow fabric, ribbon, or string; used for sashes, neckties, or decorative trim. Also called *bow knot.* **2.** See BLOUSES. **3.** Shaft attached to side of glasses, curved at one end to fit over the ear. **4.** See COLLARS.

**Bow, Clara** American film star of 1920s, called the "It Girl" in 1926. A round-eyed beauty with small cupid's-bow lips who typified sex appeal and inspired several hats of the late 1920s. See CLARA BOW HAT.

**bow dye** 17th-c. term for a scarlet dye.

**bow headdress** See ALSATIAN BOW.

**bow knot** See BOW #1.

**bowl crop** Men's hairstyle of 15th c. with hair shaved at back and sides, and longer hair hanging from crown of head in round basin-shaped fashion; a fashion revived in 1970 for young men. Also see PUDDING-BASIN CUT.

**bowler hat** First worn about 1860, made of hard felt with a domed crown and narrow stiff brim rolled up on the sides. Usually black, but brown and fawn colors were worn with *Norfolk jacket*. *Der.* Named for the hatter, William Bowler, about 1850 to 1860, although shape dates from 1820s. For contemporary adaptation, see HATS.

**bowling** Recreational sport played at a bowling alley—a long hardboard runway with ten pins set up at the end. For special clothing worn see SHIRTS and SHOES.

**bowstring hemp** Strong fiber obtained from the leaf of a plant called *Sansevieria trifascita*. Native to Asia and Africa.

**bow tie** See TIES.

**box bag** See HANDBAGS.

**box bottoms** Men's close-fitting below-the-knee breeches made with stiffened lining; worn in 19th c.

**box calf** See LEATHERS.

**box cape** Straight cut, elbow- or hip-length cape with broad padded shoulders and square silhouette. Made of fur or wool and fashionable in late 1930s.

**box coat** **1.** Woman's straight coat with wide shoulders, popular in late 1920s and 1930s. Also see CARRICK. **2.** Heavy, warm overcoat with single or multiple shoulder capes worn throughout 19th c. particularly by coachmen and travelers riding outside coach on the "box." **3.** Hip-length woman's double-breasted jacket styled like a REEFER, worn in early 1890s. **4.** Unfitted large sleeved jacket coming to below waistline, styled with MEDICI COLLAR and side closing. Worn in mid-1890s. **5.** See EMPIRE

jacket. **6.** Three-quarter-length unfitted coat of early 1900s made with shawl collar, unfastened in front. Sometimes trimmed lavishly with braid. **7.** Double-breasted girl's coat sometimes made with shawl collar, or an extra cape, worn in early 20th c.

**boxer** Adjective used for *panties* or *shorts* styled similar to those worn for sport of boxing. See PANTIES, SHORTS, and SWIMSUITS.

**boxes** 17th-c. term for GALOSHES.

**box jacket** **1.** See BOX COAT #3 and #4. **2.** See JACKETS.

**box loom** Loom with two or more shuttles used to weave structural designs in various colors, *e.g.*, checked gingham, or to weave fabrics that have alternating yarns of different types.

**box pleat** See PLEATS and SKIRTS.

**Boy George** See ANDROGYNOUS LOOK.

**boyish bob** See HAIRSTYLES.

**boy shorts** See SWIMSUITS.

**boys' sizes** Sizes 8 to 20, each size available in slim, regular, and husky. Sizes are determined by height, weight, and circumference of chest and waist.

**bra** A shaped undergarment worn by women to mold and support the breasts. Usually consists of two cups held in place with straps over the shoulders and elastic in center back. Bra is shortened form of word *brassiere*, a garment first popularized in the early 20th c. Also called *bandeau*. Also see DEBEVOISE BRASSIERE in alphabetical listing.

===== **BRAS** =====

**backless b.** Bra made with cups but no back. Elastic straps fasten at shoulder and at bottom of bra. These are worn crossed in back, brought around waistline, and hooked in center front. Shoulder straps may be unhooked and fastened at back of neck in halter style.

**bare b.** Bra constructed of a framework of straps with sewn-in uplift bands. There is no fabric over upper part of breasts.

**built-in b.** Bra used in swimsuits and sundresses which is a part of the item of clothing.

**bustier b.** Tight-fitted strapless bra usually waist length often laced up the front. Sometimes used for the top of a dress. Also see FOUNDATIONS.

**Cadoro® b.** Trademark for decorative metal bra worn with scarf or bikini underneath, consisting of metal cups, frequently filigreed, held

**PLUNGE BRA**

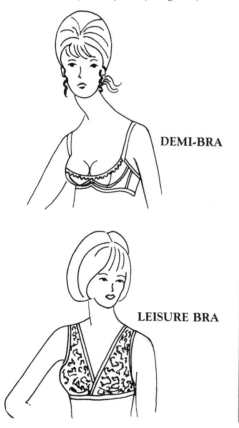

**DEMI-BRA**

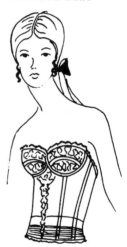

**STRAPLESS BRA**

**LEISURE BRA**

**STRETCH BRA**

on with chains. Introduced in late 1960s as an item of body jewelry.

**contour b.** Rounded bra padded with fiber-fill or foam.

**crossover b.** Bra which has reinforced straps, usually of elastic, which form an "x" in center front.

**décolleté b.** (deh-coll-eh-tay) Low-cut bra for wear with low necklines.

**demi-b.** Half bra that exposes upper part of breasts, for wear with low necklines. Also called *half bra.*

**French b.** Bra that fits under bust as an uplift but has no cups, worn with low-necked dresses for natural look.

**front-closure b.** A bra that closes in the front, usually with hooks and eyes, sometimes has built-up straps.

**half b.** See DEMI-BRA.

**leisure b.** Lightweight unconstructed bra, often of stretch lace, designed to be worn at home or when sleeping. Also called *sleep bra.*

**long-line b.** Bra that fits the bust or rib cage, extends to waist or below. Worn with girdle to eliminate waistline bulges. Sometimes boned and wired to be worn without straps.

**minimal b.** See NUDE BRA.

**natural b.** Bra which is lightweight, un-boned, unpadded, unwired, and unseamed. Also see NUDE BRA.

**nude b.** Bra made of lightweight nude-colored fabric with no bones, wires, or padding. Also called NATURAL BRA or *minimal bra.*

**one-size b.** See STRETCH BRA.

**pasties 1.** Individual cups that adhere to breasts; same as POSTS. **2.** Small decorative coverings that adhere over nipples, worn by dancers.

**pin-in b.** Two bra cups fastened together in the center with a piece of elastic, and with two tabs at the sides for pinning to clothing.

**plunge b.** Bra with deep V-shaped open section in front, separated cups are attached to a band; worn with plunging necklines.

**posts** Cups for the breasts that have no straps or back, fastened in place with adhesive. Also see PASTIES.

**push-up b.** Low-cut front and removable foam bust pads to raise the breasts.

**sleep b.** See LEISURE BRA.

**sport b.** A bra with built-up straps, coming over shoulders forming a crab-like back, secured by an elastic band around the body. Worn for active sports. Also trademarked a V-back bra.

**strapless b. 1.** Bra constructed so that it stays in place without straps over the shoulders. Popular since 1940s using boning or wire cups. **2.** See LONG-LINE, TUBE and WIRED BRAS.

**stretch b.** Bra made of fabric knitted with spandex. Elastic straps permit great freedom of movement. Often made in only one size, sometimes in pullover style with no fastening. Also called ONE-SIZE BRA.

**swimbra** Molded cups, attached or separate, used inside a bathing suit to shape the bosom.

**teardrop b.** Minimal bra with triangular cups, often the upper part of a bikini swimsuit.

**teen b.** Bra with shallow cups designed for the young girl whose breasts are not fully developed.

**tube b.** Strapless circular stretch bra with no closing; must be put on over the head.

**V-back® b.** See SPORT BRA.

**wired b.** Bra with fabric-covered wire under or over the breasts to give added support, often strapless.

---

**braccae** Loose-fitting pants or hose worn by the Romans after the Gallic conquest. See BRAIES and BROC. Also spelled *bracco.*

**bracelet** Decorative band or circlet worn on the arm, wrist, or ankle as an ornament since Biblical times. Made of metal, chain, plastic, wood, leather, or Lucite, either in one piece or in links. *Der.* Latin, *bracum,* "arm." Also see HANDBAGS, RINGS, SLEEVES, and WATCHES. In alphabetical listing see MOUSE JEWELRY #1.

## BRACELETS

**ankle b.** Ornament worn around the ankle, may be a chain or I.D. bracelet. Worn in Eastern countries and Egypt since earliest times. Also called *anklet.* Also see KHALKHAL in alphabetical listing.

**anklet** See ANKLE BRACELET.

**armband** Bracelet for the upper arm frequently made of a band of metal. Fashionable in matching sets with anklets in ancient Egypt and reintroduced in 1969.

**bangle b.** Narrow, round, rigid bracelet of

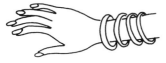

**BANGLE BRACELETS**

**TOE-ANKLE CHAIN**

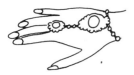

**RING BRACELET**

metal, plastic, wood, or other material, worn singly or several at a time. Popular since 1900s and originally worn in sets that jingled when the arm moved. Also called *hoop bracelet.*

**boot b.** Linked bracelet, sometimes with dangling charms, worn either around the ankle or calf of the boot.

**bracelet ring** See SLAVE BRACELET.

**chain b.** One or more chains of varying width worn on the wrist.

**charm b.** A metal (often gold or silver) chain bracelet on which one or more matching metal "charms", *e.g.,* disks, zodiac signs, or hearts— are hung often to commemorate personal events. Popular in 1940s and 1950s.

**coiled b.** Bracelet made from a long gold- or silver-tone finished strip of metal curled like a spring to fit the arm.

**cuff b.** Oval-shaped rigid bracelet styled with opening in back. May be wide or narrow and usually made of metal.

**SNAKE BRACELET**

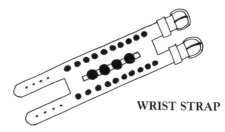

**WRIST STRAP**

**diamond b.** Bracelet made of expensive metals, *e.g.*, gold or platinum, set with many small faceted diamonds and other precious gems. Also worn as watch bracelet with diamond watch. Fashion started in 18th c. and very popular in late 19th and early 20th c.

**elastic b.** Bracelet made of beads or sectional motifs of various types strung on elastic that slips over the hand.

**expandable b.** Spring-link metal bracelet that stretches and needs no clasp. Since 1940s frequently used as watch bracelet.

**go-go watchband** Wide buckled watchstrap of brightly colored leather or plastic with watch attached by snapped tabs at either side so that band can be changed easily. Introduced in late 1960s.

**hinged b.** Any bracelet with a hinge allowing it to open wide for removal.

**hoop b.** See BANGLE BRACELET.

**Hopi b.** Narrow sterling silver cuff bracelet with American Indian symbols of Hopi tribe in black. *Der.* From Hopi Indians of Southwestern U.S.

**I.D./identification b.** Bracelet of large links attached to oblong metal plaque engraved with name or initials. First used by soldiers in wartime, later adapted for adults and children.

**Mali b.** Handmade bracelet made of leather approximately 1″ wide and decorated with very small European glass beads (called *American Indian beads* in U.S.) in a variety of colors and designs. Introduced from the Republic of Mali in Africa in 1980s.

**medic alert b.** Bracelet worn to indicate blood type and allergies to certain drugs.

**mesh b.** Metal bracelet made of minute links or a continuous piece of woven metal. Used in gold for expensive watches and bracelets.

**ring b.** See SLAVE BRACELET.

**scarab b.** Bracelet made of several oval semi-precious stones, *e.g.*, lapis lazuli or chalcedony, engraved to look like beetles, outlined in gold, and connected by gold links. *Der.* Ancient Egyptian sacred beetle. See SCARAB in alphabetical listing.

**slave b.** **1.** Ornate ring connected by a chain to a bracelet worn around the wrist. Also called a *bracelet ring* and a *ring bracelet.* Copied from bracelets worn in Eastern countries for centuries. Also popular in 1880s. **2.** A *toe-ankle chain* is also called by this name.

**sleeve b.** Ornate bracelet worn around upper arm over full sleeve to make a double puffed sleeve. Fashionable in England in late 1960s.

**slide b.** Bracelet with small piece of pierced metal through which fine flat chains are threaded. Needs no clasp as it is adjusted by pulling the chains. Popular in late 19th c., and revived by using antique watch chains in 1960s.

**snake b.** Metal bracelet in form of a serpent worn coiled around the arm. Worn by ancient Greeks and fashionable in 1880s and in late 1960s.

**spring b.** Beads strung on flexible wire in a spiral that expands to permit entry of hand.

**toe-ankle chain** Unusual ankle bracelet with chain attached to toe ring, worn in 1970. Also called SLAVE BRACELET.

**watch b.** Band or strap attached to wristwatch made of all types of metals, leather, plastic, or fabric. Also made in various styles, *e.g.*, *bangle, flexible, chain,* and *link.*

**wrist strap** Wide band of leather buckled around wrist, usually trimmed with metal studs. Introduced in late 1960s.

**bracelet ring** See SLAVE BRACELET under BRACELETS and RINGS.

**bracelet-tie shoe** Woman's ankle-strap shoe with loop extending on rim in center back to hold the strap; worn in 1930s and 1940s, and again in early 1970s.

**braces** British term for SUSPENDERS, first worn about 1787. Also called GALLOWSES.

**bractiates** Type of pin used to fasten garments from 6th to mid-8th c.

**Bradford system** Special process for spinning worsted yarns that results in more sleek, compact yarns than those made on the FRENCH SYSTEM.

**bragon braz** Full breeches, sometimes accordion-pleated, reflecting 16th-c. influence. Worn as native dress by men in Brittany, France.

**braguette** See BRAYETTE.

**braid** **1.** Narrow woven band for use as trimming, binding, or for outlining lace and embroidery. **2.** (verb) To form a plait of hair, fabric, or straw. **3.** See HAIRSTYLES.

## ■ BRAIDS ■

**coronation b.** Firmly woven mercerized cord braid, alternately wide and narrow, used to outline a pattern in embroidery or lace. Also used for COUCHING.

**diamanté b.** (dee-a-mont-ay) **1.** Fake sparkling jewels, *e.g.*, rhinestones, sewn on strips of fabric. Used as trimming on dresses, blouses, evening wear, etc. **2.** *Diamanté headband* worn around head, low on forehead during Edwardian period (1890–1910) and in late 1920s. *Der.* French, "set with diamonds."

**embroidered b.** Tape with rosebuds or other motifs embroidered at regular intervals used for trimming.

**galloon** **1.** Narrow tape or braid made of cotton, silk, rayon, wool, or man-made fibers (sometimes with metallic threads added) used for trimming. **2.** Double-edged lace made in various widths. **3.** Double-edged wide braid frequently made of gold or metallic yarn with jewels sometimes spaced at regular intervals. A highly decorative rich braid used profusely in 1969. *Der.* French, *galon*, "braid."

**gimp** Braid made from heavy core yarn arranged in a pattern and stitched to create a raised effect.

**Hercules b.** Worsted braid heavily corded from ½″ to 4″ in width; several widths often used together.

**horsehair b.** Permanently stiff coarse braid made originally from horsehair, now of nylon. Used for stiffening bouffant skirts at the hemline and in millinery.

**ladder b.** Braid with open stitches crossed by bars creating a ladderlike effect, made with a bobbin.

**middy b.** Narrow, flat white braid originally used to trim collars and cuffs on MIDDY BLOUSES and SAILOR COLLARS.

**military b.** Flat ribbed worsted or gold braid sometimes in twill weave in various widths. Used to designate rank on military uniforms.

**rat-tail b.** Silk braid of tubular shape used for trimming.

**rice b.** Firmly woven highly mercerized braid with wide parts alternating with narrow, to give the appearance of grains of rice. Used for trimming. Similar to CORONATION BRAID.

**rickrack** Cotton braid, sometimes with polyester added, made in several widths in zigzag form.

**Russian b.** See SOUTACHE BRAID.

**soutache b.** (soo-tash) Narrow flat decorative braid of mohair, silk, or rayon. Used for borders and for allover ornamental patterns. Also called *Russian braid. Der.* Hungarian, *sujtas*, "flat trimming braid."

**braided belt**   See BELTS.

**braider**   Machine used to make braid, consisting of several bobbins which intertwine yarns to form pattern.

**braie-girdle** (bray)   Also spelled *bregirdle, bray girdle*. See BREECH GIRDLE.

**braies** (brays)   Loose-fitting trousers, frequently cross-gartered, worn under the tunic as an undergarment by Romans after the Gallic conquest and in France during the Middle Ages. Also see BRACCAE.

**bra-kini**   See FOUNDATIONS.

**Brandenburg**   Man's long, loose winter coat made in military style with frog closings worn in last quarter of 17th c. Also spelled BRANDEN-BOURG, BRANDENBURGH. *Der.* Named for braid-trimmed uniforms worn by Brandenburg troops of Prussia during the Napoleonic War.

**Brandenburgs**   Term used after 1812 for military trimming consisting of transverse crocheted cording and tassels similar to *frog closings* worn by women. *Der.* Named for braid-trimmed uniforms worn by Brandenburg troops of Prussia during the Napoleonic War. Also see OLIVETTE.

**bra-shift**   See DRESSES.

**bra-slip**   See SLIPS.

**brassart**   **1.** Piece of armor worn on upper arm for protection from mid-14th to 15th c. **2.** 15th-c. French term for part of the sleeve extending from wrist to elbow attached by ribbons to upper sleeve called *mancheron*. **3.** Fur-lined half sleeve. **4.** Wide white silk ribbon bow with streamers worn by first communicants. **5.** 19th-c term for mourning band of black cloth worn on upper left arm. **6.** Ribbon bow worn in the 19th c. on the elbow of an evening dress.

**brass button**   See BUTTONS.

**brassiere**   See BRA.

**bratt**   **1.** Mantle or cape made of coarse material worn by peasants in Ireland in 9th and 10th c. Also called IRISH MANTLE. **2.** Term used in latter part of 14th c. for wrap or blanket for an infant.

**brayette**   Metal *codpiece* worn as armor in 16th c. Also spelled *braguette*.

**braygirdle**   See BREECH GIRDLE.

**Brazilian emerald**   See GEMS.

**Brazilian peridot**   See GEMS.

**Brazilian sapphire**   See GEMS.

**breacan-feile**   Another name for the early Scots tartan, described as a five-foot width of fabric sixteen yards long, wrapped and pleated first around the waist to form a skirt, with the remainder brought up around the shoulder to form a shawl.

**breaker pants**   See PANTS.

**breakfast cap**   See MORNING CAP.

**breakfast coat**   See BRUNCH COAT under ROBES.

**breakfast wrapper**   See ROBE DE CHAMBRE.

**breasted heel**   See HEELS.

**breast hook**   See STAY HOOK.

**breast kerchief**   Kerchief worn under doublet or gown, wrapped around neck and shoulders for warmth, in late 15th to mid-16th c.

**breastknot**   Bunch of ribbons or ribbon bow worn at bosom of woman's dress in 18th and early 19th c. Also called *bosom knot*.

**breastplate**   **1.** Solid metal bra or metal breast ornaments worn by women as body jewelry in late 1960s. **2.** Ornament made of two sets of long bone beads worn on chest by Plains Indians of U.S. **3.** Square ornament worn on chest by Jewish high priests described in Exodus. Believed to have been ornamented with 12 jewels set in four horizontal rows. These stones represented the 12 tribes of Israel and the names used in the Bible are sardius, topaz, carbuncle, emerald, sapphire, diamond, ligure, agate, amethyst, beryl, onyx, and jasper.

**breast pocket**   See POCKETS.

**breasts**   18th-c. tailoring term for men's waist-coat buttons. COATS was term used for coat buttons.

**breech/breeches**   **1.** Early medieval term for TROUSERS. Originally called by Anglo Saxons *brōoc* with plural being *brēec*. Same as BRAIES and Latin BRACCAE. **2.** From late 14th to early 16th c. used to indicate upper part of hose fitting trunk of body. In 16th c. upper part of breech was of contrasting color or fabric. Waist-band called BREECH BELT. **3.** From 16th c. on called *breeches, trunk hose* or *hose*. Words were synonymous until 1660 when hose indicated stockings. Worn for English court functions until about mid 1800s. For various styles see CLOAKBAG BREECHES, GALLIGASKINS, KNEE BREECHES, PETTICOAT BREECHES, SLOPS, SPANISH HOSE, and VENETIANS. **4.** See RIDING BREECHES and PANTS. Synonym: *britches*.

**breech belt**   Waistband of the BREECH or BREECHES. Also see BREECH GIRDLE.

**breechcloth**   LOINCLOTH worn by American Indians of cloth or leather about *6″ x 18″* decorated with beads and fringe. Worn draped between legs and pulled through belt in front and back leaving hanging ends.

**breech girdle**   Belt or string pulled through wide hem at top of breech in drawstring fashion—at waist or a little below. Worn from 13th to 15th c. by men. Also called *braie girdle, bray girdle, bregirdle*.

**bretelles**   (breh-tell)   **1.** Band trimming for blouse or dress bodice extending from shoulder and narrowing to waist on front and back of garment; used particularly from 1814 to 1835. Also called *suspender trimming*. **2.** Revers reaching to waistline front and back, extending over shoulders to resemble capelets. Worn in first half of 19th c. *Der.* French, "suspenders."

**Breton**   See HATS.

**Breton costume**   See BRETON JACKET.

**BRETON JACKET**

**Breton jacket**   Fitted hip-length woman's jacket buttoned on either side to a front panel, with tailored collar and lavishly trimmed with wide braid. Frequently shorter in center back. In the late 1870s, when worn with matching skirt, called a *Breton costume.*

**Breton lace**   See LACES.

**Breton work**   See EMBROIDERIES.

**Brewster green**   Dark blue-green color used for coachman's livery in Victorian era. Also called *coachman green.*

**brick stitch/brick work**   See STITCHES.

**bridal**   Adjective used for clothing and accessories worn by bride at wedding. See LACES, RINGS, VEILS, and WEDDING DRESS under DRESSES.

**bride lace**   Term used in 16th and 17th c. for blue ribbon used to tie sprigs of rosemary given as wedding favors, to the arm; later used on hat.

**brides**   **1.** Term used in 1830s and 1840s for ribbons attached to inside brim of bonnet, or broad-brimmed hat, that were loosely tied or hung free. Sometimes by extension to bonnet itself. **2.** Connecting threads joining lace designs where there is no net ground.

**bride's garter**   See WEDDING GARTER.

**bridesmaid's dress**   See DRESSES.

**bridles**   18th-c. term for strings attached to mobcap for tying under the chin. Also see KISSING STRINGS.

**briefcase**   See HANDBAGS.

**briefers**   See SWIMSUITS.

**briefs**   **1.** Men's knitted underwear shorts with elastic top. **2.** See PANTIES.

**Brigadier wig**   Military wig with two queues, worn in the second half of the 18th c. Term used in France for MAJOR WIG.

**Brigance, Tom**   See APPENDIX/DESIGNERS.

**brilliant cut**   See GEM CUTS.

**brim**   Rim of hat attached to crown and shading the face. May be narrow to wide—worn level, turned down, up or to a variety of angles.

**brin**   See RAW SILK.

**Bristol blue**   Intense blue color of Bristol glass, similar to peacock blue.

**britches**   See BREECHES.

**British look**   Conservative, elegant look for men reflecting the influence of London tailors of Savile Row. Also see LOOKS.

**British warm**   British army or navy officers' heavy double-breasted overcoat, knee-length or shorter, copied for civilian wear in 1950s and 1960s.

**Brittany work**   See BRETON WORK under EMBROIDERIES.

**broadbrim**   Wide-brimmed, low-crowned hat worn by members of the Society of Friends, called Quakers. "Broadbrim" is a soubriquet for one of these members.

**broadcloth**   **1.** Medium-weight fabric of cotton or cotton/man-made blended yarns, characterized by fine crosswise ribs. Heavier two-ply combed yarns used in filling to produce the ribs in best qualities. May be bleached, dyed, or printed. Used for dresses, shirts, blouses, and sportswear. **2.** Rayon and polyester blended fabric similar to broadcloth. **3.** Woolen fabric. See WOOL BROADCLOTH.

**broad-stitched seam**   See SEAMS.

**broadtail lamb**   See FURS.

**brōoc**   Anglo-Saxon term for trousers similar to Roman BRACCAE. Plural, *brec*, developed into BREECH, then BREECHES. Also called BRACCOS. Also see BRAIES.

**brocade**   Classification of fabric woven on the Jacquard loom giving design a raised appearance. Design is usually satin weave with background in satin, rib, or plain weave. Made with all types of yarns including gold, silver, silk, rayon, cotton, acetate, or man-made fibers. Fabric is not reversible. Embossed acetate patterns set with heated rollers are made in imitation of this fabric and should not be called *brocade* but *embossed acetate*.

**brocade embroidery**   See EMBROIDERIES.

**brocatelle**   Medium-weight dress fabric woven on Jacquard loom with pattern which stands out in high relief giving a blistered effect. Some fabrics give the appearance of being quilted. Made of silk, rayon, and acetate yarns with cotton backing yarns.

**broché** (bro-shay)   **1.** Paisley-type shawl made in Scotland, woven in alternating stripes of pattern and plain color. Very popular in 1830s. **2.** A French term for pattern produced by *swivel* or *lappet* weave. **3.** A fabric decorated with special threads introduced into the wrap or weft but not really part of the structure.

**brodekin**   **1.** Lightweight shoe worn in Middle Ages inside boots. **2.** Scottish term for man's calf-length boot worn from 15th to late 17th c. called *buskin* in England. Also spelled *brodkin, brotiken.*

**broderie anglaise**   See EMBROIDERIES.

**brogan**   Originally men's ankle-length shoe worn in Scotland. Made of leather and fastened to foot by side flaps either buckled or tied over short tongue.

**brogue**   See OXFORDS.

**broken hat**   See CHAPEAU BRAS.

**broken twill weave**  See HERRINGBONE WEAVE.

**bronzed leather**  Copper-colored kid or calf-skin.

**brooch**  Synonym for pin. See PINS.

**Brooks Brothers look**  Look of classic well-tailored clothes for both men and women. Sold at traditional trademarked Brooks Brothers® retail store. Also see LOOKS.

**Brooks, Donald**  See APPENDIX/DESIGNERS.

**broomstick skirt**  See SKIRTS.

**brow band**  Ribbon, fabric, beaded band, or braid of hair worn around head—low on forehead.

**brown belt**  See JUDO BELT under BELTS.

**brown George**  Late 18th-c. colloquial term for man's brown wig said to look like coarse brown bread.

**Bruce tartan**  See TARTANS.

**Bruges lace**  See LACES.

**BRUMMEL, BEAU**

**Brummel, Beau**  English dandy, George Bryan Brummel (1778–1840), arbiter of men's fashions during the Regency Period. Leader of the beaux who advocated unobtrusive dark-blue fitted coats, cream-colored trousers, elaborately tied cravats, absence of showy fabrics or excessive decoration, and impeccable grooming.

**Brummel bodice**  Whalebone WAIST CINCHER, or corset, worn by English dandies of Regency period (1810–1820). Also see APOLLO CORSET and CUMBERLAND CORSET.

**brunch coat**  See ROBES.

**Brunswick**  Close-fitting riding coat-dress with mannish collar worn by women in 18th c. *Der.* Said to have originated in Brunswick, Germany.

**Brunswick gown**  Sack-backed gown with front-buttoned bodice and long sleeves worn by women from 1760 to 1780. Also called *German gown.* Also see SACK #2.

**brush**  Bushy tail of an animal, usually a fox, used as trimming.

**brush cut**  See CREW CUT under HAIRSTYLES.

**brush-dyeing**  Coloring of leather by placing skins flesh side down on metal table and applying dye to grain side with brush. Desirable for black kidskin gloves as inside remains white.

**brushed fabrics**  Extremely soft knitted or woven fabrics vigorously brushed to form a warm fuzzy nap. Made of wool, cotton, or man-made fibers, *e.g., brushed rayon, brushed nylon.* Used for women's and children's sport shirts, robes, nightgowns, and pajamas.

**brushed wool**  **1.** Extremely soft knitted or woven fabric. Made of loosely twisted yarns brushed to form the nap. **2.** Term used for wool which has been brushed or cleaned while still attached to the pelt.

**brushing**  Finishing process used on fabrics to raise a NAP. SEE BRUSHED FABRIC.

**Brussels lace**  See LACES.

**Brussels net**  See LACES.

**brüsttüch** Elaborately embroidered, oblong plastron fastened around neck worn by Jewish women in Poland in 19th c.

**Brutus head/wig** Man's own hair worn closely cropped or brown unpowdered wig, both worn disheveled. Popular from about 1790 to 1820 and inspired by the French Revolution.

**bruyère** (bru-yer) Pinkish-purple, the color of heather. *Der.* French, "heather."

**Bruyère** See APPENDIX/DESIGNERS.

**buba** See DRESSES.

**bubble** Balloonlike shape, popular for many fashions in 1950s. See BEADS, CAPES, CURLS, DRESSES, HAIRSTYLES, SILHOUETTES, and SKIRTS.

**bubble beret** See HATS.

**bubble cover-up** See NIGHTGOWNS.

**Buchanan tartan** See TARTANS.

**buck clothes** 16th- and 17th-c. term for clothes placed in buck baskets to be laundered. Some clothes were sent to Holland from France for laundering.

**bucket-top boot** Man's boot with very wide, exaggerated cuff top worn in early 17th c. Compare with FRENCH-FALL BOOT.

**Buckingham/Buckinghamshire lace** See LACES.

**buckle** A decorative or functional clasp, usually of metal, wood, or plastic. Consists of a rectangular or curved rim, often with one or more movable tongues. Also a clip device fixed to end of a strap used to fasten to other end of belt or to another strap. Used since earliest times for belts, shoes, and knee breeches. Also see CLOSINGS and JUMPERS.

**buckled wig** 18th-c. man's wig with tightly rolled sausage curls arranged horizontally near ears. *Der.* French, *bouclé,* "curl."

**buckles d'Artois** Shoe buckles of enormous size worn from 1775 to 1788. *Der.* Named after the Comte d'Artois, later Charles X of France.

**Bucko calf** See LEATHERS.

**buck oxfords** See OXFORDS.

**buckram** Loosely woven, heavily sized fabric in a plain weave used for stiffening. Similar to crinoline but heavier and much stiffer. Sizing will wash out, making fabric unsuitable for washable garments. *Der.* From costly material made in Bokhara, south U.S.S.R.

**bucksain** Man's padded overcoat with wide sleeves, worn in 1850s.

**buckskin** 1. Deerskin tanned by buckskin method, then buffed. See JUMPERS and LEATHERS. 2. Sheepskin treated to resemble above.

**buckskin fabric** 1. Durable woolen or worsted fabric made in the buckskin weave, a variation of the satin weave; then napped and fulled. Winter weights are heavy and thick and made with woolen yarns. Summer weights are of worsted yarns mixed with silk or rayon. Also see MOLESKIN FABRIC. 2. Fabric made in cream color in 19th c. and used especially to imitate leather buckskin riding breeches.

**buckskins** 1. Term used from 15th to 19th c. for buckskin gloves, breeches, or riding gaiters. 2. See SPORT JACKETS. 3. See VESTS.

**buckskin tannage** Type of primitive tannage of animal skins used by American Indians. Hair and skin were scraped, skins immersed in solution of lye made from wood ashes, lubricated with brains and liver of animals, and hung in smoke-filled tepee.

**bucky pelts** Fur peltry taken in spring months when skins are not fully furred and tend to be tough and unyielding. Also called *springy pelts.*

**budget** Wallet or extra pocket hanging from belt used in 17th c.

**buff coat** Man's leather jacket made of ox or buffalo hides. Sometimes with shoulder wings and sleeves of fabric, sometimes sleeveless. Worn in 16th and 17th c. Originally a military garment worn during civil wars in England, adopted by civilians and American Colonists. Also called *buff jerkin* or *leather jerkin*.

**buffing** Finish produced on leather by abrading with emery wheel.

**buffins, pair of** English colloquial term for men's *trunk hose* similar to *slops* or *round hose* worn in 16th c.

**buff jerkin** See BUFF COAT.

**buffon** Woman's large scarf or neckerchief of gauze or fine linen draped around neck, shoulders, and puffed out over the chest. Sometimes supported by wire framework in 1780s. Also spelled *buffont*. Also see BOUFFANT NECKWEAR.

**bug-eyed glasses** See GLASSES.

**bugle beads** See BEADS.

**bugle chain** See CHAIN.

**bui-bui** A black calf-length outer garment worn by Moslem women as the traditional costume in Tanzania and its province Zanzibar.

**built-in bra** See BRAS.

**built-up heel** See STACKED HEEL under HEELS.

**built-up slip** See SLIPS.

**built-up straps** Shoulder straps constructed in continuous curve as part of garment, usually used for a slip or swimsuit.

**bulaki** A small gold nose ring worn by Hindu, or Pahari, women of western Nepal.

**bulgare pleat** Term used in mid-1870s for double box pleats kept in place with elastic on inside of skirt.

**bulking** Several procedures used for crimping, curling or looping yarn to make it bulkier.

**bulky knit** Any type of knit using special "air-bulked" yarns. Done with large stitch on large knitting needles. Very popular for handmade sweaters made from the 1960s through 1980s.

**bulky yarn** Textured, stretch, or lofted yarns suitable for hand and machine knitting.

**bulldog toe** See TOES.

**bulletproof jacket** See SPORT JACKETS.

**bull head** Woman's hairstyle with fringe of thick curls across forehead worn in late 17th c. Also called *bull tour* and *taure*. *Der.* French, *taureau*, "bull."

**bullion** Adjective meaning gold color. See EMBROIDERIES and LACES.

**bullion-hose** See BOULOGNE HOSE.

**bully-cocked** 18th-c. term for man's cocked hat, usually broad-brimmed and three-cornered.

**bum** See BUM ROLL.

**bumper** **1.** Cap worn in the Netherlands by children, fitted at back of head, with wide thick roll of yarn around the face for protection. Also see CHILD'S PUDDING. **2.** See HATS.

**bumper brim** Term for hat brim that rolls back from the face, used in various widths on different styles of hats.

**bumper collar** See COLLARS.

**bum roll** Padded roll worn around hips to hold out skirt in the tub-shaped FRENCH FARTHINGALE style. Worn in England during 16th and early 17th c. Also called *hausse-cul* in Netherlands, about 1600. Also see BOURRELET #2 and ROLL FARTHINGALE.

**bun** See HAIRSTYLES.

**bunad** National costume of Norway. Ankle-length embroidered jumper-type dress worn over a full-sleeved, high-necked blouse. Embroidered designs vary in different locales.

**bundle** Garment-trade production term for cut-out pieces of dresses, shirts, etc., tied together with cord or elastic.

**bundle stitch.** See STITCHES.

**bundle system** Garment-trade term for method of production using an unorganized flow of sectionalized work with each employee bundling his finished work. Also see DEVELOPMENT BUNDLE SYSTEM.

**Bunka embroidery** See EMBROIDERIES.

**bunny suit** See DR. DENTON SLEEPERS under PAJAMAS.

**bun snood/bun-warmer** See CHIGNON CAP.

**buntal** Fiber from Philippines used for BALLI-BUNTL STRAW.

**bunting** **1.** Same as BABY BUNTING. **2.** Name of loosely woven lightweight cotton fabric in red, white, and blue flag colors used for patriotic decorations and costumes. **3.** 18th-c. English worsted fabric.

**Burberry®** **1.** Trademark for a heavy or lightweight British fabric treated to resist the congealing of snow and penetration of wind. **2.** See RAINCOATS. **3.** Clothing worn by Arctic explorers c. 1914, consisting of boots made with tops of this fabric, Burberry helmets, Burberry overalls, and Burberry jackets. **4.** Clothing made of this fabric worn in the 1920s for skiing.

**burdash** Fringed sash worn by BEAUX over the coat in late 17th and early 18th c. Also spelled *berdash*.

**burgonet** Metal helmet worn as armor in the 16th c. Has a brim which projects over the eyes, called an *umbril*, and a metal projection to protect the back of the neck. It may have hinged ear flaps and one or more combs on the crown. Some are decorated with elaborate hammered designs. Of Burgundian origin and adopted by England, Germany, Italy, and France. Compare with MORION.

**burka** Voluminous ankle-length garment completely covering the head and figure with the top fitting close to head and a veiled opening for the eyes. Worn in India by Muslim women. Also spelled *bourkha, burga, burkha*.

**burlap** Loosely constructed, plain woven fabric made of jute or other minor bast fibers. Originally considered a utility fabric for bags and sacks. Now sometimes embroidered and used for handbags and items of apparel. Also called *Hessian* in Great Britain and Europe.

**burlet** See BOURRELET #1.

**burnet** **1.** 13th- to 15th-c. term for fine black or brown woolen fabric. **2.** 17th-c. term for HOOD or HEADDRESS. Also spelled *burnette*.

**burn grace** See BONGRACE.

**BURNOOSE #3, 1857**

**burnoose** **1.** Circular-cut traveling cape of plain or striped camel's hair fabric with a square hood tasseled at the corners worn by Moors and Arabs in northern Africa. Also called a *selham*. **2.** A cloak or wrap, sometimes without front opening, worn in Palestine, Turkey, and Arabia. **3.** Woman's sleeveless evening wrap similar to a shawl with a small hood worn from 1830s to 1860s. Also spelled *albernous, albornoz, bernos, burnouse, burnose, burnus, bournouse*.

**Burnsides** Side whiskers and full moustache with clean-shaven chin worn from 1860s to end of 19th c. *Der.* Named for Major General Ambrose Everett Burnside, commander of Army of the Potomac in 1862 under General Grant.

**burnt-out fabric** Fabric of lace made on the Jacquard loom with two different yarns—one forming the pattern and part of the ground—the other the ground. When printed with chemicals, one of the sets of yarns is dissolved, leaving a lacy pattern on a sheer ground. Brocaded effects on velvet can be made by destroying part of the pile and permitting the rest to remain. Also called *etched-out fabric* or *burnt-out print*.

**burnt-out lace** See PLAUEN LACE under LACES.

**burnt-out print** See PRINTS.

**burnt sienna** (see-en-a) Dark rust-brown color.

**burnt umber** Dark yellowish color, similar to the color of mustard.

**buros** See BIRRUS.

**burse** See BOURSE.

**Burton diamond** See DIAMONDS.

**burunduki** See FURS.

**busby** See HATS.

**bush coat/jacket** See SPORT JACKETS.

**busheling** Retail-store term formerly used for the alteration or repair of men's clothing.

**bush hat** See HATS.

**bush shirt** See SAFARI SHIRT under SHIRTS.

**business suit** See SUITS.

**busk** **1.** Term used from second half of 16th through 19th c. to indicate pieces of cane, wood, whalebone, steel, and sometimes horn used as stiffeners for woman's BODICES OR STAYS. Also see BUSK POINT. **2.** Men's clothing thus stiffened.

**buskin** **1.** Calf-length thick-soled laced boot worn by men in ancient Greece and Rome. Same as COTHURNUS. **2.** High boots, sometimes to knees, often made of patterned silk, worn from 14th through 17th c. by men and women called *botews*. **3.** Leather riding boots worn in 17th c. for traveling. **4.** Women's low-cut shoe with elasticized gores at sides of instep worn in early 20th c. Also see AMERICAN BUSKINS.

**busk point** Metal tip or tag of a lacing that secures ends of the BUSK.

**bust bodice** Boned garment, laced up front and back, worn over corset to support breasts. Introduced in 1889. One of the forerunners of the bra.

**BUSTER BROWN**

**Buster Brown** Comic-strip character of early 20th c. whose haircut, collars, suit, and shoes were widely copied for children's wear. Now a trademark for children's shoes. See COLLARS and HAIRSTYLES.

**bust extenders** Ruffles used by women to pad bosom in early 20th c.

**bust form** **1.** Padding or wire covered with muslin used by women to emphasize the bust in 1890s. **2.** An older term used for DUMMY.

**bustier** (boost-e-ay) Dress or top of 1980s made in strapless style which is held in place by boning, elastic, or stretch knit fabrics. Also see BRAS, FOUNDATIONS and TOPS.

**bust improvers** Pads of wool and cotton used by women to fill out bosom introduced in 1840. Also see BOSOM FRIENDS.

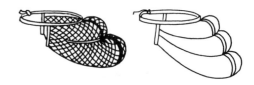

**BUSTLE**

**bustle**   Pad, cushion or arrangement of steel springs creating a bulbous projection below the waist in back of woman's dress. Called by this name about 1830, and popular in various forms to end of century. Also called DRESS IMPROVER and TOURNURE. Bustles worn prior to this date were not called by this name, words BUM ROLL, FISK, NELSON, CUSHION PAD, CUSHIONET, or QUISSIONET were used. Also see DRESSES, SILHOUETTES, and SKIRTS.

**bustle back**   Puffs of ribbon or bows at back of hat, popular in 1930s.

**bustle curls**   See CURLS.

**bust pads**   Foam-rubber or stuffed fabric pads used inside a bra to make the breasts appear larger. Also see FALSIES.

**Busvine**   See APPENDIX/DESIGNERS.

**butcher boy blouse**   Woman's blouse, hip-length or longer, shaped like a smock, usually yoked and buttoned either front or back. Popular in 1940s, and used later for maternity blouse. *Der.* Garment worn by French butchers' delivery boys.

**butcher cloth**   Low count rayon fabric imitating BUTCHER LINEN made of single or ply yarns sometimes of viscose-processed rayon with nubbed effects.

**butcher linen**   **1.** Heavyweight durable fabric made in plain weave. Originally of linen for butchers' aprons, later made in cotton. Today it must be designated by the fiber. Used for summer suits and sportswear. **2.** Spun rayon fabrics which imitate linen by using yarn of uneven thickness. Term is a misnomer and term BUTCHER RAYON should be used. Also see BUTCHER RAYON.

**butcher rayon**   Spun rayon which produce a slub effect in filling used in imitation of BUTCHER LINEN. Used for slacks, suits, sportswear.

**butcher's apron**   See APRONS.

**butch haircut**   See CREW CUT under HAIRSTYLES.

**butterfly bow**   Length of stiffly starched lace, resembling outstretched butterfly wings, fastened to front of shoe at end of 17th c.

**butterfly cap**   Woman's small lace cap wired in shape of a butterfly worn perched above forehead with lappets, jewels, and flower trimmings frequently added for court wear. Worn in 1750s and 1760s. Also called *fly cap*.

**butterfly collar**   See COLLARS.

**butterfly glasses**   See SUNGLASSES under GLASSES.

**butterfly headdress**   16th-c. term for a 15th-c. towering headdress made of sheer gauze wired to stand out like wings, and supported by a fez-shaped cap. Worn today by an order of nuns in Normandy, France.

**butterfly sleeve**   See SLEEVES.

**Butterick (Ebenezer)**   Merchant tailor is said to have invented the tissue paper pattern. In 1863 he cut out a pattern for his son's trousers using heavy paper similar to cardboard. His wife suggested women would like ready-cut-out patterns for all clothes. As the cardboard was bulky, he next tried a lighter weight paper and finally tissue paper. By 1890s patterns were available for anything made of cloth from a wedding gown to a pin cushion. There were *Butterick* designers in New York, Paris, London, Berlin, and Vienna to develop the newest ideas of great modistes. Also see DELINEATOR.

**button**   **1.** A decorative ornament used for trimming or a functional fastener. Usually made with holes punched in center or a shank on the back, made to slip through a buttonhole or loop. Introduced in the 13th c. as trim, it later became functional. In 16th c. buttons of all types were used. By the 1940s a fully dressed man wore approximately 70 buttons many of them not functional. *Der.* French, *bouton*, a round object, a bud, a knob. **2.** Term indicating the length of the glove. One button is equal to one French inch (approximately $1/12$ of an inch longer than American inch), with the measurement starting at base of thumb. A one-button glove is wrist length, a six-button glove is about halfway to elbow, and a 16-button glove is a formal length. Also see CLOSINGS.

## ■ BUTTONS ■

**abalone b.** Type of pearl button made from shell of a mollusk called an ear shell, or sea-ear, found off Pacific coast of the U.S.

**blazer b.** Distinctive brass or gold-plated brass button with a monogram, a coat-of-arms, or a crest embossed or engraved on top. Usually sold by the set which includes three large and four small sleeve buttons. Specifically used on BLAZERS.

**brass b.** Gilt button made of brass for military uniforms also made of other metals or plastic and gilded to simulate brass. Button embossed with a large eagle used on jackets and coats worn by U.S. armed forces. Also used by civilians on jackets, dresses, and coats.

**covered b.** Ball or disk-type button covered with fabric either matching or contrasting with garment. Kits of various sized disks to be covered may be purchased by the home sewer. Although first used in latter part of 16th c., the button industry in the U.S. was started in 1826 by Mrs. Samuel Williston, wife of a storekeeper in East Hampshire, Mass., who first covered wooden buttons by hand. Later she invented a machine for this purpose and her factory was credited with one-half of the world production of buttons.

**crocheted b.** Shank-type buttons made by crocheting over a disk, a ball, or a barrel-shaped object. Sometimes used on sweaters and formerly used on dresses and coats in Victorian era and early 19th c.

**glitter b.** Any type of button set with rhinestones or imitation gems.

**glove b.** Tiny buttons usually round, often pearlized, used to button long gloves, *e.g.*, formal or *mousquetaire glove*.

**gold b.** Any type of gold colored button, formerly solid gold or plated. Henry VIII had jeweled gold buttons made to match his rings. A record of the 15th c. notes 25 golden buttons, each set with seven pearls, at a cost of 200 gold pieces. In the 16th c., gold buttons set with diamonds and other precious stones were frequently used.

**mother-of-pearl b.** Button made from nacre, the inside shell of the oyster. First manufactured in U.S. in 1885 from imported mollusks and later from domestic oysters found in Chesapeake Bay.

**pearl b.** Classic button for almost any use, originally made from shells, sometimes called "ocean pearl" until development of plastic in the 1930s. Also see MOTHER-OF-PEARL BUTTON.

**poker chip b.** Extra large round flat button with a shank on the back. *Der.* From size and shape of a poker chip.

**rhinestone b.** Any button set with stones made of glass or *paste* which simulates a diamond. Same as GLITTER BUTTON.

**self-covered b.** See COVERED BUTTON.

**shank b.** Button with metal or plastic loop on the back.

**shirt b.** Small mother-of-pearl or imitation pearl button with four holes and a ridge around the edge. Originally used on men's shirts.

**sleeve b.** **1.** Button at wrist to close cuff or sleeve. **2.** Decorative trim used on sleeves of man's suit coat consisting of two or three buttons placed on outside of cuff. Fashion originated in the 18th c. when large cuffs were worn buttoned back to the sleeve.

**wooden b.** Made in all sizes and shapes—may be in ball shape with shank on back or disk-shaped. In the late 1930s larger saucer-shaped buttons tied on with matching corded fabric were used on women's coats.

---

**button-down**   See COLLARS and IVY LEAGUE SHIRT under SHIRTS.

**button earrings**   See EARRINGS.

**buttoned shoe**   Shoe with a three- or four-button diagonal closing which may have a BULL-DOG TOE or a conventional toe. Worn by men in early 1900s. See HIGH BUTTON SHOES.

**buttonhole**   Opening for button to go through in order to secure the garment. Generally classified as a bound, or a worked, buttonhole. The use of buttonholes dates from about the 15th c.

### BUTTONHOLES

**barred b.**   Worked buttonhole with straight bar embroidered across ends. May have one end rounded and a bar at the other end or have bars at both ends.

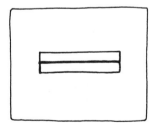

**BOUND BUTTONHOLE**

**bound b.**   Buttonhole with edges finished with stitched-on fabric or leather binding.

**eyelet**   Round opening worked with buttonhole stitches used for laced closings.

**machine-made b.**   Button hole made with a special stitch on the sewing machine.

**piped b.**   Similar to BOUND BUTTONHOLE, but *piping* is used around the opening.

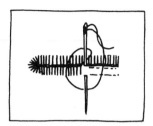

**TAILORED BUTTONHOLE**

**tailored b.**   Worked buttonhole with rounded end toward edge of garment and a bar at other end.

**worked b.**   Buttonhole finished by hand by embroidering with buttonhole stitch or with similar stitching done by a sewing machine.

---

**button hook**   Small metal hook attached to long handle formerly used to pull buttons through buttonholes of shoes or gloves.

**button hooks**   Small metal hooks first used in the 1860s instead of eyelets on shoes, the laces winding around hooks, criss-crossing to fasten shoes. Used now on skating and other types of boots and called *speed lacing* or *lacing studs*.

**button shoes**   Short boots buttoned up outer side with black japanned or mother-of-pearl buttons. Worn from 1837 to early 20th c. by men, women, and children.

**button-tab sleeve**   See SLEEVES.

**B.V.D.'s®**   **1.** Trade name for man's *union suit* popular from early 19th c. up to World War II consisting of one-piece, wide-legged, knee-length garment with U-neckline, buttoned down front, and an adjustable black flap. Usually made of checked cotton dimity. **2.** Trademark for underwear and other men's clothes made by B.V.D. Company.

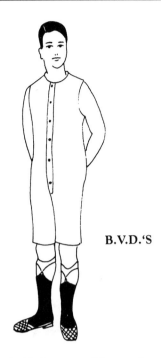

**B.V.D.'S**

**bycocket** **1.** High-crowned hat with a wide brim peaked in front, and turned up in back worn by men in the Middle Ages. **2.** Similar hat called a *student bycocket* worn by Italian students in mid-20th c. Also spelled *bycoket*.

**byesse** See BIAS.

**Byrd Cloth®** Trademark of Reeves Bros. for a high count, medium-weight reversible cotton or cotton and polyester fabric woven very tightly in twill weave. Sometimes count is 300 threads per inch, making the cloth almost completely wind resistant. May be given a water-repellent treatment and used for ski wear, snow suits, parkas and garments worn by aviators. *Der.* Fabric originally developed for Admiral Richard Byrd's Antarctica Expedition.

**Byron, Lord** *George Gordon Byron, 6th Baron* (1788–1814), English poet who became a fashion influence by 1812, especially copied were an open-necked shirt with long pointed collar and type of necktie. His travels to Turkey and Greece inspired him to wear Turkish caftans and slippers, Ottoman dressing gowns, Indian jewelry, and Oriental perfume. Also see BYRON COLLAR under COLLARS and BYRON TIE.

**Byron tie** Short, narrow string necktie made of silk worn in the 1840s and 1850s. *Der.* Named for LORD BYRON.

**byrrus** See BIRRUS.

**byzance** See NECKLACES.

**Byzantine embroidery** See EMBROIDERIES.

**Byzantine stitch** See STITCHES.

**C 1. Shoe size:** Letter indicating a width; widths run from AAAA to EEEEE with AAAA's being the narrowest and EEEEE's the widest. **2. Pajama Size:** Men's regular height (5′8″ to 5′11″) size corresponding to 41″–44″ chest measurement. For other sizes, see BIG, REGULAR, EXTRA-TALL and TALL. **3. Shirt Size:** For men's extra-tall size with 17–17½ collar measurement. **4. Bra Cup Size:** Sizes run AAA, AA, A, B, C, D, DD: AAA is the smallest size and DD the largest.

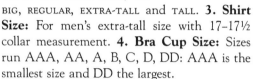

**caban 1.** Believed to have been the first fitted European coat with sleeves. Of Arabian origin, it was introduced from the East by way of Vienna in the mid-14th c. and was popular throughout the 15th c. Had a closed front and wide sleeves with underarm seam not closed. Sometimes worn with a belt. See GABARDINE. **2.** Man's coat of the 1840s. Also known as TEMPLAR CLOAK. **3.** A white scarf worn by Arabs, also spelled *cabaan.*

**cabaña set** (cah-ban-ya) See SWIMSUITS.

**cabas** (kah-bas) Version of PHRYGIAN CAP, made of beaver or velour, draped across forehead to conceal hair and ornamented in back. Created by Sally Victor, New York milliner, in 1956.

**cabbage ruff** Large ruff falling in irregular folds, like leaves of a cabbage. Worn by men in early 17th c. Also called *lettuce ruff.*

**cabbage-tree hat** Broad-brimmed hat worn in Australia made of plaited or woven leaf fibers from the cabbage tree or palm.

**cabin-boy breeches** Tight-fitting pants laced below the knees worn for sportswear by women in the late 1940s. *Der.* After uniform worn by an employee on ocean vessel who waits on officers and passengers.

**cable hatband** Band of gold yarn twisted to resemble a rope or cable; worn in the late 16th c.

**cable stitch** See STITCHES.

**cable yarn** See CORD YARN.

**cabochon** (kab-a-shon) See GEM CUTS.

**cabretta** (ka-bret-ah) See LEATHERS.

**cabriole headdress** Rare fashion of about 1755, lasting only a few years, consisting of a miniature coach-and-six, or post chaise, worn by women on head instead of a cap. Coach was made of gold thread with six dappled gray horses made of blown glass. Also spelled *caprioll. Der.* French, "two-wheeled carriage."

**cabriolet bonnet** (kab-ree-o-leh) Large bonnet popular from the late 18th c. to mid 19th c. made with brim extending forward framing the face like a carriage top, but cut away in back to show hair. *Der.* French, "two-wheeled carriage."

**cabuya** Plant similar to North American century plant which grows in the highlands of Ecuador. Fronds averaging 18″ long and 7″ in diameter are sliced lengthwise, soaked, and beaten by hand until only the fibers remain—then dried and dyed. Used by the lower classes to make clothing. In 1600 used by Spanish conquerors to make ALPARGATAS for troops. Currently used to make handbags called SHIRGA.

**cache-folies** (cash fo-lee) Short-haired wig worn by women in Paris in the early 19th c. to cover the cropped TITUS COIFFURE, of the French Revolution.

**cache-laid** (cash lade) Term used for mask worn in Paris to conceal a plain or unattractive face. Fashionable about 1650 during reign of Louis XIV. *Der.* French, "hide-ugly."

**CACHE-PEIGNE**

**cache-peigne** (cash pain)  Snood of net and ribbon worn by women to hold hair back, in the 1850s and 1860s. *Der.* French, "hide-comb."

**cack**  Heelless shoe with soft leather sole, made for infants in sizes one to five.

**caddie**  See BUSH HAT under HATS. Also spelled *caddy.*

**cadenette** (cad-net)  French term for a "lock of hair." See COIFFURE EN CADENETTES.

**cadet blue**  Light bluish-gray color, similar to color of uniforms worn by cadets at U.S. Military Academy at West Point, N.Y., and other military academies.

**cadet cloth**  Heavy, bluish-gray flannel fabric used for overcoats by cadets at the U.S. Military Academy at West Point and other military academies. Fabric is a heavily fulled double cloth.

**Cadogan**  See GEORGE under HAIRSTYLES. Also see CATAGAN #1.

**CADOGAN NET**

**cadogan net**  SNOOD, sometimes made of knotted silk yarn, worn over crown of head and enclosing the hair which hangs down the back. Popular in late 1870s and early 1880s, particularly for young women and girls. Also spelled *catagan.*

**Cadoro® bra**  See BRAS.

**café** (ka-fay)  Dark-brown coffee color. *Der.* French, "coffee."

**café au lait** (ka-fay o leh)  Brownish beige, like coffee with milk—the exact French translation.

**caftan  1.**  North African or Middle-Eastern garment (sometimes called *farasia* in Morocco) consisting of a long, full robe with slit neckline, decorated with embroidery, and long, full, bell-shaped sleeves. Worn in U.S. since 1960s as *at-home* and evening dress by women, and sometimes by men. See DRESSES, NECKLINES, ROBES, and SILHOUETTES. Compare with DAHARRA. **2.** Egyptian and Near Eastern striped coatlike garment with long sleeves worn by men with sash around waist. **3.** In Russia, a long overcoat, formerly worn by men. Also spelled *kaftan, cafetan.*

**cage  1.**  Overblouse or dress made out of latticelike or transparent fabric. See DRESSES and SILHOUETTES. **2.** Shortened name for the CAGE PETTICOAT. Also called *artificial crinoline.*

**cage-americaine**  Hoop-skirt petticoat worn from 1862 to 1869, the upper part made of hoops connected with vertical tapes and lower part covered with fabric. See CAGE PETTICOAT.

**cage empire**  Cage petticoat made with graduated hoops of steel, shaped into a slight train in back, worn under a ball gown from 1861 to 1869.

**cage petticoat**  Hoop-skirt petticoat made of a series of whalebone or wire hoops graduated in size from waist down and fastened together with vertical tapes, making it flexible and lighter in weight than layers of petticoats, worn by women from 1856 to 1868. Also called *cage* or *artificial crinoline* and *skeleton skirt*. Also see CAGE-AMERICAINE.

**caging**   Fur-cleaning process, in which furs are revolved in cagelike wire drums that permit the sawdust, used for cleaning, to fall out through the wire mesh.

**cagoule** (ka-gool)   Cloth or fur semi-circular cape with attached hood worn by peasants from 11th to 13th c.

**cai-ao**   Long chemise-type garment worn in Vietnam, by both men and women. Closes on one side and is slashed to hips revealing trousers. Worn with CAIQUAN as part of AO DAI.

**cainsil** (kane-sil)   See CHAINSE.

**caiquan** (kay-kan)   Long black trousers worn in North Vietnam by men and women under the CAI-AO to form AO DAI.

**cairngorm**   See GEMS.

**cake hat**   Man's soft felt hat of 1890s with a low oval crown creased in manner similar to ALPINE HAT.

**calamanco shoes**   Heavy twilled-cotton shoes worn by American women in Colonial days. Also spelled *calimanco, callamancoe, calliman, callimanco, calmanco.*

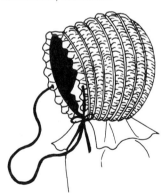

**CALASH**

**calash**   Large hood worn from 1720 to 1790 and revived 1820 to 1839, made with hinged arches of whalebone or cane covered with fabric in manner similar to folding top of convertible car. Stands away from head protect-

ing bouffant hairstyles. *Der.* After hood of "French carriage" called *calèche.* Also spelled *caleche.*

**calasiris**   See KALASIRIS.

**calcarapedes**   Self-adjusting rubber galoshes worn by men in the 1860s.

**calceus**   Roman boot coming to below ankle with long straps wrapping around leg, reaching to calf and sometimes the knee. Lower part was slit down each side to permit easy access. When worn by Roman senators called *calceus patricius.*

**calculator watch**   See WATCHES.

**calèche**   See CALASH.

**calencons**   Worn by women in early 17th c., a type of long drawers or hose worn with doublet and petticoat which later developed into the breeches and trousers of women's contemporary riding habit.

**calendar watch**   See WATCHES.

**calendering**   Running a finished fabric between hot metal rollers under pressure to make it shiny, or to give an embossed effect.

**calf-length**   See LENGTHS.

**calfskin**   Hide from young cows or bulls, tanned for use either as leather or fur. See FURS and LEATHERS.

**calico**   Cotton fabric with small distinctive designs printed on one side of the plain woven cloth. Named for Calicut, India, where printed cloth first originated. The name was originally applied to any printed cloth from India. Also see CALICO PRINT under PRINTS.

**calico button**   Metal ring covered with calico, sometimes with metal eyelets in center, used mainly for underclothes from 1840s on.

**California embroidery**   See EMBROIDERIES.

**calisthenic costume**   Knee-length dress worn with Turkish trousers similar to costume worn by *Amelia Bloomer.* Worn in late 1850s by women and girls for such sports as archery, ice

CALISTHENIC
COSTUME

skating, and exercising with dumbbells. Later version of this dress was called *gymnasium costume*.

**calk**   **1.** Device on heel, or sole, of shoe or boot to prevent slipping or give longer wear; may be a metal plate with sharp points. **2.** In Colonial America term used for CLOG with spiked sole.

**calligraphic scarf**   See SCARFS.

**Callot Soeurs**   See APPENDIX/DESIGNERS.

**calotte** (ca-lot)  **1.** Woman's small skullcap worn in 1940s and 1950s, sometimes with large jeweled pin. **2.** A cap worn by schoolboy, called BEANIE. See CAPS. **3.** Tiny, close-fitting skullcap cut in shaped gores often with a tab at center of top worn by Roman clergy, priests, and monks in early Christian orders—now worn by the Pope. Also called ZUCCHETTO. **4.** Black silk skullcap worn by Chinamen; red cord knot on top indicating a married man, a white knot worn for mourning. Also spelled *calot, callot.* **5.** See YARMULKA.

**calpac**   Large black sheepskin or felt cap worn by men in Near East, Turkey, and Armenia. Similar to COSSACK HAT.

**calypso chemise** (ca-lip-so)  Woman's dress of 1790s made of colored muslin worn under a loose robe.

**calypso shirt**   See SHIRTS.

**camail** (ka-mail)  **1.** Shoulder cape of chain mail laced to helmet worn as part of armor during first half of 14th c. **2.** Woman's waist-length or three-quarter-length capelike cloak of 1840s with small turndown collar, arm slits, and fringe trimming. Lined with wadded cashmere, satin or velvet in winter and with silk in summer.

**Camargo** (ka-mar-go)  A woman's jacket with draped fullness, pannier-style, around hips worn over waistcoat or vest in late 1870s. *Der.* After Marie Ann de Cupis Camargo (1710–1770), celebrated dancer.

**Camargo hat**   Small woman's evening hat with brim raised in front; worn in mid-1830s. *Der.* After Marie Ann de Cupis Camargo (1710–1770), celebrated dancer.

**camauro** (ka-mor-o)  Red velvet, ermine-trimmed cap slightly larger than a skullcap formerly worn by Pope of Roman Catholic church.

**cambric**   Fine closely woven cotton fabric made with mercerized yarns given a calendered finish. May also be made of linen and used for handkerchiefs. *Der.* From Cambrai, France. Also see PAPER CAMBRIC.

**Cambridge coat**   Three-button, single- or double-breasted man's suit coat of 1870, made with three seams in back and a center vent.

**Cambridge paletot** (pal-e-toe)  Man's knee-length overcoat of mid-1850s cut with wide cape collar, large turned-back cuffs, and wide lapels extending almost to hem.

**camelaurion** (kamel-lo-ree-on)  Coronet with closed crown, worn by Roman Caesars and by Byzantine emperors.

**cameleons** (ka-me-le-on)  Women's shoes and boots of late 1850s made with cutouts to show colored stockings underneath.

**camel hair** **1.** Fibers from the crossbred Bactrian camel of Asia, which produces soft luxurious yarn that is resistant to heat and cold. **2.** Cloth made of these fibers.

**cameo** **1.** A small low relief carving usually made from a banded two-layered gemstone such as onyx or sardonyx which gives a raised design, usually in white, with another color left as the background. Most common subject is a woman's head and shoulders. The opposite of INTAGLIO. **2.** Carving a two-tone shell in the same manner as above to produce a *shell cameo*. **3.** Using colored pottery material similar to that used by Josiah Wedgwood and molded to produce a WEDGEWOOD® CAMEO. Also see NECKLACES.

**Cameron tartan** See TARTANS.

**cames** See CHEMISE.

**camis** Long blouse worn by Mohammedan women of India with the baggy CHUDIDAR PA'EJAMAS.

**camisa** (kah-mee-sah) Blouse worn by women in the Philippines, made of sheer fine *rengue* cloth woven from pineapple fibers with gathered set-in sleeves hanging wide and free to the elbow, or below, and elaborately embroidered at the lower edge. *Der.* Spanish, *camis,* "blouse."

**camise** See CHEMISE.

**camisette** See FOUNDATIONS.

**camisia** Medieval British term for CHEMISE.

**camisole** (kam-ih-sole) **1.** Short bodice or vest with built-up straps worn over corset or stays. Introduced in early 1800s. Also called CHEMISE, CORSET COVER, and PETTICOAT BODICE. **2.** *Lingerie* term used to describe a waist-length, gathered, straight-cut top with straps, trimmed with lace or embroidery. Worn with a petticoat under a sheer blouse in late 19th and early 20th c. **3.** Sleeved jacket or jersey formerly worn by men.

**camisole top** Blouse of a dress, styled like a CAMISOLE, usually cut straight across, gathered with drawstring, and held up with wide straps. Also see BLOUSES, NECKLINES, SLIPS and TOPS.

**cami-tap set** Matching two-piece innerwear set in which the top, similar to a camisole, may double as a blouse. Worn over short shorts cut with a slight flare. Frequently made of satin. Also see TAP under PANTIES.

**camlet** Fine fabric of mixed materials such as silk, wool, linen, goat's and camel's hair, usually costly, used continuously for clothing from 12th through 19th c. Also spelled *camelot, chamblette*. *Der.* Place of manufacture on banks of River Camlet in England or possibly from its content of camel's hair.

**camouflage fabric** Cloth colored to resemble hues seen in surrounding terrain so that person wearing garment made from these fabrics blends into background. Originally worn by soldiers in World War II, used for clothing in 1960s and 1970s. Used for sportswear in 1980s, and very popular for suits, pants, jackets, and caps. Also see SPORT SUITS.

**camp** See SHIRTS and SHORTS.

**campagus** (kam-pa-gus) **1.** Shoe worn by bishops in Western Church, particularly Roman Catholic, sometimes Episcopal. **2.** Shoe worn during Byzantine period and the Middle Ages, high in back to the ankle and fastened with ribbon or strap over instep.

**campaign coat** **1.** Originally a long military overcoat worn by the rank and file from about 1667, and later adopted by men for civilian wear in late 17th c. **2.** Bedraggled, tattered coat worn by gypsies and beggars to arouse sympathy in the 18th c.

**campaign hat** Broad-brimmed field hat with high crown first worn by Union soldiers in Civil War and later issued to entire U.S. army. Worn by soldiers in World War II with four dents in top of crown. Same as MOUNTIE'S HAT.

**campaign wig** Periwig of bushy, wavy hair with center part, three ends tied together when traveling. Worn by European soldiers from 1675 to 1750—after that considered old-fashioned. Also spelled *campaigne.* Also called *travelling wig.*

**camyss** Shirt of linen worn by men in Turkey.

**canadienne** (ka-nah-dee-en) Woman's hip-length, double-breasted, belted coat designed in Paris during the 1940s, copied from coats worn by Canadian soldiers.

**canale/canalle** See CANNELLE.

**canary diamond** See DIAMONDS.

**cancan dress** See DRESSES.

**candlewick** Cotton fabric of loose weave to which rows of tufts of very soft cotton are attached from the back and then clipped on the face. Originally used for bedspreads; now used for robes and sportswear.

**candy pink** See BONBON PINK.

**candys** See KANDYS.

**candy stripes** See STRIPES.

**cane** Staff or stick to assist walking or to carry as a fashionable accessory, varying from rough rustic wood for country use, *e.g.,* *shillelagh,* to polished woods with elaborately decorated heads, *e.g.,* MALACCA and RATTAN CANES. Carried from 16th c. to present by men and occasionally by women. Also called *walking stick.* Also see CONSTABLE and SWAGGER.

**canale/canellee** See CANNELLE.

**canezou** (can-zoo) **1.** Woman's waist-length spencer jacket of 1820s without sleeves. **2.** In 1830s a cape, cut short and pointed, extending down center front and back but not covering the arms. Also called *canezou pelerine.* **3.** By mid-19th c. an elaborate FICHU of muslin, ribbons, and lace covering bodice of dress.

**caniche** (ka-neesh) Curly-textured wool fabric similar to hair of a poodle. *Der.* French, "poodle."

**canions** Tight-fitting cuffed tubular garments worn on the thighs as extensions of men's TRUNK HOSE from 1570 to 1620 frequently of different fabric or color.

**cannele** Warpwise cord effect in fabric with woven-in ribs, *e.g.,* PIQUÉ. Also spelled *canale, canelle, canele, canile, canellee.*

**cannetille** (can-tee) **1.** Military braid of gold or silver thread that looks like lace. Also spelled *cantile.* **2.** Fine spiral-twisted gold or silver thread, used for embroidery. **3.** French warp-ribbed dress fabric.

**cannon** **1.** See CANNONS. **2.** Piece of protective plate armor for the upper arm or forearm, cylindrical or semi-cylindrical.

**cannons** Frills of lace or bunches of ribbons that fell down over tops of wide boots worn by men during 1660s and 1670s. Also called *port canons, canons.* Also worn with low shoes and PETTICOAT BREECHES.

**cannon sleeve** Woman's padded and boned sleeve large at shoulder and tapering to wrist, giving appearance of shape of a cannon. Used in women's gowns from about 1575 to 1620. Also called *trunk sleeve.*

**canotier** (kan-o-tee-ay) **1.** See HATS. **2.** French term for fabric made in a twill weave and used for sportswear and yachting clothes. *Der.* French, "boatman."

**canteen bag** See HANDBAGS.

**cantile** See CANNETILLE.

**canton crepe** Lightweight, rippled textured crepe made of silk or rayon yarns. Surface effect is achieved by tightly twisted yarns in both directions. *Der.* Yarn came originally from Canton, China, and was called *Canton silk.*

**Canton flannel** Soft, fuzzy, cotton fabric made in twill weave. The filling yarn is lightly twisted making it possible, when brushed, to form a heavy nap covering the weave. May be dyed and printed. Used for nightgowns, robes, and pajamas. Similar to FLANNELETTE, with flannelette made in a plain weave.

**Canton silk yarn** Silk from southern China which comes from small domesticated silkworms. It is weaker than Japanese silk but is lustrous and of even diameter. It takes more than twice as much Canton silk to make a yarn of the same weight as Japanese silk. *Der.* For city of Canton, China.

**cantouche**   See KONTUSH.

**Cantrece® yarn**   Trademark of E. I. du Pont de Nemours and Co. for a resilient self-crimping nylon yarn, used for hosiery and pantyhose.

**canvas**   **1.** Classification of heavy durable cotton fabric made from coarse, hard twisted yarns used without sizing as a utility fabric. Popular in the 1970s and 1980s for raincoats, coats, handbags, and boots. **2.** May also be heavily sized and used by artists for oil painting. **3.** When woven with stripes, called *awning canvas.* **4.** *Sail canvas* is a very heavy fabric woven with two-ply linen warp and coarse cotton filling.

**Canvas embroidery**   See BERLIN WORK under EMBROIDERIES.

**cap**   Head covering fitting more snugly to the head than a hat, frequently made with a visor-type front. Usually made of felt, leather, straw, or fabric and worn for sports or informal occasions. In the 16th c. caps were worn by servants and apprentices; in the 19th c. gentlemen began to wear caps in the country or for sports, but not in town. From 1500 to 19th c. ladies wore caps indoors, *e.g., mob cap.* After that time worn only by female servants and the elderly. *Der.* Latin, *cappa,* "a hooded cloak." In alphabetical listing see CHARLOTTE CORDAY, FORAGE CAP, MONMOUTH CAP, and MORNING CAP.

===== **CAPS** =====

**applejack c.**   See NEWSBOY CAP.

**army c.**   Caps worn by U.S. Army. See GARRISON, FATIGUE, OVERSEAS and SERVICE CAPS.

**ASTRONAUT'S CAP        BASEBALL CAP**

**astronaut's c.**   Cap similar to a baseball cap with elaborately embroidered gold braid on visor, band of gold braid around edge of crown, gold button on top of crown, and adjustable back strap. Copied from caps worn by astronauts and World War II naval commanders, the gold braid is sometimes facetiously called "scrambled eggs." Also called *commander's cap* and *flight deck cap.*

**baseball c.**   Cap with dome-shaped crown, sometimes made with alternate panels of nylon net for coolness, and an adjustable band or elastic at the back. May have any type of "patch" or slogan on front, *e.g.,* major league football, baseball and Little League team names, makes of cars or trucks, sports insignia, soft-drink brands. When first introduced, cap fit more closely to the head like a skullcap. Also see BATTER'S CAP.

**bathing c.**   Tight-fitting cap made of rubber, with or without strap under chin. Often elaborately decorated with rubber flowers, fringe, or other trimmings. Worn to protect hair while swimming.

**batter's c.**   Duck-bill visored cap with hard crown for protection worn by baseball players when taking turn at bat. Also called *batter's helmet.*

**beanie**   Skullcap cut in gores to fit the head. Worn by children and by freshmen students as a part of hazing by upperclassmen. Also called *dink* or *dinky.*

**BEARSKIN CAP**     **HUNT CAP**

**CROCHETED CAP**     **JULIET CAP**

**EIGHT-POINT CAP**     **KEPI**

**GLENGARRY CAP**     **MORTARBOARD**

**bearskin c.** Tall cylindrical cap of black bearskin with a chain or strap under lower lip or the chin. Worn by some personnel of the British army, also by military guards of Buckingham Palace in London and Parliament buildings in Ottawa, Canada. Also see DRUM MAJOR'S HAT under HATS.

**bebop cap** See NEWSBOY CAP.

**bellboy/bellhop c.** Small fabric pillbox, often trimmed with gold braid, sometimes with chin strap, worn by hotel or restaurant bellboys. Also called *bellhop cap.*

**beret** Flat tam made of wool. Also see PANCAKE BERET, TAM #3 and BASQUE BERET in alphabetical listing.

**calotte** (ca-lot) **1.** Similar to beanie but frequently made of leather or suede with a small matching projection like a stem on center top. Also see SKULLCAP. **2.** Tiny skullcap with tab at center of top worn by Roman Catholic clergy. See ZUCCHETTO. Also see alphabetical listing.

**Carnaby c.** See NEWSBOY CAP.

**chapel c.** Small round cap which fits on the back of the head, sometimes lace-trimmed, matched to choir robes, and worn by women of choir for church services.

**commander's c.** See ASTRONAUT'S CAP.

**conductor's c.** Cap with crown shaped like a pillbox with visor-shaped brim, frequently trimmed with braid around the crown and an insignia in front. Worn placed straight on forehead by train conductors.

**cossack forage c.** Visored cap with soft crown set on band worn toward back of head rather than pulled down on forehead. Made in napped suede fabric in natural, black, or loden green. Adapted from caps worn by Russian Cossacks and accepted for general wear by men and women in the late 1960s. Also see FORAGE CAP.

**crocheted c.** Any type cap which is hand crocheted. Styles vary—some are helmet-shaped—others made like TAMS. Some styles are trimmed with metal or plastic paillettes attached at intervals.

**Davy Crockett c.** Coonskin (raccoon fur) cap with tail of animal hanging down back. Worn in Colonial America by woodsmen and pioneers and named after David Crockett, frontiersman and politician, who fought and died at the Alamo in Texas in 1836. Popular for young boys in 1950s and 1960s after wide exposure on television programs.

**deerstalker** Checked or tweed cap with visor on both front and back and ear laps that can be buttoned or tied to top of crown, worn from 1860s on. Associated with pictures of Sherlock Holmes, the fictional detective created by Sir Arthur Conan Doyle. *Der.* Originally worn in England for hunting including "stalking deer." Also called *fore-and-after*.

**desert fatigue c.** Visor cap of cotton poplin made with soft crown set on wide band, worn with top crushed down at sides. Copied from German forage cap worn in World War II and accepted for general wear in late 1960s.

**dink/dinky** See BEANIE.

**Dutch-boy c.** Cap with visor and soft wide crown usually made of navy-blue wool.

**eight-point c.** Policeman's cap, or utility cap, with soft crown and a stiff visor in front. Crown is made by sewing together eight straight-edged wedges of fabric making an octagon-shaped crown.

**engineer's c.** Round cap with visor worn by railroad workers, usually of blue-and-white striped cotton. The crown is box-pleated onto the band. Adopted in 1960s by young people for sportswear.

**fatigue c.** U.S. armed forces cap usually made of twill fabric in style similar to ENGINEER'S CAP.

**flight deck c.** See ASTRONAUT'S CAP.

**forage c.** A military undress cap worn in various styles in different countries, usually made of fabric in duck-billed style. No longer worn by U.S. Army. See COSSACK FORAGE CAP.

**fore-and-after** See DEERSTALKER.

**French beret** See PANCAKE BERET.

**frigate c.** Utility visored cap with flat top slanting toward back. Made of water-repellent black silky rayon with cord and buttons on front for trim. Copied from caps worn by merchant seamen in the 19th c.

**garrison c.** See OVERSEAS CAP.

**glengarry c.** Military cloth cap creased to fold flat like an OVERSEAS CAP usually with tartan band at edge, regimental badge at side front, and two black ribbon streamers in back. Part of the uniform of Scottish Highland regiments, and adapted for sportswear by women and small boys in mid-19th c. *Der.* After Glengarry, a valley in Invernessshire, Scotland.

**Greek fisherman's c.** Soft cap of denim or wool with crown higher in front than in back. Elaborately trimmed with braid on visor and at seam where visor meets crown. Styled in black wool, blue denim, or white and worn for sportswear or boating in 1980s by both men and women.

**hunt c.** Cap cut in six segments with small visor, elastic chin strap, and button on center top, sometimes of cloverleaf shape. Worn with riding habit, it is sometimes made with a plastic shell covered with velvet or velveteen and a padded lining.

**hunting c.** Bright-orange visored cap, sometimes fluorescent, enabling hunter to be clearly seen in the woods.

**jockey c.** Visored cap with crown usually of bicolored sateen cut in gores, similar to baseball cap but with deeper crown, worn by racetrack jockeys. Similar caps worn by women in mid-1960s.

NEWSBOY CAP     STOCKING CAP

NURSE'S CAP     TAM-O'-SHANTER

OVERSEAS CAP     TOURING CAP

SHAKO     TROOPER CAP

**Juliet c.** SKULLCAP of rich fabric worn for evening or with wedding veils. May also be made entirely of pearls, jewels, or chain. *Der.* Medieval costume of Juliet in Shakespeare's play *Romeo and Juliet*.

**kepi** High-crowned, flat-topped visored cap frequently worn with havelock in back as protection from sun. Worn by French Foreign Legion and French General and statesman, Charles de Gaulle. Also called *Legionnaire's cap*.

**Legionnaire's c.** See KEPI.

**miner's c.** Stiff cap with short duck-billed visor and battery-powered light attached to front of crown.

**mod c.** Cap similar to NEWSBOY CAP, popular in U.S. in mid-1960s.

**mortarboard** Large, square, flat, cloth-covered cardboard attached to a skullcap that comes down to a point in front and back. Worn with one point in center front. Large tassel, attached to the center of the hat, is worn on one side, and cap matches gown with which it is worn. Doctor's cap may have a gold bullion tassel. Cap has been worn since 16th c. with academic robe. Also see alphabetical listing.

**newsboy c.** Soft fabric cap with flat bloused crown and visor that sometimes snaps to the crown. Formerly worn by newsboys and made famous by child actor Jackie Coogan in silent films of the 1920s. Revived in exaggerated form in 1960s and 1970s. May be referred to by various names, *e.g., Carnaby, bebop, soul, applejack cap*.

**nurse's c.** White stiffly starched fabric cap received by nurses at graduation and worn pinned to the crown of the head when on duty in hospitals. Each school of nursing has an individual style of cap.

**overseas c.** Flat folding cloth cap of khaki or olive drab fabric worn by men and women in the armed services. Has a lengthwise pleat from front to back in center of crown to enable it to fold flat. Worn overseas in World Wars I and II. Also called *garrison cap.*

**painter's c.**  Lightweight duck-billed fabric cap made with a round, flat-topped crown. Sometimes imprinted with school name, team name, or resort on front of crown. *Der.* From cap worn by house painters.

**pancake beret**  Flat molded felt tam usually made in navy blue but may also come in other colors. Formerly worn tilted to one side of the head and indicated the wearer was an artist. Also called a *French beret.*

**scarf c.**  **1.** Scarf attached to visor and tied around head, worn in late 1960s. Also see SCARF HAT under HATS. **2.** Long tubular knitted or crocheted scarf with opening for head in one end, similar to STOCKING CAP.

**service c.**  Army cap worn with dress uniform, made with a stiff, round, flat top and stiff visor of leather or plastic.

**shako** (shay-ko)  **1.** Cylindrical stiff tall cap with attached visor. Top is sometimes tapered, sometimes flared, with feather cockade in front. Worn by marching bands, it was adapted from a style of military cap worn formerly. **2.** Same as DRUM MAJOR'S HAT.

**shower c.**  Plastic or waterproof cap, usually shirred into an elastic band, worn to keep the hair dry when taking a shower.

**skullcap**  Gored cap, usually made in eight sections, which fits tightly to crown of the head, often part of ecclesiastical garb or national costume. Also see CALOTTE, BEANIE, YARMULKA, and ZUCCHETTO.

**stocking c.**  A knitted or crocheted cap with a long pendant tail worn hanging down the back or side frequently with a tassel on the end. Also called *toboggan cap.*

**soul cap**  See NEWSBOY CAP.

**tam**  Flat cap made in several ways: a) out of two circles of fabric—one complete and one with hole cut in center—sewed together at the outer edge; b) crocheted with pompon on top for trim; c) made out of piece of circular molded felt and also called a BERET. *Der.* Shortened form of TAM-O-SHANTER used in U.S.

**tam-o-shanter**  **1.** Genuine Scottish tams are frequently made out of long, shaggy striped wool fabric and cut in segments so that stripes form a pattern on the top. Usually larger than other tams with a pompon at center of crown. **2.** See TAM. *Der.* From the name of the main character of Scottish poem written by Robert Burns about 1791 called "Tam O'Shanter."

**tea-cozy c.**  Cap introduced in late 1960s that fits head closely to cover hair completely. *Der.* Quilted padded cover for teapots used to keep the tea hot at the table.

**toboggan c.**  See STOCKING CAP.

**touring c.**  Leather or fabric cap with snap-down visor, frequently treated for water repellency. Popular in the 1980s, it is copied from earlier cap worn when "touring" in early 20th-c. automobiles.

**trooper c.**  Man's or boy's cap of leather or leather-like plastic with fur or pile lining and a flap around sides and back. Flaps can be folded down to keep ears warm or up to reveal lining. *Der.* Originally worn by state policemen or "troopers," now used by mailmen, policemen, etc.

**watch c.**  Knitted cap, fitting closely over head with turned-up cuff, made of navy-blue wool yarn. Worn by sailors on watch, for other work duty, or as a replacement for white duck hat. Adapted in other colors for sportswear by men, women, and children.

**YACHTING CAP**

**yachting c.** Cap, usually white, with flat crown and black or navy-blue visor, decorated with yacht-club emblem styled similar to a naval officer's cap, also worn by yacht-club members on boats.

**yarmulka** Skullcap made of embroidered, beaded, or crocheted fabric. Worn by Orthodox Jewish men for day wear and in the synagogue. Worn by other Jewish men for special occasions and religious services.

**zucchetto** Ecclesiastical skullcap worn by Roman Catholic hierarchy: white for the Pope, red for a Cardinal, and purple for a Bishop.

---

**capa 1.** Wide, circular, full-length hooded cape worn by Spanish men from Middle Ages to early 17th c. In the Romantic Era in France, it was called CAPE À L'ESPAGNOLE and worn by women. **2.** Full cape worn by bullfighters in Spain, used to attract bull's attention. *Der.* Latin, *capa,* "hooded cloak."

**cape** Sleeveless outerwear of various lengths usually opening in center front; cut in a full circle, in a segment of a circle, or on the straight—usually with slits for arms. Classic type of cloak worn in one form or another since Greek times. See PAENUAL and LACERNA. Although worn during the Middle Ages, a cape was more generally called a *mantle.* Important from then on in various eras in various lengths as a separate item or attached to coats. Also see COATS, COLLARS, SLEEVES, and SHOULDERS. In alphabetical listing see MANTLE, MANTELET, MANTELLETTA, MANTELLONE, PALATINE, and TIPPET.

## CAPES

**bubble c.** Elbow-length fur cape often made with skins worked in the round. Popular in 1950s and early 1960s.

**capelet** Any small cape, *e.g.,* a cape collar, attached or detachable, on a coat, dress, or suit. Also see TIPPET in alphabetical listing.

**capote** (kah-poat) Full circular cape with wide cape collar and red lining. Used as a working cape by matadors at Spanish and Mexican bullfights. Also spelled *capot.* Also see CAPOTE #2 in alphabetical listing.

**clerical c.** Three-quarter-length cape of wool melton with satin lining, small velvet collar, and braided frog closing worn by clergy.

**cope 1.** Ornately embroidered semi-circular mantel, fastened across the chest with an elaborate clasp arrangement worn on ceremonial occasions by the Pope and dignitaries of the Roman Catholic Church. **2.** Same style is worn as a coronation robe by English sovereigns. **3.** Originally a hooded cloak designed as a rain cape sometimes made with sleeves and fastened in center front. After adoption by clergy it was always sleeveless and richly decorated.

**ferraiolo** A full-length black circular cape worn as an outer garment by clerics over other vestments for ceremonial occasions such as receptions, academic occasions, or banquets.

**French policeman's c.** Circular-cut knee-length cape worn by French policemen made of heavy black wool and rubber. Heavy enough to be swung like a billy club. Authentic cape was sold as sportswear in boutiques and Army surplus stores in U.S. in late 1960s. Also called *gendarme cape.*

**gendarme c.** See FRENCH POLICEMAN'S CAPE.

**maxi c.** Any ankle-length cape.

**midi c.** Any calf-length cape. May be a RAIN CAPE or made of fur or fabric.

**mozetta** (mot-ze-tah) Elbow-length cape with ornamental hood hanging in back, worn by cardinals and church dignitaries. *Der.* Italian *mozzare,* "to cut short."

COPE

MIDI CAPE

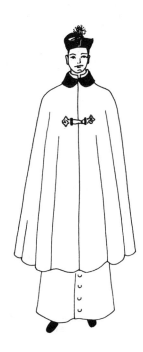

CLERICAL CAPE

OPERA CAPE

**muleta c.** Descriptive term for a Spanish-type midi cape made of felt, sometimes scarlet, and trimmed with wool tassels around the neck, down front, and around hem. Featured in late 1960s for women.

**nurse's c.** Three-quarter-length cape of navy-blue wool trimmed with brass buttons and lined in red. Worn by nurses with their uniforms.

**officer's c.** Three-quarter-length cape in navy-blue worsted with small standing collar; part of dress uniform of officers in U.S. Navy.

**opera c.** Man's full, circular calf-length black worsted cape, sometimes lined in red satin. Worn for formal occasions with tail coat and top hat. *Der.* In the 19th c. it was fashionable attire with the high silk hat for the opera. Also favored by magicians and circus ringmasters.

**rain c.** **1.** A lightweight plastic cape which may be folded, placed in a small envelope, and carried for use when it rains. See SIPHONIA in alphabetical listing. **2.** A cape of any fabric which has been treated for water-repellency.

---

**cape à l'espagnole** (les-pan-yol) See CAPA.

**capelet** See BLOUSES and CAPES.

**capeline** (cap-leen) **1.** Iron or steel skullcap worn by foot soldiers in Middle Ages. **2.** Second half of 18th c. woman's feather-trimmed wide-brimmed hat. **3.** Hood with attached cape worn in 1863 by women in country. **4.** Wide floppy brimmed hat with small round crown worn since 1920s. **5.** See HATS.

**Cape May diamond** See DIAMONDS.

**cape ruby** See GEMS.

**capeskin** See LEATHERS.

**Capezio®** See BALLET SLIPPER under SLIPPERS.

**cap of dignity** See CAP OF MAINTENANCE.

**cap of estate** See CAP OF MAINTENANCE.

**cap of maintenance** Cap carried on a cushion before British sovereigns in coronation processions; sometimes used for mayors. Usually made of scarlet velvet with ermine trim and symbolizing high rank. Also called *cap of dignity* and *cap of estate.*

**capot** (ka-pot) Man's loose coat with turn-down collar and cuffs worn in 18th c. Also spelled *capote.*

**capote** (kah-poat) **1.** See CAPOT. **2.** Hooded coat or cloak worn from Middle Ages on. **3.** Popular bonnet of 1830s with stiff brim framing the face, soft gathered crown, and ribbon bows tied at side or under chin. By 1890 worn mostly by older women. **4.** French term for fabric with napped surface used for sailors' clothes and waterproof coats. **5.** See CAPES.

**capot-ribot** Black velvet hat with long "curtain" (or veil), hanging below shoulders at sides and back. Popular in France after Napoleonic campaign in 1798 and still worn by ladies of high rank in Brittany.

**cappa floccata** (kap-pa flo-kah-ta) Round cap of hairy fabric worn by Greek shepherds.

**cappuccio** See CHAPERON.

**caprice** (ka-preece) Loose short sleeveless woman's evening jacket of mid-19th c. that tapered to rounded point below the waist in back.

**Capri-length panty girdle** See GIRDLES.

**caprioll** See CABRIOLE HEADDRESS.

**Capri pants** (ka-pree) See PANTS.

**cap sleeve** See SLEEVES.

**Capucci, Roberto** See APPENDIX/DESIGNERS.

**capuche** (cap-poosh) **1.** Cowl worn by Capuchin monks of Franciscan order. **2.** Woman's hood attached to cloak worn in 17th c. **3.** Woman's silk-lined sunbonnet of mid-19th c.

**Capuchin** (kap-yoo-chin) **1.** Hood worn outdoors in 16th, 17th and 18th c. **2.** Hood and

**CAPUCHIN**

shoulder cape or long cloak, sometimes lined in colored or striped silk, called a *redingote*, worn by women in 18th c. for traveling. *Der.* From *capuche*, "cowl worn by Capuchin monks of Franciscan order." Also spelled *capuchon, capucine, capuche.*

**Capuchin collar** Continuous roll collar on a wrap-over front bodice with a V-neckline worn by women in the late 18th and early 19th c.

**capuchon** (ka-poo-shon) **1.** See Capuchin. **2.** Woman's waist-length outdoor evening mantle with wired hood and long tight sleeves worn in 1837. Also called *carmeillette.* **3.** Tiny bonnet made of flowers. Worn in 1877.

**capucine** (kap-u-seen) **1.** Yellow-orange color. **2.** See Capuchin #2. *Der.* French, "nasturtium."

**Capulet** (cap-yew-let) Small hat conforming to shape of head and placed back from brow, sometimes with cuffed brim in front. *Der.* For cap worn by Juliet Capulet, heroine of Shakespeare's play *Romeo and Juliet.*

**caraco** (kar-a-ko) **1.** Fitted hip-length suit jacket with peplum made by French designer Yves Saint Laurent in 1969, said to derive from jackets depicted in Toulouse-Lautrec paintings. **2.** Thigh-length fitted jacket, flaring below waist, made with no waistline seams and popular for women from late 18th through 19th c. Also called *caraco corsage.* **3.** Hip-length bodice, tight-fitting and often sleeveless, worn in French provinces as part of regional costume.

**caraco corsage** See Caraco #2.

**caracul** See Karakul cloth.

**carat** Unit of weight used for gemstones. Fractions of a carat are divided into 10 points. Thus, a 1½ c. stone would be 1.5, or 1 carat and 5 points. In actual weight 1 carat equals 200 milligrams 2 grams. Not to be confused with Karat, which is related to the quality of gold. (The abbreviation used is *c.*) See Grain #2.

**caravan** Small type of collapsible bonnet of 1765 similar to the Calash. Made of semicircular hoops that, when opened, drop a veil of white gauze called *sarcenet* over the face.

**caravan bag** See Safari bag under Handbags.

**carbatina** Ancient Roman sandal made of single piece of untanned hide as sole, overlapping sides of foot, and held on by leather thongs. Copied since 1950s as barefoot summer sandal.

**carbuncle** See Gems.

**carcaille** (kar-kiyuh) 15th-c. standing collar, which flared upward to the ears. Used on Houppelande and Pourpoint.

**car coat** See Coats.

**carded yarn** Yarn made from short fibers first straightened by a process called Carding before being spun; used in making coarse cotton and woolen yarns. Compare with Combed Yarn.

**Cardigan, 7th Earl 1.** James Thomas Brudenell (1797–1868) Lieutenant General in British army who led the "Charge of the Light Brigade" in Battle of Balaklava in Crimean War in 1854 and needed an extra layer of warmth for his uniform. **2.** By 1890s a tight-fitting short jacket with, or without, a velvet collar made of knitted wool. **3.** By 1896 sometimes had a small rolled collar. Cardigan jacket and related garments are named after him. See Coats, Dresses, Jackets, Necklines and Sweaters.

**cardinal** **1.** In 18th c. three-quarter-length scarlet cloak with hood which resembled the MOZETTA worn by cardinals in Roman Catholic church. **2.** Woman's waist-length red cloak without hood or collar worn in 1840s.

**cardinal pelerine** Large lace BERTHA with collar open in center front worn on evening dresses in 1840s.

**carding** Textile term for first process used in cotton, wool, and spun synthetic fibers when making yarn in which extraneous matter and short fibers are removed, leaving a filmy weblike mass. Compare with COMBING.

**Cardin, Pierre** See APPENDIX/DESIGNERS.

**careless** Man's loose-fitting caped overcoat with spread collar and no seams at waistline worn in 1830s.

**cargo** See PANTS, POCKETS, and SHORTS.

**carma** Tall conical hat made of silver, gold, or brass—similar to the HENIN—worn by Algerian women in Tunisia in 18th and 19th c. Also see TANTOOR.

**carmagnole** (car-man-yole) **1.** Provincial ceremonial jacket worn by Italian workmen in southern France in late 18th c. *Der.* From Carmagnola, Italy. **2.** Jacket or short-skirted coat with wide collar, lapels, and rows of metal buttons. Worn with black pantaloons and red LIBERTY CAP by French Revolutionists in 1792 and 1793.

**Carmelite cloth** Loosely constructed plain woolen fabric which is heavily fulled. Used by the Carmelite Order of the Roman Catholic Church.

**carmeillette** See CAPUCHON #1.

**carmine** Rich red color with a purple cast.

**Carnaby look** Synonym for MOD LOOK. Derived from Carnaby Street in London where this look first appeared in many small boutiques catering to avant-garde young customers. Also see COLLARS, LOOKS, NEWSBOY CAP under CAPS, and CARNABY SHIFT under DRESSES.

**Carnegie, Hattie** See APPENDIX/DESIGNERS.

**carnelian** See GEMS.

**carnival collar** Collar made of wide loops of bright printed fabric arranged in an unstarched RUFF as on a clown's costume.

**carnival lace** See BRIDAL LACE under LACES.

**Caroline corsage** Woman's evening bodice of 1830s made with lace ruffles forming a V in front, extended around shoulders into small cape.

**Caroline hat** Man's hat made of Caroline beaver, imported from Carolinas in the Colonies, worn in England from 1680s to mid-18th c.

**Caroline sleeve** Woman's daytime dress sleeve worn in 1830s, full from shoulder to elbow and fitted to wrist.

**carpenter's apron** See APRONS.

**carpet bag** See HANDBAGS.

**carpet slipper** See SLIPPERS.

**carpincho** See LEATHERS.

**carriage boot** Woman's fur-trimmed winter boot usually of fabric, sometimes of leather, worn over other shoes to keep feet warm in unheated carriages or automobiles in early 20th c.

**carriage dress** Term used from about 1820 to end of 19th c. for a woman's dress or costume suitable for riding in a carriage pulled by a horse. Style varied with period and was frequently lavishly trimmed with fur.

**carriage parasol** Small umbrella, sometimes fringed, popular accessory for ladies when driving in open carriages in late 19th and early 20th c.

**carriage suit** Three-piece set for infant, consisting of jacket, pants, and hat. Worn outdoors in baby carriage since the late 1920s.

**carriage trade** Term coined by merchants during the horse-and-buggy era, 1890–1910, for wealthy customers arriving at the stores in their own carriages.

**carrick**   Man's or woman's full-length duster worn from 1877 on. Styled like a box coat with three capes similar to an ULSTER.

**Carrickmacross lace**   See LACES.

**carryall**   Open-top bag similar to a TOTE carried by women to hold small purchases when shopping.

**carryall clutch**   Woman's wallet designed to hold coins, bills, photographs and credit cards. Usually the size of U.S. paper money, with snap closing on long edge and purselike sections for coins.

**Cartier's**   Alfred Cartier and his son, Louis, established a jewelry firm in 1898 featuring the finest genuine gemstones mounted mostly in beautiful platinum settings. They became the most prestigious jewelers in the world by the beginning of the 20th c., and sold jewelry to the king of Portugal, Grand Dukes and Princes of Russia, the Brazilian Royal family, and other royalty throughout the world.

**cartoon fashions**   Fad, introduced in late 1960s becoming popular in 1980s, of imprinting comic strip and cartoon characters on clothing and accessories, *e.g.*, Mickey Mouse® shirt or wristwatch. Also see APRONS and KNIT SHIRTS.

**cartridge belt**   See BELTS.

**cartridge pleats**   See PLEATS.

**cartwheel hat**   See HATS and SLEEVES.

**cartwheel ruff**   Extremely large starched RUFF set in regular convolutions. Worn from 1580 to 1610 and somewhat later in Holland. A wire frame called a SUPPORTASSE was used for support. Also called FRENCH RUFF.

**Carven**   See APPENDIX/DESIGNERS.

**casaque** (ka-sack)   **1.** Fitted jacket buttoned down the front, worn by women from mid-1850s to mid-1870s. Early types had BASQUE effect to hips, sometimes longer; later types had

skirts draped in POLONAISE style. **2.** French term for jacket worn by jockeys, usually made in bright colors of their respective stables. **3.** Girl's coat cut on princess lines worn in 1860s. **4.** See CASSOCK #3.

**casaquin** (kas-a-kan)   One of the earliest jackets (late 18th c.) worn as top part of a dress; made fitted, long-sleeved, and waist-length in back. Similar to CARACO.

**casaquin bodice**   Tight-fitting bodice for daytime dress, similar in cut to man's *tail coat*, closing with buttons down front and worn in 1878.

**casaweck** (kasa-wek)   Woman's short, quilted outdoor mantle made with close-fitting velvet or silk collar and sleeves. Frequently trimmed with fur, velvet, or lace. Worn from mid-1830s to mid-1850s.

**cascade**   **1.** Ruffles bias-cut from fabric, in circular manner, that fall in folds. **2.** Trimming used in the 19th and early 20th c. made by cutting a narrow piece of fabric on *bias* and pleating it to form repeated shell designs. **3.** Jet pendants of beads with a zigzag edge used at waistline or bodice in 1860s. **4.** See COLLARS.

**cased body**   **1.** Man's sleeveless JERKIN worn over DOUBLET in second part of 16th c. **2.** Woman's *bodice* of early 19th c. with series of horizontal pleats or shirrings across the front, called *casings*.

**cased sleeve**   Woman's long sleeve made of sections of fabric alternating with bands of insertion worn about 1810 to 1820.

**casentino** (ca-zen-tee-no)   Red overcoat with a green lining worn by coachmen in Casentino, a section of Italy. Later adapted for winter sportswear.

**cashambles**   See CHAUSSEMBLES.

**Cashin, Bonnie**   See APPENDIX/DESIGNERS.

**cashmere**   An extremely soft luxurious fabric made from the hair of the cashmere goat—native to Kashmir in northwestern India, Tibet,

Turkestan, Iran, Iraq, and China. Wool is obtained from combing rather than clipping the animal. Yarn is used for *sweaters, suits,* and overcoats. Men's so-called cashmere overcoats are sometimes made with as little as 10% genuine cashmere, yet have a soft luxurious hand. Must be labeled correctly as to percent of wool and cashmere when sold at retail stores. Also see EMBROIDERIES.

**cashmere shawl** Shawls made in the Kashmir Valley of northwestern India from hair of the Tibetan goat which produces fine fleece called *pashm*, 18″ long in white, yellow, or black. Weaving has been under the direction of the Maharaja since 1586. For over 200 years shawls were woven for the court and never left India. At one time there were 40,000 looms each making 5 shawls a year. Two main types: a) Woven in sections and sewn together in square and oblong shapes. Often woven in pairs so that they were reversible, called *twin* or *double shawls.* b) shawls woven in plain or one color scheme of white, red, or green and later embroidered in gold and silk silver threads. The characteristic design is a cone, or palmetto, pattern. Extremely popular during French consulate (1799–1804) and Empire period (1804–1814) when a pair of the finest shawls cost about $15,000.

**casing** Fold of fabric stitched down to form a tunnel through which elastic, or a cord, is drawn. Sometimes made by a facing.

**casque** (cask) Hat shaped like a helmet. *Der.* French, "helmet."

**casquette** (kass-ket) **1.** Cap with visor, similar to military officers' caps, adapted for women's headwear. **2.** Woman's straw cap worn in 1863 and 1864 similar to a GLENGARRY with additional short brim front and back. Trimmed with black velvet ribbon and ostrich feathers.

**cassimere** Light- to medium-weight, lustrous woolen or worsted fabric made in plain or twill weave with hard spun yarns. Woven in various combinations of woolen, worsted, and cotton yarns. Frequently confused with cashmere although the appearance is quite different. Used for men's suits and trousers. Originally made at Sedan, France, in 19th c.

**CASSOCK #1**

**cassock** **1.** Full-length liturgical robe, made like a coat with standing collar worn by clergy, altar boys, and choirs, sometimes under white *surplice* or *cotta*. Also called *soutane*. **2.** Short front buttoned jacket worn by clerics. **3.** Long loose overcoat with a cape collar. Worn from late 16th through 17th c. by men and women for hunting, riding, and by foot soldiers. Also called a CASAQUE.

**cassock mantle** Woman's knee-length short-sleeved cloak, with shirring at shoulders and down the center back, of 1880s.

**Castelbajac, Jean Charles de** See APPENDIX/DESIGNERS.

**castellated** Describing a garment with "squared scallops" at edges, particularly the edge of sleeves or hem. Used in 14th and 15th c. Same as DAGGING. Also see BATTLEMENT.

**caste mark** **1.** Red mark usually worn in center of forehead by women of India originally to symbolize and identify caste membership, now serving a decorative function. **2.** Paste-on caste marks were introduced in U.S. as body jewelry for women in 1968. Also called *tilak*.

**Castle, Irene** American ballroom dancer, married to her dancing partner, Vernon Castle. Together they made tea-dancing the rage in pre-World War I. By 1914 she had started many fashion fads—short earlobe-length hair brushed back off forehead in loose weaves, Dutch lace caps, slashed hobble skirts, and dancing shoes with *ballet laces*.

**castor** **1.** Hat made entirely of beaver fur popular in 17th and 19th c. If rabbit fur was added it was called a *demi-castor*. Also see CO-DOVEC. **2.** Perfume ingredient obtained from the *castor beaver* used as fixative for spicy fragrances. *Castor caradensis*, zoological name for beaver.

**casual wear** Informal look of pants with shirts and sport jackets. **1. Men:** Started with the introduction of the sport shirt in the mid-1930s. Gained much impetus with general acceptance of Bermudas in the 1950s. Received another impetus with mod fashions of the 1960s particularly with the younger generation. **2. Women:** a look which started in the 1930s for clothes suitable for spectator sportswear. Later accepted as business dress. From the 1960s a term used for the pants look for day and evening as opposed to business and town suits for day and formal or semi-formal wear for evening.

**casula** Latin name of CHASUBLE.

**catagan** (ka-ta-gan) **1.** Woman's hairstyle with cluster of ringlets or braids of hair hanging at back of head, tied at nape of neck with wide ribbon. Worn in 1870s and resembling male CATOGAN WIG of 18th c. Bow at nape of neck revived by French couturière Gabrielle Chanel in 1960s. Also called *cadogan*. **2.** Same style worn by women with riding habit in 18th c.

Hair usually pulled back, looped up, and tied with a ribbon or the hair itself formed the band. *Der.* British General, First Earl of Cadogan, 1675–1726.

**catcher's mask** See MASKS.

**catch stitch** See STITCHES.

**cater cap** (kay-ter) Term used in 16th and 17th c. to describe a square cap worn at universities, now called MORTARBOARD.

**Catherine II** Married in 1745 to Peter III of Russia who ascended throne in 1762, was deposed, and his crown usurped by Catherine. Influenced fashion—one of her dresses, worn to receive the Turkish ambassador in 1775, was trimmed with many diamonds and 4,200 magnificent pearls. During her reign coiffures were limited in height to about 36 inches.

**Catherine-wheel farthingale** See WHEEL FARTHINGALE.

**catiole** Shoulder-length French marriage coif made of elaborate bands of lace sewed together and hanging in long LAPPETS, pinned up to half their length.

**Catlin, George** (1796–1872) American artist, traveler, and author, whose portraits and sketches of American Indians of over forty different tribes are a good source of clothing details. Collections of his works are in the National Museum in Washington, D.C. and in the American Museum of Natural History in New York.

**CATOGAN CLUB WIG**

**Catogan club wig** (ka-toe-gan) Man's wig with broad, flat, club-shaped QUEUE turned under and tied with black ribbon. Sometimes ribbon came around to front and tied in bow under chin. Worn from 1760 to 1790s. Much favored by the MACARONI in 1770s. *Der.* Misspelling of name of British General, First Earl of Cadogan, 1675–1726. Also called *club wig.* Also spelled *cadogan, catagan.*

**cat's eye** See GEMS.

**cat stitch** See CATCH STITCH under STITCHES.

**cat suit** See SPORT SUITS.

**cattlehide** See LEATHERS.

**caubeen** (caw-been) Irish slang term for any hat, particularly when shabby and old.

**caudebec** An imitation beaver hat made of felt worn from end of 17th throughout 18th c. Also called *cawdebink* or *cordybeck hat.*

**caul** (kol) **1.** Mesh cap similar to a SNOOD, frequently the work of a goldsmith. Frequently called a FRET in medieval times. Also see CRISPINE and CRISPINETTE. Usually worn by unmarried girls from late 14th to 17th c. **2.** Late 17th and 18th c., a foundation on which wig was made. **3.** In 18th and 19th c. used to describe soft crown of bonnet or cap.

**cauliflower wig** Short-bobbed wig, with tight curls allover, worn by coachmen in latter half of 18th c.

**caution fee** Fee paid by American designer or manufacturer to attend showing of a Paris couturier, which may be equal to cost of one or two items, to be applied to purchases.

**Cavalier** **1.** A partisan of Charles I of England (1625–1649), who wore an exaggerated large plumed hat, wide flared cuffs, wide cuffed boots, and a swinging hip-length cape—making these styles popular. **2.** A wide-brimmed velvet hat trimmed with ostrich plumes. **3.** Brimmed hat with one side turned up worn by Theodore Roosevelt and his Rough Riders in Spanish American War. **4.** Broad, flat, lace-edged collar falling over shoulders similar to collars worn by Cavaliers, partisans of Charles I, in early 17th c. Also called a *falling collar.*

**Cavalier sleeve** Sleeve slashed and fastened along outer edge by ribbon bows, full at shoulder, and close-fitting on forearm used on women's daytime dresses in 1830s.

**cavalry twill** Durable strong fabric made in a steep twill weave giving it a pronounced double diagonal wale on face that is coarser than ELASTIQUE. Usually made of worsted yarns and finished to give a clear hard surface. Also made in wool, cotton, spun rayon, and manmade fibers. Used for riding pants, suits, jackets, and coats.

**Cavanagh, John** See APPENDIX/DESIGNERS.

**cavu shirt** Long-sleeved man's sport shirt, popular from 1940 to 1950, with single pocket on the left and pointed collar. Closed diagonally from under collar almost to right side seam.

**cawdebink** See CAUDEBEC.

**cawdor cape** See GLENGARRY CAPE.

**caxon** Man's wig usually white or pale yellow, sometimes black styled with curls down the back and tied with a black ribbon. Worn as undress, or informal, wig by professional men in 18th c.

**ceint** (sant) Man's or woman's belt or girdle worn in the 14th and 15th c. Also spelled *seint.*

**Celanese®** A trademark of Celanese Marketing Company once used for acetate filament, yarn, staple, and fabric. Now includes fabrics made from nylon, acetate, and triacetate. Also used for Fortrel® polyester manufactured by Fiber Industries, partially owned by Celanese.

**celata** See SALETT.

**cellophane** Generic name, once a trademark, for thin transparent film made of acetate. Used in ribbon-sized strips to cover paper fibers imitating straw or used alone as synthetic straw for hats, handbags, etc.

**CELLULOID® COLLARS**

**Celluloid® collar** Detachable shirt collar made of Celluloid, trademark for a highly flammable plastic made of guncotton and camphor, popular for men in the early 20th c.

**cellulose** Basic ingredient in all vegetable fibers and certain man-made fibers including *acetate* fibers. Rayon is classified as *regenerated cellulose.*

**cendal** Silk fabric, similar to *taffeta* or *sarcinet*, widely used during Middle Ages; by 17th c. used only for linings.

**cendré** (sahn-dray) Pale-gray color. *Der.* French, "ashen."

**cerise** (se-reese) Intense pink-red color. *Der.* French, "cherry."

**cerulean** (seh-roo-le-an) Pale sky blue color, slightly greenish.

**Cerulean® mink** See MUTATION MINK under FURS.

**ceruse** Term used from 16th through 18th c. for cosmetic used by men and women to whiten the face, originally made of white lead and poisonous.

**cervellière** (ser-ve-li-air) Close-fitting steel cap usually worn under helmet during Middle Ages. *Der.* French, *cervelle*, "brains."

**ceryphalos** (ser-rif-a-los) Wide head band or fillet worn by women in ancient Greece.

**cevennes silk** (seh-ven) Top-grade French raw silk used to make laces.

**CFDA** See COUNCIL OF FASHION DESIGNERS OF AMERICA.

**chabaori** Jacket similar to the HAORI but shorter. Made popular after World War II by Osuka Sueko, Japanese designer.

**chaconne** (shak-kon) Ribbon cravat tied with ends dangling over chest. Named for dancer Pecourt, who, in 1692, danced a chaconne with his cravat tied in this manner. *Der.* Name of 17th-c. dance.

**chaddah** See CHADDAR.

**chaddar** **1.** An Indo-Iranian shawl or mantle about three yards in length. Also called *uttariya.* **2.** Indian shawls wrapped around the shoulders or waist by Hindu men. Also spelled *chadder, chaddah, chadur, chadar, chudder, chuddar.* **3.** A fabric used for Arab garments measuring about 40″ x 100″ and woven of cotton in a plain weave. Made with a wide blue or black warp stripe on one side of the fabric and narrow white filling stripes. **4.** A British fabric exported to Africa and India for loincloths. Made of half-bleached cotton with a solid color or border at one side. Also called *chadder ulaya* and *dohar.* **5.** Ancient Persian woman's shapeless black outergarment completely shrouding the figure. Also called *chadri.*

**chadri** An all-enveloping garment which covers the wearer from head to toe. Made of red pleated fabric with netting over the eyes. Worn by women of Kabul, a city in Afghanistan. No longer required dress for women by Afghan law. See CHADDAR #5.

**chadur** See CHADDAR #2.

**chaffers** (chaf-ers) 16th-c. term for embroidered hanging side flaps of ENGLISH HOOD called LAPPETS.

**chaharbagh shawl** Shawl made of KASABEH in *Kashmir* in northwestern India.

**chaharkhana** **1.** Handwoven 54″ wide dress fabric in *leno weave*, made in Kashmir and worn by the wealthy. **2.** Handmade 18″ wide checked fabric—half gray cotton, half dyed tussah silk—made in Bengal, India.

**chain** Series of connected loops or links made of gold, silver, brass, aluminum, or tortoise shell used for *closings* or worn as ornamental accessory in form of *necklace, bracelet*, or *belt*. Chains are called by various names according to shape of links—*cobra chain* is composed of two rows of triangular-shaped links which alternate in a flat effect. *Herringbone chain* is made of small slanting links giving a flat effect. *Rope chain* is composed of two (or more) pieces of chain twisted and wound together like rope. See BRACELETS, NECKLACES, EMBROIDERIES, HELMETS, STITCHES, and CHAIN LOAFERS under SHOES.

**chain mail** See MAIL.

**chainse** Full-length, fine, white linen, woman's under-tunic, sometimes pleated, made with long tight-fitting sleeves showing beneath full hanging sleeves of the dress or BLIAUT in the Middle Ages. Also spelled *cainsil*.

**chalcedony** See GEMS.

**chalk stripes** See STRIPES.

**challis** (shall-e) Sheer worsted fabric made in a firm plain weave frequently dyed and printed with small floral or geometrical designs. Originally made of silk and worsted, now made of wool, rayon staple, cotton, or man-made blends. Originally manufactured in Norwich, England, in 1832. Also spelled *challie, challi, challys*.

**chalwar** See SHALWAR.

**chamarre** (shah-mar) An academic robe made like a long full coat with sleeves full at the shoulders—usually fur-lined and decorated with braid and passementerie. Introduced about 1490 in England; later referred to a judge's gown. Also spelled *chammer, chymer, samarra, samarre, shamew*. *Also see* SIMAR.

**chambord** (sham-bor) Dress fabric woven in a ribbed, or variegated-ribbed effect. Used in France for mourning garments. Made of wool, or with silk warp and cotton, or wool, filling.

**chambord mantle** Three-quarter-length hooded woman's cloak of 1850s that resembled a shawl with fullness in back, made of satin or velvet. Also spelled *chambard mantle*.

**chambray** (sham-bray) Term given to a variety of yarn-dyed fabrics made of cotton or man-made fabrics. One type is iridescent, or frosty-looking, caused by weaving with warps of one color and fillings of another. Some fabrics are woven with cotton stripes made with heavier yarn. Some are lightweight high-count fabrics made of carded mercerized yarns giving a fine silky hand. Used for dresses, sportswear, and men's shirts. *Der.* From Cambrai, France.

**Chambre Syndicale de la Couture Parisienne** An association of Parisian couturiers founded in 1868 as an outgrowth of medieval guilds that regulates its members in regard to piracy of styles, dates of openings for collections, number of models presented, relations with press, questions of law and taxes, and promotional activities. In 1970s some prêt-à-porter firms were permitted membership. Formation of organization instigated by Charles Frederick Worth. School organized in 1930 called l'Ecole de la Chambre Syndicale de la Couture.

**Chambre Syndicale de la Mode** French official organization of milliners operating like the CHAMBRE SYNDICALE DE LA COUTURE PARISIENNE.

**Chambre Syndicale des Paruriers** An association comprised of accessory houses in Paris that produce bags, belts, feathers, flowers, gloves, and umbrellas.

**Chambre Syndicale du Prêt-à-Porter, des Couturiers et Createurs de Mode** Organization of couture and ready-to-wear designers formed in 1975 as another vehicle for promotion working within the CHAMBRE SYNDICALE DE LA COUTURE PARISIENNE.

**chammer** See CHAMARRE.

**chamois** (sha-mee, or French, shah-mawh) **1.** Sueded sheepskin tanned by the chamois method. See LEATHERS and CHAMOIS TANNING. **2.** Yellow color of chamois skin.

**chamois cloth** Soft cotton fabric which is either knitted or woven. Made with a fine soft nap in imitation of chamois-dyed sheepskin. Should not be shortened or confused with CHAMOIS as this refers to leather and a leather tanning process.

**chamois tanning** Type of primitive tannage, used by American Indians, called BUCKSKIN TANNING.

**chandelier earrings** See EARRINGS.

**Chanel, Gabrielle** See APPENDIX/DESIGNERS.

**changeable earrings** See EARRINGS.

**changeable taffeta** See SHOT CLOTH.

**change pocket** See TICKET POCKET under POCKETS.

**change purse** See HANDBAGS.

**ch'ang-fu** Informal Chinese robe worn by all classes, from Emperor down, in Manchu dynasty (1644-1912). **Men:** followed style of CHI-FU *robe*, usually made of monochrome patterned damask. **Women:** gown had wide loose sleeves finished with sleeve bands and made of fabric with woven or embroidered patterns. Contemporary Chinese dress for men and women is derived from these robes.

**chang-ot** Silk full-sleeved Korean cloak formerly worn outdoors by women—draped over the top of the head to conceal the face of the wearer, with the long full sleeves hanging loose about the face. Married women wore white and unmarried women wore bright colors.

**channel setting** See GEM SETTINGS.

**chantahi** See KASABEH.

**Chantilly lace** See LACES.

**ch'ao-fu** Long Chinese robe worn during Manchu dynasty (1644-1912) by Emperor and Mandarins and their wives for formal state occasions. **Men:** robe had kimono sleeves flared into "horse-hoof cuffs," close-fitting neckband, second attached collar with wing points extending to shoulders, and full pleated or gathered skirt attached to a set-in waistband. Prescribed colors and motifs that indicated rank included dragons, clouds, mountains, and waves. The Emperor's robe was bright yellow with 12 imperial signs embroidered on it, while other officials wore a stone-blue color. **Women:** robe was made in long straight lines with no waistline, narrow sleeves with "horse-hoof cuffs," and capelike collar with flaring upturned *epaulets*.

**chaparejos** See CHAPS.

**chapeau** (cha-po) French, hat or cap.

**chapeau à la Charlotte** See CHARLOTTE.

**chapeau bras** (sha-po bra) **1.** Man's flat three-cornered hat, evenly cocked or crescent-shaped, made expressly to be carried under arm from 1760s to 1830s in France, England, and U.S. By 1830 generally called BROKEN HAT. Also see CIRCUMFOLDING HAT. **2.** Woman's crush bonnet or CALASH which folded small enough to be carried in handbag or under the arm. Worn to concerts and opera in early 19th c. England. *Der.* French, "arm-hat."

**chapeau claque** (sha-po klack) Same as CLAQUE. Also called *crush hat* or *opera hat*. *Der.* French, *claque*, "slap." Also see GIBUS.

**CHAPEAU CLOCHE**

**chapeau cloche** Small crowned hat with wide drooping brim worn by women in 1860s to protect face from the sun.

**chapel cap**   See CAPS.

**chapel de fer** (sha-pel de fehr)  Armor for head, a skullcap of iron or steel, sometimes with brim; worn by medieval knights. *Der.* French, "cap of iron."

**chapel-length train**   See LENGTHS.

**chapel veil**   See VEILS.

**chapeo de sol**  Bright-colored parasol carried by the Portuguese woman as protection from the sun.

**CHAPERON AND LIRIPIPE**

**chaperon**   **1.** Anglo-French term for a fitted hood cut in one with a shoulder cape or GOLE, with long pendant tail called LIRIPIPE in 14th c. **2.** Draped version of the chaperon achieved by rolling the cape and tying it with the extended tail of the hood called the LIRIPIPE, popular in the 15th c. **3.** Woman's soft hood in the 17th c. Also spelled *chaperone, chaperonne.* Also called *cappuccio.*

**chapiney**   See CHOPINE.

**chapkan**   A type of ANGHARKA, worn by servants and palace guards in India. Called by this

name when made of heavy colored material and belted with a CUMMERBUND.

**chaplet**   **1.** Originally a garland of flowers for the head worn by Anglo-Saxon men and women on festive occasions. **2.** In 15th c. such a garland was worn only by a bride. **3.** Circlet, or metal band set with gems, worn by both men and women in 14th, 15th, and 16th c. Also called a *coronal of goldsmithry.* **4.** In late 14th and 15th c., a headband of twisted silk or satin wound around a padded roll. **5.** 17th-c. term used for a short rosary or set of beads worn on the neck.

**chaps**   **1.** Cowboys' leather leggings, worn over ordinary trousers to protect legs when riding. Alse see PANTS. **2.** Registered trademark owned by Polo Fashions, Inc., that designates a line of wearing apparel (not including cowboys' leather shearling leggings), various cosmetics, and fragrance products. *Der.* Spanish, *chaparajos,* "undressed sheepskin."

**chaqueta** (cha-kee-ta)  Spanish word for jacket, often of leather, worn by cowboys in the southwestern U.S.

**chargat** (shar-gaht)  Triangular indoor kerchief of sheer muslin worn fastened with pin under chin by Persian women.

**Charlie Chaplin**   See COATS and TOES.

**Charlotte**   Very large brimmed hat with lace ruffle at edge, worn drooping over forehead, sometimes worn over demi-negligee cap. Crown richly decorated with wide loops and bows of ribbon. Worn in mid-1780s. *Der.* Named for Queen Charlotte of England (1744–1818) married to George III of England. Style later returned to popularity somewhat modified in late 19th and early 20th c. Both styles also called *chapeau à la Charlotte.*

**Charlotte Corday cap**  Indoor cap worn in daytime in 1870s made with puffed muslin crown gathered into a band, sometimes had a ruffle around edge, sometimes with lappets.

**CHARLOTTE CORDAY CAP**

**Charlotte Corday fichu** Woman's long scarf of mid 1860s made of grenadine trimmed with a ribbon threaded through a wide hem placed around the neck, crossed in front, and tied in the back.

**charm** Small amulet, usually of metal, consisting of all sorts of mementos, *e.g.*, heart, disk, or zodiac signs worn on bracelet or necklace. See BRACELETS and NECKLACES.

**charmeuse** Lightweight, smooth, semi-lustrous, soft fabric with a crepe back. Made of cotton, silk, or man-made fibers and may be dyed or printed. Used for dresses. *Der.* French, "charmer."

**charro costume** See TRAJE CHARRO.

**charro pants** See PANTS.

**chartreuse** (char-troez) Tint of yellow-green, or greenish-yellow, similar to the liqueur of the same name made by Carthusian monks.

**charvet** Soft lustrous fabric woven with a faint herringbone design used for ties. Also called *Regence*.

**Chase, Edna Woolman** Editor-in-chief of American *Vogue* magazine from 1914 to 1952; also editor of *British Vogue*, first published in 1916, and French *Vogue*, 1920. Considered one of the most able and competent fashion authorities. One of her outstanding achievements was the introduction in 1914 of a society-sponsored fashion show with live models called "Fashion Fête," the beginning of her long promotion of American designers.

**chasembles** See CHAUSSEMBLES.

**chasing** Jewelry term for fine lines engraved on metals.

**CHASSEUR JACKET**

**chasseur jacket** Fitted, hip-length, military-inspired women's jacket of 1880s made with standing military collar, slashings at hem, and elaborately trimmed with braid and *Brandenburgs*.

**chastity belt** Beltlike device worn by women in the Middle Ages to ensure marital fidelity.

**chasuble** (chaz-u-behl) Sleeveless clerical garment, shaped somewhat like a *poncho*, with round neckline and open sides. Sometimes has a Y-shaped band from neck to hem called the ORPHREY. Worn as part of vestments at the celebration of Mass in the early Christian church, now worn by priests over the cassock. *Der.* Latin, *casula*, "cloak."

**chatelaine** (shat-eh-len) **1.** Ornamental chain of oxidized silver, silver-plated metal, or cut steel suspended at woman's waistline or hooked to belt to hold small items such as scissors, thimble case, tape measure, penknife, or button hook. Worn in last half of 19th c. See CORDELIÈRE. **2.** Term used in 1980s for antique silver or plated *scent bottle* worn around neck on a long chain. *Der.* French, "lady of the castle." Also see PINS and WATCHES.

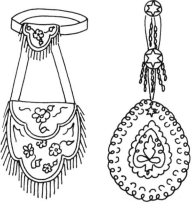

**CHATELAINE**

**chatelaine bag** Small handbag trimmed with lace or beads that hung from waist by ornamental chain and hook, popular from 1854 to 1874.

**chatoyancy** Optical properties in certain gems produced when stone is cut. As stone turns, a single streak of light reflects from needlelike crystals arranged parallel to one another. *e.g.*, CAT'S EYE or TIGER'S EYE. *Der.* French, *chatoyer*, "to change luster," as a cat's eye. Also see GEMS.

**chausons** (show-son) French equivalent of English BRAIES, or *breeches*; worn from the 5th through the 13th c.

**chausse** (shos) **1.** Stockings of CHAIN MAIL, worn by knights and soldiers in last quarter of the 13th c. **2.** Stockings and trunks cut in one piece similar to contemporary tights. First worn in Norman period (1066–1154); later in the Middle Ages, fastened to DOUBLET by means of lacers called POINTS. **3.** About mid 16th c. *chausses* were divided into two parts—upper part then called *haut de chausses*, later called

*trunk hose* and *upper stocks*. Lower part was called *bas de chausses*, then *hose* and finally *stockings*. **4.** Synonym for EPITOGA. Also called *chausse hood.*

**chaussembles** (show-som-bl) Man's hose with attached soles of leather or whalebone worn by nobility in Middle Ages. Also spelled *chausembles, chasembles, cashambles.*

**chausses en bourse** (shos awn boorce) Breeches padded so they were fuller at bottom—making a flattened balloon shape—worn in 17th c. *Der.* French, "bag breeches."

**chausses en tonnelet** (sho sawn ton-leh) See VENETIANS.

**chaussures à crics** (shaw-sir ah kree) Shoes with high heels worn in the 17th c. *Der.* French, "shoes on lifts." Also called *chaussures à Pont-Levis.*

**cheat 1.** Man's waistcoat or vest of 17th c. with expensive fabric on front and poorer quality in back. **2.** 19th-c. term for man's shirt front with collar attached worn as a DICKEY.

**chechia 1.** Felt hat with tassel worn on back of the head—similar to FEZ, but more peaked in shape—worn by Algerian and Moroccan children. **2.** Adaptation of the above hat fashionable for women in the late 1930s and early 1940s.

**check** A fabric design composed of alternate squares of colors in various sizes usually alternating with white. Design may be similar to checkerboard or any other block design which is geometrical and repeats regularly. A checked pattern may be woven or printed.

**CHECKS**

**apron c.** A gingham fabric made in even checks of white and a color, designated as 4x4 or 8x8 according to number of yarns used in each check. Originally a fabric used for aprons, by extension, a type of check.

**checkerboard c.**  Even squares of two colors alternating to form a row. Succeeding rows alternate colors. *Der.* From resemblance to a checkerboard. Also called *even checks.*

**even c.**  See CHECKERBOARD.

**gingham c.**  Yarn-dyed checks of 1″, ½″, ⅛″, or ¹/₁₆″ made in a color alternating with white. Also called APRON CHECK.

**glen/Glen Urquhart c.**  See PLAIDS.

**gun club c.**  A three-color, double check design consisting of a large check over a smaller one used in wool and worsted fabrics.

**harlequin c.**  Check made of medium-sized, diamond-shaped colored motifs alternating with white.

**hound's-tooth/houndstooth c.**  Irregular colored ½″ to 2″ check like a square with points at two corners. Consists of colored checks alternating with white, produced by a yarn-dyed twill weave. *Der.* From resemblance to pointed dog's tooth.

**pajama c.**  Dimity woven with coarser yarns at intervals in both warp and filling forming a checked design.

**pincheck**  Check made of very tiny squares.

**shepherd's c.**  Uniform checks about ¼″ wide of white and one color, usually black, made in twill or basket weave wool, worsted, or cotton. Also called *shepherd's plaid.*

**tablecloth c.**  Large checkerboard check, 1″ to 3 ″ in size, usually in red or blue alternating with white. *Der.* Originally used for tablecloths.

**tattersall c.**  Check or plaid consisting of different colored lines on a plain, light-colored ground. *Der.* Named after Richard Tattersall, English horseman, founder of Tattersall's London Horse Auction Mart established in 1776. Also called TATTERSALL PLAID.

**windowpane c.**  Dark horizontal and vertical bars crossing over light background, giving effect of a window divided into small panes. Also called WINDOWPANE PLAID.

---

**checked gingham**  See GINGHAM.

**checkerboard**  Board used when playing game of checkers or chess with alternate squares which is imitated for fabrics. See CHECKS and HOSE.

**checkered-apron man**  English barbers of 16th c. distinguished by the checked pattern of their aprons. Also see BLUE-APRONED MEN and GREEN-APRONED MEN.

**cheeks-and-ears**  See COIF #6 and ORRELET.

**cheek wrappers**  Side flaps of women's DORMEUSE or *French nightcap* worn in second half of 18th c.

**cheetah**  See FURS.

**chef's apron**  See APRONS.

**chef's hat**  See HATS.

**Chelsea look**  A changing variety of looks centering around King's Road in London worn by the Chelsea Set as a uniform, and often imitated. Also see BOOTS, COLLARS, and LOOKS.

**chemise**  1. Linen garment worn by men and women in Middle Ages next to the skin. Made with long sleeves, it was straight hanging and as long as the garment worn over it. By 14th c. man's chemise called *shirt* or *sherte*; woman's chemise called *smock.* In 17th c. called *shift*, and in late 19th c. called *combinations.* Also called *camise, camisia, cames, kemse, robe linge.* **2.** Muslin dress of the Empire period styled with high waistline, low neckline, and slim skirts. Called "chemise" because of resemblance to garment described in #1. **3.** Dress fashionable after World War I that became the basic style of the 1920s. Made in a wide variety of styles—tailored for daytime, but ornate for evening in chiffon, lace, or silk with elaborate bead-work. See FLAPPER. **4.** See DRESSES, SILHOUETTES, and SLIPS.

**chemise gown** See PERDITA CHEMISE.

**chemisette** (shem-ee-zet) **1.** Scarf or FICHU of cambric, tulle, or muslin fabric worn as fill-in for low-necked gown in 18th and 19th c. Also see PARTLET and TUCKER. Also called a *chemise tucker* and *habit shirt*. **2.** Sleeveless blouse worn under a suit in early 20th c. **3.** See VESTEE.

**chemisette à jabot** (ah zha-bo) Embroidered or pleated ruffle of 1850s and 1860s worn as a fill-in at front opening of the REDINGOTE show-ing from neck to waist.

**chemisette garter** Vertical supporter for hose attached to the corset in 1830s and 1840s.

**chemise tucker** See CHEMISETTE.

**chenille** (shah-kneel) **1.** Fabric made with very fuzzy core yarns used in the filling with plain warp resulting in a heavy material. Intro-duced for use in loose-fitting sweaters in 1980s. Compare with CANDLEWICK. **2.** Cotton, silk, woolen, or rayon yarns made with a heavy core around which are wrapped other yarns. Yarn is heavy and fuzzy like a caterpillar. *Der.* French, "caterpillar." **3.** See EMBROIDERIES. **4.** See LACES.

**cheongsam** (chong-sam) Traditional every-day dress worn by Chinese, Korean, and Hong Kong women, consisting of straight CHEMISE with side slit, standing band collar, and front closing slanted to side closed with buttons or frogs. Adapted by Westerners for housecoats and summer dresses. Also see DRESSES.

**cherkesska** See CZERKESKA.

**Cheruit, Madeleine** See APPENDIX/DESIGNERS.

**cherusse** (sher-oose) Starched lace *collarette* forming a standing border for low-cut necklines on women's gowns. Worn during the Revolu-tionary period in France and later at Napo-leon's court in Empire period. Also called *col-larette à la Lyon*. Also spelled *cherusque*.

**Chesterfield, 6th Earl of** A fashion leader in the 1830s and 1840s after whom the CHESTER-FIELD overcoat and other garments were named. Also see COATS.

**chesticore** See JUSTAUCORPS.

**chest measurement 1. Men**: distance around body at fullest part of upper torso, one of the measurements by which suits are sold. **2. Women**: measurement across front of body from armhole seam to armhole seam at point above bust; differs from the *bust measurement* taken at fullest part of bosom.

**Cheviot** (shev-ee-ot) Rugged harsh fabric made with a hairy nap. Made in plain or twill weave. Originally made of Cheviot wool; now made of all types of fibers, *e.g.*, wool, man-made, reused wool, blends, or cotton to make different fabrics of various qualities. Used for sportswear as it tends to sag and does not hold a crease well. *Der.* From Cheviot Hills on the boundary between Scotland and England.

**Cheviot shirtings 1.** Heavy, twilled cotton fabric made with heavy yarn in a variety of dobby designs, *e.g.*, single warp stripe or double warp rib in blue or brown on a white back-ground. Formerly used for work shirts. **2.** Brit-ish term for a high quality cotton shirting fabric woven with combed yarns in a medium count in plain or basket weave. *Der.* From Cheviot Hills on the boundary between Scotland and England.

**chevron 1.** Motif consisting of two straight lines meeting to form an inverted "V." **2.** Badge of these "V" stripes worn on sleeve by police-men, firemen, and the military to indicate rank.

**chevrons** Trimmings for women's clothes in-troduced in mid-1820s, usually a zigzag band near hem of skirt.

**chic** (sheek) Almost indefinable *noun* mean-ing style, or as an *adjective* meaning smart or sophisticated: a flair for assembling a costume with the proper accessories. *Der.* French, "stylish."

**chicken-skin gloves** Thin, strong leather gloves treated with almonds and spermaceti worn at night as cosmetic aid to keep hands soft and white, by women from the end of 17th to early 19th c.

**chiffon** **1.** Thin transparent fabric made in a plain weave. It drapes well and is made from tightly twisted or *creped* yarns. Originally made in silk; now also made in man-made fibers. Dyed solid colors or often printed in floral designs. Used for sheer dresses, blouses, and scarfs. **2.** A trifle or bit of feminine finery. *Der.* French, *chiffe*, "rag."

**chi-fu** Ankle-length robe worn by Chinese Mandarin men and women for regular court wear made with loose sleeves, high collar, and diagonal closing extending under right arm. Elaborately embroidered with motifs of dragons, clouds, mountains, and waves to symbolize rank. Man's robe was slit up front and back for walking. Emperor's robe was bright yellow; noblemen wore blue. Also called *dragon robes. Der.* Chi Fu, seaport of North China.

**chignon** (shee-n yon) Heavy coil or knot of hair, natural or false, worn at nape of neck or high on head. A contemporary style also popular in 1790 and from 1850s to 1870s. Revived in pin-on style in the 1960s. Also see BANGING CHIGNON and HAIRSTYLES.

**chignon cap** Small cap made in a variety of colors and fabrics worn over the chignon in the 1930s and 1940s. Popular again in the 1960s and 1970s—usually made of crocheted wool—and called a *bun-warmer* or *bun snood.*

**chignon strap** Band of ribbon fastened to woman's hat that passes around back of head and under the chignon to hold hat firmly. Worn in the 1860s and 1870s, again in the 1940s and 1950s.

**chikan embroidered cap** A white cotton cap decorated with embroidery worn by Moslem men in India.

**child's pudding** Small, round padded cap or padded band worn by infants and small children to serve as shock absorber in a fall. Also see BUMPER.

**ch'ima** Pleated moderately full skirt, worn by Korean women with waistline just under bust. Worn over petticoat and trousers with extremely short jacket, CHOGORI, and full-sleeved cloak, CHANG-OT.

**chimere** (cheh-mir) Full-length sleeveless robe, similar to an ACADEMIC ROBE worn by Anglican bishops. Extra full lawn sleeves were attached to armholes. Also spelled *chimer.*

**chimney-pot hat** Man's high-crowned hat with extremely narrow brim worn from 1830s on replacing the beaver hat. Made by felting rabbit hair on top of silk and applying steam and pressure to make a smooth and shiny surface. Also called PLUG HAT, *pot hat,* SILK HAT, and TOP HAT.

**China blue** Lavender-blue similar to that in Chelsea dinnerware.

**China grass** Bast fiber consisting of stiff ribbons of RAMIE from 3 to 6 feet in length, very strong and durable but difficult to extract. Used in Asian countries for *grass cloth.*

**China mink** See FURS.

**China ribbon** **1.** Narrow ribbon, about ⅛" wide, woven with a plain edge popular in mid-19th c. for *China ribbon embroidery.* **2.** See ROCOCO under EMBROIDERIES.

**China silk** Soft, lustrous fabric in a plain weave that may have slight texture due to irregular yarns used. Made in China and Japan; originally handmade in China as early as 1200 B.C. The name is also applied to U.S. machine-made fabrics of a similar nature.

**chinchilla** See FURS.

**chinchilla cloth** Thick, heavyweight coating fabric of all wool, or wool and cotton distinguished by curly nubs on the surface. **1.** Woven as a double cloth with a plain back and a satin face. Extra filling yarns added to the face of fabric are loosely floated over the surface. When napped and rubbed into curled tufts, these yarns form distinctive nubs on the surface. Less expensive fabric is not woven in the same manner and it may have a different surface effect. **2.** A similar fabric made by knitting and brushing surface yarns into nubs.

**chin cloak**  Term used from about 1535 to 1660s as synonym for MUFFLER or SCARF. Also called *chin clout*, *chin cloth*, and *chinner*.

**chiné**  *Der.* French, "mottled." See WARP PRINT under PRINTS.

**Chinese design**  Design composed of motifs such as dragons, lanterns, clouds, and mountains, in style typical of Chinese paintings and embroideries.

**Chinese dog**  See FURS.

**Chinese dress**  Simple, straight-lined dress with standing-band collar, closing diagonally to side, and slashed up side seams from the hem. Also see DRESSES and CHEONGSAM.

**Chinese embroidery**  See EMBROIDERIES.

**Chinese jacket**  See COOLIE COAT under COATS.

**Chinese knot**  Ornamental knot of covered cord used as trimming on apparel. Copied from traditional ornaments on Chinese robes.

**Chinese lamb**  See CARACUL under FURS.

**Chinese lounging robe**  Full-length lounging robe with standing Chinese collar, full kimono sleeves flaring at wrist, and closing to one side in Chinese manner. Worn by women in early 1900s.

**Chinese Mandarin court robes**  See CH'ANG-FU, CH'AO-FU, and CHI-FU.

**Chinese Raccoon**  See USSURIAN RACCOON under FURS.

**Chinese red**  See VERMILLION.

**Chinese shoe**  See SHOES.

**CHINESE LOUNGE ROBE, 1900**

**Chinese slippers**  See KAMPSKATCHA SLIPPER.

**Chinese styles**  See CALOTTE, CH'ANG-FU, CH'AO-FU, CHI-FU, COOLIE HAT, FINGERNAIL SHIELDS, MA-COUAL, MANDARIN HEADDRESS, MANDARIN HAT, MANDARIN ROBES, P'U-FANG, P'U-FU. Also see COLLARS, DRESSES, HAIRSTYLES, LOOKS, NECKLINES, PAJAMAS, and SILHOUETTES.

**Chinese trousers**  Trousers of blue cotton fabric cut rather wide at hems, sometimes quilted for warmth, and worn by men, women, and children in China.

**chinner**  See CHIN CLOAK.

**chino**  (chee-no)  Durable cotton, firmly woven with a fine steep twill and dyed a yellowish-tan or khaki color, now vat-dyed in many colors. Used originally for summer uniforms for the U.S. Army. In 1950s adopted by teenagers for school and general wear particularly for pants. In late 1970s used for blazers, shirts, and jumpsuits. Prior to World War I, it was made in Manchester, England, and shipped to China. From there fabric was shipped to the Philippines and sold to the U.S. Army for use in summer tropical uniforms.

**Chinon**  Very silky, man-made fiber made from *casein*, trademarked by Toyobo Co. Ltd. of Japan; wrinkle resistant, mothproof, and has a tendency to resist static electricity; therefore, does not collect lint or cling to the body. Used for blouses, lingerie, and evening wear.

**chinos** (chee-nose)  See PANTS.

**chin stays**  Term used in 1830s for ruffles of tulle or lace added to bonnet strings forming a frill when tied under chin. Also see MENTON-IÈRES #2.

**chintz**  Medium-weight printed or plain fabric with a glazed or shiny finish. Prints are frequently of floral or bird designs. Woven in a plain weave of medium-weight to fine cotton yarns. Originally a fabric for slipcovers and draperies; now also used for variety of items such as beachwear, shorts, blouses, skirts, dresses, and rainwear. *Der.* Indian, *chint*, name for a gaudily printed fabric of cotton.

**chip**  See DIAMONDS.

**chip bonnet**  Coarse, inexpensive straw bonnet made of strips or shavings of wood, or woody material, imported from Italy and used for millinery in the 19th c.

**chip straw**  Wood or straw cut in fine strips for hats or baskets. Used for women's hats in 18th c. and for women's CHIP BONNETS in the 19th c.

**chique-tades**  See SLASHINGS.

**chirinka**  Highly prized square of silk or muslin with metallic embroidery, sometimes edged with gold fringe or tassels. An accessory formerly carried by women in Russia.

**chiripa**  South American garment, made by wrapping a blanket around legs and loins. Worn by the Araucanian Indians of central Chile and formerly worn by Argentine *gauchos*, or cowboys.

**CHITON**

**chiton** (ki-tehn)  Linen, cotton, or woolen, open-sided tunic worn by ancient Greeks. Two large rectangles hung in folds from the shoulders, with back and front pinned together with FIBULAE. The *Doric chiton* was bloused and belted in a variety of ways—sometimes with two belts in a double *blouson* effect. The *Ionic chiton* was made of sheerer fabric, sewn together at the sides, and sleeves were formed by pinning with fibulae. Usually worn with the HIMATION.

**chitterlings** (chit-er-lings)  Popular term used in the 18th and 19th c. for frills or ruffles on front of man's shirt.

**chlaine** (klain)  Woolen cape worn in Greece during Homeric period by shepherds and warriors.

**chlamys** (klay-mis or klahm-is)  Oblong mantle approximately 5′ or 6′ x 3′, fastened in front or on one shoulder with a pin. Worn in ancient Greece by travelers, youths, soldiers, hunters, and in Greek mythology by the god Hermes. Chlamys continued to be worn in more semicircular shape in Byzantium and in later centuries for sports and traveling.

Chloé (klo-ee) See KARL LAGERFELD under APPENDIX/DESIGNERS.

chlorspinel See SPINEL under GEMS.

chogā Knee-length overcoat fastened with a few loops above the waist made of cotton, brocade, or cashmere, and worn by Moslem men of India.

chogori Rib-length jacket worn by Korean women with CH'IMA.

choir-boy collar See COLLARS.

**CHOIR ROBES**

choir robe Ankle-length closed robes similar to ACADEMIC GOWN worn by singers in church choirs.

choker Term used for accessories and clothing that fit high on the neck. See COLLARS, NECKLACES, and NECKLINES.

Chola derby hat Hat similar to man's derby, but with larger, higher crown and wider brim. Faced on brim with band of another color and trimmed with tailored ribbon bow on side.

Worn by Chola Indian women of Bolivia over long braided hair.

choli Short, midriff-baring blouse worn under SARI by Hindu women. See BLOUSES.

choori-dars See PANTS.

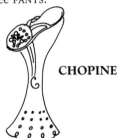

**CHOPINE**

chopine (cho-pin or chop-in) Wooden or cork CLOG, covered with leather, sometimes 18″ high, fitted with toe cap and used as a PATTEN, or overshoe; worn in 16th and 17th c. Also spelled *chopin, chapiney.*

chou (shoo) choux (pl.) **1.** Frilly pouf of fabric used at neckline. **2.** Soft, crushed-crown hat similar to MOBCAP. **3.** Large rosette used to trim gowns in late 19th and early 20th c. **4.** Late-17th c. term for CHIGNON. *Der.* French, "cabbage."

chou rouge (shoo rooz) Deep reddish-purple color. *Der.* French, "red cabbage."

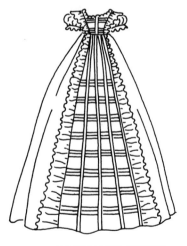

**CHRISTENING DRESS**

**christening dress** Extremely long dress elaborately trimmed with tucks, lace, beading, or hand embroidery, worn by infants for baptism. Also called *christening robe.*

**chrome tanning** A mineral type of tanning process for leather. Skins are placed in large revolving drums and are tanned in three to eight hours. The basic ingredients used are salts of chromium. This is the most used process today for tanning shoe uppers, handbags, belts, etc. Before being dyed, leather is a robin's egg blue color.

**chronometric watch** See WATCHES.

**chrysoberyl** See GEMS.

**chrysolite** See PERIDOT under GEMS.

**chrysoprase** See GEMS.

**chubby** See JACKETS.

**chu-chu** A chain of 108 stones of jade, coral, amber, etc., formerly worn around the neck by the Chinese Mandarin as reminder of his native land.

**chuddah/chudder** See CHADDAR.

**chudidar pa'ejamas** Pants, full at top, similar to JODHPURS, but tightly fitted at lower leg, worn by Mohammedan women in India with CAMIS and CHADDER. Also see CHOORI-DARS under PANTS.

**chukka** (sha-ka) Term used in a polo match for "periods" of the game. Used to describe modern clothes and accessories similar to those worn when playing polo. See CHUKKA under BOOTS and HATS, and POLO SHIRT under KNIT SHIRTS.

**chullo and Montera** (chew-yo) Helmet-shaped stocking cap with high peak and large rounded ear flaps. Worn under a black hat with wide upward-flaring brim, lined with color, and ribbons knotted under the chin. Worn by Peruvian Inca Indians.

**chunky heels** See HEELS.

**chunky shoes** See SHOES.

**chymer** See CHAMARRE.

**ciclaton** See CYCLAS.

**cidaris** Persian headdress shaped like a truncated cone and trimmed with a band or fold of fabric at the base. Worn by men B.C. 550 to 330.

**ciel** (see-el) Pale-blue color. *Der.* French, "sky."

**cinch** A tight belt around the waist. See BELTS and WAISTLINES.

**cinch buckle** See RING BUCKLE.

**cinch closing** See D-RING CLOSING under CLOSINGS.

**cincture** (sink-cher) A belt or girdle. See BELTS.

**cinglation** See CYCLAS.

**cingulum** (sin-gyeh-lehm) **1.** Belt or girdle worn under the breasts by women in ancient Rome. **2.** Belt worn by men in Rome on tunic to adjust the length of garment. **3.** Roman sword belt. **4.** Belt worn with liturgical garments since Middle Ages.

**Cipullo, Aldo** See APPENDIX/DESIGNERS.

**Circassian round robe** Early 1820s evening dress of gossamer gauze made with low square-cut neckline, short sleeves, high waistline, and skirt elaborately decorated down the front and above the hem with festoons of knotted ribbon. *Der.* Caucasian tribe of Circassia, U.S.S.R., bordering on the Black Sea.

**Circassian wrapper** Loose wrap, cut somewhat like a nightgown, worn by women for daytime in Empire Period, 1813. *Der.* Caucasian tribe of Circassia, U.S.S.R., bordering on the Black Sea.

**circassienne** Late-18th c. version of the POLONAISE worn by women just before French Revolution. *Der.* French, "circassian."

**circle** See SKIRTS and SLEEVES.

**circle pocket** See ROUND POCKET under POCKETS.

**circular** Long cape or mantle of silk, satin, or other fine fabric in extra wide widths, and frequently lined with rabbit or gray squirrel combined with bright fabric. Fashionable in late 19th c.

**circular hem** See HEMS.

**circular knit** Fabric knitted in a tubular shape with no selvages. Made either by hand or machine. Hose knitted in this manner have no seams. See SEAMLESS HOSE under HOSE.

**circular ruffle** Ruffle cut from circle of fabric rather than straight across the grain, making graceful folds less bulky than a gathered ruffle. Also see CASCADE RUFFLE.

**circular skirt** See SKIRTS.

**circumfolding hat** Man's dress hat of 1830s with low crown, made to fold flat to be carried under arm. Also see CHAPEAU BRAS.

**ciré** (sear-ray) Term used to describe a finish and a fabric. Finish is applied to sheer fabric as well as satins and heavier fabrics to give a very shiny effect. Popularized in 1969 and referred to as the WET LOOK. *Der.* French, *ciré,* "waxed," thus shiny.

**ciselé velvet** (seez-el-ay) British fabric introduced in 1876 consisting of raised velvet figures on a satin ground formed by cut, and uncut, loops—with the cut pile being higher.

**citrine** See GEMS.

**CityPants/City Shorts** Terms coined by the fashion-industry newspaper, *Women's Wear Daily,* in 1968 for women's pants or shorts suitable for town wear. Also see PANTS and SHORTS.

**civet** Perfume ingredient with a strong, musklike odor consisting of waxy substance secreted by the civet cat. Known and used since Middle Ages.

**civet cat** See FURS.

**Claiborne, Liz** See APPENDIX/DESIGNERS.

**Clamdiggers®** Trademark owned by White Stag Manufacturing Co. See PANTS.

**claque** (clack) Man's opera hat, with crown that folds flat. Also called *chapeau claque.* Same as GIBUS.

**Clara Bow hat** Trademark for various styles of felt hats for women in late 1920s. The beret and cloche styles were the most popular. *Der.* Named after *Clara Bow,* famous movie star of the 1920s.

**Clarence** Man's laced ankle-high boot of 19th c. made of soft leather with triangular gusset at the side, forerunner of ELASTIC-SIDED BOOT.

**CLARISSA HARLOWE HAT, 1857**

**Clarissa Harlowe bonnet/hat** Pictured in 1857 as a wide-brimmed, lace-trimmed hat with drooping sides and a small rounded crown with large ostrich plume placed so it curved from the crown over the back brim of hat. In 1879, described as a bonnet made of LEGHORN STRAW with a large brim lined with velvet worn tilted on the forehead—popular until 1890s. *Der.* From heroine in novel, *Clarissa, or the History of a Young Lady,* by Samuel Richardson, published in 1747–48.

**Clarissa Harlowe corsage** Evening-dress bodice with off-the-shoulder neckline, folds caught at the waist by band of ribbon, and short sleeves trimmed with two or three lace ruffles. Worn in late 1840s. *Der.* From heroine in novel, *Clarissa, or the History of a Young Lady,* by Samuel Richardson, published in 1747–48.

**classic** Apparel in such simple good taste and of a design appropriate to so many individuals that it continues to be in style over a long period of time, returning to high fashion at intervals. It retains the basic lines but is sometimes altered in minor details, *e.g., trenchcoat, polo coat, chemise, shirtwaist dress, cardigan, blazer.* Also see BROOKS BROTHERS®, AND PREPPY under LOOKS, COATS, and CLASSIC PULL-BACK under HAIRSTYLES.

**class ring** See RINGS.

**claw-hammer coat** Colloquial name for the SWALLOW-TAILED COAT named for shape of coat-tails with ends cut straight across resembling claws of a hammer.

**clayshooter's vest** See VESTS.

**clean-stitched seam** See SEAMS.

**clear-finish** Finishing process, including fulling and shearing, applied to worsteds to remove all fuzzy fibers revealing and emphasizing weave and color.

**cleats** Projections attached to soles of sport shoes, made of plastic, wood, rubber, or metal. Used particularly on football, golf, and baseball shoes to prevent slipping.

**cleavage 1.** Ability of gemstone to break along the crystalline structure lines; especially important when cutting valuable diamonds. **2.** Separation between a woman's breasts, made more obvious when a low neckline is worn.

**Cleopatra** (klee-o-pa-tra) Queen of Egypt (51–49 B.C. and 48–30 B.C.) mistress of Julius Caesar and Mark Antony, and one of the notorious beauties in history whose jewelry, hairstyles, facial makeup, and clothes sum up the exotic Egyptian style of dress. Depictions of Cleopatra on stage and screen by Vivien Leigh, 1951, and Elizabeth Taylor, 1968, influenced fashion in 1950s and 1960s.

**Cleopatra blue** Brilliant Oriental blue color with a greenish cast.

**clerical cape** See CAPES.

**clerical clothes** See ALB, CAPES, CASSOCK, COTTA, GENEVA ROBE, SOUTANE, SURPLICE, COLLARS, and SHIRTS.

**clerical front** An adjustable shirt front worn by clergymen with a black business suit or under a pulpit robe. Fits around the neck usually with black collar on top of a white collar. Ties secure the garment at the waist. Usually made in black faille or wool with or without a center pleat down the front. Also called *shirt front.*

**Cleveland diamond** See DIAMONDS.

**clip 1.** One season's growth of wool taken from a sheep. **2.** Jewelry with a spring-held fastening; an ornament similar to a BROOCH. See CLOSINGS, EARRINGS, and HATS.

**clip-on sunglasses** See GLASSES.

**clip-on tie** See TIES.

**cloak** Loose outer garment used from Anglo-Saxon times. Name used for any type of outer garment that might also be classed as *cape, mantle,* or *coat,* particularly during last half of 19th c.

**Cloak and Suit Industry** Name given manufacturers of coats and suits when first census of the clothing industry in the U.S. was made in 1860. This category made up half the total of manufacturing establishments. Originally called *Cloak and Mantilla Manufacturers,* later called *Coat and Suit Industry.*

**cloak bag breeches** Full oval-shaped man's breeches fastened above or below the knee with decorative points or bows. Worn in early 17th c. Also see BREECHES.

**cloche** (klosh) See HATS.

**clock 1.** Ornamental design, frequently embroidered, running vertically up a sock or stocking on inside or outside of ankle. **2.** Triangular gore inserted into a stocking, cape, or collar to make it wider with embroidery over the joined seams. Worn from 16th c. on. Also see HOSE.

**CLOCK #1**

**clog  1.** See PATTENS. **2.** Woman's leather-soled overshoes with instep straps generally matching the shoe, worn outdoors in 17th and 18th c. **3.** Wooden shoe. See SABOT. **4.** See SANDALS and SHOES.

**cloisonné** (kloi-zeh-nay)  An enameling technique used in the Byzantine Empire and the Middle Ages, but lost to Europeans until about 1860. Used on clocks, mirrors, and other objects in Europe, Japan, and China. Small areas of colored enamel separated by thin metal bands forming a pattern. Popular in 1980s for necklaces, bracelets, earrings, pins, and belt buckles. Also see NECKLACES. *Der.* French, "partitioned."

**cloqué** (klo-kay)  French, "blistered"; applied to a fabric, *e.g.*, MATELASSÉ. Also spelled *cloky*.

**close coat**  Term used in 18th and 19th c. for a buttoned coat.

**closed seam**  Shoe seam, similar to a simple fabric seam, stitched on the inside and edges pressed back. Usually used for joining the shoe at center back.

**close-plate buckles**  Shoe buckles of late 1660s to 1680s made of *tutania*—an alloy of tin and copper—cast in molds by street peddlers in about fifteen minutes.

**close stitch**  See BUTTONHOLE under STITCHES.

**closing**  Manner in which an item of apparel fastens—including the type of device by which it is secured. Early clothing was draped and held together by belts or pins called *fibulae*. Later lacing was used, then buttons—with men's clothing buttoning left to right and women's buttoning right to left.

### CLOSINGS

**asymmetric c.**  Closing used for a blouse, dress, or coat fastening on the side or diagonally rather than in the center.

**buttoned c.**  Conventional closing for apparel. See BUTTON category.

**chain c.**  Laced closing using a metal chain instead of a lacer. Used on vests and blouses, it was a novelty of the late 1960s.

**cinch c.**  See D-RING CLOSING.

**clip c.**  Metal fastener with a spring-backed device on one side of garment and a ring, eyelet, or slotted fastener on other side. Used mainly on raincoats, jackets, and car coats.

**double-breasted c.**  Closing lapped deeply across front of garment fastened with parallel rows of buttons on either side of center front.

**D-ring c.**  Double-ring closing, strap pulled through both rings, then back through second ring to fasten. Borrowed from fastenings on horse bridles and saddle straps and used mainly on belts and cuffs of sleeves. Also called *cinch closing*.

**fly-front c.**  Buttonholes, or zipper, inserted under a placket. Developed in latter half of 19th c. for overcoats, particularly the chesterfield, and on men's or women's trousers.

**frog c.**  Decorative closing using cording or braid through which a soft ball made of cording or a button is pulled—a typical Chinese closing. Also see BRANDENBURGS in alphabetical listing.

**galosh c.**   Closing with a metal hook on one side which clips into a metal fastener with several slots in order to adjust the degree of tightness. A closing used for raincoats, coats, and jackets. *Der.* Similar to closings for galoshes in the early 20th c.

**gripper c.**   Metal fastener in the shape of a large snap used on some types of jackets and raincoats. Also used on children's and infants' clothing, particularly at crotch of pajamas, panties, and pants to enable them to be put on more easily.

**hook and eye**   Closing using a small metal hook on one side and either an embroidered loop or a small metal loop on the other side. Used extensively for shirtwaists and dresses with back closings in late 19th and early 20th c. Almost entirely replaced by the zipper on contemporary clothing.

**laced c.**   Leather thong or cord laced through small metal or embroidered eyelets. Popular

**FROG CLOSINGS**

**LOOP-AND-BUTTON**

**DOUBLE-BREASTED CLOSING**

**TOGGLE CLOSING**

**FLY-FRONT CLOSING**

method of fastening garments in Middle Ages and in late 1960s. Also used for shoes from 18th c. on. Also see POINTS in alphabetical listing.

**loop and button** Closing with a series of corded loops on one side and covered or round buttons on the other side. Used for its decorative effect either on front or back. Sometimes used on wedding dresses.

**single-breasted c.** Conventional closing for suits, jackets, blouses, and coats. May be closed with buttons which are aligned down center front of garment. Lap is not as great as in a DOUBLE-BREASTED CLOSING.

**surplice c.** See WRAP CLOSING.

**snap c.** Metal fastener used to close the garment at places where there is little strain. Replaced almost entirely in contemporary garments by zippers and grippers.

**tabbed c.** Added pieces of fabric that lap across opening and button. Popular closing for car coats from mid-1960s. Also used on cuffs, necklines, and sleeves.

**tied c.** **1.** Type of closing used on a wrap-style garment, *e.g.*, a sash used on bathrobes, wrap dresses, and skirts to hold the garment closed. **2.** Series of ties used to fasten a garment.

**toggle c.** Rod-shaped button usually of wood attached by rope loop on one side of garment and pulled through similar loop on opposite side. Also see TOGGLE COAT.

**Velcro®** Trademark for closing consisting of a tape woven with minute nylon hooks that mesh with loops on opposite tape. Used on children's and adults' clothing, sportswear, and shoes. First used by astronauts. Also see alphabetical listing.

**wrap c.** Closing by wrapping one side of garment over the other and holding with a belt, sash, button, or snap.

**zipper c.** Used mainly on necklines, skirt plackets, coats, and jackets as a closing. Made in various lengths of metal and plastic. May be covered by fabric tape and almost invisible or made with extra-wide teeth and classified as industrial zipper. Invented in early 1890s. See ZIPPER in alphabetical listing.

**clot** Heavy shoe with thin iron plates on the sole worn by workmen in the 15th c. Also called *clout-shoen*.

**cloth** Synonym for FABRIC.

**cloth beam** Cylinder at front of the loom on which finished cloth is wound. Also called *cloth roll*.

**clothe** **1.** To put on garments. **2.** To provide with clothing.

**cloth embroidery** See EMBROIDERY.

**clothes** Items of wearing apparel. Collective term for all items of apparel worn on the body by men, women, and children. *Der.* Anglo-Saxon, *cläthas*, plural of *cläth*, "cloth." Synonyms: APPAREL, ATTIRE, CLOTHING COSTUME, DRESS, GARB, GARMENT, HABIT, RAIMENT, ROBE, UNIFORM, VESTMENTS.

**clothing industry** See APPAREL INDUSTRY.

**clothing wool** Term used in grading wool for fineness and length of fiber, applied to wool fibers which may be carded, not combed, and made into woolen fabrics.

**cloth roll** See CLOTH BEAM.

**clouded cane** See MALACCA CANE.

**clout-shoen** See CLOT.

**cloverleaf lapel** See LAPELS.

**clown suit** Popular with children for generations—a jumpsuit with full pant legs with ruffles at cuffs and ankles. A large unstarched ruff is worn at the neckline. Made of two colors, divided down center front and back, and trimmed with pompons. Worn with tall tapered DUNCE'S CAP.

**club** Heavy stick carried by men since earliest times. Fashionable in 1730s instead of a CANE, and also carried in the early 19th c.

**club wig** See CATOGAN CLUB WIG.

**Cluny lace** See LACES.

**cluster curls** Groups of false RINGLETS or SAUSAGE CURLS, mounted on netting to be pinned in place as part of an elaborate coiffure.

**cluster earring** See EARRINGS.

**cluster pleats** See PLEATS.

**cluster ring** See RINGS.

**clutch coat** Originally introduced in the mid-1920s as a low-waisted evening wrap with bagpipe sleeves and large fur collar. Also see COATS.

**clutch purse/bag** See HANDBAGS.

**coachman green** See BREWSTER GREEN.

**coachman's coat** See COATS.

**coal-scuttle bonnet** Large, stiff scoop-brim bonnet of mid-19th c. with peak in center front.

**coal tar colors** Dyes produced chemically from analine, naphthalene, phenol, and other distillate coal tar.

**coat** Hip-length to full-length outerwear with sleeves designed to be worn over other clothing. Although a coat with set-in sleeves was worn in ancient Persia, *mantles* and *capes* were more generally worn until the end of the 18th c. At this time the *redingote* and *pelisse* were introduced. *Der.* From "cloak" in use by mid-19th c., and not changed to "coat" until the late 19th c. Also see DRESSES, SWEATERS, and SPORT JACKETS. In alphabetical listing see CARRICK, CURRICULE, FROCK COAT, JUSTAUCORPS, OPERA WRAP, and PELISSE.

## COATS

**admiral c.** Double-breasted reefer-style coat, frequently with gold buttons. *Der.* Adapted from coats worn by U.S. Navy officers.

**A-line c.** Coat made close and narrow at the shoulders, flaring gently from under arms to hem like letter A, made in single- or double-breasted style with or without a collar. Introduced in 1955 by Paris designer, Christian Dior.

**all-weather c.** Waterproofed or water-repellent coat sometimes made with zip-in lining to adapt to various temperatures. Also see RAINCOAT category.

**balmacaan** (bal-ma-kan) Raglan-sleeved, loose-fitting style coat with small turned-down collar which buttons up front to neck. Frequently made of tweed or water-repellent fabric. *Der.* Named after Balmacaan, Invernessshire, Scotland.

**beach c.** See BEACH ROBE under ROBES.

**bench c.** See BENCHWARMER JACKET under SPORT JACKETS category.

**big c.** Long, full sometimes ankle length voluminous coat with long full sleeves. Worn belted, unbelted, or with a belt in the back to confine the fullness.

**bush c.** Same as BUSH JACKET or SAFARI JACKET under SPORT JACKETS category.

**cape c.** **1.** Coat with sleeves and an attached or separate cape. **2.** Combination of cape and coat with the back falling like a cape, the front having sleeves and looking like a coat. Also see DOLMAN in alphabetical listing.

**car c.** Sport or utility coat made hip- to three-quarter length. Comfortable for driving a car and popular with the station-wagon set in suburbia in 1950s and 1960s and a classic since. Also called STADIUM COAT, TOGGLE COAT, RANCH COAT, MACKINAW COAT. Also see DUFFEL COAT, BENCHWARMER and MACKINAW JACKET under SPORT JACKETS category.

**cardigan c.** Collarless coat made with plain round neckline and buttoned down center front. *Der.* Named for 7th Earl of Cardigan, who needed additional warmth for his uniform during the Crimean War, 1854.

**cashmere c.** **1. Women:** a classic style coat made of genuine *cashmere* wool or a blend of cashmere and other wool. **2. Men:** an overcoat in three-button classic style, with notched collar and large lapels, made of *cashmere* wool or a blend of cashmere and other wool. *Cashmere* is considered a luxury wool because of the extremely soft hand. *Der.* Made from hair of cashmere goat.

**Charlie Chaplin c.** Angle-length, full-shouldered, oversized coat with baggy sleeves ending in wide-buttoned cuffs and huge patch pockets. Introduced by Claude Montana, French couturier, in spring collection of 1985. *Der.* Named after Charlie Chaplin, an early silent film comedian.

**chesterfield c.** Semi-fitted, straight-cut classic man's or woman's overcoat in single- or double-breasted style, with black velvet collar. Single-breasted style usually has a fly-front closing. Originally an overcoat introduced in 1840s for men. Popular in late 1920s through 1940 and worn at intervals since. *Der.* Named after the *6th Earl of Chesterfield*, a fashion leader in 1830s and 1840s.

**classic c.** A coat style that has been popular for a long period of time with little change, *e.g.,* CHESTERFIELD COAT, POLO COAT, BALMACAAN.

**clutch c.** Woman's coat with no fasteners in front worn open or held clutched together. Popular in 1950s and early 1960s. Introduced in 1920s for day wear. The style was also used for an evening wrap with low waistline, blouson top, full bagpipe sleeves, and large rolled mink collar standing high on neck. Revived in mid-1980s for daytime.

**coachman's c.** Double-breasted coat with large, wide lapels, fitted waistline, and flared skirt. Frequently has a cape collar and brass buttons. Copied from English coachmen's coats of 19th c.

**cocoon** Wrap coat with very large shoulders, deep cuffed batwing sleeves, and standing collar which may be rolled down. Envelops the figure, tapering to the hem, like a cocoon. Used as a *rain or shine coat*. Originally introduced by Yves Saint Laurent in spring 1984 as an evening coat in velvet, it reached to thigh in back and tapered in cutaway fashion in the front.

**coolie c.** Short boxy coat reaching slightly below waist with standing band collar, *kimono sleeves* and frog fasteners. Worn by Chinese workmen and frequently copied as beach or lingerie coat. *Der.* Chinese, *kuli*, "unskilled workman."

**cutaway** Man's formal, black one-button jacket with peaked lapels and skirt cut away from waist in front, tapering to knees in back in a slanting line. Has a back vent topped by two buttons. Worn with waistcoat and striped trousers in daytime. Also called *morning coat. Der.* From 19th c. riding coat, called *Newmarket coat*, made by cutting away front of *frock coat* instead of folding the skirts back for horseback riding.

**dirndl c.** (durn-dul) Woman's coat cut with fitted torso, and skirt gathered at a low waistline, popular in the mid-1960s. *Der.* From gathered skirt and fitted bodice of the Tyrolean peasant dress called a *"dirndl."*

**dress c.** See SWALLOW-TAILED COAT.

**dressmaker c.** A woman's coat designed with softer lines and more details than the average coat. May have a waistline and unusual details, *e.g.,* tucks or pleats. *Der.* Styled more like a dress.

**duffel c.** Car coat or a shorter length coat fastened with toggles rather than buttons introduced during World War II and worn by men in British navy. In 1950s it was adopted as a sport coat. *Der.* From the original fabric used—a heavy napped wool originally made in Duffel, Belgium. Also see TOGGLE COAT.

**duo-length c.** Mid-calf- or full-length coat, sometimes made of fur, with a strip at the hem that zips off to make a shorter length. Also see ZIP-OFF COAT.

**duster 1.** Big-shouldered, big-sleeved, big-pocketed classic coat with smocked back, treated for water-repellency and introduced in 1984. **2.** Lightweight clutch coat with full swing at hem and small rolled collar usually made in black bengaline or faille worn in the 1950s. **3.** See ROBES. **4.** Fitted coat with long skirt slashed up back to waist worn when riding horseback. Has buttons and buttonholes for closing the slashed skirt. *Der.* Name used in early 20th c. as synonym for *automobile coat* as it was worn "to keep the dust off" when riding in early automobiles on dirt roads. Also see alphabetical listing.

**Edwardian c.** Man's knee-length double-breasted topcoat or overcoat with large high rolled deep-notched collar, nipped-in waistline, and deep vent in back. *Der.* Inspired by coats of Edwardian era in England, it became popular in 1960s.

**evening wrap** Any coat of fabric or fur designed to be worn primarily for formal occasions. It may be a coat designed to match or contrast with an evening dress. Very popular in the 1920s in clutch style. In 1930s, popular in black velvet in a full length with leg-of-mutton sleeves and in hip-length with batwing sleeves.

**fur fabric c.** Coat made of fabric which simulates fur, *e.g.,* modacrylic pile fabric, sometimes colored with stripes to imitate mink; sometimes stenciled to look like leopard, giraffe, tiger, and zebra. Both types very popular in 1960s and mink types continued to be popular in 1980s. Incorrectly called a *fake fur coat.*

**greatcoat** Heavy voluminous overcoat worn by men and women, originally made with fur lining and styled similar to an *ulster.* Term has been used from 19th c. to present.

**guardsman c.** Double-breasted, half-belted coat made with inverted box pleat in back, slashed pockets, and wide collar. *Der.* Adapted from coats of British guardsmen. Also called *officer's coat.*

**happi c.** See ROBES.

**hunt c.** See PINK COAT.

**Inverness c.** Knee-length coat with long removable cape or half-capes over the shoulders, like those worn by men in late-19th c. *Der.* From Invernessshire, Scotland.

**jockey c.** See SPORT JACKETS category.

**jump c.** Thigh-length coat for casual wear. Also see CAR COAT.

**mackinaw c.** As long as a car coat, but in Mackinac county, Michigan, place of origin, it is called a jacket. See MACKINAW JACKET under SPORT JACKETS category.

**mackintosh** See RAINCOATS category.

**mandarin c.** Straight-lined coat with Chinese neckline.

**maxi c.** Term for any ankle-length coat, introduced in fall in 1969, a radical change from the *mini coat* styles.

**midi c.** Mid-calf length coat introduced in 1967 in radical contrast to thigh-length MINI COAT. Made in many styles. *Der.* From term coined by *Women's Wear Daily.*

**military c.** Any coat that borrows details from military coats and jackets, *e.g.,* braid trim, epaulets, gold buttons, or high-standing collar. Usually a fitted double-breasted coat with slightly flared skirt.

**mini c.** Thigh-length coat in any style introduced in mid-1960s.

**morning c.** See CUTAWAY and alphabetical listing.

BALMACAAN

MAXI COAT

INVERNESS COAT

CHESTERFIELD
COAT,
1927

PEASANT
COAT

TENT COAT

CUTAWAY

REGENCY COAT

PANTCOAT

WRAPAROUND
COAT

CHILD'S
TOGGLE COAT

CHILD'S
PRINCESS COAT

CAR COAT        STORM COAT          CLASSIC COAT     CLUTCH COAT

MIDI COAT       SHOW COAT           COCOON           DUSTER

**officer's c.**  See GUARDSMAN COAT.

**overcoat**  Man's coat, heavier than a topcoat, designed for very cold weather. Sometimes lined with fur or modacrylic pile and made in BALMA-CAAN, CHESTERFIELD, EDWARDIAN, or other styles.

**pea c.**  See SPORT JACKETS category.

**peasant c.**  Mid-length coat lavishly trimmed down front with embroidery, sometimes with fur borders and cuffs, fashionable in late 1960s.

**pink c.**  Crimson-colored hunting jacket styled like a man's one-button suit coat with peaked lapels, back vent, and black velvet collar. Worn by men and women for fox-hunting. Also called *hunt coat.*

**polo c.**  Double- or single-breasted camel, vicuña, or camel-colored wool coat, with notched collar, buttonless, and sashed. Introduced in 1920s for men's spectator sports, for women in 1930s, and a classic since.

**princess c.**  Woman's fitted coat cut in long panels which flare at hem. Has no seam at the waistline and usually made single-breasted. *Der.* Style claimed to have been introduced by Worth about 1860 in a morning dress for Empress Eugénie.

**raccoon c.**  Long bulky coat of raccoon fur with large rolled collar worn originally by college men in the 1920s. Popular again in the mid-1960s and usually purchased from thrift shops.

**raglan c.**  Long, loose coat often of waterproof fabric with wide *raglan sleeves* cut in one with the shoulders. *Der.* From coat designed for the Earl of Raglan, who lost an arm in Crimean War, 1854, and needed an easier sleeve. Also see alphabetical listing.

**raincoat**  See separate category.

**ranch c.**  Car coat or jacket made in western style with leather side out, sometimes made of or lined with shearling.

**redingote**  Slightly fitted coat matched to a dress to make an ensemble. Also see PELISSE-ROBE and REDINGOTE in alphabetical listing.

**reefer**  **1.** Since 1960s a short double-breasted car coat. See SPORT JACKETS category. **2.** In 1930s and 1940s a woman's single-breasted fitted coat with large lapels, revived in 1983. **3.** Double-breasted hip-length boxy jacket with large revers worn by men from 1860s on, by women and girls from 1890s on. See SPORT JACKETS category. *Der.* From British brass-buttoned navy coat. Also see PEA JACKET and REEFER under SPORT JACKETS category.

**Regency c.**  Double-breasted coat for man or woman made with wide lapels and high-rolled Regency collar. Sometimes has large cuffs. Man's coat has nipped waist and deep vent in back. *Der.* Inspired by coats of the Regency period.

**riding c.**  Tailored fitted jacket worn for horseback riding, similar in cut to PINK COAT, but in other colors or plaids. Also see HACKING JACKET in alphabetical listing.

**safari c.**  Same as SAFARI JACKET or BUSH COAT under SPORT JACKET category. *Der.* East African Swahili, *safara,* "to travel."

**shortie c.**  Woman's short coat, about fingertip length, made in boxy fitted or semi-fitted styles, worn in 1940s and 1950s.

**show c.**  Longer style riding jacket or suit coat with *hacking pockets,* fitted waist, narrow lapels, three-button closing, inverted pleats at sides, and long slash in center back. Worn for semi-formal showing of horses.

**stadium c.**  **1.** Car coat of three-quarter length sometimes made with shearling collar and toggle closing introduced in early 1960s. By 1980s sometimes made with inner-zipper *sweater vest* in front. **2.** In early 1980s three-quarter-length reversible jacket made of waterproof vinyl with drawstring hood, two large pockets, and fastened with grippers at sleeves and front. *Der.* Worn at football stadiums.

**storm c.** Heavy storm coat sometimes quilted made with water-repellent finish. Sometimes styled with shearling, pile, or quilted fabric lining and collar. By 1980s entire coat was made of quilted nylon.

**suburban c.** Same as CAR COAT.

**swagger c.** Pyramid-shaped woman's coat with flared bias back. Usually with raglan sleeves and large saucer-shaped buttons attached by fabric cord. Popular in 1930s, revived in 1970s.

**swallow-tailed c.** Man's formal evening coat which does not button in front, and is cut with peaked lapels trimmed with satin or grosgrain. Made waist-length in front with two long tails in back. *Der.* Back resembles the "tail of a swallow." Also called *tails*.

**sweater c.** Knitted or cardigan-style coat.

**tail c./tails** See SWALLOW-TAILED COAT.

**tent c.** Woman's pyramid-shaped coat, widely flared at hem, popular in 1930s, 1940s, and in mid-1960s.

**toggle c.** Three-quarter-length car coat closed with loops of cord through which barrel-shaped wooden or metal "toggles" are pulled. Sometimes styled with a hood. Also see DUFFEL COAT.

**topcoat** Man's or woman's lightweight coat in any style, designed to wear over suit jacket. Also see OVERCOAT.

**topper c.** Woman's hip-length coat, often made with a flared silhouette, popular in early 1940s.

**tow c.** Three-quarter-length coat similar to a *toggle coat* or *duffel coat*, designed for winter sports.

**trenchcoat** See RAINCOATS category.

**wraparound c.** Woman's coat made without buttons or fasteners in front and held closed with long self-fabric sash. Also called *wrap coat*. Also see CLUTCH COAT.

**yachting c.** Double-breasted four-button man's jacket with lapels and collar, usually styled in navy-blue wool with brass buttons. Made similar to U.S. Naval uniforms with black braid instead of gold, and yacht club buttons instead of Navy buttons; worn onboard by yacht club members.

**Zhivago c.** Mid-calf-length coat, lavishly trimmed with fur at neck, cuffs and hem, sometimes with frog closing. Inspired by costumes worn in *Dr. Zhivago*, 1965 film of Boris Pasternak's novel about the Russian Revolution in 1917.

**zip-off c.** Long coat styled to be used in two or three lengths, achieved by placing zippers at mini and midi lengths. Also see DUO-LENGTH COAT.

---

**coated fabrics** Fabrics sometimes made nonporous and water repellent through coating with various substances such as lacquer, varnish, pyroxlin, rubber, polyethylene, or plastic resin. Achieved by dipping, impregnating, or by calendering with pressure. Fabrics frequently used for raincoats.

**coatee** Short close-fitting coat with short skirt, flaps, or coattails. Fashionable in mid-18th c. and also in 1860s.

**coating velvet** Heavy velvet with a closely woven erect pile. When the fabric is folded, no break appears in the rib. May be made with a heavy mercerized cotton back and a silk or man-made pile on the face.

**coat of mail** See HAUBERK.

**coats** 18th c. tailoring term for men's waistcoat buttons. Also called *breasts*.

**coat set** Child's coat made with matching hat, or matching pants, since 1940s sold together.

**coat shirt** Shirt that buttons down front like a coat. Introduced in U.S. in 1890s for men;

now the conventional-type shirt. Formerly all shirts were pullover placket style.

**coat-style pajamas**   Two-piece pajamas with top that opens down front like a *jacket*. See PAJAMAS.

**coattail**   Portion of coat below the back waistline, especially the long back portions of a SWALLOW-TAILED COAT or a CUTAWAY.

**cobalt blue**   Intense medium-blue color made from cobalt compounds.

**cobalt violet**   Brilliant violet, or purple, color made from cobalt compounds.

**cobbler**   Shoemaker, a term first used in Middle Ages. Also called a CORDWAINER. Also see COBBLER'S APRON under APRONS.

**cobra chain**   See CHAIN.

**coburg**   Fine, closely woven fabric made in twill weave usually with a cotton warp and a worsted filling in imitation of cashmere. Introduced in England in the 1840s after the marriage of Queen Victoria. Originally made with silk warp and worsted filling. May be piece-dyed or printed, and used for dresses. *Der.* After Prince Albert, Queen Victoria's consort, who was from Saxe-Coburg-Gotha. Also spelled *cobourg.*

**cocarde** (co-card)   French, "*cockade.*"

**cochineal** (koch-en-neel)   Brilliant red dye-stuff obtained from bodies of female insect, *Coccos cacti, Dactylopius coccus* which grow on plants in Mexico and Central America. Used to dye wools in 17th and 18th c.

**cock**   Term used from end of 17th to early 19th c. for turning up hat brim. Given various names for manner of turn-up. Also see COCKED HAT.

**COCKADE #1**

**cockade**   **1.** Ornamental ROSETTE or bow of ribbon, usually made flat around a center button. Sometimes worn as a part of a uniform or badge of office, *e.g.,* tricolor cockade of red, white, and blue worn on side of hat as patriotic symbol during French Revolution. Also called *cocarde.* **2.** Feather trimming. See FEATHERS.

**cocked hat**   Man's hat worn from late 17th to early 19th c. with wide brim. To avoid weather sag and deterioration, it became the fashion to turn up brim which was sometimes fastened with buttons and loops to crown—first one side, then two sides, and eventually three sides forming a tricorn. Many variations have developed over the years each involving individual details. Also see BULLY-COCKED, CONTINENTAL HAT, DENMARK COCK, DETTIGEN COCK, KEVENHULLER, MONMOUTH COCK, and TRICORN.

**cockers**   **1.** High boots, crudely made, worn by laborers, sailors, country people and shepherds from 14th to 16th c. **2.** In 17th c. boots worn by fishermen. **3.** From 18th c. a term used for leggings buttoned or buckled at the side with straps under the instep. Word still used today in the North of England. Also spelled *cokers, cocurs.* Also see COGGERS and OKERS.

**cock feather**   See FEATHERS.

**cockle**   **1.** Defect in fabrics that results in bumpiness or puckering in the finished goods. *Der.* French, *coquille,* "shell." **2.** 17th-c. term for woman's curl or ringlet.

**cockle hat**   Hat trimmed with a scallop shell, worn by pilgrims returning from the Holy Land during the crusades in the 11th to 13th c. *Der.* French, *coquille,* "shell."

**cockscomb**   See COXCOMB.

**cockscomb spike**   Tall cone-shaped hairstyle worn by primitive people in Africa.

**cocktail**   Any of various short alcoholic drinks served before dinner or at special parties. Extended to mean clothing and accessories worn at such parties. See APRONS, DRESSES, GLOVES, and RINGS.

**coconut straw** Braided straw, usually tan or light brown, made from coconut-palm leaves. Also called *coco straw*.

**cocoon** See COATS and ROBES.

**cocottes** (ko-kot) Courtesans or immoral women, sometimes connected with the stage, who set fashions in France from 1860s to World War I. *Der.* French, "loose woman." Also see DEMIMONDAINES.

**cocurs** See COCKERS.

**codovec** (kod-o-vec) 17th-c. trade term for a man's *castor hat*.

**codpiece** **1.** Triangular flap at front of crotch of men's *trunk hose* large enough for a pocket, frequently padded and decorated, worn during 15th and 16th c. **2.** By early 17th c. term applied to front fastening of *breeches*. Also called a *cod placket*. Compare with BRAYETTE.

**cod placket** See CODPIECE #2.

**Codrington** Man's loose-fitting single- or double-breasted overcoat resembling a chesterfield worn in 1840s. *Der.* After Sir Edward Codrington, British admiral, who led fleet to victory at Navarino in 1827.

**coffer headdress** Woman's small box-shaped headdress of 14th c. usually worn over top of hair with coiled braids over the ears.

**coggers** *Gaiters* of cloth or leather buttoned up the outside of the leg. Worn by men during the 18th and early 19th c.

**coif** (kwaf) **1.** Short for coiffure. French, "hairstyle." See HAIRSTYLES. **2.** (verb) To style or dress the hair. **3.** White headdress worn by present-day nun under the veil. **4.** Close-fitting cap—such as those worn in Brittany, France—of crisp linen or lace in various shapes to designate the region. Also spelled *coiffe*. **5.** From 12th to 15th c., linen headcovering similar to a baby's bonnet tied under chin worn by the aged and the learned professions. Also worn by soldiers and knights under metal helmets. **6.** From 16th to 19th c., an under cap worn mainly by women, sometimes embroidered, with curling sides called *cheeks-and-ears*, ORRELETS, or *round-eared cap*. **7.** See BIGGIN.

**coiffe** Women's stiffened headdress worn in French provinces. Also see COIF #4.

**coiffe de mailles** Hood of mail worn by Norman war lords from late 11th to mid-12th c. Later worn under helmet and, in 15th c., by ordinary soldiers. Also called *coif of mail*.

**coiffette** (kwah-fet) Iron or steel skullcap worn by soldiers during 14th c.

**coiffure** (kwa-fure) French term used since 18th c. for hairdressing or arrangement of hair. Also see HAIRSTYLES. *Note: coiffeur* (m.) and *coiffeuse* (f.) are the terms used for hairdressers.

**coiffure à l'Agnès Sorel** (ah-nyes sorel) Woman's hairstyle with ribbon bands in front and knot of hair at back, worn in 1830s and 1840s. *Der.* From hairdo of Agnès Sorel, mistress of Charles VIII of France.

**coiffure à la Grecque** See GREEK COIFFURE.

**coiffure à la hérisson** See HÉRISSON.

**COIFFURE
À LA INDÉPENDANCE**

**coiffure à la indépendance** French hairstyle with a sailing-ship model perched on top of wavy locks and curls. Worn in 1778 to honor Benjamin Franklin's appearance at the French court for negotiation of a treaty between the U.S. and France. Also called *Triumph of Liberty.*

**coiffure à la Maintenon** (ah la manta-naw) Woman's coiffure of late 17th and early 18th c. with hair parted in the center, curled, and piled high. *Der.* After the Marquise de Maintenon, second wife of Louis XIV of France.

**coiffure à la mouton** (ah la moo-ton) Short hairstyle fringed over forehead and crimped on sides. *Der.* French, "sheep."

**coiffure à la Ninon** (ah la nee-nonh) See Ninon coiffure.

**coiffure à la Sévigné** (say-veen-yay) Women's hairstyle of 1650 parted in center, puffed out over the ears, hanging in waves and curls to the shoulders with decorated bow at ear level. *Der.* After a witty correspondent and writer of the time, Marie, Marquise de Sévigné (1626–1696).

**coiffure à la Titus** Coiffure, worn in late 18th c. after the French Revolution that resembled the way a condemned man wore his hair, brushed forward over forehead. Also called *Titus hairstyle. Der.* From hairstyle of Roman Emperor, Titus, 79–81 A.D.

**coiffure à la zazzera** Man's long hairstyle with ends curled under—originally worn by Romans and revived by Venetians in 15th c.

**coiffure à l'enfant** (ah lon-fon) Woman's hairstyle of 1780s bobbed short like a child's.

**coiffure en bouffons** (on buff-on) Woman's hairstyle with tufts of crimped or curled hair arranged over the temples, and the forehead covered with fringe of hair called *garcette.* Worn in the Louis XIII period.

**coiffure en bourse** (on boorce) Man's wig introduced in 1730 with hair pulled back and stuffed in a black silk bag tied at nape of neck. Also called a BAGWIG. *Der.* French, "bag."

**coiffure en cadenettes** (on ka-de-net) **1.** A hairstyle worn by men and women of Louis XIII period with two long locks—called *moustaches*—falling on either side of face, wound with ribbons, and tied with bows. **2.** 17th-c. term for masculine hairstyle with two long locks pulled back and tied with a ribbon.

**coiffure en raquette** (on ra-ket) Woman's hairstyle with hair brushed up, puffed over the temples, and supported by a wire hoop. Worn in last quarter of 16th c. *Der.* French, "racket."

**coiled bracelet** See BRACELETS.

**coin de feu** (kwan de fuh) Short coat with high neck and wide sleeves made of silk, velvet, or cashmere usually worn indoors over a home dress in mid-19th c.

**coin dot** See DOTS under PRINTS.

**coin necklace** Necklace of coins representing wealth of married women in Eastern Mediterranean, North African countries, *e.g.,* ancient Palestine.

**coin purse** See CHANGE PURSE under HANDBAGS.

**coin silver** Strong silver alloy containing 90% silver and 10% copper used for jewelry. The only silver available to early American Colonists, obtained by melting down silver coins.

**cointise** (kwan-teez) **1.** Cut-out decoration used on the CYCLAS, or overgarment, worn from 13th and 14th c., also the garment itself. **2.** Lappet or scarf under the crest of helmet worn in late 12th c. Also spelled *quaintise, quintise.*

**coir** Long, coarse, reddish-brown fiber derived from outer husks of the coconut, *Cocos nucifera*, which is elastic and resistant to water. Grown in the South Sea islands and Sri Lanka, used for straw called *sennit* braid.

**cokers** See COCKERS.

**Colbert embroidery** See EMBROIDERIES.

**Colbertine lace** See LACES.

**cold mask** See MASKS.

**coleta** Mexican term for short braided hairpiece worn pinned to back of head by bullfighter.

**collar** **1.** Separate piece permanently attached to an item of clothing at the neckline. May be made of matching or contrasting fabric, or be decorative, *e.g.*, trimmed with lace or embroidery. Shape may be flat, rolled, standing, or draped. Differentiated from neckline as it is an extra piece stitched on, or turned over, at neckline. **2.** Separate piece of fabric, fur, leather, or other material which fits around the neck and is not attached to the garment. **3.** Collars were not generally worn until the 16th c. See RUFF. In 17th c. the *falling band* was introduced; in 19th c. man's coat and shirt collars were introduced. Many new styles of collars were introduced in the 20th c. In alphabetical listing see FALLING BAND, FRAISE, M-CUT COLLAR, PAPILLON COLLAR, and REBATO.

## ▬▬▬ COLLARS ▬▬▬

**angled shawl c.** Man's collar used on a tuxedo with outer edge made square cut or "angled" at waistline.

**ascot** Long narrow scarf, or *stock* attached in back to neck of blouse or shirt, the two ends brought around to the front, looped over, and falling down the front. *Der.* After race course at Ascot Heath, England. Also called a *stock collar*.

**asymmetric c.** Collar which does not appear the same on both sides of center front, *e.g.*, large collar with slanting line to one side appearing longer on one side; popular in the 1980s.

**attached c.** Any collar which is permanently attached to the clothing for which it is made, specifically a man's *shirt collar*. Originally shirt collar was separate, fastened with *studs* to neckline in back and front, and called DETACHABLE COLLARS.

**banded c.** Collar which stands up around neck and buttons. May also be turned down in either front or back, to form two distinct types of collars. Also called *stand-up collar*.

**Barrymore c.** Shirt collar with long points in front, frequently worn with string tie, popularized by the actor John Barrymore in 1930s.

**Ben Casey c.** See MEDIC COLLAR.

**Bermuda c.** Small round woman's shirt collar ending in right-angled corners in front and lies flat on the shirt. Popular since 1940s mainly on blouses.

**bib c.** Flat, rounded, or square collar fitting over top of dress or blouse and around neck like a child's bib. Also called a *plastron*. Popular in 1980s with pleating, embroidery, or lace around edge.

**bishop c.** Large collar, rounded in front, extending almost to shoulder seams.

**bolster c.** Padded circlet worn around neck as a collar.

**bow c.** Long flat stand-up band sewn to the neckline which is tied in a bow in front. Introduced in the late 1920s and continued in fashion through 1980s.

**bumper c.** Large fur collar that extends to edges of shoulders when worn flat. Becomes a high rolled collar when ends are hooked in center front. Popular on fabric coats of the late 1920s, early 1930s, and mid-1980s.

**Buster Brown c.** Medium-sized stiffly starched round white collar first worn by boys in the beginning of the 20th c. and later adopted by women and girls. *Der.* Named for *Buster Brown*, a comic strip character, drawn by Richard F. Outcault in early 20th c.

**butterfly c.** Extremely large collar extending to sleeves at shoulders. Front hangs down in two points almost to waist with outer edge having scrolled effect to shoulder, appearing open like a butterfly's wings. An innovation of early 1980s.

**button-down c.** Shirt collar with pointed ends fastened to shirt by small buttons. Popular collar of 1950s and 1960s for men and women, and part of preppy look introduced in 1980s.

**Byron c.** Collar with large points and not much roll, similar to BARRYMORE COLLAR. *Der.* Named after English poet Lord Byron. Also called *Lord Byron collar* and *poet's collar.*

**cape c.** Large circular-cut collar which extends over the shoulders and upper arms.

**Carnaby c.** Collar, usually white with rounded ends in front, worn on colored, printed, or polka dot shirt in mid-1960s. *Der.* Named after Carnaby Street, London, where *mod* fashions originated.

**cascade** Circular-cut ruffle attached to neckline of blouse with a binding which may extend to waistline in a diagonal line.

**Chelsea c.** Medium-sized flat collar with pointed ends which form a low V-neckline in front, popular in late 1960s. *Der.* For borough in southwest London where it originated.

**Chinese c.** Standing-band collar that extends up on neck not quite meeting at center front. Also called *mandarin collar* or NEHRU COLLAR.

**choir-boy c.** Flat collar with rounded ends in front similar to PETER PAN COLLAR only larger, worn over choir robes.

**choker c.** Tight band collar that stands up high on neck almost to chin and fastens in back. Often made of sheer material or lace,

boned, and edged with a narrow ruffle. Fashionable from 1890 to 1910 and revived in mid-1960s and 1980s. Also called *Victorian collar.*

**clerical c.** Stiff white *standing band* collar worn by clergy with suit or with liturgical robes. May be fastened in back as a *Roman collar* or have a narrow opening in front. White collar is sometimes half covered by a similar black collar which may be attached to the *cassock* or to a biblike RABAT. Also see VENTILATED COLLAR and GENEVA BANDS in alphabetical listing.

**convertible c.** Rolled shirt collar which can be worn open with small lapels as a sport collar. When worn fastened with small concealed button and loop, it fits close to the neck with no lapels and appears like a regular shirt collar.

**Cossack c.** High standing collar that closes on the side, frequently banded with embroidery. Also called ZHIVAGO COLLAR and *Russian collar.*

**cowl c.** Large draped collar frequently cut on the bias that extends nearly to shoulders in circular style. Popular in 1930s and revived in 1980s.

**cowl hood** Cowl collar that drapes to form a hood that can be pulled over head. *Der.* Inspired by a monk's habit.

**crossover c.** A convertible collar with two large lapels which, when buttoned up to the neck, overlap one another.

**detachable c.** **1.** Made with tiny buttonholes at lower edge of collar so that it can be buttoned onto a dress or blouse. **2.** A man's separate shirt collar usually fastened with a *stud* in back and a collar button in front. Popular men's collar until 1920s and worn later with *tuxedo* and *full dress.* Also see alphabetical listing.

**dog c.** **1.** Collar that fits tightly around base of neck or higher, sometimes used with *halter neckline.* See CHOKER COLLAR. **2.** See NECKLACES.

**dog's ear c.** Flat collar of medium size with long rounded ends. *Der.* Ends shaped like a spaniel's ear. Also called *spaniel's-ear collar*.

**double c.** Usually a large collar styled with two identical layers of fabric—one slightly larger than the other. May also be two layers with the upper one cut in an ASYMMETRIC style.

**Eton c.** Stiffened boy's collar, similar to a man's shirt collar but twice as wide, with widespread points in front. Worn by underclassmen at Eton College in England until 1967. Also see ETON SUIT in alphabetical listing.

**fichu** Originally a sheer fabric or lace triangular kerchief worn in late 18th and 19th c. with very low neckline. Reintroduced in 1968 as separate collar worn around neck, crossed in front and tied in back of waist. Also see alphabetical listing.

**funnel c.** Large, stand-up collar which stands away from the face, buttoned or zippered up the center front, used on heavy winter coats or jackets.

**fused c.** Collar of man's shirt made of two layers of fabric with adhesive between making collar easier to iron and wrinkle-free.

**horseshoe c.** Flat collar extending approximately three-quarters to seven-eighths the distance around the neck with ends not quite meeting in center front.

**Italian c.** Collar cut in one piece with front of blouse or shirt, then faced and turned over.

**jabot** (zha-bo) Standing band collar with hanging ruffle attached to front of collar.

**johnny c.** Very small collar used for woman's or girl's shirt.

**lapel** Turned-back front section of jacket, coat, blouse or shirt where section joins the collar. Folding back to form *revers* and cut in different shapes, *e.g.*, cloverleaf, fishmouth, L-shaped, notched, and peaked.

**mandarin c.** Same as CHINESE COLLAR.

**medic c.** Standing-band collar fastened with single button used on physician's white jacket with side closing. Popularized by *Ben Casey* television show in 1961. Also called *Ben Casey collar*.

**middy c.** Same as SAILOR COLLAR. Collar of a middy blouse popular for children in the late 19th and early 20th c., now widely used.

**military c.** Standing collar, high in front and hooked either front or back, *e.g.*, type used on cadet's uniform at U.S. Military Academy at West Point, New York.

**moat c.** See RING COLLAR.

**mock-turtle c.** Separate band stitched down to simulate a TURTLENECK COLLAR.

**Napoleonic c.** Collar which rolls up high on neck in back then turns over. Extends approximately three-quarters of the way around neck with wide lapels in front and double-breasted closing. *Der.* Named for *Napoleon Bonaparte* (1769–1821) as depicted by J. L. David, court painter.

**Nehru c.** (nay-roo) Standing collar similar to Chinese collar but sometimes made with rounded ends in front. Copied from the costume of Jawaharlal Nehru, Prime Minister of India 1950–1964. Also called *rajah collar*.

**notched c.** Tailored collar primarily for man's suit coat which has an indentation or "notch" cut out where the lapel joins the collar. Also called *notched lapel*.

**petal c.** Collar made of several irregularly shaped pieces that look like petals of a flower.

**Peter Pan c.** Small round flat collar with rounded ends in front. Worn originally by children, later popularized for women. *Der.* Copied from costumes worn in play *Peter Pan* written by James M. Barrie in 1904.

**Pierrot c.** Small collar made of a double ruffle or ruff. *Der.* From costume of the comedy character in French pantomime called *Pierrot*

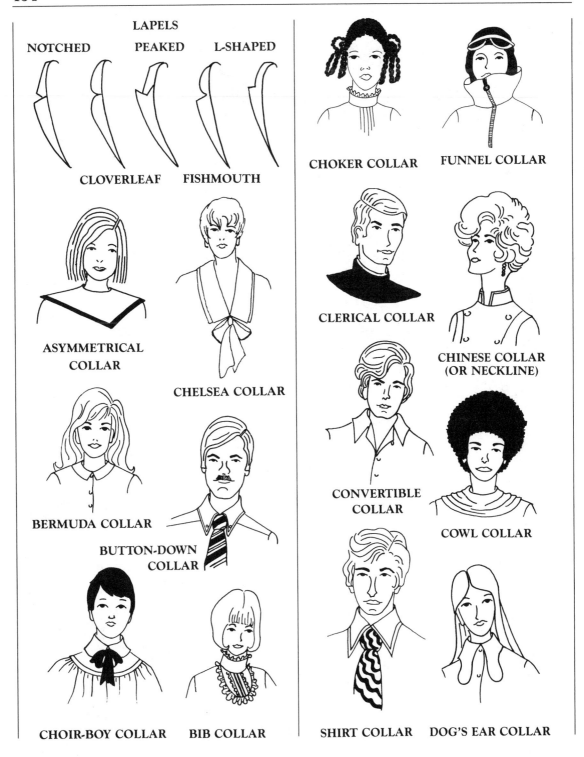

**LAPELS**

NOTCHED  PEAKED  L-SHAPED

CLOVERLEAF  FISHMOUTH

CHOKER COLLAR  FUNNEL COLLAR

ASYMMETRICAL COLLAR

CHELSEA COLLAR

CLERICAL COLLAR

CHINESE COLLAR (OR NECKLINE)

BERMUDA COLLAR

BUTTON-DOWN COLLAR

CONVERTIBLE COLLAR

COWL COLLAR

CHOIR-BOY COLLAR  BIB COLLAR

SHIRT COLLAR  DOG'S EAR COLLAR

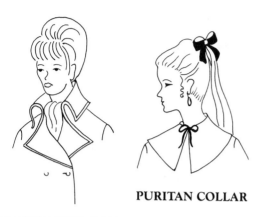

NAPOLEONIC COLLAR

PURITAN COLLAR

SHAWL COLLAR

SPREAD COLLAR

PETER PAN COLLAR

STAND-AWAY COLLAR

TURTLENECK COLLAR

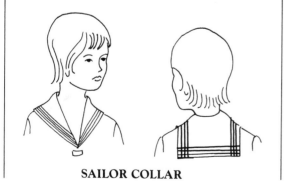

SAILOR COLLAR

WING COLLAR #2

(little Peter), especially the clown in opera *Pagliacci*, who wore a clown suit with this collar. Also see alphabetical listing.

**Pilgrim c.** Large round collar extending to shoulder seam at sides and ending in two long points at center front. *Der.* Copied from early Pilgrim costume.

**pin c.** Shirt collar fitting high on neck made with an eyelet on each side of opening through which a special collar pin is inserted.

**plastron** See BIB COLLAR.

**platter c.** Medium to large rounded collar with large rounded ends in front, worn flat on shoulders.

**poet's c.** See BYRON COLLAR.

**Puritan c.** Square-cut, wide, flat white collar, or *falling band* which extends to shoulder seam. *Der.* Copied from early Puritan costume.

**rabat** Narrow black ecclesiastical collar worn for town wear by clergy from the 17th c. to the present. Sometimes has an attached short bib. Also see CLERICAL COLLAR and CLERICAL FRONT in alphabetical listing.

**rajah c.** See NEHRU COLLAR.

**Regency c.** Similar to NAPOLEONIC COLLAR but smaller in size.

**revers** (ri-veerz) Another name for LAPELS, actually the facing of the lapels, which folds back to show the reverse side of the collar and lapels. See LAPELS.

**ring c.** Stand-away band that circles the neck at a distance about halfway to shoulder seam. Also called *moat collar* and *wedding-band collar*.

**rolled c.** **1.** Collar extending upward from neckline and turning over, the roll higher at back than in front. **2.** Any shirt collar or other collar which has a roll to it making it stand up on neck, as differentiated from a flat collar which has no roll, and lies flat at base of neck, *e.g.*, NAPOLEONIC or CONVERTIBLE COLLAR.

**Roman c.** See CLERICAL COLLAR.

**Russian c.** See COSSACK COLLAR.

**sailor c.** Large square collar hanging in back with front tapering to a V with dickey inserted. Trimmed with rows of braid and worn on *middy blouses* by the U.S. Navy. Popular style since 1860s, especially for children. Also called MIDDY COLLAR.

**separate c.** **1.** Any collar not permanently attached to the garment with which it is worn, *e.g.*, collars as worn with choir robes. **2.** See DETACHABLE COLLAR.

**shawl c.** **1.** Collar cut in one piece, or with seam in center back, that follows the front opening of garment without separate lapels. May be narrow or broad amd extend to waistline. Used on women's dresses, coats, sweaters and men's tuxedos. See ANGLED SHAWL COLLAR. **2.** Women's blouse or dress collar made in one piece with low V-neck in front and hanging ends of frilly lace. Worn in early 1980s.

**shirt c.** Turned-down collar used on a man's or woman's shirt, specifically, a small collar fitting not too high on the neck, with medium-spread points, *e.g.*, BUTTON-DOWN, CONVERTIBLE, PIN, TAB, SPREAD, and WING COLLARS.

**spaniel's-ear c.** See DOG'S EAR COLLAR.

**split mandarin c.** Similar to mandarin collar standing high on the neck. In mid-1980s called a *split mandarin collar* when it did not fasten at neckline and could be turned down to form lapels.

**spread c.** Man's shirt collar made with a wide division between points in front.

**stand-away c.** Women's collar that does not hug the neck, usually of the roll-type and popular from early 1960s.

**stand-up c.** **1.** See BANDED COLLAR. **2.** Collar similar to a banded collar extending higher on the neck and sometimes finished with a frill of lace or pleating, introduced in the early 1980s.

**stick-up c.** See WING COLLAR.

**stock c.** See ASCOT COLLAR.

**surplice c.** Flat pointed collar fastened to a neckline that crosses and wraps around. Used on a coat-style dress.

**swallow-tailed c.** Tailored collar with extremely long narrow points in front. *Der.* From resemblance to "the tail of a swallow."

**tab c.** Shirt collar fitting high on the neck with a small flap at neckband which buttons or snaps to other side of shirt.

**turndown c.** Any collar that folds over on the garment or on itself, as contrasted with standing-band or stand-up type. Also see ROLLED COLLAR.

**turnover c.** Any collar which rolls and then turns over, *e.g.*, a CONVERTIBLE COLLAR.

**turtleneck c.** High band collar, usually knitted, that fits very close to the neck and rolls over, sometimes twice. Introduced in the 1860s for men, popular in the 1920s and 1930s, and revived in the late 1960s and 1980s for men, women, and children.

**turtleneck convertible c.** Turtleneck collar with zipper down center front so collar may be worn high on neck or unzipped to a V.

**tuxedo c.** Collar that rolls over and extends down entire length of front opening in women's jacket or coat with no fasteners. Name borrowed from shawl collar of men's dinner jacket. *Der.* So named in the 1920s after the country club at Tuxedo Park, New York. Also see TUXEDO in alphabetical listing.

**ventilated c.** Stiff white standing collar punctured with holes around sides and back. Used to support the black CLERICAL COLLAR or RABAT worn by the clergy giving white trim in center front and around edge of clerical collars at the neck.

**Victorian c.** See CHOKER COLLAR.

**wedding-band c.** See RING COLLAR.

**wing c.** **1.** A tailored shirt collar with spread points. **2.** Stiff man's collar fitting high around neck with turned-down points in front; sometimes worn with man's full dress or daytime formal wear. Worn by upperclassmen at Eton College until 1967. Also called *stick-up collar*. **3.** Same type as above, introduced in 1980s of softer fabric, usually white on a colored shirt.

**wrap c.** Collar which has one end pulled around to side of neck where it buttons, introduced in 1983.

**Zhivago c.** See COSSACK COLLAR. *Der.* From 1965 film of Boris Pasternak's novel, *Dr. Zhivago*, depicting Russian Revolution of 1917.

---

**collar and cuff set** Women's separate collar and cuffs usually made of linen, lace, organdy, or other sheer fabrics—often white, trimmed with lace, insertion, embroidery, or tucks. Popular from early 15th c. until 1930s and used occasionally since.

**collar button** See STUD.

**collaret** **1.** Woman's tiny separate collar of 19th c., specifically one made of lace, fur, or beads worn like an item of jewelry. **2.** Armor worn in the Middle Ages to protect the neck. **3.** *Ruching* worn inside of high standing collar in the 16th c. **4.** In Colonial America a ruff of ribbon ending in a bow. Also spelled *collarette*.

**collarette à la Lyon** See CHERUSSE.

**collar necklace** See NECKLACES.

**collar pin** See PINS.

**collar stay** Narrow strip of plastic or metal inserted in point of man's collar from the underside to ensure a crisp unwrinkled look.

**collection** Term used by couture, ready-to-wear, or manufacturer's designer for clothing and accessories offered to customers for a specific season. Originally used only for high-priced couture clothing. Also called *line*.

**COLLEEN BAWN CLOAK**

**Colleen Bawn cloak**  Woman's cloak of 1860s to 1890s made of white grenadine with large cape pulled up in center back and caught with rosettes or bowknots. *Der.* After a melodrama by Dion Boucicault.

**collegians**  See OXONIAN BOOT.

**colley-westonward**  16th-c. slang meaning "worn awry" or "crooked," usually applied to the *mandilion jacket*, which was worn without putting arms through sleeves and turned sideways so that one sleeve hung in front, the other in back. *Der.* From a Cheshire, England, saying for "anything that goes wrong."

**colobium**  **1.** Type of undertunic or undershirt worn in ancient Rome and during the Middle Ages, also called a *sherte* by Anglo Saxons. **2.** Described as the tunic worn by Jesus under the *himation*—usually decorated with two purple vertical stripes. **3.** A liturgical garment derived from a Roman secular garment consisting of a long linen tunic, either sleeveless or with short sleeves. It was replaced by the DALMATIC.

**colombe**  Pale dove-gray color. *Der.* French, "dove."

**Colonial shoe/pump**  See SHOES.

**Colonial tongue**  Stiffened shoe tongue that extends up from vamp of Colonial shoe and is frequently trimmed with ornamental buckle.

**color blocking**  Use of large geometrical areas of contrasting color in dresses, blouses, jackets. Introduced in early 1980s to give a striking modern look.

**color-graded glasses**  See GLASSES.

**columnar heel**  See HEELS.

**comb**  **1.** An article, often of tortoise shell, ivory, plastic, wood, or metal with a row of narrow teeth. Drawn through the hair or beard to arrange or untangle it. **2.** Combs of precious metals, or those decorated with jewels, are often placed in women's hair to hold it in place and as decorations, especially at sides of head or in back when hair is set in a twist. Earliest combs are from late Stone Age.

**combat boot**  See BOOTS.

**combed yarn**  Yarn made from fibers which are given a second carding process called COMBING which eliminates the shorter fibers and makes the fibers more parallel. The resulting yarn is stronger, more durable, more tightly twisted, and less fuzzy than CARDED yarns. Used for fine quality cotton and worsted yarns.

**COMBINATIONS**

**combinations** Underwear in which two garments, *e.g.*, chemise and drawers or chemise and petticoat, are combined to make one. Introduced as the *Jaeger underclothes* for men in the 1880s. In 1920s a UNION SUIT for women was called a *combination*.

**combination tanning** Leather tanned by using both *chrome* and *vegetable* tanning methods.

**combination yarn** Two or more single yarns, of the same or different fibers or twist, combined to make a lightly twisted PLY YARN.

**combing** Additional *carding* of wool and cotton fibers that eliminates short fibers. Used in fine cotton and worsted fabrics. Also see COMBED YARN.

**combing jacket** Woman's loose jacket, usually waist-length, worn in the bedroom when brushing hair or applying makeup, in late 19th and early 20th c.

**comb morion** See MORION.

**comboy** Full-length wraparound skirt made of bright-colored printed fabric worn by both men and women in Sri Lanka. Named for the fabric which is exported from England.

**comedy mask** Mask worn by actors in ancient Greek theater with corners of mouth turned up. Exaggerated mouth needed because of distance of stage from audience.

**comforter** Woolen scarf worn around the neck in cold weather, so named from 1840 on.

**commander's cap** See CAPS.

**Commes des Garçons** See KAWAKUBO, REI under APPENDIX/DESIGNERS.

**commissionaire** Middleman who operates in foreign countries buying merchandise for American retailers.

**commode** Late 17th and early 18th c. term for a silk-covered wire frame used to support the high *fontanges headdress*. Also see PALISADE.

**commodore cap** Flat-topped cap with a visor fashionable for women for boating and sports, including bicycling, in 1890s. Similar to YACHTING CAP.

**commodore dress** Dress with nautical braid trim worn by girls and young ladies in early 1890s. Typical dress might have a wide braid-trimmed sailor collar and gathered skirt with braid trim near the hem. Usually worn with a flat SAILOR HAT or a COMMODORE HAT.

**common sense heel** See HEELS.

**Communion** Religious sacrament of the church in which people participate and share Holy Communion. Some churches require a particular type of dress for First Communion. See DRESSES and VEILS.

**compact** Cosmetic container used to hold powder, rouge, eye shadow, and sometimess lipstick. Made of metal or plastic with mirrored lid.

**compass cloak** Full circular cape worn by men in 16th and 17th c.—a type of *French cloak*. When made in semi-circular shape, called a *half-compass cloak*.

**competition stripes** See KNIT SHIRTS and STRIPES.

**computer dress** See DRESSES.

**computer pattern** Sewing pattern developed in 1960s, made to fit the individual. Salesperson in store takes customer's measurements, which are then sent to a pattern company and fed into a computer to produce a custom-cut pattern for garment.

**concierge** See POMPADOUR under HAIRSTYLES.

**conductor's cap** See CAPS.

**cone** Conical-shaped bobbin or yarn holder used as a core on which yarn is wound in preparation for weaving. Also called *cone core*.

**confidants** Woman's clusters of curls placed over the ears in late 17th c.

**CONGRESS GAITER**

**congress gaiter** Ankle-high shoe with leather or cloth top and elastic gore inset on each side popular from Civil War to early 20th c. Served as the pattern for ROMEO SLIPPERS for men and JULIET SLIPPERS for women. Also called *congress boot*.

**Connolly, Sybil** See APPENDIX/DESIGNERS.

**considerations** Lightweight PANNIERS worn to extend sides of dresses in latter part of 18th c. eliminating need for petticoats.

**constable** Small CANE with gold-plated top carried by men in 1830s and 1840s.

**continental** Term used in U.S. usually referring to the mainland of Europe. Most items are of French or Italian origin. See HEELS, PANTS, POCKETS, STITCHES, and SUITS.

**continental hat** Three-cornered hat having wide upturned brim with point placed in center front. Worn by George Washington's Continental Army. Style varied slightly according to regiment and date. Rank of officers denoted by various colors of cockades worn on left side of hat. Also see TRICORN, KEVENHULLER, and COCKED HAT.

**continental system** Yarn-making method. See FRENCH SYSTEM.

**continuous filament yarn** Man-made yarns made by pushing the spinning fluid through a nozzle, or *spinerette* with tiny holes, producing strands of indefinite length. See MONOFILAMENT and MULTIFILAMENT.

**contouche** See KONTUSH.

**contour belt** See BELTS.

**contour bra** See BRAS.

**contour clutch** *Wallet* similar to a CLUTCH

purse, but curved on top edge, sometimes with attached leather carrying loop at one end. Also called *swinger* or *swinger clutch*.

**control** Term used for women's girdles, foundations, and pantyhose made with ELASTOMERIC YARNS which provide support. See GIRDLES, PANTIES, and PANTYHOSE.

**convent cloth** **1.** Lightweight, black piece-dyed fabric used by nuns. Made wth a wool warp and silk or rayon filling in a crepe weave. **2.** A fabric with a warpwise rib made with three-ply yarns in the warp and single yarns in the filling in stripes, mixtures, and solid colors.

**conversation bonnet** POKE BONNET with rolled brim—one side extending beyond the cheek, the other side rolled back from face. Worn in 1803.

**converted goods** Fabrics which are received as *gray goods* and have had finishing processes applied to them, *e.g. sizing, dyeing, printing,* and *napping.* Finished fabrics may be known by the same name as the *gray goods,* or by different names.

**converter** Textile term for a middleman, either a firm or an individual, who takes the woven goods in an unfinished state and applies finishing processes, *e.g. dyeing, bleaching,* and *waterproofing.* After processing, fabrics are suitable for the clothing manufacturer or the yard-goods retailer.

**convertible** See COLLARS and JUMPERS.

**cony/coney** See FURS.

**coolie** Unskilled Chinese laborer who wears distinctive clothing and hat often copied by fashion designers. See COATS and HATS.

**coonskin cap** See DAVY CROCKETT CAP under CAPS.

**cop** Yarn wound on a metal, wood, or paper spindle, about 6 inches long, ready for insertion into the shuttle for weaving the filling of the fabric.

**cope** See CAPES.

**Copenhagen blue** A clear sky-blue color. Term sometimes shortened to *copen*.

**copotain** (cop-o-tan) Man's or woman's hat with a high conical crown rounded at top and medium-sized brim usually turned up at the sides and back. May be made of beaver, fur, or leather trimmed with wide band. First mentioned in 1508, but very fashionable from 1560 to 1620. Revived in 1640s to 1665; then called the *Sugarloaf hat*. Also spelled *copatain, copintank, coppintanke, copytank, coptank*.

**copped shoe** Type of PIKED SHOE worn by men in second half of 15th c.

**copper toe** See TOES.

**copyist** Person in the apparel trade who makes replicas of designs—translating a high-priced item to a lower price for a manufacturer.

**coq feathers** See FEATHERS.

**coral** See GEMS.

**corazza** Man's shirt with close-fitting sleeves, buttoned down the back, tapered to fit the body and worn from 1845 on. Usually made of cambric or cotton.

**corbeau** (kor-bo) Black with greenish reflections. *Der.* French, "raven."

**corded seam** See SEAMS.

**cordé handbag** See HANDBAGS.

**cordelière** (cor-de-lyare) Long chain, often of gold, which hung from belt, or girdle, and used to hold a cross, scissors, or other small items worn by women in the 16th c. *Der.* French, "cord or girdle worn by Franciscan friar." Also spelled *cordelier. Also see* CHATELAINE.

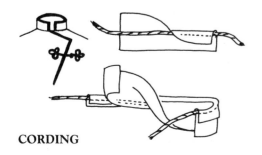

**CORDING**

**cording** 1. Trimming made by inserting a soft ropelike cord into a strip of bias-cut fabric. 2. Full-rounded trimming used for frogs and loops made by pulling the cord through a seamed tube of *bias* fabric to cover cord completely.

**cordonnet** A heavier thread used in lace usually for an outlining effect.

**cordovan** See LEATHERS.

**corduroy** Medium- to heavyweight, striped pile fabric woven with wales going predominantly warpwise and designated by size of the cords as *pinwale, regular,* or *wide wale corduroy.* Pile made by extra filling yarns forming floats which are later clipped and brushed. May be dyed or imprinted with a design. Originally a utility fabric, it is now used for coats, dresses, sportswear, men's, women's and children's wear. Sometimes used crosswise, lengthwise, and on the bias in the same garment to give an interesting effect. Now woven with blended yarn of polyester and cotton which increases washability. Very popular for car coats, pants, and jackets from late 1950s on. *Der.* French, *corde du roi,* "cord of the king."

**cordwainer** Term used in Middle Ages for shoemaker who learned his craft in Cordoba, Spain, and belonged to cordwainers' and cobblers' guild. Also called COBBLER.

**cord yarn** Heavy yarn made by twisting together two or more ply yarns. Used in bengaline, ottoman, and Bedford cord fabrics. Called *cable yarn* in Great Britain.

**cordyback hat** See CAUDEBAC.

**core yarn** Yarn made with a heavy center cord around which is wrapped with finer yarns of different fibers, *e.g.,* synthetic rubber core wrapped with rayon, cotton, or silk to improve absorption and feel. *Also see* ELASTOMERIC YARNS.

**cork** 1. Outer bark of oak, *Querous suber,* grown in Mediterranean countries. Stripped, dried, and boiled to remove sap and tannic acid, then used for fillers in shoes, for clogs, for tropical hats, and for other items that require lightweight, resilience, moisture resistance, and insulation against heat **2.** Man's PATTEN or GOLASH of 15th c. with cork rather than wooden sole.

**corkies**   See WEDGE HEEL under HEELS.

**cork lace**   See LACES.

**cork rump**   Bustle of late 18th c. made in shape of a crescent and stuffed with cork.

**corkscrew curl**   See CURLS.

**cornalia**   See ORALIA.

**corned shoe**   Broad-toed shoe worn from 1510 to 1540.

**cornercap**   Cap with four, sometimes three corners, worn with academic and ecclesiastical costume during 16th and 17th c. Also called MORTARBOARD.

**cornet**   **1.** See HENNIN. **2.** Dark-colored velvet cap similar to a BONGRACE worn from 17th to 19th c. **3.** Day cap with rounded caul; tied under the chin, in first half of 19th c. Also spelled *cornette*. **4.** Square academic cap or MORTARBOARD. **5.** Woman's skirt of early 1890s cut straight and fitted in front, and with back cut on the bias with small train. Also called *French skirt* or *cornet skirt*.

**cornet sleeve**   Close-fitting sleeve ending in a trumpet-shaped flounce.

**cornflower blue**   Bright purple-blue color of the cornflower or bachelor's-button.

**cornrows**   See HAIRSTYLES.

**cornu**   See ORALIA.

**coronal**   See CORONET.

**coronation braid**   See BRAIDS.

**coronation cloth**   Medium-weight suiting fabric of wool and unfinished worsted with warpwise striped details placed about 1″ apart. Stripes consist of single thread or decora-

tion put in with gold or metallic yarns. *Der.* First used at the coronation of King Edward VII of England in 1901.

**coronation robes**   **1.** Three capes worn by British king or queen for coronation at various times during the ceremony: a) a red cape lined with white, b) an *ecclesiastical cope*, and c) a purple velvet cloak trimmed with ermine. **2.** Ermine trimmed robes worn by British nobility attending the coronation with trains of prescribed lengths according to rank. Worn with various types of CORONETS, according to rank. Also called *robes of state*.

**coronet** (kor-o-net)   **1.** Crown that denotes rank below that of sovereign. Nobility of Great Britain have seven different styles of crowns for prince of the blood, younger son, nephew, duke marquis, earl, viscount, and baron. **2.** Band or wreath worn by women like a TIARA on the head. **3.** 14th-c. term for open crown worn by nobility. Also spelled *coronal*.

**corps** (cor)   17th-c. French term for BODICE.

**corps à baleine** (cor ah bah-lenn)   A whalebone bodice. See CORPS PIQUÉ #2.

**corps piqué** (cor pe-kay)   **1.** Quilted camisole with a *busk*, of varnished wood used as stiffening, first worn in France. **2.** In 17th and 18th c. a tightly laced underbodice, stiffened with whalebones and held on with shoulder straps. Same as French *corps à baleine*.

**corsage** (cor-sahge)   **1.** Small floral arrangement of flowers worn fastened to woman's shoulder or waist, sometimes attached to specially designed wristband and worn on wrist. Worn on special occasions or for formal events. Also see BOSOM FLOWERS. **2.** Term used in the 18th and 19th c. for a woman's bodice.

**corsage à la Du Barry**   See DU BARRY CORSAGE.

**corsage à la Maintenon** (cor-sahge ah la man-te-nah)   Fitted bodice of 1830s and 1840s trimmed with bow knots down center front.

*Der.* For Marquise de Maintenon, second wife of Louis XIV of France.

**corsage en corset** (cor-sahge on corseh) Tight-fitting evening bodice of 1830s and 1840s cut in sections with seams similar to those on a corset.

**corse** 1. Tight-fitting under-bodice, of metal or leather with center front lacings, worn under tunic by men in 12th and 13th c. 2. *Baldrick* for carrying a bugle used by men in 16th c. 3. Variant of word CORSET, in 14th and 15th c.

**corselet** 1. Tight-fitting waist-cincher belt, sometimes laced in front. Also see BELTS and WAISTLINES. 2. Originally leather armor; later in 16th c. metal-plate armor worn by pikemen, made of cast metal—lighter than the CUIRASS. 3. See FOUNDATIONS. 4. See PEASANT BODICE.

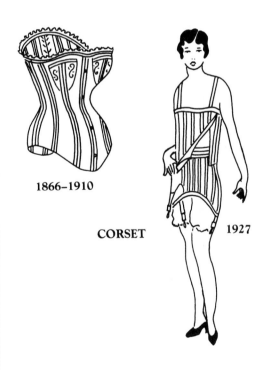

**1866–1910**

**CORSET** **1927**

**corset** 1. Woman's one-piece sleeveless, laced garment for shaping the figure. Generally a heavily boned, rigid garment worn from 1820s to 1930s. Since 1940s made of lighter-weight elasticized fabrics and called a GIRDLE or FOUNDATION GARMENT. 2. In 11th c. a leather bodice stiffened with wood or metal. 3. From 16th to 18th c., a stiffened bodice called *whalebone*, or *stays*. 4. Woman's gown laced up back and lined in fur, worn in 14th and 15th c. 5. Man's surcoat, with or without sleeves, worn in Middle Ages. Also see BRUMMELL BODICE, CORSE #3, Cumberland corset, demi-corset, foundations, and SWANBILL CORSET.

**corset à la ninon** Lightweight corset reaching to hips laced up the back and designed to wear under Empire style dresses in 1810.

**corset batiste** Fabric of heavy strong cotton, or cotton blended with polyester, woven in *Jacquard* or *dobby* designs used to make bras, foundation garments, and girdles. Rayon is sometimes used with cotton for decorative effects. Various types of fabrics are: *a)* poplinlike fabric woven in plain weave; *b)* striped rayon and cotton in dobby design; *c)* rayon warp and cotton filling in a floral *jacquard* design; *d)* poplinlike fabric with cotton filling and rayon warp in *dobby* designs; and *e)* elastomeric yarns used with cotton for stretch fabrics. The name *corset batiste* is a misnomer as these fabrics are not at all like regular batiste fabrics.

**corset cover** See CAMISOLE #1.

**corset frock** Dress of late 18th c. made with bodice of three gores of white satin in front and lacing in back, similar to a corset.

**Corsican tie** See NAPOLEON NECKTIE.

**corundum** See GEMS.

**cosmonaut look** Jumpsuits and helmets introduced when astronauts first started to explore space. *Der.* Russian, "astronaut." Also see LUNAR LOOK under LOOKS, and HELMETS.

**Cossack** Pertaining to people inhabiting the

Caucasus in southwestern Russia; men, particularly noted for their horsemanship, wore a distinctive costume including COSSACK HAT, CZERKESKA, or COSSACK COAT, full trousers, and boots. For Cossack styles see BLOUSES, COLLARS, HATS, NECKLINES, SHIRTS, and PAJAMAS, and COSSACK FORAGE CAP under CAPS.

**Cossacks** **1.** Very full trousers pleated into a waistband and fastened at ankles with ribbon drawstrings worn by Russian Cossacks. **2.** Peg-top trousers made with double straps under instep. Worn by men from 1814 to about 1850 inspired by the Czar of Russia's entourage of *Cossacks* at the peace celebration of 1814.

**costume** **1.** Dress, coat, or suit with coordinated accessories; an ensemble. **2.** Fancy dress for masquerade parties, Halloween, costume and masked balls. **3.** Dress which reflects a certain period in history. **4.** Theatrical dress worn on stage. **5.** Native dress worn for festivals and specific occasions. **6.** In the 1860s term used for outdoor day dress or afternoon dress with a long train.

**costume à la constitution** Red, white, and blue striped or flowered dress of muslin or lawn worn with a vermillion-colored sash and helmet-shaped cap. Symbolized the tricolor of the French Revolution and was worn by patriots. Also called *dress à la constitution.*

**costume jewelry** Jewelry not made of genuine gems or precious metals. Introduction is credited to French couturière *Gabrielle Chanel*, who showed imitation pearls, emeralds, and rubies for daytime in the 1920s—copies of her own real jewels. In the late 1970s new terms were introduced to describe costume jewelry. Also see FAUX JEWELS and FASHION JEWELRY.

**cote** **1.** Unfitted tunic, the main garment worn by both men and women during the 13th c. The word *kirtle* was more commonly used for women. See COTEHARDI #3. **2.** *Gipon* or *doublet* worn by men in the 14th and 15th c. **3.** Jacket or *jerkin* either sleeveless or with short sleeves worn over doublet in 16th c. Also spelled *cotte.*

**côte de cheval** French fabric characterized by a warpwise, broken-rib effect made in cotton, silk, or wool. *Der.* French *côte,* "rib" and *cheval,* "horse." Probably so called because it was used for riding uniforms and habits.

**cotehardi** **1.** Man's outergarment of 14th and 15th c. close-fitting with tight or *bagpipe* sleeves, shallow broad neckline, top buttoned to waist, and attached to full skirt of unpressed pleats. **2.** See COTE #1 and #2. **3.** Woman's close-fitting dresslike garment of same period, made of rich fabric and laced up back or front. Had long tight sleeves and slits in sides of skirt called *fitchets.* Said to have been introduced by Anne, wife of Richard II of England. Also spelled *cote-hardy, cote-hardie.* See TIPPET #1.

**COTHURNUS**

**cothurnus** Ancient Greek and Roman calf-high boot laced up the front made of colored leather with thick soles, sometimes of cork if wearer wished to appear taller. Worn by upper classes, huntsmen, and tragedians on stage in ancient Greece. Also called BUSKIN. Also spelled *kothornus..*

**cotorinas** See VESTS.

**cotta** Clerical surplice made like a full short white over-tunic, gathered into a narrow rounded yoke with long full bell-shaped sleeves. Worn by clergy over cassock and by choir members over long robes.

**cottage bonnet** Straw bonnet fitting head closely with brim projecting beyond the cheeks worn from 1808 to 1870s. Early styles were worn over a FOUNDLING CAP. Later styles had upturned pleated brim with satin lining.

**cottage cloak** Woman's hooded cloak of 19th c. tied under chin, similar to those seen in pictures of the fairy-tale character Little Red Riding Hood.

**cottage dress** High-waisted slim-lined dress of early 1820s with long apron in front made of same fabric. Necklines varied—some low with FICHU, others with white collars either trimmed with frills or VANDYKE EDGING. Sleeves were fitted. Hem of skirt was usually decorated with a ROULEAU.

**cottage front** Daytime bodice with lacings in front for decorative effect. Worn over a HABIT SHIRT, or CHEMISETTE, in early 19th c.

**cotte** See COTE.

**cotton** Soft white vegetable fiber from ½ to 2 inches long, which comes from the fluffy boll of the cotton plant, grown in Egypt, India, China, and southern U.S. American cottons include *acala*, *upland*, *peeler*, *pima*, and *Sea Island*.

**cotton batting** See BATTING.

**cotton broadcloth** See BROADCLOTH.

**cotton crepe** **1.** Crinkle-surfaced cotton fabric made with crepe-twisted yarns. **2.** A crepe fabric treated with caustic soda to form non-permanent crinkles. Also called PLISSÉ CREPE.

**cotton covert** See COVERT CLOTH #2.

**cotton velvet** **1.** Soft pile fabric woven like velvet with an extra warp yarn. A fabric distinct from velveteen with an extra filling yarn forming pile. **2.** Incorrect name for VELVETEEN.

**cotton-yarn numbering system** System used in U.S. and Great Britain for relative size of cotton yarns with lower numbers indicating heavier yarns and higher numbers indicating finer yarns. Also called *English yarn-numbering system*.

**Coty American Fashion Critics Awards** Annual awards sponsored by Coty, Inc., international cosmetics and perfume company, from 1942 to 1985, given for outstanding fashion design. Judges were magazine and newspaper fashion editors, broadcasters, and fashion retailers. The *Winnie* was awarded each year to a designer who contributed to American design and had significant effect on fashion. Originally awards were given to designers of women's fashions. In 1968 the Coty Menswear Fashion Awards were established. A designer receiving a *Winnie* or Menswear Award three times was accepted into the *Hall of Fame*.

**couched embroidery** See EMBROIDERY.

**couching stitch** See STITCHES.

**couel** **1.** British turban headdress of 15th c. of red for commoners, and black for nobility. **2.** Synonym for COWL in England.

**Council of Fashion Designers of America** A non-profit organization with a membership of over 100 American foremost designers founded in 1962 with Norman Norell as the first president. Membership is by invitation only. Accomplishments include: a) recognition for American designers both here and abroad; b) created the National Endowment for the arts with recognition of fashion as an art form; c) presents costume exhibitions annually; d) hosts the "party of the year" at the Metropolitan Museum of Art in New York City; e) contributes annually since 1963, to the Costume Institute of the Metropolitan Museum; f) supports recognized costume institutes throughout the country including the costume wing of the Smithsonian; g) was instrumental in founding the Fashion Institute of Technology in New York City. Since 1985 an annual "awards evening" is given to honor individuals who have made an outstanding contribution to fashion and fashion journalism. Also abbreviated to *CFDA*.

**counted cross-stitch embroidery**   See EM-BROIDERIES.

**countenance**   See COUTENANCE.

**counter**   Shoe-industry term for extra cup-shaped reinforcement placed at heel of shoe upper, between outer upper and lining, to add stiffness.

**counter fillet**   Late 14th and early 15th c. term for the FILLET or band securing a woman's veil.

**count of cloth**   Textile-industry term for number of WARP and FILLING yarns in a square inch of fabric. Expressed by first writing number of *warps* then number of *fillings*, e.g., 72 x 64 would mean 72 warps and 64 fillings per square inch. Knit goods are counted in warpwise loops called COURSES. Also called FABRIC COUNT.

**count of yarn**   Textile-industry term expressed in numbers given for the size of yarns in relationship to their length and weight. Also called *yarn number*. See FINENESS.

**country-western**   Style influenced by clothing worn by singers and musicians at the Grand Ole Opry® in Nashville, Tennessee. Also see LOOKS.

**coureur**   (koor-er)   Tight-fitting caraco jacket, with short *peplum* or *basques* worn by women during French Revolution.

**Courrèges fashions**   (coor-rej)   Clothes and accessories introduced in 1965 by André Courrèges, Paris designer, including A-line dress, jumpsuits, miniskirts worn with socks and Mary Jane shoes. See APPENDIX/DESIGNERS. Also see BOOTS, GLASSES, HELMETS, SOCK, A-LINE under COATS, DRESSES, SILHOU-ETTES, and SKIRTS.

**courrier dummies**   See MODEL DOLLS.

**course**   Textile-industry term for a crosswise or *fillingwise* row of loops in knitting.

**court dress**   Costume and items of apparel required to be worn for daily functions and ceremonial occasions in the presence of ruling monarchs. Also see CORONATION ROBES and COURT HABIT.

**courtepye**   Very short overgarment worn in 14th and 15th c. similar to surcoat. Made in a circle with round neckline, high collar, and slashed at the sides. Frequently *particolored* or embroidered with gems. Also spelled *courtepy*.

**court habit**   Term for men's clothing worn only at French court in 17th and 18th c. Called *grand habit* for women.

**court plasters**   Flesh-colored pieces of cotton, affixed to the face with adhesive, used to cover blemishes in early 20th c. *Der.* From cutouts of black silk or velvet adhered to the face by ladies of the English and French courts beginning in late 17th c. See PATCHES.

**court shoe**   **1.** British term for woman's shoe made in pump style. **2.** Term used in 1980s for shoe worn when playing tennis. See SHOES.

**court tie**   **1.** British term for a man's low cut oxford, generally of patent leather, worn as part of ceremonial COURT DRESS in England. **2.** British term for a woman's laced oxford of early 20th c. made with two or three pairs of eyelets in blucher style.

**coutenance**   Small muff carried in late 16th and early 17th c. Also spelled *countenance*.

**coutes**   (koot)   Armor for the elbows worn over chain mail in early 13th c. Also plate armor for elbows in latter 14th c. *Der.* French, *coude*, "elbow."

**coutil**   Durable firm cotton made in a herringbone twill weave. Used for foundation garments and bras. Also spelled *coutille*.

**couture**   French word used throughout fashion industry to describe the original styles, the ultimate in fine sewing and tailoring, made of expensive fabrics, by designers. The designs are shown in *collections* twice a year—spring/summer and fall/winter.

**couture lace**   See LACES.

**Couture Group, New York**  See NEW YORK COUTURE BUSINESS COUNCIL, INC.

**couturier** (ko-tour-ee-ay) French term for male designer or proprietor of a couture house.

**couturière** (ko-tour-ee-air) French term for female designer or proprietor of a couture house.

**coveralls**  One-piece jumpsuit worn over other clothes by mechanics and other workmen. Originally worn by gas station attendants in the 1920s. Restyled and fashionable for sportswear from the late 1960s on. Also see JUMPSUIT under SPORT SUITS.

**coverchief**  Norman term for the Saxon *head rail*, or VEIL; a draped head covering made of different fabrics and colors worn by women of all classes from medieval times to the 16th c. Also spelled *couverchief*, *couverchef*.

**covered button**  See BUTTONS.

**covered heel**  See HEELS.

**covered yarn**  See CORE YARN.

**covered zipper**  Zipper made with fabric tape covering teeth so that teeth do not show when zipper is closed.

**covert cloth**  **1.** An extremely firm durable fabric with a characteristic mottled look achieved by mock twisting worsted yarns spun from two rovings—one dark and the other light. Filling yarns are the same or of a dark color. Fabric is made with a warp-faced, left-hand twill weave of fine worsted yarns. Used for men's and women's suits and coats. **2.** Imitated in all cotton, covert is used for work clothes, caps, uniforms, and trousers.

**cover-up**  See BEACH WRAPUP under ROBES.

**cowboy/cowgirl**  **1.** Term originally used for a man or woman in western U.S. who herds or tends cattle usually going about on horseback. **2.** Easterner who imitates the above by the manner in which he/she dresses. Also called a *dude*. See BELTS, BOOTS, HATS, and SHIRTS. Also see WESTERN LOOK under LOOKS.

**cowboy suit**  Child's suit worn when playing, an imitation of the regular cowboy's costume. Consists of a shirt, pants, leather bolero, and sometimes *chaps*. Gunbelt and a wide-brimmed cowboy hat with chin cord are worn and toy guns are carried. The girl's costume is called a cowgirl's suit and sometimes has a short fringed skirt.

**cowhide**  See CATTLEHIDE under LEATHERS.

**Cowichan sweater**  See SWEATERS.

**cowl**  Cape or mantle with hood hanging over back and shoulders like a collar worn by monastic orders. See COWL COLLAR and COWL HOOD under COLLARS. Also see NECKLINES and SWEATERS.

**cowpunk look**  See LOOKS.

**coxcomb**  **1.** Woman's upswept coiffure with hair brushed to the back and pinned to form a vertical row of ringlets down center back. **2.** Hood trimmed with strip of notched red cloth at the apex worn by licensed court jesters in 16th and 17th c. **3.** A fop; a conceited foolish DANDY. Also spelled *cockscomb*.

**C.P.O. jacket/shirt**  See SHIRTS.

**crab-back bathing suit**  Man's swimsuit with top cut out very wide at armholes and a second cutout near waistline worn in 1920s and 1930s.

**Crahay, Jules-François**  See APPENDIX/ DESIGNERS.

**crakow** (kra-ko) Long-toed shoe of soft material—either a separate shoe, or cut in one piece with the hose—introduced from Poland during reign of Richard II in England. During the 14th and 15th c. toes of shoes became so long they were stuffed and fastened by gold and silver chains to bracelets below the knees. *Der.* After Cracow, Poland. Also spelled *cracow*, *crawcaw*. Later called POULAINE.

**crants**  Garland of flowers or chaplet made of gold and gems worn by women from Medieval times to 18th c. Also spelled *craunce*, *graundice*.

**crapaud** (cra-po)  See BAGWIG.

**crape**  See CREPE.

**crash**  Coarse, loosely woven fabric made in a variety of weights with irregular yarns giving it an uneven texture. Usually made in plain weaves of cotton, cotton and linen, cotton and jute, and rayon staple fibers.

**craunce**  See CRANTS.

**cravat**  **1.** Sometimes used as a synonym for a man's wide necktie worn with morning coat and pin-striped trousers. **2.** Lawn, muslin, or silk neckcloth with ends tied in a bow or knot in center front worn from 1660 to the end of the 19th c. Sometimes worn with starched collar called a STIFFENER. Also called a STEINKIRK. **3.** Necktie worn by women from 1830s on with sports costume. **4.** See TIES.

**cravate cocodes** (kra-vat ko-kod)  Large bow-tied cravat worn by women about 1863 with a HABIT SHIRT.

**cravat strings**  Piece of colored ribbon worn on top of the cravat and tied in a bow under chin. Later a ready-made bow placed behind the loosely tied cravat. Worn by men from 1665 to 1680s.

**crawcaw**  See CRAKOW.

**crawlers**  See PANTS.

**crease resistance**  The ability of the fabric to recover from wrinkles. Man-made fabrics usually have higher wrinkle recovery, but finishes applied to natural fabrics also aid wrinkle recovery.

**Creed, Charles**  See APPENDIX/DESIGNERS.

**CREEDMORE, 1908**

**creedmore**  **1.** Calf-high, laced work boot with two buckled straps at top. Worn during last part of the 19th and early 20th c. **2.** Ankle-high shoe with buckled strap over instep.

**creepalong set**  Infant's or toddler's two-piece suit usually consisting of a knit shirt with overall-type pants. Also called *creepers* and *crawlers*. See PANTS.

**creepers**  **1.** See CRAWLERS under PANTS. **2.** Small plates of metal set with spikes fastened over soles of shoes by straps. Worn when walking on ice and snow to prevent slipping.

**CREEPING APRON**

**creeping apron**  Infant's garment of early 1900s cut long and gathered at hem into a band through which a cord was drawn. Could be pushed up above knees for a romper effect.

**Cremona cravat** (kre-mo-nah kreh-vat)  Plain ribbon *cravat* edged with gathers, introduced for men in 1702 after the battle of Cremona, Italy.

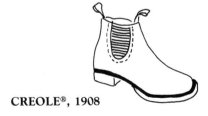

**CREOLE®, 1908**

**Creole®**  Tradename for heavy work shoe with elastic side gores. Worn by men in early 20th c.

**crepe**  **1.** A band worn for mourning. **2.** Wide variety of fabrics go under this name but usually have another name attached to define them further, *e.g.*, CREPE DE CHINE. All fabrics are related as they have a slightly pebbly texture. Some are genuine and made with CREPE YARN. Others are made by embossing or application of chemicals. **3.** A black silk fabric used for mourning. *Der.* French, *crispus*, "curled." Also spelled *crape*. For various crepe fabrics see CREPE-BACK SATIN, CRINKLE CREPE, FAILLE CREPE, LINGERIE CREPE, MATELASSÉ CREPE, MOURNING CREPE, ONE-HUNDRED DENIER CREPE, and WOOL CREPE.

**crepe-back satin** Lightweight fabric with a smooth, lustrous, shiny finish on the face and a dull crepe appearance on the back and may be used on either side. Made in a satin weave with silk, rayon, or man-made fiber for the warp, and a crepe twist filling yarn with twice as many warps as fillings. Used for dresses, blouses, and lingerie. Also called *satin-back crepe* and sometimes called *satin-faced crepe*.

**crepe charmeuse** (krepp shar-merz) All silk, dull-luster, crepe-back satin with excellent draping qualities. An expensive fabric made with grenadine-twisted warp and crepe-twisted filling yarn. Used for evening gowns, dresses, blouses, and expensive linings. *Der.* French, "charming crepe."

**crepe de chine** (krepp deh sheen) **1.** Fine, lightweight silk fabric with a crepe texture which is made by using highly twisted yarns in the filling and more warps than filling yarns. It is piece-dyed or printed and used for dresses and blouses. **2.** Crepe-textured fabric made with silk warp and worsted crepe-twisted filling. **3.** Cotton fabric made with combed two-ply yarns in warp and a crepe-twisted yarn in filling. *Der.* French, "crepe of China."

**crepe georgette** See GEORGETTE.

**crepe-soled shoes** See SHOES.

**crepe yarn** Rayon or silk yarn that is given a high twist during spinnings. The yarn is stiff, wiry, and contracts during finishing giving pebbled surface to fabrics.

**crepida** (pl. crepidae) Ancient Roman sandal similar to Greek KREPIS laced across the instep but enclosed at back and sides.

**creping** (krape-ing) Achieving a crinkled effect in the yarn by alternating twist in yarn (S- or Z-twist) or by adjusting tension on alternate warp yarns to achieve a puckered effect, *e.g. seersucker.*

**crepon** Durable crepe fabric in a heavier weight than most crepes. The crepe effect is in the warp rather than the filling. Made with silk, rayon, cotton, wool, or combination of fibers. Also made in Jacquard weave with crepe effect. Used for dresses.

**crescent** Motif copied from shape of moon in its first quarter. Also called a *lunette*. Also see TOES.

**Crete lace** See LACES.

**crève-coeur** (krev-kur) Term used at end of 17th c. for curls at nape of woman's neck. *Der.* French, "heartbreaker."

**crevés** (krev-ay) See SLASHING. *Der.* French, "slashes."

**crew cut** See HAIRSTYLES.

**crewel** (kroo-el) See EMBROIDERIES.

**crewel yarn** Two-ply, loosely twisted, fine worsted yarn used for embroidery.

**crew neckline** See NECKLINES and SWEATERS.

**crew socks** See *socks.*

**criardes** (kree-ards) Underskirt of gummed linen puffed out at the sides, forerunner of panniers. *Der.* French, "crying or scolding" because the petticoat creaked as the woman walked.

**crimp/crimping** **1.** Natural or machine-made bending or waviness in a fiber making yarn resilient, less shiny, bulkier, and suitable for knitting. **2.** To curl the hair with a hot iron. **3.** To shape leather by a machine that uses heat and pressure.

**crimson lake** Bluish-red color.

**crin** Braid used in making hats and for stiffening skirts at the hem. Same as *horsehair braid*. *Der.* French, "horsehair."

**criniere** (cran-ee-yere) See WIGS.

**crinkle crepe** Same as PLISSÉ.

**crinolette** (krin-o-let) Smaller form of woman's *cage petticoat* with hoops only in back. Made of steel half-hoops with *crinoline* or *horsehair* ruffles forming a bustle in the back. Worn from late 1860s to 1870s and revived in 1883.

**crinoline** **1.** Open weave cotton fabric which is heavily sized to be used for stiffening—similar to *buckram* but lighter in weight. Frequently used for interfacings in inexpensive fabrics, but not satisfactory as it will not wash or dry clean. **2.** A stiffened petticoat worn to extend the skirt of a dress. See CRINOLINE PETTICOAT under PETTICOATS. **3.** By extension from petticoat to include the outer skirt in hoop skirt era, 1850s to 1870s. Then by extension to entire period called CRINOLINE ERA, or age of crinoline. Also see HOOPS and SKIRTS.

**crinoline and tournure** Stiffened petticoat with bustle added in back worn under dresses in late 1860s. Also see TOURNURE and PETTICOAT.

**crinoline era** Period from 1850 to 1870 when crinoline petticoats were at their height and *Empress Eugénie* of France was called "Queen of the Crinoline."

**crisp** **1.** 16th-c. term for a woman's *veil*. **2.** 17th-c. term for a curl of hair worn by a woman.

**crispin** **1.** Cloak without a collar worn by actresses waiting in the theater wings in early 19th c., later adopted for men, women, and children. First worn in mid 1820s. **2.** Man's evening cloak, with full sleeves and quilted lining worn in late 1830s. **3.** Woman's short *mantle* of early 1840s with close-fitting back and small pelerine cape—sometimes with sleeves— made of bias-cut satin, velvet, or cashmere and often padded.

**crispine** An extra band at the forehead used during the late 14th c. to keep the elaborate CAUL or FRET in place.

**crispinette** Thought to be a veil draped over the CRISPINE and CAUL (or FRET).

**Criss-Cross® girdle** See GIRDLES.

**crochet** (kro-shay) **1.** Method of making a garment, fabric, braid, or lace with yarn and one hooked needle either by hand or by machinery. See LACES. **2.** Term used from 14th to 17th c. for a hook or fastener, *e.g.*, a hook attached at woman's waist for suspending a pomander or a fastener on a shoe. **3.** See BUTTONS, CAPS, and SHAWLS.

**crochet hook** Needle with one hooked end used for crocheting. Usually made of metal, plastic, or wood.

**crochets and loops** See HOOKS AND EYES under CLOSINGS.

**crocking** Tendency of dye to rub off fabric or leather because of improper dye penetration, dyeing methods, or treatment after dyeing process.

**crocodile** See LEATHERS.

**Cromwell collar** Wide turnover collar, with front edges nearly meeting, worn by women in the 1880s. *Der.* Named for Oliver Cromwell, Lord Protector of England, 1653–1658.

**Cromwell shoe** Woman's shoe with large buckle-trimmed tongue worn in late 1860s for croquet parties. Reintroduced in 1888 with high-cut vamp and large bow trim for daytime wear. *Der.* Named for Oliver Cromwell, Lord Protector of England, 1653–1658 .

**crooked shoe** Shoe cut specifically to fit left or right foot, first produced in volume about 1850, superseding shoes that were straight-cut and fit either foot.

**crop-doublet** Man's short-waisted doublet, popular about 1610.

**cropped** Term denoting shortened, or cut-off, when referring to clothing or hair. See PANTS and TOPS.

**cropping** See SHEARING.

**croquet boot** Woman's shoe of mid 1860s made of *Morocco leather*, frequently trimmed with fancy toe-cap, laced with colored ribbon, and trimmed with tassels. *Der.* Named for the game of croquet, a fashionable pastime of this era.

**cross** **1.** Motif of two bars intersecting at right angles used in early Christian days and in 12th c. by knights on their *surcoats* when undertaking pilgrimages to the Holy Land. **2.** European term for *bias*, or *diagonal* cut—called fabric cut "on the cross." **3.** Item of jewelry, a simple or elaborately decorated cross motif worn as a pin or as a pendant on a necklace. Also see ANKH and CRUSADER'S under NECKLACES.

**cross-boarded** Leather-industry term for skins processed to make grain more pronounced by folding leather in one direction, pressing with a cork armboard and rolling; then folding in opposite direction and repeating the process.

**crosscloth** **1.** Triangular *kerchief* of 16th and 17th c. worn by women with a *coif* or *caul* tied under chin or at back of head. Frequently embroidered to match the coif. **2.** A brow band worn in bed to prevent illness, or as a beauty aid to remove wrinkles. Worn by men and women from 16th to 18th c. Also called *forehead cloth.* Also see FRONTLET.

**cross-dyed** Term used to identify fabrics woven of two or more different fibers, such as acetate and rayon, immersed in one dyeing solution which dyes fabric into a pattern by affecting the two fibers differently. Frequently used for striped or checked fabrics.

**crosses** Fur term for small pieces of fur, such as paws and gills, sewn together to make a large piece that is cross-shaped—used particularly on varieties of lamb.

**cross fox** See FURS.

**CROSS GARTERING**

**cross gartering** **1.** Term used for binding or holding the *broc* of Anglo-Saxon, or *braie,* of the French, close to the leg by criss-crossing strips of leather around legs on top of pants. **2.** Term used from mid 16th to early 17th c. to describe the style of gartering hose by using a ribbon around leg below the knee, crossing in back, and tying with bow above knee in front or at side of knee when stockings were worn over *canions.*

**cross girdling** Style of wearing the girdle, or sash, crossed at the chest and then wrapped around the waist by ancient Greeks. Also see GREEK BELT under BELTS.

**crossover bra** See BRAS.

**crossover collar** See COLLARS.

**crossover thong sandals** See THONG #3 under SANDALS.

**cross Persian lamb** See LAMB under FURS.

**cross-stitch** See EMBROIDERIES and STITCHES.

**cross stone** See FAIRY STONE under GEMS.

**crotch** Term used for place in garment where the legs meet. British term is *crutch.*

**crown** **1.** A garland or wreath worn on the head as an ornament or sign of honor.

**2.** Circlet of precious metal and gems worn by kings and queens. **3.** Bridal headpiece worn with veil. **4.** Upper portion of a brilliant-cut faceted stone, *e.g.*, a diamond. Also called BEZEL. **5.** Portion of hat covering top of head.

**Crown diamond**    See DIAMONDS.

**crown sable**    See SABLE under FURS.

**crowsfeet**    **1.** Textile-industry term for wrinkles in finished fabric after it has been folded. **2.** Facial wrinkles at corners of eyes.

**cruches** (kroosh)   Late 17th-c. term for small curls worn on the forehead.

**crusader hood**    Snug-fitting hood cut in one piece with a small shoulder cape. Originally made of chain mail—later copied for knits for winter sportswear.

**crusader's cross**    See NECKLACES.

**crushed leather**    Leather given a crinkled surface made by hand boarding, machine boarding, or by embossing to produce an imitation of a *boarded* finish. Also called ÉCRASÉ LEATHER.

**crusher hat**    See HATS.

**crush hat**    See CHAPEAU CLAQUE.

**crutch**    British term for CROTCH.

**cryptocrystalline**    Term describing a gem with very fine crystalline structure only visible with X-rays..

**crystal**    **1.** Genuine rock crystal, a mineral. See QUARTZ under GEMS. **2.** Beads or simulated gems of faceted glass resembling *rock crystal*.

**crystalline structure**    Property possessed by most minerals and thus used as a means of identifying gems under a microscope. Principal systems are variations of hexagonal, cubic, tetragonal, orthorhombic, monoclinic, and triclinic. Minerals with no crystalline structure are called AMORPHOUS.

**crystal pleats**    See PLEATS.

**cuaran**    Knee-length boots of horsehide or cowhide held up by thongs—originally "early

Scottish bands made of rawhide." Worn by Scots Highlanders around 1500.

**Cuban heel**    See HEELS.

**Cubavera jacket**    White cotton sport jacket with four patch pockets similar to BEER JACKET. Worn with summerweight slacks for sportswear by men from 1940 to 1950.

**cube heel**    See HEELS.

**Cubic Zirconia®**    See GEMS.

**cue**    18th-c. term for the *queue*, the hanging tail of a wig, which first appeared for civilian wear about 1720.

**cueitl**    Full-length wraparound skirt made of colorful cotton of palm-leaf fabric worn by Tehuan women of Mexico.

**cue peruke** (kyu per-uke)   18th-c. term for wig with hanging *queue*.

**cuerpo**    See QUERPO.

**cuff**    **1.** Finish for a sleeve consisting of a separate sewed-on piece or a turned-back extension of a sleeve. **2.** The turned-over or stitched-on piece at the top of a glove. **3.** A turned-back piece at the hem of men's trousers; a trouser cuff. **4.** A turned-over or stitched down band at the top of a boot. **5.** See BRACELETS.

**━━━━━━ CUFFS ━━━━━━**

**banded c.**    A straight piece of fabric varying in width used on sleeves. Sometimes has an attached ruffle, sometimes a piece of elastic is pulled through band.

**barrel c.**    See SINGLE CUFF.

**detachable c.**    **1.** Cuff cut out of an additional piece of fabric rather than being an extension of the sleeve. **2.** A cuff which is buttoned or snapped to the sleeve. May be taken off, washed, and reattached to the sleeve.

**double c.** See FRENCH CUFF.

**French c.** Double cuff which turns back and is usually fastened with a cuff link. Also called *double cuff*.

**fringed c.** Leather band at the wrist which has long hanging fringe at the end. A fashion innovation of the late 1960s.

**gauntlet c.** Wide turned-back cuff that slants away from the arm, flaring wide at top and tapering to wrist.

**knit c.** Cuffs made with a rib knit stitch which gives a tight fit but is elastic enough to slip over hand easily.

**roll-up c.** Extension of the sleeve which is folded up to form a cuff. Sometimes fastened with a tab. See BUTTON-TAB SLEEVE.

**single c.** Band of material with no turnover stitched to the sleeve and usually closed with one or more buttons.

**turned-back c.** Turned-back extension of the sleeve. Sleeve is cut longer and a section is turned up to form a cuff.

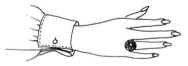

**BARREL/SINGLE CUFF**

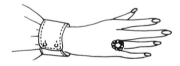

**FRENCH CUFF**

**GAUNTLET**

**cuff bracelet** See BRACELETS.

**cuff button** **1.** Small button or buttons usually of mother-of-pearl sewed on shirt cuff to fasten it. Introduced in 19th c. and used in lieu of *cuff links*. **2.** Late 17th-c. term used to describe two metal disks connected by links used to replace earlier CUFF STRING.

**cuffed** Term used in describing shorts, pants, or sleeves with very wide hems turned back to form a border called a *cuff*. On sleeves *cuffs* may be separate pieces sewn to edges.

**cuff link** Decorative jewelry consisting of two buttons or disks, joined by a link or short chain, worn to close the French cuff of a shirt. May be metal, engraved, set with stones, or made in wide variety of materials. Worn originally by men and adopted by women. Also see CUFF BUTTON.

**cuff string** String pulled through eyelets on cuff to fasten it. Used in lieu of a button in the 17th c. Also called *sleeve string*.

**cuff-top girdle** See GIRDLES.

**cuir** (queer) **1.** French, "leather." **2.** Rich warm, yellowish-brown color.

**cuirass** (kew-rass) **1.** Sleeveless leather thigh-length tunic worn as armor by ancient Greeks and Romans. **2.** Armor consisting of breastplate and back plates of steel worn either under, or over, other garments from mid 14th to mid 17th c. At first over a mail shirt and *jupel* and under a *tabard*, later worn outside with metal *tassets* forming a skirt. Similar to *corselet #3* or *breastplate*. **3.** Plain, close-fitting waist worn by women in early 1900s. *Der.* French, *cuirasse*, "breastplate."

**cuirasse bodice** Extremely tight, boned women's daytime bodice of mid-1870s extending down over hips to mold the body. Frequently made in fabric different from the dress.

**cuirasse tunic** Tight-fitting tunic skirt worn with the *cuirasse bodice* by women in mid-1870s.

**cuir savage** *Der.* French, *cuir,* "leather" and *suavage,* "fierce and untamed animal." See LEATHER LOOK and WET LOOK under LOOKS.

**cuisse** Piece of armor or padding shaped to protect the thigh worn during Middle Ages.

**culet** (ku-lit) **1.** Bottom facet of a brilliant-cut gem. **2.** Piece of armor consisting of a skirt of articulated plate fastened to backplate to protect the loins worn from mid-16th to mid-17th c.

**Cullinan diamond** See DIAMONDS.

**culottes** **1.** Term first used for tight below-the-knee pants worn during reign of Henry III of France, 1574–1589. **2.** Synonym for PETTICOAT BREECHES. **3.** Garment that hangs like a skirt, but is actually pants, *i.e.,* a divided skirt. *Der.* French, "breeches, trousers, tights, and knickers." See DRESSES, PAJAMAS, PANTS, SKIRTS, and SLIPS.

**cultivated silk** Term used in India and other countries of the Far East for silk fibers from cocoons raised in a scientific manner—the opposite of wild silk.

**cultured pearl** See BEADS and GEMS.

**Cumberland corset** Waist cincher or corset stiffened with whalebone worn by English dandies during the Regency period, 1815–1820s.

**Cumberland hat** Man's hat with 8″ high tapered crown and small brim turned up at the sides worn in 1830s. Also called *hat à la William Tell.*

**cummerbund** **1.** Sash worn by women which hooks rather than ties. **2.** Wide colorful sash worn on top of a wide leather belt by Albanian and Montenegrin men and used to hold accessories—including a pistol. Also part of native dress in India and Turkestan. **3.** See BELTS. *Der.* kamarband, "loin-band."

**Cummings, Angela** See APPENDIX/DESIGNERS.

**cupola coat** Dome-shaped petticoat made with whalebone, or cane hoops, fashionable in England from 1710–1780. Also called BELL HOOP.

**cuprammonium rayon** Filament yarn or staple rayon fiber made from wood pulp dissolved in a solution of ammonial-copper.

**curch** **1.** Untrimmed close-fitting woman's cap worn in Colonial America. Also spelled *kerche.* **2.** Scarflike woman's head covering worn in Scotland. Also called *curchef, kerchief.*

**curing** Process used on fabrics or garments previously treated with insolvent resins which are placed in an oven with temperatures of 280° or above to permanently set fabric or garment so it will retain shape after washing. Labeled DURABLE PRESS when used on garments.

**curl** Hair twisted around in a spiral fashion and worn close to the head, around the face, dangling down, or bouffant. Also see HAIRSTYLES.

## ═══ CURLS ═══

**barrel c.** Full round large curls frequently grouped at crown or back of the head.

**bubble c.** Very loose curls, back-combed slightly and turned under, appearing on head as series of rounded bumps.

**bustle c.** Long curls worn dangling at back of head.

**corkscrew c.** Free hanging curls which appear coiled, frequently lacquered to hold the shape.

**Grecian c.** Small curls around the face, copied from Napoleonic era which in turn looked to Greece for inspiration.

**guiche** (gweesh) Few strands of hair made into curl in front of ear. Also called *kiss curl.* Also see REVERSE GUICHE.

**BARREL CURLS**

**GUICHE**

**SPIT CURL**

**TENDRILS**

**jumbo c.** Very large curls similar to BARREL CURLS.

**kiss c.** See GUICHE.

**pannier c.** Curls worn at sides of face in front of the ears.

**pin c. 1.** Curls used on forehead or sides of face made by winding hair around the finger then set with bobby pins. When pins are removed, curl is left tightly twisted. **2.** Method of setting the hair by making tiny curls all over the head and securing them with bobby pins. May be combed out into either waves or curls.

**reverse guiche** GUICHE, curled back toward the ear instead of forward.

**ringlets** Loose curls that hang in dangling fashion.

**sausage c.** Tightly rolled horizontal curl usually arranged in layers around sides or back of head from ear level to nape of neck. Popular in late 1930s, early 1940s, and revived in 1980s.

**spit c.** Separate ringlets formed flat against the forehead or cheek often held in place by water, setting lotion or lacquer. Popular in 1930s, and revived in 1970s and 1980s. Also see GUICHE.

**tendrils** Long loosely curled strands of hair worn hanging at the forehead, sides, or nape of neck, popular with the *pompadour* hairstyle.

**curlyhead** See HAIRSTYLES.

**curricle coat** (kur-eh-kul) **1.** Woman's fitted full-length coat with lapels worn in early 19th c. Cut away in front from chest to waist, sloping to the back; sometimes called *gig coat.* **2.** Man's BOX COAT or *driving coat*, with one or more CAPES worn in mid-19th c.

**curricle dress** Women's thigh-length, short-sleeved, open-front *over-tunic* usually of net worn from 1794 to 1803 over a full-length dress.

**curtain drapery** American term for HIP BAGS.

**curtains** See LAMBALLE BONNET.

**cushion cut** See GEM CUTS.

**cushionet** *Bustle* worn with the FARTHINGALE from 1560 to 1630s that raised the back of a skirt. Also spelled *quissionet.*

**cushion headdress** 19th-c. term for large padded roll worn as headdress by women in first half of the 15th c.

**cushion pad** Tiny bustle stuffed with horsehair worn in late 19th c.

**cushion sole 1.** Cork, felt, or foam rubber used under the insole of shoe as shock absorber when walking. **2.** See SOCKS.

**cushion-style embroidery** See EMBROIDERIES.

**custom designer** Designer who creates an original garment that is executed by skilled seamstresses who drape the fabric on a model form, or dummy, conforming to the customer's special measurements. Clothes also called *custom-made* or *made-to-measure.*

**custom-made**   Describing garments made by tailor or couture house for an individual customer following couturièr's original design. Done by either fitting on a model form adjusted to the customer's measurements or by several personal fittings.

**cut**   **1.** Trade term used in ready-to-wear industry for cutting out fabric preparatory to sewing. **2.** Manner in which a gem is faceted or cut. See GEM CUTS. **3.** A length of GRAY GOODS, approximately 60 yards long. Also called a *bolt.* **4.** Knitting term used mainly in circular knitting for number of needles on machine in 1″ of space, *e.g.,* a 34-cut machine has 34 needles per inch.

**cutaway coat/jacket**   See COATS.

**cutaway frock**   Man's suit coat almost knee-length—similar to a FROCK COAT—and cut away from waistline to each side seam in rounded curve. Worn in 1890s and early 1900s.

**cutaway sack**   Man's loose-fitting suit jacket reaching to hips cut away in rounded lines in front to side seams. Worn in 1890s and early 1900s.

**cut-fingered gloves**   **1.** Gloves slashed to show rings on fingers worn in late 16th c. **2.** Women's gloves with tips of fingers cut off worn in early 18th c. Revived as a fad in 1985.

**cut-offs**   See SHORTS.

**cutouts**   **1.** Shoe-industry term for tiny patterns shaped like diamonds, teardrops, squares, and other shapes cut out of the upper part of shoe to give open-air effect. **2.** Holes of different sizes and shapes cut from clothing—such as rounded section at sides of waist, or round section cut from center front of dress—popular in early 1960s. Also see DRESSES, SWIMSUITS, and ACTION GLOVES under GLOVES.

**cut pile fabric**   Any fabric made with a filling, a warp, and an extra yarn to form the pile. After fabric is woven, the loops formed by the third yarn are cut. The fabric is brushed and a pile forms. (An uncut pile fabric would have surface loops similar to TERRYCLOTH.) Cut pile fabrics include CORDUROY, VELVET, and VELVETEEN.

**cut-pile weave**   See VELVET WEAVE.

**cut-steel beads**   See BEADS.

**cut-steel buckle**   Popular buckle of early 20th c. made of polished steel with jewellike facets. Used on silk or moiré afternoon or evening shoes and on belts.

**cutter**   Garment-production term for the person who cuts the fabric with an electric knife.

**cutting-up trade**   Jargon used by textile industry for clothing manufacturers.

**cut velvet**   Brocaded effect woven on a Jacquard loom in one color, or several, with a sheer background of fabric, *e.g.,* chiffon or georgette. Used for dresses and evening wear.

**cut wig**   18th-c. term for a man's small plain wig without a QUEUE.

**cut work**   See EMBROIDERIES.

**cyclas**   **1.** Robe of state with border of purple or gold worn by women in ancient Rome. **2.** Rich elaborate overgarment, sometimes fur- or silk-lined, made of a large piece of cloth with round opening for head. Worn in medieval times on ceremonial occasions by both men and women, *e.g.,* at the coronation of Henry III of England in the 13th c. **3.** Sleeveless tunic or *surcoat* worn over armor in early 14th c.—extending to waist in front and to knees in back—slashed up sides and then laced. Also spelled *ciclaton, cinglaton.*

**cycle jacket**   See MOTORCYCLE JACKET under SPORT JACKETS.

**CYCLING SUITS**

**cycling suit**   Any costume worn for bicycling in the late 19th c. **Boys:** jacket, similar to PATROL JACKET, worn with tight knee pants. **Women:** *knickerbockers* or a *divided skirt* with tailored or Norfolk *jacket, leggings,* and *a straw sailor hat.* **Men:** *knickerbockers* and *Norfolk jacket.* Also called a *cycling costume.*

**cylinder printing**   See ROLLER PRINT under PRINTS.

**cymophane**   See GEMS.

**Czechoslovakian embroidery**   See EMBROIDERIES.

**czerkeska**   Calf-length coat worn by Caucasian Cossack Army. Distinctive feature was series of cartridge pleats on either side of chest—each pleat originally held one charge of gunpowder. Also spelled *tcherkeska, cherkesska.* Also see BOURKA.

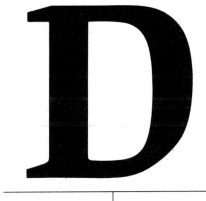

**D** **1. Shoe Size:** Letter indicating a width; widths run from AAAA to EEEEE with AAAA being the narrowest and EEEEE being the widest. **2. Pajama Size:** Men's regular height (5′8″–5′11″) size corresponding to 45″–48″ chest measurement. For other sizes, see BIG, EXTRA-TALL, REGULAR and TALL. **3. Shirt Size:** For men's extra-tall size with 18–18½ collar measurement. **4. Bra Cup Size:** Sizes run AAA, AA, A, B, C, D, DD: AAA is the smallest and DD the largest.

**dacca muslin** **1.** Handwoven fabric of fine cotton grown locally by the natives of Dacca, a town located in Pakistan. Made of yarn so fine that ten yards of the best quality fabric are reported to weigh only three or four ounces. **2.** An imitation of the above fabric made in Great Britain.

**Daché, Lilly** See APPENDIX/DESIGNERS.

**Dacron®** (day-cron) Trademark owned by E. I. du Pont de Nemours for approximately 70 types of polyester filament yarns, staple yarns, fabrics, and fiberfill all given a type number and made for various end uses, *e.g.*, with cotton for men's shirtings, and with wool for coat and suit fabrics.

**Dadaism** Movement in art and literature flourishing in Zurich during and immediately after World War I. Attempted to discredit all previous art and culture rejecting every moral, social, and aesthetic code—substituting the incongruous and accidental. Figures were distorted and the beautiful made ugly. Jean Arp and Max Ernst were the co-exponents and led the Cologne group. Flourished in Paris, Berlin, and Zurich where it was initiated.

**dagging** Ornamental borders cut on garments in shapes of leaves, tongues, and scallops; originated in 1340s. Fashionable until the end of 15th c. for hems of gowns, sleeves, and cape edge of the *chaperone*. Also called *cut work, dag, dagges, foliated, jags,* and *jagging.* Also see CASTELLATED.

**daharra** (da-har-a) Wide Moroccan full-length robe made from rectangle of striped fabric sewed up sides, leaving openings for arms, with embroidery around neckline. Compare with CAFTAN.

**Dali, Salvador** (dah-lee) (1904– ) Spanish artist, one of leading exponents of surrealism in painting, noted for his jewelry designs in fantastic shapes. His paintings influenced fashion, display, and advertising.

**dalmatic** (dal-ma-tic) Long, extra wide-sleeved, loose-fitting tunic trimmed with two vertical stripes in front worn by men and women in Byzantine period. Later worn as an ecclesiastical vestment by cardinals, abbots, and bishops, and as part of the coronation robes of Great Britain. *Der.* From *tunica dalmatica,* worn by Romans in 2nd c., starting in Dalmatia.

**damaging-out** Repairing of tears or holes in fur pelts and garments.

**damascene lace** (dam-ah-seen) See LACES.

**damascening** (dam-ah-seen-ing) **1.** Jewelry term used for engraving steel, bronze, or iron and filling up the incision with gold or silver wire. **2.** Watered pattern found on some forged items such as sword blades, armor, or gun barrels made from damascene steel. Term mentioned by Herodotus of some shields and swords of the Samites who fought against Rome. **3.** Inferior style of damascening can be made by etching the pattern on steel then depositing gold or silver in the engraved lines electronically. *Der.* Named for Damascus where it was formerly used. Also see RINGS.

**damask** Fabric made in the Jacquard weave in white or colored floral or geometric effects. Pattern may be large or small and reverses on the opposite side. Frequently made in a satin or twill weave while the background is in a plain, rib, or sateen weave. *Der.* Originally a rich silk fabric from Damascus.

**dance set** Lingerie consisting of bra and wide, flaring step-in panties worn in the 1920s.

**dance skirt** See SKIRTS.

**dandizette** (dan-dee-set) Term used from 1816 to 1820 for a female *dandy* conspicuous for her *Grecian bend*, or the manner in which she walked.

**dandy** Term used from about 1816 on for a man excessively fond of and overly concerned with clothes, exemplified by *Beau Brumell, Lord Petersham*, and *Count d'Orsay*, who greatly influenced men's fashions in England and France. Also called *beau*, or, in excessive cases, *fop*. Also see BLOUSES, BOSOM FLOWERS, DANDIZETTE, LOOKS, and SHIRTS.

**dandy hat** Woman's high-crowned, roll-brimmed hat decorated with jet embroidery, feathers, and a veil. Introduced by New York milliner Sally Victor in mid-1950s.

**Danish trousers** Pants worn by young boys in 1870s that were calf-length and open at the hems. Also called *open-bottom trousers*.

**darning** Method of reweaving threads by hand to repair a hole in a sock or garment. May also be done on sewing machine. See STITCHES and DARNED LACE under LACES.

**dart** Sewing term for V-shaped tuck used to make garment conform to the body. Used frequently at shoulders, waist, or in side seam under the arm.

**darya** Natural-colored wild silk fabric made in India.

**dashiki** African garment similar to collarless *kimono-sleeved* shirt, made in bold native-printed cotton. Introduced in U.S. in late 1960s for general wear, particularly by Afro-Americans. Also see BLOUSES and DRESSES.

**Davy Crockett cap** See CAPS.

**d.b.** British tailors 19th c. slang term for *double-breasted*.

**death's head button** 18th-c. term for domed button covered with metal thread or mohair forming an "X" on top like the cross of the "skull and cross-bones".

**DE BEVOISE BRASSIÈRE**

**De Bevoise brassière** Sleeveless low-necked waist, similar to a *corset cover*, reaching to waistline with a point in front and boned to support the bosom. Patented by the De Bevoise Company in Newark, N.J., in early 1900s. Later models were the forerunners of the contemporary bra.

**debutante slouch** Posture fashionable for young sophisticated women, starting about 1917 and very popular in 1920s, with shoulders drooping forward giving a flat-chested appearance.

**decalcomania** Process of transferring a picture or design from specially prepared paper to the skin. Fad of wearing designs of butterflies, flowers, and other motifs on legs and arms popular in mid-1960s. Also see TATTOO.

**decating** **1.** Finishing process used on wool fabric to set width and length and improve luster. Also called *potting*. **2.** Finishing process on rayon and other man-made woven fabrics and knits to improve hand, color, and luster.

**decatur ring**   See RINGS.

**deccan hemp** (dek-en)   Vegetable fiber grown in Nigeria and India used as substitute for hemp. Also spelled *decam*. Also called *ambari* or *kenaf*.

**deck**   Term used for clothing and accessories generally used for nautical sports. See PANTS, SPORT JACKETS, and BOATING SHOE under SHOES.

**décolletage** (deh-coll-eh-tahzh)   French noun meaning bare shoulders or outline of a low-cut neckline.

**décolleté** (deh-coll-eh-tay)   French adjective for garment cut very low at neckline revealing shoulders, neck, back, and sometimes part of bosom. Also see BRAS and NECKLINES.

**découpage** (deh-coo-pahg)   The art of decorating items with cutout pictures of paper or fabric pasted to surfaces and shellacked. Popular in mid and late 1960s. *Der.* French, "cutout." Also see HANDBAGS.

**Deepdeen diamond**   See DIAMONDS.

**deerskin**   See BUCKSKIN under LEATHERS.

**deerstalker**   Cap worn from 1860s on with front and back visor as worn by Sherlock Holmes. See CAPS.

**DE JOINVILLE TECK**

**de Joinville teck**   Pre-tied man's silk or satin necktie of 1890s made narrow around neck and wide like a *stock* in front. Fell in graceful folds with wide, squared, fringed ends.

**de la Renta, Oscar**   See APPENDIX/DESIGNERS.

**Delft blue**   medium-blue color, similar to color of pottery made in Delft, Holland.

**Delhi work**   See EMBROIDERIES.

**Delineator, The**   Fashion magazine originating in 1872 described as a "Journal of Fashion Culture and Fine Arts." Had many illustrations of apparel for women and children each with pattern number so that consumer could order tissue paper pattern and made her own clothing. A very successful publication edited by The Butterick Publishing Co., in New York and London.

**Dell'Olio, Louis**   See APPENDIX/DESIGNERS.

**Delphos Dress**   In 1909 MARIANO FORTUNY patented a new system for making a dress. The front and back of the dress were laced together, rather than stitched down the sides. Styles were reminiscent of ancient Greek dresses. Beautiful fabrics were used and the entire dress was minutely pleated thus molding the body like a Greek statue. Gold and silver luster effects were created on velvets. Same general style was continued until his death in 1949. Most styles were used for the theater or films as dress did not conform to usual mode of that era. Now collectors' items, selling in 1983 for $1,100. Also see FORTUNY, MARIANO under APPENDIX/DESIGNERS.

**demantoid**   See ANDRADITE GARNET under GEMS.

**demi-boot**   See BOOTS.

**demi-bra**   See BRAS.

**demi brassard**   Armor worn in early 14th c. consisting of a metal plate worn to protect the upper arm.

**demi-castor**   See CASTOR.

**demi-coronal**   16th-c. term for a *tiara* or *half coronet*.

**demi-corset**   Short corset worn by women in 1830s and 1840s.

**demi-gigot** (demee jhee-go)   Sleeve, tight from wrist to elbow but full at shoulder and upper arm. Worn from 1825 to 1830, revived in early 1890s and again by young designers in England and Scandinavia in the early 1970s. *Der.* French, "half leg-of-mutton."

**demi-habillement**   See HALF ROBE.

**demi-jamb**   Armor consisting of a metal plate over front of leg from ankle to knee connected to the *solleret*, or shoe. Worn by knights and soldiers in the early 14th c. Also see GREAVE.

**demi-maunch**   See DEMI-SLEEVE.

**demimondaines**   (demi-mon-dan) French term for mistresses of wealthy men who were dressed by famous Parisian couturiers and greatly influenced fashion from the Second Empire in France through the Edwardian era. *Der.* French, "those of the half-world."

**demi-riding coat**   See JUSTAUCORPS.

**demi-sleeve**   Full elbow-length sleeve of 16th c. Also called *demi-maunch.*

**demi-toilette**   See HALF DRESS.

**demi-vambrace**   Armor worn on front of forearm from elbow to the wrist.

**démodé**   (day-mode-ay) French adjective meaning old-fashioned, antiquated, passé, or out of style.

**Demorest, Madame**   Operator of Demorest's Emporium of Fashion with showrooms and factory located at Union Square, New York, where ladies came to select home-sewing patterns from the 1870s to 1890s. Her husband published *Demorest's Monthly Magazine* and *Demorest Fashions*, a weekly newspaper. Both were profusely illustrated with fashions.

**denier**   (den-yer) International textile and hosiery system used for numbering silk and man-made filament yarns—the low numbers represent finer yarns, the higher numbers the heavier yarns. *Der.* From old French coin, the weight used as a measure of size and number of silk.

**denim**   Sturdy, serviceable fabric woven in the twill weave in many variations of yarn coloring. Usually made with indigo-blue or brown warp and white filling. Many novelty denims are made in warp-wise striped and figured patterns. Used for sportswear, work-clothes, pants, and jackets. *Der.* French, *serge de Nimes*, a fabric made in Nimes, France. Also called *dungaree.* Also see LOOKS, BLUE JEANS under PANTS, and SPORT JACKETS.

**Denmark cock**   Man's tricorn hat of the second half of 18th c. worn with brim turned up in three sections with the back higher than the front.

**dentelle lace**   See DIEPE POINT and DENTELLE DE LA VIERGE under LACES.

**dentil**   Term for a Greek motif consisting of a series of tooth-like scallops used as a border.

**de Rauch, Madeleine**   See APPENDIX/ DESIGNERS.

**derby**   American term for British bowler hat worn from 1860s on.

**Descat, Rose**   See APPENDIX/DESIGNERS.

**desert boot**   See BOOTS.

**desert fatigue cap**   See CAPS.

**deshabillé**   (deh-seh-beeyah)   **1.** French word for *wrapper, dressing gown,* or *negligee.* **2.** Informal style of dressing with a loose careless air, originating in early 18th c. Paris and London. For examples of deshabillé dressing see BANYAN, SLAMMERKIN and MORNING DRESS. Also spelled *dishabillé.* Also see ROBE DE CHAMBRE #2.

**designer**   Person engaged in creating original clothing and accessories in various areas of the fashion industry. Some designers own their businesses, others are employed by manufacturers to develop collections of merchandise in ready-to-wear, couture, lingerie, millinery, footwear, accessories, and jewelry.

**designer collections**   See COLLECTION.

**designer label**   Woven identification on small piece of fabric usually sewed in neck of dress or left side near waist in coat. Also see DESIGNER JEANS under PANTS.

**designer scarf**   See SIGNATURE SCARF under SCARFS.

**Dessès, Jean**   See APPENDIX/DESIGNERS.

**detachable collar**   Originally a high starched, separate collar fastened to the shirt by means of studs. Invented by Hannah Montague, wife of a blacksmith in the 1820s, who cut the collars off her husband's shirts and washed them separately—thus he could wear the shirt several times with a fresh collar. During the 19th and early 20th c., the collar became taller and stiffer until it reached 4″ as worn by President Herbert Hoover. The Cluett, Peabody & Co. of Troy, New York, promoted it as the Arrow® collar from 1905 to 1931. Leyendecker was the promoter and advertisements called the *Arrow Collar Man*® appeared in newspapers, trolley cars, and magazines. This was considered the male version of the *Gibson Girl*. Also see ELLIPTICAL COLLAR under COLLARS.

**detachable cuff**   See CUFFS.

**detachable pantyhose**   See PANTYHOSE.

**detached chain stitch**   See STITCHES.

**Dettigen cock**   Man's tricorn hat worn in 18th c. with brim turned up equally in three sections.

**development bundle system**   Garment-industry term for production of sewn garments in which the items move in units or bundles in an organized manner from one operator to another. Also see BUNDLE SYSTEM.

**devotional ring**   Bronze, gold, or ivory ring with ten spherical projections around the band used in Middle Ages for saying the Creed.

**dhoti** (dough-tee)   **1.** Man's garment worn in India, consisting of a length of cotton fabric draped around the body to form trousers or a *loincloth*. The fabric, sometimes with colored striped borders or Jacquard pattern, is approximately 3½ yards long, with the width determined by the height of the wearer. **2.** A distinctive type was called a *pitambara*, of pure red or yellow silk, and is worn by Brahmins. Also see PANTS and SHORTS.

**diadem**   **1.** A crown. **2.** Decorative headdress resembling a crown. **3.** Ornamental headdress usually wider and higher toward the front worn by Oriental kings, particularly in ancient Persia.

**diadem cap**   *Bathing cap* of 1870s usually of oiled silk shaped like a shower cap with a band and upstanding ruffle in front and ties under the chin.

**diadem comb**   High, wide, curved comb with ornamental top worn for evening by women in the 1830s.

**diadem fanchon bonnet**   Lace and velvet bonnet of late 1860s with brim forming a halo. Made with two sets of bonnet strings—one tied under *chignon* in back, the other, trimmed with *ruching*, loosely tied under the chin.

**Diadem® mink**   See MUTATION MINK under FURS.

**Diaghilev, Sergei Pavlovich** (dee-ah-geh-lef) (1872–1929) Russian aristocrat and avant-garde creator of the Ballets Russes, who produced *Sheherazade*, 1910, with costumes by *Leon Bakst*. The brilliant colors and new concept of stage design started a wave of Orientalism in Paris that affected the whole couture, particularly the work of *Paul Poiret*, and banished somber Victorian fashions.

**diagonal stitch**   See STITCHES.

**diagonal weave**   See TWILL WEAVE.

**diamanté** (dee-a-mont-ay)   Term used to indicate a sparkling effect as that of the reflection of gemstones. *Der.* French, "made of diamonds." See BRAIDS, DRESSES, and TOPS.

**diamond** Transparent variety of the hardest mineral known—*corundum*, which is adamantine, or very brilliant when faceted. Colorless stones are most generally known, but diamonds also come in yellow, brown, green, red, and blue. Diamonds are graded according to color, cut, weight, clarity, and brilliance. Originally found only in India, now many come from Brazil and South Africa with 95% coming from the latter. Also see BRACELETS, EARRINGS, GEMS, GEM CUTS, and NECKLACES.

## DIAMONDS

**Arcot d.** Two diamonds weighing a total of 57.35 carats, cut in pear shape, presented to Queen Charlotte of England in 1777 by the ruler of Arcot, a district in Madras, India. When she died, they were sold to the Marquess of Westminster for about $55,000 in 1837 and mounted in a tiara with 1,421 other diamonds and a large 32-carat diamond. In 1959 sold at auction to Harry Winston, a jeweler in New York City, for $308,000.

**Borazon®** Trademark for General Electric's industrial artificial diamonds. First made in 1957, now tons are produced yearly. More suitable than natural diamonds for some industrial purposes.

**Burton d.** Pear-shaped flawless 69.42-carat cut stone bought by Cartier, a New York jeweler, in 1969 for $1,050,000, the highest auction price ever paid for a diamond. The next day Richard Burton purchased the diamond for Elizabeth Taylor.

**canary d.** Fancy diamond in a definite yellow color. As differentiated from diamonds which have a yellow tinge, genuine yellow diamonds are rare and expensive. Also see TIFFANY DIAMOND.

**Cape May d.** Misleading term for rock crystal from Cape May, New Jersey.

**chip 1.** Term used for single-cut melee, a small rose-cut diamond, or an irregularly shaped diamond. **2.** Term used for a break on the edge of a larger diamond.

**Cleveland d.** Diamond weighing 50 carats, cut in 1884 with 128 facets by S. Descu of Maiden Lane. It was the first diamond cut in New York City. *Der.* Named for President Grover Cleveland.

**Crown d.** Honey-colored 84-carat diamond which once belonged to the Russian Czars. Exhibited at the 1939 World's Fair in New York by DeBeers. Sold to Baumgold Bros. in New York then to Everts Co. of Dallas. Frequently exhibited.

**Cullinan d.** (ku-li-nan) The world's largest diamond—3,106 carats (1⅓ pounds) in the rough. Presented by the Transvaal government to Edward VII of England in 1907. Cut from it were the *Star of Africa*, a pear-shaped stone of 530.2 carats; the *Cullinan II*, a square brilliant of 317.4 carats (both are in the British crown jewels), also 9 major gems, 96 small brilliants and 9 carats of polished fragments.

**Deepdeen d.** Golden-yellow 104.88-carat diamond of cushion-cut, originally owned by publisher Carey Bok (1863–1930) of Philadelphia who sometimes loaned it for exhibits to the Philadelphia Academy of Sciences. Also spelled *deepdene*.

**Dresden Green d.** Famous apple-green flawless diamond weighing 40 carats.

**Estrella du Sud** See STAR OF THE SOUTH.

**fancy d.** Any diamond with a distinctive color and high degree of transparency. May be yellow or brown, with green, red, or blue being the rarest.

**Great Mogul d.** Largest diamond ever found in India—240 carats cut and believed to be 787 carats uncut. Not seen since 1665.

**Hastings d.**   Diamond weighing 101 carats presented to King George III of England in 1786 by Warren Hastings, Governor General of India. Caused a political scandal.

**herkimer**   Misleading term for rock crystal.

**Hope d.**   Largest blue diamond, now weighs 44.5 carats and is on display at the Smithsonian Institution, Washington, D.C. Once a part of the jewels of Louis XIV, it weighed 112.5 carats, and was recut to a heart-shaped stone. Later worn by Marie Antoinette, it disappeared during the French Revolution. Offered for sale in London in 1830 in present size, cut in a rounded oval and sold to Henry Philip Hope, a banker, for $90,000. Resold several times and finally sold by Cartier in Paris to Mrs. Edward B. McLean of Washington, D.C. for $154,000. After her death purchased by Harry Winston and given by him to the Smithsonian Institution in 1958.

**Jonker d.**   Large diamond weighing 726 carats uncut, discovered by Jacobus Jonker in 1934 at Elandsfontein, Pretoria, Africa. Bought by Harry Winston in New York City and cut into 12 stones by Lazare Kaplan. Largest stone was emerald-cut to 68 facets weighing 142.9 carats. Later recut to 58 facets weighing 125.65 carats to give it a more oblong shape.

**Jubilee d.**   Diamond weighing 650.80 carats when discovered in 1895 at the Jagerfrontein mine. Weighed 245.35 carats when cut. Named after Queen Victoria's Diamond Jubilee which took place in 1897.

**Khedive d.**   Champagne-colored diamond weighing 43 carats presented to Empress Eugènie in 1869 at the opening of the Suez Canal by Egypt. Now believed to be in Belgium.

**Kimberly d.**   Flawless, champagne-colored emerald-cut diamond weighing 70 carats. Originally a larger stone belonging to the Russian Czars. Cut down in 1921 and in 1958, it is now 55 carats and owned by Baumgold Bros. of New

York. It is frequently exhibited. *Der.* Product of the Kimberly mines.

**Koh-i-noor d.** (ko-eh-noor)   One of the oldest famous diamonds from India. Old cutting was in 187 carats, but was recut after presentation to Queen Victoria in 1850 and now weighs 108.93 carats. Now in the Queen Mother's Crown and on display in the Tower of London with the British Crown Jewels. *Der.* Persian, *koh-i-nur,* "Mountain of Light."

**Krupp d.**   Diamond weighing 33.1 carats given to Elizabeth Taylor by her husband, Richard Burton, who purchased it for $305,000.

**Lake George d.**   Misleading term for rock crystal.

**mauve d.**   Fancy diamond of a purplish hue.

**melee**   A collective term for small, brilliant-cut diamonds usually .20 to .25 carats. *Der.* French, "confused mass."

**off-color d.**   Trade term used in America for a diamond which has a tinge of an undesirable color, particularly yellow or brown, which is easily discernible.

**Pitt d.**   See REGENT DIAMOND.

**Princie d.**   Pink, cushion-cut 34.64-carat diamond bought in 1960 by Van Cleef and Arpels, Paris jewelers, for $128,000. Once belonged to Nizam of Hyderabad and christened this name in honor of the Maharanee of Baroda's son, who was nicknamed "Princie."

**Queen Elizabeth pink d.**   See WILLIAMSON DIAMOND.

**Queen of Holland d.**   Blue diamond of 136.5 carats cut in Amsterdam in 1904 and displayed at the Paris Exposition of 1924. Sold to an Indian Maharajah for $1,000,000. Present whereabouts unknown.

**Regent d.**   Indian diamond found in 1701 weighing 410 carats uncut. Owned by Thomas Pitt, it was cut to 140.5 carats and sold in 1717 to the Regent of France, Duke de Orleans, ruling for Louis XV. Later Napoleon had it set in the hilt of a sword he carried when crowned Emperor. During the Second Empire, Empress Eugènie had it set in a tiara. Now on display in the Louvre. Also known as the *Pitt diamond.*

**Russian Table Portrait d.** Portrait diamond of 25 carats said to be the largest portrait diamond in the world. Part of the Russian Crown jewels.

**Sancy d.** Almond-shaped 55-carat gem dating from 1570, which was worn by Henry III of France at front of his turban. Later worn by James I of England. Purchased from England by Mazarin, it was willed to France with 17 other diamonds, to be called "Mazarin diamonds." Louis XV wore it in his crown at his coronation. In 1791 it was valued at $250,000. Stolen during French Revolution, in 1906 purchased by William Astor who gave it to his daughter-in-law, Nancy Langhorne, as a wedding present.

**Searcy d.** Fine yellow or cape uncut diamond found in Searcy, Arkansas, sold to Tiffany's in New York in 1946 for $8,500 and now displayed there—weighs 27.2 carats uncut.

**Star of Arkansas** Diamond found in the "Crater of Diamonds" in Arkansas weighing 15.31 carats uncut. Later cut to 8.27-carat marquise. Found by Mrs. A. L. Parker of Dallas, Texas, who paid the $1.50 fee to prospect at the diamond preserve.

**Star of Africa** See CULLINAN DIAMOND.

**Star of the South** Brazilian pinkish diamond weighing 261.88 carats, found in 1853, and cut to 128.5 carats. In 1934 it was in a necklace with the DRESDEN GREEN. Also called *Estrella du Sud.*

**Theresa d.** Diamond weighing 21.25 carats found in Washington County, Wisconsin, in 1886. Cut into many small stones, the largest being 1.48 carats.

**Tiffany d.** Brilliant deep yellow diamond weighing 287.42 carats before cutting and 128.5 carats cut as a cushioned-shaped brilliant with 90 facets. Originally found in Kimberly mines and owned by Tiffany's in New York City. Also see CANARY DIAMOND.

**Uncle Sam d.** Largest diamond found in the U.S. weighing 40.23 carats. Discovered in Murfreesboro, Arkansas, in 1924, it was cut to a 12.42-carat, emerald shape. Owned by Peikin, a New York jeweler.

**Vanderbilt d.** Pear-shaped 16.5-carat diamond bought in the 1920s by Reginald Vanderbilt from Tiffany's for $75,000 for engagement ring for Gloria Morgan. After they divorced the diamond was sold to a diamond merchant in the Midwest.

**Vargas d.** Largest diamond found in Brazil in 1938, it weighed 726.6 carats. Purchased by Harry Winston, a New York City jeweler, and cut into 23 gems with the largest stone 48.26 carats, retaining the name. *Der.* Named for Brazilian president.

**Williamson d.** Pink diamond weighing 23.6 carats cut from a stone weighing 54 carats by Briefel and Lemer of London. Presented by John T. Williamson to Queen Elizabeth II of England. Also called *Queen Elizabeth Pink.*

---

**diamonds by the yard** See NECKLACES.

**Diana Vernon hat** Wide brimmed, shallow-crowned straw bonnet of the late 1870s with one side of the brim turned up and trimmed with a rosette. Wide streamers came from underside of brim to tie under the chin. *Der.* Named for the heroine of *Rob Roy*, 1817 English novel by Sir Walter Scott. Also called a *Diana Vernon bonnet.*

**diaper cloth** See BIRD'S-EYE.

**dickey 1.** Separate fill-in used inside woman's low neckline with or without an attached collar. May be knitted or woven and have many types of collars. Also see BLOUSETTE. Also spelled *dicky, dickie.* **2.** Late 18th- and early 19th-c. term for under petticoat worn by women. **3.** Man's false shirt front with attached collar, worn over a flannel shirt in the 19th c., not considered proper attire for gentlemen. **4.** *Pinafore,* or *bib,* for a child.

**Dieppe point lace** (dee-ep)   See LACES.

**Dietrich, Marlene**   German actress and entertainer, considered the supreme example of a glamorous film star—a great fashion influence in the 1930s and 1940s. Famous for her legs, arched plucked eyebrows, and screen wardrobe designed by *Travis Banton* with many clinging chiffons and feather boas. Also credited with popularizing mannish SLACKS and FEDORAS for women.

**dïmâyeh** (dee-may-a)   Long, striped coat with silken belt, a native costume of men in ancient Palestine—usually striped in combinations of red and yellow or black, blue, and yellow.

**dimensional stability**   Ability of fabric to return to its original shape and size after wear, washing, or dry cleaning.

**dimidje**   Full Turkish-style trousers of bright-colored silk worn as native dress by women of Bosnia, a part of Yugoslavia. Also spelled *dimidji.*

**dimity**   Several similar fabrics characterized by carded warpwise stripes or checks made by the addition of heavier cords spaced at regular intervals. Made by grouping several combed and mercerized yarns together to form a stripe. Woven in a plain weave; may be plain or printed. Finishes are of several types: a) lawn-type—starched and calendered; b) organdy type—given a stiff permanent finish; c) soft finishes—used for dresses, blouses, children's dresses, and formerly for underwear. Modern dimity is not necessarily the same type of fabric referred to in earlier costume references, *e.g.,* in late 18th c. was fairly sturdy weight and used

primarily for working men's shirts. *Der.* Greek, *dimitos,* "of double thread." Various variations are referred to specifically as *striped dimity, dimity cord, dimity check,* and *pajama check.*

**dink/dinky**   See BEANIE under CAPS.

**dinner**   Used as an adjective to indicate semiformal dress with man wearing *black tie* with *tuxedo* and woman wearing a semiformal or *dinner dress.* See DRESSES, JACKETS, and RINGS.

**Dior, Christian** (dee-ore)   See APPENDIX/ DESIGNERS.

**dip**   Term used in 1890s and early 20th c. for the point of a waistline that was lower in front than back.

**dip belt**   *Contour* belt, usually of stiffened fabric, cut wider in the front with a pointed lower edge. Fastened by strings attached to each end which came from back around to the front and tied under the belt. Fashionable in late 19th and early 20th c.

**dip dyeing**   Coloring by immersion in dye solution. See DYEING.

**DIPLAX**

**diplax**   Large piece of fabric, nearly square, worn folded double as a mantle by Roman women. Draped under right arm and pinned together on left shoulder—as seen in statues of Juno, or draped around hips as seen in statues of Minerva.

**diploidon** (dip-ploiy-dion) (pl. *diplois*) Mantle worn by ancient Greeks made out of a square or oblong piece of fabric folded double with the fold placed under the left arm and fastened on the right shoulder. Also see DIPLAX.

**dip-top boots** See COWBOY BOOTS under BOOTS.

**Directoire bonnet** Bonnet tied under the chin, fitting close over the ears, with a high flaring front brim. Worn in late 1870s through early 1880s. Inspired by hats worn during the French *Directoire Period* (1795–1799), but not known by this name at that time.

**Directoire coat** Woman's coat having ankle-length skirt in back and coming only to waistline in front, worn in late 1880s.

**Directoire gown** **1.** Woman's dress of muslin or similar sheer fabric with high waistline and narrow skirt. Sometimes has an overskirt forming a train in back, an extremely low neckline, and elbow-length or long sleeves. Frequently worn with a *spencer jacket* during the French *Directoire Period* (1795–1799). **2.** Slim coat-style dress with wide lapels, gauntlet-cuffed sleeves, and high-sashed waist. Worn by women in late 19th c.

DIRECTOIRE JACKET, 1889

**Directoire jacket** Woman's waist-length jacket of late 1880s. Similar to *Directoire coat* worn as top of a daytime dress.

DIRECTOIRE SKIRT, 1895

**Directoire skirt** Skirt cut in seven gores worn from late 1880s through early 1900s. The back four gores were lined, stiffened, and fluted into *pipe-organ* or *godet pleats*—the hem being four to six yards wide around. A name patented for this style by *The Delineator* magazine.

**Directoire styles** French costume of the *Directoire Period* (1795–1799). **1. Women:** high-waisted, narrow-skirted muslin dresses with low necklines. Worn with *spencer* jackets; flesh-colored stockings, shoes similar to laced ballet slippers, and ostrich plumes in the hair or on turbans. Also see DIRECTOIRE GOWN #1 and MERVEILLEUSE. **2. Men:** frock coats tapering to tails in back and left open in front to show waistcoat, tightly fitted breeches, stockings with low shoes or high boots, and top hat flaring at the top. Also see INCROYABLES. *Der.* From French Directory—five directors forming the executive power of France from 1775–1799. **3.** Styles of late 1880s to 1895 called by this name. Inspired by Sardou's drama, *La Tosca* starring Sarah Bernhardt in 1887. Some of these styles have no relationship to #1 and #2. See DIRECTOIRE COAT, DIRECTOIRE GOWN #2, DIRECTOIRE JACKET, and DIRECTOIRE SKIRT.

**Directoire waistline** See WAISTLINES.

**direct printing** Method of making printed fabrics by placing colored design on white or light-colored ground with rollers. Also see ROLLER PRINT under PRINTS.

**dirndl** (durn-dul) Full-skirted Tyrolean peasant costume originating, and still worn, in Austrian and Bavarian Alps. Also see COATS, DRESSES, PANTS, PETTICOATS, SILHOUETTES, and SKIRTS.

**discharge printing** Term used for fabric printed with a white design. Made by first piece-dyeing fabric, then making design by using rollers imprinted with a chemical which bleaches or removes the color leaving a white design, *e.g.,* white polka dots on blue background. When a basic color is added to discharge paste, a colored design is produced.

**disco clothes** Glittery fashions in bright, glowing colors styled in unrestrained fabrics. Usually made with short skirts for vigorous evening dancing at discotheques. *Der.* French, *discothèque,* "record library," as dancing is done to records rather than live music. Also see SANDALS.

**dishabille** (dis-eh-beel) American form for French DESHABILLÉ.

**dishrag shirt** Loosely knitted man's sport shirt with placket closing at neck worn in 1930s. *Der.* Resemblance of knit to knitted dishrags of that period.

**disposable swimsuit** See SWIMSUITS.

**dittos** Term for man's suit used from 1750s on with same fabric used for pants, jacket, vest, and sometimes the cap.

**divided skirt** Wide trousers that hang like a skirt, introduced in England in 1882 by Lady Harberton for bicycling. Same as *pantskirt* or *culottes.* (See illustration under SKIRTS.)

**djebba/djubba** See JUBBAH.

**djellaba** (jel-a-ba) Moroccan man's garment consisting of three-quarter length cloak with a hood worn for inclement weather. Imported and copied for men and women in the late 1960s. Also spelled *djellabah, jellaba.* Also see CAFTAN and ROBES.

**dobby attachment** Mechanical attachment for some looms to enable them to produce small repeat geometric designs of not more than 8 to 30 rows of filling. For more elaborate patterns a *Jacquard loom* is used. See JACQUARD.

**dobby fabric** Fabric made with a small geometrical pattern which repeats every 8 to 30 rows. Made with the *dobby attachment* on a regular loom. *White-on-white broadcloth* is example of a dobby fabric.

**dobby weave** Weave forming small repeat geometric patterns done on plain loom with *dobby attachment* which controls the *harnesses* handling a series of threads, *e.g.,* *diaper cloth* and *white-on-white broadcloth.*

**dōbuko** Japanese double-breasted dress formerly worn by travelers as a dustcoat. It differs from the *kimono* as it reaches only to mid-thigh, is cut larger, and is not lapped over but opens in front and fastens loosely across the chest by means of silk cords.

**Dr. Denton's®** See PAJAMAS.

**DOCTOR'S GOWN**

**Doctor's gown** Black unclosed academic gown with wide bands of velvet down the front.

The full sleeves are set in with *cartridge pleats* and have three bands of velvet at upper arm. Worn as part of academic costume by candidates for, and holders of, doctoral degrees.

**DOCTOR'S HOOD**

**Doctor's hood** Black academic hood with colored velvet band at neck to indicate type of degree. This velvet band extends down the back and is rolled over to show the school colors of the wearer. Square cut at hem and larger than Bachelor's and Master's hoods. See ACADEMIC HOOD COLORS.

**Doctor Zhivago** See ZHIVAGO.

**doeskin** **1.** Genuine doeskin is leather made by tanning female deerskins by the *chamois* process and then buffed to produce a sueded finish. **2.** Also sheepskin tanned by chamois process and sueded. Should be called *doeskin-finished lambskin.* **3.** Misnomer for *doeskin fabrics.* See GLOVES and LEATHERS.

**doeskin fabrics** Fabrics made in imitation of sueded leather doeskin of three varieties: a) woolen fabric with short nap of high count made with highly twisted yarns in the satin weave used for riding habits, uniforms, trousers, and coating; b) surface napped, medium-weight, spun rayon fabric made in twill weave, used for coats, suits, and sportswear; c) heavy,

napped-surfaced, twilled cotton fabric used for sport coats and backing for coated fabrics. Each should be called *doeskin fabrics.*

**Doeuillet, Georges** See APPENDIX/ DESIGNERS.

**dogaline** Loose-fitting, straight-cut gown with very wide sleeves—lower edge turned up and fastened to shoulder—revealing sleeve of undergown. Worn by men and women during the Middle Ages and 16th c.

**dog collar** From 1860s a small, plain, standing collar which overlapped in front. Formerly called an *all-rounder.* Later a name given to *clerical collar* which buttoned in back. See COLLARS, NECKLACES, HALTER NECKLINE under NECKLINES, and SCARFS.

**dog's-ear collar** See COLLARS.

**dohar** See CHADDAR #4.

**dollar-round toe** See TOES.

**Dolley Madison hood** Lace-trimmed opera hood resembling a *dust cap* with a deep ruffle of lace falling around the face and neck. Worn toward back of head and secured under chin with broad ribbon ties. Popular at end of 19th c. Also spelled *Dolly.* Der. Named after Dolley Madison, wife of James Madison, President of the United States, 1809 to 1817.

**doll hat** See HATS.

**dolly look** British term for BABY DOLL LOOK. See LOOKS.

**Dolly Varden polonaise** Type of woman's costume—inspired by Charles Dickens' character Dolly Varden in *Barnaby Rudge*—consisting of a POLONAISE GOWN in chintz, cretonne or foulard with silk underskirt either plain, flowered, or quilted (or cashmere in winter). Worn with wide straw hat trimmed with flowers and ribbon and tied under CHIGNON. Popular in 1870s.

**dolman** (dole-man) **1.** Woman's short mantle or full-length wrap that gives the appearance of a cape from the back but sleeved in front. Worn from 1870s through the 1880s, revived in early

**DOLMAN #1**

20th c., and returns frequently in coat collections. **2.** Full-length outer robe worn in Turkey. *Der.* Turkish, *dolamak.* Also see SLEEVES and SWEATERS.

**dolmanette** Crocheted *dolman* fastened at neck with large bow of ribbon worn in the 1890s.

**dome hat** See BUBBLE HAT under HATS.

**dome ring** See RINGS.

**dome umbrella** See BELL UMBRELLA.

**domet flannel** Soft, napped, light- to medium-weight fabric similar to OUTING FLANNEL but with a longer nap. Made of all cotton, or cotton warp with cotton and wool filling. Also spelled *domett.*

**domino** **1.** Originally, a large hood worn by monks. Later, a cloak with attached hood for men and women. **2.** A large cloak, usually black, worn with a small mask for traditional carnival and masquerade costume. Popular in 18th and 19th c. **3.** Small contemporary half-mask worn with masquerade costume. Also see MASKS.

**DOM PEDRO SHOE, 1908**

**Dom Pedro shoe** Ankle-high man's heavy work shoe fastened with laces and one buckled strap over center of lacing worn in early 1900s. *Der.* Introduced by Dom Pedro of Brazil.

**donegal tweed** **1.** Medium- to heavyweight tweed made in Ireland. Originally handwoven in the county of Donegal and made in plain or twill weave, usually of coarse yarns with a single colored warp and a blend of colors in the filling yarn. Used for coats, suits, skirts, trousers, and jackets. See IRISH TWEED. **2.** A term for tweeds made from Yorkshire yarns spun and dyed in Donegal, Ireland. **3.** Imitations of the original Irish Donegal Tweeds.

**donnilette** See DOUILLETTE.

**don't mentions** See INEXPRESSIBLES.

**door knocker** See EARRINGS.

**dopata** **1.** Shawl or scarf worn draped around the shoulders as a part of native dress of men and women in India. **2.** A fine grade of cotton muslin used for shawls as described in #1.

**dorelet** (dor-a-let) Term used in Middle Ages for woman's *hair net* ornamented with jewels. Also spelled *dorlet.*

**doriah** Term for a plain woven bleached, warp-striped cotton fabric made in Great Britain—originally made in India.

**dorino** Outer garment worn on street by Bosnian women fastened with a string belt at waist. A full garment covering a Mohammedan woman's body from head to calf of the leg—exposing striped hosiery and scarlet or blue slippers. Also spelled *dorina.*

**dormeuse** Ribbon-trimmed white cap with a puffed crown and falling *lappets* trimmed with lace, called *wings*, popularly known as *cheek wrappers*. Worn in the house by women in second half of 18th c. Also spelled *dormouse*. Also called a *French nightcap*.

**dorm shirt** See NIGHTGOWNS.

**Dorothée Bis** See APPENDIX/DESIGNERS.

**d'Orsay coat** Man's overcoat of late 1830s—similar to a *pilot coat*, but fitted at waist with darts. Made with a small collar, slashed or flapped pockets, plain sleeves trimmed with three or four buttons, and no pleats or hip buttons in the back. *Der.* Named for *Compte d'Orsay*, a 19th c. arbiter of fashion.

**d'Orsay, Count** See ORSAY, COUNT D'.

**D'ORSAY HABIT-COAT**

**d'Orsay habit-coat** Fitted, man-tailored, three-quarter-length coat for women, somewhat resembling man's cutaway style, made double-breasted with large *revers*. Introduced in early 1880s.

**d'Orsay pump** See SHOES.

**d'Orsay slippers** See SLIPPERS.

**Dorset thread button** Brass wire ring covered with cotton threads radiating from center to form a flat button; used on underwear from about 1700 to 1830.

**doschella** Fine cashmere shawls formerly worn in cold weather by Hindu gentlemen. Worn in pairs with both wrong sides placed together so that the inside was never visible. Single imported shawls from India were worn by French and English women in early 19th c.

**dotera** See TANZEN.

**dots** See PRINTS.

**dotted swiss** Crisp lightweight fabric with regularly spaced dots which are applied in various ways: *a)* May be woven in by the *swivel weave*, an expensive method which works each dot so that it cannot be pulled out; *b)* clipped spot method of embroidery, which sends extra yarns over one warp and under several warps. Yarns are carried across back of the fabric and are trimmed to dot size; *c)* by *flocking*, which secures small flecks of cotton or rayon to the fabric by means of an adhesive.

**double-breasted** Describing the front opening of a garment lapped over double and fastening with two rows of buttons. Originally both rows were functional, now one row is usually decorative. Also called *d.b.*, British tailors' 19th-c. slang. Also see CLOSINGS.

**double chignon** Woman's hairstyle of 1860s with two large rolls of hair, one above the other, at the nape of the neck. Sometimes artificial hair was used.

**double cloth** Heavy "sandwich-type" fabric consisting of two separate fabrics woven at the same time with a binder yarn connecting them. Woven in double cloth construction using five yarns. An expensive fabric usually made of fine worsted or woolen yarn. Binder yarns may be released at edges of a garment to make felled seams, that require no lining in a coat or cape.

**double collar** See COLLARS.

**double cuff** See FRENCH CUFF under CUFFS.

**double entry pocket** See POCKETS.

**double-faced satin ribbon** Ribbon woven with satin face on both sides.

**double-girdled** Describing the ancient Greek fashion of wearing a long narrow sash, or two separate sashes, wound around waist and crossed over chest to adjust fullness of garment.

**double knit** Fine rib knit in which face and back of fabric have a similar appearance. Double-needles are used on a variety of machines to give this effect. Makes a heavier knit fabric with greater dimensional stability and less tendency to sag or lose its shape. Popularized in the late 1950s.

**double mantle** See MANTLE #2.

**double ombré** See STRIPES.

**double-puffed sleeve** See SLEEVES.

**doubler** Extra layer of soft fabric placed between the leather and the lining of shoe to make leather look plumper.

**double ruffle** Strip of fabric stitched in the center and gathered to form a ruffle on either side of stitching.

**double-running stitch** See STITCHES.

**double-stitched seam** See TOPSTITCHED under SEAMS.

**doublet** **1.** Main garment for upper part of man's body worn from late 14th c. to 1670 and styled like a close-fitting short jacket of various lengths showing *trunk hose* or *breeches*. Also see GAMBESON, GIPON, POURPOINT and PEASCOD-BELLIED DOUBLET. **2.** Part of woman's riding habit from 1650 to 1670. **3.** Jewelry term for two pieces of glass or gems cemented together to form one large stone. **4.** Jacket of SCOTS HIGHLANDER'S DRESS.

**double-zipper foundation** See FOUNDATIONS.

**Doucet, Jacques** See APPENDIX/DESIGNERS.

**douillette** Woman's quilted winter *pelisse* worn from 1818 to 1830s consisting of a full-sleeved *pelerine* of *cashmere*, *merino*, or figured satin over a silk or cambric *walking dress*. Also spelled *donnilette*.

**doupioni** Fabric made from silk yarn reeled from double cocoons, or two interlaced cocoons in which the silk is intertwined. Yarn has uneven slubs, rather than smooth, giving a decorative texture to the fabric. Also spelled *douppioni*, *doppione*.

**doupioni silk** Silk yarn reeled from double cocoons, or two adjacent cocoons in which the silk is intertwined, making an uneven yarn which gives a decorative texture to *shantung* and *pongee*. Also spelled *douppione*, *doppione*.

**doup weave** See LENO WEAVE.

**down** Material used to pad winter jackets and coats to increase warmth. Genuine down comes from fluffy soft fibers under the feathers of water fowl, *e.g.*, geese and ducks. See EIDERDOWN, FEATHERS, SPORT JACKETS, and VESTS.

**downy calves** Extra padding woven into men's stockings to make calves appear more shapely; patented in 1788. Also see FALSE CALVES.

**dragon robe** See CHI-FU.

**drap d'été** Fabric used by the clergy which is made of fine wool in a twill weave. *Der.* French, "summer cloth."

**drape** The hang or fall of fabric when made into a garment is an important quality to consider in designing, *e.g.*, chiffon has a soft drape, ottoman hangs stiffly.

**draped heel** See HEELS.

**draped skirt** See SKIRTS.

**draping** **1.** Fabric falling in folds in the garment as seen on statues of ancient Greece; most outstanding modern versions made by Paris designer *Grès*. **2.** Trade term for arranging and pinning muslin cloth over a dummy to conform to the design of the intended garment. After draping, muslin is removed from dummy, stitched at seams and tried on a model. Then it is altered, refitted on model, and cut apart at seams to make the pattern.

**drawers** **1.** 19th-c. term for *underpants* worn by men and women; term used today for *thermal-type panties*. **2.** Underpants worn by men from 16th through 19th c., made of linen and footed, or with stirrup straps under instep. Later, called TROUSERS or long pants in 19th c. **3.** Underpants worn by women in early 19th c. made with separate legs joined at the waistband. See PANTALETTES and PANTALOONS. **4.** At end of 19th c. knitted or woven to-the-knee panties trimmed with lace and insertions. Also see COMBINATIONS, KNICKERS, FRENCH DRAWERS, and UMBRELLA DRAWERS.

**drawn work** See EMBROIDERIES.

**drawstring** Ribbon or cord inserted through a band of fabric, pulled and tied to form a closing for hems, necklines, pants, cuffs, handbags. Also see BLOUSES, HANDBAGS, NECKLINES, PANTS, SHIRTS, SHORTS, and WAISTLINES.

**dreadnought** See FEARNAUGHT and FEARNOTHING JACKET.

**Drécoll** See APPENDIX/DESIGNERS.

**Dresden Green diamond** See DIAMONDS.

**Dresden point** See EMBROIDERIES.

**dress** **1.** Customarily the main item of apparel worn by women and girls in the Western hemisphere. May be made in one piece, cut in two pieces and joined with a waistline seam, or made in two separate pieces with each piece finished separately. The word "dress" in its present form did not come into popular acceptance until the late 18th c. Previous to that time it was called a *robe* or a *gown*. **2.** (noun) Collective term for all clothing, *e.g.* the dress of Spain, of Eskimos, etc. Synonyms: *apparel, clothes, costume, garment, habit, robe, uniform, vestment*. **3.** Man's full dress suit or formal clothes. **4.** (verb) To put on formal clothing, *e.g.* dress for dinner. **5.** (verb) To arrange or set the hair. **6.** (verb) To tan and finish hides for leather uses. In alphabetical listing see BLOUSE DRESS, COURT DRESS, FRENCH DRESS, FOUREAU DRESS, GABRIEL DRESS, GOWN À LA FRANÇAISE, GOWN À LA LEVANTINE, GOWN À L'ANGLAISE, GOWN À LA TURQUE, OPEN ROBE, POLONAISE, ROUND GOWN, SACK, SLAMMERKIN, and SULTANE.

## DRESSES

**African d.** Straight cut or A-line dress made of African printed fabric (sometimes of raffia) elaborately trimmed with wooden beads, glass beads or sequins. Made in mini- and full-length styles, some with midriffs, others with "see-through" midriffs with strands of beads connecting top and skirt. Introduced by Paris couturier, Yves Saint Laurent, in 1967.

**Alice in Wonderland d.** See PINAFORE DRESS. *Der.* Named for dress worn by character in Lewis Carroll's book, *Alice's Adventures in Wonderland* (1865).

**A-line d.** Dress style which flares gently from under arms to hem of skirt, resembling the letter A. Usually made with narrow shoulders, a high round neckline, and is similar to SKIMMER. Introduced in 1955 by Paris couturier, Christian Dior.

**American Indian d.** **1.** Dress made of suede or buckskin with simple lines and trimming of beads and fringe, originally worn by North American Indian squaws. **2.** Modern interpretation of American Indian dress in leather, suede, or fabric. Also called *Pocahontas dress*.

**Andean shift** Native dress from Peru made in straight-cut style of native fabrics and trimmed with embroidery. Sold in U.S. in late 1960s. Also called an *ocepa*. *Der.* Dress from Andes Mountains in South America.

**apron d.** Any dress worn with a decorative apron. Also see PINAFORE DRESS.

**asymmetric d.** Dress using the principle of informal balance, rather than formal balance—

may be draped to one side, have side closing, or cover only one shoulder. Introduced in 1920s by Paris couturier, Madeleine Vionnet; variations have been in vogue since. Also see TOGA.

**baby doll d. 1.** Woman's dress cut like a smock, with a high neckline and a yoke, similar to children's, infants' and dolls' dresses of the 1930s. It was introduced in early 1960s by English designers and later in late 1970s by French ready-to-wear designers. Popularity was enhanced by film *Baby Doll* (1956) in which Carroll Baker played the lead. *Der.* Term used to refer to clothing and accessories used for children's, dolls' and infants' clothes in the early part of the 20th c. **2.** In fall 1985 *Vivienne Westwood* introduced a collection of dresses called by this name. Dresses were similar to children's and dolls' dresses of 1930s and 1940s—some with collars, cuffs and wide belts, others with full skirts over crinoline petticoats. Patou, in the fall of 1986, introduced a style with long sleeves, wrapped draped bodice and sometimes worn over petticoats made with ruffles.

**backless d.** Dress with extremely low back, sometimes below waist, used mainly for evening gowns. Made in many different styles with high front, sometimes with a cut-out.

**back-wrap d.** See WRAP DRESS.

**ball gown** See FORMAL GOWN.

**bare-midriff d.** Fashion originating in tropical countries consisting of a two-piece dress with top ending under bust, baring the ribs, with skirt beginning at the waistline or low slung. Introduced in the U.S. in the 1930s, revived in 1960s and 1970s following interest in East Indian fashions.

**basic d.** Dress simply cut with no ornamentation, usually black. Jewelry, collars, and other accessories can be added to change the appearance. Introduced in the 1930s, worn through

1940s, and revived in early 1970s. Also called "*L.B.D.*" (*little black dress*).

**bathrobe d.** Wraparound dress with shawl collar, no buttons, front lapped over and held in place with a sash. Worn since the mid-1960s.

**beach shift** Simple cover-up designed to be worn over a bathing suit, often in matching fabric. Also called *beach dress.*

**bias-cut d.** Dress cut on the diagonal of the fabric which makes a full-skirted dress hang more gracefully. When cut on the bias, a narrow dress will cling to the figure. Introduced by Vionnet in 1920s and revived in late 1960s.

**blouson** (blue-sohn) Bloused-top dress with low waistline seam. A style introduced in 1920s and reintroduced in 1950s. *Der.* French "to blouse."

**bouffant d.** (boo-fawn) Dress with tight-fitting bodice and full, gathered, pleated, or ruffled skirt. Sometimes skirt is shaped like a bubble, a bell, or a cone and may be worn with hoops or petticoats. Popular from 1830s to 1880s, and reintroduced by American designer Anne Fogarty in 1950s. *Der.* French "full" or "puffed." Also see BUBBLE and PAPER DOLL DRESSES.

**bra-shift** Sleeveless shift with top of dress fitted to the figure like a bra. An innovation of the mid-1960s.

**bridal d.** See WEDDING DRESS.

**bridesmaid's d.** Any type of dress worn by a bride's attendant at a wedding, usually selected by the bride. May match in style and color with other attendants, and selected to complement the bride's dress.

**buba** An Afro-inspired dress of 1969 worn by women. Styled in a large panel print and wide decorative borders and with same design on front and back. Sleeves are usually fitted at armholes, widely flared at wrists, and frequently ending in a long point.

ONE-SHOULDER
DRESS          BATHROBE DRESS          BUBBLE DRESS          SAFARI DRESS

BUSTLE DRESS          CAFTAN          TOGA DRESS          PANTGOWN

SHEATH, LATE 1950s     TRUMPET DRESS

TORSO DRESS

COMMUNION DRESS

GRANNY DRESS

SLIP-DRESS     THREE-ARMHOLE DRESS

WEDGE DRESS     SKATING DRESS

**bubble d.** Dress style of 1959 with fitted bodice, sometimes strapless, with skirt bubbling out at hips and tapering in closely at hem. *Der.* Literally the skirt was shaped like a "bubble." Reintroduced in 1984.

**bustle d.** Any dress with fullness protruding in back from waist to hips or waist to hem. First worn in 1870s with full skirt. Worn in 1880s with slim skirt and early 1890s with gored skirt. Also worn in 1940s and reintroduced in early 1980s. A 1980s version consisted of a knee-length dress with large pouf in back and long floor length hanging panel. Designed by Christian Lacroix for Jean Patou.

**caftan** Originally a full-length robe with embroidery around the slit neckline. In 1967 introduced in dress- or full-length for women in much the same style as worn in Morocco. Also see ROBES.

**cage d.** Made in two layers with inner layer opaque and cut close to body, and outer layer of sheer or latticed fabric hanging loosely. Introduced in late 1960s by Paris couturier, Yves Saint Laurent. Similar to dresses designed by Spanish couturier, Cristobal Balenciaga, in Paris in the 1940s.

**cancan d.** Dress with *bustier* effect for bodice laced up the back. Skirt has an overskirt in apron-like effect tapering to center back with large bow. Worn over underskirt made with rows of ruffles. Designed by Victorine for Karl Lagerfeld of Chanel for fall 1986. *Der.* Similar to dresses worn by Music Hall dancers in film and stage show *Can-Can* with setting in 1890s. Dresses also shown in paintings by Henri Toulouse-Lautrec.

**cardigan d.** Coat-dress, similar to long cardigan sweater, collarless, usually unfitted and buttoned down the front. Worn in 1960s in mini, midi, and maxi lengths. *Der.* Named for 7th Earl of Cardigan who needed additional warmth under his uniform during the Crimean War, 1854.

**Carnaby d.** Simple beltless dress made in fabrics of unusual color combinations with a large white collar. *Der.* Named for Carnaby Street, in London, England, where the "mod" fashions originated in 1960s.

**chemise** (shem-eez) Straight-cut dress with few darts and no waistline, introduced in 1957 by French couturier, Hubert de Givenchy, inspired by 1920s dresses. Also called *sack dress.* *Der.* French "shift" or "shirt."

**cheongsam** (chong-sam) A contemporary Chinese-type dress, made with mandarin collar, short sleeves, and a long slit on one or both sides of the skirt. Worn over long pants in Vietnam.

**Chinese d.** Straight lined dress, with slashes on side seams from hem to thigh. Made with *mandarin neckline* and closing that extends diagonally to the side seam. Frequently fastened with frogs of braid or fabric. Copied from traditional Chinese woman's dress and a basic style of dress since 1930 in the West. Also called *mandarin dress.* Also see CHEONGSAM.

**coat-d.** Dress fastened down front from neck to hem, like a coat, in single- or double-breasted style, either belted or unbelted. A classic since the 1930s.

**cocktail d.** Contemporary term for short evening dress with décolleté neckline made in luxury fabrics. Suitable for formal late-afternoon parties and popularized in 1950s.

**Communion d.** White dress worn with short white veil by young girls receiving First Communion in the Roman Catholic Church.

**computer d.** Dress made from discarded computer chips hooked together, sometimes made in one-shoulder style with asymmetric hemlines. Chips are collected from computers, TVs, and other electronic machines. Dresses sold in 1984 by Panages, from $2,000 to $50,000.

**culotte d.** Dress which combines pants and

blouse into one garment, usually without a waistline seam, popularized in 1967. Also called a *pantdress.*

**cutout d.**   Any dress with cutout portions revealing the body. May have enlarged armholes or be cut out at the midriff, hips, or back. An innovation of the 1960s.

**dashiki**   Contemporary dress inspired by garment worn in central Africa styled with straight lines similar to the chemise, bell-shaped or kimono sleeves, and made of a distinctive African *panel* or *border print.* Popular in U.S. in late 1960s and early 1970s.

**diamanté d.**   Dress made almost entirely of sparkling beads, sequins, or paillettes giving a glittering effect, very popular in mid-1980s. Norman Norell designed dresses in 1968 made entirely of sequins—not known by this name until mid-1980s. *Der.* French, "made of diamonds." Also see MERMAID SHEATH.

**dinner d.**   Full-length dress suitable for a formal dinner. Introduced in the 1930s, it was distinguished from an evening gown by having the shoulders covered for dinner. Frequently with a jacket which, when removed, revealed a formal dress.

**dirndl**   (durn-del) Dress with several gathers at the waistline giving a slightly belled shape to the skirt as worn in 1980s. The 1940s and 1950s version had a fuller skirt with more gathers at the waist giving a more bouffant effect. Skirt usually attached to tight-fitted bodice. *Der.* Copied from Tyrolean peasant dress.

**electric d.**   Novelty dress decorated with electric lights wired to a battery at the waist, designed to be worn to discothèques in the late 1960s.

**Empire d.**   (ahm-peer or em-pire) **1.** Dress with high waistline just under the bosom defined by an inserted piece of fabric or a seam. Derived from dress introduced by Empress Josephine of France with neckline low cut in front and back, small puffed sleeves, ankle-length straight skirt, and a sash tied under the bust. For court wear, a train usually hung from the shoulders. **2.** Any contemporary dress with high waistline, usually with a narrow skirt. *Der.* From First Empire in France, 1804–1814.

**ensemble**   Dress and coat designed to be worn together, either in matching or contrasting fabric. Also called a REDINGOTE.

**Ethiopian shirtdress**   Simple shift, with slit at neckline trimmed with embroidery, imported from Ethiopia or made domestically in same style in late 1960s.

**evening gown**   See FORMAL GOWN.

**fan-back d.**   Evening gown with slim fitting front and back of contrasting fabric made of accordion pleats caught a little below the waistline with a bow. Pleats extend upward and downward in fan shape. Featured by Guy Laroche in black and fuchsia in fall 1986 collection.

**flamenco d.**   Dress with long torso top and skirt made with a series of circular-cut flounces. In the late 1960s adaptations were accepted for general wear. *Der.* Inspired by dresses worn by flamenco dancers in Spain.

**flapper d.**   Short-skirted long torso dress first worn in the late 1920s, reintroduced in the 1960s and called by this name. Also see alphabetical listing.

**flip-chip d.**   Make-your-own dress of colored plastic chips or squares and connecting fasteners put together in any pattern, similar to a LINKED DRESS.

**float**   Dress which falls free from shoulders and neckline with a full sweep at the hem giving a *tent silhouette.* Cut in dress- or full-length with accordion pleats or cut on bias, using various types of sleeves and necklines. Style is sometimes used for leisure wear and hostess gowns.

**foil d.**   Disposable dress made in various colors of aluminum foil, sometimes quilted. Introduced in 1968 along with PAPER DRESSES, and reintroduced in 1986 in creative imaginative designs.

**formal gown** Dress designed for a formal occasion. Also called *evening gown* or *ball gown*.

**graduation d.** Traditional white dress suitable for wear under an academic robe or without the robe for school or college graduation ceremony.

**granny d.** Ankle-length dress styled with a high round or choker neckline, long sleeves, high waistline, and slightly gathered skirt—sometimes with a ruffle at the hem. Frequently made of calico fabric in a small print and trimmed with ruffles. Worn by a young person. *Der.* Copied from style worn by her grandmother or "granny."

**harem d.** Symmetrically or asymmetrically draped dress falling in loose folds to the hem where it is turned under and fastened to a lining giving the hem a draped appearance. Usually made of soft clinging drapeable fabric. *Der.* An adaptation of Eastern dress introduced by Paris designers Paul Poiret and Drécoll, in 1910 and revived at intervals.

**housedress** Term used to describe a simple inexpensive dress made of washable fabric, worn while doing household chores.

**jacket d.** Dual purpose dress with a matching or contrasting jacket. With the jacket, it is suitable for business or afternoons. Popular since the 1930s.

**Jiffy® d.** **1.** Sew-it-yourself dress with limited number of pieces that can be stitched together in a short time. **2.** Trademark for a dress knit quickly on jumbo needles from a kit or from separately purchased yarn.

**Juliet d.** Dress in medieval style with high waistline and puffed-topped sleeves that are fitted at the lower arm. *Der.* Inspired by the film of Shakespeare's play, *Romeo and Juliet*, made by Franco Zeffirelli in 1968.

**jumper d.** One-piece dress with sleeves and collar of a contrasting color giving the appearance of a two-piece blouse and jumper. Also called a *jumper shift*.

**kabuki d.** Collarless wraparound dress with *kimono sleeves*, held closed by a sash. *Der.* Copied from traditional dress of actors in Japanese popular *kabuki theater* characterized by bizarre makeup and stylized acting. Also see alphabetical listing.

**kiltie d.** Dress style is adapted from the Scottish kilt. Front of skirt is plain with wrapped side closing fastened with a safety pin, the remainder of skirt is knife-pleated and joined to a simple tailored top. Introduced in the late 1960s.

**kimono d.** Wraparound dress held in place with a sash. Made with *kimono sleeves*, usually cut in one piece with the front and the back of the dress. There are no armhole seams. *Der.* Adapted from the *Japanese kimono*, first used as a dressing robe, and adapted for a dress in late 1960s.

**kurta** **1.** Modern version of a straight-cut Hindu man's shirt which is elaborately trimmed around neck, sleeves, and hem with East Indian embroidery. **2.** Can also be a plain style shirt resembling British military uniform available in dress- or shirt-lengths.

**L.B.D.** Abbreviation for *little black dress*. See BASIC DRESS.

**Le Canned d.®** Trade name for a simple shift dress of printed nylon knit packaged in a tin can for sale. Briefly popular in 1967.

**Linde Star d.®** Jeweled full-length evening dress sprinkled with Linde Star sapphires (synthetic sapphires) set at intervals. Novelty dress of the late 1960s. Trademark called Linde Star owned by Union Carbide.

**linked d.** Dress made by linking geometrically shaped pieces of metal, leather, plastic or mirror together. Introduced by Paris couturier, Paco Rabanne in 1966.

**little black d.**  See BASIC DRESS.

**mandarin d.**  See CHINESE DRESS.

**maternity d.**  Dress designed for expectant mothers following the general style trends but made with more fullness in front.

**maxi d.**  Ankle-length dress worn for day or evening. Introduced in 1969. First time since World War I that long dresses were worn as daytime dresses.

**mermaid sheath**  Slim, fitted evening gown introduced by designer Norman Norell in late 1960s. Dress was completely covered with sequins (or paillettes) giving a dazzling effect. *Der.* Similar to way mermaids are pictured (minus the tail).

**micro d.**  Shorter version of the minidress, reaching the top part of the thigh like a tunic blouse, introduced in 1966.

**middy d.**  See SAILOR DRESS.

**midi d.**  Mid-calf-length dress introduced in 1967 in radical contrast to thigh-length MINI-DRESS. Made in many styles, usually with a waistline. *Der.* French, *midi*, "midday." Term coined in 1967 by *Women's Wear Daily*.

**midriff d.**  Similar to the BARE-MIDRIFF dress, it is a one-piece dress with a piece of fabric or elastic inserted at waistline giving a cinch-waisted effect.

**minidress**  Dress with short skirt coming to mid-thigh or about 6″ above the knee. First introduced in early 1960s by designer Mary Quant in England as part of the "mod" fashions and became a mass fashion by end of 1960s. Reintroduced in the mid-1980s.

**molded d.**  Dress made with fabric that is heat-set or molded to take on a sculptured geometrical form. Introduced by Paris couturier, Pierre Cardin in fall 1968 collection.

**Mondrian d.**  Straight unconstructed dress made with blocks of color and neutrals heavily banded with black. Introduced by Yves Saint Laurent in fall 1965 collection. *Der.* Inspired by modern linear paintings of Piet Mondrian.

**monk's d.**  Dress styled like a monk's robe with cowl neck, bell sleeves, and cord belt confining fullness.

**muumuu**  (moo moo) Loose, ankle-length dress in bold Hawaiian floral-printed fabric adapted from dresses worn on Pacific islands. *Der.* From the type of modest gown imposed on the natives by missionaries about one hundred years ago.

**ocepa**  See ANDEAN SHIFT.

**one-shoulder d.**  Asymmetric dress styled with one bare shoulder. Also called TOGA DRESS.

**panel pantdress**  Dress with free hanging panel in front and back.

**pantdress**  See CULOTTE DRESS, TORSO DRESS, PANEL PANTDRESS, PANTGOWN, and PANTSHIFT.

**pantgown**  Full-length pantdress suitable for formal occasions popular in late 1960s and early 1970s. Sometimes made with accordion pleated pants attached to a halter top.

**pantshift**  Simple pantdress cut like shift dress—made with pants instead of a skirt.

**paper doll d.**  Term used from 1950 to 1960 particularly for Anne Fogarty dresses with tight bodices, tight waistlines, and very bouffant skirts held out with nylon net and crinoline petticoats. *Der.* From the full-skirted paper dolls children played with in the 1920s and 1930s.

**paper d.**  Classification of dresses made of various types of disposable nonwoven fabrics similar to paper, a fad popularized in 1968. Worn for parties and the beach, some were hand-painted and very expensive; others were inexpensive and imprinted with funny gimmicks, *e.g.*, Yellow Pages of telephone book, a Heinz soup can, etc. Revived in 1986 as wedding dress by Susan Lane made of a nonwoven fabric that resembles paper, selling for $140.00. See FOIL DRESS.

**patchwork d.** Small pieces of various colored prints and plain colors sewed together to make the fabric from which dress is cut. Became high fashion when introduced by Saint Laurent in 1969. *Der.* Inspired by patchwork quilts sewn by Colonial American women.

**patio d.** Gay floral or abstract printed shift. Suitable for wear at a backyard barbecue or at the beach.

**pearl d.** Novelty dress adapted from Oriental fashion consisting of draped strands of pearls at top and long hanging strands for the skirt, worn over a body stocking. Introduced by a jewelry firm, Richelieu Pearls, and designed by Bill Smith in 1969.

**peasant d.** **1.** Native dress of women in many European countries consisting of snug bodice, gathered skirt, puffed sleeves, and drawstring neckline. Worn with a black front laced corselet and apron, similar to DIRNDL. **2.** Any dress cut along lines of European peasant dresses.

**peplum d.** One- or two-piece dress either fitted or belted at waistline with short ruffle or circular-cut piece of fabric extending below waistline. Popular in 1930s, 1960s, and revived in 1980s. Newest type sometimes combined two fabrics or two colors, but is actually a one-piece dress.

**pinafore d.** Dress worn with separate bib-top apron tied in back popular for children. First worn in 1870s and intermittently since. *Der.* Copied from apron worn by children. See alphabetical listing. Also called *Alice in Wonderland* or *apron dress.*

**Pocahontas dress** See AMERICAN INDIAN DRESS.

**polo shirt d.** See T-SHIRT DRESS.

**poor-boy shift** An elongated version of the poor-boy sweater. See SWEATERS.

**poster d.** Any dress imprinted with a blown-up photograph, a brief fad in the mid-1960s. Originally made of paper, later photographs were printed on fabric. In 1984 called a *toga dress* but actually with wide-shouldered "sandwich board" effect sewed up the sides and printed with posters of animals, motorcycles, and movie star faces.

**prairie d.** Dress made with stand-up or Victorian-type neckline, sleeves gathered at shoulders, a band at the wrist, and a gored skirt with a ruffle at the hem. *Der.* Adapted from dresses worn by women traveling west on the wagon trains in 19th c.

**princess d.** Fitted dress with flared skirt, frequently made like a coat-dress, styled without a waistline seam and cut in six fitted panels from shoulders to hem. Original style was claimed to be designed by Worth and introduced about 1860 for Empress Eugénie. Worn intermittently since, particularly in the 1940s and early 1950s.

**rain d.** Dress made of plastic or of fabric treated for water repellency, an innovation of the 1960s.

**redingote** Ensemble consisting of a dress with matching or contrasting full-length coat. *Der.* French, "mannish woman's frock coat" or English, "riding coat." Also see alphabetical listing.

**rhumba d.** Bare-midriff dress worn with full-length skirt split up the front, tight through the hips, flaring with a mass of circular cut ruffles from hips to hem. Popularized by movie star Carmen Miranda in 1940s, revived at intervals. *Der.* Named for South American dance.

**Russian shirtdress** Dress with high neckline banded in braid and closed on the side made with slightly full sleeves and banded at the wrist. Also called *Zhivago dress*, from clothes worn in 1965 film of Russian novel, *Dr. Zhivago*, by Boris Pasternak.

**sack d.** See CHEMISE.

**safari d.** Tailored dress introduced in Paris by House of Dior in 1960s similar to *bush coat* or *safari jacket*, with convertible neckline, two bellows pockets on the chest and two on the shirt. *Der.* Top is similar in style to jacket worn on African hunting trip.

**sailor d.** Dress with sailor collar or middy-blouse effect trimmed with rows of braid in nautical style. Very popular for girls from 1890 to 1930, and for women from 1890 on.

**sari** (sah-ree) Principal garment of Hindu women, consisting of a length of silk or cotton, often delicately embroidered and banded in gold, wrapped about the waist and pleated at one side with loose end thrown over shoulder or head. Worn with bare midriff CHOLI. ADOPTED BY WESTERNERS SINCE EARLY 1940S WITH MANY VARIATIONS. ALSO SPELLED *saree.*

**sarong d.** (seh-rong) Dress with wraparound skirt draped to one side and strapless top. Designed by Edith Head for Dorothy Lamour film, *Hurricane,* in 1937. Worn by her in many of the "Road" films of 1940s. *Der.* Copied from Indonesian native dress.

**see-through d.** Sheer dress with bands of glitter at strategic places, usually worn with body stocking underneath. Introduced by Paris designers Pierre Cardin and Yves Saint Laurent, in 1966.

**seloso** A long, flowing African dress worn by women, similar to the BUBA, introduced in 1969.

**sheath 1.** Straight, narrow fitted dress usually with no waistline but shaped to body by vertical darts, or with set-in waistline. Ease of skirt obtained by inverted pleats at sides or center back. **2.** Tight fitting dress with regular waistline seam or set-in waistline and sheath skirt which is very narrow at hem and slashed at back to facilitate walking. Both styles were popular in 1950s and early 1960s. Revived in 1986.

**shift** Straight-lined basic dress of 1960s, hanging away from body, similar to CHEMISE DRESS of 1957. The shift dress introduced a diagonal upward dart from the side seam which improved the fit. Also see SKIMMER and A-LINE DRESS.

**shirtdress** Straight-lined dress buttoned down the front cut similar to a man's shirt, worn with or without a belt. Side seams are often slashed and the hem rounded, similar to the tail of a man's shirt. Popularized in 1967, it was a variation of the classic coat-dress or shirtwaist.

**shirtwaist d.** Dress with top styled like a tailored shirt, usually buttoned from neck to waist and made with either a full or straight skirt. Introduced in the 1930s, very popular in 1940s, and now a classic. Shown by many designers in long versions for evening wear in 1980s. See SHIRTDRESS. Also see alphabetical listing.

**skating d.** Originally a close-fitting long-sleeved bodice with brief thigh-length skirt flaring from a natural waistline as worn by Norwegian skating star, Sonja Henie, in films of 1930s. Newer version with long torso and flared microskirt was worn by current popular figure skaters and Olympic® champions.

**skimmer** Term for A-LINE dress or SHIFT that hangs away from the body.

**slip-d.** Simple bias-cut dress with fitted top, straps over shoulders, and no waistline. A revival in 1966 of bias-cut dress of the 1920s and 1930s as worn by movie star Jean Harlow. Also see BIAS-CUT DRESS.

**smock d.** Dress cut with yoke which comes above the bust and straight hanging skirt attached with slight gathers to the yoke. Usually worn without a belt. The BABY DOLL DRESS is similar in cut.

**square dancing d.** Dress with puffed sleeves and a wide, full, circular skirt, frequently finished with a ruffle. *Der.* Worn for square dancing, an American type of country dancing.

**squaw d.** Full-skirted minutely pleated dress with elaborate embroidery on long-sleeved bodice and in bands on skirt. *Der.* Name of native American Indian women.

**step-in d.** Term for a coat-type dress that buttons or zips only three-quarters of the way down the front. Basic dress style since the 1940s.

**strapless d.** Décolleté dress ending just at top of bosom without shoulders or straps. Top held in place by boning, by shirring with elastic thread, or by using stretch fabric.

**suit d.** Term used in 1960s for a jacket and dress ensemble which resembles a tailored suit.

**sundress** Dress in strapless or halter style with matching or contrasting jacket worn in warm weather.

**sweater d.** **1.** Knitted dress styled like a long sweater with or without knit-in waistline, *e.g.*, POOR-BOY SHIFT or CARDIGAN DRESS. Introduced in 1940s and revived in the 1960s. **2.** Two-piece knitted dress made of matching pull-on sweater and skirt. An innovation of the 1930s, used at intervals since.

**sweatshirt d.** Extra large sweatshirt coming almost to knees worn as a tunic over a skirt or pants—or alone as a dress.

**Swirl®** Trademark for a front-wrapped housedress.

**tennis d.** Mini- or micro-skirted dress usually white, now sometimes made in colors, worn when playing tennis. Tailored shorts were worn in 1930s. Gussie Moran introduced short dresses with ruffled panties for tennis in 1940s. Also see LAWN TENNIS DRESS in alphabetical listing.

**tent d.** Pyramid-shaped dress with broad flaring hem, sometimes made with accordion pleats. Introduced by Pierre Cardin in the spring of 1966.

**three-armhole d.** An easy-to-make dress promoted by pattern companies. Made in wraparound style with the left arm going through the first and third armholes, while the right arm goes through the second. An innovation of the 1960s.

**thrift-shop d.** Term used in the 1960s for second-hand dresses of the 1920s, 1930s, and 1940s found in U.S. thrift shops, in Paris flea markets, and in London's Portobello Road antique shops. Popular with young individuals, this type clothing influenced 1970s fashions for limp fabrics, muted-color prints, and old-fashioned trimmings. In the 1980s antique dresses of other eras were described as *vintage*. See VINTAGE DRESS.

**toga d.** Asymmetric dress or at-home robe styled with one shoulder bare, the other covered, an innovation of the 1960s. *Der.* From Roman toga, which covered one shoulder. Also see ONE-SHOULDER DRESS and POSTER DRESS.

**torso d.** **1.** Follows the line of the body to the hips where skirt is attached. Sometimes with a belt at low waistline. **2.** May also be made in *pantdress* style.

**trapeze d.** Unconstructed dress made with narrow shoulders and wide swing at hem. Designed by Yves Saint Laurent for House of Dior in Paris in 1958. Same style resurfaced in fall of 1986.

**trenchdress** Shirtwaist dress with snap front closing and cinch belt at waist. Top features epaulets and free-hanging panel to rib cage, similar to back of TRENCHCOAT.

**trumpet d.** Dress with flared flounce usually starting at knees. Worn in 1930s as tight-fitting dress to knees. Reintroduced in early 1980s as full-length evening gown and shift-type dress with flounce. *Der.* So called because it flares at the hem like a trumpet.

**T-shirt d.** Simple knit dress styled like an elongated T-shirt, an innovation of late 1950s. Newer versions have extended cap sleeves, spaghetti sashes, and are often printed with silk-screen designs.

**tunic d.   1.** Two-piece dress with a long over-blouse worn over a separate narrow skirt or a one-piece dress designed to give this effect. Originally introduced in the 1850s as a ball dress with the upper skirt trimmed with lace and underskirt with a deep flounce. Popular in slim style in 1880s, 1910 to 1920, and worn intermittently since. **2.** Minidress of the late 1960s which could be worn alone or over pants to make a pantsuit.

**undershirt d.** Simple knit dress similar to T-SHIRT DRESS with a "skivvy" or buttoned placket neckline. Introduced by Courréges in 1969 and popularly accepted in 1970.

**usha** Long or mini-length dress imported from India made with high-waisted effect using native fabrics in allover prints with border designs. Fashionable in 1970.

**vintage d.** Dresses from a former era, *e.g.*, 1900s, 1920s, sold in department stores or specialty shops. Called by this name in the 1980s. See VINTAGE LOOK.

**wedding d.** Any dress worn by the bride for a wedding ceremony, traditionally long and of white satin, faille, or lace, with or without a train. Also called a *bridal dress.*

**wedge d.** Dress cut with very full, large shoulders and dolman sleeves. Entire dress tapers to hemline in a "V" or wedge shape.

**weskit d.** Tailored dress, usually full sleeved, combined with a vest.

**wrap d.** Dress wrapping either to the front, similar to the kimono dress; or to the back. In either case it has an extra lap which is approximately equal to the width of the skirt. *Der.* Term shortened from "wraparound" in late 1960s. Also see BACK-WRAP DRESS, KIMONO DRESS, SWIRL®, and BATHROBE DRESS.

**Zhivago d.** Same as RUSSIAN SHIRTDRESS.

**dress à la constitution**   See COSTUME À LA CONSTITUTION.

**dress alikes**   In 1984 it became fashionable for women who were friends to wear exactly the same dress or costume. See LOOKS.

**dress clip**   Metal hook attached at the waist-line or belt worn by women in the 1840s to lift the skirt when walking. Also see DRESS HOLDER and PAGE.

**dress coat**   See SWALLOW-TAILED COAT under COATS.

**dress elevator**   See PORTE-JUPE POMPADOUR.

**dress form**   See DUMMY.

**dress frock coat**   Man's double-breasted *cutaway frock coat*, exposing the shirt in front, worn in 1870s and 1880s.

**dress holder**   Elaborate device used for holding up skirt in the 1870s. Made with two pendant chains and clips. Also see DRESS CLIP.

**dress improver**   Polite term for *bustle* worn at intervals from 1849 to late 1880s.

**dressing gown/robe   1. Men:** Term used from 1770s to the end of the 19th c. for a loose coat-like garment made in elaborately patterned silk. From 1850s to 1860s worn for breakfast; after that relegated to the bedroom and bathroom. **2. Women:** Late 18th c. on loose garment worn at breakfast; the forerunner of the tea gown. Also see ROBES.

**dressing sacque**   Short, loose hip-length woman's jacket worn in boudoir in late 19th and early 20th c. Also spelled *dressing sack.*

**dress lounge**   British term for man's semi-formal evening jacket worn from 1888 on, only in company of gentlemen. From 1898 on, called a DINNER JACKET.

**dressmaker**   Person who makes clothing for private customers from pattern to finished garment either by hand or by machine. From 1850 through 1920s, before ready-to-wear, dressmakers often worked in customers' homes to prepare seasonal wardrobes for the family. Also called a SEAMSTRESS. Also see COATS, SUITS, and SWIM-SUITS.

**dressmaker pin**  See PINS.

**dressmaker's brim**  Hat brim, usually on a fabric hat, that has closely spaced rows of machine stitching or stitched tucks around the brim.

**dressmaker's dummy**  See DUMMY.

**dress shirt**  See SHIRTS and FORMAL SHIRT under SHIRTS.

**dress shoe**  See SHOES.

**dress socks**  See SOCKS.

**dress Wellington**  Fitted stocking reaching to the knee, attached to a shoe similar to an *evening slipper* and worn under the dress trousers or *pantaloons*. Worn by men with evening clothes from 1830 to 1850.

**drill**  Durable cotton fabric made in a warp-faced twill similar to denim. Extra strong types are made with coarse carded yarns, sometimes made in a herringbone twill. Made in two weights—medium and heavyweight. Uses: work clothes, sport clothes, shoe linings, trousers, and slacks.

**D-ring belt**  See BELTS.

**D-ring closing**  See CLOSINGS.

**drip-dry**  Describing fabric that needs no pressing after washing, achieved by weaving with man-made yarns and/or by giving a surface treatment with synthetic resins that resists wrinkles, *e.g.,* DURABLE PRESS.

**driving cape/sac**  See ALBERT OVERCOAT.

**driving coat**  See CURRIOLE COAT #2.

**driving gloves**  See GLOVES.

**drop earrings**  See EARRINGS.

**drop-front**  Descriptive of pants that are fastened by two buttoned plackets on either side of the center front allowing the front panel to drop down when unbuttoned. Used frequently on JODHPURS, other RIDING BREECHES, and in the past on U.S. Navy seamen's pants, *e.g.,* SAILOR PANTS.

**dropped shoulders**  See SHOULDERS.

**dropped skirt**  **1.** Skirt set on a low waistline; also called a *torso skirt*. **2.** Sewing term in late 19th and early 20th c. for a skirt made separate from the lining. Both are attached to the same seam at waist.

**dropped waistline**  See WAISTLINES.

**dropping**  See LETTING OUT.

**druid's cloth**  **1.** A British term used for cotton duck in Great Britain and Australia. **2.** Term used in the U.S. to refer to MONK'S CLOTH.

**drum farthingale**  See ENGLISH FARTHINGALE.

**drum major's hat**  See HATS.

**Du Barry corsage**  Bodice with a wide V-shaped front, worn by women from the 1830s to 1850, adapted from the style worn by Comtesse Du Barry (1746–1793), mistress of Louis XV of France. Also called *corsage á la Du Barry*.

**Du Barry costume**  Style of dress worn by Marie Jeanne Bécu, Comtesse Du Barry (1746–1793), last mistress of Louis XV of France. Consisted of a fitted bodice with low décolletage, long V to bodice front filled with lace ruching, elbow-length sleeves, and a full skirt.

**Du Barry mantle**  *Dolman-style* wrap of early 1880s with smocked yoke front and back, fur collar, and large full cuffs. Lavishly trimmed with ribbon bows and streamers at neck, below yoke, sleeves, and at center back. *Der.* Named for *Comtesse Du Barry.*

**Du Barry sleeve**  Double puffed sleeve, one puff above elbow and another below, worn in mid-1830s. *Der.* Named for *Comtesse Du Barry.*

**Dubinsky, David**  American labor leader active in the organization of the *International*

Ladies Garment Workers' Union and president from 1932 to 1966.

**duchess**   Late 17th c. term for knot or bow of ribbon worn as part of the *fontange* hairstyle. Often misspelled as *dutchess.*

**duchesse**   Lightweight lustrous satin fabric made of silk or rayon and dyed solid colors. Also called *duchesse satin.*

**duchesse lace**   See LACES.

**duchesse pleat**   Term used in mid-1870s for back pleats of a skirt, usually two *box pleats* on either side of center-back placket or seam.

**duchesse satin**   See DUCHESSE.

**Duchess of Windsor** (1896–1986)   The former Wallis Warfield Simpson, an American divorcee who married Edward VIII of England, causing his abdication. He assumed the title of Duke of Windsor in 1936. World famous for her impeccable taste and conservative fashion leadership, and usually dressed by French couture. Her wedding gown, designed by *Mainbocher* in Paris, became the most copied dress in the world—available at every price level.

**duck**   Term for wide range of fabrics which are closely woven in a plain weave. Made in different weights usually with single warps and ply fillings. *Army-type* duck is the lightest; *sail duck* is the heaviest. The lighter type is used for sportswear. *Der.* Dutch, *doek,* "heavy cotton fabric."

**duckbills**   Modern term for broad-toed flat shoes worn in England from about 1490 to 1540—shown in paintings of Henry VIII.

**duckbill solleret**   See SABATON.

**duck-hunter**   Striped linen jacket worn by English waiters about 1840s.

**ducks**   **1.** Trousers worn by men in late 19th c. made of DUCK *fabric.* Also see WHITE DUCKS under PANTS. **2.** See SHOES.

**duck's-foot fan**   Early *folding fan* that opened to one-fourth of a circle. Made of alter-

nate strips of mica and vellum with an ivory handle. Introduced to France from Italy by Catherine de Medici in mid-16th c.

**ducktail haircut**   See HAIRSTYLES.

**dude**   **1.** American term used at a Western ranch for someone from the city or the East Coast. Also see COWBOY/COWGIRL. **2.** Term used in 1890s for a DANDY, an affected or fastidious man.

**dude jeans**   See WESTERN PANTS under PANTS.

**duds**   Informal word for clothes in general.

**dueling blouse/shirt**   See BLOUSES and SHIRTS.

**duet pin**   See PINS.

**duffel bag**   Large utility bag of heavy fabric with drawstring top used by members of the Armed Forces to transport gear. Widely copied for civilian use. Also see HANDBAGS.

**duffel coat**   See COATS.

**Duke of Windsor** (1894–1973)   Briefly Edward VIII of England, who in 1936 married Wallis Warfield Simpson, known in international society as a fashion leader. The Duke of Windsor, as the Prince of Wales, influenced men's fashion in the 1920s by introducing several styles including the large *Panama hat, tab collar, Windsor knot tie,* double-breasted jacket with long roll lapel, *Fair Isle sweater,* white waistcoat worn as dinner jacket, guard's overcoat, seashore resort-type sportswear, and brown buckskin shoes.

**dummy**   Dressmaking form in shape of human body on which the designer or home sewer drapes clothes before sewing. Also called *dress form, dressmaker's dummy, dressmaker's form,* and *model form.*

**dunce cap**   Tall conical cap, sometimes marked with a D, formerly worn in school by students who failed in their lessons. Sometimes wrongly called *fool's cap.*

**dungaree**   See DENIM.

**dungarees** See PANTS.

**dunstable** Hat of plaited straw originally made in Dunstable, England.

**duo-length coat** See COATS.

**duplex printing** Method of printing the same design on both sides of fabric to simulate a yarn-dyed woven pattern, *e.g.*, *herringbone* or *checked design*.

**duppioni** See DOUPIONI.

**durable finish** Fabric finish that should last during the normal life of a fabric. Usually produced by resin or chemical treatment.

**durable press** Collective term for all finishes on garments and fabrics that need no pressing—even after repeated washing. Resins, fixed to garments or fabrics by a high-temperature curing oven, become an integral part of the fabric giving it complete stabilization.

**dust cap** Cap made of handkerchief, or circular piece of fabric hemmed on outer edge and gathered by elastic, worn by women or maids for housework from 19th to early 20th c.

**duster** **1.** Man's summer overcoat of 1870s. **2.** Alpaca or silk woman's long summer coat, sometimes belted and caped, worn in 1880s. **3.** Pongee-colored lightweight full-length coat worn when riding in an automobile in early 20th c. to protect clothing from dust. Also called an *automobile coat*. Worn with *automobile veil*. **4.** See COATS and BRUNCH COAT under ROBES.

**dust gown** 18th c. term for a SAFEGUARD or overskirt worn by women to protect the dress when riding horseback.

**dust ruffle** Ruffle inside of hem of full-length dress or petticoat to protect dress from becoming soiled when walking outdoors in late 19th and early 20th c. Also called *balayeuse* and *sweeper*.

**Dutch** Adjective used for various types of clothing and accessories worn in the Nether-lands. Also adopted for current use. See DUTCH BOY under CAPS, HEELS, and DUTCH BOB under HAIRSTYLES.

**Dutch breeches** **1.** Below-the-knee full trousers of dark-gray fabric worn on the Dutch island of Marken. **2.** Long full trousers worn as native costume in the Netherlands.

**Dutch cap** Cap worn by women and girls in Volendam, Holland, made of lace or embroidered muslin fitted to the head with a slight peak at the crown and flaring wings at sides of face. Made fashionable by *Irene Castle*, famous ballroom dancer in 1920s. Sometimes used as bridal cap. Also called DUTCH BONNET.

**Dutch coat** Man's short jacket worn in late 14th and 15th c., later called a jerkin. (From 14th to 16th c. "Dutch" usually meant German.)

**Dutchman** Triangular wedge placed between insole and outsole of shoe to improve posture of wearer. Also used between layers of a built-up heel to adjust heel pitch.

**Dutch neckline** See SQUARE NECKLINE under NECKLINES.

**Dutch waist** Woman's bodice without a point in center front worn with the WHEEL FARTHINGALE about 1580 to 1620.

**duvetyn** (dew-veh-teen) Soft, napped fabric with a velvet-like finish made in the twill weave of loosely twisted yarns and finished by brushing with emery rollers. It is napped, sheared, and singed to give a soft smooth nap which conceals the weave. May be made in wool, cotton, rayon, silk, or combinations of fibers. Used for dresses, coats, and sportswear. When made in cotton, sometimes called *suede cloth*. *Der.* French, *duvet*, "down-like or soft."

**Duvillier wig** (doo-vee-yee-aye) Man's wig, worn about 1700, dressed high on top of head with long, shoulder-length hair. Named after a French *perruquier* or wigmaker. Also called *long Duvillier*, *falbala wig*, or *furbelow wig*.

**dux collar** Man's narrow standing collar, with front corners turned down, worn from 1860s on.

**dyeable shoe** See SHOES.

**dyed-in-the-wool** Term for wool made of fibers dyed before yarn is spun. See STOCK-DYED YARN, HEATHER YARN, and OXFORD GRAY FLANNEL.

**dyeing** **1.** Impregnation of fibers, yarns, or fabrics with natural or synthetic coloring agents that are relatively permanent. **2.** Coloring of furs by *dip dyeing, brush dyeing, blending,* or *tipping.* **3.** Coloring of leathers by *dip dyeing* or *brush dyeing.*

**dyes** Color-producing substances, either natural or man-made, that can be permanently impregnated into fibers, fabrics, leathers or furs.

**E Shoe Size:** Letter indicating a width; widths run from AAAA to EEEEE with AAAA being the narrowest and EEEEE the widest.

**ear band** See EARRINGS.

**earclip** See EARRINGS.

**earmuffs** **1.** Two disks of wool, fur, felt, or other fabric worn to keep the ears warm in winter. Disks may be fastened to a strap which goes over top of head and ties under the chin, or fastened to a springy metal band that fits over top of the head. **2.** A pair of flaps on sides of a cap which may be turned up and buttoned at top of cap, or left down to cover the ears. **3.** A woman's hairdo. See HAIRSTYLES.

**earring** Decorative jewelry accessory worn on the ear. Ear may be pierced and small wires or posts inserted. For unpierced ears, types include screw- or clip-backs. Mentioned in the Bible and visible on carvings of ancient monarchs. Worn by kings, nobles, and soldiers, as well as women in early times. Pirates have been depicted wearing one earring. Popular during the 16th and 17th c., earrings were worn by Henry III of France and Charles I of England went to his execution wearing a drop pearl in his right ear. This seemed to end fashion of earrings for men until the 1980s. Worn by women from Biblical times to present. From mid-19th c. available in "sets" with matching necklace, brooch, and bracelet. In late 1950s piercing of ears was revived, even for pre-school children. In early 1980s double and triple piercing became a fashion with two and three sets of earrings being worn at the same time on either one or both ears. While in the 1960s earrings were often tiny, in the 1980s they became quite large and sometimes dangled to the shoulders. Also called an *earclip*.

### ■ EARRINGS ■

**Art Deco e.** Earring made in unusual geometrical forms. Popularized in the late 1960s, copied from patterns of the 1920s shown in the 1925 Paris Exhibition. See ART DECO in alphabetical listing.

**ball e.** Earring in the shape of a round bead usually suspended from a tiny linked chain, made of gemstones, plastic, glass, or other material.

**button e.** Round flat earring shaped like a button. Made in various sizes of imitation pearls, or plastic.

**chandelier e.** Long dangling oversized earring made of metal or beads hanging like crystals on a chandelier.

**changeable e.** Earring usually made with a selection of colored plastic disks that may be snapped into metal circlet. Parts of the PEEK-A-BOO EARRING can also be interchanged.

**clip-back e.** Earring that fastens to the ear by means of a spring clip that snaps against back of the ear to secure it; an innovation of the 1930s.

**cluster e.** Groups of pearls, gems, glass, or beads fastened together to make a large earring.

**diamond e.** **1.** May be a single diamond attached to a post for pierced ears. Popular wedding gift for the groom to give to the bride. **2.** Elaborate types were popular from the 1920s on for evening wear. **3.** Marie Antoinette had a handsome set made of long strings of diamonds with larger stones set at the top.

**door knocker e.** Elongated hoops hanging free from ear clips—may be interchangeable.

**drop e.**   Any earring in which the lower part swings free. Also see PENDANT EARRING.

**ear band**   Earring which clips on middle edge of ear with dangling portion.

**ear clip**   Synonym for EARRING.

**gypsy e.**   Large HOOP EARRING usually of brass or gold-colored metal, worn in pierced ear, inspired by plain brass circles worn by gypsies. For unpierced ears, hoop is suspended from a small button top which clips to the back of the ear.

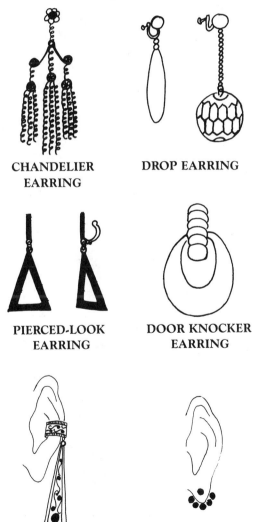

**CHANDELIER
EARRING**

**DROP EARRING**

**PIERCED-LOOK
EARRING**

**DOOR KNOCKER
EARRING**

**EAR BAND**

**PEEK-A-BOO
EARRING**

**hoop e.**   **1.** Circlet (or oval) of metal, plastic, or wood which swings free from a small button. Also see GYPSY EARRING. **2.** Incomplete circlet which fastens around the earlobe.

**jacket e.**   Earring consisting of post plus various shaped separate pieces with holes in top which may be interchanged by placing post through hole. "Jackets" may be in shape of shells, roses, hearts, butterflies, etc. Introduced in early 1980s.

**mobile e.**   (mo-beel) Delicate wire drop earring like small mobile sculpture carefully balanced so it is constantly in motion.

**peek-a-boo e.**   Earring for pierced ears with small object or stone showing where ear is pierced and three or four stones at lower edge of ear. The latter group is attached to back of earring.

**pendant e.**   One of the earliest styles and popular for single genuine gemstones or pearls. Same as DROP EARRING.

**pierced e.**   Earring designed to be worn in pierced ears. A wire or post is inserted through the ear lobe and should be made of gold or surgical steel rather than plated metals to prevent infection. Until the introduction of screw-back earrings all types of earrings were made for pierced ears. See POSTS, STUDS, and WIRES.

**pierced-look e.**   Earring designed for unpierced ears. Have a delicate band of metal coming under the ear to the front giving the appearance that it goes through the ear.

**posts**   See STUDS.

**screw-back e.**   Earring for unpierced ears, with screw behind the ear which can be tightened to hold it in place. An innovation of the early 20th c. which enabled people without pierced ears to wear earrings.

**Statue of Liberty e.**   Dangling earring with head of Statue of Liberty enclosed in circle. *Der.* Inspired by the July 4, 1986 celebration in New York harbor of the restoration of the Statue of Liberty.

**studs** Earrings similar to posts designed for pierced ears. One part of earring goes through the ear and back screws into the "post." Basic type of earring for pierced ears. Some studs are secured by pushing back piece onto straight post, notch in post secures back.

**wedding band e.** Wide gold hoop earring similar in style to a wide gold wedding ring.

**wires** Earrings for pierced ears which have a thin curved wire, usually gold, that passes through the ear. Usually dangling objects are attached to the wire or the wires may be worn separately.

---

**ear string** Black ribbon, or strands of silk, worn through pierced left ear by men from latter part of 16th c. to about 1610.

**earthquake gown** Woman's warm gown, suitable for wear outdoors, made in England in 1750 in anticipation of a third earthquake after two earlier quakes had taken place in London.

**ease** Factor taken into consideration when drafting a pattern—allowing extra measure at bust, waist, and hips, so garment will fit comfortably, not skintight.

**Easter Parade** **1.** Term coined for promenading in new spring clothes on Easter Sunday. A traditional feature in New York City since March 25, 1883. Originally people rode in carriages and strolled on Fifth Avenue after church; later centering on areas around St. Patrick's Cathedral, at 50th Street and Fifth Avenue extending north to Central Park and south to 42nd Street. Estimated crowd in 1954 was 1.5 million people—making it more like a "crush" with people wearing ridiculous hats and costumes in hopes of appearing on television. The idea of dressing in new spring finery on Easter Sunday dates back to Biblical and Roman times. **2.** Title of film and song starring Judy Garland and Fred Astaire produced in 1948 featuring New York City's Easter Parade. **3.** See BONNETS.

**ecclesiastical vestments** Garments worn by the clergy for religious services. See ALB, CASSOCK, CHASUBLE, CHIMERE, COPE, COTTA, DALMATIC, GENEVA GOWN, MITER, STOLE, and SURPLICE.

**échantillon** (eh-shawnt-e-yon) French, "sample," used to refer to a swatch of fabric.

**écharpe** (eh-sharp) Synonym for SCARF. *Der.* French, "scarf." See SCARFS.

**echelles** (eh-shell-ess) Decorative trim on front of woman's bodice made with braid, lace, or ribbon bows arranged in ladderlike effect. Popular from end of 17th to end of 18th c. *Der.* French, "ladder."

**Eclipse Tie** Trade name for woman's shoe made with one pair of eyelets and a pointed tongue usually coming up high on the instep. Worn in late 19th and early 20th c.

**écrasé** (eh-kras-zay) French word for leather crushed to reveal the grain.

**edge** **1.** Shoe-industry term for part of shoe that is visible around outside of front of shoe sole—may be rounded, beveled, or square. **2.** A late 15th- and early 16th-c. term for an ornamental border, usually made by a goldsmith, used on a headdress. Also spelled *neyge, age, oegge, egge.*

**edging** Narrow decorative border of lace, embroidery, braid, or fringe used for trimming on clothing, particularly at hem, sleeve, or neck.

**edozuma** Japanese KIMONO, worn only by married women. Originally referred to the patterned fabric on lower front from knees to hem. Later word was applied to garment decorated in this manner.

**Edwardian** Period from 1901 to 1910 when Edward VII, son of Queen Victoria, was King of England—noted for fitted frock or suit coats, top hats for men, and the *Gibson Girl* or *Merry Widow* style with large decorative hats for women. Term also applied to a revival of these styles for men's and women's suits and jackets in mid-1960s. Also see LOOKS.

**Edwardian coat**  Man's high-waisted fitted *frock coat*, usually black, double-breasted, and reaching to below knee. Made with notched satin-faced lapels showing sliver of waistcoat and stiff white collar. Worn with high silk hat and cane in Edwardian period, 1901–1910. Also see COATS.

**eelskin masher trousers**  Very tight trousers worn in mid-1880s by *mashers*, or *dandies*. *Der.* Literally, "as tight as an eel's skin."

**eelskin sleeve**  Tight-fitting lace-trimmed sleeve worn by women in the 17th c.

**eel skirt**  Woman's gored skirt of late 1890s cut on the bias, fitting very snugly over the hips, and flared slightly from the knees to hem.

**egge**  See EDGE #2.

**eggshell finish**  Dull finish given to fabric by running it between engraved rollers for a rough effect.

**Egham, Staines, and Windsor**  Nickname used in early 19th c. for TRICORN HAT. *Der.* From geographical location of three English towns that form a triangle on map.

**egret feathers**  (e-grit)  See AIGRETTE under FEATHERS.

**Egyptian collar**  Wide flat necklace made in ancient Egypt of beads, shells, seeds, faïence, or semiprecious stones in various colors. Sometimes mounted in gold or made of papyrus or fabric with geometrical lotus designs embroidered in colored wool.

**Egyptian cotton**  High-quality long-staple, strong lustrous cotton produced along the Nile River with staple averaging ⅛″ to 1½″. Imported to make threads, laces, and fine fabrics. Types include Ashmouni and Sakellarides.

**Egyptian lace**  See LACES.

**Egyptian sandal**  Thong-type sandal with T-strap coming up over instep to join two straps attached to both sides of sole. Worn by ancient Egyptians, *e.g.*, sandal found in King Tut's tomb made entirely of gold. See THONG under SANDALS.

**Egyptian styles**  Early costumes consisted of plain wraparound loincloths called SHENTI and simple wrap dresses beginning below the bust, held on with one or two straps. Later costumes were more elaborate and made of sheer accordion-pleated fabric. Also see ANKH, EGYPTIAN COLLAR, EGYPTIAN SANDALS, and UTCHAT.

**Egyptian wig**  **1.** Long black wig worn by ancient Egyptians with straight bangs, square cut at bottom, and often with intricate braiding interspersed with gold links. Wig was made on a framework that elevated it from the head creating protection from the sun. **2.** Colored short wigs in layered styles, blue or red, worn by ancient Egyptians.

**eiderdown**  **1.** Soft fine under feathers from the eider duck. Also called DOWN. **2.** A lightweight knit or woven fabric which is elastic and heavily napped on one or both sides. Made of wool, cotton, rayon, or combinations of these fibers, and used for robes and negligees. *Der.* From the feathers of the *eider duck*.

**eighths**  Height of heels of shoes are measured in eighths of an inch, *e.g.*, a ¹⁶/₈ths heel is a 2″ heel, a ⁴/₈th heel is ½″ high.

**eight-point cap**  See CAPS.

**Eiseman, Florence**  See APPENDIX/ DESIGNERS.

**Eisenhower jacket**  World War II short battle jacket bloused to waistband with large patch pockets. Worn by President Dwight D. Eisenhower when he was a general in the U.S. Army. Also see BATTLE JACKET under SPORT JACKETS.

**eisteddfod costume**  (a-steth-vod)  Costume of Wales, originating in 17th c., consisting of gown called PAIS-A-GWN BACH, striped petticoat, apron, neckerchief, and ruffled muslin cap tied on with ribbons under chin. Over the cap is worn a broad flat-brimmed polished beaver hat with tall tapered crown. Also worn with outer garment consisting of a large checked or plaid wool shawl folded diagonally or a long circular cape with a hood. Worn by women during Welsh national competitive song festivals. Also spelled *eistheddfodau*.

**eis yarn** Fine two-ply worsted knitting yarn. Also called *eis wool* and *ice wool*.

**elastic** Stretchable tape originally woven with rubber yarn—now made with *Lastex* or *spandex* yarn covered with cotton or nylon. Used at waistlines, sleeves, hems, or any other place where stretch is needed. Also see BRACE-LETS, HOSE, WAISTLINES, and ELASTIC-LEG BRIEF under PANTIES.

**elasticity** Ability of fabric or yarn to stretch and return to its original shape when tension is released. Very important for hose and panty-hose.

**elasticized** **1.** Describing fabric made with natural or synthetic rubber yarns for stretcha-bility, *e.g.*, Lastex and spandex core yarns. **2.** Use of stretch yarns on sewing machine to form rows of gathers on waistlines, sleeves, or necklines—very popular in 1970s and 1980s. **3.** Use of *elastic*, sewed to a garment, or in-serted through a tunnel of fabric, at waistband of pants, skirts, petticoats, panties, and at hems of sleeves. Also see NECKLINES and WAISTLINES.

**elastic round hat** Patented collapsible hat of 1812, which could be flattened by releasing a steel spring and carried under the arm. Fore-runner of the GIBUS.

**elastic-sided boot** Ankle-high boot, intro-duced for men and women about 1837, with India-rubber insert on each side, and patented by James Dowie.

**elastic webbing** Narrow fabric woven with elastomeric yarns for use in foundations, bras, and garters.

**elastomer** (e-las-to-mere) Textile term for a yarn with high stretch qualities made from natural or synthetic rubber—used either cov-ered or uncovered.

**elbow cuff** Turned-back cuff attached to woman's elbow-length sleeves in first half of 18th c.—wide on outside of arm and fitting more closely at elbow.

**elbow-length sleeve** See SLEEVES.

**electric** Adjective used when apparel or ac-cessories are powered by electricity. See DRESSES, SOCKS, VESTS, and WATCHES.

**electric blue** Vibrant greenish-blue color re-sembling the color of a spark of electricity.

**electric comb** Electrically powered vibrating comb for the hair that fluffs as it combs, pro-ducing a neat but not slick effect. Introduced in the early 1970s.

**electric mole** Incorrect terminology used in early 20th c. for *rabbit fur* prior to the Fur Labeling Act of 1938. Correct terminology is *electric-processed rabbit*.

**electric-processed rabbit** See ELECTRIC MOLE and ELECTRIC SEAL.

**electric seal** Incorrect terminology for *rabbit* that is sheared and then carved in ridges. Cor-rectly called *electric-processed rabbit*.

**electrified lambskin** Lambskins tanned with hair intact and given an electrical treat-ment that gives the hair a silky texture.

**electronic game watch** See WATCHES.

**elephant-leg pants** See PANTS.

**elephant sleeve** Large sleeve of early 1830s usually made of sheer fabric—full at the shoul-der, hanging down somewhat in the form of an elephant's ear, and close-fitting at the wrist.

**elevator heel** See HEELS.

**elevator shoes** See SHOES.

**Elizabethan styles** Garments and accesso-ries worn during the reign of Elizabeth I of England, 1558–1603. Men's costume consists of SLASHED and PANNED TRUNK HOSE, DOUBLET with slashed sleeves, and variations of the RUFF. Women's dress had barrel-shaped skirt, standing lace collar, and slashed sleeves. Costume of this period also called *Shakespearean costume*.

**elkside**   Misleading term for cattlehides finished to look like elk leather—should be labeled *elk-finished cowhide*.

**elliptic collar**   Patented detachable man's collar of early 1850s with the front cut higher than the back. Could be fastened either in front or in back.

**Ellis, Perry**   See APPENDIX/DESIGNERS.

**EMBA® mink**   See MINK.

**embossed leather**   See LEATHERS.

**embossing   1.** Process using metal plates to impress a pattern on leather or plastic to imitate genuine alligator, lizard, snakeskin, or turtle. **2.** Use of metal rollers to imprint a texture on fabrics, which gives a permanent finish on man-made fibers when HEAT-SET.

**embroidery**   Fancy needlework or trimming using colored yarn, embroidery floss, soft cotton, silk or metallic thread. Usually done by hand, but may be made on a *Schiffli machine*. In primitive times, straws or grasses were used to embroider with a bone needle; gold embroidery was first made by Assyrians; later copied by Egyptians, Greeks, and Romans. Each country in Europe developed its own type of embroidery. Needlework has been a popular diversion for women since medieval times. Also see BRAIDS and SWEATERS.

## ■ EMBROIDERIES ■

**aloe thread e.**   Aloe fibers, *e.g. Agave, Ceylon bowstring hemp*, and *piteira*, embroidered in a raised effect.

**Anglo-Saxon e.**   Long surface stitches *couched* with metal or silk threads in an outline effect. *Der.* Done by Anglo-Saxons in ancient times.

**Appenzell e.** (ap-en-tsell)   Fine Swiss drawn work, used chiefly on handkerchiefs and fine muslin, a cottage industry in Switzerland. *Der.* Named for town in Switzerland where it originated.

**Arrasene e.** (ar-a-seen)   Embroidery with a velvet-like effect made by using Arrasene thread, made of silk or wool, which resembles *chenille*. *Der.* Named for town of Arras, France.

**arrowhead**   Triangular-shaped embroidery used at ends of pockets, pleats, or for decorative effect.

**Ayrshire e.**   See MADEIRA EMBROIDERY.

**backstitch e.**   Outline embroidery similar to HOLBEIN work, but single-faced instead of double.

**ballpoint e.**   See LIQUID EMBROIDERY.

**Beauvais e.** (bo-vay)   Tapestry-like embroidery done in many colors. *Der.* Named after city in France where it originated.

**Berlin work**   Allover type of embroidery done on canvas, primarily using the cross-stitch. *Der.* Name dates from 1820 when Berlin wool was used. Also called *canvas* or CUSHION-STYLE embroidery.

**black work**   Embroidery done in black silk on white linen, fashionable from 16th to 17th c. Sometimes worked in an allover continuous scroll design and used to decorate collars, cuffs, smocks, and handkerchiefs. Also called *Spanish black work*.

**bonnaz** (bo-nahz)   Machine embroidery, sometimes worked on canvas-based cloth, with all types of designs possible as the operator can make the machine go in any direction. Used on sweaters, dresses, hats, gloves, and handbags. *Der.* Named after J. Bonnaz, a French inventor.

**Breton work** Peasant embroidery in colored silk and metallic threads made in floral and geometric designs, largely done in chain stitch. Also called *Brittany work. Der.* Originated in Brittany.

**Brittany work** See BRETON WORK.

**brocade e.** Embroidery made by needlework done over the designs of brocade fabric.

**broderie anglaise** (brod-e-ree onh-glase) Eyelet embroidery, made by re-embroidering holes. Also called MADEIRA EMBROIDERY. Also see MORAVIAN WORK.

**bullion e.** (bool-yon) Embroidery done with fine gold wire, also embroidery done with gold or silver threads, or cords, originating with the Phrygians in ancient times.

**Bunka e.** Japanese embroidery done with chain stitch with machine-made knitting yarn (frequently polyester) which is unraveled to reveal its textured effect. This yarn is threaded through a special needle, held like a pencil, and punched into the fabric (similar to making a hooked rug). Usually used to make scenes depicting figures, animals, birds, and floral patterns.

**Byzantine e.** Appliqué work combined with decorative stitches done in the 19th c.

**California e.** **1.** Contemporary term used for leather stitching and braiding. **2.** Primitive pre-Spanish embroidery made in California by Indians using fishbone needle and animal substance for thread.

**candlewick e.** Tufts made with thick loosely twisted cotton yarn called *candlewicking* and a large needle. Several stitches are taken in the same place making loops that are cut to form a fluffy tuft.

**canvas e.** See BERLIN WORK.

**Cashmere work** Rich, varicolored embroidery, frequently inlaid appliqué done in India, with complicated needlework covering almost entire surface, used for shawls.

**chainstitched e.** Machine embroidery worked in different designs using a chain stitch. Used lavishly at necklines, cuffs, and hems of blouses in India in 1980s.

**chenille e.** (shen-neel) Embroidery originating in France using fine chenille yarn with flat stitches producing a soft, velvet-like pattern.

**Chinese e.** Single- or double-faced embroidery which usually covers entire robe or gown with motifs of cherry blossoms, birds, butterflies, and dragons. Done in satin, chain, French knots, feather, and other stitches with silk, gold or silver threads in an elaborate and intricate design. Originally floss and metal threads were worked over a painted design.

**Colbert e.** (col-bare) Embroidery made with colored threads outlining the designs and background covered with an allover pattern done in the satin stitch.

**couched e.** Raised embroidery done by arranging threads or cords in a pattern on fabric and securing with small stitches.

**counted cross-stitch e.** Embroidery done on *aida cloth* using cross-stitch worked with embroidery floss. Design is made by following a graph pattern.

**crewel work** Coarse embroidery made with heavy colored yarns, usually of loosely twisted two-ply worsted, on a heavy plain-weave fabric. Motifs *e.g.*, leaves and flowers, are filled in with many types of stitches.

**cross-stitch e.** Embroidered x's made in a colored pattern on a plain ground.

**cushion-style e.** Canvas embroidery worked in an allover pattern. Also see BERLIN WORK.

**cut work** **1.** Embroidery made by cutting designs out of fabric and embroidering the cut edges with the purl stitch. Bars are frequently used to connect the larger areas. **2.** Term used in mid-14th through 15th c. to refer to *dagging*, or a dagged border of a garment, *e.g.*, motifs such as leaves, flames, and scallops were used.

**Czechoslovakian e.** Bright-colored cotton, silk, or wool threads worked in geometric designs on linen. Made by counting stitches or using a traced pattern.

**Delhi work** Chain- and satin-stitch embroidery made in India with metal and silk threads on satin or other fabrics.

**drawn work** Openwork embroidery made by removing some threads in each direction of the fabric and interlacing remaining yarns with simple embroidery stitches. Also see FAGOTING in alphabetical listing.

**Dresden point** German lace of drawn work type introduced in the late 16th c., on linen. Some of the threads are taken out and some left to form a pattern. Others were worked to form square meshes. After the pattern was made, it was embroidered with intricate stitchery.

**English e.** See MADEIRA EMBROIDERY.

**English work** Excellent quality of embroidery done by Anglo Saxon women from 7th to 10th c. Highly prized in England and on the Continent. Also called *opus Anglicum*.

**eyelet e.** Holes punched out and embroidery worked around the hole, by hand or on a Schiffli machine. Also see MADEIRA EMBROIDERY.

**flame e.** Canvas embroidery done in zigzag patterns of colored yarn. Also see FLORENTINE EMBROIDERY.

**Florentine e.** Embroidery done on canvas in zigzag patterns and in shaded colors. Also called FLAME EMBROIDERY, from the effect it achieved, or HUNGARIAN POINT EMBROIDERY.

**Genoese e.** Embroidery done by buttonhole-stitching over a cord on muslin or linen, then cutting fabric away from between parts of the design. Formerly used for dress and undergarment trimmings.

**gimped e.** Embroidery where the design is achieved by arranging cord or vellum on fabric and covering with silk or gold threads. Also called LAID EMBROIDERY.

**grass e.** Native American embroidery using colored grasses as threads usually done on deerskins.

**gros point** (groh pwanh) Canvas embroidery worked from right to left, working over double threads through large meshes of canvas. The same stitch worked over single threads is called *petit point*.

**hardanger e.** Needlework made in diamond or square patterns on coarse linen or open canvas. A part of the material is cut and threads are pulled out between stitches to make designs native to Norway.

**hemstitching 1.** Embroidery in which several parallel yarns are removed from the fabric and fine stitches used to catch group of three or four cross threads at regular intervals giving an even openwork arrangement. **2.** This type of embroidery done at the edge of the hem, holds and decorates at the same time.

**Holbein work** (hole-bine) Delicate reversible outline embroidery done in double-running stitch using exact geometrical or conventional designs. Popular for trimming in the 16th c. *Der.* Named after the painter Hans Holbein (1465–1524) because design was so frequently shown on his paintings. Also called *Rumanian embroidery*.

**holy work/hollie work** Fancy work in lace, cut work, and embroidery carried out in religious subjects. Used in late 16th c. and by Puritans mainly in the 17th c. to decorate shirts, smocks, wristbands, and neckbands.

**huckaback e.** Darned-type of embroidery done on huckaback toweling by working horizontal stitches between surface yarns of the toweling.

**Hungarian e. 1.** Brightly colored peasant garments and linens embroidered in conventional designs in flat or chainstitch on Hungarian peasant costumes. **2.** A type of appliqué done on blue, scarlet, or ecru linen.

**Hungarian point** Zigzag designs done on canvas, same as FLORENTINE EMBROIDERY.

**Indian e.** Oriental embroidery including embroidery on cloth, CASHMERE WORK, QUILTING, and CHAINSTITCH embroidery done by East Indian natives.

**inverted-T e.** See MATHILDE EMBROIDERY.

**inverted-Y e.** See MATHILDE EMBROIDERY.

**Japanese e.** Elaborate embroidery worked with colored silk or metallic threads in satin stitch forming an intricate design or scene. Also includes padded and shaded embroidery.

**laid e.** Obsolete term for *gimped embroidery* which was used primarily for court robes and military uniforms. See GIMPED EMBROIDERY.

**liquid e.** Not actually embroidery, but color applied to fabric with ballpoint-shaped paint tubes in special colors. Paint is squeezed from the tube to outline designs on a cloth. Creates a permanent and washable design resembling colored-thread embroidery. When seen at a distance, gives the general effect of embroidery.

**Madeira e.** (ma-deer-a) *Eyelet embroidery* cut or punched and then overcast. Made with openings arranged in floral or conventional designs on fine lawn or linen. Also called BRODERIE ANGLAISE, *Ayrshire*, *English*, or *Swiss embroidery*. *Der.* From Island of Madeira where work was originally done by nuns.

**Mathilde e.** Wide vertical band of embroidery used on front of woman's dress in early 19th c. Later a band added around hem of dress and the combination with vertical band called an *inverted-T* or *inverted-Y*.

**Moravian work** Type of cotton embroidery known from about 1850 as BRODERIE ANGLAISE. Also see MADEIRA EMBROIDERY.

**needlepoint** Allover wool embroidery worked on open canvas with yarn in a variety of tapestry stitches either horizontally across the rows or diagonally making it double-faced. Used for slippers, vests, and handbags. Regular-

sized stitches called *gros point*, small stitches called *petit point.*

**needle tapestry work** Embroidery worked in a variety of stitches on canvas to resemble woven tapestries.

**net e.** See TULLE EMBROIDERY.

**openwork** Embroidery made by drawing, cutting, or pulling aside threads of fabric to form open spaces in the design.

**opus Anglicum** See ENGLISH WORK.

**petit point** Canvas embroidery worked from right to left, working over single threads through large meshes. The same stitch worked over double threads is called *gros point.*

**Philippine e.** Handmade embroidery done in dainty floral motifs by native women in the Philippine Islands. Used on lingerie.

**piqué e.** (pee-kay) Embroidery worked on firm fabric with white thread using corded outlines and various filling stitches. Used formerly for children's garments.

**pulled work** See PUNCH WORK.

**punch/punched work** Embroidery of openwork type made by pulling certain threads aside with a needle or stiletto and securing them with embroidery stitches. Also called *pulled work.*

**raised e.** Embroidery done in the satin stitch over padding stitches to give a raised effect in the design. Used for monograms, scallops, etc. If heavily padded called STUMP WORK.

**rococo e.** Type of embroidery made with very narrow ribbon, often called *China ribbon.*

**Rumanian e.** See HOLBEIN WORK.

**Russian e.** **1.** Embroidery done mainly in outline designs on Holland linen. **2.** Cloth and canvas embroidered with wool. Then canvas is removed to leave embroidery on background of cloth.

**Schiffli e.** A form of shuttle embroidery done by a Schiffli machine that can embroider the entire width of fabric at one time, in either elaborate or simple designs. Both eyelet and quilted designs may be made in many colors simultaneously.

**seed e.** Type of German embroidery done with seeds for floral motifs and chenille yarn for stems and leaves, formerly used for handbags.

**shadow e.** Embroidery worked with a catch stitch on the wrong side of transparent fabric.

**Sicilian e.** See SPANISH EMBROIDERY.

**Spanish e. 1.** Muslin worked with herringbone filling stitches. **2.** Lacelike embroidery made on muslin or cambric with braid and closely placed buttonhole stitches. Also called *Sicilian embroidery.*

**stump work** Embroidery in high relief due to much padding, sometimes using horsehair, covered with satin stitches. Subjects are Biblical or allegorical scenes in grotesque shapes carried out with complicated stitchery. Also called RAISED EMBROIDERY.

**Swiss e.** See MADEIRA EMBROIDERY.

**tambour work** (tam-boor) Double drum-shaped frame used to hold embroidery worked with a hooked needle and a stitch similar to the chain stitch. Originally used in Eastern embroideries, replaced by *chainstitch embroidery.*

**tulle e.** Floss silk used on tulle, a net-like fabric, either by darning or by using embroidery stitches on a traced paper design. Formerly used for trimming party dresses.

**Venetian ladder work** Outline embroidery done with two parallel lines of buttonhole stitches connected with cross-stitches at intervals in ladder-style. Used mainly for border work in conventional designs.

**Yugoslavian e.** Bright-colored wool used on coarse linen in geometrical designs, done by counting threads, mainly in cross-stitch, double-purl, slanting, or satin stitch. Also spelled *Jugoslavian.*

**embroidery crash/linen** See ART LINEN.

**emerald** See GEMS.

**emerald cut** See GEM CUTS.

**emerizing** Fabric passed through rollers covered with emery that brush up a nap producing a surface resembling SUEDE or CHAMOIS.

**emperor** Lining material of Great Britain made in a twill weave of fine cotton warp with alpaca or luster worsted yarns in the filling.

**emperor shirt** A country gentleman's shirt of red flannel worn in the 1850s and 1860s.

**empiecement** Trimming effect with outer fabric cut away and edges embroidered to show a sheer fabric underneath. Popular in late 19th and early 20th c.

**Empire bodice** (ohm-peer) Dress bodice of late 1880s giving a short-waisted effect by arranging several silk scarfs around the waist and tying them on one side or in the back.

**Empire bonnet** (ohm-peer) Small outdoor bonnet of 1860s shaped like a baby's cap with no veil or curtains in back. Also called *Empire cap.*

**Empire coat** (ohm-peer) Woman's three-quarter to full-length coat of early 1900s worn for traveling or evening wear. Made with a full skirt of large unpressed pleats attached to a high waistline. Bodice is cut somewhat like an *Eton jacket* with large lapels and a standing *Medici collar.*

**Empire coiffure** (ohm-peer) Hairstyle worn in 1860s with curls in Greek manner around the face, and a band of narrow ribbon wrapped three times around the head. The back is done in a large CHIGNON with narrow ribbon wrapped around it several times ending with two ribbon streamers down the back.

**Empire cone hairstyle** See HAIRSTYLES.

**Empire dress** (ohm-peer) See DRESSES. Also see EMPIRE STYLES.

**EMPIRE HOUSE GOWN, 1895**

**Empire house gown** (ohm-peer) *Negligee* of mid-1890s with high collar and tucked yoke crossed with ribbons tied in bow at center front. Gown was floor length and fell in folds from yoke, with three-quarter length sleeves, trimmed with ruffle at wrist.

**Empire jacket** (ohm-peer) Square-yoked woman's jacket of mid-1890s made with *Medici collar*, large box pleats in front and back, and large balloon sleeves. Also called a *box coat*.

**Empire jupon** (ohm-peer zhu-pon) Gored petticoat, very full at the hem where two or three steel hoops were inserted, worn under the *Empire dress* of 1867 instead of the *cage petticoat*. Also called *Empire petticoat. Der.* Fashion of Second Empire of Napoleon III, 1852–1870.

**Empire petticoat** See EMPIRE JUPON.

**Empire silhouette** See SILHOUETTES.

**Empire skirt** (ohm-peer) **1.** Evening skirt with *train* worn in late 1880s and 1890s set on waistband with gathers and finished with wide hem ruffle. *Steels* or *half hoops* were inserted in back of skirt. **2.** Daytime skirt with ruffled flounce at hem that had a front and back panel and a triangular gore on each side. Worn from 1888 into 1890s. **3.** High-waisted skirt extending to just below the bust. **4.** See SKIRTS.

**Empire stays** (ohm-peer) Short high-waisted corset, forerunner of the bra, laced in back for wear with high-waisted *Empire dresses* in the 1890s.

**Empire styles** (ohm-peer) **1.** First Empire—Costumes worn during the First Empire in France, 1804–1815, under the reign of Napoleon I. Men wore tight-fitting Kerseymere, cassimere, or cashmere breeches; double-breasted jackets with high NAPOLEON COLLARS, short, single-breasted waistcoats—cut straight at hem—and cravats or neck cloths. Women wore high-waisted dresses with low square necklines on front and back, tiny puffed sleeves, SPENCER JACKETS, and bonnets. Also see DRESSES and WAISTLINES. **2.** Second Empire—See EUGÉNIE, EMPRESS.

**Empress Eugénie hat** See EUGÉNIE HAT.

**Empress Josephine** See JOSEPHINE, EMPRESS OF FRANCE.

**Empress Josephine gown** High-waisted dress with *surplice bodice*, full sleeves, sash ends hanging from inserted belt, and gathered skirt. Worn in the 1890s with a FIGARO JACKET. Inspired by dress of the First Empire in France.

**Empress petticoat** Evening petticoat substituted for the *cage petticoat* in mid-1860s. Made in gores to fit tightly at the waist and spread to eight yards at the hem, forming a train a yard long, and finished with a full gathered flounce beginning at the knees.

**enameling duck** Coated DUCK fabric used for oilcloth and imitation leather. Made in widths varying from 38″ to 90″ and also in a variety of weights.

**end** **1.** An individual WARP YARN, single, ply, or cord. **2.** A remnant or short piece of fabric.

**end-and-end** Men's shirting fabric with a fine colored yarn in one direction forming a pinstripe or used in both directions for checks. Usually made with a colored warp alternating with white warp. Used widely for men's shirt fabrics. *Der.* An alternate name for WARP, called *end.*

**endangered species** Term used for animals and birds which are becoming rare because of slaughter of animals for clothing, accessories, adornment, and other reasons. Animals include tigers. Birds include the *egret* and eagle. Several states and the U.S. federal government have passed protective laws. For protective legislation concerning furs see FURS. Also see AUDUBON PLUMAGE LAW.

**engageantes** 1. French term for two or three tiers of lace, or sheer-fabric ruffles, used as cuffs on sleeves from end of 17th through 18th c. 2. Detachable undersleeves, of white fabric edged with lace or embroidery, worn by women from 1840s until about 1865. Also see ISABEAU SLEEVE.

**engagement ring** See RINGS.

**engineer's boot** See BOOTS.

**engineer's cap** See CAPS.

**engineer's cloth** British term for fabrics similar to DUNGAREE. Used for work clothes.

**English chain** Form of CHATELAINE—a strand of twisted wire with attached watch, tweezer case, or other small object worn by women in early 19th c.

**English coat** 1. Woman's double-breasted three-quarter-length jacket of 1890s made somewhat like a *pea jacket* with lapels and flapped pockets. 2. Full-length coat of 1890s sometimes made with elbow-length cape.

**English cottage bonnet** See BIBI BONNET.

**English drape** 1. Style used for man's single- or double-breasted long suit jacket in 1930s and 1940s. Distinguished by fullness at top of tapered sleeve, width through the chest, and fitted waist. Worn with trousers made with

**ENGLISH DRAPE, 1930–1940**

high-rise waistline and pleats at side front. 2. Similar style jacket adopted for women's suits in 1930s and 1940s; revived in 1980s.

**English embroidery** See MADEIRA EMBROIDERY under EMBROIDERIES.

**English farthingale** Drum-shaped farthingale of 1580s to 1620s consisting of a BOURRELET or BUM ROLL around the waist permitting the skirt to hang straight down in the shape of a barrel. Also called *drum* or *tambour farthingale.*

**English hood** Woman's headdress worn from 1500s to 1540s, sometimes made of black fabric wired to form a peak or gable over the forehead with long velvet lappets at side and the back draped in thick folds over the shoulders. After 1525, the back drapery became two long pendant flaps. Also called GABLE and *pediment headdress,* by 19th c. writers. (See illustration under GABLE HEADDRESS.)

**English rib socks** See SOCKS.

**English thumb** See BOLTEN THUMB.

**English walking jacket** Woman's jacket of mid-1870s made in single-breasted style with lapels. Unfitted in front but fitted at waistline in back flaring to form a peplum. Sleeves with large turned-back cuffs.

**English work** See MADEIRA EMBROIDERY under EMBROIDERIES.

**English wrap**  Man's double-breasted *paletot sac* worn in 1840s, similar to a loose CHESTER-FIELD COAT.

**ensemble** (ahn-sahm-bl)  **1.** The entire costume, including accessories, worn at one time. **2.** More than one item of clothing designed and coordinated to be worn together. See DRESSES and REDINGOTE.

**en tablier**  Trimming arranged in crosswise rows of lace or ribbon spaced down front panel of dress, sometimes from neck to hem or from waist to hem. Used particularly in 19th c. *Der.* French, *tablier,* "apron."

**entari**  Ankle-length gown, with a rather full skirt and a sash at waistline, usually made of striped silk. Worn particularly by Hebrew men and women in Turkey, Palestine, Syria, and India in 19th c.

**en tous cas** (on too kah)  Nickname for a parasol, which could also be used as an umbrella, carried about 1870. *Der.* French, "in any case."

**entre deux** (on-tray do)  Fine narrow openwork insertion set into the seams of dainty lingerie used from late 19th c. until mid-1930s.

**envelope combination**  Man's *undershirt* and *drawers* combined into one garment—a type of loose-fitting *union suit*—with open double fold in the back. Worn in the 1920s and 1930s the best-known trade name for this garment was *B.V.D.*®

**envelope handbag**  See HANDBAGS.

**envelope pleat**  See PLEATS.

**envoy hat**  See HATS.

**eoliene/eolienne**  Lightweight ribbed fabric made in a plain weave with fine silk warp. Heavier worsted yarns form a rib in the filling. Formerly a very lightweight dress fabric made in a twill weave with organzine warp and different colored worsted yarns in the filling. *Der.* Greek God, Eolus, the god of the winds. Also spelled *aeolian.*

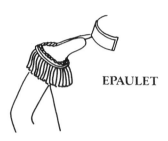

EPAULET

**epaulet** (ep-eh-let)  **1.** Ornamental shoulder trim used on military uniforms, originally consisting of gold braid looped to form fringe around the edge. **2.** Shoulder trim used in 19th c., very popular in 1860s. **3.** Flat band of fabric, sometimes fastened with a button on shoulders of uniforms; also used on military-style civilian coats and jackets, *e.g.,* TRENCHCOATS. Very fashionable in 1980s on blouses, coats, dresses, shirts, and jackets. Also spelled *epaulette.* Also see SHIRTS, SHOULDERS, and SLEEVES. **4.** See EPAULIÈRE.

**epaulière** (ep-eh-leer)  Armor consisting of single piece of unarticulated shoulder plate, first worn about 1300, smaller in size than the PAULDRON. Also called EPAULET and *shoulder cop.*

**ephebi** (ef-he-be)  Military cape similar to the CHLAMYS, worn by Greek soldiers.

**épinard** (eh-pi-nar)  Soft dark-green color. *Der.* French, "spinach."

**épinglé** (eh-pang-gl)  Fine, lustrous, dress fabric with fine ribs running either warpwise or fillingwise. Ribs may alternate in size or color being either small or large. Originally made in silk, it is now made of fine worsted or man-made yarns. *Der.* French, "pin."

**epitoga**  **1.** Originally an ancient Roman cloak worn over the toga sometimes having bell-shaped sleeves. **2.** Cloak of the 13th c. similar to above but cut more like a robe and worn as academic dress. Also called *chausse.* **3.** The medieval hood reduced to symbolic form as a part of academic and ceremonial robes. **4.** A hood covering only the shoulders worn by French officials for ceremonial dress.

**épomine hood**   See EPITOGA.

**éponge**   (eh-pongh)  Spongy woolen fabric made in the plain weave with plain yarn in one direction and a novelty yarn in the other. *Der.* French, *éponge,* "spongy."

**equestrienne costume**   Term used for riding habit for women from about 1840s. Consisted of a full-length gathered skirt worn with a tailored jacket, sometimes double-breasted with revers and peplum. Accessories included a tall TOP HAT with veiling hanging down the back, a tailored shirt, and necktie or STOCK. In early 20th c. skirt was uneven in length—shorter on right side, longer on left—looped up when walking, let down when mounted sidesaddle. By 1908 drill breeches and boots were worn under a short skirt. A DERBY, FEDORA, TRICORN, or SAILOR HAT was worn over a braided club hairstyle. By 1910 or 1912 women rode astride wearing a divided skirt which buttoned closed in front. Also see RIDING HABIT under SPORT SUITS. *Der.* Latin, "woman skilled in horsemanship."

**equipage**   See ETUI.

**eria**   Wild silk from Pakistan and East India, which is uneven and coarse like TUSSAH silk. Used for SPUN SILK.

**ermine**   See FURS.

**ermine cap**   See LETTICE CAP.

**erogenous zone theory**   (e-roj-e-nus)  Theory expounded by James Laver, noted British authority on historical costume, that emphasis in dress tends to shift from one erogenous zone of the body to another, *e.g.,* when short hemlines are worn, the legs are in focus; when plunging necklines are worn, the bosom or breasts are emphasized. The cycle is about seven years between shifts of interest from zone to zone.

**Erté**   (1892– )  Fashion designer and costume illustrator of timeless, daring, flamboyant creations touched with fantasy. Strongly influenced public taste in feminine beauty during period 1915 to 1936 by designing 240 covers for *Harper's Bazaar.* Styles were sometimes bizarre and romantically inviting, but always highly imaginative, theatrical, and unique. Faded to obscurity and returned to high popularity in 1980s by designing an imaginative line of limited edition knitwear for MagiFrance® in 1985. Born Romain de Tirtoff in St. Petersburg (Leningrad), he settled in Paris in 1912 where he took his present name from pronunciation of his initials in French (air-tay).

**escarelle**   (es-ka-rel)  Pouch or purse attached to a waist or hip belt in the 14th and 15th c. into which a knife was frequently thrust.

**esclavage**   Mid-18th c. term for a necklace composed of several rows of gold chain which fell in swags over the bosom. *Der.* French, "slave."

**Eskimo cloth**   Heavy, napped, overcoating fabric either dyed in plain colors or woven in horizontal stripes. Made in either satin or twill weave.

**Esmeralda cloak**   Waterproof wrap of the late 1860s worn in U.S. Introduced from Paris in both plain and tartan designs. In England, worn only in the rain; in Paris, the basic paletot with two capes, had no sleeves, and was ornamented with bows, frills, fringe, satin braid, and rosettes.

**espadrille**   See SHOES.

**Estrella du Sud diamond**   See STAR OF THE SOUTH under DIAMONDS.

**étamine**   Lightweight fabric made with an open weave of coarse tightly twisted yarns. Made in many different qualities and of various fibers. Used for sportswear and sport jackets. *Der.* French, "sieve" (originally fabric was used as a sifting cloth).

**etched-out fabric**   See BURNT-OUT FABRIC.

**eternity ring**   See RINGS.

**Ethiopian shirtdress**   See DRESSES.

**ethnic**   During the second half of the 1960s all types of native clothing, particularly from the East and Near East, were introduced and worn. From Africa—the *dashiki, buba, seloso, djellaba, caftan,* and *burnoose.* From India—the *kurta, usha,* and *choori-dars.* From Pakistan—the *Pakistani wedding vest.* From Japan—adaptations of *karate, judo,* and *kimono* styles. From China—*cheongsam* and *pajamas.* Also see PEASANT and HAREM LOOKS under LOOK.

**Eton cap**   Close-fitting cap with a short visor, modeled after those worn at Eton College in England. Popular in fabrics to match coats for young boys in the U.S. in 1920s and 1930s.

**Eton collar**   See COLLARS.

**Eton crop**   See HAIRSTYLES.

**Eton jacket**   See JACKETS and ETON SUIT.

**Eton jacket bodice**   Woman's waist-length jacket similar to boy's Eton jacket worn open in front over a waistcoat in 1889. In the late 1890s the front was trimmed with braid and frogs and rounded at waistline.

**ETON SUIT**

**Eton suit**   Uniform worn by junior school-boys at Eton College, Eton, Buckinghamshire, England, from 1798 until 1967, consisting of a waist-length square-cut jacket with wide lapels and small turned-down collar. Worn with a white shirt having a white starched collar, nar-row dark tie, and single-breasted vest. Jacket was originally blue or red, becoming black in 1820 when mourning for George III; trousers were usually gray. Adaptation became a peren-nial dress-up suit for very young boys in U.S. and England from late 19th through early 20th c. Also see ETON JACKET under JACKETS.

**être á la mode**   French, "to be in fashion."

**etui** (a-twe)   An ornamental case worn hang-ing from the waist by women in the 17th and 18th c., to hold thimble, scissors, or scent bottle. Also called *equipage.*

**Eugénia, The**   Voluminous woman's cape of early 1860s, of seven-eighths length. Usually black with second cape reaching to waist in back and shorter in front. Both capes were edged with fancy box-pleated ribbon.

**Eugénie collarette**   Crocheted collar of late 1860s made in two-tone yoke effect, pointed in center back and front, and closed in center front with loops and buttons. *Der.* Named for EMPRESS EUGÉNIE.

**Eugénie dress**   Full skirted dress of 1850s made with three-tiered skirt, tight fitting waist, and short or PAGODA style sleeves. *Der.* Named for EMPRESS EUGÉNIE.

**Eugénie, Empress** (oo-jshe-ne)   Marie Eugé-nie de Montijo de Guzmán (1826–1920), wife of Napoleon III, and Empress of France (1853–1871), exerted great influence on fashion dur-ing the Age of Crinoline, with her constant desire for innovations. *Worth* was her couturier and is credited with designing the PRINCESS STYLE DRESS for the Empress.

**Eugénie hat**   Small hat, with brim rolled back on either side, popular in 1930s. Worn tilted sideways and to the front, and often trimmed with one long ostrich plume in the side roll. *Der.* Named for EMPRESS EUGÉNIE.

**Eugénie paletot**   **1.** Tailored three-quarter-length woman's coat of 1860s made in unfitted double-breasted style with notched collar and bell sleeves having false cuffs. The sides of cuffs and rounded patch pockets were decorated with buttons. **2.** Shorter length sack-type jacket, collarless or with a small collar, closing at neck with one button. *Der.* Named for EMPRESS EUGÉNIE.

**Eugénie petticoat** Petticoat worn in the early 1870s made full-length in back and a little below waist in front. Semicircular steel *hoops* in the back and *bustle* held out skirt in the back. *Der.* Named for EMPRESS EUGÉNIE.

**even checks** See CHECKERBOARD under CHECKS.

**evening** Clothes worn primrily in the evening especially for formal and informal occasions. See FORMAL DRESS under DRESSES, PETTICOATS, SHOES, SKIRTS, SLIPS, EVENING WRAP, and SWALLOW-TAILED COAT under COATS. Also see FORMAL ATTIRE and TUXEDO.

**even twill weave** Twill or diagonal weave which produces wales of equal sizes.

**evening wrap** **1.** Wrap worn for formal functions, may be styled like a shawl, a cape, a stole, or a coat. **2.** See COATS.

**even plaid** See PLAIDS.

**Everett** See SLIPPERS.

**Everglaze®** See CHINTZ.

**examining gown** Simple wraparound gown, or one slit up the back and fastened with ties, used by patients in doctors' offices. Originally made in coarse muslin, now in disposable materials.

**exercise sandals** See SCHOLL'S® EXERCISE SANDALS under SANDALS.

**exercise shorts** See ATHLETIC SHORTS under SHORTS.

**exercise suit** See SAUNA SUIT under SPORT SUITS.

**expandable bracelet** See BRACELETS.

**express stripes** Sturdy fabric, similar to denim, woven with dyed yarns in warpwise even stripes. Usually made in the twill weave with twelve white warps—then twelve indigo-blue warps with a white or unbleached filling. Used for sportswear and workclothes. Also see STRIPES.

**extended shoulder** See SHOULDERS.

**extract printing** See DISCHARGE PRINTING.

**extra large** **1.** Size range used along with SMALL, MEDIUM, and LARGE for women's sweaters, housecoats, nightgowns, panties, girdles, and panty girdles. **2.** Size for men's sport shirts, sport jackets, sweaters, and robes.

**extra long knit shirt** See KNIT SHIRTS.

**extra-tall** Men's size corresponding to a chest measurement of 38″ to 48″ and a height of 6′3″ to 6′6½″.

**extruded latex** Round elastomeric yarn made by forcing latex into a coagulating bath and drawing off solid round yarn.

**eye agate** See AGATE under GEMS.

**eyelet** **1.** Circular metal ring pressed through fabric or leather and cinched on garments or shoes, through which a lacer is pulled; first used about 1828. See BLIND EYELET. **2.** Punched holes embroidered in fabrics for lacings or as decoration. Also see BUTTONHOLES and EMBROIDERIES. **3.** Embroidered cloth with allover embroidered pattern made on the Schiffli machine on fabrics such as batiste, lawn, or piqué. Also called EYELET EMBROIDERY.

**ezor** An item of apparel mentioned in the Bible, Book of Isaiah, as worn by Hebrews. Believed to have been a loincloth although often translated later as a girdle. Also see KÉTHONETH and SIMLAH.

**fabala** See FURBELOW.

**Fabergé, Carl** (1846–1920) (Russian name Karl Gustavovich.) Russian goldsmith, jeweler, and brilliant designer, who used precious and semi-precious gems, *e.g.,* jade, lapis lazuli, and malachite—plus gold and silver to make conventional jewelry and gift objects of fantasy including celebrated Easter eggs commissioned by Czars Alexander III and Nicholas II of Russia. Also made ingenious and exquisite masterpieces of flowers, figure groups, animals, and bibelots. Established workshops in Moscow, Kiev, and London. Inherited family business in 1870 which he operated until Russian Revolution of 1917. Died in exile in Switzerland.

**fabric** Cloth made of textile yarns by weaving, knitting, lace making, braiding, netting, or felting. Also cloth made by bonding or nonwoven methods. *Der.* Latin *fabrica,* "workshop."

**fabric count** See COUNT OF CLOTH.

**fabric finishes—basic** The processes required to convert gray (or greige) goods into final fabric by mechanical or chemical means. These processes include *beetling, brushing, calendering, crimping, embossing, glazing, mercerizing, moiréing, napping, pressing, printing, singeing, sizing,* and *starching.* Also see FABRIC FINISHES—SPECIAL.

**fabric finishes—special** Treatments applied to fabrics to suit them to specific uses. These treatments include crease resistance, flame resistance, mildew resistance, moth repellent, shrinkage control, waterproofing, water repellent, wrinkle resistance (durable press). Also see FABRIC FINISHES—BASIC.

**face** Right side of fabric with better appearance—as opposed to back, or reverse side. Some fabrics are reversible and may be used on both sides.

**face cone** Long megaphone-type cone held over face while wig was being powdered in 18th c. Also see POWDERING JACKET.

**faced hem** See HEMS.

**face-finished fabric** Textile industry term applied to fabrics finished on right side or FACE of fabric, *e.g., chinchilla, bouclé,* and *melton.*

**facet** Jewelry term for a small plane cut in a gemstone to enhance its ability to reflect light—the more facets, the more brilliance.

**facing** Sewing term for self-fabric lining used on curved or irregularly shaped area of garment, *e.g.,* neckline, lapels, collars, cuffs, or hem. Also called *parament.*

**facing silk** Term for fabrics such as silk, rayon, heavy satin, and grosgrain used primarily for facing lapels of men's formal wear or for linings.

**façonné** (fa-so-nay) French term for figured fabrics with Jacquard designs, usually small. Term sometimes applied to Jacquard fabrics.

**façonné velvet** (fa-so-nay) Pile fabric with a pattern design made by the BURNT-OUT FABRIC method.

**facts** See FAX

**fad** Short-lived fashion that becomes suddenly extremely popular, remains for a short period of time, and fades quickly.

**Fade-Ometer®** Trade name for textile laboratory machine that tests amount of light that fabric can take before color changes or fading occurs.

**fading** Loss of color in fabrics from exposure to light from washing, dry cleaning, or from ordinary household fumes. Also see FUME FADING.

**fagoting** **1.** Open-work embroidery done by drawing out horizontal threads of a fabric, then tying the vertical threads in groups to produce open spaces. **2.** Method of joining two fabric edges together by means of embroidery stitches to produce a lacelike effect. Also see HEM-STITCHING and FAGOTING under STITCHES. British spelling is *fagotting*.

**faïence**   Small pieces of glazed pottery in rich colors fitted together to form large circular collars by Egyptians.

**faille** (fie)   Fabric with a flat-ribbed effect running fillingwise which is flatter and less pronounced than *grosgrain*. Warps are finer and there are more of them in order to cover the heavier filling yarns. Originally made in silk—now made of silk, wool, cotton, man-made, yarns, or combinations of yarns. Used for women's suits and dresses, robes, trimmings, and hats.

**faille crepe**   Fabric with a fillingwise flat rib similar to *faille*, but lighter in weight, used for dresses. Made in silk and man-made fabrics.

**Fair Isle sweater**   See SWEATERS.

**fairy stone**   See GEMS.

**faja**   Broad brilliant-colored sash of silk worn by men in Spain and Latin America as a part of their native dress.

**fake fur**   Soft pile fabric made to imitate fur. Name is a misnomer as the word "fur" should not be used; correct term *furlike fabric*.

**fake fur coat**   See COATS.

**falbala**   See FURBELOW.

**falbala wig**   See DUVILLIER WIG.

**faldetta**   **1.** Native headdress of Malta consisting of hood and cape in one piece made of black silk with stiffened whalebone hood making an arched frame for face. **2.** Waist-length colored taffeta women's mantle trimmed with wide lace ruffle worn in 1850.

**fall**   **1.** Long straight hairpiece fastened to head with ribbon headband or pinned in place so that it hangs down over natural hair. Popular in late 1960s. Purchased by length; short length

**FALL #1**

fall is called a *mini fall*; shoulder-length fall is called a *midi fall*; and long-length fall is called a *maxi fall*. **2.** A collar, same as FALLING BAND.

**fal-lals**   Term for any trifling decoration on a garment or accessory, *e.g.*, ribbons and bows, used from 17th c. on.

**FALLING BAND**

**falling band**   Large flat turned-down collar attached to the shirt, later made as a separate collar. Usually edged with lace and worn instead of the *ruff* by men and women from 1540s to 1670s. Also called a *fall*.

**falling ruff**   Unstarched *ruff* falling around the neck in unregulated folds. Worn in England from about 1615 to 1640 by men and women. Worn by men in France during reign of Henry IV (1589–1610) and then called *fraise à la confusion*.

**falling tucker**   Fabric fill-in hanging over front of low-cut bodice of gown in early 19th c. Also see TUCKER.

**fall lift**   Late 1960s term for dome-shaped piece of wire mesh placed under the hair, frequently used when wearing a hairpiece called a FALL.

**falls** Term for the front opening of men's trousers from 1730 on, *e.g.*, *whole falls* were flaps extending across front to side seams; *small* or *split falls* meant a central flap similar to that formerly used on SAILOR PANTS. Also see SPAIR.

**false bosoms** Term introduced in early 1800s for padding used to extend the bust. Also see BOSOM FRIEND, BUST IMPROVERS, and FALSIES.

**false calves** Padding inserted in men's stockings to make legs more shapely—worn during 17th, 18th, and 19th c. Also see DOWNY CALVES.

**false doublet** Jewelry industry term for stone made from two pieces cemented at the girdle—a genuine stone for the *crown* or top, and a cheaper stone or glass is used for the *pavilion* or bottom part.

**false eyelashes** Eyelashes made of synthetic fibers or animal hair attached to a very narrow band that is fastened to the eyelid with adhesive. Each lash may also be glued in place by a skilled technician.

**false face** See MASKS.

**false gown** **1.** 18th-c. woman's dress style borrowed from dresses worn by little girls in France featuring a tight bodice, gathered skirt, and wide ribbon sash. **2.** Dress worn during French Revolution made without PANIERS and tight bodice with skirt which was not split in front.

**false hips** Term used for side hoops or *paniers* worn in England from the 1740s to 1760s. (Term PANIERS was not used in England in 18th c.) Also see *oblong hoops*.

**false rump** See RUMP FURBELOW.

**false hanging sleeve** See HANGING SLEEVE #2.

**falsies** Bust pads, usually of foam rubber, inserted into bra to give a fuller appearance. Originally made in 19th c. of lace ruffles and sometimes called *fluffy ruffles* or *gay deceivers*. Height of popularity was in 1950s when a large bosom was the desired shape.

**family ring** See RINGS.

**fan** A hand-held implement for creating a breeze. Made rigid—either wedge-shaped, round, flat. Some were pleated, collapsible, and attached to a handle. Made of carved ivory in early Egypt, China, and Japan. In common use by women in the Western world from mid-16th c. Made of paper, fabric, lace, tortoise shell, feathers, hand-painted silk, or woven palm. The fan was considered a weapon for coquetry with definite rules for flirtation from 17th through 19th c. Also see DUCK'S FOOT FAN and FOLDING FAN.

**fan-backed dress** See DRESSES.

**fanchon** (fan-shon) Small lace-trimmed head scarf, or the lace trimming on sides of an outdoor bonnet or day cap, worn from 1830s on.

**FANCHON CAP**

**fanchon cap** (fan-shon) Small indoor cap of tulle or lace with side pieces covering the ears worn by women from 1840s to 1860s.

**fancies** Term used from 1650s to 1670s for ribbon trimmings used on men's *petticoat breeches* or other types of open-legged breeches.

**fan collar** Standing collar of Elizabethan times shaped like an open fan, and placed at back of neck. Usually lace-edged, starched, and wired to stand up.

**fancy diamond**  See DIAMONDS.

**fancy leather**  Industry term for leather having a natural grain or a distinctive pattern, *e.g.,* alligator, lizard, and snakeskin. Also includes embossed effects simulating reptile patterns or leathers given a decorative finish, *e.g.,* metallic kid.

**fancy sapphire**  See CORUNDUM under GEMS.

**fancy work**  Type of EMBROIDERY or needlework. See EMBROIDERIES.

**fan hoop**  HOOP petticoat, cone-shaped but compressed front and back, mentioned in England in 1713 but not popular until 1740s and 1750s.

**fanny sweater**  See SWEATERS.

**fanons**  Two decorative LAPPETS, attached to back of *miter*, worn by the Pope, which hung down over the shoulders. These may originally have been used to hold the miter on the head.

**fan pleat**  See ACCORDION PLEAT under PLEATS.

**fantail hat**  *Tricorn* hat with wide brim, *cocked* or turned up at sides, with point in front; the back somewhat shaped semicircular resembling a fan. Worn in the last quarter of 18th c. by men and women for horseback riding.

**fantail wig**  Man's wig of early 18th c. with QUEUE hanging loose in many small curls in back.

**fan tucks**  See SUNBURST TUCKS.

**farasia**  See CAFTAN #1.

**farmer's satin**  **1.** Glossy durable lining fabric used for men's suits. Made with a cotton warp with a worsted, rayon, or cotton filling in the satin weave. **2.** Term sometimes used for *Italian cloth* and *Venetian cloth.*

**farous**  Loincloth worn in Iraq.

**farthingale**  Woman's coarse linen petticoat stretched over iron, wire, cane, bone, or whalebone in a cone-like shape. Introduced in Spain in late 15th c. and worn in France in 16th c. and in England 1545 to 1620s. For other FARTHINGALES see: BUM ROLL, DRUM FARTHINGALE, ENGLISH FARTHINGALE, FRENCH FARTHINGALE, GUARD INFANTA, SPANISH FARTHINGALE, VERDUGADO, VERTUGALE, and WHEEL FARTHINGALE.

**farthingale sleeves**  Sleeves cut in *bishop* shape held out with wire, reed, or whalebone. Worn in late 16th and early 17th c. by men and women.

**fascia**  Lengths of cloth wrapped around legs, arms, or head for warmth by ancient Romans.

**fascinator**  See SHAWLS.

**fashion**  **1.** The contemporary mode in wearing apparel or accessories as interpreted in textiles, fur, leather, and other materials. In the broader sense it also involves the designing, manufacturing, promotion, and selling of such items. *High fashion* denotes the mode of the moment; the current styles in apparel and accessories. These styles usually change from one season to the next. **2.** All the clothes and accessories worn during a given historical period, *e.g., Elizabethan fashions.*

**fashion babies**  See MODEL DOLLS.

**fashion boot**  See BOOTS.

**fashion calendar**  **1.** General term for a schedule for the current year which indicates the market weeks, or dates, when the designers' or manufacturers' new lines may be seen by buyers. **2.** Retail store schedule listing all fashion promotions for the store including fashion shows, advertising, and special promotions.

**fashion dolls**  See MODEL DOLLS.

**fashion forecast**  Prediction of the colors and styles of apparel and accessories which the majority of people will want to buy at a given time and place.

**Fashion Group Inc., The**  An international professional association of women executives in fashion manufacturing, marketing, retailing, communication, and education. Founded in

1931 with Mary Brooks Picken as the first president. Originally formed to promote more careers for women in fashion and serve as a "clearing house" for information and ideas. Based in New York, the Group circulates information among its members by means of fashion shows, exhibits, speeches, career courses, and discussion panels.

**fashion helmet** See HELMETS.

**fashion industry** The production of all clothing and accessories for men, women, and children plus all the related trades necessary to produce these items; considered one of the main industries in New York City.

**fashion jewelry** Term coined in 1980s for high quality costume jewelry with expensive price tags. Styles include PAVÉ collars, flashy brooches, lapel pins, necklaces, earrings, and hat pins made of imitation gems. When made in identical imitation of jewelry called *paste*. Also see COSTUME JEWELRY and FAUX JEWELS.

**fashion marks** Term used for the marks seen in seamed or full-fashioned hosiery, particularly at the back of the leg, Stitches are decreased in this area to shape the hose to the ankle.

**fashion plate** 1. Illustration depicting the prevailing or new styles in clothing and accessories first introduced in last quarter of 18th c. 2. Individual who consistently dresses in the current mode.

**fashion press** Reporters and/or periodicals specializing in reporting news on fashion for trade or consumer magazines, newspapers, and broadcast media.

**fashion promotion** Sales promotion of fashion merchandise in a retail store accomplished by newspaper and magazine advertising, window and interior display, publicity, fashion shows, and broadcast media.

**fashion research** 1. Conducting of fashion counts, consumer surveys, and the study of past performance of an item in order to forecast the demand for various types of fashion merchandise. 2. Study of historical costume to suggest ideas for contemporary styles.

**fashion show** Parade of fashions on live models usually on a runway or stage given by a retail store, a designer, or a manufacturer to promote fashion merchandise. Frequently given to introduce the clothes for a new season or as a benefit performance for charity. Same as *style show*. First fashion show with live models was staged by *Vogue* magazine under Edna Woolman Chase in November, 1914, and started the idea of fashion shows for charity which spread over the country. The current trend in fashion shows includes TV, videotapes and film.

**fashion trend** Direction in which styles, colors, and fabrics are moving. Influenced by political events, films, personalities, dramas, social, and sports events.

**fashion watch** See WATCHES.

**fast-color** Describing dyed fabric that will not fade when subjected to sunlight, washing, dry cleaning, perspiration, or atmospheric fumes.

**fastener** Small device used for a closing on clothing and accessories including: *button, D-ring, frog, gripper, hook and eye, lacer, snap, toggle,* and *zipper.* Also see CLOSINGS.

**fatas** (fah-tus) Sheer silk or cotton veil elaborately embroidered in gold or silver. Frequently made with gold fringed edge and formerly worn in U.S.S.R. over an ornate headdress.

**Fath, Jacques** See APPENDIX/DESIGNERS.

**fatigues** Military clothing worn when doing chores at camp. Some items have been adopted for wear by civilians. See FATIGUE CAP under CAPS, FATIGUES under PANTS, and FATIGUE SWEATER under SWEATERS.

**Fauntleroy** See LITTLE LORD FAUNTLEROY SUIT.

**fausse montre** (foss mawn-tre) Term used at end of 18th c. when two watches were worn.

One was a snuff box disguised as a watch. *Der.* French, "false watch."

**fausse Valenciennes** (foss va-lhan-see-en) See LACES.

**Faust slipper**   See ROMEO under SLIPPERS.

**faux** (fo)   False or counterfeit, imitation; used in connection with gems, pearls, and leathers.

**faux jewels** (fo je-wels)   Term used for fashion jewelry when it is obviously fake.

**favourites   1.** Term for women's curls worn near the temples from 1690 to about 1720. **2.** Man's small tuft of hair worn on the chin from 1820 to 1840.

**fax**   Term used from Middle Ages to early 17th c. for hair on the head. Also spelled *facts*, *feax*.

**fearnaught**   Heavy, shaggy, British overcoating fabric similar to *Cheviot*. Usually *shoddy* and REWORKED WOOL are combined in the bulky yarn which forms the filling. When napped, this gives the fabric a long shaggy effect. May be called *fearnothing* or *dreadnought*. Also see FEARNOTHING JACKET.

**fearnothing jacket**   Man's jacket similar to a waistcoat with sleeves worn by sailors, sportsmen, laborers, and apprentices in the 18th and early 19th c. Made of heavy woolen fabric called FEARNAUGHT.

**feather**   Individual unit from a bird's plumage, consisting of a quill or hollow shaft surrounded by closely arranged parallel barbs usually tapering to the tip. Used from earliest times as decorative hair ornament, necklace, or body ornaments. Also used for fans or to decorate hats from 16th c. on, *e.g.*, plumes on *Gainsborough*, *Robin Hood* or *mousquetaire hats*. In late 1960s and 1970s whole dresses, pants, shawls,

and jewelry were made of feathers. Songbird and eagle feathers, as well as other wild bird feathers are not permitted by law to be used for clothing or accessories in the U.S.

**▬▬▬▬ FEATHERS ▬▬▬▬**

**aigrette f.** (ai-gret)   **1.** Extremely long, delicate, white feathers with plume at the tip, from the egret, a member of the heron family—a long-legged wading bird which became almost extinct from the excesses of fashion. Popular in the 1920s, it is now illegal in the U.S. to use these feathers on clothes or accessories. Also spelled *aigret*. **2.** Jeweled ornament imitating feathers, attached to a headband worn in the 1920s.

**Amazon plume**   Early term for an ostrich feather, generally taken from the wing of the bird with the tips of the barbs curled so shaft is concealed.

**bird-of-paradise f.**   Long plume brilliantly colored, often golden-orange. Taken from beneath the shoulder or tail of full-grown male birds of paradise. Used on hats or headdresses. Illegal to import into U.S. Introduced on evening wear by Yves Saint Laurent in 1969.

**cockade**   Tuft of feathers used as trim.

**cock f.**   Long curly feathers from the tail of the rooster, often black, blue, and green with iridescent highlights.

**coq f.**   French for "cock or chicken feathers."

**down**   Basic term for soft fluffy feathers from ducks and geese. The first plumage of young birds or the underfeathers of adults. Used as interlining for insulation and warmth in vests, jackets, and coats.

**egret f.**   See AIGRETTE.

**grebe f.**   Feathers from waterfowl, similar to ducks, ivory-colored flecked with brown used for millinery in early 20th c.

**guinea f.** (gin-ee)   Small, flat feathers from the guinea hen characterized by black, white, and gray striated markings used in 1960s for pants and stoles.

**jabiru** (jab-ih-roo)  Soft fuzzy plumage from a storklike South American bird. The white, pale smoke-colored, and black-and-white feathers were popular for trimming on women's hats, muffs, and collars in early 20th c.

**marabou**  Delicate, fluffy, fine feathers from tail and wing of a species of stork made into trimmings that sell by the yard in black, white and all colors. Popular in the 1920s and 1930s for trim on lingerie and boudoir slippers. Also used for trim on dresses or cape collars, sleeves, and hems. Returned to fashion in early 1980s. Because of the expense of these feathers, less expensive feathers are sometimes substituted.

**osprey f.**  Feathers from the osprey or fish hawk, the breast feathers white, other feathers brown or gray-brown crossed by brown bars, used for trimming on hats in early 20th c.

**OSTRICH FEATHER**

**ostrich f.**  Long curly plume feathers from the ostrich, a native African bird. Natural color of the feathers from the female bird is beige barred with white. Most feathers are dyed in colors and used in 1960s for whole dresses, capes, stoles, or pants. Popular decoration on hats for men and women in time of the Cavaliers, Louis XIV, and in Edwardian era for women.

**paradise f.**  See BIRD-OF-PARADISE FEATHERS.

**peacock f.**  Long thin dark feather with brilliantly marked "eye" in greenish-blue at the tip, from upper tail of peacock. Individual feathers became a fad of the hippies, carried in the hand, in the late 1960s.

**pheasant f.**  **1.** Long stiff tail feather from the domestic game bird, with striated markings of orange, black, and brown. **2.** Small soft body feathers of the same bird, sometimes used to cover hats or hat bands.

**rhea f.**  Either of two South American *ratite* birds, resembling *African ostrich*, having long draping feathers.

**FEATHER BOA**

**feather boa**  Long cylindrical scarf, made of feathers, worn by women in late 19th and early 20th c.; revived in early 1970s. See BOA under SCARFS.

**feather boning**  Light boning used particularly at hem of skirt to extend it. Compare with BONES and STAYS.

**featherbrush skirt**  Daytime skirt of sheer material, with overlapping flounces below knees, worn in 1898.

**feather cloth**   **1.** Soft novelty fabric made by mixing wool yarn with feathers when it is processed. **2.** Feathers, such as chicken or ostrich feathers, sewed to cloth before a garment is made. Popular in the 1960s for evening dresses, pants, jackets, stoles, and shawls.

**feather cut**   See HAIRSTYLES.

**feathering**   Applying extra dye delicately to guard hairs of fur by means of a feather dipped in dye. Used to improve appearance of the fur.

**feather stitch**   See STITCHES.

**feax**   See FAX.

**Federal Trade Commission**   U.S. agency that investigates and enforces laws concerning fair competition and proper labeling of such items as furs, cosmetics, and fiber content of fabrics.

**fedora**   See HATS.

**feed bag**   See HANDBAGS.

**feldspar**   See GEMS.

**fell stitch**   See FLAT-FELLED SEAM under SEAMS.

**felt**   Nonwoven fabric made by compressing wool and hair fibers by means of heat and steam into sheet form. No adhesives are used. Some felts are left hard and smooth; others are napped to give a softer hand. When used for hats, the felt is shaped into an object called a *hood* which has a crown and a floppy shapeless brim. Hats are made by placing the hood in a metal mold. Steam and pressure are used to achieve desired shape. Felt is also used for apparel, handbags, bedroom slippers, and trimming. *Der.* Anglo-Saxon, *filt*, "filter." Also see FIELTRO, FUR FELT, and VELOUR.

**felts**   See SLIPPERS.

**femoralia**   Short pants or drawers, reaching from waist to knees, worn by Roman troops in northern climates; probably imported by Emperor Augustus from Gaul. Also called *feminalia* or *Roman leggings*.

**fencing**   Sport using foils or epees for which special clothing is worn. See MASKS, SPORT JACKETS, SPORT SUITS, SHIRTS, and DUELING under BLOUSES.

**Fendi**   See APPENDIX/DESIGNERS.

**feradjé**   Long, loose, caped cloak of silk or wool formerly worn in Turkey. Jewish women wore specially shaped feradjé to distinguish themselves from Moslems. Also spelled *feridjee, feridgi, ferigee, ferijee*. Later replaced by the *tcharchaf*.

**feredeza**   Loose coat or cape with large sleeves worn out of doors to completely cover the body from neck to feet. Formerly worn by Moslem women of Bosnia.

**feridgi**   See FERADJÉ.

**fermail**   Term used in 15th c. for buckles or pins used to hold *slashes* of the garments together *e.g.*, as on sleeves and *doublets*. Also called *fers*. Also spelled *fermayll*.

**Ferragamo, Salvatore**   See APPENDIX/DESIGNERS.

**ferraiolo**   See CAPES.

**Ferré, Gianfranco**   See APPENDIX/DESIGNERS.

**Ferris waist**   Trade name for an item of underwear worn by young girls in the late 19th and early 20th c. consisting of a straight sleeveless cotton vest extending to the hips. Made with buttons at the waist to which underpants and petticoats were buttoned. Also had elastic tabs or garters to hold up long stockings. Also called *pantywaist*.

**ferronnière** (fehr-on-ee-air)   **1.** Delicate chain worn as *brow band* with single jewel hanging in center of forehead. Fashion originated by La Belle Ferronnière, a favorite of Francis I (1515–1547), as shown in portrait attributed to Giovanni Boltraffo or Leonardo da Vinci. **2.** Narrow brow band, with jewel in center, worn on the forehead with evening dress by women in the 1830s. Also called *La Belle Ferronnière*.

**fers** See FERMAIL.

**festoon** Term used for garlands of flowers, braid, or other decorative trimmings arranged in loops. Sometimes used on dresses worn by Marie Antoinette and on hoop-skirted ball dresses in 1860s.

**festul** Veil made of an oblong red scarf decorated with embroidery hanging to below hips and sometimes to hem of skirt. Frequently held in place by a jeweled tiara. Worn by Hebrew women in Morocco.

**feuille morte** (fueheeyh mort) Dark grayish-brown color. *Der.* French, "dead leaf."

**fez** See HATS.

**fiber** Basic filament or strand from which yarns are made—either with short natural materials such as cotton, wool, silk or linen; or man-made materials such as rayon, acetate, or polyester which are made in long continuous filaments. See MONOFILAMENT and MULTIFILAMENT.

**fiberfill** Generic term for a material consisting of fluffy short fibers. Frequently made of polyester and used between two layers of fabric to make fine quality quilted fabrics, padded bras, less expensive coats, and vests of the quilted type. Will wash without matting.

**fiber lace** See LACES.

**FIBULAE**

**fibula** (pl. *fibulae*) Pin or brooch shaped like a long straight *stiletto*, or hinged like a *safety pin*. Used by the Greeks and Romans to secure garments, especially at the shoulder. Also see CHITON.

**fichu** (fish-u) **1.** Term used in 18th c. for neckwear usually consisting of a large square of muslin folded diagonally to form a triangle. As time progressed became more elaborate— shaped to fit the neck, trimmed with ruffles, lace, and ruching. Frequently fastened or tied in front with hanging ends. Continued to be worn until about 1871. *Der.* French, "handkerchief." **2.** Term applied to a triangle of net edged in lace worn in early 19th c. as a capelet. Also see ANTOINETTE FICHU, CANEZOU, CHARLOTTE CORDAY FICHU, and COLLARS.

**fichu lavalliere** (fish-u la-va-leer) Woman's shoulder scarf of 1868 with sides not crossed in front and fastened with a button. *Der.* From Duchesse de La Vallière.

**fichu menteur** Scarf worn by women in 1780s at neck of coat or low bodice. Draped so it puffed out to increase apparent size of bust. Also see BUFFON.

**fichu-pelerine** Large cape or shawl-like covering for woman's shoulders worn from mid-1820s to 1860s. Usually white and frequently made with a double cape and turned-down collar and tied in front with the ends reaching to the knee.

**fichu-robings** Term used in 1820s for flat trimming used on the bodice of gown from shoulders to waist to give the effect of a *fichu*.

**field glasses** See GLASSES.

**field pants** See FATIGUES #1 under PANTS.

**fieltro** Spanish hooded cape of 16th c. made of *felt* in two layers—upper layer extended to the hips, while second layer extended to below the knees. Hood was cone-shaped, standing away from the face. Worn particularly by men when riding horseback.

**fiesta shirt** See SHIRTS.

**fifties look** See LOOKS.

**Figaro jacket** Variation of the ZOUAVE or BOLERO JACKET, with or without shoulder epaulets, worn by women in 1860s and again in 1890s.

**fig leaf** Small black silk apron worn by women in 1860s and 1870s.

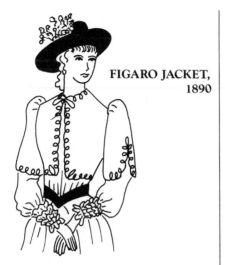

**FIGARO JACKET,
1890**

**figure improver**   Small BUSTLE worn by women in the 1890s.

**figure skate**   See BOOTS.

**filament**   **1.** See FIBER. **2.** See MONOFILAMENT and MULTIFILAMENT YARNS.

**filature**   Textile industry term referring to a good grade of RAW SILK reeled by machinery as opposed to hand-reeled; a product of cottage industry.

**filet**   **1.** Net with a square mesh formed by knotting at right angles. **2.** Embroidery thread made of fine raw silk fibers twisted together. **3.** See LACES.

**filet de Bruxelles**   See BRUSSELS NET under LACES.

**filigree**   Ornamental metal work for jewelry or accessories made of fine silver, gold, or copper wire intricately arranged—or similar pierced metal openwork. See RINGS.

**filled gold**   See GOLD-FILLED.

**fillet**   **1.** Narrow band tied around the hair, usually as a brow band, worn from 13th to 19th c. **2.** Stiffened band of linen worn with the *barbette*, *fret*, or both in 13th and 14th c. **3.** In 18th c. a hairnet worn at night. **4.** 19th c. evening *hairstyle* made by wrapping a satin band, embroidered with pearls, spirally around the head. **5.** See MITER #4.

**filleting**   Term used in 17th c. for narrow tape used as trimming.

**filling**   *Crosswise* yarn of a fabric which runs at right angles to the *selvage*. Also called PICK, *woof*, or *weft*. Opposite of WARP, the vertical yarns.

**filling stitch**   See STITCHES.

**fillingwise**   Textile industry term meaning across the fabric or at right angles to the selvage. Also called WEFT- or WOOFWISE.

**findings**   Sewing or trade term for all the smaller items and trimmings that complete a garment, *e.g.*, buttons, hooks, bindings, laces.

**fineness**   **1.** Term applied to the measurement of the diameter of yarns or fibers. Also see DENIER and COUNT OF YARN. **2.** Term used in reference to purity of gold. **3.** Term used for sewing machine stitches—meaning number of stitches to the inch.

**Finger-Free® gloves**   See GLOVES.

**fingering yarn**   **1.** Combination of woolen and worsted yarn, usually two or more ply, used for hand-knitted garments. **2.** Loosely twisted wool yarn used in Great Britain for *Berlin work*.

**fingernail shields**   Gold or jade devices worn to protect extraordinarily long fingernails by Chinese Mandarin men and women; the long nails indicated freedom from household chores and manual labor.

**fingerwave**   See HAIRSTYLES.

**finished width**   Measurement in inches across woven cloth after all operations have been completed.

**finnesko boot**   Boot of tanned reindeer hide used with fur side out, in the Arctic. Also spelled *finnsko*.

**fins**   See FLIPPERS.

**fire opal**   See GEMS.

**firmla** Heavily embroidered vest, extending to below the hips, worn indoors by the Berber women of Morocco and by women of Tunis over a linen shirt.

**fish** Term used in the first half of 19th c. for a dart cut off close to the seam on reverse side. Used to reduce bulk and give better fit.

**fishbone braids** See HAIRSTYLES.

**fishbone stitch** See STITCHES.

**fisher** See FURS.

**fisherman's clothes** Various items of clothing worn by fishermen for the sport of fishing. Items adapted from fisherman's clothing and accessories used for everyday wear. See SWEATERS, VESTS, WADERS under BOOTS, and FISHING PARKA under SPORT JACKETS.

**fisherman's ring** Gold ring used at investiture of the Pope of the Roman Catholic Church. The figure of St. Peter in a fisherman's boat is engraved along with name of the Pope on the ring.

**fishmouth lapel** See LAPEL.

**fishnet** Coarse mesh cotton fabric made in LENO WEAVE. Used for dresses, scarfs, and trimming. See HOSE, KNIT SHIRTS, and PONCHOS.

**fishnet underwear** Lightweight 100% cotton string yarn in net-like weave, acting as an insulator against zero temperatures and 90° heat. Originally worn by Norwegian explorers and Norwegian Army. Worn by athletes and by general public as sportswear in 1970s and 1980s.

**fishtail** See GEM SETTINGS and SKIRTS.

**fishwife costume** Blouson dress of 1880s made with shawl collar, dickey insert, and full sleeves. Double skirt was gathered at waistline with overskirt turned up revealing a lining of contrasting fabric. Underskirt made of a third fabric, frequently striped to match dickey. Imitated the dress worn with several petticoats by Portuguese fishermen's wives.

FISHWIFE COSTUME, 1891

**fitch** See FURS.

**fitchet** French term used from 13th to mid-16th c. for vertical slit made in side front of skirt of the gown to enable woman to reach her pocket located in an undergarment.

**fitted** Describing a garment that conforms closely to body lines. See SLEEVES.

**fitting** Trade term for dressmaker's or tailor's session with customer for altering garment to fit the figure.

**Fitzherbert hat** Modified form of *balloon hat*, with wide oval brim and low crown of puffed fabric, worn by women in mid-1780s.

**five-language watch** See WATCHES.

**fixing** Textile term for process of steaming or washing. Used to set the dye in fabric or fiber.

**flag blue** Light blue color as found in the iris flower, or dark blue as the blue of the American flag.

**flame embroidery** See EMBROIDERIES.

**flamenco dress** See DRESSES.

**flame resistance** Fabric treated with a flame retardant. Fabric will burn only when placed in a flame, but self-extinguishes rapidly when the ignition source is removed. All sleepwear labels cite precautions for proper care. Also see FLAMMABLE FABRICS ACT.

**flame stitch** See BARGELLO STITCH under STITCHES.

**Flammable Fabrics Act** Bill signed by President Eisenhower on June 30, 1953, and effective July 1, 1954, prohibiting certain flammable fabrics or clothing from importation or interstate commerce in the U.S. Amended in 1967 to include building interior furnishings. Act is enforced by the Consumer Products Safety Commission.

**flammeolum** Small veil worn by ancient Roman brides.

**flammeum** Dark, flame-colored, full-length wedding veil worn by Roman brides. Removed by bridegroom when couple arrived at new home.

**flandan** Late 17th-c. term for a *pinner* or *lappet* fastened to woman's day cap.

**flange heel** See HEELS.

**flange shoulder** See SHOULDERS.

**flannel** 1. Fine soft fabric made in tightly woven twill or plain weave and finished with a light napping. May be made of woolen, worsted or combinations of yarns. Comes in colors or plaids which are yarn-dyed. 2. Same type of fabric in cotton is called FLANNELETTE. Used for women's and girls' coats, suits, and dresses or men's trousers and sport shirts. *Der.* Welsh, *Gwlanen* from *Gwlān,* "wool." Also see FLANNEL SHIRT under SHIRTS and NIGHTGOWNS.

**flannelette** Soft medium- to-lightweight fabric with a fuzzy surface. Made of cotton yarns lightly twisted and brushed so that a nap is raised to conceal the plain weave. May be dyed plain colors, printed in stripes, or made with small floral designs. Used for winter nightgowns and pajamas. Similar to *Canton flannel.*

**flannel petticoat** Infant's and woman's winter petticoat worn for warmth under fancy petticoats from 1870s to early 1920s. Usually made of wool flannel, sometimes of cashmere. Also called a *flannel skirt.*

**flannel shirt** See SHIRTS.

**flannel skirt** See FLANNEL PETTICOAT.

**flapper** 1. Style featured by *Butterick Fashions* in spring of 1914 with dresses tapered to narrow hemlines. Bodices usually had surplice closing with kimono, raglan, or dropped-shoulder sleeves. Skirts were fuller at hips, sometimes with draperies, *peplums,* or *peg-tops.* Other skirts were made in tiers. Most skirts had a slashed side seam at hem to facilitate walking. Accessories included small pouch handbags, spats, and hats with large crowns and small brims. 2. Term used to describe a young girl of 1920s wearing lipstick, makeup, bobbed hair, short skirt, a long strand of pearls, and walking in a *debutante slouch*—the type pictured by cartoonist John Held, Jr., and described by F. Scott Fitzgerald in his novel *This Side of Paradise.* Also see DRESSES and LOOKS.

**flap pockets** See POCKETS.

**flared leg panties** See PANTIES.

**flares** See PANTS.

**Flashdance** Styles adapted from 1983 film *Flashdance* starring Jennifer Beal. See LOOKS, TOPS, and FLASHY NIGHTSHIRT under NIGHTGOWNS.

**flat crepe** 1. Soft silky fabric made of silk or man-made fibers with only a slight crinkle. Creped or S- and Z-twisted yarns used in the filling to give the crinkled appearance. 2. A similar fabric that does not use crepe-twisted yarns. Also called *mock crepe.*

**flat-felled seams** See SEAMS.

**flat heel** See HEELS.

**flat knit** Fabric knitted flat with selvages—in contrast to *circular knit.* Also see FULL-FASHIONED HOSE under HOSE.

**flats/flatties** See SHOES.

**flat-top** See CREW CUT under HAIRSTYLES.

**flax** Vegetable or bast fiber from tissue between bark and woody fiber of a flax plant which produces fibers 12″ to 40′ long. Long fibers are called *line linen*; shorter fibers are called *tow*. Grown in Europe and Egypt.

**flea fur** Fur scarf made of any small animal with head, tail, and paws attached to a jeweled muzzle and chain. Worn by women during late 16th c. as decoy for obnoxious insects. *Der.* From fact that "fleas" were attracted to it. Also called *Flohpelzchen*.

**flea-market clothes** Clothing sold at markets held continuously or occasionally in large barns, buildings, or in the open. All types of clothing, either used or new, are sold, *e.g.*, shirts, shorts, and dresses purchased in job lots from manufacturers. Also see VINTAGE LOOK under LOOKS.

**fleece** **1.** Wool sheared from the sheep usually taken off in one piece. **2.** Heavy wool coating fabric with an extremely soft napped finish. Usually made of soft twisted woolen yarn that is brushed, sheared, and singed. The surface finish completely conceals the weave. Fleece varies in thickness and length of nap. *Fleece* should be used to describe only fabrics made of wool. **3.** See SHEARLING.

**fleece-lined fabric** Soft fabric with a heavily napped surface on one side. Usually knitted with floats on back which are brushed with wire brushes to form a nap. Used for *sweatshirts*, *sweatpants*, and *jogging suits*.

**Flemish hood** See BEGUIN.

**fleshing** **1.** Processing the skin side of hides, with a machine that has rollers fitted with sharp spiral knives, to remove excess skin and flesh making hide appear even in thickness. **2.** Hand process of smoothing reverse side of fur by scraping with a sharp knife.

**fleur-de-lis** Lily motif used in heraldry and part of the coat-of-arms of France's royal family. Also see PRINTS.

**flight** Term used for flying in an airplane—extended as adjective for clothing and accessories used or connected with flying. See HANDBAGS, SPORT JACKETS, and FLIGHT DECK CAP under CAPS.

**flip** See HAIRSTYLES.

**flip-chip dress** See DRESSES.

**flip-down glasses** See GLASSES.

**flippers** Rubber extensions shaped like a duck's webbed foot which fit over the feet and attach with straps around heels. Worn for scuba diving, underwater swimming, and water sports. Also called *fins*.

**flip-tie blouse** See BLOUSES.

**float** **1.** *Filling* or *warp* yarn which extends over several rows without being interlaced. **2.** In knitting, a yarn which extends for some distance across back of fabric without being interlaced. **3.** See DRESSES.

**floating pedestal wedge** See HEELS.

**floats** See BOOTS.

**flocked ribbon** Ribbon given a pile-like surface by means of *flocking*, an electrostatic process, rather than woven in a pile weave like *velvet ribbon*.

**flocking** **1.** Adding weight to woolen fabrics by pressing short fibers into back of fabric. **2.** An electrostatic process used to produce a velvet effect. See FLOCK PRINTING.

**flock printing** **1.** Method of applying a design by first printing fabric with an adhesive and then causing minute pieces of fibers to adhere to the design. See DOTTED SWISS. **2.** See PRINTS.

**Flohpelzchen** See FLEA FUR.

**flokati** See SLIPPERS.

**floral print** See PRINTS.

**Florentine** Alpaca dress fabric woven in Great Britain in a fancy weave with cotton warp and alpaca filling.

**Florentine embroidery** See EMBROIDERIES and STITCHES.

**Florentine neckline** See NECKLINES.

**Florentine stitch** See BARGELLO STITCH under STITCHES.

**Florodora costume** Dress with tight-fitted lace-trimmed bodice with bishop sleeves and long full skirt trimmed with ruffles. Worn with an off-the-face picture hat trimmed with ostrich feathers. Popularized by chorus of the musical *Florodora*, a hit of 1900.

**flotation vest** See VESTS.

**flounce** 1. Piece of material either circular and bias-cut or straight-cut and gathered. Used on skirt of dress, usually at hem, singly or in series. First introduced in 16th c. 2. In 18th and 19th c. called a *furbelow*.

**flouncing** 1. Decorative lace or embroidered fabric usually gathered at upper edge. 2. See LACES.

**flower bottle** 1. Fresh flower in small bottle of water worn in buttonhole and held in place under lapel by broad ribbon. Worn by men in the mid-1860s. 2. See BOSOM BOTTLES.

**flowered mink** Term used to describe a mink coat worked in a floral design, usually consisting of a six-petal arrangement, *e.g.*, a daisy. Used in color or white against colored background. An innovation of the late 1960s.

**flower-pot hat** Man's hat of 1830s with crown shaped like a truncated cone, or upside-down flower pot, with large turned-up brim. Also called *turf hat*.

**flow-flow** Term used in mid-1880s for bodice trimming consisting of a graduated cascade of ribbon loops.

**fluffy ruffles** See FALSIES.

**flush setting** See CHANNEL SETTING under GEM SETTINGS.

**fluted hem** See HEMS.

**fluting** Tiny pleats in sheer fabrics that give a corrugated effect. Those set in man-made fabrics may be permanently heat-set. A late 19th c. trimming popular again in 1960s through 1980s. Also called *goffered*. Also see FLUTED HEM under HEMS.

**flutter sleeve** See SLEEVES.

**flyaway jacket** Very short jacket, with a full back worn by women in the late 1940s and early 1950s.

**fly boy glasses** See AVIATOR under GLASSES.

**fly cap** See BUTTERFLY CAP.

**fly-fringe** 18th-c. term for fringe, consisting of strands of silk floss knotted in clumps, used for trimming a gown.

**fly front** See CLOSINGS.

**flying panel skirt** See SKIRTS.

**fly shuttle** Term for a device carrying the *filling* yarn across the *warps* when weaving; devised in 1738 by John Kay. *Der.* So called because it "flies" through the warp yarns.

**fob** See WATCH FOB.

**fob pocket** Small horizontal *welt pocket*, near waistband of man's pants, designed to hold pocket watch. Popular from 17th c. until the 1920s when wristwatches began to be fashionable. Also called *watch pocket*. See POCKETS.

**fob ribbon** Term used from 1740s to 1840s for ribbon attached to watch carried in the *fob pocket*. The ribbon end hung outside of pocket and held a fob, seals, or watch key. Worn only with *breeches*, or *pantaloons*.

**Fogarty, Anne** See APPENDIX/DESIGNERS.

**foil button** Silk pasted on paper and glued to reverse side of glass button; patented in 1774.

**foil dress** See DRESSES.

**folding** Adjective used when size of object is reduced by doubling over. See GLASSES, SLIPPERS, FOLD-OVER CLUTCH under HANDBAGS, FOLD-UP hat under HATS, and FOLD-UP RAINCOAT under RAINCOATS.

**folding fan** Half- or quarter-circle fan pleated to close narrowly. Introduced to France in mid-16th c. by Catherine de Medici. Also called a *duck's foot fan*. Also see FAN.

**folette** (fall-et) Loose scarf or *fichu* in triangular shape of soft light-colored fabric, worn with ends tucked into neckline of bodice during first half of 18th c. Also spelled FOLLETTE.

**foliated** See DAGGING.

**follow-me-lads** Long ribbon streamers of 1850s and 1860s hanging from back of girl's bonnet.

**folly bells** Tiny bells suspended from chains used to decorate belts, shoulder belts, or neckbands in 15th c.

**Fontana Sorelle** See APPENDIX/DESIGNERS.

**fontanges** (fawn-tanjz) Woman's starched, pleated, lace-and-ribbon headdress placed on top of upswept hairstyle in late 17th and early 18th c. Originated by Marie Angélique de Scorraille de Roussilles, la Duchesse de Fontanges, a favorite of Louis XIV. While out riding with the King about 1679, she used her lace and jeweled garter to fasten back her hair. Also called *tower headdress* and *high head*. The *commode* was used to support the headdress. Sometimes spelled *fontange*. Also see DUCHESS.

**fontanges hat** (fawn-tanjz) Tiny hat covering crown of head trimmed with lace, ribbon, and flowers with a sheer veil or curtain in back. A band of ribbon, edged with fluting, went under the chin. Featured in *Godey's Magazine* in 1876.

**fool's cap** Of three types: *a)* forward-curved peaked cap with donkey's ears; *b)* a cockscomb in place of peak and without ears; *c)* two horn-like peaks at sides of head. Bells were added to each style. Also called *jester's cap*. Also see JESTER'S COSTUME.

**football helmet** See HELMETS.

**football jersey** **1.** Shirt worn for football games in 1870. Made with long sleeves of knitted jersey with horizontal stripes. **2.** Official jersey shirt, with striped drop-shoulder sleeves and large identifying numerals on front and back, worn by football players. **3.** Similar shirt worn as sportswear. See KNIT SHIRTS.

**footed pajamas** See PAJAMAS.

**footing** Term for trimming used on edges of garments, *e.g.*, elaborate ruffles, pleating, lace, net, insertion, and ribbon. Widely used on women's dresses and undergarments in late 19th and early 20th c.

**foot-mantle** **1.** An outer, or extra, woman's skirt, worn in American Colonial days to keep dress clean when riding horseback. **2.** An overskirt worn by country women when riding horseback in the 14th c. Also spelled *fotemantle*. Also see SAFEGUARD #1.

**footwarmers** See BED SOCKS under SOCKS.

**fop** Term used to describe a vain man preoccupied with the exquisiteness of his dress or showiness of his person, *e.g.*, affected eccentricities such as the carrying of fans in the late 16th and late 18th c. *Der.* Middle English *foppe*, "fool." Also see DANDY.

**forage cap** **1.** *Visor cap* adapted from the military for small boys in first half of 19th c. Made with circular felt crown, head band stiffened with cane, a tassel from center of crown, and sometimes japanned leather straps under the chin. **2.** Small cap similar to a KEPI, formerly worn by soldiers in U.S. Army. **3.** See CAPS.

**ford** Apparel industry slang for a style that has mass acceptance. *Der.* From the similarity to mass appeal of the inexpensive early Ford automobiles.

**fore-and-after cap** See DEERSTALKER.

**forehead cloth** See CROSSCLOTH #2 and FRONTLET #2.

**forepart** **1.** Term used from 16th c. to 1630 for a decorative panel made of expensive or elaborate fabric sewed to an underskirt of coarse fabric. The expensive fabric showing through the split skirt of the gown. **2.** 19th-c. term for the part of a man's waistcoat extending across the chest.

**foresleeve** Sleeve covering the arm from wrist to elbow. Also see HALF SLEEVE.

**forestry cloth** Fabric of olive green color made in a twill weave of cotton, wool, worsted, and mixtures. Used by the Forestry Service and the U.S. Army for uniforms, overcoats, shirts, and trousers. Also see KHAKI #2.

**foretop** Term used from 13th to end of 18th c. by men and women for the hair or wig just above the forehead. Also called TOUPEE.

**forks** See FOURCHETTES.

**formal attire** Clothes worn by men and women at formal social functions. For specific items see: ASCOT, BLACK TIE, CUMMERBUND, CUT-AWAY COAT, DINNER JACKET, FORMAL GOWN under DRESSES, FORMAL SHIRT under SHIRTS, FULL DRESS, MORNING COAT, SWALLOW-TAILED COAT under COATS, TUXEDO under SUITS, white tie under TIES, and WING COLLAR under COLLARS.

**Fortrel®** Trademark for a polyester fiber jointly owned by Imperial Chemical Industries Ltd. and Celanese Corp.

**Fortuny, Mariano** See DELPHOS DRESS and APPENDIX/DESIGNERS.

**fote-mantle** See FOOT-MANTLE #2.

**fotoz** Headdress resembling a large off-the-face turban worn by Jewish women in Turkey. Consists of an enormous cushion of parti-colored fabrics, ornamented with jewels and strings of pearls, worn with a large veil out-of-doors. Also spelled *hotoz.*

**foulard** Soft lightweight silk, rayon, or acetate fabric made in a twill weave. Usually surface printed in a small design. It is lighter in weight than SURAH and sometimes made in plain weave. Used for scarfs, neckties, and dresses. Also see SCARFS. Also called *gum twill.*

**foundation** Undergarment combining a *bra* and *girdle* in one piece to mold the figure. Made with or without straps over the shoulders and optional supporters for the hose. Frequently made with alternating panels of flexible elastic fabric and non-stretch fabric. Formerly called a *foundation garment* or *garment* from about 1920 to early 1980s. Evolved from the *corset* (see alphabetical listing).

### ▬▬▬ FOUNDATIONS ▬▬▬

**all-in-one** Another name for a foundation with bra and girdle combined into a one-piece garment.

**body briefer** **1.** Two-way stretch garment made in panty style without garters for hose. Usually made in Lycra power-net, sometimes with lace inserts for bra. **2.** Lace trimmed garment styled like a TEDDY with high cut legs made of lightweight stretch fabric with V or camisole-type top.

**boned f.** Foundation garment that contains thin metal or plastic strips called *bones* for stiffening inserted under cotton tapes making a firm garment for more control. *Der.* So called because "bones" were originally made of whale-bone.

**bra-kini®** Minimal foundation garment composed of bra and bikini panties joined through midriff by see-through fabric. Sometimes made in two pieces.

**bustier** One-piece support garment which is a combination bra and waist cincher. Reaches to a few inches below the waist or to the hips. Frequently made without straps and with removable garters, it has flexible boning and is sometimes lace trimmed. Also called *torsolette*. Also see BRAS.

**camisette** Minimal support foundation with a natural bra top made close-fitting to hips with long attached garters. Sometimes worn with bikini panties.

**corselet** Foundation with firm support achieved by boning, power-net side panels, and front panel of non-stretch nylon taffeta. Sometimes has an inner belt which hooks separately to help flatten abdomen. Bra top is often of nylon lace with *marquisette* lining and adjustable shoulder straps. Foundation is fastened by hooks underneath zipper and has 6 garters. Appearing first in America in 1921 and then spelled *corsellette*. Also see alphabetical listing.

**double-zipper f.** Easy-to-get-into foundation garment with one zipper extending from under arm to below waist, a second zipper on opposite side extends from thigh to waistline.

**front-zipper f.** Foundation with zipper placed in center front rather than at side.

**laced f.** Foundation closed by lacing through eyelets, an early method of fastening still used in some support-types of foundations.

**merry widow** Bra and short girdle combined into a minimal support garment. Made of elastic power-net in lacy pattern with ruffle at lower edge and hose supporters.

**panty f.** Lightweight garment with crotch, usually made of two-way stretch elastic.

**teddy** Feminine one-piece foundation introduced in the 1960s and translated in the 1980s to a garment with minimal support. Popular in the 1980s with low-cut front and back, and high-cut leg openings. Also see alphabetical listing.

**torsolette** See BUSTIER.

**two-way stretch f.** Stretch garment made of Lycra spandex with a satin panel in front.

**ALL-IN-ONE FOUNDATION**      **TEDDY**

**foundation pattern** See SLOPER.

**foundling bonnet** Small, soft-crowned, stiff-brimmed bonnet of 1880s usually made of plush and fastened with ties under chin.

**fourchettes** (foor-*shet*) Narrow pieces forming the sides of the fingers of gloves ending in points at tips of fingers and joining the back to the front of the glove. Also called *forks*.

**four-gore slip** See SLIPS.

**fouriaux** (foor-e-o) Silken sheaths worn over long braids by ladies of rank in first half of 12th c.

**four-in-hand tie** See TIES.

**fourragère** (foor-ah-zher) Braided cord worn usually draped around left shoulder as a military award or decoration. Compare with AIGUILLETTE.

**fourreau dress** (foor-o) Princess-style dress of mid-1860s made with no waistline seam and buttoned down front. Usually worn with a peplum tied around the waist. *Der.* French, "scabbard."

**fourreau skirt** (foor-o) Gored skirt made without pleats at waistline and worn over a crinoline in 1864. *Der.* French, "scabbard."

**fourreau tunic** (foor-o) Double-skirted dress with bodice and overskirt cut in one piece and worn as a tunic over underskirt in 1865. *Der.* French, "scabbard."

**fox** See FURS.

**foxing** Shoe-industry term for extra fancy-cut piece of leather sewed on at the top of the back seam of the shoe for reinforcement and decoration.

**frac** French term for the English *frock coat* made with turned down collar, full skirt, and without pockets. Worn by men from about 1767. By mid-19th c. the jacket was cut away in front and long narrow tails hung down in back.

**fraise** **1.** Embroidered muslin scarf, folded across the chest and kept in place by an ornamental pin, worn by women in 1836 with a carriage dress. **2.** Fashionable neckpiece worn by women from about 1877 to 1885. Had a *frilling* or *ruching* around a high neckline which continued down front of dress nearly to waistline, trimmed with bow and frilled at edges.

**fraise à la confusion** See FALLING RUFF.

**frame** **1.** Metal top of handbag around which the bag is constructed. See SQUARE-BOTTOM CHANNEL FRAME, SIDE-CHANNEL FRAME, INVERTED FRAME. **2.** Term for machine used in yarn making.

**framing** Handbag-industry term for securing the frame to the handbag. Material and lining are fitted into frame and secured permanently by machine. See FRAME #1.

**France, point de** See LACES.

**franchise** Privilege granted to one retailer in an area or city by a wholesaler or manufacturer to sell manufacturer's entire line of merchandise exclusively.

**frangipani** (fran-ge-pa-knee) Perfume from the flowers of the plumeria shrub introduced during the reign of Louis XIII in the 16th c. Created by an Italian nobleman, the Marquis Frangipani, and at first used to scent gloves.

**fraternal rings** See RINGS.

**fraternity** See PINS and RINGS.

**Frazer tartan** See TARTANS.

**free-form ring** See RINGS.

**frelan** Late 17th-c. term for woman's *bonnet* and *pinner* worn together. Also spelled *freland, frelange.*

**French antelope lambskin** See LEATHERS.

**Frenchback** **1.** Fabric with a dull surface made with two warps and one filling forming a twill weave on the right side and a satin weave on the reverse side. Usually made of worsted yarns and given a clear finish on the right side to reveal the weave. Used for men's suits and trousers. Also called *Frenchback serge.* **2.** Similar cotton fabric made with two-ply warp yarns and ply- or single-filling yarns.

**French back** Back of dress made with three seams—one in center and one on either side curving into the armhole. Fashionable in late 19th and early 20th c. and still used. See SIDE BODIES.

**French beret** See BERET under CAPS.

**French boa** Tubular length of swansdown fabric, fur, or feathers worn as a neckpiece by women from 1829 on. Also fashionable in 1890s, 1930s, and 1970s. Also see BOA under SCARFS.

**French bottoms** 19th-c. term for men's trousers flaring at the hems.

**French bra** See BRAS.

**French braid** See FISHBONE BRAID under HAIRSTYLES.

**French cinch** See GIRDLES.

**French cloak** Long circular or semi-circular cape, sometimes with a square flat collar or shoulder cape worn in 16th and 17th c. Also see COMPASS CLOAK.

**French corsage** Woman's BASQUE waist worn in 1860s with wide tight-fitting corselet extending to middle of bust made of different fabric with boat-shaped neckline and double ruffled sleeves. Skirt was of contrasting fabric.

**French crepe** Originally a silk fabric with a flat smooth surface made in France of crepe-twisted yarns. Now applied to a large group of similar plain woven fabrics called *lingerie crepes* made of rayon and man-made fibers.

**French cuff** See CUFFS.

**French drawers** Flared, knee-length panties lavishly trimmed with lace, ruffles, and *insertion* at the hems. Set on a band at waist with ties or buttons in back to adjust the size. With split crotch, called "open," or with seàm sewed, called "closed." Made of fine cambric, lawn, muslin, and worn in late 1890s and early 1900s.

**FRENCH DRESS**

**French dress** Little girl's long waisted dress, worn in late 19th and early 20th c. Usually made with square or round neckline accented with a large BERTHA. Sleeves may be short, ruffled or puffed, or of long LEG-OF-MUTTON style. Skirt was full with wide ribbon sash at low waistline.

**French-fall boot** Leather boot of 17th c. with extravagantly wide top crushed down to reveal elaborate lace cannons. Also called *bucket-top boots.* Also see BOOT HOSE and BOOT-HOSE TOPS.

**French farthingale** Drum-shaped skirt, mounted on stiff frame, with widened sides and slightly flattened front. Worn by women in England from 1580 to 1620s.

**French flannel** Solid color, striped, or checked fabric made in twill weave of slightly napped wool.

**French frock** Man's FROCK COAT worn from 1770 to 1800 for full dress and usually trimmed with gold embroidered buttons.

**FRENCH GIGOT SLEEVE**

**French gigot sleeve** (zhee-go) Woman's sleeve full at top, and fitted at forearm, made with a point over back of hand. Worn from 1890 to 1897 and popularized by actress Sarah Bernhardt. *Der.* French, *gigot,* "leg of lamb." Compare with LEG-OF-MUTTON SLEEVE under SLEEVES.

**French gores** Term used in 1807 for panels introduced into skirts to eliminate gathers at the waist.

**French heel** See HEELS.

**French hood** Woman's headdress, consisting of a small bonnet over a stiffened frame, worn at back of head and trimmed with *ruching.* Front border was curved forward to cover the ears and had two ornamental gold bands or *billiments.* A back flap was folded forward over head, projecting above forehead. Fashionable from 1521 to 1590 and worn by some until 1630.

**French hose** See BOULOGNE HOSE.

**French jacket** See PETENLAIR.

**French kid**   See LEATHERS.

**French knot**   See STITCHES.

**French lace**   See LACES.

**French lock**   See LOVE LOCK.

**French maid sleeper**   See PAJAMAS.

**French nightcap**   See DORMEUSE.

**French opening vest**   Man's vest of 1840s cut low enough to reveal a large part of the shirt front.

**French panties**   Short, flared, lacy panties made of silk and cut with wide legs, worn in 1920s.

**French policeman's cape**   See CAPES.

**French polonaise**   See IRISH POLONAISE.

**French portrait buttons**   Buttons worn about 1790 with profiles of famous people in light color mounted against a black silk background and surrounded with a rim of tin, *e.g.*, profiles of Lafayette, Mirabeau, and Louis XVI.

**French purse**   See HANDBAGS.

**French Revolution styles**   During the French Revolution in 1789, fashions changed immediately from elaborate to simple, *e.g.*, powdered wigs, *panniers*, and costly fabrics disappeared and a careless, unkempt style prevailed including muslin dresses and little underwear. Dress *à la constitution*, became fashionable.

**French roll**   See HAIRSTYLES.

**French ruff**   Extremely wide ruff, also called *cartwheel ruff*, worn by men from late 16th to early 17th c.

**French sailor dress**   Girl's long-waisted tailored dress of early 20th c. with *blouson* effect, short pleated skirt, and *sailor collar*.

**French sailor hat**   See HATS.

**French seam**   **1.** See SEAMS. **2.** Shoe seam which starts with a simple or closed seam, restitched on either side on the outside. Used for closing back of shoe.

**French skirt**   See CORNET #5.

**FRENCH SAILOR DRESS, 1905**

**French sleeves**   Detachable sleeves worn by men in England in second half of 16th c.

**French system**   One of three main systems for making worsted yarns, originating in Alsace, France, and now used in Europe and U.S. The process uses short fibers and resultant yarn is springier or loftier than other worsteds. Also called *Continental* and *Alsatian system*.

**French twist**   See HAIRSTYLES.

**French vest**   Man's high-buttoned vest of the 1860s with small lapels not turned over.

**French wig**   See FULL-BOTTOM WIG.

**freshwater pearls**   See PEARLS under BEADS and GEMS.

**fret**   **1.** Mesh snood or skullcap made of gold mesh or fabric worked in an openwork lattice design and sometimes decorated with jewels. Worn by women from the 13th to early 16th c. Also called a *caul*. **2.** Headdress of gold or silver trelliswork worn by Jewish women in Germany in the 18th c. **3.** Trelliswork sometimes used to ornament a garment in a lattice design in the 16th c. *Der.* French, "trelliswork." **4.** Greek design consisting of a series of incompleted rectangles in a repeat design. Also called the *Greek key, Greek fret,* or *Grecian border.*

**friendship pin** See PINS.

**friendship ring** See RINGS.

**frieze** Very heavy rough fabric made in a variety of qualities. Frequently made of wool combined with reworked or reprocessed wool, best qualities come from Ireland. Used for overcoats for soldiers. *Der.* First made in Friesland, Holland, in the 13th c. of coarse wool with a napped surface. Also spelled *frisé*.

**frigate cap** See CAPS.

**frileuse** Woman's cape or *pelerine* wrap, with a fitted back and loose sleeves, made of quilted satin or velvet. Used indoors or at the theater in 1847.

**frill** Term used since the 16th c. for narrow piece of fabric or lace gathered to form a ruffle and attached as trimming to a dress or blouse.

**frilling** Term used for ruffles of gathered, stiff, white muslin worn at the wrist and neck, specifically on widows' dresses of 1870s and 1880s.

**fringe** **1.** Ornamental trim used since medieval times, consisting of loose strands of thread, yarn, or beads, fastened to a band. **2.** Fabric or leather slashed into narrow strands, used for trim, *e.g.*, on BUCKSKIN JACKETS.

**fringed cuff** See CUFFS.

**fringed tongue** Shoe tongue finished with saw-toothed edge at top.

**friponne** See JUPE #1.

**frisé** See FRIEZE.

**frisette** **1.** 19th-c. term for crimped bangs of hair, either real or false, worn on the forehead. **2.** In the 1860s a sausage-shaped pad over which back hair was rolled.

**frisk** Small BUSTLE worn by women from 1815 to 1818 to produce the Grecian bend posture. Compare with NELSON.

**frizze** See FRIZZ-WIG.

**frizzle** **1.** See FRIZZ-WIG. **2.** Term used for 17th c. small ruff.

**frizz-wig** Man's wig, closely crimped all over, worn from 17th to 19th c. Also called a *frizze* or *frizzle*.

**frizzy** Describing hair in tight kinky curls.

**frock** **1.** Term used generally as synonym for woman's dress. In 16th and 17th c. an informal gown; by 19th c. usually a dress of thin fabric; and in 20th c. a term usually used for a child's dress. **2.** From medieval times, a man's loose-fitting, sleeved outer garment of coarse fabric, derived from a monk's *habit* and worn by farm workers or laborers. Also called *smock frock*. **3.** From 16th to end of 18th c., a man's loose-fitting, frocked jacket or informal coat. Also see FRENCH FROCK, FROCK COAT, and JEMMY FROCK.

**FROCK COAT #1**

**frock coat** **1.** Man's close-fitting suit coat, single- or double-breasted, buttoned to waistline with full skirt, flapped pockets, and vent in back with two buttons at waistline. At first with a *Prussian collar* and no lapels. Worn with minor variations for many years and called *morning frock coat*. Worn from end of 18th c. through the 19th c. when it extended to knees.

Also see FRAC. **2.** Hip-length fitted tailored jacket worn by women in 1890s.

**frocked jacket**   See FROCK #3.

**frock greatcoat**   Man's coat worn from 1830s on, similar in cut to a *frock coat* but usually double-breasted, longer, and styled for outdoor wear. Also see TOP FROCK.

**FROCK OVERCOAT**

**frock overcoat**   Boy's calf-length overcoat, worn in late 1880s and 1890s, made with fitted lines, usually with a large *cape collar*.

**FROG**

**frog**   **1.** Ornamental fastener made of *braid* or *cording* used for closing garments, especially military uniforms and some Chinese clothes. When introduced in the West from China in last quarter of 18th c., called BRANDENBURGS. Also see CLOSINGS. **2.** See LEATHERS.

**frog button**   Braided button made in a spindle shape for use with frog fasteners. Also called an OLIVETTE. See BRANDENBURGS.

**front**   17th-c. term for *hairpiece* consisting of a fringe of false hair worn on the forehead.

**frontayl/frontel**   See FRONTLET.

**front-closure bra**   See BRAS.

**frontier pants**   See PANTS.

**frontlet**   **1.** Decorative *brow band* worn in medieval times under a *coverchief* or *veil*. Also worn in 16th and early 17th c. with COIF or CAUL. **2.** In 18th c. called *forehead cloth* or *crosscloth*. A *brow band* covered with face cream, worn at night to remove wrinkles. Also spelled *frontayl, frontel*.

**front-zipper foundation**   See FOUNDATIONS.

**froufrou**   Fluffy trimmings such as ruffles, ribbons, and laces. *Der.* French, "rustle" or "swish."

**froufrou dress**   Daytime dress of 1870 made with low-necked bodice and worn under a short muslin tunic. Skirt was cut away in front revealing a silk underskirt trimmed with many tiny pinked flounces. *Der.* From the name of the comedy *Froufrou* written by Henri Meilhac and Ludovic Halévy in 1869.

**froufrou mantle**   Woman's shoulder cape or *pelerine* of late 1890s made in three tiers trimmed with *ruching*. Closed with a choker neckline having rosettes and long ribbon streamers in front. Also called *froufrou cape*. *Der.* From the name of the comedy *Froufrou* written by Henri Meilhac and Ludovic Halévy in 1869.

**frouting**   17th-c. term for process of rubbing perfumed oil into a garment to freshen it.

**frouze**   Term used in late 17th and early 18th c. for curled *false hair* or *wig* worn to conceal baldness. Also spelled *fruz*.

**F.T.C.**   See FEDERAL TRADE COMMISSION.

**full-bottom wig**   Extremely large man's wig with center part, small *sausage* curls all over, and long locks on shoulders. Worn from 1660 to early 18th c. on formal occasions by lawyers and learned professional people. Still worn by judges in Great Britain in 20th c. for ceremonial occasions. Also called *French wig*. Also see BINETTE.

**full dress** Term used to indicate *formal attire—formal evening dress* for women and *white tie* and *tails* for men. See DRESSES and SUITS.

**full-fashioned hose** See HOSE.

**full grain** Grain side of leather. Also see FULL TOP GRAIN.

**fulling** Finish applied to woolen and worsted fabrics to compress or shrink the fabric by use of heat, moisture, pressure, and friction to give the appearance of felt.

**full length** See LENGTHS.

**full lining** Finishing of the inside of the garment with a complete lining, so that no seams of the outer fabric are showing. Used mainly for coats, jackets, and sometimes dresses.

**full piqué/full P.K. seam** See GLOVE SEAMS.

**full skirt** See SKIRTS.

**full tee** See KNIT SHIRTS.

**full top grain** Leather industry term for the side of the skin or hide from which the hair has been removed.

**fully let-out** Fur industry term for a fur coat with pelts cut so that one let-out strip goes from neck to hem of coat. Also see LETTING-OUT.

**fume fading** Fading of acetate fabrics caused by acid gases in the atmosphere. Also see FADING.

**fun furs** Term popularized in 1965 for long-haired and unusual furs worked in an interesting manner into a coat or other garment suitable for sports or informal occasions.

**funk fashion** See FUNKY LOOK under LOOKS and PRINTS.

**funnel** Adjective used for accessories and parts of apparel made in the shape of a flaring cone. See COLLARS, NECKLINES, and PAGODA SLEEVE under SLEEVES.

**funnel hat** Brimless tall conical hat of felt or fabric worn by women in the 1930s and 1940s.

**fur** 1. Pelt of an animal, raw or processed, with the hair attached as differentiated from leather, which is tanned without the hair. All furs usually have dense short hairs which are called *underfur*, and much longer, silky hairs which are called *guard hairs*. Best, or *prime pelts*, are secured in coldest time of year with the exception of beaver, a water animal, where water is coldest in early spring from melting snow. 2. An item of wearing apparel, accessory, or trimming made from such pelts, *e.g.*, a fur coat, scarf, hat, or muff. Furs were used since earliest times for clothing, preceding woven cloth. Popular for trim and linings in the Middle Ages, with certain furs, *e.g.*, *ermine*, reserved for the nobility. Popular in the latter half of the 19th and early 20th c. for matching collar and cuffs on full-length coats. From 1900 through 1950s fur scarfs with head, tail, and feet of animal were fashionable. In the early 1930s all types of furs were fashionable. During the 1940s, mink became the most generally used fur with the fur stole increasing in popularity. In 1964 *fun furs* were introduced. Later, furs worked in herringbone, grooved, plaid, and tweed patterns were introduced. In the mid-1980s full-length coats of long-haired furs, *e.g.*, lynx, fox (including silver fox), fisher, fitch and tanuki were popular along with mink and sheared beaver. According to Federal Fur Products Labeling Act of 1952, furs must be labeled as to name of fur; proper origin; processing (sheared, dyed, etc.); and marked as to made of whole skins or pieces, *e.g.*, flanks, paws, tails, gills, etc. Secondhand or used furs must be so labeled. Also a Label Authority Tag must be attached stating that product was made by manufacturer who supports code of Fair Labor Standards. In 1969, U.S. Congress passed Endangered Species Act which banned importation and sale of pelts of tiger, snow leopard, polar bear, and jaguar. In 1970, New York State passed two laws: 1) Harris Act, similar to federal law, and 2) Mason Act of September 1, 1971, which prohibited sale or importation of several species of leopards, tigers, cheetahs, and red wolves. Also extended protection to ocelots, marmots, and jaguars and provided for the seizure of the goods. Other animals protected by law in other countries are: *Northern kit fox* of Canada, *Giant otter* of the Amazon basin, *fur seal* of Argentina and Ecuador, and *Spanish lynx* of Spain. See DYEING #2, GROOVING, GUARD HAIR, LEATHERING, LETTING-IN, LETTING-OUT, NAILING, PLATES, PLUCKING, PRIME PELT, SHEARING, STAPLING, TIPPING, and UNDERFUR in alphabetical listing.

## FURS

**Alaskan seal**  See FUR SEAL.

**American marten**  Least expensive marten with long guard hair and underfur ranging in color from blue-brown to dark-brown.

**antelope**  Stiff flat hair, similar to calf, in beautiful soft brown color; rarely used for fur as the number of antelopes is very limited.

**Armur raccoon**  See USSURIAN RACCOON.

**Australian opossum**  Woolly-type fur usually gray in color; best quality comes from Australia and Tasmania.

**badger**  Heavy, warm, durable fur with long silvery gray guard hairs and dense white or tan underfur.

**baum marten**  Medium-length brown guard hairs and yellow-brown underfur; resembling sable, but guard hairs are coarser, shorter, and not as lustrous. Best pelts are obtained from Europe. Used primarily for jackets, scarfs, and trimmings. Fair to good durability; expensive. Also see MARTEN and STONE MARTEN.

**beaver**  Rich velvety brown fur that, when sheared, reveals a wide silvery stripe down the center. Preferred color is blue-brown; sometimes left natural or bleached beige for "blonde beaver." Most beaver is sheared and coarse guard hairs are plucked out. Peltries are large, requiring only five to seven for a *let-out* coat. Best qualities from Canada, particularly the Laurentian Valley in Quebec, and the U.S., including Alaska. *Der.* From Middle English *bever*, "brown."

**black fox**  Fur with long silky guard hairs and thick underfur, a color phase of the RED FOX belonging to the same genus. SILVER FOX and PLATINUM FOX are color phases of the black fox. It is possible to raise all types by fur farming with the best qualities obtained from this source as well as from Alaska, eastern Canada and northern Europe.

**blue fox**  Dark brown fur with a bluish cast, long silky guard hairs, and thick underfur. Some pelts also have silvery hairs. This fox is a color phase of the Arctic WHITE FOX, but its habitat is more southerly. Best qualities from Alaska and Greenland. It is possible to dye the white fox this color.

**broadtail lamb**  Natural, unsheared, flat moiré pattern, with silky texture. Colors may be natural brown, grays, or black or possibly dyed.

**burunduki**  Usually small, lightweight delicate skins with nine alternate stripes of white and black on a yellow or orangish background. Skin obtained from rodent native to Russia similar to American chipmunk. Frequently imported in *plates*. Used for linings and trimmings.

**calf**  Flat, short, stiff-haired fur from young cattle, usually brown spotted with white, also may be black and white, all black, or brown. Used for trimmings, handbags, belts, shoes, and vests.

**caracul**  Lamb pelt with a *moiré* appearance—best peltries are the flattest. Majority of skins are white and may be dyed; or may be rusty brown, dark brown, or black. Best quality from Russia. When skins are from China, called *Chinese lamb* or *Mongolian lamb*. Used for coats, jackets, and trimmings. Durability is moderate.

**cheetah**   Flat fur from the cat family from Africa or Southern Asia, with black spots on a tawny ground. Hair is softer and lighter than leopard. Used for coats, jackets, hats, etc. No longer permitted by law to be used in U.S.

**China mink**   Yellowish mink found in China dyed to imitate North American mink which is much more expensive. Also see KOLINSKY.

**chinchilla**   Silky-haired fur which has a very delicate skin. Best quality has slate-blue underfur and guard hairs that are white and darker at the tips, center back is gray. This small rodent is native to the Andes Mountains in South America. May also be raised on fur ranches. Mutation colors are now available.

**Chinese dog**   Fur with long guard hairs and thick underfur from Mongolia and Manchuria. Used as trimming on inexpensive coats. Sewed into mats for shipment.

**Chinese lamb**   See CARACUL.

**Chinese raccoon**   See USSURIAN RACCOON.

**civet cat**   Spotted fur characterized by elongated black marks against a dark gray background with a greenish cast. Not widely used. Comes from southern China and the Malay Peninsula. The little spotted skunk of South America is sometimes incorrectly called the civet cat.

**coney**   Synonym for RABBIT. The word "rabbit" originally meant "the young of the coney." This term is accepted as a synonym for rabbit for proper fur labeling. Coats may be labeled beaver-dyed coney or beaver-dyed rabbit.

**cross fox**   Fur with long silky guard hair and dense underfur in a dark reddish color. Named for the marking between the gills in the shape of a "cross" rather than a product of cross breeding. It is a color phase of the RED FOX.

**ermine**   Pure white fur from weasel family with short guard hairs and silky soft underfur. Best quality from the far north—Siberia, in particular. As the animal roams further south, it develops a protective coloration which changes to light shades of brown. Traditionally used by royalty since Middle Ages and still used on ceremonial robes of British peerage.

**fisher**   Color shading from brown to blackish tones with long guard hairs and dense underfur. Used primarily for scarfs and jackets usually in its natural state. Best quality pelts come from Labrador. Very good durability; fairly scarce and expensive.

**fitch**   Moderately priced fur, with yellow underfur and black guard hairs with a silky texture; found in Europe. *White fitch*, another type, is found in Ural Mountains of southern Russia. Used for coats, jackets and trimmings. Durability is very good; relatively inexpensive. Color ranges from ecru with black markings to orange tones.

**fox**   Fur with long lustrous guard hairs and deep dense underfur. There are four primary types of foxes and many miscellaneous types. Main groups are: (a) *red fox*—includes black, silver, platinum, and *cross fox* (yellowish with a black cross marking) as color phases; (b) *white fox*—with blue fox a color phase; (c) *gray fox*; and (d) *kit fox*. Northern kit fox is protected by Canadian government. Found in every continent except South America, and also raised on fur farms. Used for coats, jackets, scarfs, muffs, jackets, and trimmings. See other fox furs listed separately: BLACK, BLUE, CROSS, GRAY, PLATINUM, RED, SILVER, and WHITE FOX.

**fur seal**   Soft velvety fur from the genuine Alaska seal. All pelts are sheared and dyed either black or brown and other colors. Sealing is controlled by the U.S. government with pelts coming from the Pribilof Islands, off the coast of

Alaska. Used for coats, jackets, hats, and muffs. Durability is high. Expensive because of the limited quantity available. Argentina and Ecuador protect species.

**golden muskrat**  Side portions of the southern muskrat pelt. Also see MUSKRAT.

**gray fox**  Long-haired fur with silky guard hairs and dense underfur of a gray color. Used mainly for trimmings; best qualities are from the U.S.

**gray muskrat**  The belly part of the southern muskrat. Also see MUSKRAT.

**guanaco**  Reddish-brown fur from the young guanaco or guanaquito found in Argentina. Inexpensive and not durable, it is used for jackets and trimmings, and is the only member of the llama family used for fur.

**hair seal**  Stiff rather short-haired fur with a natural blue-black or blue-and-black mottled effect that may be dyed various other colors. Comes from two varieties of seals, the *harp seal* and the *hooded seal*, whose habitat is the North Atlantic. Baby hair seals are white in color, and used to make sealskin leathers as the fur is slightly woolly.

**hamster**  Small soft golden-brown pelts of rodent found in the Rhine River Valley and in Siberia. Similar in appearance to the American muskrat. Used most often for linings. Rarely used in America.

**hare**  Soft short-haired fur, similar to rabbit but with more tendency to mat. Arctic hare from northern Europe and Asia has a long guard hair and is sometimes used to imitate the Arctic fox. Durability is low but higher than rabbit fur.

**Hudson Bay sable**  See MARTEN.

**Hudson seal**  Proper name is *Hudson seal-dyed muskrat*. Also see MUSKRAT.

**jaguar**  Flat spotted fur with dark rosette markings with two dots in centers against tawny background. Popular for coats and two-piece suits for women in the early 1960s. In comparatively short supply. No longer permitted by law to be used in U.S.

**Jap/Japanese mink**  Muddy yellow-colored mink from Japan which is always dyed in imitation of more expensive American mink.

**Jap fox**  See USSURIAN RACCOON.

**Jap raccoon**  See USSURIAN RACCOON.

**kidskin**  Short-haired flat gray fur with wavy pattern, inexpensive fur with low durability. The best peltries come from young goats of India, China, Ethiopia, and South America.

**kolinsky**  Brownish fur with medium-length silky guard hair and slightly yellowish underfur. Best qualities from Manchuria. Used primarily for scarfs and trimmings, and used in imitation of American and Canadian mink. Durability is fair. Also see CHINA MINK.

**lamb**  Many types of lamb are processed for fur, but three main types stand out: *Persian lamb, broadtail lamb*, and *caracul lamb*—differentiated by luster, and tightness of the fur curl. Other lamb variations include *Afghan, Astrakhan, Argentine, Bessarabian, Iranian, Kalgan, Soviet Union, India, China*, and *Southwest Africa*. Crimean lamb is called *crimmer* or *krimmer*. Also see BROADTAIL, CARACUL, MOUTON, and PERSIAN LAMB.

**leopard**  Spotted jungle-cat fur judged by: (a) flatness; (b) contrast between spots and background; (c) shape of rosettes or spots. There is no underfur in the best qualities, and better qualities have shorter hair. Best quality are from African Somaliland. Although leopard fur was used as early as Egyptian times, it was not popular for women's wear until after World War I. Good durability; very limited in supply and expensive. No longer permitted by law to be used in U.S.

**lynx**  Long silky-haired delicately spotted fur. Colors vary from white, blue gray, pale gray, and brown. Best quality of white comes from the Hudson Bay area and Alaska. Peltries also come from other parts of Canada, Scandinavia, and Siberia. Used for coats, jackets, and trimming. Spain protects the *Spanish lynx*.

**lynx cat** Differs from lynx being darker in color with darker spots and shorter guard hairs, similar to the American wildcat. Best qualities are from Nova Scotia, other qualities from Canada and U.S. Used mainly for trimmings.

**marmot** Fur with guard hair and underfur similar to MUSKRAT and MINK. Blue-black color is preferred, other peltries are dyed brown and frequently processed to simulate mink; moderately priced. Marmot comes mainly from the Soviet Union, Manchuria, and China. Used mainly for coats, jackets, and trimmings for cloth coats. No longer permitted by law to be used in U.S.

**marten** Soft rich fur with fairly long guard hair and thick underfur similar to sable; blue-black or brown colors preferred, but ranges to canary yellow. Best qualities found in eastern Canada and the Hudson Bay area. Incorrectly called the *Hudson Bay sable*. Also see BAUM MARTEN, STONE MARTEN, and AMERICAN MARTEN.

**mink** Fur with silky to coarse guard hairs and dense, soft underfur. Best qualities of the dark pelts are lustrous with the guard hairs giving off a blue reflection. Originally only WILD MINK was available, with best qualities coming from eastern Canada; northeastern U.S. pelts ranked second. Animal also exists in Europe, but pelts are usually of less value. Zoological name is *Mustela vison* and animal is from the weasel family. *Vison* is the European name for mink. Since the 1940s much mink is raised by fur farming in the U.S. Many color variations are now available due to the development of new strains, or MUTATIONS, on ranches. Most mink is used in the NATURAL color and the fur is of good durability. In the 1930s the mink coat became a status symbol. With the growth in popularity of the stole during the 1950s, and the production of more pelts by fur farming,

mink became available to the masses. Usually made in *let-out* style for coats until the 1960s when it was worked *in-the-round*. In mid-1960s patterned and patchwork minks became fashionable. These were made of paws, gills, and small bits pieced together to form *blankets* of flowered, herringbone, plaid, tweed and windowpane patterns from which a garment was cut. In the late 1960s and early 1970s painted, sheared, hand-screened, and tie-dyed mink became fashionable. Also see CHINA MINK, JAPANESE MINK, NATURAL MINK, WILD MINK, and MUTATION MINK.

**mole** Extremely soft gray fur, rather flat with a wavy appearance, and a very delicate skin. Best qualities come from Asia. Popular for jackets and trimmings in early 1900s. Poor durability. Always dyed to avoid white skin from showing through.

**Mongolian lamb** See CARACUL.

**monkey** Very long lustrous black fur with no underfur. Used for trimmings and jackets. Obtained primarily from the colobus monkey on the east and west coasts of Africa.

**mouton-processed lamb** Woolly fur with a dense pile, made by shearing the merino sheep rather than "hair" sheep. Used for coats, jackets, and hats. Inexpensive, warm, and durable. Generally dyed brown, frequently water-repellent.

**muskrat** Fur with long guard hairs and dense underfur, processed three different ways: (a) dyed and striped to resemble mink and sable; (b) sheared and dyed to imitate Alaskan seal and called *Hudson seal-dyed muskrat*; and (c) left natural and finished to improve the coloring. Best qualities of northern muskrat, which is brown or black, are used for *Hudson seal dyed muskrat* and come from the Great Lakes region in the U.S. Southern pelts, which vary in color, are used for natural muskrat coats. Durability is moderate to high. Natural muskrat skins are split into five parts, each part used separately as "back coats," "golden sides coats," and "silver belly coats."

**mutation mink** Term for strains of mink developed scientifically on fur farms by carefully mating the animals. Original wild pelts were brown. From mating the odd animals, many new colors were produced. EMBA trademark names for these colors are: *Aeolian*, taupe; *Arcturus*, lavender-beige; *Argenta*, gray: *Autumn Haze*, medium brown; *Azurene*, blue-gray; *Cerulean*, blue; *Diadem*, pale brown; *Jasmine*, white; *Lutetia*, gunmetal; *Morning Light*, pale blue-beige; *Rovalia*, rose; *Tourmaline*, pale beige; *Tyrian Glo*, dark brown. *Blackglama* is the GLMA trademark for very dark brown mink. Also during the 1960s mink with longer hair was produced through breeding. A trade name for this type was *Kojah*. In order to market pelts, associations of mink breeders were formed. Some of these are CMBA, Canadian Mink Breeders Association; EMBA, Mink Breeders Association (American); GLMA, Great Lakes Mink Association (American); and SAGA, Scandinavian Association.

**natural mink** Mink which has not been dyed or colored in any manner.

**nutria** Fur with a velvety appearance after long guard hairs have been plucked with color ranging from cinnamon brown to brown with gray stripes. Fur is similar to beaver although not as thick, lustrous, and rich in color. Animal is a water rodent of northern Argentina, usually wild but some attempts at breeding were made in 1950s. Used for coats, linings, and trimmings. Durability is moderate. Sometimes kept in natural state with long guard hairs and short underfur in lustrous brown. When produced on a ranch, it is bluish-beige in color and slightly coarser. May also be dyed.

**ocelot** Spotted fur with elongated dark markings against a tan background. Flatter-haired peltries are the best qualities and come from Brazil and Mexico. Used mainly for coats and jackets. This durable fur is in short supply, relatively expensive.

**opossum** Long straight guard hairs and dense underfur which in the natural color is either black or gray. Best qualities come from Australia and the U.S. Used for coats, linings, trimmings or dyed to imitate other furs such as skunk and fitch; moderately priced. Australian varieties have short, dense, plushlike fur ranging from yellow-gray to blue-gray.

**otter** Relatively short-haired fur with silky lustrous guard hair and dense underfur—the most durable fur for the weight and thickness. Preferred color has blue-brown guard hairs and underfur slightly lighter with the base being gray to white color. Best qualities come from eastern Canada. Some otter is sheared and plucked. *Giant otter* of Amazon protected by Brazil. Also see SEA OTTER.

**Persian lamb** Curly lustrous fur which is usually black but occasionally brown or white. Dark colors are always dyed to color the white skin. Quality is determined by the tightness of the "knuckle" curl and formation of interesting patterns called "flowers." Best quality comes from Bokara, Russia, from Karakul Sheep. Others come from Afghanistan, Southwest Africa, and Iran. Popular for coats and trimmings. Durability is high. Now available in new mutation colors. Also see LAMB.

**Persian paw** Fur of the Persian lamb which is left after a coat is made—the paws, head, and gills. Small pieces are sewed together to make larger pieces called *plates*. Another coat, collar or garment is then cut from the *plate*.

**platinum fox** Silvery long-haired fur with long guard hairs and dense black underfur. The reverse of the silver fox it has much silvery hair and little black hair. First discovered in 1935, and later raised on fur farms in the U.S. and Norway, where the trade name is *Platina*. Originally one of the rarest furs.

**pony** Short-haired flat fur with a wavy moiré appearance. Used in natural color, bleached, or dyed pale colors. Best quality comes from Poland and Russia. Durability good, but short bristly fur has a tendency to wear "bald."

**rabbit** Soft light fur in a variety of colors used in natural state or can be dyed or processed as follows: a) striped to imitate muskrat, b) sheared to imitate beaver, and c) sheared and stenciled to resemble leopard. Best qualities come from Australia and New Zealand. Poor durability; inexpensive. Also see CONEY.

**raccoon** Long light-silvery guard hair and dark-brown underfur. Lighter weight peltries from the southern part of the U.S. are used for coats. Northern U.S. provides heavy-skinned pelts used primarily for hats and trimmings. Popular for men's and women's coats in 1920s, revived in 1960s. Also see SHEARED RACCOON.

**Raccoon dog** See USSURIAN RACCOON.

**ranch mink** Color ranges from true rich brown to brownish-black.

**red fox** Fur with long silky guard hairs and dense underfur, which is red-orange in color. As the fur becomes more yellowish, it is less valuable. A red fox may have different colored foxes in its litter, *e.g.*, BLACK, SILVER or CROSS FOX. Best qualities come from Alaska, Siberia, and Labrador.

**sable** Luxurious fur with lustrous long silky guard hairs and soft dense fluffy underfur; preferred color, a blue-black-brown. Skins that are light brown in color are tipped, blended, and called *dyed sable*. Used for coats or scarfs, with best quality, called *Russian crown sable*, coming from Siberia. Animal is also found in China, Korea, and Japan. Durability is good and very expensive. Golden sable in amber tone is less expensive.

**seal** See HAIR SEAL and FUR SEAL.

**sea otter** Fur with silky guard hairs and silky underfur in a deep blue-black or brown with sprinklings of white hairs. Almost extinct, one pelt brings an extremely high price. Extremely large pelts measure 5′ to 11′ in length are found in Arctic region.

**sheared raccoon** Velvety-textured fur similar in appearance to beaver, but not as soft or silky and more cinnamon brown in color with lighter stripes. Raccoon is processed by plucking and shearing. Durable fur, much less expensive than beaver.

**shearling** Pelts from "wool" lambs, which have been processed with the hair intact, therefore classifying them as "fur" rather than "leather." Used for jackets, collars, and coats. Usually sueded on the leatherside.

**silver fox** Black long-haired fur with long silky silvery guard hairs and dense underfur. Best quality has the greatest amount of "silver" in it. Silver fox may be found in litters of the red fox. Also raised by fur farming.

**skunk** Black fur with long guard hairs and thick underfur with characteristic white stripe down back. Quality of fur depends on ability of the underfur to remain black rather than take on a brownish or rust-colored appearance. For an all-black fur, peltries have white streaks removed and are dyed to darken the skin. Used extensively in the 1930s for jackets and coats; best qualities are from the Dakotas and Minnesota. Also found in Canada and South America. Better U.S. types have high durability. Zorina South American skunk is similar with flatter fur and silky texture.

**snow leopard** Spotted long silky guard hair with long underfur in a pale yellow-gray color with white belly and markings which are more like spots than rosettes. Found in high altitudes of the Himalaya Mountains of central Asia. No longer permitted by law to be used in U.S.

**spotted cat** Variety of spotted fur which comes from three main types of South American cat: the *chati cat*, the *marguay*, and *long-*

tailed cats. Markings are more rounded than those of the OCELOT; fur is less expensive.

**squirrel**　Very soft gray or brown relatively short fur that takes dye readily and may be made any color or worked into a two-toned pattern. Best qualities come from Europe, Asia, Russia, Poland, Finland, and Canada. Used mainly for jackets, capes, and trimmings. Low durability; moderately priced.

**stone marten**　Fur with brown guard hairs and grayish-white underfur judged for quality by the contrast of two colors. Best qualities come from Europe, particularly Russia. Used primarily for scarfs. Also see MARTEN.

**tanuki**　Japanese name for raccoon-dog which must be labeled and sold under name *Ussurian raccoon* in U.S. according to Federal Trade Regulations. Also see USSURIAN RACCOON.

**Ussurian raccoon**　Long-haired, yellowish-brown peltry with shoulder and tail tipped with black, slightly coarse guard hair and long, dense underfur. May be dyed, sheared or used in natural state mainly for collars and trim. Comes from a species of dog which resembles a raccoon in appearance. The Japanese species, known as TANUKI, has the most silky, fully-furred pelt (but is not the largest). Other qualities come from Manchuria, Korea, Siberia, and parts of Europe. Also called *Raccoon dog, Amur raccoon, Chinese raccoon, Jap fox, Jap raccoon.* These names cannot be used when merchandising pelts in U.S. Color is similar to red fox with distinctive cross markings.

**vison**　See MINK.

**weasel**　Soft silky short guard hairs and silky underfur similar in texture to ERMINE, a close relative. Color varies with the seasons—winter, white; spring, yellowish; summer, streaked with brown or gray; and brown all year in southern climates.

**white fox**　Pure white fur with long silky guard hairs and dense underfur. Comes from the *Arctic fox*, which lives north of the timber-line and remains white the entire year. The BLUE FOX is a color phase of this fox living south of the timberline.

**wild mink**　Skins procured from animals which run wild in the forest. Very expensive because skins must be matched in color. Under controlled conditions on a mink farm, color is more uniform and is usually brown.

**wolf**　Long-haired fur with long silky guard hairs and dense underfur. Pale-colored skins are sometimes stenciled to imitate LYNX; others are used in natural state or dyed brown, black, or gray. Quality depends on fluffiness and density of underfur that supports the long guard hairs. The best quality comes from the timber wolf of Canada. Used for coats, capes, jackets, trimmings, and scarfs. The red wolf is protected in U.S.

**wolverine**　Coarse fur with long brown guard hairs and dense gray underfur. Very durable; best qualities found in the Arctic regions, also found in the Rocky Mountains and Siberia. Used mainly for sportswear and trimming. Used in the far north to trim the edges of parkas as moisture will not condense on it.

**zebra**　Flat, stiff fur with wide, black irregularly shaped stripes against a light-colored background. Comes from Africa; used infrequently for coats. Calf is sometimes stenciled to imitate zebra.

**zorina**　See SKUNK.

---

**furbelow**　Term for skirt ruffles used as trim on women's skirts and scarfs in the 18th c. Usually made of same fabric or lace. Also called *falbala* or *fabala*.

**furbelow wig**　See DUVILLIER WIG.

**fur blended yarn**　Any yarn made from mink, muskrat, rabbit, or raccoon fur blended with other yarns, *e.g.*, wool or nylon, used for knitted clothing. See HAIR FIBERS.

**fur fabric coat** See COATS.

**fur farming** Raising and scientific breeding of animals for their pelts. Originated in the 1920s with raising of *silver foxes*; later same method was used to raise *ranch mink* and *mutation mink*. See FURS.

**fur felt** Best grade of felt obtained from underfur, especially from beaver and rabbit, used for hats. Also see BEAVER HAT.

**fur fiber** See UNDERFUR.

**furisode** Kimono with large flowing sleeves.

**Fur Labeling Act** Legislation passed by Congress in 1938, amended in 1952, in regard to labeling of fur items sold to consumers. All furs must be labeled with correct name of animal, country of origin, and whether dyed, stenciled, etc. See FURS.

**fur lining** Lining a garment with fur for warmth and fashion appeal. If the garment is meant to be reversible, the sleeves are lined; otherwise sleeves are not fur-lined in order to reduce bulkiness.

**fur scarf** Neckpiece made of several skins of a small animal such as *mink*, or one large fox skin complete with head, tail and paws. Popular in the 1930s in black, platinum, or silver fox. In the late 1940s and early 1950s made of *mink*, *sable*, *fisher*, *kolinsky*, and *baum marten*. A fashion revived in 1973, continuing into 1980s.

**fur seal** See FURS.

**fur stole** Term used in 20th c. for waist-length fur cape with elongated ends in front, sometimes trimmed with tails of animals. Formerly called PELERINE or TIPPET. Very popular in late 1940s, 1950s, and 1960s, especially in mink.

**fused collar** Collar for a man's shirt, preferably made by bonding the interlining with the right side of the collar using solvents, heat, and pressure. Two methods are used: *a)* the dry process uses a coating of acetate film on the interlining which melts and fuses to other fabric, and *b)* the wet process involves an interlining fabric woven with some acetate yarns which melt and fuse when heated.

**fused fabric** Nonwoven fabric which is made up of more than one fiber. One of the fibers is man-made and has a low melting point. When heat is applied the man-made fiber melts and bonds with the other fibers, *e.g.*, PELLON.

**fused hem** See HEMS.

**fused ribbon** Ribbon which is made of acetate and woven like piece goods. It is then cut with a hot knife melting the edges enough to keep them from fraying.

**fused seam** See SEAMS.

**fustanella** (foo-sta-knell-a) Knee-length, stiffly pleated full skirt worn by palace guards in Greece.

**gabardine** **1.** Durable, closely woven fabric with definite ridges caused by the warp-faced twill weave. *Cotton gabardine* is made with carded or combed yarns—with single yarns used in the filling and single or two-ply yarns in the warp direction. *Wool gabardine* has a firm hand, is made with worsted yarns, and given a clear finish. Also made of rayon. Used for tailored suits and coats for men and women, pants, sportswear, and riding breeches. *Der.* From word used for a cloak or mantle in the Middle Ages. **2.** See GARBERDINE.

**gabbia** Italian term for hair accessory, often called a *rat*, consisting of a roll over which hair is wrapped for high round effect, *e.g.*, in the POMPADOUR manner. *Der.* Italian, "cage."

**gaberdine** (gab-er-deen) Long, loose-fitting cloth overcoat, sometimes made of felt, with wide sleeves and belted. Worn particularly by fashionable men until 1560, and by commoners until early 17th c. *Der.* Eastern *gaba*, "coat." Also spelled *gabardine*. Also see CABAN.

**gable bonnet/hat** Woman's hat of 1884 with front brim angled like a Gothic arch.

**GABLE HEADDRESS, c. 1515**

**gable headdress** See ENGLISH HOOD.

**Gabrielle dress** (ga-bree-el) **1.** Daytime dress of 1865 with bodice and front of skirt cut in one piece. Back was made with two large box pleats on either side and another in center. **2.** Girl's jumper-type dress of early 20th c. made in princess style and worn over bracelet-length, full-sleeved, high-necked blouse.

**1906**

**GABRIELLE DRESS #1**

**Gabrielle sleeve** (ga-bree-el) **1.** Type of sleeve used in *spencer jackets*, and dresses in 1820s and early 1830s. Made with *mancherons* at shoulder, full to elbow, narrowed to wrist, and ending in a deep cuff. **2.** Sleeve composed of series of puffs extending from shoulder to wrist worn from late 1850s to 1870s.

**Gabrielle waist** (ga-bree-el) Woman's fitted waist of 1870s buttoned down center front. Sometimes made with a small fluted ruff and sleeves in a series of puffs.

**GABRIELLE WAIST**

**Gainsborough hat** Large, graceful brimmed hat worn from late 1860s to 1890s. Made of velvet, straw, or beaver, frequently turned up on one side and trimmed with ostrich plumes. *Der.* Named after the 18th c. British painter, *Gainsborough*, who painted many portraits of ladies in this type of hat including portrait of *Duchess of Devonshire.*

**gaiter** **1.** Cloth or leather covering for leg and ankle, buttoned or buckled at side, often held on by straps under foot. Worn by men from end of 18th to early 20th c. **2.** Fashionable for women from 1820s to 1840s, and from 1890s to early 20th c. Revived in 1960s in vinyl, leather, or cloth. Fashionable in 1980s in Gor Tex® with Velcro® closing for cross-country skiing. Also called *leggings.* Also see SPATS.

**gaiter boots** Woman's buttoned or elastic-sided, ankle-high leather shoes worn from 1835 to 1870. Made with cloth tops and fastened at side—simulating low shoe worn with GAITERS.

**galabijeh** Dress worn formerly by an Egyptian native laborer called a *fellah.*

**galage** See GALOSH.

**Galanos, James** See APPENDIX/DESIGNERS.

**Galashiels** **1.** Term used to describe tweeds made in the Galashiels, a section of Scotland. **2.** Yarn numbering term designating size of yarns used in these fabrics.

**galatea** Striped blue and white shirting fabric made in Great Britain.

**galatea fichu** Large ruffled *fichu* of mid-1890s with unpressed vertical pleats ending at center front waistline in a point and two ruffles around the outside edge.

**galatea hat** Child's hat of plaited straw with sailor crown and turned-up brim worn in 1890s.

**Galitzine, Princess Irene** See APPENDIX/DESIGNERS.

**gallants** Small ribbon bows worn in hair or on sleeve, bodice, or skirt in mid-17th c.

**galligaskins** (galli-gas-kins) **1.** *Trunk hose,* similar to stuffed or *bombasted barrel hose,* worn from 1570 to 1620 and rarely to 17th c. by men. Also spelled *gally-gascoynes.* Also called *gaskins* or *gregs.* **2.** 19th-c. term for gaiters of leather worn by sportsmen.

**Gallo-Greek bodice** Bodice style of 1820s made with narrow flat trim running diagonally from shoulders to waist in front and back.

**galloon** See BRAIDS.

**galloses/galloshes** Plural of GALOSH.

**gallowses** See BRACES.

**galosh** **1.** Waterproof ankle-high boot worn over the shoe, fastened with a snap, buckle, or zipper. Also spelled *goloshe, golosh.* Also see ARCTICS under BOOTS and GALOSH CLIP under CLOSINGS. **2.** Wooden platform elevating foot above street, worn in 15th and 16th c. Also called a *patten.* **3.** In the 17th c. also called *boxes.* **4.** In 16th and 17th c. wooden-soled low overboots. **5.** In 17th c. became "covers for shoes." **6.** In 18th c. called CLOGS. **7.** Rubber galoshes were patented in 1842. Also spelled *galoche, galage, galoss, galossian*; plurals: *galloses, galloshes, gallotives.*

**galuchat** See LEATHERS.

**galungan** Crown-shaped headdress, with wing-shaped projections over the ears, worn low on the forehead by Bali temple dancers. Made

**GALUNGAN**

of stenciled, colored, and gilded leather. Trimmed with fresh lotus flowers on top, metal rosettes, and dangles in front of ears.

**gambeson** (gam-bee-son) Sleeveless leather or quilted fabric garment worn under armor in Middle Ages. Adapted as regular civilian garment in knee lengths, forerunner of DOUBLET, GIPON, or POURPOINT. Also see ACTON and HAUBERK.

**gambeto** Thick woolen overcoat worn by men in Catalonia, a region of Spain.

**gamin** See HAIRSTYLES.

**gaming purse** Drawstring bag of kid, velvet, or embroidered fabric used in 17th c. Made with flat stiffened circular base and pleated sides. *Der.* Used to hold counters and coins when "gaming," *e.g.,* playing cards for money.

**gamp** 19th-c. slang for umbrella. Named after Mrs. Sarah Gamp, character in Charles Dickens' 1843 novel, *Martin Chuzzlewit.*

**gandourah** (gahn-doo-rah) Loose ankle-length garment worn by Arabian women. Made of brocade or satin for winter and calicos or muslin for summer. Sometimes matched to SHALWAR trousers. Also spelled *gandoura, gondura.*

**ganges** Term used for leather embossed to imitate snakeskin.

**gangster suit** See SUITS.

**Ganymede look** (gan-e-meed) Look of Ancient Greece popularized in 1969 consisting of a short tunic worn with unusual sandals. *Der.* From the Greek myth about a Greek boy, named Ganymede, carried off by an eagle to become a cup bearer for Zeus. Also called *Greek boy look.* Also see SANDALS and LOOKS.

**garb** See APPAREL #1.

**Garbo, Greta** Swedish-born MGM film star of great beauty who gave unforgettable performances from 1925–1939 in such movies as *Mata Hari* (1932), *Grand Hotel* (1932), *Anna Karenina* (1935), *Camille* (1936), and *Ninotchka* (1939). At age 36 she retired to a secluded life in New York City. Publicity shy, she was frequently seen in trenchcoat, slacks, and slouch hat, the latter now called by her name. Also see GARBO HAT under HATS.

**garcette** (gar-cett) Fringe of hair over forehead worn in Louis XIII period. Also see COIFFURE EN BOUFFONS.

**garconne look** (gar-sown) Current French term for flapper look or boyish look of 1920s with straight-cut dresses de-emphasizing the bust and boyish bob. *Der.* French, "boy." See FLAPPER and HAIRSTYLES.

**garde-corps** (gard cor) Full, unbelted outer tunic with hood and long full hanging sleeves, frequently worn with arms passed through slits above elbows. Worn by men and women in 13th and early 14th c. England.

**GARDEN HAT, 1860**

**garden hat** **1.** Woman's hat of 1860s made of muslin with flat top cut in oval shape. Ruffles or long pieces of muslin hung down to protect the wearer from the sun. Hat was frequently made with ribbon trim. **2.** Large-brimmed floppy hat of horsehair or straw worn in 1920s and 1930s for afternoon teas and garden parties. **3.** Large-brimmed straw hat currently worn when gardening to protect face from the sun.

**Garibaldi jacket** (gar-ih-bawl-dee) Woman's square-cut waist-length jacket of 1860s made of red cashmere trimmed with black braid. *Der.* Inspired by clothes worn by Italian patriot Giuseppe Garibaldi.

**GARIBALDI SHIRT, 1862**

**Garibaldi shirt/blouse** (gar-ih-bawl-dee) Red merino high-necked shirt of 1860s trimmed with black braid, bloused, and belted. Made with full sleeves gathered into wristband, small collar with black *cravat*, and *epaulets* on shoulders. *Der.* Inspired by clothes worn by Italian patriot Giuseppe Garibaldi.

**Garibaldi suit** (gar-ih-bawl-dee) **1.** Little boy's collarless suit of 1860s consisting of thigh-length overblouse with dropped shoulders, belted at waistline, and worn with calf-length trousers. Trimmed with braid, rickrack, and buttons down center front, around hem of blouse, at sleeves, and down sides of trousers.

**GARIBALDI SUIT**

**2.** Little girl's collarless two-piece dress of 1860s with full blouse, sleeves set into dropped shoulders, and a full skirt. Trimmed at neck, down front, around waist, wrists, and hem with bands of leather and steel buttons.

**garland** Wreath of flowers or foliage worn on the head as ornament or as an honor.

**garment** **1.** See APPAREL #1. **2.** Shortened form of the term *foundation garment*.

**garment trade** See APPAREL INDUSTRY.

**garnache** Tunic worn for extra warmth from 13th to mid-14th c. Made of a long rectangle of fabric with a hole in the center for the head. Sides were either joined at waist, from waist to hem, or left open. Cut wide across the shoulders so that tunic fell like a cape over upper arm to elbow. Similar to HOUSSE. Also see TABARD.

**garnet** See GEMS.

**garniture** Term used in 19th and early 20th c. for trimmings, *e.g.*, ruffles, lace, ribbons, and bows.

**garrison cap** See CAPS.

**garter** **For Women:** Elastic supporters attached to *girdle* or *garter belt*, used to hold up hose. **For Men: 1.** Buckled around calves of legs to hold up socks, a custom starting in early 19th c. **2.** Since Medieval times a strip of fabric tied spirally around leg or buckled below knee worn by men through 18th c. **3.** Band of elastic worn below the knee to hold up hose. **4.** Round

**GARTER, 1930s**

elasticized band worn around the sleeve to shorten it. Also see CHEMISETTE GARTER.

**garter belt** Elasticized band, which fits either around the hips or waist, with four or six elastic garters attached to hold up hose. Some are styled like a girdle to give added support. Some are lacy and provocative when worn over tiny *bikini panties*. Also see HOSE.

**garter briefs** See GIRDLES and PANTIES.

**gascon coat/gaskyn** See JUPE #3.

**gaskins** See GALLIGASKINS.

**gassing** Finish used on fabrics and yarns which removes all fuzzy ends and short fibers. Fabric or yarn is passed over a gas flame or a heated copper plate to singe off short fibers. Also called *singeing*.

**gathered skirt** See SKIRTS.

**gathering** Drawing up fullness by tightening of several threads in a row of stitching. Also see SHIRRING.

**gatyak** Full pantaloons extending to below the knee, cut to resemble a divided skirt, formerly worn by the peasant men of Hungary. Made of white linen or white woolen fabric and frequently finished at the hem with coarse handmade lace or fringe.

**gaucho** (gow-cho) Clothing and accessories worn by South American cowboys. *Der.* Spanish, "cowboy" of Argentina, Chile, and Uru-

guay. Also see BELTS, HATS, LOOKS, PANTS, SILHOUETTES, and SUITS.

**gaufré** (go-freh) Raised surface effect, *e.g.*, honeycomb or waffle pattern on cotton, produced by embossed patterns with heated rollers. *Der.* French, "crimped."

**gauge** Knitting term for number of stitches per unit of width and length in a knitted fabric.

**gauging** See SHIRRING.

**Gaultier, Jean-Paul** (Go-tea-ay) See APPENDIX/DESIGNERS.

**gauntlet** 1. Armor of *mail*, or plate, worn on the hand from 15th to 17th c. 2. See CUFFS and GLOVES.

**gauze** 1. Net-like sheer, open weave fabric used for trimmings and costumes made in the *leno* or *plain weave* of silk, cotton, rayon, and other man-made fabrics. 2. Plain open weave fabric, similar to lightweight muslin made of loosely twisted cotton yarns. Sometimes given a crinkled finish, used for blouses, and worn unpressed. 3. See LENO WEAVE. *Der.* From Gaza, a city in the Middle East.

**gay deceivers** See FALSIES.

**Gay 90s** Period in history from 1890 to 1900 when society relaxed from prim and staid Victorianism. More women were employed, thus requiring more tailored clothing. See TAILOR-MADE and GIBSON WAIST. Sports and recreation became more popular necessitating divided skirts for bicycling and special clothing for yachting, tennis, canoeing, and swimming. Men wore less formal clothes, *e.g.*, the STRAW BOATER and BLAZER. Also see GAY 90S BATHING SUIT under SWIMSUITS.

**Gaze, point de** See LACES.

**geisha** (gay-sha or gee-sha) Japanese hostess trained in art of entertaining men by singing and dancing while dressed in traditional Japanese headdress and *kimono*.

**gele** See SCARFS.

**gem** Mineral which is rare, beautiful, durable, and is in demand because of fashion. It must also be portable and suitable for personal adornment. Divided into PRECIOUS STONES, SEMIPRECIOUS STONES, ORNAMENTAL STONES, and MARINE GEMS. Gems are classified as TRANSPARENT, SEMI-TRANSPARENT, or OPAQUE. Also classified as to CRYSTALLINE, CRYPTOCRYSTALLINE, or AMORPHOUS. Only a qualified gemologist can determine accurately the name of a gem. This is done by testing the gem for hardness, specific gravity, light reflection, and crystalline structure. The *mohs scale* is used to rate the degree of hardness of precious gems. The diamond, the hardest gem, has a hardness of 10 and will scratch any gems which rate below it. A set of minerals used to test gems was invented by Friedrich Mohs and is as follows:

| Mineral | Hardness |
| --- | --- |
| Talc | 1 |
| Gypsum | 2 |
| Calcite | 3 |
| Fluorite | 4 |
| Apatite | 5 |
| Orthoclase (feldspar) | 6 |
| Quartz | 7 |
| Topaz | 8 |
| Sapphire | 9 |
| Diamond | 10 |

## GEMS

**agate** Variety of CHALCEDONY quartz consisting of bands of color either arranged in curved or wavy parallel bands and thus called *banded agate* or in widening circular rings and called *eye agate*. Also with fern or foggy effect called *moss agate* or *mocha stone*.

**alexandrite** Transparent or translucent variety of the mineral CHRYSOBERYL, which appears one color in daylight and another color under artificial light. May appear emerald green in daylight and columbine-red at night. Found in Russia in 1833 on the same day which Czar Alexander II celebrated his attainment to majority and named after him.

**almandine spinel** See SPINEL.

**almandite garnet** Transparent to opaque semiprecious garnet in deep-red, violet-red, brownish-red to almost black. Includes the CARBUNCLE.

**amber** Exists in colors and is translucent. Most popular is called "clear" in a yellow which varies from colorless to brownish-red. It is an amorphous fossil resin which was exuded from prehistoric trees found in deposits along the southern coast of Baltic Sea in Poland. Also found in marine deposits in East Germany, Rumania, Sicily, and Burma.

**amethyst** Transparent purple or violet-colored quartz of the crystalline variety. Rated as a semiprecious stone because it exists in large quantities. Best qualities are a clear even color in the darker tones. The finest qualities come from Uruguay, Ural Mountains, and Brazil. Other sources include Sri Lanka, Japan, South America, and Mexico.

**andradite garnet** Transparent to opaque garnets called by various names: *topazolite*, yellow and transparent; *demantoid*, grass-green and transparent also known erroneously as *olivine* and as *Ural emerald*; *melanite*, black opaque garnets formerly used for mourning jewelry.

**aquamarine** Transparent variety of *beryl* from which the emerald comes. Has the same crystalline structure and hardness but color is aqua rather than green. A 737 carat oval aquamarine owned by the Museum of Natural History in New York City figured in a jewel robbery in 1965. Comes from Ural Mountains, Brazil, and Madagascar. One large aquamarine found in Minas Gerais, Brazil weighed 243 pounds.

**Arizona ruby**   See RUBY.

**balas ruby**   See SPINEL.

**banded agate**   See AGATE.

**beryl**   Mineral from which the EMERALD, a precious gem, is secured. Semiprecious stones include: AQUAMARINE, GOLDEN BERYL, HELIDOR, MORGANITE, and GOSHENITE. Hardness is from 7½ to 8 on *mohs scale*.

**black opal**   See OPAL.

**bloodstone**   Opaque variety of the mineral quartz characterized by red spots on a dark green background. The early church frequently used it to engrave sacred objects, the red spots simulating the blood of Christ. Found in India and Siberia. Also called *heliotrope*.

**Brazilian emerald**   Misleading term for a green TOURMALINE used as a gemstone.

**Brazilian peridot**   Misleading term for a yellow-green TOURMALINE used as a gemstone.

**Brazilian sapphire**   Misleading term for a blue TOURMALINE used as a gemstone.

**cairngorm**   Popular stone in Scotland. See SMOKY QUARTZ.

**cape ruby**   Gem from the *garnet* group, ruby red to black in color and found in deposits with diamonds in Africa. No relationship to genuine ruby.

**carbuncle**   Variety of ALMANDITE GARNET which varies from deep red and violet-red to brownish-red and black. Transparent red varieties are used for gems. Before scientific testing, often believed to be a ruby or spinel.

**carnelian**   Transparent to translucent reddish variety of chalcedony which may be pale red, deep clear red, brownish-red, or yellow-green. Also called *sard*. *Der.* Latin, "flesh-colored."

**cat's eye**   1. Variety of opalescent greenish

*chrysoberyl*, which is chatoyant when cut cabochon. Light seems to fluctuate lengthwise across the stone as it is turned under the light. Also called *cymophane* and *oriental cat's eye*. **2.** Variety of *quartz*, also chatoyant, which is grayish, brownish, or green in color. Not as valuable as #1.

**chalcedony**   Transparent to translucent varieties of quartz which are known by different names for each color. Red is called *carnelian*, apple green called *chrysoprase*, dark green with red spots is called *bloodstone* or *heliotrope*, black and white banded is called *onyx*, and brown banded with white called *sardonyx*.

**chlorspinel**   See SPINEL.

**chrysoberyl**   A mineral with a hardness of 8.5 from which these striking gems are obtained—the chameleon-like *alexandrite*, *oriental cat's eye*, and *chrysolite*.

**chrysolite**   See PERIDOT.

**chrysoprase**   Apple-green variety of *chalcedony quartz* which comes from California, Oregon, and Silesia.

**citrine**   Yellow crystalline *quartz* which resembles topaz in color and transparency, sometimes erroneously sold as topaz. Comes from Brazil.

**coral**   Translucent substance made up of calcareous skeletons secreted by tiny marine animals found in tropical seas. Precious coral of red or pink "grows" in branchlike formations. Used for necklaces, rosaries, and bracelets; may also be cut into beads.

**corundum**   Extremely hard mineral rating 9 on mohs scale, which produces the precious gems RUBY and SAPPHIRE. Also comes in other colors, but these are not so valuable and are called *fancy sapphires*. All red corundum gems are called rubies.

**cross stone**   See FAIRY STONE.

**cubic zirconia**   Man-made synthetic stone made to imitate the diamond.

**cymophane** See CAT'S EYE.

**diamond** See separate category.

**emerald** Precious gem from the mineral BERYL. Hardness is 7½ to 8. Best stones are transparent to translucent green, and large stones of clear color are rare, thus making them very valuable. Comes from Colombia and Brazil, also found in Ural Mountains and Australia.

**eye agate** See AGATE.

**fairy stone** Mineral frequently found in the shape of a cross caused by twin crystals. Usually reddish-brown in color and translucent to opaque. Used for crosses for the clergy or for curiosity items. Also known as *staurolite* and *cross stone.*

**fancy sapphires** See CORUNDUM.

**feldspar** A transparent to opaque mineral with vitreous to pearly luster and a hardness of 6½. Various colors of gem varieties are called by the following names: opalescent called *moonstone* comes from Switzerland, Elba, and Sri Lanka; green, called *amazon stone*, comes from the Urals and Pennsylvania; blue, called *Labradorite*, comes from Labrador; yellow, called *orthoclase*, comes from Madagascar; and reddish, called *sunstone* or *aventurine* comes from Norway and Siberia.

**fire opal** Semi-transparent to transparent variety of opal which is yellow, orange, or red in color. May show a play of color.

**garnet** Gems with a hardness of 6½ to 7½, which exist in too large a quantity to be considered precious gems. Exists in all colors except blue and ranges from transparent to opaque. Varieties include ANDRADITE and ALMANDITE.

**golden beryl** Yellow semiprecious transparent variety of the mineral BERYL.

**goshenite** Colorless transparent variety of the mineral BERYL.

**harlequin opal** White opal which displays uniform patches of colors resembling a mosaic.

**helidor** Yellow transparent variety of the mineral BERYL from southwest Africa.

**heliotrope** See BLOODSTONE.

**hematite** Iron mineral which is opaque black, or black with red streaks and metallic luster. Comes from England, Norway, Sweden, and Lake Superior region.

**Hope Star®** Trademark for a synthetic star sapphire.

**hyacinth** Name used for clear transparent zircons of yellow, orange, red, and brown varieties. Also called *jacinth.*

**jacinth** See HYACINTH.

**jade** Includes two minerals of similar appearance, *nephrite* and *jadeite*. The former is the most common variety with hardness of 6 to 6½, and color variations from white to leaf green. Often found in China, Turkestan, Siberia, and Alaska. *Jadeite* is lustrous, transparent to opaque, and more rare with a hardness of 6½ to 7. Color is white or greenish white to emerald green, translucent to opaque, and found in upper Burma, Yunnan in southern China, Tibet, Mexico, and South America. In 1965, boulders weighing as much as 10,000 pounds containing gem quality jade (nephrite) were found in Alaska. Popular in China for centuries either carved into objects or used for jewelry.

**jargon** See ZIRCON.

**jasper** Form of *opaque quartz* available in brown, dark green, grayish-blue, red, or yellow colors.

**jet** An opaque mineral made largely of carbon, a variety of lignite or coal, which polishes easily. Comes from England, Spain, France, and the U.S. Black varieties of quartz, obsidian, and glass also masquerade as this mineral. All were used for pins, earrings, and beads in mourning jewelry during Victorian era.

**lapis lazuli**   Translucent to opaque mineral in tones of blue, deep blue, azure blue, Berlin blue, and greenish-blue. It is a mixture of lazurite and other minerals. Comes from Afghanistan, Siberia, and Chile. In contemporary times, used for beads, brooches, pendants, and cuff links.

**Linde Star®**   Trademark for a synthetic gem which imitates the star sapphire. Also see LINDE STAR® DRESS.

**malacite**   Ornamental opaque stone which exists in too large a quantity and is too soft to be a precious or semiprecious gem, mainly from Ural Mountains. May have irregular rings of various tones or be banded. Primary color is green—from emerald green to grass-green.

**marcasite** (mar-ka-sight)   Mineral with a metallic luster having the same composition as iron pyrite, but crystals are different. Cut material sold as marcasite is usually pyrite.

**marine gems**   Gems which are found primarily in the sea, *e.g.*, pearls, amber, and coral.

**melanite**   See ANDRADITE GARNET.

**mocha stone**   See AGATE.

**moonstone**   Opalescent gem variety of *feldspar*, which is cut cabochon.

**morganite**   Transparent pink to rose variety of the mineral BERYL. *Der.* Named after J. P. Morgan, financier and collector of gems.

**moss agate**   See AGATE.

**nephrite**   See JADE.

**obsidian**   Volcanic glass rather than a mineral. Usually black in color, but also comes in red, brown, and greenish-black. Attractive colors are cut as gems. Comes from Mexico, Greece, California, and Wyoming.

**olivine**   The gemologists' term for PERIDOT.

**onyx**   Variety of *chalcedony quartz*, which consists of parallel straight bands of black and white. Used for cameos and stones for rings. A popular ring for many years is composed of a large onyx with small diamond mounted on it.

**opal**   Transparent to opaque gem, which is amorphous and has a pleasing play of color, or opalescence, when cut cabochon. Comes in many colors including the valuable dark gray, blue, and black colors called *black opal*. Also see FIRE OPAL and HARLEQUIN OPAL.

**oriental cat's eye**   See CAT'S EYE.

**ornamental stones**   Gems which exist in such large quantities that they are not considered precious or semiprecious gems, *e.g.*, MALACITE and TURQUOISE.

**pearl**   Divided into three groups: GENUINE PEARLS, CULTURED PEARLS, and SIMULATED PEARLS. *1)* GENUINE PEARLS are secured from oysters, which have made a deposit over a grain of sand. The grain of sand is an irritant to the oyster, which secretes a deposit over it making it a pearl. Very expensive and rare, pearls must be matched in size and color. They are translucent to opaque, are most often white or faintly yellowish or bluish, but they may be pink, yellow, purple, red, green, blue, brown, or black. Genuine pearls also include: (a) *baroque pearls* which are irregular in shape; (b) *freshwater pearls* of chalk-white color found in mussels in freshwater streams in U.S.; (c) *Oriental pearls* the most beautiful and expensive natural pearls from Japan, Pacific Islands, Persian Gulf, Australia, Venezuela, and Panama; (d) *seed pearls*, tiny irregular-shaped real pearls. *2)* CULTURED PEARLS are secured by artificially implanting oysters with a tiny round piece of mother-of-pearl, placing oysters in cages, and lowering them into the ocean. Pearls are formed around the irritant. Pearls formed this way do not have many layers of coating, and can only be distinguished from genuine pearl by x-ray. *3)* SIMULATED PEARLS are not gems, but plastic or glass beads coated with a solution called "pearl essence" made from an adhesive combined with fish scales giving an iridescent luster.

**peridot** Transparent gem which is bottle green to olive green in color and comes from Burma, Ceylon, Brazil. Also called *chrysolite*. Called OLIVINE by minerologists.

**precious stone** Term applied to a gem which is not only beautiful, durable, and portable, but also rare—diamonds, rubies, sapphires, and emeralds fall into this category.

**quartz** Mineral used for gems existing in both crystalline transparent varieties, and cryptocrystalline, transparent or opaque varieties. Crystalline varieties include *rock crystal, amethyst, rose quartz, smoky quartz, citrine, tiger's eye,* and *cat's eye.* Cryptocrystalline quartz appears to the unaided eye to be amorphous, but revealed as crystalline under the microscope. Usually regarded as chalcedony although various colors go by different names, *e.g., carnelian* or *sard, chrysoprase, bloodstone* or *heliotrope, agate, onyx, sardonyx, jasper.*

**rhinestone** Artificial or imitation stones made of glass, called *paste* or *strass.* See PASTE in alphabetical listing.

**rock crystal** Clear transparent crystalline variety of the mineral *quartz.* Exists in such large quantities that it is inexpensive. May be carved for beads. May also be imitated by glass poured into molds to make beads.

**rose quartz** Transparent crystalline variety of *quartz* in rose-pink color.

**rubicelle** See SPINEL.

**ruby** Transparent precious gem which comes from the mineral CORUNDUM. Pigeon's blood red is the preferred color. Some stones have an asterism and are called STAR RUBIES. Best quality comes from Burma. The terms *cape ruby* and *Arizona ruby* are misleading and refer to garnets. The term *balas ruby* is misleading and refers to a *spinel.*

**sapphire** All-precious transparent corundum mineral of a color other than red. Preferred color is cornflower blue and called "Kashmir blue." Other sapphires may be white, pink, or yellow. May also be asterated and then called a STAR SAPPHIRE. Rates next to the diamond in hardness.

**sapphirine** See SPINEL.

**sard** See CARNELIAN.

**sardonyx** Variety of *chalcedony quartz* which is composed of banded layers of *sard* or *carnelian,* and layers of white.

**semiprecious stones** Gems too plentiful to be considered rare, *e.g.,* topaz, garnet, tourmaline, spinel, zircon, opal, amethyst, and quartz.

**smoky quartz** Transparent variety of *crystalline quartz* in smoky yellow to dark brown. The national gem of Scotland. Also called CAIRNGORM. Sometimes mistaken for TOPAZ.

**spinel** Transparent to opaque semiprecious mineral which closely resembles the ruby. Softer and lighter in weight than a ruby with hardness of 8 on mohs scale. Preferred color is deep ruby-red; comes in a great variety of other colors including violet and purple. Misleading terms for the above include: *balas ruby, rubicelle, almandine, sapphirine,* and *chlorspinel.* Properly spinels should be identified by color name. A large red stone on the English Crown, called the Black Prince's *ruby,* was later proved to be a *spinel.*

**star ruby** Genuine ruby from corundum mineral which shows a five- or six-pointed star or *asterism* when cut cabochon.

**star sapphire** Genuine sapphire from corundum mineral which shows a five- or six-pointed star or *asterism* when cut cabochon. Color varies from blue to gray and transparent to translucent. The 116-carat Midnight Star Sapphire and the 563-carat Star of India, the largest star sapphire in the world, were recovered after a jewel robbery at the Museum of Natural History in New York City in 1965.

**staurolite** See FAIRY STONE.

**synthetic gems** Gems manufactured in a laboratory having the same physical and chemical properties as genuine gems. Virtually all types of gems can be manufactured, including synthetic diamonds, emeralds, and sapphires. These gems are used in watches and sold for fine jewelry when mounted in necklaces, bracelets, and rings.

**tanzanite** First discovered in the foothills of Mount Kilimanjaro in Tanzania, Africa. In 1968 was confirmed to be blue zoisite by gemologists—the first ever found. Name was changed by Tiffany's of New York to tanzanite, from place where it was found. Not a precious stone, but beautiful when cut. Changes color when held in light to a blue, richer than a sapphire; purple, similar to amethyst; and pinkish-salmon brown or flesh-colored. One gem found was 2500 carats and when cut weighed 360 carats.

**tiger's eye** Semiprecious variety of *quartz* is chatoyant when cut cabochon. Yellowish-brown, bluish, or red in color. Found in South Africa.

**topaz** Transparent gem of which the most precious is wine-yellow in color. Other colors include colorless, yellowish-brown, gray, pale tints of green, blue, lavender, and red. The hardness is 8 with only the diamond, ruby, sapphire, and chrysoberyl being harder, the emerald and spinel are of equal hardness. Found in Europe, South America, Sri Lanka, Japan, Mexico, Utah, Colorado, and Maine.

**topazolite** See ANDRADITE GARNET.

**tourmaline** Transparent semiprecious mineral which comes in many colors: achroite, colorless; rubellite, rose-red; siberite, violet; indicolite, dark blue, green, blue, and yellowish-green. Sometimes erroneously called *Brazilian emerald*, *Brazilian peridot*, *Brazilian sapphire*, and *peridot of Ceylon*.

**turquoise** Opaque amorphous ornamental stone, which comes in sky blue, greenish-blue, or apple green. Used for jewelry, but exists in too large a quantity to be rare. Popular for jewelry made by Indians of Arizona and Mexico usually set in silver for bracelets, necklaces, pins, and earrings.

**Ural emerald** See ANDRADITE GARNET.

**zircon** Transparent gem which has a luster approaching the diamond when brilliant cut is used. White colorless stones resembling diamonds are sometimes referred to as *matura diamonds*, a misleading term. Yellow, orange, red, and brown zircons are called *hyacinth* or *jacinth*; all other colors including colorless gray and smoky are called *jargons*, while blue are called *blue zircon*. 103-carat zircon is in The Smithsonian Institution in Washington, D.C.

**gem cuts** Methods of cutting gemstones to be mounted into gold and other metals, *e.g.*, rings, bracelets, necklaces, tiaras, etc.

### GEM CUTS

**baguette c.** Small stones cut in oblong shape with facets. Usually placed horizontally along the side of a larger center diamond. *Der.* French "rod."

**brilliant c.** A faceted cut used particularly for iamonds and transparent gems cut with 58 facets which may be increased to 64, 72, and 80 facets. Usually it appears with a flat surface on top, called the *table*, sloping outwardly to *girdle* or widest point, and tapered to a point at bottom where a small facet called the *culet* is cut. When mounted only about one-third of gem is visible. The number of facets and the expertise in cutting increase the brilliancy of the stone. It can be round, oval, pear, marquise, or heart-shaped.

**cabochon c.** **1.** Type of cut used for gemstones which involves rounding off the top of the stone so that it is higher in the center and slopes to the rim. Used particularly for star rubies and sapphires. **2.** A *high cabochon* cut is a stone with a flat base and a higher elongated top. Also called a *tallow top cut.*

**cameo c.** A raised design carved out of a stone, *e.g.*, onyx or *banded sardonyx* which has more than one layer. The foreground color is carved away leaving a white design exposed on a colored surface, usually of black or orange. Cameos carved by the Greeks about the 4th c. had a perfection which has never been equalled.

**cushion c.** Variation of the BRILLIANT CUT—shaped square with the corners cut off and rounded at the widest part of the stone or girdle. Used particularly for large diamonds and transparent stones.

**emerald c.** A type of STEP CUT with all four square corners cut off diagonally. Used particularly for emeralds and large diamonds. Also see CUSHION CUT.

**heart-shaped c.** Variation of the BRILLIANT CUT in heart shape used for large diamonds.

**intaglio c.** Method of cutting gems by engraving the surface of the gem. Engraving is incised into the gem similar to a signet ring.

**marquise c.** (mar-keez) Variation of the BRILLIANT CUT, basic shape is oval with pointed ends. Introduced during reign of Louis XV, and named for his mistress Marquise de Pompadour.

**old mine c.** Brilliant cut of the 19th c. which retained much of original stone and had a larger culet and smaller table when compared to modern cuts.

**oval c.** Variation of the BRILLIANT CUT made in oval shape.

**pear c.** Variation of the BRILLIANT CUT, similar to MARQUISE CUT, but with one pointed and one rounded end. Shaped somewhat like a pear. Used particularly for large diamonds.

**rose c.** Simple faceted cut, used for inexpensive gems.

**square c.** See EMERALD CUT.

**step c.** Rectangular stone cut with facets that are oblong and placed in horizontal positions in steps, or rows, both above and below the girdle, or widest part of the stone.

**tallow top c.** See CABOCHON #2.

**gemel ring** A ring fashionable in the Middle Ages which was really two identical rings joined together and worn together. Popular style had clasped bands on the front. Traditionally the rings were separated at betrothal—the man and woman each wearing one. After marriage the rings were joined together and worn by the woman. Later, triple and quadruple rings of this style were worn. Revived in the mid-1980s. *Der.* From the word *gemelli*, or Latin, *gemini*, "twins." Also spelled *gemmel*, *geminal*, *gimmel*.

**gem setting** The manner in which a stone is mounted in an article of jewelry. Metals used for genuine jewelry are usually 14k or 18k gold, silver or platinum. Costume jewelry uses any type of metal, sometimes gold-washed or gold-plated.

### GEM SETTINGS

**channel s.** Grooves of metal used to hold stones. Also called *flush setting.*

**fishtail s.** Series of scallops (like fish scales) holding stone in place.

**flush s.** See CHANNEL SETTING.

**paste s.** Stone is glued in place; method used for inexpensive stones.

**pronged s.** Stone held in place by narrow projecting pieces of metal.

**square s.** Four prongs forming corners for *emerald-cut* stones.

**Tiffany s.** High pronged setting for solitaire stone introduced by Tiffany & Co., New York jewelers, in 1870s and often imitated. In 1971 Tiffany introduced a modernized version of its famous setting.

---

**gendarme** (john-darm) Term for a French policeman whose uniform has been copied for fashion items. See FRENCH POLICEMAN'S CAPE under CAPES, and GENDARME JACKET under JACKETS.

**Geneva bands** Collar consisting of two short white linen tabs: hanging down from neckline, attached to string tied around the neck worn mainly by clergy. Also called *short bands* and *bäffchen*. *Der.* Originated by Swiss Calvinist clergy in Geneva, Switzerland. Also see GENEVA GOWN. Also see BÄFFCHEN.

**GENEVA GOWN**

**Geneva gown** Black clerical gown worn by Calvinists and later by other Protestant clergy, similar to an ACADEMIC ROBE and often worn with two vertical white linen bands at neck called GENEVA BANDS.

**Geneva hat** Wide-brimmed, high crowned hat worn in late 16th and early 17th c. by Puritan ministers and others.

**Genoa cloak** See ITALIAN CLOAK.

**Genoese embroidery** See EMBROIDERIES.

**George** See BOOTS and HAIRSTYLES.

**genouillère** See POLEYN.

**genuine pearl beads** See BEADS and GEMS.

**geometric design** Pattern of circles, squares, triangles, oblongs, or straight-lined forms which are taken from figures, and parts of figures, used in geometry. Also see GEOMETRIC PRINT under PRINTS.

**georgette** 1. Fine sheer silk fabric made in the plain weave with twisted or creped yarns in both the warp and filling. Yarns may be two-ply with one made in Z-twist and the other in an S-twist, or two alternating yarns of S-twist may be followed with two Z-twist yarns. Used for dresses, evening gowns, blouses, and nightgowns. 2. British term for a fine cotton fabric made with crepe-twisted yarns. Also called *georgette crepe* and *crepe georgette*.

**George Washington wig** See WIGS.

**German gown** See BRUNSWICK GOWN.

**German helmet** See HELMETS.

**German hose** See ALMAIN HOSE.

**Germantown yarn** Coarse woolen yarn, usually four-ply, slackly twisted. Used for hand-knitting.

**German wool** See BERLIN WOOL.

**Gernreich, Rudi** See APPENDIX/DESIGNERS.

**gertrude** Infant's slip worn in early 20th c. styled with round neck, built-up shoulders, and sometimes long in length. Also called a *gertrude skirt.*

**geta** See SANDALS.

**ghlila** Jacket style, hip-length North African vest with low neckline and short or long full sleeves. Worn mostly by women, sometimes by men, in Morocco and Algeria over a blouse and under the JUBBAH.

**Gibson, Charles Dana** (1867–1944) American illustrator, master of black and white drawings published in *Scribner's, Harper's,* and *Century* magazines depicting the "shirtwaist girl," or idealized American girl, of this era with POMPADOUR hairstyle which became so popular that the "look" of the late 19th and early 20th c. was dubbed "The Gibson girl." See GIBSON PLEAT and GIBSON WAIST. Also see LOOKS.

**Gibson pleat** Wide 2″ pleat at the shoulder of blouse in front and back covering the armhole seam and sloping to waistline to give a narrow-waisted effect. *Der.* Named after Charles Dana Gibson who portrayed "The Gibson girl."

**Gibson waist** **1.** Blouse styled like a man's shirt with a small turned-over collar, small black bow tie, and LEG OF MUTTON SLEEVES. Popularized in the 1890s and worn with separate skirt and belt. **2.** Blouse with high CHOKER NECKLINE, buttoned down the back, LEG OF MUTTON SLEEVES, and GIBSON PLEATS. Made in lawn, satin, bobbinette, and other fabrics, it was elaborately decorated with lace, insertion, and tucks. *Der.* Named after Charles Dana Gibson who portrayed "The Gibson girl."

**Gibus** (jy-bus) Man's collapsible OPERA or TOP HAT with sides containing metal springs that snapped open to hold it upright. *Der.* From Antoine Gibus, who invented the hat in 1823, patented in 1837. Also see CHAPEAU CLAQUE, and ELASTIC ROUND HAT.

**gig** Textile-industry term for machine used to raise nap on fabrics, usually a cylinder covered with wire brushes or *teasels.*

**gig coat** See CURRICLE COAT.

**gigot sleeve** See FRENCH GIGOT SLEEVE.

**GILET**

**gilet** (zhee-lay) **1.** Term for vest or short waistcoat worn by men in the 1850s and 1860s. **2.** Woman's lacey or frilly PLASTRON worn from mid-19th through mid-20th c., revived in 1980s.

**gillie** See OXFORDS.

**gills** Colloquial term for upstanding points of men's shirt collars in the 19th c. Also called *shirt gills.*

**gimmel ring** See GEMEL RING.

**gimp** **1.** See BRAIDS. **2.** See WIMPLE.

**gingham** **1.** Yarn-dyed checked or plaid fabric made of cotton or cotton blended with polyester. May be made of coarse uncarded yarn or of combed yarns in a high count fabric. *Checked ginghams* are two-colored effects made by using two colors, or one color and white, for groups of yarns in both the warp and filling. *Plaid ginghams* are yarn-dyed designs of several colors. *Zephyr ginghams* are made with fine, silky, mercerized yarns. Used for dresses, children's wear, sportswear, swimsuits, blouses, and beachwear. **2.** 19th-c. colloquial term for an umbrella. So called because the less expensive types were made out of gingham fabric.

**gingham check/plaid** See CHECKS or PLAIDS.

**gipcière**  See GIPSER.

**gipon/gippon** (jee-pon)  Military garment of 14th c. variation of *gambeson*, a close-fitting, sleeveless, leather or padded jacket. It was laced down front, extending to knees, sometimes belted, and with long tight sleeves buttoned from wrist to elbow; forerunner of DOUBLET. Also spelled *jupe, jupel, jupon*.

**gipser**  Bag for alms, usually silk, worn by men in late Middle Ages. Also spelled *gipcière, gypsire*. Compare with AULMONIERE.

**girdle**  **1.** Undergarment worn by women and girls designed to mold lower torso and sometimes legs. May be flexible two-way stretch, or one-way stretch elastic with non-stretchable fabric panels, and extends from hip- to ankle-length, with or without garters. Introduced in the 1930s as a rigid support garment. **2.** See BELTS. **3.** Jewelry term for circumference of largest portion of faceted stone.

## GIRDLES

**Capri-length panty-g.**  Very long two-way stretch panty girdle extending about four inches below knees.

**control-brief**  See GARTER-BRIEF.

**Criss-Cross® g.**  Trademark of Playtex Corp. for a girdle which has a lapped over front with each side going diagonally to thigh—thus permitting easier walking or sitting.

**cuff-top g.**  Pull-on zippered girdle that extends above waistline with wide band of elastic at top. Also called HI-RISE GIRDLE.

**French cinch**  Short girdle designed to accentuate a small waist starting at the ribs and stopping above the hips with or without long garters. Also see GUEPIERE.

**garter-brief**  Stretch panty or girdle with detachable garters offering light control. Also called *stretch brief* or *control-brief*.

**guepiere** (geh-pee-air)  Short girdle worn to narrow the waist into hourglass shape, sometimes with attached garters. Designed by Marcel Rochas, Paris couturier, in 1947. Also called FRENCH CINCH or WAIST-CINCHER.

**hi-rise g.**  Girdle extending above the waistline. See CUFF-TOP GIRDLE.

**long-leg panty-g.**  Girdle with longer legs to eliminate bulges.

**pants liner**  Tight-fitting control panties coming over the knee to the calf or the ankle and worn under pants for a sleek fit.

**panty-g.**  Girdle with closed crotch, resembling panties, coming in lengths from hip joint to ankle.

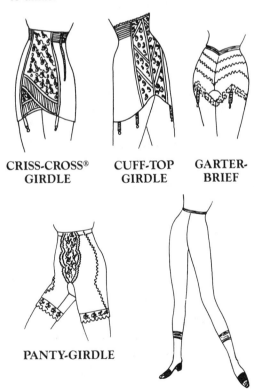

CRISS-CROSS®      CUFF-TOP      GARTER-
GIRDLE           GIRDLE         BRIEF

PANTY-GIRDLE

PANTLINER

**pull-on g.**   Girdle without zipper or other opening, that is pulled on over the hips like panties.

**Sarong**® (seh-rong) Trademark for a girdle similar to a CRISS-CROSS® GIRDLE.

**stretch-brief**   See GARTER-BRIEF.

**waist-cincher**   Not actually a girdle, but a wide strip of fabric with six or eight vertically placed *bones* or *stays* that hook in front. Worn to make waistline appear smaller. Also see GUEPIERE.

**waist watcher**   Wide band, reaching from ribs to top of hips made of spongy stretch fabric secured with Velcro®. Worn by men and women to pull in the waist and as an aid in reducing the size of the waistline.

**zippered g.**   Girdle usually made of two-way stretch and non-stretch panels closed with zippered placket worn for firmer support.

---

**girdlestead**   Term used from Middle Ages to 17th c. to indicate waistline of a garment.

**girls' sizes**   Size range from 4 to 6X and from 7 to 14.

**Givenchy, Hubert de**   See APPENDIX/ DESIGNERS.

**glacé** (gla-say) Shiny finish applied to kidskins by using a glass roller. Also called *glazed*. *Der.* French, "frozen."

**gladiator sandal**   See SANDALS.

**Gladstone**   Man's short double-breasted overcoat of 1870s made with shoulder cape and borders of ASTRAKHAN. Also see ULSTER.

**Gladstone collar**   Standing collar with sides flaring up towards cheeks. Worn with a wide black scarf-like tie in latter half of 19th c. *Der.* Named for William Ewart Gladstone, Prime Minister of England at intervals, between 1868 and 1894, during Queen Victoria's reign.

**glasses**   An accessory worn over the eyes to improve the vision or to protect the eyes from the glare of the sun. Conventional glasses are made with plastic or glass lenses that fit into metal or plastic frames with bows that extend over top of ears. Photochrome® lens, which darkens as the light increases and vice versa, was one of the innovations of the 1980s. Glasses were first introduced in Italy in the late 13th c. They were an indication of wisdom as few people could read. During the 17th c. colored lenses were introduced for protection from the sun. In the 1960s glasses, previously considered a mar to beauty, suddenly became a fashion item. Originally called SPECTACLES. Also see QUIZZING GLASS in alphabetical listing.

---

### GLASSES

**aviator's g.**   Sunglasses with lens wider at sides of face and sloping toward nose. Made in imitation of goggles worn by early airplane pilots. Also called *flyboy glasses. Der.* From style worn by aviator pilots.

**Ben Franklin g.**   Small elliptical, octagonal, or oblong lenses with delicate metal frames, worn perched on the middle of the nose. A fad started in 1965 imitating the glasses seen in paintings of Benjamin Franklin, U.S. statesman. Also called *granny glasses*.

**bifocals**   Glasses with lenses divided in two parts for near vision and distance. The line dividing the two fields of vision was made invisible in the early 1980s.

**binoculars**   See FIELD GLASSES.

**bug-eyed g.**   Bulging convex sunglasses shaped like the eyes of an insect. Some glasses are made of a solid piece of plastic shaped to head and face. Unusual colors such as red are sometimes used to give a psychedelic appearance to viewer. An innovation of the late 1960s.

**butterfly g.** Large rimless sunglasses with lenses made in the shape of a butterfly's wings, an innovation of the late 1960s.

**clip-on sunglasses** Sunglasses without frames made with a V-shaped projection to fit over the top of prescription glasses. Some have a hinge which permits them to flip up.

**color-graded g.** Tinted glasses with the lenses made of colors varying from light at the bottom to dark at the top. Designed for use in a car; maps can be read through the clear section at bottom.

**Courréges g.** Sunglasses introduced by André Courréges in 1966 made of a strip of opaque plastic which circled the face extending to the ears. Through the center of the plastic was a tinted sliver of glass or plastic. Copied widely, they became known by the name of the French couturier who invented them.

**field g.** Compact, easily portable binocular telescope for use out-of-doors. Also called *binoculars*.

**flip-down g.** Ben Franklin-type glasses with separate hinged lenses which pull down so that eyeshadow or mascara can be applied. Also used for inserting contact lenses.

**flyboy g.** See AVIATOR'S GLASSES.

**folding g.** Glasses with both bridge and bows folding to a 3″ size for easy carrying.

**goggles** Protective glasses, usually with shatterproof lenses in wide frames wrapped around temples, held on by strap around head and worn by auto racers, skiers, etc. Goggles for underwater swimming are watertight.

**granny g.** Same as BEN FRANKLIN GLASSES. *Der.* So called because they resemble glasses formerly worn by grandmothers.

**half-g.** Glasses for reading with shallow lenses allowing wearer to look over top for distance viewing.

**harlequin g.** Glasses with diamond-shaped lenses.

**horn rims/horn-rimmed g.** Eyeglasses with heavy frames of dark horn, or mottled brown plastic imitating horn, very popular in the 1940s and 1950s.

**instant sunglasses** Lightweight, shatterproof shaped plastic which is placed behind regular glasses when outdoors.

**Lennon specs** Sunglasses with circular metal-rimmed lenses and thin metal bows. *Der.* John Lennon, member of the English rock group, The Beatles, popularized this style. Originally English workmen's sunglasses.

**lorgnette** (lorn-yet) A pair of eyeglasses attached to a handle, or a pair of opera glasses, similarly mounted; usually hinged so eyeglasses may be folded when not in use. Used since late 19th c. *Der.* French *lorgner*, "to spy or peep."

**louvre sunglasses** Molded plastic sunglasses made with tilted slats similar to Venetian blinds. Introduced from France in mid-1980s.

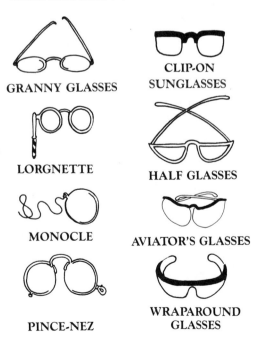

GRANNY GLASSES

CLIP-ON SUNGLASSES

LORGNETTE

HALF GLASSES

MONOCLE

AVIATOR'S GLASSES

PINCE-NEZ

WRAPAROUND GLASSES

**monocle**  Man's single eyeglass used for one eye. When not in use, suspended on a ribbon around the neck.

**opera g.**  Two small telescopes mounted for viewing with both eyes. Used to provide close-up view at the opera or theater. Usually a fashionable accessory decorated with mother-of-pearl, gold, brocade, etc. *Der.* Used to view "opera."

**owl g.**  Extra large sunglasses with very wide heavy rims which give the look of a surprised owl.

**pince-nez** (pants-nay)  Eyeglasses without ear pieces, kept in place by spring gripping the bridge of the nose. *Der.* French "nose-pincher."

**Polaroid® g.**  Trademark for special sunglasses with lenses coated with a substance that polarizes light, especially effective in cutting down glare.

**rimless g.**  Lenses attached to metal nose piece and ear pieces but not outlined by a frame. Popular from 1930s to 1940s, and revived in 1960s.

**safety g.**  Glasses made of unbreakable glass worn by industrial workers. Also called GOGGLES.

**shades**  Slang for SUNGLASSES.

**specs**  Slang for SPECTACLES.

**spectacles**  Older term for glasses.

**sunglasses**  Eyeglasses with dark-colored lenses to cut glare invented about 1885, popularized by movie stars in Hollywood in 1930s and 1940s, prevalent fashion from 1960s to 1980s in various shapes and sizes. Some made with mirrored lenses. Also see SHADES, AVIATOR'S, CLIP-ON, INSTANT, and COURRÉGES GLASSES.

**tortoise-shell g.**  Glasses with frames made from tortoise shell or from plastic imitating tortoise shell, usually mottled brown. Heavy tortoise-shell frames became very popular in 1940s and 1950s replacing metal frames and rimless glasses worn earlier.

**trifocals**  Prescription glasses worn to correct vision made similar to BIFOCALS, but with three sections—the middle section being for intermediate vision for drawing, playing the piano, or playing cards.

**wraparound g.**  Sunglasses made of a molded piece of plastic shaped like a headband which is cut out for insertion of the lenses. Similar to Courréges glasses but with a wider viewing area.

---

**glazed chintz**  See CHINTZ.

**glazed kid**  See GLACÉ.

**glazing**  Process of pressing fabric with heated rollers to give it a high gloss. Finish may be permanent or non-permanent. See CHINTZ.

**glen check/Glen Urquhart check**  See CHECKS.

**glengarry**  **1.** Scottish cap similar in shape to an OVERSEAS CAP trimmed with a cockcade of GROSGRAIN ribbons at the side and a band of Stuart plaid around the head in memory of Bonnie Prince Charles. Developed around 1805 as a different form of the BLUEBONNET. Now more generally worn. **2.** Fabric of the homespun tweed type made in England woven of varicolored woolen yarns containing waste fibers. *Der.* For Glengarry, a valley in Inverness-shire Scotland.

**Glengarry cape**  Three-quarter length cape worn by women in the 1890s made with a tailored collar and single-breasted closing. A hood, sometimes plaid lined, was attached at neckline under the collar. Also called *cawdor cape*.

**glen plaid**  See PLAIDS.

**glissade**  **1.** Cotton lining fabric usually made with black ground and narrow white or colored stripes. Made in the satin weave with polished cotton yarns in the warp and ordinary yarns in the filling. **2.** Sateens which are printed in comparable stripes then mercerized and schreinerized to give a high sheen.

**glitter button**   See BUTTONS.

**glitter hose**   See HOSE.

**glocke** (glokka)   Medieval poncho-type outer garment made of LODEN fabric, with hole in center of large circle of fabric. Still worn today, especially in mountainous Alpine regions of Europe. *Der.* German, "bell."

**gloria**   **1.** Ornament for the hair in imitation of a halo, a nimbus or aureole. **2.** Tightly woven lightweight fabric used mainly for umbrellas. Plain weave is usually used but some fabrics are made in twill or satin weaves of nylon, rayon, acetate, or cotton.

**Glospan®**   Trademark owned by Globe Manufacturing Co. for fused multifilament spandex yarn made by extrusion. Claimed to have high elasticity and resistant to chlorine bleach. Used for knitted elastic fabrics.

**glove**   A covering for the hand, usually divided into separate stalls for the thumb and fingers, worn as a decorative accessory or for warmth in cold weather. *Mittens*, however, have only a stall for the thumb and another compartment for the fingers. Both types may be knitted, crocheted, or die-cut out of leather or vinyl and then stitched together. Gloves were known to ancient Egyptians, Greeks, and Romans but did not become an important accessory until the Middle Ages. As many people could not write, the glove was used as a substitute for a signature. Throughout the Victorian era and early 20th c. gloves were the mark of a lady or gentleman. In the 1960s, gloves declined in use for social occasions and by 1970s were very seldom worn except for protection from the cold. *Button* is the term used to indicate the length of the glove. One-button is equal to one French inch, approximately $1/12''$ longer than the American inch, with the measurement starting at base of thumb. A one-button glove is wrist length, a six-button glove is about halfway to elbow, and a 16-button glove is a formal length. *Der.* Origin of the word is disputed, believed to have been from Anglo-Saxon, *glof,* "palm." See TRANK, QUIRK, and FOURCHETTE in alphabetical listing.

### GLOVES & MITTENS

**action g.**   Gloves with cut-outs on back of hand or over knuckles to increase flexibility. Originally used for sports such as golf or race car driving, adopted for women's daytime wear in mid-1960s. Also called *cutout gloves* or *racing gloves.*

**biarritz g.**   Slip-on glove with no vent usually of two- or four-button length.

**bicycle g.**   Wrist-length knitted glove with leather palm padded with two layers of foam for comfort. Mesh knit is used for remainder of glove leaving the tips of the fingers and thumb exposed.

**cocktail g.**   Dressy suede gloves with wide stand-up accordion pleated taffeta cuffs.

**cutout g.**   See ACTION GLOVES.

**doeskin g.**   **1.** Gloves made of suede-finished sheepskin. Properly it should be "doeskin finished sheepskin" but the term doeskin is permissible. **2.** Gloves made from the skin of the female deer frequently sueded. As there are few deerskins available for commercial usage, real doeskins usually come from areas where deer are plentiful, *e.g.,* northern Michigan and where skins are usually processed on Indian reservations.

**driving g.**   Knitted gloves with leather palms made for a good grip on the steering wheel of the car.

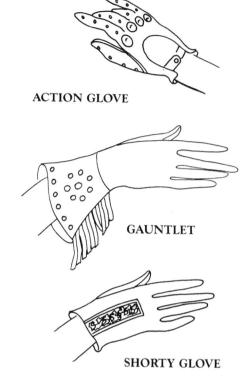

**ACTION GLOVE**

**GAUNTLET**

**SHORTY GLOVE**

**Finger-Free® g.** Trademark for gloves made with one long strip of material forming all the *fourchettes* between fingers. Designed by Merry Hull in 1938 for greater flexibility.

**gauntlet** Above-the-wrist glove with wide flaring cuff.

**insulated g.** Glove lined for protection against cold with fur, fleece, wool or acrylic knit used for lining.

**kid g.** Gloves made of genuine kidskin and also of sheepskin, including *cabretto*. Originally all were kid and as the leather became more scarce, other leathers were used. Fashionable from early 19th c. and still used.

**lace g.** Made by hand or machine in white and used for dress-up summer wear.

**mittens** Gloves with a thumb and one other compartment for fingers. Worn mainly by children and skiers for warmth.

**mitts** Fingerless gloves, reaching above wrist, often of kid or sheer fabric and worn with bridal dresses, etc. Originally a hand-covering in wool worn in Colonial America.

**money mitt®** Knitted glove with fingers and thumb made with vinyl palm and back. Has zippered slot in center of palm for keys or money.

**mousquetaire g.** (moos-keh-tare) Woman's long loose glove made in pull-on style or with buttoned slit at wrist in 14- or 16-button length. Worn crushed down or with hand out of slit, remainder of glove crushed up to elbow with formal evening dress.

**opera g.** Long-length glove, sometimes made without a thumb.

**pull-ons** Glove without placket or fastening that slips easily over the hand. Also called *slip-on gloves*.

**racing g.** See ACTION GLOVES.

**shorty g.** Any two-button glove coming to the wrist.

**slip-ons** See PULL-ON GLOVE.

**snowmobile g.** Similar to SNOWMOBILE MITT made with fingers.

**snowmobile mitt** Water-repellent gloves with polyester fiberfill or down as insulation. Made with suede-leather palms, rubberized nylon back, knitted cuffs, and leather pull-on tabs.

**table-cut g.** *Tranks* from which these gloves are cut, are hand-pulled to determine the amount of stretch in the leather and then cut. Women's fine kid gloves are made in this manner to ensure proper stretch but no bagginess.

**thermal g.** Short gloves made of glacé leather with silk lining and inner lining of polyfoam. Worn for warmth especially for riding or driving.

**glove band** Ribbon or plaited horsehair band tied near elbow to keep a woman's long glove in place. Used from 1640 to about 1700. Also called *glove string*.

**glove button** See BUTTONS.

**glove fabric** Term used for any fabric, knitted or woven, used for gloves. Made of many different fibers—wool, silk, cotton, and man-made fibers. Some fine-gauge knit fabrics of man-made yarns are also used for lingerie.

**glove length** Glove term indicating the length of a glove. One button is equal to one French inch (approximately $\frac{1}{12}''$ longer than an American inch), with measurement starting at base of thumb. A 1 button glove is wrist length, a 6-button glove is halfway to elbow, and a 16-button glove is a formal length.

**glover's stitch** See WHIP and SADDLE under STITCHES.

**glove seam** Manner in which gloves are stitched together. Seams must be flexible and sturdy. The *trank* of the glove is cut in one piece and the *fourchettes* (or pieces for the sides of the fingers) and *quirks* (small pieces for base of fingers and thumb) are stitched to it by various seams.

### ▬▬▬ GLOVE SEAMS ▬▬▬

**full piqué/full P.K. s.** Used on expensive kid gloves, all fourchettes are inserted with one piece of leather lapped over the other and stitched on the right side. Also called *kid seam* and *overlapped seam*.

**half piqué/half P.K. s.** Finger seams connecting trank and fourchettes on the outside of hand are made in *piqué* manner; seams toward the palm of the hand are stitched with *inseams*.

**inseam** Gloves stitched together inside out and then turned so that no stitching shows on the right side. Used on sheer nylon, lace, and cotton gloves.

**kid s.** See FULL PIQUÉ GLOVE SEAM.

**outseam** Gloves are stitched by machine on the right side, leaving edges exposed. Used on sport gloves, *e.g.*, pigskin and sometimes cotton gloves.

**overlapped** See FULL PIQUÉ GLOVE SEAM.

**overseam** Gloves stitched on the right side with an *overcast stitch* which covers the two raw edges. Used on men's gloves. Also called *round seam*.

**piqué/P.K. s.** See FULL PIQUÉ and HALF PIQUÉ GLOVE SEAMS.

**prixseam/PXM s.** *Outseam* stitched on a flat machine which moves horizontally instead of vertically. Used on heavier gloves instead of piqué seam.

**round s.** See OVERSEAM.

**saddle-stitched s.** Small running stitches visible on the outside of glove used to close fingers of the glove.

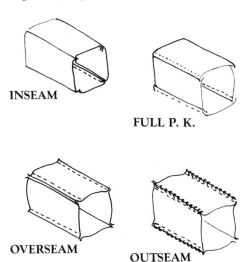

INSEAM

FULL P. K.

OVERSEAM

OUTSEAM

**glove silk**  Tricot knit fabric made on a warp knitting machine with two sets of yarns. See TRICOT.

**glove string**  See GLOVE BAND.

**goatee**  Small pointed *beard* similar to tuft of hair on a goat's chin.

**goatskin**  See LEATHER.

**GOBELIN CORSET**

**gobelin corselet**  Woman's belt in form of a *corselet* worn in mid-1860s coming up high under the bust to a point in front at waistline, narrowing in back and trimmed with a ruffle of lace.

**gob hat**  See SAILOR HAT under HATS.

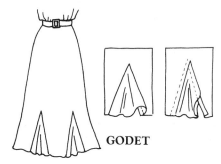

**GODET**

**godet**  (go-day)  Triangular piece, sometimes rounded at top and flaring at the base, set into a skirt or sleeve to give added fullness. See GORE and GUSSET. Also see PLEATS and SKIRTS.

**Godey, Louis Antoine**  (1804–1878)  American publisher who, with Charles Alexander, published the first woman's periodical in the U.S. Distributed monthly, it contained stories, music, needlecraft, poetry, and fashions. Each month there was a hand-colored engraving

showing fashions as well as many black and white illustrations. Started in 1830 as the *Lady's Book* it was later called *Godey's Lady's Book*. *Sarah Josepha Hale* acted as editor for many years.

**Godey's Lady's Book**  The first American periodical for women, published by Louis Antoine Godey. Edited by Sarah Josepha Hale from 1837 to 1877. Featured one colored fashion plate a month and several engravings. Also see GODEY, LOUIS A. and HALE, SARAH JOSEPHA.

**goffer**  (goff-er)  **1.** An ornamental pleating used for frills and borders as on women's caps. **2.** To press ridges or narrow pleats into a frill.

**goffered veil**  19th-c. term for linen headdress, with fluted or *goffered* frill surrounding the face. Has back drapery to shoulders, worn from 1350 to 1420. Also see NEBULA HEADDRESS.

**goggles**  See *glasses*.

**go-go**  Term coined in late 1960s particularly for a dancer at a discotheque called a go-go dancer. Term extended to mean "flashy" or "hip" accessories of this era. See BOOTS, WATCHES, and BRACELETS.

**gold**  Precious metal which in its pure state is too soft to be durable; it is usually made into alloys called *karat gold*, used for *plating*, or gold washed jewelry items. See KARAT, ROLLED GOLD, FILLED GOLD, GOLD PLATED and GOLD WASHED. Also see BEADS and BUTTONS.

**golden beryl**  See GEMS.

**golden casque**  See OORYZER.

**golden muskrat**  See FURS.

**gold filled**  Gold of 10 to 22 karats fused to a base metal, *e.g.*, nickel, silver, or brass. Layer of gold should weigh at least 1/20th of the entire metal used. 1/10 18K means that the gold used is 18 karat and that it represents 1/10th of the weight of the metal. Compare with ROLLED GOLD.

**gold leaf**  Pure gold hammered so thin it takes 300,000 units to make a stack 1″ high. Used for jewelry and gold leather.

**gold-plated**  Describing jewelry with a thin surface of gold which is electrolytically plated to a base metal.

**gold-washed**  Describing jewelry with a thin coating of gold applied to a base metal by dipping or washing it in a solution of gold.

**gole**  Medieval term for cape part of the *chaperon* which hung around the shoulders. Also spelled *golet*. See CHAPERON. Also see GORGET #3.

**golf clothes**  By 1890s golf was a sport enjoyed by both men and women. Men wore KNICKERS, a NORFOLK JACKET, and a cap with a visor; by the 1920s they wore PLUS FOURS and a SWEATER. Women in the early days wore a version of the NORFOLK JACKET, the GLENGARRY CAP, and sometimes shorter skirt or a DIVIDED SKIRT; in pre-World War I days, a COAT SWEATER was worn; in the 1930s the *action-back dress* was introduced. Also see SHOES and SPORT JACKETS.

**golf vest**  Man's knitted, wool single-breasted vest of mid-1890s made with braid-trimming, without a collar, and with three pockets—one on each side plus watch pocket.

**gondolier's hat**  Straw hat with a medium-sized brim and a shallow, slightly tapered crown with a flat top. Wide ribbon trims the crown and long streamers extend down the back; the color of the ribbon denoted length of service. Worn formerly by gondoliers of Venice, Italy.

**gonel** (gon-el)  Synonym for *gown* in 14th c.

**goose-bellied doublet**  See PEASCOD-BELLIED DOUBLET.

**Gordian knot**  Decorative square knot used as trimming in the last half of 18th c.—sometimes on bracelets, sometimes a length of false hair used as a *chignon*. *Der.* From Greek mythological founder of Phrygia (now Turkey) called *Gordius*. An oracle pronounced that he would be master of Asia until the knot he tied was undone. Alexander the Great severed the knot with one blow of his sword.

**gore**  **1.** Skirt section, wider at hem than top, providing fullness and shaping to waist without using darts. A four-gore skirt has seams at sides, center front, and center back; six-gore skirt has side-front and side-back seams as well as side seams. There may be as many as twenty-four gores in a skirt. Also see FRENCH GORES. **2.** Sewing term for a triangular insert of fabric that creates fullness, greater width, or desired shape. Used in skirts and bell-bottom pants. Also used in gloves at wrist, to make a flared cuff and facilitate opening. Also called GODET. Also see GORED SKIRT under SKIRTS.

**gorge**  Men's tailoring term used to indicate seam where collar meets lapel—may be either high or low.

**gorget** (gorge-et)  Term for variety of neck and shoulder coverings: **1.** Armor worn on throat in Middle Ages. **2.** Variant of WIMPLE in 12th and 13th c. Also spelled *gorgette*. **3.** Shoulder cape of the chaperon in 14th and 15th c. Also called *guleron* and *gole*. **4.** Small ruffle at neck of smock in 16th c. Also spelled *gorgette*. **5.** Second half of 17th c. a large falling collar. Also called a WHISK. **6.** Chain with crescent-shaped ornament worn around the neck by officers during 17th and 18th c. as a badge of rank. **7.** High collar, cut low in front, worn by women in late 19th and early 20th c.

**Gore-Tex® fabric**  Trade name for rainwear and sportswear fabric with Teflon®-based membrane sandwiched between nylon outer fabric and soft inner fabric. Has many minute pores—nine billion per square inch—which makes it "breathable" yet water and vapor proof. Sometimes made in camouflage print, used for hunting, fishing, and outdoor sportswear.

**goshenite**  See GEMS.

**gossamer**  **1.** British term, originally a trade name, for a light silk hat. **2.** Veiling fabric made of fine sheer silk used in 19th c. **3.** Coated lightweight fabric made of cotton, silk, or wool treated with a rubber composition to make it waterproof.

**Gothic costume** Usually includes early Gothic referring to costumes from 13th to mid-14th c. Late Gothic refers to costume from mid-14th through mid-15th c.

**gown**  **1.** See NIGHTGOWN and ROBES. **2.** See DRESSES. **3.** Term used from 11th c. on for woman's dress and for loose-fitting, wide-sleeved outer garment or robe worn by judges, scholars, clergy, and for ceremonial occasions. Also see ACADEMIC GOWN, GENEVA GOWN and GONEL.

**gown à la francaise** (ah la frawn-saiz) Sack dress fashionable in 18th c. made with close-fitting bodice. Front closing was filled in with decorative *stomacher*, and two wide box pleats fell from shoulders to hem in back. *Der.* French, "French gown." Also called *robe à la française.*

**gown à la levantine** (ah la levan-teen) A loose open robe fastened at the chest with a pin or ties revealing a waistcoat and petticoat of contrasting color and fabric worn from 1778 on. Wrist-length undersleeves matched the petticoat. The overdress had wide turned-back collar and wide draped sash with long hanging ends, sometimes fur-trimmed. Also called *levite gown.*

**gown à l'anglaise** (ah long-glaze) Dress worn in late 18th c. without *panniers*. Bodice was shaped to long point in back and closed in front over a *waistcoat*. Skirt was slashed in front to show matching petticoat. *Der.* French, "English gown." Also called *robe à l'anglaise.*

**gown à la polonaise** (po-lo-nayz) See POLONAISE #1.

**gown à la sultane**  See SULTANE.

**gown à la turque** (ah la toork) Dress with a tight-fitting bodice, turned-down collar, flared sleeves at wrist, and draped large sash knotted on one hip with long hanging ends. Worn over contrasting petticoat in 1780. *Der.* French, "Turkish gown."

**graduation dress**  See DRESSES.

**graffiti**  Street art form found originally in words scratched and painted on old buildings and subways. Now a mishmash of fantasy art consisting of odds and ends of everything including street scenes, water scenes, and printed words all jumbled together with dots and squiggly lines. See LOOKS. *Der.* Archeological term *graffito*, "ancient drawings or writings scratched on a wall or other surfaces."

**grain**  **1.** Leather term for the markings which appear on the skins and hides when the hair or feathers are removed. Pigskin shows small markings in groups of three. Ostrich skins show a rosette where the quill has been removed. **2.** Measure used to determine the weight of pearls and sometimes diamonds equal to 50 milligrams or 1/4 carat. Not the same as the troy grain. Also see CARAT. **3.** Textile and sewing term which means *warpwise* or lengthwise of the fabric. To cut "against the grain" means fillingwise or across the fabric. **4.** Historical term applied to reddish dye used for *kermes* and occasionally *cochineal*—broadened to include any dye, particularly a fast one. In France in 14th and 15th c. it referred to scarlet dye.

**grande-assiette sleeve** (grawn ass-ee-ette) Extra cap sleeve, crescent shape, extending over top curve of shoulder on the GIPON or DOUBLET from 14th to mid-15th c.

**grand habit**  See COURT HABIT.

**grand vair**  See VAIR.

**granite cloth**  Any fabric woven in a granite weave, with a crinkled or pebbly effect on the surface, used in particular for wool fabrics.

**granite weave**  Weave characterized by pebbly effect somewhat similar to crepe. See GRANITE CLOTH. Also called *momie weave* and *pebble weave.*

**granjamers**  See PAJAMAS.

**granny bonnet**  Child's bonnet of early 1890s with ribbon ties under the chin, broad flaring brim, and gathered conventional crown decorated with ribbons. *Der.* Styled after the bonnets that grandmothers wore.

**GRANNY BONNET (CHILD'S), 1895**

**granny look** Term introduced for young people in early 1960s. See BLOUSES, BOOTS, DRESSES, GLASSES, LOOKS, NIGHTGOWNS, GRANJAMMERS under PAJAMAS, PRINTS, SILHOUETTES and SKIRTS.

**granny waist** **1.** Fitted bodice of 1890s with lace insert in front, large lace ruffle around a low neckline, and optional large lace ruffles falling over the arms from puffed sleeves. *Der.* Named for the styles worn by one's grandmother. **2.** See GRANNY BLOUSE under BLOUSES.

**grass cloth** Term for fabrics made of *ramie*, *flax*, *hemp*, etc., which have a smooth lustrous surface and are loosely woven in a plain weave. Made in the Far East on hand looms. Used for sportswear and blouses. Also see CHINA GRASS.

**grass embroidery** See EMBROIDERIES.

**graundice** See CRANTS.

**gray flannel** See OXFORD GRAY FLANNEL.

**gray fox** See FURS.

**gray goods** Textile term to describe unfinished fabrics as they come from the loom. Some fabrics may be mill-finished but most are sent to *converters* for the finishing processes. Originally called *greige goods*. *Der.* French, *grege*, "raw."

**gray muskrat** See FURS.

**greatcoat** See COATS.

**Great Mogul diamond** See DIAMONDS.

**greave** Metal-plate leg covering reaching from ankle to knee. Worn from 11th to 17th c. as armor. Also called *jamb (jambe)*. When made of leather in the 14th c. called a *jambeau*. When worn just on the front of the leg, called a *demi-jamb (jambe)*.

**grebe feathers** See FEATHERS.

**Grecian bend** Fashionable stance of woman from 1815 to 1819 and again from 1868 to 1870. Body was tilted forward from a wasp waist with bustle in back emphasizing the derrière.

**Grecian border** See FRET.

**Grecian curls** **1.** Hairstyle of the 1860s with rows of *fingercurls* hanging down the back from the nape of the neck. Sometimes arranged in two rows, one shorter than the other. **2.** See CURLS.

**Grecian sandal** See GANYMEDE SANDAL under SANDALS.

**Greek belt** See BELTS.

**Greek boy look** See GANYMEDE LOOK under LOOKS.

**Greek coiffure** Woman's hairstyle of 1860s with center part, hair braided and wrapped around the crown of the head, made to form three hanging loops in back, and wound around the loops at nape of neck. Also called *coiffure à la Grecque*. Also see GRECIAN CURLS.

**Greek fisherman's cap** See CAPS.

**Greek fret** See FRET.

**Greek handbag** See HANDBAGS.

**Greek key** See FRET.

**Greek lace** See RETICELLA under LACES.

**Greek lounging cap** See LOUNGING CAP.

**Greek point lace** See RETICELLA under LACES.

**green-aproned men** London porters of 18th c. distinguished by green aprons worn by members of this trade. Also see BLUE-APRONED MEN.

**Greenaway, Kate** Popular British children's book illustrator of late 19th c. whose characters wore early 19th-c. high-waisted, ankle-length dresses with ribbon sashes, *pantalettes* showing, and *mob caps* or *poke bonnets*. These dresses were widely copied for children's wear through end of 19th c. and are still a fashion inspiration. Also see KATE GREENAWAY STYLES.

**greenery-yallery** See AESTHETIC DRESS.

**grego** Short jacket or coat with attached hood made of coarse fabric worn by Greeks and Levantines.

**gregs** *Trunk hose* or *chausse* first worn in last quarter of 16th c. Usually slashed to reveal lining and elaborately trimmed with gold and silver. Also spelled *gregues*. Also called GALLI-GASKINS.

**greige goods** See GRAY GOODS.

**grenadine** 1. Openwork fabric of *leno weave* made of cotton, wool, silk, or man-made fibers tightly twisted. Sometimes checked, striped, or made with other patterns. Sometimes a black filling is used and these are called *black lenos*. 2. Silk yarn given a hard twist used formerly in hosiery and still used in laces.

**Grès, Alix** See APPENDIX/DESIGNERS.

**grey goods** See GRAY GOODS.

**gripper closing** See CLOSINGS.

**grisaille** (gree-zah-yeh) French term for pepper-and-salt effects or grayish mixtures in fabrics.

**grommet** (grom-it) Reinforced eyelet in garment through which a fastener may be passed.

**grooving** Method of shearing a deep pile of fabric or furs in lines which have a shorter pile than the rest of the surface.

**gros de Londres** (groh dee loan-dreh) Lightweight fabric with flat fillingwise ribs which vary in size. Made of silk or rayon and may be piece-dyed, warp-printed, or made with colored yarns for iridescent effect. Used for dresses.

**grosgrain** (groh-grain) Ribbon with rib more rounded than FAILLE that is made with several filling yarns used together. Made originally in silk, now made mostly with rayon or acetate warp and cotton or rayon filling. Also made entirely of cotton. Used for ribbons, sashes, trim on dresses, bows, neckwear, hatbands, and millinery trimming.

**gros point** (groh pwanh) See EMBROIDERIES, LACES, and STITCHES.

**Grosvenor gallery costume** See AESTHETIC DRESS.

**Groult, Nicole** See APPENDIX/DESIGNERS.

**grow bag** Synonym for a BABY BUNTING.

**grow sleepers** See PAJAMAS.

**G-string** Brief band, worn low on the hips, with a decorative ornament on front. Originally worn by striptease dancers.

**guanaco/guanaquito** See FURS.

**guard hair** Long silky hair of animals *e.g.*, mink, muskrat, and fox, which shed water to protect the animal from rain while the shorter underfur provides warmth. All animals do not have guard hairs, particularly those in the sheep and lamb families.

**guard Infanta** FARTHINGALE, or frame under skirt, very wide at sides and flattened front and back. Worn in Spain in 17th c., *e.g.* as in Velasquez' portrait of the Infanta.

**guards** 16th-c. term for decorative bands of rich fabrics, plain or embroidered, used to conceal garment seams.

**guardsman coat** See COATS.

**guayabera shirt** See SHIRTS.

**Gucci** (goo-chee) See APPENDIX/DESIGNERS.

**Gucci® loafer** (goo-chee) See SHOES.

**guepiere** See GIRDLES.

**guiches**  See CURLS.

**guimpe**  **1.** Separate blouse worn under a low-necked dress, similar to a *chemisette* or blousette. **2.** Piece of fabric draped around the face falling over the neck and chest. Worn by women in the 14th and 15th c., particularly by widows and nuns and still worn by the latter. Also spelled *guimp*.

**guimpe dress**  Jumper-dress with *guimpe* or blouse under short-sleeved, low-necked dress. Worn from 1880s to early 20th c.—first by children, later by older girls and women. Sometimes took the form of a suspender-type jumper with blouse called GUIMPE underneath. Also called *guimpe costume*.

**guimple**  See WIMPLE.

**guinea feathers** (ginny)  See FEATHERS.

**guipure/guipure de Bruges**  See LACES.

**guleron** (goo-ler-on)  See GORGET #3.

**gumshoe**  **1.** Colloquial term for rubber overshoe, or sneaker. **2.** Slang term meaning a detective or private investigator alludes to the quiet tread of *sneakers*.

**gum twill**  See FOULARD.

**gun-club checks**  See CHECKS.

**gusset**  **1.** Sewing term for diamond-shaped piece of fabric inserted under the arm of sleeve to permit greater movement. **2.** Triangu-

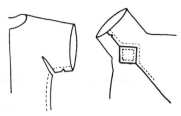

**GUSSET**

lar piece used at sides of handbag, at sides of men's shirttails, and sides of shoes for wider opening.

**gym bloomers**  Black sateen or navy-blue serge bloomers bloused below knee and pleated into waistband. Worn by women for gym classes from about 1900 to late 1920s. Also worn for camping. Also see BLOOMER, AMELIA.

**gymnasium costume**  Woman's costume worn from 1890s until early 20th c. consisting of full-cut blouse, buttoned down the front, with small tailored collar and long full cuffed sleeves. Collar and cuffs were braid trimmed. Worn with braid-trimmed calf-length skirt or BLOOMERS with unpressed pleats at the waist. Compare with CALISTHENIC COSTUME.

**gym suit**  See SPORT SUITS.

**gypsy look**  Styles copied from those worn by nomadic gypsy tribes. Also see BLOUSES, EARRINGS, LOOKS, SHAWLS, and BAYADÈRE under STRIPES.

**haba** See ABA.

**haberdashery** A store that sells men's apparel and furnishings.

**habiliment** (heh-bil-eh-ment) Term used for clothing, garb, attire, or dress. Also see BILLIMENT. *Der.* French, *habillement,* "clothing."

**habit** Characteristic apparel of a calling, rank, or function, *e.g., clerical clothes, court dress* or *riding habit.*

**habit à la française** (ah-beet ah la fran-sayz) See JUSTAUCORPS.

**habit d'escalier** (ah-beet des-kahl-yaye) Late 18th and early 19th c. evening dress made with an overtunic or *half robe.* The short sleeves were slit open and trimmed with ribbons tied in ladder-like fashion.

**habit-redingote** Woman's dress of 1879 made in princess style with front closed from neck to knees. Lower front of skirt was cut away and rounded to reveal the underskirt.

**HABIT SHIRT**

**habit shirt** **1.** Linen shirt with standing collar, ruffled front, and wrist ruffles. Worn under a vest as part of woman's *riding habit* in 18th and 19th c. **2.** Shirt worn as fill-in under low necklines in early 19th c. Also called *chemisette.*

**habutai** (ha-boo-tie) Soft, lightweight, plain silk fabric first woven in Japan (without the impurities removed from yarn). Originally made on hand looms—now made on power looms. Also spelled *hautae, habutaye.*

**hacking** Riding for pleasure, as opposed to riding to hounds, for which a specific type of clothing is worn. See POCKETS, SCARFS, and SPORT JACKETS.

**hacking scarf** Scarf, originally 72″ long, worn by four-in-hand coach drivers (coach with four horses) in Old England. Popular at Oxford and Cambridge Universities in England in 1931 when it was worn by the Prince of Wales—becoming a fad for U.S. college students in 1932.

**haik** Voluminous wrap made of large oblong of fabric which covers entire head, face, and body. Worn by Moslem women in northern Africa when out of doors. Also spelled *haick, hike, hake. Der.* Arabic, *hyak,* "to weave."

**haincelin** (han-se-lin) Short *houppelande,* the difference was embroidery on both sleeves instead of one. *Der.* After Charles VI's jester, Haincelin Coq.

**hairband** **1.** From 15th to 17th c. a *hair ribbon* or *fillet.* **2.** See HEADBAND #1 and #2.

**haircut** Trimming and shaping of hair with scissors or razor. See HAIRSTYLES.

**hairdo** See HAIRSTYLES.

**hair fibers** Animal fibers with a silky hand, *e.g.* MOHAIR from angora goat; ALPACA from cashmere goat, *camel's hair, guanaco, llama,* and *vicuña.*

**hairline stripe** See STRIPES.

**hair net** Fine cap-shaped net worn over the hair to keep it in place. Sometimes made of knotted human hair and nearly invisible. Also made of chenille, gold, or silver threads and worn as decoration. Also see SNOOD.

**hairpiece** Additional pieces of hair, either natural or of synthetic fibers, worn to complete a hairstyle. From 1840 to end of 19th c. elaborate hairstyles demanded extra hairpieces. See

WATERFALL. Many new styles were introduced during the 1960s and 1980s. Focus on hairstyles increased the use of hairpieces. Also see CADOGAN, CHIGNON, GUICHES, PIN-ON CURLS, POSTICHE, PUT-ON, SWITCH, TOUPEE and WIGS.

**hairpin** A two-tined device usually of tortoise shell, plastic, or metal. Used to hold the hair in place, especially hair styled in a bun or knot. The classic hairpin is a wire bent double with crimps halfway down each side to give flexibility. Pins of very fine wire tinted to match hair are called *invisible hairpins*. Decorated hairpins are worn as jewelry and made of exotic materials or jeweled. Also see BOBBY PINS.

**hairpin lace** See LACES.

**hair seal** See FURS.

**hair sticks** Long stiletto-like pieces of wood, plastic, or metal worn for decorative effect. Usually thrust through hair knotted at the back of the head.

**hairstyle** Manner in which the hair is worn. Also called *hairdo, coiffure,* or *coif.* Elaborate hairstyles were popular in ancient times, particularly with the Greeks and Romans. Popular throughout history with most elaborate styles worn during Marie Antoinette's time. In alphabetical listing see BENOITON COIFFURE, COIFFURE À LA GRECQUE, COIFFURE À LA INDEPENDENCE, COIFFURE À LA MAINTENON, COIFFURE À LA MOUTON, COIFFURE À LA NINON, COIFFURE À LA SÉVIGNÉ, COIFFURE À LA TITUS, COIFFURE À LA ZAZZERA, COIFFURE À L'ENFANT, COIFFURE EN BOUFFONS, COIFFURE EN BOURSE, COIFFURE EN CADENETTES, and COIFFURE EN RACQUETTE. First permanent wave introduced in about 1909. Hair spray became generally used in the 1950s, thus making possible more elaborate hair arrangements. Hairstyles from the 1960s on re-vived many old styles as well as introducing totally new ones. Styling gel and mousse were in general use by 1980s. Also see CURLS.

## ▬▬ HAIRSTYLES ▬▬

**abstract cut** Straight short geometric haircut, often asymmetric, with one side of hair cut different from other. Introduced by English hairstylist Vidal Sassoon in mid-1960s.

**Afro** Style adopted from African-Americans in 1960s with natural kinky hair combed straight out from the head; the size varying with the length of hair. There were many interesting variations of this style. Also see AFRO PUFFS and CORNROWS.

**Afro puffs** Afro-style hairstyle made by parting hair in center, pulling to sides tying near ears, and teasing to form puffs over ears.

**American Indian h.** Hair worn straight and long—below shoulder length—and parted in center. A headband worn low on the brow is usually added. The long hair may be tied in two pony tails, made into braids, or hang free. When braided called *American Indian braids*.

**ape drape** See SHAG.

**artichoke** Short, back-combed layered hair, not worn too bouffant popular in early 1960s.

**bangs** Hair combed forward over forehead and cut straight across, the remainder is left smooth or waved. Called FRINGE in England.

**Bardot h.** Long hair, loosely curled and arranged in tousled disarray with loose tendrils around face. Popularized by French film star, Brigitte Bardot, in 1959.

**Beatle cut** Man's haircut worn full with sideburns and well down the neck in back. First style to revive longer hairstyles for men. Introduced in the 1960s by the Beatles, avant-garde rock music group from Liverpool, England.

**beehive** High, exaggerated bubble hair shape, achieved by back-combing into a rounded dome. First worn by Teddy girls in

London in late 1950s, popular until mid-1960s. Also called *bubble bob.*

**bingle** British term for very short haircut. *Der.* Combination of the words BOB and SHINGLE.

**bob** Short blunt-cut hair, either with bangs or bared forehead, introduced in 1920s by Irene Castle. Also called *Twenties bob.* Also see BUSTER BROWN, BOYISH BOB, and GAMIN HAIRSTYLES. See IRENE CASTLE BOB in alphabetical listing.

**Boldini** Also called *Belle Epoque, concierge,* and *onion. Der.* For Italian society painter Giovanni Boldini (1845–1931), who often painted women wearing this style. See POMPADOUR #1.

**bouffant** Hair exaggeratedly puffed out by means of back-combing and held there by use of hair spray. Fashionable in early 1960s for medium-length and long hair. *Der.* French "full" or "puffed."

**boyish bob** Woman's extremely short hairstyle, shingled in back and short on sides. Originally popularized by Beatrice Lillie, British actress in the mid-1920s, and worn since at intervals, revived in 1980. Also see ETON CROP, GAMIN, and GARÇONNE.

**braids** Hairstyle made by plaiting three sections of hair together. Braids may be worn hanging down on shoulders, looped up, tied or pinned together, wound around the head in a coronet, or wound in a *bun* at the nape of the neck. Popular style for children in the early 20th c., also very popular in the 1960s and early 1980s. Also see AMERICAN INDIAN HAIRSTYLE, FISHBONE BRAIDS, MINI-MINI BRAIDS, QUEUE, and RASTA DREADLOCKS.

**brow-banded h.** Hair worn in various styles with headband or braid worn low on the forehead. Similar to AMERICAN INDIAN HAIRSTYLE.

**bubble bob** See BEEHIVE.

**bun** Large mass of hair confined neatly at crown of the head or at the nape of the neck.

**bush cut** See CREW CUT.

**Buster Brown** Straight short hairstyle with bangs over forehead. *Der.* Named for early 20th c. comic-strip character and popular for little boys. Also called DUTCH BOB. Also see alphabetical listing.

**Butch cut** See CREW CUT.

**cadogan** See GEORGE. Also see CATOGAN in alphabetical listing.

**chignon** Large roll of hair twisted into a circle or figure eight on the back of the head or at the nape of the neck, often enclosed in decorative net or held by fancy hairpins. Classic style in 1860s, in 1920s, 1930s, and revived in 1980s.

**China doll h.** Typical Chinese hairstyle with short straight hair, sometimes shingled in back, and bangs at forehead.

**classic pull-back** Long hair worn combed neatly to the back and tied with a ribbon. In the 1940s worn with a barrette in the back. Also see GEORGE.

**coif** Another name for hairstyle or shortened form of the world *coiffure.*

**concierge** See LA GOULUE. *Der.* Named for French caretaker of an apartment house, "concierge," who often wore this hairstyle in not too neat a fashion. Also called *La Belle Epoque,* BOLDINI, and ONION. SEE POMPADOUR #1.

**cornrows** Hair braided in horizontal rows by adding more hair after each plait to the braid. *Der.* From African styles worn by Southern Blacks in the 19th c., revived in early 1970s by fashionable Blacks.

**crew cut** Man's hair closely cropped so that hair on crown of head stands erect. Originally worn by oarsmen to keep hair out of eyes. Adopted by college men in 1940s and 1950s. At that time it was similar to Army haircuts. Also called *bush cut, Butch cut,* or *flat-top.* Also an outré fashion worn by women in 1980s.

AFRO         AFRO PUFFS         GAMIN         MOHAWK

LA BELLE ÉPOQUE

BRAIDS

PONY TAILS         PORCUPINE

CORNROWS

EARMUFFS

SASSOON

SPIKEY

FINGERWAVE         FLIP

UPSWEEP

**curls**   See separate category.

**curlyhead**   See POODLE CUT.

**ducktail haircut**   Short hairstyle combed to come to a point at the nape of the neck. Worn by both men and women in the 1950s.

**dutch bob**   **1.** See BUSTER BROWN HAIRSTYLE. **2.** Same style worn by girls with back cut straight or shingled.

**earmuffs**   Hair parted in center, braided on each side, and wound around to form buns over the ears.

**Empire cone**   Cone-shaped ornament, frequently wound with braids, and placed on crown of head. Hair is pulled back smoothly from the forehead, brought through the cone, and allowed to hang in a ponytail from top of cone or wound into a cockscomb spike.

**Eton crop**   Variation of BOYISH BOB worn in England.

**feather cut**   Short lightly curled woman's bob, cut in layers, popular in 1950s and 1960s.

**fingerwave**   Short hair set in flat waves by means of setting lotion and held until dry by bobby pins, or sometimes by combs. Popular in 1930s and revived in early 1970s. Also called *water wave*.

**fishbone braid**   Hair is braided so that the interlacing of hair down center back looks similar to the spine of a fish with small bones on each side. Also called *French braid*.

**flat-top**   See CREW CUT.

**flip**   Medium-length woman's hairstyle with hair turned up on ends to form an incomplete curl. Front is often cut in bangs.

**French braid**   See FISHBONE BRAID.

**French roll/twist**   Upswept hairstyle with side and back hair combed and twisted in roll at the center back. Popular in 1940s and classic style since.

**fringe**   British term for BANGS.

**gamin**   Short boyish cut with shingled back and sides and irregularly cut bangs, popular in 1940s. Also called *urchin* and *garçonne*. Der. French "street urchin."

**garçonne**   Boyish bob adapted by the flappers in 1920s. *Der.* French, "fast flapper."

**George**   Long hair pulled back and secured at the nape of the neck with a twist of hair, ribbon, or scarf. Named for hairstyle as seen in 18th c. portraits of U.S. President George Washington. Classic style for women, adapted by men in early 1970s. Also called a *cadogan*. Also spelled *catagon*.

**Gibson Girl**   Hair worn in high puffy POMPADOUR with small bun on top of head. Fashionable in 19th and early 20th c. popularized in drawings of Charles Dana Gibson. Similar to LA GOULUE but not as many loose tendrils.

**ironed hair**   Long straight hair, achieved by placing hair on an ironing board and pressing with a warm iron to remove all waves; a fad with young girls in the late 1960s.

**La Belle Époque**   Variant of POMPADOUR hairstyle. *Der.* For the period 1890–1910, called "La Belle Époque" in France. Also called BOLDINI, CONCIERGE, LA GOULUE, and *onion*. See alphabetical listing.

**La Goulue**   Variant of POMPADOUR. Also called BOLDINI, CONCIERGE, and *onion*.

**layered cut**   Hair cut in graduated lengths in a horizontal fashion around the head. With this cut, a bouffant hairstyle is easier to style.

**lion's tail**   A long piece of hair or a switch hanging down the back which is twined with cord to about 6 inches from the bottom, thus appearing like a lion's tail. Also called *queue de lion*.

**Mandinko**   Exaggerated Mohawk-type hairstyle with sideburns connected to beard and moustache as worn by "Mr. T.", television star of early 1980s.

**mini-mini braids** Extremely minute braids introduced in 1968. May be natural hair styled in this manner or an attached hairpiece. Also called *mini-plaits*.

**Mohawk** Style in which entire head is shaved except for upstanding fringe of hair, about 3″ high and 2″ or more wide, running from brow to the nape of the neck. Sometimes left long and made to stand up in "Spikes" with gel. See PORCUPINE. *Der.* Adapted from style worn by Mohawk Indians.

**onion** See POMPADOUR #1.

**page-boy** Straight hair shoulder length or shorter, with ends curled under at back and sides very smoothly. Popular style of 1940s, revived in 1970s. *Der.* From hair of medieval "pages."

**pigtails** **1.** Hair worn in two side braids, sometimes with ribbon bow tied on ends. Popular style for young girls since 1940s. **2.** Child's hairstyle for short hair with tiny, ribbon-tied braids all over head.

**pixie h.** Short hairstyle cut in layered style close to head and combed in points around forehead and face.

**pompadour** **1.** Woman's hair brushed up high and smooth from forehead and temples, sometimes teased or rolled over false stuffing and tucked into a small bun on top of head. Copied from style worn in late 19th and early 20th c. See GIBSON GIRL. Variations of this style called *La Belle Epoque, concierge, onion, Boldini,* and *La Goulue* in late 1960s. **2.** Hair rolled up in front with back worn straight and curled on ends, popular in 1940s. **3.** Man's hair worn rather long and brushed straight up and back from forehead with no part. Also see QUIFF. *Der.* From Marquise de Pompadour, mistress of Louis XV of France.

**ponytail** **1.** Hair pulled to crown or center back of head and tied with a ribbon or held with an elastic band. Ends left hanging loose like a horse's tail. **2.** Hair parted in the center

and two ponytails made—one on either side of the face near the ears.

**poodle cut** Allover short curled effect similar to hair of a poodle. Also called *curlyhead.*

**porcupine h.** Man's 1985 hairstyle with center portion from forehead to neck left longer with even longer strands about 8″ in length made to stand up on top of head with gel or mousse.

**pouf** See BOUFFANT.

**punk h.** A variety of outré hairstyles including MOHAWK, PORCUPINE, and SPIKY HAIRSTYLES, sometimes dyed a variety of colors.

**queue** (kew) Long single braid hanging down the back. Similar to hairstyle worn by Chinese men. Also see CUE and CUE PERUKE in alphabetical listing.

**queue de lion** See LION'S TAIL.

**quiff** Hairstyle brushed forward first, then back, giving a somewhat *pompadour* effect in front. Similar to style affected by Elvis Presley, a rock-music superstar of the 1950s and 1960s.

**Rasta dreadlocks** Man's or woman's long hair styled with a profusion of mini-braids. May be shoulder length or longer. Sometimes hair spray is used to make braids stand up on top of head in a tousled mass, introduced in 1980s. *Der.* From the style worn by Rastafarian Negro sect from Jamaica, founded in 1930 when Ras Tafari (Haile Selassie) became Emperor of Ethiopia.

**Romeo** Modified *page-boy* cut with bangs falling to eyebrows, sides cut sloping backward to reveal the face as an oval, and hair gently turned under at back and sides.

**Sassoon** Short, straight boyish hairdo, combed forward from crown, cut in low bangs, shaped to points in front of ears, and shingled in back to deep V. *Der.* First abstract cut, designed by British hairdresser, Vidal Sassoon in 1964.

**sculptured h.** Hair covered with mousse so that it may be arranged in fan-shaped design or brushed straight up from face and cut in scalloped design at top. Styles were introduced by Patti LaBelle, a rock singer in mid-1980s.

**shag** Longish bob, layered for a shaggy look, with bangs and "shaggy" in front of ears. An innovation of the late 1960s. Also called *ape drape*.

**shingle** Tapering of hair up back of head, and sometimes around to the sides, in imitation of a man's conventional haircut. Style introduced in 1920s for women, achieving new popularity in the 1960s and 1980s. Also see BINGLE.

**spiky h.** Short or medium-length hair, segmented and twisted to form pointed projections which are stiffened with hair spray, gel or mousse. Sometimes dyed different colors., *e.g.*, blue, orange, and pink.

**Statue of Liberty h.** Outré hairstyle of 7 spikes of hair, sprayed to stand erect, framing face like Statue of Liberty crown. *Der.* Inspired by the July 4, 1986 celebration of the restoration of the Statue of Liberty in New York harbor.

**topknot** Hair twisted into a knot or bun at the crown of the head.

**twenties bob** See BOB.

**upsweep** Popular 1940s woman's hairstyle with medium-long hair brushed upward from the sides and nape of neck, then secured on top of the head in curls or a *pompadour*. Also called *updo*.

**urchin** See GAMIN.

**Veronica Lake h.** Long hair parted on side with heavier section hanging down almost covering one eye. Popularized by star Veronica Lake in 1940s, revived after interest for older movies in 1960s.

**wash and wear h.** Hair with permanent, worn in a tousled mass, achieved by washing hair and allowing it to hang uncombed. Popularized in early 1980s.

**water wave** See FINGERWAVE.

**wedge** A style where hair is tapered close to the head at the nape of the neck, almost to a V. Above this the hair is full and all one length. The front and sides are all one length, squared off at middle of ear, and short bangs are informally styled. *Der.* Popularized by Dorothy Hamill, an Olympic figure skating champion in 1976.

**wind-blown bob** Popular 1930s woman's hairstyle which was cut short and shingled, so that hair fell softly about the face as if blown by the wind.

---

**hakama** (hak-e-ma) **1.** Stiff silk trousers, slashed up sides, made by pleating fullness into stiff belt using six pleats in front and two in back. A belt with cords attached is tied around the *obi*. Formerly worn by Japanese men. **2.** Loose divided skirt worn by Japanese women as part of a so-called "reform dress."

**hakimono** (hak-e-mo-no) Japanese term for footwear which consists mainly of sandals, *e.g.*, *geta* and *zori*.

**hakoseko** Silk purse or compact, placed in folds of Japanese kimono by women.

**haku no gohō** Japanese robe. See HŌ.

**Hale, Sarah Josepha** (1788–1879) As editor of *Godey's Lady's Book* from 1837 to 1877, she was responsible for the establishment of Thanksgiving as a national holiday and advocated women teachers in public schools. As a friend and adviser of Matthew Vassar, she helped in organizing Vassar College, the first college for women. She stressed physical education, better working conditions, and wages for women. Also wrote 24 books and hundreds of poems including *Mary Had a Little Lamb*. Also see GODEY, LOUIS A.

**half** Adjective used for smaller or incomplete items of apparel or accessories. The prefix "demi" is a synonym. See APRONS, BELTS, glasses, slips, demi-boot under BOOTS, DEMI-BRA under BRAS, and DOMINO under MASKS.

**half-compass cloak**   See COMPASS CLOAK.

**half coronet**   See DEMI-CORONAL.

**half dress**   Late 18th and 19th c. term for daytime or semiformal evening dress. Also called *half-toilette* or *demi-toilette*.

**half gaiters**   See SPATS.

**half gown**   See HALF ROBE.

**half handkerchief**   Neck or head scarf worn by women in 18th and early 19th c. made of decorative fabric in triangular shape. From 1830s on, called *fanchon*.

**half jack boot**   See JOCKEY BOOT.

**half kirtle**   See KIRTLE.

**half lining**   Lining of only part of the garment, *e.g.*, front completely lined but only the shoulders lined in the back. Frequently used in men's jackets and topcoats.

**half-moon pocket**   See POCKETS.

**half mourning**   Costume worn for a time following the period of deep *mourning*, usually consisting of gray, purple or black costume with touches of white. Worn until 20th c.

**half piqué/half P.K. seam**   See GLOVE SEAMS.

**half robe**   Low-necked, short-sleeved, thigh-length tunic worn over long gown with fullness pulled in at waist by narrow ribbon. Worn from late 18th to early 19th c. Also called *half-gown* or *demi-habilliment*.

**half shirt**   Man's short shirt, with decorated panel down front, worn over plain or soiled shirt from 16th to 18th c. Also called *sham*.

**half sizes**   Women's garments cut for a fully developed figure: short-waisted in back, larger in waist and hips, height about 5'2" to 5'8"—usually sized 10½ to 24½.

**half sleeve**   **1.** Protective sleeve covering the sleeve on forearm, held on by an elastic garter. Worn in early 20th c. particularly by clerical workers. **2.** Sleeve covering forearm made of richer material than rest of garment, attached by lacings. Worn from late 14th to mid-17th c. Also called *foresleeve*.

**half-toilette**   See HALF DRESS.

**Hall of Fame**   See COTY AMERICAN FASHION CRITICS' AWARD.

**halo hat**   See HATS.

**Halston**   See APPENDIX/DESIGNERS.

**halter**   Strap encircling the neck used to support front of blouse or dress, leaving shoulders and back bare. Popular in 1930s and revived in early 1970s. Also used on evening wear and swimsuits. Also see NECKLINES and TOPS.

**Hamburg lace**   See LACES.

**hamster**   See FURS.

**hand**   Qualities of a fabric revealed through sense of touch., *e.g.*, crisp or soft, smooth or rough.

**handbag**   Accessory carried primarily by women and girls to hold such items as money, credit cards, and cosmetics. Comes in many styles and made of a variety of materials, *e.g.*, leather, fabric, vinyl, metal, plastic, canvas, straw, and patent leather. The word is often shortened to "bag."* Also called a *purse* or *pocketbook*. From 13th to 16th c. the *aulmoniere*, a small leather pouch, was worn suspended from man's girdle in order to have alms for the poor. From late 19th to early 20th c. women carried a small elongated bag called a *reticule*. In late 19th c. various types of handbags began to be carried mainly for traveling. By 1920s it was

---

*The abbreviation "b" is used for the word *bag* in the following category listing.

a necessary accessory. In 1968 the MANBAG was introduced for men.

## ■■■■■■■ HANDBAGS ■■■■■■■

**accordion b.** Bag made like an expandable filing envelope which is narrow at the top and pleated at sides and bottom. Usually made with a handle and frequently with a zipper compartment in the center. *Der.* From resemblance to pleats on the musical instrument of this name.

**American Indian b.** See SQUAW BAG.

**Apache b.** See SQUAW BAG.

**attaché case** See BRIEFCASE.

**back pack** Nylon bag with straps fitting over shoulders so that it can be worn on the back. Used since 1970s to carry books and sometimes used in lieu of a handbag in the 1980s.

**barrel b.** Handbag shaped like a stubby cylinder with a zipper closing and handles attached to the sides. *Der.* From the shape similar to a small "barrel."

**basket b.** Term covering many types of handbags. Originally woven only of reed in typical basket shapes. Now made of reed, straw, cane, or interwoven plastic strips in many styles. Most popular style is one which resembles a small picnic hamper. Made in natural color or painted, and sometimes decorated with shells, beads, sequins, brass or leather.

**beaded b.** Any ornate small bag generally used for evening which may be entirely encrusted with varicolored pearls or glass beads. Also a fabric bag, usually satin, with a design worked in beads. Popular in the early 1900s, one type was usually hand-crocheted in small elongated pouch style with a drawstring top and a beaded tassel at the bottom. Another style, made in France, was oblong in shape with beaded fringe on the bottom and sterling silver frame and handle. Latter type was revived in 1968.

**belt b.** **1.** A small bag worn at waist having slots in the back through which a belt is drawn. Usually has a flap closing and is worn with sportswear. **2.** A pouch bag with handle through which belt is drawn. **3.** Handbags of Middle Ages were fastened to the belt, worn primarily by men, and called *pockets*. Also see AULMONIERE in alphabetical listing.

**book b.** Slim oblong bag the size of a notebook cinched around center with strap that forms loop handle; introduced in 1970s.

**box b.** Handbag with rigid frame, similar to small suitcase or lunchbox, made in leather, metal, or vinyl.

**bracelet b.** Type of handbag with one or two *bangle bracelets* as handles. May be a soft pouch bag made of leather or fabric, or it may be made with a frame.

**briefcase** Handbag for woman executive which is of briefcase size and features small outside pockets for purse items. Also called *attaché case*.

**canteen b.** Circular-style bag frequently made with a shoulder strap and zipper closing. Made in the shape of a flat canteen used to carry water in dry climates.

**caravan b.** See SAFARI BAG.

**carpet b.** Handbag made of patterned carpeting or heavy tapestry, in a large satchel style. Popular in late 1960s and revived in mid-1980s in lighter weight fabrics. *Der.* From carpet valises popular with Northerners for travel just after the Civil War and alluded to by the derisive term "carpetbaggers."

**carryall** See TOTE BAG.

**change purse** Small purse that closes by a snap clasp on the rigid frame or by a zipper. Usually carried inside handbag to hold coins and made in leather, clear plastic, or matched to the larger handbag. Also called a *coin purse*.

**clutch b.** **1.** Regular-sized handbag without a handle. **2.** Type of handbag frequently used for an evening bag. Sometimes has a strap on back through which hand may be inserted, or a fine gold chain attached in such a manner that it is of optional use. Frequently made in envelope style. *Mini-clutch* bags are tiny versions of this style.

**coin purse**   See CHANGE PURSE.

**cordé b.**   Any type of handbag made out of a fabric composed of rows of *gimp* stitched to a background fabric to make a pattern. Popular style in the 1940s and still used.

**drawstring b.**   Any handbag which is closed by pulling a cord, usually of pouch type.

**duffel b.**   **1.** Large barrel-shaped canvas bag with a drawstring top. Used originally by sailors and soldiers to transport their clothing and other items. When used by sailors, called a *sea bag*. **2.** Copied in smaller style for handbags or beach bags. May have an extra piece of fabric on outside which forms large pockets around outside of bag. **3.** Small taffeta evening bag in pouch style with large ruffled top closed with tasseled drawstring.

**envelope b.**   Long narrow handbag made in the shape of a correspondence envelope, usually of clutch-type without handle. Newer styles have a handle which may be snapped on.

**feed b.**   Cylindrical leather or canvas bag with flat round bottom and top handles copied from horse's feed bag. Forerunner of many open tote bags.

**flight b.**   **1.** Soft canvas satchel with zippered top closing and two handles copied from standard carryall issued by airlines to passengers. **2.** Any handbag used for traveling, larger than a handbag and smaller than a suitcase. Also called a *travel bag*.

**fold-over clutch**   Small envelope bag may be open at the top or with zippered closing. Bag is folded over double and carried in the hand or under arm.

**French purse**   Fold-over wallet for bills, one

half of which incorporates a change purse with metal clasp closing at the top which is actually one end of the wallet.

**Greek b.**   Square or rectangle wool open-top bag. Handwoven in Greek-key designs, trimmed around edge with cable yarn which also forms the handle.

**hippie b.**   See SQUAW BAG.

**Indian b.**   See SQUAW BAG.

**interchangeable b.**   Complete handbag with extra covers that snap or button over frame to change colors. Very practical when traveling.

**Kikuyu**   Open-top straw tote bag with leather handles. Handwoven of natural sisal in horizontal strips of red and blue alternating with natural color. Made by Kikuyu craftsmen of Kenya.

**knapsack**   A carryall made in heavy fabric usually about 4″ deep, 12″ to 14″ long, and nearly square, with webbing around edge which also forms the handle. Originally used by hikers, now used as a school bag.

**lunchbox b.**   Identical in shape to the traditional deep lunchbox with a curved lid. Introduced from Italy in 1967, it was first made in paper-mâché and later in metal. Distinctive feature is a collage effect of decorative pictures pasted on the outside and then shellacked. Later "do it yourself" *découpage* kits were sold.

**manbag**   Handbag, usually a shoulder bag style, carried by a man. A fashion which gained in popularity in early 1970s as an outgrowth of wide use of camera bags by men.

**mesh b.**   Tiny links of metal joined to make a flexible bag. Popular in early 1900s in small size with sterling silver top and chain with the metal frequently enameled in a floral design. In the 1940s, mesh handbags were made with larger white enameled links and white plastic frames.

**minaudiere**   (min-ode-ee-air) Small rigid metal evening bag used to hold cosmetics made in oval, oblong or square shapes. Carried in hand or by short chain. Decorated by engraved designs or set with jewels, this expensive jeweler's product was popularized by Cartier in New York. *Der.* French, *simper*, "to smirk."

**mini b.** Small bags became important in the 1960s with the introduction of miniskirts. Tiny bags were introduced in all styles. Some had double and triple frames, usually with attached shoulder chains or straps.

**mini-clutch b.** See CLUTCH BAG.

**Moroccan b. 1.** Tooled leather handbag made in Morocco of Moroccan leather. Decorated with elaborate designs and color combinations, such as saffron and wine. **2.** Handbag made with stitched allover design in saffron on wine-colored leather.

**muff b.** Basically a muff, an accessory used to keep the hands warm, frequently styled in fur. In the 1930s a zippered compartment to hold small items was added to the muff and this became a classic item used by little girls.

**newsbag** *Tote bag* style with separate section on the outside to slip in a rolled magazine or newspaper.

**pannier b.** A bag with zipper compartment in the center and two open compartments on either side. A single broad handle extends from one side to the other on the outside of bag at the middle.

**pianta b.** Small evening bag introduced from Italy in mid-1960s resembling a tiny umbrella made from a square of fabric with four corners folded to the center and a looped center handle.

**pokey** Small drawstring pouch made of sueded leather, sometimes with tiny pocket on front. Popularized in the late 1960s. *Der.* Copied from a small leather bag used by '49ers to carry gold nuggets and gold dust.

**pouch** Basic style originally made of soft shirred leather or fabric with a drawstring closing. Now also made with a frame and handles.

**saddle bags** Pair of soft leather bags joined to central strap handle. *Der.* From large bags thrown over horse's saddle to carry provisions.

**safari b.** Double-handled bag made like a small flight bag with a zippered closing. Characteristic features are the small pockets placed low on the outside of the bag. One of the most popular bags of the late 1960s. Also called *caravan bag.*

**Sally Jess® b.** Trademarked by English designer Sally Jess, this bag was a favorite with British younger set in the 1960s. Made of fabric in simple tote design with fabric handle and two cut-out crescent sections at the top.

**satchel** Leather bag with a rigid flat bottom, sides slope to close on metal frame hinged about halfway down bag. Often fastened with extra snap locks and with metal reinforcements at corners and rigid curved handle. Sides are usually recessed.

**sea bag** See DUFFEL BAG.

**shigra** Handmade handbag of tote type sold to American tourists or exported to U.S. from Ecuador. Made from fibers of the *cabuya* plant using a looping system done with a needle to form distinctive patterns with natural and colored yarns. Originally used for storage of grain and flour. Made in patterns characteristic of different communities in Ecuador.

**shoulder b.** Handbag in any shape or size with long chain or strap to place over the shoulder. Some types of shoulder straps convert to double chain handles, others may be shortened by unbuckling a section of the strap.

**signature b.** Handbag of leather or canvas with designer's initials or signature stenciled or printed in an allover repeat pattern. Originating with Louis Vuitton in Paris, later copied by Hermés, Saint Laurent, Mark Cross, Gucci, etc., and considered a fashion "status symbol."

**sporran b.** (spor-an) Adaptation for women of *sporran* as worn by the Scots Highlander.

**ACCORDION BAG**

**BARREL BAG**

**NEWSBAG**

**POKEY BAG**

**BELT-BAG**

**BRACELET BAG**

**SADDLE BAGS**

**SHOULDER BAG**

**ENVELOPE BAG**

**LUNCHBOX BAG**

**TOTE BAG**

**SQUAW BAG**

**MINAUDIERE**

**SAFARI BAG**

**MANBAG**

**UMBRELLA TOTE**

**BACK PACK**

Shoulder bag with metal frame made of leather with long strands of horsehair hanging from it. Also see alphabetical listing.

**squaw b.** Handbag inspired by native Americans. May be made of genuine doeskin in natural color or made of tiny geometric contrasting patches of colored leather. Most bags are trimmed with fringe. Popular handbag of the late 1960s. Also called *American Indian bag*, *Apache bag*, and *hippie bag*. *Der.* Name for native American woman.

**suitcase b.** Handbag made of metal and shaped like a miniature suitcase complete with lock and reinforced corners.

**swagger pouch** Distinct type of bag with double handles and two open sections on either side of zippered compartment. Classic style since the 1930s.

**swinger b.** Bag styled like a large wallet with attached loop handle. May have outside pockets for keys and change.

**tooled leather b.** Typical Western-type handbag made of natural colored cowhide with handstamped pattern. Each individual character is stamped with a metal die.

**tote b.** **1.** Utility bag, large enough to carry small packages, sometimes with inner zippered compartment for money. Copied from shape of common paper shopping bag. Made with open top and two handles, sometimes with outside loop to hold umbrella. **2.** Any large bag with open top and two handles.

**travel bag** See FLIGHT BAG.

**triplex** Triple-framed bag with three separate clasps. Each section is an individual compartment. Introduced in 1967, many were styled as tiny MINI BAGS. Also called *triple-framed bag*.

**umbrella tote** **1.** Similar to a TOTE BAG, but with a pocket at side for holding an umbrella. **2.** Bag shaped like a briefcase with a zipper around it and the umbrella attached to the side with a plastic loop. **3.** Conventional satchel-type bag with zippered compartment at bottom for umbrella.

**vanity b.** Stiff-framed box-shaped bag usually fitted with a large mirror and sometimes other accessories.

---

**hand-blocked print** See PRINTS.

**handcoverchief/hand cloth** See HANDKERCHIEF.

**hand cuff** See HAND FALL.

**hand fall** Term for lace-trimmed, turned-back, flared starched *cuff* frequently made double. Worn by men and women in 17th c. with *falling band, falling ruff,* and *standing band.* Also called *hand cuff.*

**handkerchief** **1.** 16th-c. square of linen or silk, often edged with lace, carried about the person and used for wiping the face or nose, called a *napkin.* **2.** Men's usually larger than women's often colored for day use, black for mourning. In 1870 plain white cambric was correct for day or evening. In 1890s fashionable to wear in the cuff of the left sleeve—copied from the military. Also see BANDANNA. At one time called *handcoverchief* or *hand cloth.* Also see HEMS, SKIRTS, and SLEEVES.

**handkerchief dress** Dress of the 1880s with a tunic made from, or resembling, a bandanna handkerchief. Two were arranged diagonally on the front of the dress with one point reaching nearly to the hem of dress. A long-skirted jacket with shaped *revers* and waistcoat comprised the bodice of the dress. Also see HANDKERCHIEF TUNIC.

**handkerchief lawn** High count lawn given a soft finish. Woven with borders along the selvage and cross borders to match. Usually woven 51 inches wide to make three handkerchiefs—then torn apart and hemmed. If torn, rather than cut, handkerchiefs will wash better and fold evenly. Cut handkerchiefs, not cut

**HANDKERCHIEF DRESS, 1882**

precisely along the warp and filling yarns, become irregular in shape when washed.

**handkerchief linen** Lightweight, sheer fine fabric used for handkerchiefs and infants' wear.

**handkerchief tunic** Dress of 1917 with peplum made from large square of fabric, like a handkerchief. Made with center opening for waist and pointed ends hanging down over skirt.

**hand knitting** Knitting apparel, accessories, or trimming made entirely by hand as opposed to MACHINE KNITTING.

**hand sleeve** 16th-c. term for lower part of sleeve.

**handspun yarn** Yarn made with different types of hand-spinning wheels—making yarn which is less regular in appearance than machine-made yarns—adding texture and interest to the woven fabric.

**hang** **1.** Term used in clothing construction to describe how fabric drapes on the figure after it is sewn. **2.** Term used for marking hem of skirt with pins or chalk for straightening.

**hanger** See SHOULDER BELT.

**hanging sleeve** **1.** Long sleeve worn from 1400 to 1630 made in a wide tubular shape with a slit extending from upper arm to below elbow through which the arm could be placed to make short sleeves. The remainder of the sleeve hung free, sometimes to the calf of leg. Sometimes made open from upper arm to wrist with a cuff. **2.** *Sham hanging sleeve* Long hanging pendant piece of fabric attached to a short sleeve or set in armhole in back which fell sometimes to ankle-length in 1560s to 1630s. In 17th and 18th c. pendant fabric became more like a ribbon streamer—representing *leading strings* worn by children and young women for a decorative effect. Also called *false hanging sleeve.*

**hank** **1.** Unit by which knitting yarn is sold—usually comes in coiled form. See SKEIN. **2.** Unit of yarn of a definite length varying for different types of yarn. For linen it is 300 yards; for cotton, 840 yards; for spun silk, 840 yards, and for worsted, 560 yards.

**hanseline** (han-sa-lyn) Man's extremely short *doublet*, fashionable in late 14th and early 15th c. Also called *paltock*. Also spelled *hanslein*, *haunseleyns*, *hense lynes*, and *henselyns*.

**hanten** Short, dark blue, front-closed coat with no belt and narrow sleeves worn by Japanese male workers. Usually stenciled with name on the back between the shoulders or on the lapels with badge of employer.

**han-yeri** Embroidered collar, worn by Japanese, attached to the undergarment and worn pulled out over *kimono* at neck. See JUBAN and SHITA-JUBAN.

**haol** Full length robe worn by Chinese women.

**haori** (hah-o-ri) Loose knee-length Japanese coat.

**happi** **1.** Originally a Japanese sleeveless, stiffly starched undergarment worn under the hō. Had a neckline which crossed in V in front and did not show under outergarment. **2.** For contemporary version see HAPPI COAT under ROBES.

**happy face**   Stylized face made up of a yellow circle with black dots for eyes and nose and a single black line for mouth. Used on *sweatshirts*, buttons, jewelry, and in prints, since early 1970s.

**Hardanger bonnet**   Native Norwegian cap, shaped to head like baby's bonnet and tied under chin. Cap is cut in three sections—with white center and red sides—edged with black velvet, decorated with braid and colored beads in eight-pointed star designs.

**Hardanger embroidery**   See EMBROIDERIES.

**hard hat**   See HATS.

**Hardwick, Cathy**   See APPENDIX/DESIGNERS.

**hare**   See FURS.

**harem**   **1.** Adjective used for a draped dress with skirt attached to an underskirt. Hem is turned up and attached to underskirt making an irregular hemline. **2.** Turkish trousers. See SHALWAR. **3.** Look of the Near East using full ankle-length harem pants or skirt. See DRESSES, LOOKS, PAJAMAS, PANTS, SILHOUETTES, and SKIRTS.

**harlequin**   **1.** Costume made of vari-colored diamond-shaped patches on tunic and tights, a flaring brimmed black bicorn hat decorated with pompons, and a black mask. **2.** A pattern of lozenge-shaped checks in multi-color used on fabric. **3.** Eyeglasses slanting up to corner peaks. See GLASSES. **4.** Hat with brim, wide at sides and cut straight across front and back, worn in 1938. *Der.* From *Harlequin*, a part played by an actor, in 16th to 18th c. Italian comedies called *commedia dell'arte*.

**harlequin opal**   See GEMS.

**harlot**   Garment, similar to tights, worn by men in England in the late 14th c. Stockings and pants were made in one piece and tied to the upper and outer garments by strings known as POINTS. Also spelled *herlot*.

**Harlow, Jean**   Platinum-blonde Hollywood film actress of the late 1920s and early 1930s. A sex symbol, associated with soft, bias-cut clothes worn over natural body—a fashion influence in the late 1960s. Also see LOOKS, PANTS, SHOES, SLIPPERS and SLIPDRESS under DRESSES.

**harness**   Part of a loom which regulates the weave of the fabric. Each warp yarn is threaded through HEDDLES attached to a HARNESS. The individual harnesses are raised to alternate the yarn shot through by the SHUTTLE. See LOOM.

**Harper's Bazaar**   Ladies' fashion magazine started in 1867 as a weekly tabloid-style newspaper containing many fashion engravings. Became a monthly magazine in 1901. William Randolph Hearst bought the magazine in 1913. Former editors were *Edna Woolman Chase, Carmel Snow,* and *Diana Vreeland.*

**Harris Tweed®**   Trademark of Harris Tweed Association for tweed fabric. Defined by the British Board of Trade and Federal Trade Commission as handwoven woolen fabric from the Hebrides Islands, off the coast of Scotland, consisting of Harris, Lewis, Uist, Barra, and other smaller islands. There are two types *a)* made from hand-spun yarn, and *b)* made from machine-made yarn. Used mainly for women's coats styled in a classic manner.

**Hartnell, Sir Norman**   See APPENDIX/DESIGNERS.

**Harvard crimson**   Deep cherry color with a violet cast; official color of Harvard University, Cambridge, Massachusetts.

**harvest hat**   Believed to be the term used for the first straw hats worn by farmers in the U.S.

**hasp**   Decorative silver fastening, similar to *hook and eye.* Used for fastening coats in 17th and 18th c.

**Hastings diamond**   See DIAMONDS.

**hat**  An accessory worn on the head consisting of a crown and a brim. Designed to complete a costume or worn for warmth and made of felt, straw, fur, fabric, leather, vinyl, etc. Worn since 10th c., early hats were designed to show the importance of the wearer. *Men:* until 1660 worn indoors as well as out and in church. *Women:* rarely worn until late 16th c. except for traveling. Flat straw hats were worn in church from approximately 1750 to the mid-1830s. At that time, bonnets took over and hats were not again considered proper for church until 1875 when they almost replaced bonnets as headgear. From the late 1950s, bouffant hairstyles and later the use of wigs and falls, made it difficult to wear hats. Also see BONNETS, CAPS, and in alphabetical listing BEAVER, BICORNE, CHAPEAU BRA, CHARLOTTE, MUFFIN HAT, and TRICORN.

## ══════ HATS ══════

**Alpine h.**  **1.** Various types of hats adapted from Bavarian and Austrian Tyrolean hats. One contemporary version for men is of pile fabric of fur felt with slightly peaked crown and upturned brim in the back. Popular since 1940s for man's sport hat, it was first introduced in the late 1890s. Also called a *Tyrolean hat.* **2.** Woman's hat with high crown and medium-sized brim worn in 1890s. See alphabetical listing. *Der.* Named for alpine Tyrol region in Austria and Bavaria where this type hat is worn by natives.

**beach h.**  Hat used as a sunshade on the beach or at a resort usually made of bright-colored straw, either natural or synthetic, in a variety of shapes. Frequently has a wide brim, conical crown, and sometimes decorated with felt, sequins or shells.

**beefeater's h.**  Distinctive hat worn by Yeomen of the Guard in England, consisting of a narrow brim and soft high crown pleated into headband with crown flaring slightly at the top. Also see BEEFEATER'S UNIFORM in alphabetical listing.

**beret**  See BUBBLE BERET.

**bicycle-clip h.**  Tiny half-hat fastened over crown and side of head by piece of springy metal. *Der.* From metal clip worn around leg when riding a bicycle to keep trousers from catching in chain or wheel spokes.

**boater**  **1.** Straw hat with flat oval crown, flat brim, and ribbon band originally worn for boating. Popular for men in late 19th c. Used for summer wear until about 1930. See alphabetical listing. Also see CANOTIER. **2.** Style copied in plastic for wear at political conventions.

**bobby's h.**  Hat with domed high crown and narrow turned-down brim worn by English policemen. *Der.* From slang term "bobbies," used for English policemen.

**bowler**  Man's hat of hard felt, with domed crown and narrow brim turned up at sides, usually black. Worn originally by London businessmen or with formal riding habit. Similar to American DERBY. *Der.* From design of William Bowler in 1850s. See alphabetical listing.

**Breton**  Woman's off-the-face hat made with medium-sized rolled-back brim worn on back of head. Copied from hats worn by peasants of Brittany, France.

**bubble beret**  Large bouffant beret, usually without a brim, worn tilted to side of head in the early 1960s.

**bubble h.**  Puffed-out felt or straw hat, usually stiff rather than soft, made with tiny brim in early 1960s. Worn perched on top of head over bouffant hairstyles. Also called a *dome hat.*

**bumper**  Hat with thick rolled-back brim, surrounding various styles of crowns. Also see BUMPER BRIM in alphabetical listing.

**busby**  Tall cylindrical black fur or feathered military hat with cockade at top of center front. A bag-shaped drapery hangs from crown and is draped to the back. Worn by Hussars and certain guardsmen in the British army.

**bush h.**  Large-brimmed Australian-type hat worn turned up on one side. Worn in Australia and in Africa for safaris, also worn as part of uniform by Australian soldiers in World War II. Also called *caddie* or *caddy*.

**caddie/caddy**  See BUSH HAT.

**canotier**  (ka-no-tee-ay)  Man's stiff flat oval crowned straw hat with straight brim. Fashion of early 20th c. and identified with actors Maurice Chevalier, Buster Keaton, and Harold Lloyd. Also called a *boater*. Also see GONDOLIER'S HAT in alphabetical listing.

**cape h.**  Woman's half-hat made by attaching felt or fabric capelet to a springy metal clip which crosses the head from ear to ear letting capelet fall over back of head.

**capeline**  (cap-leen)  Fitted skullcap with large floppy brim worn since 1920s.

**cartwheel h.**  Woman's hat with extra wide stiff brim and low crown frequently made of straw.

**chef's h.**  Tall, white full-crowned fabric hat starched to stand up stiffly. Set into the headband with 100 pleats which originally indicated that the chef could cook eggs 100 ways. Also called *hundred pleater*. The more important the chef—the taller the hat.

**chukka h.**  Domed hat with small brim copied from hats worn by polo players. Similar to, but not as high as, English policeman's hat. *Der.* Named for divisions of polo game called chukkars.

**clip h.**  Half-hat mounted on a spring-metal clip worn across the crown of the head often used for a child's hat of fur. See BICYCLE-CLIP HAT.

**cloche**  (klosh)  Deep-crowned hat with very narrow brim fitting head closely, almost concealing all of the hair. Worn pulled down almost to eyebrows, fashionable in 1920s and again in 1960s. *Der.* French, "bell."

**coolie h.**  **1.** Chinese hat made of straw which may take many forms—mushroom-shaped with knob at top, bowl-shaped, conical flared shape, and a flared shape with a peak in the center. All are made of bamboo, palm leaves, or straw and stand away from the head forming almost a parasol against the sun. **2.** Copies of the above styles made in felt and straw for general wear. *Der.* Chinese, "kuli," an unskilled worker.

**Cossack h.**  Tall brimless hat of fur worn by Russian horsemen and cavalrymen. Copied for men's winter hat in U.S. and England in 1950s and 1960s.

**cowboy h.**  Large wide-brimmed felt hat with crown worn creased or standing up in cone shape with the brim rolled up on both sides and dipping in front. Sometimes with hatband of leather and silver. Worn in U.S. by Western cowboys to shade face and neck. Also called TEN-GALLON HAT. Also see STETSON.

**crusher h.**  Comfortable man's snap-brim felt hat which can be made into a compact roll to fit in pocket or pack for travel. Introduced about 1900 and popular in the 1920s and again in the 1980s.

**derby**  **1.** Man's stiff black or brown felt hat with high rounded crown and narrow brim curved up at sides. Worn as semiformal hat by businessmen in England. Also worn for riding. **2.** American name for English BOWLER. *Der.* Named for Earl of Derby and English horse race called the Derby; pronounced *darby* in England.

**Doll h.**  **1.** Miniature hat worn attached to the back of head with combs or pins. Sometimes had a veil; in early 1960s. Also worn in the late 1930s, pushed forward on the head

BEEFEATER'S HAT

SCOTTIE

MOUNTIE'S HAT

SNAP-BRIM HAT

BUBBLE BERET

GAUCHO HAT

PICTURE HAT

REX HARRISON HAT

HARD HAT

DERBY

HALO HAT

SAILOR HAT

SAILOR HAT, 1898

FEDORA          GARBO/SLOUCH HAT

TENNIS HAT

TOP HAT, LATE 1840s

TURBAN          WILLIAM PENN HAT

and held on with an elastic band around back of head. Popularized by Jacqueline Kennedy when she was First Lady. **2.** Reintroduced in 1984 to perch on the front of the head in various shapes—square, round, etc.

**dome h.**   See BUBBLE HAT.

**drum major's h.**   Very tall hat with chin band, frequently made of fur in black or white, worn by the leader of a band or drum major for parade functions. Similar to BEARSKIN CAP.

**envoy h.**   Man's winter hat similar to CosSACK HAT with leather or fur crown and fur or fabric edge. Popular in late 1960s.

**fedora**   Felt hat with medium-sized brim and high crown with lengthwise crease from front to back. Originally worn by men but now also styled for women with turned-up back brim. *Der.* Popularized for men after Victorian Sardou's play *Fedora* was produced in 1882.

**fez**   **1.** Red felt hat shaped like truncated cone with long black silk tassel hanging from center of crown worn by Turkish men until 1925; also worn in Syria, Palestine, and Albania. Also worn by the "Shriners" an auxiliary order of the Masons. **2.** Basic shape, without tassel, copied for women's hats in the West. *Der.* Named for town of Fez in Morocco.

**fold-up h.**   Straw sun hat with pleated brim and crown which folds to a 6-inch roll for carrying in pocket or purse.

**French sailor h.**   Large navy-blue or white cotton tam, stitched to stiff navy-blue headband and trimmed with red pompon at center of crown. Originally worn by French seamen pulled down on forehead with top exactly horizontal.

**Garbo h.**   Slouch hat worn so frequently by Greta Garbo in the 1930s that it is sometimes called by her name. See SLOUCH HAT. Also see GARBO, GRETA in alphabetical listing.

**gaucho h.**   (gow-cho) Wide-brimmed black felt hat made with medium-high flat crown.

Fastened under chin with leather thong. Originally worn by South American cowboys, it was adapted for women in late 1960s and worn with gaucho pants. Also called *sombrero córdobes*. Also see WESTERN HAT. *Der.* Spanish "cowboy" of Argentina, Chile, and Uruguay.

**Gibus**   See OPERA HAT.

**gob h.**   See SAILOR HAT.

**halo h.**   Hat with upturned brim forming circle around face popular in 1940s and still worn by children.

**hard h.**   Protective covering for the head. Made of metal or hard plastic in classic PITH-HELMET shape or similar to a baseball BATTER'S CAP. Held away from the head by foam lining to absorb impact. Worn by construction workers and others subject to work hazards. In late 1960s, the term "hard hat" took on political connotations when U.S. construction workers expressed their sentiments against peace advocates.

**high h.**   See TOP HAT.

**homburg**   Man's hat of rather stiff felt with narrow rolled brim and lengthwise crease in the crown worn from 1870s on for formal occasions. Made fashionable by Prince of Wales, later Edward VII, who visited Bad Homburg in Germany many times. *Der.* Homburg, Prussia.

**hundred pleater**   See CHEF'S HAT.

**hunt derby**   Stiff protective derby made with reinforced strong plastic shell covered with black felt worn with riding habit.

**leghorn h.**   Woman's hat in leghorn straw, a yellowish-colored straw, usually styled similar to a broad-brimmed PICTURE HAT. Fashionable at intervals since latter half of 19th c. *Der.* Named for place of export for the straw, Livorno, Italy.

**matador h.**   (mat-ah-door) Hat shaped like the top of a bull's head—rounded over forehead with two projections like bull's horns covered with black tufts of fabric, with the center of crown of embroidered velvet. Worn by bullfighters in Spain and Mexico.

**Mountie's h.**   Wide-brimmed hat with high crown creased into four sections with a small peak at the top. Similar to World War I army hat worn with dress uniform. Worn by state policemen, Forest Rangers, and by the Royal Canadian Mounted Police.

**open-crown h.**   Woman's hat made without a crown—may be of the HALO or TOQUE type.

**opera h.**   Man's tall silk hat with collapsible crown worn formerly for full dress occasions. Also worn by ringmasters, magicians, and performers. Differs from a TOP HAT by being completely collapsible and made of dull, rather than shiny fabric. *Der.* Invented by a Parisian, Antoine Gibus, in 1823. Also called a *Gibus*.

**padre h.**   Shovel-shaped hat with turned-up brim on the sides and long square cut brim in front and back. Worn by some orders of Catholic priests. *Der.* Italian, "father."

**Panama h.**   **1.** Genuine Panama hats made of fine, expensive straw of the *jipijapa* plant handwoven in Ecuador. Very popular at the end of 19th c. and beginning of 20th c. Worn in different styles from 1855 on. **2.** A large Panama hat was worn by the Prince of Wales in 1920s at Belmont Park, Long Island, where more than 50,000 people were gathered, thus reviving the wearing of Panama hat. **3.** By extension, any man's summer hat regardless of type of straw.

**picture h.**   Hat with large brim framing the face frequently made of straw. Also see LEGHORN HAT.

**pillbox h.**   Classic round brimless hat sometimes worn forward on the head, sometimes on the back of the head. Introduced in late 1920s and worn since with slight variations. *Der.* From small round pillboxes formerly used by chemists or druggists.

**planter's h.**   Wide-brimmed white or natural handwoven straw hat with high dented crown, banded with dark ribbon. Worn by Southern gentlemen in the U.S. and popular for women in late 1960s.

**polo h.**   See CHUKKA HAT.

**pork-pie h.**   **1.** Classic snap-brim man's hat, flat on top with crease around edge of crown, made of fabric, straw or felt. Worn in 1930s and copied for women in the 1940s. Still a basic hat for men. **2.** Introduced in 1860s as a hat for women made of straw or velvet with a low flat crown and turned-up narrow brim.

**profile h.**   Woman's hat with brim turned down sharply on one side, silhouetting the profile, popular in late 1930s.

**Puritan h.**   Black, stiff, tall-crowned man's hat with medium-wide straight brim trimmed with wide black band and silver buckle in center front. Worn by Puritan men in America in early 17th c. and copied for women in 1970s. See WILLIAM PENN HAT.

**rain h.**   Any waterproof hat worn in the rain. Some hats are made of vinyl and styled with a high crown and a floppy brim. Also see SOU'WESTER.

**Ranger's h.**   Hat worn by U.S. Forest Rangers similar to MOUNTIE'S HAT.

**Rex Harrison h.**   Man's snap-brim hat of wool tweed with narrow brim and matching tweed band. Popularized by actor Rex Harrison in his role as Professor Henry Higgins in the musical *My Fair Lady*, in 1956.

**roller**   Hat with close-fitting crown and narrow curved brim worn rolled up or with the front turned down. Popular for women and girls in 1930s and 1940s, revived in early 1970s.

**safari h.**   Lightweight straw or fabric hat shaped somewhat like a shallow soup dish with medium-sized brim. Hat is somewhat similar to a TOPEE/PITH HELMET with a shallower crown. Worn to deflect heat in warm weather. *Der.* Shape of hat is similar to those worn on African hunting trips called "safaris."

**sailor h.**   **1.** Hat worn by naval enlisted personnel made of white duck fabric with gored crown and stitched upturned brim worn either on the back of the head or tilted over the forehead. Also called *gob hat* and *tennis hat*. **2.** Women's straight brimmed hat with shallow flat crown worn since 1860s. Very popular in 1890s for sportswear and bicycling and worn intermittently since. **3.** Popular hat for small boys in the 1880s, sometimes embroidered with fictitious name of a ship on a ribbon band at the base of the crown, similar in style to the brimless FRENCH SAILOR HAT.

**scarf h.**   **1.** Woman's soft fabric hat made by tying a scarf over a lining or base, sometimes shaped like a PILLBOX, and sewed in place. **2.** A triangular piece of colorful print or plain fabric quilted on long side. Worn with quilted part in center front and tied on the head like a *kerchief*.

**Scottie**   A brimless hat styled somewhat like the Glengarry with narrow recessed crown. Veiling, ribbon, or feathers are sometimes placed on top toward the back.

**silk h.**   See TOP HAT.

**skimmer**   SAILOR HAT or BOATER, with exaggerated shallow crown and wide brim.

**slouch h.**   Woman's hat similar to a man's FEDORA made with a flexible brim which may be turned down in front. Also called a GARBO HAT.

**snap-brim h.**   Man's or woman's hat with the brim worn at several different angles according to the preference of the wearer. Also see REX HARRISON HAT.

**sombrero** (som-bray-yo)   Mexican hat with a tall, slightly tapered crown and large upturned brim. Worn in Mexico by peons in straw and by wealthier citizens in felt lavishly trimmed around the edge, sometimes with silver lace. Also worn in Spain and southwestern U.S. where it is made of felt and somewhat similar to a *ten-gallon hat*. *Der.* Spanish, *sombre*, "to shade."

**sombrero córdobes**   See GAUCHO HAT.

**sou'wester/southwester** Rain hat made with a dome-shaped sectioned crown and broad stitched brim—larger in back. Originally made of yellow oiled silk—now made of any waterproof fabric for children's rainwear and fishermen. *Der.* First worn by New England fishermen where a wind from the southwest meant rain.

**Stetson®** Trade name for a man's hat manufacturer of all types of hats, but often used to mean a wide-brimmed Western-style hat, especially the COWBOY or TEN-GALLON style.

**swagger h.** Informal sports hat, often felt, with medium-sized brim turned down in front. Popular in 1930s and 1940s for men and women.

**ten-gallon h.** Extra tall COWBOY HAT made of felt and worn uncreased, similar to a SOMBRERO.

**top h.** Man's tall hat made of shiny silk or beaver cloth with narrow brim. Differs from an OPERA HAT in that the latter is always collapsible and made of dull silk. Also called a *silk hat* or *topper*. Also see alphabetical listing.

**topper** See TOP HAT.

**toque** Draped fabric hat which fits the head closely, sometimes made with an open crown.

**turban 1.** Contemporary draped hat worn by women. **2.** Oriental head covering consisting of a long piece of fabric wrapped around the head. See PAGRI in alphabetical listing.

**Tyrolean h.** See ALPINE HAT.

**western h.** High-crowned hat with a flat top and wide brim frequently trimmed with a leather thong pulled through holes punched at regular intervals around the crown. Has a leather adjustable strap worn under the chin to secure the hat, or permit it to hang down the back. Similar to GAUCHO HAT.

**wig h.** Soft hat, often crocheted, which fits tightly around the face but blouses in the back. Some hats are entirely covered with feathers,

some with flowers. No hair shows from beneath the hat. Popular in mid-1960s.

**William Penn hat** Medium-sized brim with high-rounded crown worn forward on the head. Introduced in late 1960s. *Der.* Similar to hat worn by William Penn (1644–1718) when he colonized Pennsylvania.

---

**Hat à la William Tell** See CUMBERLAND HAT.

**hatband** Decoration, usually of ribbon, around the base of the crown of a hat. In former years men wore black hatbands for mourning.

**hatbox 1.** Circular-shaped item of luggage with a strap handle and flat bottom. Originally made to carry large hats in the 1920s. At one time used as a general item of luggage. Now carried by fashion models in particular. **2.** Special box used by stores when selling a hat, may be round, oval, hexagonal, or square in shape. **3.** See BANDBOX.

**hat cap** 18th-c. term for .a day cap worn under a hat mainly by women. Also called *under cap.*

**hat fawr** Distinctive hat, a part of the *eisteddfod costume* of Wales, made of polished beaver with a wide flat brim and extremely tall tapered crown.

**hat mask** See MASKS.

**hat pin** See PINS.

**hauberk** (ho-berk) Knee-length shirt made of *mail* worn as armor in 11th, 12th, and 13th c. Sometimes covering hands ending in mail mittens. Sides were split from waist down in front and back for convenience in riding horseback and worn over quilted *gambeson*. Sometimes called *coat of mail*. Also see VAMBRACE.

**haunseleyns** (hon-se-len) See HANSELINE.

**hausse-cul** See BUM ROLL.

**hautae** See HABUTAI.

**haut de chausses** (oh de shos)  See CHAUSSES. *Der.* French, "top of hose."

**haute couture** (oht koo-toor)  Top designers of custom-made clothes. Term originally applied to top designers in France. *Der.* French, "highest-quality dressmaking." Also see CHAMBRE SYNDICALE DE LA PARISIENNE.

**HAUT TON, 1889**

**haut ton** (oh ton)  Patented bustle of the late 1880s made of three pendant spirally coiled springs with small pad at back of waist. Secured by a belt around the waist which fastened in the front.

**havelock**  Cloth covering for military cap extending to shoulders in back protecting neck from sun. *Der.* Named for Sir Henry Havelock, British general in India.

**havelock cap**  See AUTOMOBILE CAP.

**Hawaiian shirt**  See SHIRTS.

**Hawes, Elizabeth** (1903–1971)  American designer and an author who studied at Vassar and Parsons School of Design. In 1925 she went to Paris and worked in a French design studio. Later became a stylist at Paris offices of Macy's

and Lord & Taylor. Returned to New York in 1928 and opened a dressmaking business with Rosemary Harden making bias-cut draped clothes which attracted the attention of Mary Lewis of Best and Co. and Dorothy Shaver of Lord & Taylor, who both realized that American designers should be encouraged. In 1931 designed for manufacturers, but withdrew from designing in 1938. She is best known for her autobiography, *Fashion is Spinach*, which gave an insight to the construction of clothing as done by a Parisian couture house to the American public, and especially to students interested in fashion careers.

**headband**  **1.** Strip of leather, cord, or fabric bound around the head horizontally across the forehead. Also called a *brow band*. **2.** Band worn over top of the head from ear to ear as an ornament or to keep hair in place since ancient times. **3.** Band at bottom edge of hat crown.

**head cloth**  Medieval term for KERCHIEF.

**headdress**  A covering or decoration for the head. See BALZO, BATTANT L'OEIL, BOURRELET, FONTANGES, ENGLISH HOOD, FRENCH HOOD, and HENNIN.

**head end**  See HEADING #3.

**heading**  **1.** Small *hem* through which *elastic* is pulled. **2.** Decorative borders woven on fabric, shipped to Africa and the East from England, trademarked until 1882. **3.** Beginning of piece of fabric as it comes from loom. Also called *head end*.

**head rail**  *Kerchief,* usually in colors and sometimes edged with lace, worn by women in 16th and 17th c. Draped from left side over the head, around the neck, and tied under chin.

**head wrap**  In 1980s a scarf, bandanna, ribbon, or piece of fabric worn in carefree manner around the head to frame the face or as a BROW BAND.

**heart breaker**  See CRÈVE-COEUR and LOVE LOCK.

**heart-shaped cut**  See GEM CUTS.

**heart-shaped headdress**  Rolled woman's headdress of 1420 to 1450, forming a heart-shaped peak in center front. Raised on sides to show netting coming down over the ears. Usually worn with a long *veil* called a *miter* by 19th c. writers.

**heather yarn**  Purple and white wool stock-dyed fibers blended together to produce a lavender colored yarn. *Der.* Named for color of flower found on English moors.

**heat setting**  Process used to set permanent pleats or creases in fabrics made of man-made fibers, *e.g.*, nylon and polyester, by heat and pressure.

**Hechter, Daniel** (Esh-tar) See APPENDIX/DESIGNERS.

**heddle**  Small needle-like pieces attached to each harness of the loom through which each warp yarn is threaded. The manner in which the warps are threaded through the heddles varies the weave. See LOOM.

**hedgehog**  See COIFFURE À L'HERISSON.

**heel**  **1.** Part of the shoe which elevates the back of the foot. Heels may be flat, medium, or high and are measured in ⅛", *e.g.*, a 16/8 heel is 2" high. Inside edge of heel is called the *breast of the heel*. Extra replaceable piece on bottom is called the *heel lift*. Heels may be made of wood, plastic, Lucite, or metal. **2.** Term used for portion of the hose which fits the heel of the foot.

━━━━━━━━━ **HEELS** ━━━━━━━━━

**baby Louis h.**  See LOUIS HEEL.

**ball h.**  Spherical heel made of wood or Lucite, popular since 1960s.

**bell-bottom h.**  Chunky medium heel, curved inward and then flaring at the bottom, an exaggerated version of a LOUIS HEEL.

**block h.**  Straight heel similar to CUBAN HEEL but set further back and approximately the same width at top and base.

**boulevard h.**  Sturdy high heel similar to a CUBAN HEEL is tapered at sides and back, has straight front, and a flange where heel joins with sole.

**breasted h.**  Any heel made with a curved section where it attaches to the sole of the shoe at the *shank*.

**built-up h.**  See STACKED HEEL.

**chunky h.**  High or medium heel that has exaggerated width—a shoe fad of late 1960s and early 1970s.

**columnar h.**  High circular-styled heel graduating from wide width at sole of shoe to small base.

**common sense h.**  Low heel used on children's or infants' shoe made by increasing size of outsole at heel.

**Continental h.**  High narrow heel made straight in front with square corners at base and slight curve at back. Has a slight edge extending forward where it joins the sole. Exaggeratedly high and narrow version is called a SPIKE HEEL.

**corkies**  See WEDGE HEEL.

**covered h.**  Heel of wood or plastic covered with leather or another plastic.

**Cuban h.**  Medium to high broad heel with slight curve in back, popular in 1930s and 1940s.

**cube h.**  Square-backed heel made of leather or Lucite.

**draped h.**  Heel on woman's shoe with leather or fabric from *counter* arranged in folds over the back.

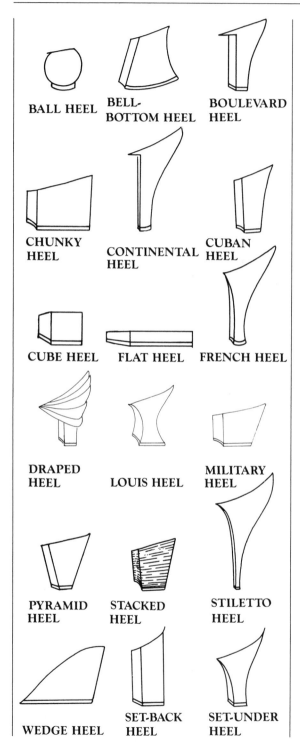

BALL HEEL • BELL-BOTTOM HEEL • BOULEVARD HEEL • CHUNKY HEEL • CONTINENTAL HEEL • CUBAN HEEL • CUBE HEEL • FLAT HEEL • FRENCH HEEL • DRAPED HEEL • LOUIS HEEL • MILITARY HEEL • PYRAMID HEEL • STACKED HEEL • STILETTO HEEL • WEDGE HEEL • SET-BACK HEEL • SET-UNDER HEEL

**Dutch boy h.** Low heel with medium-sized base, back slants slightly and inside edge is slanted toward front where it joins the edge.

**elevator h.** Man's heel worn to make him appear taller. Inside of shoe is built up at the heel making the outside of shoe appear higher. Attached heel lift is higher than average.

**flange h.** Heel which flares or angles to make a wider base.

**flat h.** Broad low heel originally used on children's shoes, now popular on women's shoes. Shoes with this heel are called FLATS or FLATTIES.

**floating pedestal wedge** Medium broad heel similar to a wedge, but cut out under the arch making it wider at the base of the heel and slanting toward the sole.

**French h.** High heel that curves inward at back then flares slightly outward at base.

**hooded h.** Heel slanting into shank of shoe, usually covered in one piece with upper.

**ice cube h.** Low, square-cut heel of clear Lucite introduced in 1970. *Der.* The shape and size of an ice cube.

**Louis h.** Heel of medium height curved sharply inward around sides and back, then flared slightly at base, similar to heels worn in Louis XV period. Low version called *baby Louis heel.*

**military h.** Medium to low heel with a broad base. Slants slightly in back and usually has an attached rubber lift. Used on comfort shoes and walking shoes for women.

**museum h.** Medium-height heel with front and back curving inward and then outward to make a flared base. Also called *shepherdess heel.*

**pinafore h.** Flat leather or rubber heel made in one piece with the sole with a curve under arch of the shoe. Made in the same manner that rubber heels and soles are joined on *saddle oxfords.*

**pyramid h.** Medium-high heel with squared base flaring toward the sole—like an inverted pyramid.

**sculptured h.** Broad medium-high heel made with a see-through center introduced in 1960s. Similar to some free-form pieces of sculpture. Used on wooden clogs in late 1970s.

**set-back h.** Heel with straight back joined to the sole as far back as possible.

**set-under h.** Heel with outside edge curving forward under heel.

**shepherdess h.** See MUSEUM HEEL.

**Spanish h.** High heel with a curve similar to a FRENCH HEEL but has a straight inside edge.

**spike h.** High curved slender heel with tiny base; usually 3″ to 3½″ high. Also see CONTINENTAL HEEL.

**spring h.** Low broad heel with extra layer of leather inserted between heel and sole. Used primarily on children's shoes.

**stacked h.** Heel built up of horizontal layers of leather. Also called *built-up heel.*

**stiletto h.** Set-back heel which ends in a tiny rounded base, usually fitted with a metal tip. As the walking surface is small, there is an enormous amount of weight on the heel. Used mainly from 1950s until mid-1960s.

**wedge h.** Slanted heel made in one piece with the sole of the shoe. Comes in low, medium, and high heights. Introduced in 1930s. Some heels are cut in one piece with a slight platform sole and are usually covered with jute, fabric, urethane, or leather. Some are made of cork and called *corkies.*

---

**heelless hose** See HOSE.

**heel lift** See HEELS and LIFT.

**Heim, Jacques** See APPENDIX/DESIGNERS.

**heko-obi** Sash of soft white crepe, 15″ to

24″ wide, worn by Japanese men over kimono for informal occasions. Wrapped around waist three times and tied in loose bow. Compare with KAKU-OBI.

**Helanca® yarn** Trademark, owned by Heberlein & Co., licensed on worldwide basis, for textured man-made yarn with considerable elasticity used for knits, woven fabrics, and hosiery.

**heliodor** See GEMS.

**heliotrope** See BLOODSTONE under GEMS.

**helmet** **1.** Protective covering for the head worn primarily to prevent injury, particularly by armed forces and for various sports. First worn by Greeks and Romans with feathered crests; *chain mail* was used during the Crusades; cast metal used from 14th c. on for knights' helmets which usually had a visor. **2.** In the late 1950s space helmets were introduced for astronauts. **3.** In 1960s the helmet was introduced as a fashion accessory. See BURGONET and MORION in alphabetical listing.

## ═══ HELMETS ═══

**aviator's h.** **1.** Helmet made of high-impact plastic, sometimes fitted with an oxygen mask, worn by a pilot and crew of planes flying at high altitudes. **2.** World War I helmet fitting the head snugly and fastened under the chin. Made of leather with wool or shearling lining for warmth. Goggles were worn on top. Also called a RED BARON HELMET.

**batter's h.** Duck-billed visored cap with hard crown for protection worn by baseball players when taking turn at bat. Also called *batter's cap.*

**bicycle h.** Helmet not covering the ears, with dark adjustable visor and air inlets for

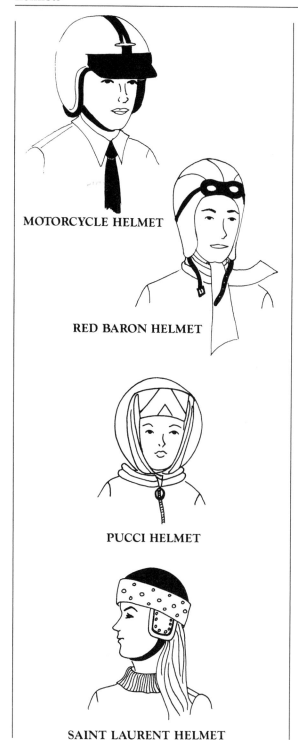

**MOTORCYCLE HELMET**

**RED BARON HELMET**

**PUCCI HELMET**

**SAINT LAURENT HELMET**

ventilating and cooling, held on by a strap under the chin. Shell is high-impact PVC plastic lined with polystyrene, and foam-lined for comfort.

**chain h.** Decorative close-fitting cap made with lengths of chain—some linked together, others dangling. Decorative item of body jewelry introduced in the late 1960s.

**Courrèges h.** Fashion helmet shaped similar to World War I aviator's helmet. Introduced in 1964 by French couturier André Courrèges as a result of universal interest in astronauts.

**fashion h.** Any helmet designed as a fashion item rather than for protection. May be made of leather, fabric, fur, plastic or other materials. Types include *Courrèges, Paco Rabanne, Pucci,* and *chain* helmets.

**football h.** Molded plastic helmet which conforms closely to the head covering the ears. Made with nose guard, consisting of curved plastic strips attached to sides, and decorated with symbols indicating team. Worn by all football players.

**German h.** Metal helmet made with small visor and a spike on the top decorated with large gold eagle on front. Worn by Germans in World War I and adopted by teenage boys in the late 1960s. Also called a *pickelhaube.*

**hard h.** See HATS.

**motorcycle h.** Molded plastic helmet with foam lining worn when riding a motorcycle. Usually has a large dark-colored plastic shield which snaps on to protect eyes and face.

**Paco Rabanne h.** Unusual cap fitted to conform to the head and covered with tiny diamond-shaped mirrors linked together. Introduced in late 1960s and named for French couturier, *Paco Rabanne.*

**pickelhaube** See GERMAN HELMET.

**pith h.** See TOPEE.

**Pucci h.** Plastic glass bubble with cut-out for the face which stands away from the head to keep hair from blowing. Designed by Emilio Pucci, Italian couturier, as part of wardrobe for airline stewardesses.

**Red Baron h.** World War I aviator's helmet named after a famous ace. Also see AVIATOR'S HELMET.

**Saint Laurent h.** Cap designed by French couturier Yves Saint Laurent in 1966 made of leather studded with nailheads and styled similar to World War I aviator's helmet.

**space h.** Helmet made of molded plastic covering the head and neck completely and fastening to collar around the top of the space suit. Front section is made of see-through plastic with mirror-like reflective finish.

**topee** Tropical helmet shaped more like a hat with a wide brim, originally made of cork ½" thick. Worn particularly in the jungles as a protection from the sun. Does not fit close to the head, because constructed with an air space between head and helmet. Also called *pith helmet. Der.* Name refers to European cork.

**World War I h.** Cast metal helmet with a shallow crown and narrow brim, which did not cover the ears or conform to the shape of the head, held on by a chin strap.

**World War II h.** Cast metal helmet conforming closely to the shape of the head with slightly upturned edge. When worn in battle, sometimes covered with a piece of multi-colored fabric for camouflage.

**hem** The finished portion of sleeves, or the lower edge of an item of clothing.

## HEMS

**asymmetric h.** Hem of uneven length—may be long in back and short in front or slanted diagonally from one side to the other. The latter has been popular since the late 1960s. All types of uneven hemlines are popular in the 1980s.

**circular h.** Hem put in a full circular or gored skirt. If narrow, hem is machine-stitched or hand-rolled. Deeper hems have fullness worked in with tiny darts.

**faced h.** Use of another piece of fabric, usually lighter in weight and bias cut, sewed on at base of hem, turned up, and finished like a plain hem. Usually used when dress or pants are to be made longer.

**fluted h.** Tiny hem finished with picot edge in a sheer nylon fabric which is set in crystal pleats. The edge gives a serpentine effect winding outward and inward.

**fused h.** Hem created with special tape which when pressed with a hot iron melts and adheres to the fabric. Sometimes loosens when garment is washed or dry cleaned. Introduced in the 1960s.

**handkerchief h.** Hem which falls in points similar to when a handkerchief is held in the center and allowed to fall.

**lingerie h.** Rolled hem with overcast stitches at intervals forming minute puffs between stitches. Handmade hem popular in the 1920s and still used occasionally.

**petal h.** Hem which falls in rounded sections similar to petals of a flower.

**picot h.** Hem finished with a row of machine hemstitching—then cut apart—used on ruffles to reduce bulkiness. Popularized in the 1920s. See HEMSTITCH #2 under STITCHES.

**plain h.** Hem folded up and hand sewn with slip or overcast stitch. When seam binding is used, machine stitching is used first, then hand, stitches are used to finish hem.

**rolled h.** Handmade hem used on sheer and delicate fabrics. First rolled between the fingers, then sewed with tiny stitches. Used for chiffon evening gowns of the 1920s and 1930s, and still used occasionally.

**saw-toothed h.** Faced hem made with edges pointed in zigzag fashion.

**scalloped h.** Faced hem made with indentations simulating a shell design.

---

**hematite** See GEMS.

**hemispherical hat** Hat with bowl-shaped crown and narrow brim. Worn in 1850s and 1860s. By 1858 had knob in center of crown and then sometimes called a bollinger.

**hemmer** **1.** Commercial machine for sewing hems. **2.** Attachment for home-sewing machine for hemming.

**hemp** The tough fiber of a tall Asiatic plant of the nettle family, *Cannabis sativa*. Used in cordage and sometimes sailcloth.

**hemstitch** See EMBROIDERIES and STITCHES.

**Henley boater** Blue felt hat in the shape of a straw *boater*. Worm from 1894 on.

**Henley shirt** See KNIT SHIRTS and NECKLINES.

**henna** **1.** Orange-colored dye, one of the earliest dyes discovered, comes from the plant by the same name. Egyptians used it to dye their fingers to the first joint simulating our nail polish. Also used on toes in some Eastern countries in early days. Used to dye fabrics in primitive times. **2.** Basic hair dye or rinse. **3.** An orange color.

**hennin** French term for woman's tall steeple-shaped headdress worn in second half of 15th c. Supported by a wire frame and worn tilted back with a long sheer veil hanging from tip down to floor, or caught up as drapery at waist. Also called *steeple headdress* and *cornet*.

**Henrietta jacket** Loose three-quarter-length woman's jacket of 1890s with large collar

**HENNIN**

falling over chest in front, frequently lined with quilted satin.

**Henry II collar** **1.** Small, medium, or large collar standing up high on the neck in back and rolling over to form points in front. Larger collars had a shawl-collar effect in front. Worn by women in 1890s. **2.** Medium-sized *ruff* with a large ribbon bow and ends in front worn by women in 1890s.

**Henry IV collar** Standing collar around which are placed loops of ribbon forming a small *ruff* worn by women in 1890s.

**hense lynes/henselyns** See HANSELINE.

**Hercules braid** See BRAIDS.

**herlot** See HARLOT.

**hérisson** (air-ee-sonh) **For women:** Late 18th c. short hairstyle with loose curls in back and frizzled ends at front and sides. **For men:** Same cut in front, but worn with a *cadogan* or *pigtail* in back. Also known as *coiffure à la hérisson*. *Der.* French, "bristly, shaggy."

**herkimer** See DIAMONDS.

**Hermés** See APPENDIX/DESIGNERS.

**herringbone** Pattern made of short, slanting parallel lines adjacent to other rows slanting in reverse direction, creating a continuous V-shaped design like the bones of a fish. Used in tweeds, embroidery, and in working of fur skins.

**herringbone chain** See CHAIN.

**HERRINGBONE WEAVE**

**herringbone weave** Chevron pattern produced in a fabric by using the twill weave for several rows in one direction, then reversing the direction. Usually made of yarns of two colors in yarn-dyed woolen fabric with thick yarns producing a large pattern. Also called *broken twill weave*.

**hessian** Synonym for BURLAP in England, India, and parts of Europe.

**Hessian boot** Man's black leather riding boot, calf-length in back, curving upward to below knee in front and ending in a point decorated with a tassel. Often made with narrow top border of another color. Worn from 1790s to 1850s.

**heuke** *Veil* enveloping wearer to knees or ankles—sometimes with the top stiffened by wire—worn over head forming a cage. Worn in Flanders in 16th and 17th c. Also spelled *hewke, heyke, hewk*.

**heuse** (huse) Mid-thigh length leather riding boot with thick sole, fastened with buttons, buckles, or straps on outer side of leg. Worn by men from 1240s to end of 15th c. Later called *housel* or *huseau*.

**hezaam** Long woolen sash worn as part of native dress by Bedouin women. Similar to *hizaam*, worn by Arabian men.

**Hickory stripes** See STRIPES.

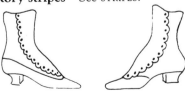

**HIGH BUTTON SHOE**

**high button shoe** Shoe coming to ankle or above which is closed to side of center front with a row of small *shoe buttons*. Worn by both men and women from late 19th through early 20th c. Also called *buttoned shoe*.

**high hat** See TOP HAT.

**high head** See FONTANGE.

**HIGHLAND DRESS**

**Highland dress** Traditional man's costume of Scots Highlander, consisting of *kilt*; *plaid* over one shoulder fastened by *brooch*; scarlet jacket; wide belt with *sporran* attached; feather bonnet or *Glengarry cap*; plaid-top socks; and buttoned *gaiters* over shoes. Costume was forbidden by law from 1747 to 1782. Also see TARTANS.

**Highland suit** Boy's suit of 1880s and early 1890s consisting of jacket, kilts, Glengarry cap, and plaid socks copied from *Highland dress*. Also called a *Scotch suit*.

**HIGHLAND SUIT**

**high-rise** A term used to describe any waistline higher than the natural waistline. See PANTS and WAISTLINES.

**high tech clothes** Clothing and accessories featuring high technology of 1980s. Also see COMPUTER DRESS under DRESSES, LOOKS, NEON SOCKS under SOCKS, GORE-TEX®, and THINSULATE®.

**hikers** See BOOTS.

**HIMATION**

**hiking costume** Costume worn by women in 1890s consisting of serge or lighter weight bloomers, pleated or gathered at the waist and pulled down below the knee. Worn with a tight-fitting Eton-type jacket with large lapels; a white shirt; man's necktie; serviceable shoes with flat heels worn with *puttees* or high top laced boots to below the knee; and hat similar to a cowboy hat with high uncreased crown and wide brim. Worn for mountain climbing and hiking.

**himation** (him-mah-tee-on) Greek mantle in form of a rectangular shawl, 3½ to 4 yards long and about 1½ yards wide. Made of wool or linen—usually white with border. Worn alone or over *chiton* by men and women in ancient Greece. Usually draped over left shoulder and wrapped under right arm, sometimes one end was pulled over head. Also see PALLIUM.

**hinged bracelet** See BRACELETS.

**hip bags** Slang term in 1883 for folds of skirt forming *panniers* at hips. Also called *curtain drapery* in U.S. and *pompadour* in England.

**hip boot** See BOOTS.

**hip buttons** Term used from late 17th to end of 19th c. for pair of buttons placed on either side of center back pleats of man's suit coat.

**hip-hugger** Contemporary term for *low-slung* pants, skirt, or belt worn below normal waistline, resting on hip bones. Also see PANTIES, PANTS, SHORTS, and SKIRTS. Compare with NATURAL and HIGH-RISE WAISTLINES.

**hip length** See LENGTHS.

**Hiplets®** See PANTYHOSE.

**hippie** Term coined in mid-1960s for young person who defied established customs and adopted an unconventional mode of dress, *e.g.*, long uncombed hair, aged blue jeans, miscellaneous tops, fringed jackets, strings of beads, symbolic pendants, pouch bags, bare feet, or sandals. Started a trend toward *ethnic* fashions and unusual mixtures of dress. Also see BEADS, HANDBAGS, LOOKS and NECKLACES.

**hip-rider swimsuit**   See SWIMSUITS.

**hipsters**   See HIP-HUGGERS under PANTS.

**hi-rise girdle**   See GIRDLES.

**his and hers look**   Clothing and accessories styled for both men and women. Also see LOOKS. Compare with ANDROGYNOUS and UNI-SEX LOOKS.

**hive bonnet**   See BEEHIVE HAT #1.

**hizaam**   White sash worn by Arabian men on top of the ankle-length shirt (*kamis*) or on top of the *caftan*. Dagger is frequently worn tucked in the sash.

**H-line**   Straight silhouette, or dress, marked by a low horizontal belt or seam called "H" by Paris designer Christian Dior in 1957.

**hō**   General designation for a class of below-the-knee ancient Japanese robes worn by court nobles down to 9th rank and occasionally by emperor and princes. White silk hō worn for Imperial wear known as *haku no gohō*; red hō worn by retired emperor for formal wear; black hō with damask pattern varying with family of wearer worn by everyone above 5th rank on certain occasions; yellow hō worn only by emperor and empress for court functions such as coronations. Worn since the 7th c. in the Japanese court. Hōyeki-hō (sewn-side hō) worn by everyone above 5th rank; *ketteki-hō* (open-side hō) worn by military court officials.

**hobble skirt**   Woman's skirt rounded over hips, tapered to ankle so narrowly that walking is impeded. Fashion designed by Paris designer *Paul Poiret* about 1912. Later called PEG-TOP SKIRT.

**hogger/hoker**   See OKER.

**hockey skate**   See BOOTS.

**Holbein stitch**   (hole-bine)   See DOUBLE-RUNNING STITCH under STITCHES.

**Holbein work**   (hole-bine)   See EMBROIDERIES.

**HOBBLE SKIRT**

**hollow-cut velveteen**   Velveteen fabric which resembles ribbed corduroy. Differs from corduroy in that some wales of the corduroy have no pile while the velveteen variety is entirely a piled surface which has been carved in ridges by various methods. Also called *velvet cord*.

**Hollywood top slip**   See SLIPS.

**holster pockets**   See POCKETS.

**holy work/hollie work**   See EMBROIDERIES.

**homburg**   See HATS.

**homespun**   **1.** Name for a great variety of fabrics which are made at home on a loom. **2.** Machine-made homespuns imitate these fabrics by being loosely woven in a simple weave and having coarse uneven yarns not too tightly twisted. Originally made of wool, now made in spun rayon, wool blends, and bulky man-made fibers.

**honan**   (hoe-nan)   Fabric similar to pongee from Honan, China, of fine quality wild silk that takes dye better than other wild silk. Also called *Honan Pongee*.

**hondorgo** Ankle-length native dress worn by Hungarian women. Skirt is bell-shaped and worn instead of older type skirt which was worn with 10 to 20 petticoats underneath.

**honeycomb** Any fabric made in honeycomb weave which forms a series of recessed squares similar to a waffle. Made on the dobby loom of carded or combed yarns either plied or single in a variety of weights. Cotton fabrics are frequently called *waffle cloth*. They are sometimes erroneously called *waffle piqués*.

**Honiton gossamer skirt** Lightweight summer petticoat of 1850s made with strips of fabric attached to a waist belt by means of several vertical tapes as far as the hips where three circular ruffles of fabric were attached.

**Honiton lace** See LACES.

**HOOD, 1870**

**hood** 1. Hat term for a preliminary shaped piece of FELT or straw from which the milliner works. Has a high rounded nondescript crown and an extra large floppy brim. 2. Accessory worn on the head and sometimes the shoulders frequently attached to a jacket or coat. Differs from a hat in that it has no specific shape and usually covers the entire head sometimes tying under the chin. Popular item for winter wear, it is made in all types of fabrics and fur. Al-

though there are a great variety of styles, there are no specific names for these items. Worn from 11th c. on but replaced generally by caps and hats in the early 17th c. Revived in the 1860s, 1870s, and for winter sportswear in the 1920s and 1930s. Very popular from late 1960s through 1980s. Also see ENGLISH HOOD, FRENCH HOOD, ACADEMIC HOOD, CAPUCHIN, and CHAPERON.

**hooded heel** See HEELS.

**hook and eye** See CLOSINGS.

**hoop bracelet** See BANGLE under BRACELETS.

**hoop earrings** See GYPSY under EARRINGS.

**hoops** 1. A framework of whalebone, wire or cane, made as a petticoat, used to extend the skirt. For specific types see BELL HOOP, FAN HOOP, FARTHINGALE, and OBLONG HOOP. 2. Usually a full-length petticoat consisting of a series of circular bands held in place with vertical tapes making the skirt flexible enough to permit one to sit down. Introduced in 1850s and worn at intervals since—whenever full skirts are popular. Revived in 1950s. See CAGE, CAGE AMERICAINE, CAGE PETTICOAT, Empire jupon, Empress PETTICOAT, and PETTICOATS.

**hoop skirt** See SKIRTS.

**Hoover apron** See APRONS.

**Hope diamond** See DIAMONDS.

**Hope Star®** See GEMS.

**Hopi bracelet** See BRACELETS.

**hopsacking** Sacks made originally from coarse undyed jute or hemp to contain hops when harvesting. Now a term for a broad classification of fabrics made in loosely constructed plain weave of coarse uneven yarns. Made in cotton, spun rayon, and man-made fibers. Coarse varieties also called BURLAP.

**hoqueton/houqueton** See ACTON.

**Horn, Carol** See APPENDIX/DESIGNERS.

**horned headdress** Wide headdress consisting of two horns extending horizontally at either side of face with a veil draped over top and hanging down back. Worn from 1410 to 1420, and rarely to 1460.

**horn rims** See GLASSES.

**horsehair** **1.** Hair fiber obtained from a mane and tail of horse. **2.** Fabric made from this fiber used in combination with mohair, linen, cotton, and other fibers woven in an openwork weave. Used for interfacing in suits, coats, and also for stiffening. See BRAIDS and CRINOLINE under PETTICOATS.

**horsehide** See LEATHERS.

**horseshoe** Term for U-shape, used as neckline or yoke on blouses, sweaters, and dresses. Also see COLLARS, JUMPERS and NECKLINES.

**hose** Knitted item of wearing apparel covering the foot and leg; also called *hosiery* or *stockings*. Current usage suggests that hose refers to the more transparent and decorative varieties, while "stockings" is used for heavier varieties of a more utilitarian nature. Originally a type of leg covering worn in the 15th and 16th c. which covered the foot and leg and extended to the waist. See CHAUSSES in alphabetical listing. When divided into two parts, lower part was called a stocking in 1660. Queen Elizabeth I wore the first pair of knitted silk hose. In the 1920s silk hose became fashionable in a beige color; nylon hose were introduced in 1940. Textured hose became fashionable in the 1960s. Also see PANTYHOSE. *Der.* Anglo-Saxon *hosa*. See LISLE HOSIERY and SILK STOCKINGS in the alphabetical listing.

━━━━━━━━ **HOSE** ━━━━━━━━

**ankle-length h.** Sock-length hosiery made out of conventional nylon yarn. Worn by women with full-length slacks or pants.

**Art Deco h.** Hose printed with geometric designs, popularized in the late 1960s. *Der.* French, *art decoratif*, "decorative art."

**Art Nouveau h.** Stylized single or multiple printed designs placed on the calf or climbing the leg, usually on opaque or colored hose. An innovation of the late 1960s. *Der.* French, "new art."

**astrolegs h.** Hose imprinted with signs of the zodiac introduced in the late 1960s.

**checkerboard h.** Hose knitted in a checked design with some squares sheer and some opaque, or knitted in two colors.

**clocked h.** Hose or stockings which have designs running part way up the sides of the legs. First worn in the 16th c. and intermittently since. Designs may be knitted in or embroidered on after hose are knitted.

**fishnet h.** Openwork hose in a diamond-shaped pattern.

**flat-knit h.** See FULL-FASHIONED HOSE.

**full-fashioned h.** Hose knit in flat pieces and seamed up the back, leaving fashion marks where knitting is increased or decreased. Also called *flat-knit hose.*

**garter belt h.** Hose attached to two elastic strips which connect at waistline to an elastic band around waist.

**glitter h.** Hose made of shiny yarn—some are made with metallic yarn which reflects silver, gold, and copper tones. Introduced to wear with minidresses in the 1960s. Also called *silver, gold* or *metallic hose.*

**gold h.** See GLITTER HOSE.

**heelless h.** Hosiery without a double reinforcement at the heel.

**Jacquard h.** Hosiery knit on a Jacquard knitting machine which permits much variation in colors and patterns. Argyle and herringbone designs would be examples of jacquard patterns. Popular in the 1920s for children and fashionable since.

**knee-high h.** Hose of conventional nylon yarn which come to below the knees and are finished at the top with elastic. First made in beige and worn when dresses were long, now worn with various types of pants and in the 1980s featured in black, white and colors. Sometimes abbreviated to *knee-hi*.

**lace h.** Knitted lace in rose, Chantilly, and Spanish lace patterns used to make hosiery. Introduced in 1960s and popular for children and women in 1980s.

**mesh h.** Nylon hose which is knit with a milanese stitch forming tiny diamond designs which make hose run-resistant.

**metallic h.** See GLITTER HOSE.

**nylon h.** Trademarked nylon yarn was introduced in 1939 making possible a much sheerer type of hose which was also more durable than the silk hosiery worn previously. In great demand during World War II, nylon hosiery became a "black market" item. The word "nylons" later became a synonym for hose.

**opaque h.** Fine knit lisle hose first made in white. Later in all colors including fuschia, chartreuse, and kelly green. Popular from the 1960s.

**patterned h.** Hosiery woven in a design, usually on a Jacquard knitting machine, *e.g., point d'esprit, checkerboard,* and *argyle hose.*

**point d'esprit h.** (pwan des-pree) Netlike machine made hose of cotton or nylon which has some of the holes made solid to form a decorative pattern.

**proportioned h.** Hosiery designed to fit different types of legs, *e.g.,* extra long, full above-the-knee, long, short, and average.

**ribbed h.** Textured hose knit with vertical wales.

**sandalfoot h.** Hosiery with no reinforcement at the toe.

**seamed h. 1.** Full-fashioned hose with a seam up the back, originally made by the flat-knit process and sewed together. Popular type hose generally worn until the 1960s when textured yarns were invented with more "stretch," making it possible to make well-fitting hose without the seam. By 1968 very few seamed hose were sold. **2.** Reintroduced in 1970s but made in circular knits usually with black lines up the back.

**seamless h.** Circular-knit hose without seam in back, *e.g.* STRETCH, MESH, OPAQUE, and SHEER HOSE. See CIRCULAR KNIT in alphabetical listing.

**sheer h.** Nylon hose made with a fine or low denier yarn thus making them more translucent.

**silver h.** See GLITTER HOSE.

**stay-up h.** Regular hose knitted with a special top which holds the hose up without garters. Also called *stretch top.*

**stretch h.** Hosiery made with textured nylon yarns such as Agilon or Cantrece nylon. When such hose are not on the leg they look very tiny.

**support h.** Knit Lycra Spandex hose which keep pressure on the blood vessels so they will not dilate. This improves the circulation and prevents leg fatigue.

**textured h.** Any style of hose patterned with thick and thin sections, *e.g.* LACE, STRIPED, or WINDOWPANE HOSE. First introduced by Rudi Gernreich in 1964 and later popularized by couturiers including Givenchy in 1969.

**windowpane h.** Textured hose made in geometric squares in thin and thick sections. Heavier part looks like the frame of the window, sheerer section looks like the glass. *Mini-pane* hose have smaller squares. Made in white, black, and all colors, *e.g.,* shocking pink, chartreuse and orange. Popular in the mid-1960s.

**hostess** A term used to describe informal apparel worn at home while entertaining. Also called *at-home wear*. See ROBES and CULOTTES under PAJAMAS.

**hot mask**   See MASKS.

**hotoz**   See FOTOZ.

**hot pants/HotPants**   See SHORTS.

**hounds' ears**   Large turned-back cuffs with rounded corners used on men's coats from 1660s to 1680s.

**hound's-tooth/houndstooth check**   See CHECKS.

**houppelande** (hoop-land)   **1.** Man's voluminous outer robe of late 15th and 16th c., introduced by Richard II of England, made with high funnel-shaped neckline—later V-shaped. Sleeves were long, full, and *dagged* at edge or of *bagpipe-type*. Varied from thigh-length to trailing on the ground when worn as ceremonial robe. **2.** Woman's dress worn from late 14th through the 15th c. with fitted bodice, V-neckline with revers and dickey, or scooped neckline. Sleeves were long and tight-fitting or voluminous with fur lining. Frequently trained in back and so long in front that skirt had to be lifted when walking.

**hourglass silhouette**   See SILHOUETTES.

**housecoat**   See ROBES.

**housedress**   See DRESSES.

**housel**   See HEUSE.

**house slippers**   See SLIPPERS.

**housse** (oos)   Tunic worn during 14th c. with short caped sleeves which was put on over head and fastened with two little tabs at neck. Also see TABARD #2.

**howling bags**   Slang term for men's *trousers* made of colorful patterned fabrics worn in mid-19th c.

**hōyeki-hō**   Japanese robe. See HŌ.

**huarache** (wa-rach-ee)   See SANDALS.

**Hubbard blouse**   Loose-fitting tunic blouse with ruffles at hem, sleeves, and neck with a

cord used to pull in fullness at waist. Worn by young girls in 1880s over KILT-PLEATED SKIRT.

**huckaback embroidery**   See EMBROIDERIES.

**huckaback stitch**   See STITCHES.

**Hudson seal**   See MUSKRAT under FURS.

**huepilli**   Sleeveless blouse worn by Aztec Indians and Mayan women made of handwoven fabrics.

**HUIPIL GRANDE**

**huipil grande** (we-peel-li)   Mexican Indian woman's headdress consisting of a white ruffled child's dress worn over head, with neck ruffles framing the face; and the remainder of blouse hanging loose over shoulders. Copied from dress worn by a child, the sole survivor of a shipwreck off the Gulf of Tehuantepec.

**hug-me-tight**   See VESTS.

**huke**   See HUQUE.

**hula skirt**   Mid-calf length skirt, made of long grasses fastened together at low waistline, worn by native Hawaiian women for hula dances. Also see SKIRTS.

**human hair wig**   See WIGS.

**hundred pleater**   See CHEF'S HAT under HATS.

**Hungarian cord**   Heavy silk cord of 1860s used as border on hem of skirt with train, most fashionable in 1867 and 1868.

**Hungarian point**   See EMBROIDERIES.

**Hungarian suit**   A boy's belted double-breasted tunic, worn from late 1860s with a small turned-down collar and fastened on the side in a double-breasted manner. Trimmed with braid down the side front, on the flapped pockets, and cuffs. Worn with matching full or fitted trousers to below the knees with *jockey boots.*

**hunt**   Adjective used for clothing and accessories used by equestrians when hunting on horseback. See CAPS, LOOKS, HUNT BREECHES under PANTS, HUNT DERBY under HATS, and PINK COAT under COATS.

**hunter's pink**   Fabric made for riding coats distinguished by its color—a crimson red—rather than pink. See PINK COAT under COATS.

**hunter's watch**   See WATCHES.

**hunting calf**   British term for *reverse calf.* See LEATHERS.

**hunting necktie**   Man's broad, high necktie worn from 1818 through 1830s with three horizontal pleats on each side angled toward center front. Worn with ends brought to front, tied, and hidden by coat.

**hunting plaid**   See PLAIDS and TARTANS.

**hunting shirt**   See SHIRTS.

**hunting stock**   Man's long *scarf* folded double, wrapped twice around neck, and tied.

Worn instead of *necktie* for sports in 1890s. Also see TIES.

**hunting vest**   See VESTS.

**huque**   Man's flowing outergarment, worn throughout 15th c., generally calf-length—sometimes longer or shorter—slashed up sides, and fur-trimmed around edges. Sometimes slashed up front and back for ease in riding horseback. Also spelled *huke.*

**hurluberlu** (her-loo-bare-loo)   Woman's hairstyle with short curls all and over and long ringlets in back, first worn by Madame de Montespan about 1671.

**huseau**   See HEUSE.

**Hush Puppies®**   See SHOES.

**husky sizes**   Boys' sizes—8 to 20—cut with more generous proportions.

**hussar boots**   Man's calf-length boots coming to a slight point in front, sometimes having turnover tops and iron soles. Style borrowed from the military and worn by men from 1800 to 1820.

**hussar jacket**   Woman's short jacket of 1880s fastened with *frogs* and trimmed with braid and worn over waistcoat. Inspired by uniforms of British troops returning from a campaign in Egypt.

**hyacinth**   See GEMS.

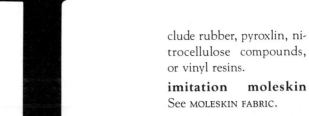

**ice dyes** See AZOIC DYES.

**Icelandic sweater** See SWEATERS.

**ice silk** British term for loosely twisted silk yarn used for knitting.

**ice wool yarn** Same as EIS YARN or EIS WOOL.

**ichella** Long cape, fringed around hem, worn by Araucanian Indian women of Chile. Fastened with distinctive brooch consisting of a large silver disk attached to a long pin.

**I.D./identification bracelet** See BRACELETS.

**igloo mitt** Shaggy fur mitten, frequently with leather palm, worn for sportswear.

**ihram** (ee-rahm) Two piece white cotton dress consisting of two pieces of fabric: one forming a wraparound skirt and the other a shawl over the left shoulder. Worn by Moslem pilgrims to Mecca. *Der.* Arabic, "forbid."

**ikat** (ee-cat) A method of yarn dyeing. *Der.* Malayan, *mengikat*, "to tie, bind, knot or wind around."

**I.L.G.W.U.** Abbreviation for INTERNATIONAL LADIES' GARMENT WORKERS' UNION.

**illusion** See SILK ILLUSION.

**imbecile sleeve** Very full balloon sleeve set in at a dropped shoulder and gathered to narrow cuff at wrist. Worn from late 1820s to mid-1830s. Also called *sleeve à la folle*.

**imitation gems** Reproductions of fine gemstones in colored glass or other inexpensive material as distinguished from man-made SYNTHETIC GEMS. The latter, although man-made, are chemically identical to gems occurring in nature.

**imitation leather** Fabrics such as drill, sateen, and duck which have been coated, dyed, and embossed to simulate leathers such as alligator, snakeskin, or lizard. Coatings used include rubber, pyroxlin, nitrocellulose compounds, or vinyl resins.

**imitation moleskin** See MOLESKIN FABRIC.

**imitation pearls** See PEARL under GEMS.

**Imperial 1.** Man's coat worn in 1840s similar to loose-fitting, fly-front *paletot* overcoat. **2.** Man's small pointed tuft of hair under lower lip. Popular with DANDIES. Fashion set by Emperor Napoleon III of France from 1852 to 1871.

**Imperial Skirt** Patented cage-type *hoop* skirt of late 1850s with as many as 32 hoops hung on fabric strips to provide a flexible, lightweight crinoline.

**inchering** 18th-c. term for taking measurements of a person in order to make a garment.

**incroyable bow** Large bow of lace or *mousseline de soie* worn at the neck by women in 1889 with revival of *Directoire costume*.

**incroyable coat** Woman's coat of 1889 made with long coattails and wide lapels. Worn with lace *jabot* and waistcoat for afternoons. Adapted from the SWALLOW-TAILED COAT. *Der.* Copied after styles of INCROYABLES.

**incroyables 1.** Extreme French fashions worn by men during the *Directoire Period* (1795–1799) which reflected a contrived carelessness, *e.g.*, sloppy-looking cravats draped high around neck, unkempt hair, and ridiculously large lapels. **2.** Term revived in late 1880s for similar look.

**incrustation 1.** Set-in piece of embroidery, lace, or trimming on women's and children's garments. **2.** Covered or studded with gems.

**Indian 1.** Term used for articles of clothing and accessories copied from North American Indian tribes. See AMERICAN INDIAN under DRESSES, HAIRSTYLES, LOOKS, and NECKLINES. **2.** Adjective used for country in southern Asia.

**Indian beadwork** See AMERICAN INDIAN BEADWORK.

**Indian blanket** See AMERICAN INDIAN BLANKET.

**Indian dimity** Fabric with fine cords at intervals either in the warp or filling made in India, and finer than domestic dimity.

**Indian embroidery** See EMBROIDERIES.

**Indian gown** See BANYAN.

**Indian handbag** See APACHE under HANDBAGS.

**Indian Head®** Trademark of Textron, Inc., for a cotton fabric woven to imitate *linen crash*. Introduced in 1831 by Nashua Manufacturing Co., and still in use today. Used for sportswear and children's clothing.

**Indian headband** See AMERICAN INDIAN HEADBAND.

**Indian lamb** See LAMB under FURS.

**Indian meditation shirt** See MEDITATION under SHIRTS.

**Indian moccasin** See MOCCASIN under SHOES.

**Indian necktie** Muslin *cravat*, worn by men from 1815 to 1830s, secured in front with a sliding ring. Also called a *maharatta tie*.

**Indian nightgown** **1.** See BANYAN. **2.** Term used occasionally in 17th and 18th c. for a woman's *negligee* attire.

**Indian print** See PRINTS.

**Indian war bonnet** See AMERICAN INDIAN WAR BONNET.

**Indian wedding blouse** See BLOUSES.

**India silk** Handloomed, plain woven silk fabric made in India.

**Indienne** **1.** Term previously used for printed fabric from India. **2.** French cotton fabric with a small design **3.** Cotton fabric made with alternating warpwise colored stripes and printed patterns.

**indigo** **1.** Blue dye made since earliest time from stems and leaves of *Indigofera tinctoria*, *Indigofera anil*, and woad plants; a similar synthetic dye now made from coal tar. **2.** Deep violet-blue color of this dye. **3.** Type of wool cloth used in Civil War by the Union Army.

**indispensible** Small handbag of silk or velvet, frequently square- or diamond-shaped, fastened at top with drawstring to form a cord handle. Carried by women from 1800 to 1820. Also see RETICULE.

**industrial mask** See MASKS.

**industrial zipper** Large-sized zippers, originally used for upholstery and industrial uses, adopted for decorative trim on clothing in mid-1960s.

**ineffibles** See INEXPRESSIBLES.

**inexpressibles** Late 18th and early 19th-c. polite term for men's *breeches* or *trousers*. Also called *ineffibles*, *don't mentions*, *nether integuments*, *unmentionables*, and *unwhisperables*.

**infanta style** Costumes as shown in paintings by Velâsquez of Philip IV of Spain's daughter showing extremely wide *vertugales*. Used as inspiration for evening gowns by *Balenciaga*, *Givenchy*, and *Castillo*, in 1950s.

**informal habit** See SPORT SUITS.

**initial ring** See RINGS.

**inlay** Shoe-industry term for piece of leather or fabric placed underneath a cut-out layer of leather and stitched into place for a decorative effect.

**inner-vest jacket** See SPORT JACKETS.

**innerwear** Trade term used to describe UNDERWEAR or LINGERIE.

**inseam** **1.** The seam in men's trousers, from the crotch to the hem. Leg length for men's pants is measured by this seam. **2.** See GLOVE SEAMS.

**insertion** Trimming made in straight bands and set between pieces of fabric in a garment.

Popular from 1890 to 1910 when bands of beading, embroidery, braid, or lace were often set in between rows of tucks and ruffles. Used particularly on white lawn dresses, blouses, petticoats, and drawers.

**insole**   Inside of shoe on which sole of foot rests; usually covered by *sock lining*.

**instant sunglasses**   See GLASSES.

**instita**   Flounce or narrow border on the lower edge of ancient Roman matron's robe, *e.g.*, the *stola*.

**insulated**   Describing a garment constructed to protect against cold. Materials used to insulate include DOWN, FIBERFILL, wool, and sheepskin. Also see BOOTS, GLOVES, SPORT JACKETS, THERMAL UNDERWEAR, HUG-ME-TIGHT under VESTS, and QUILTING.

**intaglio** (in-tal-yo)   Method of cutting gems by engraving design into the surface. Compare with *cameo* carving. Also see GEM CUTS.

**intarsia** (in-tar-sea-a)   Decorative colored motifs knitted into a solid color fabric giving an inlay effect. Patterns on both sides of fabric are identical.

**interchangeable bag**   See HANDBAGS.

**interfacing**   Canvas of linen, linen and hair, unbleached muslin, and crinoline fabric inserted between the outside and the facing of a tailored garment to give body and shape. See INTERLINING #2.

**interlining**   **1.** Fabrics used between the lining and the outer fabric of a coat, collar, or suit to give shape to the garment. Best types have permanent stiffening and will dry clean or wash, *e.g. tailor's canvas, linen canvas*, or *Pellon®*. Unbleached muslin and crinoline fabric are used in less expensive fabrics and will not wash or clean satisfactorily. **2.** Open weave woolen or cotton fabric used between the lining and outer fabric in a winter coat to give warmth. Same as INTERFACING.

**interlock**   Knit made on a machine having alternate units of short and long needles. Thicker than plain rib knits with good lengthwise elasticity, firm texture, and less tendency to curl at the edges.

**interlock fabric**   Tubular knitted fabric made on a circular knitting machine by interlock method. Similar to jersey but both the face and back of the fabric look alike.

**International Ladies' Garment Workers' Union**   A semi-industrial union founded in 1900 of U.S. and Canadian needle-trades workers. Originally an affiliate of the American Federation of Labor. The union is famous for the militancy of its early organizational drives, fight against sweatshop conditions, housing, educational, cultural programs, and medical services to members. David Dubinsky, elected president of the union in 1932, remained in office for thirty-four years and became a major figure in U.S. politics.

**intimate apparel**   Department-store term for *lingerie* and *underwear*.

**Inverness** (in-ver-ness)   **1.** Man's loose-fitting overcoat with below-elbow removable cape, introduced in 1859, a variation of *cape paletot*. In 1870s, sometimes had a separate cape over each shoulder. In 1880s, the sleeves were sometimes omitted. In 1890s armholes were very large and a "sling" was used to support or rest arm. **2.** Man's full cape, usually long, and made of wool or worsted. Was close-fitting at neck and fell loose from shoulders—often made in plaid patterned fabric. **3.** See COATS. *Der.* From county of Invernessshire, Scotland.

**inverted frame**   Handbag industry term for type of frame covered with fabric, or leather, so metal frame does not show at top of bag.

**inverted leg-o'-mutton sleeve**   Woman's sleeve of early 1900s with tiny darts at shoulder, close-fitting at upper arm, bouffant on lower arm, and a tight-fitting cuff. Compare with LEG-OF-MUTTON under SLEEVES.

**inverted pleats**   See PLEATS and SKIRTS.

**INVERTED LEG-O' MUTTON SLEEVE**

**inverted-T/-Y embroidery** See MATILDA under EMBROIDERIES.

**invisible zipper** See ZIPPER.

**Irene Castle bob** Short bob with hair brushed back off the forehead and hanging in loose waves. *Der.* After *Irene Castle*, the ballroom dancer who made bobbed hair fashionable prior to World War I.

**Irene jacket** Short, fitted, collarless woman's jacket of late 1860s cut away in front above waistline and sloping to below waistline in center back. Lavishly trimmed with braid around neckline, on sleeves, and in back.

**Iribe** (1883–1935) Paul Iribarnegaray, a Parisian illustrator and designer who was an important figure in artistic and fashionable circles of Paris in early 20th c. In 1908 he illustrated *Les Robes de Paul Poiret*, a limited edition of the couturier's oriental fashions. His original and imaginative style changed the type of drawings used as illustrations in magazines. In 1914, he came to U.S. and in 1919 worked in Hollywood with de Mille. In Paris in 1906 he published the newspaper, *Le Démoin*, which failed and was later revived in 1930s. Also see LEPAPE.

**iridescent fabric** Any fabric made of yarn-dyed rayon, silk, cotton, or man-made fibers woven with one color in the warp and another color in the filling. Reflects both colors in the light, *e.g., chambray.*

**iridium** (i-rid-i-em) Metal frequently alloyed with platinum to make a more durable metal for use in jewelry.

**Irish crochet** See LACES.

**Irish knit** Hand-knit in traditional patterns usually including cables, bobbles, and unusual stitches. Knit on large needles with natural wool yarns (without the oil removed from yarn). Used for Irish fishermen's bulky sweaters imported by U.S. for general sportswear in 1950s and 1960s. Also, similar knits of man-made yarns imitating the authentic Irish knits. Also see FISHERMAN'S SWEATER under SWEATERS.

**Irish linen** Fine quality of linen fabric woven from flax grown mainly in Northern Ireland. Used for handkerchiefs and apparel.

**Irish mantle** **1.** 15th-c. cloak, formerly called *bratt.* **2.** Blanket used for wrapping an infant.

**Irish point lace** See YOUGHAL under LACES.

**Irish polonaise** (po-lo-nayz) Woman's dress worn from 1770 to 1775 with square-cut neckline, bodice buttoned to waist, fitted at back, and elbow-length sleeves. A long pleated skirt, split in front to show shorter underskirt and caught up at waist by buttons or vertical cords into puffed sides. Also called *Italian nightgown, French* or *Turkish polonaise.* See POLONAISE.

**Irish poplin** **1.** Fabric with a slight crosswise rib made with a silk warp and a woolen filling in Ireland; originally made in China. **2.** Fine shirting fabric of linen or cotton made in Ireland.

**Irish tweed** Another name for tweed fabrics known to the trade as DONEGAL TWEEDS.

**ironed hair** See HAIRSTYLES.

**iron ring** Finger ring worn by ancient Romans with gold rings being reserved for badges of civil and military rank.

**Isabeau bodice** Black or colored silk, woman's evening bodice of 1869 ending at the waistline with a wide ribbon sash having long ends and large bow in front. Made with low square neckline, short puffed sleeves, and trimmed with two lace ruffles.

**Isabeau corsage**   Bodice worn in mid-1840s made like a jacket with the front cut away just below the hips. Also had a high neckline with a falling collar; long sleeves with open *mancheron* below each shoulder; and was trimmed with horizontal bands of *galloon lace*, braid, and silk buttons.

**Isabeau sleeve**   Triangular-shaped sleeve of 1860s with one point at the shoulder and widening to wrist. Used as an oversleeve with *engageantes* on dresses, on the *pardessus*, and on the *Maintenon cloak*.

**Isabeau style dress**   Daytime dress of 1860s cut in *princess style* and trimmed down front with a row of buttons or rosettes.

**THE ISABELLA**

**Isabella (The)**   Hip-length collarless cape of mid-1850s made with slashes for arms and extra capelets at dropped shoulders to cover arms.

**Isabella peasant bodice**   Close-fitting decorative corselet bodice decorated with long strands of beads hanging down from waistline. Worn over a dress in early 1890s.

**Isabella skirt**   Underskirt worn in late 1850s with three small hoops extending one-third of the distance from waist to hem. The remainder of skirt was made with three widely spaced hoops with quilted fabric between.

**ISABELLA SKIRT**

**istle**   Mexican-grown fiber from leaves of various plants, *Agave, Yucca,* and *Faircroza,* which is strong, coarse, and stiff. Used for hats and bags. Also called *ixtle, Tampico fiber* or *Mexican fiber. Der.* From Mexican Indian tribe, Nahauatlans, *ixtle,* "fiber producing plant."

**Isotoner® slipper**   See SLIPPERS.

**Italian bodice**   Corselet bodice laced up the front with straps over shoulders, flat fitted collar, and embroidery in front. Worn over a blouse in early 1870s.

**Italian cloak**   Short hooded cloak worn by men in the 16th and 17th c. Also called *Spanish cloak* or *Genoa cloak.*

**Italian cloth**   **1.** Glossy lining fabric made in a twill or satin weave in all cotton, or cotton warp with a wool filling—usually dyed black. Some types are also called *Albert, farmer's satin,* or *Venetian.* **2.** Lining fabric used in the uniforms of the U.S. Marine Corps. Made of combed cotton dyed black or green. Also called *Albert.*

**Italian collar**   See COLLARS.

**ITALIAN CORSAGE**

**Italian corsage** Woman's low-cut BASQUE bodice of mid-1860s laced up the front and worn over a blouse. *Peplum* was made up of decorative tabs. Sleeves of bodice were slashed and trimmed with bows of ribbons pulled through openings.

**Italian farthingale** See WHEEL FARTHINGALE.

**Italian heel** Shoe heel worn from 1770s on that curved inward at back, similar to LOUIS HEEL. Also had a wedge-shaped extension at top of heel extending under the sole nearly to ball of foot.

**Italian hose** See VENETIANS.

**Italian nightgown** See IRISH POLONAISE.

**Italian stitch** See DOUBLE-RUNNING STITCH under STITCHES.

**ivory 1.** Hard opaque substance—creamy white to pale yellow—from the tusks of elephants and other mammals. Carved for fans and other ornaments for many centuries and very popular for jewelry in early 1970s and 1980s. **2.** The color of ivory—a creamy white.

**Ivy League look** Style originally worn by college men at Eastern universities in Ivy League intercollegiate sports *e.g.,* Brown, Columbia, Cornell, Dartmouth, Harvard, Pennsylvania, Princeton, and Yale. Suit jacket was slim cut with natural shoulders, narrow lapels, and skinny sleeves. Pants were also slim cut. Popular look in 1940s and 1950s, often in medium-gray flannel. *Der.* The name was originally popular slang alluding to the old and ivy-covered buildings on these campuses. Also see PANTS, SHIRTS, and SUITS.

**ixtle** See ISTLE.

**iznak** Heavy gold chain worn as necklace as part of native dress in Palestine.

# J

**jabiru feathers** (jab-ih-roo) See FEATHERS.

**jabot** (zha-bo) Ruffle of lace, embroidery, or sheer fabric made in a *cascade*, attached to front of dress, blouse, or a *cravat*-like neckpiece. Popular in 18th c. for men and revived for women in late 19th c., 1930s, 1940s, and 1980s. Also see BLOUSES and COLLARS.

**JABOT #2, 1891**

**jacerma** Velvet or silk, sleeveless close-fitting jacket worn as native costume by women of Bosnia—now a part of Yugoslavia. Another embroidered jacket is sometimes worn on top.

**jacinth** See HYACINTH under GEMS.

**jack** Padded tight-fitting military DOUBLET worn from late 13th to late 15th c. Sometimes made of 30 layers of fabric and worn over the HAUBERK. Also worn by civilians in 14th c. as a short jacket made of rich fabrics.

**jack boot** **1.** Man's heavy leather riding boot made with square toes and heels with expanded bucket tops extending over knees. Worn by cavalry and civilians from 1660 to 18th c. **2.** Lightweight boots of 18th c. made of soft leather, sometimes laced or buttoned on outside. Also called *light jack boots*. For HALF-JACK BOOT see JOCKEY BOOT.

**jack chain** Chain made of links like a figure eight worn as an ostentatious decoration by men in 17th c.

**jacket** **1.** Item of apparel, usually shorter than hip-length, designed to be worn over other clothing either indoors or outdoors. Some are made in double-breasted or single-breasted manner; others have no closing, and some are closed with a zipper. **2.** Part of a suit which covers the upper part of the body—a suit jacket. *Men:* worn in France and England in 15th c. and by mid-17th c. called a *jerkin*. In 18th c. worn by country people, laborers, seafarers, and apprentices, thus becoming a mark of social inferiority. In mid-19th c. accepted by gentlemen replacing the suit coat for some occasions. *Women:* adopted by American women in 1860s in the form of the *Zouave jacket*. In the 20th c. many styles, for both formal and informal occasions, were introduced for both men and women. *Der.* Old French, *jackquette,* the diminutive of *jacque,* a coat. Also see SPORT JACKETS. In alphabetical listing see: BENJAMIN JACKET, COTEHARDI, DIRECTOIRE JACKET, FIGARO JACKET, GARIBALDI JACKET, and OXONIAN JACKET.

## JACKETS

**bellboy/bellhop j.** Waist-length jacket with standing collar, two rows of brass buttons on front in V-style, frequently connected with gold braid. Originally worn by messenger boys, pages, and bellboys at hotels. Now used mainly for band uniforms and occasionally adapted for men's, women's, and children's wear.

**blouson j.** (blue-sohn) Jacket with a bloused effect at a normal or low waistline, either gathered into knitted waistband or pulled in by drawstring. *Der.* French, "blouse."

**bolero** Waist-length or above-the-waist jacket, usually collarless and often sleeveless, with rounded front, and no fastenings. Copied from the Spanish bullfighter's embroidered jacket and worn by women since late 19th c. *Der.* From name of Spanish dance and also music for the dance.

**box j.** Any straight unfitted jacket, waist-length or longer; popular since 1940s and 1950s as woman's suit or dress jacket.

**cardigan j.** Straight box-type jacket with no collar, usually long sleeved, and may have binding around neckline and down front. *Der.* Named for the 7th Earl of Cardigan who needed an extra layer of warmth for his uniform during the Crimean War in 1854.

**Chinese j.** See COOLIE COAT under COATS.

**chubby** Woman's straight-cut waist- to hip-length jacket of long-haired fur, made collarless, with straight sleeves. Popular in late 1930s and revived in early 1970s.

**cutaway j.** See CUTAWAY COAT under COATS.

**dinner j.** **1.** Man's white semiformal jacket with shawl collar worn in summer. **2.** See TUXEDO.

**Edwardian j.** Fitted jacket made with some flare at back and sides and vents at sides or center back. Styled with double- or single-breasted closing and NAPOLEON or REGENCY COLLAR. Introduced in the 1960s, it was similar in cut to jackets of the Edwardian period. *Der.* After Edward VII, King of England, 1901–1910.

**Eton j.** Straight-cut jacket with collar and wide lapels worn unbuttoned or with only top button closed, reaching to waist or a little below. Adapted from jackets worn by under-classmen at Eton College in England until 1967, popular for women in early 1890s and a perennial style for small boys. Also see ETON SUIT in alphabetical listing.

**gendarme j.** Conventional jacket buttoned and adorned with brass buttons on sleeves, pockets, and down center front. Inspired by jackets worn by French policemen. *Der.* French, *gendarme*, "an armed policeman."

**lounging j.** See SMOKING JACKET.

**mandarin j.** Jacket with standing-band collar copied from styles of Chinese Mandarin costume. Also see NEHRU JACKET.

**man-tailored j.** **1.** Woman's suit jacket tailored similar to a man's suit jacket made in fabrics of pinstripes, tweeds, and other men's

**BOLERO**      **DINNER JACKET, 1971**

**NEHRU JACKET**      **TUXEDO JACKET, 1972**

wear fabrics. Style may be made with one, two, or three buttons or may be double-breasted. **2.** First jackets with mannish-type tailoring were introduced for women as suit jackets in the late 19th c. and called *tailor-mades.* Continued in various styles as a type of jacket suitable for the "working woman;" returning to popularity in early 1980s.

**mess j.**   White waist-length jacket made with large revers in front and no buttons. Back section is cut in three pieces with center section extending to shoulders in a modified "T," center waistline pointed in back. Worn by busboys and waiters. Formerly worn in white as a summer semiformal for men. Originally worn as part of naval formal evening dress. *Der.* From Naval "mess room."

**Nehru j.**   (nay-roo) Single-breasted jacket, slightly fitted, with a standing band collar introduced in late 1960s. Adapted from type of coat worn by Indian maharajahs. *Der.* From type worn by Jawaharlal Nehru, Prime Minister of India, 1947–1964.

**rajah j.**   **1.** *Men:* similar to NEHRU JACKET. **2.** *Women:* usually a tunic-length jacket, with NEHRU COLLAR worn with pants. *Der.* Shortened form of "maharajah."

**sack j. (or coat)**   See STROLLER.

**shirt-jac**   See SHIRTS.

**smoking j.**   **1.** Man's jacket of velvet or other luxurious cloth, or with velvet or satin shawl collar, buttonless, tied with sash, and worn at home for informal entertaining, since 1850. **2.** English version of American *tuxedo,* a short black semiformal *dinner jacket* made with satin lapels, called by the French "le smoking." Adapted for women by Paris designer, Yves Saint Laurent, in mid-1960s.

**Spencer**   Short open jacket, usually to above the waistline, with lapels and long sleeves reintroduced in mid-1980s for women. Originally introduced by Lord Spencer and worn by men from 1790 to 1850 and by women from 1790 until about 1820. Three tales vary about the introduction: a) Lord Spencer burned one of the coattails of his jacket and cut off the other; b) He was out riding and tore one of the coattails, so tore off the other; and c) He made a wager he could start a new fashion and proceeded to cut off the coattails of his jacket, thus creating a new popular fashion. *Der.* Named for Lord Spencer. Also see alphabetical listing.

**sport j.**   See SEPARATE CATEGORY.

**stroller j.**   A semiformal man's suit jacket similar to a *tuxedo* with satin lapels and peaked collar. Also called a *sack coat.*

**toreador j.**   Waist-length woman's jacket with epaulet shoulder trimming frequently braid-trimmed and worn unfastened. Adapted from jackets of bullfighters in Spain and Mexico. Also see SUIT OF LIGHTS under SPORT SUITS.

**tuxedo j.**   Man's semiformal jacket made in one-button style with shawl collar usually faced with satin or faille. Until the late 1960s, it was conventionally black or navy for winter and white for summer. Now styled in any color or pattern, *e.g.,* red, green, blue, or plaid fabrics, sometimes with notched collar. Introduced in 1886. *Der.* After Tuxedo Park Country Club, Tuxedo Park, New York, where it was first worn by Griswold P. Lorillard. Also called a DINNER JACKET.

---

**jacket dress**   See SUIT DRESS under DRESSES.

**jacket earring**   See EARRINGS.

**Jackson, Michael**   Originally of the Jackson Five he became famous as an individual rock singer in 1983 and set the first record for winning eight Grammy awards. Also see LOOKS and SPORT JACKETS.

**Jack Tar suit**   Sailor suit with bell-bottom trousers worn by boys—younger boys wore knickers in 1880s and 1890s. *Der.* "a sailor."

**Jack Tar trousers** Man's trousers, close-fitting at knees, flaring widely around ankles, and worn for yachting in 1880s. *Der.* "a sailor."

**jaconet** **1.** Gray goods made in a variety of qualities. Best types are fine sheer cottons finished for use in dresses, children's clothes, and summer clothing. **2.** Lightweight cotton dress fabric, sheerer and thinner than CAMBRIC. Originally made in India. Also spelled *jaconnet, jaconnette, jaconnot.*

**Jacquard** (jack-card) Elaborate woven or knitted pattern made on Jacquard loom. Invented by Joseph Marie Jacquard in France in 1801. Each warp yarn is controlled separately by use of a pattern on a punched card. Fabrics may have a background of plain, rib, satin, or sateen weave with design usually in satin weave. Some fabrics have specific names such as BROCADE, DAMASK, and TAPESTRY. These are referred to by their name, but others with no specific name are simply called by the name of the weave. Also may be knitted and then called *Jacquard knit.* Also see HOSE and SWEATERS.

**jade** See GEMS.

**Jaeger underclothes** (yea-ger) Type of wool UNION SUIT made with hygienic principles in mind. Introduced for men and women by a German, Dr. Gustave Jaeger, in 1880s.

**jagging/jags** See DAGGING.

**jaguar** See FURS.

**Jamaicas** See SHORTS.

**jamb** See GREAVE. Also spelled *jambe.*

**jamboy** See TONLET.

**jambeau** (zham-bow) Leather armor worn to protect leg in 14th c. See GREAVE.

**James, Charles** See APPENDIX/DESIGNERS.

**Japanese costume** For clothing and accessories as worn in Japan see the following: FURISODE, GEISHA, GETA, under SANDALS, HAKAMA, HAKIMONO, HAKOSEKO, HAN-YERI, HAORI, HAPPI COAT under ROBES, HEKO-OBI, HŌ, JUBAN, JUNIHITOYE, KAKU-OBI, KASA, KIMONO, KOSHIMAKI, MINO, MOFUKU KIMONO, OBI, OBIAGE, PARASOL, SHITAGI, SHITA-JUBAN, YUKATA, ZORI, and ZUKIN.

**Japanese parasol** Parasol or umbrella made of brightly colored glazed paper with bamboo ribs. Also made of oiled silk for wet weather.

**Japanese sandals** See ZORI under SANDALS.

**Japanese style** Clothing and accessories worn in Japan many of which have been adopted in the Western Hemisphere. For fashion influences: see EMBROIDERIES, LOOKS, PRINTS. Also see KIMONO, and JAPANESE MINK under FURS.

**JAPANESE WRAPPER, 1905**

**Japanese wrapper** Woman's lounging robe of early 20th c. made in wraparound style with long wide sleeves and a square yoke. Styled after a Japanese *kimono.*

**Jap fox/Jap raccoon** See USSURIAN RACCOON under FURS.

**jargon** See ZIRCON under GEMS.

**jasey** (jay-see) **1.** Late 18th and 19th c. man's wig made of worsted jersey yarn. **2.** Slang term for judge. Also spelled *jazey, jazy.*

**1**

**2**

**1.** Egyptian: copy of a wall painting from the Tomb of Kenamun, XVIII Dynasty (1436–1411 B.C.). See CUFF BRACELET, SHENDYT, NECKLACE.

**2.** Greek: man's costume, 5th c. B.C. See CHITON, CHLAMYS, COTHURNUS, PETASUS.

**3.** Roman emperor's costume, 3rd c. A.D. See TOGA, TUNIC.

**3**

4

5

6

**4.** Byzantine Empress Theodora, 6th c. A.D. See DIADEM, PALUDAMENTUM, STOLA.

**5.** Carolingian costume, 9th and 10th c. See BRAID, CRAKOW, HEADBAND, MANTLE.

**6.** English costume of the Middle Ages, 1250. See CROWN, MANTLE, SURCOAT, TUNIC.

**7.** Costume worn in battle during the Middle Ages, c. 1349. See ARMOR, COUTES, FLEUR DE LIS, GORGET, MEDIEVAL.

**8.** French costume of the Middle Ages, 1395–1422. See CROSS, FUR, HENNIN, VEIL.

**9.** English costume of the late Middle Ages, 1440–1450. See BLIAUT, MEDIEVAL.

**10.** Italian noblewomen, 15th c. See HANGING SLEEVE, HEART-SHAPED HEADDRESS.

**11.** Queen Elizabeth I, British painter, unknown, 16th c. See BOMBAST, DROP EARRING, ELIZABETHAN STYLES.

**12.** English costume of the Elizabethan Age, 1580–1590. See DOUBLET, BOMBAST, ELIZABETHAN STYLES, FUR.

11

**13**

**14**

**15**

**13.** Costume worn during the reign of Louis II, France, 15th c. See ARMOR, CHAUSSE, DOUBLET.

**14.** During the reign of Henry IV, France, 16th–17th c. See ARMOR, DOUBLET, MALTESE CROSS.

**15.** Woman's costume worn during the reign of Henry III, France, (1574–1589). See BEADING, FAN, FALLING BAND.

16

**16.** English costume of the 18th c., 1730. See BAGWIG, BREECHES, CRAVAT, FAN, TRICORNE, WAISTCOAT.

**17.** *George Washington* painted by Charles William Peale (1741–1827). See BREECHES, EPAULET, JABOT, STOCK, UNIFORM, VEST.

**18.** French costume, 18th c., c. 1770. Ivory-colored ball gown in ribbed silk with light blue and pink stripes overlaid with serpentine garlands and floral sprays brocaded in polychrome silk, trimmed with self-fabric and multicolored fly fringe. See FLY FRINGE, PANNIER, ROBE À LA FRANÇAISE.

17

18

**19**

**21**

**20**

**19.** Japanese woodcut, 18th c. Kitao Shigemasa (1739–1820). Two geishas out walking. See GEISHA, HŌ, JAPANESE COSTUME, KIMONO, OBI.

**20.** English costume of the 19th c., 1810. See NAPOLEON, PELISSE, TROUSERS.

**21.** French costume, 1831. See BONNET, FRENCH GIGOT SLEEVE, RUFF.

22

24

23

**22.** French costume, 1843. See CAPE, LACES, SAUSAGE CURLS, BRIDAL DRESS.

**23.** French costume, 1888. See BUSTLE, PARASOL, SILHOUETTE.

**24.** American costume, 19th c., c. 1882. Dolly Varden dress—polonaise or shepherdess style. Bodice of ivory sateen with a tiny printed rose pattern; skirt of rose-colored chambray. See DOLLY VARDEN POLONAISE.

**jasmine gloves** See JESSAMY GLOVES.

**Jasmine® mink** See MUTATION MINK under FURS.

**jasper** 1. See GEMS. 2. Fabric with a salt and pepper effect made by using white yarns in one direction and black yarns in the opposite direction. British fabric may have alternating yarns of black and white in the warp.

**Java canvas** See AIDA and LINEN CANVAS.

**Java lizard** See LEATHERS.

**jazerant** (jazz-er-ant) Armor worn in 14th c. consisting of a leather or cloth tunic covered with overlapping plates of leather, metal, or horn. Also spelled *jazeran, jazerine, jesseraunt*.

**jazz garter** Elaborate, wide, round-elastic garter covered with colored satin and sometimes trimmed with lace rosettes. Worn for decorative effect with very short skirts in the late 1920s. *Der.* From jazz music of this era.

**jazz oxford** See OXFORDS.

**jazz suit** Narrow shouldered, tight-waisted three-button jacket made with long 12″ center vent and vertical slashed pockets. Worn with pipe-stem pants by men in post World War I era. *Der.* From jazz music of this era.

**jean** Durable fabric made of carded yarns, primarily of cotton, in a twill weave similar to *drill*, but lighter in weight and made of finer yarns. It may be bleached, dyed solid colors, or printed. Used in blue for overalls and work pants, it gave the pants the name of *blue jeans*. Used for uniforms, slacks, shoe linings, and sportswear.

**jeanette** Women's necklace of 1836 made of a narrow braid of hair or velvet from which a small heart or cross is suspended.

**jeans** See BLUE JEANS under PANTS.

**jellaba** See DJELLABA.

**jellies** See SHOES.

**jellybag** See NIGHTCAP.

**jemmy** Man's shooting coat of 19th c. styled like a many pocketed short FROCK COAT.

**jemmy boot** 18th-c. term for man's lightweight riding boot, a fashionable type of JOCKEY BOOT.

**jemmy frock** Man's FROCK COAT fashionable in 18th c.

**Jenny** See APPENDIX/DESIGNERS.

**JENNY LIND CAP, 1849**

**Jenny Lind cap** Crocheted band crossing the crown of the head coming down over ears and around to the back where it fastened. Sometimes made of scarlet and white wool. Worn as a woman's MORNING CAP in late 1840s and early 1850s. *Der.* Copied from style worn by Jenny Lind (1820–1887), famous coloratura soprano, called the "Swedish Nightingale."

**Jenny Lind dress** Hoop-skirted dress of mid-19th c. with three lace ruffles on skirt and off-the-shoulder neckline. *Der.* Copied from style of dress worn by Jenny Lind (1820–1887), coloratura known as the "Swedish Nightingale."

**jerkin** 1. Jacket similar to *doublet* with slightly longer skirt, sometimes with *hanging sleeves* worn from 1450 to 1630. 2. Sleeveless jacket, with *wings* on shoulders, worn in 16th and 17th c. 3. See VESTS.

**jersey** 1. Synonym for knitted shirt worn by seamen, or for sports, from 1860s on—called *football jersey* in 1870s. 2. See JERSEY COSTUME. 3. Classification of knitted fabrics that are knitted in a plain stitch without a distinct rib. Originally made of wool but now made of many natural and man-made yarns, some textured. Made by circular or warp knitting processes, they may be printed, embroidered or napped. *Der.* From Isle of Jersey, off the coast of England, where it was first made. Also see KNITS.

**Jersey costume** Long, tight-fitted torso-like blouse reaching to the thigh worn over a serge or flannel pleated skirt. Top was made of red or blue knitted silk or wool jersey. Fashion popularized by actress *Lillie Langtry*, the "Jersey Lily," about 1879.

**jessamy gloves** Perfumed gloves given by bride and groom as wedding presents in 17th c.; jasmine being most popular scent. Also called *jasmine gloves*.

**jester's costume** *Coati-hardi* (doublet) and *chausses* (tights) worn with *fool's cap* having bells attached to peak. Bells sometimes worn on garters below knee or attached to dangling sleeves. Usually the entire costume was of *particolored* fabric.

**jet** See BEADS and GEMS.

**jewel** **1.** Precious stone that has been cut and polished—a *gem*. **2.** Natural or synthetic precious stone used as a bearing in a watch.

**jeweled pantyhose** See PANTYHOSE.

**jewel neckline** See NECKLINES.

**jewelry** A purely decorative accessory, *e.g.*, bracelet or necklace, made of genuine or simulated stones mounted in precious or plated metals. See BRACELETS, EARRINGS, NECKLACES, PINS, and RINGS. Jewelry of less precious materials is called COSTUME JEWELRY. Also see FASHION JEWELRY.

**jibba** (jib-eh) See JUBBAH.

**jiffy dress** See DRESSES.

**jiffy-knit sweater** See SWEATERS.

**jigger button** 19th-c. term for button concealed under lapel on man's double-breasted coat which was used to fasten back a wide lapel.

**jipijapa** (he-pe-ha-pa) Palm-like plant of South America from which *Panama* hats and braid are made. Also see PANAMA STRAW.

**Joan** Woman's small, close-fitting indoor cap shaped like baby's bonnet tied under chin with narrow frill of muslin or lace around face. Worn from 1755 to 1765. Also called *Quaker cap*.

**Joan-of-Arc bodice** Woman's tight-fitting bodice worn in 1875, reaching to hips and covered with jet or steel beads. Made with tight-fitting sleeves and ruffles at wrists.

**jobba** See JUBBAH.

**Jocelyn mantle** Knee-length, double-skirted, sleeveless woman's mantle of 1852 made with three capes trimmed with fringe.

**jockey boot** **1.** See BOOTS. **2.** Child's high boot of 19th c. often with cuff of contrasting material trimmed with a tassel. **3.** Man's below-the-knee boot with turned-down top of soft light-colored leather with loops on either side of top to aid in pulling on. Worn from 1680s to end of 18th c. Also called *half-jack boot*. After 1780s, called *top boot*.

**jockey silks** Costume of racehorse rider who wears a colorful shirt and cap to designate stable that owns his horse. Also called *racing silks*. Also see BOOTS, CAPS, COATS, PANTS, and SHIRTS.

**jockey waistcoat** Straight-hanging man's vest or waistcoat with a low standing collar, similar to *Chinese collar*. Worn from 1806 and revived in 1880s.

**jodhpurs** (*jod*-perz) Riding breeches popular after World War I, wide and loose at hips, tight from knees to ankles. Also see BOOTS and PANTS. *Der.* From Jodhpur, a city in India.

**jogging** Exercising by running at a slow steady pace. A type of *sweatsuit* is usually worn; or shorts and top. See SHORTS and SPORT SUITS.

**Mr. John** See APPENDIX/DESIGNERS.

**johnny collar** See COLLARS.

**Johnson, Betsey**  See APPENDIX/DESIGNERS.

**joinville**  Man's neckwear of mid-1840s to mid-1850s made by tying a 5″ wide scarf around neck in a bow. Usually had square-cut fringed ends.

**Jonker diamond**  See DIAMONDS.

**joobeh**  see JUBBAH.

**jornade**  See JOURNADE.

**Joseph**  **1.** Woman's green riding coat worn in the mid-18th c. **2.** Woman's outdoor wrap worn from 1800 to 1810 with loose sleeves, similar to Hebrew man's long tunic.

**Josephine knot**  Ornamental knot used for trimmings—made by looping two ribbons leaving the four ends hanging free.

**journade**  (zhur-naad)  Short circular jacket with large full sleeves, or with sleeves long and slit. Worn in 14th and 15th c. for riding. Also spelled *jornade*.

**juban**  An undershirt of silk or cotton worn by the Japanese under a *kimono* called a *shitagi* to which is attached the *han-yeri*, or collar, which is pulled out over the outer kimono—collar is black for winter, white for summer. Also see SHITA-JUBAN.

**jubbah**  (joob-a)  Long-sleeved, ankle-length, loose outer garment worn in Mideast—primarily Turkey, and northern African countries; mainly Algiers, Morocco, and Egypt. When used for winter in cold climates, sometimes fur-trimmed. *Der.* Arabic, *jubbah.* Also spelled *jubba, joobeh, jibba, djubba.*

**Jubilee diamond**  See DIAMONDS.

**judo clothes**  Special clothes worn by participants in Japanese method of self-defense without weapons—now considered a sport. Clothing includes short kimono-cut jacket; *white, brown, or black belt* that denotes degree of skill; and loose, mid-calf-length trousers. Judo clothes were copied for casual wear for men and women in 1950s and 1960s. See BELTS and SPORT SUITS.

**Jugoslavian embroidery**  See YUGOSLAVIAN under EMBROIDERIES.

**juive tunic**  (zweeve)  Hip-length princess-style *overdress* of 1875 made with large armholes, V-neck front and back, and overskirt forming a train in back. Worn over regular dress as outdoor costume. *Der.* French, "Jewish."

**Julian, Alexander**  See APPENDIX/DESIGNERS.

**Juliet**  Heroine of Shakespeare's drama *Romeo and Juliet.* For fashion influences see CAPS, DRESSES, NIGHTGOWNS, SLEEVES, and SLIPPERS.

**jumbo curl**  See CURLS.

**jump**  **1.** Thigh-length 17th c. soldier's coat, buttoned down front with long sleeves and vent in back, adopted by civilians. Also called *jump-coat* and *jumpe.* **2.** British name for woman's jacket. **3.** See COATS.

**jumper**  **1.** Women's and children's sleeveless garment, similar to a dress but usually beltless, worn over a sleeved blouse, sweater, or shirt. Also see DRESSES. **2.** British term for pullover sweater. **3.** British term for loose jacket-blouse worn to protect clothing. **4.** Sailor's overblouse or *middy blouse.*

### ━━━━ JUMPERS ━━━━

**A-line j.**  Jumper styled similar to a sleeveless dress, it can be worn with or without a blouse or shirt underneath.

**bib j.**  Jumper styled similar to a skirt with the front extending up to form a bib similar to the top of overalls. Straps are attached to the bib, extend over the shoulders, cross in the back, and attach to the skirt.

**buckled j.**  Bib-type jumper with two buckles placed at the neckline through which straps coming over the shoulder from the back are fastened.

**buckskin j.** Made similar to a sleeveless fringed Native American dress fastened with a laced closing in center front.

**coat-j.** Single- or double-breasted jumper styled similar to a sleeveless coat dress.

**horseshoe j.** Jumper made with a very low horseshoe neckline in front and back and large armholes. The straps which extend over the shoulders are cut in one piece with the skirt of the garment.

**pantjumper** **1.** Jumper similar to a sleeveless pantdress, worn with or without a blouse. **2.** Jumper worn over a long sleeved blouse combined with full-length pants.

**pinafore j.** Jumper similar to a BIB JUMPER. Also see PINAFORE APRON under APRONS.

**sandwich-board j.** A jumper made by joining two oblong pieces of fabric at the shoulders and at the waistline. So called because it resembles a sign previously worn over the shoulder with advertising copy in front and back called a "sandwich-board sign."

**shift j.** Jumper similar to a sleeveless shift dress, may be worn with or without a blouse.

**suspender j.** Any jumper with straps extending over the shoulders usually hooked to waistband of the skirt. A popular style for young girls. Also see SUSPENDER SKIRT under SKIRTS.

**tunic j.** Thigh-length jumper worn over a blouse. Usually made with matching full-length pants. Can be worn as a minidress or as a pantsuit.

**wrap j.** A jumper which wraps around the body and ties in front or back.

**BIB JUMPER**

**PANTJUMPER**          **SANDWICH-BOARD JUMPER**

**A-LINE JUMPER**

**jumper coat**   See BEAUFORT COAT.

**jumper shift**   See JUMPER under DRESSES.

**jumper suit**   Jumper dress with matching jacket.

**jumps**   Unboned bodice of 18th c. worn by women for comfort or during pregnancy.

**jumpshorts**   See SHORTS.

**JUMPSUITS**

**jumpsuit**   Combination shirt and trousers in one piece, zipped or buttoned up front. Introduced in World War I for flyers, worn during World War II by parachute troops, aviators, and adopted by civilians during air raids. Adapted for sports and leisure wear by men and women in 1960s and 1970s—especially for skiing, after-swim-wear, and loungewear. Continued in popularity during 1980s. Also see COVERALLS, PAJAMAS, SIREN SUIT, and SPORT SUITS.

**jungle**   See BOOTS and PRINTS.

**juni-hitoye**   Former court costume of empresses of Japan worn at coronations and formal court functions. Consisted of many robes, worn on top of each other, with four described as outer robes. Costume also worn by princesses and high court officials' wives. *Der.* Japanese, "twelve single robes."

**junior petite sizes**   Women's garments cut for adult, well-proportioned figure, about 5' to 5'1" tall. Usually sized 3JP to 13JP.

**junior sizes**   Women's garments cut for a well-proportioned adult figure, about 5'4" to 5'5" tall and short-waisted. Usually sized 5 to 15.

**jupe** (zhoop)   **1.** French term used from late 17th c. on for woman's skirt, sometimes in three layers: *modeste* on top, *friponne* in middle, and *sècrete* underneath. Also see SKIRTS. **2.** See GIPON. **3.** 16th and 17th c. British term for woman's riding coat worn with protective skirt or *safeguard*. Also called *gascon coat* and *jupon*. **4.** Scottish woman's jacket or bodice.

**jupel**   See GIPON.

**jupes**   Stays or stiffeners.

**jupon**   **1.** See GIPON. **2.** Woman's *underskirt*, that contrasted or matched fabric of bodice, worn between 1850 and 1870. Also see EMPIRE JUPON. **3.** See JUPE #3.

**justaucorps** (zhust-o-kor)   **1.** Man's tight-fitting, knee-length coat worn over waistcoat. Borrowed from a military coat and worn from mid-17th to early 18th c. in England and France. **2.** Woman's riding coat, styled like a man's FROCK COAT, worn from mid-17th to early 18th c. Also called *demi-riding coat* and *habit à la française*. Also spelled *justacor*, *juste*, *justico*, *just-au-corps*.

**jute**   A bast fiber obtained from the round-pod jute, *Corchorus capsularis*, or the long-pod jute, *Corchorus olitorius*. Grown extensively in Pakistan and India. Used in coarse yarns for *buckram*, *hessian*, and *scrim*.

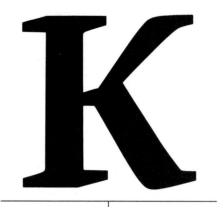

**K** Abbreviation for KARAT.

**kabaya** (kay-bay-yah) Straight white jacket, frequently trimmed with lace or embroidery, worn by Javanese women with the SARONG and SLENDANG.

**kabuki** Traditional theater of Japan beginning in early 17th c. with women dancers and actors. In mid-17th c. (1652) the government decreed that there should only be men as actors—doing all the female parts, too. Plots fall in three groups: historical plays, domestic plays, and dance drama. Costumes used are elaborate and include exaggerated brocaded *kimonos*, wide jeweled belts, wigs, and mask-like face makeup. Also see DRESSES, ROBES, and SLEEVES.

**KAFFIYEH-AGAL**

**kaffiyeh-agal** (ka-fee-ya ah-gal) Headdress consisting of a large square of plain or striped cotton which is folded diagonally and placed on head. Sometimes has hanging tassels at corners, and held by a circlet of twisted cord called AGAL. Worn by Arabs in Middle East. Also spelled *kaffiyah, kaffieh, keffiyeh, kuffieh*.

**kafsh** Low heelless slipper worn in ancient Persia.

**kaftan** See CAFTAN.

**Kahn, Robin** See APPENDIX/DESIGNERS.

**kaku-obi** Stiff silk sash tied in a double knot worn over the kimono by Japanese men for formal occasions, replaced by the soft HEKO-OBI for informal wear in the house.

**kalasiris** (kah-lah-seer-iss) Long, tight-fitting sheath-type dress reaching from under bust to calf or ankles made with one or two shoulder straps. Usually made of repeat geometric patterned fabric. Worn by early Egyptians and in archaic Greek period.

**kaleidoscope** Tubular optical instrument made of plexiglass, carved wood or copper in sizes ranging from a vest-pocket cigar to a 500 pound giant tube operated with pulleys. Held loosely together at one end of the tube are bits of colored glass, gems, beads or stained glass, which form symmetrical patterns as the tube is revolved from the reflection caused by three mirrors placed at 60° angles to one another. May be viewed from the other end of the tube through a peephole. These designs are sometimes the inspiration for fabric designs. Old and new kaleidoscopes are now collectors' items.

**Kalgan lamb** Named for city in China. See LAMB under FURS.

**kall** See CAUL.

**kalso** See SANDALS.

**kalyptra** (ka-lip-tra) Sheer veil worn over head and face by women in ancient Greece.

**Kamali, Norma** See APPENDIX/DESIGNERS.

**kamarchin** Gold embroidered silk or velvet TUNIC worn over the shirt by ancient Persian men with length varying with importance of wearer. Pockets are located in *alkalouk*, an undergarment, and are reached through lengthwise slits on either side of front of garment.

**kamelaukion** (kam-e-law-ki-on) Brimless, cone-shaped, tall flat-topped hat worn by clergy of the Greek Orthodox Church, in ancient times by various early Mohammedan sects.

**kamik** (kah-mick)   Knee-high handmade boot of smooth leather elaborately decorated at top and down center front with beads, feathers, and colored leather in geometrical patterns. Worn by Greenland Eskimo women.

**kamis** (ka-meece)   Ankle-length white cotton shirt embroidered around neck and across front with red or white silk worn by Arabian and Moroccan men. Usually dyed blue when worn by Egyptians. Also spelled *gamis*.

**kampskatcha slipper** (kamp-skat-cha) Woman's shoe of late 18th c. with pointed upturned toe, moderately high *vamp*, and low curved French heel frequently made of Spanish leather with fur lining. Also called *Chinese slipper*.

**kandys** (can-dis)   *Caftan* with tight sleeves worn by Byzantine emperors; Persian in origin. Also spelled *candys*.

**kangara**   Bold colors of red, green, black and yellow used in large squares of cotton fabric for scarfs in Saudi Arabia.

**kangaroo**   See LEATHERS and POCKETS.

**kangaroo skirt**   Term used for maternity skirt designed by Elsie Frankfurt in early 1940s with a circular cutout in center top front. This portion was not filled in with stretch fabric as in later maternity skirts.

**kapa**   **1.** Small black pillbox hat with red silk crown, sometimes embroidered, part of native dress in Montenegro worn by men and young girls until they are married. **2.** Handmade fabric of Hawaiian Islands. Sometimes applied to TAPA CLOTH.

**kappel**   Skullcap worn in Poland in 18th c. Also called *keppelche* and YARMULKA.

**kapta**   Thigh-length, full-cut slip-on tunic with fullness pulled in with narrow sash. Made of fur for winter, and worn by Laplanders.

**Karaca sweater**   See SWEATERS.

**karakul cloth**   Heavyweight pile fabric, similar to *astrakan*, woven in imitation of *broadtail* fur or *Persian lamb*.

**karakul lamb**   See CARACUL under FURS.

**Karan, Donna**   See APPENDIX/DESIGNERS.

**karat**   Relates to the quality or fineness of gold used particularly in jewelry. Gold of 24K is 100% gold with no alloys added; however, gold of this quality is too soft for jewelry. When alloys are added to gold, the resultant alloys are labeled as 12K, 14K, or 18K gold meaning that 12/24, 14/24, or 18/24 of the metal is gold, the remainder is the alloy. The letter K is used as an abbreviation. Compare with CARAT, which is the weight of a gemstone.

**karate costume**   Clothes worn by participants in unarmed man-to-man combat developed in Okinawa during 17th c. as means of self-defense. Now a popular sport in Japan and U.S. For fashion influences see SPORT JACKETS, SPORT SUITS, and PAJAMAS.

**karcher**   Medieval spelling for KERCHIEF.

**kasa**   Straw hat, shaped like a deep basket, worn by Japanese men and women for traveling.

**kasabeh**   Cashmere woven in Kashmir, of fine mesh in plain weave in many qualities. Used for veils and shawls called *chaharbagh* and *chantahi*.

**Kate Greenaway costume**   Children's dress, popular in 1880s and 1890s inspired by illustrations of children in empire costumes drawn by the artist, Kate Greenaway. Dress was made of lightweight fabric printed with flowers and styled with a high waistline, puffed sleeves, and skirt trimmed with narrow ruffles. *Der.* Named after the artist, Kate Greenaway (1846–1901). Also see GREENAWAY, KATE.

**kat-no**   Korean rain hat made of oiled silk or paper shaped like miniature half-folded parasol. Worn to protect high horsehair hat worn over top-knots and tied under chin.

**kaveze** (ka-veeze) Tall, tapered, brimless hat, draped with plaid or plain fabric to appear more like a turban. Worn by Hebrews in Turkey from 18th until end of 19th c.

**Kawakubo, Rei** See APPENDIX/DESIGNERS.

**Keds®** Trademark for *sneakers* and other rubber-soled shoes. See SHOES.

**keffieh** See KAFFIYEH-AGAL.

**kelle** Woman's CAUL. Also spelled *kall.*

**Kellerman, Annette** (1888–1975) Swim star of early 1900s who appeared in a one-piece wool jersey bathing suit, considered very daring, which came to be called by her name and was worn by women in early 1920s. She was arrested in Boston for appearing on beach in her one-piece suit. See ANNETTE KELLERMAN for description of swimsuit.

**kemes/kemise/kemse** Synonyms for CHEMISE in England during the Middle Ages.

**kenaf** See DECCAN HEMP.

**Kenyan tobe** Wraparound dress made of printed fabric with large border design, appears like two large scarfs joined together. Worn by women in Kenya, East Africa.

**Kenzo** See APPENDIX/DESIGNERS.

**kepi** See CAPS.

**keppelche** See KAPPEL.

**kercher/kercheve** Medieval spelling of KERCHIEF.

**kerchief** **1. (modern)** Large triangle of cloth, or square folded in triangular fashion, worn as a headcovering (see SCARFS), or around the neck. Also see NECKERCHIEF under SCARFS. **2. (antique for head)** Covering for the head from Medieval times to end of 16th c. Also spelled *karcher, kercher, kercheve, kersche.* Also see COVERCHIEF and HEADCLOTH. In 16th and 17th c. called a *head rail.* **3. (antique for neck)** After 16th c. used around the neck as a neckerchief. See SCARFS. **4.** See CURCH #2.

**kermes** Natural dyestuff known in ancient times in Asia Minor and used for scarlet dye. Obtained from dried bodies of a tiny insect known as kermes found on certain oak trees (*Quercus coccifera*). After the discovery of *cochineal*, became less important. *Der.* Persian, "little worm."

**kersche** Medieval spelling for KERCHIEF.

**kersey** **1.** Heavy durable woolen fabric with a long lustrous nap similar to *melton* and *imitation beaver cloth.* Used for uniforms and overcoats. **2.** Fabric which originated in the 11th c. in the English town of Kersey. Made in a twill weave of coarse yarns in wool, or with cotton warp and wool filling, finished by fulling.

**kerseymere** Fabric similar to CASSIMERE made of fine quality wool in a twill weave finished by napping.

**keswa el kbira** Dress of Moroccan Hebrew woman worn since 18th c. Early version was made with long skirt and *plastron* under a low-necked tight-fitting *corselet.* Voluminous elbow-length sleeves were brought to center back where they tied. By 1880 became a ceremonial costume with highly ornate gold embroidery. Skirt was of wraparound style, corselet had short sleeves with long patterned silk undersleeves with plastron showing in front. By 1900 skirt did not wrap—by 1940 worn with long shawl.

**kethoneth** Ancient Hebrew garment similar to a calf-length tunic or Greek CHITON decorated at the hem with tassels. Mentioned in the Bible as a basic garment along with the *simlah* and/or *salmah*, and the *ezor.*

**Ketteki-hō** Japanese robe. See HŌ.

**kevenhuller hat** Man's tricorn hat worn from 1740s to 1760s cocked with front forming a peak and turned up higher in back. Also called *kevenhuller cock.*

**keyhole neckline** See NECKLINES.

**key pocket** See POCKETS.

**khaddar** Handwoven cotton of coarse texture woven in India from native yarns. Sometimes spelled *khada, khadi*.

**khaki** (ka-key) **1.** Dull yellowish-tan color. **2.** Fabrics of this color, whether they are serges, drills, or whipcords, are called by this name. Used by the Armed Services of France, England, and U.S. as far back as 1848. After World War I, U.S. added an olive drab tint which is now government issue for Armed Forces. *Der.* Hindu, "dust color or earth color."

**khalak** Large veil worn over a tall conical native headdress by Moslem women in Bethlehem.

**khalat** (ka-lat) Long dark-colored wrap, once worn by Moslem women in Turkestan, that completely enveloped the person. Shaped like a coat, but worn like a cape with sleeves tied in back.

**khalkhal** (kal-kal) Large gold and silver ankle bracelets worn by Persian women.

**Khanh, Emmanuelle** See APPENDIX/ DESIGNERS.

**Khedive diamond** See DIAMONDS.

**kho** Kimono-shaped knee-length coat, either plain-colored or striped, bloused at the waist, and secured with a sash. Made with a small shawl collar and kimono sleeve cut all-in-one with the rest of the garment. Worn by the men of Bhutan, a small country north of India near Tibet.

**khurkeh** (ker-ka) A long linen dress, bloused over a figured belt, with sleeves narrow at shoulder and flaring to wrist. Elaborately embroidered at top of dress and in bands on sleeves and skirt. Worn by women in ancient Palestine.

**kick pleat** See PLEATS and SKIRTS.

**kid/kidskin** See FURS, GLOVES and LEATHERS.

**kikoi** (key-koy) Large rectangle about 1½ yards wide and 2 yards long of cotton fabric from Kenya, Africa, handwoven in stripes and various patterns. Introduced to the U.S. by high-fashion model, Iman, in 1987 and used as a skirt in various ways: a) draped to the back to form a bustle-like fullness, b) doubled lengthwise and tied in front to form a short skirt over a swimsuit, and c) draped to one side like a SARONG. May also be worn as a shawl or a head wrap. The original item has been worn in Africa since the 14th c.

**kidney belt** See BELT.

**kid seam** See FULL PIQUÉ under GLOVE SEAMS.

**Kieselstein-Cord, Barry** See APPENDIX/ DESIGNERS.

**kikuyu** See HANDBAGS.

**kilt** Man's knee-length, knife-pleated, wrap-around skirt with plain front, made in a *tartan* or plaid design, distinctive for each Scots Highland clan. Worn by members of clan, army regiments, and bands, *e.g.,* Carnegie-Mellon University. See HIGHLAND DRESS. Widely copied as basic skirt for women and children. For fashion influences, see KILTIE LOOK.

**kiltie look** Clothing and accessories derived from those worn by Scots Highlanders. See CAPS, DRESSES, LOOKS, OXFORDS, PINS, PLEATS, SKIRTS, and TARTANS.

**Kimberly diamond** See DIAMONDS.

**kimono** Loose, straight-cut cotton or silk robe made in various lengths and sashed at waist with an OBI. Loose straight sleeves are either cut on or set-in at right angles. A traditional costume of Japan, either in dark colors for men or in bright colors and floral patterns for women. Also see MOFUKU. For types of obis, see KAKU-OBI and HEKO-OBI. For fashion influences, see DRESSES, ROBES, SILHOUETTES, and SLEEVES.

**kimono silk** Lightweight silk usually printed in Chinese and Japanese pictorial scenes and motifs. Used for robes and pajamas.

**kip/kipskin** Leather-industry term for pelts of young steers, cows, or horses that weigh between 15 and 25 pounds, as distinguished from *skin* or *hide* of older animals.

**kipper** See TIES.

**Kirk, Alexis** See APPENDIX/DESIGNERS.

**kirtle** **1.** From 9th to end of 14th c., a knee-length tunic with sleeves worn by men. **2.** Full-length sleeved garment worn by women from 10th to 16th c. as basic garment over the smock and under the gown. **3.** Worn under gown by women in the 16th c., as an underskirt, to make a dress. **4.** From mid-16th to mid-17th c. called *half-kirtle* and became a *petticoat*. **5.** Short jacket worn in 18th and 19th c. **6.** An outer petticoat worn when riding.

**kiss curl** See GUICHE under CURLS.

**kissing strings** 18th-c. term for strings attached to mobcap to tie under the chin. Also called *bridles*.

**kiss-me-quick** Popular name for tiny bonnet fashionable in late 1860s.

**kit fox** See FOX under FURS.

**Klein, Anne** See APPENDIX/DESIGNERS.

**Klein, Calvin** See APPENDIX/DESIGNERS.

**knapsack** See HANDBAGS.

**knee breeches** Type of pants worn by men from 1570s to about 1820. Made to fit the leg, blousing slightly below knee, where they fastened with a button on outside of leg. From end of 17th c. on, buckles were usually worn.

**knee cop** See POLEYN.

**knee-fringe** Fringe of ribbons around bottom edge of open-style breeches, worn by men from 1670 to 1675.

**knee/knee-high/knee-hi** See HOSE and SOCKS.

**knee length** See LENGTHS.

**knee pants** Short, tight pants extending to knees worn by boys from age 8 to 16 popular from latter part of 19th c. until after World War I. During the 1920s became wider, more like shorts, and worn by younger boys age 2 to 8.

**knee-piece** **1.** Upper part of boot hose. **2.** Armor worn to protect the knee. Called POLEYN or *knee cop.*

**knee-string** Drawstring used in 17th and 18th c. for tightening breeches below knee.

**knee warmers** Pair of knitted cuffs that slip on over legs to cover knees worn under hose in winter.

**knickerbockers** **1.** Loose breeches gathered or pleated into buckled band at knee, introduced for men about 1860 originally for country wear. **2.** Worn by women for bicycling in early 1890s. Also see RATIONALS. **3.** Used by men for golf and sportswear in late 19th and early 20th c. Also see PLUS FOURS. **4.** Fashionable for boys from 1863 and worn with short collarless jacket, older boys wore a waistcoat. By 1890s worn with NORFOLK JACKET. In the early 20th c. usually called KNICKERS.

**knickers** **1.** Woman's underpants, originating in 1890s, of below-the-knee length at that time. English term still current and synonymous with PANTIES. **2.** Woman's below-the-knee pants similar to KNICKERBOCKERS, but not as wide. Worn for hiking, gym, and sportswear after World War I. **3.** Boys below-the-knee pants narrower than knickerbockers worn particularly in corduroy for school in 1920s. **4.** Worn for golf by men in 1920s. Also called PLUS FOURS. *Der.* Shortened form of KNICKERBOCKERS.

**knife pleats** See PLEATS and SKIRTS.

**knightly girdle** Decorative belt made of sections of metal joined together and buckled around hips with ornamental buckle in front. Worn only by nobility from about 1350 to about 1420.

**knit/knitting** Process of making a fabric, or an item of apparel, by the interlacing of loops either by machine or by hand. A crosswise row of loops is called a *course* while a vertical row is called *wale*. A great variety of stitches and yarns may be used to give textured effects and surface interest. Knitted stockings were introduced about 1530 with Queen Elizabeth I wearing the first pair of knitted silk hose. Knits were used in colonial days but not widely used for clothing until late 1870s when the *jersey costume* was introduced by *Lillie Langtry*. Popular in handknits for sweaters for men from 1860s and women from early 20th c. In the 1920s, knits became fashionable for women's dresses. Knits have also been important for lingerie and underwear since the 1880s. In the 1950s, the Italians introduced double-knit fabrics which gave knits better shape retention. Also see JERSEY and CUFFS.

**knit shirt** Sport shirt made of knitted fabric usually in pullover style. First introduced in mid-19th c. and called a *jersey*. Made of worsted wool and so-called because the fabric was first knitted on the Isle of Jersey, off the coast of England. Early shirts were worn for football, rowing, and for other sports. In 1920s worn for tennis. See LACOSTE® under KNIT SHIRTS. In 1930s knit shirts with placket necklines and convertible collars were introduced for casual wear at resorts for men. In the 1950s and 1960s knit shirts increased in popularity for men, women, and children due to improvements in knitting and acceptance of less formal style of dress. In the 1980s became more popular—accepted at schools and some offices as proper attire.

## ▬▬▬ KNIT SHIRTS ▬▬▬

**A-shirt** See ATHLETIC SHIRT.

**athletic s.** **1.** Sleeveless shirt with large arm-holes and scooped neckline, worn for track and active team sports, copied for men and women in 1960s and early 1970s. Also called TANK TOP or *A-shirt*. **2.** Man's undershirt of similar style.

**baseball s.** Knit shirt with three-quarter-length raglan sleeves usually made in contrasting color to the body of the shirt. May have a round neckline bound with contrasting color or slit neckline with buttons. Became popular in 1980s. *Der.* From shirt worn by major league baseball players under uniforms.

**big tee s.** Extremely large mini-length shirt with placket neckline, tailored collar and all-in-one sleeve. Worn as a beach coverup. Can also be worn as a minidress or tunic over pants. Also called *oversized shirt*.

**cardigan s.** Identical to *cardigan sweater*, but usually made in lighter weight knits. *Der.* Named for the 7th Earl of Cardigan who needed an extra layer of warmth under his uniform in the Crimean War in 1854.

**cartoon T-shirt** Conventional T-shirt with round neck, short sleeves, and screen-printed with slogan or cartoon, *e.g.*, pictures of individuals, self-portraits, names, comic strip characters, motorcycle names, baseball team names, and such slogans as "follow your dreams."

**chukka s.** See POLO SHIRT.

**competition-striped s.** Sport shirt designed with wide colored stripes alternating with white. Also see RUGBY SHIRT.

**crew-neck s.** Plain pullover knit shirt, usually made with short sleeves and a crew neckline. *Der.* From knit shirts worn by members of a "crew" of a racing shell.

**extra-long s.** T-shirt to knee or below styled with ribbed or placket neckline in plain or striped fabric worn with below-the-calf matching skirt.

**fishnet s.** Round-necked, raglan-sleeved shirt made of a loose, openwork, diamond-shaped knit. Designed to keep warm air next to skin, but allow perspiration to evaporate. Undershirt originally used by Norwegian army made of 100% cotton for protection against 0° cold and 90° heat.

**football jersey/football s.** **1.** Knit shirt with round neck, long or short sleeves set on dropped shoulders, and large numerals printed on front and back. Copied from shirts worn by football players and popular for children and teenagers in 1960s. Also called *numeral shirt*. **2.** In early 1980s made with very long dropped shoulders in short rib-tickler style of mesh fabric. Also see alphabetical listing.

**full tee** Shirt cut out of a circular piece of fabric gathered into waistband in front and back and stitched at the sides to form deep dolman-like sleeves. Finished with a wrapped peplum below waistline. Design originated with Paris couturier, Pierre Cardin, in mid-1980s.

**Henley s.** Lightweight knit shirt with buttoned placket at neckline, made in striped or plain knits with contrasting lining at placket and around ribbed neck. Popular in early 1960s and again in the 1980s for men, women and children. *Der.* Copied from shirt worn originally by rowers in crew races at Henley, England.

**Lacoste**® An internationally recognized trademark used extensively on apparel as well as other goods. The term originally identified the knit shirts manufactured by La Chemise Lacoste of Paris, marked with a small alligator symbol on left front. The shirts were designed of piqué knit with the shirt tail being slightly longer in back so that it would not pull out when worn during active sports. *Der.* René Lacoste, an international tennis champion, nicknamed "le Crocodile" by French sports writers in the 1920s. Lacoste had his friends in a textile company produce a new style of short-sleeved cotton knit shirts which he designed and sold to replace the uncomfortable long-sleeved woven shirts then worn by tennis play-

ers. He adopted the alligator symbol as the logo for knit shirts of this design because of his nickname.

**muscle s.** **1.** Descriptive term for a tight-fitting knitted shirt usually made in black or dark color, banded with white around the neck, short sleeves, and on underarm seams. Popular in late 1960s. **2.** 1980s version is sleeveless with rib-knit band around upper arm. Made in white and colors with printed designs or words on front. *Der.* Fitted tightly to reveal "muscles" of upper arm.

**numeral s.** See FOOTBALL SHIRT.

**oversized s.** See BIG TEE SHIRT.

**pocket T-shirt** Simple knit shirt worn for sports with crew neck and tiny rounded pocket on left breast.

**polo s.** A knitted shirt with placket neckline and collar usually made with short sleeves originally used when playing polo in 1920s and introduced for men's sportswear in the 1930s.

**prospector's s.** Shirt worn next to the skin made of knitted silk fabric which insulates. Similar in style to WALLACE BEERY knit shirt and ideal for traveling.

**pullover** Any light knit shirt without neck placket or fastening, *e.g.* T-SHIRT or FOOTBALL SHIRT.

**rugby s.** Knit shirt with broad stripes in two contrasting colors with small white rib knit collar and cuffs. The placket neckline closed with a zipper or buttons. *Der.* So called in imitation of shirts worn in Great Britain when playing rugby.

**skivvy** Knit shirt, copy of undershirt worn by sailors, made with bound neckline and tiny placket opening in front. *Der.* Scot-Gaelic, *skivvy* or *skivvies*, slang term for sailors' underwear.

**sweatshirt** Long-sleeved, fleece-backed, cotton-knit pullover or zipped-front knit shirt made with rib-knit crew neck, rib-knit cuffs and waistband. Sometimes has attached hood

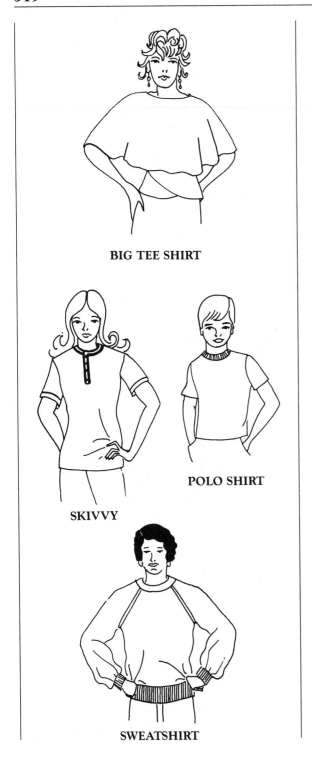

**BIG TEE SHIRT**

**SKIVVY**

**POLO SHIRT**

**SWEATSHIRT**

**WALLACE BEERY SHIRT**

**ATHLETIC SHIRT**

**FOOTBALL JERSEY**

and often worn with matching SWEATPANTS, as a SWEATSUIT. Originally worn after exercising to prevent chilling. In late 1960s adopted for jogging. Became more popular in 1980s for school and sportswear, sometimes with cartoon pictures, slogans, or name of school or club printed on front or back.

**tank top** Similar to ATHLETIC SHIRT, but styled in colors. Also see TOPS.

**T-shirt/tee s.** **1.** White undershirt worn by men with round neck and set-in sleeves. **2.** Knitted pullover sport shirt made in any color, frequently screen-printed with names, slogans, or cartoons. In early 1980s became so popular that some were trimmed with lace, embroidery, and ruffles. The name in 1980s was extended to include simple woven blouses. See T-SHIRT DRESS.

**Wallace Beery s.** Narrow rib-knit shirt for men and women with self-binding at neck and buttoned placket closing. Copied after *skivvies*, or government surplus underwear. *Der.* Called by this name because a shirt of this type was sometimes worn by Wallace Beery, the Hollywood actor, in films of the 1930s.

---

**knitted fabric** Fabric knitted by hand or machine. See KNIT/KNITTING.

**knitted velour** See VELOUR.

**knitting yarn** Man-made or natural yarn used for making knitted fabrics or garments either by hand or by machine. Includes *bulky, fingering, Germantown, Orlon acrylic, Shetland, worsted,* and *zephyr* yarns.

**knob toe** See TOES.

**knock-off** Trade term for the copying of an item of apparel, *e.g.,* a dress or a coat, in a lower price line. Compare with PIRACY.

**knot** **1.** Interlacing of threads, cords, ribbons and joining them together to fasten a garment,

or ends of a belt. **2.** Ornamental *bow* of ribbon, fabric, or lace. Also see CHINESE KNOT, MACRAMÉ KNOT, SAILOR KNOT. For historical knots see JOSEPHINE KNOT, LOVE KNOTS, LOVER'S KNOT, MOURNING KNOT, SHOULDER KNOT. **3.** See CHIGNON under HAIRSTYLES.

**knot stitch** See FRENCH KNOT under STITCHES.

**knotted lace** See LACES.

**knuckle curl** Fur-industry term for tight natural curl in *Persian lamb.* See FURS.

**Kodel®** Polyester fiber trademarked by Eastman Kodak Co.

**kodpeased doublet** See PEASCOD-BELLIED DOUBLET.

**Koh-i-Noor diamond** See DIAMONDS.

**kohl** (coal) Black substance similar to lamp black made from powdered antimony sulphide. Used in ancient Egypt and the Near East by women for eyeshadow and eyeliner. The look of kohl was revived in early 1970s for women's eye makeup. True kohl not sold legally in U.S.

**Kojah mink** See MUTATION MINK under FURS.

**kokochnik** See POVOINIK.

**kolah** (ko-la) Lambskin or cloth brimless hat with tall tapered crown wound with 10- to 20-yard strip of varicolored fine muslin to make a turban. Worn by ancient Persian men.

**kolbe** (kol-be) Man's hairstyle worn in mid-16th c. with bangs in front and hair the same length at sides and back, usually above the ears. Also called *kolbenschmitt.*

**Kolhapuri sandals** See SANDALS.

**kolinsky** See FURS.

**kolobion** Shirtlike garment worn by men in ancient Greece, opening at the side seam rather than along the top. See COLOBIUM for Roman variation.

**kolpos** Greek term for blousing of fabric at

waistline of the CHITON. A second belt, worn at hips, made a *double kolpos*.

**kontush** **1.** German name for woman's gown, specifically *gown à la française* of the 18th c. Also spelled *cantouche, contouche.* **2.** Robe with hanging sleeves worn by Polish nobility in 1810.

**Korean dress** National costume of Korean women. See CH'IMA, a high-waisted pleated skirt; CHOGORI, an extremely short jacket; and CHANG-OT, a full-sleeved cloak.

**koshimaki** (kosh-e-ma-ki) Long petticoat made of patterned crepe or muslin in gay colors worn by Japanese women over the *shita-juban* and *yumoji,* and under the *kimono.*

**kotény** (ko-ten-yee) Decorative apron worn by Hungarian women as part of native dress on festive occasions. Used in plainer styles for everyday wear.

**kothomos** See COTHURNUS.

**krama** A shawl or piece of fabric of checkered cotton cloth used by the men and women of Kampuchea, formerly Cambodia, for several purposes: a) May be folded several times and placed on the head so it appears to be in a turban shape with two ends hanging down. b) Used to carry things. c) To cover the body when bathing in a stream for modesty. d) Used by men as a loincloth. e) Embroidered by girls and given to young men as a love token.

**krepis** (kray-pees) Man's toeless sandal with sides and straps crossing in center front, worn in ancient Greece. Similar to Roman sandal called CREPIDA.

**krimmer** See LAMB under FURS.

**Krizia** See MANDELLI, MARIUCCIA under APPENDIX/DESIGNERS.

**Krupp diamond** See DIAMONDS.

**k'sa** Length of material, about 6 yards long, draped to form a garment worn by Moorish men in Morocco.

**kulah** (koo-lah) **1.** Red velvet brimless cap with gold-embroidered crown slightly peaked with fabric wound around the velvet part making a turban. An *aigrette* was sometimes added by royalty. Part of native costume in states of Delhi and Punjab, India. **2.** Similarly styled cap of lambskin or felt worn by Moslem monks in Persia and India.

**kulijah** (koo-lee-jah) Overcoat with rolling collar, lapels, and pleats in back. Made of camel's hair and lined in silk or fur worn by ancient Persian men.

**kumya** Shirt which closes down the front with many buttons and loops worn by Moorish Moroccan men.

**kurta** **1.** See DRESSES. **2.** Hip-length shirt fastened on left side with long sleeves buttoned at the wrist. Worn by Moslem and some Hindu men in India. **3.** Sleeveless shirt worn by Moslem women of southern India with the ANGIYA, a short-sleeved bodice.

**L** Letter designation for size LARGE used along with SMALL, MEDIUM, and EXTRA LARGE for men, women and children. See LARGE.

**L-85** Law enforced during World War II by U.S. government War Production Board on March 8, 1942 restricting the use of fabric and limiting yardage: under 3 yards for a dress, jackets no longer than 25 inches; limiting sweep of hem, number of extra pockets, linings, and other restrictions.

**lab coat** See LABORATORY COAT.

**label** Small piece of cloth stitched to neck or facing of garment identifying manufacturer or fabric used in clothing, *e.g.*, ILGWU label, indicating garment was made under union conditions in the U.S. Custom of labeling started in early 1820s with men's tailored garments.

**La Belle Époque** (ee-pock) Period of time between 1871 and 1914 when peace prevailed in Western Europe. Social life was especially carefree and clothes were elegant. Also a period noted for progress in literature, the arts, and technology. *Der.* French, "the beautiful epoch."

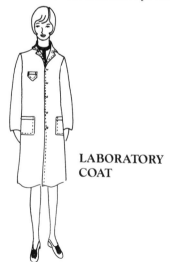

**LABORATORY COAT**

**La Belle Ferronière** (ferr-on-ee-air) See FERRONIÈRE.

**labels** 14th-c. term for two LAPPETS of silk or fur that were part of the hood worn with academic costume.

**laboratory coat/smock** Single-breasted coat, usually with turned-down collar and revers, made of white cotton. Worn to protect street clothes while working in chemical or medical laboratory. Also called *lab coat*.

**lace** Decorative openwork fabric made by hand or machine by looping, braiding, interlacing, knitting, or twisting of cotton, silk, wool, nylon, or other types of thread to form a pattern. Motifs are sometimes joined by bars called *brides*. Sometimes uses a heavier outline thread called a *cordonnet*. Classified according to method as *needlepoint* or *point* lace, *pillow* or *bobbin* lace, and *tatting*. Lace-making developed from embroidery in the 15th c. and was an important industry for centuries. Cities of Venice, Antwerp, and Brussels developed distinctive techniques and patterns. Became very popular for collars, cuffs, and ruffs in 16th c. Fashionable in 17th and 18th c. for trimmings and flounces. By early 19th c., John Heathcoat invented the *bobbinet* machine and John Leavers started a factory to make lace by machine in England. First lace factory in the U.S. was started in Medway, Massachusetts, in 1818. Machine-made lace was used for *shawls, parasols, berthas*, and trimmings. In 20th c., lace is used especially for lingerie trim, collars, cuffs, and wedding veils. See GLOVE and SHOES.

## ▰ LACES ▰

**Alençon l.** (a-lonh-sohn) Fine handmade or machine-made needlepoint lace with solid designs on sheer net ground outlined with cordonnet. First made in 1665 and called *point de France*, later in 1678 called *point d'Alençon. Der.* For town of Alençon, France.

**allover l.** Term for wide lace with repeat patterns extending entire width of fabric. Lace purchased by the yard used for clothing.

**aloe l.** Tatting and bobbin lace made from aloe, agave, Ceylon bowstring, and bast-like fibers in the Philippines, Italy, South America, and the Barbados Islands.

**Angleterre, point d'** See POINT D'ANGLETERRE LACE.

**antique l.** Darned bobbin lace made by hand with heavy linen thread on knotted square net with large irregular or square openings. Also called *araneum, opus araneum,* and *spider work.*

**Antwerp l.** **1.** Rare handmade bobbin lace similar to Alençon with a vase or basket effect in design first made in 17th c. Also called *Antwerp pot lace* or *potten kant.* **2.** All Belgian laces, including MECHLIN and BRUSSELS, made before 17th c.

**appliqué l.** Type of lace made by attaching previously made bobbin or needlepoint handmade designs to machine-made mesh ground. Also called *point d'appliqué.*

**araneum l.** (a-ray-nee-um) See ANTIQUE LACE.

**argentan l.** (ahr-jen-tan) Flat-patterned French needlepoint lace of *Alençon* type but with bolder designs, larger mesh background, and no cordonnets. Popular for aprons, cravats, sleeve ruffles, and caps in 18th c. Also called *point d'Argentan* or *point de France.*

**Armenian l.** Hand- or machine-made knotted lace made in narrow widths with sawtoothed edge.

**baby Irish l.** Narrow fine hand-crocheted lace made in Ireland.

**baby l.** Any narrow, fragile, dainty lace used to trim infants' garments, *e.g.,* baby caps and baptismal gowns.

**Battenberg l.** Lace made by applying a coarse linen Battenberg tape to the design and connecting tape with decorative linen stitch by hand or machine. Similar to RENAISSANCE LACE, but coarser.

**Bavarian l.** Simple type of TORCHON LACE.

**beggar's l.** Inexpensive type of TORCHON LACE.

**Belgian l.** Classification for *pillow laces* with machine-made grounds from Belgium, including *Antwerp, Valenciennes, Brussels,* and *Mechlin laces.*

**Binche** (bansh) Flemish bobbin lace similar to *Valenciennes* with scroll floral patterns and snowflakes sprinkled on net ground. Used for cuffs and fichus since 18th c. *Der.* Named for town of Binche, Belgium.

**bisette** (bee-set) Inexpensive narrow, coarse bobbin lace of *torchon* type, made in France since 17th c. Same as *beggar's lace.*

**blonde de Fil** See MIGNONETTE LACE.

**blonde l.** Fine French bobbin lace with floral pattern on net ground, originally made of unbleached Chinese silk in Bayeux, Caen, and Chantilly; later bleached and dyed black or colors. Fashionable at French court from mid-18th to mid-19th c.

**bobbinet** Mesh fabric base for lace with hexagonal holes made by hand or machine.

**bobbin l.** General category of handmade lace made with small bobbins holding each yarn attached to a small pillow. Paper design is placed on pillow, pins inserted, and yarns interlaced around pins to form pattern. Designs may also be made separately and appliquéd to handmade net. Types include: *Brussels, binche, Cluny,* and *duchesse*. Also called PILLOW LACE. Also see BONE LACE.

**Bohemian l.** Bobbin lace characterized by tapelike designs on net ground. Originally handmade in Bohemia from old Italian patterns, now machine-made.

**bone l.** Bobbin lace made by fastening threads to pillow by thin fish bones when pins were scarce in Elizabethan times. See BOBBIN LACE.

**bourdon l.** (boor-dohn) Machine-made net lace with cord outlining pattern and outer edge.

**Breton** **1.** Lace made by embroidering with colored yarns on net, rather than weaving design, in imitation of *Alençon* lace. **2.** Net fabric with larger holes than Brussels net.

**bridal l.** **1.** Contemporary industry term for lace used to make a wedding dress, for trimming, or for the veil. **2.** Reticella-type of lace worn by brides of France and Spain in the 16th and 17th c. The designs consisting of heraldic devices relating to owner. Also called *carnival lace*.

**Bruges l.** (broozh) Fine *guipure* tape lace of bobbin-type similar to DUCHESSE, but coarser. *Der.* For city of Bruges, Belgium.

**Brussels l.** Formerly needlepoint lace made with cords outlining designs made separately and appliquéd to fine net, now machine-made.

**Brussels net** Handmade bobbinet, made in Belgium, with hexagonal holes, two sides of holes braided, the other four sides twisted. Also called *filet de Bruxelles*.

**Buckingham l.** Fine bobbin lace with simple pattern on a fine clear ground worked all in one piece. *Der.* For Buckinghamshire, England, where it was first manufactured in 16th c. Also called *Buckinghamshire lace*.

**bullion** Antique heavy lace made of silver or gold thread in a simple design. Also called *bullion lace*.

**burnt-out l.** See PLAUEN LACE.

**carnival l.** Also spelled *carnaval*. See BRIDAL LACE #2.

**Carrickmacross l.** (kar-ik-ma-cross) Two types of lace: a) *guipure type* with design cut from fine cambric or lawn and embroidered with fine needlepoint stitches connected by brides, b) *appliqué type* with designs embroidered, then superimposed on machine net. *Der.* Made in or near Carrickmacross, Ireland, since 1820.

**Chantilly l.** (shan-til-ee or shon-tee-yee) Delicate fragile-looking bobbin lace first made by hand in early 18th c. Later made by machine with hexagonal mesh and a design of scrolls, branches, and flowers outlined with cordonnets. Made with a scalloped edge in white and used for contemporary bridal dresses. Also comes in black. Made in Caen and Bayeux during the last half of the 19th c., Chantilly lace was very fashionable for shawls and parasols. *Der.* For town of Chantilly, France, where it was first made.

**chenille l.** 18th-c. French needlepoint lace made with hexagonal mesh and designs outlined in white chenille yarn.

**Cluny l.** **1.** Coarse bobbin lace, similar to *torchon*, usually made of heavy ivory-colored linen thread in wheel or paddle designs. **2.** Machine-made cotton lace of similar design.

**Colbertine l.** A coarse, French bobbin lace with a square mesh ground. Produced in France in 17th c. under royal patronage when Colbert was prime minister. Sometimes spelled *Colberteen, Colbertan*.

**Cork l.** Older types of Irish lace formerly made in Cork, Ireland, are identified by this term. Includes flat needlepoint lace copied after Italian laces and *Youghal lace*.

**Crete l.** Silk or linen bobbin lace usually made with geometrical designs on colored ground with colored chain stitch along the edge. Made in Crete.

**crochet l.**   Lace made by looping single threads together by means of a hook. Best quality comes from Ireland.

**damascene l.** (dam-ah-seen)  Lace made with sprigs and braids of lace joined together by corded bars in imitation of *Honiton lace*.

**darned l.**   Term applied to all filet-type lace made by pulling out groups of warps and fillings from fabric and inserting stitches with a needle. Background may also be reworked in buttonhole stitch. See FILET LACE.

**dentelle de la vierge** (donh-tell de la vee-airzh)  See DIEPPE POINT LACE.

**Dieppe point l.**   French bobbin lace similar to *Valenciennes* but simpler, made in 17th and 18th c., narrow variety is called *poussin*; wider type called *dentelle de la vierge*. *Der.* For town of Dieppe, France.

**duchesse l.**   Type of bobbin lace characterized by floral designs and a tapelike effect made with fine thread and much raised work. Designs are made first then connected by means of brides or bars. When joined together, it gives an allover effect with irregularly shaped spaces between the designs. Frequently handed down from one generation to next for use on bridal dresses. Originally called *guipure de Bruges*.

**Egyptian l.**   Knotted lace frequently made with beads placed between meshes.

**fausse Valenciennes**   A term used for lace similar to *Valenciennes* but not made in the city of Valenciennes.

**fiber l.**   Delicate lace made of banana and aloe fibers.

**filet de Bruxelles**   See BRUSSELS NET.

**filet l.**   Hand-knotted lace with square holes frequently filled in with colored yarns in darning stitch. Also imitated by machine. Also called *darned filet lace*.

**flouncing**   Lace wider than edging lace, used for ruffles or trimmings, with one straight edge, the other scalloped. Usually made with one strong thread along straight edge that can be pulled to make gathers.

**French l.**   Machine-made lace fabrics made in imitation of handmade French lace. Lingerie laces of the *Alençon, Chantilly, Valenciennes* types. Couture laces used for garments, grouped into: *a)* re-embroidered lace, *b)* Chantilly of the fine type, *c)* guipure lace, *d)* veiling and tulle.

**Greek l.**   See RETICELLA LACE.

**gros point** (groh-pwanh)  Venetian needle-point lace made in large designs with high relief work. Also called *gros point de Venise* and *point de Venise*.

**guipure** (gee-poor)  **1.** Heavy tape lace characterized by large showy patterns in needlepoint or bobbin fashion worked over a coarse mesh ground. **2.** Lace with designs, with or without bars or brides, to hold pattern in place. **3.** Early name for gold and silver lace.

**guipure de Bruges**   See DUCHESSE LACE.

**hairpin l.**   Insertion-type lace with a looped edge made by winding the thread around a hairpin. Crochet hook is used to catch the threads together.

**Hamburg l.**   Heavy embroidered effect carried out on cambric or muslin fabric.

**Honiton l.**   Bobbin lace, similar to *duchesse*, made in England with either motifs made first and appliquéd to machine-made net ground, or lace with round heavy motifs made of fine braid joined together like *guipure*. *Der.* From town of Honiton, Devonshire, England, where lace has been made since time of Queen Elizabeth I.

**Irish crochet l.**   Handmade lace characterized by raised designs of roses, shamrocks, or other patterns set against a coarse diamond-shaped mesh with heavy scalloped edge. Made in the chain stitch. Copied from needlepoint lace of Spain and Venice and made in Ireland originally. Later made in France, Belgium, China, and Japan. Popular for collars and cuffs in early 20th c.

**Irish point l.** See YOUGHAL LACE.

**knotted l.** Lace made by hand-tied knots to form a mesh-like pattern, *e.g.*, *macrame* and *tatting*.

**lacis** (lay-sis) Original term for square-mesh net that is darned or embroidered; a forerunner of lace.

**Leavers** (leevers) Term applied to all laces made on Leavers machine invented by John Leavers in 1813 and used in factories, particularly in Nottingham, England, and in the U.S. Also spelled *Levers*.

**Lille l.** Fine bobbin lace of simple pattern outlined by heavy cordonnets on net background with hexagonal holes, similar to *Mechlin lace*. First made in 16th c. *Der.* From town of Lille, France.

**Lyons l.** *Maline-type* of lace with pattern outlined in silk or mercerized cotton. *Der.* From British name for town of Lyons, France.

**machine-made l.** Any type of lace made by machine. See LEAVERS LACE and NOTTINGHAM LACE. Most contemporary laces of all types are made by machine.

**macramé l.** One of the oldest types of hand-made knotted lace, made of coarse thread, cord, or yarn in Italy. Originally of Arabic origin, woven in geometrical patterns from selvage down. Revived popularity in early 1970s for belts, bags, etc. *Der.* Turkish, *magramah*, "napkin or facecloth."

**maline l.** **1.** Stiff bobbin lace with hexagonal mesh ground similar to *Mechlin lace*. **2.** General term for all light Flemish laces before 1685. Also spelled *malines*.

**Mechlin l.** (meck-lin) Fragile bobbin lace with ornamental designs outlined with shiny cordonnets and placed on hexagonal net ground. Used in Regency and Louis XV period;

greatest vogue about mid-18th c. *Der.* From city of Mechlin, Belgium, where it was made.

**Medici l.** (me-dee-chee) French bobbin lace, combining closed and open work, one edge finished in scallops similar to but finer than *Cluny lace*. Also spelled *Medicis* in France. *Der.* For royal Italian family in power from 14th to 18th c.

**mignonette l.** (mee-yon-et) Narrow, light, fine, French bobbin lace made in linen thread and worked in small patterns on six-sided mesh ground that resembles tulle. Also called *blonde de fil*.

**Milan l.** Type of bobbin lace, originally made with flat tapelike circular designs connected with brides or bars. Popular in 17th c. and earlier made of gold, silver, and silk thread. Later, elaborate designs such as flowers, animals, and figures were used on a mesh ground and made in shaped pieces for collars. *Der.* From Milan, Italy. Also called *Milan point lace*.

**Moscow l.** A copy of Italian lace made in Russia.

**needlepoint l.** Handmade lace made by outlining design with a single linen or cotton thread on parchment paper, holding it with tiny stitches to be cut away later, then working the background entirely with a needle.

**Northamptonshire l.** Bobbin lace with fine mesh ground imitating Flemish laces, similar to *Lille*, *Valenciennes*, and *Brussels laces*. Made in England in 17th and 18th c. and popular in U.S. in 19th c.

**Nottingham l.** **1.** Cotton lace made on Nottingham machine. Has a V-shaped mosaic-like pattern and is made in wide widths. **2.** Originally a classification of machine-made laces made in Nottingham, England. Now used for laces made on Nottingham machines anywhere. *Der.* From place of origin.

**opus araneum** See ANTIQUE LACE.

**orris l.** (or-iss)   18th-c. lace of gold and silver. *Der.* From Arras, France. Also spelled *orrice*.

**passement**   French term used in 16th c. for all types of lace, finally developed into *passementerie*.

**pillow l.**   Same as BOBBIN LACE. Made in two different ways: a) motifs or designs made first then connected by brides; b) made in one piece with same thread forming design and background.

**Plauen l.**   Lace made by *burnt-out* method— the design is embroidered by Schiffli machine in a fiber different from the ground fiber, so when chemically treated, the ground dissolves, leaving lace. *Der.* From Plauen, Germany, where method was invented. Also called *St. Gall* and *Saxony laces*.

**point l.**   Shortened form for NEEDLEPOINT LACE.

**point d'Alençon**   See ALENÇON LACE.

**point d'Angleterre** (pawnh donh-gla-tare) Fine handmade Brussels bobbin lace with pattern of floral, bird, or geometrical motifs worked separately and applied to handmade mesh. Introduced into England and Belgium in 17th and 18th c. and used for collars, fichus, handkerchiefs, aprons, petticoats, fans, and to trim gloves Revived in the 19th c. when applied to good Belgium lace, a coarse mixed Belgium lace, or a type of tape lace.

**point d'appliqué**   See APPLIQUÉD LACE.

**point d'Argentan**   See ARGENTAN LACE.

**point d'esprit l.**   Open stitch used in guipure lace with loops forming a pattern on a mesh ground.

**point de France**   Needlepoint lace similar to *Venice* and *Milan* laces of same era. Manufacture was encouraged by French government under supervision of Colbert, who imported workers from Italy and started a factory in 1665 at Alençon. Also see ARGENTAN LACE.

**point de Gaze** (pwanh de gahz)   Belgian needlepoint lace with flower designs appliquéd on fine bobbin net, later cut away under the designs.

**point de Paris** (pwanh de pa-ree)   **1.** Narrow bobbin lace with hexagonal mesh and flat design. **2.** Machine-made lace similar to *val lace* with design outlined with *gimp*.

**point de rose**   See ROSE-POINT.

**point de Venise**   Type of Venetian needlepoint lace made with padded, raised cordonnets, and edges of designs trimmed with many picots. By late 17th c. also made in France and England. Most sought after lace of 17th c. Cavaliers. Also called *gros point de Venise*.

**potten kant l.**   See ANTWERP LACE.

**poussin l.**   Lace of narrow, delicate Valenciennes type produced at Dieppe, France. See DIEPPE POINT LACE.

**princesse l.** (pranh-sess)   Imitation of *duchesse lace*, done in a fine delicate manner with machine-made designs joined together or applied to net ground.

**punto**   Term for Italian laces of 16th c. Also applied to Spanish laces. *Der.* Italian, "stitch."

**Renaissance l.**   Heavy flat lace made with tape laid out in pattern and joined together in a variety of stitches. First made in 17th and revived in late 19th c. for fancy work and then called *Battenberg lace*.

**reticella l.** (reh-tee-chella)   First needlepoint lace made by cutting and pulling out threads, then re-embroidering. Developed from cut-work and drawn work done on linen. Early patterns were geometrical and connected by picot brides or bars. First mentioned in 1493 in a Sforza inventory. Very fashionable in 16th c. and widely imitated; still made in Italy. Also called *Greek lace*, *Greek point*, *Roman lace*, *Roman point* and *Venetian guipure*.

**Roman l.**   See RETICELLA LACE.

**rose-point l.** Venetian needlepoint, similar to Venetian point but finer and with smaller motifs of flowers, foliage, and scrolls. Has more design repeats and connecting brides, or bars and is padded with buttonhole edges and a heavy cordonnet. Also called *point de rose.*

**Saxony l.** See PLAUEN LACE. *Der.* From Saxony, Germany.

**shadow l.** Machine-made lace that has flat surface and shadowy indistinct designs.

**Shetland l.** Bobbin lace made of black or white Shetland wool. Formerly used for baby covers and shawls.

**Spanish blonde l.** Lace characterized by heavy pattern on fine net ground. Made in Catalonia and Barcelona or frequently imported from France to Spain for use in mantillas, scarfs, and flounces.

**Spanish l.** **1.** Lace with a flat design of roses connected with a net background. Used for mantillas. **2.** Coarse pillow lace made with gold and silver threads.

**spider work** Coarse open bobbin lace, same as ANTIQUE LACE.

**St. Gall l.** A term for Swiss laces and embroideries, specifically *Plauen lace. Der.* From Saint Gall, Switzerland.

**stretch l.** Machine-made lace of narrow or full width knitted with extra core yarns which are expandable. Used in narrow width for hems; wider widths used for girdles and foundations.

**tambour work** See EMBROIDERIES category.

**tatting** Knotted lace, usually narrow, made by winding thread on small hand-held shuttle with the fingers making small loops and patterns. Used for edging lingerie, handkerchiefs, etc.

**teneriffe l.** Lace with wheel designs made by winding thread around the top of a small spool about 2½″ in diameter then working

back and forth across the circle with a needle and thread. Made chiefly in the Canary Islands. Sometimes called *teneriffe work.*

**torchon l.** Coarse inexpensive bobbin lace made of cotton or linen in simple fanlike designs, produced in Europe and China. Also made by machine. Also called BEGGAR'S LACE and BISETTE LACE.

**Valenciennes l.** (va-lhan-see-en) Handmade French fine bobbin lace first made in time of Louis XIV. Distinguished by small floral and bow designs made in one with the ground of square, diamond-shaped, or round mesh. *Der.* From Valenciennes, France.

**Val l.** Abbreviated form for *Valenciennes.* This term usually applies to machine-made copies.

**Venetian l.** Many types of laces and embroidery from Venice including cut work, drawn work, *reticella,* raised point, and flat point.

**Venetian point l.** Heavy needlepoint lace with floral sprays, foliage, or geometrical designs made in high relief by buttonhole stitches with motifs connected with brides or bars and decorated with picots. Originally made in Venice; later made in Belgium and other countries. Also called *Venetian raised point.* Also see POINT DE VENISE.

**Youghal l.** Irish flat needlepoint lace inspired by Italian laces, particularly Venetian types. *Der.* First made in Youghal, County Cork, Ireland. Also called *Irish point lace.* Also see CORK LACE.

---

**laced closing** See FOUNDATIONS and CLOSINGS.

**lace insertion** Narrow lace finished with straight edges used on blouses, dresses, and lingerie. Very popular in 1890s, early 20th c., and reintroduced in 1980s.

**lacer** Rounded or flattened string or thong often with reinforced tips of metal or plastic. Usually threaded through *eyelets* as a fastener for a *laced closing* or shoes. Also called *shoe lacer* and *shoestring*.

**lacerna** Semi-circular knee-length cape fastened in center front or on right shoulder by a FIBULA (pin). Worn by ancient Romans from 2nd c. B.C. to A.D. 5th c. Made of wool in white, natural, amethyst, and purple decorated with gold.

**lacet** Term for a braid of silk or cotton woven in various widths, frequently with looped edges. Used for trimming and edging, and sometimes combined with crochet work or tatting.

**Lachasse** See APPENDIX/DESIGNERS.

**lacing studs** Oval brass hooks, rather than eyelets, used on boots since 1897 for speed skating. Also see SPEED LACING.

**Lacoste®** See KNIT SHIRTS.

**lacquer** (lak-er) **1.** Orange-red color of lacquer used by Chinese. **2.** Fingernail polish.

**Lacroix, Christian** See APPENDIX/DESIGNERS.

**ladder braid** See BRAIDS.

**ladrine** See LANDRINE.

**Lagerfeld, Karl** See APPENDIX/DESIGNERS.

**La Goulue** See POMPADOUR under HAIRSTYLES.

**laid embroidery** See EMBROIDERIES.

**laid fabric** Type of nonwoven fabric made with warp yarns and no filling yarns. Warp yarns are held together by latex rubber or another type of adhesive.

**laisse-tout-faire** Long apron worn over the dress for home wear in 17th c.

**Lake George diamond** See DIAMONDS.

**Lalique, René** (la-leak, Rah-nay) (1860–1945) Presented at Salon du Champ de Mara

in Paris in 1895 such unique and artistic jewelry that he became known as the foremost *Art Nouveau* jeweler-artist. He used subjects, *e.g.*, the snake, owl, octopus, and bat set with blue-green colored stones including opals to carry out his highly personalized jewelry. Also used mysterious female figures carried out in enamel, ivory, vitreous paste, or engraved glass to obtain pictorial effects.

**lamba** A long, narrow piece of white or striped material worn wrapped around the shoulders like a SCARF or SHAWL by women of Madagascar. Wrapped from the right arm across the back, over the left shoulder, across the front of the body, over the right shoulder and hung to the knees in back.

**lamballe bonnet** (lam-bahl) Saucer-shaped straw bonnet of mid-1860s worn flat on head with sides pulled down slightly and tied under chin with large ribbon bow. Some had lace LAPPETS, others had small *veils* in back called CURTAINS.

**lamboy** See TONLET.

**lambskin** See LEATHERS and FURS.

**lame** (lah-may) **1.** Armor composed of thin overlapping plates used for a GAUNTLET. **2.** (*lamé*) Textile fabric with metallic yarns woven to form either the background or the pattern. May be made in Jacquard or rib weave. In the 1930s metallic yarns tarnished and became black. Now they are frequently coated with a fine polyester film which prevents tarnishing. **3.** Knitted fabric made with metallic yarns. *Der.* French, *lamé*, "leaves of silver or gold."

**laminated fabric** **1.** "Sandwich-type" fabric made by a process permanently securing polyester foam to back of a fabric. **2.** Layers of fabric bonded together with resins under heat and compression.

**lampas du japon** French silk brocade fabric with ribs in the warp. Used for dresses, evening coats, and gowns.

**lampshade beads** See BEADS.

**landlady shoe** See WOOLWORTH® shoe under SHOES.

**landrine** Louis XIII boot with wide flared cuff reaching halfway up leg with top turned up for riding horseback. Also called *lazarine*. Also spelled *ladrine*.

**Lane, Kenneth Jay** See APPENDIX/DESIGNERS.

**langet** **1.** Term used for a *thong* or *lacer* used to fasten garments together in 15th c. Also see POINTS. **2.** Plume worn on a knight's helmet.

**langettes** Term for string of beads in 16th c.

**Langtry bustle** Woman's patented, lightweight collapsible bustle, worn in late 1880s. Made of a series of semicircular hoops fastened to a *stay* on either side. *Der.* Named after actress *Lillie Langtry*.

**Langtry hood** Detachable hood on woman's outdoor garment of 1880s with a colored lining. *Der.* Named after actress *Lillie Langtry*.

**Langtry, Lillie** (1852–1929) Famous British actress and beauty born on the Isle of Jersey, located in English Channel. Also called the "Jersey Lily." Popularized the *jersey costume* and gave her name to many items of apparel. See LANGTRY BUSTLE and LANGTRY HOOD.

**languette** (lang-get) Flat, tongue-shaped piece of cloth appliquéd as trimming on woman's cloak or skirt, either singly or in series, from 1818 to 1822. *Der.* French, *langue*, "tongue."

**languti** Fabric used for DHOTIS in India.

**lansdown** Fine soft lightweight fabric woven in a twill weave in such a manner that the silk warp yarns appear on the face of the fabric and the cotton or worsted filling yarns appear on the reverse side. Also spelled *lansdowne*.

**lantern sleeve** See SLEEVES.

**Lanvin, Jeanne** See APPENDIX/DESIGNERS.

**lanyard** Cord, usually braided in contrasting colors, used suspended around neck or from belt to hold an accessory such as a whistle or pocket knife.

**lapel** Turned-back front section of blouse, jacket, coat or shirt where it joins the collar. Each side folds back to form REVERS, or LAPELS which are cut in different shapes.

LAPELS NOTCHED PEAKED L-SHAPED CLOVERLEAF FISHMOUTH

**lapels** Types include *cloverleaf*—both collar and lapel are rounded where they meet. *Fishmouth*—with lapel cut slanted and collar rounded. *L-shaped*—with lapel cut straight across and narrow collar rounded. *Notched*—with lapel cut slanted and collar having a notch; also called notched collar. *Peaked*—with V-shaped ending at lapel and collar fitting into it.

**lapidary** Person who specializes in cutting of gems other than diamonds. Same as a *gem cutter*.

**lapin** French word for rabbit. Not used in the U.S. except in a descriptive form, *e.g.*, lapin-processed rabbit.

**lapis lazuli** See GEMS.

**la pliant** (la plee-awnt) Invention of 1896 for holding out back of skirt by inserting steel strips in casings eliminating the need for many petticoats. *Der.* French, "flexible."

**lapot** Crude laced shoes made of the inner bark of the birch or lime tree formerly worn by peasants in Russia.

**lappets** **1.** See FANONS. **2.** 18th- and 19th-c.

term for drapery or long ribbon-like strips of fabric often lace trimmed, hanging at sides or back of an indoor cap.

**lapponica**   See PONCHOS.

**lap seam**   See SEAMS.

**large**   Size used along with *small; medium,* and *extra large* for men, women, and children in such categories as: *gloves, girdles, knit shirts, nightgowns, pajamas, panty girdles, robes, shirts, sport jackets,* and *sweaters.* Abbreviation is *L.*

**Laroche, Guy**   See APPENDIX/DESIGNERS.

**last**   Carved wooden or molded plastic form on which a shoe is made. There is a right and left form for each pair in each size. A *combination last* has heel of narrower width than toe.

**Lastex® yarn**   Trademark of Uniroyal for yarn with a central core of Lastex wrapped with other fibers for use in woven or knitted fabrics. High in elasticity, it is used for bathing suits, girdles, foundations, and bras.

**lasting**   **1.** Fabric made in various widths used mainly for shoe and bag linings. Made of tightly twisted cotton or worsted yarns in the twill weave, it is strong and durable. **2.** Another variety of fabric made in plain weave is piece-dyed and given a stiff finish, and is exported to the Philippine Islands and South America to use for trousers.

**lasting boots**   Term for late 19th c. boots made with black cashmere uppers.

**latch buckle**   Round, square, or oblong metal plates attached to each end of belt and closed over one another. A swivel from one end of belt slips through a slot in the other end and turns to fasten.

**latchet**   Term used from Middle Ages on for strap used to fasten a shoe.

**latex**   Rubber in natural or synthetic liquid form which may be extruded or cast to form core of elastomeric yarn. May be used bare or wrapped with another textile yarn.

**lattice**   Decorative openwork made from crossed pieces of fabric, leather, or *bias binding.* Pieces are crossed at right angles to look similar to "lattice work" on old houses. Used for decorative trimming on clothing and shoes.

**Laura Ashley**   See LOOKS and PRINTS.

**laurel wreath**   Symbol of victory worn by victorious Caesars of Rome and Olympic athletes of Greece.

**Lauren, Ralph**   See APPENDIX/DESIGNERS.

**lava-lava**   **1.** Rectangular piece of colored printed cloth worn as a skirt or loincloth as the principal item of clothing for men and women of Polynesia. Adaptations popular in U.S. as beach fashion in 1950s. Also called *pareu.* **2.** Plain woven, highly sized cotton fabric printed in Great Britain in special designs for export to South Sea Islands where it is used for dresses.

**lavaliere**   *Der.* Named after François Louise de la Baume Le Blanc La Vallière, mistress of Louis XIV of France. See NECKLACES.

**lavender**   **1.** Perfume of lavender, a fragrant European mint, with a pale-purple flower. **2.** A pale-purple color.

**Laver, James**   Outstanding English fashion historian and writer who developed theories on relation of costume to advancement of society. Head of the British Museum's costume division for many years. Has written many historical and philosophical books on fashion from 1937 to 1983. Some of these titles include: *Dress* (1950), *Costume* (1963), *Modesty in Dress* (1969), and *Costume and Fashion* (1983). Also see ANDROGYNOUS.

**lawn**   **1.** Sheer, lightweight, high-count cotton fabric made in a plain weave of fine combed yarns. May be dyed or printed, given a soft or a starched finish, and calendered. **2.** Basic fabric called by other names when given different finishes—called *organdy* where given a stiff finish. Originally it was a fine linen fabric made in

Laon, France. Used mainly for handkerchiefs. Also see HANDKERCHIEF LAWN.

**LAWN-PARTY DRESS, 1896**

**lawn-party dress** Afternoon dress suitable for an outdoor reception in 1890s, frequently made with CHOKER collar, GORED full-length skirt, and sash at waist. Worn with floppy straw hat trimmed with flowers, ribbon, and veiling.

**lawn-tennis apron** Drab-colored bib apron worn for tennis by women in 1880s with skirt pulled up on left side and draped at back where there was a large patch pocket for holding tennis balls. Another pocket was placed low on the right side of the skirt. Both pockets were decorated with embroidery.

**lawn-tennis costume** Woman's fitted jacket and full skirt coming to boot tops made with bustle-back. Sometimes embroidered with racquets and tennis balls at hem. Worn by women for playing tennis in the 1880s. See TENNIS CLOTHES for listing of modern clothing.

**layered** Adjective used from late 1960s for clothing and sleeves of varying lengths worn one on top of the other. See HAIRSTYLES, LOOKS, and SKIRTS.

**layette** Garments and accessories collected by prospective mother for a new baby. Includes such items as diapers, *sacques*, and *undershirts*—formerly included *pinning blankets* and *gertrudes*.

**lazarine** See LANDRINE.

**lazy daisy stitch** See STITCHES.

**L.B.D.** Abbreviation for *little black dress*. See BASIC DRESS under DRESSES.

**LCD quartz watch** See WATCHES.

**lea** **1.** Measure for linen yarn which has been wet spun—based on 300 yards weighing one pound. Twelve *leas* make a *hank* and 16½ hanks or 200 leas make a *bundle*. **2.** A unit of length for other yarns, *e.g.*, for *cotton* or *spun silk*, 120 yards equals a *lea*; for *worsted*, 80 yards equals a *lea*.

**leading strings** Term used in the 17th and 18th c. for long narrow ribbons or strips of fabric attached to shoulders of children's

**LAWN-TENNIS COSTUME**

dresses, developed from *hanging sleeves* or *tippets*. Used to guide child when learning to walk. Also called *tatas*. Also see HANGING SLEEVE #2.

**leaf**   British term for turned-down part of a *stand-fall* or *rolled collar*.

**leather**   Skin or hide of an animal with the hair removed and the grain revealed by process of tanning. Usually dyed and finished by *glazing*, *buffing*, *embossing*, or *sueding*. Sometimes split into several layers with top layer called the *grain*, others called *splits*. Leather has been used for shoes and clothing since primitive times, *e.g.*, buckskins in Colonial America. Now used extensively for all types of clothing including coats, jackets, skirts, vests, pants, suits, handbags, shoes, and other accessories. Also used as trim on fabric apparel. Fabric and vinyl used as a substitute for leather must be labeled "manmade materials." Real leather may be labeled "genuine leather." In alphabetical listing see ALUM, CHROME, COMBINATION, and VEGETABLE TANNING.

### ▰▰▰▰ LEATHERS ▰▰▰▰

**alligator**   Leather from alligators with characteristic markings of blocks, rectangles, and circles with cross markings between. Used for shoes, handbags, and belts. Law passed by Congress in 1970 prohibited use in U.S., later rescinded.

**alligator lizard**   Leather from a large lizard with markings like grains of rice and elongated blocks, similar in appearance to hides of small alligators.

**antelope**   Rare soft velvety leather made from antelope skins, usually sueded. Used for fine shoes, bags, and jackets.

**box calf**   Calf that has been boarded in two directions to give it squared markings on the grain side.

**Bucko® calf**   Trade name for cattlehides processed to look like buckskin for shoe uppers.

**buckskin**   Deer or elk skins with the grain given a suede finish similar to early skins cured by native Americans. Second *splits* of deerskin must be called *split deerskin* or *split buckskin*.

**cabretta**   Fine, smooth, tight-grained leather made from Brazilian sheepskins used mainly for women's dressy gloves.

**calf/calfskin**   Supple, fine-grained, strong leather from skins of cattle a few days to a few weeks old finished in many ways, *e.g.*, glazed, sueded, boarded, embossed, waxed, or made into patent leather. Used for shoes, handbags, belts, and wallets. Best qualities come from the U.S.

**capeskin**   Light, flexible fine-grained leather made from skin of the South African hair sheep. *Der.* Frequently shipped from Capetown, South Africa, hence the name.

**carpincho**   Leather tanned from a water rodent. Often sold as pigskin and used mainly for sport gloves.

**cattlehide**   Heavy leather, usually vegetable-tanned, from cow, bull, and steer hides. Used for sole leather. Also called *cowhide*.

**chamois skin**   Originally leather made from an Alpine goat or chamois; now undersplits of sheepskins which are oil-dressed and suede-finished are correctly called by this name.

**cordovan**   Durable, almost completely non-porous leather, made from the shell of horse-butts used for uppers of fine men's shoes. It is given a characteristic waxy finish in black and reddish-brown colors. *Der.* Named for Cordoba, Spain, where tanning of leather was highly perfected under the Arabs.

**cowhide**   See CATTLEHIDE.

**crocodile** Thick-skinned leather, from a large water reptile, characterized by black markings and a scaly horny surface; very similar to *alligator.*

**deerskin** See BUCKSKIN.

**doeskin** Trade term for sheepskin and lambskin tanned by the alum or formaldehyde processes. When finished white, often used for gloves. When tanned by *chamois process,* used mainly for jackets and vests.

**embossed l.** Leather impressed with engraved metal rollers to imitate another leather, *e.g., alligator, lizard* or *snakeskin.*

**French antelope lambskin** Lambskin, tanned in France, that has been given a lustrous suede finish to make it look like antelope skin.

**French kid** Originally KIDSKIN imported from France, now refers to any alum- or vegetable-tanned kidskin which resembles the original.

**frog** Leather with a distinctive grain and pattern made from the skin of a species of giant frog found in Brazil. Limited in availability and used for women's accessories and trimmings. May be simulated by *embossing* other leathers and called *frog-grained leathers.*

**galuchat** Leather made from tough outer layer of sharkskin. Used for handbags and novelty items.

**glazé kid** Kidskin given a very shiny surface by means of heavy rollers. Also called *glazed kidskin. Der.* French, "shiny."

**goatskin** Leather made from the skin of the goat. Used for gloves, shoe uppers, and handbags. Also see KIDSKIN.

**horsehide** A durable fine-grained leather from horses and colts. Usually imported and used flesh side up with grain used for inside surface of shoe uppers. Also see CORDOVAN LEATHER.

**hunting calf** See REVERSE CALF.

**Java lizard** Lizard skins with black, white, and gray coloring. Imported from Java in Indonesia, and used for handbags, shoes, and belts.

**kangaroo** Durable scuff-resistant leather made from kangaroo and wallaby hides. Similar to KIDSKIN in appearance and imported mainly from Australia.

**kid/kidskin** Leather made from young goat skins. Used for women's shoe uppers, handbags, belts, and fine gloves.

**lambskin** Leather made from skin of a young sheep.

**lizard** Reptile leather with pattern similar to grains of rice. Often named for place of origin in India and Java. Used for shoe uppers, handbags, belts, and ornamental trimmings.

**mocha** Fine-sueded glove leather made from skins of blackhead or whitehead sheep from Somaliland, Sudan, and Egypt. Used for women's fine gloves and shoes.

**Moroccan 1.** Fancy goatskins with a pebbly grain, often dyed red. Originally tanned in Morocco and mainly used for handbags and slippers. See HANDBAGS.

**napa** Glove leather from sheepskins or lambskins of domestic New Zealand or South American origin that have been tanned by *chrome, alum,* or *combination methods.*

**ostrich** Leather with a distinctive rosette pattern caused by removal of plumes from ostrich skins. Used for fine shoes and handbags.

**patent l.** Leather processed on the grain side to form a bright hard brittle surface. Done by degreasing, stretching on frames, coating with paint and linseed oil, then alternately baking in the sun and rubbing with pumice stone. Vinyl is used to make imitation patent leather.

**peccary** Leather processed from the skin of the wild boar of Central and South America. Used mainly for pigskin gloves.

**pigskin** Leather made from the skin of the

pig which has groups of three tiny holes forming a distinctive pattern caused by removing the bristles.

**pin seal** High-grade skins from hair seal with fine pebbly grain. Imitated widely by embossing patterns on calfskin, cowhide, goatskin, and sheepskin, and then called pin-grain calfskin, etc.

**python** Leather processed from skin of a large non-poisonous snake with medium-sized scales and distinctive markings. Available in black and white, tan and white. It is sometimes dyed bright red, yellow, blue, and other colors. Used for handbags, shoes, and trimmings.

**rawhide** Leather in natural pale beige or yellowish color made from cattlehides not actually tanned but dehaired, limed, stuffed with oil and grease. Used mainly for thongs.

**reverse calf** Calfskin finished with flesh side out, grain side inside. Called *hunting calf* in England.

**Russian 1.** Leather tanned with birch bark which has a distinctive odor. Usually finished in brown and originally from Russia. Term now used for any similar brown calfskin.

**saddle 1.** Natural tan leather made from vegetable tanned steerhides or cattlehides and used for tooled-leather handbags, belts, and saddles for horses.

**sealskin** Leather made from genuine Alaska fur seal hides; rare, because the Alaska fur seal is protected by the U.S. government. Also see PIN SEAL.

**sharkskin** Almost scuff-proof leather made from the skin of certain species of sharks. The "outer armor," or *shagreen*, is removed before the skins are tanned. Used for shoes, belts, handbags, wallets, and cigarette cases. Also see GULUCHAT.

**shearling** Short curly wool skins of sheep or lambs sheared before slaughter and tanned with the wool left on. Used for slippers, gloves, coats, and jackets, with the sueded flesh side out.

**sheepskin** Leather from sheep, characterized by more than average sponginess and stretchability, frequently sueded. Small skins with fine grain are called LAMBSKINS. Used for shoes, handbags, coats, and jackets. Sheepskin tanned with wool left on is often used leather side out for coats and sport jackets. See SHEARLING.

**snakeskin** Diamond-patterned leather with overlapping scales processed from skin of a number of species of snakes, *e.g.*, diamond-backed rattlesnake, python, cobra, or boa.

**sole l.** Heavy stiff leather usually cattlehide used for the soles and built-up heels of shoes.

**split buckskin/deerskin** See BUCKSKIN.

**steerhide** Heavy leather from skins of castrated male cattle, usually used as SOLE LEATHER for shoes or to make SADDLE LEATHER.

**suede** Leather, usually lambskin, doeskin, or splits of cowhide (sometimes called REVERSE CALF) that has been buffed on the flesh side to raise a slight nap. Sometimes buffed on grain side or on both sides of a split to cover small defects. Used for skirts, pants, jackets, vests, and accessories.

**vici kid** Term used for all GLAZÉ KID. Formerly trade term for a chrome tanning process.

**wallaby** Leather made from the skins of small species of kangaroo family. Similar to KANGAROO LEATHER but sometimes finer grained.

---

**leatherette** Misnomer for fabrics made in imitation of leather.

**leathering** Fur-industry term for using narrow strips of leather between strips of fur in order to make the fur less bulky and give it a more graceful hang.

**leather jerkin**   See BUFF COAT.

**Le Canned Dress®**   See DRESSES.

**Lectra-Sox®**   Trademark of Timely Products Corp, for *electric socks.* See SOCKS.

**Lederhosen**   See SHORTS.

**le dernier cri**   French, "the last word," the utmost in fashion.

**le dernier mode**   French, "the latest fashion."

**Leek button**   Shank-type button with metal edge surrounding a metal shell or mold of pasteboard made at Leek, England, and patented in 1842.

**left-hand twill weave**   See TWILL WEAVE.

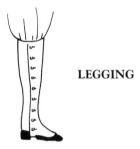

**LEGGING**

**legging**   Covering for leg and ankle extending to knee or sometimes secured by stirrup strap under arch of foot. Worn in 19th c. by armed services and by civilian men. See PUTTEE and GAITER. Worn by women in suede, patent, and fabric in late 1960s.

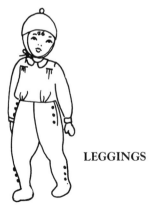

**LEGGINGS**

**leggings**   Outer *pants* for children worn in cold weather. Made with tight-fitting legs and usually matched to a coat making a leggings set. Also spelled *leggins.* See PANTS.

**leghorn**   **1.** Fine, smooth straw braid plaited with thirteen strands. Made from upper part of wheat stalks grown near Livorno, a town in Tuscany, Italy. **2.** Any style woman's hat made of *leghorn straw.*

**legionnaire's cap**   See KEPI under CAPS.

**leg-of-mutton/leg-o'mutton sleeve**   See SLEEVES.

**Legroux, House of**   See APPENDIX/DESIGNERS.

**legwarmers**   Knitted coverings for legs extending from the ankle to the knee or above. Originally worn by ballet and toe dancers when exercising. In the 1980s became a fashion item—worn for "looks" as well as warmth.

**lei** (lay)   See NECKLACES.

**Leicester jacket**   Englishman's suit or lounge jacket with *raglan sleeves.* Worn in 1857.

**leisure bra**   See BRAS.

**leisure suit**   See SUITS.

**Lelong, Lucien**   See APPENDIX/DESIGNERS.

**length**   Lower edge of item of apparel—the hem of a coat, jacket, skirt, or dress. Dresses were generally floor length until World War I. In late 1920s they were knee length; dropping in the 1930s to calf length. Knee length again in the early 1940s, and dropping in 1947 to below the calf. In late 1960s the MINI, MAXI and MIDI lengths were introduced. Since then, skirt length has become a matter of personal choice rather than being dictated by fashion. In the 1980s skirts of all lengths from ankle length to mini-length were worn.

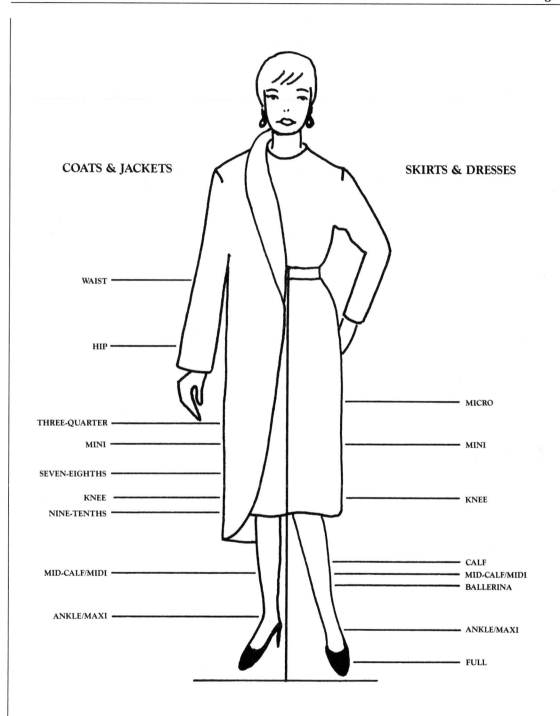

**COATS & JACKETS**

**SKIRTS & DRESSES**

WAIST

HIP

MICRO

THREE-QUARTER

MINI

MINI

SEVEN-EIGHTHS

KNEE

KNEE

NINE-TENTHS

CALF

MID-CALF/MIDI

MID-CALF/MIDI

BALLERINA

ANKLE/MAXI

ANKLE/MAXI

FULL

# LENGTHS

**ankle l.**   Length which clears the floor by a few inches reaching to the ankle. Popular for evening dresses, daytime skirts, coats, and pants since the late 1960s. Same as MAXI LENGTH.

**ballerina l.**   Skirt reaching to the center of the calf of the leg or a little below, worn particularly by ballet dancers. Popular for evening dresses in the late 1940s and 1950s.

**calf l.**   Hem of skirt, dress, or coat reaching below the knee at the widest part of the calf. Compare with MIDI LENGTH, which is longer. Most popular length during 1930s, 1950s, and early 1980s.

**chapel-length train**   Skirt made with back cut longer, ending in a short train of about one yard, primarily used for informal wedding dresses.

**full l.**   Term indicated floor length. Most dresses were this length until early part of the 20th c. Evening gowns were floor length until late 1940s.

**hip l.**   Popular length for suit coats for men and women, ending at hip bone.

**knee l.**   Skirt or coat reaching to the middle of the knee cap or to the top of the knee.

**longuette**   Term coined by *Women's Wear Daily* in January 1970 to describe the radically longer lengths on coats, skirts, and dresses reaching from below-the-knee to ankle-length that were an abrupt change from the miniskirts of the late 1960s. Styles were introduced simultaneously in Paris and New York. *Der.* French diminutive for "long."

**maxi l.**   Term coined in 1968 for hem of dress, skirt, or coat reaching to the ankles, worn for daytime. Also see ANKLE LENGTH, COATS, DRESSES, SILHOUETTES, and SKIRTS.

**micro l.**   Dress or skirt reaching to upper thigh; an exaggerated mini. Worn by ultra-mod young girls in the late 1960s.

**midi l.**   Mid-calf length introduced for coats and dresses in 1967. *Der.* Term coined by *Women's Wear Daily.*

**mini l.**   (minn-ee) Dresses, skirts and coats reaching to mid-thigh, introduced in England in the early 1960s as part of mod fashions, with credit for introduction often going to Mary Quant, the English designer. In late 1960s became an accepted fashion in U.S.

**nine-tenths l.**   Coat length made a few inches shorter than the dress or suit worn underneath.

**seven-eighths l.**   Woman's coat length made several inches shorter than the dress or suit it covers. Popular for coats and *redingotes* in the 1940s and 1950s.

**three-quarter l.**   Woman's coat or jacket approximately halfway between hip and thigh. Popular length for jackets in the 1940s and 1950s.

**waist l.**   Jacket length reaching to the natural waistline. Fashionable length for suit jacket used at intervals since 1890s. Also a popular length for a jacket matched to a dress from the 1930s on.

**waltz l.**   Calf length usually used for nightgowns and robes.

---

**Lennon specs**   See GLASSES.

**leno**   Net-like transparent fabric made of cotton or man-made fibers in LENO WEAVE.

**leno weave**   Open weave with two warps locking around each filling in figure-eight design, *e.g.* MARQUISETTE. Also called *doup* and *gauze weave.*

**leopard**   See FURS.

**leopard print**   See ANIMAL PRINT under PRINTS.

**LEOTARD**

**leotard**  Form-fitting one-piece knitted garment with high or low neck, long or short sleeves, and ending in brief panties. Worn alone or over ankle-length *tights* as practice garment by dancers, acrobats, and for exercising. *Der.* Named for Jules Leotard, 19th c. French aerial gymnast. Also see SHIRTS and AEROBIC ENSEMBLE under SPORT SUITS.

**Lepape**  (1887–?)  An illustrator who studied at École des Beaux Arts and became famous when asked by Paul Poiret, Parisian couturier, to illustrate his publication *Les Chose de Paul Poiret* in 1911. After that his fashion drawings were in demand by periodicals such as *Gazette du Bon Ton, Vanity Fair, Femina, Harper's Bazaar,* and *Vogue.* Did many covers for *Vogue* during the 1920s and early 1930s. Also designed sets and costumes for plays. He used bold color with original and inventive designs rather than naturalistic portrayals in his fashion illustrations. He was influenced by the *Ballets Russes,* and famous artists of that time. Also see IRIBE.

**Leroy**  See ROY, HIPPOLYTE under APPENDIX/ DESIGNERS.

**Leser, Tina**  See APPENDIX/DESIGNERS.

**let-out**  See LETTING OUT.

**letter/letterman sweater**  See SWEATERS.

**lettice**  Term used for *ermine* or *miniver,* specifically white ermine or other white or gray fur, in 16th and 17th c.

**lettice cap/bonnet**  **1.** 16th c. term for woman's outdoor cap or bonnet of triangular shape that covered the ears. Made of *lettice,* a fur resembling ermine. **2.** In 16th and 17th c., man's nightcap of lettice fur worn to induce sleep. Also called *ermine cap* or *miniver cap.*

**lettice ruff**  Ruff of 17th c. made with flattened convolutions that looked like crinkled lettuce leaves. Also see CABBAGE RUFF. *Der.* Old spelling of "lettuce."

**letting-in**  Fur-industry term for process of intricate cutting and resewing a fur skin to make it shorter and broader.

**letting-out**  Fur-industry term for process of intricate cutting and sewing a fur skin to make it longer and narrower. The pelt is cut down center back, slit into tiny diagonal pieces, and each piece dropped when joined to next pieces. Process makes the pelt long enough that a skin may extend from neck to hem of the garment. Also called *dropping.*

**Letty Lynton dress**  Dresses styled by ADRIAN and worn by Joan Crawford in the 1932 MGM film *Letty Lynton.* One particular style was fitted to the hips with a full skirt, the outstanding feature being very full balloon sleeves covered with ruffles. Another style designed for the movie was a slim sheath, tight to the knees, with a halter neckline and flaring trumpet skirt. *Der. Letty Lynton,* a film of 1932.

**levantine**  **1.** Glazed cotton fabric in a twill weave with a high count made with combed yarns used for linings. Originally made of silk and imported to Great Britain from the Levant, an area surrounding the eastern end of

Mediterranean and Aegean Sea. **2.** An early 19th-c. velvet.

**leviathan** Soft woolen yarn used for embroidery and knitting.

**Levi's®** See PANTS.

**levite gown** See GOWN À LA LEVATINE.

**lhenga** (ee-heng-a) Short, full skirt worn by Hindu women in India.

**liars** Wire framework worn during latter half of 18th c. under the *fichu*, to give the effect of a larger bosom. Also called *menteurs* and *trompeurs*.

**libas** Knee-length or full-length full *trousers* worn by contemporary Egyptian men as part of native dress.

**Liberty®** Trademark for Liberty Ltd., a London fabric manufacturer which produces cotton prints called *Liberty Prints*. Also produces a *Liberty Satin*, and *Liberty Lawn*, and some silk fabrics. All have the trademark attached.

**liberty cap** Red wool peaked-top cap worn by Roman slaves when freed. Later adopted as a symbol of liberty in the U.S. and by French Revolutionists of the 1790s. Compare with PILEUS and PHRYGIAN CAP. Also called BONNET ROUGE. *Der.* Worn as a symbol of liberty.

**liberty stripes** See HICKORY STRIPES under STRIPES.

**life mask** See MASKS.

**lift** The replaceable part on the bottom of the heel of the shoe. Also called *heel lift*. Also see HEELS.

**light jack boots** See JACK BOOTS #2.

**Lille lace** See LACES.

**Lilly®** Trademark for a simple printed-cotton shift dress designed and sold by Lilly Pulitzer of Palm Beach, Florida, from late 1960s. Pulitzer began designing these printed dresses after spilling orange juice on her dress. Company was liquidated in mid-1980s. Also see PULITZER, LILLY under APPENDIX/DESIGNERS.

**lily Benjamin** Colloquial term for man's white overcoat worn by workmen in first half of 19th c. Also see BENJAMIN.

**Limerick gloves** Short or long *lambskin* gloves made from very young or unborn lambs. Worn by women during latter half of 18th and first half of 19th c.

**limousine** **1.** Full-length circular woman's evening cape of late 1880s with shirring around neck so fullness falls in folds over the arms forming sleeves. **2.** Hairy, rough woolen fabric produced in England in last quarter of 19th c. It was thicker, heavier and coarser than *cheviot*. **3.** Striped *herringbone* fabric made in England of worsted yarn. Fulled and napped, sometimes with fancy loop yarns added for decoration.

**Lincoln lamb** See FURS.

**Lindbergh jacket** Waist-length heavy woolen or leather jacket with large pockets, lapels, and rolled collar. Made with waistband and cuffs of stretchable rib-knit wool. *Der.* Type of jacket worn by Colonel Charles A. Lindbergh, who made the first solo flight from New York to Paris across the Atlantic in 1927.

**line** See COLLECTION.

**linecloths, pair of** Linen *drawers* worn by men in the 15th c.

**line fibers** See LINEN.

**line-for-line copy** American interpretations of Parisian and Italian couture dresses made expressly for American stores. The retail dress buyer may purchase a *toile*, or pattern, for the dress from the original designer in Paris. May also purchase the identical fabric, but the dress is produced and sold in America at a much lower price than the Parisian original. Compare with KNOCK-OFF.

**lineman's boot** See BOOTS.

**linen** **1.** Fibers of the flax plant, either the short fibers called *tow* or the longer fibers called *line*, used to make linen yarn. **2.** Fabrics made of linen yarns in many qualities and many weights which are cooler, stronger, and more absorbent than cotton. Finishing processes may include beetling (to make the yarns appear flatter), bleaching, dyeing, and printing. Non-crush finishes are frequently applied to dress linen and crease-resistant linen fabrics. Softer finishes are used for handkerchiefs. *Der.* French, *linge*, "linen."

**linen cambric**    See CAMBRIC.

**linen canvas    1.** Firm linen fabric used as an interfacing for collars and fronts of jackets and coats. Contains no sizing and must be completely shrinkproof to permit dry cleaning or washing. Also called *tailor's canvas.* **2.** An open-work fabric with large spaces between yarns used for embroidery purposes. Also called *Java canvas* and *aida canvas.*

**linen crash**    Fabric with an uneven textured effect usually made with yarn-dyed yarns, particularly a white and black combination. Woven in the plain weave of a combination of linen and cotton yarns. Extremely popular for *knickers* in the 1920s.

**line yarn**    Linen yarn made of longer fibers as differentiated from *tow* which uses the shorter length linen fibers. See LINEN.

**lingerie** (lan-zha-ree)    **1.** Collective term for women's underwear including SLIPS, NIGHT-GOWNS, PANTIES, and BRAS. Sometimes called *intimate apparel* by the trade. **2.** Fabric used for underwear from Middle Ages to 20th c. *Der.* French, *linge*, "linen," as originally of linen.

**lingerie crepe**    Flat smooth lightweight silky crepe originally made of crepe-twisted silk yarns in France and called *French crepe.* Now used in rayon, acetate, nylon, and blends for slips and other lingerie. Yarns are not as tightly twisted as originally and all are twisted in the same direction. Also see FRENCH CREPE.

**lingerie hem**    See HEMS.

**lining**    Fabric, pile fabric, or fur used to finish inside of garment. The extra layer is used for warmth, to retain shape of outer layer, or for appearance. Fashion for stiff or limp linings fluctuates. Use of linings popular for dresses in first quarter of 20th c. and in 1950s. Unlined garments prevalent in 1920s and 1930s, and again from 1960s through 1980s. See HALF LIN-ING and ZIP-IN/ZIP-OUT LINING.

**linked**    See DRESSES.

**lion's tail**    See HAIRSTYLES.

**lipstick    1.** A crayon-like stick of lip coloring, usually in a metal or plastic tube. **2.** Term sometimes used to describe a bright crimson red.

**liquid embroidery**    See EMBROIDERIES.

**liripipe    1.** Long pendant tail of the *chaper-one*, a hood worn in 14th and 15th c. **2.** Part of a hood worn by graduates from 1350 to 15th c. Also spelled *liripipium, lirapipe, liripoop.* Also called *tippet.*

**lisle**    Two-ply cotton yarn made of long staple fibers which are combed, tightly twisted, and sometimes given further treatment to remove all short fuzzy fibers. Used for knitwear, hosiery, and men's undershirts. *Der.* Early spelling of Lille, France. See LISLE HOSIERY.

**lisle hosiery**    Socks and hose made of cotton *lisle*, nearly as fine as silk, usually white, brown, or black. Worn by men, women, and children throughout 19th and early 20th c. until replaced by silk in 1920s and nylon in 1940s. *Der.* Early spelling of Lille, France.

**list/listing**    See SELVAGE.

**little black dress**    See BASIC DRESS under DRESSES.

**little bodkin**    See PONYET #2.

**little-boy shorts**    See SHORTS.

**little girl look**    Style introduced in 1967 for women which imitated the dress of a 12-year-old girl. Also see LOOKS.

**Little Lord Fauntleroy suit**    Young boy's costume consisting of black velvet tunic and knee pants worn with wide sash. Blouse had wide white lace trimmed collar and cuffs, and was worn with black stockings, pumps, and shoulder-length hair. Worn by boys in U.S. for special occasions from 1886 to 1914. *Der.* Inspired by popularity of book, *Little Lord Fauntleroy*, by Mrs. Frances Hodgson Burnett published in 1886.

**Littleway shoe construction** Process of shoe construction or manufacturing which uses a staple to attach the insole to the upper. The outsole may be sewed on with a lock stitch or cemented to the insole.

**Little Women dress** Child's dress made with plain, fitted, front-buttoned bodice, short or long plain sleeves, small turned-down collar with ribbon bow tie, and full-gathered skirt. *Der.* Inspired by dresses described in Louisa May Alcott's book, *Little Women*, published in 1868.

**linked dress** See DRESSES.

**livery** Characteristic clothes or uniform worn formerly by servants, now chiefly used in reference to chauffeurs' uniforms.

**lizard** See LEATHER.

**llama** Fibers similar to *alpaca* obtained from an animal related to *camel*, native to high altitudes in Andes mountains of South America with color ranging from white, gray, and light brown to black. Outer coat of animal is coarse and under fiber is soft.

**L.L. Bean® clothes** All types of sportswear suitable for fishing, hunting, mountain climbing, bicycling, etc. Clothes and shoes are of the best quality and such items as shorts, jackets, turtleneck shirts, oxford shirts, sweaters, chino pants, and swim trunks are sold. Many of the items have become a status symbol for city wear. Clothes are sold under the trademark, L.L. Bean®, a mail-order store in Freeport, Maine, open 24 hours daily, organized by Leon Leonwood Bean (1872–1967) in 1912. The third generation of the family now heads the business.

**loafer** See SHOES.

**locket** See NECKLACES.

**lockstitch** See STITCHES.

**loden cloth** Thick, fulled, water-repellent coatings and suitings woven by people of the Tyrol, a section of Austria and Germany. Made in deep olive green color of local wool, sometimes with the addition of camel's hair. Ideal for winter sportswear, skiwear, and coats.

**loft** Term to describe the resiliency of wool and man-made fibers that imitate wool, *e.g.*, *Orlon acrylic*.

**loincloth** Garment wrapped around the lower torso by primitive people, American Indians, and ancient Egyptians; still worn in some countries. Length may vary from very short to ankle-length. Sometimes made of long piece of fabric which goes between legs and is brought up and pulled under a belt in front and back. Part of the fabric is left hanging down in front and back. Also see BREECHCLOTH, DHOTI, and LUNGI.

**London Fog® raincoat** See RAINCOATS.

**London look** Conservative elegant look for men reflecting influence of London tailors of Savile Row. See BRITISH LOOK under LOOKS.

**long-bellied doublet** See PEASCOD-BELLIED DOUBLET.

**long clothes** From second half of 17th c. the dress of infants, replacing SWADDLING CLOTHES. Dress was approximately 3 feet long, usually decorated with embroidery, and worn with a matching petticoat. A style still used for modern CHRISTENING DRESSES.

**long Duvillier** See DUVILLIER WIG.

**long handles** See LONG JOHNS.

**longhee** See LUNGI #2.

**long hood** 18th c. term for a woman's hood similar to the PUG or *short hood*. Sides were made with long tabs to facilitate tying under chin.

**long johns** Slang term for *union suit* or *thermal underwear* with long legs. Also called *long handles.*

**Long John trunks** See SWIMSUITS.

**long-leg panty girdle** See GIRDLES.

**long-line bra** See BRAS and SLIPS.

**long lock** See LOVE LOCK.

**long stocks** Stockings attached at thigh to *trunk hose* worn by men in 16th and 17th c. Also called *long stockings.*

**long-torso** Describing a garment with waistline placed near the widest part of the hips. See SILHOUETTES and TORSO under DRESSES.

**longuette** (long-get) Term coined by the fashion-industry newspaper, *Women's Wear Daily*, January 1970, to describe the radically longer coats, skirts, and dresses reaching from below-the-knee to ankle-length that were an abrupt change from the miniskirts of the late 1960s. Styles were introduced simultaneously in Paris and New York. *Der.* French diminutive for "long." Also see LENGTHS.

**longyi** See LUNGI #2.

**look** Term used to describe the complete accessorized costume. Term was first introduced in 1947 with Christian Dior's *New Look* a radical change in fashion from short sheath styles made with a minimum of fabric, due to World War II restrictions on use of fabrics, to long skirts with fitted waists and tops. Since 1950s looks have been influenced by protest of the younger generations against traditional styles, social evolution, civil rights movements, and political events. Some looks evolved from clothes and accessories worn on stage, as well as movies and TV shows. Still other looks evolve from clothes and accessories worn by celebrities in the limelight, *e.g.*, Jackie Kennedy Onassis and Princess Diana of England. All looks are not worn by everyone but general trends find their way eventually into the mainstream of fashion.

### LOOKS

**Afro l.** Use of colorful African garments of either domestic or imported origin including the BUBA, DASHIKI, and SELOSO (see DRESSES) made in characteristic African prints. Hair is worn "au naturel" or an AFRO WIG is worn. Popularized in the late 1960s and early 1970s for both men and women. Also see HAIRSTYLES, NECKLACES, PRINTS, and WIGS.

**American Indian l.** Styles inspired by bead-trimmed, fringed, sueded doeskin dresses, pants, tunics, and accessories used by American Indians. Made in fabrics as well as leather with hems and sleeves cut at edges to resemble fringe. Also see BEADS, BELTS, HAIRSTYLES, NECKLACES, SHOES (INDIAN MOCCASIN), SQUAW BOOTS under BOOTS, SQUAW HANDBAG under HANDBAGS, SQUAW DRESS under DRESSES, APACHE SCARF under SCARFS, and APACHE SHIRT under SHIRTS.

**androgynous l.** (an-drodg-e-nus) Possessing both male and female characteristics. James Laver, fashion historian, says ideal fashion figure of 1920s and late 1960s and 1970s is the androgynous female who resembles a boy. Some boys of the 1970s and 1980s are also androgynous. **Women:** Illustrated in mid-1980s by return to short boyish bob hairstyles; man-tailored suits of men's wear fabrics; tailored trousers; trenchcoats, slouch hats, neckties, and button-down collars. **Men:** some men adopted more feminine styles including long hair, makeup, clothes with more drapery and more color, including kimonos, *e.g.*, Boy George, British rock singer and entertainer. Also see UNISEX LOOK.

NEW LOOK          HAREM LOOK          PUNK LOOK     ANDROGYNOUS LOOK

GAUCHO LOOK       HUNT LOOK          FLAPPER LOOK        RETRO LOOK,
                                                        EARLY 1930s

**Annie Hall l.** Look that introduced baggy pants, challis skirts, shawls, and the idea of wearing clothes in an uncoordinated manner, *e.g.*, a cowboy shirt over a long evening skirt or a silk blouse and earrings with jeans. *Der.* From the Academy Award winning movie, *Annie Hall*, 1977, by Woody Allen, starring Diane Keaton.

**aprés ski l.** Look popularized at ski resorts featuring in 1960s colorful glamorous sports-wear items such as vests of fur and native type; pants of velvet, prints, and suede; sweaters in jacquard knits; and unusual boots. Popularized first during the 1950s at famous resorts such as Sun Valley, Lake Placid, and San Moritz. With more general acceptance of skiing (due mainly to development of artificial snow), this look increased in popularity from 1960s to the 1980s. Also see BOOTS and SLIPPERS. *Der.* French, "after skiing."

**Arabian Nights l.** See HAREM LOOK.

**Art Deco l.** Geometric non-representational style of jewelry and fabric designs popular in late 1920s. Inspired by *Exposition International des Arts Décoratifs et Industriels Modernes*, Paris, 1925. Revived in late 1968, continuing into the 1980s as inspiration for fabric and jewelry design. *Der.* French, *art decoratif*, "decorative art." Also see EARRINGS, PRINTS, and HOSE.

**Art Nouveau l.** (ar noo-vo) Decorative style popular for jewelry and fashion from late 19th to early 20th c. and reintroduced in late 1960s and 1980s for fabric and jewelry designs. Characterized by use of natural forms in curving, stylized designs of climbing vines, leaves, flowers, and women's long hair. *Der.* French, "new art." Also see HOSE.

**attic l.** Term introduced in early 1970s for old clothes and accessories found in the attics of old houses. Also see FLEA MARKET and VINTAGE LOOKS.

**baby doll l.** **1.** Childish look with dress (and sometimes coat) styled with gathers or pleats hanging from a tiny yoke. Accessories included baby doll shoes, with straps over instep and CHARLIE CHAPLIN toes, and mini purses on long chains. Carried over to very short pajamas and nightgowns. *Der.* Term used to refer to clothing and accessories used for children's dolls and infants' clothes in the early 20th c. Popularity enhanced by movie *Baby Doll* (1956) in which Carroll Baker played the lead. **2.** Look revived in 1986 by Vivienne Westwood, English designer, featuring dresses similar to children's and dolls' dresses of 1930s and 1940s some with collars and cuffs and wide belts, others with full skirts over crinoline petticoats. Patou, in the fall of 1986, introduced a style with long sleeves, wrapped draped bodice sometimes worn over petticoats made with ruffles. See DRESSES, NIGHTGOWNS, PAJAMAS, SILHOUETTES, and SLEEVES.

**bare l.** Look of the 1970s, continuing in 1980s, baring various parts of the body. Achieved by tiny halters, tiny bikinis, halter necklines on dresses and evening gowns, bare-midriff styles, and low, plunging décolletage. Achieved by *cutouts* and tiny halters. Also see TOPS and TOPLESS LOOK.

**bare midriff l.** Fashion originating in tropical countries consisting of two-piece dress with top ending under the bust, baring the ribs, with skirt or pants starting at waistline or low-slung. Introduced in the U.S. in the late 1920s and early 1930s, popularized by Carmen Miranda, revived in the 1960s and 1980s following interest in fashions of India, mainly the CHOLI and SARI. See BLOUSES and DRESSES.

**big l.** See V-LOOK.

**Bonnie and Clyde l.** Look becoming popular in 1967 which was a revival of the 1930s silhouette with late-1960s, above-the-knee, skirt length. Characteristics included three-piece suit with V-neck, long waistline, and unbuttoned jacket; pinstriped *gangster suits*; and the beret worn on the side of the head. *Der.* Named after movie by the same name with costumes designed by Theadora Van Runkel.

**Boy George l.** See ANDROGYNOUS LOOK.

**British l.** **1.** Conservative elegant look for men reflecting the influence of London tailors of Savile Row included narrow shoulders, three-button suit coats with narrow lapels, and narrow trousers without cuffs popular in 1960s. **2.** Current mode of men's wear as reflected by London tailors of Savile Row, a street in London's West End where many of the finest men's custom tailoring shops are located, catering to wealthy internationals, stressing quality and conservatism since Henry Poole & Co. opened in 1843. Also called *London look* and *Savile Row look.*

**Brooks Brothers® l.** **1.** Traditional well-tailored look of successful businessman featuring items such as button-down collar, Ivy League suit, trenchcoat, balmacaan coat, as sold by *Brooks Brothers®*, a famous New York specialty store. **2.** Women's classics including tailored suits, shirts with button-down collars, and tailored skirts. *Der.* Trade name and name of famous store in New York City originally catering only to men.

**Carnaby l.** Look popularized in London first in connection with the mod look. Introduced in U.S. in 1964 it featured such items as mini-skirts; capes for men; polka dot shirts with large flat white collars; low-slung, bell-bottomed trousers; newsboy caps; and wide vinyl neckties one day—stringbean ties the next. Started the trend by young men away from traditional styling, influenced skirt lengths for women, and also influenced styling of children's wear. *Der.* After Carnaby Street, a London back street, behind the grand shopping thoroughfare of Regent Street, where these fashions originated. Also called *mod look.* Also see COLLARS.

**casual l.** Informal look of pants with shirts and sport jackets. **1. Men:** Look started with the introduction of the sport shirt in the mid-1930s. Gained much impetus with general acceptance of Bermudas in the 1950s. Received another impetus with mod fashions of the 1960s particularly with the younger generation. **2. Women:** Look started in the 1930s for clothes suitable for spectator sportswear. Later accepted as business dress. From the 1960s a term used for the pants look for day and evening as opposed to business and town suits for day and formal or semiformal wear for evening.

**Chelsea l.** A changing variety of looks centering around King's Road in London worn by the Chelsea Set as a uniform and imitated other places. In late 1940s and 1950s, it was tight jeans from U.S. In the late 1960s, old uniforms including nurses' or policemen's uniforms, red guardsmen's tunics, and navy overcoats were all featured. Trends changed from time to time and were usually copied in other countries as items chosen by this group had wide influence on general fashion trends. Also see COLLARS and BOOTS.

**Chinese l.** Adaptations of Chinese styles in U.S. for many years including items such as COOLIE COATS and HATS, CHINESE PAJAMAS, MANDARIN COATS, MANDARIN NECKLINES, and Chinese dresses with side slit called CHEONGSAM. When China opened its doors to West in early 1970s there was a revival of interest in Chinese fashions resulting in such styles as the basic worker's suit—or MAO SUIT, quilted jackets, the CHINESE SHOE, and denim coolie coats. St. Laurent featured Chinese ensembles in 1977 which included small versions of red coolie hats, coolie-type jackets of red and gold brocade with frog closings and mandarin collars; pants which tapered to hem worn with boots having flared tops. Also see COATS, DRESSES, HATS, HAIRSTYLES, NECKLINES, PAJAMAS, and SHOES.

**classic l.** See BROOKS BROTHERS® and PREPPY LOOKS.

**cosmonaut l.** Jumpsuits and helmets reflecting this look influenced by the attention drawn to the first space astronauts. Featured by St. Laurent in 1963. Started the trend toward pantsuits and jumpsuits for women. *Der.* Russian, "astronaut." Also see LUNAR LOOK.

**country-western l.** **1.** Look initiated by country-western musicians at the Grand Ole Opry® in Nashville, Tennessee which ranges from overalls, straw hats, and gingham dresses to ultra dressy rhinestone and sequin-studded western garb as displayed by Dolly Parton, Barbara Mandrell, and Kenny Rogers. *Der.* From style of music. See WESTERN LOOK for individual items. **2.** The costumes worn by square dancers in rural U.S. which features women in dresses and skirts (sometimes gingham) with many petticoats, and men in western pants, plaid or fringed shirts, and neckerchiefs, *e.g.*, as seen on characters in the musical *Oklahoma*. *Der.* Type of dancing originating in rural U.S. usually done to the music of a fiddler. Also see SQUARE DANCE DRESS under DRESSES, SQUARE DANCE SKIRT under SKIRTS.

**Courrèges l.** Above-the-knee skirts worn with white calf-length boots. Cut of dress or skirt had hard geometric lines, standing away from the body in A-line shape. Introduced by French couturier, André Courrèges, in fall of 1963. The next year his whole collection was done in shorter length skirts. Responsible for starting the general trend in U.S. toward shorter length skirts and wearing of boots, this trend actually originated with the *mod* and *Carnaby looks*. Also see BOOTS, COATS, DRESSES, GLASSES, HELMETS, SKIRTS, SILHOUETTES, and SOCKS.

**cowpunk l.** An uncoordinated medley of PUNK and WESTERN LOOKS popularized in Los Angeles in 1986. Style includes western fringed jackets or leather jackets worn over miniskirts, chain jewelry, three western belts worn at same time, Boy George hats and hairstyles, ragged-looking shirts, all type of hairstyles including spiky, mini braids, mohawk and Indian braids. *Der.* Combination of cowgirl and punk looks.

**cuir savage** See LEATHER LOOK and WET LOOK.

**dandy l.** Similar to the Edwardian look but characterized by ruffles at neck and wrists. Worn by both men and women in the late 1960s and early 1970s. Complete costume might include an Edwardian suit with Regency collar and shirt with ruffled front and cuffs. Also see BLOUSES, SHIRTS, and EDWARDIAN LOOK.

**denim l.** Look becoming important with the acceptance of jeans for daytime and school wear in early 1970s. Matching skirts, jackets, and shorts, as well as men's tailored suits were introduced. Although denim was originally a cotton fabric, polyester and stretch fibers were combined to give a more comfortable feel and in order that pants could be worn skin tight. *Der.* From name of fabric used. Also see JEANS under PANTS, and JACKETS.

**Dolly l.** See BABY DOLL LOOK.

**dress alikes** Fashionable look for women who were friends to wear identical dresses or costumes not only in inexpensive price lines but also in designer price lines. At one designer's spring showing in 1984 11 women wore the identical suit. At a charity dinner dance 8 women appeared in identical dresses. At an evening affair 33 women appeared in beaded evening dresses designed by Fabrice—8 were identical but of different colors while the remainder were very similar variations of the same theme. This look is in opposition to former trend that women wanted to dress in an individualistic manner.

**Edwardian l.** Return to fashions of early 1900s including nipped waistlines regency collars, capes, and neck ruffles worn by both men and women. *Der.* From period 1901–1910 when Edward VII was King of England. Also see COATS, JACKETS, and SUITS.

**ethnic l.** Trend among young people in 1960s through 1980s to adopt clothing and accessories reflecting native or national styles of many countries, including many types of clothing of Africa, Asia, South America, Europe, as well as American Indian clothing. Also see AMERICAN INDIAN, GYPSY, HAREM, PEASANT, ARABIAN NIGHTS, AFRO, and KILTIE LOOKS.

**fifties l.** Retro fashion growing in popularity since mid-1970s and definitely a fashion influence in mid-1980s. Important features include nipped-in waistlines, swing skirts, ruffled petticoats, strapless bodices, high-heeled shoes, and hats. The slim *sheath silhouette* was also popular.

**flapper l.** Look reflecting style of late 1920s as pictured by cartoonist John Held Jr., described by F. Scott Fitzgerald in his novel *This Side of Paradise*. Typical styles of dresses were knee-length long-waisted blouson- and chemise-types lavishly decorated with beads. Coats were unwaisted, or long-waisted, wrap-style with exaggerated fur collars. Hair was worn in short bob frequently with brow band, and long ropes of pearls were worn. Also called *twenties style*.

**flashdance l.** Various items of dancewear adapted for fashion designed by Michael Kaplan for the 1983 movie *Flashdance*, which included loose oversized shoulder-baring sweatshirts, tank tops, cardigans, dresses, and exercise pants. Also see NECKLINES, FLASHY NIGHTSHIRT under NIGHTGOWNS, and TOPS.

**flea market l.** Old clothing and accessories adopted from former eras sold and worn as contemporary items of clothing. Flea market shops opened in Paris and England in late 1960s. In U.S. term refers to markets held outdoors. Also see ATTIC and VINTAGE LOOKS.

**funky l.** **1.** Descriptive term first used in the title of a record and later, in 1969, as a fashion term for an antique-attic look which included limp faded dresses in old-fashioned prints, accompanied with clunky platform shoes and antique-like jewelry and accessories. **2.** In 1983, the designer Kenzo used "funky factor" to describe hobo styles and baggy oversized suspender pants worn with clown-like makeup. Also called *funk fashion*.

**Ganymede l.** (gan-e-meed) Look of ancient Greece popularized in 1969 consisting of a tunic shirt slashed to hip with a one-shoulder neckline and unusual sandals which reached nearly to the knee with straps up center front and other straps around the leg. *Der.* From the Greek myth about a Greek boy named Ganymede carried off by an eagle to become a cup bearer for Zeus. Also called *Greek boy look*. Also see SANDALS.

**gaucho l.** Pant look of 1960s and 1970s with calf-length full culotte-type pants usually worn with a full-sleeved blouse, bolero, and distinctive broad-brimmed gaucho hat similar to the Spanish CORDOBES HAT. Style trend was influenced by Andalusian riding suit worn by Jacqueline Kennedy on her trip to Spain in 1966. Shown in 1967 but not widely accepted until 1969 and 1970. *Der.* Spanish, "cowboy" of Argentina, Chile, and Uruguay. Also see BELTS, BOOTS, HATS, and PANTS.

**Gibson Girl l.** Romantic look introduced in 1967 with high choker collars, tucked and lace-trimmed blouses with leg-of-mutton sleeves, gathered skirt in maxi style, and hair worn in pompadour style. Style still used in 1980s, particularly for blouses. *Der.* For Charles Dana Gibson's magazine sketches of fashionable women of the 1895–1910 era. Also see HAIRSTYLES.

**graffiti l.** Abstract designs used for clothing and accessories made by drawings on fabric, leather or vinyl; piecing bits of fabric, leather, and vinyl together and studding with fake jewels or dabbing with blobs of paint, used for *jackets, blouses, shoes, handbags,* and *belts*. Developed from copying street-art forms painted or scratched on buildings. *Der.* Latin, graffito, an ancient drawing or writing scratched on a wall or surface.

**granny l.** Introduction of ankle-length dresses for girls. Made of small calico-printed fabrics and styled with high ruffled necklines and ruffled hem. Popularized in England in early 1960s and accepted in U.S. in mid-1960s. Also adopted for sleepwear in late 1960s. Also see BLOUSES, BOOTS, DRESSES, GLASSES, NIGHT

GOWNS, GRANJAMMERS under PAJAMAS, and PRINTS. *Der.* Worn by a young person copying style worn by her grandmother or "granny."

**Greek boy l.**   See GANYMEDE LOOK.

**gypsy l.**   Colorful garments in bright shades—full skirts, blouses, scarfs, boleros, shawls, head scarfs, and hoop earrings—characteristic apparel of nomadic tribes of gypsies in Europe. A popular style for Halloween costumes since mid-19th c. and high fashion in late 1960s. Also see BLOUSES, EARRINGS, SHAWLS, and STRIPES. *Der.* Originally worn by *gypsies*, a nomadic people of Europe, Asia, and North America.

**harem l.**   Look of the Near East primarily using full ankle-length harem pants gathered at the ankle combined with blouse and bolero or in bare-midriff effect. Much jewelry and chains are used to complete the costume. Sandals are generally worn. Featured in late 1960s to 1980s. Also called *Arabian Nights look.* Also see DRESSES, PAJAMAS, PANTS, SILHOUETTES, and SKIRTS.

**Harlow l.**   Adaptation of styles of late 1920s and early 1930s including bias-cut dresses, wide-legged cuffed trousers for women, shoes, and slippers of this era. Dress was introduced in 1966, pants popularized in 1968, and shoes popular in 1969. *Der.* Named for Jean Harlow, Hollywood star of the late 1920s and 1930s. Also see SLIPDRESS under DRESSES, PANTS, SHOES and SLIPPERS.

**high tech l.**   Clothing and accessories with unusual features made of easy-care man-made fibers; polyurethane, man-made leather substitutes; clothing with built-in stretch as a result of technology of crimped yarns; water-repellent fabrics treated with modern finishes; new fabrics in neon colors that glow; and fashions made of discarded computer chips which in 1984 ranged from $2,000 to $50,000. Look represents high degree of technology in 1980s. Also see COMPUTER DRESS under DRESSES.

**hippie l.**   Disheveled look with long unkempt hair and ragged clothing. Characteristic items including: bleached and frayed jeans, tank tops, batik T-shirts, beads, ragged clothing, fringed suede vests and handbags, bare feet, and Indian headbands. Hair became longer for both sexes and young men grew bushy beards and side burns. Also see HANDBAGS, NECKLACES, and BEADS. Other items featured were the *peace symbol, love beads,* and *miniskirts.* In 1986 there was a revival of the hippie look in California.

**his and hers l.**   Garments made one for a man, the other for a woman—as distinct from "unisex-look" where garments were actually interchangeable. Popular for pajamas during the 1950s. During the late 1960s popular for all types of clothing particularly pantsuits with matching vests, caped coats, shirts, and sweaters. Also see UNISEX LOOK.

**hunt l.**   **1.** Look popularized in 1984 consisting of the wearing, for daytime or evening, of either full attire or individual items of apparel worn when riding or for a formal fox hunt, *e.g. jodhpurs* or *stirrup pants* in tweeds or flannels with a *stock shirt* or any other type blouse; *Derby* worn with *stock tie, weskit* (sometimes with sleeves), pleated trousers, and a full-length coat similar to a *Chesterfield;* a narrow midi-length skirt with side slit worn with boots and *hacking* or velvet jacket. **2.** Riding habit as worn for a formal fox hunt or hacking in Great Britain, Massachusetts, or Virginia. Also see HUNT CAP under CAPS; HUNT DERBY under HATS; BREECHES and JODHPURS under PANTS; RATCATCHER®, STOCK and ASCOT SHIRT under SHIRTS; PINK COAT under COATS; HACKING JACKET under JACKETS; RIDING BOOTS under BOOTS.

**Japanese l.**   **1.** Styles, as exemplified by Rei Kawakubo and Issey Miyake, are constructed with few seams, and are not fitted to the body—sometimes one size fits everyone. Although the basic KIMONO is not used, its "ease" is borrowed. Emphasis is also on originality of fabrics, sophisticated colors, and dramatic simplicity. Most styles are bulky, such as the 1983 style of very full harem pants shirred in front from ankle to knee, worn with a big top which has large kimono-cut sleeves. Also an oversized knee-length coat of bulky fabric which is draped in front rather than buttoned. Some styles have ASYMMETRIC NECKLINES, COLLARS, and HEMS. **2.** Style of the Japanese kimono as adapted by U.S. and European designers for dresses, robes, and sportswear. A style for negligees used since the 19th c. Also see DRESSES, ROBES, and SLEEVES.

**kiltie l.** Wearing of skirts cut like *kilts, knee socks, tams, glengarries,* plaid fabrics, and *gillie shoes,* in imitation of Scots Highlanders' garb. First adopted for boys in about 1880, revived at intervals, and fashionable since late 1960s. Also see CAPS, DRESSES, OXFORDS, PINS, PLEATS, and SKIRTS.

**Laura Ashley® l.** Style using small Victorian floral designs on cotton fabric for everything from garden overalls to nightgowns and dresses. Designed and trademarked by Laura Ashley of England, and sold in Laura Ashley stores in France, The Netherlands, Switzerland, Great Britain, and U.S. Also see PRINTS.

**layered l.** Look of several garments worn one on top of the other all being of different lengths. Popular from the late 1960s, early 1970s, and 1980s. Also see MIX AND MATCH LOOK.

**leather l.** Classic tailored look of natural, sueded, or simulated leather used for coats, jackets, pants, skirts, or accessories. First introduced in 1920s for jackets, and in 1960s for coats, skirts, and pants. Not called by this name until 1968 when it started the trend toward the slick, shiny, or wet look. Popularized again in 1984 which also included patchwork leather patterns in various colors. Also called *cuir savage.* Also see WET LOOK.

**little girl l.** Fashions for adults introduced by designers in 1960s which imitated the dress of a 12-year-old girl with undeveloped figure included above-the-knee skirts, some knee-high socks for day and evening wear, and ankle socks worn with Mary Jane shoes. Also see BABY DOLL LOOK.

**London l.** See BRITISH LOOK.

**lunar l.** Descriptive term used after the first landing of the American astronauts on the moon on July 20, 1969. During the same month Italian designers Baratta, Eleanor Carnett, and Tiziani showed metallic jumpsuits. Parisian designer, Cardin, showed a moon cape. Space suits were introduced for children in imitation of the astronauts' suits. For earlier interpretations of this same look see COSMONAUT LOOK.

**maxi l.** Ankle-length style popularized in 1968 for *dresses, skirts, coats,* and *silhouettes.* The GRANNY LOOK is an early example of this style.

**men's wear l.** Women's style of dress using men's suit and overcoat fabrics in an uncoordinated way, *e.g.,* using stripes and different-sized plaids and checks together. Introduced in 1969 starting a trend toward mixing of fabrics previously thought to be unharmonious. In 1984 look was further implemented with oversized coats, similar to men's overcoats; man-tailored blazers; pinstriped suits; men's tailored dress shirts worn with neckties; tailored cuffed trousers in silk and linen tweed; and well-cut jodhpurs worn with a Victorian blouse.

**Michael Jackson l.** Look popularized by Michael Jackson, rock singer, which swept the entire country becoming almost a "must" for back-to-school students of all ages in September 1984. Included multi-zippered jackets, pants of polyurethane, white socks, and black loafers. Some students even copied the wearing of one white rhinestone-studded glove which he wore as his mark of distinction. Also see MICHAEL JACKSON® JACKET under SPORT JACKETS.

**midi l.** Mid-calf style popularized in 1967 used for COATS, DRESSES, SKIRTS, and SILHOU-

ETTES. The ZHIVAGO LOOK best illustrates this look. *Der.* French, *midi*, "midday."

**military l.** **1.** Clothes and accessories, inspired by military uniforms of officers and enlisted men, frequently trimmed with brass buttons often featured by designers. **2.** Fad starting in late 1960s with college men wearing army jackets of previous wars and sometimes helmets for daytime wear. See PICKELHAUBE under HELMETS. **3.** Wearing of items purchased from Army/Navy surplus stores of all types of military clothing and accessories. Also see CARTRIDGE BELT, SAM BROWNE BELT, and WEBBED BELT under BELTS; COMBAT BOOT under BOOTS; ASTRONAUT CAP, DESERT FATIGUE CAP, FORAGE CAP, GARRISON CAP, KEPI, and OVERSEAS CAP under CAPS; BATTLE JACKET and C.P.O. under JACKETS; CAMOUFLAGE PANTS and FATIGUES under PANTS; TRENCHCOAT under RAINCOATS; FLIGHT JACKET under SPORT JACKETS; and CAMOUFLAGE SUIT under SPORT SUITS.

**mini l.** The look of short thigh-length skirts, fashionable in 1960s. Also see BABY DOLL, COURRÈGES, MOD, CARNABY and LITTLE GIRL under LOOKS, DRESSES, COATS, SILHOUETTES, and SKIRTS.

**mix and match l.** Use of coordinated prints or plaids with plain-colored fabrics for blouses, skirts, jackets, pants, vests, etc. Look popularized in the 1950s which resulted in increased sales of "separates" in retail stores. In the late 1960s, generally called the *put-together look.* Also see LAYERED LOOK.

**mod l.** **1.** Look which originated in England in the early 1960s and came to mean the miniskirt for girls and long neat hair for men along with clothes varying from traditional styles—exemplified by the Beatles. Mary Quant, the British designer, with her imaginative and unconventional designs gained wide acceptance for the *mod look.* Clothes were sold on side streets such as King's Row and Carnaby Street—away from Savile Row and Bond Street. See CARNABY LOOK for specific items. **2.** In

England, the concept of mod was entirely different. This clean, neat look consisted of close-cut hair, ankle-length skirts worn with *granny boots, Edwardian suits,* etc. *Der.* From word "modernist" meaning someone who appreciated the music of the times—the Beatles.

**nautical l.** Items of clothing and motifs borrowed from navy uniforms or seamen's clothes, frequently using a red, white, and blue color scheme and symbols such as stars, chevrons, or stripes. In 1966 St. Laurent showed clothes of this type. Used since the 1860s particularly for boys' sailor suits, it is a classic look for yachting and boating as well as sportswear. See MIDDY BLOUSE under BLOUSES; SAILOR DRESS under DRESSES; SAILOR CAP and YACHTING CAP under CAPS; SAILOR HAT under HATS; PEA JACKET and MESS JACKET under JACKETS; BELL-BOTTOMS, DUNGAREES, and SAILOR PANTS under PANTS; and SAILOR SUIT under SUITS.

**New L.** See generic definition.

**no bra l.** Look accompanying the *see-through look.* Originally a sheer lightweight bra designed by Rudi Gernreich in early 1960s. Later by extension transferred to advocating of wearing nothing, or bikinis, under see-through clothes in late 1960s and early 1970s. Also see SEE-THROUGH LOOK.

**nomad l.** Look copied after clothing worn by nomadic tribes of Middle East countries. Unusual patterned fabrics, use of shearling and embroidered leather as exemplified by the *Afghanistan jacket* and *vest* popularized in 1968. See AFGHANISTAN VEST and JACKET.

**nude l.** Shedding of clothes and showing more of the body or use of beige or natural-colored BODY STOCKINGS which give a nude effect. Introduced in 1966 by St. Laurent and Cardin with sheer transparent dresses worn over nude-colored body stockings. Later in the 1960s the body stocking was not worn and then called SEE-THROUGH LOOK.

**paper doll l.** Style featured by Anne Fogarty from 1950 to 1955 with tight-fitted waist or bodice and very bouffant skirt held out by many petticoats. Miss Fogarty won many awards for this style. *Der.* From full-skirted paper dolls children played with in 1920s and 1930s.

**patchwork l.** A style introduced by St. Laurent, Parisian couturier, in 1969 of cutting up various colored and printed fabrics into small pieces and sewing them back together to form larger yardage from which the dress, skirt, coat, etc., is cut. From this style printed fabrics evolved, *e.g.*, gingham of all sizes printed on one piece of fabric. Old antique American patchwork quilts were found and used to make coats and skirts. Also featured in leather of different colors and patterns in 1980s. *Der.* From *patchwork quilt*—a country craft practiced in the U.S. since colonial days. Also see DRESSES and PRINTS.

**peasant l.** Originally a costume worn for festive occasions by peasants in various countries, *e.g.*, Bavaria and Poland. Dress usually had a full skirt gathered at the waist, full puffed-sleeves, and drawstring neckline trimmed with embroidery. Sometimes an apron or black-laced corselet was added. Also see DIRNDL under COATS, DRESSES, PETTICOATS, SKIRTS, SILHOUETTES; and PEASANT under BLOUSES, COATS, DRESSES, SKIRTS, and SLEEVES. Also see RICH PEASANT LOOK and TYROLEAN LOOK.

**prairie l.** Look introduced in early 1970s featuring long dresses, usually of calico-like printed fabric, styled with two-gored skirts and bodices with high neckline and long sleeves. In 1980s shown in full skirts with ruffle at hem and Victorian-styled collars. *Der.* From dresses worn by American settlers moving westward in mid and late 19th c. Also see DRESSES and SKIRTS.

**preppy/preppie l.** A dress code which emphasizes well-known trademarks from high-quality stores; classics such as Ivy League shirts, wool and cashmere sweaters, *A-line* skirts, conventional-style pants in fabrics such as chino, wool, and corduroy; and shoes such as oxfords, loafers, or classic pumps in expensive leathers. Also see BROOKS BROTHERS® LOOK.

**punk l.** **1.** Punk fashion originating in London in the late 1970s was a demand for attention and a protest against the establishment by working class teenagers who were largely unemployed. Their idea was to scare and frighten their elders who responded with feelings of rage, guilt, compassion, and fear. It included pasty white makeup, blackened eyes, and much lipstick; hair was cut short and dyed or painted startling colors, *e.g.*, red, yellow, orange, green, or lavender. Clothing included black leather jackets, stud-decorated jeans, and T-shirts printed with vulgar messages or pornographic pictures. Clothing was torn and soiled, held together by safety pins. Favorite accessory was a bicycle or dog chain worn around the neck, sometimes used to fasten one leg to the other. Their girlfriends dressed the same or wore hot pants, skirts with side slits, tight sweaters, and spike-heeled sandals. **2.** American version called *New Wave Punk* was an exaggerated theatrical look not associated with the working class. Look included ripped shirts, leather clothing, and extreme hairstyles, *e.g.*, Mohawk, wild, spiky, or frizzy hair dyed in patches of various colors, *e.g.*, blue, orange, pink. Worn mainly by rock entertainers and their followers. *Der.* From punk rock music, popularized in late 1970s. Also see MOHAWK, PORCUPINE, PUNK, and SPIKY under HAIRSTYLES.

**put-together l.** Use of separate items such as blouse, pants, and skirt plus jewelry and accessories worn by each person in an individual manner rather than a formula for conformity. Popular in late 1960s and continuing through 1980s. Also see LAYERED and MIX AND MATCH LOOKS.

**retro l.** Term used when fashions from past eras are updated and used as current styles.

Sometimes the date is attached, *e.g.*, *retro-thirties, retro-forties, retro-fifties.*

**rich peasant l.**   In the late 1960s this look referred to the use of peasant and native fabrics. Clothes of midi-length, made of elaborate prints or plain colored silks, velvets, and rich fabrics ornately decorated with colorful embroidery and rich bands of braid. Yves Saint Laurent, Oscar de la Renta and Giorgio Sant' Angelo designed many clothes of this type.

**rocker l.**   Tough look of British young men in late 1950s, mixture of storm trooper and motorcyclist costume with crash helmet, tight jeans or drain-pipe trousers, black leather jacket, and knee-length boots or short boots with high heels. Rockers liked rock and roll music and admired Elvis Presley, movie star and singer, imitating his hairstyle.

**romantic l.**   Return to frilly, fluffy ruffles, choker-necked Victorian blouses, and softer fabrics in 1967 after the rigid lines and geometric look of the Courrèges style. Also see EDWARDIAN LOOK.

**Russian l.**   In fall-winter 1976–77 St. Laurent introduced a collection of Russian dresses—evening dresses had long sleeves and tight-fitting bodices to a little below hips; usually made in black with bouffant gathered skirt in colored satins, *e.g.*, red, green. A coat with high waistline made of elaborate gold brocade was also shown with fur Russian Cossack hat. Also see HATS and ZHIVAGO LOOK.

**safari l.**   Restyling in 1967 by Dior of African bush jacket—a belted hunting jacket buttoned down the front, two bellows pockets with flaps on chest, and two toward hem—for daytime wear. In 1980s this look resurfaced with popularity of film *Out of Africa*, 1986, starring Meryl Streep and Robert Redford. *Der.* From name of African hunting trip. Also see BELTS, COATS, DRESSES, HANDBAGS, SHIRTS, SPORT JACKETS and BELLOWS under POCKETS.

**Savile Row l.**   See BRITISH LOOK.

**see-through l.**   Look dating from 1967 with flowered pantdress introduced by Courrèges. In 1968 sheer see-through blouse was introduced by St. Laurent and called by this name. Rudi Gernreich had shown a sheer "at home" blouse in 1964. St. Laurent showed sheer dresses in spring of 1966. At that time called *transparent dresses* and worn over flesh-colored body stockings; also called NUDE LOOK. By 1969 the *see-through blouse* either with, or without, a bra was an accepted fashion. Also had an effect on sleepwear including the introduction of bikini-type p.j.s with transparent overblouse. Also see BLOUSES, DRESSES, PANTS, and SHIRTS, NO-BRA LOOK and NUDE LOOK.

**Teddy Boy l.**   Tough young man's fashion appearing in London in early 1950s consisting of exaggerated Edwardian jackets, high stiff collars, tight pants, pointed-toed shoes called WINKLE PICKERS, long hair carefully greased and waved, and no hats. Starting trend to individualized style of dress, a protest against the establishment by teenagers of working class. Fashion came up from the streets rather than set by designers. *Der.* Teddy is nickname for "Edward," or Edwardian fashions. Also see WINKLE PICKERS under SHOES.

**Teddy Girl l.**   British girls fashion fad in early 1950s (counterpart of Teddy boys) consisting of short tight skirts, high-heeled pointed-toed shoes, and high beehive hairstyles, forerunners of the new wave of youth-created fashions. Also see HAIRSTYLES.

**topless l.**   The baring of the body to the waist by women. In 1964 Rudi Gernreich introduced the sensational topless swimsuit. Women who attempted to wear it on American beaches were arrested, although it was accepted on the beaches of France. Topless style was accepted in nightclubs for dancers and waitresses. Also see SWIMSUITS.

**twenties l.**   See FLAPPER LOOK.

**Tyrolean l.**   (tee-roll-ee-an) Type of dress worn by natives of Austrian Tyrol and Bavarian region, including dirndl skirts, embroidered vests, and aprons worn by women; Lederhosen, knee socks, and feather-trimmed felt Alpine hats, worn by men. Also see PEASANT LOOK and EMBROIDERIES, ALPINE HAT under HATS, and DIRNDL under DRESSES and SKIRTS. *Der.* Named for alpine region in Austria and Bavaria called the "Tyrol."

**unisex l.** Garments designed so that they may be worn by either men or women. Included shirts laced at the neckline, pants with drawstrings, and double-breasted jackets with buttons and buttonholes on both sides so they could be buttoned to the right or left. Introduced in 1968, it became a popular look particularly with young people. In the 1980s popular for sweatsuits and sweaters. Items were featured both in department stores and boutiques. Also see HIS AND HER LOOK.

**vintage l.** Clothes and accessories from another era refurbished and sold in department stores or specialty shops, *e.g.,* Victorian, Edwardian, and twenties dresses—plus items such as beaded bags and antique jewelry. Called by this name in 1980s. Formerly called FLEA MARKET LOOK and ATTIC LOOK.

**V-l.** Look of huge shoulders and oversized blouse tapering to a narrow skirt at the hem. Shoulders and dolman (or batwing) sleeves were sometimes cut in one piece so that sleeve at elbow sloped into side seam at waist. Other styles were made with extended padded shoulders and large armseye seams usually with sleeves of generous proportions. Introduced in 1983 causing tops of clothing to be very full and blousey. See COCOON COAT under COATS; WEDGE DRESS under DRESSES; OVERSIZED under BLOUSES and TOPS.

**western l.** A look popularized all around the world inspired by movies taking place in the old western frontier in the U.S. Tight jeans, high-heeled boots, cowboy shirts, and western hats of various styles were accepted for city wear in the late 1960s; also resurfaced in early 1980s.

Also see COUNTRY-WESTERN LOOK; TOOLED-LEATHER BELT under BELTS; COWBOY and DIP-TOP under BOOTS; COWBOY, TEN-GALLON, and WESTERN under HATS; CHAPS, DUDE JEANS, and WESTERN under PANTS; NECKERCHIEF under SCARFS; COWBOY and WESTERN DRESS under SHIRTS; BUCKSKIN, DENIM, WESTERN and WRANGLER JACKET under SPORT JACKETS.

**wet l.** Look of 1968 achieved by very shiny, glistening fabrics—sometimes of cira satin—worn for pants, jackets and shirts. Frequently in black and with a high amount of reflection from the shiny surface. First impetus came with wearing of black leather motorcycle jackets in 1950s. Also called *cuir savage look.* Resurfaced in the 1980s in bold neon colors, *e.g.,* red, chartreuse, and light pastels of pink, lavender, and lime. Also see LEATHER LOOK.

**Zhivago l.** Look featuring Russian-inspired clothing and accessories included Russian-type overblouses with high standing collar closing at the side rather than center front. Coats were usually midi length and lavishly trimmed with fur at neck, sleeves, and hem. Boots were also featured. Look was introduced by Dior in 1966–67. *Der.* Inspired by costumes worn in *Dr. Zhivago,* 1965 film of Boris Pasternak's novel set in Revolutionary Russia in 1917. Also see RUSSIAN LOOK, BLOUSES, COATS, COLLARS, SHIRTS, and COSSACK HAT under HATS.

---

**loom** A mechanical device on which cloth is woven. On one end is the *warp beam* which holds the warp yarns. These are threaded through *heddles* attached to *harnesses* which are raised and lowered alternately to produce the desired weave. A *shuttle* goes across and back, between sheds raised by each harness, to form the filling of the cloth. Finished cloth is collected on a large roller called the *cloth beam.* Also see JACQUARD and BOX LOOM.

**loo mask** Half mask hiding upper part of face, worn by women from mid-16th to early

18th c. on the stage or as a disguise. Also spelled *lou*. Also see LOUP and DOMINO under MASKS.

**loonghie**   See LUNGI #2.

**loop and button closing**   See CLOSINGS.

**LOOPED DRESS, 1886**

**looped dress**   *Hoop-skirted* dress worn in 1860s made with skirt in two layers. Outer layer was gracefully looped up in four, five or six places by fabric tabs called LYONS LOOPS to show the underskirt. Also see PAGE, DRESS CLIP, and DRESS HOLDER.

**looped yarn**   See BOUCLÉ YARN.

**Lord Byron shirt**   See SHIRTS.

**Lord Fauntleroy suit**   See LITTLE LORD FAUNTLEROY SUIT.

**lorgnette** (lorn-yet)   See GLASSES.

**Louiseboulanger**   See APPENDIX/DESIGNERS.

**Louis XIV sleeve**   Woman's oversleeve, flared as it descends from the shoulder and edged with rows of fluting. Worn with undersleeve or ENGAGEANTES in 1850s. *Der.* Named after Louis XIV who ruled France from 1639 to 1715.

**Louis XV basque**   Woman's fitted tailored jacket of 1890s worn open down center front revealing waistcoat or vest. Usually hip length with a standing collar and cut tabs extending from waistline to hem. *Der.* Named after Louis XV who ruled France from 1710 to 1774.

**Louis XV bodice**   Dress bodice of 1850s and 1860s made with long point in front tapering to waistline with a short *peplum* in back. Had several rows of *ruching* around neck and a V-shaped neckline in front which was filled in with bows of ribbon. *Ruching* also the *peplum* and sleeves. *Der.* Similar to bodice worn by Marquise de Pompadour, mistress of Louis XV of France in mid-18th c.

**LOUIS XV HAT**

**Louis XV hat**   Woman's hat of mid-1870s with large high crown and wide brim turned up on one side. Fastened to crown with velvet bows and trimmed elaborately with ostrich feathers. *Der.* Named for Louis XV of France, 1710–1774.

**Louis XVI basque**   Woman's fitted jacket of late 1890s made with a point in front at waistline. Had a standing lace-edged *Medici collar* extending to two squared lapels and moderate-sized leg-of-mutton sleeves with cuffs that fell over the wrists. Skirt flared over hips, had pleats in center back, and was open at center front. *Der.* Named for Louis XVI of France, 1754–1793.

**Louis heel**   See HEELS.

**Louis Philippe costume**   Style of woman's dress fashionable in 1830s and 1840s. Made with sloping shoulders accentuated by ruffles, capes, or *berthas*. Had a fitted waistline in front, extremely large puffed sleeves, and wide full skirt. Usually worn with elaborate straw bonnet. *Der.* Named for Louis Philippe, King of France from 1830 to 1848.

**lou mask**  See LOO MASK.

**lounger**  See BOOTS.

**lounge suit**  British term for man's suit worn for informal occasions from 1860s on, consisting of lounging jacket, vest, and trousers all of same fabric.

**loungewear**  Clothes designed to be worn primarily at home when relaxing or entertaining—may include *lounging pajamas* or *hostess robes*. See PAJAMAS, ROBES, and SLIPPERS.

**LOUNGING CAP, 1857**

**lounging cap**  Gentleman's at-home cap, worn in mid-1860s, made in pillbox or dome shape with silk tassels fastened at center. Also called *Greek lounging cap*.

**lounging jacket**  **1.** Man's suit jacket with rounded corners in front, flapped or slit pockets at sides, and one breast pocket. Sometimes made with waistline seam, sometimes without. Introduced about 1848 and worn from then on with modifications; the forerunner of present-day suit jacket. **2.** Contemporary man's jacket for at-home wear. See SMOKING JACKET under JACKETS.

**lounging pajamas**  See PAJAMAS.

**lounging robe**  **1.** Term used until 1920s for a DRESSING ROBE. In the 1890s was full length, had leg-of-mutton sleeves, and may be trimmed with lace or ruffles. **2.** See ROBES.

**LOUNGING ROBE, 1895**

**loup**  Black velvet mask worn during 16th and 17th c. by fashionable women on the street to protect face from sun, rain, dust, and eyes of passing men. A full mask was worn in 16th c. as a fashion item or when riding. When not being worn, mask hung from the belt by a string. Also see LOO MASK. *Der.* French, "wolf," because it frightened children. Also see DOMINO under MASKS.

**louvre sunglasses**  See GLASSES.

**love beads**  See BEADS.

**love knot**  **1.** Decorative bow used in 16th c. tied across puffs in vertically slashed sleeves. **2.** Ornamental knot of ribbon originally worn as a love token.

**love lock**  Long lock of curled hair brought forward from nape of neck and worn hanging over chest popular from 1590 to 1650s for men and sometimes women. Also called a *Bourbon lock, French lock, long lock, heart breaker*, COIFFURE EN CADENETTES. and CRÈVE COEUR.

**love ribbon** Gauze ribbon with narrow black and white satin stripes, formerly worn as a mourning band.

**lover's knot** Decorative knot made of intertwined loops of two or more cords. Originally symbolized constancy of true love.

**lower stocks** Stockings made of silk or wool cloth worn by men from mid-16th to 17th c. Also called NETHER SOCKS, formerly called *bas de chausses*. Worn with UPPER STOCKS. See CHAUSSES.

**low-slung** See PANTS and WAISTLINE.

**lozenge front** Daytime dress bodice with front trimmed with strips of net, ribbon, and lace arranged in crisscross fashion to form a diamond-shaped pattern. Worn at the end of 18th and beginning of 19th c. Similar to dresses worn by the Marquise de Maintenon, second wife of Louis XIV of France. *Der.* French, *lozenge*, "diamond shaped."

**L-shaped lapel** See LAPELS.

**luau pants** See PANTS.

**Lucile** See APPENDIX/DESIGNERS.

**Lucite®** Trademark of E.I. du Pont de Nemours and Company for transparent acrylic plastic material used for handbags, sandals, shoe heels, and jewelry.

**lumberjack** Waist-length jacket with a bloused effect and rib-knitted bands at waist and sleeves, made of woven plaid wool fabric. Originally worn by woodsmen in the lumbering trade. In the late 1920s worn by both children and adults. Also called *lumber jacket*. Also see PRINTS.

**lumber jacket** See SPORT JACKETS and LUMBERJACK.

**lumberman's over** Man's heavy laced 10″ high boot with oiled-leather top, rubber vamp, and sole worn over felt inner boot. Worn by men in early 20th c. especially when working in lumber industry. *Der.* Boot originally worn in lumbering trade.

**LUMBERMAN'S OVER, 1902**

**Lunardi hat** See BALLOON HAT.

**lunar fashions** Clothes and accessories imitating those used by astronauts introduced after American astronauts landed on the moon July 20, 1969. Also see LUNAR LOOK under LOOKS. *Der.* Latin, *lundris*, "of the moon."

**lunchbox bag** See HANDBAGS.

**lunette** See CRESCENT.

**lungi** **1.** Short wraparound skirt or *loincloth* composed of single length of fabric worn by men of lower castes in India. **2.** Fabric used for scarfs, turbans, and loincloths in India. Also spelled *longhee, longyi, loonghie, lungee*.

**Lurex®** Trademark of Dow Badische Company for a decorative metallic fiber and yarn which is made of aluminum-coated plastic to make it tarnish-proof.

**luster cloths** British term for fabrics made with shiny woolen yarns in the filling, *e.g.* mohair, alpaca, or other luster wools. Cotton is used in the warp. Fabric is usually made in a plain weave, but sometimes has designs made with floating fillings, *e.g. brilliantine* and *sicilian*.

**lustering** Any finishing process that gives glossy appearance to yarn or fabric produced by heat, steam, pressure, or calendering.

**Lutetia® mink** See MUTATION MINK under FURS.

**Lycra®** Trademark of E. I. Du Pont de Nemours and Company for filament *spandex* fiber. Fabrics are not composed entirely of Lycra, since only a small amount is needed to provide stretch and recovery. Used for *foundations, girdles, bras,* and *swimsuits.*

**lynx/lynx cat**   See FURS.

**Lyons lace**   See LACES.

**Lyons loops**   Term used in 1865 for velvet straps used to pull up and loop the overskirt in three or four places, revealing the underskirt. Also see LOOPED DRESS and PAGE.

**Lyons satin**   **1.** Originally a French silk satin with twill showing on face, usually all silk, but some British fabrics use silk and plied cotton yarn. Used for linings. **2.** A good quality satin with a dull face having a silk back and a cotton face used for trimmings. *Der.* Named for Lyons, France, famous silk weaving center since the reign of Louis XIV.

**Lyons velvet**   Velvet fabric with an erect pile and more body than transparent velvet. Has excellent draping qualities and good resistance to crushing. Originally made of silk with a silk pile in Lyons, France. Now made in silk or man-made fibers with silk, cotton, or linen back. Used for high quality millinery and dresses. *Der.* Named for Lyons, France, a famous silk weaving center since the reign of Louis XIV.

**M** Letter designation for size *medium* used along with SMALL, LARGE and EXTRA LARGE for men, women and children. See MEDIUM.

**Mac** See MACKINTOSH #2.

**Macaroni** Fashionable man of George III's reign who belonged to the *Macaroni Club* formed in 1764 with membership based on having traveled to Italy. Style of dress did not develop until 1770s and included the Macaroni suit which had a thigh-length, tight-fitting jacket with very tight-fitting sleeves; an extremely high, dangerously tight *stock* or *cravat* breast pocket for handkerchief, and low flapped pockets; large nosegay on left shoulder; and breeches worn with hose of various colors. Shoes were low-cut with enormous buckles, and a tiny *tricorn hat* was carried. Also see BOSOM FLOWERS.

**Macaroni collar** Dangerously tight high collar worn in the 1770s by English DANDIES, members of the *Macaroni Club*.

**Macaroni cravat** Man's lace-edged muslin cravat of 1770s tied in a bow under the chin. Named for *Macaroni Club*.

**Macbeth tartan** See TARTANS.

**Macclesfield silk** **1.** Textile trade term used for fabrics woven in Macclesfield, England **2.** Term used to refer to tie silks in small yarn-dyed dobby patterns which are typical of this area but made in U.S. for neckties, sometimes for dresses.

**MacDonell of Glengarry tartan** See TARTANS.

**Macfarlane** Man's overcoat made with separate cape over each sleeve and side slits to permit access to pockets of inner garment. Worn from 1850s to end of 19th c.

**MacGregor (Rob Roy)** See TARTANS.

**machine knitting** See KNITTING.

**machine-made buttonhole** See BUTTONHOLES.

**machine-made lace** See LACES.

**Macintyre and Glenorchy tartan** See TARTANS.

**Mackie, Bob** See APPENDIX/DESIGNERS.

**mackinaw** See COATS and SPORT JACKETS.

**mackinaw cloth** Heavy napped cloth similar to texture of blankets from which the original Mackinaw coat was first made. Woven in double cloth or single cloth construction of all wool with plaid on one side and a plain color on the other. Also made in wool with cotton warp or cotton and rayon blended yarns in various weights. Finished by fulling and napping. *Der.* From Mackinaw City, the name of the town located in northern Michigan facing the Straits of Mackinac. Also spelled *Mackinac* which is the name of the island, the fort and the straits. Also see COATS and SPORT JACKETS.

MACKINTOSH, 1895

**Mackintosh** **1.** Loose-fitting, waterproof coat made of patented India rubber cloth of olive drab or dark green with proof straps over the seams. Introduced in 1836 and named for the inventor, Charles Macintosh, who patented fabric in 1823. **2.** British slang for various types of raincoats, often abbreviated to *mac*. **3.** Long coat with single or double detachable cape introduced for women at end of 19th c. for a raincoat. Made either of "single texture" with printed or woven fabric on outside and heavy rubber coating on inside or "double texture" with a layer of rubber between two fabrics. **4.** See RAINCOATS.

**ma-coual  1.** Wide-sleeved, short jacket made of fur for winter and silk or satin for other seasons, worn by Chinese gentleman over ankle-length silk robe. **2.** Silk coat, knee-length or shorter, made with narrow standing collar and fastened under right arm, worn by Chinese women.

**MacPherson hunting tartan**   See TARTANS.

**macramé** (mak-rah-may)  Two, three, four or more strands of cord, string, or yarn knotted in groups to form patterns. Craft used by sailors as a pastime producing belts and ornaments. Revived in early 1970s by young adults making neckwear, vests, belts, and other accessories. In 1980s used for belts, handbags, and shoes. *Der.* Turkish *magramah*, "napkin or facecloth." Also see LACES.

**Mad Carpentier**   See APPENDIX/DESIGNERS.

**madder**   Natural dyestuff obtained from root of the *Eurasian herbaceous* perennial *Rubis tinctoria* used since ancient times to produce a rich red color on cotton and sometimes wool. Now usually replaced by synthetic dyes. Also see ANCIENT MADDER.

**Madeira embroidery**   See EMBROIDERIES.

**made-to-measure**   Dress or suit made according to an individual's measurement. This type of clothing is primarily made in Hong Kong; no fittings are necessary. See CUSTOM-MADE and TAILOR-MADE.

**madras**   Shirting fabric woven in a variety of structural patterns, *e.g.* stripes, cords, plaids,

*dobby* and *Jacquard* patterns. All are made of fine woven cotton from good quality long fibers which are combed and mercerized. Stripes and plaids are yarn-dyed and may BLEED. Sometimes this is considered an asset as it tends to soften the sharp plaid effect. Also see WHITE-ON-WHITE. *Der.* Imported from the city of Madras in India. When made domestically, the origin of manufacture must be stated on label. Also see PLAIDS.

**madras turban**   Turban worn by women in 1819 made of a blue and orange Indian handkerchief.

**mafors**   Long narrow veil worn by women from 6th to 11th c. which usually covered head and draped over shoulders.

**magenta** (mah-jen-tah)  Purplish-red color, first chemical dye to be used for dress fabrics. *Der.* Named after Magenta, a town in northern Italy, where dyes to make the color were developed in 1860.

**Magyar costume**   Hungarian native costume consisting of man's shirt or woman's blouse of white linen, lavishly embroidered, worn with long aprons over pants or skirts by both sexes. Men also wear the felt or leather SZÜR, elaborately decorated. *Der. Magyar*, an ethnic group of Hungary.

**maharatta tie** (ma-ha-ra-ta)  See INDIAN NECKTIE.

**mahoitres** (ma-hoy-treh)  Term used in France from end of 14th c. and in England from 1450 to 1840 for shoulder pads used as trim on sleeves of GIPON. Also spelled *maheutres*.

**mail**   Early form of armor consisting of metal rings sewn to foundation of leather in parallel rows, worn since earliest times by Persians, Etruscans, Normans, and Saxons. Also called *chain mail*. *Der.* Middle English, *maille*, one of the "rings" from which it was made.

**mail-coach necktie**   Man's large scarf, sometimes a cashmere shawl, loosely folded twice around neck, tied in knot in front with ends falling over chest like a waterfall. Worn as neckcloth from 1818 to 1830s by dandies. Also called *waterfall necktie*.

**maillot**   See SWIMSUITS.

**Mainbocher**   See APPENDIX/DESIGNERS.

**Maintenon cloak** (man-te-non)  Woman's wide-sleeved, black velvet coat of 1860s sometimes embroidered and usually trimmed with a wide pleated flounce covered with *guipure lace*. *Der.* Named for the *Marquise de Maintenon.*

**Maintenon coiffure** (man-te-non)  Woman's hairstyle of early 1860s with two long hanging curls at either side of face, tiny curls on the forehead, and a *chignon* at the back of the neck. Filmy lace decorated with foliage and flowers went over the crown of the head and hung down each side to shoulders in form of *lappets*. The *Maintenon toupet* could be added to secure proper effect of curls on the forehead. *Der.* Named for the *Marquise de Maintenon.*

**Maintenon corsage** (man-te-non)  Woman's evening dress bodice of 1839 and 1840s trimmed with ribbon bows down center front in ladder-like effect with lace ruffle at waist. *Der.* Named for the *Marquise de Maintenon.*

**Maintenon, Marquise de** (man-te-non)  Françoise d'Aubigne, (1635–1719), mistress and second wife of Louis XIV of France, married in 1685; a retro-fashion influence in the 19th c.

**Maintenon toupet** (man-te-non)  Band of false curls attached to ribbon that tied at nape of neck. Worn by women in mid-1860s pulled over the forehead to imitate the hairstyle worn by the Marquise de Maintenon. Also called *toupet Maintenon*. Also see MAINTENON COIFFURE. *Der.* Named for the *Marquise de Maintenon.*

**majorette boot**   See BOOTS.

**Major wig**  Man's hairpiece consisting of a *toupee* with two *corkscrew curls* tied at the nape of neck to make a double *queue* in back. Origi-

nally a military style, but adopted by civilians and worn during latter half of 18th c. Term used in England for French BRIGADIER WIG.

**malabar**   **1.** Cotton handkerchiefs from India printed with bright colors. **2.** A general term used for variety of printed cotton fabric exported to East Africa from Great Britain and India. *Der. Malabar*, region of southwest India.

**malacca cane** (ma-lak-a)  Man's cane carried in 18th c. made from the mottled stem of the malacca palm. Also called *clouded cane*.

**Mali bracelet**   See BRACELETS.

**maline**   **1.** Extremely fine, soft silk, rayon, or cotton net with hexagonal holes used primarily for millinery. Sometimes used over feathers on hats to keep them in place. **2.** See LACES. *Der.* Originally the lace was made in Maline, Belgium.

**Malmaison** (mal-ma-zon)  Pale rosy-pink color of a rose by this name grown at Malmaison, Napoleon's home, where the Empress Josephine had a famous rose garden.

**malo**  A loincloth worn by native Polynesian men in Hawaii.

**Maltese cross**  Cross with four arms of equal length shaped like arrowheads decreasing in size as they approach the center. Used as a motif for jewelry, particularly for necklaces and pins. *Der.* Emblem of the Knights of Malta. See CRUSADER'S CROSS under NECKLACES.

**mama shoe**   See SHOES.

**Mameluke sleeve** (mama-luke)  Full sleeve finished with a large cuff of thin fabric used in daytime dresses of the late 1820s. *Der.* Mamelukes were originally slaves brought to Egypt, later trained as soldiers. Ruled Egypt from 1250 to 1517 and remained powerful until 1811 under Turkish viceroys.

**Mameluke tunic** (mama-luke)  See TUNIC À LA MAMELUKE.

**Mameluke turban** (mama-luke)  White satin woman's turban of 1804 trimmed with one large ostrich feather, with the front rolled back like a hat brim over a dome-shaped crown. *Der.* Mamelukes were originally slaves brought to Egypt, later trained as soldiers. Ruled Egypt from 1250 to 1517 and remained powerful until 1811 under Turkish viceroys.

**manbag** See HANDBAGS.

**mancheron** **1.** Late 15th and early 16th c. half sleeve reaching from elbow to shoulder, lower part of sleeve called *brassart*. Two parts held together with pins and ribbons. **2.** 16th-c. false sleeve attached only at shoulder and worn hanging down back. **3.** 19th-c. very short oversleeve, similar to a large epaulette, worn by women. Term replaced by word EPAULETTE in 1860s.

**manchette** (mon-chet) Wrist ruffle of lace worn by women on afternoon dresses from 1830s to 1850s.

**Manchu headdress** (man-chew) Elaborate Chinese woman's headdress with hair shaped into two upswept winglike projections on each side with long gold bar extended across top of the head. Headdress was decorated with flowers, black satin loops of ribbon, and jewels.

**Mandarin collar** See CHINESE COLLAR under COLLARS, and COATS.

**Mandarin floss/tassel hat** Ancient Chinese man's hat for summer made of silk or bamboo in dome shape, topped by a button that indicated the rank of the man at the Chinese Mandarin Court. Red silk floss extended from the button completely covering hat.

**Mandarin hat** **1.** Ancient Chinese court hat for winter with wide, flaring, upturned brim and decorative button at crown indicating rank of wearer. Made of fur and satin for winter and decorated with a peacock feather. See MANDARIN FLOSS. **2.** Woman's black velvet *pork pie hat* of early 1860s with feather trim over the back of the flat crown.

**Mandarin headdress** Tall ornate headdress, studded with jewels, which stood away from the head worn by Chinese Mandarin's wife before 1912.

**Mandarin robes** Costume worn by one of the nine ranks of officials of the Chinese empire during the Manchu period from 1643 until 1912 (when China became a republic). The three-quarter length coat was distinguished by patches of embroidery called PU-FU. For descriptions of robes see CH'ANG-FU, CH'AO-FU, and CHI-FU. For modern adaptations of mandarin style see COATS, COLLARS, DRESSES, JACKETS, NECKLINES, and SLEEVES.

**Mandelli, Mariuccia** See APPENDIX/DESIGNERS.

**mandilion** (man-dill-yun) Loose hip-length jacket with narrow long sleeves worn by men from late 16th to early 17th c. Often worn *colley westonward, e.g.*, worn by soldiers around shoulders as a cape, with sleeves hanging free. Later worn with short sleeves, sometimes slit, for *livery*. Also called *mandeville*.

**maniakes** A large, elaborate, gold-embroidered, jewel-encrusted collar worn in the Byzantine court from 4th to 6th c. as a part of ceremonial costume. Collar was of Persian derivation and signified royalty.

**Mani-Hose®** See PANTYHOSE.

**manikin** See MANNEQUIN.

**Manila hemp** See ABACA.

**maniple** Narrow ornamental band about 3½ feet long worn by Catholic priests on the left arm near the wrist.

**man-made fiber** Fibers made totally by chemical means as well as fibers made of regenerated cellulose. U.S. Textile Fibers Products Identification Act of 1960 states that these fibers must be labelled in accordance with generic groups as follows: ACETATE, ACRYLIC, METALLIC, MODACRYLIC, NYLON, RAYON, SARAN, SPANDEX, TRIACETATE, and VINYL. See individual listings.

**mannequin** **1.** A model of the human body,

used to display clothes in department stores, etc. **2.** A woman whose job is wearing clothes in *fashion shows.* Also spelled *manikin.*

**Manon robe** Daytime dress of 1860s with front cut in one piece from neck to hem. Back with double *box pleat* or *Watteau pleats* hanging from under collar to hem of skirt. *Der.* Named for Manon, heroine of 1733 book by Abbe Prevost.

**mant** 17th or 18th c. term for MANTUA.

**manta** (man-teh) **1.** In Chile and Central America, a woman's square shawl of thin fabric draped over head and shoulders covering most of dress. Made of silk or lace for upper class women, and of alpaca and cashmere for other women. Similar to the Spanish *mantilla.* Also called a *manto.* **2.** Plaid wrap worn by men of Valencia, Spain. **3.** Coarse *unbleached muslin* used in Mexico for items of clothing and sometimes for shawls. Also a gray cotton sheeting made in Central America.

**man-tailored** Term usually applied to women's suits or coats, implying that garment is tailored similar to a man's suit, coat, or shirt, as contrasted with tailoring of the softer type used in *dressmaker suits.* Also see JACKETS and SUITS.

**manta suit** Two-piece men's suit made out of *manta* fabric worn in Mexico.

**manteau** (man-tow) **1.** 16th c. term for man's *French cloak, compass cloak* or *half compass cloak.* **2.** Woman's gown. See MANTUA.

**mantee** Woman's coat of 18th c. worn open in front showing *stomacher* and *petticoat* underneath.

**mantelet** **1.** A short cape mentioned by Chaucer in 1386. **2.** Small cloak worn by women in 18th c. **3.** Scarf of fur, lace, or silk worn around shoulders, crossed over chest, and ends tied in back from 1814 to 1835. **4.** 19th c. woman's rounded shoulder cape with long end tucked under belt in front. Also spelled *mantelot, mantlet.*

**mantella** See MANTILLA.

**mantelletta** Sleeveless thigh-length circular-cut garment opened in front with small collar worn by prelates of Roman Catholic Church over the *rochet.* Made of silk or wool with two vertical slits for arms. For cardinals it is red, purple, or rose-colored.

**mantellone** Purple ankle-length ecclesiastical mantle, worn over the *cassock,* by lesser prelates of Papal court of the Roman Catholic Church.

**mantelot** See MANTELET #4.

**MANTILLA #4, 1877**

**mantilla** **1.** See VEILS. **2.** Shawl or veil worn by Spanish women, usually of black lace—white lace worn for festive occasions. Worn draped over head, sometimes over a high comb placed in hair, wrapped around neck, and falling over shoulders. **3.** Mexican and South American women wear the black lace mantilla usually over the high comb similar to those worn in Spain for festive occasions. **4.** Lightweight *shawl* of silk, velvet, or lace worn by women from 1840s to 1880s. Shawl hung long in back and had long ends in front. Also spelled *mantella. Der.* Diminutive of Spanish *manta,* "shawl."

**mantle** **1.** Long, loose, cape-like cloak originally cut square, oblong, or as a part of a circle.

Worn from 12th through 16th c. by men and women. Fastened by a pin or clasp on one shoulder or tied at neck. **2.** In 14th c. usually a ceremonial cape. Sometimes lined and called a double mantle. **3.** By 19th c. term for a *cape* without sleeves. **4.** Wrap for infants in 17th and 18th c. *Der.* Latin, *mantellum,* "cloak."

**mantlet**   See MANTELET.

**mantlet Matilda**   Type of shawl-like woman's garment trimmed with fringe or taffeta in front worn in 1850s. Also spelled *mantlet Matilde.*

**manto**   See MANTA #1 and MANTUA.

**manton de manilla**   Large embroidered square of silk crepe made in China and sent to Manila in the Philippines (formerly a Spanish port) and from there to Spain where the fringe was added. Worn by women in early 20th c. Also see SPANISH SHAWL under SHAWLS.

**mantua**   (man-tu-a)   Woman's overdress or gown worn over underskirt. Made with a loosely fitted unboned bodice joined to overskirt with long train. Split in front to expose petticoat. Worn on social or formal occasions from mid-17th to mid-18th c. Also called *manteau, manto, manton,* and *mantua gown.*

**mantua maker**   17th and 18th c. term for *tailor* or *dressmaker,* either man or woman.

**manule**   Elaborately embroidered high heeled slipper or sandal worn as native dress by women of Bosnia, now a part of Yugoslavia.

**marabou**   See FEATHERS.

**marama**   Rumanian matron's native headdress consisting of a long sheer veil of cotton or silk decorated with embroidery and sequins. One end is wound around the head the other hangs down the back.

**marcasite**   (mar-ka-sight)   See GEMS.

**marcel**   Artificial wave put in woman's hair with heated curling irons, devised by Marcel of France in 1907 and popular in the 1920s.

**Marguerite dress**   Dress of early 1890s with

STOCK NECKLINE made with full sleeves gathered into a wide cuff reaching halfway to elbow. Blouse was full and gathered at neckline and worn with full gathered skirt trimmed with bands of braid. Contrasting low-necked sleeveless peasant bodice, laced up the front and back, is worn over the dress.

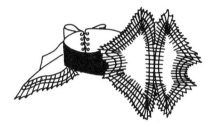

**MARGUERITE GIRDLE**

**Marguerite girdle**   Stiff belt laced in back and wider in front, forming two points above and below waistline. Sometimes made with butterfly arrangement in front and ruffle, *peplum,* or bow in back to give a *bustle* effect. Popular in 1860s and worn at intervals since.

**Marie Antoinette fichu**   See ANTOINETTE FICHU.

**Marie Antoinette skirt**   Skirt worn from 1895 on made with seven gores—three in front, four in back—with two back panels pleated in large *box pleats* stitched down to hips, making the skirt 4 to 6 yards wide at the hem. Named for Marie Antoinette (1755–1793), wife of Louis XVI of France.

**Marie sleeve**   Full sleeve tied at intervals to form several puffs. Worn from about 1813 to mid-1820s and revived in the early 1870s—then called the *Marie Antoinette sleeve.*

**Marie Stuart bodice**   Tight-fitting, boned evening bodice ending in a deep point at waistline worn in late 1820s. *Der.* Similar to bodice of dress worn by Mary, Queen of Scots, also called Mary Stuart (or Stewart) (1542–1587).

**Marie Stuart bonnet/cap**   Bonnet with heart-shaped peak or brim projecting over center of forehead, popular from 1820 to 1870, especially for widows. A derivative of the *attifet* headdress worn by Mary, Queen of Scots, also called Mary Stuart (or Stewart) (1542–1587).

**MARIE STUART CAP**

**MARIE STUART HOOD**

**Marie Stuart hood**   Separate hood of 1860s with heart-shaped peaked brim in front extended over the face with crown cut round and gathered at edge. Tied with ribbons under chin and lavishly trimmed with ruching, embroidery, braid, and ribbon.

**marin anglais bonnet**   Woman's bonnet worn on the back of the head like a child's sailor hat in 1870s. Trimmed with ribbon and feathers and tied under chin. *Der.* French, "English sailor cap."

**marine gems**   Gems which are found primarily in the sea, *e.g.*, *pearls*, *amber*, and *coral*. See GEMS.

**mariner's cuff**   Man's coat cuff worn in second half of 18th c. consisting of a small turned-back cuff decorated on outside with a curved flap, similar to a pocket flap, and three or four buttons that matched those of the coat.

**Marino Faliero sleeve**   Full hanging sleeve of first half of 1830s secured with ribbon band at elbow, and long point hanging to wrist. *Der.* After drama of the same name written by Lord Byron.

**mark stitch**   See TAILOR'S TACKS under STITCHES.

**marlota**   Spanish man's long coat with *hanging sleeves* similar in cut to a *caftan*; worn only for tournaments and bullfights in late 16th c.

**marlotte**   16th-c. woman's outer garment, similar to short *mantle*, open in front with back falling in folds. Made with short puffed sleeves and a standing collar or ruff.

**marmot**   See FURS.

**marmotte bonnet**   Tiny bonnet of early 1830s with narrow front brim similar to *bibi bonnet*.

**marmotte cap**   Triangular handkerchief, placed on back of head and tied under chin, worn indoors by women in early 1830s.

**marocain**   Fabric with a wavy ribbed effect in the filling caused by using spiral yarns. May be made in silk, wool, rayon, man-made fibers, or combinations of various fibers. Used for dresses and women's suits.

**maroon**   Dark purple-brown-red color.

**marquis**   (mar-kwiss or mar-kee) A three-cornered hat worn by women.

**marquise**   (mar-keez) **1.** See GEM CUTS. **2.** See MARQUISE MANTLE.

**marquise bodice**   (mar-keez) Evening bodice of mid-1870s with low heart-shaped neckline forming two large scallops and trimmed with ruching or lace frill. Also called *bodice en coeur*.

**marquise mantle** (mar-keez) Short lace-trimmed taffeta woman's mantlet of mid-1840s with short sleeves. Made with fitted back and flounce below the waist. Also called *marquise*.

**marquisette** (mar-kee-set) Fine, transparent net-like fabric with good durability. Made with cotton, silk, and polyester yarns in the leno weave which prevents the filling from slipping. Cottons are made with best quality combed single yarns and may be plain or show dobby effects. Used for evening gowns, cocktail dresses, and sheer blouses.

**marseilles** (mar-say) Reversible fabric made in a jacquard weave with a raised woven pattern in all white, or white with colored raised designs. Usually made with a fine warp and two fillings—one coarse and one fine. Ground is formed by interlacing the fine yarns. Raised design is made with coarser filling yarns. Formerly used for men's fancy vests. *Der.* From city in France where it was first manufactured.

**marten** See FURS.

**MARTHA WASHINGTON FICHU**

**Martha Washington fichu** Large draped *fichu* of mid-1890s extending to shoulders with pointed ends fastened by a rosette of lace in front, and two wide ruffles of lace extended around the edge. *Der.* An adaptation of style worn by Martha Washington, wife of the first U.S. President, George Washington.

**Martha Washington waist** V-necked blouse of late 1890s with dickey having an inserted choker collar. Surplice front gathered at shoulder seams, draped to one side, and tied in back with a bow. Sleeves varied from full double puff,

to single puff coming to elbow and fitted to wrist. *Der.* For Martha Washington, wife of first U.S. President, George Washington.

**martingale** See BELTS.

**Mary cap** See MARY, QUEEN OF SCOTS CAP.

**Mary Jane®** See SHOES.

**Mary, Queen of Scots cap** Indoor cap worn by women, mainly matrons and widows, from 1750s to 1760s. Made with a heart-shaped peak in center front edged with beads, may have side frills and lappets. Also called *Mary cap*. Also called MARIE STUART BONNET/CAP.

**masher** Term used for an elaborately dressed *dandy* of 1880s and 1890s. Also called *Piccadilly Johnny*.

**masher collar** Extremely high collar worn by ultra-fashionable men in 1880s and 1890s.

**masher dust wrap** Tight-fitting man's *Inverness coat* of 1880s having large armholes with a separate cape over each shoulder.

**masi cloth** See TAPA CLOTH.

**mask** Covering for the face used as a disguise for Halloween or masquerades. Also worn as a protection for the face for active sports and industrial purposes. Primitive people used masks in ritual dances. Greeks used the *comedy* and *tragedy masks* in the theater. In the 16th and 17th c., masks were used for purposes of disguise when going out on the street at night. See LOUP in alphabetical listing. In the American colonial period, masks were fashionable for protection of face from the sun in the daytime. Called a LOO. See alphabetical listing.

**━━━━ MASKS ━━━━**

**catcher's m.** Mask made of wire or plastic covering the face fastened with a strap around the head. Worn in baseball games by the catcher to prevent face injury.

**cold m.**   See HOT MASK.

**domino**   Small mask covering upper half of the face leaving the mouth exposed, worn for masquerades. Also called a *half-mask*. See alphabetical listing.

**false face**   Mask molded out of heavily sized fabric or rubber, covering the entire face for Halloween. Also see RUBBER MASK.

**fencing m.**   Protective mask of fine wire screening fitting over the face to prevent injury from foil when fencing.

**half-m.**   See DOMINO.

**hat m.**   Hat extending part way down over the face with cut-outs for the eyes used for beach hats, later for helmet-type hats in 1960s.

**hot m.**   Mask shaped like a *domino* which ties at back of head. Chill mask is used for puffy eyes, tension or hangover; heat mask is used to relieve sinus pain and stuffy noses. Also called *cold mask*.

**industrial m.**   Large fiberglass mask with clear see-through window. Worn for soldering or doing dangerous industrial tasks.

**life m.**   Mask similar to a surgical mask with carbon filter. Worn on the street as a protection against air pollution and smog.

**rubber m.**   Mask fitting over the entire head—worn for Halloween. Molded of latex and painted various colors in a realistic representation of characters from comic strips, cartoons, stories, films, and television. Also see FALSE FACE.

**scarf m.**   Fashion item of the early 1970s consisting of a scarf tied across the face revealing only the eyes.

**scuba m.**   See-through mask covering eyes and nose worn when swimming underwater or for scuba diving.

**ski m.**   Knitted hood fitting snugly over the

**DOMINO MASK**

**SKI MASK**

head and neck with openings for the eyes, nose, and mouth. Worn for skiing, winter sports, and in cold climates to prevent frostbite. *Der.* Inspired by similar hoods worn in the mountains of Peru.

**sleep m.**   Soft cushioned mask fitting closely to eyes and nose made of black rayon with elastic band fitting around head. Worn when sleeping in daylight to block out the light.

**surgical m.**   Sanitized cloth mask tied over nose and mouth by physicians and nurses to prevent spread of germs to patients. Sometimes used outdoors by people affected by allergies or air pollution.

**master pattern**   See SLOPER.

**MASTER'S GOWN**

**Master's gown**   Black open-front gown with square yoke and long closed HANGING SLEEVES with crescents cut out near hems. Arms emerge through slits above elbows. Full back and sleeves are joined to yoke by CARTRIDGE PLEATS. Worn with *Master's hood* and *mortarboard* by candidates for, and holders of, Master's degrees.

**Master's hood**   Black cowl-drape 3½ feet long in back with band of colored velveteen around edge which is turned over in back to show lining denoting institution granting degree. Worn with MASTER'S GOWN. Also see ACADEMIC HOOD.

**matador hat** (mat-ah-door)   Hat shaped like top of bull's head—rounded over forehead with two projections on sides like bull's horns. Part of hat is covered with black tufts of fabric, and center of crown is of embroidered velvet. Worn by bullfighters in Spain and Mexico. Also called *toreador hat*. Also see SUIT OF LIGHTS.

**matador's jacket**   See BOLERO #2.

**matelassé** (mat-lass-ay)   Luxurious fabric with a blistered or embossed effect made on the Jacquard or dobby loom in a double cloth weave. Front and back of cloth are actually separate fabrics which are fastened together with extra crepe yarns that form the raised pattern. Genuine matelassé will not become flat-looking as the raised portion is woven in, and quite different from an inexpensive embossed design. Made in cotton, silk, rayon, and acetate. Cotton may have a quilted effect, others a blistered effect. Used for formal dresses, cocktail dresses, evening wraps, blouses, and robes. *Der.* French, "cushioned or padded." Also spelled *matellassé*.

**maternity clothes**   Garments designed to be worn by expectant mothers. See BLOUSES, DRESSES, PANTS, SKIRTS, SLIPS, and TOPS. Also see KANGAROO SKIRT.

**Mathilde embroidery**   See EMBROIDERIES.

**Matilda**   **1.** Term used in 19th c. for velvet decoration around hem of a woman's skirt.

**2.** Term used in 1840s for a bouquet of flowers worn in the hair by women.

**matinee** (mah-tin-aye)   **1.** A jaconet hooded pardessus worn with morning dress in early 1850s. **2.** Another name for a *tea jacket* worn in 1890s and early 20th c. **3.** Lace-trimmed simple jacket to hips worn only in the boudoir from about 1915 to 1930s.

**matinee-length necklace**   See NECKLACES.

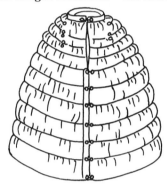

**MATINEE SKIRT**

**matinee skirt**   Woman's lightweight patented hoop skirt of 1859 made by inserting 11 lightweight hoops into a petticoat.

**matte finish**   **1.** Textile-industry term for any dull finish. **2.** Make-up that has no shine.

**mattress-ticking**   See TICKING and TICKING under STRIPES.

**Maud**   Woman's fringed wrapper of plaid fabric worn in mid-1850s.

**mauve** (mohv)   Grayed-lilac color.

**mauve diamond**   See DIAMONDS.

**maxi**   Word coined in 1968 for daytime wear reaching the ankles. See CAPES, COATS, DRESSES, LENGTHS, LOOKS, SILHOUETTES, and SKIRTS.

**Maxwell, Vera**   See APPENDIX/DESIGNERS.

**mazamet** (maz-a-may)   Melton fabric made in France.

**mazarin hood** (mas-a-rhan)   Woman's hood worn in the last quarter of the 17th c. *Der.* Named after the Duchesse de Mazarin, niece of

Cardinal Mazarin (1602–1661), Minister to Louis XIV.

**McCardell, Claire**   See APPENDIX/DESIGNERS.

**McFadden, Mary**   See APPENDIX/DESIGNERS.

**McKay shoe construction**   Shoe manufacturing process in which the upper is pulled around the last and fastened to the insole by means of tacks. The outsole may be attached by stitching or by cementing. Invented by Lyman Blake in 1861.

**M-CUT COLLAR**

**M-cut collar**   Man's coat collar of first half of 19th c. with M-shaped notch at the *lapel*. Worn for day wear, continuing until 1870 for evening coats.

**Mechlin lace** (meck-lin)   See LACES.

**Mecklenburg cap**   Turban-style indoor cap worn by women in 1760s. *Der.* Named after Charlotte of Mecklenburg, who married George III of England in 1761.

**medallion**   **1.** See NECKLACES. **2.** See PRINTS. **3.** Shoe-industry term for ornamental pattern punched in leather in center of man's WING-TIP OXFORD.

**medic**   See COLLARS and SHIRTS.

**medic alert bracelet**   See BRACELETS.

**Medici collar** (meh-dee-chee)   **1.** Large standing fan-shaped collar, usually of net or lace wired to stand up in back, and sloping to join low square neckline in front. Worn by Marie de'Medici, (1573–1642), second wife of Henry IV of France. Reintroduced in 18th and 19th c. **2.** Smaller woman's standing collar of 1890s rolled over at top, sometimes nearly meeting in front.

**Medici dress** (meh-dee-chee)   Trained *princess dress* of early 1870s with *tablier* front and short sleeves. *Der.* Inspired by clothes worn by Marie de' Medici.

**Medici lace** (meh-dee-chee)   See LACES.

**Medici sleeve** (meh-dee-chee)   Full sleeve, puffed to elbow and tight from there to wrist worn by women in 1830s. *Der.* Inspired by clothes worn by Marie de' Medici.

**Medici vest** (meh-dee-chee)   Woman's fitted blouse of mid-1870s with double-puffed sleeves ending in three fluted ruffles at elbow and V-neck trimmed with a single pleated ruffle. Had a short basque below waistline with fullness in back. *Der.* Inspired by clothes worn by Marie de Medici.

**medieval**   In a broad sense, usually refers to period 500–1450; same as Middle Ages. For costume the terms *Byzantine* (400–1100), *Romanesque* (900–1200), *Early Gothic* (1200–1350), and *Late Gothic* (1350–1450) are sometimes used.

**meditation shirt**   See SHIRTS.

**medium**   Size used along with SMALL, LARGE, and EXTRA-LARGE for men, women, and children for such items as sweaters, knit shirts, sport jackets, nightgowns, pajamas, robes, gloves, girdles, and panty girdles. Abbreviation M.

**Medusa wig** (meh-doo-sa)   Woman's wig of early 19th c. made of many hanging *corkscrew curls*. *Der.* From the Greek mythical Gorgon, Medusa, slain by Perseus.

**melanite**   See ANDRADITE GARNET under GEMS.

**melee**   See DIAMONDS.

**melon sleeve**   See SLEEVES.

**Melrose** Fabric with a silk warp and a wool filling woven in a double twill weave. *Der.* Named for Melrose, a town on the Tweed River in Scotland where it was first produced during the 18th c.

**melton** Heavy, durable coating fabric which looks somewhat like wool broadcloth and has a hand similar to felt. Originally made of heavy woolen yarns or wool filling and cotton warp. Now made in combinations and man-made fibers. Finishing processes include fulling, napping, shearing, and pressing to conceal the twill weave. Best qualities are the most lustrous. Compactness of the fabric makes it warm and protective against wind penetration. Used by the U.S. Armed Forces. Also used for men's, women's, and children's coats and snowsuits. *Der.* Named for Melton Mowbray, a town in Leicestershire, England.

**meltonette** Fabric similar to *melton* but lighter in weight. Used for women's coats and suits.

**men's wear look** Use by women of men's suit and overcoat fabrics in an uncoordinated way, *e.g.*, using stripes and different-sized plaids and checks together. Also see LOOKS.

**menteurs** See LIARS.

**mentonnière** (mohn-ton-ee-ehr) Protective armor for lower part of face or chin worn in tournaments in Middle Ages.

**mentonnières** (mohn-ton-ee-ehrz) Lace or tulle ruffles sewn to bonnet strings in 1820s and 1830s making frill around lower face and neck when tied. Same as CHIN STAYS.

**menu vair** See VAIR.

**Menzies Black and White tartan** See TARTANS.

**Menzies hunting tartan** See TARTANS.

**mercerization** Finishing process with caustic soda applied to cotton yarn, fabric, or thread to make fibers more nearly parallel and to increase the luster. *Der.* Named for John Mercer, calico printer in Lancashire, England, who discovered this process in 1844.

**mercerized yarn** Yarn which has been immersed in caustic soda to increase the luster. Used in fine cotton fabrics.

**merino wool** High-quality wool yarn made from fleece of merino sheep which is short, fine, strong, resilient, and takes dyes well.

**mermaid sheath** See DRESSES.

**Merry Widow** See FOUNDATIONS.

**Merry Widow hat** Very wide-brimmed hat, sometimes a yard across, frequently of velvet and ornately trimmed with ostrich plumes. *Der.* Named for 1905 light opera, *The Merry Widow*, with music by Franz Lehár.

**merveilleuse** (mare-vay-yez) French styles worn by women in the *Directoire Period*, 1795–1799. Affected Grecian styles by wearing high-waisted, low-necked, sheer muslin dresses with shawls or *spencers*; and exaggerated *poke* bonnets flaring high in center front. Sometimes flesh-colored stockings were worn with shoes similar to laced ballet slippers. *Der.* French, "marvelous." Also see MERVEILLEUX #2.

**merveilleux** (mare-vay-yer) **1.** Lining fabric made in the satin weave of silk and cotton, all silk, or all rayon. Used for linings in men's outer apparel. Masculine for MERVEILLEUSE. **2.** Term used during French Revolution for *fops* or *dandies*. *Der.* French, "marvelous." Also see MERVEILLEUSE.

**mesh** **1.** Metal links joined together to form a flat flexible unit. See BRACELETS, CHAIN MAIL, MESH BELTS, and HANDBAGS. **2.** Knitted or woven fabric in an open weave, such as *leno*, producing a net or a screen-like effect. Also see MILANESE KNIT and HOSE.

**messaline** (messa-lean) Lightweight, soft silk satin dress fabric first made in France in early 20th c. of very fine organzine warp yarns and tram. Now made in rayon. *Der.* Named after

Messalina, third wife of Claudius, Emperor of Rome.

**mess jacket** 1. See JACKETS. 2. Waist-length jacket with standing collar and *leg-of-mutton* sleeves worn by women in 1890s.

**mest** Turkish socks worn inside the PABOUDJ SLIPPER.

**metallic cloth** Any type of fabric made with metallic yarns, *e.g.*, *Lurex*, or using metallic yarns in the filling and other yarns in warp. Formerly yarns such as silver tarnished, but now they may be coated with a fine film of polyester which resists tarnish. Some metallic fabrics have a cross rib, others are knit, and some have Jacquard designs. Used for blouses, formal wear, cocktail dresses, and knitwear.

**metallic yarn** 1. See LUREX. 2. *Core yarn* made by twisting thin metal foil around cotton, silk, linen, or rayon yarn.

**Metternich sack** (meh-ter-nick) Woman's collarless, knee-length wrap of mid-1860s made of black velvet with three *box pleats* at center back. Trimmed at neck, front, shoulders, and cuffs with wide velvet ribbon embroidered with white cord. *Der.* Named for Prince von Metternich, Austrian statesman of the mid-19th c.

**Mexican wedding boot** See BOOTS.

**Mexican wedding shirt** See SHIRTS.

**Michael Jackson** See SPORT JACKETS and LOOKS.

**micro** Fashion term coined in late 1960s as a synonym for tiny or very short. See DRESSES and LENGTHS.

**middy** Term used for blouse worn by sailors in U.S. Navy. Extended to mean dress with top styled like a *middy blouse*. See BLOUSES and SAILOR under COLLARS and DRESSES.

**middy suit** Three-piece sailor suit for children introduced in the mid-1890s. Boy's suit had waist-length jacket with large sailor collar, close-fitting collarless blouse, and short or knee-

**MIDDY SUIT**

length pants. Girl's suit had hip-length jacket with sailor collar, leg-of-mutton sleeves, and unpressed-pleated skirt.

**middy-top pajamas** See PAJAMAS.

**midi** (mee-dee) Originally a French term for a skirt length coming to the mid-calf of the leg, later applied to anything that length. Also see CAPES, COATS, DRESSES, LENGTHS, LOOKS, PONCHOS, SILHOUETTES, and SKIRTS. *Der.* French, *midi*, "midday."

**midinette** (mee-dee-net) French working girl or seamstress. *Der.* French, *midi*, "midday."

**midnight blue** Very dark blue, almost black, used for men's formal suits.

**midriff style** See BARE-MIDRIFF, DRESSES, and SHIRTS.

**mignonette lace** (mee-yon-et) See LACES.

**Milan bonnet** (mee-lan) Man's cap of first half of 16th c. usually black with soft puffed crown. Rolled-up brim was sometimes slit on the sides and trimmed with crimson satin lining pulled through slashes.

**Milanese knit** Machine-made warp knit with diagonal yarns at intervals giving run-resistant openwork effect. Used particularly for women's panties and hose.

**Milan lace** See LACES.

**Milan straw** Plaited straw using seven strands in each braid. Made from lower part of wheat stalk, called *pedal straw*, grown near the city of Milan in Tuscany, Italy.

**mildew resistance** Finish applied to KHAKI and other cottons to make them resist mildew or dampness. Not always permanent.

**military** Adjective used for clothing, accessories, and trim inspired by military uniforms of officers and enlisted men. Frequently trimmed with brass buttons. See BRAIDS, COATS, COLLARS, HEELS, LOOKS, and ARMY/NAVY CLOTHES.

**military folding hat** See OPERA HAT #2.

**military frock coat** Man's frock coat, worn from early 1820s on, made with standing collar, no lapels, and no flaps on pockets. Later styles had rolled collars and lapels.

**military stock** Man's made-up neckcloth, frequently of black corded silk edged with kidskin, stiffened with cardboard or leather, and tied or buckled in back. Worn from mid-18th to mid-19th c.

**military tunic** 1. Term used first in France in 1670 for long tunic worn by army over a full sleeved waistcoat. 2. Man's long tube-like coat with skirts lapped over in front; adopted by British army in 1855.

**milkmaid hat** See BERGÈRE HAT.

**milkmaid skirt** Term used from 1885 to 1895 for double skirt with plain overskirt gathered and pulled up on one side by cord or loop at waistband to reveal a striped underskirt.

**millefiore** (meel-eh-fee-o-reh) Italian word describing tiny-flowered print. *Der.* Italian, "thousand flowers."

**mille-fleurs** (meel-flhur) French name for a pattern of tiny flowers. *Der.* French, "thousand flowers."

**mill end** Short lengths of fabric which are usually sold at reduced prices. May have imper-

fections or be the last piece on the bolt. Usually sold in a store at the textile mill, or sold to retailers which deal mainly in discount fabrics. Also see REMNANT.

**millinery** Any covering for the head, specifically *hats, bonnets, caps, hoods,* and *veils.*

**minaudiere** (min-ode-ee-air) See HANDBAGS.

**miner's cap** See CAPS.

**mini** (minn-ee) Originally a French term for a skirt length reaching to mid-thigh. Later applied to any fashion item that is tiny or short. See COATS, DRESSES, HANDBAGS, LENGTHS, LOOKS, MINI-JEANS under SHORTS, SILHOUETTES, and SKIRTS. Also see MINI-MINI BRAIDS under HAIRSTYLES and MINI-PETTI under PETTICOATS.

**minimal bra** See NUDE BRA under BRAS.

**mini-pettipants** See PETTIPANTS under PANTIES.

**miniver** 1. White or spotted gray and white fur, used for linings and trimmings in the Middle Ages. 2. White fur, especially ermine, used to trim "robes of state" in various countries. Also see LETTICE CAP and VAIR.

**miniver cap** See LETTICE CAP.

**mink** See FURS.

**mino** 1. Straw skirt or sometimes a collar worn in Japan as protection from rain. 2. Straw *raincoat* made of long pieces of plaited straw leaving long fringe from knees down. Shaped like a cone with square-cut window to see through. Worn in rural Japan by children and adults.

**Miranda pump** See SHOES.

**misericord** Man's dagger worn on right side as costume accessory in 14th and 15th c. Also spelled *misericorde. Der.* Named "pity-heart" because it was used to give the death stroke to a mortally wounded knight.

**miser purse** Small tubular silk purse closed at each end, with slit in center, and two movable rings to keep money at one end or other. Carried from latter half of 17th through 18th c. Compare with STOCKING PURSE.

**misses sizes** Women's garments cut for a well-proportioned adult figure about 5′5″ to 5′6″ tall, usually sized 6 to 18.

**Missoni** See APPENDIX/DESIGNERS.

**mistake hat** Woman's hat with tall flat-topped crown and brim cut in blunt point in front and turned up. Back brim was turned down. Worn on the back of the head in 1804.

**mistral** Sheer lightweight fabric made with nubby worsted yarns used for dresses.

**miter** 1. Very tall ornamental headpiece worn by Catholic and Episcopal church dignitaries with high separate pointed arches in front and back. 2. (mitre) Judaism: High priest's official headdress with gold plate on front engraved "Holiness to the Lord." Mentioned in Ex. 28:36–38. 3. Tall conical headdress with flaring top worn by Assyrians. 4. Woman's *fillet* worn in ancient Greece. 5. Name given by 19th c. writers to heart-shaped headdress worn in 15th c. Also spelled *mitre*.

**mitering** Making a square corner when sewing by cutting the two edges in a diagonal manner and stitching them together.

**mitons** See MOUFLES.

**mitre** See MITER.

**mittens** Gloves with a thumb and one other compartment for remaining fingers worn mainly by children and skiers for warmth. So called since 14th c.

**mitten sleeve** Woman's tightly fitted sleeve of lace or net reaching to the knuckles; used in the early 1890s in theater and dinner dresses.

**mitten-sleeve gown** 1. Infant's nightgown with drawstrings at the ends of the sleeves to cover the hands to prevent scratching. 2. In

1980s made with small mitten, with slit for hand, at end of sleeve.

**mitts** Fingerless gloves, reaching above wrist, often of lace or sheer fabric and worn with bridal dresses. Originally a hand-covering in wool worn in Colonial America.

**mix and match** The use of *separates* in coordinated prints and plaids with plain colors. Also see MIX AND MATCH LOOK under LOOKS.

**mixed suit** Man's suit with contrasting jacket and pants. Popularized in early 1930s, and developed into sport jacket and slacks look.

**mixture** 1. Term applied to a fabric woven with mixture yarns, or yarns composed of fibers dyed different colors. Fabric may also be made of yarns which vary in luster. 2. U.S. manufacturers of man-made fibers limit the term to fabrics with warp of one type yarn and filling of another, *e.g.*, a nylon warp with a rayon filling. Also see BLEND and COMBINATION YARN.

**Miyake, Issey** See APPENDIX/DESIGNERS.

**mizpah medallion necklace** See NECKLACES.

**mizz** Foot covering of soft cordovan leather worn inside shoes by people in the Mideast. Kept on at mosques and indoors when outer shoes (*papush*) were removed.

**Moabite turban** Woman's crepe turban draped in many folds and trimmed with an *aigrette* on one side. Worn tilted to back of head in early 1830s.

**moat collar** See RING COLLAR under COLLARS.

**mob cap** Woman's indoor cap of 18th and 19th c. made of white cambric or muslin with gathered crown and ruffled edge forming a bonnet. Had side *lappets*, called *kissing strings* or *bridles* which tied under the chin.

**mobile earrings** (mo-beel) See EARRINGS.

**moccasin** See INDIAN MOCCASIN and MOCCASIN-TYPE SHOE under SHOES, and SLIPPERS.

**mocha** (mo-ka) Milk-chocolate brown color.

**mocha leather**  See LEATHERS.

**mocha stone**  See AGATE under GEMS.

**mockador**  **1.** Term used for handkerchief or child's bib in 15th c. Also spelled *mockadour, moctour, moketer.* **2.** From 16th to early 19th c. spelled *mocket, mocketer.* **3.** See MUCKINDER.

**mock crepe**  See FLAT CREPE.

**mock pocket**  See POCKETS.

**mock romaine**  Dress fabric with a viscose rayon warp and filling of creped viscose rayon plus acetate filaments all twisted together to form one yarn. Compare with ROMAINE.

**mock seam**  Hosiery industry term for seam sewed into circular-knit hose to give appearance of *full-fashioned hose.*

**mock turtleneck**  See COLLARS and SWEATERS.

**mock-twist yarn**  Two colored rovings are fed into the spinning frame at the same time to make the yarn. Resembles a two-ply spiral yarn in the two-tone effect, but is only a fancy single yarn.

**moctour**  See MOCKADOR #1.

**mod**  British slang for a particular pseudo-Edwardian style adopted by the group of young men known as the Teddy boys and their girl friends about 1958. The mods opposed the rockers, who wore leather jackets, other motorcycle gear. Also see ROCKER LOOK, TEDDY BOY, CARNABY LOOK, BOOTS, CAPS, and LOOKS.

**modacrylic**  Generic term for a man-made fiber made from acrylic resins characterized by soft hand, warmth without bulk, resistance to moths and mildew, and high wrinkle recovery. Used for sweaters, other knitwear, and fur fabrics.

**mode**  French word for FASHION.

**model**  **1.** American term for person who is paid to wear a garment in a fashion show or for a photograph. **2.** French term for the garment itself.

**model dolls**  Full-sized dolls made of wax, wood, or fabric were a means of sending the current fashions to various places to show styles as early as the 14th c. The word "doll" was not used until about 1750—previously referred to as MOPPETS or *courrier dummies.* In America during the 18th c. called *little ladies* or *fashion babies.* At the Hotel Rambouillet in Paris two dolls were dressed in current styles—*La grande Pandora,* showing dresses and cloaks, while *la petite Pandora* showed underwear. Other dolls in the 17th and 18th c. were used by milliners, dressmakers, and hairdressers. Appeared in America in early 18th c., some where only 12 inches high. After 1850 paper-mâché heads were used. In the latter part of the 19th-c. fashion plates replaced the dolls. Also called *fashion dolls, fashion babies,* and *moppets.*

**model form**  See DUMMY.

**modeste**  See JUPE #1.

**modesty piece**  Piece of lace or lace-edged linen pinned to front of corset covering the cleavage of the bosom. Worn with décolleté bodices in 18th c.

**modiste**  (mow-deest)  **1.** French, milliner. **2.** In Great Britain a *dressmaker.*

**mofuku kimono**  Mourning kimono worn in Japan, usually black silk although sometimes white.

**mogadore**  Tie fabric similar to *faille* with fine crosswise ribs in a striped pattern. *Der.* Named for the Moroccan seaport town, *Mogador,* where similar colorful striped fabrics are worn by the natives. Also spelled *mogador.*

**mohair**  **1.** Hair of the angora goat. **2.** Coarse, wiry yarn of mohair fibers popular for sweaters in the mid and late 1960s. **3.** Fabric made of 100% mohair or of mohair and other fibers; the fiber must be indicated by percentage on the label. *Der.* Arabic, *mukhayyar,* "goat's hair."

**Mohawk hairstyle**  See HAIRSTYLES.

**Mohs scale** Used to rate degree of hardness of precious gems. The diamond, the hardest gem, has a hardness of 10 and will scratch any gems which rate below it. A set of minerals used to test gems was invented by Friedrich Mohs (1773–1839), a German minerologist. See GEM.

**moiles** See MULES.

**moiré** (more-aye) **1.** Fabric finish that achieves a wave-like watered effect by means of embossed heated rollers. **2.** Stiff, heavy-ribbed fabric with a watered effect. Made with warps of silk, rayon, or acetate, and filling of corded or ply yarns made of cotton or man-made fibers. The design is applied with heated rollers which flatten some of the heavy fillings thus changing the light reflection and making the pattern not permanent except on acetate. Used for evening dresses, skirts, and women's coats. *Der.* French, "watered."

**moiréing** See MOIRE #1.

**moiré pattern** (mo-ray) Fur term for appearance of Persian broadtail and American processed broadtail—flat furs with a wavy surface.

**mokadour/moketer** See MOCKADOR.

**mola** A blouse of multilayered cloth with elaborate multicolored primitive appliquéd designs. Worn by Cuna Indian women, who live on San Blas Island off Panama's northeastern coast.

**Moldavian mantle** Full-length woman's mantle of mid-1850s with long capes over the shoulders forming "elephant sleeves."

**molded** See BOOTS and DRESSES.

**molded felt** Hat industry term for the felt *hood* made into hat shape by placing over a wooden block shaped like a head.

**moleskin fabric** Durable cotton fabric with a suede-like nap in a satin weave made with coarse cotton yarns and a large number of filling yarns. Used for sportswear and work clothes. *Der.* Arabian, *molequin,* "old fabric." Also see BUCKSKIN FABRIC. Fabric should be called *moleskin fabric* to distinguish it from the fur by the same name. See FURS.

**molleton** French name for MELTON. Also spelled *molliton.*

**momie cloth** Classification of fabrics characterized by a special weave used to create a crinkled or pebbly surface peculiar to crepes. Also see MUMMY CLOTH. Weave is called a *momie weave.* See GRANITE WEAVE.

**Mondrian, Piet** (1872–1944) Dutch painter who was an exponent of neo-plasticism. Best known for his geometrics using only vertical and horizontal lines intersecting to form colored compartments of color. From about 1921 on, his palette held only red, yellow, and blue colors plus neutrals of white, black, and gray. Paintings include: *Broadway Boogie-Woogie,* or *Victory Boogie-Woogie,* and *Composition in Red, Blue, and Yellow.* See DRESSES.

**money belt** See BELTS.

**monkey** See FURS.

**monkey jacket** Short jacket made of heavy fabric like a *pilot coat.* Worn by sailors in rough weather from 1850s on.

**monk's** Adjective used for apparel and accessories worn by monks in monasteries since early Christian times. Extended to mean similar items copied from their vestments and used since. See BELTS, DRESSES, and SHOES.

**Monmouth cap** Man's knitted cap with high rounded crown and small turned-down brim worn by soldiers, sailors, and civilians. Listed as necessary item for new settlers in America. Most common in 17th c. although also worn from 1570s to 1625. Made at Monmouth and Bewdley in Worcestershire,

England. Also called *Bewdley cap* and worn by country folk by that name as late as 19th c.

**Monmouth cock**   Broad-brimmed man's hat of second half of 17th c. turned up or *cocked* in back.

**monocle**   See GLASSES.

**monofilament yarn**   Man-made yarns produced by pressing a mixture through a spineret with only one hole. Yarn comes out in a single strand. To be strong, yarn must be large in diameter. Compare with MULTIFILAMENT YARNS.

**monogram**   **1.** Marking of a single initial for person wearing the garment or the designer who created the garment. **2.** A person's initials worked into a design, engraved on earrings, cuff links, or a locket. **3.** Term meaning two or three initial letters of name embroidered on an item of clothing.

**monokini**   See SWIMSUITS.

**monster shoe**   See SHOES.

**Montague curls** (mon-ta-hue)   Woman's evening hairstyle with a fringe of crescent-shaped curls gummed to forehead in 1877.

**montero** (mon-tar-o)   Spanish hunting cap with round crown and ear flaps worn from 17th c. on. Also called *mountie cap* in England. Also spelled *mountera, montere*. *Der.* Spanish, *monte*, "hill."

**Montespan corsage** (mon-tes-pan)   Tight-fitting woman's evening bodice of 1843 with deep square-cut neckline and pointed waistline in front and back. *Der.* Named for Marquise de Montespan (1641–1707), mistress of Louis XIV of France.

**Montespan hat** (mon-tes-pan)   Woman's small round velvet evening hat of 1843 with brim turned up in front, trimmed with plume. *Der.* Named for Marquise de Montespan (1641–1707), mistress of Louis XIV of France.

**Montespan pleats** (mon-tes-pan)   Large, flat, double or triple *box pleats* used at waistband of skirt. Popular in 1859 and 1860s. *Der.* Named for Marquise de Montespan (1641–1707), mistress of Louis XIV of France.

**Montespan sleeve** (mon-tes-pan)   Woman's puffed sleeve of early 1830s made with upper part caught in band at elbow and lace Vandyke ruffle falling down from the band. *Der.* Named for Marquise de Montespan (1641–1707), mistress of Louis XIV of France.

**Montgomery beret**   Military cap, a bit larger than the conventional *basque beret* but set on a band like a Scottish *tam-o-shanter* and decorated with regimental insignia. Popularized by field marshal Bernard Law Montgomery, 1st Viscount Montgomery, commander of British ground forces in World War II.

**mont-la-haut** (mont-la-oh)   Framework used to support headdress. Same as COMMODE.

**montpensier mantle** (mon-pon-see-ay)   Woman's cape-like *mantle* of 1840s, long in back, with front ending in a point, and slit up sides leaving arms free.

**moonstone**   See GEMS.

**moppet**   See MODEL DOLLS.

**Moravian work**   See EMBROIDERIES.

**morganite**   See GEMS.

**Mori, Hanae**   See APPENDIX/DESIGNERS.

**morion**   Lightweight *helmet*, with brim forming peaks front and back. Turned down on sides with high comb in center extending from front to back over crown of head. Popular in 16th c. throughout Europe, and associated with Spanish conquistadors in Mexican conquest. Also called *comb morion*. Compare with BURGONET.

**morning cap**   Dainty cap of muslin, lace, tulle, and ribbon worn on the back of the head indoors in the morning by women from 1820s to end of 19th c. Also called a *breakfast cap*.

**MORNING CAP**

**morning coat** Term dating from 1870s for man's formal jacket with peaked lapels, formerly called a riding coat, and a Newmark coat when tapered from waist in front to knees in back. Called a *cutaway* in 1850s. See COATS.

**morning dress** **1.** Formal daytime attire for men consisting of *striped pants, cutaway coat, ascot tie*, and sometimes *top hat*. **2.** Term used in the 19th c. for any dress suitable for wear in the morning—for visiting, shopping, or at home. As differentiated from a more formal afternoon dress. Also called *morning gown* or *morning robe*. **3.** Term used in early 20th c. for a *house dress* of inexpensive fabric.

**morning frock coat** See FROCK COAT.

**morning-glory skirt** *Gored* skirt of early 20th c. fitted through hips, then flaring in trumpet fashion. Also called *serpentine skirt*.

**morning gown** **1.** Long, loose dressing gown with a sash at the waist worn indoors by men from 18th c. to 1830s. Similar to BANYAN. **2.** See MORNING DRESS #2.

**Morning Light® mink** See MUTATION MINK under FURS.

**morning robe** **1.** Type of *robe de chambre* worn in last half of 19th c. by women. **2.** See MORNING DRESS #2.

**Moroccan handbag** See HANDBAGS.

**Moroccan leather** See LEATHERS.

**Moroccan slippers** Leather slippers with turned-up toes; yellow worn by Moroccan men, red worn by women.

**Morris bells** Tiny bells attached to leather or ribbon trim worn for Morris dancing in 16th c. Tudor England. Bells were attached to ribbon-trimmed garters worn below knees, hat bands, sleeves, or special leggings.

**Morris, William** (1834–1896) Creator of printed and painted fabrics in intricate designs first produced in the 1870s. From 1881 until 1940 made in a large workshop in Merton Abbey, England. These prints used in fashionable clothing helped liberate the prim and sedate Victorian and Edwardian women to a gentler mode called the Pre-Raphaelite woman. He was an artist, an architect, social reformer, and writer—instrumental in changing Victorian taste and launching the Art Nouveau movement. The William Morris Society founded in 1956 for the preservation of his work and precepts has its headquarters in the Old William Morris house in Hammersmith, London.

**mortarboard** Academic headgear consisting of large, square black brim attached horizontally to a cap. Large tassel in center of flat top hangs to right side before graduation, to the left after. Worn all over U.S. today and since 14th c. at universities such as Oxford and Cambridge in England. Formerly called CATER CAP, CORNERCAP, CORNET, *Oxford cap*, and *trencher cap*. Also see CAPS.

**mosaic print** See PRINTS.

**moschettos** (mos-ket-os) Pants similar to men's *pantaloons* of early 19th c. but fitted to leg and worn over boots like *gaiters*.

**Moscow** **1.** Overcoating fabric made of heavyweight wool with a shaggy nap, similar to *Shetland*, used in very cold climates. Made in various qualities and usually piece dyed. **2.** Term used for lace made in Moscow in imitation of Italian lace.

**Moscow wrapper** Man's loose-fitting overcoat of 1874 with *pagoda sleeves*, fly front, narrow turned-down collar of astrakhan fur, and other fur trimming.

**moss agate** See GEMS.

**Mother Hubbard** Comfortable, plain housedress or wrapper, fitted only at the square yoke. Used for morning wear at home in late 19th and early 20th c. *Der.* Named for nursery-rhyme character.

**Mother Hubbard cloak** Woman's or girl's three-quarter length cloak of 1880s made of brocade, velvet, satin, or cashmere with quilted lining, high collar tied at neckline, full sleeves—often in *dolman* style with shirring over shoulders. Sometimes the back section was draped over a *bustle* and tied with ribbon bow.

**MOTHER HUBBARD WRAPPER, 1892**

**Mother Hubbard wrapper** Negligee or morning dress first worn by girls and women about 1890s. Styled for girls in ankle-length, full-length for women. Usually made with a square yoke with buttons or ties down the front. Later became a shapeless housedress called MOTHER HUBBARD. *Der.* Named for nursery rhyme character.

**mother-of-pearl** Shiny, iridescent substance lining shell of the pearl oyster, abalone, or other mollusks. Also called NACRE. See BUTTONS.

**mothproofing** A special finish used on wool fabrics or clothing to make them resistant to moths. Can also be purchased in a spray can for use at home.

**motorcycle** Adjective used for clothing and accessories worn for motorcycling. Some of the items are used for general wear. See HELMETS and SPORT JACKETS.

**motoring veil** See AUTOMOBILE VEIL.

**mouche** (moosch) *Der.* French, "fly" or "speck." See PATCH.

**moufles** **1.** Fingerless gloves or mittens worn in Merovingian Period for hunting or working. **2.** Late 14th-c. term for extensions of sleeves covering hand. Also called *mitons.*

**moulds** Men's *drawers*, padded with horsehair and other fibers, worn under *bombasted* or *balloon* trousers in England in latter half of 16th c. Also spelled *mowlds.*

**mountain climbing boot** See HIKING BOOT under BOOTS.

**mountera** See MONTERO.

**Mountie's hat** **1.** See HATS. **2.** See MONTERO.

**mourning bonnet** Any black bonnet worn to complete a mourning costume—especially in the 1870s and 1880s. An off-the-face bonnet, sometimes with a *Marie Stuart* peak, made of black silk, lavishly trimmed with *ruching* and ribbon, and tied under the chin. The veil was arranged over the face or allowed to hang down the back.

**mourning clothes** **1.** Clothing, usually black, worn for funeral or during mourning period after funeral since 14th c. Sometimes extended for one year. **2.** Clothing was black for mourning in 14th and 15th c. In 16th c. usually black but sometimes white was worn, particu-

**MOURNING DRESS, 1884**

larly by widows. **3.** During 19th and early 20th c., deep mourning of black was worn for six months, followed by half mourning, with purple or lavender added. See MOURNING CREPE.

**mourning crepe**   Collective term for black fabrics, usually crepe, worn for funerals or for mourning. During the 19th and early 20th c. deep mourning or black was worn for six months after the death of a close member of the family. *Half mourning*, a purple or lavender color, was worn for six months longer.

**mourning garland**   17th-c. term for a willow hat band or garland of willow worn for mourning.

**mourning jewelry**   Jet and black-enameled jewelry worn by women instead of regular jewelry during a mourning period from mid-19th through early 20th c.

**mourning knot**   Term for armlet with attached bunch of black ribbons worn on left arm for mourning by men in 18th c.

**mourning ribbon**   17th-c. term for black ribbon worn by men on the hat for mourning.

**mourning ring**   Massive ring, frequently black, later blue enamel, sometimes given to guests at funerals. Sometimes included portrait of deceased, emblems, motto, *e.g.*, "be prepared to follow me," or hair of the departed plaited in a design.

**mourning scarf**   Scarf of lawn about 3¼ yards long presented along with hat bands to principal mourners at funerals in 17th and 18th c.

**mourning tire**   17th-c. term for a *mourning veil* worn by women.

**mourning veil**   See VEILS.

**MOUSE JEWELRY, 1880**

**mouse jewelry**   **1.** Bracelets, brooches, rings, and earrings made of metal and decorated with replicas of mice worn by women during the 1880s. Bracelet consisted of a metal ring with three mice placed along the outer edge, their tails winding around the ring of metal. **2.** In the late 1960s and early 1970s jewelry for children was made with enameled metal or plastic mice, usually to look like Mickey Mouse®, a Walt Disney creation.

**mousers**   See BOOTS OR PANTS.

**mousquetaire collar**   (moose-ke-tare) Medium-sized turned-down collar, usually linen, with the front ends pointed. Fashionable for women about 1850. *Der.* From uniform of French musketeers or royal bodyguards of Louis XIII in 17th c.

**mousquetaire cuff**   (moose-ke-tare)   **1.** Deep, wide cuff flaring above the wrist, used on men's coats in early 1873. **2.** Sleeve of mousquetaire-type worn in late 1880s with flaring top and cuff sometimes trimmed with Vandykes. *Der.* From uniform of French musketeers or royal bodyguards of Louis XIII in 17th c.

**mousquetaire gloves** (moose-ke-tare) See GLOVES.

**mousquetaire hat** (moose-ke-tare) **1.** Wide-brimmed hat usually trimmed with three ostrich plumes. Also called *Swedish hat. Der.* From hats worn by French musketeers or royal bodyguards of Louis XIII in 17th c. **2.** Brown mushroom-shaped woman's straw hat edged with black lace hanging from the brim worn in late 1850s.

**mousquetaire mantle** (moose-ke-tare) Braid-trimmed black velvet mantle of mid-19th c. with short deep cuffs lined with quilted satin. Worn by women in 1847. *Der.* From cape worn by French musketeers or royal bodyguards of Louis XVIII in 17th c.

**mousseline de laine** (moose-a-lean dee lain) Lightweight worsted dress fabric made in plain weave which comes in several qualities and is usually printed. Sometimes made with a cotton warp and worsted filling. First made in France in 1826. Made in Massachusetts in 1840. *Der.* French, "wool muslin."

**mousseline de soie** (moose-a-lean dee swa) Transparent, fine, lightweight fabric made in the plain weave similar to *chiffon.* Best qualities are made of silk and are fine and glossy—other qualities are made of rayon. Perishable and not very durable, it is used for millinery and as a foundation fabric in women's clothing. *Der.* French, "silk muslin." This fabric, however, is much finer softer and lustrous than muslin.

**moustaches** See COIFFURE EN CADENETTEE.

**mouton-processed lamb** See FURS.

**mowlds** See MOULDS.

**mowles/moyles** See MULES.

**mozambique** (moe-zam-beak) **1.** Light-weight net-like fabric made in plaids, checks, and other openwork patterns with a combed cotton warp and a mohair filling. **2.** Woolen fabric characterized with a nap raised in geometrical patterns of squares and dots. **3.** An English fabric used in the last half of 19th c. similar to wool grenadine embroidered with silk.

**mozetta** See CAPES.

**muckinder** **1.** Term for a child's bib from early 16th to 19th c. **2.** Term for handkerchief in 17th c. Also see MOCKADOR. Also spelled *muckender, muckiter, muckinger.*

**muff** Warm tubular covering for the hands open at each end, frequently of fur or rich fabrics—usually round or oblong in many sizes—sometimes with concealed inner pockets. Carried by women as accessory matched to material of coat or trimming. Carried by men from second half of 16th to 19th c. See COUTENANCE, MUFFETEES, and ROXBURGH MUFF. Also see HANDBAGS.

**muffettees** **1.** Pair of small wrist muffs worn for warmth or when playing cards to protect wrist ruffles by both men and women in 18th and 19th c. **2.** Pair of small muffs worn for warmth in mid-18th c. closed at one end and sometimes with separate stall for thumb. **3.** Coarse mittens of leather or wool knit worn by old men in early 19th c.

**muffin hat** Man's fabric hat with round flat crown and narrow standing brim used for country wear in 1860s.

**muffler** See SCARFS.

**muff's cloak** Man's coat of late 16th and early 17th c. Same as *Dutch coat.* (Note: the "Dutch" meaning German.)

**Muir, Jean** See APPENDIX/DESIGNERS.

**mukluks** Adaptation of an Eskimo boot. See BOOTS and SLIPPERS.

**mulberry silk** Silk obtained from silkworms

that are fed on leaves of cultivated mulberry tree.

**mules    1.** Slippers that fit over toes but have no back or quarter. A term used since 16th c. Also spelled *moiles, moyles, mowles.* **2.** See SLIP-PERS.

**muleta**    See CAPES.

**Muller cut-down**    Man's hat of 1870s made like top hat with crown cut to half the height. *Der.* Named after English murderer whose hat led to his arrest in 1864.

**multifilament yarn**    Term used for rayon and man-made continuous yarns composed of many extremely fine strands twisted together.

**mummy cloth    1.** Dull finish crepe-like fabric used for mourning when dyed black. Cotton or silk is used for the warp and wool for the filling. **2.** Heavy linen or cotton fabric made in the plain weave and used unbleached for embroidery work. **3.** An early Egyptian cloth used for wrapping mummies. Woven with two or three warps to each filling. Sometimes confused with MOMIE CLOTH.

**Munro tartan**    See TARTANS.

**muscle shirt**    See KNIT SHIRTS.

**museum heel**    See HEELS.

**mushroom hat**    Woman's straw hat with small round crown and downward-curved brim, shaped like the cap of a mushroom. Worn in 1870s and 1880s, trimmed with ribbons,

flowers, and birds. Worn again in early 1900s and in the 1930s and 1940s usually made of felt.

**mushroom pleats**    See PLEATS.

**mushroom sleeve**    Woman's short sleeve pleated into the armhole with the lower edge trimmed with lace. Used in evening dresses of the mid-1890s.

**musk apples/muskballs**    See POMMES DE SENTEUR.

**muskrat**    See FURS.

**muslin**    Plain weave fabric made in many weights from very fine and sheer to coarse and heavy. Fine qualities have combed mercerized yarns which may be dyed and printed. Fabrics are lustrous, long wearing, very washable, and soft to the touch, *e.g.,* powder puff muslin. Coarser qualities have carded yarns, may have a variety of construction counts, and are used for sheets and pillowcases. Lightweight fabrics are used for summer dresses and blouses.

**muslin pattern    1.** Complete garment made in an inexpensive fabric, *e.g.,* muslin, usually draped on a dummy and, after muslin garment is finished, taken apart to provide a pattern for actual garment. **2.** Process used for fur designing. Also called a *toile.*

**mutation mink**    Term for strains of mink developed scientifically on fur farms by carefully mating the animals. See FURS.

**muumuu**    See DRESSES.

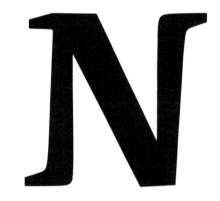

**nabchet** 16th c. slang term for *cap* or *hat*.

**nacre** (nah-creh) See MOTHER-OF-PEARL.

**nacré velvet** Velvet fabric with an iridescent or changeable effect caused by using one color for the background yarn and another color for the pile. Used for evening wear.

**naga-juban** Japanese woman's kimono-styled shift worn over a *shita-juban* in cold weather.

**nailing** Process used in making of fur garment which involves fastening strips of fur with thin nails to a board on which shape of garment is outlined. Currently called STAPLING because now staples are used in the process.

**nail sandals** Eastern sandals held on with a knob between the first and second toes. Sometimes raised in high cloglike fashion similar to Japanese GETA, frequently painted gold and highly ornamented.

**nainsook** Soft, lightweight cotton fabric slightly heavier than *batiste* woven with a plain weave. Better qualities are made with finer yarns, mercerized, and calendered on one side to increase glossiness. May also be bleached, dyed, or printed. French nainsook is given a calendered finish while English nainsook is given a soft finish. Formerly widely used for infants' clothing, now used for blouses.

**nakli daryai** Handloomed cotton fabric made in plain weave of fine yarns in India in imitation of *darya* silk and usually dyed light-green or yellow.

**nankeen** **1.** Rumanian term for a cotton fabric made with a white warp and colored filling—usually pink, red, or yellow. **2.** Fabric of brownish-yellow natural cotton finished without bleaching or sizing. Originally made in Nanking, China, later imitated in France and England. Also spelled *nankin*.

**nap** A fuzzy finish raised on cloth, made of loosely twisted yarns, by brushing the surface on one or both sides. When cutting a garment, pieces of the pattern should be placed so that the nap runs in the same direction.

**napa leather** See LEATHERS.

**nap finish** **1.** Leather finish that *suedes* the grain side of the leather. **2.** See EMERIZING.

**napkin** 16th and early 17th c. term for handkerchief used for the nose.

**napkin-cap** Man's 18th c. house cap or plain *nightcap* worn at home when wig was removed.

**napkin hook** Ornamental hook of 17th c., attached to woman's waistband, used to suspend a handkerchief.

**Napoleon** See BONAPARTE, NAPOLEON.

**NAPOLEON COAT**

**Napoleon coat** Woman's man-tailored hip-length jacket of mid-1890s with standing *military collar*, full *leg-of-mutton* sleeves, *military braid* down the front, and fastened with large *Brandenburgs*. *Der.* Named for Napoleon, who wore a similar style during his military career.

**Napoleonic collar**   See COLLARS.

**Napoleon necktie**   Man's medium-wide necktie of about 1818 in violet color worn passed around neck, crossed over chest, and ends tied to suspenders or continued around to tie at back of neck. *Der.* Reported to have been copied from necktie worn by Napoleon on his return from Elba. Later by about 1830 called *Corsican necktie.*

**Napoleons**   Long military boots, reaching above knee in front, with piece cut out in back. Worn by civilians on horseback in 1850s. *Der.* Named for Napoleon III, Emperor of France, 1851–1871.

**nappe/napperon**   See NAPRON.

**napping**   See NAP.

**napron**   Term used in 14th c. and first half of 15th c. for APRON. *Der.* Old French, *naperon,* diminutive of *nape* or *nappe,* "tablecloth" or "apron." From about 1460 words *apron* or *appurn* were used.

**narrow fabric**   Any non-elastic fabric such as tape, ribbon, or webbing, not more than 12″ wide, woven on narrow looms with selvages on both sides. Bias binding and seam binding are not included in this classification. British term for such items is small wares or narrow wares.

**narrow goods**   Term once used for fabrics woven 27″ wide or less.

**Nast, Condé** (1874–1942)   Publisher of *Vanity Fair* from 1913 to 1936 and of *Vogue* Magazine, including English and French Vogue from 1909 to 1942. President of The Condé Nast Publications Inc. which also published the *Vogue Pattern Book, Glamour,* and *House and Garden* during his lifetime. Other magazines were acquired later.

**National Press Week**   Semiannual event when newspaper fashion editors across the country are invited to New York by the *New York Couture Group* to see collections of Seventh Avenue designers. Idea originated with New York manufacturer Ben Reig in 1942.

**natté**   Loose basket-weave fabric made with different colored yarns in the warp and filling. *Der.* French, *natte,* "mat, matting, plait."

**natural bra**   See BRAS.

**natural fibers**   Fibers that are of animal, vegetable, or mineral origin, as opposed to man-made chemicals used to make yarn, *e.g., wool, linen, silk, cotton, jute, sisal, hemp, ramie, cashmere,* and *mohair.*

**naturalistic print**   See PRINTS.

**natural mink**   See FURS.

**natural shoulder**   See SHOULDERS.

**natural straw**   Straw made from any vegetable plant or tree grown in the soil, *e.g.,* bark, coconut fibers, grass, hemp, or palm tree fibers.

**natural waistline**   See WAISTLINES.

**Naugahyde®**   Trademark of U.S. Rubber Co. for a fabric with a vinyl resin coating on the face and a knitted fabric back. The knitted back gives stretch to the vinyl. Used for handbags, shoes, and rainwear.

**nautical**   Motifs and garments borrowed from naval or seamen's clothes usually emphasizing the use of a red, white, and blue color scheme. This style has been popular at intervals since 1865 and is a classic look for yachting and boating as well as townwear. Also see MIDDY BLOUSE under BLOUSES; SAILOR DRESS under DRESSES; SAILOR CAP and YACHTING CAP under CAPS; SAILOR HAT under HATS; PEA JACKET and MESS JACKET under JACKETS; BELL-BOTTOMS, DUNGAREES, and SAILOR PANTS under PANTS; LOOKS; JACK TAR SUIT; SAILOR SUIT; and PILOT COAT.

**Navajo**   American Indian tribe of Southwestern U.S. living in Arizona and New Mexico, noted for metalworking in iron, copper, and silver; blankets woven in distinctive geometric designs; and for handmade silver jewelry often set with turquoise, the latter a classic fashion in the West, and popular throughout the U.S.

**Neapolitan bonnet** (nee-a-poll-i-tan) *Leghorn* bonnet of 1800, trimmed with straw flowers and matching ribbons attached at the crown loosely tied over the chest. *Der.* Greek, *Napolis,* "old town," present day Naples.

**Neapolitan hat** (nee-a-poll-i-tan) Sheer lacy conical hat made in Naples of horsehair braid. Later, any hat made of this braid. *Der.* Greek *Napolis,* "old town," present day Naples.

**Nebula headdress** 19th c. term for GOFFERED HEADDRESS, worn from mid-14th to early 15th c.

**neckatee** Mid-18th c. term for neckerchief. See KERCHIEF and SCARFS.

**neck button** Decorative button of mid-17th c. worn at neck of doublet and held closed by loop on opposite side to reveal the fine shirt underneath.

**neck-chain** Decorative gilded brass or gold chain worn by men from Middle Ages to mid-17th c. Sometimes worn by travelers in Middle Ages who used a few links of it for money. For late 17th c. variation, see JACK CHAIN.

**neckcloth** **1.** General term from about 1660 to mid-19th c. for any type of man's neckwear or *cravat* wrapped around neck. Also see STOCK. **2.** Previous to 1660s indicated a *neckerchief* for women. Also see SCARFS.

**necked bonnet** Lined or unlined cap with wide flap fitted around back of neck worn by men in first half of 16th c.

**neckerchief** See KERCHIEF and SCARFS.

**neckerchief slide** Ring of metal, plastic, or woven braid used to hold *neckerchief* in place, *e.g.,* those used by Boy Scouts or cowboys.

**neck handkerchief** Synonym in 18th and 19th c. for man's NECKTIE or CRAVAT.

**necklace** Decorative accessory worn around the neck. Frequently made of beads or chain and sometimes of real or imitation gems set in gold, silver, or other metals. Primitive man wore necklaces of seeds, nuts, shells, teeth and claws of animals strung on grass or thong. Bronze Age necklace was of heavy ring-type called a *torque.* Egyptians wore amulets such as the *scarab* and the *utchat.* Greeks wore metal necklaces with a "fringe" of small vaselike drops of diamonds, sapphires, garnets, etc. Romans introduced the rope pearl necklace. From 16th c. on heavy chains and all types of necklaces were worn. In contemporary times an expensive necklace is frequently a status symbol. Also see BEADS and GEMS.

## NECKLACES

**Afro choker** Necklace made of strand of springy metal wound around the neck many times. *Der.* Copied from necklaces worn by Ubangi tribe in Africa. Also called UBANGI NECKLACE.

**American Indian n.** **1.** Long, flat necklace made with tiny glass beads of various colors, usually woven on small loom. **2.** Necklace of tiny colored beads worked in rope effect with American Indian motif as center pendant, also made by American Indians. American Indian jewelry was popular in late 1960s and early 1970s.

**ankh** Cross with top bar forming a loop worn attached to a chain. *Der.* Egyptian symbol for eternal life. Also called an *ansate cross.*

**ansate cross** See ANKH.

**beaded n.** See AMERICAN INDIAN NECKLACE

**beads** See separate category.

**bib n.** Necklace fitting close to base of neck

and extending in the shape of a child's bib. Sometimes made of linked metal looking like a short triangular scarf, sometimes made of several irregular strands of beads or chains arranged like a fringe.

**birthstone n.    1.** Medium-length fine-linked chain with individualized birthstones in the form of a bead placed about every three to four inches. Also see DIAMONDS BY THE YARD. **2.** A short fine-linked chain with an attached pendant containing a colored gem representing an individual birthstone. See alphabetical listing.

**byzance** Beads alternating with chain in long necklace with dangling ends similar to a rosary. Created by Christian de Gasperi (nephew of former prime minister of Italy) and given this name by Pierre Cardin in 1968 when it was popularized at St. Tropez, France.

**chain n.** Necklace consisting of links of metal sometimes interspersed with gems or imitation stones. May be short or long and looped around neck several times. Worn at intervals since 16th c. and very popular during the late 1960s and 1980s. See alphabetical listing for types of chain.

**charm n.    1.** Gold- or silver-toned chain worn around the neck with a cluster of metal objects attached in center front, *e.g.*, hearts, initials, animals, sports motifs, some engraved with slogans or names. **2.** Young girls' plastic chain necklace with dangling miniature plastic replicas of keys, telephones, tennis rackets, roller skates, pencils, and other ornaments.

**choker** Necklace fitting snugly around base of neck, may be one or more strands of beads, a suede or ribbon band, or a dog collar. Popular in 1930s and also in 1960s.

**cloisonné n.    1.** A medallion made of brass enameled with luminous colors and fired. Usually attached to a braided cord of nylon or polyester with an additional cord pendant from base of medallion. **2.** Necklace of beads with

some of the beads being made in the cloisonné manner.

**coin n.** Antique coin, *e.g.*, a five dollar gold piece, a silver dollar, an Indian head penny, or a buffalo nickel, worn on a chain around the neck, sometimes enhanced by a circlet of gold, silver, or other metal around edge.

**collar n.    1.** Necklace shaped and fitted to neck like a collar. Frequently of metal and popular in late 1960s. **2.** Tiny beads interlaced to form a separate collar.

**cross** Pendant made of metal, *e.g.*, gold or silver, the basic symbol of Christianity. The most common cross worn by both Protestants and Catholics is the *Latin cross*—an upright or vertical bar crossed near the top by a shorter horizontal bar. Dates from Roman times—predating Christianity. The *Greek cross* with both bars of the same length is also worn.

**crusader's cross** Name given in 1960s to a large Maltese cross used as a pendant for a necklace. Also called *St. George cross*.

**diamond n.    1.** Any necklace made of genuine diamonds. May be single or large diamonds set in pavé fashion in a band of precious metal, or diamonds set in precious metals and mounted in medallions linked together with chains of the same metal. **2.** Single large diamond suspended from a chain. **3.** Historic necklace of Marie Antoinette made entirely of diamonds which aided in precipitating the French Revolution.

**diamonds by the yard** Chain of 18k gold interspersed with a diamond at intervals, sold by the yard. Worn wrapped around the neck, wrist or waist. Introduced in 1974 by Elsa Peretti of Tiffany's, New York City. In 1984 sold for $2,500 per yard depending on size of diamonds. Also made of rubies, emeralds, or sapphires.

**dog collar    1.** Wide choker, similar to a dog's collar, often consisting of pearls or of band of metal set with diamonds or rhinestones. Introduced in early 20th c., popular in 1930s, and again in 1960s. **2.** CHOKER band of colored suede or leather worn tightly around neck, popular in early 1970s.

**hippie n.**   See BEADS category.

**lariat n.   1.** Long strand of beads or metal, sometimes ending in tassels, that is not fastened by a clasp. Worn looped into a knot or uses a slide so that the two ends hang free. **2.** Man's short necklace (or tie) usually made of leather that has a silver slide and two ends tipped with silver hanging free.

**lavaliere**   Pendant, sometimes set with precious stones, worn as a necklace on a fine chain. *Der.* Named after Louise de la Baume Le Blanc La Vallière, mistress of Louis XIV of France.

**lei**   Hawaiian garland of flowers, frequently orchids, worn around the neck. Often presented to visitors on arrival in Hawaii.

**locket**   Thin chain necklace with a gold or silver disk which opens to reveal picture of loved one or lock of hair. Very popular from mid-19th to early 20th c. and still worn, especially by children.

**love beads**   See BEADS category.

**matinee-length n.**   Bead necklace, usually of pearls or simulated pearls, 30″ to 35″ long.

**medallion n.**   Heavy chain necklace with large disk as a pendant, worn by women during various eras and introduced for men in late 1960s.

**mizpah n.**   Large medallion with a quotation from Genesis cut in half in zigzag fashion to form "his" and "hers" medals worn on a chain.

**neck ring**   Single narrow band of springy metal worn as choker, sometimes with dangling ornament. An innovation of late 1960s.

**opera-length n.**   Necklace of beads, usually of pearls or simulated pearls, 48″ to 120″ long, usually worn wrapped twice around the neck. Originated in 1890s for wear to the opera

or for other formal occasions. Also see ROPE NECKLACE.

**pearls**   Pearl beads, *e.g.*, natural, cultured, or simulated, all of one size or graduated in size. Usually strung on thread, often with a knot after each bead, made in a variety of lengths and worn in single strand or several strands. A classic fashion for many centuries. See CHOKER,

**CRUSADER'S CROSS**          **LAVALIERE**

**DOG COLLAR**

**MEDALLION**          **NECK RING**
**NECKLACE**

MATINEE, OPERA, ROPE NECKLACES, and GEMS category.

**pendant n.** Ornament such as a locket, medallion, or single jewel suspended around neck from a chain, thong, or cord worn since the Renaissance.

**religious medal** A pendant necklace worn by Christians of various sects, *e.g.*, the St. Christopher medal worn predominantly by Catholics.

**rope n.** Extra-long beaded necklace, usually of pearls, that may be wrapped around neck several times or worn long and knotted. Very popular in 1920s and worn continuously since then.

**rosary** See BEADS category.

**St. George cross** See CRUSADER'S CROSS.

**sautoir** (sow-twar) Pendant-type necklace with a dangling piece in front which may appear to be fringed at base. *Der.* French, woman's watch chain or a medal of honor worn around the neck.

**squash blossom n.** Traditional necklace made of tiny pieces of turquoise set in sterling silver. Stones are mounted in a manner to imitate flowers with many petals. *Der.* Hand-crafted by Zuni Indians of southwestern U.S. Some necklaces are in the collections of the Museum of Natural History and the Smithsonian Institution.

**tassel n.** Long linked chain necklace with cluster of as many as twelve short chains forming a tassel at the end.

**throat belt** Another name for DOG COLLAR of 1960s.

**Ubangi n.** See AFRO CHOKER.

**worry beads** See BEADS category.

**zodiac n.** Any necklace, usually of the pendant type, with medallion engraved with a personal sign of the zodiac. Popular in late 1960s and early 1970s.

**neckline** Contour or shape of clothing at neck, shoulders, or above the bust—ranging from high, to low, to strapless. A variety of necklines were not worn until the 20th c. Previous to that time, most clothing in one period had a similar style of necklines. Since the 19th c. evening dresses have usually had low necklines. Also see COLLARS category.

### ■ NECKLINES ■

**ascot n.** Long scarf approximately 4″ to 8″ wide attached to center back of neckline with ends brought around to the front and looped over. Popularized in the late 1920s, reintroduced in late 1960s, and popular since for both men and women. *Der.* Fashionable horse-racing spot, Ascot Heath, England. Also called ASCOT COLLAR, *stock neckline*, and *stock collar*.

**asymmetric n.** Any neckline which appears different on either side of center front, or closes to one side of center front of blouse or shirt, *e.g.*, a slit at left side closed with a loop and button which, when opened, makes one lapel on right.

**banded n.** Narrow band attached to neckline and buttoned in front. Introduced in early 1980s, it looks somewhat like neckbands of shirts of the 1890s and early 1900s without the ATTACHED COLLAR.

**band n.** See CHINESE, MANDARIN, and NEHRU NECKLINES.

**bateau n.** (ba-toe) Boat-shaped neckline slit over to shoulders but high in front and back. Popular neckline in 1930s and 1940s and revived in 1980s. Also called *boat neckline*. *Der.* French, "boat."

**boat n.** See BATEAU NECKLINE.

**CREW NECKLINE**

**NEHRU NECKLINE**

**DRAWSTRING NECKLINE**

**ONE-SHOULDER NECKLINE**

**KEYHOLE NECKLINE**

**OFF-THE-SHOULDER NECKLINE**

**SABRINA NECKLINE**

**SWEETHEART NECKLINE**

**SCOOP NECKLINE**

**V-NECKLINE WITH DICKEY**

**caftan n.** Round neckline with slit down center front and frequently finished with embroidery, beading, or diamanté bands. Fashionable in late 1960s and adapted from the African CAFTAN.

**camisole n.** Neckline cut straight across above the bust with straps over the shoulders. Also see CAMISOLE in alphabetical listing.

**cardigan n.** Plain, round, collarless neckline with center front opening, as on cardigan sweaters. *Der.* Named for the 7th Earl of Cardigan who needed an extra layer of warmth for his uniform during the Crimean War of 1854.

**Chinese n.** Classic standing-band collar attached to apparel with ends not quite meeting in front. Also called a CHINESE COLLAR.

**choker n.** Standing neckline coming up high on throat and fastened in back. Very fashionable from 1895 to 1910 on Gibson girl blouses and reintroduced in 1968, continuing in popularity in 1980s. Also called a CHOKER COLLAR.

**Cossack n.** Standing band, closing on one side, usually decorated with embroidery. *Der.* From shirts worn by Russian Cossacks.

**cowl n.** Draped neckline falling in soft folds. Blouse or dress is usually bias cut for better drape. Popular style of the 1920s, 1930s, and 1980s.

**crew n.** Round neckline finished with knit ribbing. *Der.* From neckline on crew-racing shirts.

**décolleté n.** (day-coll-e-tay) Any neckline cut very low. *Der.* French, "to bare the neck."

**dog-collar n.** See HALTER NECKLINE.

**drawstring n.** Neckline with cord threaded through a casing to be gathered and adjusted high or low. Inspired by peasant styles. Introduced for little girls in the 1930s and used intermittently since.

**Dutch n.** See SQUARE NECKLINE.

**elasticized n.** Low neckline cut very wide and finished by turning fabric over a narrow band of stretched elastic making a wide scooped neckline in front and back. Used for nightgowns and blouses.

**Florentine n.** Wide square-cut neckline extending to shoulders which is cut straight across front and back. *Der.* Inspired by Florentine paintings of the Renaissance.

**funnel n.** Neckline coming up high on the throat cut in one with garment. Made with shoulder seams slanted upward toward neck in the shape of an inverted funnel.

**halter n.** Sleeveless front of garment held by a strap around neck leaving back and shoulders bare. May be gathered by a drawstring at neck and tied in a bow, or held by a jeweled band like a dog collar.

**Henley n.** Round neckline made with ribbing and front placket opening. *Der.* From crew racing shirts worn at Henley, England.

**horseshoe n.** Scooped neckline made low in front in shape of a horseshoe.

**jewel n.** High round neckline made with or without binding as a simple background for jewels.

**keyhole n.** High round neckline made with wedge-shaped or keyhole piece cut out at center front.

**mandarin n.** Same as CHINESE NECKLINE. *Der.* For neckline used on the Chinese mandarin robes. Also called MANDARIN COLLAR.

**Nehru n.** (nay-rue) Standing-band neckline similar to *Chinese* and MANDARIN necklines, sometimes with curved edges in front, popular in mid-1960s. Also called NEHRU COLLAR. Also see RAJAH NECKLINE. *Der.* For Jawaharlal Nehru, Prime Minister of India, 1947–1964.

**off-the-shoulder n.** Low neckline, usually elasticized, extending around upper part of arms baring the shoulders, sometimes with straps, sometimes without. Frequently finished with a wide ruffle around the edge. Popular for evening gowns in 1930s and 1940s, and used intermittently since. Popular in 1980s for nightgowns, blouses, and evening dresses.

**one-shoulder n.** Asymmetric neckline starting under one arm and continuing diagonally over opposite shoulder leaving one shoulder bare. Popular for evening dresses, swimsuits, and nightgowns. Also called *sling neckline.*

**peasant n.** Low round neckline gathered into a bias band, or made with a drawstring. Sometimes worn in off-the-shoulder fashion. See DRAWSTRING NECKLINE.

**placket n.** Slit at neckline bound with bias binding, or made with a facing, sometimes in a contrasting color. Bias may continue around neck or a simple collar may be added.

**plunging n.** Neckline made with low V in center front, sometimes extending to the waist or below. Fashionable for extreme styles in the 1960s and continued in popularity in 1980s.

**rajah n.** Variant of NEHRU NECKLINE. *Der.* From rajahs in India who wear garments with this type of neckline. Also called a RAJAH COLLAR. Fashionable in mid and late 1960s.

**Sabrina n.** High boat neckline fastened together at shoulders with spaghetti strings that are tied in bows. Originally designed by Edith Head and worn by Audrey Hepburn in film *Sabrina* in 1950s.

**scoop n.** Low curved neckline extending to shoulders or cut deep in front, back, or both. Introduced for evening wear in late 1930s, used on daytime dresses in 1950s, and blouses since late 1960s.

**sling n.** See ONE-SHOULDER NECKLINE.

**square n.** Moderately low neckline cut square in front. Also called *Dutch neckline.*

**stock n.** See ASCOT NECKLINE.

**strapless n.** Boned or elastic bodice which requires no shoulder straps. An innovation of the 1930s popular for evening wear as well as sportswear, revived in 1970s, and continuing into 1980s.

**surplice n.** Neckline of wraparound blouse, dress, or robe with one side lapping over other to form a V in center front. Introduced in 1920s and used since.

**sweetheart n.** Moderately low neckline with heart-shaped center front. Sides of neckline slant toward neck in front with back rounded. Introduced in 1930s and used intermittently since.

**turtleneck** See TURTLENECK COLLAR under COLLARS.

**Ubangi n.** Extremely high choker-type neckline covering the entire neck. Sometimes made of fabric, sometimes of chain or springy wire wrapped around the neck. Popularized in late 1960s. *Der.* Inspired by women of the Ubangi, a native tribe of Africa.

**U-n.** See HORSESHOE NECKLINE.

**V-n.** Cut down in front or back to a sharp point, resembling the letter V.

**neckpiece** *Boa* or *scarf*, usually of fur.

**neck ring** See NECKLACES.

**neck ruche** Woman's neckpiece of early 20th c. made of frilled *mousseline* pleated, sewed to a ribbon, and worn around the neck with long hanging streamers of silk or ribbon in front.

**neckstock** Stiffly folded made-up cravat buckled in back worn by men in 18th and 19th c. See STOCK.

**necktie** See TIES.

**necktie pin** See STICKPIN under PINS.

**neckwear** Accessories worn around neck exclusive of jewelry, includes *neckties, scarfs,* and *collars.*

**neck whisk** **1.** Small wired or stiffened fan-shaped man's sheer standing collar worn inside standing collar of the doublet in late 16th c. **2.** Flat round man's collar with pointed ends open in front. Worn in Spain in 17th c.

**needle** **1.** Small thin spike, usually of polished steel, with one end pointed and an eye at the other end through which the thread is drawn for sewing. **2.** A long implement without an eye that has a hook at one end used for knitting or for crocheting.

**needlepoint** See EMBROIDERIES, LACES, REP and PETIT POINT under STITCHES.

**needle tapestry work** See EMBROIDERIES.

**needle toe** See TOES.

**needle trades** See APPAREL INDUSTRY.

**negligee** (neh-glee-zheh) See ROBES.

**negligee costume** (neh-glee-zheh) Informal costume, worn primarily in privacy of home or bedroom. Usually a long easy robe of supple material, ranging from simple cotton to elaborately trimmed silk. Worn by both men and women from 18th through 19th c. and developing into the TEA-GOWN for women in last quarter of 19th c. Also see BANYAN, ROBE, NIGHT COIF and NIGHTGOWN. *Der.* French, *négligée*, "neglected."

**NEGLIGEE SHIRT**

**negligee shirt** (neh-glee-zheh)  Term used for a man's shirt, either white or striped, with white stiff separate collar and white cuffs. Worn from early 1900s to about 1925.

**Nehru styles** (nay-roo)  See COLLARS, JACKETS, NECKLINES, and SUITS.

**Nelson**  Bustle worn by women about 1819 and 1820 to achieve the *Grecian bend* stance. Compare with FRISK.

**neon socks**  See SOCKS.

**net**  See BOBBINET.

**net embroidery**  See TULLE under EMBROIDERIES.

**nether integuments**  See INEXPRESSIBLES.

**nether stocks**  See LOWER STOCKS.

**Netsuke** (net-sue-keh)  Miniature, palm-sized fastener used by Japanese to secure pouches, purses, and other articles to kimonos which are pocketless. Made in any material, *e.g.*, wood, bone, glass, or leather and lavishly sculptured in form of plants, animals, mythological deities, folk heroes, and men in all vocations and occupations. Used to express the religions, history, and society of Japan. *Der.* Japanese, *ne* "root" (as originally made of roots and gourds) and *tsuke*, "to fasten."

**Newgate fringe**  Colloquial term in 19th c. for men's short whiskers that formed a fringe around the jaw.

**New Look**  Style introduced by couturier CHRISTIAN DIOR in Paris in 1947. See generic definition in LOOKS.

**Newmarket coat**  Man's long *tail coat*, worn from 1838 on, made single- or double-breasted with front skirts cut away and rounded, often with flap pockets and cuffed sleeves. Formerly called a *riding coat*; from 1750 to 1800 called a *Newmarket frock*. After 1850, generally called a *cutaway*. *Der.* Named for racing center of Newmarket, England. Also see CUTAWAY under COATS.

**Newmarket frock**  See NEWMARKET COAT.

**Newmarket jacket**  Woman's close-fitting hip-length jacket with turned-down collar, silk-faced lapels, flapped pockets, and cuffed sleeves. Frequently part of the "masculine" *tailor-made* fashions of the 1890s.

**NEWMARKET OVERCOAT #2, 1891**

**Newmarket overcoat** **1.** Man's long single-breasted overcoat of 1880s similar to a *frock overcoat*. Usually made with velvet collar and cuffs and frequently made of *homespun*. **2.** Woman's long single- or double-breasted winter coat with velvet collar, lapels, tight sleeves, cuffs, and flapped pockets. Made of heavy fabric for winter from mid-1880s to 1890s.

**Newmarket top frock** Man's overcoat of 1895 similar to a *frock coat* made of rough *cheviot* fabric with velvet collar, pockets on waist seams, and the lower part lined with checked fabric—upper part with silk or satin.

**Newmarket vest** Plaid or checked vest, buttoned high, made with or without flapped pockets, worn by sportsmen in mid-1890s.

**newsbag** See HANDBAGS.

**newsboy cap** See CAPS.

**New York Couture Business Council, The** An organization of manufacturers of ready-to-wear clothing serving as a trade council and mediating disputes between retailers and manufacturers. The promotional arm of this organization is called *The New York Couture Group* and is responsible for *National Press Week*.

**neyge** See EDGE #2.

**niced** See NYCETTE.

**NIGHTCAP, 1867**

**nightcap** **1.** Plain washable cap worn in bed by men and women from earliest times sometimes made like stocking cap of knitted silk with tassel on top. In 19th c. called a *jellybag*. Also see BIGGIN. **2.** 14th to mid-19th c. skullcap

with upturned brim, worn indoors by men when wig was removed. **3.** See NAPKIN CAP. **4.** See MOBCAP.

**night clothes** An older term referring to apparel worn to bed, *e.g. nightgowns, pajamas*, and *nightshirts*.

**night coif** Woman's cap worn with *negligee costume* or in bed in 16th and 17th c. Frequently embroidered and usually worn with FOREHEAD CLOTH.

**nightgown** **1.** An item of apparel, styled similar to a dress, worn by men, women and children for sleeping. Sometimes abbreviated to *gown* or *nightie*. Also called a *sleeper*. Meaning of the word and use of the item dates from the early 19th c. **2.** From the 16th to the 19th c. an informal coat for men cut on contemporary lines which could be worn outdoors as well as indoors. See INDIAN NIGHTGOWN or BANYAN in alphabetical listing. **3.** In the 18th c. a comfortable women's dress, without stays, worn either outdoors or indoors. See MORNING GOWN in alphabetical listing.

### ▬ NIGHTGOWNS & NIGHTSHIRTS ▬

**baby doll n.** Bouffant hip-length nightgown made with short puffed sleeves and matching bloomers. Usually made of sheer fabric, and popular in 1940s and 1950s.

**bubble cover-up** Loose-fitting, mini-length blouson-type gown gathered below hips into wide band forming a very short shirt.

**dorm shirt** Above-the-knee nightshirt made of knitted fabric and styled like a T-shirt.

**flannel n.** Traditional full-length winter nightgown styled with a square yoke accented with a ruffle made of flannelette or cotton flannel.

**NIGHTSHIRT/NIGHTSHIFT**

**TOGA NIGHTGOWN**

**BABY DOLL SHIFT**    **JULIET GOWN**

**PEIGNOIR SET**

**flashy nightshirt**   Low, scoop-necked, raglan-sleeved, above-the-knee nightshirt made with curved hem split at sides. Made of sweatshirt gray polyester knit. Similar to FLASHDANCE KNIT SHIRT.

**granny gown**   High-necked, long-sleeved, full-length gown made with ruffle-trimmed yoke, no waistline seam, and sometimes a ruffled flounce at hem. *Der.* Worn by a young girl who copied styles worn by her grandmother or "granny."

**Juliet gown**   Nylon gown, usually made full length with a high or Empire waistline. May be lace-trimmed, have tiny puffed sleeves, and have ruffle at hem.

**nightshift/nightshirt**   **1.** Sleeping garment worn by both men and women. Frequently made in "his or hers" style like a man's shirt in mini, knee, or calf length, usually with rounded hem and a slash at side seams. Formerly worn by men and boys before introduction of pajamas about 1880. **2.** Mid-1980s versions for women made in tank top, shirt, or T-shirt styles double as day wear.

**peignoir set** (pai-nwar)   A matching robe and gown set usually made full length. Gown may be made of knit nylon with robe of sheer nylon. Originally a *negligee costume*, with an unboned bodice and full sleeves worn in 1830s and 1840s. Also see NEGLIGEE COSTUME and SACK DRESS in alphabetical listing.

**shortie**   Term for mini-length gown.

**sleepcoat**   Styled like a man's pajama top but longer in length.

**slip gown**   Bias-cut full-length gown made with no waistline seam and slip-like top with V-neck and narrow shoulder straps. Sometimes made of satin with matching jacket.

**slouch gown**   Thigh-length gown of knitted fabric styled like a long sweatshirt with a band at hem.

**toga n.**   Gown styled with one shoulder or with conventional top and one or both sides split to hips. Introduced in the late 1960s. *Der.* From draping of Roman toga.

**waltz-length n.**   Gown made in mid-calf length, popular since 1950s.

---

**nightie**   See NIGHTGOWN.

**night rail**   **1.** Term originally used for a nightgown. Also spelled *night rayle.* **2.** Loose-fitting dress or robe made of plain drab-colored fabric worn in the morning by women in Colonial America. **3.** Woman's shoulder cape of lawn, silk, satin, or lace. Worn from 16th to early 18th c. as boudoir jacket or in bed.

**nightshift/nightshirt**   See NIGHTGOWNS.

**nine-tenths length**   See LENGTHS.

**ninon**   Lightweight, somewhat crisp, translucent to transparent open weave fabric made of very fine yarns in a plain weave of silk, nylon, polyester, acetate, and other man-made fibers. Used primarily for curtains, but often for blouses, dresses, evening gowns, and petticoats.

**Ninon coiffure**   Hairstyle with ringlet curls over the forehead, shoulder-length curls at sides (sometimes wired), and back hair pulled into a knot. Introduced in England in mid-17th c. *Der.* Style was later given this name after Anne de Lenclos (1620–1705), known as Ninon de Lenclos, a legendary courtesan and Parisian fashion leader.

**no-bra look**   Discarding of the bra by women particularly under *see-through* clothing. Also see LOOKS.

**nomad look**   Look of roaming nomadic people of Middle East. Also see AFGHANISTAN JACKET and VEST, and LOOKS.

**nonwoven fabrics**   **1.** Fabrics constructed by means other than weaving, braiding, knitting, crocheting, and lacemaking. **2.** Newer terminology describes *nonwoven* as interlocking or bonding of fibers (or both) by chemical, mechanical, thermal, solvent methods, and combinations.

**Norell, Norman**    See APPENDIX/DESIGNERS.

**Norfolk jacket**    Man's informal jacket introduced in 1880s for sports. Made with tailored collar and one or two box pleats down front and back with belt of the same fabric sliding under or over the pleats at waistline. See SPORT JACKETS.

**Norfolk shirt**    Man's lounging jacket styled like a shirt made of rough tweed with box pleat down center back and two box pleats on either side of front. Worn with matching belt. Had a tailored collar and bands at wrist. Worn from 1866 to 1880.

1914                 1905

**NORFOLK SUIT**

**Norfolk suit**    **1.** Little boy's suit with top styled like *Norfolk jacket* with one or two box pleats in front and back, usually worn belt at waist continuing under pleats. Worn with *knickerbockers* to above knee, BUSTER BROWN COLLAR, BOW TIE, and large off-the-face hat in early 1900s. **2.** Man's suit with matching coat and pants, jacket styled in *Norfolk*

manner, worn from about 1912 to about 1930. Also see NORFOLK JACKET under SPORT JACKETS.

**Norfolk suiting**    Woolen or worsted fabric made in Norfolk County, England. Popular for use in *Norfolk suits* and *jackets.*

**Normandie cape**    Lightweight, hip-length woman's cape of late 1890s made with ruffles extended down center front, around the hem, sometimes around yoke, and a standing collar or a double-tiered ruff at the neck.

**Northamptonshire lace**    See LACES.

**Norwegian morning cap**    Woman's cerise and white striped Shetland wool, knitted kerchief-shaped head covering of 1860s. Tied under the chin with a ribbon and trimmed with bows over crown and back of the head. Also called *Norwegian morning bonnet.*

**notched collar**    See COLLARS.

**notched lapel**    See LAPEL.

**Nottingham lace**    See LACES.

**nouch**    See OUCH.

**novelty yarn**    Yarns made of more than one color with a nub, a slub, a loop, or some other variation. Also see BOUCLÉ, CHENILLE, NUB, SLUB, and RATINÉ YARNS.

**nub yarn**    Yarn made with lumps, knots, or flecks of fibers at intervals—sometimes of different colors giving a mottled effect to the finished fabric.

**nude bra**    See BRAS.

**nude look**    Wearing of flesh-colored body-stocking or nothing at all under *see-through* clothes. Also see BRAS, NUDE LOOK and SEE-THROUGH LOOK under LOOKS.

**nugget ring**    See RINGS.

**numbered duck**    Firm, heavyweight fabric woven in yarns varying in weight. Given various numbers according to their weight, *e.g.,* #1 duck weighs 18 ounces per yard, #2 weighs 17 ounces per yard. Also see DUCK.

**numeral shirt** See FOOTBALL JERSEY/SHIRT under KNIT SHIRTS.

**nun's habit** Apparel worn by nuns, women members of convents of the church, dating from Middle Ages. Usually a covered-up ankle-length black dress, often with white collar and belted with a long cord. Head and neck are wrapped in starched white cotton like a *wimple*, with shape varying according to the convent or order. Usually covered by a long black veil. Many changes have been made in Roman Catholic nuns' habits since 1965, *e.g.*, simpler headdresses, shorter skirts, brown, navy, and gray colors added to conventional black color.

**nun's tucks** Tucks, usually of 2″ or more in width, placed around the hem of a dress or used on sleeves in a series of three, five, or seven.

**nun's veiling** Sheer lightweight fabric woven in a plain weave of fine silk, cotton, worsted yarns or combinations. Usually dyed black for use by nuns of various orders, particularly for veils. Also used for mourning.

**Nureyev shirt** See SHIRTS.

**nurse's cap** See CAPS.

**nurse's cape** See CAPES.

**nutria** See FURS.

**nycette** Late 15th and early 16th c. term for light scarf worn at neck. Also spelled *niced*.

**nylon** **1.** Generic term for a man-made fiber made of long chain of synthetic polyamides extracted from coal and petroleum. Introduced in 1939 by DuPont and later produced by other manufacturers. Qualities include a silky hand, strength, crease resistance, washability, and resistance to mildew and moths. **2.** Yarn as used in knitted and woven fabrics for hosiery, dresses, gloves, nightgowns, shoes, etc.

**nylons** Synonymous with women's hosiery. Also see HOSE.

**obi** (o-bee) Sash approximately 15″ wide and 4 to 6 yards long, worn by Japanese men, women, and children on top of *kimono*. Obi is folded lengthwise with fold toward hem wrapped twice around waist, and tied in flat butterfly bow in back. Style of tying and design of fabric vary according to age and sex. Sometimes spelled *obe*. Also see HEKO-OBI, KAKU-OBI, and OBIAGE. Also see OBI-STYLED SASH under BELTS.

**obiage** (o-be-ege) Small pad that supports upper loop of obi or sash held by silk cord tied in front.

**obi hat** Woman's hat of 1804 with high flat-topped crown and narrow brim rolled up in front. Ribbons come over crown and brim of hat tying under chin.

**oblong hoops** British term used from 1740s to 1760s for PANNIERS on women's gowns which were flattened from front to back and projected sideways over hips. Sometimes hinged to permit passage through narrow doorways. Also called *square hoops* and FALSE HIPS.

**obsidian** See GEMS.

**ocelot** (ah-seh-lot) See FURS.

**ocepa** See ANDEAN SHIFT under DRESSES.

**ocher/ochre** (o-ker) Muddy earthy yellow or reddish-yellow color of a clay containing iron ore.

**octagonal hat** Cap shaped like a *tam* made of six wedges stitched together forming an octagonal-shaped crown. Sometimes made of two contrasting fabrics and usually trimmed with two short streamers hanging in back. Popular for girls and young women in mid-1890s.

**octagon tie** Man's made-up scarf or cravat worn from 1860s on with long wide piece of fabric folded to form an X in front and attached to a narrow band fastening at back of neck with hook and eye.

**oegge** See EDGE.

**off-color diamond** See DIAMONDS.

**officer's cape** See CAPES.

**officer's coat** See GUARDSMAN under COATS.

**officer's collar** Woman's collar of mid-1880s with stiff standing band around neck, sometimes with frill of lace at neck. A tri-layered *jabot* with *vandyke* edges was worn in center front.

**off the peg** British expression for buying ready-made clothes from retail stores rather than custom-made clothing.

**off-the-shoulder** See NECKLINES.

**oilet** (oy-let) Term for EYELET used in 18th and 19th c.

**oilskin** **1.** Yellow waterproof fabric made by coating cotton with linseed oil. Used originally for raincoats worn by fishermen, sailors, and children. Term also used for fabrics given waterproof finish. **2.** Garments made of this or similar fabric, *e.g.*, raincoats, pants, and jackets, worn by sailors in rainy weather.

**oker** 16th-c. term for boot worn by ploughman. Also spelled *hogger*, *hoker*. Also see COCKER.

**old mine cut** See GEM CUTS.

**old rose** Dull rosy-pink color with a grayish cast.

**olefin** Generic term for a man-made fiber made from petroleum by-products. Used for women's knitted underwear and hosiery.

**olive button** Long, oval-shaped, silk-covered button worn from mid-18th c. on.

**Olive, Frank** See APPENDIX/DESIGNERS.

**Oliver, André** See APPENDIX/DESIGNERS.

**Oliver Twist dress** Young girl's dress worn about 1919. Made with double-breasted wrap-front and skirt pleated at sides and back. Had a fluted frill at neckline and at end of three-quarter length sleeves.

**OLIVER TWIST SUIT & DRESS, 1919**

**Oliver Twist suit** Little boy's suit worn about 1919 similar to girl's *Oliver Twist dress*. Made with wrap closing, double-breasted effect on blouse, and knee pants buttoned to blouse. Made with a frill at neck and sleeves.

**olivette** (o-lee-vet) Oval-shaped button, same as FROG BUTTON, used with BRANDENBURGS from mid-18th c. on.

**olivine** See GEMS.

**Olympics®** Sporting contests held both in the winter and summer, every four years, with participants from around the world. All types of sport clothes are worn. See DRESSES and SPORTS SUITS. *Der.* From the games and festivals held in honor of the god Zeus on the plain of Olympia in ancient Greece, where a laurel wreath was presented to the victor.

**ombré** (om-bray) Closely related tones of color with monochromatic shading from light to dark of single color, *e.g.*, pale pink to red, or in several colors like a rainbow. *Der.* French, "shaded." Also see STRIPES.

**ondé** **1.** Cross-dyed French fabric made with cotton warp and bright colored filling yarn. **2.** French term used for a moiré effect first used in the 14th c.

**one hundred pleater** See CHEF'S HAT under HATS.

**one-piece bathing suit** See MAILLOT under SWIMSUITS.

**one-shoulder** See DRESSES, NECKLINES, and TOGA NIGHTGOWN under NIGHTGOWNS.

**one-size bra** See STRETCH BRA under BRAS.

**onion** See POMPADOUR under HAIRSTYLES

**onyx** See GEMS.

**ooryzer** Ancient helmet, similar to a gold skullcap fitted to head, worn by Frisian women in the Netherlands. Earrings were attached near temples to spiral ornaments. Lace cap was placed over top toward back of head showing gold in front. Also called *golden casque.*

**opal** See GEMS.

**opaque** Term applied to gems and fabrics through which no light passes, *e.g.*, turquoise, onyx, and denim fabric. Also see HOSE and PANTYHOSE. Compare with TRANSLUCENT and TRANSPARENT.

**op art print** See PRINTS.

**open-back shoe** See SLINGBACK under SHOES.

**open-crown hat** See HATS.

**open robe** Term used in 19th c. for dress with overskirt split in front revealing an ornamental underskirt or petticoat. Worn since 16th c. but not called by this name. Worn during 18th c. but most fashionable, mainly for daytime and evening wear, in 1830s and 1840s.

**open-shank** See SANDALS and SHOES.

**open-toed shoe** See SHOES.

**open-welt seam** See TUCKED under SEAMS.

**openwork** Knitting, weaving, or embroidery in which threads are used in such a manner that holes in fabric give a lacy effect. See EM-BROIDERIES.

**opera** Adjective used for apparel and accessories designed to be worn to musical renditions of operas. See CAPES, GLASSES, GLOVES, LENGTHS, SHOES, SLIPPERS, and OPERA WRAP.

**opera hat** **1.** Small tricorn hat carried under the arm rather than worn from mid-18th c. on. Also called *chapeau bras.* **2.** Bicorn hat worn from 1800 to 1830 with a crescent-shaped brim front and back which could be compressed and carried under the arm. Also called a *military folding hat.* **3.** After 1830 the CIRCUMFOLDING HAT, and later the GIBUS were worn. **4.** See HATS.

**opera length** See NECKLACES.

**OPERA WRAP, 1900**

**opera wrap** Term used in early 1900s for women's full-length opera cape usually made of elaborate fabric trimmed with fur or feathers.

**opossum** See FURS.

**opus Anglicum** See ENGLISH WORK under EMBROIDERIES.

**opus araneum** See ANTIQUE under LACES.

**oralia** (o-ray-lee-a) Early medieval term for pointed veil. By first quarter of 14th c., known as *cornalia* or *cornu.* Also spelled *orales. Der.* Latin, "veil."

**Oreilles de Chien** (or-ray de she-en) Nickname for two long curls worn at either side of face by men from 1790 to 1800. *Der.* French, "dog's ears."

**organdy** Light sheer cotton fabric with a permanent crispness. Made in an open weave of fine, high-quality combed yarns. Compared to the fillings, the warp yarns are greater in number and heavier. Finished fabric may be dyed, printed, or embroidered. Eyelet organdy is embroidered on a *schiffli machine* around a previously cut pattern. The fabric is permanently stiff, but not necessarily crease resistant. Also made of man-made fibers and more crease resistant. Used for dresses, collars, cuffs, millinery, aprons, interfacing, and neckwear. Also see LAWN.

**organza** Lightweight, thin, transparent fabric which is stiff and wiry. Made in the plain weave of rayon or silk yarns, given an organzine twist. Has a tendency to crush, but easy to press. Used for dresses, millinery, trimmings, neckwear, and blouses.

**organzine yarn** Ply yarns of raw silk made of two or more single yarns which are then doubled and twisted in the reverse direction to form the ply yarn.

**orhna** Head veil worn by women of India when sari is not pulled over head.

**Oriental cat's eye** See CAT'S EYE under GEMS.

**Oriental pearls** See PEARL under BEADS and GEMS.

**Oriental stitch** See STITCHES.

**orle** See OURLE.

**Orlon®** Trademark of DuPont for acrylic staple and tow. Fabrics of Orlon can be crisp and springy, soft and luxurious, bulky or fine, firm or light and airy. There are many types of Orlon manufactured. Each type possesses certain specific characterics for special end uses.

**ornamental stones** Gems which exist in such large quantities that they are not considered precious or semiprecious gems, *e.g., coral* and *turquoise.*

**orphrey** (or-free) Y-shaped band of embroidery decorating the *chasuble,* an ecclesiastical garment, which extends from each shoulder meeting vertical stripe in center front and back. Also spelled *orfray, orfrey.*

**orrelet** (or-let) Term used in latter half of 16th c. for hanging side pieces of woman's *coif* that covered ears. Also called *cheeks-and-ears.* Also spelled *oreillett, oreillette, orilyet.* See COIF #6.

**orris/orrice lace** See LACES.

**Orsay, Count d'** Alfred Guillaume Gabriel (1801–1852). French society leader in Paris and London at the time of William IV. A *dandy* or "arbiter elegantiarum" of fashion. Described as a wit, a sculptor, and a conversationalist. He attempted to take BEAU BRUMMELL's place. See D'ORSAY under SHOES and SLIPPERS.

**Osbaldiston tie** (os-bald-stun) Necktie tied in front with a barrel-shaped knot worn by men from 1830s through 1840s. Also called *barrel knot tie.*

**Osnaburg** Coarse medium- to heavy-weight fabric of low count. Made of coarse yarns, sometimes cotton waste is used with the abbreviation *P.W. (part waste).* Called *clean Osnaburgs* if waste is not added. Used in *gray* state for bagging or in dyed state for sportswear linings, workshirts, and overalls. *Der.* Osnaburg, Germany, where it was first made of flax and tow, and sometimes made in yarn-dyed checks and stripes.

**osprey** See FEATHERS.

**ostrich** See FEATHERS and LEATHERS.

**otter** See FURS.

**ottoman** Heavy luxurious fabric with broad, flat crosswise ribs or wales. Made from silk, acetate, rayon, cotton, or wool with filling cord yarns of cotton. Warp yarns are finer and more are used so that they cover the filling completely on both sides. Also knitted and called OTTOMAN RIBBED KNIT. Used for coats, evening wear, suits, and trimmings.

**ottoman ribbed knit** Double-knit fabric with a pronounced wide crosswise *rib.*

**ouch** Term used from 13th to 15th c. for a collection of jewels or a jeweled clasp or buckle. Also spelled *nouch.*

**ourle** Term used in 13th and 14th c. for a fur border. Later spelled *orle.*

**outing cloth** See OUTING FLANNEL.

**outing flannel** Light- or medium-weight, soft, fuzzy cotton fabric. Made with lightly twisted yarns which are napped to conceal the plain or twill weave completely. May be made in yarn-dyed stripes, piece-dyed, or printed. Used for winter pajamas, nightshirts, and gowns. Also called *outing cloth.*

**outline stitch** See STITCHES.

**outré** (o-treh) French adjective meaning exaggerated, strained, excessive.

**outseam** See GLOVE SEAMS.

**oval cut** See GEM CUTS.

**oval ruff** Woman's large plain ruff, oval shaped rather than round, made with large PIPE-ORGAN PLEATS. Worn from about 1625 to 1650.

**oval toe** See TOES.

**oval trunk hose** See BOULOGNE HOSE.

**overalls** See PANTS.

**overblouse** See BLOUSES and SWIMSUITS.

**overboot** Crocheted or fabric woman's boot of 1860s worn over the shoes for warmth in carriages in winter. Also used as bedsocks for warmth in winter.

**overcast** See SEAMS and STITCHES.

**overcoat** See COATS.

**overdress** **1.** *Transparent dress* worn in late 17th c. constructed with an attached opaque underdress. **2.** Term used in 1870s for a hip-length *bodice* worn with a separate skirt. Some were formal in style with low-cut neckline, peplum, and fancy decorative trim of lace and ribbons. See CAGE under DRESSES.

**overlapped seam** See FULL PIQUÉ under GLOVE SEAMS and LAP SEAM under SEAMS.

**overlay** In the shoe industry, a piece of leather or other material stitched on shoe in decorative manner. Usually made of a contrasting color or a textured leather such as lizard or snakeskin.

**overplaid** See PLAIDS.

**overseam** See GLOVE SEAMS.

**overseas cap** See CAPS.

**overshirt** See SHIRTS.

**overshoe** Waterproof fabric or rubber shoe worn over other shoes in inclement weather. Also called *rubbers.* Also see ARCTICS, GALOSHES, and RAIN BOOTS under BOOTS.

**oversized** See LOOKS, SHIRTS, TOPS and BIG TEE under KNIT SHIRTS.

**overskirt** See SKIRTS.

**over-the-knee socks** See SOCKS

**owl glasses** See GLASSES

**oxford** **1.** Basic style of low shoe usually fastened with shoe laces, but may be closed with buckles, Velcro®, or other type of fasteners. **2.** Originally a shoeman's term to differentiate low-cut shoes from boots. **3.** Historically a half-boot introduced in England about 1640 and worn by university students. *Der.* Named for Oxford University. Some shoes that lace are not specifically called oxfords. Also see SHOES category, VAMP, COUNTER and QUARTER.

═══ **OXFORDS** ═══

**bal/Balmoral** Basic style of oxford with the tongue cut in a separate piece from the vamp of the shoe and joined with stitching across the vamp. *Der.* First worn at Balmoral Castle in Scotland in early 1850s.

**blucher** Man's basic type of oxford with the tongue and vamp cut in one piece. *Der.* Named after Prussian Field Marshal Gebhard Leberecht von Blucher, who devised this type of shoe for army wear in 1810.

**blucher bal** Modified BLUCHER OXFORD with vamp stitched over quarter at sides, but not stitched over tongue.

**brogue** Men's heavy oxfords, usually with wing tip decorated with heavy perforations and pinkings. Frequently worn for golf but also for city wear. *Der.* From coarse heelless shoe of untanned hide, with hair left on, worn by men in Ireland in 1790.

**buck o.** A blucher-type oxford made with sueded split-leather upper. Typically has a red cushion-crepe rubber outsole.

**gillie** **1.** Laced shoe, usually without a tongue, with rounded lacer pulling through leather loops and fastened around the ankle. Worn with Scottish kilt. *Der.* Popularized by Edward VIII and sometimes called *Prince of Wales shoe.* **2.** Many adaptations of this style, particularly for women's shoes, include some styles with high heels. *Der.* Scottish, *gille,* "an attendant or personal servant to a Highland chieftain."

**jazz o.** Flat-heeled oxford made with vamp line curved and stitched extending downward to arch. The remainder of shoe is cut in one piece with front lacing.

**kiltie o.** Laced shoe with a shawl or fringed tongue projecting over front of shoe through which laces may be tied. Adopted from Scottish type shoes and popular in 1930s, 1960s, and 1980s.

**plug/plugged o.** Low laced shoe cut with vamp and quarters in one piece and a separate lace stay, *e.g.*, SADDLE OXFORDS.

**Prince of Wales shoe** See GILLIE.

BAL/
BALMORAL

KILTIE OXFORD

SADDLE OXFORD

WING-TIP
OXFORD

**saddle o.** Sport or school shoe usually made of white buck calf with a brown or black leather "saddle" shaped section over the middle of the shoe. Usually made with rubber soles, it has been a basic style since the 1920s, very popular in the 1940s, and still worn.

**side-laced o.** Oxford laced at side front rather than center front, made with low wedge heel, reinforced counter, side perforations near sole for ventilation, and cushioned arch support. Often made in white and popular with nurses.

**Sperry Topsiders®** Trademark of the Stride Rite Corp. for shoes with a specially designed rubber sole that provides good traction on a wet boat deck; often made in sneaker style with canvas upper.

**Theo tie** An open-throated, tongueless shoe with ribbon or cord lacings introduced in early 20th c.

**white bucks** White leather oxfords, styled like BUCK OXFORDS.

**wing-tip o.** Laced shoe decorated at toe with wing-shaped overlay perforations, sometimes trimmed with perforations.

---

**Oxford bags** See PANTS.

**Oxford button-overs** Men's shoes of 1860s covering the instep and closed with buttons instead of laces.

**Oxford cap** See MORTARBOARD.

**oxford cloth** Men's shirting fabric made in a basket weave sometimes 2 x 2 and sometimes 4 x 2. Yarns may be all combed or all carded with filling yarns coarser than warp. Better grades are *mercerized*. May be bleached, dyed, have yarn-dyed strips, or small fancy designs. *Der.* Originally produced by a Scottish firm along with fabrics labeled Yale, Harvard, and Cambridge which are no longer important.

**Oxford coatee**   See OXONIAN JACKET.

**Oxford gloves**   Perfumed gloves, worn from mid-16th to mid-17th c., scented with Earl of Oxford's favorite perfume.

**Oxford tie**   Straight narrow necktie worn in 1890s by men with informal lounge suit and by women with shirtwaist.

**Oxonian boots**   Man's short black boots worn in 1830s and 1840s often made of patent leather with wedge-shaped portion cut out of either side at top so they pull on easily. Also called *Oxonians* or *collegians*.

**Oxonian jacket**   Two- or three-button single-breasted tweed jacket worn by men in 1850s through 1860s. Made with many pockets and a back shaped by three seams. Also called *Oxford coatee*.

**Oxonians**   See OXONIAN BOOTS.

**Oxonian shoe**   High laced shoe with seam at instep worn by men in 1848.

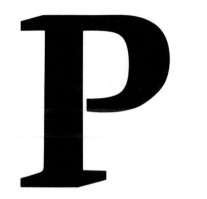

**paboudj** See BABOOCHE.

**pac** See BOOTS.

**Paco Rabanne** See HELMETS and APPENDIX/DESIGNERS.

**padding** Any stuffing material used between two layers of fabric or leather to give a rounded effect to clothing or accessories, *e.g.*, horsehair in 16th c. for man's *busk* and for *bombasted hose*. In latter part of 19th c. used for *false calves*. In contemporary times, padding is used mostly for warmth in the form of *down* for coats and jackets or *fiberfill* for shaping in bras. Also see SHOULDERS and STITCHES.

**paddock** Lightweight worsted coating fabric made in Great Britain in a twill weave. Piece-dyed in tones of brown and given a water-repellent finish.

**paddock coat** Man's long semi-fitted overcoat worn from 1892 on, made with single- or double-breasted fly-front closing, large pockets, and pleat-covered back vent.

**padre hat** See HATS.

**pa'ejamas** Pants worn by Moslem men in Persian and India. Either: *a*) tight-fitting to ankles, or *b*) very full at waist and knees and tight at lower leg—resembling cut of jodhpurs. *Der.* Hindu words *pae*, "leg," and *jamah*, "garment." Also see PAJAMAS.

**paenula** (pie-new-la) Hooded cape or poncho-shaped garment, made of heavy woolen fabric or leather. Worn by ancient Romans for traveling or inclement weather.

**PAGE**

**page** Belt with long loop of ribbon, cord, or velvet placed in either side. Used to loop up overskirt of dress from 1850 to 1867. Compare with DRESS CLIP and DRESS HOLDER.

**page-boy bob** See HAIRSTYLES.

**pagne** (panye) Tight wraparound skirt or loincloth draped at right side made of hand-woven cotton in striped, chevron, or other designs. Worn in Guinea, the Belgian Congo region, and other parts of Africa.

**pagoda sleeve** See SLEEVES.

**pagri** East Indian turban divided into two types: *a*) *short*—made from a strip of fabric 20″ to 30″ wide and from 6 to 9 yards long, and *b*) *long*—made from fabric 6″ to 8″ wide and varying from 10 to 50 yards long. The color, fabric, design, and method of wrapping are used to indicate rank, prestige, and other information about the wearer. Also spelled *pugree*, *puggree*.

**pa-hom** Length of fabric wound around the body with end thrown over left shoulder to form a dress. Worn by Siamese women of the lower classes. Also see SLENDANG.

**pah-poosh** Velvet slippers with high heels, decorated with embroidery and studded with jewels, worn indoors by Persian women.

**paille** Yellowish straw color. *Der.* French, "straw."

**paillette** (pai-yet) Spangle made of metal or plastic, usually a round disk larger than a *sequin*. Used as trimming on evening clothes and handbags. *Der.* French, "speck or spangle."

**painter's** See CAPS and PANTS.

**pair of bodies** Stays or corset worn in the 17th c. stiffened with whalebone, steel, or wood—frequently padded.

**pais-a-gwn bach** Welsh native dress consisting of tight-fitting bodice, an *overskirt* turned back to show striped *petticoat*, and full apron. Worn as part of the *eisteddfod costume. Der.* Welsh *pais,* "country or people," and *gwn,* "dress."

**Paisley shawl** Worsted shawl of fine quality, popular in 19th c., made square or oblong. Sometimes woven double with a different pattern on each side. *Der.* Made in Paisley, Scotland. Also see PRINTS and SHAWLS.

**pajama checks** Fabric similar to checked dimity made of carded yarns with cords at intervals in both the warp and filling to form a checked effect. Used for men's underwear in 1920s and 1930s.

**pajamas** One- or two-piece item of apparel originally designed for sleeping; later for lounging; and in late 1960s for entertaining, evening parties, and dining out. The word pajamas is often abbreviated to "p.j.s." Originally introduced about 1880 from India for men to wear for sleeping instead of nightgowns. Introduced for women for sleeping in mid-1920s. Popular for lounge- and beachwear in the late 1920s and 1930s. *Der.* Hindustani "pajama" which came from the Persian words *pai,* "leg," and *jaman,* "a garment." Note: British spelling is *pyjamas.*

=== **PAJAMAS** ===

**baby doll p.** Very short, micro-mini or mini-length pajamas consisting of a tent-shaped top, usually gathered into the neckline or yoke, worn with brief panties.

**bare-midriff p.** Two-piece pajamas with a brief top worn by women since late 1960s for lounging or sleeping.

**blanket sleepers** Children's winter pajamas made in two pieces or in one piece with front buttoned or zippered, of napped fabric similar to that used for blankets.

**bunny suit** Form-fitting knitted jumpsuit buttoned or zippered down the front and made in footed-pajama style. Sometimes made in wide crosswise stripes of red and white.

**Chinese p.** Hip- or thigh-length jacket with side seams slashed to waist, mandarin collar, and closing—sometimes diagonal with frogs—worn with straight-legged pants. *Der.* From work garments worn in China by men and women.

**coat-style p.** Classic pajama style made like a single- or double-breasted coat with tailored convertible collar, frequently trimmed with piping, and worn with drawstring or elastic-top pants.

**Cossack p.** Pants plus tunic top closing at side front with standing-band collar. Introduced in 1930s and revived in late 1960s.

**culotte p.** Floor-length pajamas with wide legs, resembling a long dress, worn for dining in mid- and late 1960s and early 1970s. Also called *hostess culottes* and PARTY PANTS.

**Dr. Denton Sleepers®** Trademark of Denton Mills, Inc., New Albany, Massachusetts, established in 1865, for one-piece knitted pajama with covered feet, buttoned down the front, and with buttoned drop seat originally worn by children. Similar style now worn by adults called a BUNNY SUIT.

**footed p.** One- or two-piece child's sleeping garment with attached slipper-like coverings for the feet with soles often made of non-skid plastic.

**French maid sleeper** Provocative two-piece pajamas consisting of a lace-trimmed sheer top, styled like a French maid's apron, with bikini panties worn underneath.

**granjamer** Granny-style top with yoke, a placket neckline, and ruffle trimming worn with matching pants in 1960s for sleeping.

SKI PAJAMAS

COAT-STYLE
PAJAMAS

KARATE PAJAMAS (HIS AND HERS)

HAREM PAJAMAS

LOUNGING PAJAMAS

CHINESE PAJAMAS

PAJAMA SET

**grow sleepers** Children's pajamas with several rows of snaps at waist that extend the length as the child grows taller.

**harem p.** Very full trousers gathered at ankle, which may be paired with tunic or Oriental bolero. Fashionable for at-home wear in late 1960s.

**hostess culottes** See CULOTTE PAJAMAS.

**jumpsuit p.** Fitted pajamas in one piece usually buttoned or zipped at center front similar to BUNNY SUIT but lacking feet.

**karate p.** Two-piece pajamas styled like a karate costume, with pants and Japanese-type wrap top, introduced in late 1960s and early 1970s.

**knitted knickers** One-piece, sleeveless knitted pajamas with fitted top, round neck, and pants shirred at hem making a ruffle below the knee.

**lounging p.** Full-length pajamas cut in tunic or one-piece style. Legs are wide and long giving the appearance of a skirt when not in motion. Introduced in the 1930s and used for lounge- and beachwear. Reintroduced in mid-1960s for evening or entertaining at home. Also called *hostess pajamas*.

**middy-top p.** Man's two-piece pajamas styled with a slip-on top having no buttons. So named because of the resemblance to a MIDDY BLOUSE.

**pajama set** Tailored pajamas with a matching robe styled for men or women.

**party p.** Type of pajamas, pants, or culottes with styling suitable to wear for dining and dancing. Also called *hostess pajamas* or *culotte pajamas*.

**rompers** One-piece pajamas styled like a jumpsuit with short legs. Usually knitted, sometimes made of terry cloth.

**shortie p.** Two-piece pajamas with legs coming to knee. Worn primarily in summer by both men and women.

**ski p.** Any two-piece pajamas styled with full legs gathered into knitted cuffs at the ankles.

**sleep set** Two-piece seductive sleepwear consisting of jacket or camisole-type top worn over brief bikinis. Top can also double for streetwear.

**sleep shorts** Man's pull-on shorts, sometimes with two piped pockets, worn for sleeping.

**tailored p.** Any pajamas which are not excessively decorated or trimmed, usually finished with piping.

**teddy** One-piece sleep garment with low-cut wrap-style front, high-cut legs, and elasticized waistline; sometimes with a short skirt. Often made of nylon satin or georgette trimmed with lace or ruffles. Can also be worn as an undergarment. Also see alphabetical listing.

**t-shirt p.** Two-piece pajamas with a knitted t-shirt top.

**tunic p.** Two-piece pajamas styled with a long overblouse top. Also see COSSACK PAJAMAS.

**pajama set** See PAJAMAS.

**pajama stripes** Group of bold striped fabrics made of cotton, wool, silk, blends, and mixtures of fibers. Many varieties of colored stripes are used.

**Pakistani vest** See VESTS.

**palatine** 1. Fill-in or small scarf of tulle worn around the neck to cover the low neckline of dresses of mid-17th c. 2. Woman's small fur or lace shoulder cape of the 1840s with long flat ends in front reaching below the waist. *Der.* Named after Charlotte of the Palantine (Liselotte) who tried to induce more modesty in dress. Also spelled *pallatine*.

**palatine royal** A fur cape of 1851 with a quilted hood and short ends in front. Also called *victorine*.

**palazzo pajamas/pants** See PANTS.

**paletot** (pal-e-toe or pal-tow) Term for variety of coat styles for men and women used loosely from 1830s to end of century. **1.** In 1830s, a man's short overcoat made without a waistline seam, with or without, a short back vent. Sometimes pleated at side seams. **2.** Late 1830s to end of 19th c., woman's caped three-quarter length cloak which hung in stiff pleats form the shoulders. By mid-1840s had three capes and armholes trimmed with flaps. **3.** From 1860s to 1880s, woman's short paletot also called a *yachting jacket*. **4.** Long fitted outdoor coat worn by women from mid-1860s to mid-1880s—reaching to below the knees frequently trimmed with lace and having tight sleeves. **5.** Short women's paletot worn in 1870s with wide cuffed sleeves and WATTEAU PLEATS in the back. *Der.* Dutch *paltrok*, from *pals*, "palace" and *rok*, "garment."

**paletot-cloak** (pal-e-toe or pal-tow) Man's hip-length cape of the 1850s made in single- or double-breasted style with armhole slits.

**paletot-mantle** (pal-e-toe or pal-tow) Woman's three-quarter-length cloak with hanging sleeves and a cape collar worn in late 1860s.

**paletot-redingote** (pal-e-toe or pal-tow) Woman's long, fitted, outdoor coat of late 1860s made in Princess style with no seam at the waistline. Made with buttons down the front and revers. Sometimes made with circular shoulder capes.

**paletot-sac** (pal-e-toe or pal-tow) Single- or double-breasted paletot cut short and straight, sometimes made with a collar, sometimes with a hood. Worn by men in 1840s and 1850s.

**palisade** Wire framework worn by women to support the FONTANGES HEADDRESS from 1690 to 1710. Same as COMMODE.

**palla** Rectangular shawl-like garment resembling ancient Greek HIMATION. Worn by Roman women draped around body, sometimes with one end draped over head.

**pallatine** See PALATINE.

**pallium** Rectangular shawl worn by Roman man. Also see HIMATION.

**palmering** Finish applied to taffetas, twills, and satins by inserting fabric between two layers of felt and pressing with steam-heated rollers to give fabric a smooth hand.

**Palmerston wrapper** Man's single-breasted, loose-fitting *sac overcoat* of mid-1850s made with wide collar and lapels. Sleeves were full at wrists with no cuffs and pockets had side flaps. *Der.* Named after British statesman 3rd Viscount Palmerston, Henry John Temple, who was Prime Minister of England between 1855 and 1865.

**palmetto** Term used for a variety of fibers obtained from leaves of the palmetto or cabbage palm grown along south Atlantic coast in the Bahamas, Cuba, and Mexico. Used for hats and baskets.

**paltock** (pal-tock) Man's short outer jacket worn from 14th to mid-15th c. similar to the *doublet*. The hose were fastened to it by means of lacers, called *points*. Later called POURPOINT. Also spelled *paltok*, *paultock*. Compare with HANSELINE.

**paludamentum** **1.** Purple mantle of rich fabric fastened with clasp at shoulders. Worn by Roman emperors and military officers. **2.** Same item worn by Byzantine emperors but changed to ankle-length by 5th c.

**Pamela bonnet** Straw bonnet worn from 1845 to late 1860s, made of a "saucer-shaped" piece of straw or fabric placed on top of the head. Fastened with bonnet strings which bent it into a U-shape around the face. Trimmed on top with foliage, flowers, or feathers.

**panache** (pa-nash) Plume or erect bunch of feathers worn on hat—originally used on military helmets.

**Panama hat** See HATS.

**Panama straw** Leaves of the jipijapa plant, the *Carludovica palmata*, a palm-like plant cultivated extensively in Colombia and Ecuador. Young leaves are collected, split into thin pieces, cleaned, bleached, and handwoven. Only these fibers are used for genuine Panama hats. Although made in Ecuador, they are distributed from a port in Panama.

**Panama suiting** Men's summer suiting fabric made in a plain weave with a cotton warp and worsted filling or combinations of yarns. Usually piece-dyed in solid colors. Smooth and somewhat wiry, it is wrinkle resistant and somewhat soil resistant.

**pancake beret** See CAPS.

**Pandora** See MODEL DOLLS.

**panel** See PRINTS, SKIRTS, and PANEL PANTDRESS under DRESSES.

**panes** Term used from 1500 to 1650s for series of vertical slashes in a garment, *e.g.,* hose, *doublet,* or sleeves, with the contrasting lining pulled out through these slashes. Also see PULLINGS OUT.

**paneva** Traditional Russian shirt, usually of striped or checked wool, sometimes embroidered and worn with RUBAKHA or under a sleeved tunic or apron.

**panier/paniers** (pan-yehr) French spelling for *pannier* worn in France from about 1718 or 1720 until the French Revolution. First styles were *en coupole* (domed-shaped) and *en guéridon* (round-shaped). Toward the middle of the 18th c. made in two pieces. By 1750 half paniers, or *pocket hoops* were worn only for court functions while *considerations* were worn for other occasions.

**paniers à bourelet** (pan-yehr a boor-lay) French panier hoop petticoat with a thick roll at the hem to make the skirt flare.

**paniers à coudes** (pan-yehr a could) French paniers of late 1720s which extended wide at the sides and were narrow from front to back.

*Der.* French, "elbows" because the woman's elbows could be rested on them.

**paniers anglais** (pan-yehr ong-glaze) French term for the hoop petticoat. This term and the term *pannier* (English spelling) were rarely used in England in the 18th c. English panniers of the 18th c. were called the *oblong hoop, square hoop,* and *false hips.*

**panne satin** Glossy heavyweight satin which may be made of a variety of yarns—all silk, fine cotton, acetate, rayon, or combinations of acetate and rayon.

**panne velvet** Velvet which has had the pile pressed down in one direction giving it a glossy appearance. Originally made with wool or silk pile and organzine silk yarns; later with silk ground and flattened rayon pile. Used for dresses and sportswear.

**pannier/panniers** (pan-yehr) **1.** Structure of metal, cane, wire, or wooden hoops for extending a woman's dress at both sides at hip level. Popular from about 1720 to 1789 in France. The word *pannier* was seldom used in England. See OBLONG HOOP. **2.** Petticoat or overskirt extended at sides of the hoops. Popular from late 1860s to 1880s. **3.** Puff formed over the hip by looping up the underskirt. *Der.* Latin *panarium,* "a basket for bread."

**pannier bag** See HANDBAGS.

**pannier crinoline** Underskirt for extending the dress in 1870s which combined a CAGE CRINOLINE petticoat with a BUSTLE. Also called *Thomson's pannier crinoline.*

**pannier curls** See CURLS.

**pannier drape** **1.** See PANNIER. **2.** In late 1860s, puff formed over hip by looping up outerskirt of dress. **3.** In 1880s, fullness or drapery on hips made by an extra piece of fabric attached to bodice or waistline draped over hips with remainder pulled to the back in POLONAISE style. **4.** In World War I era, drapery over hips sometimes made in tunic effect, or sometimes cut as part of the dress to give a *peg-top* look.

**PANNIER DRAPE #4, 1919**

**pannier dress**   Daytime dress of the late 1860s with an overskirt looped up and puffed out at back and sides. Worn over an underskirt with train trimmed with a flounce.

**pannier skirt**   **1.** Skirt which is extended at the sides but frequently narrow from front to back. Popular in the 18th c. and again in the 1870s. **2.** Skirt with an overskirt draped at the hips to form puffs, popular in the 1850s and 1860s, and again in the 1880s. Also called a *pannier puff.*

**pant**   An adjective used as a prefix to words when pants became accepted for the office, daytime, and evening wear in the late 1960s. See PANTCOAT under COATS; PANTDRESS, PANT-SHIFT, and PANTGOWN under DRESSES; PANTJUM-PER under JUMPERS; PANTSKIRT under SKIRTS; and PANTSUIT under SUITS.

**Pantacourt®**   See SHORTS.

**pantalettes**   **1.** Women's and girls' underpants with long straight legs covered with ruf-

fles, tucks, and embroidery worn showing below the dress. From early 1800s to 1840 worn by women and until 1865 by girls. The woman's version of *pantaloons.* James Monroe's daughter, Maria Hester, is said to have been first person to wear pantalettes in Washington, D.C. in 1807 (she would have been about 8 years old). **2.** Contemporary style of late 1960s. See PANTS.

**pantaloons**   **For Men: 1.** Same as PETTICOAT BREECHES. **2.** From 1790 to about 1850 tight-fitting pants ending at calf to 1817, later to ankles with strap under the instep. Known as *tights* about 1840. **3. For Women:** Long straight-legged drawers worn from 1812 to 1840, called *trousers* in 1830s. Also called *pantalettes.* *Der.* French, *pantalon*; Italian, *pantalone.*

**panties**   Abbreviated term for women's and children's underpants; garments worn under outer clothing covering torso below the waist. Word came into popular usage in the 1930s. Previously called *drawers.* In the 1980s some types of briefs and panties were higher cut revealing all of the leg. The word "underpants" is a synonym but more frequently used in reference to men's and boys' underwear. Also see PANTYHOSE.

### ■■■ PANTIES & UNDERPANTS ■■■

**band briefs**   Short panties finished at the legs with knitted bands. Also called *band-leg pant-ies.*

**band-leg p.**   See BAND BRIEFS.

**bikini p.**   Below-the-navel brief panties introduced in early 1960s, modeled after BIKINI SWIMSUIT. *Der.* Named for the island of Bikini in the Pacific.

**bloomers**   Full panty with thigh-length leg gathered into elastic. Popular since 1920s for little girls, and worn by older women from 1930s to present. *Der.* Named for Amelia Jenks Bloomer, early-19th c. American reformer, who wore full gathered pants instead of a skirt when lecturing. Also see alphabetical listing.

**boxer p. 1.** Women's and children's loose-legged panties of pull-on type. **2.** Rather loose-fitting short woven underpants worn by men and boys. *Der.* Similar to men's shorts worn for the sport of boxing.

**briefs 1.** Woman's or girl's very short panties, sometimes made of control stretch fabric with garters added. **2.** Tight-fitting short knitted underpants worn by men and boys.

**cami-tap set** See TAP PANTIES.

**control p.** Briefs, long-leg panties, or pantsliners knitted with elastomeric yarns to provide support.

**drawers** Cotton knitted ankle- or knee-length, fitted underpants worn for warmth. Introduced for men in 16th c. and for women in early 19th c. Also see UMBRELLA DRAWERS and TIGHTS in alphabetical listing.

**elastic-leg brief** Short panty finished with elastic around the leg rather than a band.

**flared-leg p.** Longer panties which flare and hang loose on the leg introduced in the 1920s.

**garter briefs** Short panties with attached supporters to hold up stockings.

**hip-huggers** Low-slung panties starting at hip bone level, intended to be worn with hip-hugger pants and bare-midriff dresses.

**BAND BRIEFS**

**BIKINI PANTIES**

**BLOOMERS**

**BRIEFS**

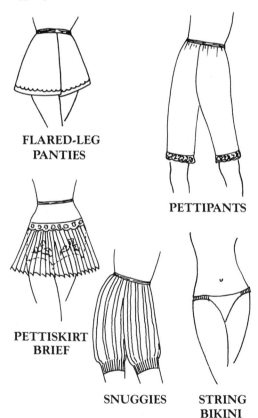

**FLARED-LEG PANTIES**

**PETTIPANTS**

**PETTISKIRT BRIEF**

**SNUGGIES**

**STRING BIKINI**

**mini-pettipants**   See PETTIPANTS.

**pantsliner**   Tight-fitting control panties coming over the knee to the calf or the ankle, worn under pants for sleek fit.

**pantyslip**   Short petticoat with panties attached at waistband; a popular style for little girls.

**petticulottes**   Slip and panties combined in one garment which has flared legs and an inverted pleat in center front and back, frequently lace-trimmed.

**pettipants**   Long dress-length panties made of plain or bright-colored knits with ruffles and lace trimming, introduced in late 1960s. Also came in mini length, called *mini-pettipants*.

**pettiskirt brief**   Combination petticoat and short panties joined by elastic waistband.

**Rhumba p.**®   Little girls' panties with several rows of ruffles across the seat. *Der.* From ruffled costume worn for South American dance.

**snap p.**   Waterproof panty for infants with snaps at the crotch.

**Snuggies**   Knee-length or over-the-knee panties made of knitted cotton, worn for warmth with matching tank-top undershirt.

**string bikini**   Minimum panties consisting of two small triangular pieces attached to a band of elastic worn low on the hips.

**tap p.**   Panties styled like short shorts with a slight flare at hem. May be made of satin or floral print with lace-trim. Frequently made with matching camisole and then called *cami-tap set.*

**tights**   **1.** Underpants and stockings knit in one piece, worn originally by athletes, circus performers, and dancers in late 19th c. with *leotard.* Now worn by women and children in variety of textured cotton, nylon, or wool knits in many colors for all occasions. **2.** A LEOTARD with legs and sometimes feet added.

**trunks**   Loose-fitting panty cut similar to men's shorts.

**pantile**   Term used for the *sugar-loaf hat*, popular from 1640s to 1665 for men and women.

**pantofle** (pan-tof-l)   **1.** Slipper worn from end of 15th to mid-17th c. by men and women. Also spelled *pantoffle, pantoffel.* **2.** Overshoe similar to a patten, with a cork sole worn in late 16th c. Also spelled *pantables, pantacles.* **3.** Term used for bedroom slippers. *Der.* French, *pantoufle,* "slipper."

**pants**   **1.** Clothing for the lower torso made to fit around each leg, may be any length and width, some have cuffs, some do not. In early times various styles were worn by Persian and Anglo-Saxon men, and also worn by women in China and mid-Eastern countries. Not known, however, by this name until late 19th c. when first used as a colloquial term for items worn by men and boys—now it is an all-inclusive term for all types of TROUSERS, BREECHES, BLUE JEANS, etc., worn by children and adults. *Slacks* were popularized in the 1930s for women by Hollywood stars such as Marlene Deitrich and Katharine Hepburn and also worn in war plants during World War II. All types of pants became very popular for women in late 1960s when pants became acceptable for business, townwear, school, and evening wear. Also see SHORTS. See BREECHES, PANTALETTES, PETERSHAM COSSACKS, and TRUNK HOSE in alphabetical listing. **2.** Shortened form of the word *underpants* and *panties.*

**════ PANTS ════**

**accordion-pleated p.**   See PARTY PANTS.

**athletic p.**   See SWEATPANTS.

**baggy p.** Pants cut fuller through hips with legs tapering and becoming narrow at ankles. Term used originally for jeans in late 1970s, adopted for all types of pants in 1980s. Also called *baggies*.

**bell-bottoms** **1.** Pants cut with fullness on both the outer and inner seams to give a "bell" flare at the hem. Style most generally worn by young people in late 1960s and early 1970s. Also called FLARES. **2.** Traditionally the navy-blue or white trousers worn by seamen in the Navy, also known as SAILOR PANTS.

**bib-top p.** See OVERALLS.

**bloomers** **1.** Wide cut, above-the-knee pants gathered with elastic at hem. Originally popular for little girls under dresses in 1920s. **2.** Black sateen pleated bloomers worn for gym and camp by women from early 20th c. to late 1920s. **3.** See PANTIES. *Der.* Name applied in 1851 to young ladies wearing rather narrow, ankle-length pants with elastic at the bottom in imitation of costume worn by Amelia Bloomer. Also see alphabetical listing.

**blue jeans** Ankle-length pants traditionally made in faded blue or indigo denim. Originally worn by farmers and workmen, pants were styled with top-stitching, two hip pockets, two side pockets, a V-shaped yoke in back, and rivets reinforcing points of strain. In the late 1960s adapted as a general fashion with flared legs in same cut but made of many fabrics including denim, bleached denim, printed fabrics, suede, stripes, corduroy, and even velvet. *Bleached jeans* became popular in the 1960s, to give a faded worn look. *Stone washed jeans* were popularized in 1980s to give a pale look. By mid-1980s *acid-washed jeans* were introduced which gave an almost white look with splotches of navy. In the 1970s accepted for school wear with a small watch pocket added to carry money. Leg styles conform to the current mode. In 1980s sold in four widths: bell-bottoms, flared, boot cut, and straight cut. Also called DUNGAREES, LEVIS®, JEANS, DUDE JEANS, and DESIGNER JEANS. Also see BAGGY PANTS.

**boot-cut p.** Refers to the width at hem of pants—cut wide enough so that pants can be pulled on over western boots with pant leg worn outside of boots.

**breaker p.** Straight-legged pants with zipper at side seam which shows contrasting lining when opened. May have zippered back pocket and grommet trim. *Der.* From break-dancing which requires a lot of movement.

**breeches** An all-inclusive term for pants reaching to below the knee worn particularly for horseback riding. *Der.* From word "breech" which was plural of "broc." Also see HUNT BREECHES, RIDING BREECHES, and CANARY BREECHES.

**camouflage p.** Pants adapted for general wear in 1980s printed with greens and browns in abstract pattern. Originally used as camouflage wear for the Army because colors blended with scenery.

**canary breeches** Riding breeches made in pale yellow-colored fabric.

**Capri p.** **1.** Tight-fitting three-quarter-length pants, with short slit on outside of leg. Worn in 1950s. **2.** Tight-fitting jeans trademarked by Lee with slit on outside of leg called *Capri®* jeans. Worn in 1980s. *Der.* Named for Italian resort, Island of Capri, where style first became popular.

**cargo p.** Pants with large bellows pockets in back and two extra large patch pockets in front that have extended tops which form large tunnel loops through which a webbed belt with brass buckle is pulled.

**chaps** Covering for the legs worn over pants, made with legs and a front, but no seat. Originally worn by cowboys, made of leather or shearling. Adopted by women as fashion item in the late 1960s. *Der.* Shortened form of Spanish word *chaparejos*, "undressed sheepskin."

**charro p.** Wide Mexican-inspired pants in midi length, similar to GAUCHO PANTS. *Der.* Mexican, "rancher."

**chinos** Washable man's sport pants made of chino cloth, a durable close-woven khaki-colored cotton fabric. Popular in 1950s for sportswear and for school wear in early 1960s. *Der.* Adapted from Army summer uniforms made of fabric that originally was purchased in China before World War I.

**choori-dars** Pants with full-cut top and tight-fitting legs which are extra long and worn rumpled from knee down. Worn in 1960s, increasing in popularity in 1980s. *Der.* From pants worn in India called by the same name.

**CityPants** Term coined by fashion industry newspaper, *Women's Wear Daily*, in 1968 for women's trousers considered suitable for wear in town as well as at home or for sportswear. Also see CitySHORTS under SHORTS.

**Clamdiggers®** Trademark owned by White Stag Manufacturing Co. for mid-calf slacks and snug-fitting calf-length pants. Originating from cut-off BLUE JEANS, worn while wading to dig for clams. Adopted for sportswear in 1950s.

**continental p.** Man's trousers styled with fitted waistband and no belt. Front pockets are placed horizontally, or curved to waistband seam rather than placed in the side seams. Popular in late 1960s, the style originated in Italy.

**crawlers** Slacks for infants and also sizes 1 to 3, frequently made in bib-overall style of corduroy and other fabrics. Formerly called *creepers*.

**creepers** See CRAWLERS.

**cropped p.** Pants cut at varying lengths between ankle and knee. The most common type was cut just below the knee. Newer versions in 1984 were full cut, longer, and sometimes pleated into the waistband.

**cuffed trousers** See PRE-CUFFED TROUSERS.

**cut-offs** See SHORTS category.

**culottes** Pants of any length cut to look like a skirt which hangs similar to a divided skirt. Worn from 1930s to 1940s and again in 1960s,

and very popular in the 1980s. In 1986 some culottes were worn knee length in a pleated style sometimes with a matching jacket. *Der.* French, *culotte*, "pants." Also see alphabetical listing.

**deck p.** Fitted pants ending below the knees; worn by men, women and children particularly on boats in late 1950s and early 1960s.

**designer jeans** After blue jeans became widely worn at schools and some offices, noted designers such as Calvin Klein and Gloria Vanderbilt produced them in higher price lines usually attaching their names to the hip pocket and trademarking their product.

**dhoti** Pants with many gathers at waistband made long between the legs and tapering to ankle. *Der.* From pants worn in India called by the same name. Also see alphabetical listing.

**dirndl p.** (durn-del) Culottes or pants styled with gathers at the waistline introduced in early 1980s. Sometimes made in seven-eighths length with large pockets in side seams and decorative braided belt.

**drawstring p.** Pull-on pants, usually of cotton, with drawstring at top. A unisex fashion of the late 1960s. Also called *unisex pants*.

**dude jeans** Similar to WESTERN PANTS. Also see BLUE JEANS.

**dungarees** Work pants or overalls named for the coarse blue fabric from which they are made. Also see BLUE JEANS.

**elephant-leg p.** Trousers with extremely wide legs similar to HARLOW PANTS. Introduced in late 1960s.

**fatigues** **1.** Pants of tough fabric worn by U.S. Army for work details. Also called *field pants*. **2.** Coveralls for work worn by Army men and WACS during World War II, sometimes made in olive drab or camouflage colors.

**field p.** See FATIGUES #1.

**flares** **1.** Synonym for BELL-BOTTOMS popular in the late 1960s and early 1970s. **2.** Pants with slight flare at hem in early 1980s.

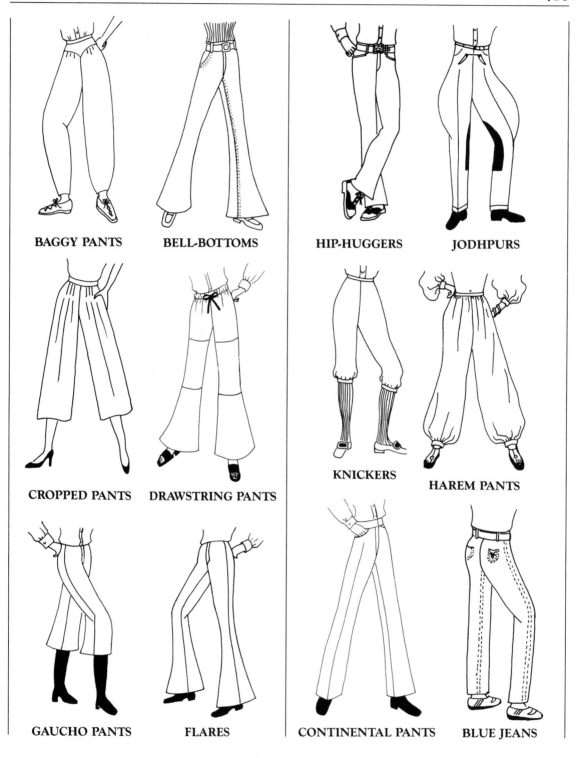

BAGGY PANTS     BELL-BOTTOMS          HIP-HUGGERS     JODHPURS

CROPPED PANTS   DRAWSTRING PANTS

                                      KNICKERS        HAREM PANTS

GAUCHO PANTS    FLARES                CONTINENTAL PANTS   BLUE JEANS

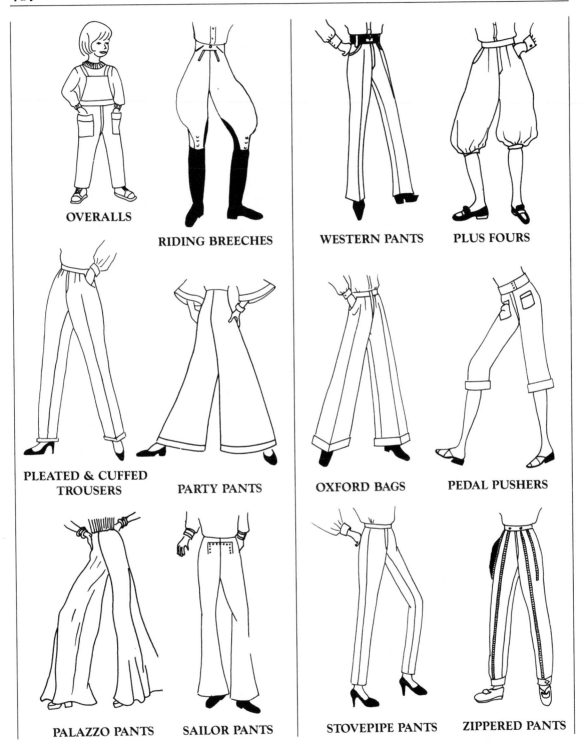

OVERALLS

RIDING BREECHES

WESTERN PANTS

PLUS FOURS

PLEATED & CUFFED TROUSERS

PARTY PANTS

OXFORD BAGS

PEDAL PUSHERS

PALAZZO PANTS

SAILOR PANTS

STOVEPIPE PANTS

ZIPPERED PANTS

**frontier p.**  See WESTERN PANTS.

**gaucho p.**  Wide calf-length women's pants, frequently made of leather, copied from pants worn by Spanish as a part of Andalusian riding suit and adapted by South American cowboys; a fashion in the late 1960s. *Der.* Spanish, "cowboy" of Argentina, Chile, and Uruguay.

**harem knickers**  Knee-length bouffant harem pants similar to *bloomers*, introduced in late 1960s.

**harem p.**  Bouffant pants gathered into bands at the ankles, popular at-home fashion of late 1960s. *Der.* Copied from Near Eastern styles. Also see SHALWAR.

**Harlow p.**  Trousers wide from hips to hem, introduced in late 1960s. *Der.* Copied from slacks worn in 1930s by Jean Harlow, a popular film star.

**high-rise p.**  Pants which extend to above the waistline, as opposed to HIP-HUGGERS.

**hip-huggers**  Low-slung pants of any style starting below the normal waistline, usually with belt resting on hip bones, popularized in mid-1960s. Also called *hipsters* and *low-slung pants*.

**hipsters**  See HIP-HUGGERS.

**hunt breeches**  Riding breeches with drop front, legs cut wide from thighs to hips and tight at knees. Usually made in canary or tan cavalry twill with buckskin patches at inside of knees.

**Ivy League p.**  Type of men's trousers with "skinny" legs, usually without cuffs, cut somewhat shorter in length. Worn first by college men and introduced for general wear in 1950s. *Der.* From a group of eastern colleges which are called "the Ivy League."

**jeans**  See BLUE JEANS. *Der.* Originally pants made of jean fabric worn by sailors since 1810.

**jockey p.**  Below the knee breeches with drop front and jodhpur-type legs worn tucked into boots by jockeys in horse races.

**jodhpurs**  Riding pants, with drop front or zipper closing, that flare at thighs and have narrow straight-cut legs below knee with cuffs at ankles. Similar to men's breeches worn in India and popular for men and women horseback riders since 1920s. *Der.* Jodhpur, city in India. Also see RIDING BREECHES.

**knee p.**  See KNICKERS.

**knickers**  **1.** Pants of varying widths fastened below knee with buttons, buckles, or elastic; popular for boys in early 20th c. for school. Reintroduced in late 1960s for women and men. **2.** See PANTIES category. *Der.* Shortened form of word *knickerbockers*. Also called *knee pants*. Also see alphabetical listing.

**leggings**  **1.** Pants which are wide at the top but conform to the leg from the knee down, sometimes cut like JODHPURS. **2.** Another style is full to the ankle where it is held by a knitted band. Both styles worn by children for warmth in winter. Also spelled *leggins*. **3.** Skintight pants to ankles worn in thin Lycra spandex knit fabrics in brilliant colors for dancers and entertainers or in regular knits sometimes worn with *leotards* in place of tights for exercising. Some have *stirrup straps* at foot. Popular in late 1980s.

**Levis®**  Trademark for type of *dungarees* or *blue jeans*. Distinguishing characteristics are a label stitched to the outside on one hip pocket, also the placing of rivets at places of most strain, and patch pockets placed at hips. First made by Levi Straus in California for miners prospecting for gold in 1840s out of cloth used for sails—later *denim* was used. A distinct American fashion, it developed into a multimillion dollar industry with many pairs exported yearly. The Costume Institute of the Metropolitan Museum in New York and the Smithsonian Institution, Washington, D.C., have included Levis in their *Americana Collection.*

**low-slung p.**   See HIP-HUGGERS.

**luau p.**   Man's calf-length pants styled in colorful Hawaiian print. *Der.* From Hawaiian luau parties where this type of pants were first worn.

**maternity p.**   Pants worn by expectant mothers with either a cut-out section at top center front or a section of stretch fabric inserted over the abdomen.

**mousers**   Women's leather stocking pants reaching to waist made of shiny wet-look leather with attached chunky-type shoes. Introduced by Mary Quant, British designer, in 1969.

**overalls**   Pants with a bib top and suspender straps over the shoulders which cross in back. Traditionally worn by farmers in blue denim. House painters and carpenters wore them in natural or white. See PAINTER'S PANTS. Also worn by railroad workers in striped fabrics. In late 1960s styled in many fabrics for all occasions and worn by adults and children. Also called *bib-top pants* and *suspender pants. Pleated overalls* introduced in early 1980s are similar in style but cut all in one piece in front with much fullness at top which was pleated into a band. *Der.* So called because originally worn over clothing.

**Oxford bags**   Men's long trousers with very wide cuffed legs. Popular in the 1920s, beginning at Oxford University in England, and revived for men and women in early 1970s.

**painter's p.   1.**   Natural-colored or white pants styled with one or more loops on legs to hold brushes, originally worn by house painters. Adapted as a fashion item in late 1970s and worn for school and sportswear. In 1980s also made in colors. **2.** See OVERALLS.

**pajamas**   See SEPARATE CATEGORY.

**palazzo p.**   Women's long, wide pajamas or culottes with voluminous flared legs and gathered waist. Worn for lounging or evening dress in the late 1960s and early 1970s.

**parachute p.**   Straight-legged pants with zipper (of about 6 inches) from hem up leg to give tight fit at ankles. Three zip pockets are placed at side of leg, and another zip pocket on hip.

**party p.**   Name adopted in late 1960s for women's pants and pajamas made in more elaborate fabrics and sometimes accordion-pleated. Styled to wear for dining and dancing in the evening.

**pedal pushers**   Below the knee straight-cut women's pants, often cuffed. Popular during World War II for bicycling and reintroduced in 1980s.

**peg-top p.**   Pants which are pleated at the waistband and narrow at the ankles.

**pleated overalls**   See OVERALLS.

**pleated p.**   Trousers with pleats at waistband in front giving more fullness through the hips.

**plus fours**   Wide baggy knickers popularized by Duke of Windsor in 1920s when he was Prince of Wales. Worn by men, usually with patterned wool socks and *brogues,* for golfing and other sports. Reintroduced for men in late 1960s. *Der.* When introduced, these knickers were 4 inches longer than usual knicker length.

**pre-cuffed trousers**   Men's trousers sold in various lengths, *e.g.,* 27″, 29″ and 31″ for inside seam, with cuff already finished. As contrasted with trousers bought with unfinished hems, tailored to length, and finished in retail store workroom.

**proportioned p.   1. Women:** Any pants for women made in petite, average, and tall sizes. Particularly women's stretch pants since 1950s. **2. Men:** Trousers sold by inseam lengths of 27″, 29″ and 31″ as short, regular, and long.

**pull-on p.**   Stretch pants which do not have a placket but have an elasticized waistband.

**riding breeches**   Pants full-cut at hips and thigh and tightly fitted at knee, sometimes made of stretch fabric, some with zipper closure, and others with buttoned drop front.

Worn by men and women with high boots for horseback riding. Also called CANARY BREECHES, HUNT BREECHES and *show breeches*. Also see JODHPURS.

**sailor p.** Worn by sailors in navy blue for winter and white for summer. Now made in conventional style with zip-closing. Originally made in bell-bottom style with drop-front closing having thirteen buttons for the thirteen original states. Seven buttons went across horizontally with three additional buttons extending vertically at each side. A functional lacing went across center back. Also called BELL-BOTTOMS.

**see-through p.** Women's pants of sheer fabric or lace worn over bikini pants—a style of the late 1960s.

**seven-eighths p.** Any style pants coming to just below the calf of the leg.

**shalwar** Very full ankle-length pants gathered into a band at waist and ankle, similar to HAREM PANTS. Customarily worn by women in Turkey, Albania, and by all Persian women until 1890 when the ruler Nair-Ne-Din visited Paris. After seeing the Parisian ballet he ordered all women to wear short skirts in place of trousers. Also spelled *chalwar*, *salvar*, *salwar*.

**shorts** See separate category.

**show breeches** See HUNT BREECHES.

**ski p.** Pants or leggings worn for skiing and other winter sports. The styles vary with the general trend in legs of trousers from wide to tight-fitting, often with straps under feet. First introduced with jodhpur-type legs in the late 1920s; narrow styles in stretch fabrics appeared in 1950s. For downhill racing and jumping competitions see UNITARD under SPORT SUITS.

**slacks** Synonym for *pants*.

**slim jeans** Blue jeans cut with very narrow legs frequently made of stretch denim worn literally "skintight."

**stirrup p.** Pants usually made in a narrow

style having an extension under the instep which can be worn inside or under the shoe.

**stovepipe p.** Tight-fitting pants with narrow legs the same width from knees down. Worn by men from 1880 until 1920, reintroduced in mid-1960s, and popular in 1980s.

**straight cut p.** Pants straight cut from knee down. See STOVE PIPE PANTS.

**stretch p.** Pants made from knitted stretch fabric, which conform closely to the body, very popular from 1950s to mid-1960s. In 1980s popular for jeans made of stretch denim.

**surfers** Close-fitting pants extending to knee popular in early 1960s. *Der.* Introduced for beachwear and surfboard riding in California.

**suspender p.** **1.** See OVERALLS. **2.** Children's pull-on pants with straps made of same fabric as pants.

**sweatpants** Pants of cotton knit with fleece backing to absorb moisture. Worn by athletes before and after exercising. Also called WARM-UP PANTS.

**tapered p.** Full-length pants with legs becoming narrower toward the ankle, popular in early 1960s and 1980s.

**tights** See PANTIES category.

**toreador p.** Tight-fitting below-the-knee pants patterned after those worn by Spanish bullfighters, popular for women in late 1950s and early 1960s. Also see SUIT OF LIGHTS under SPORT SUITS.

**trousers** Synonym for all full-length pants.

**tuxedo p.** **1. Men:** Conventional black trousers, usually with narrow satin stripe down each side, worn with TUXEDO JACKET and CUMMERBUND for semiformal wear. **2. Women:** Pants made with gathers at waistline, worn with a cummerbund and introduced in 1980s.

**unisex p.** See DRAWSTRING PANTS.

**warmup p.** **1.** Interlined overpants worn for skiing with zippers down the sides for easy removal. **2.** See SWEATPANTS and WARMUP SUIT under SPORT SUITS.

**western p.** Low-waisted, slim fitting pants made of denim or gabardine, characterized by double-stitched seams and rivets placed at points of strain. Often with pockets opening at both top and side, producing right-angle front flaps that are buttoned at the corners. Also see BLUE JEANS. Worn originally by ranchers and cowboys in American West. Popular for general wear since mid-1960s. Also called *dude jeans* and *frontier pants*.

**white flannels** Slacks made of white wool, especially flannel, worn by men in 1980s. Reminiscent of those worn from 1890s through 1930s for sportswear with striped blazer and straw hat.

**work p.** Durable full-length trousers with patches at knees, triple-stitched main seams, and rivets at points of strain. Worn by auto mechanics and other workmen. Styled with watch pocket, tool pockets on legs, and hammer loop. Made of durable washable fabric.

**Wranglers®** Trademark for type of WESTERN PANTS or BLUE JEANS.

**zippered p.** Straight-legged pants with one zipper from waist to ankle and second zipper from waist to upper thigh on each leg. Snap tabs hold pants tightly at ankle.

---

**pants boot** See BOOTS.

**pantliner** See GIRDLES.

**panty** See PANTIES.

**panty dress** Girl's dress with matching bloomers, worn in the 1920s. Also called BLOOMER DRESS.

**panty foundation** See FOUNDATIONS.

**panty girdle** See GIRDLES.

**pantyhose** Term introduced about 1963 to describe stockings and panties cut in one piece and made in textured and sheer nylon yarns such as Cantrece and Agilon. First made in sizes for tall, medium and petite heights, later made in larger sizes. Introduced for men in fall 1970. Originally called *tights*, usually made in cotton and worn mostly by children and dancers. In 1958 the firm called Societe de Bonneterie De Tergnier in France patented a brand of sheer pantyhose called *mitoufle* (or tights). Mary Quant, British designer, also was influential in trying to find a suitable hose and girdle combination for wear with her short-skirted dresses of early 1960s. In mid-1980s interest in unusual pantyhose was revived. Made in many patterns including those used for *hose*.

### ■ PANTYHOSE ■

**all sheer p.** Pantyhose of sheer nylon yarn made with no reinforcements. Also called *sheer pantyhose*.

**bikini p.** Pantyhose with low-slung top for wear with bare-midriff dresses, hip-hugger skirts or low-slung pants.

**control p.** Pantyhose made with the panty portion knit of nylon combined with *elastomeric yarn* to give the control of a lightweight girdle.

**detachable p.** Three-piece pantyhose made with patented bands on panties to attach replacement stockings.

**Hiplets®** Separate hose for each leg with cut-out sections over the hips and an elastic band around the waistline to hold hose in place. Introduced in late 1960s.

**jeweled p.** Sheer pantyhose with embroidery at ankle trimmed with rhinestones. Introduced in 1986.

**lace p.** Pantyhose made of patterned stretch lace in openwork styles.

**Mani-Hose®** Trademark for pantyhose for men introduced in 1970. Made of stretch nylon, with lower leg made in rib-knit.

**opaque p.** Textured or plain pantyhose which are not sheer and come in all colors.

**Patternskins®** Trademark for women's pantyhose made in bright-colored geometric designs of Jacquard knits by designer Giorgio Sant'Angelo in early 1970s.

**sandalfoot p.** Sheer pantyhose with no reinforcements at toes or heels. May have an opaque panty portion, or be sheer to the waist.

**DETACHABLE PANTYHOSE**

**CONTROL PANTYHOSE**

**HIPLETS®**

**SANDALFOOT PANTYHOSE**

**seamed p.** Conventional pantyhose with black seam up the back.

**sheer p.** See ALL SHEER PANTYHOSE.

**support p.** Pantyhose made with support for the legs.

**tattoo p.** Very sheer pantyhose with legs painted in twining floral designs which appear at a distance to be tattooed on the leg.

**tights** Knitted pants and stockings made in one piece usually made of opaque textured yarns. Worn originally by athletes and dancers, later worn by children. In the early 1960s worn primarily by women and girls as a substitute for hose. In 1980s also worn with leotards for dancing, exercising, etc.

**ultra-sheer p.** See SHEER PANTYHOSE.

---

**pantyslip** See PANTIES, PETTICOATS, or SLIPS.

**pantywaist** Child's cotton undergarment worn from early 20th c. consisting of fitted sleeveless top buttoned down front. Made with buttons around waistline to attach panties and *suspender garters*. Also called *underwaist*. Also see FERRIS WAIST.

**pañuelo** (pa-knew-eh-lo) Square scarf, usually made of fine sheer rengue cloth, worn around the shoulders by women in the Philippines.

**panung** (pah-nung) Length of fabric approximately 3 yards long and 1 yard wide, draped like an Indian DHOTI to form loose-fitting trousers or skirt. Worn by men and women in Thailand. *Der.* Siamese, *pa*, "cloth" and *nin*, "one."

**paperbag waistline** See WAISTLINES.

**paper cambric** Loosely woven fabric of coarse yarns which is heavily sized and given a non-permanent glazed finish. Becomes limp if washed. Used mainly for costumes. Also called *lining cambric*.

**paper doll style** Full-skirted, cinched-waisted fashions designed by Anne Fogarty in 1950–55. See DRESSES and LOOKS. Also see ANNE FOGARTY under APPENDIX DESIGNERS.

**paper dress** See DRESSES.

**paper pattern** Dress pattern sold by pattern companies such as *Vogue, Butterick, McCalls,* and *Simplicity.* Made in various sizes and sold to individuals for home sewing. First paper patterns were not made in sizes, but offered to subscribers of magazines such as *Harper's Bazaar* in supplements. Patterns for eighteen garments were sometimes placed on one large sheet of paper. Pieces for each pattern were made with different types of lines, *e.g.,* .----..----..---- or .....-.....-.......--. To make a pattern, women copied these lines with a tracing wheel on tracing paper and enlarged pattern to the proper size. Butterick invented "sized patterns" in 1872. These were sold through fashion magazines such as *The Delineator* and *Demorest's Magazine.* Also see BUTTERICK.

**paper taffeta** Crisp lightweight taffeta fabric.

**papier-mâché** Lightweight material molded of combination of tissue paper, bits of newspaper, or paper pulp fastened together with glue or various binders. May be painted and shellacked. Used for jewelry, particularly bracelets, beads, and pins in late 1960s. *Der.* French, "chewed paper." Also spelled *paper-mâché.*

**papillion** (pa-pi-yon) See BONNET À BEC.

**PAPILLON COLLAR
& CUFF, 1869**

**papillon collar** (pa-pi-yon) Small standing collar, decorated with pleated fabric in front to form a small butterfly, worn by women in late 1860s. Cuffs were also decorated with small pleated butterflies. *Der.* French, "butterfly."

**papillotte comb** Decorative tortoise shell comb, 3 to 4 inches long, used on either side of head to puff out hair by women in late 1820s. *Der.* French, *papilloter,* "to flutter," and *papillon,* "butterfly."

**papush** Elaborately embroidered yellow or red flat leather sandal worn by Arabian men and women.

**Paquin** See APPENDIX/DESIGNERS.

**parachute fabric** Lightweight strong fabric previously made of silk, now made of nylon and used for parachutes by skydivers and military airborne troops. Sometimes used for bridal gowns in the 1940s—for sentimental reasons and because of the shortage of fabrics during World War II.

**parachute hat** See BALLOON HAT.

**parachute pants** See PANTS.

**parachute sleeve** Long full sleeve made without a cuff with the lower edge gathered to a lining cut shorter than the sleeve.

**paradise feather** See BIRD-OF-PARADISE under FEATHERS.

**parament** (pa-ra-ment) **1.** Early term for a *facing.* **2.** Ornamental cuff at wrist, turned up over sleeve and stitched. Also spelled *parement.* **3.** Trimming used on *gown à la française* in 18th c., usually a long decorated band, wider at hem. **4.** Ecclesiastical vestment.

**parasol** **1.** Sun umbrella, sometimes made of fabrics matched to dresses with ruffles and embroidered trim. Made in various shapes, *e.g.,* pagoda or dome, sometimes with folding handle. An accessory popular in 19th and early 20th c. **2.** Japanese umbrella made of glazed waterproof paper and bamboo in bright colors and printed with large decorative motifs. Used to protect elaborate high headdresses, as a sunshade, and against rain and snow. **3.** Also carried by Burmese women and by men in royal ceremonies. Also called *sunshade*. *Der.* Latin, *parare*, "to shield," and *sol*, "sun."

**parasol skirt** Skirt cut with many gores, stitched in same manner as seams in a parasol. Worn by women in late 19th and early 20th c.

**parchment calves** Padding of parchment worn inside stockings to make legs shaplier. Worn by men in latter half of 18th c. Also see FALSE CALVES.

PARDESSUS #2

**pardessus** (par-de-soo) **1.** French term for man's overcoat. **2.** Generic term used from 1840s to end of 19th c. for woman's outdoor garment of half or three-quarter length. Made with sleeves, fitted waistline, and frequently with a cape trimmed with lace or velvet. Also called MANTELET and PALETOT. *Der.* French, "for on top." Also see POLONAISE PARDESSUS.

**pareu** (pah-ray) See LAVA-LAVA.

**paridhana** Type of DHOTI worn in India.

**Paris, point de** See LACES.

**parka** **1.** Hooded fur jacket worn by Eskimos, usually of flat fur with fluffy fur on hem and around hood. Sometimes had an embroidered *yoke*. Sometimes spelled *parkeh*. **2.** See SPORT JACKETS. *Der.* Russian-Aleutian, "pelt."

**Parnis, Mollie** See APPENDIX/DESIGNERS.

**parta** Native headdress worn by single girls in Hungary, consisting of a *halo-type hat* trimmed with metallic lace and often studded with semiprecious stones.

**parti-colored** Bicolored garment divided vertically with each side made of a different color—or striped on one side, plain on the other. Popular from mid-14th to mid-15th c. for hose and clothing. Also see PIED HOSE.

**partlet** **1.** Decorative covering for upper part of chest and neck showing under low-cut doublet worn by men in first half of 16th c. **2.** Fill-in for low-cut *bodice* worn by women in 16th and 17th c. Also called CHEMISETTE and TUCKER. Also spelled *patlet*.

**party** See PAJAMAS and PANTS.

**parure** (par-oor) Matched set of jewelry that may consist of a necklace, earrings, pin, or bracelet. *Der.* French, "adornment."

**pashm** See CASHMERE SHAWL.

**passé de mode** French term, "out of fashion"; "unfashionable."

**passement** See LACES.

**passementerie** (pas-mehn-tree) Trimmings *e.g.* heavy embroideries, braid, tinsel, beads, lace, and guimp used as edging in 19th c.

**paste** Highly reflective transparent types of flint glass faceted or molded to make *imitation gems*. One variety is called *strass*, named for Josef Strasser, a German jeweler. Used in making replicas of expensive jewelry. Also see FAUX JEWELS and FASHION JEWELRY.

**pasties** See BRAS.

**patch** **1.** Extra piece of fabric sewed or bonded by heat to clothing for mending a tear or for decorative effect, *e.g.*, suede elbow patches on sweaters and knee patches on blue jeans. **2.** Insignia sewed to sleeve of uniform to indicate rank. **3.** From 1590s to end of 18th c., a decorative cutout of black silk or velvet shaped like moon, star, etc., applied to the face. Placement of patch denoted the wearer's mood, *e.g.*, the "coquette" was placed on the lip; the "roguish" was placed on the nose; the "impassioned" was placed at the corner of the eye. From 1702 to 1714 in England the patch indicated the political party of the wearer. Also called *assasin*, *beauty spot*, or *mouche*. See COURT PLASTER.

**patch box**   Small box carried by women in 17th c. to hold various types of decorative cutouts called *patches* which were applied to face.

**patchouli** (pat-chew-lee)   Oil used as fixative in perfumes very popular in 19th c. Used in Oriental blends and made from Malaysian, Indian, and Indonesian plant leaves.

**patch pocket**   See POCKETS.

**patchwork**   A method of sewing small pieces of various colors and patterns together to form a fabric or quilt. See DRESSES, LOOKS, and PRINTS.

**patent leather**   Leather with a shiny hard surface. See LEATHERS.

**patio dress**   See DRESSES.

**patlet**   See PARTLET.

**Patou, Jean**   See APPENDIX/DESIGNERS.

**patrol jacket   1. Men:** Jacket of military cut made with five-button single-breasted closing and Prussian collar. Worn in late 1870s with tight knee pants for bicycling. **2. Women:** Tight-fitting hip-length jacket of late 1880s trimmed with military braid across front. Also had a standing collar at neck and tight-fitting sleeves finished with cuffs.

**patte**   Term for earliest form of *lapel*, resembling a narrow collar with tabs, worn on *garnache* in 13th and 14th c. Also called *paw*.

**patten   1.** Shoe fitted with iron blades for skating in Middle Ages. **2.** Overshoe worn over regular shoes to raise feet above muddy streets. Consisted of a wooden sole raised about three inches with bands of iron forming the walking surface. Another type had a wooden sole with top portion indented for the heel and secured

by strap fitting over regular shoe. Worn by men and women from 14th to mid-19th c. Also called CLOG. Also see CHOPINE.

**pattern book**   Large volume issued regularly (and updated) by the publisher of paper patterns for home sewers showing all of the designs available. Available where *patterns* are sold for convenience of customers. Also called *counter book*.

**patterned hose**   See HOSE.

**Patternskins®**   See PANTYHOSE.

**pauldron**   Armor worn in late 15th c. consisting of single large rigid shoulder plate lapping over armor at chest and back. Also called ÉPAULIÈRE and *shoulder cop*.

**paultock**   See PALTOCK.

**pavé**   A jewelry term for a setting of stones placed close to each other so that no metal shows between them.

**pavilion**   Jewelry industry term for lower portion below the girdle of a brilliant cut gem. Also called the *base*. See GEM CUTS.

**paw   1.** See PATTE. **2.** Fur term for small pieces of fur from paws of animals.

**paw crosses**   See CROSSES.

**peace symbol**   Circle or oval enclosing a vertical staff with two bars projecting at about a 60° angle down to left and right from center of staff. Introduced in 1960s by opponents of U.S. involvement in Vietnam War. Used for rings and medallions.

**peacock feathers**   See FEATHERS.

**Peacock Revolution**   A term used in 1967 concerned with radical change in men's wear from the conventional type of clothing, *i.e.*, the gray flannel three-button suit worn with buttoned-down shirt and necktie, to clothing of the more relaxed, more creative, nonconventional type. New styles accepted for men's wear included *turtleneck knits shirts, Nehru jackets, flared pants, Edwardian coats, medallion neck-*

*laces,* rings, perfumes, and less conservative hairstyles.

**pea jacket/coat** From 1830s on, man's double-breasted, unfitted thigh-length jacket with wide lapels and notched collar. Worn either as an overcoat or as a suit jacket. In 1850s had large buttons, usually six. Also called a *pilot coat.* See SPORT JACKETS. *Der.* So called because it was made of "pilot cloth." From 1860 known as a REEFER.

**peaked lapel** See LAPEL.

**peaked shoe** See PIKED SHOE.

**pear cut** See GEM CUTS.

**pearl** See BEADS, BUTTONS, DRESSES, GEMS, and NECKLACES.

**peasant bodice** *Corselet* bodice of mid-1880s laced up the front to bustline with straps extending over outermost edge of shoulder, and worn over a blouse by women. Also see NECKLINES.

**peasant fashions** Styles originating from various peasant costumes worn in Europe for festive occasions. See BLOUSES, COATS, DRESSES, LOOKS, SKIRTS, and SLEEVES. Also see DIRNDL, RICH PEASANT and TYROLEAN LOOKS under LOOKS.

**peascod-bellied doublet** Man's *doublet,* with a false front stuffed with cotton into a horn-shaped projection over waistline. Introduced into France from Spain and popular from 1570 to 1600. Originally a Dutch style. *Der.* Said to be in imitation of the *cuirasse* to deflect bullets. Also called *bellied doublet, goose-bellied doublet, kodpeased doublet, long-bellied doublet,* and *shotten-bellied doublet.*

**peau de soie** (po de swah) Heavyweight satin with a fine filling ribbed effect on the reverse side made of silk or man-made fibers. Piece-dyed and given a dull luster—better grades are reversible. Used for shoes, dresses, evening gowns, and wedding dresses. *Der.* French, "skin of silk."

**pebble Cheviot** Shaggy, nubbed, heavy fabric made in a twill weave of worsted, woolen, or combinations of these yarns. Used for overcoats and sport jackets.

**pebbled finish** An embossed leather finish similar to tiny cobblestones or pebbles.

**pebble weave** See GRANITE WEAVE.

**peccary** See LEATHERS.

**pedal pushers** See PANTS.

**pediment headdress** 19th-c. term for the gabled or peaked hood worn in 16th c. Called the ENGLISH HOOD.

**pedlar dolls** See MODEL DOLLS.

**Pedlar, Sylvia** See APPENDIX/DESIGNERS.

**Peds®** See SOCKS.

**peek-a-boo earrings** See EARRINGS.

**peek-a-boo waist** Woman's waist made of eyelet embroidery popular in early 20th c.

**peeler** See COTTON.

**Peggy collar** Rounded collar with scalloped ends similar to PETER PAN COLLAR.

**peg-top** Pants or skirts which have fullness through hips and taper to hem. See PANTS and SKIRTS.

**peg-top sleeve** Sleeve worn by men from 1857 to 1864, full at shoulder and tapered to wrist. A modified form of the *leg-of-mutton* sleeve.

**peg-top trousers** Man's trousers wide and pleated at top, tapered on lower leg, and close fitting at ankles. Popular from 1857 to 1865 and revived in 1892. Also see PANTS.

**peigne Josephine** (pai-nyeh) Woman's high comb, ornamented with small gilt balls. Worn at the back of head for evening in 1842.

**peignoir** (pai-nwar) **1.** See ROBES. **2.** See NIGHTGOWNS. **3.** Loose wrapper, or loose jacket and skirt worn by woman for informal morning wear from late 18th c. on. In 1840s styled with *Bishop sleeves.*

**PELERINE**

**pelerine** (pel-er-reen) **1.** Woman's short shoulder cape of fur, velvet, or other fabric worn from 1740 to end of 18th c. Sometimes worn with long scarf ends crossed and tied around waist. **2.** A muslin cape-shaped collar trimmed with lace worn from 19th c., in 1825 reverted to former style.

**pelisse** (pe-leese) **1.** Full-length, sometimes sleeveless, fur-lined coat trimmed with fur down the front, at neck, and armholes. Worn open in front by Jewish men in Palestine in late 17th c. over the *entari.* **2. Women:** 18th-c. caped, or hooded, three-quarter length cloak with armhole slits and entire collar, hem, and front usually edged with fur, sometimes with silk or satin. **3. Women:** 1800 to 1810 fitted three-quarter length lightweight silk coat having one or more capes. Later ankle-length. **4. Women:** In 1880s full-length winter mantle gathered on the shoulders and having loose sleeves, often made of silk, velvet, or satin. **5. Men:** Late 19th and early 20th c. heavy fur-lined coat with fur collar worn particularly with formal clothes. Also spelled *pellice.*

**pelisse-robe** (pe-leese) Daytime dress in coat style, worn from about 1817 to 1840, fastened down the front with ribbon bows or with hidden hooks and eyes.

**pellice** See PELISSE.

**pellison** Fur-lined outer tunic or gown for men and women worn throughout 14th to 16th c. Also called *pilch.*

**Pellon®** Trademark of Pellon Corp. for a nonwoven fabric used for interlining and made by fusing natural fibers and man-made fibers together. Retains its shape through laundering and dry cleaning. Several types are as follows: *a)* with a stretch similar to regular fabrics; *b)* bias Pellon® used where more stretch is needed; *c)* Pellon® fusable web which, when pressed with a steam iron, fuses to the fabric. Used as interlining in collars and facings.

**pelt** Skin of an animal with the hair attached used for making fur garments and accessories. Also called a *peltry.*

**Pelt-Belt®** See BELTS.

**peltry** See PELT.

**pembroke paletot** (pal-e-toe) Man's calf-length, long-waisted overcoat worn in mid-1850s made with wide lapels, double-breasted with eight buttons and easy fitting sleeves with turned-back cuffs. Also had flapped side pockets and vertical breast pocket.

**penang lawyer** Walking stick used by men in 19th c. made from a palm stem with a bulbous top.

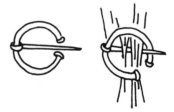

**PENANNULAR BROOCH**

**penannular brooch** A moveable pin set on an incompleted ring used to fasten clothing from 11th through 13th c.

**pencil pocket** See POCKETS.

**pencil stripe** See STRIPES.

**pendant** An ornament that hangs or dangles. See EARRINGS, NECKLACES, PINS, and WATCHES.

**pendicle** Term for single pendant earring worn by men in 17th c.

**Penelope** (peh-naell-o-pee) **1.** British term for knitted jacket without sleeves. **2.** Type of fine mesh canvas used for needlework and embroidery. *Der.* Named after the legendary Greek queen of Ithaca, the faithful wife of Odysseus, who wove cloth during the day and unraveled work at night to forestall suitors during his absence.

**penny loafers** See SHOES.

**pentes** Distinctive woman's skirt of mid-1880s cut in two layers. The overskirt was draped to reveal an underskirt trimmed with alternating silk and velvet strips which were pyramid-shaped and graduated in size.

**peplos** Earliest form of Greek *chiton* worn in Homeric period by women. Made of a rectangle of woolen fabric, sometimes heavily embroidered at edges. Wrapped around body and fastened on shoulder with a *fibula* (pin). Tied with a rope-type sash at the waist. Sometimes one breast was exposed and garment hung open on one side.

**peplum** Extension of bodice of dress that comes below waistline, sometimes pleated, sometimes flared. Can be made in one piece with bodice, cut separately and joined to bodice by a seam, or attached to a belt. Popular in mid-1860s, 1890s, and 1930s. Revived in mid-1980s. Also see BLOUSES and DRESSES.

**peplum basque** (bask) Woman's dress of mid-1860s with peplum attached to belt. Peplum was usually short in back and front with long hanging ends at sides.

**peplum bodice** Bodice of evening dress worn in 1870s cut with long side panels draped to form *panniers* at hips.

**peplum dolman** *Dolman* worn by women in the early 1870s with long points hanging at sides.

**peplum rotonde** Woman's waist-length circular cloak, made with back vent and fringed border, worn in 1871.

**percale** Plain lightweight fabric made in a great variety of qualities. Originally cotton, better qualities now use blended yarns of polyester staple with the cotton. Finest qualities are high count and made with combed yarns. Other percales are of low count, made of carded-yarns, and sized to add body to the fabric. All types may be dyed or printed. Best qualities are used for drip-dry dresses and blouses.

**percaline** **1.** Lustrous, cotton lining fabric similar to lawn. Usually dyed dark colors and used to line clothing, particularly furs. **2.** Mercerized, combed cotton fabric given a *bettled* and a *moiré* finish. Also called *cotton taffeta*.

**percan** See BARACAN/BARRACAN.

**perdita chemise** British term for daytime dress of 1873 made with close-fitting bodice and V-neck with large falling collar, sometimes double. Also had long tight sleeves, buttons or ribbon ties down front, and sash at waist tied with long ends in back. Also called *chemise gown. Der.* Named after Perdita Robinson, the actress.

**Peretti, Elsa** See APPENDIX/DESIGNERS.

**perforations** Small holes punched through leather of shoe to achieve decorative effect. Used particularly for SPECTATOR PUMPS and BROGUES. Also called *perfs* in shoe trade slang.

**perfume cone** Small cone of perfumed wax worn on top of head by ancient Egyptians during parties and dinners. When the cone melted, it gave off a pleasant scent.

**perfume ring** See RINGS.

**peridot** See GEMS.

**periwig** A wig, specifically an extremely large powdered wig, with raised peaks on top and long hanging loose curls—as worn by Louis XIV of France. Also called *peruke.*

**perkan**   See BARACAN/BARRACAN.

**permanent press**   See DURABLE PRESS.

**permanent wave**   Waves or curls that last until hair is cut off, originally created by chemicals and heated rollers, later by means of only chemicals. First permanent wave was invented by Charles Nestlé in 1906. First machine wave, introduced in beauty shops, required electrical wiring to each roller. In 1930s, new machineless wave used chemicals and heated rollers. In the early 1940s, the first *cold wave,* in which chemicals curled the hair without heating it, was introduced. This made home permanents possible. In 1960s a soft version called a body wave gave hair more fullness for non-curly coiffures. Popularized for men in late 1970s. Name usually shortened to *permanent.* British slang, called *perm.* Also see MARCEL.

**perraje**   Shawl worn in Guatemala.

**perruque à l'enfant**   Man's wig of 1780s with tiny curls over most of the head, larger horizontal curls above ears and neck, and long queue hanging down back. Also called *perruque naissante.*

**perruquier** (perook-kee-ay)   Term used for a person who arranged and set wigs in the 18th c.

**Persian lamb**   See FURS.

**Persians**   Leather industry term for hairsheepskin leather tanned in India.

**peruke**   See PERIWIG.

**Peruvian hat**   Term for woman's rain hat made from plaited palm leaves worn in early 19th c.

**petal collar**   See COLLARS and SLEEVES.

**petal hem**   See HEMS.

**petasus**   **1.** Felt hat with a large floppy brim and nondescript crown worn in ancient Greece when traveling. Also worn in ancient Rome. **2.** Close-fitting winged cap as seen in represen-

**PETASUS #1**

tations of Roman god, Mercury. Also spelled *petasos.*

**petenlair**   Dress worn by women from 1745 to 1770s, made with separate thigh-length bodice with fitted *stomacher* front, full back, and elbow-length sleeves. Worn with long petticoat to make a dress. Also spelled *pet-en-l'air.* Also called *French jacket.*

**Peter Pan collar**   See COLLARS.

**Peter Pan hat**   Small hat with brim extended in front and turned up in back. Made with a conical crown trimmed with long feathers. *Der.* Named after the hat worn by actress Maude Adams in 1905 when starring in James M. Barrie's play, *Peter Pan.*

**Petersham Cossacks**   Trousers worn by men from 1814, modified in 1820s, and worn into the 1830s. Very bouffant and worn spread out over the foot, drawn in with ribbon tied in bows on outside of leg, and worn with flounces at ankles. Also called *Petersham trousers. Der.* Named for Viscount Charles Petersham.

**Petersham frock coat**   *Frock coat* of 1830s with slanted flapped pockets on hips and collar, lapels, and cuffs of velvet. *Der.* Named for Viscount Charles Petersham.

**Petersham greatcoat**   Man's overcoat, with short shoulder cape worn in 1830s. *Der.* Named for Viscount Charles Petersham.

**Petersham, Viscount Charles** (1780–1851) Fashionable figure from Regency period to

1850, classified between an eccentric and a true *dandy,* for whom various items of men's clothing and fabrics were named. See Petersham cossacks, Petersham frock coat, and Petersham greatcoat.

**Peter Thomson dress** One piece dress with *middy collar* and box pleats from yoke to hem. Worn as uniform by many school children and older girls (through college) from 1900 to 1920. *Der.* Named for designer Peter Thomson, who was once a tailor for the Navy.

**petit casaque** (pe-tee ca-sack) French name used in 1870s for polonaise dress.

**petite** **1.** Size range for women who are below average height—usually sized from 6 to 16. Junior petite sizes for short-waisted women run from 5 to 15. **2.** Smallest size, along with *small, medium,* and *large* for pantyhose, bodysuits, and nightgowns.

**petit point** See embroideries and stitches.

**petits bonshommes** (peh-tee bun-zum) Bands of fabric with several ruffles—often of lace—used to edge sleeves of gown *e.g.,* gown à la française from early 1720s to 1780s.

**petti** Prefix used to mean little or small. See pants, slips, and pettiskirt under petticoats; petticulottes and pettiskirt brief under panties.

**pettibockers** Ankle-length silk-jersey pantaloons worn as underwear by women in early 20th c.

**petticoat** **1.** Undergarment for a woman or girl similar to a slip, but starting at the waist. Depending on overgarment, it may be full or narrow, lace-trimmed or tailored, and long or short. Originally called an *under-petticoat,* from 16th to 18th c.; called a petticoat since the

19th c. **2.** Term used in 17th and 18th c. for the skirt of the dress, not the underskirt. **3.** Waist-length under-doublet worn by men from last half of 15th to end of 16th c. Also called a *waistcoat.*

## ▰▰▰ PETTICOATS ▰▰▰

**bouffant p.** Any full petticoat made with gores or ruffles worn under a wide-skirted dress.

**crinoline** **1.** Stiffened petticoat intended to hold out a bouffant skirt—may be made of stiff

DIRNDL PETTICOAT

CRINOLINE

HALF-SLIP

EVENING PETTICOAT

PETTICULOTTES

nylon, either plain or ruffled. **2.** Underskirt, worn in 1840s and 1850s, made of fabrics called *crinoline* or horsehair. **3.** Term applied to any underskirt, *hoops*, that support a full skirt. See HOOPS in alphabetical listing.

**dirndl p.** (durn-dul) Petticoat fitting smoothly over hips with gathered fullness to hem. Sometimes made with tiers or ruffles. *Der.* From Austrian Tyrol full-skirted peasant costume.

**evening p.** Narrow ankle-length petticoat made with slash in center front or slashes on side seams.

**half-slip** Narrow slip which begins at the waistline, hence a petticoat.

**hoop p.** Full-length petticoat consisting of series of circular metal bands held by vertical tape, making skirt flexible to permit one to sit down. Introduced in late 1850s and worn at intervals since. Also see HOOPS in alphabetical listing.

**mini-petti** Mid-thigh-length petticoat. Introduced in late 1960s for wear with MINISKIRTS.

**pantyslip** Short petticoat with panties attached at waistband.

**petticulottes** Short petticoat and panties combined in one garment. Also see CULOTTES in alphabetical listing.

**pettiskirt** Synonym for PETTICOAT.

**pettiskirt brief** Combination petticoat and short panties joined by elastic waistband.

---

**petticoat bodice** **1.** Petticoat joined by waistline seam to sleeveless bodice worn from about 1815 until 1890. **2.** In 1890, a type of corset cover. See CAMISOLE.

**petticoat breeches** Wide-legged *culottes*, fashionable court fashion worn by men in England and France in 1660s and 1670s,

made pleated or gathered to waistband, full to knees, and trimmed with ribbon loops at waistband and near hem on sides. Worn as livery for "running footmen" until mid-18th c. Also called *Rhinegraves*.

**pheasant feathers**   See FEATHERS.

**Philippine embroidery**   See EMBROIDERIES.

**photographic print**   See PRINTS.

**Phrygian cap** (frij-i-an) **1.** Cap with high rounded peak curving forward with lappets hanging at sides, sometimes made of leather. Worn in ancient Greece from 9th to 12th c. and copied from 18th c. on as LIBERTY CAP. **2.** See PILEUS #2. Also called *Phrygian bonnet*.

**PHYSICAL WIG, 1755–56**

**physical wig**   Short wig, brushed back from forehead, bushy at sides and back, worn by professional men during latter half of 18th c., replacing FULL BOTTOMED WIG. Also called *pompey*.

**piano shawl**   See SHAWLS.

**pianta bag**   See HANDBAGS.

**Picadill/Piccadilly**   See PICKADIL.

**Piccadilly collar**   Man's detachable high wing collar of 1860s fastening to the shirt with a stud in front and a button in back. By 1895, collar was cut larger to allow a scarf to pass underneath.

**Piccadilly Johnny**   See MASHER.

**pick**   Textile term for one yarn which runs at right angles to the selvage. Also called FILLING, WEFT, or WOOF.

**pick-a-devant** See PIQUÉ DEVANT.

**pickadil**  **1.** Standing collar with tabbed or scalloped edge worn in 16th c. **2.** Notched edge on sleeve, bodice front, or neck opening worn from late 16th through early 17th c. **3.** Stiffened band to support ruff or collar in back in early 17th c. Also spelled *piccadill*, *pickardil*, *Piccadilly*. *Der.* From Piccadilly, a street in London.

**pickelhaube** See GERMAN HELMET under HELMETS.

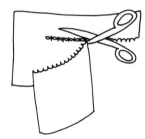

**PICOT #2**

**picot** (pee-ko)  **1.** A row of small loops woven along selvage of fabric made of ribbon or a part of the edge design on lace. **2.** Machine-made edge on fabrics produced by cutting through center of *hemstitching*, each edge becoming a *picot* edge. See HEMSTITCH under STITCHES. **3.** Run-resistant loops on edge of welt in hosiery. **4.** See HEMS.

**picture hat** See HATS.

**piece**  Mill term for fifty yards of fabric—or the amount that can be dyed in one vat.

**piece goods**  Fabric sold by the yard. Piecegood departments in retail stores sell fabrics by the yard to customers for home sewing. In the early days of retailing few ready-made dresses were sold so this department was one of the largest in the store. Also called *yard goods*.

**pied hose**  Hose, similar to tights, with each leg made in a different color. See PARTI-COLORED.

**Piedmont gown**  Type of *sack gown* worn about 1775 with fitted bodice and box pleats

hanging free from shoulders in back as far as waistline where they became a part of the overskirt. Also called *robe à la Piedmontese*.

**pierced earrings** See EARRINGS. Also see PIERCED-LOOK EARRINGS.

**Pierpont collar** (peer-pont)  Man's collar ending in sharp points extended over tie, worn in 1840s and 1850s. Also called *pinpoint collar*.

**Pierrot** (pee-ehr-o)  Close-fitting, low-necked bodice, extending to slightly below the waist worn with a matching flounced skirt from 1780s to 1790s.

**Pierrot cape** (pee-ehr-o)  Woman's three-quarter length cloak of 1892 with additional shoulder cape and satin ruff at neckline similar to that worn with Pierrot costume. Also see PIERROT COLLAR under COLLARS.

**PIERROT COSTUME**

**Pierrot costume** (pee-ehr-o)  Clown suit worn by the comedy character in French pantomime called *Pierrot* (Little Peter) and interpreted by the Italian clown Pagliacci in Leoncavallo's opera. Face is whitened, the suit loose and baggy similar to clown suit—usually white with large buttons or pompons on the jacket front. Usually worn with slippers with pompons and tall hat. Also see COLLARS.

**pigeon-wings** Man's hairstyle or wig with single or double horizontal curls over the ears, smooth at top and sides, worn from 1750s to 1760s. Wig also called *pigeon-winged toupee* or *aile de pigeon*.

**pigskin** See LEATHERS.

**Piguet, Robert** See APPENDIX/DESIGNERS.

**pigtails** See HAIRSTYLES.

**pigtail wig** Wig with a queue worn by men in 18th c., interwoven with black ribbon, tied with ribbon bow at nape of neck, and smaller bow at end of queue.

**piked shoe** Extremely long-toed shoes worn in late 14th and early 15th c. and again from 1460 to 1480. Also called *peaked shoe*. Also see CRAKOW.

**pilch** 1. Close fitting fur-lined outer gown worn by men and women from 14th to 16th c. in winter; later worn by clergy in drafty churches. 2. See PELLISON.

**pile** Loops or other yarns which stand erect on fabric to form all or part of the fabric surface. Either warp or filling produce this thick soft surface. May be uncut as in *terry cloth* or cut as in *velvet*, *velveteen*, and *corduroy*.

**pileolus** Skullcap worn by Catholic priests and Pope under the *miter* and *tiara*. Also spelled *pilleolus*. *Der*. Latin, "skullcap."

**pileus** (pil-ee-us) 1. Ancient Roman skullcap worn at games and festivals. 2. Felt brimless cap with peak folded over, similar to *Phrygian* or *liberty cap*, worn by freed Roman slaves. Also spelled *pilleus*. Also see PILOS. *Der*. Latin, "skullcap."

**Pilgrim collar** See COLLARS.

**pillbox hat** See HATS.

**pilleolus** See PILEOLUS.

**pilleus** See PILEUS.

**pilling** Tendency of woven fabrics and knits, especially wools, nylons, and acrylics, to form surface nubs or bunches of fibers resulting from rubbing during normal wear and washing. Pilling is caused by loosely twisted yarns unwinding and interlocking with each other.

**pillow lace** See LACES.

**pillow-slip dress** Straight-cut *chemise* dress of 1920s, usually short in length with short *kimono* sleeves.

**pilos** (pi-los) Conical cap worn by Greek peasants or fishermen, derived from those worn by ancient Greeks and Romans, similar to PILEUS. *Der*. Latin, "skullcap."

**pilot cloth** Coarse heavy fabric woven of woolen yarns in a twill weave. Finishing processes include fulling, napping, and dyeing—navy-blue—or other dark colors. Used for seamen's jackets, which were called *pilot coats* or *pea jackets* in late 19th c.

**pilot coat** See PEA JACKET.

**pilot shirt** See EPAULET SHIRT under SHIRTS.

**pilot's suit** Early woman's two-piece aviatrix suit of 1912 made with knee-length knickers, fitted blouse with long full sleeves at wrist, and high neckline with attached hood. Worn with bulky knee-length socks, high laced boots, and gauntlet gloves. Costume was designed by Harriet Quimby who was the first woman to fly across the English Channel on April 14, 1912.

**pima cotton** Fine quality long-staple cotton raised in Arizona, Texas, New Mexico, and California, a development of American-Egyptian cotton. *Der*. From Pima County, Arizona.

**pin** **1.** Useful device used as a temporary fastener or when sewing. **2.** Ornamental jewelry made with pin fastener on back usually having a safety catch. Made in all types of materials, *e.g.*, gold, silver, plated metals, and frequently set with gems or imitation stones. In Anglo-Saxon, Greek, and Roman times used to fasten clothing. See PENANNULAR BROOCH and FIBULA. Later became more decorative. The word *brooch* is a synonym.

=========== **PINS** ===========

**bar drop p.** Long narrow pin made with attached pendants.

**bar p.** Long, narrow pin secured by back fastener the same length as the pin. Fashionable since early 20th c. mainly in platinum set with diamonds.

**brooch** Synonym for PIN.

**cameo p.** Single, double, or triple profiles carved out of onyx or sardonyx which comes in layers. Top is usually white while black and shades of orange are popular for the background. See alphabetical listing. Also see WEDGWOOD CAMEO®.

**chatelaine** (shat-eh-len) Pin worn on the lapel or chest with hook on back to secure a watch, or two decorative pins joined by a chain. Also called *fob pin*. *Der.* Keys worn at the waist on a chain by medieval mistress of the castle or "chatelaine."

**clip** Ornament similar to a pin but with spring clasp on back that snaps closed over the edge of fabric. Set with diamonds or rhinestones introduced in 1930s and 1940s.

**collar p.** **1.** Pin which is placed through holes embroidered into the points of shirt collars. **2.** Stud first used in late 19th c. by men for attaching separate shirt collar.

**dressmaker p.** Fine straight pin with head used when sewing on delicate fabrics usually sold in small box by the pound. Also called *silk pin.*

**duet p.** Two pins worn together as a set.

**fob p.** See CHATELAINE.

**fraternity p.** Pin selected and specially made for a high school or college fraternity group. Usually contains the Greek letters of the fraternity in gold on an onyx background. Tiny pearls may be mounted around the edge. Sometimes a small guard chain is attached with individual symbol.

**friendship p.** Tiny colored beads threaded on small safety pin and worn fastened to shoelaces. Exchanged as tokens of friendship or love, colors of the beads have various meanings, *e.g.*, red, best friend; pink, sweetheart; green, enemy; purple, good friend; yellow, pal; blue, going steady. A school fad of the 1980s.

**hat p.** Straight pin from 3″ to 12″ long with bead or jewel at top. Used by women to secure their hats in late 19th through early 20th c., becoming less common after hair was bobbed in the 1920s.

**kilt p.** See SAFETY PIN #3.

**lapel p.** Woman's pin originally worn on the lapel of a suit. Almost all medium-sized pins are now called lapel pins.

**necktie p.** See STICKPIN.

**pendant p.** Pin with a clasp at back and a hook at center top so it can be worn on a chain, cord, etc., as a necklace or a pin.

**safety p.** **1.** Utilitarian pin, shaped somewhat elliptical with large head on one end. **2.** An item of jewelry of similar shape, may have beads hanging suspended from the long bar. **3.** Similar shaped pin used on front of kilt. Also called *kilt pin.*

**scarf p.** See STICKPIN.

**CAMEO PIN**

**SAFETY PIN #2**          **STICKPIN**

**silk p.** See DRESSMAKER PIN.

**sorority p.** Similar to FRATERNITY PIN, but worn by high school and college girls as an emblem of their club or sorority.

**stickpin 1.** Straight stiletto-type pin with an ornamental top worn by a man to secure a four-in-hand necktie or ascot. Popular from late 19th c. to 1930s. Now *tie tacks* are more usually worn. Also called *scarf pin* and *tie pin*. **2.** Same type of pin styled as a lapel pin for women.

**straight p.** Functional device consisting of a sharp pointed shaft with flattened head used when cutting out pattern, pinning cut out pieces together before sewing, or as a temporary fastening. Used since the 14th c., pins were scarce and sold only on January 1 and 2. Originally heads were hammered on top, after 1830 made in one piece. Also see DRESSMAKER PIN and PIN MONEY in alphabetical listing.

**tie p.** See STICKPIN.

**Wedgwood® cameo p.** Usually blue in color with the head of a woman in raised design on the surface. Made by casting Wedgwood pottery material. Can be distinguished from cut cameos by the tiny air bubbles on the surface. *Der.* Made by the Wedgwood China Company in England.

**pinafore** Sleeveless garment like an *apron* worn over dress as protection against soil by women and children since last half of 19th c. See APRONS, DRESSES, JUMPERS, and SWIMSUITS.

**pinafore heel** See HEELS.

**pince-nez** See GLASSES.

**pinchbeck** Alloy, composed of five parts copper and one part zinc, used for pins and buckles cast with a surface design and then plated with a thin layer of silver or gold; frequently set with colored glass or paste. *Der.* From invention of Christopher Pinchbeck, London watchmaker, about 1700.

**pin check** See CHECKS.

**pin collar** See COLLARS.

**pin curl 1.** See CURLS. **2.** Term used from 1840 to 1860s for curl pinned on to underside of bonnet. Also called *pin-on curl*.

**pin dot** See DOTS under PRINTS.

**pin-in bra** See BRAS.

**pink coat** See COATS.

**pinked seam** See SEAMS.

**pinking 1.** Unhemmed border of fabric cut with saw-toothed edge to prevent raveling by using special *pinking scissors* or shears that have saw-toothed blades. **2.** Decorative effect made by cutting short slits to form a pattern in shoes or garments, in late 15th to 17th c. Also called *pouncing*. **3.** Saw-toothed trimming on edges of leather used in contrasting color on extra pieces applied to toes and heels of *spectator* and *golf* shoes for a decorative effect.

**pinner**  **1.** Term for LAPPET of woman's indoor cap frequently worn pinned up and, by extension, term for cap itself in 17th to mid-18th c. **2.** 17th c. term for TUCKER.

**pinning blanket**  See BARROW #2 and LAYETTE.

**pin-on curl**  See PIN CURL.

**pinpoint collar**  See PIERPONT COLLAR.

**pin seal**  See LEATHERS.

**pinson**  Lightweight indoor slipper, often furred, worn from end of 14th to end of 16th c. by men and women. Also called *pinsnet*. From 17th c. referred to as *pump*.

**pinstripe**  See STRIPES.

**pinwale**  Narrow rib in CORDUROY. Also spelled *pin wale*.

**pinwale piqué**  See PIQUÉ.

**Pipart, Gerard**  See APPENDIX/DESIGNERS.

**piped buttonhole**  See BUTTONHOLES.

**pipe-organ pleats**  See GODET under PLEATS.

**pipes**  Small rolls of clay pipe heated and used to tighten curls of man's wig in 17th and 18th c. Also called ROULETTES.

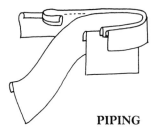

**PIPING**

**piping**  Narrow piece of bias-cut fabric folded over and stitched into seam between fabric edge and facing to form decorative trim, *e.g.*, navy-blue blazer with white piping on *revers* and pockets. See PIPED under BUTTONHOLES, POCKETS, and SEAMS. Compare with CORDING.

**pipkin**  Woman's small hat worn about 1565 to 1600 made with flat crown pleated into narrow brim. Usually trimmed with a narrow jeweled band and feathers. Also called *taffeta pipkin*.

**piqué**  (pee-kay) Group of durable fabrics characterized by corded effects either warpwise of fillingwise. *a)* Plain piqués in the U.S. are made with warpwise cords similar to *bedford cord* by which name they could more properly be called. *Pinwale piqué* is a variation with smaller ribs. *b)* Piqués made in England have cords in the filling. *c)* *Waffle piqué* is made in the *honeycomb weave*. *d)* *Birds-eye piqué* has a diamond-shaped woven-in dobby pattern. *e)* *Embroidered piqué* is plain piqué which has been embroidered with the *Schiffli machine*. All types are used for dresses, blouses, pants, sportswear, handbags, and neckwear.

**piqué devant**  Short pointed beard worn by men from 1570s to 1600 with a moustache. Also called *pickadevant* and *barbula*.

**piqué embroidery**  See EMBROIDERIES.

**piqué seam**  See FULL PIQUÉ under GLOVE SEAMS.

**piracy**  Stealing of an idea for a dress by making sketches of it. Punishable as a crime in France where dress designs are protected by the French government. Not considered a crime in the U.S. unless the design is patented. Viewers at couture showings are permitted to mark their programs, but not permitted to make sketches.

**pirahan**  Embroidered shirt studded with pearls worn in ancient Persia by women.

**pirn**  See QUILL #2.

**pith helmet**  See TOPEE under HELMETS.

**Pitt diamond**  See REGENT DIAMOND under DIAMONDS.

**pixie hairstyle**  See HAIRSTYLES.

**pizazz**  (pih-zazz) Word coined in 1930s to express the quality of audaciousness or daring; credited by the fashion magazine, *Harper's Bazaar*, to students at Harvard University.

**p.j.s** Abbreviation for PAJAMAS.

**p.k. seam** See FULL PIQUÉ under GLOVE SEAMS.

**plackard** **1.** Chest piece or stomacher, used to fill in gap made by open neckline of man's doublet in late 15th to mid-16th c. **2.** Front panel of woman's open-sided surcoat, often trimmed with fur and embroidery, from mid-14th to early 16th c. Also spelled *placcard, placart, placcate.* Compare with PLASTRON #1.

**PLACKET**

**placket** Word used since the 16th c. for slit at neck, side, front, back, or wrist in dress, blouse, pants, or skirt to facilitate taking garment on and off. Fastened in early times by lacings, buttons, or hooks and eyes; since 1930s by zippers, and since 1970s by *Velcro®.* Also see NECKLINES.

**plahta** Wraparound skirt formerly worn by Ukrainian women of Russia. Made of two strips of wool or silk material with a woven plaid pattern worn wrapped around the body, lapped in front, and held in place with a belt. Also spelled *plakhta.*

**plaid** **1.** Common term for tartan pattern woven of various colored yarns in stripes of different widths running at right angles to form blocks. *Der.* From Scottish fabrics woven to designate different clans. See TARTANS. **2.** Fabric design printed or woven of yarns dyed

in various colors. Bands of color of different widths run both horizontally and vertically, crossing at right angles to form a series of boxes which are slightly longer warpwise.

## PLAIDS

**argyle p.** Made with various colored diamond-shaped designs—usually a larger diamond pattern of dark or light lines is superimposed over other solid colored diamonds. Popular in 1920s, 1940s, and revived in the late 1960s. *Der.* Tartan of Duke of Argyle and Clan Campbell of Argyll, a county in West Scotland. Also spelled *argyll, argyl.*

**blanket p.** Very large plaid with dark colored ground and lighter overstripes, or white ground and colored overstripes used originally in woolen and cotton blankets.

**even p.** Design which starts with a central box and repeats in the same manner on each side of the central motif. Popular for shirts, suits, and dresses because it is easier to match when sewing than an UNEVEN PLAID.

**gingham p.** Woven design in a cotton fabric made with stripes and boxes of various sizes in three or more colors. Gingham with only two colors is called a *gingham check.* Fabrics used for aprons, dresses, and shirts.

**glen p.** See GLEN URQUHART PLAID.

**Glen Urquhart p.** Woven design which pairs small checks with larger checks made with similar colored yarns in warp and filling in a combination of subdued color and white. Used particularly for men's worsted suits. Also called *glen plaid* or *glen check. Der.* Named for Glen Urquhart, a valley in Invernessshire, Scotland.

**hunting p.** Everyday version of a Scottish clan's tartan made in subdued colors to blend with landscape, in contrast to dress plaid worn on ceremonial occasions.

**lumberjack p.** Distinctive plaid similar to a *blanket plaid* but smaller in size. Usually combines tones of green and tan on a beige background. *Der.* From early plaids used for jackets by lumbermen.

**Madras p.** (mad-dres) East Indian woven cotton in multicolor crossbar patterns with red. Bleeds after washing giving a blurred effect.

**overplaid** Lines of another color superimposed over a plaid or a checked design.

**shepherd's p.** See CHECKS category.

**tattersall p.** Plaid consisting of narrow lines in two alternating colors, crossed to form a checked design on a plain light-colored ground, often uses red and black lines on white ground. *Der.* Named after Richard Tattersall, British horseman, founder of Tattersall's London Horse Auction Mart established in 1776. Also called TATTERSALL CHECK.

**uneven p.** Similar to EVEN PLAID, but designs on either side of central box are different.

**windowpane p.** Fine cross stripes, widely spaced, making a design like a multipaned window. Popular in wool for women's coats and suits in 1960s and for knits in 1970s. Also called WINDOWPANE CHECKS.

---

**plain hem** See HEMS.

**plain knit** Simplest type of knitting done in flat or circular knit. On the right side loops run lengthwise, on the reverse side crosswise. Used extensively for hosiery and pantyhose. Also called JERSEY KNIT. Also see STITCHES.

**plain seam** See SEAMS.

**plain weave** Weave with *filling yarn* going over one *warp*, then under one *warp*; second row alternates creating a checkerboard pattern.

**plait** (plate) **1.** A *braid* of hair. See BRAIDS under HAIRSTYLES. **2.** (verb) To weave three or more strands into a single strip or braid, *e.g.*, bands of straw for hats or ribbons for trimming. **3.** Variant of PLEAT.

**planter's hat** See HATS.

**plastic patent** Simulated or imitation *patent leather* made from a vinyl compound which is durable and will not split or crack like genuine patent. May have a crushed surface or be embossed with a design, *e.g.*, alligator or snakeskin. Used for shoes and handbags and in lighter weights for jackets, coats, and trimmings. Popular from 1960s on.

**plastron** **1.** Iron breastplate worn as armor between *hauberk* and *gambeson*. **2.** Front center portion set into a woman's dress, usually made of a contrasting fabric for a decorative effect. Used in the 19th and early 20th c. Formerly called the PLACKARD and STOMACHER. **3.** See KESWA EL KBIRA. **4.** See BIB COLLAR under COLLARS. *Der.* French, "breastplate."

**plated** As applied to jewelry, *e.g.*, gold-plated, a thin film of precious metal applied to an inexpensive base metal—usually by electrolysis.

**plated knit** Reversible double-knit fabric knitted with two different colored yarns, one forming background on front and design on back, the other color reverses. Popular in mid- and late 1960s with one side used for jacket, the other for skirt or pants.

**plates** Small pieces of fur joined together to make a larger unit, *e.g.*, *Persian lamb plates* made from *paws* and *gills* that are left over from other garments.

**platform sole** Mid-sole of shoe, often made of cork or sponge rubber, raising the foot off ground on a platform varying in height from 1/4″ to 3″. Popular in 1940s for women's shoes, reintroduced in late 1960s by Roger Vivier in Paris, and popular in U.S. from early 1970s. See SANDALS and SHOES.

**platinum** **1.** Rare white metal used for mounting jewels, usually alloyed with 10% iridium to increase hardness. **2.** Very pale silvery blond; popular shade of hair in 1930s and 1940s.

**platinum silver fox** See FURS.

**platter collar**   See COLLARS.

**platypus toe**   See TOES.

**Plauen lace**   See LACES.

**playsuit**   See JUMPSHORTS under SHORTS and SPORT SUITS.

**pleat**   **1.** (*noun*) Fold of fabric usually pressed flat but sometimes left unpressed. When used in a skirt, blouse or dress, it is sometimes stitched down at the top of the garment to make it hang better. In polyester and nylon fabrics pleats may be put in permanently with a heat-setting process. **2.** (*verb*) To set in folds. Formerly spelled *plait*.

### ▬▬▬ PLEATS ▬▬▬

**accordion p.**   Pressed in pleats, sometimes heat-set, small at top but larger at bottom. Lower edge of hem shows a zigzag pattern. For an accordion-pleated skirt it takes a full circle of fabric. First used in the late 1880s. Also called *sunburst* and *fan pleat*. *Der.* From bellows of accordion.

**bias p.**   Pressed down pleats made in fabric cut on the diagonal which are usually stitched down a few inches at top to make them hang better.

**box p.**   Fabric folded and pressed with larger areas forming the top and an *inverted pleat* located between each box pleat.

**cartridge p.**   Small rounded pleats used for trimming, copied from cartridge loops on military belts.

**cluster p.**   Pressed or unpressed pleats arranged in groups. Usually consisting of a large BOX PLEAT with several small *knife pleats* on either side.

**crystal p.**   Very fine heat-set ridges usually used in sheer nylon or polyester fabrics. Also see MUSHROOM PLEAT.

**envelope p.**   Large *inverted pleat* placed on side seam of dress which reveals a pocket underneath when one edge is pulled aside.

**fan p.**   See ACCORDION PLEAT.

**godet p.**   Pleats that hang in a series of rolls forming a gored skirt, popular in 1890s. Also called *pipe-organ pleats*.

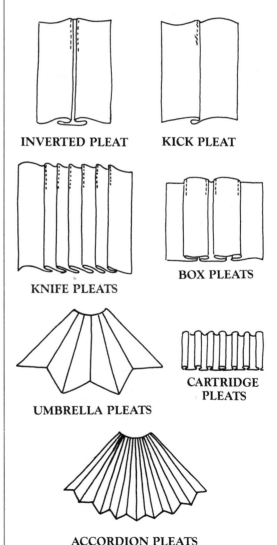

INVERTED PLEAT        KICK PLEAT

KNIFE PLEATS        BOX PLEATS

UMBRELLA PLEATS        CARTRIDGE PLEATS

ACCORDION PLEATS

**inverted p.** Two folds brought to a center line and pressed. Reverse side of several pleats will look like box pleats.

**kick p.** Single flat pleat or one *knife pleat* at the back or front of a narrow skirt to make walking easier.

**kilt p.** Flat pleat covering half of next pleat, all folded in the same direction as in a Scottish kilt.

**knife p.** Pressed in pleats usually placed one-half inch to 1″ apart. All pleats going in the same direction.

**mushroom p.** Very fine, heat-set pleats similar to CRYSTAL PLEATS. *Der.* From appearance of the inside cap of the mushroom.

**pipe organ p.** See GODET PLEAT.

**sunburst p.** See ACCORDION PLEAT.

**umbrella p.** Similar to ACCORDION PLEATS but larger, like the folds of an umbrella.

**Venetian blind p.** A pleat formed by a wide stitched tuck made in the fabric. Each tuck slightly overlaps the previous one in the fashion of Venetian blind slats.

**Watteau p.** Box pleats hanging free from back shoulder yoke to hem of dress or dressing gown. *Der.* For 18th c. French painter who often depicted women wearing dresses with this style pleat.

---

**plissé** (plee-say) Lightweight cotton with a pebbly surface given a creped finish by applying caustic soda with rollers. Pressing will remove the crinkle. Used for pajamas, nightgowns, and children's clothing. Also known as *crinkle crepe* and *plissé crepe*.

**plucking** Fur-industry term for the process of removing some of the longer *guard hairs* which may mare the beauty of the final product.

**pluderhose** German and Swiss unpadded *trunk hose* worn by men in latter half of 16th c. Characterized by broad slashes with loose silk linings protruding. Also see ALMAIN HOSE.

**plug hat** American term for TOP HAT, worn by men from 1830s on. Same as CHIMNEY-POT HAT.

**plug/plugged oxford** See OXFORDS.

**PLUMET PETTICOAT**

**plumet petticoat** Narrow, back-buttoned petticoat of 1870s with ruffles forming bustle at back and continuing to form a detachable train.

**plummet** Term used in 17th c. for PENDANT EARRINGS. Also see PENDICLE.

**plumpers** Lightweight, thin round balls of cork used by women inside mouth to make cheeks look rounder from late 17th to early 19th c.

**plunge bra** See BRAS.

**plunging neckline** See NECKLINES.

**plus fours** Full baggy *knickers* popularized by Duke of Windsor in 1920s when he was Prince of Wales. Worn by men, usually with patterned wool socks and brogues, for golfing and other sports. *Der.* When introduced, these knickers were 4″ longer than usual length. Also see PANTS.

**ply yarn**   A number of individual yarns, or singles, twisted together to form a heavier yarn.

**Pocahontas dress**   See AMERICAN INDIAN DRESS under DRESSES.

**pocket**   Piece of fabric shaped to fit either on the outside or inside of clothing. Used for decorative purposes or to carry small articles, *e.g.,* handkerchiefs or coins. From 15th c. on, small pouches were worn fastened to the belt. **Men:** In mid-16th c. pockets added to *trunk hose;* by end of the 16th c. added to *breeches.* Waistcoat pocket introduced in early 17th c. In late 17th c. flaps were added to coat and waistcoat pockets. **Women:** 18th-c. pouches were worn suspended from waist under dress and reached by means of placket holes. In 19th c. a pouch called a *railway pocket* was worn under the dress and reached by a slit in the dress. In late 19th c. pockets were put in dresses and shirtwaists.

## POCKETS

**angled p.**   See HACKING POCKET.

**bellows p.**   Outside pocket made with center BOX PLEAT or INVERTED PLEAT that expands when pocket is used. Type of pocket used on BUSH JACKET and SAFARI DRESS. Also called *safari pocket.*

**besom p.**   Tailoring term for an inset pocket on a man's suit jacket made with a narrow welted edge above the pocket opening. It is called a *double-besom* pocket if both edges have welts. If a flap is added it is called a *flapped besom.* Also called a WELT POCKET.

**bound p.**   Interior pocket made with slit finished like a bound buttonhole on outside providing access to inner concealed pocket. Also called *piped, slash, slit* or WELT POCKET.

**breast p.**   Man's pocket placed on left side of chest on suit coats and overcoats.

**cargo p.**   Large patch pocket used on shorts and pants. Curved top of pocket extends to waist and forms a loop through which belt is pulled.

**change p.**   See TICKET POCKET.

**circle p.**   See ROUND POCKET.

**continental p.**   Pocket cut away at the top, usually in a curved manner, used on men's western or continental trousers. Also called a *western pocket.*

**double-besom p.**   See BESOM POCKET.

**double-entry p.**   Pockets which may be entered from the top or side.

**flap p.**   Pocket with separate piece of material covering the opening. May be of bound, welt, or patch pocket type.

**flapped-besom p.**   See BESOM POCKET.

**fob p.**   A small pocket in the side front of a man's trousers, usually of the welt style, used to carry a watch. Also called a *watch pocket.*

**hacking p.**   Flap pocket placed on an angle used on jackets and coats, especially on hacking jackets.

**half-moon p.**   Curved semicircular bound pocket used primarily on cowboy shirts. Usually reinforced at ends with embroidered arrowheads. Also called a *smile pocket.*

**holster p.**   Novelty pocket shaped like a gun holster, used on sportswear.

**kangaroo p.**   **1.** Extra-large pocket placed on center front of garment, *e.g.,* a sweatshirt. **2.** Any extra-large pocket.

**key p.**   Small patch pocket sewn inside of larger right-front pocket in jeans-style pants, just large enough for a key or a few coins.

**mock p.** Flap sewed on outside of garment to suggest a real pocket.

**patch p.** Pocket stitched on outside of garment, either made plain or with a flap.

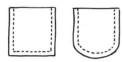

**PATCH POCKETS**

**RAILWAY POCKET**

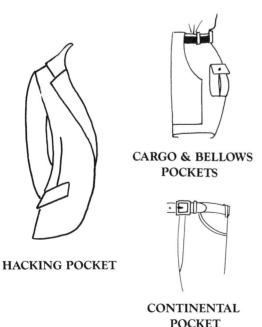

**HACKING POCKET**

**CARGO & BELLOWS POCKETS**

**CONTINENTAL POCKET**

**pencil p.** Zip pocket placed on upper sleeve of sport coat or SNORKEL JACKET, used to hold small items or a pencil.

**piped p.** See BOUND POCKET.

**round p.** Full circular patch pocket bound around the edge with opening in the center, top, or side for access. Also called a *circle pocket*.

**safari p.** See BELLOWS POCKET.

**seam p.** Pocket inserted in seam of skirt, dress, or pants, which is not visible from outside.

**slash p.** See BOUND POCKET.

**slit p.** See WELT POCKET.

**smile p.** See HALF-MOON POCKET.

**ticket p.** British tailoring term for a small pocket, usually flapped, placed above regular pocket on right side of a man's suit coat or overcoat. Introduced in late 1850s for a railroad ticket and used at intervals since. Also called *change pocket*.

**vest p.** Welt pocket placed on side chest of waistcoat or vest, originally used to carry a pocket watch. In the Louis XV period men carried two watches, therefore, a pocket was made on either side of garment. Also called a *waistcoat* or *watch pocket*.

**waistcoat p.** See VEST POCKET.

**watch p.** See FOB and VEST POCKETS.

**welt p.** An inset pocket with the lower lip finished by an upstanding welt that may be from ⅜″ to 1″ wide. Usually a breast pocket placed on the left front of a man's suit coat or overcoat. Also see BESOM POCKET. Also called *slit pocket* or BOUND POCKET.

**western p.** Same as CONTINENTAL POCKET.

**zip p.** Any pocket closed with a zipper used particularly on sportswear.

**pocketbook** Synonym for HANDBAG.

**pocket handkerchief**   **1.** See HANDKERCHIEF. **2.** From 16th to mid-19th c., handkerchiefs were carried for display, often made of fine lace, silk, or linen.

**POCKET HOOPS, c. 1760**

**pocket hoops**   British term for very small *panniers* popular in early 1720s when side hoops were coming into fashion. Also popular in 1770s when the style was waning.

**pocket siphonia**   See SIPHONIA.

**pocket T-shirt**   See KNIT SHIRTS.

**poet's collar**   See BYRON under COLLARS.

**poet's shirt**   See LORD BYRON under SHIRTS.

**point**   Shortened form for NEEDLEPOINT.

**point d'esprit** (pwan des-pree)   **1.** Net-like machine-made fabric of cotton or nylon which has some of the holes made solid to form a decorative pattern. Used for evening gowns and veiling. First handmade in France in 1834. Compare with BOBBINET. **2.** Open-stitch used in *guipure lace* with loops forming a pattern on a mesh ground.

**pointing**   Glove-industry term for ornamental stitching on back of glove, same as *silking*.

**Point l'Abbe coif**   Woman's high-crowned cap of voile or lace, with long streamers tied under right side of chin. Worn in fishing village of Point l'Abbe on Brittany coast of France.

**point noué**   French lacemakers' term for button hole stitch, the basis of all needlepoint lace.

**points**   Cords with metal tips used to fasten garments together from 15th to mid-17th c., *e.g.*, *trunk hose* attached to DOUBLET. Also see LANGET #1.

**Poiret, Paul**   See APPENDIX/DESIGNERS.

**POISON RING #1**

**poison ring**   **1.** Finger ring designed to hold a dose of poison worn from Roman period through the 17th c. Made in Roman times with the setting a mere shell and the poison behind it. Cesare Borgia's ring, dated 1503 and still in existence, has a small sliding panel which opened into a small cavity in which poison was placed. **2.** Similar novelty item of the late 1960s sometimes used to contain perfume.

**poke**   Large pouch used as pocket in late 16th and early 17th c. Word still used for a bag in southern U.S. *Der.* French, *poche*, "bag" or "pocket."

**poke bonnet**   Bonnet of 19th c. made with wide brim slanting forward from small crown to frame and shadow the face. Also called *poking bonnet*.

**poker chip button**   See BUTTONS.

**pokey**   See HANDBAGS.

**poking sticks**   Term used in 16th c. for heated bone, wood, or metal sticks used to set pleats of a *ruff*.

**Polaroid® glasses**   See GLASSES.

**poleyn**   Piece of armor consisting of a metal plate (originally leather) worn over knee cap, introduced in 13th c. Also called *knee cop* and *genouillière*.

**police boot**   See BOOTS.

**Polish boot**   Woman's high front-laced boot of 1860s decorated with colored high heel and tassel in front.

**polished cotton**   Most any plain weave cotton fabric *e.g., sateen, chintz*, given a glazed finish to make it shiny and lustrous. Some finishes are permanent, particularly those of the resin-type. If the finish is made by *sizing* and *calendering*, it is not permanent. Used for blouses, dresses, and sportswear.

**Polish greatcoat**   Full-length tight-fitting man's coat with collar, cuffs, and lapels of Russian lambskin. Closed with *frog* fasteners or loops. Worn with evening dress in early 19th c.

**Polish jacket**   Woman's waist-length jacket made with *revers* and collar. Sleeves were wide at wrist, squared off, and slit to elbow on inside seam. Usually made of cashmere lined with quilted satin. Worn outdoors for informal occasions in mid-1840s.

**Polish mantle**   Knee-length woman's cloak of mid-1830s with attached cape made of satin edged with fur.

**POLISH TOQUE, c. 1866**

**Polish toque**   Woman's hat of mid-1860s somewhat similar to *pillbox*, trimmed in front with foliage and in back with a large bunch of velvet ribbon loops.

**polka**   **1.** Woman's short outdoor jacket of mid-1840s made with full sleeves, cashmere or velvet fabric and lined with silk. A variety of CASAWECK. **2.** Woman's knitted close-fitting jacket. **3.** Woman's *French cap* of cream-colored tulle with crocheted edges appliquéd with lace floral designs, with lappets covering ears, and tied under chin.

**polka dot**   See DOTS under PRINTS.

**pollera**   A handwoven, many-layered skirt with embroidered borders worn by women in Peru. Usually black with red borders.

**polo**   Game played on horseback with long-handled wooden mallets and a ball. Periods of the game are called *chukkas*. Distinctive clothing worn has been much copied for sportswear. See BELTS, COATS, DRESSES, HATS, and SHIRTS.

**Polo cloth®**   Trademark of Worumbo Mfg. Co., for an overcoating fabric, usually made in a camel color, with a soft thick nap on both sides. May be made of wool, camel's hair, or a blend of both. Used for polo coats and other overcoats.

**polo collar**   Man's white starched collar worn in late 1890s with points sloping toward shoulders. Could be worn either standing or turned down.

**polonaise** (pol-on-nays)   **1.** Boned bodice and overskirt made in one piece with low neckline and several types of sleeves. *a)* Elbow-length puckered at cuff with or without a frill; *b)* three-quarter length with short frill; *c)* long and buttoned at wrist with a frill, and *d) sabot sleeves* trimmed with *petite bonshammes*. In 1770s overskirt was looped up to form three large puffs by drawstrings at hips and back to reveal the petticoat or underskirt. Worn over a separate ankle-length or trained skirt, sometimes contrasting in color, or with one skirt plain the other striped. Popularized by Marie Antoinette as an informal costume. In 1870s style was revived. Also called a *gown à la polonaise* and *à la polonaise. Der.* Named after a Polish national dance and also the music for such a dance. **2.** In 1750s a cape or small hooded cloak drawn

**POLONAISE #1**

back like a polonaise dress. Also called *polonaise pardessus.* **3.** Man's jacket of early 1770s also called a *polonese frock.* **4.** In 1830s a military redingote, usually of blue fabric worn by civilians. Also called a *redingote.*

**polonese frock**   See POLONAISE #3.

**polyester**   Generic name for man-made fibers made of ethylene glycol and terephthalic acid, having the following qualities: shrinkproof, retains shape, wrinkle and moth-resistant. Yarns are knitted or woven, often in blended fabrics with cotton or rayon. See DACRON®, KODEL®, and FORTREL®.

**pomander**   See POMMES DE SENTEUR and POUNCET BOX.

**pommel slicker**   Raincoat worn when riding horseback in early 20th c. Similar to other raincoats but with long vent in back. Also called a *saddle coat.*

**pommes de senteur** (pum de sawn-tehr) Small balls of gold or silver filigree set with precious stones used to hold scent, carried or

hung from belt from 1500 to 1690s. Also called *musk apples, pound-box, musk balls,* or *pomander. Der.* French, "perfumed apples."

**pompadour**   **1.** See HAIRSTYLES. **2.** See POMPON #2. **3.** See HIP BAGS.

**POMPADOUR BAG, 1885**

**pompadour bag**   Drawstring bag in circular or oblong shape popular in mid-1880s made of satin, plush or velvet with floral embroidery heightened by edgings of gold or silver thread. *Der.* Named after Marquise de Pompadour, mistress of Louis XV of France.

**pompadour bodice**   Bodice for daytime dress worn in the 1870s with a low square neckline and tight, elbow-length sleeves trimmed with lace or ruffles. Worn as part of the *polonaise* in 1870s. See POLONAISE #1. *Der.* Named for Marquise de Pompadour, mistress of Louis XV of France.

**Pompadour, Marquise de** (1721–1764)   Née Jeanne Antoinette Poisson. Mistress of Louis XV of France (1745–1764) who had great influence over him. Promoted the arts during this period. Paintings of her by Boucher epitomize the beautiful costume of this era. Many items of fashion have been named after her. See POMPADOUR, POMPADOUR BAG, POMPADOUR BODICE, and POMPADOUR SLEEVE.

**pompadour sleeve**   Adaptation in 1830s and 1840s of elbow-length sleeve edged with ruffle worn by the Marquise de Pompadour, mistress of Louis XV of France.

**Pompeian silk sash** Wide black silk belt woven with allegorical figures, usually worn by women with a bodice, colored skirt and white summer jacket in 1860s.

**pompey** See PHYSICAL WIG.

**pompon** **1.** Round ball of cut ends of yarn used as trimming. **2.** Hair or cap ornament composed of feathers, tinsel, butterflies, etc., worn in center part of hair by women from 1740s to 1760s, originally called *pompadour*. **3.** Same as TOP KNOT. **4.** See SOCKS.

**poncho** **1.** Fashion item shaped like a square or a small oblong blanket with hole in center for the head, frequently fringed. Popular in late 1960s. **2.** Utilitarian garment consisting of waterproofed fabric with a slash in the center for the head. When worn it was used as a rain cape; when not worn could be used as a tarpaulin or a blanket. **3.** Woman's loose three-quarter length cloak worn in the 1860s with buttons from neck to hem, a small standing collar, full sleeves—narrower at the wrist—with capes over the sleeves.

## ▬▬▬ PONCHOS ▬▬▬

**all-purpose p.** See RAIN PONCHO.

**beach p.** Oblong terrycloth poncho which can be laid flat for use as a towel at the beach.

**fishnet p.** Square medium-sized poncho made of fishnet or see-through fabric with a high large turtleneck collar. The edge of the collar and the hem is trimmed with ball fringe.

**lapponica** Poncho of plaid wool with fringed edges imported from Finland. Colorful plaids are of all varieties, some being in large squares of color; some being more complicated similar to the *Stewart tartans*; and some in smaller checks similar to *glen plaids*.

**rain p.** Poncho made of nylon fabric, 54″ × 80″, laminated with polyvinyl chloride, which slips over the head and snaps closed at the sides to make a partial sleeve. One size fits everyone. Usually styled with an attached hood. Originally made of a rubberized fabric and worn by policemen on a rainy day. Also called an *all-purpose poncho*.

**ruana** **1.** Small square poncho worn by bullfighters in South America, particularly Colombia. **2.** General purpose wrap worn in Colombia, South America. Also a part of uniform for hostesses on Colombian airlines.

**skoncho** A do-it-yourself style poncho made from a brushed wool plaid blanket or striped with a fringe on two ends, similar to a blanket used at football games. A 16″ slash is cut diagonally in the center. May also be worn as a skirt.

**space blanket** Insulated blanket with one side aluminized, the other brightly colored. Worn on one side to insulate from the cold, the other side protects from the heat of the sun. Folds to pocket size for easy carrying. *Der.* Developed for NASA space program in late 1960s.

**RUANA**

**pongee   1.** Light- to medium-weight rough-textured silk fabric made from wild silk and usually left in natural color. Originally made on handlooms in China, later machine made. Warp yarns are finer than the filling, causing a slight rib formed by the uneven texture of the yarn. *Der.* Chinese, *penchi,* "woven at home." **2.** Cotton fabric which has little resemblance to the above except that it has a slight crosswise rib. Fabric is light to medium in weight and may be *schreinerized* or *mercerized.*

**pony**   See FURS.

**ponyet   1.** Doublet sleeve on lower part of arm, frequently of different fabric from upper sleeve worn from 14th to 16th c. Also spelled *poynet.* **2.** Long pin with decorative head worn by men in 17th c. Also called *little bodkin.*

**pony tail**   See HAIRSTYLES.

**poodle cloth**   Knitted or woven fabric characterized by small curls over the entire surface. Similar to *astrakan* fabric but made with looser curls like the coat of a poodle dog.

**poodle cut**   See HAIRSTYLES.

**poor-boy**   Descriptive term used in mid-1960s referring to type of shrunken casual clothing influenced by that worn by newsboys in early 20th c. See DRESSES, SWEATERS, and NEWSBOY CAP under CAPS.

**popcorn stitch**   See STITCHES.

**Pope, Virginia** (1885–1978) Promoted to fashion editor of *The New York Times* in 1933 from a member of Sunday staff hired in 1925. In 1955 became fashion editor of *Parade* magazine. She also held the Edwin Goodman chair, established by Bergdorf Goodman, at Fashion Institute of Technology. She changed fashion reporting by seeking news in the wholesale markets of New York; encouraged young American designers; and originated the *Fashion of the Times* fashion show in 1942 which featured clothes from American designers. Cosmopoli-

tan, statuesque, and beautifully dressed in her later years she became the "grande dame" of American fashion.

**poplin**   Medium-weight durable fabric with crosswise rib effect made with cotton yarns, or blends of cotton and polyester, which are heavier in the filling. Originally poplin had a silk warp and wool filling. Better qualities use combed yarns in both directions and are finished by piece-dyeing or printing. A water-resistant or water-repellent finish may also be applied to fabrics used for raincoats. Also used for sportswear, pants, shorts, blouses, dresses, and men's shirts.

**popover**   Denim wraparound dress with short sleeves, a large patch pocket on the front of slightly flared skirt, and trimmed with decorative double topstitching. Designed by Claire McCardell in 1942 for *Harper's Bazaar.* Intended as an inexpensive, protective, yet stylish cover-up for household work. Original dress sold for $6.95, different $30 versions were shown in her collection for several years.

**porc-epic**   See PORCUPINE HEADDRESS.

**porcupine hairstyle**   See HAIRSTYLES.

**porcupine headdress**   Hairstyle, with short hair standing up like bristles, worn at end of 18th c. Also called *porc-epic.*

**pork-pie hat**   See HATS.

**port canons**   See CANNONS.

**PORTE-JUPE POMPADOUR**

**porte-jupe Pompadour** (port-zhupe pomp-pa-door) Belt worn under dress in 1860s made with eight suspenders for looping up outer skirt when walking. Also called *dress elevator*.

**PORTE-MONNAIE, 1859**

**porte-monnaie** Embroidered handbag carried by women in the 1850s made with metal frame sometimes made with chain handle, sometimes in clutch styles. *Der.* French, "purse."

**Porter, Thea** See APPENDIX/DESIGNERS.

**posh** British slang term meaning rich or luxurious, derived from the acronym for preferred quarters on ships sailing between Britain and India. *Der.* "Port Out, Starboard Home," *i.e.*, the shady side of the ship.

**postboy hat** Woman's small straw hat of 1885 styled with high flat crown and narrow brim sloping down all around. Trimmed with plume in front and worn perched on top of head.

**poster dress** See DRESSES.

**postiche** (pos-teach) *Der.* French, "false." See WIGLET under WIGS.

**postillion** (poce-till-yun) **1.** Hat with tall tapered crown and narrow brim, usually beaver, worn by women for riding. **2.** Dress bodice extending below back waistline, usually with pleats or ruffles that flare outwards. Worn by women in latter half of 19th c. Also called *postillion basque*. *Der.* From clothes worn by *postillions*, "men on horseback accompanying carriages."

**postillion coat** (poce-till-yun) Double-breasted fitted greatcoat with flap pockets, high Regency collar, and broad revers. *Der.* From clothes worn by *postillions*, "men on horseback accompanying carriages."

**POSTILLION CORSAGE**

**postillion corsage** (poce-till-yun) Tight-fitting jacket-type waist with long sleeves worn by women in early 1860s and early 1880s. Made with high neck and a series of double box pleats in back, one over the other to form fullness over hips; or made with long tabs over the bustle in back. Usually worn with contrasting skirt in 1880s. Also spelled *postilion corsage*. *Der.* From clothes worn by *postillions*, "men on horseback accompanying carriages." Also see BALMORAL BODICE.

**posts** **1.** See BRAS. **2.** See EARRINGS.

**posy/poesy ring** See RINGS.

**pot derby** Colloquial term for DERBY or BOWLER.

**pot hat** See CHIMNEY-POT HAT.

**potholder vest** See VESTS.

**potten kant lace** See ANTWERP LACE.

**Potter, Clare**   See APPENDIX/DESIGNERS.

**potting**   See DECATING #1.

**poturi**   Wide white serge breeches decorated with black braid worn by men of Bulgaria.

**pouch**   **1.** See HANDBAGS. **2.** Bag or purse of 12th to 16th c. worn suspended from gentleman's belt, often with dagger thrust through the pendant strap.

**pouf**   See BUBBLE DRESS under DRESSES and HAIRSTYLES.

**pouf au sentiment**   (poof o sont-eh-mont) Extravagantly high hairstyle elaborately decorated with flowers and other objects, worked over a framework of gauze. Worn by women in 18th c. before the French Revolution, *e.g.*, by Marie Antoinette.

**poulaine**   (poo-lan) French term for shoe in England called PIKED SHOE or CRAKOW. Also spelled *poulain, pullayne.*

**pouncet-box**   A type of POMANDER, consisting of a dry-scent box which contained fragrant herbs and flower petals, carried during the late 16th c. Compare with POMMES DE SENTEUR.

**pouncing**   See PINKING.

**pound-box**   See POMMES DE SENTEUR.

**pourpoint**   French term for the stuffed and quilted *doublet* or jacket worn by men from 14th to 17th c. and formerly called PALTOCK or GIPON. Also see DOUBLET and GAMBESON.

**poussin lace**   (poo-sahn)   See LACES.

**povoinik**   Headdress of cloth stiffened with cardboard and trimmed with imitation or paste jewels or freshwater pearls. Worn by unmarried girls in Russia. The trim varied with region and affluence of wearer. Married women wore a similar headdress called *kokochnik.*

**powder blue**   Pale gray-blue color.

**powdering jacket/gown**   A loose wrap worn by men in 18th c. to protect clothing while the wig was being powdered. Also see FACE CONE.

**poyas**   Red sash worn by Bulgarian men.

**poynet**   See PONYET.

**prairie styles**   Copying of style of dress worn by American pioneer women. See DRESSES, LOOKS, and SKIRTS.

**prayer veil**   See VEILS.

**precious stones**   Term applied to a gem which is not only beautiful, durable, and portable but also rare—the diamond, ruby, sapphire, and emerald fall into this category. See GEMS.

**pre-cuffed trousers**   See PANTS.

**Premet**   See APPENDIX/DESIGNERS.

**première main**   (prem-ee-erman) French term for head of workroom in French couture house. *Der.* French, "firsthand."

**preppy/preppie**   See LOOKS.

**pressing**   **1.** Finishing process used on fabrics using heavy heated rollers to smooth and improve appearance. **2.** Finishing process used at home or by garment manufacturers to improve appearance and remove wrinkles. Garment manufacturers use a steam pressing machine while individuals use a conventional iron.

**prêt-à-porter**   (pret-ah-por-tay) French term for ready-to-wear clothes. *Der.* "ready to be carried."

**pre-walkers**   See SHOES.

**prime pelt**   Fur term for a best quality peltry. Animals must be hunted during the season when the pelt is the most fully furred. For most animals this is during the coldest winter months. *Beaver*, being a water animal, has a fuller pelt in the early spring when the streams are cold with water from melting ice and snow. *Marmot* pelts are best before animal hibernates for the winter.

**primitive print**   See PRINTS.

**Prince Albert coat**   **1.** Double-breasted long *frock coat* worn in late 18th c., with flat collar, usually of velvet. Worn for formal occasions, *e.g.,* weddings and funerals until about 1920. **2.** Adaptation of this coat for women worn in late 1890s—a double-breasted fitted, knee-length coat with turned-down collar and *revers,* flared skirt seamed at waistline, with two unpressed pleats with button trim at center back. *Der.* Named for Prince Albert of Saxe-Coburg-Gotha, consort of England's Queen Victoria.

**Prince of Wales jacket** Man's jacket of late 1860s similar to *reefer.* Cut in double-breasted style with three pairs of buttons. Named for Edward VII of England before he became king.

**Prince of Wales shoe** See GILLIE under OXFORDS.

**Prince Rupert** Woman's full-length fitted coat of late 19th c. made of velvet or plush, worn with a blouse and skirt.

**princess chemise** Woman's undergarment with corset cover and petticoat made in one piece with no waistline seam. Sometimes lavishly trimmed with lace at neckline, armholes, and hem. Worn in late 19th and early 20th c.

**princesse lace** See LACES.

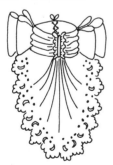

**PRINCESS STOCK, 1894**

**princess stock** High choker collar, usually made of shirred fabric with two bows extending at sides. When a *plastron* was attached at center front neckline, collar was called *princess stock collarette.* Worn by women in mid-1890s.

**princess style** Basic cut for women's clothing characterized by continuous vertical panels, shaped to body through torso without waistline

seam. Used in dresses, coats, and slips, from about 1860 on, especially in late 1930s and 1940s. Called *Agnès Sorel style* and *Isabeau style* in early 1860s. French form, *princesse.* See COATS, DRESSES, SILHOUETTES, SLIPS, and WAISTLINES.

**Princeton orange** Brilliant orange color, official color of Princeton University.

**Princie diamond** See DIAMONDS.

**print** Design reproduced on fabric in color either by mechanical means or by hand. Prints are repeat patterns, border designs, or large panel designs. Most countries no matter how primitive, have prints native to their land. Also see PRINTING in alphabetical listing.

### ■ PRINTS ■

**abstract p.** Stylized designs of a non-naturalistic type, *e.g., op art* or *geometric print.*

**African p.** Bold geometric designs frequently carried out in browns, blacks, and whites.

**allover p.** Print covering the entire surface of the fabric from selvage to selvage in a repeat design as opposed to a BORDER PRINT or a PANEL PRINT.

**American Indian p.** Bold, stylized, geometric designs from native American sources carried out in bright colors, popular in late 1960s.

**animal p.** Designs imprinted on fabrics in imitation of fur of the leopard, giraffe, ocelot, tiger, or zebra. Used on cotton, jersey, or on modacrylic pile fabric to resemble furs. Popular from mid-1960s on.

**Art Deco p.** Small geometric prints, frequently outlined in black, inspired by Exposition International des Arts Décoratifs et Industriels Modernes, Paris, 1925, reintroduced in the late 1960s. Used for fabrics and knits for dresses, sweaters, etc. *Der.* French, *art décóratif,* "decorative art."

**Art Nouveau p.**   Flowing prints of stylized leaves, flowers, and intertwined vines popular in late 1960s, inspired by early 20th-c. French art movement. *Der.* French, *nouveau,* "new art."

**Aztec p.**   Designs based on Mexican Indian geometric motifs in bright colors usually banded in black, popular in late 1960s.

**bandanna p.**   Designs, usually in black and white on a red or navy-blue background in imitation of bandanna handkerchiefs. *Der.* Indian, *bandhnu,* "method of tie-dyeing cloth."

**batik p.**   Designs, usually in dark blue, rust, black or yellow, copied from Indonesian technique of painting with wax before dyeing. See BATIK in alphabetical listing.

**block p.**   See HAND-BLOCKED PRINT.

**bookbinder p.**   Designs copied from multicolored abstract, swirled, and wood grain designs used formerly on end papers of expensively bound books.

**border p.**   Print designed so that one selvage forms a distinct border which is used at the hem of a dress or shirt, or worked into the garment in some other way.

**burnt-out p.**   Print made by weaving the design and background of two different types of fibers. Chemicals are applied to dissolve one fiber, leaving the design in high relief against a sheer background.

**calico p.**   Allover print usually of tiny naturalistic sprigs of flowers on a colored background of red, blue, yellow or black.

**chiné**   See WARP PRINT.

**discharge p.**   Design made on piece-dyed fabric by applying chemicals with copper rollers which dissolve and remove the dye in the design area. A white polka dot design on a navy ground is made in this manner.

**dots**   Round spots used as a pattern in regular rows or a random arrangement; *e.g., coin dots,* larger than a dime; *pin dots,* as small as the head of a pin.

**duplex p.**   Fabric with same design printed on both sides to imitate a woven pattern.

**fleur-de-lis**   French stylized lily design used in heraldry and part of the coat-of-arms of France's former royal family. Often used in formal repeat designs.

**flocked p.**   Design made by applying glue to lightweight fabric, *e.g.,* organdy, and dusting with tiny fibers that adhere to form a pattern. Frequently used to make border prints or flocked dotted Swiss.

**floral p.**   Any design using flowers in either a natural or stylized manner, *e.g.,* a daisy, a rose, or sprigs of flowers arranged together in a repeat design.

**geometric p.   1.** Circles, oblongs, squares, triangles, or other geometrical forms used in a printed design. **2.** Print with background broken up by using a repeat design of rectangular forms then imprinting another design within each unit.

**granny p.**   Small floral print similar to a calico print. *Der.* Named after prints formerly worn by grandmothers for housedresses at the turn of the 20th c.

**hand-blocked p.**   Pattern made by cutting design on wood or linoleum blocks (one for each color in the print) inking the blocks, then printing colors individually with a hand press.

**hand-painted p.**   A contradiction of terms, not a print at all but a pattern painted directly on fabric. A technique used by American Indians, revived in early 1970s and used since by fashion designers.

**hand-screened p.**   See SILK-SCREEN PRINT.

**ikat**   See WARP PRINTING.

**Indian p.**   May be a hand-blocked print or a batik as long as it originates in Madras or another city of India. Frequently made with inferior dye which *bleeds* or runs when the fabric is washed.

**Japanese p.** Usually a scenic print featuring pagodas, foliage, and mountains, in a repeat design. Fabric is frequently used to make garments in the kimono style.

**jungle p.** Designs using animals found in the jungle, *e.g.*, leopards, tigers, and lions.

**Laura Ashley® p.** Provincial, small floral designs typically Victorian, copied from antique designs printed on cotton fabrics and wallpapers. Originally used for home furnishings, now used for clothing. Trademarked by Laura Ashley of England where they are manufactured in Carno and sold in Laura Ashley stores in France, The Netherlands, Switzerland, Great Britain, and U.S.

**Liberty® p.** Trademark of Liberty, London, for wide range of printed fabrics. The best known are small multicolored floral designs.

**medallion p.** Repeat round or oval design sometimes connected with realistic swags of foliage.

**mosaic p.** Print introduced in early 1970s made by tiny square blocks of color arranged in a manner imitating a Byzantine mosaic.

**naturalistic p.** Representation of flowers, shrubs, trees, and birds, arranged in a realistic manner in a repeat design.

**Op Art p.** Design, basically geometric, in which lines are "bent" or "warped" to give optical illusion, *e.g.*, a checkerboard design formed with some curved lines and squares not all of equal size. *Der.* Became popular in 1964 after an exhibit of Op Art paintings at the Museum of Modern Art in New York City.

**paisley p.** Allover design featuring a design shaped like the side of the hand with a curved little finger included (or like a teardrop with a curved top). Frequently features rich colors with bold designs outlined in delicate tracery and swirls. Although of Persian origin, popularized in Paisley, Scotland, where paisley shawls were introduced in the late 1780s. Also see PAISLEY SHAWL in alphabetical listing.

**panel p.** A large design intended to be used in one length, without repeating, *e.g.*, one panel used for front—one for back of a dress. Usually made with hand-screened process and expensive.

**patchwork p.** A print designed to mimic a patchwork quilt design. Design is printed on fabric, not made with "patches."

**photographic p.** Large design covering entire front of the garment and reproduced in such a manner as to look like a black and white photo. Prints in 1960s included pictures of Beethoven and Bach imprinted on sweatshirts. Later rockets, tigers, and pictures of movie stars were imprinted on the front of a T-shirt-type dress.

**primitive p.** A classification of prints which includes those worn by early and unsophisticated civilizations. Also see AMERICAN INDIAN and AFRICAN PRINTS.

**psychedelic p.** Unconventional designs done in extremely vibrant, full-intensity colors, *e.g.*, chartreuse, fuchsia and purple in bizarre combinations forming flowing patterns on the fabric. *Der.* Inspired by the hallucinations seen when under the influence of the drug LSD.

**Pucci p.** Design introduced by Emilio Pucci, an Italian couturier, which is highly original and hard to imitate. Pattern is abstract and composed mainly of brilliant unusual color combinations outlined in black, usually printed on knitted fabric. White space is also utilized but the distinguishing feature is the use of exciting and unusual color combinations. *Der.* Prints are inspired by medieval and late Renaissance designs still used in flags and costumes of the famous Pallio in Sienna.

**resist p.** Process in which chemicals are used to prevent certain areas of fabric from being colored by dyes. Also see RESIST PRINTING in alphabetical listing.

**roller p.** Use of engraved copper cylinders to produce a colored design, using as many as 16 separate rollers—one for each color.

**screen p.** See SILK-SCREEN PRINT.

**silk-screen p.** Made by etching a design for each color on separate pieces of pure dye silk enclosed in wooden frames. Fabric to be printed is stretched on a long table; each screen is placed individually over the fabric; and paint, applied with a squeegee, is pushed through the etched sections. Process produces especially vibrant colors and unusual designs.

**stenciled p.** Design made by using cardboard or metal cut-outs over fabric, spraying paint or roller printing over them. The uncovered portions absorb the color and form the pattern.

**stylized p.** Ideas presented in an abstract, rather than naturalistic, manner reducing the objects to a design. Artistically considered a better design than representing natural elements too realistically.

**tie-dyed p.** Handmade primitive print made by gathering the fabric and tying at intervals, then immersing in dye which does not penetrate the tied areas. When untied reveals a pattern of irregular designs. Method originated in Dutch East Indies and became popular as a handicraft in U.S., in late 1960s and early 1970s. Used on pants, knit shirts, dresses, and even furs. Also imitated commercially by other methods. Called BANDANNA in India.

**wallpaper p.** Tiny floral stripes alternating with plain colored stripes, frequently of pastel colors. *Der.* Made in imitation of 19th-c. wallpaper.

**warp p.** Design printed on warp yarns before fabric is woven, producing a watered effect with fuzzy edges. Also called *chiné* and *ikat.*

**printing** Method of applying a pattern to a fabric in color. A variety of methods may be used, *e.g., duplex, direct, flock,* and *roller printing.* Designs may also be applied to fabric by photographic means and air brushing to give shaded effects by blowing color on a fabric.

**Priscilla apron** Young girl's apron of 1890s styled with full skirt shirred into waistband. Bib top extended around neck in broad, lace-trimmed, sailor-collar effect. Had straps from shoulder blades to waistband in back. Frequently made of DOTTED SWISS, NAINSOOK, or lightweight MUSLIN.

**prixseam** See GLOVE SEAMS.

**profile hat** See HATS.

**PROMENADE COSTUME**

**promenade costume/dress** Term used in last half of 19th c. for clothes suitable for walking and shopping as contrasted with *carriage dress* worn for riding in a carriage. Also called *walking costume* or *dress.*

**promenade skirt** Petticoat of 1850s with steel hoops set into muslin worn to support dress.

**PROMENADE SKIRT**

**pronged setting** See GEM SETTINGS.

**proportioned** See HOSE and PANTS.

**prospector's shirt** See KNIT SHIRTS.

**Prussian collar** Man's coat with narrow standing collar of 19th c. with ends nearly meeting in front, or worn turned down.

**psychedelic print** See PRINTS.

**Psyche knot** (si-kee) Copy of Greek hairstyle for women with hair pulled back and twisted to form a knot at back of head. *Der.* Named for Greek mythological maiden, Psyche, the lover of Cupid, made immortal by Jupiter.

**Pucci, Emilio** (poo-chee) An Italian designer whose fabrics were among the most widely imitated in the 1960s. See APPENDIX/ DESIGNERS. Also see HELMETS and PRINTS.

**pudding-basin cut** Bowl-shaped hairstyle for men consisting of hair combed from crown of head into bangs in front. Fashionable in England, France, and Italy in 15th c. Also see BOWL CROP.

**p'u-fang** **1.** Embroidered circular medallions, reference is to "heaven" as the Emperor of China is traditionally called "son of heaven," worn by highest nobility of China. **2.** Square patch of embroidery in gold and bright colors sewn to front and back of Chinese *Mandarin court robe* indicating rank. Also see P'U-FU.

**puff** **1.** (verb) To make full, particularly in a sleeve. **2.** 19th-c. term for a V-shaped gore of thin fabric, that filled in space at back of waistband of men's trousers. Lacing was used to close gap, and fabric was pulled out through laces. See PULLINGS OUT. Also see PUFF SLEEVE under SLEEVES.

**puffs** **1.** Term used for hair when *back-combed* to form bouffant effect at sides of face in early 20th c. by women. **2.** See PULLINGS OUT.

**p'u-fu** Three-quarter-length coat of purple-black silk, worn in China during Imperial period from 1644 to 1912, during Ch'ing dynasty made with embroidered patches, or P'U-FANG.

**pug hood** Woman's soft hood of 18th c. with pleats radiating from back where it fitted the head. Made with or without an attached cape. Usually black with colored turned-back lining and tied under the chin with matching ribbons. Same as *short hood.* Compare with LONG HOOD.

**pugree/puggree** **1.** See PAGRI. **2.** Scarf tied around a hat or sun helmet with ends hanging down the back. Worn for protection from sun, particularly in India.

**Pulitzer, Lilly** See LILLY®.

**pull** British abbreviation for PULLOVER SWEATER.

**pullayne** See POULAINE.

**pullback** Skirt of 1880s, with the fullness drawn to the back and draped.

**pulled work** See PUNCH WORK under EMBROIDERIES.

**pullings out** Decorative effect used from 16th through mid-17th c. made by drawing out colored lining fabric through slashes in the outer garment, *e.g.,* the *doublet, trunk hose,* or sleeves. Also called *puffs.* Also see PANES.

**Pullman slipper** Man's lightweight, glove leather flat slipper that folds into small envelope for traveling. Also made in patterned stretch fabrics for women. *Der.* Named for railroad sleeping cars designed by George Pullman and Ben Field in 1858–59 and owned since 1864 by Pullman Palace Car Co. Also see FOLD-ING SLIPPER under SLIPPERS.

**pull-on**   See BLOUSES, GIRDLES, GLOVES, PANTS, SHORTS, and SWEATERS. Also called a PULLOVER.

**pullover**   A garment without full-length opening, can be pulled over the head, *e.g.*, a pullover sweater as opposed to a cardigan. Also called PULL-ON. Also see BLOUSES, KNIT SHIRTS, and SWEATERS.

**pultney cap**   Woman's heart-shaped indoor cap of 1760s with wired peak, worn on the back of the head.

**pumps**   See SHOES.

**punched**   Shoe or leather industry term for leather perforated for decorative effect. See PER-FORATIONS.

**punch work**   See EMBROIDERIES.

**Punjab silk**   **1.** Silk fabrics made in checks, stripes, changeable effects, and Jacquard weaves. **2.** Trade name for heavy, lustrous, rough decorative silk made in U.S. Both fabrics should be labeled as to country of origin.

**punk**   *Avant-garde, outré style* adopted by males and females in late 1970s. *Der.* From punk rock music, popularized in late 1970s. Also see HAIRSTYLES and LOOKS.

**punto lace**   See LACES.

**pure dye silk**   Soft, lustrous, high-quality silk fabric from which the gum, or impurities, have been removed. So called because less than 10% (15% for black goods) metallic salts have been added to give the fabric more weight. Pure dye silk has a very good affinity for dye and may be printed, dyed, or screen-printed.

**Puritan**   See COLLARS and HATS.

**purl stitch**   See STITCHES.

**purse**   Synonym for HANDBAG.

**push-up bra**   See BRAS.

**put-on**   Thick hairpiece, sometimes 18″ long, made of modacrylic matched to hair. May be worn in a multiplicity of styles, *e.g.*, *ponytail*, *double braid*, *fall*, *bun*, *chignon*, *wiglet*, *Empire cone*, and *French twist*.

**PUTTEES, 1927**

**puttee**   **1.** Legging worn by U.S. Army in World War I consisting of long strip of khaki-colored wool fabric, about 4″ wide, wrapped around leg from ankle to knee. **2.** Legging worn by U.S. Army made of shaped piece of fabric or leather, usually closed with buckles, similar to GAITER. Also see LEGGINGS.

**put-together look**   Individuality in dressing rather than conforming to a dress code. See LOOKS. Compare with LAYERED and MIX AND MATCH LOOKS.

**PXM**   See GLOVE SEAMS.

**pyjamas**   British variant of PAJAMAS.

**pyramid coat**   Tent-shaped woman's coat of late 1940s and early 1950s made with narrow shoulders and wide hem.

**pyramid heel**   See HEELS.

**python**   See LEATHERS.

**qatrah**  A large gold *nose ring* worn by women of Mandisha in the Bahariya Oasis of Egypt. May be three inches in diameter, with an elaborate metalwork design and filigree edge covering the lower half, plus a smaller solid disk at one side. *Der.* Of southern Saharan origin.

**Qiana®** (key-a-na) Registered trademark of E. I. du Pont de Nemours Co. for filament nylon with unusual molecular units in chemical linkage. Trademark is restricted to fabrics meeting quality standards set by the producer. Qualities of the fabric include: lightweight, luxurious silklike hand, good drapability, easily dyed with colors appearing clean and brilliant, and will not yellow or water spot. Used for woven and knitted fabrics.

**quail-pipe boot**  Man's high soft leather boot worn pushed down and wrinkled on the leg. Fashionable in late 16th and early 17th c.

**quaintise**  See COINTISE.

**Quaker bonnet**  Small close-fitting, undecorated woman's bonnet with a puffed crown and stiff brim tied under the chin. Made in same fabric as the dress (often gray), and worn over a ruffled white muslin cap. In 17th through 19th c. prescribed for women of Quaker faith by the Society of Friends.

**Quaker cap**  See JOAN CAP.

**Quaker hat**  **1.** TRICORNE HAT with open cock and tall crown, worn in 18th c. **2.** Hat with large, slightly rolled brim, low crown, and no ornamentation worn in the 19th c. by Quaker men.

**Quant, Mary**  See APPENDIX/DESIGNERS.

**quarter**  Back portion of shoe upper covering the sides and back of the foot.

**quartered cap**  Boy's cap with flat circular crown divided into four segments and attached

to stiff band. Made with or without a visor from mid-18th to mid-19th c.

**quarter socks**  See SOCKS.

**quartz**  See GEMS.

**quatrefoil**  Geometrical four-lobed design derived from heraldry.

**Queen Elizabeth pink diamond**  See WILLIAMSON DIAMOND under DIAMONDS.

**Queen of Holland diamond**  See DIAMONDS.

**queen's cloth**  Cotton shirting made of fine yarns, bleached after it is woven in Jamaica in the West Indies.

**Queen size**  Term used for large size women's wear particularly used for pantyhose.

**queen's mourning**  Black suiting fabric made in England about the time of the coronation of Edward VII in 1901. It was an unfinished worsted or wool with a fine hairline stripe approximately every inch. *Der.* Used for clothes worn for mourning Queen Victoria's death.

**querpo**  (kwer-po) 17th-c. term for a man without cloak or jacket. *Der.* Spanish, *cuerpo,* "body."

**queue**  (kew) See HAIRSTYLES.

**queue de lion**  (kew de le-ohn) See HAIRSTYLES.

**queue-peruke**  (kew pear-ook) Man's small wig worn from 1727 to 1760 with fluffed or curled sides and long ends tied back with black bow to make a QUEUE.

**quiff**  See HAIRSTYLES.

**quill**  **1.** Long stiff shaft of a feather with many thin projections called *barbs.* Used as ladies' hat trim, especially in 1940s. **2.** Bobbin used in weaving to hold filling yarn. Also called *pirn.*

**quilling** **1.** Trimming made of narrow fluted fabric, used in 19th c. **2.** Process of winding filling yarns on bobbins or *quills*.

**quill work** Decorative designs made on fabric and leather by native American Indians using porcupine quills.

**quilting** Technique of joining together layers of fabrics, sometimes with BATTING or other filling between. Done by hand or machine topstitching in crisscross lines, in diamonds, or in other patterns. Used to provide added bulk or warmth, *e.g.*, quilted petticoats worn as underskirts in 18th and 19th c. Used for robes, raincoats, sport jackets, coats, handbags, and linings.

**quintise** See COINTISE.

**quirk** Small triangular insert placed in glove at base of each finger and at thumb. Used to give a close fit yet permit flexibility.

QUIRK

**quissionet** See CUSHIONET.

**quizzing glass** MONOCLE, a single magnifying eyeglass, suspended from a neckchain in the 18th and early 19th c. The *dandies* of the 1820s had the glass fixed in the head of a cane.

**quoif** (kwaf) See COIF.

**qutn/quoton/qutun** Arabic, "cotton."

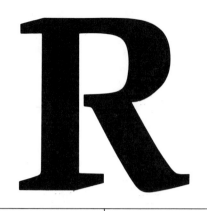

**Rabanne, Paco** See APPENDIX/DESIGNERS and HELMETS.

**rabat** (rab-e; ra-bat) **1.** Black *dickey* or *shirt front* to which the white *clerical collar* is attached. Worn with suits or with liturgical robes by Catholic and Protestant clergy. **2.** A linen and lace collar worn over the *doublet* in 17th c. Also called *rabbi*.

**rabato** (rah-bah-toe) **1.** White collar wired to stand up at back of neck, worn with low-cut neckline by women from late 16th to mid-17th c. **2.** 17th-c. term for a support of wire or wood used for the ruff. Also spelled *rebato*. Also called a SUPPORTASSE or *underpropper*.

**rabbi** See RABAT.

**rabbit** See FURS.

**raccoon** See COATS and FURS.

**racing** Adjective used for items of apparel and accessories borrowed from various forms of competitive racing, *e.g.*, foot racing, auto racing, and horse racing. See SHOES, SPORT JACKETS, ACTION GLOVE under GLOVES, and JOCKEY SILKS.

**raffia** Fiber from species of Madagascar palm used for making hats, bags, and fabrics.

**rag business** Slang term for APPAREL INDUSTRY.

**raglan boot** Thigh-length, soft black leather boot worn by men for hunting in late 1850s. *Der.* Named after Lord Raglan.

**raglan cape** Fly-front or double-breasted overcoat of 1857 with slit pockets and *raglan* sleeves which extended in V-shaped form to neck rather than having a seam at the shoulder. *Der.* Named for Lord Raglan.

**Raglan, Lord** (1788–1855) Fitzroy James Henry Somerset, British General in Crimean War. After losing an arm in the Charge of the Light Brigade in 1854, had a coat designed with special sleeve, later called *raglan sleeve*. Also see COATS, SHOULDERS, and SLEEVES.

**ragyogo** Very ornate headdress of jewels and feathers worn as native costume by Hungarian bride.

**rail 1.** Folded *neckerchief* worn like a shawl around neck by women from late 15th to late 17th c. Also see HEAD RAIL. **2.** In the 17th and 18th c. a *nightgown*. Term also applied to gown worn at home in morning. See NIGHT RAIL. Also spelled *rayle*.

**railroad trousers** Term for men's trousers with stripes, horizontal or vertical, worn from late 1830s to 1850.

**railway pocket** Flat bag with side opening tied on with tape around waist and reached by slit in skirt. Worn by women under dress when traveling, from late 1850s.

**railway stitch** See CHAIN and TRICOT under STITCHES.

**raiment 1.** Older term used to denote clothing. **2.** Biblical term for clothing.

**rainbow stripes** See STRIPES.

**raincoat** Clothing originally designed to be worn in rainy weather, now also worn as *top coat* in fair weather. Made of waterproof material or regular fabric given a special surface finish to make it water repellent. Raincoats were introduced in 1830 after the perfection of a rubberized fabric by Charles Macintosh in 1823. Original fabric was waterproof but had an objectionable odor. *Trenchcoats* were introduced in World War I. Modern technology in the development of water-repellent finishes in recent years has made it possible to use a greater number of fabrics for raincoats. Another new innovation is Gore-Tex®. See SIPHONIA in alphabetical listing.

### ▰▰▰▰ RAINCOATS ▰▰▰▰

**all-weather r.** Raincoat which can be worn year-round as it is made with a zip-out lining, usually of acrylic pile.

**Burberry®** Trademark of Burberry's International, Ltd., London, for an expensive unisex trenchcoat-type raincoat. Made in lightweight polyester and cotton fabric with an optional plaid zip-out lining. Skirts, scarfs, and umbrellas are made to match the lining. Details include handstitching on collar, handmade buttonholes, and D-rings on belt for holding objects. First used by British officers in 1914. Also see alphabetical listing.

**fold-up r.** Any raincoat which folds to small size, specifically a lightweight raincoat frequently of clear vinyl which folds to pocket size. Introduced as early as 1850 and then called *pocket siphonia*. Also see alphabetical listing.

**London Fog®** Trademark for London Fog, a division of Interco, Inc., for men's and women's raincoat of classic style.

**mackintosh** **1.** Rubberized or plastic yellow waterproof raincoat made with a cape worn by policemen and firemen. **2.** British slang for any raincoat. Sometimes abbreviated as *mac.* **3.** Women's coat of 1880s. Also see alphabetical listing. *Der.* Named after Charles Macintosh who first invented the rubberized fabric in 1823.

**rain cape** Cape of mini-, midi-, or maxi-length with slits for arms, made of water-repellent fabric or vinyl.

**rain or shine coat** Fabric coat treated with

**MACKINTOSH #3, 1895**

**TRENCHCOAT**          **SLICKER**

water-repellent finish so that it can be worn as an all-purpose coat.

**slicker** **1.** Bright-yellow oilskin coat, or similar coat of rubberized fabric in other colors, usually fastened with clips in front. Originally worn by sailors, now often worn with sou'wes-TER HAT by fishermen and children. **2.** A type of yellow rubber raincoat with slash in back to waist and extra insert so that each side can be fastened around legs to form protection when riding horseback in rainy weather.

**trenchcoat** In World War II the trenchcoat became an all-purpose coat made of a water-repellent fabric in double-breasted style with a convertible collar, large lapels, epaulets, fabric belt, slotted pockets, and a vent in the back. Over the shoulders in back it had an extra hanging yoke and an extra flap hung from the front right shoulder. In the 1940s women adapted the trenchcoat and it has been worn as a classic since. Also see BURBERRY®. *Der.* Origi-nally worn by British officers in World War I.

**vinyl r.** **1.** Waterproof raincoat usually made of heavy clear vinyl. Special attention must be paid to the seams or it will tear where the sewing machine perforates it. **2.** Fabric given a vinyl finish and used to make a raincoat.

---

**rainwear** Clothing and accessories that are waterproofed or water-repellent. See BONNETS, BOOTS, CAPES, COATS, DRESSES, HATS, and RAIN-COATS.

**Rainy Daisy skirt** Tailored, ankle-length walking skirt fashionable from about 1902. Also worn for roller skating. *Der.* A nickname given to women who were members of the "Rainy Day Club" and wore skirts of this type. Also called *rainy day skirt.*

**raised embroidery** See EMBROIDERIES.

**rajah collar** (rah-jah) See NECKLINES and NEHRU under COLLARS.

**rajah jacket** (rah-jah) See JACKETS.

**ramie** Strong soft fiber from inner bark of *ramie* plant, formerly imported from China. Used for dress goods and hats. Also called *rhea* or CHINA GRASS.

**Ramillies wig** Man's wig of 18th c. puffed at sides with long, tapered, braided *queue* tied with black ribbon at end and nape of neck, or looped up and tied only at neck. *Der.* Named for English victory over French in Ramillies, Belgium, in 1706. Also spelled *Ramilet, Ramille.*

**Ramsey tartan** See TARTANS.

**ranch coat** See COATS.

**ranch mink** See MINK and MUTATION MINK under FURS.

**ranelagh mob** Woman's cap of 1760s made with a *kerchief* folded diagonally and placed over the head with two long ends tied under chin. Then ends were pulled back and pinned or left to hang down.

**Ranger's hat** See HATS.

**rank swell** See HEAVY SWELL.

**Raphael's body** Woman's fitted *bodice* worn from late 1850s through mid-1860s with a low square neckline. Sometimes worn with a high-necked *chemisette* underneath and matching skirt.

**rapolin** (rap-o-lin) Swiss millinery braid made in triple rows and having an uneven surface.

**raschel knit** Type of warp knitting done with plain or Jacquard patterns in a lacy effect—popular since 1960s.

**Rasta dreadlocks** See HAIRSTYLES.

**rat** Sausage-shaped padded roll of hair or felt worn by women under natural hair to create high *pompadour* effect in early 20th c. Also see POMPADOUR under HAIRSTYLES. Compare with GABBIA.

**Ratcatcher** See SHIRTS.

**ratiné** (rat-in-ay) Spongy, rough feeling fabric loosely woven in a plain weave. The rough, nubby appearance is made by using *ratiné yarn* which has nubs or knots at intervals. In best qualities the ratiné yarn is used in both direc-tions. In less expensive variations, it is used only in the filling. *Der.* French, "frizzy" or "fuzzy."

**rationals** Popular name for full pleated serge bloomers or knickerbockers worn by women for bicycling in 1890s.

**rat-tail braid** See BRAIDS.

**rat-tail comb** Comb for the hair with fine teeth and a long pointed handle used for shaping curls.

**rattan** **1.** Flat reed-like stem from tropical palm woven to form *basket handbags* and other items. **2.** Man's *cane* carried in 17th and 18th c. made from East Indian palm.

**ratting** See BACK-COMBING.

**rawhide** See LEATHERS.

**raw silk** Silk fiber reeled from cocoon while still containing the gum or sericin, wound into reels for sale. It may have two filaments and be called *bave* or one filament and called *brin.*

**rayon** Generic term for man-made fibers derived from trees, cotton, and woody plants. Originally known as *artificial silk* until 1927. First produced by Count Hilaire de Chardonet in 1889, it was worn at Queen Victoria's funeral in 1901. Rayon fabrics both knitted and woven are widely used primarily because of low cost. Characteristics include a silky hand, shiny lustrous appearance, good dyeability, and good drapability qualities. Disadvantages include wrinkles easily and must be ironed. Used for lingerie, dresses, shirts. *Der.* French, "ray of light."

**ready-to-wear** Apparel that is mass produced in standard sizes. Records of ready-to-wear industry tabulated in U.S. Census of 1860 included *hoop skirts*, *cloaks*, and *mantillas*; from 1890 on, *shirtwaists* and wrappers were added; and, after 1930, dresses. First ready-to-wear dresses appeared in Paris in 1792. Also abbreviated *RTW.* Also see PRÊT-À PORTER and OFF THE PEG.

**rebato** See RABATO.

**Reboux, Caroline** See APPENDIX/ DESIGNERS.

**rebozo** (re-bow-zo) Veil or scarf worn over head by Spanish or Mexican women in place of lace *mantilla.* See SHAWLS.

**rebras** (ray-bras) 13th to 17th c. term used when apparel or accessory was turned back to reveal lining, *e.g.*, revers of coat, upturned *brim* on hat, or cuff of glove.

**Rècamier hairstyle** (ray-cahm-ee-ay) Hairstyle of 1870s and 1880s arranged with *chignon* high on back of head and curls at neck. *Der.* Named after hairstyle worn by Madame Rècamier.

**Rècamier, Madame** (ray-cahm-ee-ay) Jeanne Françoise Julie Adelaide (1777–1849), famous beauty of Napoleonic era. Painted by both David and Gérard, her mode of dress and hairstyles were widely imitated.

**reclaimed wool** Term required by U.S. Wool Labeling Act of 1939 to be used when referring to REPROCESSED or REUSED WOOL.

**Red Baron helmet** See HELMETS.

**RED CROWN**

**red crown** Outward flaring crown with long extension up back worn by kings of Upper Egypt in ancient times. When kingdom became united both the *red crown* and the WHITE CROWN were worn together.

**Redfern, House of** See APPENDIX/ DESIGNERS.

**redingote** (red-in-gote) **Men:** **1.** A full overcoat having a large collar worn for riding in France about 1725. **2.** In 1830 a greatcoat of blue cloth in military style closed with frogs, had sloping pockets, and a fur collar. Also called a *polonaise*. **Women: 3.** Coat adapted from man's coat in 1790s in lighter-weight fabrics and worn as part of a dress rather than an outdoor coat. **4.** During the Empire period, it was an outer coat. **5.** From 1820s on it was essentially a variation of the *pelisse robe*, a dress most fashionable from 1835 to 1860s. See ROBE REDINGOTE. **6.** By late 1840s name replaced the PELISSE ROBE. **7.** In 1890s became an ensemble with matching coat and dress with the coat usually being cut a little shorter than the dress. **8.** Contemporary term referring to a matching or contrasting coat and dress worn together as an ensemble. Also see COATS and DRESSES. *Der.* French, "mannish woman's frock coat" or English, "riding coat."

**REEFER, 1919**

**reefer**    **1.** Double-breasted, thigh-length boxy jacket introduced for men in 1860 with small collar, short lapels, and three or four sets of buttons. Originally called a *pea jacket* or *pilot coat* from 1830s. See SPORT JACKETS. **2.** Women's and children's short jacket of 1890s and early 20th c., frequently worn with matching skirt as a suit. Made with unfitted double-breasted front and fitted back. **3.** Fitted full-length coat with large lapels either double- or single-breasted. See COATS.

**refajo**    Guatemalan skirt in wrap or pleated style worn by women.

**regard rings**    Rings worn in 16th c. set with stones having initials spelling out such words as L-O-V-E or name of the beloved.

**regatta shirt**    Man's cambric or oxford striped shirt with plain front. Worn as informal summer wear in 1840s.

**Regency coat**    Man's short-waisted coat cut away to show waistcoat with knee-length tails, high rolling NAPOLEONIC or REGENCY COLLAR revealing close-wrapped *cravat*. Worn by *dandies* such as BEAU BRUMMELL during English Regency period, 1811–1820. Also see COATS.

**Regency collar**    See COLLARS.

**Regency costume**    **1.** French period during regency of Philip, duc de Orleans, 1715–1723 for Louis XV. Characterized by lightweight dresses with *basque bodices*, *sabot sleeves*, and *panniers*. **2.** English period during the regency of the Prince of Wales, 1811–1820 for George III. Noted for fashions of the DANDIES and BEAU BRUMMELL. Also see REGENCY COAT under COATS.

**Regent diamond**    See DIAMONDS.

**regimental stripe**    See STRIPES.

**Regny, Jane**    See APPENDIX/DESIGNERS.

**regular**    The ordinary size range for clothing as opposed to special sizes, *e.g.*, regular boys sizes as opposed to slim or husky.

**regular twist**    See Z-TWIST.

**religious medal**    See NECKLACES.

**remnant**    **1.** Short length of fabric remaining after yardage has been cut off a bolt or roll of fabric. Too short to make an entire garment, these pieces are sold at a special prices. **2.** Short lengths of fabric left at mill after winding bolts to be sold at retail. Also called *mill ends*. **3.** Short lengths of lace or trimming sold at reduced prices.

**Renaissance lace**    See LACES.

**rep** **1.** Fabric with fillingwise ribs, less distinct than in *bengaline* and more pronounced than in *poplin*. May be made from a variety of fibers in several ways: *a)* using a *rib weave;* *b)* using heavy filling yarns; or *c)* relaxing tension at intervals. Used for neckties and women's wear. **2.** Late 19th c. term for a strong warp-ribbed fabric made with a heavy cotton warp and fine wool filling. Sometimes made double-faced. **3.** Warp-ribbed silk fabric originating in 18th c. In mid-19th c. ribs were sometimes placed fillingwise. Also spelled *repp.*

**reprocessed wool** Wool formerly made into cloth or garments but not used by the ultimate consumer. May consist of small pieces remaining after garments are cut out. Wool is garnetted or shredded, then respun into yarn, and woven into fabrics. Must be labeled in accordance with the *Wool Labeling Act* of 1939 when sold to the ultimate consumer.

**rep stitch** See STITCHES.

**rerebrace** Plate armor worn on the upper arm; an upper CANNON or VAMBRACE.

**reserve wig** See WIGS.

**resist dyeing** Piece-dyeing process in which some of the yarns are chemically treated. These yarns remain undyed while other, untreated yarns, take the dye, resulting in a two-toned fabric. Also see RESIST PRINTING.

**resist printing** Method of printing fabric by first applying design to fabric with chemical paste that will not take dye, and then dying the fabric. When chemical is removed, design is left white against colored background, *e.g.,* white polka dot on navy ground.

**reticella lace** (reh-tee-chella) See LACES.

**reticulation** (re-ti-cu-lay-shun) Decorative *netting* holding hair on either side of face worn with horned headdress by women in 15th c. See CAUL.

**reticule** (ret-ih-kewl) Woman's small purse made of satin, mesh, velvet, red morocco

**RETICULE**

leather, and other materials. Took many shapes, *e.g.,* shaped like an envelope, an urn, a lozenge, a circle, a shell or a basket. Used from 19th to early 20th c. Also called INDISPENSIBLE and BALLANTINE. Also spelled *ridicule.*

**retro fashions** Shortened form of word "retrogressive" meaning looking backward to distinctive styles of former eras. See LOOKS.

**reused wool** Wool that has been previously made into a garment, worn, and discarded; collected, cleaned, and reduced to a fibrous state. After some new fibers are added, it is respun into yarn, woven into fabric, and again made into a garment. Reused wool is composed of short fibers and generally has a harsh feel or *hand.* The *Wool Labeling Act* of 1939 requires that such wool be labeled properly.

**revers** (ri-veerz) See COLLARS.

**reverse calf** See LEATHERS.

**reverse guiches** (gweeshes) See CURLS.

**reverse twist** See S-TWIST.

**reversible clothing** Any item of clothing made so that it can be worn on either side. Usually of different color, pattern, or style on reverse side. Popular for capes, ponchos, and coats. Also see SPORT JACKETS and VESTS.

**reversible fabric** Any fabric which may be used on either side, *e.g., double cloth* or *crepe-back satin.*

**Rex Harrison hat** See HATS.

**Reykjavik sweater** (rye-k-vic)   See SWEATERS.

**rhea**   Indian name for RAMIE.

**rhea feathers**   See FEATHERS.

**Rhinegraves**   See PETTICOAT BREECHES.

**rhinestone**   A colorless transparent artificial gem made of glass or paste, usually cut like a diamond and used widely for costume jewelry and buttons. *Der.* Originally made in Strasbourg, France, on the Rhine River. Also see BUTTONS and GEMS.

**Rhodes, Zandra**   See APPENDIX/DESIGNERS.

**rhodium**   White-colored metal of the platinum group used for plating jewelry.

**rhumba**   Latin or South American dance costumes usually using ruffles. Also spelled *rumba*. See DRESSES, PANTIES, and SLEEVES.

**rib**   **1.** Textile-industry term for corded effect in fabrics caused by weave or by use of heavier yarns in either warp or filling, *e.g., bengaline, grosgrain, ottoman,* or *faille*. **2.** Individual strip of metal that forms part of frame of umbrella, *e.g.,* usually there are six to sixteen ribs in an umbrella. Also see HOSE.

**riband**   **1.** The border of an item of apparel from 14th to 15th c. **2.** Narrow band of decorative material or silk from 16th c.

**ribbon**   Long narrow strip of silk, cotton, or rayon woven with selvages on both sides. Also made of acetate and then sliced into narrow strips with heated knives that fuse the edges. Used mainly for trimming and for tying hair. Made in a variety of weaves: *a)* cross-ribbed, called *grosgrain; b)* with looped edges, called *picot; c)* cut-pile surface, or *velvet* (sometimes satin-backed); *d)* satin, very narrow pink or blue satin is called *baby ribbon.*

**rib knit**   Knitted fabric which shows alternate lengthwise rows of ribs and wales on both sides. More elastic, heavier, and durable than plain knitting. Used frequently on cuffs and necklines of sweaters and sport jackets. Also see KNITTING.

**rib-tickler**   Term used to describe short top that just reaches to rib-cage—similar to *bare-midriff* top. See SWIMSUITS.

**Ricci, Nina**   See APPENDIX/DESIGNERS.

**rice braid**   See BRAIDS.

**rich peasant look**   Midi-length styles emphasizing embroidery and elaborate fabrics. See LOOKS.

**rickrack**   See BRAIDS.

**ridicule**   See RETICULE.

**riding coat**   **1.** See COATS. **2.** Man's suit coat worn from 1825 to 1870s made with skirt slanting from waist to thigh in back. Also called NEWMARKET COAT. Also see MORNING COAT and CUTAWAY COAT.

**riding coat dress**   Woman's dress cut in coat-style worn from 1785 to 1800 with buttons down front, large collar and lapels, long tight sleeves, and skirt with slight train.

**riding habit**   **1.** Riding costumes for women are mentioned in the early 17th c. composed of long hose, or *calencons,* worn with doublet and petticoat. **2.** In mid-17th c. women wore the man's *justaucorps.* For 18th and 19th c. women's riding dresses see AMAZONE, BRUNSWICK, JOSEPH, and EQUESTERIENNE *costume.* **3.** Riding trousers were introduced in the early 1880s for women and worn under the riding dress or skirt. *Breeches* without the skirt were worn with a longer jacket about 1914. By the early 1920s, *jodhpurs* were popular. **4.** Contemporary habits are determined by the occasion—for riding clothes see RIDING BOOT under BOOTS; HUNT CAP under CAPS; HUNT COAT, PINK COAT and SHOW COAT under COATS; HACKING JACKET under JACKETS; HUNT BREECHES and JODHPURS under PANTS; RATCATCHER under SHIRTS; and INFORMAL HABIT and RIDING HABIT under SPORT SUITS.

**riding skirt**   Calf-length wraparound skirt worn by women who rode side-saddle in late 19th and early 20th c.

**riding smalls**   Man's riding *breeches* worn

from 1814 to 1835 made of light-colored doe-skin made with wide hips but tight from knees down.

**riding stock**   See STOCK under TIES.

**riding suit**   See RIDING HABIT.

**right twist**   See Z-TWIST.

**rimless glasses**   See GLASSES.

**ring**   Decorative jewelry worn on the finger, sometimes on the thumb, and infrequently on one of the toes. Before the mid-1960s, rings were worn on the third finger and the little finger. After this time, it was fashionable to wear rings on any of the fingers. This was a revival of styles of the 16th c. when many rings were worn and two rings were sometimes worn on the same finger. Since earliest times a ring has been a pledge or a seal of faith, and also used as a stamp of authority. See DEVOTIONAL RING, FISHERMAN'S RING, GIMMEL RING, and POISON RING in alphabetical listing.

## ▬▬▬ RINGS ▬▬▬

**adjustable r.**   Ring made with band made of overlapping ends so that it can be fitted to any finger size. Usually an inexpensive costume or fashion ring.

**ankh r.**   Gold or gold-finished ring made in the shape of the ancient Egyptian symbol of life—a cross with a loop at the top.

**birthstone r.**   Ring set with a stone representing the birth month, *e.g.,* an amethyst for February. For stones see BIRTHSTONES in alphabetical listing.

**bracelet r.**   Ring and bracelet combined. Also called a *slave bracelet* and a *ring bracelet.* See BRACELETS category.

**bridal set**   Matching *engagement ring* and *wedding band.*

**class r.**   High school or college ring of individual design for each school with class year included. Sometimes uses large stones, crests or individual initials. Also called a *school ring.*

**cluster r.**   Type of ring set with many large and small stones grouped together. Sometimes made of precious stones, frequently diamonds.

**cocktail r.**   Large showy ring, either a piece of costume jewelry or made of fine jewelry, set with precious or semiprecious stones. Sometimes called *dinner ring.*

**damascene r.**   Blackened metal inlaid with fine gold-tone wire to form a delicate design.

**Decatur r.**   Gold band, similar to a wedding ring, with two inset bands of black enamel. Copied from ring given to Stephen Decatur, American naval officer, by Lieutenant Richard Somers in 1804 as a friendship ring. Original ring is in the Smithsonian Institution, Washington. D.C.

**dinner r.**   See COCKTAIL RING.

**dome r.**   Ring with a high rounded top, similar to a dome, usually set with many stones or made of metal.

**engagement r.**   Ring given to a woman by a man signifying that they plan to be married—

**SIGNET RING**

**SOLITAIRE**

for many years a diamond *solitaire*—now most any type of ring.

**eternity r.** Full or half circlet of diamonds, rubies or sapphires set in a narrow band of gold or platinum sometimes given by husband to wife as a pledge of love on a special occasion, *e.g.*, birth of a child or wedding anniversary. This tradition started in England in 1930s.

**family r.** Rings for all members of the family, *i.e.*, father, mother, daughter, grandmother, etc. Rings are of various sizes and shapes, but all incorporate several birthstones representing birthdays of various members of the family.

**filigree r.** Gold or silver wire twisted in a lacy intricate pattern to make a ring, usually protruding upward to make a dome.

**fraternal r.** Emblematic ring only used by members of fraternal organizations, *e.g.*, Masons, Elks, and Knights of Columbus. Frequently made of gold or silver with an onyx setting on which symbols of the organization are placed in gold, silver, and gems.

**free-form r.** Contemporary ring which may be almost any shape other than the conventional round ring. Frequently made of a long piece of metal shaped to the finger but having the two ends lapped over each other, often made with gemstones at the ends. *Der.* From free-form sculpture.

**friendship r.** An older term for a simple metal ring exchanged by good friends and worn for sentimental value. Formerly called a *talisman ring*.

**initial r.** See SIGNET RING.

**nugget r.** Ring with stone made from a piece of metal in its natural shape, *e.g.*, a gold nugget.

**peace r.** Simple ring designed of metal with "peace symbol" consisting of a circle intersected with straight bar down the center and Y-shaped bars to the outer edge.

**perfume r.** **1.** Large costume ring which is hinged under the stone so that solid perfume

may be placed inside. **2.** Ring similar to above used at Court of Louis XIV.

**posy/poesy r.** Plain gold band, sometimes with small decorative design in center, given as a love token. Inside was inscribed "let love endure" or "faithful and true." Popular in the 16th c., revived in the 1980s.

**ring bracelet** See BRACELET RING.

**rolling r.** Bands of three circlets of gold in different colors of gold—rose, yellow, and white—interlocked to make a ring. Designed and made by Cartier since the 1920s. Also made with six interlocking circles.

**school r.** See CLASS RING.

**serpent r.** Ring shaped like snake curled around the finger. Similar rings were worn in ancient Rome.

**signet r.** **1.** Ring with large stone cut intaglio. Formerly used to make an impression in sealing wax to seal letters. **2.** Ring with king's seal used by Egyptians before the lock and key was invented.

**slave bracelet** See BRACELET RING or BRACELETS category.

**solitaire** Ring set with a single stone, frequently a diamond, sometimes a pearl or another gem.

**spoon r.** The handle of a small sterling silver spoon molded to wrap around the finger to form a ring.

**talisman r.** See FRIENDSHIP RING.

**toe r.** Any ring worn on one of the toes, usually the big toe. In 1967 plastic, papier-mâché, or felt rings were popular. Also see TOE-ANKLE CHAIN under BRACELETS category.

**wedding band** See WEDDING RING.

**wedding r.** Ring or rings used in a wedding ceremony. Traditionally a band of gold in various widths worn by both men and women on third finger of left hand. Although worn since Egyptian times, not adopted by Christians until second half of 9th c. Plain gold band of modern times dates from the time of Mary Tudor and her marriage to Phillip II of Spain in 1554. Also called a *wedding band.*

**wedding trio** Woman's engagement ring and wedding band—plus men's wedding band, similarly styled and sold together. Also see BRIDAL SET.

**Zuni snake eye r.** Sterling silver ring set with 25 turquoise stones, mounted five to a row in five rows, alternating with rounded silver beads. Copied from ring in the Smithsonian Institution. *Der.* Originally made by Zuni Indians of southwestern U.S.

---

**ring and pin** See ANNULAR and PENANNULAR BROOCHES.

**ring bracelet** See BRACELET RING under RINGS and SLAVE BRACELET under BRACELET.

**ring buckle** Two rings on one end of belt through which opposite belt end threads—first through both, then back through one—and pulls tight. Sometimes in the shape of a "D." Also called *cinch buckle* or *cinch closing.*

**ringlets** See CURLS.

**ripple cape** In the 1890s a woman's short ruffled cape extended beyond the shoulder by shirring three layers of fabric or lace onto a yoke trimmed with ribbon.

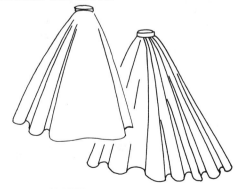

**RIPPLE SKIRT**

**ripple skirt** *Gored* skirt worn in 1890s sometimes with as many as eleven gores. Fitted snugly over hips but flared at hem to a width of six yards or more. Lined with horsehair stiffening and pressed to hang in rounded PIPE-ORGAN PLEATS.

**rise** Men's tailoring term for distance from crotch to top of waistband in pants, *e.g., hip-hugger pants* have a *low rise.*

**robe** **1.** Informal clothing usually styled like a loose coat; may be sashed, buttoned, zipped, or hang loose. Worn over pajamas or nightgown, at the beach, or for informal entertaining at home. Current meaning of the word is a shortened form of the word *bathrobe* or *dressing robe.* **2.** Ceremonial garment made in long, loose, flowing style; *academic robe, clerical robe,* or *coronation robe.* **3.** In Middle Ages a long loose flowing gown or tunic worn as an outergarment. **4.** From 1817 to 1830, an outergarment or wrap; synonym for the *pelisse. Der.* Originally the robe meant all furniture and personal effects belonging to a person. Later it meant his collection of clothes; still later a *gown.*

=== **ROBES** ===

**bathrobe** **1.** Wraparound robe usually styled with long sleeves, a shawl collar, and held closed with a sash. Worn primarily by men and children, popular styles are made of plaid, plain wool or bathrobe cloth. **2.** Synonym for various types of robes.

**beach toga** Cover-up worn over a bathing suit, styled to match or contrast with bathing suit. Frequently made of terrycloth, sometimes of lace fabric. Also called *beach coat.*

**beach wrapup** Large square or rectangle of fabric frequently of terrycloth, wrapped around the body in various ways for protection after swimming or as fashion beachwear item.

**bed jacket** Waist-length jacket worn when sitting up in bed for breakfast or when recuperating from an illness. May match or contrast with nightgown. Popularized in 1920s and still used.

**breakfast coat** Contemporary name for BRUNCH COAT or DUSTER.

**brunch coat** Knee- or mid-calf-length, front-buttoned robe often in printed cotton worn in the daytime at home, popular since 1950s. Also called DUSTER or BREAKFAST COAT. *Der.* Named for meal combining "breakfast" and "lunch".

**caftan** Moroccan or mid-eastern-inspired garment similar to a long full dress with slit neckline decorated with embroidery, and long bell-shaped sleeves. Introduced for at-home wear for men and women in mid-1960s. Also spelled *kaftan.* Some original robes are imported from Morocco; others are made domestically.

**cocoon** Luxurious hip-length robe with large batwing sleeve and blouson back with the open front usually banded in a constrasting color. Also see COATS category.

**djellaba** (jel-a-ba) Loose garment, sometimes hooded, derived from Moroccan man's cloak. It was popular in 1960s along with the *caftan*, still worn by women as a housecoat or hostess robe.

**dressing gown** See DRESSING ROBE.

**dressing r. 1. Men:** Term more generally used for a man's bathrobe usually lined and styled in a silk, rayon, or nylon fabric. Made in wraparound style with long shawl collar and sash. **2. Women:** Voluminous wraparound always worn in the boudoir. Also called a *dressing gown.*

**duster** Housecoat, usually made in short length of lightweight fabrics with zipper, buttons, or snaps in front. See BRUNCH COAT. Also see COATS category.

**happi coat** Hip-length jacket made in kimono style of brightly printed fabric, copied from knee-length jackets worn by Japanese laborers. Frequently with printed medallion on back in imitation of original Japanese jackets which had symbol of employer on the back. Used in U.S. as beach coats from 1950s to 1960s. Also spelled *happie.*

**BATHROBE** **BRUNCH COAT**

**HOUSECOAT** **KIMONO** **SHAVE COAT**

**hostess r.** Full-length robe fastening in front, frequently with zipper, made in elaborate fabrics and worn for entertaining at home. Also called *hostess gown* or *hostess coat.*

**housecoat** Informal robe worn at home. See BRUNCH COAT and LOUNGING ROBE.

**kabuki r.** Short-length man's or woman's wraparound robe styled like a kimono closed with a sash.

**kimono** Type of robe cut like the Japanese kimono with *kimono sleeves* and generally made in a scenic or floral printed fabric reminiscent of Japan. Sometimes closed with frogs rather than buttons. Very popular in the early 19th c. and used continually since. Also see alphabetical listing.

**lounging r.** Term applied to any woman's robe, often a long one, worn informally at home for relaxation.

**monk's r.** Full-length, flowing robe with bell sleeve, frequently made with a hooded cowl neckline and a rope belt. *Der.* Inspired by a monk's habit.

**negligee** (neg-le-zhay) Flowing informal woman's robe of delicate fabric with trimming of lace, ruffles, etc., often worn with a matching nightgown.

**peignoir** (pai-nwar) Feminine type of robe made in a sheer or elaborate fabric only intended for the boudoir; usually made with a matching gown. *Der.* French, *peignoir,* "to comb," as it was originally worn when combing the hair.

**shave coat** Man's knee-length wraparound bathrobe frequently matched to pajamas.

**travel coat** Nylon jersey robe which packs easily and does not wrinkle.

**wraparound r.** Any robe made in wraparound style.

**robe à l'anglaise** (ah long-glaze) See GOWN À L'ANGLAISE.

**robe à la française** (ah la frawn-saiz) See GOWN À LA FRANÇAISE.

**robe à la Piedmontese** See PIEDMONT GOWN.

**robe de chambre** **1.** 17th c. term for man's informal style of dressing intended for occasions other than court functions, receptions, and ceremonies. Considered a *deshabille* style of dress. **2.** 19th c. term for woman's dress suitable for informal occasions or in the boudoir. Also called a *breakfast wrapper* in 1880s.

**robe gironnée** Loose-fitting dress worn in 15th c. with *pipe-organ pleats* at waistline.

**robe redingote** Dress of 1830s and 1840s with collar and lapels on bodice, and skirt opening in front to show an *underskirt.* Also see REDINGOTE.

**robes of state** See CORONATION ROBES.

**Robespierre collar** (robes-pee-air) Man's coat collar worn about 1790, coming up high at back of neck and then turned down with jabot showing in front, similar to REGENCY COLLAR on a double-breasted coat. *Der.* Named for Maximillian François Marie Isadore de Robespierre, French lawyer and Revolutionist, executed in 1794.

**robin front** 19th c. term for bodice with trimming from shoulder to waist forming a deep V.

**robings** See ROBINS.

**Robin Hood hat** Hat with high peaked crown, brim turned up in back, down in front, and trimmed with one long feather. *Der.* From hat worn by Robin Hood, legendary British outlaw of the 12th c.

**robins** Wide flat trimmings used in 18th and 19th c. around neck and down front of woman's bodice, sometimes continued down sides of open overskirt. Also spelled *robings.*

**roccelo** See ROQUELAURE.

**Rochas, Marcel** See APPENDIX/DESIGNERS.

**rock crystal** See GEMS.

**rocker** British young man of late 1950s who wore special styles. *Der.* So called because "rockers" liked the rock and roll music of Elvis Presley. See LOOKS.

**rocklo** See ROQUELAURE.

**rococo embroidery** See EMBROIDERIES.

**roculo** See ROQUELAURE.

**rodeo suit** See SPORT SUITS.

**roll** **1.** 15th c. term for the circular pad made when converting the man's chaperon into a hat. Also see BOURRELET #1. **2.** 16th and 17th c. term for pad used to raise the front hair up from forehead. Also spelled *rowle*.

**rolled collar** See COLLARS.

**ROLLED HEM**

**rolled hem** See HEMS.

**roller** See HATS.

**roller print** See PRINTS.

**rollers** See ROLLUPS.

**roller skate** See BOOTS.

**roll farthingale** Tubular-shaped skirt supported by means of a BUM ROLL tied around the waist.

**rolling ring** See RINGS.

**rolling stockings/hose** See ROLLUPS.

**rollio** See ROULEAU.

**roll point collar** Similar to wing collar but overturned point is not pressed down. Worn by men in late 19th and early 20th c.

**roll sleeve** See SLEEVES.

**roll-up** See CUFFS and SLEEVES.

**ROLL-UPS**

**rollups** Man's stockings pulled up over knee of breeches and folded over in wide band. Worn in late 17th to mid 18th c. Also called *rollers*, *rolling stockings*, or *hose*.

**romaine** Semi-sheer, dull lustered fabric having a crepey texture made in plain weave. Crepe twisted ply yarns made of acetate and rayon are used in warp and filling. Originally made of silk, wool may also be used. Also called *romaine crepe*.

**Roman collar** See COLLARS.

**Roman lace** See RETICELLA under LACES.

**Roman leggings** See FEMORALIA.

**Roman stripes** See STRIPES.

**romantic styles** Feminine styles for women with lace, frills, and ribbon. See ROMANTIC LOOK under LOOKS.

**Romeo hairstyle** See HAIRSTYLES.

**Romeos** See SLIPPERS.

**rompers** See PAJAMAS, PANTS, and SPORT SUITS.

**rope chain** See CHAIN.

**rope necklace** See NECKLACES.

**Roquelaure** (roke-lowr) Man's knee-length to full-length heavy cloak of 18th c. often fur-trimmed and lined with bright-colored silk. Usually made with cape collar and back vent for riding horseback. *Der.* From Antoine Gastone Jean-Baptiste, le duc de Roquelaure (1656–

1738), minister of wardrobe under Louis XIV. Also spelled *roculo, roccelo, rocklo.*

**rosary**   See BEADS.

**Rosebery collar**   Man's detachable collar of mid-1890s of white linen, 3″ high in back, with rounded points in front. *Der.* Named for 5th Earl of Rosebery, British statesman, author and Prime Minister, 1894–1895.

**rose cut**   See GEM CUTS.

**rosehube**   See ROSENKÄPLI.

**Rosenadel**   Two-pronged, curved, ornamental hat pin used by Schwyz women of Switzerland to hold the *Rosenkäpli.*

**Rosenkäpli**   Native lace cap worn by Schwyz women in Switzerland. Cap shaped like two open upstanding fans dipping down in the front to show the central portion which was decorated with flowers. The *rosehube*, a small box, is placed in the center to hold long braids of hair were coiled underneath. See ROSENADEL.

**rose-point lace**   See LACES.

**rose quartz**   See GEMS.

**Roser, Maud**   See APPENDIX/DESIGNERS.

**rosette   1.** Ornament arranged like a rose, usually ribbon arranged in standing loops or flattened into a formal pattern. Used to trim shoes in 17th c. and from then on to trim dresses and hats. See SHOE ROSES. **2.** Spotted marking on leopard fur, resembling a paw mark. **3.** Mark left on ostrich skin when quill is removed.

**rotonde**   Woman's short or three-quarter length circular *cape* of 1850s and 1860s made of lace or of same material as dress.

**rouche**   See RUCHING.

**Rouff, Maggy**   See APPENDIX/DESIGNERS.

**Rough Rider shirt**   Khaki shirt buttoned down the front and made with standing collar, breast pockets with flaps, and epaulets, *Der.* Similar to shirts worn by Theodore Roosevelt,

**ROTONDE**

Leonard Wood, and their volunteer cavalry regiment in Cuba during Spanish-American War in 1898.

**rouleaux** (roo-low)   Tubular-shaped trimming stitched at regular intervals to make puffs of fabric. Used around hems of women's skirts in the 1820s. Also called *rollio.*

**roulettes**   See PIPES.

**ROUND DRESS, 1870**

**round dress** Term used in 18th to mid-19th c. for a full-length dress cut without a train, as differentiated from a dress slit up the front with underskirt showing. In the 18th c. occasionally had a train, in the 19th c. always without a train. Also called a *round gown, closed robe,* or *closed gown.*

**round-eared cap** Woman's white cambric or lace indoor cap worn from 1730s to 1760s which curved around face and was finished with a ruffle. The shallow back was pulled together with a drawstring. Sometimes with side LAPPETS pinned up or tied loosely under chin. Sometimes called COIF.

**round hat** Term used for hat that was worn in place of the *tricorn* in 1770s.

**round hose** *Trunk hose* worn from 1550s to 1610 which were padded in an onion-shaped style. Also see BOMBAST.

**roundlet** **1.** 17th c. term used to describe the roll of the 15th c. *chaperon* worn with a stuffed roll encircling the head and tail of *becca* hanging at side of face. Also called *berretino.* **2.** Man's small round hat of the 18th c. with attached streamer for carrying it over shoulder.

**round pocket** See POCKETS.

**round seam** See OVERSEAM under GLOVE SEAMS.

**Rovalia®** See MUTATION MINK under FURS.

**rowle** See ROLL.

**Roxalane bodice** Term used from late 1820s on for low-necked bodice trimmed with wide pleated folds meeting at an angle at the waistline. Bodice had a central bone which held pleats in place.

**Roxalane sleeve** Bouffant sleeve worn from the late 1820s on made by tying a fringed band around a long full sleeve above the elbow—dividing it into two puffs.

**Roxburgh muff** Woman's muff carried in 1816 made of swansdown fabric sometimes gathered at intervals and trimmed with bands of white satin.

**royal blue** Bright purplish blue.

**Royal George stock** Man's black velvet stock worn in 1820s and 1830s, made with satin over the velvet at base of neck and tied in bow in front.

**Royal Stewart tartan** See TARTANS.

**Roy, Hippolyte** See APPENDIX/DESIGNERS.

**RTW** Abbreviation for the READY-TO-WEAR clothing industry.

**ruana** See PONCHOS.

**rubakha** Traditional loose-fitting cotton or linen blouse worn by Russian women. Made with long sleeves gathered at wrist with cuff or frill. Embroidered on standing band collar, on upper sleeve, and sometimes on center front slit. Embroidery has regional variations. Worn with SARAFAN or PANEVA.

**rubber boot** See BOOTS.

**rubber mask** See MASKS.

**rubbers** Waterproof lightweight shoes which pull on over regular shoes in inclement weather. Also called *overshoes.* Also see STORM RUBBERS and TOE RUBBERS.

**rubber shoes** See DUCKS® under SHOES.

**Rubens hat** High-crowned woman's hat of 1870s and 1880s with brim turned up on one side, sometimes trimmed with feathers and bows. *Der.* Named for hats painted by Flemish master, Peter Paul Rubens, 1577–1640.

**ruby** See GEMS.

**Ruby Keeler shoe** See SHOES.

**ruching** Trimming made by pleating a strip of lace, ribbon, net, fine muslin, or silk so that it ruffles on both sides. Made by stitching through the center of pleating. Also spelled *rouche, ruche.*

**ruff** **1.** Pleated stiff white collar of varying widths, usually edged in lace, projecting from

**RUFF #1**

neckline like a wheel around neck. Worn by men and women from 1560s to 1640s supported underneath by RABATO, SUPPORTASSE, or UNDER-PROPPER, usually made with *pipe-organ pleats* or regular convolutions. See FALLING RUFF, BETSIE RUFF, CHERUSSE, and CARTWHEEL RUFF. **2.** Narrower versions of ruff used at wrist.

**ruffle** Strip of cloth, lace, or ribbon gathered along one edge or cut in a curve to produce a ripple. Used to trim neckline, wrist, or hem of apparel. Also see FLOUNCE.

**rugby shirt** See KNIT SHIRTS.

**rugby shorts** See SHORTS.

**Rumanian embroidery** See HOLBEIN under EMBROIDERIES.

**Rumanian stitch** See ORIENTAL under STITCHES.

**rumba** Variant of RHUMBA. See DRESSES, PANTIES, and SLEEVES.

**rummage sale clothes** Used and antique clothing usually gathered and sold under church sponsorship. Sales are usually held in spring and fall for fund raising.

**rump furbelow** Stuffed pad forming a bustle worn in the late 18th c. Also called *rump*. Compare with CORK RUMP and FALSE RUMP.

**running shoe** See SHOES.

**running stitch** See STITCHES.

**run proof** Hosiery and knit term for items made with specially interlocked stitches which withstand runs.

**run resistant** Hosiery and knit term for stitches with locked or displaced loops which inhibit runs, but do not prevent them.

**Russell, Lillian** (1861–1922) American singer and actress noted for her spectacular costumes with tiny waists, full bosoms, and hips—also for her large hats. She represented the fashion ideal at the turn of the 20th c.

**Russian blouse** See COSSACK BLOUSE under BLOUSES.

**Russian blouse suit** **1. For boys:** A long belted blouse with box pleats in front, sometimes made with a sailor collar, sometimes with a turndown collar. Worn with knickers which came below the knees. **2. For girls:** A long overblouse, sometimes with Russian styling, worn over a full circular skirt. Worn during the early 20th c.

**Russian braid** See SOUTACHE BRAID.

**Russian collar** See COSSACK COLLAR under COLLARS.

**Russian embroidery** See EMBROIDERIES.

**Russian leather** See LEATHERS.

**Russian style dress** Two-piece dress of 1890s with knee-length tunic over full-length skirt, high *Russian collar*, and embroidery trim around neck, cuffs, down side of blouse front, and around hem. Also see RUSSIAN SHIRTDRESS under DRESSES.

**Russian styles** Clothing and accessories copied from those worn in Russia. See COSSACK under BLOUSES, COLLARS, DRESSES, HATS, and NECKLINES. Also see ZHIVAGO and RUSSIAN under LOOKS, and SOUTACHE under BRAIDS.

**Russian Table Portrait diamond** See DIAMONDS.

**Rykiel, Sonia** See APPENDIX/DESIGNERS.

**S** Letter designation for *small* size used along with MEDIUM, LARGE, and EXTRA LARGE for men, women and children. See SMALL. Also see SHORT.

**S.A.** **1.** Abbreviation for *Seventh Avenue*, New York City garment district, coined by trade newspaper *Women's Wear Daily.* **2.** In 1940s term for sex appeal, as exemplified by Lana Turner, in the movie "sweater girl."

**sabaton** Broad-toed armor of mid-16th c. strapped over top of foot. Also called *bear paw* or *duckbill solleret.* Also spelled *sabatayne.* Also see SOLLERET.

**sable** See FURS.

**sabot** (sa-bo) **1.** Shoe carved from one piece of wood, worn by peasants in France, Belgium, Spain, and Portugal. Also worn with Dutch national costume. **2.** Clog shoe with thick wood sole made with closed leather vamp or leather bands across instep and open heel.

**sabot sleeve** (sa-bo) **1.** Sleeve used on 18th c. dresses, *e.g., gown à la polonaise,* tight-fitting to elbow, flared below elbow and trimmed with ruffles. **2.** Sleeve with single or double puff above elbow used on women's evening dresses from late 1820s to 1836. Also used from 1836 to 1840 on day dresses and then called *Victoria sleeve.*

**sabot-strap shoe** See SHOES.

**Sabrina neckline** See NECKLINES.

**sack** **1.** 16th c. loose-fitting gown for country wear. **2.** Dress mentioned in *Pepy's Diary* in 1669. Fashionable in France at beginning of 18th c. (about 1704) and popular until 1755. Popular in England from 1720 to 1780. Main feature was the full back or *sack-back* with two large box pleats stitched from neckband to shoulders and then hanging free to make a full skirt. From 1720 to 1730 the bodice was fitted at sides and front. After 1750, skirt was split up the front to reveal an underskirt. From 1770s pleats in back were sometimes stitched to the waist as in *robe à l'Anglaise,* or loose as in *robe à la Piedmontese.* Also called *Adrienne* and *sack gown.* Compare with WATTEAU BACK and WATTEAU DRESS. **3.** Woman's or child's loose-fitting jacket of 1896. Also spelled *sac, sacque.*

**sack-back** See SACK #2.

**sack coat** See STROLLER under JACKETS.

**sack dress** See CHEMISE under DRESSES.

**sack overcoat** Man's above-the-knee, loose-fitting overcoat worn from 1840s to about 1875. Made with sleeves wide at wrist, *welt pockets,* and back cut in one piece with center slit. The edges of coat were double-stitched or bound. In 1860s closed higher and styled with three- or four-button closing, narrow lapels, optional

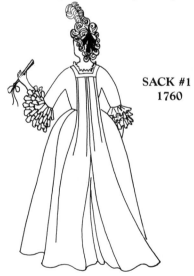

**SACK #1**
**1760**

pockets, and sometimes trimmed with velvet at collar, cuffs, and lapels.

**sack suit**   Man's single-breasted daytime suit of early 20th c. Made with unfitted long jacket having wide shoulders. Pants were cut wide in legs and at hems.

**sacque**   **1.** See SACK #1, #2, and #3. **2.** Layette item of late 19th and early 20th c. for an infant. Styled like a small jacket usually having ribbon ties for closing. **3.** See DRESSING SACQUE.

**saddle**   Extra piece of leather sewed over in-step of oxford shoe, usually of contrasting color or texture, *e.g.*, black or brown on white shoes. See SADDLE under OXFORDS. ALSO SEE HAND-BAGS, SEAMS, SHOES, SLEEVES, and STITCHES.

**saddle coat**   See POMMEL SLICKER.

**saddle leather**   See LEATHERS.

**saddle shoulder**   See SHOULDERS.

**saddle-stitched seam**   See GLOVE SEAMS.

**sadra**   Sacred shirt worn by the Parsis men and women of India.

**safari clothes**   Garments adapted from, or similar to the *bush jacket* worn in South Africa by hunters on safaris. See BELTS, COATS, DRESSES, HANDBAGS, HATS, LOOKS, SPORT JACK-ETS, SHIRTS, and BELLOWS under POCKETS.

**safeguard**   **1.** Overskirt worn by women when riding horseback to protect regular skirts from soil. Term used from 16th to 18th c. Also called FOOT MANTLE and in western England called *seggard*. **2.** Man's colored apron worn by bakers and tradesmen from 16th to 18th c. **3.** Term for *swathing band* for infant in early 18th c. Also see SWADDLING CLOTHES.

**safety**   See GLASSES, SHOES, and TOES.

**safety pin**   Elliptical pin with covered head to sheath the point, introduced from Denmark in late 1870s. Also see PINS.

**saffron**   Bright orange-yellow color with the dye obtained from dried pistils and stamens of the flower of the Autumn crocus.

**sagum**   Woolen blanket made out of a rectangle of cloth worn as a cape pinned on shoulder. Originally worn by ancient Celts and Germanic peoples. Later worn by Roman soldiers in daytime and used as a cover at night.

**sailcloth**   **1.** Durable heavy canvas fabric made in a rib weave. Previously made of all cotton or cotton and linen. **2.** Medium-weight fabric usually made in all cotton, sometimes striped. Used for sportswear.

**sailor**   Term used to describe clothes and ac-cessories popular since 1860s inspired by uni-forms worn by British, French, and U.S. Navy. See JACK TAR SUIT, SAILOR SUIT, COLLARS, DRESSES, HATS, PANTS, SCARFS, SHORTS, and MIDDY BLOUSE under BLOUSES.

**sailor's reef knot**   Common double knot or square knot used on sailor ties in U.S. Navy. Used for men's neckties from 1870 on, most fashionable in 1890s.

**sailor suit**   **1.** Boy's suit inspired by French and British sailors' uniforms consisting of *middy blouse* with braid-trimmed square collar in back, plus baggy *knickerbockers*, or Danish *trousers* introduced in 1860s. Also see JACK TAR SUIT. **2.** Girls' two-piece dress with similar *middy blouse* and pleated skirt popular from 1880s until 1930s and worn at intervals since.

1891        **SAILOR SUIT**        1906

**Saint Cyr, Claude**   See APPENDIX/DESIGNERS.

**St. Gall**   See LACES.

**Saint George cross** See CRUSADER'S CROSS under NECKLACES.

**Saint Laurent, Yves** See APPENDIX/ DESIGNERS and HELMETS.

**St. Tropez skirt** See SKIRTS.

**sakellarides** See EGYPTIAN COTTON.

**sallet** Helmet worn in 15th c. by Germans, French, and British, usually cast in one piece in pot-like shape flaring somewhat at neck in front and sometimes in back. Covered entire face with small slit to see through, sometimes had a moveable visor. Also spelled *celata, salade, salet*.

**Sally Jess® bag** See HANDBAGS.

**salmah** See SIMLAH.

**salon dresses** Department-store term for expensive dresses made by well-known designers sold in a special room in department store. Dresses are not hung on view in salesroom but brought out by salespeople and sometimes shown on live models.

**salt-box pocket** Term used in 1790s for man's narrow rectangular flapped waistcoat pocket.

**salvar** See SHALWAR.

**Salvation Army bonnet** High-crowned black straw bonnet with short front brim raised off forehead to show a pale-blue lining. Had dark-blue ribbon around crown and tied under chin worn by women of Salvation Army, a religious and charitable organization.

**salwar** See SHALWAR.

**samarra/samarre** See CHAMARRE.

**Sam Browne belt** See BELTS.

**samite** Rich heavy silk brocade fabric, sometimes made with gold and silver yarns, used in Middle Ages for robes of state.

**sampot** Length of colored silk, wrapped about waist and draped to form trousers. Worn by men and women in southern Cambodia (Kampuchea) as part of national dress.

**Sanchez, Fernando** See APPENDIX/ DESIGNERS.

**Sancy diamond** See DIAMONDS.

**sandal** **1.** Type of shoe held on the foot by means of straps or a projection between the toes. Usually made with an open shank and frequently toeless and heeless, or consisting of a sole held to the foot with straps. Worn since earliest times—gold sandals have been found in Egyptian tombs. Greeks and Romans wore many types of sandals. See CREPIDA. During the Middle Ages sandals were worn only by the peasants. In the 16th c. worn only by monks in monastic orders, pilgrims, and by sovereigns at coronations. During the 1920s and 1930s introduced for evening wear, sportswear, and day wear. **2.** Popular foot covering worn in Japan. Also see GETA and ZORI. *Der.* Greek, *sandalon*.

■■■■■■ **SANDALS** ■■■■■■

**alpargata** (ahl-par-gah-ta) Sandal worn in Spain and South America with rope sole and canvas upper only around the heel. Fastened to foot by cord coming from sole in front, crossing at instep, threaded through holes in upper and fastened around ankle.

**ankle-strap s.** Medium- to high-heeled sandal held on with a strap around the ankle. Frequently has a platform sole. Popular in the 1930s and 1940s, and worn at intervals since.

**clog** **1.** Thick wooden or cork sole fastened to foot by various strap arrangements, popular for beachwear in late 1930s and for street wear in late 1960s and 1970s. Also see SHOES. **2.** Heelless shoe with thick wooden sole resembling *sabot*, imported mainly from Sweden during late 1960s and early 1970s. **3.** From medieval times to the 19th c., a term synonymous with PATTENS. See alphabetical listing.

**crossover thong s.**  See THONG SANDAL #3.

**discotheque s.**  Actually a sole with a small heel, fastened to the foot by means of a few narrow straps. Popular for dancing at discotheques in the mid and late 1960s. *Der.* French, "record playing."

**exercise s.**  Vinyl sandal held on with two straps. Foot rests on sole made up of tiny rounded projections which massage the foot. Introduced in early 1980s. Also see SCHOLL's® EXERCISE SANDAL.

**flip-flops**  See ZORI.

**Ganymede s.** (gan-e-meed)  Open sandal derived from Ancient Greek style, with vertical straps from the sole extending up the legs and crossed at intervals around the leg with additional straps. Introduced in 1960s to wear with minidresses. *Der.* Named for the beautiful boy who was the cupbearer of the gods in Greek mythology.

**geta**  Japanese sandal elevated by means of wooden blocks under the sole and fastened to foot by two straps, meeting between first and second toes, curved to fasten at sides of sole. Adapted for beachwear in 1960s.

**gladiator s.**  Flat sandal with several wide cross straps holding sole to foot, and one wide strap around ankle. Introduced in late 1960s. *Der.* Copied from sandals worn in Roman arena by "gladiators."

**huarache** (wah-rah-chee)  Mexican sandal consisting of closely woven leather thongs forming vamp, made with sling back and flat heel.

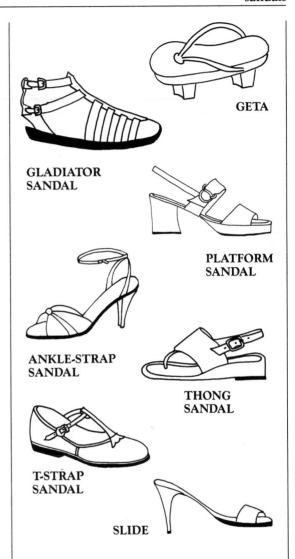

GLADIATOR SANDAL

GETA

PLATFORM SANDAL

ANKLE-STRAP SANDAL

THONG SANDAL

T-STRAP SANDAL

SLIDE

Popular casual shoe in the U.S. for all ages and both sexes.

**kalso**  Danish open sandal with platform sole, carved from laminated mahogany, finished with rubber walking sole and held on with two wide straps—one over instep and one around heel.

**kolhapuri s.**  Leather thong-type sandal imported from India, made of hand-tooled water buffalo hide. When sandals are first worn in the shower, the leather becomes permanently shaped to the sole of the foot. Also spelled *kolhapure, kolhapur.*

**open-shank s.** High-, medium-, or low-heeled sandal shaped like a *d'Orsay pump* with a strap around the ankle or over the instep frequently heelless and toeless. Popular style since the late 1930s.

**platform s.** Open-type sandal with platform sole usually made with high heel. Popular in 1940s and 1970s.

**Scholl's® exercise s.** A trademark of Scholl, Inc. for a wooden sandal with sole shaped to fit foot and special carving underneath the ball of the foot for gripping the foot when walking; made with only one wide strap over front of foot, buckled to adjust the size, and an outer sole of ridged rubber. Action of foot on carved sole when walking provides healthful exercise. Introduced in late 1960s, continuing into 1980s.

**slide** Toeless open-back sandal with wedgie sole of various heights or regular heel in all heights made of wood or leather.

**slingback thong s.** See THONG SANDAL #2.

**tatamis** Thong-type sandal with non-flexible rubber sole having a slight wedge. Top of sole is made of woven straw matting. Thong straps are made of wide pieces of durable velvet. *Der.* Japanese, *tatami,* "woven straw mat."

**thong s. 1.** Flat, often heelless sandal, held to the foot by narrow strips of leather coming up between first and second toes and attached to sole at either side. Popular for beachwear since 1960s. **2.** In early 1980s strap was added around heel then called *slingback thong.* **3.** Thong sandal with complete strap around big toe is called *crossover thong sandal.*

**T-strap s.** Sandal made with a strap coming up from the vamp to join second strap across the instep forming a T. May have high or low heel with open or closed shank. Popular since 1920s.

**zori** Sandal made with sponge rubber sole fastened to the foot by two straps which come up between the first and second toes and fasten to the side of the sole. Copied from the original Japanese *zori.* Also called *flip-flops.* Also see alphabetical listing.

---

**sandalfoot hose** See HOSE and PANTYHOSE.

**sandwich-board jumper** See JUMPERS.

**Sanforized®** Registered trademark of The Sanforized Company, a division of Cluett, Peabody & Co., Inc., appearing on fabrics with a residual shrinkage of not more than one percent, despite repeated laundering.

**sans-culottes** (sahn koo-lon) Nickname for those opposing the monarchy during the French Revolution, *i.e.,* those who wore *trousers*—the common people, instead of *breeches*—the aristocrats. *Der.* French, literally "without breeches."

**Sant'Angelo, Giorgio** See APPENDIX/DESIGNERS.

**santon** Colored silk cravat worn with small *ruff,* by women in 1820s. Also called a *sautoir.*

**sapphire** See GEMS.

**saradi** Sleeveless waistcoat worn over the *anga* by Mohammedan men of India.

**sarafan** Dress formerly worn by women in Russia made with a full pleated skirt gathered to a high-waisted, sleeveless bodice with either a high round or low square neckline, and buttoned down front to hem. Usually made of brocade and worn by "boyâr class," latter by upper classes on their estates. Peasants wore the same style in wool. Also see RUBAKHA.

**sarape** See SERAPE.

**sard** See CARNELIAN under GEMS.

**Sardinian sac** Loose-fitting single-breasted man's overcoat of mid-19th c. Made with square-cut collar, no lapels, and full bell-shaped sleeves. Worn flung over shoulders and secured by cord with tassel in front.

**sardonyx**   See GEMS.

**sari** (sah-ree)   **1.** Woman's outer garment consisting of a long length of cotton or silk wrapped around the waist and pleated at the side to form a skirt. One end is thrown over shoulder or used to cover head. Worn mostly in India and Pakistan. **2.** The fabric from which the Indian garment is made. A sheer, lightweight, lustrous fabric made predominantly of silk with some cotton added. Made with beautiful borders, frequently in gold, which run along one side and one end of the fabric. Woven about 12′ long and 36″ to 50″ wide. May be hand or machine made. Less expensive ones may be woven in cotton in a long length and cut to individual lengths. Also spelled *sarrie, saree.*

**sarmah**   See CARMA.

**sarong** (seh-rong)   Long straight wraparound skirt made of bright-colored *batik-printed* fabric with deep fold in front, held on by scarf around waist. Worn by men and women of the Malay Archipelago. Adapted as a beach style and popularized by actress Dorothy Lamour in films of the 1930s and 1940s. Also see DRESSES, GIRDLES, SKIRTS, and SWIMSUITS. *Der.* Copied from Indonesian native dress.

**sash**   See BELTS.

**sash ring**   Large ring on a chain suspended from a belt at the hip in late 1860s. Overskirt was pulled through ring to drape the skirt.

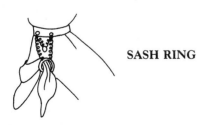

**SASH RING**

**Sassoon hairstyle**   See HAIRSTYLES.

**satchel**   See HANDBAGS.

**sateen**   Smooth glossy cotton fabric made in the sateen weave with floating fillings on the right side, given a lustrous finish, and used mainly for linings. Formerly spelled *satine.* Also see SATEEN WEAVE under SATIN WEAVE.

**sateen weave**   See SATIN WEAVE.

**satin**   Smooth lustrous silk fabric woven with floating yarns in the warp in many variations: *a)* woven with a crepe back, and called *crepe-back satin; b)* finished to be rather stiff in texture and called *panne satin; c)* finished with a dull nubbed surface and a satin back and called *antique satin.* Made of silk, rayon, acetate, nylon, or combinations of these yarns. *Der.* Name derived from *Zaytoun,* now Canton, China, from which fabrics were shipped in the Middle Ages.

**satin-backed ribbon**   See RIBBON.

**satine**   See SATEEN.

**satin stitch**   See STITCHES.

**satin stripe**   See STRIPES.

**satin weave**   Weave in which the warp, and sometimes the filling, float over several yarns going in the opposite direction. For smooth satin fabrics, the *warp* yarns float over five to eleven *filling* yarns. In *sateen fabric* the *filling* floats over four warps. This construction is sometimes called the *sateen weave.*

**SATIN WEAVE**

**sauna suit**   See SPORT SUITS.

**sausage curl**   See CURLS.

**sautoir** (sow-twar)   **1.** See NECKLACES. **2.** See SANTON.

**Savile Row**   Street in London's West End where many of the finest men's custom tailoring shops are located. They cater to wealthy internationals, stressing quality and conservatism, since Henry Poole & Co. opened in 1843.

**Savile Row look**  Conservative, elegant look for men reflecting influence of London Savile Row tailors. Also see BRITISH LOOK under LOOKS.

**saw-toothed hem**  See HEMS.

**saxony**  **1.** Superior merino wool from Saxony, Germany. **2.** Type of knitting yarn made of tightly twisted three-ply yarns which are vegetable dyed. Imported to U.S. in 1850s from Saxony, Germany, where manufactured. **3.** Soft luxurious fabric made in England and Scotland originally of woolen or worsted yarns from Saxony, Germany. Now fine, soft-finished woolen fabrics made from fine wools. *Der.* From Saxony, Germany.

**Saxony lace**  See PLAUEN under LACES.

**saya**  Bright-colored skirt with train worn with the *camisa* blouse by Philippine women.

**Scaasi, Arnold**  See APPENDIX/DESIGNERS.

**scabilonians**  Man's *underpants* worn in latter half of 16th c. Also spelled *scavilones*.

**scaling hose**  *Trunk hose* similar to *Venetians*, popular in latter half of 16th c. Also called *scalings*.

**scallop**  **1.** The shell of a mollusk used in ornamentation. See COCKLE HAT. **2.** One of series of curves or circle segments—like one edge of the scallop shell—forming an ornamental edge on fabric or lace. See HEMS.

**scalpette**  (scal-pet) Term used in mid-1870s for woman's hairpiece composed of extra curls attached to an invisible net worn on top of head.

**scarab**  A beetle, regarded as the symbol of immortality by the ancient Egyptians, used in stylized designs on fabrics or carved from gemstones with inscriptions on the undersides. Semi-precious stones carved with scarabs are

still used in *rings* and *bracelets*, especially popular in the U.S. in the late 1940s.

**Scarborough ulster**  Caped and hooded man's *ulster* without sleeves worn in early 1890s.

**scarf**  (pl. *scarfs* or *scarves*) **1.** Decorative or utilitarian accessory worn draped around the shoulders, the neck, or over the head for warmth or adornment. May be square, oblong, or triangular and made of knitted, crocheted, or woven fabric. **2.** A decorative sash worn diagonally from shoulder to opposite hip, like a BALDERICK. **3.** Extremely large *cravat* which spread over shirt front and fastened with a decorative tie pin worn by men in 1830s. **4.** Tradename for late-19th c. necktie which was narrow in back and had wide hanging ends.

### ▰▰▰ SCARFS / SCARVES ▰▰▰

**Apache s.**  Man's small square or triangular scarf introduced in late 1960s for wear instead of a necktie. Worn knotted or pulled through a slide. *Der.* French slang for gangster or thug, especially as depicted by French nightclub dancers. The French word taken from the southwest American Indian tribe, thought to be very fierce.

**ascot s.**  Oblong scarf, frequently white, lapped over and worn loosely around neck by men and women. Reintroduced in late 1960s by St. Laurent, the Paris couturier, who emblazoned it with his initials, making it a status symbol. *Der.* Named for a scarf worn at Ascot racetrack in England.

**babushka**  (bah-boosh-ka) Triangular-shaped scarf or square folded diagonally, worn draped over head and tied under chin in manner of

Russian peasant woman. *Der.* Russian, "grandmother." So called because it was worn by older Russian immigrants to this country. Also called a KERCHIEF.

**bandanna** Large square cotton handkerchief, either red or blue with distinctive black and white design. Worn in late 19th and early 20th c., tied around the head or neck by workmen later adopted in all colors for wear with sport clothes. Also see alphabetical listing.

**boa** Woman's long tubular scarf usually made of feathers or fur. In 1890s made of lynx, fox, or sable worn with matching muff. Revived in late 1920s and again in early 1970s, especially in fur, *ostrich feathers*, or *marabou.*

**BOA**

**calligraphic s.** Letters of the alphabet arranged to form a pattern in much the same manner a picture is "drawn" on a typewriter by using x's and other characters. Introduced in late 1960s.

**designer s.** Scarf made in an elaborate design using beautiful or unusual colors. In the late 1960s it became popular to print the name of a famous company or designer on the scarfs which were then called SIGNATURE SCARFS.

**dog collar s.** Triangular or oblong scarf folded to go around neck twice bringing ends

back to the front where they are knotted or looped over.

**écharpe** (eh-sharp) Synonym for scarf. *Der.* French, "scarf."

**foulard s.** **1.** Scarf of silk twill, often made with small designs on plain ground. Originally imported from India. **2.** Originally a scarf, cravat, or necktie fabric.

**gele** Scarf 2½ yards long and ½ yard wide used as a headwrap. Inspiration comes from Yoruba, in west Africa, where wrapping of the scarf has different meanings, *e.g.*, indicating whether the woman is single or looking for husband.

**hacking s.** Long oblong scarf doubled and placed at back of neck. Both ends are then pulled through loop and hang down in front. *Der.* Long scarf, originally 72″ worn by four-in-hand coach drivers in Old England; popular at Oxford and Cambridge Universities in England in 1931 when it was worn by Prince of Wales, becoming a fad for U.S. college students in 1932.

**kerchief** Scarf worn as head or neck covering, usually a square folded into triangle with crossed ends fastened on chest. Also called NECKERCHIEF. Originally spelled *kerchner, kercheve, karcher.* See COVERCHIEF, FICHU, and NECKATEE in alphabetical listing.

**mantilla** See VEILS.

**muffler** **1.** Long scarf approximately 12″ wide; usually knitted, or woven of plaid or plain-colored wool, silk, or rayon. Worn from 19th c. to present. **2.** Fashionable for men made out of *foulard,* tie silk, and white silk for evening wear from 1920s to 1940s. **3.** See CHIN CLOAK in alphabetical listing.

**neckerchief** **1.** Triangular scarf, either cut in shape of a triangle or a square folded diagonally, worn by men and women in late 1960s

GELE

HACKING SCARF

MUFFLER

and early 1970s. Worn from 19th c. on by cowboys instead of a necktie. Also worn by Boy Scouts with uniforms. **2.** Late 14th to early 19th c., a square or oblong of fabric folded around the neck by women. **3.** In 19th c. term sometimes used for a large silk *cravat* worn by men and women.

**Paisley s. 1.** Square or oblong scarf made with paisley designs, featuring imprint of closed fist with little finger extended and delicate tracery, done in rich reds, rusts, beiges and browns. Usually made in an allover design. **2.** Unusual scarf featuring a shell design with elongated blocks around edge, Paisley print inside, and plain cream-colored center sprinkled with a few designs. Comes in 18″ × 62″ size and is copied from shawl in National Museum of American History's Costume Division of the Smithsonian Institution.

**ring s.** Oblong scarf with ends stitched together to form a circle. Worn with jewelry to form a collar on a dress in early 1950s.

**sailor s.** Square NECKERCHIEF, folded diagonally, worn under sailor collar and slipped through loop front of blouse or tied in a knot. Also called *sailor tie*.

**signature s.** Pure-silk scarf with couturier's name printed in one corner. The fashion started in Paris in 1960s by Balenciaga, Dior, and Saint Laurent—spread to Italy and U.S. as a status symbol for most prestigious designers. Also called DESIGNER SCARF.

**souvenir s.** Large square scarf, usually made of silk or rayon, imprinted with scene, picture, symbol, or words depicting a special place, *e.g.*, Miami, Paris. Usually bought by tourists to remind them of a special holiday spent at that place.

**stock** Oblong scarf worn loosely lapped over rather than tied. During 1968 introduced to be worn instead of *neckties* by men. See alphabetical listing.

**scarf pin** See STICKPIN under PINS.

**scarf slide** See NECKERCHIEF SLIDE.

**scavilones** See SCABILONIANS.

**scenic print** See PRINTS.

**scent bottle 1.** Small cut-crystal bottle of 1880s made with bronze stopper and attached to belt with sterling silver chain. **2.** Bottles used from Egyptian times for perfume. Made of glass by Venetians in 13th c. Made of glass in Bohemia, Silesia, and England in 16th c. Jewelers and goldsmiths made them in 17th and 18th c.

**SCENT BOTTLE, 1880**

In middle of 18th c. made of porcelain by Chelsea and Staffordshire china manufacturers. Made of pressed or molded glass and etched or engraved in late 19th c.

**schenti** Ancient Egyptian loincloth, sometimes pleated in center front and attached to narrow belt. Frequently shown in illustrations of Egyptian pharaohs. Also spelled *shendot*, *shenti*, *shendyt*.

**Scherrer, Jean-Louis** See APPENDIX/ DESIGNERS.

**Schiaparelli, Elsa** See APPENDIX/DESIGNERS.

**Schiffli embroidery** (sif-lee) See EMBROIDERIES.

**Scholl's® exercise sandals** See SANDALS.

**Schön, Mila** See APPENDIX/DESIGNERS.

**schoolgirl look** See LOOKS.

**school ring** See CLASS RING under RINGS.

**school sweater** See LETTER SWEATER under SWEATERS.

**schreinerizing** Finish used on cotton fabrics to produce a high luster. Done by passing fabric through two sets of heated rollers—one engraved with fine lines the other a plain roller. The engraved roller makes ridges on the fabric which increase the reflection of light but are invisible to the eye.

**scissoring** See SLASHING.

**scoop bonnet** Bonnet popular in 1840s with wide stiff brim shaped like a flour scoop attached to soft crown. *Der.* From old-fashioned "flour scoop."

**scoop neckline** See NECKLINES.

**scooter shorts/skirt** See SKORT® under SHORTS or SKIRTS.

**Scotchgard®** Registered trademark of Minnesota Mining and Manufacturing for a fluoride-based finish used on fabrics to repel grease and water stains.

**Scotch plaid** Yarn-dyed fabrics woven in plaids which represent the various clans of Scotland. See TARTANS.

**Scotch suit** See HIGHLAND SUIT.

**Scottie** See HATS.

**Scottish Highlander costume** See HIGHLAND DRESS.

**scrambled eggs** See ASTRONAUT'S CAP under CAPS.

**scratch wig** Man's *bob wig* worn from 1740 to end of 18th c. made with one long hanging curl, covering only back of head. Arranged with the natural hair brushed over top of wig. Also called *scratch bob.*

**screen print** See SILK SCREEN PRINT and TOPS.

**screw earrings** See EARRINGS.

**scrub suit** Pants and long tunic top with round or V-neck and long sleeves, slit down entire back, with ties at neck and waist in back. Worn with matching pants. Made of 100% cotton and worn by physicians when operating on patients and sterilized after each wearing. In early 1970s adapted in modified form—slip-on top with short sleeves and pants—used for casual wear by men.

**scuba mask** See MASKS.

**scuba suit** See WET SUIT under SPORT SUITS.

**scuff** See SLIPPERS.

**sculptured heel** See HEELS.

**scye** (ski) See ARMSEYE.

**Sea Island cotton** Excellent grade of long staple cotton raised in hot, humid climates. Originally brought from the West Indies to islands off the coast of southeastern U.S. Also see ANGUILLA COTTON.

**seal/sealskin** See FUR SEAL and HAIR SEAL under FURS and LEATHERS.

**sea legs** See SWIMSUITS.

**seam**   Two edges of fabric, leather, or other material joined by sewing in a variety of stitches, sometimes incorporating *bias binding, cording, piping* and other decorative trimming. Before sewing machines were invented, all seams were sewn by hand. Also see GLOVE SEAMS.

## SEAMS

**bound s.**   Edges of PLAIN SEAM bound with *bias binding.* Used particularly on seams of unlined jackets and around necklines, armholes, and jackets in contrasting color for decoration.

**broad-stitched s.**   Similar to TOP-STITCHED SEAM with two rows of top-stitching on either side of seam.

**clean-stitched s.**   PLAIN SEAM pressed open on wrong side of garment with the raw edges turned under and stitched so they will not ravel.

**corded s.**   Plain seam with cord inside bias binding inserted in seam before basting so that covered cord appears as decoration along the seam.

**double-stitched s.**   See TOP-STITCHED SEAM.

**fell s.**   See FLAT-FELLED SEAM.

**flat fell s.**   Two edges of fabric stitched together on right side. One edge is then cut close to seam, the other edge folded over cut edge. Both are then pressed flat and top-stitched showing two rows of stitching on outside. Also called *fell seam.*

**French s.**   Seam first stitched on right side of garment, trimmed, then stitched on inside of garment to cover raw edges. Used on transparent and lightweight fabrics that ravel.

**fused s.**   Seam made in plastic or vinyl by heating edges to be joined.

**lap s.**   Simplest seam used on shoe uppers made with one edge of leather placed on top of another and top-stitched. Also used for gloves. Also called *overlapped seam.*

**open-welt s.**   See TUCKED SEAM.

**overcast s.**   **1.** Plain seam pressed open on wrong side and each raw edge finished by overcast stitches to prevent raveling. **2.** Seam made on inside of garment with both raw edges overcast together either by hand or machine.

**overlapped s.**   See LAP SEAM.

**pinked s.**   Plain seam pressed open on wrong side and finished by trimming raw edges with a pinking shears to make saw-toothed edges that prevent raveling.

**piped s.**   Seam decorated by inserting piece of bias binding between two layers of fabric before stitching. Similar to a CORDED SEAM but with a flat rather than a rounded edge.

**plain s.**   Simple seam stitched on wrong side of garment usually pressed open. Used on a fabric that will not ravel.

**saddle s.**   Hand or machine-stitched seam used on shoes when two raw edges of leather stand up on outside, as on the vamp of a moccasin.

**slot s.**   Seam showing two rows of stitches with tape showing in between.

**strap s.**   Plain seam stitched with wrong sides together, pressed open, and covered on right side by bias tape that is stitched on each edge.

**top-stitched s.**   Plain seam pressed open and stitched on either side of seam on right side of garment or pressed to one side and stitched on reverse side. Also called *double-stitched seam.*

**tucked s.**   Seam finished with tucks stitched about ¼″ to 1″ from either side of seam and pressed to meet over seam. Also called *open-welt seam.*

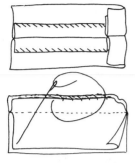

**OVERCAST SEAMS**

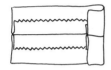

**PINCKED SEAM**

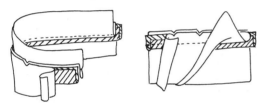

**PIPED SEAMS**

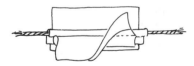

**CORDED SEAM**

**welt s.** Plain seam stitched on wrong side, one edge trimmed, both edges pressed in same direction, and top-stitched to catch wider edge.

**seam binding** Narrow tape woven on the straight used at hem of garment to cover raw edge. Also stitched to seams on wrong side to prevent stretching. Sometimes used to bind cut edges of ravelled seams.

**seamed hose** See HOSE and PANTYHOSE.

**seamless hose** See HOSE.

**seamless knit** See CIRCULAR KNIT.

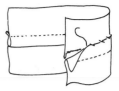

**WELT SEAM: SINGLE STITCHED**

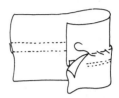

**WELT SEAM: DOUBLE STITCHED**

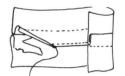

**FLAT FELL SEAM**       **FRENCH SEAM**

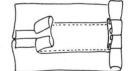

**STRAP SEAM**   **TOP-STITCHED SEAM**

**seam pocket** See POCKETS.

**seamstress** Same as DRESSMAKER.

**seam tape** See SEAM BINDING.

**sea otter** See FURS.

**Searcy diamond** See DIAMONDS.

**seaside costume** Clothing suitable for children and women to wear at "watering places" and seaside resorts, *e.g.*, Asbury Park and Atlantic City, in New Jersey. Included are bathing suits, *promenade dresses, sailor dresses,* and *yachting dresses,* from about 1860s to early 20th c.

**SEASIDE DRESS, 1854**

**seconds** Merchandise having slight flaws, some barely discernible, which is sold at lower prices.

**secrete** See JUPE #1.

**seed embroidery** See EMBROIDERIES.

**seed pearl** See BEADS and GEMS.

**seed stitch** See STITCHES.

**seersucker** **1.** Medium-weight fabric made with warpwise crinkled stripes alternating with plain woven stripes. Puckering is achieved by releasing the tension at intervals on the warp yarns. Effect is permanent and will not wash out. Compare with PLISSÉ CREPE. **2.** Seersucker is also made of acetate and rayon yarns then *cross-dyed*. Used for slacks, shorts, suits, shirts, skirts, and jackets.

**see-through** Fashion started by American designer, Rudi Gernreich, in 1964 with sheer blouses over bare skin. In 1966 developed by French couturier, Yves Saint Laurent, with sequined chiffon dress over body stocking. In 1968 transparent blouses were introduced. In late 1960s transparent voile shirts were introduced for men. This fashion was part of a general trend toward nudity. See BLOUSES, DRESSES, LOOKS, PANTS, and SHIRTS.

**seggard** See SAFEGUARD.

**self-covered** A sewing term used when belts and buttons are covered with same fabric from which the item of clothing is made. See BELTS and BUTTONS.

**self-edge** See SELVAGE.

**self sash** See SELF-COVERED BELT under BELTS.

**selham** See BURNOOSE #1.

**seloso** See DRESSES.

**selvage** Term used since 14th c. for narrow tightly woven band on either edge of fabric parallel to the warp that prevents fabric from raveling. Originally called *self-edge*. Also spelled *selvedge*. Also called *list* and *listing*.

**semiformal suit** See SUITS.

**semiprecious gems** Gems too plentiful to be considered rare, *e.g.*, *topaz, garnet, tourmaline, amethyst,* and *quartz*. See GEMS.

**sempstress bonnet** Woman's bonnet of 1812 with long, wide ribbons crossing under chin and brought up to top of crown where they tied in a bow.

**sennit** Braided rough straw, grass, or leaves used for men's hats in Japan and China.

**señorita** Woman's waist-length, bolero-style jacket of mid-1860s made with three-quarter or full-length sleeves and lavishly trimmed with braid, fringe, buttons, or lace. Worn over a blouse with full sleeves. Also called a *Spanish jacket*.

**separate collar** See COLLARS.

**separates** Retail term for sportswear items—shirts, blouses, sweaters, and pants—designed to wear in combination with other items from same line.

**sequin** (sea-qwin) Small shiny iridescent disk of metal or plastic pierced in the center and sewn on garments in a decorative design or in rows to cover a portion or the entire surface. Often used for evening dresses or sweaters. See SUIT OF LIGHTS under SPORT SUITS and MERMAID DRESS under DRESSES.

**serape** (se-rah-pee) Woolen blanket, folded lengthwise like a wide scarf, worn by Mexican peasants over one shoulder or wrapped around body. Also spelled *sarape, zerape*. Also see SHAWLS.

**serge** Suiting fabric made in an even twill with worsted yarns. Occasionally some woolen yarn is used in the warp or filling to provide greater softness. Generally piece-dyed navy blue and given a clear finish which becomes shiny with wear. Used for suits, skirts, and pants. *Der.* Latin, *serica,* "silk," indicating it was first a silk fabric; later Italian, *sergea,* "cloth of wool mixed with silk," probably appearing as early as the 12th c.

**serpentine belt** See BELTS.

**serpentine skirt** See MORNING-GLORY SKIRT.

**serpent ring** See RINGS.

**serul** Long, full, Turkish-type trousers worn by women in Northern Africa. Also spelled *serual.*

**set-back heel** See HEELS.

**set-in** See SLEEVES and WAISTLINES.

**setting** See GEM SETTINGS.

**set-under heel** See HEELS.

**seven-eighths** See LENGTHS and PANTS.

**seventeen-jeweled watch** See WATCHES.

**Seventh Avenue** Nickname for garment district of New York City, roughly from 40th Street to 34th Street and from Avenue of the Americas (6th Avenue) to 9th Avenue, where much of American ready-to-wear is produced. Abbreviated *S.A.*

**sew** To join together by *stitches.*

**sewing machine** Machine for stitching invented in late 18th c. patented by Thimonnier in France in 1830, improved on and patented by several others, most widely known was I. M. Singer in mid-19th c. It was responsible for rapid growth of *ready-to-wear* garment industry.

**shade** **1.** Color term for hues with black added to darken, *e.g.,* navy blue is correctly called a "shade of blue." Light blue, however, with white added is called a "tint of blue." **2.** Sheer scarf of lace, net or gauze worn by women over the bosom of a low-necked bodice. Sometimes had a small ruff attached at the neck. Worn from latter half of 18th to early 19th c. **3.** Piece of knitted or woven fabric usually attached to a hatband and arranged to fall over the back of the head and neck to prevent sunburn. Worn by women in 1880s. Also see UGLY.

**shades** See GLASSES.

**shadow** See EMBROIDERIES, LACES, and STRIPES.

**shadow-panel slip** See SLIPS.

**shag** See HAIRSTYLES.

**shagreen** Untanned leather of the shark and similar fishes usually dyed dark green or black and highly polished. Used in 18th and 19th c. for snuff boxes, medallions, and watch cases.

**Shakespeare collar** **1.** Standing collar of medium width, flaring away from face. Made of a curved pleated strip of stiffened lawn. *Der.* Similar to those shown in portraits of 16th-c. dramatist, William Shakespeare. **2.** Similar collar with longer points, sometimes trimmed with *lace* and *insertion,* worn by women in mid-1860s.

**Shakespearean costume** See ELIZABETHAN STYLES.

**shakespere collar** Small collar with points turned down in front worn by men from 1860s on.

**shakespere vest** Man's single- or double-breasted vest of mid-1870s with narrow lapels and a turndown collar similar to *shakespere collar.*

**shako** (shay-ko) See CAPS.

**shal** **1.** Indian term for *chaddar*, made with small figured borders. See CHADDAR #2. **2.** Large woolen scarf tied under the chin worn by Russian women in the winter.

**shale** **1.** Full loose wrap worn by Arabian women. Frequently made of black silk embroidered at the edges in silver or gold threads. **2.** French shawls with handspun warp and machine-spun merino filling made in Rheims.

**shalwar** **1.** Very full ankle-length pants worn by Turkish women at home. Frequently called *harem pants* in the U.S. **2.** Extremely full, puffed Turkish-style pants very full at the waist and gathered at the ankle. Worn by Albanian women with a *cummerbund*. **3.** Customarily worn by all Persian women until 1890. When the ruler Nair-Ne-Din visited Paris, and saw the Parisian ballet, he ordered all the women to wear short skirts in place of trousers. Also spelled *clalwar, salvar, salwar, shulwar.* Also see BERUNDJUK.

**sham** See HALF SHIRT.

**sham hanging sleeve** See HANGING SLEEVE #2.

**shamew** See CHAMARRE.

**shamiya** (sham-i-ya) Headscarf of red, white, or green worn in Bulgaria by married women knotted under chin and by single girls knotted at back of head.

**shank** **1.** The narrow part of the shoe under the arch of the foot between the heel and the ball of the foot. **2.** The narrow strip of metal inserted under arch of shoe between insole and outsole to give strength to the arch.

**shank button** See BUTTONS.

**shantung** **1.** Medium-weight fabric woven with irregular, elongated slubs in the filling caused by yarns of uneven diameter throughout. Originally *tussah silk yarn* was used which varied in thickness. **2.** Texture has been imitated with yarn of rayon and cotton. Frequently dyed various colors or discharge printed in polka dots. Used for dresses, sportswear, men's shirts, and a wide variety of items.

**shantung straw** See BAKU.

**shapka** Brimless hat, ranging up to two feet tall and two feet across with peaked or creased crown, made of fur, *e.g., caracul* or *Persian lamb*. Traditional hat worn by Russian Tatar horsemen. Also called *Cossack hat.*

**sharkskin** **1.** Worsted fabric woven in a twill weave with alternating black and white yarns in both the warp and the filling to give a grayed effect. Characteristic feature is the smooth, sleek, clear finish. Used for men's suits. **2.** Lightweight acetate (sometimes rayon) sharkskin uses filament yarns in a plain, basket, or sometimes *Jacquard*, weave to get a smooth sleek appearance. Usually made in white but sometimes dyed, used for sportswear and uniforms. **3.** Leather processed from the skins of sharks. See LEATHERS.

**shatweh** Palestinian woman's conical fez-like hat, stiff and hard with a recessed top for carrying things on the head, made of elaborately striped fabric and trimmed with beads and embroidery, two rows of coins on front, and a veil.

**shave coat** See ROBES.

**Shaver, Dorothy** President from 1946 to 1959 of Lord & Taylor, a specialty store in New York City, one of the first women to hold such a position. A backer of American designers during World War II, when French couture was in eclipse. An important person in the development of clothing design in the U.S.

**shawl** Decorative or utilitarian wrap, larger than a scarf, worn draped over the shoulders and sometimes the head. May be oblong, square, or a square folded diagonally. Believed to have originated in Bukhara, it was worn in Kashmir as early as late 16th c. Also worn in Persia and India, and worn by country people for utilitarian purposes. Did not become fashionable in Europe until second half of 18th c. Very popular throughout the 19th c., particularly the *Paisley shawl*, and worn intermittently since. *Der.* Persian and Hindu, "shal." See PAISLEY SHAWL in alphabetical listing.

## SHAWLS

**crocheted s.** Fringed shawl made by hand crocheting usually in a lacy pattern. Popular in late 1960s and early 1970s in oblong, semi-circular, or diagonal shapes.

**fascinator** Large long woolen scarf made in a lacy knit worn over the head or around the shoulders by women particularly at seashore resorts. First fashionable in the early 1890s and worn at intervals since.

**piano s.** Another name for the SPANISH SHAWL, so called because in the early 20th c. this type of shawl was draped on the top of grand pianos.

**rebozo** (re-bow-zho) **1.** An oblong shawl made of native fabric worn originally by South American Indians and introduced as a fashion item in late 1960s. **2.** Veil or scarf of dark-colored cotton worn by Mexican women in place of the *mantilla.*

**serape** Bright-colored oblong rectangle worn by Mexicans over the shoulder. Handmade in horizontally striped patterns, it resembles a small blanket. Usually made with fringed ends.

**Spanish s.** Large embroidered silk shawl usually made in China then shipped to Spain where the long silk fringe is added. Style of wearing shawl is of Spanish origin. When used as a wrap, folded diagonally with point in center back and ends thrown loosely over the shoulders. A fashionable accessory of the early 20th c., revived in the late 1960s and early 1970s. Also called PIANO SHAWL.

SPANISH SHAWL

FASCINATOR

**shawl collar** See COLLARS.

**shawl-collared cardigan** See TUXEDO SWEATER under SWEATERS.

**shawl tongue** Extra-long tongue on an *oxford shoe* folded over the lacing, sometimes made with decorative fringed end. Shoe made fashionable when Prince of Wales wore it with kilts in Scotland in mid-1920s. Shoe with shawl tongue sometimes called KILTIE SHOE.

**shawl waistcoat** **1.** Man's vest with *shawl collar* worn in the 19th c. **2.** Man's vest sometimes cut out of a fabric with a printed or woven design normally used for shawls. **3.** A man's vest, sometimes actually made from a woman's shawl.

**sheared raccoon**   See FURS.

**shearing**   **1.** Process used on furs, *e.g.*, beaver, lamb, muskrat, raccoon, and seal to cut hairs to same length to give them a velvety appearance. **2.** Textile process of clipping nap of fabric to desired length.

**shearling**   See FURS, LEATHERS, and SPORT JACKETS.

**sheath**   See DRESSES, SILHOUETTES, SKIRTS, and SWIMSUITS.

**sheepskin**   See LEATHERS and SPORT JACKETS.

**sheer**   **1.** Term applied to any fabric which is fine and transparent or semi-transparent. May be made of silk, wool, cotton, or man-made yarns—with yarns usually finer than average. Fabrics include sheer crepe, sheer wool, *georgette*, and *chiffon*. **2.** See HOSE. **3.** See PANTY-HOSE.

**sheeting**   Group of fabrics which vary in quality made predominately of cotton yarns but also of blends of cotton/polyester and sometimes of linen or nylon. In the gray it is used for handbag and shoe linings. Heavier qualities are bleached or dyed and used for work clothes. Medium- and lightweight qualities are used for uniforms, aprons, pocketing, sportswear, and interlining.

**shell**   See BLOUSES, SHOES, and SWEATERS.

**shell cameo**   See CAMEO.

**shell lining**   Lining for only part of a coat or jacket, similar to a *half-lining*. Also see ZIP-IN/ZIP-OUT LINING.

**shell stitch**   See STITCHES.

**shenti/shendot/shendyt**   See SCHENTI.

**shepherdess hat**   See BERGÉRE HAT.

**shepherdess heel**   See MUSEUM HEEL under HEELS.

**shepherd's check**   Small checked patterned fabric usually made of black and white or of white and another color. Made in a twill weave of fine to medium quality yarns. Originally of wool, now cotton and rayon are also used. Originated from a checked length of fabric about 4 yards long and 1½ yards wide worn in a draped manner by Scottish shepherds in Scotland. Also called *shepherd's plaid*. Also see CHECKS.

**sheriff tie**   See TIES.

**sherte**   Chief male undergarment worn by men from 12th to 16th c., forerunner of modern shirt. Usually called *chemise* until 14th c. Also called *camise*.

**Shetland**   **1.** Soft suiting fabric made of fine wool from Shetland sheep of Scotland. Usually woven in *herringbone weave*, the term refers to the type of wool used. **2.** 19th c. overcoating fabric of coarse wool with long shaggy nap. **3.** Knitted fabric, or item such as a sweater, made from Shetland wool. Also see LACES and SWEATERS.

**shift**   **1.** See DRESSES, JUMPERS, and SILHOU-ETTES. **2.** Undergarment worn in 18th c. by women, replacing word *smock*. Called a *chemise* in the 19th c.

**shigra**   See HANDBAGS.

**shillelagh**   See CANE.

**shingle**   See HAIRSTYLES.

**shirring**   **1.** Three or more rows of *gathers* made by small running stitches in parallel lines. Used to produce fullness at tops of gloves, skirts, sleeves, and swimsuits. Also called *gauging*. **2.** May be made by using a large stitch on the sewing machine and then pulling the bobbin thread to form gathers. **3.** May be made on sewing machine by using elastic thread on the bobbin. See ELASTIC WAISTLINE.

**shirt**   **1.** Clothing for the upper part of the body usually more tailored than a blouse. May be closed in front or back or pulled on over the head; some are worn tucked in while others are of overblouse type. *Women and girls*: worn with pants, skirt, jumper, or suit, and buttoned right over left. *Men and boys*: worn with pants or suit and buttoned left over right. Worn since early Middle Ages the shirt was originally of slip-on type worn next to the skin; neckband was added in 14th c.; *standing collar* added in 15th c.; embroidery, frills, and lace added in 17th and 18th c. Usually white although colors, including pink, were introduced in mid-19th c., printed shirts with white collar introduced in 1860s and stripes were introduced in late 19th c. The *attached collar* popularized in 1920s. See BOSOM SHIRT in alphabetical listing. **2.** In 1890s term applied to a summer blouse worn by women. See SHIRTWAIST in alphabetical listing. In 1920s and 1930s shirts became popular for sportswear for women. Also see BLOUSES and KNIT SHIRTS. See GARIBALDI SHIRT, CORAZZA SHIRT, and HALF-SHIRT in alphabetical listing.

## ■■■ SHIRTS ■■■

**Afghanistan wedding tunic** 18th c.-style velvet tunic-blouse, lavishly decorated with gold embroidery, worn in early 1970s by men in U.S. in both original and copied styles.

**aloha s.** See HAWAIIAN SHIRT.

**Apache s.** Overblouse or tuck-in shirt of pullover type. Neckline is cut in low V, sometimes laced, sometimes with *Italian collar*. Sleeves are sometimes long, full and gathered into band at the wrist. *Der.* Named for Indian tribe of the southwestern U.S.

**barong tagalog** Man's *overblouse*-type shirt worn for informal occasions made with no buttons and a vent at the neckline. Made of fine sheer fabric and frequently trimmed with embroidery; worn in the Philippines. Introduced for casual wear in U.S. in late 1960s. Sometimes called *barong*.

BODYSHIRT #1

COWBOY SHIRT

DRESS SHIRT

HAWAIIAN SHIRT

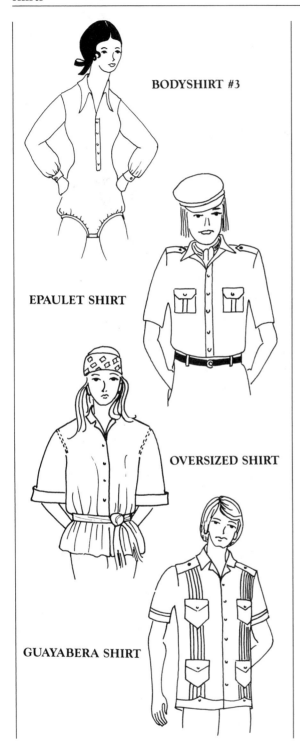

BODYSHIRT #3

EPAULET SHIRT

OVERSIZED SHIRT

GUAYABERA SHIRT

**Ben Casey s.** See MEDIC SHIRT. *Der.* Named for television series *Ben Casey*, popular in early 1960s.

**big s.** See OVERSIZED SHIRT.

**bodyshirt** **1.** Shirt fitted by shaping side seams to conform to body lines, introduced in early 1960s. Also called *tapered shirt.* **2.** Long shirt with rounded tails worn by girls over short shorts in 1960s. **3.** Woman's leotard or bodysuit combination often made with a snap crotch. Introduced in 1960s in stretch fabrics. Also see LEOTARD SHIRT.

**boiled s.** See alphabetical listing.

**bowling s.** Shirt designed to be worn by men and women for bowling—personalized with name of individual on front and team name on back.

**bush s.** See SAFARI SHIRT.

**button-down s.** See IVY LEAGUE SHIRT.

**calypso s.** Tailored collar or V-neck shirt which ties in center front giving a bare-midriff effect. *Der.* Style of music characteristic of the West Indies where shirt was originally worn.

**camp s.** Conventional front-buttoned shirt with a notched collar. Usually made of woven cotton and polyester blends in solid colors, prints, or blocks of color.

**cavu s.** Long-sleeved man's sport shirt with single pocket on the left and pointed collar, closing diagonally from under collar almost to right side seam. Popular from 1940 to 1950.

**clerical s.** Black or gray shirt with short or long sleeves styled with a fly-front and standing *clerical collar* worn by clergymen. A second collar of white may be inserted inside the neckline. Frequently has white cuffs. Formerly made of lightweight wool, now made in wash-and-wear fabrics.

**Cossack s.** **1.** Russian-type shirt with standing collar and neck placket placed to one side. Often made with braid trimming at neck, down front, and at cuffs. **2.** Similar style with turtle-neck called *turtleneck Cossack shirt.* Same as Zhivago shirt, Cossack blouse, and Russian blouse.

**cowboy s.** Shirt with a convertible collar sometimes worn with a *neckerchief* or a *string tie,* often closed with grippers. May have pockets in front and V-shaped yoke in front and back. Sometimes made of contrasting fabrics. Originally worn by cowboys in western U.S. and now worn by women and children in all parts of the U.S. and some foreign countries. Also called a *western shirt.*

**C.P.O.** Navy-blue shirt of lightweight wool worn by chief petty officer in U.S. Navy made with buttoned front and patch pockets. Adapted for civilian wear, sometimes in wool plaids, and worn open as a jacket over shirt or T-shirt by men, women, and children in late 1960s.

**dandy s.** Shirt with lace or self-ruffles down front and at cuffs, popular in late 1960s for women and worn with dinner suits in evening by men. *Der.* From shirts worn by Beau Brummell, and other 18th- and 19th-c. dandies.

**drawstring s.** Hip-length shirt with drawstring at bottom giving a bloused effect. Designed to be worn over a bathing suit and frequently made of terrycloth or cotton knit. Introduced in 1940s and 1950s and still used.

**dress s.** **1.** Traditional buttoned-down-the-front shirt usually worn with a necktie and a traditional suit by men. Made in tuck-in style with *tab, spread, buttoned-down,* or *pin collar* and with conservative sleeves with *single* or *French cuffs.* Popular for men since 1920s replacing shirt with separate collar. Originally made in woven cotton, now made in cotton/polyester blends, and in fine knitted nylons and polyesters. **2.** See formal shirt.

**dueling s.** Man's full-sleeved shirt of slip-on type sometimes worn with long stock around the neck. *Der.* Named after full-sleeved shirts shown in movies depicting era of the Three Musketeers. Similar to fencing shirt.

**epaulet s.** Shirt which has long sleeves, buttoned front, convertible collar, patch pockets with bellows pleats, and buttoned-down flap. The characteristic feature is a separate epaulet tab on each shoulder with button near neckline. Also called *pilot shirt.*

**fencing s.** Unisex shirt, with large full sleeves and pointed collar, frequently laced at neck. *Der.* Similar to those worn in old swash-buckling movies by Errol Flynn and Tyrone Power. Similar to dueling shirt.

**fiesta s.** Man's white cotton sport shirt trimmed with a wide band of eyelet embroidery down either side of front. Popularized in Acapulco, Mexico, in late 1960s. Also see Mexican wedding shirt.

**flannel s.** Shirt of colored or plaid flannel fabric with one or two patch pockets and conventional or convertible neckline. Worn originally by woodsmen, later for sports, *e.g.*, hunting. From early 1960s popular in lighter-weight washable fabrics for general wear. In the early 1980s a lining was added and shirt was frequently worn as a jacket.

**formal s.** **1.** Man's conventional white shirt with pleated front, wing collar and long sleeves usually finished with french cuffs. Worn with tuxedo jacket and black bow tie, or tails and white tie. **2.** A similar men's shirt styled with ruffles made in white or colors. Fashionable particularly for weddings or semi-formal wear since late 1960s. **3.** Formerly a shirt with highly starched bib front and detachable stiff starched collar called a boiled shirt. (see alphabetical listings.)

**guayabera s.** (gwah-ya-bare-a) **1.** Lightweight overshirt made with convertible collar, short sleeves and four large patch pockets. Has two sets of pin tucks in front running from small shoulder yokes to hem, and three sets of pin tucks in the back from yoke to hem. Small white pearl buttons are used for the front closing, pocket flaps, and at the top and bottom of the sets of tucks. Copied from shirts worn by the well-dressed businessmen in pre-Castro Havana. **2.** Another style is similar with embroidered stripes down front instead of tucks styled for men and women. *Der.* Shirt worn in Cuba by guava tree growers.

**Hawaiian s.** Man's sport shirt printed with colorful Hawaiian floral designs, made with convertible collar and worn outside of trousers; introduced in 1936, became fashion item in 1950s when President Harry Truman wore one and appeared on the cover of *Life* magazine in 1951; popular in 1980s. Also called *aloha shirt.*

**hunting s.** Bright-red wool shirt worn by hunters, so they are visible for long distances in woods.

**Ivy League s.** Traditional shirt with buttoned-down collar, front buttoned, and styled with a yoke in back with a loop at center of yoke. Worn first by college men in the 1950s and later by girls and boys. *Der.* Named for a group of eastern colleges which is called "the Ivy League."

**jockey s.** Woman's shirt with contrasting colored inserts, similar to *jockey silks.* Introduced as sportswear in late 1960s after first woman was accepted as a professional jockey.

**knit s.** See separate category.

**leotard s.** Fitted shirt with a long tail which snaps between the legs making a leotard-type garment.

**Lord Byron s.** Shirt with full sleeves and long pointed collar worn open at neck in shape of a V. Popular in 1920s and late 1960s. Also called *poet's shirt. Der.* Named for the 6th Baron Byron, early 19th-c. English poet.

**medic s.** White shirt-jacket with standing-band collar and shoulder closing worn by mem-

bers of medical profession. Also called *Ben Casey shirt.*

**meditation s.** Loose, open-sleeved, pullover tunic-blouse, usually made of Indian printed cotton or of solid colors and banded with embroidery around slit neck, across shoulders and at hem. *Der.* Part of late 1960s ethnic look inspired by eastern gurus.

**Mexican wedding s.** Tailored shirt of a crisp white fabric usually made with wide bands of embroidery down either side of front and on collar, popular in Acapulco, Mexico, for men and women in late 1960s. *Der.* Inspired by shirts worn by Mexican peasant grooms at weddings. Also see FIESTA SHIRT.

**midriff s.** Shirt for women cut to just below bustline, revealing rib cage. Often improvised from a conventional shirt by tying the tails in a knot under the bosom.

**nightshirt** See NIGHTGOWN category.

**Nureyev s.** Shirt with long full sleeves gathered in bands at wrists and a low round neckline finished with bias binding, popularized in late 1960s. *Der.* Named for Rudolf Nureyev, ballet performer who defected from his native Russia to the West in 1961.

**overshirt** Any shirt styled to be worn outside of trousers or skirt, rather than tucked in, *e.g.,* HAWAIIAN SHIRT, COSSACK SHIRT.

**oversized s.** Shirt cut extra large and extra long usually made with button closing and convertible collar. Also called *big shirt.*

**pilot s.** See EPAULET SHIRT.

**poet's s.** See LORD BYRON SHIRT.

**polo s.** See KNIT SHIRT category.

**Ratcatcher®** Trademarked tailored shirt that has detachable self-fabric collar with long ends to lap or tie in front. Worn by men or women with informal riding habit. *Der.* From informal hunt shirt worn at English "rat hunts," when foxes are out of season.

**safari s.** African-inspired shirt introduced by Dior in mid-1960s for women. Styled with lapels, buttoned center-front closing, and four large pockets—usually of bellows-type. Same as *bush shirt. Der.* Named after an African hunting trip.

**see-through s.** **1.** Shirt of transparent fabric worn by women with no underwear underneath. Introduced by Parisian couturier, Saint Laurent, in spring 1968 and popularly accepted in 1969 and 1970. Presented by Rudi Gernreich in 1964 for "at-home" wear but not called by this name at that time. Also called *see-through blouse.* **2.** Voile and sheer fabric shirts as worn by men in the late 1960s and early 1970s.

**shirt-jac** Front-buttoned shirt worn outside the trousers for sportswear. May have side slits, FLAP POCKETS, and sometimes worn open over another shirt or knit shirt. *Der.* Combination of words "shirt" and "jacket."

**sport s.** **1.** Any type of shirt which is worn without a necktie by a man. At first a woven-fabric shirt with a CONVERTIBLE COLLAR, worn outside or tucked in trousers, popularized in mid-1930s. Now any shirt, other than a DRESS SHIRT, whether it is woven or knitted. **2.** Tailored or knitted shirt worn by women as sportswear since 1940s.

**stock-tie s.** Plain shirt with *Ascot neckline.* Also called STOCK-TIE BLOUSE and FLIP-TIE BLOUSE.

**tapered s.** See BODYSHIRT #1.

**tchamir** (cha-meer) Moroccan shirt or overblouse with heavily embroidered caftan neckline. Imported as a current style in late 1960s for men and women in black with white embroidery and white with multicolored embroidery.

**Tom Jones s.** Pullover shirt made with STOCK-TIE, yoke, full body, and full sleeves with ruffled wristband gathered into dropped shoulders. Some adaptations omit yoke and have slit neckline with pointed collar. *Der.* Inspired

by costumes worn in *Tom Jones,* 1963 film of Henry Fielding's novel, about an 18th-c. hero.

**T-shirt** See KNIT SHIRT category.

**tuxedo s.** **1.** See FORMAL SHIRT #1 and #2. **2.** Women's version made with bib front frequently tucked, popularized in the early 1980s. Sometimes worn with a black bow tie and a version of the man's tuxedo jacket. Also called *tuxedo blouse.*

**unisex s.** Shirt designed to be worn by a man or woman. Has no buttons, and is usually laced at neckline.

**Western dress s.** Western shirt which is elaborately decorated and worn at rodeos. May be trimmed with fringe, elaborate embroidery, leather, beads, or sequins. Special shirt worn by cowboys for important rodeos.

**Western s.** See COWBOY SHIRT.

**Zhivago s.** Same as COSSACK SHIRT. *Der.* Inspired by costumes worn in *Dr. Zhivago,* 1965 film of Boris Pasternak's novel, set in Revolutionary Russia in 1917.

---

**shirt-drawers** Man's combination undershirt and underpants worn in 1890s.

**shirt front** Term used from 1860s on for a man's false shirt or *bosom,* which had a complete front but tapered into a band in back and buttoned in center back of collar. Compare with CLERICAL FRONT.

**shirt gills** See GILLS.

**shirt-jac** See SHIRTS.

**Shirtmaker®** Trademark of Best & Co., New York specialty store, for tailored shirt-dress, popular in 1940s and 1950s.

**shirtwaist** **1.** Term originating in 1890s for women's blouses styled like men's shirts with buttons down front, tailored collar, and sometimes worn with a black tie. **2.** A woman's blouse with a high choker neckline buttoned in back—one of the first items produced by the ready-to-wear industry. After 1920, term BLOUSE was more common.

**SHIRTWAIST**

**shirtwaist dress** See DRESSES.

**shitagi** (shi-taag-e) Inner *kimono* with attached collar (HAN-YERI) that folds over top of outer *kimono* worn by Japanese men.

**shita-juban** (shee-ta-joo-ban) Short undergarment worn by Japanese women with attached collar called HAN-YERI that folds over neckline of outer *kimono*.

**shoe/shoes** Outer covering for the foot which does not reach higher than the ankle. Shoes are basically made up of the *sole* or part under the foot, the *vamp* or front part of the shoe; the *quarter* or back of the shoe, and the *shank* or portion under the instep. Shoes may be of the slip-on variety or closed with lacers or buckles. *Velcro*® was introduced in the early 1980s for closings. See SOLLERET and CALAMANCO, COPPED, CRAKOW, Eclipse tie, PINSON, and POULAINE in alphabetical listing. Also see BOOTS, HEELS, OXFORDS, SANDALS, SLIPPERS, and TOES.

## SHOES

**aerobic s.** Laced shoe of nylon mesh with suede outside counter, toe band, and trim. Somewhat higher cut than a sneaker with shock-absorbing mid-sole and non-skid rubber sole.

**ankle-strap s.** Shoe, frequently of the sandal-type, having a strap attached at the top of the heel which goes around the ankle. Frequently made with platform sole. Very popular in the 1930s and 1940s, revived in late 1960s, and very popular in 1980s.

**baby doll s.** Low-heeled shoe with wide rounded toes similar to MARY JANE SHOE, sometimes with straps over instep, popular for women in 1960s with miniskirts for little-girl look. Popularity enhanced by film, *Baby Doll* (1956) in which Carroll Baker played the lead. *Der.* Term used to refer to clothing and accessories used for children's dolls and infants' clothes in the early part of the 20th c.

**ballerina s. 1.** Soft low kid shoe with thin sole and flat heel, sometimes made with drawstring throat. Inspired by shoe worn by ballet dancers. Popular in 1940s for school girls. Also see BALLET SLIPPER under SLIPPERS. **2.** Plain, low-cut pump made with flat or wedge heel and a crepe or man-made sole, introduced in 1980s.

**basketball s.** High or low oxford laced to the toe made of canvas or army duck with non-slip molded rubber sole, frequently made with reinforced toe and backstay. Originally used only for sports, in 1970s accepted for school wear. In 1980s sometimes made in leather with a padded collar added at top.

**Bass Weejun**® Trademark of G.H. Bass & Co., a division of Chesebrough Pond's, Inc., for a high-quality moccasin-type loafer with tasseled bow in front using the same type last since 1936. Originally copied from a Norwegian-type moccasin. *Der.* Word originally from shortened form of Norwegian-Injun.

BALLERINA SHOE          BASKETBALL SHOE          COLONIAL SHOE

1902          1970

ESPADRILLE          GOLF SHOE          LOAFER

MARY JANE®          MIRANDA PUMP          MOCCASIN-TYPE SHOE

RUBY KEELER SHOE

OPEN SHANK SHOES          PLATFORM SHOE, 1973          SPECTATOR PUMP

SABOT-STRAP SHOE          SLING PUMP          CLOG

**boating s.** Canvas shoe similar to TENNIS SHOE, but made with a special non-skid rubber sole for walking on slippery boat decks. Also called *deck shoes.* Also see SPERRY TOPSIDERS® under OXFORDS.

**boots** Shoes extending to above the ankles. See separate category.

**bowling s.** Soft, supple shoe of oxford or other type with cushioned insole for comfort. Made with hard rubber sole and heel with an added leather tip on the sole of the right shoe (or left, for left-handed bowlers).

**chain loafer** Moccasin-type shoe of the slip-on variety trimmed with metal links or hardware trim over the instep. A classic shoe since the 1960s. Also see GUCCI® loafers.

**Chinese s.** Fabric flat-heeled crepe-soled shoe of *Mary Jane* type made with one strap and rounded toe in many colors, sometimes with embroidery. The national shoe of China which was imported by the U.S. and sold first at Oriental and later at other stores in late 1970s and 1980s.

**chunky s.** Shoes of all types made in exaggeratedly heavy shapes with bulbous toes and massive heels, often with very thick platform soles. A fad in late 1960s and early 1970s.

**clog** Shoe made with thick sole of wood or cork. Usually the upper is made in sandal-style, sometimes with closed toe and open heel similar to *sabot.* Very fashionable during late 1960s and a classic since. Also see SANDALS.

**colonial s.** Medium-heeled slip-on shoe with stiffened tongue standing up over instep, frequently decorated with large ornamental buckle. Worn in the 17th and 18th c. in U.S., and revived often.

**crepe-soled s.** Shoe made with crepe rubber sole and heel. Originally worn for sportswear, they were so comfortable that they were adopted for everyday wear particularly by men and school children, fashionable for women since early 1970s.

**court s.** **1.** See TENNIS SHOE. **2.** British term for a *pump.*

**court tie** **1. Men:** Oxford which is low-cut, usually made of patent leather, used with ceremonial court dress in England. **2. Women:** Two- or three-eyelet shoe that ties.

**deck s.** See BOATING SHOE.

**d'Orsay pump** Pump with closed heel and toe, cut down to the sole at the sides leaving shank bare. Often made with high heel. Popular in 1940s as evening shoe or at-home shoe. Also see SLIPPERS.

**dress s.** **1.** Man's shoe worn for formal occasions, general wear, and business. Does not include sport shoes or crepe-soled shoes. **2.** Girl's shoes worn on Sunday or for special occasions, not for school or sportswear.

**ducks®** Trademarked oxford or slip-on style shoe usually made in two colors, *e.g.,* brown with tan, navy with yellow, of man-made waterproof materials with chain-tread rubber soles. Also called *rubber moccasin.*

**dyeables** Shoes made of white fabric such as satin, faille, or silk which may be dyed to match a dress, worn primarily for evening parties or weddings.

**Elevator® s.** Trademark for a man's shoe with a wedge inserted inside the shoe toward the heel to make the man appear taller. Usually made to order.

**espadrille** **1.** Rope-soled shoe with canvas upper tied on with long shoelaces threaded through top of shoe, crossed, and tied around the ankle. Originally worn for bathing shoe and later for sportswear. Popular in 1940s and reintroduced in 1970s. **2.** Restyled in 1980s as an oxford, or pump cut high and straight across instep with medium-high wedge heel covered with jute, made with crepe sole, and no lacers.

*Der.* French, shoe made of canvas with cord sole.

**evening s.**   Delicate shoe worn with evening clothes. Women's styles include pumps or sandals in gold, silver or metallic kid or luxurious fabrics; men's style is usually a patent-leather pump or slipper.

**flat/flatties**   Any shoe with broad low heels worn by children and women for school or general wear.

**golf s.**   Oxford-style shoe made of oil-treated leather usually given a water-repellent finish, and having a foam-cushioned inner sole. Original shoes had replaceable golf spikes, located on heel and sole, attached to two metal sole plates. Popularized in 1920s in two-toned black and white style which returned to fashion in late 1960s and early 1970s. In the 1980s soles of shoes were made with solid rubber sole with rubber spikes.

**Gucci® loafer**   Most popular of the fine shoes sold by Italian firm Gucci in U.S. since early 1960s. Slip-on shoe of modified moccasin type with distinctive gold-metal harness hardware decoration across vamp. Man's shoe has low heel, woman's, a medium heel. Widely copied throughout the 1960s and early 1970s. Also see CHAIN LOAFER.

**Harlow pump**   Sabot-strap pump with high chunky heel popular in early 1970s. *Der.* Named after shoes worn by Jean Harlow, Hollywood actress of the 1920s and 1930s.

**Hush Puppies®**   Trade name for casual oxford or slip-on shoes with sueded leather uppers and crepe soles. Popular for men, women, and children.

**Indian moccasin**   True heelless moccasin in which the sole is made of leather and comes up to form the quarter and part of the vamp of the shoe. A tongue-like curved piece is hand-stitched to complete the vamp of the shoe. Thong is threaded around the collar of the shoe and ties on the instep. Fringe and bead trimming is frequently used. *Der.* Made by American Indians in the same style since colonial times.

**jellies**   Molded footwear of soft plastic or rubber made in many styles, *e.g.*, wedgies, multi-strapped sandals, flat-heeled thongs, high-heeled pumps, and booties. Some have cut-out "portholes" or lattice strips, and are worn with bright-colored contrasting socks. All are made in a great variety of bright colors and high fashion in 1983–84. Originally introduced for children. They appeared several years ago from Brazil, China, Japan, Greece, and Mexico. Also made in U.S. Style was basically a practical fisherman's sandal made of soft plastic. Also called *jelly beans. Der.* Named for soft translucent look of jelly in jelly-bean colors.

**Keds®**   Trademark of U.S. Rubber Company for rubber-soled shoes. See SNEAKERS.

**kiltie flat**   A low-heeled shoe with a fringed tongue and shoelace tied over top in a bow usually made with crepe sole. Compare with KILTIE OXFORD under OXFORDS.

**landlady s.**   See WOOLWORTH® SHOE.

**loafer**   Slip-on shoe of moccasin-type construction with a slotted strap stitched to the vamp. Also called PENNY LOAFER, CHAIN LOAFER, and *tassel-top loafer.* Introduced first for wear by college girls in the 1940s, now a classic worn by adults and children. Also see GUCCI® loafer.

**Mamma s.**   Retail store and trade name for shoes worn by older women which stress comfort rather than style. Usually made in an oxford style with medium-high broad heel.

**Mary Jane®**   **1.** Low-heeled slipper made of patent leather with blunt toe and single strap over the instep buttoned or buckled at center or side. A trademarked shoe for children, popular since early 20th c. **2.** In 1980s a *flattie* or *wedgie* in pump style with buckled strap coming high over the instep. *Der.* Named for shoes worn by character Mary Jane in comic strip Buster Brown drawn by R. F. Outcault in early 1900s. Compare with BABY DOLL SHOE.

**Miranda pump** Platform pump with high, heavy, flared heel worn in 1969. *Der.* Named after Carmen Miranda, a popular movie star of the late 1930s and 1940s.

**moccasin-type s.** Shoe construction based on the INDIAN MOCCASIN, in which the upper starts under the sole of the foot and forms the quarter with the toe stitched to an oval vamp. Hard soles, sometimes of rubber, are added to produce a more durable shoe than the soft Indian moccasin.

**monk s.** Closed shoe with wide buckled strap over tongue at instep rather than lacings. Popular for women in 1940s and for men during World War II when this style was favored by U.S. Army Air Corps officers. Revived in late 1960s and early 1970s.

**monster s.** Clumsy bulky shoe with wide bulbous toe and large clunky heel popularized in 1968.

**open-back s.** See SLINGBACK SHOE.

**open shank s.** Woman's shoe with closed toe and heel portions but open on sides down to sole; sometimes with side straps connecting vamp and quarter. Also see D'ORSAY PUMP.

**open-toed s.** Women's shoe with the toe section cut out. Popular in the 1920s, 1940s, mid-1970s, and 1980s.

**opera pump** Plain, undecorated woman's pump with medium to high heel. Upper is cut from a single piece of leather or fabric. Introduced in 1920s and a basic style during 1940s and 1950s, revived in 1970s.

**oxfords** Shoes which fasten with shoe lacers. See separate category.

**penny loafer** Loafer with a slot in the strap across each vamp into which a coin is sometimes inserted. Pennies were originally worn but

dimes and quarters are now more generally used. Originally in brown but featured in colors in 1980s.

**platform s.** Shoe with thick mid-sole, usually made of cork and covered so that the wearer appears taller. Popular for women in 1940s and revived by Paris designer, Yves Saint Laurent in 1960s. Worn by men in 1970s.

**pre-walkers** Infant's shoe with very soft soles worn before child begins to walk.

**pump** Slip-on shoe with low-cut, rounded, or V-shaped throat, usually a medium to high heel sometimes covered with the same material as the upper. Toes vary from rounded to pointed with current style. Sometimes made with open toe and/or open heel in SLINGBACK style. A classic style for women for day or evening since 1920s. Also see SPECTATOR PUMP, COURT SHOE, and OPERA PUMP. *Der.* Pump replaced the word *pinson* used in 17th c.

**racing s.** See RUNNING SHOE.

**Ruby Keeler s.** Low-heeled pump tied across instep with ribbon bow similar to tap shoes. Popular for teenagers in early 1970s. *Der.* Named after tap dancer, Ruby Keeler, popular star of 1930s films, who made a stage comeback on Broadway in 1971 in a revival of the 1917 musical, *No, No Nanette*.

**running s.** Sport shoe with crepe or rubber sole and upper made of two or three colors of contrasting leather or fabric. Sometimes laced to the toe and sometimes styled like a regular oxford. Style inspired by the track shoes worn by athletes, which sometimes have contrasting stripes of colored leather on the sides of the shoe. Also called *racing shoe*.

**sabot-strap s.** Woman's shoe with a wide strap across instep usually buckling to one side. May be used on a SPECTATOR PUMP type of shoe.

**safety s.** Work shoe with a heavy metal reinforced toe, or another protective feature, worn by industrial workers.

**sandals**   Open-type shoes usually held on foot by means of straps. See separate category.

**shells**   See SKIMMER.

**side-gore s.**   Slip-on shoe, usually with high vamp, that has triangular insertions of elastic at sides.

**skimmer**   Very low-cut pump for women with shallow sides set on low or flat heels, usually made of very soft leather. Also called *shells*.

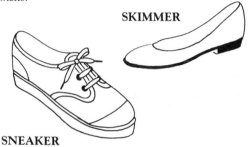

**SKIMMER**

**SNEAKER**

**slingback s.**   Any shoe with an open back and a strap around the heel of the foot to hold it in place. May be made in pump or sandal style.

**sling pump**   Pump with open back, held on heel by slender strap, sometimes buckled at side. Also called SLINGBACK PUMP.

**slip-on s.**   Any shoe which stays on the foot without using straps or fasteners, *e.g.*, a PUMP, LOAFER, or MOCCASIN. Also called a *step-in shoe*.

**slippers**   Shoes usually worn indoors. See separate category.

**sneakers**   Term formerly used to refer to gym shoes or tennis shoes of white canvas. Now refers to a type of low shoe similar to tennis shoes or a high canvas shoe worn by men, women and boys for school, sportswear, or gym. See KEDS®.

**Space® s.**   Trademarked name for side-laced leather orthopedic shoes, with extra moving space for each toe, custom-made over casts of the wearer's feet. Made with thick crepe soles and low wedge heels for comfort.

**spectator pump**   Two-toned pump frequently made in contrasting colors of black, navy, red, or brown on white. Extra sewed-on toe and heel pieces of another color sometimes have perforations and are pinked at edges. Introduced in 1920s.

**Sperry Top-Siders®**   See OXFORDS category.

**step-in s.**   See SLIP-ON SHOE.

**stocking s.**   Shoe covered with knitted fabric and attached to a long stocking. Introduced in late 1960s by shoe designer Beth Levine.

**tap s.**   Any shoe worn by a tap dancer. Made with metal plates at tip of toe and back edge of heel to increase sound when dancing. Men's style is usually a patent-leather pump or oxford; women's is usually a low-heeled patent-leather pump with ribbon tie at instep. Also see RUBY KEELER SHOE.

**tassel-top loafer**   Loafer with leather tassle on instep.

**tennis s.**   Canvas or drill low-cut oxford with a circular cut vamp. Made with special type of rubber sole for use on tennis courts. Also see SNEAKERS. Also called *court shoe*.

**track s.**   Oxford-type shoe with no heel usually laced to toe, made of kangaroo leather with cushioned insole. Has four detachable metal spikes on sole under the front of the foot. Extra sets of spikes are given for wear on a hardwood floor for indoor track meets.

**tuxedo pump**   Low-heeled pump with rounded toe usually made of patent leather with grosgrain trim around the collar of the shoe and a broad flat grosgrain bow on the vamp. Introduced in mid-1980s.

**walkers**   Ankle-high laced shoe, usually made of white leather, with man-made or leather soles. Worn by children when first learning to walk.

**WALKERS**                    **WALKING SHOE, 1940**

**walking s.** Any comfortable shoe with a relatively low heel, sometimes made with a cushion or crepe sole, worn more for comfort than style.

**wedgies** Shoes with wedge-shaped heels completely joined to soles under arches, made in all styles and heel heights. Popular for women in late 1940s, revived for women and also worn by men in 1970s. Originally made with high wedge, now made with low- and medium-sized wedges.

**WEDGIE**

**WOOLWORTH® SHOE**

**winkle pickers** British slang for exaggeratedly pointed shoes worn by *Teddy Boys*, in early 1950s. *Der.* From suggestion that pointed toes can dig out snails or periwinkles from the sand.

**Woolworth® s.** Shoe which has been sold in millions by Woolworth stores. Made of cotton canvas, in sandal style, in red, navy, paisley, black, or white. This shoe has sold for 50 years and has been entered in the permanent collection in the Metropolitan Museum of Art Costume Collection. Also called *landlady shoe.*

---

**shoe buckle** Buckles worn on the shoe were very popular in France and Italy about 1660 and in England during reign of Charles II (1660–1685). Also fashionable in colonial America until about 1770. At first intended to hold shoe in place, the buckle was small in size and worn with *butterfly bows*, later reached larger dimensions. Also see BUCKLE and PINCHBECK. Revived in 1870s and at end of 19th and early 20th c., but limited to women's shoes. Revived for both men's and women's shoes in late 1960s.

**shoe button** See BUTTONS.

**shoe cloth** Any fabric used in making of fabric shoes, shoe linings, or any other part of the shoe. Silk, cotton, wool, and man-made fabrics are all used. Many fabrics are used to make white *dyeable shoes.* Other fabrics such as brocade, tapestry, slipper satin, faille, nylon mesh, crepe, and shantung are used. Better shoes are lined with leather. Drill and similar fabrics are used for less expensive shoes.

**shoelace** **1.** Synonym for SHOESTRING since 19th c. **2.** When jogging-type shoes became popular, shoelaces became more decorative and included such woven designs as small hearts, animals, or strawberries. Also called a *lacer.* **3.** See BOLO TIE under TIES.

**shoe rose** Large ornamental rosette of lace or ribbon, frequently jeweled, used by men and women to trim shoes in 17th c. Sometimes also used on garters and hat bands.

**SHOE
ROSE**

**shoestring** Lace for tying a shoe. At first not acceptable to society—some invitations stating that shoe buckles were required—but fashionable by the end of 17th c. when made of ribbon. From mid-19th c. on, term *shoelace* more commonly used. See SHOELACE.

**shoestring tie** Man's extremely narrow necktie of 1850s, tied in bow in front or fastened by pulling ends through a small ring. Also see BYRON TIE.

**shooting coat** Term used from 1860s to 1890s for *morning coat*.

**short** Woman's size group for various proportioned garments along with AVERAGE and TALL. Abbreviated S.

**shortalls** See SHORTS.

**short bands** Collar consisting of two narrow white linen bands hanging in front, fastened by strings around neck, and tied in back. Worn in 16th and 17th c. by clergymen, barristers, and collegians. Also called GENEVA BANDS, BANDS, or BÄFFCHEN.

**short hood** See PUG HOOD.

**shortie/shorty** See COATS, GLOVES, NIGHTGOWNS, and PAJAMAS.

**short paletot** See YACHTING COAT #1.

**shorts** **1.** Pants shorter than knee-length worn mainly by adults and children for sportswear. Worn by little boys from late 19th c. but not called by this name until 1920s. See KNEE-PANTS in alphabetical listing. In early 1930s worn by children and adults for camping. In 1933 worn by Alice Marble for a professional tennis match. Later became generally accepted for tennis and sportswear for women. In 1940s became a children's wear item—a substitute for dresses and rompers. In 1950s Bermuda shorts were accepted by men for leisure and city wear but not for business. In the late 1980s accepted for school wear and accepted as day wear but not for business. In 1986 the shorts suit was introduced with jackets matched to various types of shorts worn with contrasting tops giv-

ing the appearance of a minidress. **2.** Men's underpants usually made in boxer style.

## ▬ SHORTS ▬

**athletic s.** Pull-on cotton twill men's shorts with elastic top worn for gym and exercise. Also called *exercise shorts*, *running shorts*, and *track shorts*.

**balloon s.** Wide shorts set into waistband with large pleats and gathered at the legs into wide bands. Similar to BLOOMERS.

**Bermuda s.** Just-above-the-knee shorts that fit close to leg. First worn with knee socks as streetwear by men on the island of Bermuda, introduced in U.S. in early 1950s, as sportswear for women, later adopted by men for summer casual wear both in country and in town. Also called *walking shorts*.

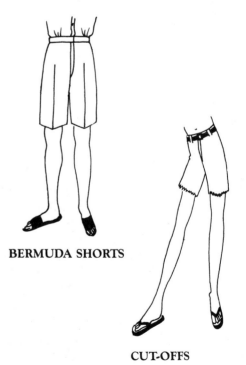

**BERMUDA SHORTS**

**CUT-OFFS**

**bib s.** Women's and children's shorts made with a bib top and straps over the shoulders attached to pants at the back of waist. Popular for women in 1940s and again in 1960s and 1980s. For children in the 1980s the word SHOR-TALL was used for this type of shorts.

**bike s.** Thigh-length shorts of durable fabric with fitted waistband, inside drawstring, and zip-fly closing with button at waist. Cut to fit snugly, but not to restrict movement, seat has an extra lining of terrycloth with back cut higher to prevent shirt from pulling out. Also have specifically designed pockets on sides of legs for wallet and maps. Tight-fitting shorts sometimes knitted with Lycra spandex. *Der.* Shortened form of word *bicycle*.

**body s.** Woman's tight-fitting shorts cut to top of leg, like leotards, with horseshoe-shaped straps in front and back. Worn with a knit shirt for dancing and exercising.

**boxer s.** **1.** Shorts made with elastic in a casing around waist, similar to those worn by prize fighters. Worn as underwear and for sportswear. **2.** See PANTIES.

**camp s.** **1.** Shorts with large patch pockets on the front and back. Belt is run through tunnel loops formed by tops of pockets. Also called *trail shorts*. **2.** Any shorts worn at a summer camp by children and counselors, sometimes of a required style or color constituting a uniform.

**cargo s.** Thigh-length shorts similar to CAMP SHORTS with two very large patch pockets in front—extending almost to hem and up and over belt in a tunnel loop; has one large box-pleated pocket in back with buttoned flap. Usually made in twill fabric in a blend of polyester and cotton.

**CityShorts** Term coined in 1969 by fashion-industry newspaper, *Women's Wear Daily,* for women's tailored shorts worn instead of skirt with matching jacket for town wear.

**cut-offs** Full-length pants, often BLUE JEANS, cut off above knee and fringed. Fad among teenagers in early 1960s. Became so popular

CARGO SHORTS

HOT PANTS

that stores began selling this style shorts.

**dhoti s.** Thigh-length shorts with many gathers at waistband which hang longer between the legs. *Der.* From Indian loincloth of the same name. Also see PANTS and alphabetical listing.

**drawstring s.** Pull-on shorts fastened with a drawstring at the waist similar to short pajama pants, introduced in late 1960s.

**exercise s.** See ATHLETIC SHORTS.

**hip huggers** Low-slung shorts resting on hips rather than coming to waistline.

**hot pants/HotPants** Slang term given a new meaning and spelling by fashion-industry newspaper, *Women's Wear Daily,* in early 1971 to describe women's short shorts made of luxury fabrics and leather, worn with colored tights and fancy tops as evening wear and on city streets.

**Jamaica s.** Shorts ending at mid-thigh, shorter than Bermudas. *Der.* Named for shorts worn in resort areas on island of Jamaica.

**jogging s.** See SWEATSHORTS.

**jumpshorts** Jumpsuit with legs reaching to knee or above, worn in late 1960s. Similar to style worn in 1930s and 1940s called a *playsuit.*

**lederhosen** Leather shorts usually made with bib top, originally a Tyrolean style, adopted for children and young people in the U.S. in late 1960s. *Der.* German plural of *Lederhose,* from *leder,* "leather" and *hose,* "trousers."

**little-boy s.** Short-length shorts made with turned-back cuffs. Popular in early 1960s for sportswear and bathing suits.

**mini-jeans** Very short shorts made by cutting off BLUE JEANS. Introduced in late 1960s.

**Pantacourt® s.** White wool belted close-fitting shorts coming a few inches above the knee embroidered with navy-blue stripes. Made with white binding at hems, waistline, and slashed pockets. Introduced by Andrè Courréges, Parisian couturier, in 1967.

**pleated s.** **1.** Woman's shorts styled to resemble a short skirt with inverted pleats in front and back and knife pleats in between. **2.** Shorts with several small unpressed pleats in front for added fullness.

**pull-on s.** Shorts made with an elasticized waistband.

**rugby s.** Thigh-length shorts precisely cut for unrestricted leg movement with elastic waistband only over hips, inner drawstring, lap-over closing with fly-front, and double-stitched side pockets. Made in colors and white of strong cotton twill. *Der.* Inspired by British shorts worn when playing rugby.

**running s.** See ATHLETIC SHORTS.

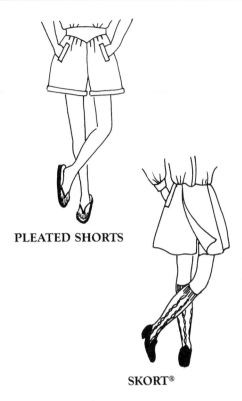

**PLEATED SHORTS**

**SKORT®**

**sailor s.** **1.** Shorts that fasten up back with lacings made with square buttoned flap closing in front like *sailor pants.* **2.** Woman's shorts with a zipper at front or side and a decorative, but not functional, lacing in back.

**scooter s.** Shorts made with a panel attached in front making them appear like a skirt. Also called a *scooter skirt.*

**shortall** Term introduced for children's and infants' bib shorts in the late 1960s. Used for adults in the 1980s. *Der.* Combination of words "shorts" and "overalls."

**short s.** Very brief shorts.

**Skort®** Trade name for shorts combined with miniskirt. Similar to *scooter shorts. Der.* Combination of words "skirt" and "shorts."

**suspender s.** Any style shorts worn with suspenders of felt, fabric, or other material.

Style was inspired by Tyrolean costume. Also see LEDERHOSEN.

**sweatshorts** Pull-on shorts made of cotton fleece fabric used for running and jogging in warmer weather. Also called *jogging shorts*.

**trail s.** See CAMP SHORTS and CARGO SHORTS.

**tennis s.** Conservative type of shorts, traditionally white, worn for playing tennis and general sportswear. Colored shorts were promoted in the late 1960s, but white was still first choice on the courts. Originally women players wore skirts but when length of skirts got longer in the 1930s, Senorita de Alvares played in a below-the-knee divided skirt in 1931, and in 1933 Alice Marble appeared in the above-the-knee shorts.

**track s.** See RUNNING SHORTS.

**trunks** Man's brief loose shorts worn (originally over tights) for swimming, boxing, and track.

**walking s.** See BERMUDA SHORTS.

**western s.** Shorts styled like dungarees with zipper fly in front, patch pockets on hips, and tight-fitting legs. Popular in late 1960s.

**short shorts** See SHORTS.

**shorts suit** See SPORT SUITS.

**shot cloth** Term for fabrics woven with different colored yarns in warp and filling which achieve a changeable or iridescent effect when held in the light. May be made of silk, rayon, or man-made fibers. Same as CHANGEABLE TAFFETA.

**shot silk** See SHOT CLOTH.

**shotten-bellied doublet** Man's *doublet* worn from 1560s to 1570s and also in 1600s made short waisted with a long point in front. See PEASCOD-BELLIED DOUBLET.

**shoulder** Manner of cutting an item of apparel in order to fit over the shoulder. In most early historical periods, shoulders followed normal body lines; however, in the 16th c. shoulders were extremely wide, and from 1825 to 1860 dropped shoulders were fashionable. In 1895 shoulders appeared very wide, returning gradually to natural shoulders during World War I period. In the late 1930s both men and women wore exaggerated, padded shoulders, and by late 1940s returned to natural shoulderline. Wide padded shoulders were again fashionable in 1980s.

## ▬▬ SHOULDERS ▬▬

**cape s.** Shoulder cut in shape of a cape with the sleeve set-in at a dropped shoulderline to give more freedom of movement. Used on sport jackets in mid-1980s.

**dropped s.** Shoulder of garment extended over upper arm. Sleeve seam comes on the upper arm rather than at the natural armhole. Style was very popular from 1825 to 1860, used occasionally since, becoming fashionable again in the mid-1980s.

**epaulet** Wide flat band extending along top of shoulder to sleeve seam, frequently trimmed with braid. *Der.* Borrowed from military uniforms. Also see alphabetical listing.

**extended s.** Plain shoulder seam extending down over arm to form a cap sleeve of longer length. Very popular in 1980s.

**flange** Extension of shoulders over armhole seam. Top sometimes made by using a wide band at edge, sometimes by making a deep pleat in front of blouse at the shoulders.

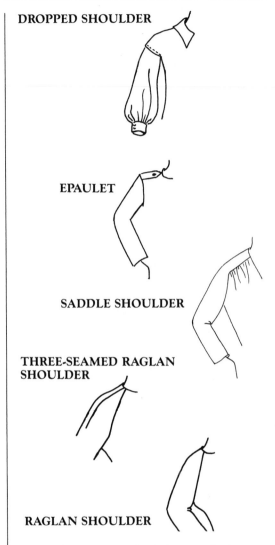

**DROPPED SHOULDER**

**EPAULET**

**SADDLE SHOULDER**

**THREE-SEAMED RAGLAN SHOULDER**

**RAGLAN SHOULDER**

**natural s.**   Follows body lines with sleeve set in at natural armhole without padding. Fashionable for men's suits in 1950s and 1960s.

**padded s.**   Pads sewn inside garment to make shoulder appear broader. Introduced for women in 1930s by Schiaparelli and also popular in mid-1980s.

**raglan s.**   Traditionally the raglan sleeve has no seam across the shoulder as seams come from under the arms directly to the neck in

front and back. *Three-seamed raglan* sleeves are similar to above but have an additional seam coming from the neck, across the shoulder and down the arm. *Der.* Lord Raglan, Fitzroy James Henry Somerset, British General in Crimean War, who after losing an arm in the Charge of the Light Brigade in 1854, had a coat designed with this special sleeve.

**saddle s.**   Shoulder with small yoke made by not bringing the raglan sleeve to the neck in a point, but by widening it so that it is 3 to 4 inches in width at the neck, thus forming a "saddle" over the shoulder.

**shoulder bag**   See HANDBAGS

**shoulder belt**   Sword belt worn diagonally from right shoulder to left hip by men in 17th c., formerly called *baldrick*. Also called *hanger.* See BELTS.

**shoulder cop**   Small plates covering front of shoulder. Later they were small pieces of articulated metal. Still later consisted of a single large plate called a *pauldron*. Also called *épaulière*.

**shoulder dart**   V-shaped dart, extending from mid-shoulder seam to bust, or from shoulder seam to shoulder blade in back.

**shoulder heads**   British term for shoulder straps of low-cut dresses used from 17th c. on.

**shoulder knot**   **1.** Ribbon loops, sometimes jeweled, worn by men on right shoulder from 1660 to 1700. **2.** 18th-c. decoration used on footman's livery. **3.** One of a pair of detachable flaps, decorated with braided metallic cord insignia, worn on the shoulder by commissioned and warrant officers of the U.S. Armed Forces to designate rank.

**shoulder pad**   Triangular-shaped or rounded pad filled with wool, cotton, or synthetic fibers used as a separate piece and tacked to the shoulder seam of clothing such as coats, dresses and blouses. Designed to create the illusion of broad or square shoulders. Introduced in late 1930s and also popular in 1940s, and 1980s.

**shoulder wing** Decorative projection at shoulder attached at armhole seam like a wing covering the *points* (laces) by which the sleeve is fastened to the armhole. Worn from 1545 to 1640 by both men and women.

**show** See COATS and SHOW BREECHES under PANTS.

**shower** See CAPS and SLIPPERS.

**showing horn** See SHOE HORN.

**shrink** See SWEATERS.

**shrinkage control** Fabrics woven and finished with processes that make them have less of a tendency to reduce their dimensions after washing and dry cleaning.

**shrug** See SWEATERS.

**shtreimel** Sable-trimmed hat worn by married male Hasidic Jews on the Sabbath and holidays.

**shuttle** Weaving term for the device which carries the *filling* yarn through the *warp* yarns on the *loom*. Usually a boat-shaped wooden object having an opening in the center for a *pirn* or a *quill* of yarn. Also see FLY SHUTTLE.

**Sicilian bodice** Evening-dress *bodice* of mid-1860s made with square décolletage and four knee-length panels attached—two in front and two in back—giving *tunic* effect.

**Sicilian embroidery** See SPANISH under EMBROIDERIES.

**side** 15th to 16th c. term for the term *long*, e.g., a *side gown* is a long gown.

**side boards** Slang term for side whiskers.

**side bodies** In tailoring, the two side pieces in the back of a man's coat. The seams that join these side panels to center back piece curve outward at the shoulder blades ending at arm-

hole seams. This construction gives better fit and flexibility than a one- or two-piece back and was used from 1840s on.

**side-channel frame** See FRAME.

**side-gore shoe** See SHOES.

**side-laced shoes** See OXFORDS.

**side leather** Cattlehides, too large to process in one piece, are cut down center back into two parts—each part is called a *side*. Used for sole leather or for shoe uppers and belts.

**sideless surcoat** Full-length, pullover woman's gown worn from mid-14th c. to end of 15th c. with boat-shaped neckline and huge armholes (like a jumper) extending to below hips showing *kirtle* and jeweled belt underneath. Usually fur-trimmed around neck, armholes, and on front *plackard*. Skirt was full, very long, and trained. Sometimes had family coat of arms on skirt—husband's family on right, wife's family on left. Also called *sideless gown*. Also spelled *sideless surcote*.

**side placket** Opening placed in side seam of a dress or blouse to facilitate putting on a fitted dress. Extends about 4″ above and below waistline. Originally fastened with *snaps*, later by a special type of zipper. Most dresses had this type of opening from 1930s to 1950s. Replaced by long back zippers extending from neckline to hips.

**signature** Practice started by Parisian couturiers in late 1960s of using their own name printed on scarfs and handbags. See HANDBAGS and SCARFS.

**signet ring** See RINGS.

**silhouette** Contour or outline of ensemble as shown in solid black on a white background.

Similar to a black shadow cast on a white wall. Formerly a term widely used to indicate trend in length and general outline for the coming seasons. *Der.* Named after French author and statesman, Étienne de Silhouette, 1709–1767, who first made portraits in black with no background.

## ▬▬▬ SILHOUETTES ▬▬▬

**A-line s.** Shape styled close and narrow at the shoulders, flaring gently away from the body from under arms to hem—resembling letter "A." Usually made in sleeveless or short-sleeved styles. One of the most popular silhouettes used for coats, dresses, skirts, and jumpers during the 1960s. *Der.* Originated by Paris couturier Christian Dior in 1955. Also see COATS, DRESSES, and SKIRTS.

**asymmetric s.** Silhouette using the principle of informal balance rather than formal balance with each side of the garment giving a different silhouette. Used for dresses, coats, blouses, nightgowns, skirts, and swimsuits, particularly of the toga or one-shoulder style.

**baby/baby doll s.** Short silhouette, styled bouffant from neckline or made with a shoulder yoke, gathered on skirt, and undefined waistline. Gives an outline similar to children's and infant's dresses of the 1930s. Used for dresses and nightgowns, particularly in the 1960s. Popularity enhanced by movie *Baby Doll* (1956) in which Carroll Baker played the lead. *Der.* Term used to refer to clothing and accessories used for children's dolls and infants' clothes in the early part of the 20th c.

**blouson s.** (blue-sohn) Bloused effect at the waistline, often below the natural waist, used in various types of dresses, jackets, shirts, and blouses. Introduced for children's dresses and boys' blouses in late 19th and early 20th c., used intermittently since, and popular in 1980s.

**A-LINE SILHOUETTE**

**BUBBLE SILHOUETTE**

**bouffant s.** (boo-fawn) Full-skirted dress shape usually combining fitted bodice and tight waistline with skirt in gathered, bell, or cone shape sometimes supported by means of hoops, ruffles, or stiff under-petticoats. Also see BUBBLE and DIRNDL SILHOUETTES.

**bubble s.** Bouffant shape that balloons from cinched waist and curves in again at hem to give a rounded contour. Popular for evening dresses in 1950s and used occasionally in mid-1980s.

**BUSTLE SILHOUETTE**

**CAGE SILHOUETTE**

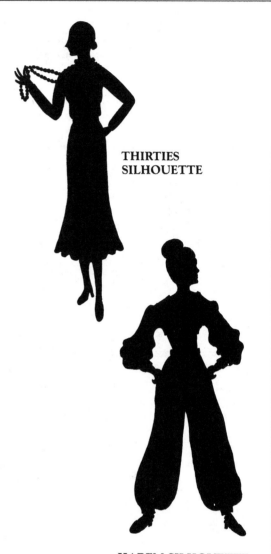

**THIRTIES SILHOUETTE**

**HAREM SILHOUETTE**

**bustle s. 1.** Straight front with fullness drawn to the back giving a bouffant effect in rear. Worn in 1880s, and revived in the 1930s, 1950s, and 1980s. **2.** Straight front with very full skirt in back ending in a train worn in 1870s.

**caftan s.** Loose, long flowing silhouette with undefined waistline and long sleeves, wide at the wrist. Adapted from Near East fashions in the late 1960s.

**cage s.** Dual silhouette formed by two layers of fabric with the outer layer of an openwork lace or a "latticed" type of fabric. Inner silhouette is made of opaque fabric or a body stocking is used. *Der.* Gives the appearance of a person standing within a "cage." Used for dresses, evening gowns, swimsuits and sport tops, it was introduced in late 1960s.

**chemise s.** See SHIFT SILHOUETTE.

MAXI SILHOUETTE          MIDI SILHOUETTE          MINI SILHOUETTE

TENT SILHOUETTE          TRUMPET SILHOUETTE          V-SHAPE SILHOUETTE

**Chinese s.** Straight-lined dress, coat, or robe silhouette fitted through the bust and waistline and made with slashes on the side seams from the hem to the thigh. Usually made with a mandarin-style neckline.

**dirndl s.** (durn-del) Modified bouffant silhouette with the skirt gathered at waistline. Worn in 1940s and 1950s. Same silhouette with modified, less full, skirt worn in 1980s. *Der.* Adapted from Tyrolean peasant dresses.

**Empire s.** (em-pire or om-peer) High-waisted silhouette with waistline directly under bust, and skirt hanging straight and narrow. Popular for dresses and nightgowns. *Der.* From style worn by Empress Josephine during First Empire in France, 1804–1815.

**gaucho s.** Calf-length, divided skirt silhouette with bolero worn over a full-sleeved blouse. Worn with wide flat, brimmed hat with a high, flat crown. *Der.* Spanish cowboy of Argentina, Chile, and Uruguay.

**granny s.** Ankle-length silhouette with a high waistline and slightly gathered but not bouffant skirt; usually with trimmed with ruffle at hem. Used particularly for dresses and nightgowns. Style was introduced from England in mid-1960s and worn particularly by young girls.

**harem s.** Near Eastern woman's silhouette, consisting of loosely draped skirt or full pants gathered in at ankle, first popularized in the West by Paris designer Paul Poiret, in 1912.

**hourglass s.** Woman's dress shape with full bust, pinched in waist, and full curving hip. The height of fashion in late 19th and early 20th c., popularized by Lillian Russell. Revived during late 1960s and 1980s. *Der.* From glass used to measure time in the same shape.

**kimono s.** Slim silhouette with narrow skirt—frequently full length—natural shoulders, high waistline effect, and wide sleeves—sometimes of hanging type. Used for dresses in late 1960s and for robes since late 19th and early 20th c.

**long-torso s.** Closely fitted silhouette on the torso to hips with low waistline and skirt in circular, pleated, or straight style.

**maxi s.** Ankle-length silhouette introduced in the late 1960s particularly for coats and skirts fitted at waistline with flaring skirt.

**midi s.** Variety of silhouettes distinguished by length which is mid-calf.

**mini s.** Variety of silhouettes defined by the length of the skirt which reaches to mid-thigh. Top usually conforms to body lines, the skirt may be flared, of long-torso, or dirndl-type. Introduced in England in early 1960s, the mini shape became one of the most popular silhouettes in the late 1960s.

**princess s.** Classic silhouette, snug-fitting through rib cage and waistline, with a flared skirt and no waistline seam. Dresses and coats are frequently made in this style. Popular in 1870s, the late 19th and early 20th c. revived in 1930s and 1940s and worn at intervals since. *Der.* Claimed to have been introduced by Worth about 1860 in a morning dress for Empress Eugénie.

**sheath s.** Silhouette following body lines made with a fitted waistline and simply cut narrow skirt, usually with pleat or vent in back of skirt. Basic style of the 1950s.

**shift s.** Straight-lined unfitted tube-shaped silhouette falling from the shoulders to the hem, not fitted at the bust or waistline. Worn in 1920s, reintroduced in 1957, and revived in the late 1960s and early 1970s. Also called *chemise.*

**tent s.** Pyramidal silhouette with fullness starting at neckline and flaring to hem. Popular for coats in 1930s and 1940s, revived in mid-1960s for dresses and coats.

**thirties s.** **1.** Early 1930s silhouette featured long lean bias-cut dress with intricate drapery, unusual sleeves and frequently U or round necklines. **2.** In late 1930s extremely broad shoulders were featured with small waistline and more tailored silhouette.

**tiered s.** Silhouette composed of series of flounces on the skirt. Worn in 1840s, 1930s, late 1960s, and revived in 1980s.

**torso s.** See LONG-TORSO SILHOUETTE.

**trapeze s.** Shape created for House of Dior in Paris by Yves Saint Laurent in 1958. Styled with narrow shoulders, unfitted waist, and flaring to hem.

**trumpet s.** Silhouette with long fitted-torso, flared from mid-thigh to hem in the shape of an inverted lily or trumpet. Popular in 1920s, 1930s, 1960s, and 1980s.

**twenties s.** Silhouette of straight-hanging shape to knees, sometimes bloused on top, with belt at hips. "FLAPPER" LOOK of 1920s, revived in the late 1960s and 1980s.

**V-shape s.** Silhouette of huge shoulders and oversized blouse tapering to a narrow skirt at hem. Shoulders and dolman or batwing sleeves sometimes cut in one piece so that sleeve at elbow slopes into side seam at waist. Other styles made with extended padded shoulders and large armhole seams—usually with sleeves of generous proportions. Introduced in 1983.

---

**silk** Fiber from larvae of insects produced when spinning their cocoons, specifically fiber from cocoon of the silkworm. Noted for its resiliency, elasticity, and strength. Primarily grown in Japan and China. Also see DOUPIONI, RAW SILK, SPUN SILK, and TUSSAH SILK.

**silk batting** Use of silk fibers instead of down for insulation in jackets and coats. Provides 20% more warmth than down.

**silk hat** High cylindrical-shaped hat with flat top and silk-plush finish used by men on formal occasions and with formal riding dress by men and women. Invented by John Hetherington, a haberdasher of London, provoking a riot when first worn by him on January 15, 1797. He was charged in court for "breach of peace" for frightening timid people. Hat subsequently became the *top hat* in 1830. Also see CHIMNEY-POT HAT.

**silk illusion** Very fine net, similar to *tulle*, used for wedding veils.

**silking** See POINTING.

**silk-screen printing** Method of printing designs on fabric by blocking out motifs for each color on separate screens made of silk or man-made fabric. Screens are laid over the flat fabric and each color is squeezed through by hand or machine. Also see SILK SCREEN PRINT under PRINTS. *Der.* Made by individual "silk screens."

**silk stocking** Hosiery knit of silk yarn, with first pair said to have been worn by Queen Elizabeth I. In early 1900s hosiery was made of heavy pre-dyed silk yarns with cotton tops and sold for $12.50 per pair. After World War I, perfection of machinery plus the use of gum silk in knitting, and improved methods of dyeing, produced hose which were much sheerer and lower in price. Very popular until early 1940s when replaced by nylon. In early 1900s term "Silk Stocking District" coined for a high-rent congressional district on New York's East Side, and still referred to as such.

**silver** Metal used for jewelry. See STERLING SILVER and COIN SILVER.

**silver fox** See FURS.

**silver pantyhose** See PANTYHOSE.

**silvertone and goldtone effects** Textile term for introducing an iridescent quality or silvery effect by using a few white yarns at intervals in velours or velvets. Also made by working silver and gold threads into the napped surface of wool coating fabric.

**simar** (si-mar) **1.** Woman's loose-fitting jacket

with side flaps, or skirts, extending to knees, sometimes worn over petticoat to make a dress in 17th and 18th c. Also spelled *samarre*. **2.** Clerical robe, similar to full-length cassock, but having short button-on false sleeves and a shoulder cape that does not fasten in front. Worn at home or on the street, but not worn for high church services, particularly by prelates of the Catholic church. Made of white wool for the Pope, black wool with scarlet trimmings for Cardinals, black wool with amaranth red or purple trim for Penitential or mourning days for Bishops, and ash-gray wool for Franciscans. Also worn by seminarians without the false sleeves (thus indicating inferior dignity). Italian spelling is *zimarra*. Also see CHAMARRE. **3.** Robe worn by chancellors and magistrates in Italy which takes its name from full-length long-sleeved robe worn by senators of Venice in 14th and 15th c. Also spelled *simarra*. **4.** French Justice's robe. Also spelled *simarre*.

**simlah** Basic Hebrew garment consisting of a rectangular shaped piece of cloth wrapped around the body as an outer garment. Similar to the Greek HIMATION and Roman PALLIUM. Also spelled *samlah*.

**Simpson, Adele** See APPENDIX/DESIGNERS.

**simulated gems** Term applied to copies of precious gems made of *paste*, or other inexpensive materials. Sometimes confused with synthetic gems, which are man-made but chemically identical to natural gems. Also see BEADS and GEMS.

**singeing** Process used on yarn or fabric which involves passing it over a gas flame to remove the shorter fibers.

**single-bar tricot** See TRICOT KNIT.

**single-breasted** Conventional closing, usually aligned down center front of garment. See CLOSINGS.

**single cuff** See CUFFS.

**single knit** Knit fabric made on one set of needles.

**single yarn** Refers to one strand of yarn. When two single yarns are twisted together the result is a *two-ply yarn*.

**siphonia** (sy-fo-ni-a) Long weather-proof overcoat worn by men in 1850s and 1860s. The *pocket siphonia* was short and thin enough to be rolled up and carried in case of rain.

**siren suit** British one-piece *coverall* worn during World War II. Designed for fast dressing in case of emergencies signaled by air-raid sirens.

**sisal** (sy-sal) Finely woven smooth straw with linen finish made from Philippine sisal hemp shipped to China. Also spelled *sisol, sissol*.

**sisi** A girdle-like belt, about 6″ wide, made of various colored beads with strands of small beads hanging down in loops. Worn by women in the Fiji Islands.

**sivlonoth** Marriage or wedding belt worn in 16th and 17th c. by Jewish bride and groom as gifts to one another. Made of gold or silver gilt and brocaded velvet with rosettes set with precious stones.

**Siwash sweater** See COWICHAN SWEATER under SWEATERS.

**sizing** **1.** Measurements of body used as guide for cutting garments to fit a variety of body types. **2.** Non-permanent finishing process applied particularly to cotton fabrics to increase weight, crispness, and luster by means of starch, gelatin, oil, and wax.

**skating** See BOOTS, DRESSES, and SKIRTS.

**skein** **1.** Unit by which knitting yarn is sold, usually comes packaged in loosely coiled form. Also called a *hank*. **2.** Originally the form in which silk and other yarns were sent from spinning plant to weaving plant. Now yarn is frequently delivered in *tubes, cones, warps*, and *cake*-form.

**skeleton suit** Boy's suit worn from 1790 to 1830 consisting of tight jacket decorated with two rows of buttons extending over shoulders, and ankle-length trousers buttoned to jacket at waist.

**SKELETON
WATERPROOF**

**skeleton waterproof** Woman's full-length front-buttoned raincoat of 1890s made with large armholes, instead of sleeves, covered by a hip-length circular cape.

**skelton skirt** Another name used for the CAGE PETTICOAT.

**ski clothing** Clothes worn for the winter sport of skiing. Also clothing copied from ski-wear. See BOOTS, MASKS, PAJAMAS, PANTS, SPORT JACKETS, SPORT SUITS, and SWEATERS.

**skimmer** See DRESSES, HATS, and SHOES.

**skin socks** Socks made by Greenland Eskimos of hides with fur on the inside.

**skirt** **1.** Lower part of dress; the section below the waistline. From medieval times to 1795 and from 1830 to late 19th c. dresses usually made with separate skirts and bodices; in early 20th c. made in one piece with seam at waistline. **2.** Separate item of clothing starting above, below, or at natural waistline. In 1870s tailor-made suits were introduced for women with separate skirts and jackets. Emphasis on shirtwaists in the 1890s also made separate skirts popular. In the 1920s the sweater and skirt became a popular combination. **3.** Term used for lower part of a coat or jacket, particularly in Great Britain. See DIRECTOIRE SKIRT, FOOT MANTLE, FUSTANELLA, MORNING-GLORY SKIRT, PULLBACK, RAINY DAISY SKIRT, and SUNRAY SKIRT in alphabetical listing.

## ■ SKIRTS ■

**accordion-pleated s.** Skirt made from a full circle of fabric with pressed-in ridges which are wider at the hem and taper to waistline, giving a flare to skirt. When the body is in motion pleats flare at the hem like the bellows of a half-open accordion. Introduced in late 1880s by Loie Fuller for "skirt dancing" and popular at intervals since. Also called *sunburst-pleated skirt.* Also see SUNRAY SKIRT in alphabetical listing.

**A-line s.** Slightly flared skirt introduced in the early 1960s. In silhouette it appears like the letter A.

**asymmetric s.** Any skirt which differs on either side of an imaginary line drawn down the center front. Sometimes has ruffles or flounces attached diagonally across center front from waist to hip; frequently has an ASYMMETRIC HEMLINE.

**bell s.** Skirt usually gathered at waistline, making it full over hips and flared at hem. Popular from the 1830s to late 1860s and sometimes worn with crinoline or hoops underneath. Popular for evening gowns from 1930s to 1960s.

**bias s.** Any skirt cut on the diagonal or *bias* of the fabric. The bias cut was introduced by Madeleine Vionnet in 1920s and was popular through the 1930s, worn at intervals since, and revived in 1980s.

**bouffant s.** Any full skirt; more specifically a gathered skirt.

**box pleated s.** Two flat folds meeting underneath to form box pleats which extend around the waist, alternating with inverted pleats. Popular in 1940s and 1950s, and at intervals since.

**broomstick s.** Full skirt which, after washing, is tied tightly with a string around a broomstick. When dry, it contains vertical ridges or wrinkles. Popular in the 1940s and somewhat revived in the late 1960s.

**bubble s.** Skirt gathered to small waistline, ballooning out and tapered in at hem, popular in 1950s. Also called *tulip skirt.*

**bustle-back s.** Any skirt with puffed fullness, ruffles, or large bow in the center back. Starting in late 1860s skirt fullness was pulled to the back but skirt was full. During the late 1870s skirt became slim with accent in back. In mid-1880s skirt was full with large bustle. Style was somewhat revived in the 1930s, 1940s, and 1980s.

**circle/circular s.** Skirt made by cutting a semicircle out of a piece of fabric folded lengthwise. The selvages are then joined to make a full circle. Popular for skating and general wear in the 1930s, it has remained a basic type of skirt becoming very popular in mid-1980s.

**crinoline** Underskirt made of stiffened fabric which holds out the main skirt. Used in 1850s before hoop skirts were invented and popular again under dresses from 1940s to 1950s. Reintroduced in 1986.

**culottes** **1.** Skirt divided into two sections so that it is actually a pair of pants but looks like a skirt when not in motion. Also called *split skirt, pantskirt,* DIVIDED SKIRT, *scooter skirt,* or SKORT®. **2.** See DRESSES. *Der.* French, *culotte,* "knee breeches"; *des culottes,* "trousers."

**dance s.** Short skirt worn over leotard and tights by dancers for practicing.

**dirndl s.** (durn-del) Skirt cut full and gathered into band at waist, popular in 1940s, and 1950s. In 1980s a modified style with only a few gathers at waist was popularized. *Der.* Copied from Tyrolean peasant skirts.

**divided s.** Contemporary skirt similar to CULOTTES. First worn in England by Lady Haberton for bicycle riding in early 1880s. Also worn by women for riding horses in western U.S. Popular in 1890s, again in 1930s, and revived in 1980s. Also called CULOTTES.

**draped s.** Any skirt with additional fullness pleated or gathered into one side seam or forming a drapery which hangs down.

**Empire s.** Straight skirt starting at a high waistline under the bust. Originated in *Empire Period,* 1804–1815, and worn at intervals since.

**evening s.** Any type of separate skirt worn for a formal occasion. Popular in the 1930s, 1940s, 1970s, and 1980s for semiformal occasions.

**fishtail s.** Skirt with additional stitched on free-hanging panel in front or back simulating the tail of a fish.

**flying panel s.** Complete skirt made with an extra panel attached at the waistline which hangs free. Basic type skirt for dresses in 1940s and 1950s, and revived with pants-type dress of late 1960s.

**full s.** Any skirt made with several widths of fabric, may be cut in a complete circle, made with many gores, or gathered.

**gathered s.** Skirt made straight with panels of fabric sewed together, shirred (or gathered) at the top, and attached to a waistband or bodice of dress. Popular at intervals since 1830.

**godet s.** A triangular piece of fabric inserted upward from the hem of the skirt to give more fullness. Popular in 1930s and used occasionally since.

**gored s.** Skirt which fits through the waistline and flares at the hem. May be made of from four to twenty-four shaped sections. Dates from 14th c. and much used in 19th c. Very popular in the late 1860s, mid-1890s, early 20th c., 1930s, 1940s, and worn intermittently since.

**granny s.** Full-length gathered skirt usually with a ruffle at hem introduced in 1960s. *Der.* Worn by a young girl in imitation of skirt worn by her grandmother or "granny."

**handkerchief s.** Skirt with hemline cut to fall in points as if made of handkerchiefs. Popular in 1920s, 1960s, and 1980s.

**harem s.** Draped skirt with hem gathered, turned up, and fastened to lining. Worn in the Near East and introduced to the West by Paris designer Paul Poiret in 1912.

**hip-hugger s.** Any skirt, usually belted, that rides low on hips below the natural waistline, popular in late 1960s.

**hoop s.** A skirt held out with crinoline, a stiffened underskirt, or hoops. May be bell-, cone-, or pyramid-shaped. Very fashionable from 1850 to 1870 and worn at intervals since, particularly for evening gowns.

**hula s.** Grass skirt worn originally in Hawaii. Also copied in plastic strips for costumes. *Der.* Named for skirts worn by hula dancers in Hawaii.

**inverted pleated s.** Skirt made by bringing two folds of fabric to a center line in front and/or back. May be cut straight at sides or be slightly flared. Has been a basic type of skirt since 1920s.

**jupe** French word for skirt. A *mini-jupe* is a miniskirt. Used in 1960s as a synonym for skirt.

**kangaroo s.** Term used for maternity skirt designed by Elsie Frankfurt in early 1940s with a circular cutout in center top front. This portion was not filled in with stretch fabric as in later maternity skirts.

**kick-pleated s.** Straight skirt with only one pleat in either front or back to make walking easier. Popular when narrow silhouettes are worn.

**kilt** Scottish skirt made in wraparound style. Center front is plain with *knife pleats* starting at side front and wrapping around to other side or front. Hanging end may be fringed and fastened with a large decorative safety pin. Originally worn by Scots Highlanders in various tartans. Copied for children and women at intervals since the 1860s.

**knife pleated s.** **1.** Skirt made with single pleats about 1″ wide all going in the same direction completely around the skirt. **2.** Skirt made with single pleats starting from a center *box pleat* and going around to center back where they form an *inverted pleat*. Both are basic types of skirts introduced in the 1920s. Also popular in 1940s and late 1960s when heat-set pleating was introduced.

**layered s.** Skirt made of tiers in varying lengths, placed one on top of the other.

**maternity s.** Skirt worn by expectant mothers with either a cut-out section at top center front or a section of stretch fabric inserted over the abdomen.

**maxi s.** Term used for ankle-length daytime skirt, popular with women in late 1960s as reaction against miniskirts.

**midi s.** Skirt with hem halfway between ankle and knee, below the widest part of the calf.

Introduced by designers in 1967 as a reaction to very short miniskirts.

**miniskirt**   Term used for extremely short skirt, any length from 4″ to 12″ above the knee. Popular for day and evening in the 1960s, credited to London designer, Mary Quant.

**overskirt**   **1.** A second skirt or drapery often looped up or split at sides, front, or back. Also an entire skirt of a sheer fabric constructed over a more opaque *underskirt*. **2.** See POLONAISE #1 in alphabetical listing.

**panel s.**   See FLYING PANEL SKIRT.

**pantskirt**   Synonym for CULOTTES, *split skirt*, SKORT®, DIVIDED SKIRT, and SCOOTER SKIRT. All popular since mid-1960s.

**peasant s.**   **1.** Full gathered skirt which may be trimmed with bands of embroidery; plain gathered skirt; or skirt worn with an embroidered apron. **2.** In the 1960s referred to skirt decorated with bands of embroidery rather than style of skirt. *Der.* Adopted from national costume of European countries.

**peg-top s.**   **1.** Basic skirt cut full at the waistline with darts, gathers, or small unpressed pleats used at waistline. From hips to hem skirt tapers inward becoming very narrow at hem. Sometimes made with center front seam with each panel rounded at hem. Usually made with a *knife pleat* or slit on center back seam. Popular in 1950s and 1960s, used occasionally since. **2.** Skirt made with fullness from waistline to hips, tapering narrowly to hemline. Popular during World War I and revived at intervals. *Der.* Name borrowed from boy's cone-shaped spinning top.

**prairie s.**   Flared skirt gathered at the waistband with one or two ruffles at the hem made in plain or calico-patterned fabrics. *Der.* Adapted from skirts worn by women traveling West on the wagon trains.

**St. Tropez s.**   Ankle-length full skirt made with diagonal bands of various printed and plain-colored fabrics—may be as many as eight different fabrics used.

**sarong** (seh-rong)   Wrapped skirt, usually made of bold floral-print cotton, used as beach coverup. Popularized by actress Dorothy Lamour in film, *Hurricane*, late 1930s. *Der.* Copied from Indonesian native dress. See DRESSES category.

**scooter s.**   See SKORT®.

**sheath s.**   Straight skirt with no flare. Usually has a kick pleat or slit in back to facilitate walking. Popular style in the 1950s and early 1960s.

**skating s.**   Very short full circular skirt. First popular in late 1930s after films by Norwegian-American ice-skater Sonja Henie. See DRESSES category.

**Skort®**   Trademark for miniskirt with shorts, popular in late 1960s. Also called *scooter skirt*. *Der.* Combination of words "skirt" and "shorts."

**slit s.**   **1.** Straight-lined skirt with slashes on each side seam to knee or thigh. Copied after styles worn by Chinese and Vietnamese women. Also see CHEONGSAM under DRESSES and AO DAI in alphabetical listing. **2.** Straight skirt with slash at center front or center back.

**split s.**   Synonym for PANTSKIRT, DIVIDED SKIRT, or CULOTTES.

**square-dance s.**   Full skirt with large ruffle at hem. Popular in rural areas for square dancing and barn dances.

**squaw s.**   Full skirt set with tiny pleats which may have horizontal embroidered bands at intervals and a ruffle at hem. Originally worn by American Indian women with embroidered blouse. In late 1960s accepted for wear by other women.

**straight s.**   Any slim skirt without fullness, *e.g.*, a SHEATH SKIRT.

**sunburst-pleated s.**   See ACCORDION PLEATED SKIRT.

ASYMMETRIC SKIRT    FLYING PANEL SKIRT    CULOTTES    GRANNY SKIRT    PEG-TOP SKIRT

MINISKIRT    DIVIDED SKIRT, 1895    PRAIRIE SKIRT

SLIT SKIRT    SQUAW SKIRT    WRAP SKIRT    YOKE SKIRT

**suspender s.** Any skirt with attached suspenders frequently worn by young girls.

**swing s.** Flared skirt, circular or cut in gores, fitted at hips with a wide flare at the hem. Popular in the late 1930s, and at intervals since. Very popular in mid-1980s.

**tiered s.** Straight-lined skirt with a series of flounces cut either in circular style, or on the straight of the material. Each flounce is usually cut larger than the previous one. Popular in the 1840s, 1860s, 1930s, and at intervals since.

**torso s.** Pleated or gathered skirt attached to a yoke at hips.

**trumpet s.** Straight-lined skirt with one large circular flounce at the hem which flares like an inverted trumpet.

**tulip s.** See BUBBLE SKIRT.

**tunic s.** Double-layered skirt with the overskirt cut shorter than the underskirt. Originally introduced in the 1850s as a ball dress with the upperskirt trimmed with lace and underskirt with a deep flounce. Popular in slim style in the 1880s, 1910 to 1920, and worn intermittently since.

**umbrella-pleated s.** Circular-cut or gored skirt with widely spaced pleats similar to accordion pleats only larger, simulating folds in an umbrella

**underskirt** **1.** Simple basic skirt over which an overskirt, or drapery, hangs. **2.** Term for a woman's *slip* or *petticoat.*

**wrap s.** A skirt open from waist to hem which wraps around the body and fastens with buttons or ties, usually lapped across the front or back.

**yoke s.** Skirt with small fitted piece, sometimes straight, pointed, or scalloped attached at waistband. Lower part of skirt attached to yoke may be gathered or gored. Yoke may be placed at front or back of skirt, or both.

**skirt belt** See BELTS.

**skirt supporter** Patented elliptical metal *hoop* of late 1850s with two moon-shaped wire metal cages inserted within the hoop—one on either side. Fitted over woman's petticoat just below the waistline to hold out a full skirt.

**skivvies** Slang term for a man's underwear consisting of shorts and top. Also see KNIT SHIRTS.

**skivvy** Slang term for a man's undershirt, especially as worn by a sailor.

**skoncho** See PONCHOS.

**Skort®** See SHORTS or SKIRTS.

**skullcap** See CAPS.

**skunk** See FURS.

**slacks** Term is usually applied to loose-cut casual pants, not part of a suit. See PANTS and TROUSERS.

**slammerkin** Loose-fitting, unboned *morning gown* worn without hoops by women from 1730 to 1770. If worn outdoors, hoops were added. Also called *trollopee.*

**slant/slanted toe** See TOES.

**slap-shoe** Woman's shoe of the 17th c. styled like a *mule,* usually with high heel.

**slashed sleeve** See SPANISH SLEEVE.

**slashing** 15th and 16th c. term for vertical slits in clothing that enabled the contrasting lining to be pulled through. Used on *doublets,* sleeves, and *trunk hose.* Also called *scissoring, chique-tades,* and *creves.* Called BLISTERED during late 16th and 17th c.

**slash pocket** See BOUND POCKET under POCKETS.

**slave bracelet** See BRACELETS.

**sleepwear** Department-store term for nightgowns, pajamas, and robes. See SLEEP BONNET under BONNETS; LEISURE BRA under BRAS; NIGHTSHIRT, SLEEPCOAT, SLEEPER, and SLEEP SHIRT under NIGHTGOWNS; and SLEEP SET and SLEEP SHORTS under PAJAMAS.

**sleeve** Part of an item of clothing which covers the arm. In early times sleeves were cut in one with garment, *kimono style*. In the Middle Ages *set-in sleeves* were used; in 16th and 17th c. sleeves were *puffed, padded,* or *slashed*; in 18th c. women wore plain, elbow-length sleeves with ruffles, and coat sleeves for men were made with large turned-back cuffs. In the 19th c. Regency Period short puffed sleeves were worn by women and tailored plain set-in sleeves by men. In the Victorian Era large puffed and *leg of mutton* sleeves were worn by women. In the 20th c. a great variety of sleeves for both men and women were worn. See IMBECILE SLEEVE, MARINO FALIERO SLEEVE, and VIRAGO SLEEVE in alphabetical listing.

### ■■■■■ SLEEVES ■■■■■

**all-in-one s.** Sleeve with no armhole, cut in one piece with front and back of blouse with seams down the inside and outside of the arm. Resembles the batwing sleeve and kimono sleeve but not cut as full under the arm. May be combined with a raglan or set-in sleeve with the front cut in either manner and the back cut all-in-one.

**angel s.** Any type of long flowing sleeve. May fit smoothly into the armhole or be gathered. Sometimes split up outer arm to shoulder like a HANGING SLEEVE.

**baby doll s.** Another name for a tiny PUFFED SLEEVE.

**balloon s.** Very large puff sleeve extending to elbow set into a regular armhole and frequently made of crisp fabrics. Popular in 1890s and since for evening and wedding dresses.

**barrel s.** Sleeve that fits at armhole and at wrist but is full at the elbow.

**batwing s.** Long sleeve cut with deep armhole almost to waist, made tight at wrist, giving wing-like appearance when arm is extended.

**bell s.** Sleeve made narrow at the top, set into normal armhole, and flaring at lower edge like a bell. Introduced in the second half of the 19th c.

**beret s.** Short sleeve, often used on evening dresses, made from two circles of fabric seamed at outer edges with holes cut in centers for armhole and arm. Usually lined to stand out stiffly. Popular from 1820 to 1850 and again in 1930s. Also called *melon sleeve.*

**bishop s.** Full sleeve set into normal armhole and gathered into band at wrist.

**bracelet s.** Three-quarter length fitted cuffless sleeve allowing a bracelet to show.

**butterfly s.** Wide flaring sleeve set in smoothly at armhole, extending to elbow or wrist, giving a caped effect.

**button-tab s.** A convertible roll-up sleeve made in long sleeve style with buttonholed tab sewed on above elbow. Sleeve is rolled up and fastened to tab with button sewn on underside of sleeve.

**cape s.** **1.** Circular, or semi-circular, piece placed over each shoulder and stitched to the blouse giving a caped effect over each arm. **2.** Flared piece of fabric cut to extend to neck in raglan style. Introduced in 1920s and featured in late 1960s for *cape coats.*

**cap s.** Small extension cut on the front and back of a blouse to cover the shoulder. Has a seam at the shoulder fastening front and back of garment together but no armhole seam. Popular in the 1940s and worn at intervals since. In the 1980s flat turn-over cuffs were sometimes added to this type of sleeve.

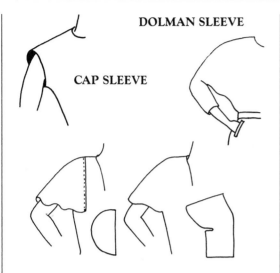

**DOLMAN SLEEVE**

**CAP SLEEVE**

**CAPE SLEEVES**

**cartwheel s.** Short sleeve composed of two circles joined together around the outer edge. One circle fits into armhole, the other fits around the arm. Copied from the BERET SLEEVE. Also called *circle sleeve*.

**circle s.** See CARTWHEEL SLEEVE.

**dolman s.** Sleeve fitted at wrist but cut with deep armhole so that it somewhat resembles a cape from the back. So called because it looks somewhat like sleeve in original DOLMAN. Also see alphabetical listing.

**double-puffed s.** Full sleeve with band around arm that divides it into two puffs. In 1960s, a bracelet was sometimes worn around upper arm over full sleeve to give same effect.

**elbow-length s.** Any sleeve which stops at elbow. Popular length used for dresses in 1940s and 1960s.

**epaulet s.** Sleeve with yoke across top of shoulder cut in one piece with sleeve.

**fitted s.** Full-length, bracelet, or three-quarter length sleeve set into the normal armhole.

**French gigot s.** See LEG-OF-MUTTON SLEEVE.

**funnel s.** See PAGODA SLEEVE.

**handkerchief s.** Sleeve made with square piece put over shoulder in such a manner that it falls in points like a handkerchief.

**hanging s.** Any sleeve with long piece of drapery starting at shoulder, at the upper arm, or at the elbow. Also see alphabetical listing and ANGEL SLEEVE.

**Juliet s.** Long sleeve with short puffed top, fitted on lower arm. *Der.* Named after heroine of William Shakespeare's drama *Romeo and Juliet*.

**kabuki s.** **1.** See KIMONO SLEEVE. **2.** In 1984 a version of kimono sleeve was made with wide hanging piece under the arm which tapered to close-fitting at wrist.

**kimono s.** Wide sleeve cut in one piece with front and back of the garment and seamed down outer and under arm like a Japanese KIMONO. Also called KABUKI SLEEVE and *mandarin sleeve*.

**lantern s.** Sleeve which is plain at top and wrist but balloons out halfway between the wrist and the elbow. Cut in two pieces with a seam going around the sleeve at the fullest part.

**leg-of-mutton s.** Sleeve with full top gathered or pleated into armhole and tapered to wrist where it looks like a regular sleeve. Size may vary—in 1895 very full sleeves requiring a yard or two of fabric were popular. Also spelled *leg-o'mutton*. Also called a FRENCH GIGOT SLEEVE. See alphabetical listing. *Der.* French, "leg of lamb."

**mandarin s.** See KIMONO SLEEVE.

**melon s.** See BERET SLEEVE.

**pagoda s.** Funnel-shaped outer sleeve flaring at wrist, falling over a puffed undersleeve. *Der.* Named for the shape of a Far Eastern temple's flaring roof. Also see alphabetical listing.

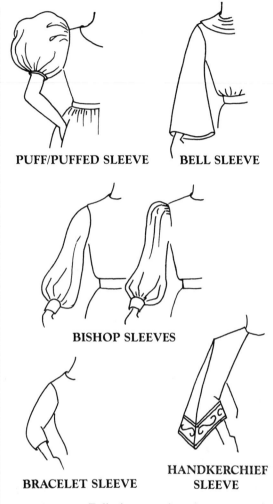

**PUFF/PUFFED SLEEVE**     **BELL SLEEVE**

**BISHOP SLEEVES**

**BRACELET SLEEVE**     **HANDKERCHIEF SLEEVE**

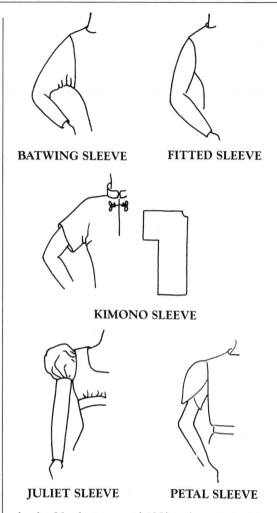

**BATWING SLEEVE**     **FITTED SLEEVE**

**KIMONO SLEEVE**

**JULIET SLEEVE**     **PETAL SLEEVE**

**peasant s.** Full sleeve gathered at top and bottom. May be either short and puffed or long and full.

**petal s.** Short sleeve curved at hem and overlapping to give a petal-shaped effect in front.

**puff/puffed s.** Short sleeve gathered, either at the armhole or at the cuff band or both, producing a rounded shape. Popular in 1920s and 1930s, revived in late 1960s, and still used for babies and children's wear.

**raglan s.** Sleeve that extends to neckline, set in by seams slanting from underarm front and back. Used since mid-1850s. A variation is made with an additional seam down outside of arm called a *three-seamed raglan. Der.* Lord Raglan, or Fitzroy James Henry Somerset, British General in Crimean War, who, after losing an arm in the Charge of the Light Brigade in 1854, had a coat designed with a special sleeve.

**rhumba s.** Barrel-shaped sleeve covered with rows of small horizontal ruffles. *Der.* From shirts worn by men dancing South American rhumba.

**roll/roll-up s.** Sleeve, approximately elbow length, finished only with a narrow hem, de-

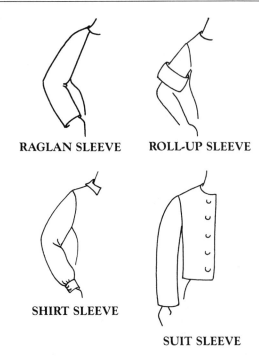

**RAGLAN SLEEVE**  **ROLL-UP SLEEVE**

**SHIRT SLEEVE**

**SUIT SLEEVE**

**THREE-QUARTER SLEEVE**

signed to be folded—or rolled up—at least twice in lieu of a cuff. Popular for women's tailored shirts in 1950s and 1960s, an outgrowth of earlier fad for wearing long sleeves folded up in this manner.

**saddle s.** Variation of RAGLAN SLEEVE in which shoulder portion forms a straight band cut in one piece with the sleeve and seamed to front and back parallel to shoulder, instead of at an angle as in raglan style. Also see EPAULET SLEEVE.

**set-in s.** Any type of sleeve which is sewed into the natural armhole.

**shirt s.** Tailored wrist-length sleeve with flat-felled seams set smoothly into the armhole. Sometimes has one or two small unpressed pleats where it joins the cuff. Basic sleeve for men's shirts since late 19th c., may have BARREL or FRENCH CUFF—women's style may have band at cuff.

**suit s.** Sleeve cut in two pieces—one for under the arm—one for top of arm. Cut to allow for the bend at the elbow, it is generally used in tailored suits for men and women.

**three-quarter s.** Sleeve ending between elbow and wrist.

**three-seamed raglan s.** See RAGLAN SLEEVE.

**Tom Jones s.** Full sleeve, gathered into cuff or ruffle, used on men's shirts, sometimes set into dropped shoulder. *Der.* Named for style of shirts worn in 18th c. popularized by costumes worn in 1963 film of Henry Fielding's 1749 novel *Tom Jones*.

**trumpet s.** Sleeve fitting into natural armhole, falling straight to elbow where it flares in the shape of a trumpet.

**tulip s.** Set-in sleeve with bell shape made in several pieces like petals on a flower.

---

**sleeve à la folle** See IMBECILE SLEEVE.

**sleeve hand** 17th c. term for opening in sleeve through which hand is thrust.

**sleeveless blouse** See BLOUSES.

**sleeve string** See CUFF STRING.

**sleeve tongs** Ornamental metal tongs used to position large sleeves inside coat sleeves in mid-1890s.

**sleevings** See SLIVINGS.

**slendang** (slen-dahng) **1.** Cotton scarf of brightly colored woven pattern with fancy headings and fringed ends. **2.** Fabric manufactured in England and exported to Java, Siam, and Philippines where it was used for clothing. Compare with PA-HOM.

**slicker**   See RAINCOATS.

**slide**   See SANDALS.

**slide bracelet**   See BRACELETS.

**slide fastener**   See ZIPPER.

**slim jeans**   See PANTS.

**slingback shoe**   See SHOES.

**slingback thong**   See THONG #2 under SANDALS.

**sling-duster**   British term for coat worn by women in mid- and late 1880s. Made with *dolman* or *sling sleeves*. Frequently made of black and white checked silk.

**sling neckline**   See ONE-SHOULDER NECKLINE under NECKLINES.

**sling pump**   See SHOES.

**sling sleeve**   Sleeve cut in one with upper part of garment like a cape, frequently with attached horizontal piece of fabric, similar to a *sling*, on which to rest the arm. Worn by women in mid-1880s and used in SLING-DUSTER.

**slip**   **1.** Undergarment worn by women and girls beginning above the bust usually held in place with shoulder straps. Length is long or short in relation to the dress worn on top. Current meaning of the word dates from the early 19th c. **2.** 17th c. lining for semi-transparent dresses. **3.** 18th c. type of corset cover. **4.** Late 19th c. term for a man's white piqué edging for a morning vest called a *white slip.*

=== SLIPS ===

**bias s.**   Slip cut on the diagonal of the fabric to give a closer fit, it stretches to conform to the movements of the body. Introduced in the 1920s, popularized in the 1930s, and a classic since.

**blouse-s.**   Combination slip and blouse with top cut like a blouse and lower part serving as a slip under the skirt. Also called *slip-blouse.*

**bra-s.**   Slip made with a fitted top. One garment replaces two—the bra and the slip. Popularized in 1960s.

**built-up s.**   Slip made with U-neckline, deep armholes, and wide straps.

**camisole s.**   Slip of a lace or embroidered top to be worn under a sheer blouse—often cut straight across at neckline with wide straps. Also see CAMISOLE in alphabetical listing.

**chemise s.**   Thigh-length slip of the late 1960s which hangs straight and is not fitted.

**culotte s.**   Slip styled like wide panties cut knee length or shorter.

**STRAPLESS SLIP**

**CAMISOLE SLIP**

**evening s.** Slip made to be worn under an evening dress with the back of the slip and the length conforming to the dress worn over it.

**four-gore s.** **1.** Slip with no waistline, cut in four panels with two side seams, one seam down center front, and another in center back. **2.** Slip with a plain top, a waistline seam, and a four-gored flared skirt made to wear with bouffant dresses.

**half-s.** Straight-cut slip beginning at the waist. Another name for a *petticoat*. Introduced in 1940s, becoming a classic substitute for a regular slip.

**Hollywood-top s.** Slip with a fitted V-top, introduced in 1920s. Previous to this time slips were cut straight across in front or made with wider built-up straps.

**long-line bra-s.** A long-line bra attached to a petticoat or half-slip.

**maternity s.** Slip with an elastic panel at mid-section in the front worn by expectant mothers.

**panty s.** Actually a short petticoat with attached panties.

**petti-s.** Same as HALF-SLIP or PETTICOAT.

**princess s.** Slip made in fitted panels from top to hem having no waistline seam, may be flared or straight cut. Called *princess petticoat* in 1870s.

**shadow-panel s.** Slip made with an extra layer of fabric in a panel in front or back to diffuse the light when worn under a sheer dress or skirt.

**slip-blouse** See BLOUSE-SLIP.

**snip s.** Slip finished with three rows of hemstitching around bottom. One or more rows may be cut off to adjust length.

**strapless s.** Bra-top slip made with elastic, boning, and detachable straps.

**suit s.** Slip with white top and dark skirt worn under dark suit and sheer or white blouse.

**tailored s.** Slip made with cording, appliqué, or tucks as trim, rather than lace. Popular in 1940s, revived in early 1970s.

---

**slip-on** Term referring to clothing that pulls on over the head without use of extra slashes or plackets. Also called PULLOVER and *slip-over*. See BLOUSES, GLOVES, SHOES, and SWEATERS.

**slip-over** See SLIP-ON.

**slippage** **1.** Textile term for openings in the fabric due to shifting of either warp or filling yarns. Occurs because fabric is poorly constructed or *balance of cloth* is poor. **2.** Sewing term for shifting of warp or filling yarn at seams of a sewed garment.

**slipper** **1.** Low shoe usually worn indoors. **2.** In 16th c. the word meant a low shoe easily slipped on and off as differentiated from boots and oxfords. **3.** Sometimes used as a definition for some delicate types of shoes, *e.g.*, evening slipper.

**■■■■■ SLIPPERS ■■■■■**

**acrobatic s.** Soft flexible slipper made out of sueded splits of leather. Vamp comes up high in center front and a piece of elastic connects it to the quarter or back of shoe. Worn by dancers and gymnasts and also adopted by avant-garde for streetwear in the 1960s.

**after-ski s.** Same as SLIPPER SOCKS.

**après-ski s.** Same as SLIPPER SOCKS. *Der.* French, "after ski."

**ballet s.** **1.** Soft flexible slipper made of kid.

Upper is pulled around to form part of the sole which is very thin and has no heel. Worn by ballet dancers and children for dancing and in late 1940s for streetwear. Most slippers for professional dancers have been made since 1887 by Capezio, trademark of Capezio Ballet Makers, a division of U.S. Shoe Corp. **2.** Any similarly styled slipper worn indoors or outdoors usually with a heavier type sole. Reintroduced in 1984 with outer sole for streetwear styled in leather or fabric and sometimes worn with ballet laces.

**bedroom s.** An older term used for shoes made of fabric, felt, or leather usually in heelless style.

**bootee** **1.** Bedroom slipper edged with fur or fake fur. **2.** Infant's fabric or knitted shoe. **3.** Type of sock worn by astronauts in flight.

**boudoir s.** Early 20th c. term usually referring to slippers without backs made in fancy fabrics, and sometimes trimmed with marabou. Also see MULES.

**carpet s.** 19th c. informal slip-on house slipper made of carpeting, cut in pump style with a standing rounded tongue cut in one piece with toe and soft padded leather sole with flat heel made in one piece. Style still made in other fabrics and in felt. Also see FELTS.

**d'Orsay s.** Pump-shaped open-shank slipper cut down to the sole at either side. Women's styles have heels of varying heights, men's have flat heels. *Der.* Named for *Count d'Orsay.*

**evening s.** Delicate shoe worn with evening clothes. Man's style is usually a patent-leather pump.

**Everett** Man's house slipper with low back and high tongue curving over instep.

**Faust s.** See ROMEO SLIPPER.

**felts** Slippers with soft sole and upper frequently made of felt.

**flokati** Handcrafted Greek slipper sock in above-ankle length, made of fuzzy wool in

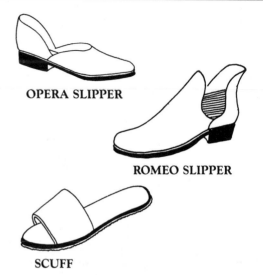

OPERA SLIPPER

ROMEO SLIPPER

SCUFF

bright colors and used as AFTER-SKI SLIPPER. Also see SLIPPER SOCKS.

**folding s.** Lightweight leather or fabric slippers with flexible leather or rubber soles which fold into a small case to carry when traveling. Formerly called a PULLMAN SLIPPER.

**Harlow s.** Boudoir slippers, similar to toeless slides with medium to high heel, trimmed with marabou. Copied from slippers worn by Jean Harlow, the Hollywood actress, in the late 1920s and 1930s.

**house s.** Older term for any type slippers worn indoors.

**Isotoner® s.** Trademarked soft lightweight washable slipper in ballet style made of fabric that stretches four ways for perfect fit and comfort. Made with soft leather split-sole® near the heel.

**Juliet s.** Woman's slipper with a high front and back, and V-shaped elastic gores at the sides. *Der.* Named for heroine of William Shakespeare's play *Romeo and Juliet.*

**moccasins** True heelless moccasins in which the sole is made of leather and comes up to form the quarter and part of the vamp. A tongue-like curved piece is hand-stitched to complete the vamp. Thong is threaded around the collar of the slipper and ties on the instep. Frequently is fleece-lined. May have fringe, beadwork, or tassel trim.

**mukluk s.** Slipper socks made in moccasin construction.

**mule** **1.** High-heeled slipper with vamp but no back often made of fancy leathers and fabrics. **2.** Term used since 16th c. for slipper without a quarter. Also spelled *moile, moyle, mowle.*

**opera s.** Man's bedroom slipper similar to D'ORSAY SLIPPER but front and back sections overlap at shank.

**Pullman s.** Man's lightweight, glove-leather flat slipper that folds into small envelope for traveling; also made in patterned stretch fabrics for women. *Der.* Named for railroad sleeping cars designed by George Pullman and Ben Field in 1858–59 and owned since 1864 by Pullman Palace Car Co.

**Romeo s.** Man's pull-on, boot-type slipper with elastic side gores. Also called *Faust slipper. Der.* Named for hero of William Shakespeare's play *Romeo and Juliet.*

**scuff** Open-back, sometimes open-toe, slipper with flat heel. May be of fur, shaggy fabric, lightweight kid, terrycloth, or other fabrics.

**shower s.** Plain heelless pump with upper of fishnet and sole of rubber or crepe. Worn at home, in the shower, or at the beach.

**slipper socks** Bulky knit socks frequently handmade with lightweight leather or urethane soles worn after skiing or around the house. Also called *after-ski slippers, après-ski slippers,* MUKLUK SLIPPERS, and FLOKATI.

**toe s.** Lightweight kid slipper reinforced with a hard toe and usually tied on with satin ribbons crisscrossing halfway up leg. Worn by ballerinas and toe dancers. Made by Capezio, trademark of Capezio Ballet Makers, a division of U.S. Shoe Corp.

**slipper satin** Lustrous, stiff satin fabric made primarily of acetate. May be combined with rayon, with silk and cotton, or made in brocaded effect. Used for formal gowns and shoes.

**slipper socks** See SLIPPERS and SOCKS.

**slip-shoe** Man's *mule* worn from 16th to mid-18th c. Made with flat heel that produced a shuffling step from which came the word "slipshod."

**slip stitch** See STITCHES.

**slit** Slashed opening in front of clothing used from 14th c. on to facilitate entry. When used at back of jacket, called a *vent.* Also see POCKETS and SKIRTS.

**slit trank** Trade term used in glove production. Piece of leather large enough for one glove is called a *trank.* When a die is pressed on the *trank* to cut out the glove, the process is called "slitting the trank."

**SLIT TRANK**

**slivings** Wide breeches worn by men in late 16th and early 17th c. Also see SLOPS. Also spelled *slivers, slives, sleevings.*

**slop** **1.** Short jacket worn by men in 14th and early 15th c. over a *doublet.* **2.** Term for slipper in 15th c. **3.** Cloak or nightgown worn by men and women in first half of 16th c. **4.** Term for laborer's *smock* worn by men in 18th and 19th c. Also see SMALL SLOPS and SLOPS.

**sloper** Basic pattern for a garment section, without style lines or seam allowances developed from *model form* (or dummy), live model, specific measurements, or manufacturer's specifications. Used to develop original patterns and create new designs. Also called *standard pattern*, *foundation pattern*, *block pattern*, and *master pattern*.

**slops** **1.** Knee-length unpadded *trunk hose*, worn during second half of 16th and early 17th c. Also see SMALL SLOPS and SLIVINGS. **2.** Term used until late 18th c. for sailor's trousers carried in a sea chest or "slop chest." **3.** From 17th to 19th c. a term for ready-made or old clothes and also the bedding and supplies sold in stores known as "slop shops."

**slot seam** See SEAMS.

**slouch** See HATS, NIGHTGOWNS, and SOCKS.

**slub yarn** Yarn which has a thick and thin texture. When used as filling in *shantung* fabric, it produces an uneven appearance with elongated thickened places at intervals.

**small** Size used along with MEDIUM, LARGE, and EXTRA LARGE for men, women, and children in such categories as sweaters, knit and sport shirts, sport jackets, nightgowns and pajamas, robes, gloves, girdles, and panty girdles. Abbreviated *S*.

**smallclothes** Polite term for men's breeches used from 1770 to mid-19th c.

**small falls** See FALLS.

**small slops** Trunk hose large at top, without band at hem, and reaching just to knees. Required for Cambridge University students in England from 1585 to about 1610.

**Smith, Willi** See APPENDIX/DESIGNERS.

**smock** **1.** Utility garment with sleeves fastened down front or back meant to protect clothes while wearer is working. Also see ARTIST'S SMOCK and TOPS. **2.** Garment worn next to skin by women from 11th to end of 18th c. See SMOCK-FROCK DRESSES, and TOPS.

**smock blouse** Child's dress of 1880s with the top bloused below the waistline by gathering with a ribbon pulled through insertion.

Knee-length skirt sometimes consisted of two ruffles.

**smock-frock** **1.** 18th- and 19th-c. term for man's knee-length, loose-fitting homespun gown worn by farmers. Sometimes made with a sailor collar, or yoke. Usually smocked in various patterns indicating the locality of the worker. Also called *smock*. **2.** In 1880s, a women's garment cut like a farmer's smock. See AESTHETIC DRESS.

**smocking** Decorative needlework used to hold gathered cloth together. The stitches catch alternate folds in elaborate honeycombed designs. Used especially on infants' and children's yokes and on waists and sleeves of dresses in late 19th and early 20th c., revived in early 1970s.

SMOCKING

**smoking jacket** See JACKETS and SUITS.

**smoky quartz** See GEMS.

**snail button** Covered button ornamented with *French knots* used on men's coats and waistcoats in 18th c.

**snake bracelet** See BRACELETS.

**snakes** Term for 17th-c. LOVE LOCKS.

**snakeskin** See LEATHERS.

**snap** See CLOSINGS and PANTIES.

**snap-brim hat** See HATS.

**sneaker** See SHOES and SOCKS.

**snip slip** See SLIPS.

**snood** **1.** Hairnet made from chenille, mesh, or other material worn at the back of the head and nape of neck to confine the hair—sometimes attached to a hat. In 15th and 16th c. nets decorated with pearls and jewels were worn. During the Second Empire (1852–1870) snoods of chenille or fine silk cord decorated with steel beads were worn over the *chignon*. Revived in 1930s and 1940s. Also see CADOGAN NET. **2.** Headband formerly worn by unmarried women in Scotland and northern England.

**snorkel coat/jacket** See SPORT JACKETS.

**Snow, Carmel White** (1888–1961) Worked for *Vogue* magazine from 1921 in fashion department. Made editor of American *Vogue* from 1929 to 1932. In 1932 she became fashion editor of *Harper's Bazaar*—later becoming editor until her retirement in 1957. Originally from Ireland, she was in the firm of Fox and Co. owned by her mother. A personality of wit, intelligence, and strong views, she was tiny and well-dressed in Parisian clothes. She had an instinct for fashion today and what would come tomorrow. Awards include 1941, Neiman Marcus Award; 1949, French Legion of Honor; 1954, Italian Star of Solidarity. Author with Mary Louise Aswell of *The World of Carmel Snow.*

**snow leopard** See FURS.

**snowmobiling** A winter sport using a small vehicle mounted on skis to glide over the snow. Distinctive clothing was designed for protection against the wind and cold temperatures. See SNOWMOBILE BOOT under BOOTS, SNOWMOBILE GLOVES under GLOVES, SNOWMOBILE SUIT under SPORT SUITS.

**snowsuit** See SPORT SUITS.

**snuggies** See PANTIES.

**soccus** (pl. socci) **1.** Light slip-on slipper worn in ancient Greece, especially the low shoe worn by the comic actors on the stage. Compare with COTHURNUS worn by Greek tragic actors. **2.** Ceremonial and coronation cape fastened on the right shoulder worn during Middle Ages by kings and dignitaries. Also spelled *socq.*

**sock boot** British term for *slipper socks.*

**socklets** See SOCKS.

**sock lining** Sole-shaped piece of leather or fabric covering shoe *insole.*

**socks** Knitted covering for the foot and part of the leg. In medieval times socks were worn with footless hose; in the 16th c. worn with *boot hose* and *stirrup hose*. From 1790 worn by men mainly with *pantaloons*, and in the 19th c. with trousers. Kept in place from about 1890 to 1940s with garters of the suspender-type fastened below the knee. In 1920s introduced for women and children for sportswear. *Der.* Latin, *soccus,* "a sock-like shoe."

## ▬▬▬ SOCKS ▬▬▬

**ankle s.** Short sock reaching only to the ankle; may be worn turned down or have elastic top with no cuff. Introduced for women in 1920, causing a sensation when first worn at Forest Hills, New York, for an amateur tennis match in 1931 by Mrs. Fearnley-Whittingstall. Worn today by women and children and infrequently by men. Also called *anklet.* Also see BOBBY SOCK.

**anklet** See ANKLE SOCK.

**argyle s.** Sock knitted in a diamond pattern of several colors by hand or on a jacquard loom. Heel, toe, and top areas are of solid color while the other part is of a multi-colored, diamond-patterned plaid. Also see alphabetical listing. *Der.* Tartan of Duke of Argyle and Clan Campbell of Argyll, a county in West Scotland. Also spelled *argyll, argyl.*

**athletic s.** Gym sock of cotton knit with heavy yarn worn for track meets, competitive sports, and for general wear by boys and girls. Also see SWEATSOCK.

**bed s.**   Wool knit sock worn when sleeping to keep foot warm. Often hand-knit in a variety of fancy stitches. Also called *foot warmer*.

**blazer s.**   Boys' and girls' socks decorated with bands of color. Similar in effect to competitive stripes on knit shirts.

**bobby s.**   ANKLE SOCK, usually with turned-down cuff, worn by children and popular with teenagers during 1940s and 1950s, so universally that young girls were called "bobby soxers."

**Courrèges flower s.**   Dainty feminine sock coming to several inches below the knee usually styled in white with lacy top, embroidered with flowers. Introduced by Paris couturier, Andrè Courréges, in 1967.

**crew s.**   Heavy sock extending to lower calf with foot knitted in plain stitch, upper part with rib stitch. Originally white and worn for rowing and other sports. Now made in colors, especially for men and boys.

**cushion-sole s.**   Sock worn for active sports knit with a special sole that keeps the foot from blistering—often a layer of cotton and stretch-nylon terry cloth. Frequently given a special finish to help protect the foot from fungus, bacteria, and odor.

**dress s.**   Man's sock in lightweight, silky type, non-bulky yarns in conservative colors.

**electric s.**   Heavyweight knee-high sock, usually made of a combination of fibers, with a specially designed heating element operated by a battery held on by strap around the leg. Worn by spectators at winter sports events. Trade-marked by Timely Products Corp. and called *Lectra-Sox®*.

**English rib s.**   Man's sock knit with a wide rib or wale and a narrow depression between the wales.

**foot warmer**   See BED SOCK.

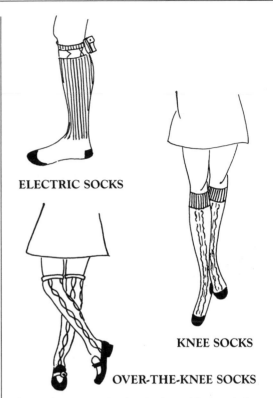

ELECTRIC SOCKS

KNEE SOCKS

OVER-THE-KNEE SOCKS

**knee-hi s.**   **1.** Sock which reaches to below the knee. Popularized by boys in early 1900s with knickers and accepted for girls in 1920s and 1930s. Worn by children from 1940 on. Adopted by teenagers and adult women in the 1960s as the popularity of the *miniskirt* increased. Featured by the couturier Courrèges in his collection in 1965. Also called *knee sock*. **2.** Traditional sock worn by Scottish Highlanders with kilts.

**knee s.**   See KNEE-HI SOCKS.

**Lectra-Sox®**   Trademark of Timely Products Corp. for ELECTRIC SOCKS.

**neon s.**   Ankle- or knee-length sock styled with ribbed tops in extremely bright colors of 100% nylon.

**over-the-knee s.**   Sock or stocking with an elastic top that reaches above the knee. Elastic top holds up the stocking without a garter.

**Peds®** Trademark for the first widely available SOCKLETS made in a number of fibers and styles.

**Pompon® s.** Sneaker sock with colored ball of yarn attached to top at back.

**quarter s.** Sock, shorter than ankle length, made of Orlon acrylic and nylon with colored terry knit top in colors.

**slipper s.** Crocheted or knit sock attached to soft, moccasin-type sole. For further description see SLIPPERS.

**slouch s.** Anklet with shirred tri-colored top, made of Orlon acrylic and stretch nylon.

**sneaker s.** Type of SOCKLETS which are shaped higher in front to conform to laced instep of the sneakers. Worn instead of socks for the bare-legged look.

**socklets** Very low-cut socks usually lightweight and not visible above pumps or other shoes, styled to keep feet comfortable while maintaining bare-leg look in summer. Also see PEDS®.

**stretch s.** Man's sock knit with textured yarns, *e.g.*, Banlon, nylon or Orlon acrylic. Made so flexible that one size usually fits any size foot. Also made for women and children.

**support s.** Knee-length sock knitted with an elastic-type fiber, *e.g.*, Lycra spandex, and worn by men to prevent leg fatigue.

**sweatsock** Sock made of combination of fibers, *e.g.*, wool, rayon, cotton, sometimes with cushioned sole. When this type of sock was first worn, it was always white and made of coarse cotton yarns which stretched out of shape easily. Worn instead of wool socks for active sports and gym because of washability. Blends now make these socks more washable and shape retentive.

**tube s.** Calf or knee-length sock made of stretch yarn with no indentation for the heel.

---

**sock suspenders** British term for men's *garters*, introduced in 1895, to hold up calf-length socks. Consisted of a band of elastic with attached garter clip.

**socq** See SOCCUS.

**soft goods** Retail-trade term for fashion and textile merchandise, *e.g.*, dresses, lingerie, coats, as contrasted with *hard goods, e.g.*, home appliances, hardware, or furniture.

**solaret** See SOLLERET.

**sole** Bottom part of the shoe, under the foot, usually consisting of three parts—*out-sole, mid-sole*, and *innersole*.

**solea** (pl. *soleae*) Simple form of sandal worn by the Romans consisting of a wooden sole held on with thongs or a cord.

**sole leather** See LEATHERS.

**solers** Early form of slippers used from the 12th c. on. Made of leather or cloth in various unlined styles, worn strapped on the foot. *Der.* Roman, *solea*.

**solitaire** **1.** See RINGS. **2.** Necktie worn with man's bagwig from 1730s to 1770s, tied in various ways, *e.g.*, in a bow under chin and pinned in place, or loosely knotted with free hanging ends. **3.** Narrow colored scarf, worn by women in mid-1830s, loosely tied with ends hanging to knees—usually worn with a white dress.

**solleret** Piece of armor worn to protect foot during Middle Ages. Consisted of jointed flexible pieces of iron. In the 15th c. had a long pointed toe—then called *solleret à la poulaine*. Also spelled *soleret, solaret*. Also see SABATON.

**SOLLERET**

**solution-dyed yarn** Man-made fibers which are made by mixing the pigment directly into the spinning solution. The mixture is then forced through the spinneret. When used for acetate fabric, this process reduces the tendency to fade.

**sombrero** (som-bray-yo)  See HATS.

**sombrero Córdobes** (som-bray-yo cor-do-base)  See GAUCHO HAT under HATS.

**sontag** (sonn-tag)  Woman's small cape of 1850s and 1860s worn for warmth, often knitted or crocheted with ends crossed in front and worn under a cloak. *Der.* Named for German opera singer, Henriette Sontag.

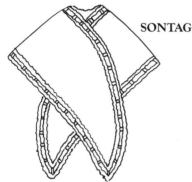

**SONTAG**

**Sorel, Agnès** (1422–1450) Mistress of Charles VII of France (1444–1459), called "La Dame de Beauté" (Lady of Beauty), wore jewel-studded robes, was the first commoner to wear diamonds, and made the king a waistcoat embroidered with pearls and precious stones. Acted as a model for the financier and merchant Jacques Coeur who brought linen, silken gowns, sables, and pearls from the Orient. Painted by Fouquet. See AGNÈS SOREL COIFFURE, AGNÈS SOREL CORSAGE, and AGNÈS SOREL DRESS.

**sorority pin**  See PINS.

**sorquenie**  Woman's *tunic* worn from 13th to 19th c. fitted tightly over bust. Also spelled *soucanie*.

**sortie de bal** (sor-tee de bal)  Woman's evening *cloak* with attached hood worn from 1850s to 1870s. Made of silk or cashmere and lined with a quilted fabric.

**sottana**  Striped undertunic worn by women in Italy in 13th c. Also worn as an outer gown by young girls.

**soucanie**  See SORQUENIE.

**SORTIE DE BAL, 1859**

**soufflé** (soo-flay)  Textile-industry term used to describe fabrics with puffed surface, *e.g.,* matelassé.

**soul**  See NEWSBOY under CAPS.

**soulette** (soo-let)  Early 17th-c. term for leather band crossed over instep and under arch of foot to hold the *patten* to the shoe. Fitted over a *surpied*, a quatrefoil of leather, used as trimming on the instep of boot. Also spelled *solette*.

**soutache** (soo-tash)  See BRAIDS.

**soutane**  See CASSOCK #1.

**Southern Colonel tie**  See STRING under TIES.

**souvenir scarf**  See SCARFS.

**sou'wester/southwester**  See HATS.

**space blanket**  See PONCHOS.

**space clothes**  Since the entrance of the U.S. into the space program in the 1960s, the development of clothing and accessories for astronauts has been essential. New fabrics have been designed which withstand extremes of heat and cold. Velcro® was introduced for use on soles of booties and floor of space cabin to keep astronauts feet on the floor when in weightless condition. French and U.S. designers were inspired by space clothes. See COURRÈGES HELMET under HELMETS and COSMONAUTS and LUNAR under LOOKS. Also see SHOES and VELCRO®.

**space-dyed yarn**   Yarns which are colored or dyed various colors at intervals. When woven into a fabric, they produce a random design.

**spaghetti sash**   See BELTS.

**spaier**   Medieval term for vertical slash in garment, similar to a slit, used to reach pocket on inner garment.

**spair**   Term used from 1840s on for closing on men's trousers. Also called FALLS.

**spandex**   Generic term for man-made fibers, composed largely of segmented polyurethane, which are stretchable, lightweight, and resistant to body acid. Used primarily for girdles, foundations, and bras.

**spangle**   Another term for SEQUIN or PAILLETTE.

**spaniel's-ear collar**   See DOG'S EAR COLLAR under COLLARS.

**Spanish**   See LACES and SHAWLS.

**Spanish blonde lace**   See LACES.

**Spanish breeches**   Narrow high-waisted below-the-knee breeches worn by men from 1630s to 1645 and from 1663 to 1670. Loose at hems, trimmed with rosettes, buttons, and ladder-like trim. Hooked to doublet lining and similar to *small slops* but longer. Also called *Spanish hose.*

**Spanish cape**   See CAPA.

**Spanish comb**   Comb with ornamental top, sometimes five inches high, worn at crown of head to support a MANTILLA or separately for decorative effect.

**Spanish embroidery**   See EMBROIDERIES.

**Spanish farthingale**   Dome-shaped *under-skirt,* worn in England in last half of 16th c., made either with graduated *hoops* of wood or

wire or with just one hoop at the bottom. Also called *vertingale.*

**Spanish flounce**   Deep gathered ruffle joined to hem of short skirt worn in late 19th and early 20th c.

**SPANISH FLOUNCE, 1898**

**Spanish heel**   See HEELS.

**Spanish hose**   See SPANISH BREECHES.

**Spanish jacket**   **1.** See SENORITA. **2.** Short sleeveless jacket worn in 1862, somewhat similar to a bolero with no fasteners in front. Sometimes has a collar attached to a low neckline and often has rounded edges at hem in front.

**Spanish kettledrums**   English colloquial term for *trunk hose,* particularly of *round hose type,* worn from 1555 to 1570s.

**Spanish sleeve**   Puffed sleeve, with vertical slashes revealing colored silk lining, worn by women from 1807 to 1820 and in late 1850s and 1860s. Also called a *slashed sleeve.*

**sparterie**   Straw fabric made of esparto grass, *Stipa tenacissima,* from North Africa and Spain. Inexpensive and used for basketbags, sandals, and for experimental shapes in millinery designs. Also called *esparto.*

**spats**   Short cloth or leather *gaiter* reaching over ankle, buttoned at sides, and held on by strap under instep. First worn by the military, later adopted by civilian men in 1878 to wear with *morning coat* in white, tan, or gray. Also worn by women from 1914 to 1920. Reintroduced at intervals, including the late 1960s for women. Also see SPATTERDASHES.

SPATS

**spatterdashes** High leggings worn by men from 1670s on, made mainly of leather or canvas reaching to knees. Fastened down outside of leg with buttons or buckles.

SPATTERDASHES

**spectacles/specs** See GLASSES.

**spectator pump** See SHOES.

**speed lacing** Closing on boot consisting of metal hooks replacing eyelets for upper part of lacing. Used particularly on ice skates, ski boots, and *hiking boots*. Also see BUTTON HOOKS.

**Spencer** **1.** Man's waist-length double-breasted jacket with rolled collar and cuffed sleeves worn from 1790s to 1850. **2.** Woman's waist-length jacket with shawl collar often fur-trimmed, sleeveless, or made with long sleeves covering hands, and sometimes collarless. Worn from late 18th to early 19th c., revived in 1860s, late 19th and early 20th c., and in 1980s. See JACKETS. **3.** Sleeveless knitted jacket worn by elderly women in 1860s. Three tales vary about the introduction: a) Lord Spencer burned one of the coattails of his jacket and cut off the other; b) he was out riding and tore one of the coattails, so tore off the other; and c) he made a wager he could start a new fashion and proceeded to cut off the coattails of his jacket, thus

creating a new popular fashion. *Der.* Named for Lord Spencer (1758–1834).

**Spencer cloak** Woman's cloak of early 19th c. made of embroidered net with elbow-length sleeves.

**Spencerette** Woman's fitted jacket with low-cut neckline edged with lace worn at end of Empire Period, about 1814.

**Spencer waist** Woman's fitted blouse with a band at the waistline worn in 1860s and 1890s.

**spere** Late 16th and 17th c. term for *placket*. Also spelled *speyer*.

**Sperry Top Siders®** See OXFORDS.

**spider work** See LACES.

**spiked shoe** Shoes with spikes on the soles used for playing cricket in 1861.

**spike heel** See HEELS.

**spike-tail** Slang term for man's SWALLOW-TAILED COAT.

**spiky hairstyle** See HAIRSTYLES.

**spindle** **1.** Tapered rod used to hold bobbin when winding yarn. **2.** Yarn unit of measurement: for cotton, 18 hanks, or 15, 120 yards; for linen, 48 cuts, or 14,400 yards. Generally spelled *spyndle* for yarn measurement.

**spinel** See GEMS.

**spinneret** Textile-industry term for nozzle with holes through which man-made liquids are pressed to form filaments of yarn.

**spinning** **1.** Process of twisting natural fibers together to form a yarn. **2.** The extrusion of the solution into a coagulation bath to form man-made fibers.

**spired headdress** Elaborate filigree headdress with votive spire, similar to those seen on Buddhist temples, worn by royal temple dancers of ancient Siam.

**spit-boot** Man's boot combining *shoe* and *gaiter* worn in northern England from 18th to

**SPIRED HEADDRESS**

mid-19th c. Closed down outside of leg with interlocking fasteners. The last fastener was an iron spike or "spit" that fastened through an iron socket.

**spit curls**   See CURLS.

**splinter-hat**   See SPLYTER-HAT.

**split**   One of several layers or *cuts* sliced from thick cattlehide with the grade of leather determined by the split: *top-grain* is the smooth hair side of the skin; other splits have a rough surface, called deep-buff, split, and slab. The latter cuts mainly used to make *suede*.

**split falls**   See FALLS.

**split mandarin collar**   See COLLARS.

**split skirt**   See SKIRTS.

**splyter-hat**   16th c. term for hat made of braided split pieces of straw rather than whole rounded stalks. Also spelled *splinter*.

**spoon back**   Term used in mid-1880s for circular folds of drapery formed at back by the overskirt of a walking dress.

**spoon bonnet**   Small-crowned bonnet of early 1860s with brim narrow at sides and projecting upward above forehead in elliptical shape.

**spoon rings**   See RINGS.

**sporran** (spor-an) Purse worn by Scottish Highlander at center front over kilt on low-slung belt. Originally made of leather with a thong as drawstring. Later made with silver clasp top and covered with long strands of horsehair in white with two long black tassels. Worn by Scottish army regiment with kilts. Also see HANDBAGS.

**sport**   See BRAS, CAPS, and GLASSES. Also see separate categories SPORT JACKETS and SPORT SUITS.

**sport jacket**   **1.** Conventional tailored jacket made in tweed, plaid, or plain colors worn with contrasting pants for business and general wear since 1920s. Also see BLAZER in alphabetical listing. **2.** Outerwear worn for school and general wear in place of coat as lifestyles became more informal. **3.** Outerwear designed for specific sports, *e.g.*, golf, skiing, and cycling, sometimes accepted for general wear.

### SPORT JACKETS

**Afghanistan j.**   Jacket of lambskin, tanned with hair left on, made with leather side out giving a shaggy border around edge, sometimes embroidered on the smooth side. Popular in late 1960s as part of trend toward ethnic clothes.

**anorak** (an-no-rack) **1.** Hooded waist-length jacket of sealskin or printed cotton worn for warmth by Greenland Eskimos. Also spelled *anora*. **2.** Hip-length jacket with zip-front and drawstring hem made of water-repellent fabric, sometimes lined with fur, worn for winter sports. Introduced in World War II for pilots. *Der.* Name of Eskimo origin.

**baseball j.**   **1.** Waist-length zippered or snap-closed jacket with ribbed cuffs and waist worn by major league and Little League baseball players in team colors with team name on the front and player's number on the back. **2.** Similar jacket worn by children with sewed-on emblems of major league baseball teams. **3.** Jacket with similar styling made as a woman's fashion item.

**battle j.** Copy of waist-length Army jacket worn in World War II, having two breast pockets, fitted waistband, zippered fly-closing, and turn-down collar with revers. Also called *Eisenhower jacket.*

**benchwarmer** Hooded knee-length jacket slipped over head and zipped at neck. Copied for young people from jackets worn by football players waiting on the bench. Also called *bench coat.*

**bike j.** Waist-length sport jacket. Styling is not specific. May be similar to WINDBREAKER or BATTLE JACKET.

**blazer** Fitted, single-breasted, patch-pocketed jacket worn with contrasting trousers or skirt. Some made with inch-wide stripes in two colors with white. Worn by college students, singing groups, and for general wear. *Men:* In late 1960s many were made in navy or gray in double-breasted style with brass buttons. In early 1980s became conventional suit jacket for men with matching pants. *Der.* Originally scarlet-colored, it was introduced for cricket and boating in England in 1890. Later, term was used for any brightly striped jacket. Both jackets were worn at Henley boat races in 1983, the former one in a muted crimson color.

**bomber j.** See FLIGHT JACKET.

**buckskin j.** Western-style jacket of sueded doeskin or sheepskin trimmed with long fringe. A standard style in the American West from colonial days, it was adapted for citywear in the late 1960s.

**Bulletproof® j.** Trademarked lightweight jacket with zipper front and three bulletproof panels—two in front and one in back—which slip into pockets in the lining that is closed with zippers. Comes in two styles (a) *safari-type* short-sleeved jacket and (b) a long-sleeved *flight-type* jacket. Has two levels of protection with panels constructed of layers of Kevlar® a strong and ballistic-resistant fiber. Made by Emgo U.S.A. Ltd., the American division of Eagle International, an Israeli manufacturer.

**bush j.** Jacket originally worn in Africa on hunting expeditions made of khaki-colored cotton with peaked lapels, single-breasted front, belt, and four large bellows pockets. Made in all types of fabrics and worn by men, women and children in mid and late 1960s. *Der.* From clothes worn on hunting trip into the African bush country. Also called BUSH COAT or SAFARI JACKET.

**C.P.O.** Also called C.P.O. SHIRT. See SHIRTS category.

**cycle j.** See MOTORCYCLE JACKET.

**deck j.** Short hooded water-repellent jacket, sometimes made with nylon pile lining, closed with zipper and with attached ribbed knitted trim at wrists and neck. Worn onboard sailboats and other craft.

**denim j.** Jacket of overblouse-type, often Western style, made of blue denim with fitted band at waist. Usually snap-fastened down front and styled with yoke in front and back.

**down j.** **1.** Usually a zippered jacket with long sleeves, knitted cuffs and waistband, interlined with *down* quilted to the outer fabric and lining. Worn for warmth and popularized for everyday use and sportswear in the 1970s. **2.** A similar jacket with zip-off sleeves which can also be worn as a vest.

**Eisenhower j.** See BATTLE JACKET.

**fencing j.** Close-fitting waist-length jacket, usually padded or quilted, made with high standing collar and fastened diagonally to right side with a red heart embroidered on left chest.

Worn for sport of fencing and sometimes copied for general wear.

**fishing parka** Knee-length slip-on jacket styled with attached hood and one large kangaroo pocket across the chest. Made of waterproof fabric and worn for fishing in inclement weather.

**flight j.** Waist-length jacket, sometimes made of leather, worn by commercial airline pilots. First worn as part of uniform by U.S. Army Air Corps pilots in World War II, and adapted for sportswear in 1960s. In early 1980s made in a variety of styles, mainly of nylon, with standing collar, ribbed or elastic waistband, patch or slot pockets, and zip-front. Also called *bomber jacket.*

**golf j.** Any type short waist-length jacket, frequently made of lightweight nylon with zip-front worn when playing golf.

**hacking j.** Single-breasted fitted jacket similar to man's suit coat made with slanting flap pockets and center back vent. Used for informal horseback riding and for general casual wear.

**inner-vest j.** Short jacket, sometimes with hood, snapped or buttoned down front. Attached to the side seams in front is a vest usually similar to a sweater with front zipper.

**insulated j.** Lightweight jacket usually made of tightly woven high count 70 denier nylon, frequently quilted with padding of Dacron polyester fiberfill. Usually made with zip-front and rib-knit at neck and wrists, and frequently given soil-resistant and water-repellent finish.

**judo j.** See JUDO CLOTHES in alphabetical listing.

**karate j.** An indoor jacket styled like a Japanese kimono but short in length. Worn when engaging in sport of karate and also adopted for at-home wear by men and women in late 1960s. *Der.* Named for sport for which it is used.

**lumber j.** Waist-length jacket with a bloused effect and rib-knitted bands at waist and cuffs. Made of woven plaid wool fabric. Originally worn by woodsmen in the lumbering trade. Introduced for sportswear in the late 1920s and worn by both adults and children. Reintroduced in early 1980s. Also called *lumberjack.*

**mackinaw j.** Hip-length sport jacket of heavy wool woven in patterns similar to those used for blankets. Improvised in the winter of 1811 when Captain Charles Roberts, a British officer, became stranded with his patrol on St. Martin's Island in the Straits of Mackinac. When reinforcements failed to reach him, warm coats were made from blankets of wide strips and various patterns. Became popular for explorers and woodsmen of the north and continued in popularity to present. *Der.* Named after Mackinaw City, Michigan, located at tip of Michigan facing the Straits of Mackinac. Also called MACKINAW COAT.

**Michael Jackson j.** Red leather jacket designed by Claude Montana for Michael Jackson in the video "Beat It." Copied in polyurethane buttoning down the front in windbreaker-style with stand-up collar and as many as twenty-seven short zippers placed in unusual places, *e.g.,* three placed diagonally on each side of chest and on shoulder blades in back, vertically at midriff, two placed at armholes so that sleeves are detachable. Trademarked and licensed for sale by Stadium Management Corp. and introduced in 1984. *Der.* Named for Michael Jackson who won 8 Grammy awards in 1983.

**motorcycle j.** Close-fitting black leather jacket waist-length, fastened to one side of center front with zipper, snap fasteners, or buttons. Popularized in the 1960s and worn by both children and adults, continuing into the 1980s. Also called a *cycle jacket.*

**Norfolk j.** Belted hip-length jacket with two box pleats from shoulders to hem, on front and back. Matching fabric belt is either threaded

**BLAZER**

**BUCKSKIN JACKET**

**INNER-VEST JACKET**

**LUMBER JACKET**

**MACKINAW JACKET**

**NORFOLK JACKET, 1914**

**PEA JACKET**

**SAFARI JACKET**

**SHEARLING JACKET**

through slots under pleats or worn over them. Worn by men for sport and travel since 1880s and associated with the character Dr. Watson of Sir Arthur Conan Doyle's Sherlock Holmes' stories. Popular for young boys from 1890s to about 1920 and revived in late 1960s for men and women, and again in 1980s. See NORFOLK SUIT in alphabetical listing.

**parka**   Loose-fitting pull-on jacket made with an attached fur-trimmed hood. Worn originally by the Eskimos and introduced during the 1930s for winter sportswear, *e.g.*, skiing and skating. Still worn in all cold climates.

**pea j.**   Copy of U.S. sailor's hip-length, straight, double-breasted navy-blue wool coat with notched lapels, vertical slash pockets, and vent in back. Inspiration for coats designed by Yves Saint Laurent in Paris in 1960s and a classic coat style for men, women and children. Also called *pea coat* and formerly called a *pilot coat.*

**PVC j.**   Hip-length simulated leather-look jackets made with conventional styling including a convertible collar, sometimes a yoke, buttoned- or zip-front, long sleeves, and tied or buckled belt. Made of polyvinyl chloride, a leather substitute which is soft and supple, washable, and water resistant.

**racing j.**   Lightweight two-ply nylon jacket with zip-front and drawstring hem. Made in various official colors with a wide stripe outlined with two narrow stripes of red, running from shoulder to hem on left side. Jacket is wind-resistant, water-repellent and made of wash-and-wear fabric that is colorfast. Originally worn for auto stock racing, now available for men and women. Usually has a patch printed on right chest with automobile brand emblems.

**reefer**   1. Semi-fitted navy-blue jacket, usually double-breasted, made with collar, revers and brass buttons. Often has shoulder tabs and two lower patch pockets. Worn by men from

1860 on, and from 1890s by men, women, and children. Also see alphabetical listing. **2.** See COATS.

**reversible j.**   1. Any jacket which can be worn on either side. **2.** Short down-quilted nylon jacket with zip-out sleeves and zip-front made with knitted cuffs and waistband. Reverses to a knitted jacket with removable sleeves.

**safari j.**   Similar in all respects to the BUSH JACKET, but called by this name in the mid and late 1960s when introduced as a fashion item for women by Dior, the French couturier. Newer versions in 1980s styled without belt, sometimes with epaulets. *Der.* From name of African hunting trip, *safari*, for which similar style jacket is worn.

**shearling j.**   Jacket in a variety of casual shapes, made of a sheepskin tanned with wool attached. Leather side is sueded or buffed and used for the outside of the coat, with woolly side worn inside. Collar is made with wool side out. Also called *sheepskin jacket.*

**sheepskin j.**   See SHEARLING JACKET.

**ski j.**   Any type of wind-resistant jacket worn when skiing. Conventional type zips up front and may be made of nylon, wool, fur, or quilted fabric. Frequently has an attached hood. Usually made waist- or hip-length with zippered pockets.

**snorkel j.**   Warm hooded parka, made with front-opening zipper extending up over the wearer's chin, giving the hood the look of a "snorkel" (a submarine's air-intake or exhaust tube). Made hip- to knee-length usually of water-repellent nylon satin or taffeta with quilted or pile lining and fake-fur edging around hood. Characterized by an inside drawstring waistline and knitted inner cuffs. Also has a multiplicity of zippered and snapped pockets, including one for pencils on the sleeve and a flap fastened with buttons and loops to keep snow out of the front zipper. Very popular in early 1970s for men, women, and children.

**sweatjacket**   Made of cotton knit jersey with cotton fleece lining originally gray-colored. In late 1970s made in any color and fabric with matching pants. Also see SPORT SUITS. Similar to a sweatshirt but opens down the front with buttons or a zipper.

**tweed j.**   **1.** Man's conventional sport jacket of textured wool usually made with traditional single-breasted styling. **2.** Women's jacket of almost any style made out of yarn-dyed wool of a textured nature and usually worn with matching skirt or pants. Popular in the 1920s and 1930s for women as suitable for the "country" rather than town wear.

**western j.**   Jacket like those worn by American cowboys, made of buckskin or fabric with breast pockets, a yoke, and sometimes having a fringe of leather on yoke, sleeves, and hem. Also called *Wrangler*®, DENIM, or BUCKSKIN JACKET.

**Windbreaker**®   Trademark for a warm lightweight nylon jacket zipped up front with close-fitting waistband and cuffs often made with attached hood.

**Wrangler® j.**   Trademark for WESTERN JACKET.

**yachting j.**   See COATS category.

---

**sport set**   Trade term for two or more items of sportswear made to match or contrast and sold as a set, *e.g.*, bathing suit with cover-up, top with shorts or skirt, twin sweaters and skirt, child's bloomers with pinafore.

**sport shirt**   See SHIRTS.

**sport suit**   Clothing designed to be worn for specific sports, *e.g.*, a suit used for horseback riding, exercising, scuba diving. Special cloth-

ing for active sports started at end of 18th c. with clothing for hunting; *ice skating clothes* for men and women in 1870s; *lawn tennis dresses* for women in 1880s; *bicycling suits* for men and boys and *divided skirts* for women in mid-1880s; and golf suits for men and dresses for women in 1890s. *Hiking costume* for women in 1890s; later consisting of knickers, sweater or shirt, and boy's cap introduced in World War I period. *Ski pants*, then suits, introduced for women in late 1920s and early 1930s. Since then each new sport has demanded special clothing with scuba diving, judo, karate and jogging being some of the more recent sport suits introduced. See CYCLING SUIT, LAWN TENNIS COSTUME, and YACHTING COSTUME in alphabetical listing.

---

### ■ SPORT SUITS ■

**aerobic ensemble**   Headband, leotards, tights, and leg warmers worn for aerobic dancing. *Headband* is a brow band of terry cloth; *leotards* are a tight-fitting, torso garment with high or low neck and long or short sleeves; *tights* are one-piece pantyhose with or without feet and/or stirrups usually made of stretch nylon; *leg warmers* are knitted leg coverings without feet. Also called *workout suit* or *exercise suit*.

**bike s.**   Tight fitting leggings worn with colorful tops worn for bike riding. Also see TRI-SUIT and SHORTS.

**camouflage s.**   Two-piece suit consisting of a hip-length jacket, tapered pants and sometimes a matching cap with ear flaps. Made of soft waterproofed duck fabric printed in abstract pattern of greens and browns to blend with surrounding terrain. Used by combat soldiers in World War II. Accepted for sportswear, particularly for duck hunting in mid-1960s. In early 1980s accepted for general wear.

**cat s.**   One-piece skin tight, long-sleeved suit with feet similar to UNITARD.

**exercise s.**   See AEROBIC ENSEMBLE and SAUNA SUIT.

**fencing s.** Two-piece white suit with close-fitting pants and waist-length jacket made with a standing collar, diagonal closing, and small red heart on left breast. Top is quilted or padded to prevent injury from the fencing foil.

**gymnastic s.** Suit worn for gymnastic competitions. Women wear *leotards*. Men wear athletic shirts and long slim tapered pants with a stirrup strap under the instep.

**gym s.** Suits worn by students for physical education classes. Style is determined by individual school. When gym was first introduced women wore blue serge or sateen pleated *bloomers*, white *middy blouses*, and long black stockings. During the 1930s *romper suits* were worn. Since mid-1970s any type pull-on shorts and T-shirts are acceptable.

**informal habit** Suit worn by adults and children for horse shows consisting of a *riding coat* and *jodhpurs*, sometimes matched as to fabric, sometimes contrasting. Colors worn are usually black, tan, blue, and gray. *Derby* may be worn to complete costume. Also see RIDING HABIT.

**INFORMAL HABIT**

**JUMPSUIT**

**jogging s.** Suit worn for exercising by a slow type of running called "jogging," popularized in 1960s. Various types of suits are worn: (a) SWEATSUIT *type*, (b) suit consisting of a zippered jacket, crew-necked sweater, and pants. Made of fleece, terrycloth, or velour. Also see WARMUP SUIT.

**judo s.** Two-piece suit consisting of pants and jacket made of lightweight fabric, usually white. Pants are three-quarter length with full tops and taper to calf. Wrap jacket is hip-length and made in kimono style. A belt of white, brown, or black is worn to denote proficiency. Also see JUDO BELT under BELTS and JUDO CLOTHES in alphabetical listing.

**jumpsuit** **1.** Shirt and ankle-length pants in a one-piece suit with zip-front and long or short sleeves. Originally worn by flyers in World War I, also by parachute jumpers and flyers in World War II. In the late 1960s adopted for sports- and leisurewear by men and women. **2.** Sleeveless one-piece suit with tank or V-top combined with shorts. Introduced in 1985.

**karate s.** Similar in style to JUDO SUIT with a kimono-styled jacket. Belts of different colors are worn to indicate degree of proficiency. Worn for karate, a form of Japanese wrestling.

**leotards** See AEROBIC ENSEMBLE.

**pantsuit** See SUITS category.

**playsuit** Shorts and shirt combined to make a suit with a waistline seam, worn with a coordinating skirt. Introduced in early 1940s and fashionable at intervals since.

**riding habit** Any combination of jacket and breeches or jodhpurs worn for horseback riding. The occasion determines the type of costume worn. Also see INFORMAL HABIT.

**rodeo s.** Suit worn at a western-type rodeo. Combination of western shirt, western pants, neckerchief, cowboy hat, and boots. Some suits

**AEROBIC ENSEMBLE**

**RODEO SUIT**

**SUIT OF LIGHTS**

**SUNSUIT**

**SNOWSUIT**

**SAUNA SUIT**

**SNOWMOBILE SUIT**

**SWEATSUIT**

are very elaborately trimmed with embroidery, fringe, or beads.

**rompers**  One-piece sport suit or sleepwear with shirt and shorts, or *bloomers*, joined by waistline seam. Originally bloomer-type rompers were introduced for children's playwear during World War I period.

**sauna s.**  Exercise suit made of soft flexible vinyl in jumpsuit or two-piece style with zip-front and knitted cuffs at wrists and ankles. Worn around the house, it seals in body heat acting like a steambath and encouraging loss of

weight. An innovation of the late 1960s. Also called an *exercise suit*.

**shorts s.**  **1.** Shorts and tops made of matching or contrasting material for sportswear. **2.** Suits accepted for city wear with longer jackets and shorts ending above-the-knee in a variety of styles.

**ski s.**  Any type jumpsuit or two-piece pantsuit worn for winter sports. First ski pants made their appearance for women in late 1920s styled similar to *jodhpurs*. In the 1930s ski suits were made of wool with medium-width trousers and knitted bands at the ankles. Jackets were close-fitting and usually zippered. In the 1968 Winter Olympics® fitted jumpsuits with a contrasting stripe extending down the side were introduced. In 1984 Winter Olympics®, *unitards* were worn. Quilted nylon insulated jackets may be added for extra warmth. Bulkier jumpsuits with high collars and belted waistlines were worn in mid-1980s by non-competing skiers.

**snowmobile s.**  Jumpsuit with attached hood made of wind-resistant nylon and polyester fiberfill insulation. Made with two-way zippers to hips or one-way zipper to knees. Has snap closed pockets on chest, self-fabric belt, and knitted cuffs at wrists. Sometimes has stripes around sleeves which reflect lights of cars. Worn with *snowmobile boots* and *gloves*.

**snowsuit**  Two-piece suit, or one-piece jumpsuit, worn by infants up to two years of age. Jumpsuit has a zipper which extends part way up the leg making access easier. Suits have attached hoods and ribbing at ankles and wrists, some are insulated and waterproofed.

**stormsuit**  Two-piece sport suit made of rubberized nylon consisting of pants and jacket with hood worn for hunting and fishing in inclement weather.

**suit of lights**  Working costume of banderilleros and matadors for Spanish and Mexican bullfights, consisting of waist-length, long-sleeved, heavily embroidered jacket open in front and trimmed with elaborate epaulets. Worn with tight-fitting below-the-knee pants with elaborate embroidery down outside of leg. Also called *suit of sequins, toreador suit,* and *traje de luces.* Also see MATADOR'S HAT under HATS.

**sunsuit**  Child's or infant's summer playsuit made with romper pants and a bib top.

**surfing s.**  See WETSUIT.

**sweatsuit**  Two-piece cotton knit suit with cotton fleece lining. Consists of a sweatshirt which pulls over the head or a sweatjacket which zips, plus sweatpants with legs gathered into ribbing or elastic at the ankles. Used by athletes for practicing running and also worn after boxing, or other exercise, to prevent sore muscles. Also worn for jogging.

**swimsuit**  See separate category.

**toreador s.**  See SUIT OF LIGHTS.

**tri-suit**  Tight fitting suit of Lycra Spandex made in color-blocked style similar to a *tank suit* but with mid-thigh length legs. Worn particularly by athletes participating in Triathlon competitions which include swimming, bike riding, and running. *Der.* Shortened form of "Triathlon."

**unitard**  One-piece *bodysuit* made of patterned knitted fabric. Combines *leotards* and *tights* into one suit. Worn for exercising and aerobics, sometimes with small bikini pants on top. Suits of this type, screen-printed and made-to-order, were worn by various participants in skiing events in the 1984 Winter Olympics® at Sarajevo, Yugoslavia. *Der.* From *uni* meaning "one," and *leotard.*

**UNITARD**

**warmup s.**  *Jumpsuit* or two-piece suit of quilted and napped fabric worn by athletes and skiers while warming up or while resting to avoid cooling too quickly. Also see SWEATSHIRT under SHIRTS, SWEATPANTS under PANTS. In the

1980s made of terrycloth and velour adopted for outdoor sports, beachwear, indoor exercises, and casual wear. Also see JOGGING SUIT.

**wetsuit** **1.** Three-piece suit made of black rubber backed with nylon consisting of skin-tight pants, jacket, and hood shaped to fit closely over head with Plexiglass® window for eyes and nose. Fastened by zippers at center front and down each arm and leg. Used for underwater sports and scuba diving. **2.** Long-sleeved one-piece black rubber suit with knee-length pants zipped up front is worn for surfing.

**workout s.** See AEROBIC ENSEMBLE.

**sportswear** **1.** Originally a term for clothing worn for tennis, golf, bicycling, bathing, ice skating, yachting and hunting in 1890s. See generic definition under SPORT SUITS. **2.** Term popularized in 1920s and 1930s for casual wear when participating in spectator sports, *e.g.*, sweaters, skirts, blouses, pants, and shorts. **3.** Since the late 1960s the concept of sportswear has changed somewhat and is now considered a fashion for day as well as evening based on the original concept of sports clothing. This has occurred primarily in the U.S. due to the adoption of less formal lifestyles by Americans. It has been stated that sportswear is the American contribution to the history of costume.

**spotted cat** See FURS.

**spread collar** See COLLARS.

**spring-bottom trousers** Trousers of 1870s and 1880s that flare at the ankles.

**spring bracelet** See BRACELETS.

**spring heel** See HEELS.

**spun silk** See SILK.

**spyndle** See SPINDLE.

**square** See NECKLINES, GEM SETTINGS, and TOES.

**square-bottom channel frame** See FRAME.

**square cut** See EMERALD CUT under GEM CUTS.

**square dance** Dance popular in rural U.S. See DRESSES, SKIRTS, and COUNTRY-WESTERN LOOK under LOOKS.

**square hoop** See OBLONG HOOPS.

**squash blossom necklace** See NECKLACES.

**squaw** Clothes influenced by those worn by native American Indian women. See BLOUSES, BOOTS, DRESSES, HANDBAGS, and SKIRTS. *Der.* Female American Indian called a "squaw."

**squirrel** See FURS.

**stacked heel** See HEELS.

**stadium** See BOOTS and COATS.

**standard pattern** See SLOPER.

**stand-away collar** See COLLARS.

**stand-fall collar** 19th c. term for ROLLED or TURNOVER COLLAR.

**standing whisk** See WHISK.

**stand-up collar** See COLLARS.

**staple** Trade term for short natural or man-made fibers long enough to be spun into yarns.

**stapling** A fur industry term used for wetting, blocking, and fastening pieces of a fur garment to a board to make them conform to the shape called for in the pattern. Formerly this process was called NAILING because nails were used. Now staples are used because of their smaller size.

**starcher** Man's starched cravat of 19th c.

**starching** Finishing process for fabrics which involves dipping fabric into a solution. When pressed with heated rollers, the fabric becomes stiff. Not a permanent finish.

**Star of Africa** See CULLINAN DIAMOND under DIAMONDS.

**Star of Arkansas** See DIAMONDS.

**Star of the South** See DIAMONDS.

**star ruby/star sapphire** See GEMS.

**startup** High shoe reaching above the ankle worn by country men, American colonists, and sometimes by women in late 16th and early 17th c. Frequently laced or buckled on outside of leg, made of untanned leather, and worn for sports or by country people. Sometimes had velvet or silver trim for women. When loose-fitting, it was called a *bagging shoe*. Also spelled *startop, styrtop, stertop*.

**Statue of Liberty visor** Headband with seven spikes and visor in front worn during "Liberty Weekend" in 1986 in celebration of the renovation of the Statue of Liberty in New York harbor. Also see EARRINGS and HAIRSTYLES.

**staurolite** See FAIRY STONE under GEMS.

**Stavropoulos, George** See APPENDIX/ DESIGNERS.

**stay** 1. Sewing term for strip originally of bone, now usually thin metal or plastic, inserted in seam to stiffen a woman's *foundation* garment, fabric belt, strapless bodice, or corners of shirt collar. 2. Piece of fabric stitched under pleats or gathers to hold fullness in place. Also see FEATHER BONING.

**stay hook** Small ornamental hook attached to bodice in 18th c. to hold watch. Also called *breast hook* or *crochet*.

**stays** Earlier term for corset made very rigid with iron or whale bone. Made like a bodice laced up back with scoop neckline in front, higher in back, with shoulder straps set wide in front.

**stay-up hose** See HOSE.

**steeple headdress** See HENNIN.

**steerhide** See LEATHERS.

**Steinkirk** Long lace-edged cravat loosely knotted under the chin with the ends pulled through a buttonhole, pinned to side, or left hanging. Worn by men from 1692 to 1730 and unfashionably to 1770. Women wore it with their riding habits. *Der.* From the Battle of Steinkirk in 1692 when soldiers were surprised in battle with cravats untied.

**stem stitch** See STITCHES.

**stenciled print** See PRINTS.

**stenciling** Applying dye to fur or fabric by painting through a cut-out stencil, *e.g.*, used to make pile fabric look like leopard. In late 1960s and early 1970s applied to sheared mink and all kinds of fur and fur fabrics to simulate giraffe, tiger, leopard, jaguar, and zebra. Practice continued into the 1980s.

**step cut** See GEM CUTS.

**stephane** 1. Decorated crescent-shaped headdress worn in ancient Greece and Rome either as a badge of office or wreath used as a symbol of victory. 2. Ancient Greek term for anything which encircles the head; a *coronal*, *diadem* or the brim of a helmet. 3. Crown sent by Byzantine Emperors to other monarchs and important dignitaries. Also spelled *stephanos*.

**step-in dress** See DRESSES.

**step-ins** Woman's underpants with widely flared legs and narrow crotch popular in 1920s and 1930s. Also see DANCE SET.

**step-in shoe** See SLIP-ON under SHOES.

**sterling silver** Metal containing 92.5 parts silver and 7.5 parts copper, a standard set by law. Used for jewelry it is "silvery" in color and lustrous. One disadvantage is that it tarnishes. This can be easily remedied with silver polish.

**stertop** See STARTUP.

**Stetson** See HATS.

**Stewart dress and hunting tartan** See TARTANS.

**stickpin** See PINS.

**stick-up collar** See WING COLLAR under COL-LARS.

**stiletto** (stil-let-o) **1.** Narrow pointed stick used in ancient Greece as a hairpin. **2.** Pointed instrument similar to a large needle used to punch holes in embroidery. **3.** See HEELS.

**stirrup hose** Stockings with no foot, fitted with strap under arch of foot and laced through eyelets at top to connect with breeches. Worn by men in 17th and 18th c. over finer stockings for protection when riding. Also called BOOT HOSE and STIRRUP STOCKINGS.

**stirrup pants** See PANTS.

**stirrup tights** See AEROBIC ENSEMBLE under SPORT SUITS.

**stitch** One complete motion of a threaded needle or other implement, *e.g.*, a knitting needle or crochet hook, which, when used in a series, results in decorative or utilitarian work such as sewing, embroidering, knitting, crocheting, or tatting. May be made by hand or machine with thread, yarn, embroidery floss, string, straw fiber, or other material. Also see EMBROIDERIES category.

■ STITCHES ■

**afghan s.** Simple crochet stitch made with a long hooked needle and yarn in various colors used to make garments and afghans. Also see TRICOT STITCH.

**arrowhead s.** Embroidery consisting of two stitches slanted to form an arrow, used singly or filled in with the satin stitch. Often used as reinforcement at top of a pleat.

**Aubusson s.** See REP STITCH.

**back s.** Stitch used for hand sewing to pre-

vent seam from ripping out. Also used for embroidery. Each stitch goes back over space left by previous stitch giving the appearance of a machine stitch.

**bargello s.** Stitch worked vertically on canvas over a given number of threads forming a zigzag pattern. Also called *flame* and *Florentine stitch*.

**basket s.** Embroidery stitch resembling series of overlapped cross-stitches used to fill in backgrounds.

**basket weave s.** Needlepoint stitch in which a series of diagonal stitches is used to fill background of canvas.

**basting** Loose running stitches, often alternating long and short, used to hold sections of garment together before machine stitching.

**blanket s.** Embroidery stitch that looks like a series of connected U's. Originally used to finish edges of binding on blankets, now used for decorative effect. Also called PURL STITCH.

**blind s.** See SLIP STITCH.

**brick s.** Blanket stitch used on flat fabric in continuous rows resembling brick wall. Also called *brickwork*.

**bundle** Embroidery stitch resembling a small bow knot. Made by taking 3 or 4 long loose stitches side by side, then placing a small stitch across at the center, drawing them together.

**buttonhole s.** Embroidery stitch similar to BLANKET STITCH worked close together with an extra purl at the edge. Used for worked buttonhole. Also called *close stitch*.

**Byzantine s.** Slanting embroidery stitch, similar to SATIN STITCH, worked on canvas as a background filler over 3 or 4 vertical and horizontal threads in diagonal pattern.

**cable s.** **1.** Embroidery stitch, similar to *chain stitch*, with extra stitch connecting the links. **2.** Hand-knitting stitch that produces a vertical cable pattern by crossing groups of knitting stitches over each other. **3.** Type of stitch used for smocking which consists of extra stitches between the dots.

**catch s.** Loose stitch, like a series of X's crossed near their top, used for bulky hems and for pleats in linings. Also called *cat stitch.*

**cat s.** See CATCH STITCH.

**chain s.** **1.** Embroidery stitch making connected loops that form a chain on the front. **2.** Machine stitch made by a commercial sewing machine done with a single thread, forming a chain on the back, used for hems and shoes—easy to remove. **3.** Basic crochet stitch.

**close s.** See BUTTONHOLE STITCH.

**continental s.** Diagonal stitch used on canvas worked over 2 threads used to make the pattern or to fill in needlepoint backgrounds.

**couching** Decorative embroidery stitch with long piece of yarn or embroidery floss laid flat while tiny stitches are worked around this yarn at intervals to fasten it tightly.

**cross-s.** Decorative stitch which forms an X worked in various colored yarns on a plain background. Also used in canvas work.

**darning** Vertical stitches woven through horizontal stitches in a one-to-one checkerboard pattern to resemble plain woven cloth. Used for mending holes or as an embroidery stitch.

**detached chain s.** See LAZY DAISY STITICH

**diagonal s.** Embroidery stitch worked diagonally over double threads of canvas with stitches varying in lengths.

**double-running s.** Tiny running stitch, worked and then reversed, so that new stitches fill spaces and make pattern similar to machine stitch. Also called *two-sided stitch, Holbein stitch,* and *Italian stitch.*

**fagoting** Stitch, similar to single FEATHER STITCH, used to join two edges of fabric together in decorative openwork effect.

**feather s.** Decorative stitch which looks like a double row of V's, branching out first to one side then to the other in a continuous line.

**filling s.** Any type of embroidery stitch used to fill in part of an outlined design.

**fishbone s.** Embroidery stitch resembling the backbone of fish made with a series of blanket stitches. Stitches worked to right and left, branching from unmarked center line, similar to FEATHER STITCH, but worked closer together.

**flame s.** See BARGELLO STITCH.

**Florentine s.** See BARGELLO STITCH.

**French knot** Decorative stitch used for embroidery. Embroidery floss is looped around the needle, usually 5 times, needle is pulled through the material forming a small nub or ball of yarn on the surface.

**gros point** (grow-pawn) Diagonal stitches worked on canvas over 2 threads. Used to make pattern or fill in background. Also see PETIT POINT.

**hemming s.** Long loose slanting stitch placed through hem and caught to fabric with very small stitch.

**hemstitch** **1.** Ornamental stitch made by drawing out several parallel threads, then fastening together groups of vertical threads at regular intervals making hourglass shapes. Used as borders on blouses, handkerchiefs, etc. **2.** *Machine hemstitching* is done with a special attachment on sewing machines which gives the same effect as above. When cut through the middle, each edge forms a *picot edge.*

**herringbone s.** Name of the CATCH STITCH, when used for embroidery work.

**Holbein s.** See DOUBLE-RUNNING STITCH.

**honeycomb s.** **1.** Similar to BRICK STITCH. **2.** Machine zigzag stitch used for smocking, mending, overcasting, attaching elastic, stretch lace, and blanket binding. Looks like 3 rows of diamond-shaped stitches.

**huckaback s.** Darning stitch worked horizontally on huck toweling, a fabric which has ridges at intervals. Stitches are worked underneath the ridges across the fabric to make geometrical motifs.

**Italian s.** See DOUBLE-RUNNING STITCH.

**laid s.** Embroidery stitch made by first placing yarn or floss on area and then working small stitches over it to hold it in place.

**lazy daisy s.** Single chain stitch used in embroidery with extra stitch added at outer edge to hold loop in place to form a petal. Also called *detached chain stitch.*

**lock s.** Machine stitch done with one thread coming across the top of the machine around the tension and through the needle. Other thread comes from a bobbin on the underside of the machine.

**mark s.** See TAILOR'S TACKS.

**Oriental s.** Series of long straight stitches placed side by side with each stitch intersected in center by short diagonal stitch. Also called *Rumanian stitch.*

**outline s.** Variation of STEM STITCH. Used to outline stems, leaves and other motifs in embroidery.

**overcasting 1.** *By hand:* diagonal edging stitch that enters the fabric always from the same side and goes around raw edge to keep it from fraying. **2.** *By machine:* a similar finish for raw edges made by a special sewing-machine attachment.

**padding s. 1.** Running stitch sometimes used in rows to provide a base for embroidery stitches, *e.g.,* satin stitch, worked on top. **2.** Diagonal rows of basting stitch. Used in tailoring to hold interfacing in place.

**petit point** Tiny diagonal stitches worked on canvas over single thread of canvas. Used to make pattern or fill in background.

**picot stitching 1.** See HEMSTITCH. **2.** Stitch used in lacemaking which forms loops of thread extending from the edges.

**plain knitting s.** Basic stitch used in knitting. Made by putting one needle through a previous stitch, putting yarn around needle, and pulling stitch through.

**popcorn s.** Knitting or crocheting stitch which projects like a round pompon.

**purl s. 1.** Knitting stitch made to give a ribbed effect. **2.** See BLANKET STITCH. **3.** Double purl stitch is used in making buttonholes and is formed by throwing thread over the needle as it crosses.

**railway s.** See CHAIN and TRICOT STITCHES.

**rep s.** Needlepoint half-stitch worked vertically on double thread canvas. Also called *Aubusson stitch.*

**Rumanian s.** See ORIENTAL STITCH.

**running s.** Very tiny even stitches placed close together and used for seams, tucking, gathering, and quilting.

**saddle s.** Running stitch made in contrasting or heavy thread. Frequently used for trim on coats, sport dresses, and gloves.

**satin s.** Embroidery stitch with straight, usually long, stitches worked very close together either vertically or slanted to fill in a large area, *e.g.,* leaf or flower.

**seed s.** Embroidery stitch consisting of tiny individual back stitches, worked at random to fill background.

**shell s. 1.** Stitch taken at intervals on a tuck to produce scalloped effect. **2.** A crochet stitch forming a shell design.

**slip s.** Small almost invisible stitches with connecting thread hidden under fabric. Used to join an edge to a single layer, *e.g.*, a hem or facing.

**stem s.** **1.** Embroidery stitch with overcast stitches placed close together making a rounded, raised, ropelike effect. **2.** Outline stitch used in crewel work.

**tailor's tacks** Large stitches taken through 2 thicknesses of fabric with a loop left between the layers. Later cut apart, leaving tufts in each piece, used for guide marks in tailoring. Also called *mark stitch*.

**tapestry s.** Short vertical stitches used in canvas work to imitate tapestry fabric.

**tent s.** See Continental stitch.

**top-s.** Machine stitching showing on the right side of the garment, *e.g.*, the edge of a shirt collar.

**tricot s.** Simple crochet stitch usually made with a hooked needle. Also called afghan or *railway stitch*.

**two-sided s.** See double-running stitch.

**whip s.** Short overcast stitch used on rolled or raw edges.

**zigzag s.** Sewing machine stitch giving a saw-toothed effect used to connect 2 flat pieces of fabric together. Also used on edges of fabric to eliminate fraying.

---

**stitchdown shoe construction** Manufacturing process for shoes which involves flange lasting, or turning of the shoe upper to the outside rather than around and under the last. Outsole is stitched to the extended edge around the shoe. Simple flexible low-cost shoe construction used primarily for infants' shoes, now used for all types of shoes. Sometimes made with two soles and called *double stitchdown*. Sometimes made with three soles and called *triple stitchdown*.

**stock** **1.** Man's made-up neckcloth, sometimes stiffened with pasteboard, which fitted high on the neck. Worn from about 1735 to end of 19th c. Also see military stock, hunting stock, neckstock, and Osbaldiston. For contemporary items see stock-tie blouse under blouses, collars, necklines, scarfs, shirts, and ties. **2.** From about 1590 the word *stock* was occasionally used as a synonym for stockings. **3.** Term used for leather in shoe manufacturing. **4.** Retail store synonym for merchandise.

**stock collar/neckline** See Ascot under necklines and collars.

**stock-dyed yarn** Yarns made from wool fibers which have been dyed and blended with colored fibers before they are made into yarn.

**stocking** See hose. Also see boots and caps.

**stocking bodice** Knitted or shirred elastic tube pulled over woman's *torso* as a *strapless top* to wear with pants, shorts, or an evening skirt. Popular in the 1940s, revived in late 1960s and 1980s.

**stocking purse** Small tubular purse shaped like a stocking closed at each end, but slit in center to provide entry, and often crocheted in elaborate designs. Two movable rings in the center kept money at one end or the other. Carried by both men and women in latter half of 18th and mid-19th c. Compare with miser purse.

**STOCKING PURSE**

**stocking shoe**  See SHOES.

**stocks**  Part of men's hose which were worn on the legs from about 1400 to 1610. Hose were originally styled like tights. When made in two separate pieces the upper part was known as *trunk hose, overstocks, haut de chausses,* or *upper stocks;* lower part was often called *bas de chausses, lower stocks, nether stocks, hose,* and later *stockings.*

**stock-tie blouse/shirt**  See BLOUSES.

**stola**  (stow-la) Long belted outer garment usually made of wool worn by Roman matrons and resembling the Doric *chiton* of ancient Greeks.

**stole**  **1.** Long wide scarf, often fringed at ends, made of fabric, knit, or fur worn as woman's wrap since 19th c. **2.** A short fur cape with long ends in front, popular in 1940s and 1950s instead of a jacket. **3.** Long wide scarf matched in fabric to woman's dress worn with bare-top dress in 1950s, especially in the evening. **4.** Long narrow scarf, part of *ecclesiastical vestments* worn over the *cotta* by clergymen.

**stomacher**  **Men: 1.** An ornamental chest piece worn under a V- or U-shaped doublet from late 15th to early 16th c. **Women: 2.** Heavily embroidered or jeweled V-shaped panel over chest, extending down to point over stomach held in place by busks. Either a part of the dress or a separate *plastron,* worn with low cut décolletage from late 15th c. to 1770s. **3.** Same type of inserted front panel made of shirred fabric used on dresses in first half of 19th c. Also see COTTAGE FRONT and WAIST-COAT BOSOM DRESS.

**stone marten**  See FURS.

**storm**  See BOOTS and COATS.

**storm rubbers**  Waterproof overshoes with rounded flap coming up over the instep.

STORM RUBBER, 1916

**storm suit**  See SPORT SUITS.

**stovepipe hat**  Man's black silk dress hat. Evolved from hat style of the 1790s made with high crown, flat on top, similar to tall hat worn by Abraham Lincoln. See PLUG HAT. *Der.* So called because of its resemblance to "stove pipe" of kitchen stove.

**stovepipe pants**  See PANTS.

**straight**  See PINS and SKIRTS.

**strapless**  Woman's apparel that bares the shoulders. See BRAS, DRESSES, NECKLINES, SLIPS, and TOPS.

**strapped trousers**  Man's trousers fashionable from 1820s to 1850s made with one or two straps under the instep.

**strap seam**  See SEAMS.

**strass**  See PASTE.

**straw**  Vegetable substance or synthetic imitation used for hats, bags, shoes, and trim. Natural straw comes from dried stems of grains, *e.g.,* barley, oats, rye, and wheat which are pulled, laid on the ground, and bleached. Outer layer is removed, bleached a second time with chemicals, then woven or plaited either by hand or on mechanical looms. Straws may be woven into bodies of hats or made into narrow "straw braid" which is stitched together in a circular manner to make a hat. Also used for handbags, particularly of the basket type. Sometimes used for shoes.

**streaking**  A fad popular during the winter of 1973–74 for running across a college campus or other public place nude except for shoes and possibly a hat. "Classic" college streaker's costume consisted of knit ski mask and tennis shoes.

**stretch** Classification of fabrics of various types. *a)* Knitted fabrics which stretch because of the elasticity of the knit. *b)* Fabrics made with *textured yarns* which have been crimped or curled. Such yarns give more resiliency and elasticity to fabrics and clothing, *e.g.,* knit shirts, sweaters, and dresses. *c)* Fabrics with piece-goods stretch—given special finishes permitting fabrics, *e.g.,* denim, to have more resiliency and elasticity. *d)* Fabrics woven with *elastomeric* yarn. See BOOTS, BRAS, GIRDLES, LACES, PANTS, SOCKS, and TOPS.

**stretch knit fabrics** Fabrics knitted with textured or stretch yarns. Also see STRETCH.

**string bikini** See PANTIES and SWIMSUITS.

**string tie** See TIES.

**stripes** **1.** Bands of color or texture of varying widths, making a design in a fabric, either printed on or woven in; may go in horizontal, vertical or diagonal direction. **2.** Narrow bands of braid, bias binding, ribbon, or fabric applied in rows. **3.** See PAJAMA STRIPES in alphabetical listing.

━━━━━━ STRIPES ━━━━━━

**awning s.** Wide even bands of one or more bright colors and white, woven or printed on coarse canvas. Formerly used for window awnings, now copied in lighter fabrics for sportswear.

**bayadère s.** (by-yah-deer) Horizontal stripes of varying widths in brilliant colors of red, green, blue, and gold. Also called *gypsy* or *Romany stripes. Der.* Hindu, "dancing girl."

**blazer s.** Inch-wide bands of one or several colors alternating with white. *Der.* From original blazer jackets.

**candy s.** Narrow bands of red on white background, imitating peppermint candy sticks.

**chalk s.** Narrow lines of white, widely spaced, frequently used on gray, navy, or black flannel—a classic for men's business suits.

**competition s.** Brightly colored single or cluster stripes across front of garment borrowed from competitive-sports uniforms, *e.g.* football jerseys.

**double ombré s.** Stripes of two colors shaded from light to dark, usually run horizontally, either printed or woven.

**express s.** Twill weave fabric made with even stripes of blue and white running warpwise. Originally used for janitors' uniforms, caps, and railroad workers' overalls. *Der.* From overalls worn by railroad workers.

**gypsy s.** See BAYADÈRE STRIPES.

**hairline s.** See PINSTRIPES.

**hickory s.** Structural warpwise stripes, usually blue and white with the blue two times the size of the white, woven in a denim-type fabric. Fancy hickory stripes are white stripes of varying widths on a blue ground. Also called *Liberty stripes* and *victory stripes.* Originally used for janitors' uniforms and work clothes, now used for sportswear.

**Liberty s.** See HICKORY STRIPES.

**mattress-ticking s.** See TICKING STRIPES.

**ombré s.** Bands of color either woven or printed, usually composed of monochromatic tones of one color running from light to dark.

**pencil s.** Vertical stripes as wide as a pencil line, with wider stripes of background color in between.

**pinstripe** Very narrow stripes the width of a straight pin woven or printed in vertical stripes placed close together, either white stripes on dark ground or vice versa. Also called *hairline stripes.*

**rainbow s.** Full range of the spectrum hues arranged in bands on the fabric; a multi-striped effect made by weaving or printing.

**regimental s.** Wide even colored stripes on plain dark background. Used for men's tie fabrics. *Der.* Taken from insignia on British military uniforms in which colors of stripes identify the regiments.

**Roman s.** Horizontal stripes, varied in size and color, grouped together with no contrast in background.

**Romany s.** See BAYADÈRE STRIPES.

**satin s.** Satin-woven stripes alternating with bands of plain fabric.

**shadow s.** Indistinct narrow stripes, all in tones of one color family, woven vertically, *e.g.,* navy, light blue, and gray-blue used together.

**ticking s.** Narrow woven dark-blue stripes, sometimes spaced in pairs, on a white ground, ground made in a twill weave. *Der.* Originally a heavy fabric called *ticking* used to cover mattresses, now used for sport clothes and copied in lighter weights and other colors for clothing.

**victory s.** See HICKORY STRIPES.

---

**stroller** **1.** See JACKETS. **2.** Casual mannish felt hats worn by women for town and spectator sports in 1930s and 1940s.

**strophium** **1.** Type of corset worn by ancient Roman women made with three supporting bands for the bust, waist, and hips held on by shoulder straps. Made of wool, linen, or leather. **2.** A *chaplet*; a *headband*. *Der.* Greek *strophos,* "a swaddling band."

**structural design** **1.** Term used by dress designers for lines of dress which are concerned with the functional design of the dress, *e.g.,* a

zipper down the back of the dress, pleats, as contrasted with *decorative design.* **2.** Textile term for a fabric, motif, or pattern achieved by weaving rather than surface treatment, *e.g.,* fabric woven on a *Jacquard* loom.

**stud** Small ornamental button used since mid-18th c. mounted on a short post with a smaller button-like end. Inserted through eyelet to fasten shirt front, neckband, or cuffs. Also called *collar button.*

**student bycocket** See BYCOCKET.

**studs** See EARRINGS.

**stump work** See EMBROIDERIES.

**S-twist** Yarn twisted so that, when held vertically, the spirals slope in the direction of the center of a letter S from upper left to lower right. Also called *left-hand twist.* Also see Z-TWIST.

**style** **1.** (noun) Fashion term for an individual and distinctive type of dress, coat, blouse or other item of apparel or accessory. **2.** (verb) Style, styling. Usually used with "to," *e.g.* "to style a line." Term used by a manufacturer when making or selecting the specific types of apparel for seasonal collections. **3.** "To have style" meaning to have a certain flair which is specific and individualistic.

**stylized print** See PRINTS.

**styrtop** See STARTUP.

**suba** Long circular-cut sheepskin coat made with shoulder yoke worn by Hungarian men on either the leather or the wooly side. Long seams are decorated on the leather side with appliqué or embroidery. A shorter version is worn by women.

**subucula** Ancient Roman man's garment similar to a shirt.

**suburban coat** See CAR COAT under COATS.

**succinta** Wide belt worn by men and women in ancient Rome around waist so garments could be bloused when walking.

**suede** See LEATHERS.

**suede cloth** Knitted or woven fabric of wool, cotton, or rayon having a nap on one or both sides. Heavier than *duvetyne*, it has a shorter nap. Used for suits, coats, vests, pants, and sportswear in imitation of genuine *suede* made from lambskin or doeskin.

**sugarloaf hat** Man's and woman's high tapered-crown hat with broad brim worn in 1640s. *Der.* Crown is made in a shape formerly used for loaf sugar. Also see CAPOTAIN.

**suit** Two, three, or more items of apparel, either of matching or contrasting fabric, designed to be worn together. **1. Women:** *e.g.*, jacket and skirt, or vest, blouse, and pants, etc. **2. Men:** Conventional attire usually consisting of trousers and jacket made in single- or double-breasted style, sometimes including a vest. **3.** Term used in 16th and 17th c. for *doublet* and *hose*. Current meaning of the word suit dates from late 19th c. See DITTO SUIT, ETON SUIT, JACK TAR SUIT, LITTLE LORD FAUNTLEROY SUIT, SAILOR SUIT, TAILOR-MADE, and ZOOT SUIT in alphabetical listing.

## SUITS

**black tie** See TUXEDO.

**business s.** Man's suit, conservative in style and color, suitable for daytime wear at the office and also worn for other occasions—with exception of formal and semi-formal occasions. So called and cut to distinguish it from a sport suit which may be made of plaids and brighter colors. May be single- or double-breasted and made in one-, two-, or three-button style.

**continental s.** Man's suit with natural shoulderline, easy fitting jacket, and narrow tapered trousers with no belt. Pockets in trousers are slanted from waistline to side seams. Style originated in Italy in 1950s.

**dressmaker s.** Woman's suit that is made with soft lines and fine details, as contrasted with man-tailored styles that have the sharply defined lines of a man's suit made by a tailor. Fashionable in 1950s and revived in the mid-1980s.

**Edwardian s.** Man's suit with close-fitting fingertip-length jacket, with high notched lapels, and narrow stovepipe pants. Copied from styles of 1900 to 1911, reign of Edward VII, and popular in exaggerated form by London *Teddy boys* in late 1950s. Made in velvet for women in late 1960s and early 1970s.

**formal s.** See TUXEDO and FULL-DRESS SUIT.

**full-dress s.** Man's formal suit consisting of *swallow-tailed coat* and matching trousers frequently trimmed with satin lapels and satin stripes down side of pants. Worn with formal shirt, white vest, and white tie. Also called *white tie and tails*.

**FULL-DRESS SUIT**

**gangster s.** Wide-shouldered, single- or double-breasted suit with wide lapels, inspired by movie *Bonnie and Clyde* in 1967. Usually made of black or gray pinstriped flannel; re-creation of 1930s man's fashion.

**gaucho s.**  Woman's pantsuit with wide-legged calf-length *culottes* and a matching *bolero*, frequently made in leather. A full-sleeved blouse is usually worn under the sleeveless bolero. Introduced in mid-1960s. *Der.* Spanish, "cowboy" of Argentina, Chile, and Uruguay.

**Ivy League s.**  Man's suit with natural shoulders, narrow lapels, three-button closing, and narrow trousers. Popular in 1950s, spreading from the eight Eastern college campuses in the Ivy League as reaction against exaggeratedly wide padded shoulders and wide trouser legs of the 1940s.

**leisure s.**  Man's suit styled in knit or woven fabric in more casual style with jacket made more like a shirt having a convertible collar, more "sporty" buttons, and sleeves with no cuffs or with single cuffs.

**man-tailored s.**  Woman's suit made similar to a man's business suit, sometimes made in men's wear fabrics. May be a one-button suit in pinstripe fabric *e.g.*, GANGSTER SUIT.

**Nehru s.** (nay-roo)  **1.** A suit with a high stand-up Nehru collar introduced in 1967. Made in various fabrics for both men and women. **2.** Woman's pantsuit with a tunic top made with Nehru collar. Top may be worn separately as a dress. *Der.* Named after Jawaharlal Nehru, Prime Minister of India 1950–1964.

**pantsuit**  Term introduced in mid-1960s for woman's suit with pants, instead of skirt, styled for town wear and evening wear. Some are of traditional styling with jackets. Others are composed of a thigh-length tunic and pants. Some formal pantsuits are styled in elaborate fabrics. Also made with matching vest or coat, and with various types of pants including knickers. Also see CITYPANTS under PANTS and SMOKING SUIT.

**semiformal s.**  Suit suitable for BLACK TIE or semi-formal occasions. **Men:** TUXEDO, or DINNER JACKET is required. **Women:** any type dressy suit or dress made in a more elaborate style or fabric, appropriate for semiformal dinners, dances or weddings.

**smoking s.**  Woman's lounging suit with jacket styled similar to man's smoking jacket, usually styled with matching velvet pants. Introduced in late 1960s, and attributed to St. Laurent, Paris couturier.

**tails**  See FULL-DRESS SUIT.

**theatre s.**  Woman's two-piece dressy suit suitable for late afternoon or evening. Made in two or three pieces with short jacket or regular length coat. May be made in luxurious fabrics, trimmed with beading or fur.

**tuxedo**  Man's semiformal fingertip-length jacket and pants made with satin or faille lapels and side stripes on pants. Made in black or midnight blue in winter, white jacket with dark pants in summer. Sometimes made in other colors, or plaids since 1960s. Worn with *cummerbund* and *black bow tie*. Abbreviated as *tux*. Also called *black tie*. *Der.* Worn by Griswold P. Lorillard at Tuxedo Park, N.Y., in 1886.

**TUXEDO**

**WEEKENDER          VESTSUIT**

**vestsuit**  Pants and vest designed to be worn together. A full-sleeved blouse or shirt is worn underneath the sleeveless vest. Popular in 1960s.

**walking s.   1.** Woman's three-quarter-length coat, sometimes fur-trimmed, worn with straight skirt; usually made of tweed. **2.** Woman's suit worn in 1901 with skirt just brushing the ground.

**wash-and-wear s.**  Any washable suit worn by men or women which does not need to be pressed, *e.g.,* suits made of polyester fibers blended with cotton or types made of nylon fabrics.

**weekender**  Woman's three- or four-piece suit including coordinated pants, skirt, jacket, and blouse suitable for weekend trips.

**western s.   1.** Man's or woman's suit with jacket cut longer and more fitted through waistline worn with straight-legged pants. Reminiscent of the American west in late 19th c. **2.** A suit for formal occasions styled with similar lines, called a *western formal.*

**white tie and tails**  See FULL-DRESS SUIT.

**suitcase bag**  See HANDBAGS.

**suit dress**  See DRESSES.

**suiting   1.** Term which applies to any fabric used for men's and women's suits. Includes mainly worsteds and woolens made in a variety of weaves and patterns which have no specific name but tailor well. **2.** Term used for mercerized plain woven fabric made in a solid color. Formerly called linen and crash suiting. **3.** British term for all striped cotton fabrics, usually made with yarn-dyed stripes, shipped to South America and Far East.

**suit of knots**  Term used from 17th to mid-18th c. for set of matching bows, used to trim a dress or to wear in the hair.

**suit of lights**  See SPORT SUITS.

**suit of ruffs**  Term for matching neck and wrist ruffs, worn by men and women from 1560 to 1640.

**suit of sequins**  See SUIT OF LIGHTS under SPORT SUITS.

**suit sleeve**  See SLEEVES.

**suit slip**  See SLIPS.

**suit vest**  See VESTS.

**sultana scarf**  Scarf of oriental colors worn in mid-1850s over *canezou jacket* tied below waistline with long hanging ends.

**sultana sleeve**  Full *hanging sleeve* of late 1850s slit open down outside. Sometimes fastened with ribbons around upper and forearms. Also spelled *sultan sleeve.*

**sultane**  Dress worn in the late 17th c. and again in the 1730s and 1740s, trimmed with buttons and loops. Worn for traveling. In 18th c. it was a dress with short *robings*, a *stomacher*, and a plain back.

**sultane dress**  *Princess-style* daytime dress of late 1870s with scarf elaborately draped to one side.

**sultane jacket**  Very short, sleeveless bolero-type woman's jacket worn in late 1880s. Similar to ZOUAVE JACKET.

**sun bonnet**   See BONNETS.

**sunburst-pleated skirt**   See ACCORDION-PLEATED under SKIRTS.

**sunburst pleats**   See ACCORDION PLEAT under PLEATS.

**sunburst tucks**   Used in a series these are darts which taper to nothing. May be arranged around the neckline of a dress, on the front of the blouse, or at the front of the waistline. Provide a decorative effect and reduce fullness without gathers. Also called *fan tucks.*

**Sunday clothes**   Term used in 19th and early 20th c. for clothing worn especially for church and special occasions, as opposed to *work clothes.* Also called *Sunday best.*

**sundress**   See DRESSES.

**sunglasses**   Eyeglasses with dark-colored lenses to cut glare invented about 1885, popularized by movie stars in Hollywood in 1930s and 1940s, prevalent fashion from 1960s to 1980s in various shapes and sizes. Some made with mirrored lenses. Also see GLASSES.

**sunray skirt**   An older term for an accordion pleated skirt of late 1880s made from a full circle of fabric.

**sunshade**   See PARASOL.

**sunsuit**   See SPORT SUITS.

**super tunic**   Overgarment made with or without sleeves. From 9th to end of 14th c. worn by men and women and also called *surcoat.*

**supportasse**   Wire framework of mid-16th to first half of 17th c. used to tilt enormous starched ruff up on back of neck. Also called *underpropper.* The RABATO was similar.

**support legwear**   Hosiery for men or women knit of stretch nylon combined with elastic yarns to provide support to the muscles and veins of the legs. See HOSE, PANTYHOSE, and SOCKS.

**surah**   Lightweight, soft silky fabric made in a twill weave of silk or man-made yarns. May be woven in yarn-dyed plaids, printed, or dyed in solid colors. Similar to *foulard,* but heavier. Used for dresses, scarfs, neckties, and blouses.

**surcingle belt**   See BELTS.

**surcoat**   **1.** Man's outer garment, usually knee-length with wide sleeves, worn over armor by knights or over tunic or *cote* in Middle Ages. **2.** Woman's long, loose outer garment with full tubular or bell-shaped sleeves, worn over *kirtle* in Middle Ages. Also spelled *surcote.* Also called SUPER TUNIC and SIDELESS SURCOAT.

**surfing**   Sport of riding ocean waves on a surfboard. For clothing used for this sport see PANTS, SWIMSUITS, and WET SUIT under SPORT SUITS.

**surgical mask**   See MASKS.

**surpied**   See SOULETTE.

**surplice**   **1.** Loose white overblouse, either waist or knee-length, gathered to flat yoke with full open sleeves worn by clergy and choir singers. Sometimes a style copied for children's wear, blouses, and nightgowns. Also see COTTA. **2.** Neckline that overlaps diagonally in front making a V-neckline. Sometimes wrapped and fastened in back. See COLLARS, NECKLINES, and WRAP CLOSING under CLOSINGS.

**SURPLICE #1**

**surplice bodice** A day bodice, worn in 1881, the top of the dress wraps rather than buttons. May be plain or pleated at shoulders and waistband. Also called *surplis front*.

**Surrealism** Movement in art and literature starting in the 1930s which was greatly influenced by psychoanalysis. Art has a "dream-like" quality which suggests the expression of the subconscious and reflects the imagination uncontrolled by reason. *Salvadore Dali* is one of the main exponents of this style.

**surtout** (ser-too) **1.** Contemporary French and British term for man's cloak or overcoat. *Der.* French, literally "overall." **2.** Term for BRANDENBURG overcoat from 1680s to 1840s. **3.** From 1730 term for WRAP-RASCAL. See WRAP-PER #2. Also called *surtout greatcoat* in 19th c. **4.** Called *surtout greatcoat* from 1820s to 1840s. **5.** Caped coat worn by women in late 18th c.

**suspenders** **1.** Detachable straps of elasticized fabric passed over shoulders and clipped or buttoned to trousers or skirt front and back, same as British *braces*. **2.** British term for woman's garters for stocking attached to corset called a *suspender garter*. **3.** Shoulder straps on bodice or bib top. Also see JUMPERS, PANTS, SHORTS, and SKIRTS.

**suspender trimming** See BRETELLES #1.

**Svend** See APPENDIX/DESIGNERS.

**swaddling clothes** Term used from earliest times to end of 18th c. for narrow strips of fabric wrapped around infant in place of clothing. Also called *sweath-bands*, *swaddling bands*, and *swathing band*.

**swag** Draped folds of fabric used on women's gowns in latter part of 18th c., *e.g.*, shown in illustrations of gowns worn by Marie Antoinette.

**swagger** See COATS and HATS.

**swagger pouch** See HANDBAGS.

**swagger stick** Short stick, usually leather covered and shaped somewhat like a baton, sometimes carried by Army officers.

**swallow-tailed** See COLLARS and COATS.

**swanbill corset** Back-laced woman's corset of mid-1870s with long metal bone in front which curves outward over lower abdomen.

**swan's down** Soft underfeathers of swans, used to trim negligees, dresses, and cloaks, especially in late 19th and early 20th c. Also spelled *swansdown*. Compare with MARABOU.

**swatch** Textile and sewing term for a small sample of fabric.

**swathing band** See SWADDLING CLOTHES.

**sweatband** **1.** Band, usually made of sheepskin leather, placed around the inside of a man's hat where crown joins the brim to protect hat from sweat. **2.** A stretch terrycloth band worn around the head during exercise to absorb sweat in 1980s. See AEROBIC ENSEMBLE under SPORT SUITS.

**sweatclothes** Apparel worn primarily for exercising and jogging. Also worn as leisure wear. See KNIT SHIRTS, PANTS, SHORTS, SOCKS, SPORT JACKETS and SPORT SUITS.

**sweater** Clothing for the upper part of the body worn either as an outer garment or under a coat or jacket. Usually hand- or machine-made by knitting or crocheting in cable, ribbed, or lacy patterns. Sweaters are frequently called by yarns used: (a) wool—Shetland or lambswool; (b) hair fibers—mohair or angora; and (c) man-made yarns—Orlon acrylic, or Antron nylon. Also called by specialized types of yarns, *e.g.*, bouclé, chenille, or high bulk (called bulky). The sweater was introduced as the jersey, in mid-19th c. In early 1890s turtleneck jerseys were introduced. Later a collar was added and the jersey was worn for golf and sports. In the 1920s accepted by students and later widely adopted for general wear. At first only made of wool, washability was improved when new yarns, *e.g.,* Orlon acrylic and nylon, were introduced in 1950s and 1960s. Also see BLOUSES, COATS, DRESSES and VESTS categories.

## SWEATERS

**Aran Isle s.** Pullover with round or V-neck knit in traditional Irish designs including raised cable knit, and interlaced vertical diamond-shaped patterns. *Der.* Named for island off coast of Ireland where sweaters of this type were originally made. See FISHERMAN'S SWEATER.

**argyle s.** Jacquard-knit sweater using several colors to make diamond-shaped designs, either knit by hand or machine, often matched to socks. Popular in 1920s and 1930s, and revived in late 1960s. See PLAIDS. *Der.* Tartan of Duke of Argyle and Clan Campbell of Argyll, a county in west Scotland. Also spelled *argyll, argyl.*

**award s.** See LETTER SWEATER.

**Aztec s.** Long bulky coat sweater with shawl collar closed with matching sash. Usually made in white with predominantly black Jacquard-knit Aztec Indian motifs running in wide bands across chest, below waist, around upper arm, and wrist.

**beaded s.** Woman's sweater with decorative beading, sometimes of seed pearls, often worn for evening in 1940s and 1950s, and worn at intervals since.

**big easy s.** Extra large long sweater, one style made in lacy bouclé knit with extended shoulder making a short sleeve in loose-fitting style with rib-knitted hem.

**blazer s.** Double-breasted cardigan with wide lapels and collar styled similar to BLAZER JACKET.

**bolero s.** Short sweater to the waist or above, styled with rounded ends in front and no fasteners. *Der.* A lively Spanish dance; also the music for this dance.

**cardigan s.** Coat-style sweater known by various names. "Classic cardigan" is made of Shetland-type yarns with crew neck, ribbed cuffs and hem, closed with pearl buttons. "Belted cardigan" usually made in longer length, sometimes in *Norfolk* style. "Shawl collar cardigan" made in tuxedo-collared style with no buttons. Another type of cardigan is the *coat sweater.* Also see *coat sweater. Der.* Named after *7th Earl of Cardigan* who needed an extra layer of warmth under his uniform in the Crimean War in 1854.

**cashmere s.** Sweater in any style knitted of yarn spun from the hair of the cashmere goat. Extremely soft and luxurious, usually imported from England or Scotland. See CASHMERE in alphabetical listing.

**coat s.** Cardigan-style sweater, usually made in a longer style with or without a ribbed waistband. Frequently styled with a long V-neck and buttons. From 1930s to 1960s usually restricted in usage to men or older people. In 1980s worn by adults and children. Also see TUXEDO SWEATER.

**Cowichan s.** Sweater using North American Indian pattern—black on white or gray background—made by Cowichan Indians of Vancouver Island. Used in the late 1940s and early 1950s and revived in early 1970s. Also called a *Siwash sweater.*

**cowl-neck s.** Pullover sweater with extra large rolled collar which forms a cowl drapery, popular in 1980s.

**crew-neck s.** Pullover sweater with a round rib-knit neck. *Der.* Named for knit shirts worn by members of college rowing teams or "crews."

**dolman s.** Pullover sweater with *batwing sleeves,* may have a turtleneck, a boatneck, etc., with ribbing at waist. In early 1970s worn with a belt—in 1980s became loose and full with ribbed band at waist. Also see SLEEVES.

**embroidered s.** Sweater which is knit first and then decorated with embroidery, usually in large floral allover designs in many colors, as opposed to a Jacquard-knit sweater where the design is part of the knit.

**Fair Isle s.** Sweaters, both pullovers and cardigans, imported from Fair Isle off the coast of Scotland. Characterized by soft heather yarns, and bright-colored knit in traditional patterns. Name also applied to sweaters imitating this style. Popularized in 1920s by Duke of Windsor, at that time Prince of Wales, as a short-waisted sweater with V-neck, worn instead of a vest.

**fanny s.** Long coat sweater coming to below the hips with ribbing or sash at waistline, introduced in early 1970s and still worn.

**fatigue s.** Slip-on sweater made in firm rib knit with long sleeves, small V-shaped yoke, round turnover collar, and five-button closing. Originally worn in World War II and restyled in cotton for men and women in 1980s.

**fisherman's s.** Bulky hand-knit sweater, made of natural color, water-repellent wool in characteristic patterns including wide cable stripes, bobbles, seed stitch, and other fancy stitches—imported from Ireland. Popular in early 1960s and widely imitated in man-made yarns. *Der.* From Irish fishermen who wear hand-knit sweaters in a pattern indicating locale in which they live.

**Icelandic s.** Hand-knit sweater in individual designs made in natural-colored wool of browns, blacks, whites, and grays. Fleece is from the rare *heath sheep*. Rich in lanolin, the wool is said to be almost entirely water repellent. Designs consist of bands around the neck in yoke fashion copied from beaded collars worn by Icelandic Eskimos. Also called *Reykjavik sweater*.

**Jacquard s.** Sweater knit with an elaborate design by hand or machine in many colors. May be made of a geometrical repeat pattern or one large design such as a deer either on front, back or both sides of sweater. Popular type of sweater for winter.

**jiffy-knit s.** Sweater hand-knit of bulky yarn on very large needles, which takes only a few hours to knit. Popular in late 1960s.

**Karaca s.** Turtleneck pullover sweater with elaborate Turkish embroidered panel down center front and lines of embroidery down sleeves. Imported from Black Sea region.

**letter s.** Bulky shawl-collared coat sweater with service stripes, on upper sleeves and school letter on chest. Formerly given to varsity sports team members in high schools and colleges, now copied for general sportswear. Also called *award, letterman, school* or *varsity sweater.*

**mock turtleneck s.** See TURTLENECK SWEATER.

**poor-boy s.** Ribbed knit sweater made with high round neck or turtleneck. Revived in the mid-1960s. *Der.* From type of sweater worn by newsboys of the early 20th c.

**pull-on s.** See PULLOVER.

**pullover** Sweater with round, crew, or V-neck pulled on over the head as contrasted with a cardigan or coat sweater which opens down the front. Also called *pull-on* or *slip-on sweater.*

**Reykjavik s.** *Der.* Capital of Iceland. See ICELANDIC SWEATER.

**school s.** See LETTER SWEATER.

**shawl-collared cardigan** See TUXEDO SWEATER.

**shell** Sleeveless collarless pullover sweater usually made in solid colors, worn instead of blouse. Introduced in 1950s.

**Shetland s.** Originally a sweater knit of fine worsted yarn from the Shetland Islands off the coast of Scotland. Usually made in classic style, in a medium-sized stockinette stitch. By extension, name now used for same type of sweater made in man-made yarns.

**CARDIGAN**  **COAT SWEATER**  **COWL-NECK SWEATER**

**CREW-NECK SWEATER**  **DOLMAN SWEATER, 1970**  **FISHERMAN'S SWEATER**

**shrink** Waist-length sweater sometimes made with ribbing from below bust to hem, sometimes sleeveless, sometimes has short sleeves. *Der.* Entire sweater looks as if it "shrunk" when washed.

**shrug** **1.** Shawl and sweater combined, fitting over the back like a shawl. From elbow to wrist edges are drawn together to form brief sleeves. Formerly popular at seaside resorts. **2.** Short-sleeved sweater baring midriff with long V-neckline and fastened with one hook under the bust.

**Siwash s.** See COWICHAN SWEATER.

**ski s.** Classification of elaborately patterned sweaters made in Jacquard knits in many colors either domestically or imported, particularly from Norway, Sweden, Switzerland, or Iceland. Worn outdoors for skiing and sometimes indoors for after-ski wear. Also see ICELANDIC SWEATER.

**slip-on** See PULLOVER.

**sweater-for-two** Extremely wide sweater made of stretch Orlon acrylic with wide horizontal strips. Designed with two necks, a sleeve on each side, and a single slit for arms in center. A fad of the early 1960s worn by two people for warmth at football games.

**sweater set** Two sweaters made to be worn together. One usually of short-sleeve PULLOVER type and the other in CARDIGAN style.

SHRINK

SWEATER SET

**sweater-vest** See VEST SWEATER.

**tennis s.** Pull-on, long-sleeved sweater sometimes made in cable-knit. Usually white and trimmed with narrow bands of maroon and navy blue at V-neck and wrists. Worn since 1930s.

**turtleneck s.** A pullover sweater with a very high rib-knit roll collar that folds over twice to form a flattened roll around the neck. *Mock turtleneck* may fold only once or be knitted double to give turtleneck effect without folding.

**tuxedo s.** Coat-style sweater with no buttons, and collar that rolls around neck and down each side of front. Also called *shawl-collared cardigan*.

**undershirt s.** Pullover with tank top, similar to man's undershirt, sometimes tunic length. Popular in early 1970s.

**vest s.** Sleeveless coat style sweater made double- or single-breasted with a V-neck. Also called a *sweater-vest*.

**wraparound s.** Hip-length cardigan-type sweater with one side lapping over the other, held closed with a matching rib-knit sash.

**sweater clasp** Two decorative clasps connected with a short chain used to hold a sweater together at the neckline.

**sweater-for-two** See SWEATERS.

**sweater girl** In 1940s slang for shapely film stars who wore tight pullovers to emphasize the bosom, *e.g.*, Lana Turner.

**sweater-knit clothing** Apparel knitted and styled in the same manner as a sweater. See BLOUSES, COATS, DRESSES, and VESTS.

**sweater set** See SWEATERS.

**sweater-vest** See VEST SWEATER under SWEATERS.

**sweath-bands** See SWADDLING CLOTHES.

**sweatshop** Slang term for turn-of-the-century clothing manufacturing plant where workers were paid low wages and worked long hours under unfavorable conditions.

**Swedish hat** See MOUSQUETAIRE HAT.

**sweeper** See DUST RUFFLE.

**sweet coffers** Term used in Elizabethan times for boxes used by women to hold cosmetics.

**sweetheart neckline** See NECKLINES.

**swim bra** See BRAS.

**swimsuit** Sportswear designed to be worn at the beach, the swimming pool, for sunbathing, or swimming. Not generally known by this name until 1950s. In the 1980s swimsuits for women were cut so that they came higher on the sides revealing all of the leg. Suits for men generally cut with shorter legs, and some trunks were as small as bikinis. Formerly called a *bathing suit* (see alphabetical listing).

# SWIMSUITS

**apron s.** See PINAFORE SWIMSUIT.

**asymmetric s.** Swimsuit with strap over only one shoulder.

**bandeau s.** Elasticized strapless swimsuit for women, cut straight across top usually made without a skirt, popular in 1980s.

**bathing dress** See SWIMDRESS.

**bathing suit** Synonym for SWIMSUIT.

**bikini** **1.** Woman's brief two-piece swimsuit with tiny bra top and brief pants cut below navel. Designed by Jacques Heim and introduced in Paris, 1946, at the Piscine Molitar, coincidental with the explosion of the first atomic bomb at island of Bikini in the Pacific. Named for its shock value and a sensation on Riviera beaches, but not accepted on U.S. public beaches till early 1960s. By the 1980s became tinier than originally. **2.** Man's very brief swim trunks.

**bloomer s.** Swimsuit made in the romper style with bouffant pants gathered into elastic bands at legs. Fashionable in 1940s and also in the 1960s, particularly for little girls. *Der.* See AMELIA BLOOMER in alphabetical listing.

**blouson s.** (blue-sohn) One- or two-piece swimsuit with a bloused effect coming below natural waistline with top having a built-in bra. Fashionable in the 1960s and revived in 1980s.

**boxer shorts** Man's *trunks* with thigh-length legs and elastic waistband, frequently styled with three contrasting stripes down side.

**boy-shorts** Girl's two-piece swimsuit designed with shorts or cuffed shorts and brief top.

**briefers** Very short trunks worn by men and boys made of elastic or knitted fabric. In 1980s became similar to *bikini pants.*

**cabana set** Swimsuit for men and boys with trunks and jacket cut out of the same fabric or made in contrasting fabrics designed to be worn together. *Der.* Spanish, *cabaña,* "a small tent-like shelter placed on the beach."

**cutout s.** Fitted *maillot*-type of swimsuit with sections cut out at sides, center front, or anywhere. May have fishnet inserted in cutouts or have lacers connecting the cutout parts. Introduced in mid-1960s.

**dressmaker s.** Any swimsuit made of knitted or woven fabric, rather than lastex and styled with a skirt. Sometimes shirred across back using elastic thread on bobbin of sewing machine. Basic type of swimsuit since 1940s.

**Gay 90s s.** Two-piece, circular-striped knitted suit with knee-length pants and hip-length short-sleeved top. Offered for sale in late 1960s, it imitated jersey suits of the 1890s.

**hip-rider s.** Two-piece swimsuit for women with low-slung pants or skirt, showing the navel. An innovation in the 1960s.

**Long John Trunks** Man's swimsuit made with rope sash and just above-the-knee knit pants with wide stripes alternating with bright red, green, or black. *Der.* Worn in imitation of boxing trunks worn by late John L. Sullivan (1858–1918), heavyweight boxing champion (1882–1892).

**maillot** (my-yo) Classic one-piece knitted or jersey swimsuit without skirt, form-fitting and usually backless. Sometimes with detachable strap tied around neck or buttoned to back of suit. Popular since 1930s and very popular in 1980s with high cut legs. *Der.* French, *maillot,* "tight garment."

**mono-kini** Woman's topless swimsuit consisting only of brief *bikini panties* worn with pasties. Introduced by Rudi Gernreich in 1970.

**one-piece s.** Any swimsuit for women or children made all in one piece. Sometimes has an attached skirt. Classic type of suit since the 1920s. Also see MAILLOT and TANK SUIT.

BIKINI         BLOOMER SUIT        BLOUSON SWIMSUIT     CABANA SET

**overblouse s.** Woman's two-piece bathing suit with brief trunks and a separate blouse often with a tank-top neckline and unfitted waist.

**pinafore s.** Bikini swimsuit with extra pinafore which fits tightly over bust and has free-hanging skirt curving from sides up to center back revealing the bikini pants underneath. Also called *apron swimsuit*.

**rib tickler s.** Two-piece bare midriff suit for women made in knits or woven fabrics.

**sarong s.** (seh-rong) Dressmaker-type swimsuit with rounded ends on wrap skirt which drapes to one side. *Der.* Copied from dress designed by Edith Head for Dorothy Lamour for film *Hurricane* in 1937, similar to Indonesian dress.

**sea legs** Man's long tightly fitted beach pants coming to below calf made with elasticized waist. Made in brilliant horizontal stripes in varying widths and many colors.

**sheath s.** Similar to a MAILLOT with a tiny skirt panel added in front, but not in back, usually made of stretch fabric. Classic style since the late 1930s.

**string bikini** Minimal halter bra with bikini panties worn low on hips made of two triangular shaped pieces attached to an elastic band or string ties.

**surf trunks** Swim trunks for men longer in length than regular trunks with a hip pocket for surfboard wax. Introduced in the late 1960s.

**MAILLOT**        **STRING BIKINI**        **TUNIC SWIMSUIT**        **TANK SUIT**

**swimdress** Swimsuit which looks like a micro-mini length dress. Same as *bathing dress.*

**tank s.** Classic maillot swimsuit without skirt made with scooped neck and built-up straps. *Der.* Early indoor swimming pools were called "tanks."

**teardrop bikini** Bikini pants worn with a teardrop bra composed of two tiny triangles with straps at neck and around the body.

**Thread® The** Very small string bikini, similar to G-string with minimal bra.

**topless s.** Swimsuit that starts below bust or at waist held up by two straps from the back meeting in a V in center front. Introduced by American designer Rudi Gernreich in 1964. Forbidden on most U.S. beaches, but started topless waitress style in California nightclubs.

**trunks** Synonym for men's or boys' swimsuits.

**tunic s.** Two-piece swimsuit cut like a dress with straight lines, slashed on the side seams with panties worn underneath.

**swinger/swinger clutch** See CONTOUR CLUTCH.

**swinger bag** See HANDBAG.

**swing skirt** See SKIRTS.

**Swirl®** See DRESSES.

**Swiss belt** Broad woman's belt pointed at center top and bottom and sometimes laced up front in corselet style. Worn at various times throughout the 19th c. Also called *Swiss girdle.*

**Swiss bodice** Sleeveless velvet bodice worn with *Swiss belt* worn over sleeved blouse in late 1860s.

**SWISS DRESS, 1865**

**Swiss dress** Child's two-piece costume worn in mid-1860s with tailored waist-length jacket and full skirt with fitted corselet at waistline.

**Swiss embroidery** See MADEIRA EMBROIDERY under EMBROIDERIES.

**Swiss girdle** See SWISS BELT.

**switch** Long hank of hair which may be braided in a plait and worn as a *coronet* or twisted into a *chignon*.

**swivel weave** Plain weave background with embroidered dot effect woven in circular effect around a few warps. Used on expensive *dotted* swiss, this dot will not pull out.

**sword** Weapon of various types, typically with a long straight or slightly curved blade—sharp on one or both sides—with an ornamental handle, fashionable man's accessory from 16th to end of 18th c.

**syglaton** See CYCLAS.

**synthetic fiber** Man-made *fibers* including acrylic, nylon, polyester, and vinyl.

**synthetic gem** A gem chemically identical to those found in nature but man-made in the laboratory. Compare with SIMULATED GEM. See GEMS and BEADS.

**synthetic straw** Man-made fibers or materials used to make straws.

**szür** White felt full-length man's coat with large lapels and broad collar lavishly decorated with embroidery and appliqué in flower motifs. Worn like a cape fastened with a leather strap across chest. Part of Hungarian national costume. Also see MAGYAR COSTUME.

**T** Abbreviation designating *tall* size range. See TALL.

**tab** An extra flap, strap, or loop of fabric, used with buttonhole, buckle, or snap to close coats, collars, sleeves, and cuffs. See CLOSINGS.

**tabard** **1.** *Tunic* with loose front and back panels and short winglike sleeves, sometimes with heraldic coat-of-arms embroidered on back. Worn by heralds for tourneys and knights over armor from 13th to 16th c. See GARNACHE. **2.** 14th-c. overgarment. **3.** Short heavy cape of coarse cloth worn outdoors in 19th c. by men and women.

**tabbed closing** See CLOSINGS.

**tabby weave** Synonym for PLAIN WEAVE.

**tab collar** See COLLARS.

**tabi** Ankle-length white woven cotton socks with separate division for big toe. Worn by Japanese indoors and with the *zori* outdoors.

**table** The top surface of a brilliant-cut diamond. Also see BRILLIANT CUT under GEM CUTS.

**tablecloth check** See CHECKS.

**table-cut gloves** See GLOVES.

**tablet mantilla** Watered or plain silk wrap of mid-1850s made with a yoke that falls low on the shoulders. Trimmed with cut-turret edging, narrow braid, and fringe.

**TABLET MANTILLA, 1854**

**tablier skirt** (tab-lee-ay) Skirt worn from 1850s to 1870s with decorated free-hanging panel in front suggesting an apron. Sometimes trimming was applied directly to skirt. *Der.* French, "apron."

**tablion** Elaborate decorative oblong of gold embroidery on both the front and back of the Byzantine Imperial robes. Worn by the Emperor Justinian and his wife, Theodosius, during the Byzantine period. High court officials wore a purple tablion on a white mantle. Depicted in mosaics of *Church of Ravenna.*

**tabs** Term used in 19th c. for one of several loose-hanging pieces of fabric with a border of square or round edges forming a peplum or used as trimming. See VANDYKE and TURRET BODICE.

**tack** To sew together lightly with invisible stitches or to join by sewing loosely at just one point.

**taffeta** Term used for a classification of crisp fabrics with a fine, smooth surface usually made in the plain weave, sometimes with a small crosswise rib. Originally made in silk, now made in man-made fibers. *Der.* Persian *tuftah*, "fine, plain woven silk fabric." Also see ANTIQUE TAFFETA, PAPER TAFFETA, and SHOT CLOTH.

**taffeta pipkin** See PIPKIN.

**tagilmust** A long piece of fabric wrapped around the head and the lower part of the face to make a turban and veil combined. Worn by all Tuareg men of the Sahara before strangers, women, and especially in-laws.

**Taglioni** (tah-gyee-oh-nee) Man's fitted *greatcoat* reaching to knees worn from 1839 to 1845. Usually double-breasted with wide turned-back lapels, large flat collar and cuffs of satin or velvet. Also had a back vent, and slit pockets bound with twill fabric. *Der.* Named after Italian ballet master Flippo Taglioni (1777–1871).

**Taglioni frock coat** Man's single-breasted *frock* coat worn from 1838 to 1842 made with short full skirt, broad notched collar, slashed or flapped pockets, and back vent. *Der.* Named after Italian ballet master Flippo Taglioni (1777–1871).

**tail coat** See SWALLOW-TAILED COAT under COATS.

**tailleur** (ty-yer) French for tailored costume—a suit. *Der.* French, "tailor" or "cutter."

**tailor 1.** Person who makes either men's or women's clothes, mends clothing, or does alterations. Originally men did all of the commercial clothing production of men's wear, coats, and suits, especially those made of wool. **2.** (verb) To fit clothing for one individual; to fashion a garment. **3.** To alter a ready-made military uniform for a better fit.

**tailored** Fashion term used to indicate that an item of apparel is relatively plain without decoration and depends on the line and fit of the item for style. See BLOUSES, BUTTONHOLES, PAJAMAS, and SLIPS.

**tailoring** Process of cutting, fitting, and finishing a garment to conform to the body by means of darts, linings, hems, and pressing, *e.g.*, a man's suit or coat. Same techniques applied to women's suits, slacks, shirts, with simple clear lines—no fancy details. Garments are called *custom-made* or *tailor-made* when garment is made to order for an individual in a special shop, *e.g.*, as at tailoring establishments in *Savile Row*, London. The opposite of "tailored" for a woman's dress, suit, or coat is *dressmaker.*

**tailor-made 1.** Garment made specifically for one individual by a tailor—customer's measurements are taken and several fittings are necessary. Also called *custom-made* or *custom-tailored.* **2.** In the late 19th c., a woman's costume for morning or country wear, usually a suit consisting of a jacket and skirt made by a

**TAILOR-MADE, 1898**

tailor rather than a dressmaker. Introduced by Redfern in late 1870s.

**tailor's canvas** See LINEN CANVAS #1.

**tailor's chalk** Hard chalk made in flattened form about one inch square. Used in white, black, and colors to mark hems, darts, etc., when sewing. Brushes off when garment is completed. Chalk in powdered form is used in skirt markers to mark hems.

**tailor's ham** Pillow, shaped like a ham used to press shoulders and other rounded surfaces when tailoring clothing.

**tailor's tack** See STITCHES.

**tails** See FULL DRESS under SUITS.

**tāj** Headdress, or high cap, worn by Mohammedan Dervishes in Persia.

**taj toe** See TOES.

**talaria** (ta-lay-ree-a) Winged sandals, as seen in representations of Roman god Mercury and Greek god Hermes.

**tali**  Item of jewelry worn by women in India consisting of a gold ornament worn suspended from a slender cord around the neck. Takes the place of a wedding ring in India.

**talisman ring**  "Charm" ring worn in Ancient Greece and the Middle Ages to ensure the wearer of good health, the strength of ten, love, wealth, and happiness. Worn in recent times as a pledge of friendship. Also see FRIENDSHIP RING under RINGS.

**tall**  **1.** Men's size corresponding to a chest measurement of 38″ to 48″ and a height of 5′11″ to 6′2½″. Also see EXTRA-TALL. **2.** Women's size range corresponding to a height of 5′8″ to 6′.

**Talleyrand collar** (tal-i-ranh)  Collar standing up at back of neck and turned over, similar to ROBESPIERRE COLLAR. *Der.* Named after French statesman Charles Maurice de Talleyrand-Perigord, active in politics from 1775–1815.

**Tallien redingote** (tal-ee-en red-in-goat)  Outdoor coat worn by women in late 1860s created by French couturier Worth. Matched to dress or made of black silk. Coat had a heart-shaped neckline, full back, and a sash tied in large bow with long ends in back. Small bows were tied to ends of sash. *Der.* Named for Theresa Tallien, Princess de Chimay, (1773–1835) a fashionable woman, who is said to have owned 30 wigs of different colors.

**tallith**  Prayer shawl with tassels, usually blue, at the four corners called *tsitsith*, worn by Jewish men after age 13. Believed to have been derived from Roman *pallium.* Took various shapes throughout the ages. Modern tallith is made of wool or silk in white with black or blue stripes. Silk types vary from 54″ to 90″ long and 32″ to 72″ wide. Woolen type is larger and made with two lengths joined together. Narrow silk ribbon covers place where it is pieced. At the neck is the *ata,* a narrow ribbon or band woven with silver or gold thread. Also see ARBA KANFOTH and TSITSITH.

**tallow-top cut**  See CABOCHON under GEM CUTS.

**Talma**  **1.** Woman's long *cape* or *cloak,* frequently hooded, worn in 1860s. **2.** Woman's knee to hip-length *cape* of embroidered satin, lace, or velvet with fringe at hem used as an outer garment from 1850s to mid-1870s. **3.** In 1890s, a woman's full-length coat with loose sleeves and lace cape or deep velvet collar. *Der.* Named for François Joseph Talma (1763–1826), a French tragic actor of Consulate and Empire period. Also called *Talma mantle.*

**TALMA**

**Talma cloak**  Knee-length man's cloak, worn for evening in 1850s.

**Talma lounge**  A jacket worn by men in 1898 made with raglan sleeves, straight fronts, and curved or slanted pockets. Worn as an informal jacket. *Der.* Named for François Joseph Talma (1763–1826), a French tragic actor of Consulate and Empire period.

**Talma overcoat**  Raglan-sleeved greatcoat with large armholes worn by men in 1898. *Der.* Named for François Joseph Talma (1763–1826), a French tragic actor of Consulate and Empire period.

**tam**  See CAPS.

**tambour farthingale**  See ENGLISH FARTHINGALE.

**tambour work**   See EMBROIDERIES.

**tamein**   Wrapped garment worn by women of Burma, made of a length of cotton or silk, 4½′ x 5′, woven in two pieces in different patterns, worn wrapped around bust and secured by twisting the ends. Also spelled *tamehn.*

**tam-o-shanter**   See CAPS.

**tank suit**   See SWIMSUITS.

**tank top**   See TOPS and KNIT SHIRTS.

**tanning**   The process of making leather from hides. Methods include: vegetable tanning with tannin, mineral tanning with chrome or alum, and artificial methods. Also see BUCKSKIN TANNAGE.

**tantoor**   Bridal headdress, shaped like a spike about a yard high, formerly worn by Druse sect in Syria. Headdress was fixed in position on top of the bride's head by the groom and worn thereafter, night and day. Style indicated home district of husband. Also spelled *tantoura.*

**TANTOOR**

**tanzanite**   See GEMS.

**tanzen**   Fabrics from which robes are made—fine striped silk or cotton.

**tapa cloth**   Fabric made from fibers of the inner bark of the paper mulberry tree, *Brousonnetia papyrifera,* of the tree *Pipturus albidus,* varying from a muslinlike to a leatherlike fabric. Made by natives in the South Pacific Islands by beating bark to form a weblike fabric. Used for clothing by the natives of Pacific Islands and eastern Asia. In Hawaii sometimes called *kapa,* and in Fiji, called *masi.* Also see BARKCLOTH.

**tapered pants**   See PANTS.

**tapered shirt**   See BODY SHIRT under SHIRTS.

**tapestry**   **1.** Heavy fabric, usually with a pictorial design, woven of multi-colored yarns on a Jacquard loom. Has two warp yarns and two or more fillings of various colors, carried across the back when not needed, giving a striped effect on the reverse side. Cotton, silk, wool, and other fibers are used. Fabric is heavy for dresses, so used mainly for shoes, bags, and handbags. **2.** Handmade textile similar to #1. **3.** See STITCHES.

**tapis**   Three-quarter length overskirt of net worn over the bright-colored *saya,* or underskirt, by women in the Philippines.

**tap panties**   See PANTIES.

**tap shoe**   See SHOES.

**tarboosh** (tar-boosh)   Tall headdress with flat topped, brimless felt cap, shaped like a truncated cone, usually red with black tassel from center of crown—similar to the *fez,* sometimes worn under a turban. Also spelled *tarbush.* Also see BETHLEHEM HEADDRESS.

**tarlatan**   **1.** Netlike, sheer, transparent fabric of low quality used for costumes. Made of heavily sized cotton it becomes limp after washing. **2.** *Glazed tarlatan* is coated on one side and used for theatrical purposes. Originally a coarse fabric with linen and wool warp made in Italy. Also spelled *tarlatane, tarleton, tarlton.*

**tartan** Each clan in Scotland has adopted a specific plaid fabric in individual colors used for the *kilt*, or short pleated skirt worn by men, and the *shawl*, a drapery worn hanging from the shoulders, across back, and tucked into belt. Although Scots are reported to have used stripes as early as the 5th c. and were fond of "mottled" fabrics, the real origin of the tartan is controversial. Various historians mention plaids as early as 1594 and 1645, but it was not until early 18th c. (1703) that they began to emerge as a clan symbol which designated a place of residence. After the defeat of Bonnie Prince Charles in 1747, plaids were banned by British law. Revived in 1822 when George IV visited Scotland—from that time on there were specific tartans for each clan. A brief list of better known tartans follows. Also see PLAIDS and HIGHLAND DRESS in alphabetical listing. *Der.* Believed to have come from Flemish word *tire-taine.* Also see KILT under SKIRTS and KILTIE LOOK under LOOKS.

## ═══ TARTANS ═══

**Balmoral t.** Predominantly gray with two narrow black stripes and one red stripe grouped together and running vertically with two red stripes running horizontally plus wider stripes of black and gray used in both directions.

**Black Watch t.** Very dark blue and green squares with wide and narrow black lines in both directions and no overplaid. Worn by members of the Black Watch.

**Bruce t.** Bold red plaid crossed by dark green stripes of various sizes forming a central box consisting of four green boxes outlined with narrow green stripes. Large yellow and white overplaid encloses the design.

**Buchanan t.** Intricate bold plaid consisting of dull green bands combined with red, orange, green, and yellow checks arranged in squares, having a fine overplaid of white and black.

**Cameron t.** Predominantly bright red with four dark green stripes crossed at right angles making a central section of sixteen blocks of green. Yellow overplaid outlines each pattern.

**Frazer t.** Similar to the CAMERON CLAN TARTAN, but smaller in size with navy and green stripes crossing at right angles making a central section of sixteen navy and green blocks. Also includes an overplaid in white.

**Macbeth t.** A more complicated patterned tartan made with cobalt blue ground and colored stripes in red, yellow, green, and black, some outlined in white.

**MacDonell of Glengarry t.** Dark green and navy ground crossed with narrow red lines of two widths making a smaller design than most tartans. Has a large overplaid in white.

**MacGregor (Rob Roy) t.** Combination of vivid red blocks and wide black bands in a small block design.

**Macintyre and Glenorchy t.** Red ground crossed with medium-sized bands of green and navy running vertically and horizontally with narrow bands of green and blue in between—making a squared pattern with large overplaid of light blue.

**MacPherson hunting t.** Bold black block alternating with gray and beige blocks, and outlined with two narrow red stripes with bright blue stripe between them.

**Menzies Black and White t.** Similar in design to MENZIES HUNTING TARTAN. but woven only in black and white.

**Menzies hunting t.** Predominantly wide blocks of solid green alternating with red blocks divided into checks by green bands—other blocks are striped.

**Munro t.** Vivid red ground plaided in dark green and navy with fine yellow lines running in both directions at intervals.

**Ramsay t.** Brilliant red ground with wide black bands in both directions and double lines in white overplaid. Also has fine purple stripes running in both directions. Dates back to the 17th c.

**Rob Roy t.** See MacGregor tartan.

**Royal Stewart (Stuart) t.** Similar to Stewart dress tartan with bold red ground and central box of nine squares of red outlined with green, black and blue bands. Fine navy lines run through center of boxes with fine white and yellow overplaid.

**Stewart (Stuart) dress t.** Central box contains nine red squares outlined by wide black bands, alternating with white blocks, and green, red, and black striped blocks with fine yellow and white stripes defining the squares.

**Stewart Hunting t.** Very dark blue or green ground crossed at right angles with black bands making a central section of sixteen blocks. An overplaid of red and yellow outlines the pattern.

---

**tasar** See TUSSAH.

**tasseau** **1.** Type of pin or clasp used to fasten *mantel* in late Middle Ages. **2.** Triangular scarf, usually black, used to fill in the low bodice neckline worn by women in the late 15th c. Also called *tassel. Der.* Latin, *tassa,* "clasp."

TASSEAU #1

**tassel** **1.** Bundle of threads, bound at one end, hung singly or in groups as ornament on belts, hats, shawls, etc. **2.** See TASSEAU. **3.** See NECKLACES.

**Tassell, Gustave** See APPENDIX/DESIGNERS.

**tassel-tie** Bows ending in tassels on *moccasins, wing-tip oxfords,* and *loafers.* Also see LOAFERS under SHOES.

**tasset** Armor for the upper thigh made either of a single plate or of several narrow flexible plates joined together by rivets. Also spelled *tace, tasse.*

**tatamis** See SANDALS.

**tatas** See LEADING STRINGS.

**tattersall** Fabric with an over-check, approximately one-half inch square made with colored lines in both directions, on a white or contrasting ground. Also called *tattersall checks.* Sometimes called *tatersall plaid.* Used for vests, sport shirts, and coats. *Der.* Named after Richard Tattersall, English horseman, founder of Tattersall's London Horse Auction Mart established in 1776. Also see CHECKS, PLAIDS, and VESTS.

**tatting** See LACES.

**tattoo** (tat-oo) **1.** Permanent design made on skin by process of pricking and ingraining indelible pigment. Of Polynesian origin and practiced by aboriginal tribes. Adopted by western world and popular with sailors. **2.** Fashion fad in early 1970s of decorating body with transfer designs of ships, hearts, etc., imitating those tattooed on sailors' skin. Also see BODY PAINTING and DECALCOMANIA. See PANTYHOSE.

**taupe** (tope) Brownish-gray color with a purple cast.

**taure** See BULL HEAD.

**tchamir** See SHIRTS.

**tcharchaf** Informal wrap worn by Turkish women which replaced the *feradjé.* Cut similar to two skirts of different lengths open down the front. Shorter one is pulled up over the head as a scarf and fastened under the chin. A *yashmak* or face veil is also worn.

**tchapan** (cha-pan) Man's long loose outer

robe worn in Turkestan with full sleeves made of quilted silk or cotton fabric striped red, orange, and green.

**tcherkeska**   Knee-length coat worn in central Caucasus. Distinguished by cartridge pleats on either side of chest. A narrow leather belt is worn around the tight-fitting waistline. The *bourka* is worn on top. Also spelled *cherkesska*.

**tea-cozy cap**   See CAPS.

**tea apron**   White lawn apron with small pocket, which ties around waist, and is trimmed with ruffles, Valenciennes lace, and hem-stitching. Used when sewing, or to protect the dress, in early 20th c.

**tea gown**   **1.** Loose-fitting long gown in pale colors worn from 1877 to early 20th c. Usually made of thin wool or silk trimmed with ruffles and lace down front opening and on sleeves. Worn without corset as an informal hostess gown. **2.** Term used in 1920s and 1930s for semiformal dress suitable for an afternoon tea or garden party.

**TEA GOWN**

**tea jacket**   Loose informal jacket or bodice with close-fitting back. Sometimes made with tight sleeves and loose-hanging front profusely trimmed with lace. Worn by women from late 1880s to end of 19th c. replacing the tailor-made bodice of the dress for afternoon tea. Also called MATINEE.

**TEA JACKET**

**teardrop bikini**   See SWIMSUITS.

**teardrop bra**   See BRAS.

**teasel**   Dried burr of plant called *Dipsacus* used in England to brush up nap of woolen fabrics. Also see GIG.

**teasing**   See BACK-COMBING.

**tebenna**   Etruscan semi-circular cloak in purple, white, or black (for funerals) worn by King and important citizens—short at first, later knee-length, and finally full-length. The Roman TOGA developed from this cloak.

**teck scarf**   Man's wide necktie of 1890s somewhat shorter than average. Tied in *four-in-hand-knot* with ends cut straight across or ending in center point with slanted sides. Also see DE JOINVILLE TECK.

**teddy**   **1.** Straight-cut garment of 1920s combining a chemise with short slip, or long vest with panties. Wide strap is attached to the front

**TECK SCARF, 1893**

and back at the hem thus making separate openings for each leg. **2.** Revived in late 1960s, and in 1980s, becoming a one-piece tight fitting minimal garment. See FOUNDATIONS and PAJAMAS.

**teddybear coat** Bulky coat of natural-colored alpaca-pile fabric worn by men, women, and children in 1920s. *Der.* Named after the teddy bear, a child's toy of early 20th c., which was named for President Theodore Roosevelt.

**Teddy boy** British youth who wore unusual styles in protest against traditional fashion. *Der.* Teddy is nickname for Edward. Also see LOOKS, and WINKLE PICKERS under SHOES.

**Teddy girl** British girl, counterpart of Teddy boy, who wore distinctive clothes in protest against traditional current fashions. Also see LOOKS and BEEHIVE HAIRSTYLE under HAIRSTYLES.

**teen bra** See BRAS.

**tee shirt** See T-SHIRT under KNIT SHIRTS.

**templar cloak** Cloak or *paletot-sac* of 1840s cut wide with large bell-shaped sleeves, sometimes hooded or with small shoulder cape. Also called CABAN.

**templers** Ornamental nets or bosses worn by women in first half of 15th c. at sides of face to conceal the hair. Sometimes connected by band above forehead, sometimes part of headdress. Also spelled *templettes, temples.*

**tendrils** See CURLS.

**teneriffe lace** See LACES.

**ten-gallon hat** See HATS.

**tennis clothes** Although first played in France in the middle ages, tennis was introduced in the U.S. as lawn tennis in 1874 with the basic rules, height of net, and dimensions of court not changing since this time. See DRESSES, SHOES, SHORTS, and SWEATERS. Also see LAWN-TENNIS COSTUME.

**TENNIS COSTUME, 1892**

**tensile strength** Textile term for the ability of a fiber or fabric to withstand strain and resist breaking. Swatch of fabric is placed between jaws of a tensile tester machine and pulled until it rips. A gauge records this point as the "tensile strength" of the fabric. Fabrics are measured in the warp direction in pounds per inch and grams per *denier.*

**tent** Term used for item of apparel with much fullness. See COATS, DRESSES, and SILHOUETTES.

**tentering** Finishing process used on fabrics which involves straightening and holding it to desired width.

**tent stitch** See CONTINENTAL under STITCHES.

**terai hat** Riding hat of fur or felt with red lining, shaped somewhat like a *derby*, with large brim which had a metal vent through crown.

Made with two hats sewed together at edges of brims and worn by British women, sometimes men, in tropical climates since 1880s.

**Teresa**   See THÉRÈSE.

**terno**   Grand-occasion dress worn by Filipino women in Hawaii, frequently elaborately embroidered or beaded. Made with flared sleeves shaped to stand up from shoulders, and a high-waisted slim cut skirt.

**terrycloth**   **1.** Absorbent fabric made in the pile weave with uncut loops and a background weave of plain or twill. Usually made in cotton but now also made with man-made yarns. Sometimes woven in plaid, dobby, or Jacquard patterns of two or more colors. May be yarn-dyed, bleached, piece-dyed, or printed. **2.** A similar pile weave fabric made by knitting, usually called *knitted terrycloth*. Both fabrics are used for shorts, jumpsuits, pants, beachwear, summer dresses, robes, and sport shirts.

**tête de mouton**   Woman's short curly wig worn in Paris from 1730 to about 1755. *Der.* French, "sheep's head."

**tethered studs**   Man's evening jewelry of 1830s and 1840s consisting of three ornamental shirt *studs* joined with small chains.

**textured hose**   See HOSE.

**textured yarn**   **1.** Man-made continuous-filament yarns permanently heat-set in crimped manner, or otherwise modified to give more elasticity, used to make stretch fabrics. **2.** Man-made filament yarns processed to change their appearance, *e.g., abraded.*

**T.F.P.I.A.**   Textile Fiber Products Identification Act: Federal law enacted setting labeling requirements for clothing made of textiles.

**theatre suit**   See SUITS.

**Theo tie**   See OXFORDS.

**Theresa diamond**   See DIAMONDS.

**Thérèse** (ter-eece)   **1.** Large hood, held out

with wire, designed to go over tall bonnets and hairstyles. Worn in France from mid-1770s to 1790, later with an attached shoulder cape. Also spelled *Teresa.* **2.** Scarf of light gauze fabric often worn over an indoor cap in the 1770s and 1780s.

**thermal gloves**   See GLOVES.

**thermal underwear**   Long-sleeved undershirt and long-legged pants or one-piece *union suit* made of knitted cotton or cotton-and-wool mesh, woven in a manner to contain air cells which act as insulators to keep body heat close to skin. Worn for winter, particularly for sports.

**thick and thin yarn**   Yarns, particularly rayon and acetate, which are of uneven texture at intervals. When woven into cloth, they add interest. Used for fabrics such as *shantung*.

**Thinsulate®**   A 60% polyolefin, 40% polyester microfilament insulation providing warmth equal to down or polyester insulations of close to twice the thickness. Does not absorb water.

**Thirties look**   **1.** Early 1930s style that featured long, lean, bias-cut dress with intricate drapery, unusual sleeves, and frequently V or round necks. **2.** In late 1930s extremely broad shoulders were featured with small waistline and more tailored styles. Also see RETRO under LOOKS, and SILHOUETTES.

**thong**   Narrow strip of rawhide or other leather used for a lacer braided into a belt, or wound around foot and leg as a fastening for sandals. See BELTS and SANDALS.

**thread**   Yarn twisted tightly for use with needle or a sewing machine, in various fibers and strengths.

**Thread®, The**   See SWIMSUITS.

**thread count**   See COUNT OF CLOTH.

**threads**   British slang term of young "trendy" people in 1960s for mod clothes on Carnaby Street, London.

**three-armhole dress**   See DRESSES.

**three-decker**   Term used from late 1870s on for man's or woman's triple-caped ULSTER. Also see CARRICK.

**three-quarter**   See LENGTHS and SLEEVES.

**three-seamed raglan sleeve**   See RAGLAN SLEEVE under SLEEVES.

**three-seamer**   British tailoring term for man's jacket with center back seam and two side seams, contrasted with coat having *side bodies* and five seams. Used from 1860 on.

**three-storeys-and-a-basement**   Amusing name given to woman's hat of 1886 with very high crown.

**thrift shop**   Secondhand clothing or fur store. In the 1960s, a popular source of fashion of 1920s, 1930s, and 1940s. Also see DRESSES and VINTAGE under LOOKS.

**throat belt**   See NECKLACES.

**thrum**   **1.** Short tufts of wool left on loom after fabric is cut away which was knitted into workmen's caps in U.S. and England in 18th c. **2.** Long-napped felt hat worn in 16th c. Also called a *thrummed hat.*

**tiara**   (tee-ar-a)   **1.** Curved band, often of metal set with jewels or of flowers, worn on top of woman's head from ear to ear giving effect of a crown. Sometimes used to hold a wedding veil. Also see DEMI-CORONAL. **2.** An ancient headpiece worn by the Pope of the Roman Catholic church, consisting of three coronets placed one on top of the other, each successively smaller. **3.** An ancient Persian headdress. Also see DIADEM #2 and CORONET #1.

**Tice, Bill**   See APPENDIX/DESIGNERS.

**ticket pocket**   See POCKETS.

**ticking**   Sturdy durable fabric woven in a close satin weave or a twill weave with soft filling yarns. Originally used for covering pil-

lows and mattresses, now used for sport clothes and pants.

**ticking stripes**   **1.** Mill finished, firm durable fabric woven with narrow blue stripes on a natural colored ground in the twill weave. **2.** See STRIPES.

**tie**   Long band made in various widths of double-thick fabric or rounded braid worn around the neck under the shirt collar and tied in various ways. May be made of fabric, suede, leather, chain mail, and beads. Term came into use about 1820 but did not entirely replace the term *cravat* used earlier. Originally worn only by men, women adopted ties in 1890s to wear with the shirtwaist.   Since 1930s the width varies, *e.g.*, wide in 1930s, narrow in 1950s, wide again in 1970s, and more moderate width in the 1980s. See DE JOINVILLE TECK, OCTAGON TIE, OSBALDISTON TIE, and TECH SCARF in alphabetical listing.

━━━━ **TIES** ━━━━

**ascot**   **1.** Wide necktie worn looped over with ends cut diagonally and held in place by scarf pin. Introduced in 1876 and worn since with morning coat. **2.** Scarf looped under the chin. *Der.* Fashionable horse-racing spot, Ascot Heath, England. Also see SCARFS category.

**black t.**   **1.** Man's black *bow tie* worn with dinner jacket or tuxedo, for semiformal occasions. **2.** Denotes type of dress expected at a semiformal occasion. "Black tie" indicates a tuxedo is required for men.

**boater t.**   Man's FOUR-IN-HAND TIE, shorter than average, made with extra large knot, and usually with square-cut ends. Introduced in late 1960s from England.

**bolo t.** Western-type tie made of heavy rounded braid with metal-tipped ends fastening with a slide. Also called *shoelace tie*.

**bootlace t.** See STRING TIE.

**bow t. 1.** Man's tie, square-cut or with shaped ends, tied in a bow under the chin. Originally introduced in late 19th c. and worn with *full dress* since. **2.** Man's tie, already tied in a bow, which clips to the collar. **3.** Short bow tied by hand on the front of a woman's dress or blouse. See BLACK TIE and WHITE TIE.

**clip-on t.** Tie, either pre-tied in a knot like a four-in-hand or a bow tie, that is fastened to the collarband by a metal clip.

**cravat 1.** Sometimes used as a synonym for a man's wide necktie worn with morning coat and pinstriped trousers. **2.** Lawn, muslin, or silk neckcloth with ends tied in a bow or knot in center front worn from 1660 to the end of the 19th c. Sometimes worn with starched collar called a *stiffener*. See alphabetical listing.

**four-in-hand t.** Long necktie which goes around the neck with one end looping over the other end twice, then pulled through loop making a slip knot. Usually made of bias-cut fabric or knit, narrow in the center back and wider at the ends. Width varies, very wide ties in the 1930s, becoming very narrow in the 1950s, wide again in 1970s, and of more moderate width in 1980s. Worn continuously since the 1890s. Also worn by women with tailored suits.

**hunting stock** Type of wide tie or *stock*. Worn folded over once to fill in neckline of jacket. Used by equestrians when riding in hunt field or show ring.

**kipper** Necktie 4″ or 5″ wide with ends like a bow tie usually of striped or patterned fabric. Introduced from England in late 1960s.

**sailor t.** Large square scarf of black silk folded diagonally and worn under square *sailor collar*, and either tied in sailor knot or pulled through strap on front of *middy blouse*. Formerly

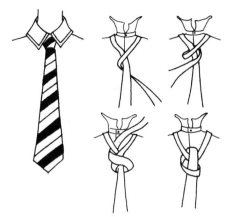

**HOW TO TIE FOUR-IN-HAND**

                            **BLACK TIE**

worn by U.S. Naval enlisted personnel, and adopted by women and children in late 19th c. to wear with middy blouse.

**sheriff t.** British term for STRING TIE.

**shoelace t.** See BOLO TIE.

**Southern Colonel t.** See STRING TIE.

**stock** Long wide straight tie worn looped over once at the neckline sometimes fastened with a pin. Ends hang free or are tucked inside jacket. For historical information see alphabetical listing.

**string t.** Necktie, usually not more than one inch wide, often black, worn in a bow with ends hanging down. Also called *bootlace tie* and *Southern Colonel tie*.

**white t. 1.** Man's white bow tie worn for formal occasions with tails, usually hand tied.

**2.** Denotes a type of dress for a special occasion. "White tie" means formal dress or *tails* for a man and a formal gown for a woman.

**Windsor t.** **1.** Regular man's necktie tied in four-in-hand style with a more complicated knot which is larger. *Der.* Called a *Windsor knot* after Duke of Windsor who popularized it in early 1920s. **2.** Large flowing bow tie worn by men in 1870s and 1880s.

---

**tie-back skirt** Skirt with a train pulled back and looped to form puffs at sides by means of a drawstring inserted through tapes. Gave a silhouette which was flat in front and puffed at back and hips. Worn from mid-1870s through early 1880s.

**tie clasp/clip** Jewelry consisting of a decorative metal bar bent double that slides over a man's tie and behind his shirt front placket clipping the tie in place. May also have spring-clip back.

**tied closing** See CLOSINGS.

**tie dyeing** Hand method of coloring a fabric by first dyeing the background color, then tying strings tightly around puffs of fabric and dipping in a second color to get a two-color design, repeating to add more colors. Designs are usually circular with feathered or blended edges. A technique originating in Indonesia and popular in the 1920s mainly for scarves. Revived in 1960s for blue jeans, T-shirts, dresses, and furs. Also see PRINTS.

**tie pin** See STICKPIN under PINS.

**tiers** Several layers of ruffles or bias-cut sections placed one above the other and overlapping. Used mainly on skirts, full sleeves, or pants. See SILHOUETTES and SKIRTS.

**tie shoe** See OXFORDS.

**tie silk** All inclusive term for fabrics used for making neckties and scarfs. Usually distinguished by small designs or stripes and woven

in narrower widths than other fabrics. Since neckties are now made of fabrics with all types of fibers including cotton, polyester, and nylon, the term *tie fabrics* is more accurate.

**tie tack** Small ornament with a sharp-pointed back worn pierced through both parts of a man's necktie to hold them together. Back portion is usually screwed into a round metal stud.

**Tiffany, Charles Lewis** Made silverware in New York City in 1850. In 1886 introduced the *Tiffany setting*, a simple pronged setting used for diamonds and large stones. His son, Louis Comfort (1848–1933), was one of the most imaginative of Art Nouveau jewelers. Their store on Fifth Avenue has been a landmark for years, and noted for the finest quality gems, jewelry, and silver craftsmanship. Among his famous clients were Abraham Lincoln and Sarah Bernhardt. Also see TIFFANY DIAMOND under DIAMONDS and TIFFANY SETTING under GEM SETTINGS.

**tiger's eye** See GEMS.

**tights** **1.** Ankle-length, tight-fitting men's trousers usually white or light-colored, introduced at end of 18th c. and worn until 1850. Also called PANTALOONS. **2.** Knitted pants and stockings made in one piece, usually made of opaque-textured yarns, worn by athletes, circus performers, and dance hall girls in latter part of the 19th c. **3.** Women's and girls' below-the-knee underpants made in fine ribbed knit in either black or white worn in early 20th c. **4.** See PANTYHOSE.

**tilak** Mark painted on center of forehead by East Indian women, originally of caste significance, now *ornamental*. Also called CASTE MARK.

**tilari** A long necklace with about 24 strands of small beads ending with each three strands going through a series of larger beads. In the center is a group of hand-fashioned silver ornaments. Worn by women of Nepal.

**tilbury hat** Man's small hat with high tapered flat-topped crown and narrow rounded brim worn in 1830s.

**Tilley, Monika** See APPENDIX/DESIGNERS.

**timiak** Shirt lined with skins of birds cured with the feathers attached. Worn by Greenland Eskimos with feathers next to the skin for warmth.

**Tinling, Teddy** See APPENDIX/DESIGNERS.

**tinsel yarn** Metals such as gold, silver, aluminum, or copper cut into fine strips and used alone or made into core yarn for use in brocades and glitter fabrics.

**tippet** **1.** Streamer hanging from sleeve of the *cotehardi.* **2.** A white streamer worn around arm and hanging from elbow in Middle Ages. **3.** See LIRIPIPE #1. **4.** Shoulder cape of fur or cloth worn by women from 16th c. on. See PALATINE. **5.** See ALMUCE.

**TIPPET #1**

**tipping** Fur-dyeing process in which only the tips of the guard hairs are colored.

**tire** See ATTIRE #2.

**tissue** Descriptive of lightweight, semi-transparent fabric, *e.g.,* tissue gingham, tissue taffeta.

**Titus coiffure/wig** See COIFFURE À LA TITUS.

**tobe** **1.** Outer garment worn in northern and central Africa consisting of a long piece of fabric draped around the body and fastened on shoulder or worn as a skirt. **2.** Skirt worn by Bedouin men and women—man's garment is dark blue, ankle-length and made in slip-on style with an opening at the neck. Woman's garment is large and loose, and may be made in dark blue, black or red fabric.

**toboggan cap** See STOCKING CAP under CAPS.

**Toby ruff** Woman's small ruff of 1890, made of two or three layers of frills tied at the throat with ribbon.

**toc** Man's broad-brimmed felt hat worn by the Bretons of France (Brittany).

**toca** White cotton headcloth worn over red cap by Hebrews and Moors in Algeria.

**toddlers** Size range from 1 to 4 for very young children.

**toe** Front portion of the shoe covering the toes. In the Middle Ages toes of shoes became extremely long and pointed—some were two feet longer than the foot and were held up by chains attached to a band worn below the knee. See POULAINE and CRAKOW in alphabetical listing. In the 16th c. extremely wide toes were worn on duckbilled shoes. Fashion fluctuates between the extremes, while in the early 1960s very narrow needle toes were worn, by the mid-1960s broad-toed shoes became fashionable.

## TOES

**bulldog t.** Bulbous toe popular on a man's buttoned ankle-high shoe before World War I. Also see KNOB TOE.

**BULLDOG TOE**

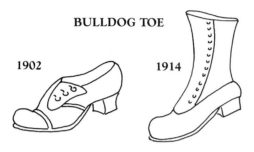

1902          1914

**Charlie Chaplin t.** Wide round toe used on a Mary Jane shoe. Featured by Courrèges in his spring 1967 collection. Also see MARY JANE SHOE under SHOES category.

**copper t.** Term for a metal cap placed on children's shoes to keep them from scuffing and wearing out. Used at the turn of the 20th c.

**crescent t.** Narrow-toed shoe ending with a curved rather than a needle tip.

**dollar-round t.** Old trade term for a toe of a shoe whose shape coincided with the rounded edge of half a silver dollar.

**knot t.** Bulbous toe introduced in the early 1970s. Similar to BULLDOG TOE.

**needle t.** Long narrow extremely pointed toe. Narrower and more pointed variations are called *double-needle* and *triple-needle toes*. Also see WINKLE PICKERS under SHOES category.

**oval t.** Woman's shoe toe, narrower than a round toe but not an extreme point.

**platypus t.** Squared-off tip of toe shaped like a duck's bill. *Der.* Named for animal with snout shaped in this manner.

**safety t.** Steel toe box inserted between shoe upper and lining. Used on shoes worn by workmen in industrial plants for protection.

**slant/slanted t.** Rather wide toe which slants diagonally toward the little toe.

**taj t.** Tiny pointed and turned-up oriental-type toe used on a shoe.

**walled t.** Deep toe cap with vertical edge at least ¾" high.

**toe-ankle chain** See BRACELETS.

**toe ring** See RINGS.

**toe rubbers** Overshoes worn by women which fit over the toes and have either a strap around the heel or snap together over the instep.

**toe slippers** See SLIPPERS.

**tog** Medieval term for coat. *Der.* Shortened form of *toga*.

**toga** **1.** Outer garment, consisting of large rectangle of cotton, wool, or silk cloth, either all white or royal purple. Often rounded at corners and decorated along one side, worn draped about the body by ancient Romans. **2.** Large rectangle of printed cotton, pinned on one shoulder and draped under opposite arm, worn in African countries. For fashion influences see DRESSES, NIGHTGOWNS, and ROBES. Also see TEBENNA.

**toggle** See CLOSINGS.

**togs** Slang for clothing, especially fancy garments.

**toile** (twal) **1.** French term for *muslin* pattern for a garment. **2.** Lace-makers term for pattern of lace as distinguished from the background. *Der.* French, "cloth."

**toile de Jouy** Floral or scenic design printed on fabric. Christopher Philip Oberkampf was the first person to produce fabric printed with copper rollers. Most famous of his prints are single colors beautifully engraved and finely colored characterized by classic motifs. Mainly used for interior decoration, some were used for apparel. *Der.* Factory established at "Jouy," near Versailles, in France.

**toilet/toilette** (twa-let) **1.** Late 19th-c. term for a woman's entire costume, *e.g., afternoon toilette.* **2.** Process of a woman dressing, *e.g.,* combing her hair, applying her makeup. Term used especially in 19th and early 20th c. **3.** Term used in 18th c. for loose *wrapper* worn by women while having hair arranged. Also spelled *twillet.*

**tom-bons** Long cotton trousers worn by Afghanistan men and women, styled very full at the hips tapering to the ankle.

**Tom Jones** 1963 film of Henry Fielding's novel about an 18th c. hero which inspired clothes in mid-1960s. See SHIRTS and SLEEVES.

**tongue** Part of *oxford* shoe under the lacing. Sometimes made with an ornamental flap that is fringed or perforated, and hangs over lacing of shoe called *shawl tongue.*

**tonlet** Flaring skirt of metal plates or of solid metal, sometimes fluted with deep vertical folds, worn as armor in 16th c. Also called *lamboy, jamboy,* or *base.*

**tooled-leather** See BELTS and HANDBAGS.

**top** Clothing worn as a blouse or shirt substitute with pants or a skirt mainly for sportswear, and sometimes for evening. First introduced in the 1930s when halter tops were popular for both sportswear and evening. A synonym for BLOUSE and TOUPEE.

## ═══ TOPS ═══

**bare-midriff t.** Top cropped below bust baring rib cage with strapless halter, or tank neck-line. Also see CHOLI under BLOUSES category.

**bare t.** Strapless evening bodice tightly fitted and boned.

**bib t.** Bare-back top, just covering front of body, like top of overalls.

**bikini t.** Brief top, using a minimum of fabric, covering the bust and tying in back and around neck in halter fashion.

**bustier** Tight-fitting top sometimes laced similar to a corset or camisole. Used separately or for the top of a dress.

**camisole t.** **1.** Top made with straps over the shoulder, or strapless, cut straight across with elastic drawn through a heading. May hang free or have elastic at waistline. Sometimes made with built-in bra. **2.** Top with spaghetti straps and low scoop neckline in front and back. *Der.* From word *camisole,* formerly a lingerie item.

**cropped t.** Top baring the midriff section similar to bare-midriff top. May be a cut-off NUMERAL SHIRT, T-SHIRT, or SWEATSHIRT. Style adopted by men, as well as women and children, since early 1980s.

**diamanté t.** Top made entirely (or partly) of sparkling sequins, beads, or paillettes. Very popular in mid-1980s. *Der.* French, "made of diamonds."

**flashdance t.** Knit shirt styled similar to conventional sweatshirt with sleeves cut short and neckline cut low in various styles. Both are left in unfinished state with seams overcast on right side of shirt. *Der.* From designs by Michael Kaplan for the movie *Flashdance,* 1983.

**halter t.** Top with front supported by tie or strap around the neck, leaving back bare.

**maternity t.** Any top worn by expectant mothers.

**oversized t.** Extra large slip-on top made in many styles, sometimes hip-length with full sleeves.

**BARE-MIDRIFF
TOP**

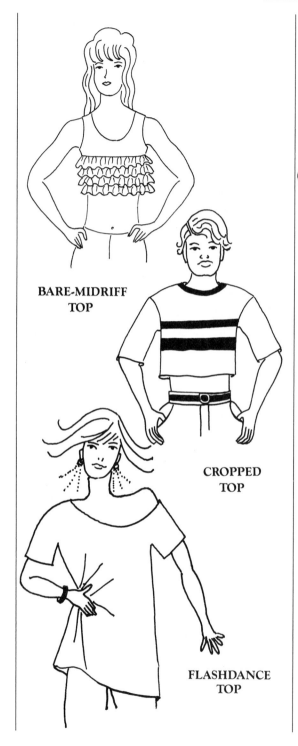

**CROPPED
TOP**

**FLASHDANCE
TOP**

**TANK TOP**

**SCREEN-PRINT
TOP**

**screen-print t.** Knit top screen-printed with animals, hearts, and other designs—often popular cartoon characters, idols, or slogans are used.

**smock t.** Full overblouse with full sleeves, similar to a smock.

**strapless t.** An elastic or stretch top made without straps. Also see TUBE TOP.

**stretch t.** Close-fitting blouse made of stretchy knit fabric. Also see BODY SUIT in alphabetical listing.

**tank t.** Similar to men's undershirt with U neckline and deep armholes shaped toward shoulder to form narrow straps. Similar to ATH-

LETIC SHIRT. *Der.* From top of tank suit, a bathing suit worn in early indoor swimming pools called "tanks."

**tube t.**   Strapless top made of fabric shirred with elastic.

**wrapped t.**   Diagonal piece of fabric, about 1½ to 2 yards long and 1 yard wide, worn folded in half and wrapped around the body with ends tied in front to make a strapless top. Two long ends hang down at waist. May be stitched to front of shorts to make rompers or attached to pants to make a jumpsuit.

---

**topaz**   See GEMS.

**topazolite**   See ANDRADITE GARNET under GEMS.

**top boot**   Variant of JOCKEY BOOT.

**topcoat**   **1.** Term for any form of coat worn over the suit when outdoors. See COATS. **2.** Woman's tailored, full-length straight-cut coat worn in 1890s, with moderate leg-of-mutton sleeves, tailored collar, and fly-front closing. Had large flap pockets on hips and small ticket pocket above.

**TOPCOAT, 1891**

**topee/topi**   See HELMETS.

**top frock**   Man's overcoat cut like a *frock coat* but longer, worn from 1830 on. Usually double-breasted and intended to be worn without a suit coat.

**top grain**   Leather-industry term for first *split* from grain side of leather. Used for shoes and handbags.

**top hat**   **1.** Term used since about 1820 for a high crowned hat with a flat top and narrow brim, sometimes slightly rolled at the sides. Also called *pot hat, silk hat, plug hat,* and *chimney pot hat.* **2.** See HATS.

**topknot**   See HAIRSTYLES.

**topless**   A style introduced by Rudi Gernreich in 1964. See SWIMSUITS and LOOKS.

**topper**   **1.** See TOP HATS under HATS. **2.** See COATS.

**tops**   See BOOT-HOSE TOPS.

**top stitch**   See STITCHES.

**topstitched seam**   See SEAMS.

**toque**   **1.** Woman's coif or head scarf worn in the 16th and early 17th c. **2.** From 1815 to 1820 a triangular cushion worn by women on top of the head to extend the hair. **3.** Turban-like hat worn from about 1817 to end of 19th c. (except for the 1850s). Worn outdoors and sometimes with evening dress, made of many different fabrics. **4.** See HATS.

**toquet** (tow-ket)   Woman's small draped evening hat worn on back of head in 1840s. Made of satin or velvet with small turned-up brim in front and trimmed with ostrich feather.

**torchon lace**   See LACES.

**toreador**   See JACKETS and PANTS.

**toreador hat**   **1.** See MATADOR HAT. **2.** Woman's hat of the 1890s with flat, shallow circular crown made of felt or straw and worn tilted. Inspired by the opera "Carmen," starring Emma Calve.

**toreador suit** Two-piece suit plus cape and hat worn by bullfighters in Mexico and Spain. See SUIT OF LIGHTS under SPORT SUITS, and MATADOR HAT.

**torque** Twisted metal collar or necklace fitted close to the neck worn by ancient Teutons, Gauls, and Britons.

**torsade** Coronet of pleated velvet or tulle with long *lappets* worn for evening by women in 1864.

**torso** Fashion term for apparel which fits the body tightly from neck to hips. See BLOUSES, DRESSES, and LONG TORSO under SILHOUETTES, and SKIRTS.

**torsolette** See BUSTIER under FOUNDATIONS.

**tortoise shell** **1.** Mottled yellowish to brown substance from horny back plates of sea turtles native to Cayman Islands, Celebes, and New Guinea. Used for ornamental combs, jewelry, buckles, eyeglass frames, etc. **2.** Pattern similar to genuine tortoise shell used for printed fabrics and plastic eyeglass frames.

**tote** See HANDBAGS.

**Totes®** See BOOTS.

**toupee** (too-pay) **1.** Man's small partial wig used to cover baldness. **2.** Front roll of hair on man's *periwig* from 1730 to end of 18th c. Also called *toupet*, *foretop*, and *top*.

**touring cap** See CAPS.

**tourmaline** See GEMS.

**Tourmaline® mink** See MUTATION MINK under FURS.

**tournure** **1.** Bustle of early 1870s made from six rows of horsehair ruffles mounted on a calico foundation stiffened with whalebone. Attached to a band around the waist which tied

in front. **2.** A foundation piece worn in 1870s which hung down back from waist with ruffles at hem to hold out the train of dress. Made with ties to fasten in front at intervals. **3.** In the 1880s, a polite term for BUSTLE.

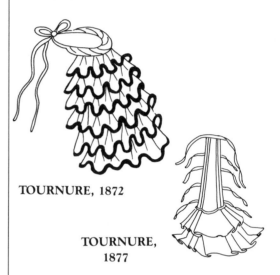

**TOURNURE, 1872**

**TOURNURE, 1877**

**tournure and petticoat** *Bustle* combined with *petticoat* worn from about 1875 to 1885. Some made all in one piece, some with buttons and buttonholes at hip-level so that *tournure* or *bustle* could be used separately.

**TOURNURE AND PETTICOAT, C. 1875**

**tournure corset** Laced *foundation garment* with straps over shoulders and hip-length underskirt of stiff fabric intended to hold out the skirt. Worn in late 1850s over the *chemise*.

**tow 1.** Tangled broken flax fiber less than 10″ long, as distinguished from *line*—flax fiber more than 10 inches long. **2.** Man-made fibers before being twisted into yarn.

**tow coat** See COATS.

**tower** False curls, worn by women above the forehead from 1670s to 1710, usually with the FONTANGES headdress. *Der.* French, "tour."

**toyo** Hat body material made of cellophane-coated rice paper of fine quality produced in Japan, Okinawa, and Taiwan.

**track** See SHOES and SHORTS.

**Trafalgar turban** British woman's evening turban of 1806 embroidered with Admiral Nelson's name. *Der.* Named for British naval victory near Cape Trafalgar, off Spanish coast, in 1805.

**tragedy mask** Mask with corners of mouth turned down used in Greek theatre.

**trail shorts** See CAMP SHORTS under SHORTS.

**train** Elongated back portion of woman's skirt that lies on the floor and is pulled along behind by wearer. Worn for formal evenings, especially in late 19th and early 20th c., and traditionally a part of bridal gowns. Dates from Middle Ages when length of train, worn only at court, indicated rank.

**traje charro** Mexican riding costume consisting of ruffled shirt, short jacket, ankle-length fitted trousers, and elaborately trimmed large *sombrero*. Front of jacket and side seams of trousers were trimmed with silver or gold buttons.

**traje de corto** Traditional Andalusian, crimson waist-length riding jacket with a black collar and lavishly trimmed with black braid around lapels, slit pockets, and sleeves. Disks with hanging fringe decorate the buttonless front.

**traje de luces** Spanish for *suit of lights*. See SPORT SUITS.

**trank** Rectangle of leather from which a glove is cut.

**transformation** Term used in early 20th c. for a natural-looking wig or hairpiece worn by women.

**translucent** Semi-transparent quality applied to gems and fabrics.

**transparent** Term used to describe gems and fabrics through which light passes so that object behind may be seen clearly.

**transparent dress** Dress worn during the last quarter of the 17th c. consisting of a layer of lace over a complete dress of gold or brocade. Lace was usually black *point d'Angleterre*.

**transparent velvet** Lightweight velvet which reflects light changing color to be somewhat iridescent. Has excellent draping qualities. Usually made with rayon pile, and given a crush resistant finish. See CHIFFON VELVET.

**trapeze** See DRESSES and SILHOUETTES.

**trapunto** Type of quilting in which design is outlined and then stuffed from the back of the fabric to achieve a raised or embossed effect.

**travel coat** See ROBES.

**travelling bag** Large handbag consisting of two somewhat circular pouches made of fabric fringed around the edges and joined together at the top. Used when traveling in the 1860s.

**TRAVELLING BAG, 1864**

**travelling wig**   See CAMPAIGN WIG.

**trenchcoat**   See RAINCOATS.

**trench dress**   See DRESSES.

**trencher cap**   See MORTARBOARD.

**trencher hat**   Woman's silk hat with triangular brim coming to point above forehead worn in first decade of the 19th c.

**trend**   See FASHION TREND.

**Trevira®**   Trademark of Hoeschst Fibers for polyester fibers.

**trews** (trooz)   **1.** Narrow tartan (plaid) trousers worn in Scotland. Originally breeches and hose in one piece worn by Highlanders. **2.** British slang term for TROUSERS.

**triacetate**   Man-made fiber made from regenerated cellulose. Differs from acetate in that a much higher percentage of the cellulose has been acetylated—not less than 92%. Used particularly for knitted fabrics which have elasticity with good return, are easily washed, dry quickly, and need little or no pressing. Packable, as does not wrinkle easily. Disadvantages: dimensional stability depends on type of knit and stitch.

**Triangle Shirtwaist Fire**   A fire at the New York City women's garment manufacturing shop, Triangle Waist Co., on March 25, 1911 which took 146 workers' lives. Consequently, public opinion was aroused to demand reforms for fire protection, better working conditions, sanitation, and unionization.

**tricorn**   19th c. term for variation of the *cocked hat*, turned up to form three equidistant peaks with one peak in center front. Also see CONTINENTAL HAT and KEVENHULLER HAT. Also spelled *tricorne*.

**tricot** (tree-co)   **1.** Warp knit fabric made with two sets of yarns characterized by fine vertical wales on the face and crosswise ribs on the back. When made with one set of yarns, it is called *single-bar tricot*. *Two-bar tricot*, made with yarns crossing, is run-resistant. Also called *double warp tricot, glove silk*. *Three-bar tricot* has an open-work effect. When a plain knit is used, it is called JERSEY CLOTH. Man-made fibers, of rayon, or acetate yarns are used—with acetate tricot used frequently for backing on bonded knits. **2.** Knitted woolen or worsted fabric characterized by a horizontal rib on the face. **3.** See STITCHES. *Der.* French, *tricoter*, "to knot."

**tricotine** (tree-co-teen)   Durable fabric similar to cavalry twill, but with double diagonal wales on the surface caused by the steep twill weave. Yarns used for warp and filling may be carded or combed and made of cotton, worsted, or blended man-made fibers. Also called *cavalry twill* and *elastique*.

**trifocals**   See GLASSES.

**Trigère, Pauline**   See APPENDIX/DESIGNERS.

**trilby**   Man's soft felt hat with supple brim worn from 1895 on. Also see HATS. *Der.* Inspired by George de Maurier's 1894 novel *Trilby*. The following year *Trilby* was made into a play in which Beerbohm Tree played the character "Svengali," in this type of hat.

**triple-needle toe**   See TOES.

**triplex**   See HANDBAGS.

**tri-suit**   See SPORT SUITS.

**trollopee**   See SLAMMERKIN.

**trompe l'oeil** (trump loy)   Generally applied to embroidery and painting which fool the eye; also applied to dress and clothing. *Der.* French, "to fool the eye."

**trompeurs**   See LIARS.

**trooper cap**   See CAPS.

**tropical suiting**   Lightweight fabric originally used for men's summer suits, now used for suits for all seasons. Made of all types of yarns including blends of wool/polyester and cotton/polyester. Usually tightly woven of highly twisted yarns.

**tropical worsted**   Lightweight worsted fabric made in an open weave to permit circulation of air. Finished by singeing to give a clear finish. Packs well and is popular for dresses and suits for cooler days in the summer.

**trousering**   General term for fabrics used to make pants. May be woolen, worsted, or cotton made in stripes or plain colors and given a variety of finishes.

**trousers**   **1.** Term used in 18th and 19th c. for loose-fitting pants worn particularly by sailors, soldiers, and town workers. **2.** At beginning of 19th c. worn for day and evening by men, although not general for evening until after 1850. Also see INEXPRESSIBLES. **3.** In the late 19th c. worn by women under riding habit. **4.** Term also applied to *pantaloons* from 1830 to 1840. **5.** See PANTS. *Der.* From *trouse*, a variation of *trews*.

**trouser skirt**   Tailored skirt split at side front to reveal matching bloomers attached at waistline. Worn from 1910 to 1920 by avant-garde women.

**trouses** (trouz)   Underpants or drawers worn by Englishmen under the *trunk hose* in 16th and 17th c. Also spelled *trowses*.

**trousses** (trouz)   French *tights*, similar to *greques*, worn by pages and knights of king's order in 17th c.

**trowses**   Variant of TROUSES.

**trucker's apron**   See APRONS.

**trumpet**   See DRESSES, SILHOUETTES, SKIRTS, and SLEEVES.

**trunk hose**   *Breeches* covering legs from waist to middle of thigh. Varied in style from tight to loose fitting and frequently *paned*. Styles include *haut de chausses*, *bombasted breeches*, *round hose*, *slops*, *trunk breeches*, and *Venetians*. Also see CHAUSSES. Also called *upper stocks*.

**trunks**   **1.** Man's shorts made loose-legged with drawstring at waist. Worn from late 19th c. on for boxing and other sports, sometimes over full-length *tights*. **2.** See TRUNK HOSE. **3.** See SWIMSUITS. **4.** See PANTIES.

**trunk sleeve**   See CANNON SLEEVES.

**truss** (verb)   To tie up, used from 14th c. to about 1630. Phrase "to truss the points" meant to fasten *hose* to *trunk hose* and *doublet* by means of *points* (lacers) which ended in decorative metal tip called an *aglet*.

**trusses**   See VENETIANS.

**tsarouchia** (tsar-ooch-ee-a)   Pointed shoes with upturned toes decorated with pompons, formerly worn by Greek palace guards. Also see FUSTANELLA.

**T-shirt**   Man's *undershirt* with short sleeves and high round neck forming a T-shape, usually made in white cotton knit. Adapted for sportswear by men, women, and children. Also spelled *tee-shirt*. See DRESSES, KNIT SHIRTS, and PAJAMAS.

**tsitsith**   Tassel, usually blue, worn on prayer shawl called *tallith* or on the *arba kanfoth* by Jewish men, prescribed in Numbers 15:38 in the Bible. Also see TALLITH.

**T-strap**   See SANDALS.

**tsuzure-ori**   Japanese art of finger weaving dating from 15th c., done by inserting shuttle by hand under several warps and then combing the filling with the fingernails.

**tube**   See BRAS, SOCKS, and TOPS.

**tubular knit**   See CIRCULAR KNIT.

**tuck**   Narrow pleat in fabric of even width usually stitched in place and used for decorative effects on blouses, shirts, and dresses, particularly children's and babies' dresses.

**tucked seam**   See SEAMS.

**tucker**   Narrow strip or frill of plain or lace-trimmed fabric, used by women from 17th c. to about 1830s, to fill in low dècolletage. Also called *pinner* or *falling tucker* in 19th c. when it hung down over bodice. Also see PARTLET and CHEMISETTE.

**tucks**   Usually tucks are arranged in a series and designated by width, *e.g.*, inch, half-inch, quarter-inch, or *pin tucks*. The latter are only wide enough for a row of stitching. Tucks were used particularly from 1890 to 1910, especially in fine white lawn dresses with sleeves and bodices sometimes completely covered with tucks. Revived in early 1980s particularly for blouses. Also see NUN'S TUCKS and SUNBURST TUCKS.

**Tudor cape**   Woman's short circular cape of 1890s, usually using embroidered fabric. Made with pointed *yoke* front and back, an *epaulet* on each shoulder, and velvet *Medici collar.*

**tuft**   **1.** Variant of POMPON; a cluster of threads or fibers tied together to form a ball. **2.** See CANDLEWICK.

**tulip**   See BUBBLE under SKIRTS; and SLEEVES.

**tulle** (tool)   **1.** Fine sheer net fabric made of silk, nylon, or rayon with hexagonal holes. Used unstarched for wedding veils and millinery, and starched for ballet costumes. **2.** In the 18th c. all hexagonal netlike fabrics were called by this name. *Der.* First made in 1768 in England by machine; in 1817 a factory was opened in the city of Tulle, France. Also see EMBROIDERIES.

**tunic**   **1.** Straight, loose-fitting, knee-length basic garment with full sleeves worn in ancient Greece and Rome. **2.** A full-length outer or undergarment worn by all classes for centuries, elaborately decorated for emperors and dignitaries. **3.** Garment similar to *kirtle* of varying lengths worn by men and women from 9th to 14h c. **4.** Knee-length coat similar to *surcot* with buttoned-down front and loose sleeve worn by men from 1660s to 1670s. Introduced from France by Charles II of England. **5.** Long plain, close-fitting *military* jacket. **6.** Young boy's costume of 1840s and 1850s consisting of close-

fitting jacket to just above the knees worn with ankle-length trousers. **7.** Short loose skirted garment worn in late 19th and 20th c. by women and girls over bloomers for athletics. Often called *gym tunic.* **8.** Long overblouse of sheer decorated fabric used as upper part of long evening gowns, first shown by designer Worth in Paris, 1868, worn from 1890s to 1914. **9.** Thigh-length sleeved or sleeveless *overblouse,* usually slightly fitted and belted or beltless, worn over skirt, slacks, or alone as short dress; popular in 1940s, revived from 1960s through 1980s. Also see DRESSES, BLOUSES, JUMPERS, PAJAMAS, SKIRTS, and SWIMSUITS. Also see TUNIC À LA MAMELUKE and TUNIC À LA ROMAINE.

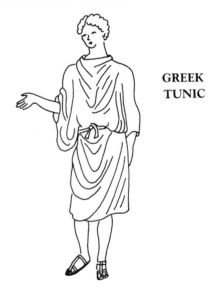

**GREEK TUNIC**

**tunic à la mameluke**   Woman's knee-length tunic with long sleeves fashionable at beginning of 19th c. Later called *tunique à la juive.* Inspired by Napoleon's Egyptian campaign, 1798. *Der.* Mamelukes were originally slaves brought to Egypt in 19th c., later trained as soldiers. Ruled Egypt from 1250 to 1517 and remained powerful until 1811 under Turkish viceroys.

**tunic à la romaine**   Tunic worn by women in late 18th c. which was full-length, high-waisted, long-sleeved, and made of gauze or lawn.

**tunnel loops** Loops of matching fabric placed at waistband of pants or skirt for belt to pull through. Loops may be 1″ to 3″ wide—larger than regular belt loops.

**tunnel waistline** See DRAWSTRING under WAISTLINES.

**turban** **1.** Man's headdress of Moslem origin consisting of long scarf of linen, cotton, or silk wound around the head. Sometimes with one loose end hanging down, or decorated with a jewel in center front. Sometimes consists of fabric wrapped around a *fez* with crown showing. Also see PAGRI. **2.** See HATS.

**Turkey bonnet** Term used in the 15th and 16th c. for man's or woman's tall cylindrical hat without a brim introduced to Italy, France, and England from the East. Woman's style was shaped like inverted flower pot with veil from crown passing under chin. Also called *Turkey hat.*

**Turkey gown** **1.** Man's long black velvet gown bordered with lynx and decorated with 77 gold and black-enameled buttons made for Henry VIII who ruled England from 1515 to 1548. **2.** Long gown open in front with long narrow sleeves slit above elbow so arm could come through, remainder of sleeve hung down. Worn from 1530s on becoming style for Puritan ministers.

**Turkish polonaise** See IRISH POLONAISE.

**turndown collar** See COLLARS.

**turned-back cuff** See CUFFS.

**turned shoe construction** Lightweight shoe, usually in pump style, constructed by stitching sole to upper inside out then "turning" to right side with seams on inside.

**turnip pants** Bicycling knickers that could be turned down to make full-length pants worn in 1890s.

**turnover collar** See COLLARS.

**turn-ups** British term for man's *cuffed trousers* first worn in House of Commons in 1893.

**turquoise** See GEMS.

**turret bodice** Bodice with peplum, cut in square tabs below waistline, popular in early 1880s.

**turtleneck** See COLLARS, NECKLINES, and SWEATERS.

**turtleneck convertible** See COLLARS.

**turumagi** Korean man's wraparound overcoat extending to lower calf of leg. Worn wrapped to right and fastened by tying with attached fabric into bow making one loop on right breast. Made of grass cloth or calico for lower classes, of white silk for upper classes. Also spelled *turumaggie.*

**tussah** Coarse, irregular reeled silk from undomesticated Asian silkworms used to make *pongee* and *shantung.* The silkworm, the fiber, the yarn, and also the fabric made from the yarn are all called by this name. *Der.* Hindu, *tasar,* from the Sanskirt *trasara,* "a shuttle." Also spelled *tasar, tusser, tussas, tussus.*

**tutu** **1.** Ballet dancer's costume designed in 1832 by Eugene Lami for Maria Taglioni, a great Italian ballerina of the Romantic period. Consisted of a tight-fitting bodice leaving the shoulders bare worn with a bell-shaped, sheer, white gathered skirt reaching midway between knee and ankle. **2.** Multi-layered very short skirt of net or tulle. Pale pink *tights* were worn underneath and pale pink satin *ballet slippers* were worn with both versions.

**tutulus** **1.** Tall cone-shaped hat worn by ancient Etruscan women with, or without, upturned brim or coronet across the front. **2.** Hairstyle of Etruscan women made by plaiting the hair and then winding it around the head tapering at crown.

**tuxedo** **1.** Man's dinner jacket. See JACKETS. **2.** Semiformal evening suit. See PANTS and SUITS. *Der.* Introduced by Griswold P. Lorillard at Tuxedo Park, N.Y., in 1886 who suggested copying the Prince of Wales' velvet smoking jacket for semiformal wear. **3.** Jacket-style sweater. See SWEATERS. **4.** Woman's blouse made in imitation of man's formal shirt. See BLOUSES and SHIRTS. **5.** See SHOES. **6.** See COLLARS.

**tweed** Term applied to rough textured fabrics made of coarser wool in yarn-dyed effects. Made in plain, twill, or herringbone weave in various weights for coats, jackets, and suits.

**tweeds** Clothing made of tweed fabric. *Der.* Scotch, *tweed*, "twill," because they were at first handloomed in homes along the Tweed River in Scotland. See DONEGAL, HARRIS, IRISH, SCOTCH, and COTTON TWEED. Also see SPORT JACKETS.

**twenties bob** See HAIRSTYLES.

**twenties look** See FLAPPER LOOK under LOOKS, and SILHOUETTES.

**twillet** See TOILET/TOILETTE #1.

**twill fabric/twills** Fabrics which show a distinct diagonal wale on the face, *e.g.*, *denim*, *elastique*, *gabardine*, *middy twill*, *surah*, *tricotine*, and *whipcord*. Difference between drills, jeans, and twills in the U.S. is based on type of yarn used. In England difference is based on the weave used, *e.g.*, warp twills are called *drills* and filling twills are called *twills*.

**twill weave** Basic weave characterized by diagonal wales produced by staggering the points of intersection of warp and filling, generally upward from left to right called *right-hand twill*. A *left-hand twill* goes from lower right to upper left. Both make a firm, durable fabric, *e.g.*, *denim*, *ticking*, *serge*, and *gabardine*.

**LEFT-HAND TWILL WEAVE**

**twinset** See BLOUSES.

**two-bar tricot** See TRICOT.

**two-ply yarn** **1.** Yarn which is made by combining two lightly twisted single yarns into one yarn. The resultant yarn is stronger and more durable and is used in fabrics such as *broadcloth*. **2.** Also *cord yarn* made by first twisting two sets of singles or doubles, and then twisting both into one yarn.

**two-sided stitch** See STITCHES.

**two-way stretch foundation** See FOUNDATIONS.

**tye** 18th c. term for man's tied-back wig.

**tyes** American term for girl's apron in late 19th c.

**Tyrian Glo® mink** See MUTATION MINK under FURS.

**Tyrian purple** Red-purple color originally obtained from shellfish found off the shores of Tyre in ancient Palestine, and reserved for royalty from Biblical to medieval times.

**Tyrolean look** (tee-roll-ee-an) Type of peasant style worn in Austrian and Bavarian Alpine region. See LOOKS; ALPINE HAT under HATS; and DIRNDL under DRESSES and SKIRTS.

# U

**Ubangi** See NECKLACES and NECKLINES.

**ugly** British term for collapsible brim worn from late 1840s to mid-1860s over a *bonnet* as a sunshade to protect weak eyes or when traveling. Made of series of cane half-hoops covered with silk. When not is use, folded up like a *calash*.

BOY'S ULSTER

WOMAN'S ULSTER

UGLY

**Ukrainian peasant blouse** White cotton peasant blouse with full, puffed sleeves and narrow standing-band collar, embroidered in vivid-colored geometric designs on upper sleeves and around shoulders. Trimming extended down front in narrow bands. Worn by peasant women in Russian Ukraine.

**ulster** **1.** Man's heavy overcoat introduced in late 1860s. Usually made in single- or double-breasted style with a belted back or with a complete belt and detachable hood. By the 1870s a cape was more usual. By 1875 a TICKET POCKET was placed in left sleeve above cuff. By 1890 a *fly-front* closing was used. Length varied being ankle length in 1870s. **2.** Woman's coat similar to man's worn from late 1870s on. When made with a triple cape it was called a CARRICK. Sometimes made of waterproof fabric, sometimes with a train. **3.** An overcoating fabric similar to *frieze* from which ulsters were made in Belfast. **4.** Heavyweight napped fabric made of low grade wool mixed with shoddy used for overcoats. Piece- or stock-dyed and finished with a long pressed down nap. *Der.* Named after a northern province of Ireland in which the cities of Belfast and Londonderry, manufacturing centers for heavy coats, are located.

**ultramarine** Rich deep purple-blue color made from powdered lapis lazuli, or made chemically to reproduce this color.

**ultra-sheer pantyhose** See SHEER PANTYHOSE.

**ultrasonic sewing** Sewing accomplished by special machines using ultrasonic sound waves that fuse, or weld, fabrics together without the

591

use of needles and thread. In early 1970s used on most synthetic fabrics but most often used on double-knit polyesters. Advantages: eliminates use of needles and thread, also eliminates seam slippage.

**Ultrasuede®** Registered trademark of Springs Mills, Inc. for luxury suedelike fabric.

**umbrella** Accessory used as a protection against the rain or sun. Canopy is made of silk, rayon, or plastic with six to sixteen collapsible ribs for convenience in carrying. Original purpose was as a sun shade and restricted for use to kings, priests and high-ranking dignitaries. Used in ancient Egypt, China, Japan, and India. Not used as protection from the rain until late 18th c. Jonas Hanway carried one in 1780 in England for the rain. He was ridiculed, and it was 1787 before it was generally accepted. *Der.* Italian, *umbra,* "shade." Also see DOME UMBRELLA, EN TOUS CAS, and PARASOL. Also see HANDBAGS, PLEATS, and SKIRTS.

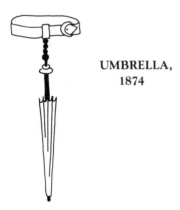

**UMBRELLA, 1874**

**umbrella brim** Brim of woman's hat set in *umbrella pleats,* opens out to resemble an umbrella.

**umbrella drawers** Women's wide bell-shaped *drawers* of late 19th and early 20th c., trimmed with *tucks, insertion,* and *lace* filled to waistband.

**umbrella pleats** See PLEATS and SKIRTS.

**umbrella tote** See HANDBAGS.

**unbleached muslin** Coarse heavily sized cotton utility fabric woven in a plain weave of carded yarns and sold in the unbleached or *gray* state. Used by fashion designers when draping garments on *dummies.* After garment is designed, seams are ripped and muslin is used as a pattern. Also used for interfacings in low-quality suits and coats. Also see PRINT CLOTH and SHEETING.

**Uncle Sam diamond** See DIAMONDS.

**underarm dart** See DARTS.

**under cap** **1.** Indoor cap made like a skullcap worn under hat by elderly men in 16th c. **2.** Woman's indoor cap usually shaped like a COIF (#6) worn under outdoor hat from 16th to mid-19th c.

**underfur** Short fur fiber of animals such as mink, muskrat, and fox as contrasted with the GUARD HAIRS which are long and silky. Formerly called *fur fiber.* See FURS.

**undergarment** Term used for garments worn next to the skin. More commonly now called UNDERWEAR.

**underground fashion** Weird way out clothes in bizarre colors and extreme shapes worn in 1965 by avant-garde people who attended private showings of unconventional "underground movies" of the day shown in beatnik-type bars and coffee houses.

**underpants** See PANTIES generic definition.

**under petticoat** Term for white cambric, flannel, or skirt of poorer quality fabric worn under dress skirt or under hoops from 16th through 18th c.

**underpropper** See RABATO and SUPPORTASSE.

**undershirt** **1.** Man's knitted shirt, usually white cotton, with U-neckline continued into *built-up straps,* or with short sleeves and crew or V-neckline, worn underneath outer shirt or sweater. Also called A-SHIRT or T-SHIRT.

**2.** Woman's knitted *undervest*, usually of cotton or cotton and wool, shaped like a man's undershirt. Also see DRESSES, KNIT SHIRTS, and SWEATERS. **3.** Infant's knitted wool or cotton shirt, in four styles: *a)* double-breasted, fastened with grippers; *b)* high-necked cardigan-style, usually with long sleeves; *c)* *pullover*, similar to man's undershirt; *d)* sleeved *pullover* with lapped shoulders that stretch to permit easy passage over head.

**undershirt dress** See DRESSES.

**underskirt** **1.** Term used for a SLIP or PETTICOAT. **2.** See SKIRTS.

**undersleeve** See ENGAGEANTES.

**undervest** British term from 1840s for UNDERSHIRT (see #1).

**underwaist** See PANTYWAIST.

**under waistcoat** **1.** Man's short sleeveless vest, introduced in 1790, fashionable in contrasting fabrics from 1825 to 1840, worn under the waistcoat. Survives in England for men's formal wear as waistcoat with WHITE SLIP. **2.** Undergarment worn by men in last half of 18th c. for warmth. Usually made of flannel.

**underwear** **1.** Term used for women's *lingerie*, e.g., *panties, slips, bras*. **2.** Men's *A-shirts, T-shirts, shorts, trunks*, worn beneath outer clothes. See THERMAL UNDERWEAR. **3.** Infants' and children's vests and panties.

**undress** Ordinary or unceremonial dress for man or woman as contrasted with formal wear. Term used in 18th and 19th c. particularly in England. Also see NEGLIGEE COSTUME.

**U-neckline** See NECKLINES.

**uneven plaid** See PLAIDS.

**Ungaro, Emanuel** See APPENDIX/DESIGNERS.

**uniform** **1.** Any specific type of apparel required for wear by the armed forces of any country; for a specialized occupation, by a school, or for competitive team sports such as baseball, football, and hockey. Probably originated in antiquity with costumes worn by personal bodyguards of monarchs. Worn by the Greek and Roman armies and since then by armed forces throughout the world. **2.** Worn throughout history to denote status or trade of an individual. See BLUE-APRONED MEN. **3.** Worn as *livery*, particularly in France and England.

**uniform cloth** Collective name for many fabrics used to make uniforms for police, firemen, the armed services, and other organized groups. *Woolens* and *worsteds* used for winter include *meltons, whipcords, gabardines, serges*, and fabrics made with blends of wool/polyester. Summer fabrics include *broadcloths, ducks, poplins, twills, tropical worsteds*, and fabrics made of blended yarns, mainly polyester/cotton.

**union suit** One-piece knitted undergarment buttoned up center front introduced in 1880s and made with short or long legs, short or long sleeves, a drop seat. Worn for warmth. See JAEGER SUIT. For summer wear see B.V.D.s. Worn by all ages until 1940s, now mainly used under ski or other winter sports' clothing. Long-legged underwear is often nicknamed *long johns* or *long-handles*. Also see THERMAL UNDERWEAR.

**unisex fashions** See LOOKS, SHIRTS, and DRAWSTRING under PANTS.

**unitard** See SPORT SUITS.

**university coat** See ANGLE-FRONTED COAT.

**university vest** Double-breasted *waistcoat* of early 1870s made with sides cut away from lowest button and fashionable with *university coat*.

**unmentionables/unwhisperables** See INEXPRESSIBLES.

**Upland** See COTTON.

**upper** Shoe industry term for all parts of

shoe above the sole. Includes the *counter, quarter, vamp,* and *lining.*

**upper garment** British term used from 17th c. for outer garments such as a cloak, cassock, or gown which indicated dress of a gentleman. Without upper garment, gentleman was said to be "in querpo."

**upper stocks** See TRUNK HOSE.

**upsweep** See HAIRSTYLES.

**urchin cut** See HAIRSTYLES.

**usha** See DRESSES.

**utchat** Sacred eye of the ancient Egyptians, worn as pendant on necklaces to ward off evil.

**uttariya** Irano-Indian mantle or cloak. See CHADDAR #1.

25

27

26

**25.** Costume worn for bicycling, 1896. See HATS, LEG-OF-MUTTON SLEEVE, SHIRTWAIST, SPORTSWEAR.

**26.** Children's clothing, England, 1890. See KATE GREENAWAY, REEFER COAT, SMOCK.

**27.** English costume, 19th c., c. 1870. See HATS, SACK COAT, TROUSERS.

28

**28.** French costume, 20th c., c. 1911. Fancy dress costume designed by Paul Poiret (1879–1944). Silver lamé and green silk gauze trimmed with colorful tinfoil and celluloid beads. See BEADS, HAREM, APPENDIX/DESIGNERS.

**29.** French costume, 20th c., 1911–12. Evening gowns designed by Jeanne Hallée. Silk with beaded trim. See FEATHERS, HOBBLE SKIRT, SILHOUETTES.

**30.** Fashion plate from *The Delineator*, 1910. See FASHION PLATE, THE DELINEATOR, RETICULE, WRAP COAT.

30

29

**31**

**32**

**33**

**31.** Easter bonnets advertised in *The Ladies Home Journal*, 1912. See BONNETS, HATS, EASTER PARADE.

**32.** Hats by Jean Blanchot, 1924–25. See MUFF, SCARFS, TURBAN, APPENDIX/DESIGNERS.

**33.** Gown by Lucille, 1925. See GODET, NECKLINES, APPENDIX/DESIGNERS.

36

**34.** Furs by Revillon, 1925. See FUR, JACKET, TWENTIES SILHOUETTE.

**35.** Gown by Bernard, 1925. See CLUTCH COAT, HATS, SILHOUETTES.

**36.** French costume, 20th c., 1932. Evening gown designed by Madeleine Vionnet. Red-orange, bias cut, silk velvet with attached black feathered cape. See BIAS CUT, FEATHERS, THIRTIES SILHOUETTE, APPENDIX/DESIGNERS.

**37.** French costume, 20th c., 1938. Short cloak designed by Elsa Schiaparelli. A circular design of chariots and horses, surrounded by fountain sprays and clouds, inspired by the Neptune Fountain in the Parc de Versailles. Black silk velvet, embroidered with gold sequins, bugle beads and bullion. See BEADS, EMBROIDERY, SURREALISM, APPENDIX/DESIGNERS.

**38.** French costume, 20th c., 1964. Evening gown in blue silk and linen gazar designed by Balenciaga. See APPENDIX/DESIGNERS.

**39.** *Left:* Multicolored silk plaid playsuit, Bonnie Cashin, 1950s. Dark rattan hat with ribbon trim, Lilly Daché, 1950s. *Center:* Multicolored cotton plaid playsuit, Claire McCardell, 1950s. *Right:* Black and white cotton plaid romper with red elastic belt with brass fasteners, Claire McCardell, 1950s. See CINCH BELT, PLAYSUIT, RATTAN, ROMPERS, SPORTSWEAR, APPENDIX/ DESIGNERS.

39

**40.** French costume, 20th c. *Left:* Minidress of linked plastic discs by Paco Rabanne, 1965. *Center:* Evening dress in black velvet with black plastic discs designed by Christian Dior, 1969. *Right:* Evening gown completely embroidered with multicolored paillettes in stylized design by Chloe, c. 1968. See MINIDRESS, BEADS, PAILLETTE, APPENDIX/DESIGNERS.

**41.** Yves Saint Laurent's fuchsia cape over a black velvet dress for his couture collection, 1980. See CAPE, COLLECTION, HAUTE COUTURE, APPENDIX/DESIGNERS.

**42.** Gold-trimmed evening panel dress in multicolored silk Jacquard by Geoffrey Beene, 1981. See PANEL DRESS, JACQUARD, APPENDIX/DESIGNERS.

41

42

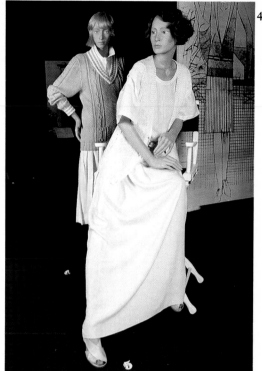

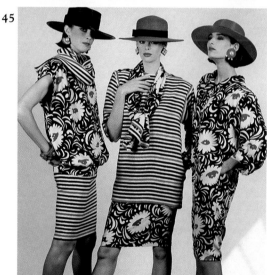

**43.** Wool camel twinset and long satin skirt for evening by Bill Blass, 1984. See TWINSET, APPENDIX/DESIGNERS.

**44.** *Left:* White cotton knit polo shirt, white pleated skirt and blue and white cotton knit pullover, Ralph Lauren, 1985. *Right:* White handkerchief linen shirt, white linen skirt, handknit white vest, Calvin Klein, 1984. See POLO SHIRT, PULLOVER, READY-TO-WEAR, SPORTSWEAR.

**45.** Above-the-knee chemise dresses in a mix of stripes and florals by Oscar de la Renta, 1984. See CHEMISE, APPENDIX/DESIGNERS.

**46.** Calvin Klein's tailored leather suit for fall 1986, worn with a cashmere mock turtleneck. See LEATHER, MOCK TURTLENECK, APPENDIX/DESIGNERS.

**47.** Ralph Lauren's kilim-rug color, one-shoulder sweater over a long pleated linen skirt with matching shawl, 1984. See CUFF BRACELET, SHAWL, ONE SHOULDER, ETHNIC FASHION, APPENDIX/DESIGNERS.

**48.** Perry Ellis' pink linen-chambray duster over khaki and white herringbone linen pants, 1984. See CHAMBRAY, DUSTER, HERRINGBONE, PANTS, APPENDIX/DESIGNERS.

48

47

50

49

**49.** Three ways to wear a wool jersey bodysuit by Donna Karan, 1985: with matching skirt and pants, side-draped wool crepe skirt, and cuffed-waisted skirt. See BODYSUIT, SARONG, SKIRTS, APPENDIX/DESIGNERS.

**50.** Strapless dress in gingham-checked taffeta with modern interpretation of panniers by Christian Lacroix, 1988. See PANNIER, STRAPLESS DRESS, APPENDIX/DESIGNERS.

**vair** Name for highly prized fur worn by kings and magistrates in 13th and 14th c., used for linings and trimmings.

**Val/Valenciennes lace** See LACES.

**Valentino** See APPENDIX/DESIGNERS.

**vallancy** (va-lan-si) Extremely large wig worn in 17th c. which shaded the face.

**Valois hat** Velvet or beaver hat with brim of equal width all around worn by women in 1822.

**Valois, Rose** See APPENDIX/DESIGNERS.

**vambrace 1.** *Armor* consisting of metal plate worn on forearm, under the *hauberk* or over it, in early 13th c. **2.** Later, plate armor for entire arm made up of upper and lower CANNONS and COUTES for the elbow.

**vamp 1.** Term for front part of shoe, covering toes and instep, used since 15th c. Formerly called *vamprey*. **2.** Term used to describe seductive woman. See THEDA BARA.

**Vanderbilt diamond** See DIAMONDS.

**vandyke** Name given to various collars and trims as illustrated in portraits of early 17th c. Flemish artist Sir Anthony Van Dyke, who painted portraits of Charles I. **1.** Saw-toothed lace or fabric borders. **2.** 17th-c. ruff-edged with points of saw-toothed lace. **3.** Lace-bordered handkerchief. **4.** Small pointed beard. *Der.* Named for Flemish painter, Sir Anthony Van Dyke (1599–1641).

**vanity 1.** Small metal or plastic case carried in woman's handbag containing face powder and sometimes rouge or other cosmetics. **2.** See HANDBAGS.

**varens** Woman's short outdoor jacket of 1847 with loose sleeves made of cashmere or velvet with silk lining, a variation of the *casaweck* and *polka*.

**vareuse** (va-reuz) Rough woolen overblouse or jacket, similar to PEA JACKET.

**Vargas diamond** See DIAMONDS.

**varsity sweater** See LETTER SWEATER under SWEATERS.

**vasquine** See BASQUINE.

**Vassar blouse** Woman's blouse worn in 1890s similar to a peasant blouse. Had a *drawstring* neckline with upstanding ruffle and bouffant sleeves—either three-quarter or full-length—ending in a ruffle. Sometimes decorated with embroidery, ribbon suspender straps, or with clusters of bows on the shoulders.

VASSAR BLOUSE

**V-back bra** See SPORTS® BRA under BRAS.

**vegetable tanning** Tanning process which produces various shades of orange- and beige-colored leathers. Basic ingredients include vegetable products such as bark, leaves, nuts, tannic acid, and twigs. Great disadvantage is the length of time involved for tanning which runs between four and six months.

**veil 1.** Decorative accessory usually made of

lace, net, tulle, or sheer fabric placed on the head and usually draped down the back. May also drape over the face and shoulders. **2.** Piece of net or tulle attached to a hat. Introduced in medieval times and called a *coverchief*. From late 18th to end of 19th c. a piece of net, lace, or gauze worn attached to an outdoor bonnet or hat worn by women. Arranged to cover part or the entire face or draped to back as trimming. From 1890s veils extended to the chin. Worn intermittently since, mostly as trim. Particularly worn in 1930s, 1940s, and 1950s. See AUTOMOBILE VEIL in alphabetical listing.

## ▬ VEILS ▬

**bird cage** Dome of stiff wide-mesh veiling pinned to crown of head covering face and ears. Worn in place of hat, especially in late 1950s.

**bridal v.** Traditionally a length of white net, lace, tulle, or silk illusion reaching to waist, hips, ankles, or floor in back. Chest length in front and worn over face during wedding—turned back after ceremony.

**BRIDAL VEIL**

**chapel v.** Small circle of lace or tulle, frequently edged with a ruffle, worn by women over top of head while inside a church. Also called a *chapel cap.*

**communion v.** A sheer net elbow-length veil worn by girls for first communion in the Catholic Church.

**mantilla** Large oblong fine lace veil, usually in rose pattern of black or white, worn wrapped over head and crossed under chin with one end thrown over shoulder. Frequently worn to church instead of a hat in Spain and South America. Popularized in early 1960s by U.S. President's wife, Jacqueline Kennedy. Also see alphabetical listing.

**mourning v.** Semi-sheer black veil to the shoulders, usually circular, sometimes edged with wide band of black fabric worn under or over hat at funerals or during periods of mourning.

**prayer v.** Small triangular lace veil worn instead of hat for church services.

▬▬▬▬▬▬▬▬▬▬▬▬▬▬▬▬

**veiling** Nets of various sizes made in different constructions to form open weave fabrics that are used for trimming on hats.

**Velcro®** See CLOSINGS.

**velour** **1.** Soft velvety thick pile fabric originally made with all wool yarns now made of various fibers and yarns. Used for coats, warm-up suits, knit shirts, and dresses. **2.** Velvet-like felt used for good quality hats. **3.** Term used in Rumania for *flannelette*. **4.** Knitted fabric similar to woven velour used for warmup suits and knit shirts.

**velvet** Textile term applied to several fabrics made of various fibers in different weights woven with an extra yarn in the warp. These are cut and brushed to form a pile or left uncut. Background may be in a plain, twill, or satin weave. May be woven in *double-cloth construction* and cut apart to form two pieces of fabric. Some velvets are also woven on a Jacquard loom in colored patterns. Originally pile was silk, now made with cotton or man-made fibers. For various velvets, see BAGHEERA, COATING VELVET, LYONS VELVET, PANNE VELVET, and TRANSPARENT VELVET.

**velveteen** Cut-pile cotton fabric made with an extra filling yarn. Pile is not more than

⅛″ high. Best qualities have a twill background. May be piece-dyed or printed. Used for dresses, suits, and sportswear.

**vendeuse** (von-derz) French term for saleswoman employed at couture house in Paris.

**Venetian** **1.** Lining fabric with a two-ply worsted warp and woolen or worsted filling made in a satin weave. **2.** Smooth strong sateen fabric made of cotton with combed ply yarns used in best qualities. Fabric is finished by *mercerizing* and *schreinerizing*. Formerly used for linings, now made with all rayon or cotton warp and rayon filling. Also called *farmer's satin*.

**Venetian-blind pleats** See PLEATS.

**Venetian cloak** Woman's black satin cloak of late 1820s with collar, cape, and wide hanging sleeves.

**Venetian lace** See LACES.

**Venetian ladder work** See EMBROIDERIES.

**Venetian point lace** See LACES.

**Venetians** Man's pants or breeches, worn from 1570 to 1620, being most fashionable in 1580s. Made in form of pear-shaped *trunk hose*, often bombasted and fastened below knee by garter-ribbons. When voluminous throughout, called *Venetian slops*, when tightly fitted called *Venetian galligascoines*, *galligaskins* or *chausses en tonnelet*. Also called *trusses* and *Italian hose*.

**Venetian sleeve** Full sleeve of late 1850s fitting into armhole, slashed nearly to shoulder, worn by women over puffed ENGAGEANTES.

**Venet, Philippe** See APPENDIX/DESIGNERS.

**Venise, point de** See LACES.

**vent** Term used since 15th c. to indicate vertical slit in garment, usually from hem upward. Used *e.g.*, in coats, jackets, shirts, and suit coats.

**ventail** Armor for lower part of face on 16th c. helmet. If face guard is made in three pieces *ventail* is middle piece.

**ventilated collar** See COLLARS.

**verdigris** Brilliant blue-green color similar to color of deposit seen on copper, brass, or bronze that has been exposed to the atmosphere.

**verdugale/verdugalle/verdugado/verdugo** See SPANISH FARTHINGALE.

**vermillion** Brilliant red-orange color. Also called *Chinese red*.

**Veronese cuirasse** (ver-o-naiz-e cure-ass) Jersey bodice laced up back fashionable in 1880s.

**Veronese dress** Daytime dress of 1880s with knee-length *princess-style* woolen tunic ending in deep points over silk *underskirt* with large box pleats around hem.

**Veronica Lake hairstyle** See HAIRSTYLES.

**Versace, Gianni** See APPENDIX/DESIGNERS.

**vertically worked** Term for fur skins which are first let out, and then sewn together so that each skin runs from top of fur coat to hem.

**vertugale** (var-tu-gal-leh) See SPANISH FARTHINGALE and INFANTA STYLE. *Der.* Spanish, "rod" or "hoop." Also spelled *vertugadin*, *verdugale*, *verdyngale*, *vertugade*, *vertingale*.

**vest** **1.** An item of wearing apparel extending to the waist or longer similar to a sleeveless jacket. Usually worn over a blouse or shirt and sometimes under a suit jacket. Also called a *waistcoat* and *weskit*. **2.** Woman's undershirt usually made of knitted rayon or nylon styled with built-up straps or a *camisole top*. **3.** A knitted undergarment worn by infants from late 19th c. to about 1940 See UNDERSHIRT #3. **4.** An accessory worn by women as a fill-in for a low neckline, or as a substitute for a blouse in 19th and early 20th c.

====== VESTS ======

**adjustable v.** Term for a man's front-buttoned vest which fits around the neck halter style and is held on by a band around the waist fastening in center back with a buckle. Worn by men with formal wear, *e.g., dinner jacket* or *tuxedo.*

**Afghanistan v.** Vest made of curly lamb tanned and worn with smooth embroidered skin side out showing edges of curly lamb. An ethnic fashion popular in the late 1960s. *Der.* Copied from vests worn by natives in Afghanistan.

**buckskin v.** Vest made of sueded deerskin or sheepskin, frequently laced rather than buttoned, trimmed with self fringe at hem and shoulders. Style popular in America since colonial days. Also see BUCKSKIN in alphabetical listing.

**clayshooter's v.** Sleeveless jacket designed by Bob Lee with belted back, leather piping, and large side pockets; suitable for sportswear or shooting mark or clay pigeons. Main feature is a quilted leather pad at shoulder to absorb recoil of gun. Vest features a secret pocket for holding wallets, and keys.

**cotorinas** Descriptive term for a Mexican-inspired vest made of brilliant-colored horizontal stripes in handwoven fabric similar to those used for *serapes* in Mexico.

**down v.** Quilted vest fastened with snaps, toggles, or a zipper. Interlined for warmth with down quilted to the lining and outer fabric. Popularized in late 1970s for general outerwear. Also see DOWN JACKET under SPORT JACKETS.

**electric® v.** Vest with a lining that reflects 80% of body's heat. Special built-in electric heating system operated by batteries is located at the center of the lower back with batteries concealed in left pocket.

**fisherman's v.** Waist-length sportsman's

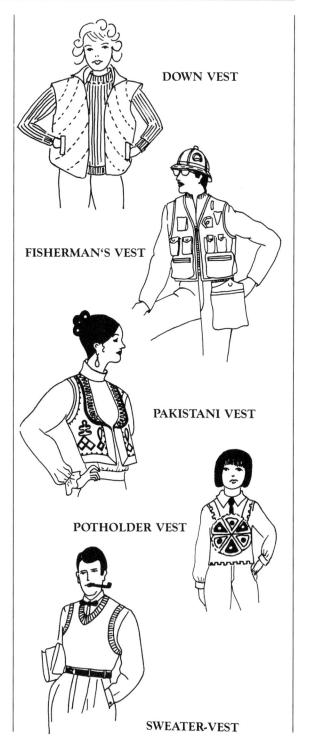

DOWN VEST

FISHERMAN'S VEST

PAKISTANI VEST

POTHOLDER VEST

SWEATER-VEST

vest usually made of khaki-colored cotton duck worn over other clothes when fishing. Has many pockets—two larger zip or snap pockets near hem and small pockets on chest to stow gear when fishing.

**flotation v.**   Lightweight flexible vest with zip front made with shell of tear-resistant nylon filled with polyethylene foam quilted together in wide vertical panels. Worn for all recreational boating purposes as a life-saving device.

**hug-me-tight**   Knitted or quilted vest with V-neck buttoned down front. Usually worn by older people under coats for extra warmth.

**hunting v.**   Front-buttoned sportsman's vest of cotton duck fabric with large rubber-lined game pocket worn over HUNTING SHIRT.

**jerkin   1.**   Contemporary synonym for *vest*, *waistcoat*, and *weskit*. First made in buckskin by American colonists. **2.** Man's sleeved jacket worn over doublet, sometimes laced or buttoned up front, sometimes sleeveless with shoulder wings; worn from late 15th through 16th c.

**Pakistani v.**   Fitted vest with long gold-braided shawl collar, fastened in front with invisible hooks, and elaborately trimmed around edges with wide gilt braid, mirrors, and tassels. Originally called *Pakistani wedding vest*—part of fad for ethnic fashions in late 1960s.

**potholder v.**   Handmade sleeveless crocheted vest made with built-up straps over the shoulders and crocheted "granny squares" in front and back.

**reversible v.**   Any vest which can be worn on both sides using fabric combinations, *e.g.*, plain and plaid or corduroy and paisley print. Man's four-piece suit usually has a reversible vest with each side made to match the different fabric of the two pairs of trousers.

**suit v.**   Matching or contrasting vest sold with a man's suit. Usually styled with V-neck, six buttons, and two or four pockets. The back

is made of lining material and has an adjustable belt. Sometimes copied for women and children.

**sweater-v.**   Knitted vest without sleeves made in slip-on style with a V-neck or buttoned down the front. Also called a *sleeveless sweater*.

**tattersall v.**   Man's vest in small checked fabric made single-breasted with six buttons, no collar, and four flapped pockets. Worn by sportsmen in mid-1890s and later worn with riding habit or with man's sport coat. *Der.* Named after Richard Tattersall, British horseman, founder of Tattersall's London Horse Auction Mart established in 1776.

**vestido   1.**   Long, handwoven wool, thigh-length vest with a fringed hem. **2.** Spanish and Mexican word for *vest*.

**waistcoat/weskit**   Synonyms for VESTS.

**white v.**   Vest worn by men for dress under a *swallow-tailed coat*. It is cut low in front showing the formal shirt and white tie.

---

**vestee**   Woman's decorative front or half vest attached around neck and by ties around waist. Worn under a jacket instead of a blouse in 19th c. Also called *chemisette*.

**vestido**   See VESTS.

**vesting**   Term applied to fabrics formerly used to make men's vests. Especially applied to fancy silks and Jacquards, Bedford cord, piqués, and dobby-figured fabrics.

**vestment cloth**   See ACCA.

**vestments   1.**   Items of wearing apparel worn particularly for ecclesiastical services and by clergy. See ECCLESIASTICAL VESTMENTS. **2.** Ceremonial or official robe.

**vest pocket**   See POCKETS.

**vestsuit**   See SUITS.

**vest sweater**   See SWEATERS.

**Vibram**®   Trademark for durable synthetic rubber usually used as a lug-type sole on hiking shoes.

**vici kid**   See LEATHERS.

**Victoria** (1819–1901)   Queen of Great Britain 1837–1901, married Albert of Saxe-Coburg-Gotha, who took the title of Prince Consort. She assumed the British throne when only eighteen and reigned for sixty-four years. Era is called "Victorian" after her. Period was noted for primness and excessively decorated costumes.

**Victorian**   See BLOUSES and COLLARS.

**Victoria sleeve**   See SABOT SLEEVE.

**Victorine**   See PALATINE ROYAL.

**victory stripes**   See HICKORY STRIPES under STRIPES.

**vicuña**   Hair fiber from the vicuña, a species of llama, extremely soft with colors ranging from golden chestnut to deep fawn. Marketed exclusively by Peruvian government.

**vinaigrette** (vi-nah-gret)   Small bottles attached to metal chains carried by women or attached to handbags in 19th c. Used to hold some aromatic, *e.g.*, vinegar or smelling salts, used by women when they fainted in a fashionable manner.

**vintage fashions**   Used clothing and accessories from other eras refurbished and sold. See VINTAGE, FLEA MARKET, and ATTIC under LOOKS.

**vinyl**   Man-made material that is non-porous plastic, tough, flexible, shiny, elastic, and can be transparent. Used for fabric coating and to produce materials resembling leather for *boots, capes, gloves, raincoats, shoes*, etc. See P.V.C JACKET under SPORT JACKETS.

**violin bodice**   Long bodice, reaching to the knees in back, worn over the dress in 1874. Made in princess style with violin-shaped dark fabric insert in the back.

**Vionnet, Madeleine**   See APPENDIX/DESIGNERS.

**virago sleeve**   Puffed sleeve worn by women in first half of the 17th c. made with many slashes. Tied at intervals to the wrist, sometimes tied only at elbow and wrist making two large puffs.

**viscose rayon**   Type of rayon fiber made from regenerated cellulose. Produced in large quantities and suitable for many uses in clothing manufacture.

**visite** (vee-zeet)   General term for woman's loose cape-like outdoor garment worn in last half of 19th c.

VISITE, 1883

**visiting dress**   Term used throughout the 19th c. for woman's costume worn especially for making calls in the afternoon. Also called *visiting costume* and *visiting toilette*.

**vison**   European name for *mink*. See MINK under FURS.

**visor**   Stiffened part of a semi-circle attached to a headband or to front of a cap to protect eyes from the sun. *Der.* From ancient armor—movable part of helmet which could be lowered to cover the face.

**Viyella**®   Trademark of Williams Hollins and Co. for a lightweight British fabric made of a yarn blended of 50% cotton and 50% wool. Also made in a twill weave in several weights and used for shirts, dresses, pajamas, and underwear. Also called *Viyella® flannel.*

**V-look**   See LOOKS.

**V-neckline**   See NECKLINES.

**Vogue**   Fashion magazine first published as a weekly in December of 1892—in 1910 became a bi-monthly. Arthur Baldwin Turnure was its founder and publisher. Bought by Condé Nast in 1909. Published both in France and Great Britain in the 1920s. Edna Woolman Chase was the editor from 1914 until 1951. See CONDÉ NAST, EDNA WOOLMAN CHASE, CARMEL WHITE SNOW, and DIANA VREELAND.

**voile**   Lightweight open-weave fabric made of tightly twisted combed yarns giving it a grainy feel. Originally made only of cotton but now popular in blends of cotton/polyester. Yarns are gassed to remove short fibers. Used for dresses, blouses, and some men's shirts.

**Volendam cap**   See DUTCH CAP.

**Von Furstenberg, Diane**   See APPENDIX/ DESIGNERS.

**Vreeland, Diana Dalzial** (1906–    ) Dynamic fashion authority who went to work for *Harper's Bazaar* in 1937 becoming fashion editor in six months. Left to become associate editor of *Vogue* magazine in 1962, becoming editor-in-chief until 1971. Since then acted as consulting editor to *Vogue* and consultant to the Costume Institute of Metropolitan Museum of Art, where she supervised outstanding exhibitions including subjects such as *Balenaiaga, American Women of Style, The Glory of Russian Costume, Vanity Fair,* and *Yves Saint Laurent.* Born in Paris she has been awarded in 1970 the French Order of Merit; in 1976 the French Legion of Honor; in 1976 the Dorothy Shaver "Rose" award from Lord and Taylor; and in 1977 Honorary Doctor of Fine Arts Degree from Parsons School of Design. She is the author with Irving Penn of *Inventive Paris Design* and of an autobiography entitled *D.V.*

**V-shape**   A silhouette and look with broad shoulders and no waistline which tapered to very narrow skirt at hem. See LOOKS and SILHOUETTES.

**Vuitton, Louis**   See APPENDIX/DESIGNERS.

**vulcanized shoe construction**   Shoe construction which involves bonding a rubber outsole and heel to a shoe. Upper is tacked or staple-lasted to insole and cement is applied to the shoe bottom. Sole is then inserted into a mold which was previously prepared for individual widths, sizes, and sole pattern. Heat and pressure hold the soling compound to the shoe.

**vulture-winged headdress**   Egyptian queen's headdress with two wings hanging down on either side of the face with the uraeus, or cobra design of the sacred asp, usually attached to center front. The vulture wings are a symbol of protection used by the Egyptians.

**W** Large-size pictorial fashion newspaper featuring American and couture fashions, fashionable personalities, social events, and other articles of particular interest to women. Published biweekly by Fairchild Publications.

**wad** See WOAD.

**wadded hem** Hem that has been padded with wide band of *cording*. Used in 1820s and used occasionally on contemporary dresses and robes.

**wadding** Loosely connected cotton fibers in sheet form used for shoulder pads in coats and suits. Also see FIBERFILL.

**waders** See BOOTS.

**waffle cloth** Cotton fabric made in a honeycomb weave. Also called HONEYCOMB.

**waffle weave** See HONEYCOMB WEAVE.

**waist** **1.** Term used for narrowest part of the torso. Also called *waistline*. **2.** Term for *blouse* or *shirtwaist* used from 1890 to the 1920s.

**waistband** **1.** Band of fabric, usually faced and interfaced, seamed to waistline of skirt or pants. Buttoned or fastened, along with the *placket* to hold garment firmly around waist. **2.** See SET-IN WAISTLINE under WAISTLINES.

**waist-cincher** See GIRDLES.

**waistcoat** **1.** Term synonymous with *vest* in contemporary styles. Other synonyms include *jerkin* and *weskit. Men:* **2.** From 16th c. to 1668 an under-*doublet* which was waist-length, quilted, and worn for warmth. Also worn to complete a costume—and then made of decorative fabric. Also called a *petticoat.* **3.** From 1668 on, an undercoat cut similar to the *justaucorps* made with sleeves until 1750, unfashionable until 1800. Gradually became shorter until it just reached the waist in 1790. Single-breasted until 1730s. Double-breasted in 1780s and 1790s with both styles common in the 19th c. See JOCKEY WAISTCOAT, SHAWL WAISTOCAT, and

FRENCH VEST. *Women:* **4.** 17th c. bodice buttoned in front worn with a dress. **5.** Latter half of the 18th c., clothing similar in style to a man's *waistcoat* of the same date worn with a riding habit. **6.** First half of 19th c., a woman's flannel undergarment worn for warmth. **7.** In 1851, elaborately brocaded outergarment worn by women with a *carriage dress.* **8.** In 1880s and 1890s a fill-in *vestee* worn by women with a suit or *tailor-made* costume. Also see VESTS.

**waistcoating** See VESTING.

**waistcoat paletot** Woman's knee-length coat of 1884 in tailored style buttoned only at neckline, made with hip-length waistcoat showing in front.

**waistcoat pocket** See VEST POCKET under POCKETS.

**waisting** Former grouping of several fabrics all used to make *waists* or *shirtwaists.* This industry thrived in late 19th and early 20th c. and represented the beginning of the ready-to-wear industry.

**waist length** See LENGTHS.

**waistline** **1.** Place on the torso where the belt is located. **2.** Horizontal seam joining the top and skirt of a dress if the garment is made in two pieces. During most historical periods waistlines were located at the normal waistline. During the early Middle Ages and the 1920s, however, long torso waistlines were popular. During the French Directoire, Empire, and English Regency periods high waistlines were favored. Since the 1940s many types of waistlines have been worn concurrently.

=========== **WAISTLINES** ===========

**cinched w.**    Waistline pulled in very tightly, usually with a wide belt.

**corselet w.**    Pulled in waistline usually made by wearing a wide belt usually laced in the front, frequently used on *peasant dresses.*

**Directoire w.**    See EMPIRE WAISTLINE. *Der.* Named for Directoire period in France, 1795–1799.

**drawstring w.**    Waistline with a cord or belt drawn through a casing, heading, or beading, to gather the fullness when tightened and tied in a bow or knot. Also called *tunnel waistline.* See APERBAG WAISTLINE.

**dropped w.**    Waistline seam placed below the natural waistline.

**elasticized w.**    A waistline used for pull-on pants, skirts, and also dresses. May be made in three ways: a) fabric shirred to the elastic with two or more rows of stitching. b) a piece of elastic inserted through a casing. c) elastic stitched directly to the fabric at waistline; used mainly for dresses and undergarments.

**Empire w.**    High-waisted effect with seam placed directly under bust. Used from the late 18th c. to 1820s during Empire and Directoire periods in France, popular since for women's dresses, coats, and lingerie.

**high-rise w.**    Term used for pants coming above the natural waistline.

**low-slung w.**    Term for waistline placed below the normal waistline, usually for hip-hugger skirts or pants. Popular in the mid-1960s.

**natural w.**    Belt or seam placed at narrowest part of the midriff—the usual place for the waistline.

**paperbag w.**    Waistline made by inserting a drawstring through a casing creating a small stand-up ruffle around the waist. Introduced for pants and shorts in early 1980s.

PRINCESS WAISTLINE        EMPIRE WAISTLINE

HIGH-RISE WAISTLINE        LOW-SLUNG WAISTLINE

CINCHED WAISTLINE

**princess w.**    Fitted waistline with no seam. Garment cut in panels from neck to hem and fitted by vertical seams. Worn by Empress Eugénie in 1860s, and popular at intervals since. *Der.* Claimed to have been introduced by French couturier, Charles Frederick Worth, about 1860 in a morning dress for Empress Eugénie.

**set-in w.**    Horizontal panel of fabric used at waistline of dress, fitted between top and skirt, making two seams—one at normal waistline and one higher.

**tunnel w.**    See DRAWSTRING WAISTLINE.

---

**waist watcher**    See GIRDLES.

**wale    1.** Textile term for woven ridge in fabric running vertically, *e.g.,* in *Bedford cord* and *corduroy;* crosswise in *faille;* and diagonally in twills, *e.g., gabardine* and *whipcord.* **2.** Knitting term for row of loops or stitches running warpwise.

**walkers**    See SHOES.

**walking costume dress**    See PROMENADE COSTUME.

**walking shorts**   See BERMUDA under SHORTS.

**walking stick**   See CANE.

**walking suit**   See SUITS.

**wallaby**   See LEATHERS.

**Wallace Beery shirt**   See KNIT SHIRTS.

**walled toe**   See TOES.

**wallet**   **1.** Accessory used to carry money, credit cards, and photographs. Sometimes with change purse attached and/or space for checkbook and note pad. Originally used only by men, now also used by women and children. **2.** In 1980s smaller sizes, closed with *Velcro*®, were introduced to wear on wrist, ankle, or belt, primarily when engaging in sports, *e.g.*, jogging.

**wallpaper print**   See PRINTS.

**walrus mustache**   Mustache with long drooping ends hanging at either side of the mouth. *Der.* Similar to tusks of a walrus.

**waltz length**   See LENGTHS and NIGHTGOWNS.

**wampum belt**   See AMERICAN INDIAN under BELTS.

**wamus**   (wah-muss)   Heavy outdoor jacket or cardigan of coarse cloth, buttoned at collar and wrists worn in U.S. Also spelled *wammus, wampus*.

**wardrobe**   **1.** All the clothing of an individual. **2.** 15th-c. term for room where clothing was kept. **3.** From 19th c. on, piece of furniture used to contain clothing called an ARMOIRE.

**wardrober**   See SUITS.

**warmup**   See PANTS and SPORT SUITS.

**warp**   Basic weaving term for yarns in fabric that run parallel to selvage.

**warp-backed fabric**   See BACKED CLOTH.

**warp beam**   Roller containing warp yarns placed on loom for weaving.

**warp-faced fabric**   Fabric with more warp yarns, or ends, than filling yarns showing on the surface on the right side, or face, of the fabric, *e.g.*, *slipper satin*.

**warp print**   See PRINTS.

**warp printing**   Method of printing design on the fabric by printing the warp, or vertical yarns, before the fabric is woven. Used particularly for cretonne fabric and silk ribbon.

**wash-and-wear**   See DURABLE PRESS, HAIRSTYLES, and SUITS.

**washed gold**   Thin coating of gold applied to a base metal by dipping or washing it in a solution of gold salts.

**watch**   Decorative timepiece usually carried in pocket or worn on a band at wrist. Fashionable accessory since 16th c. mainly worn in pocket. In late 19th c. dangled from pins and worn by women. Wristwatch was developed before World War I. In 1960s and 1970s worn with novelty straps and face designs and considered costume jewelry. There have been many technical developments in recent decades which include watches powered by small replaceable batteries, self-winding batteries, waterproof, and shock-resistant. *Digital watches* have digital printouts which not only show date, time and seconds, but are also designed with alarms and other technical features which remember appointments, read pulses, and tell the temperature.

## ■■■ WATCHES ■■■

**alarm w.**   Wristwatch which rings at a set time; sometimes the alarm is musical and called *musical alarm watch*.

**ankle w.**   Large watch with wide band worn strapped to the ankle.

**bangle w.**  See BRACELET WATCH.

**bracelet w.**  Watch with an ornamental band with the face of the watch sometimes covered with a small hinged piece of metal frequently set with stones, acting as both a decorative bracelet and a watch. Also called *bangle watch*.

**calendar w.**  Watch which also shows month and day of year in addition to indicating time.

**calculator w.**  Watch which, in addition to giving the time in eight different time zones of the world, is a stop watch, has an alarm, and will do mathematical problems of sixteen types.

**cartoon w.**  Children's watch with trade-marked cartoon characters, *e.g.*, Mickey Mouse®, Star Wars® characters, and Smurfs®, popular since 1930s.

**chatelaine w.**  Watch suspended from a lapel pin. Popular in 19th and early 20th c. and revived intermittently. Also called a *lapel watch*. *Der.* Keys worn at the waist on a chain by medieval mistress of the castle or "chatelaine."

**chromometric w.**  Watch equipped with aviation computer to calculate speed, distance, conversion of miles into kilometers or knots, and fuel consumption. Used when flying, auto racing, and boating. First used by space pioneers in flight of May 1962.

**diamond w.  1.**  Wristwatch decorated around the dial with diamonds and other precious gems. Introduced in the 1920s, the watchband was made with diamonds set in a platinum band. **2.**  In the 1960s semiprecious gems *e.g.*, sard, onyx, or turquoise were used for the face with diamonds set around the edge.

**digital w.**  A watch which shows the time in hours, minutes, and seconds in numbers which constantly change, rather than having a dial with hands pointing to the time.

**fashion w.**  Watch which is a decorative accessory as well as a functional one. In the 1950s bracelet, pendant, and ring watches were de-

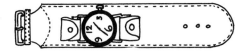

**GO-GO WATCH**

**WATCH ON CHAIN**

signed, some set with jewels, others in antique mountings. Previous to this, women owned one watch—now they may own several and wear them as decorative or genuine jewelry.

**go-go w.**  Watch which snaps into very wide interchangeable, colorful bands, matching or contrasting with the costume. Introduced in 1966, they were at first considered a fad, but later influenced the introduction of larger-sized watches and watchbands for women.

**hunter w.**  Large gold pocket watch with covered face depicting a hunting scene.

**lapel w.**  See CHATELAINE WATCH.

**LCD quartz w.**  Digital watch which displays time and date by *Liquid Crystal Display*; powered by a small replaceable battery.

**pendant w.** Watch suspended from a chain worn around the neck. May be decorated on the back and worn on either side or made with a hinged cover. Made in all shapes and sizes in antique as well as modern designs and in *LCD calendar watches.*

**pocket w.** Man's watch worn either in the vest pocket or in a small watch pocket in the trousers. First worn during Louis XIV period. Sometimes two watches were worn in small pockets of the waistcoat. Popular until the introduction of the wrist watch in World War I period.

**ring w.** Watch in ring style—popular in 1960s and 1980s, sometimes decorated with stones and made with hinged cover. Other very simple styles were made of lucite.

**seventeen jeweled w.** Fine watch using genuine or imitation rubies and sapphires at points of friction inside the case. Originally stones were genuine but now synthetic stones are more frequently used.

**wristwatch** Watch worn on the wrist. Introduced before World War I. Made in all sizes and types of faces, sometimes made with interchangeable bands. Some are set with diamonds and called DIAMOND WATCHES.

**wristwatch wardrobe** Women's watch sold with several interchangeable watchbands in several colors.

---

**watch bracelet** See BRACELETS.

**watch cap** See CAPS.

**watch chain** A decorative chain attached to a man's pocket watch often embellished with seals or emblems. When watch is worn in vest pocket, chain may be pulled through vest buttonhole and end tucked into pocket on opposite side.

**watch coat** Short heavy, windproof coat worn by sailors on watch. Also see PEA COAT under SPORT JACKETS.

**watch fob** Short chain, ribbon, or charm frequently engraved with *initials* attached to man's pocket watch. Named for the trouser pocket in which the watch is carried, called a *fob pocket.*

**watch pocket** See VEST and FOB POCKETS under POCKETS.

**waterfall** Woman's hairstyle of the 1860s and 1870s usually made with a piece of false waved hair hanging down in a confined mass, or in form of loose chignon with braid pulled tight at center making two loops of hair.

**waterfall back** Skirt of mid-1880s worn over bustle made with series of cascading puffs down center back. Fullness was held in place with series of drawstrings inside dress.

**waterfall necktie** See MAIL-COACH NECKTIE.

**waterproof** Describing clothing, usually of rubber, plastic, or heavily coated fabric, that cannot be penetrated by water, especially boots and coats. Also see WATER RESISTANT/REPELLENT.

**waterproof cloak** Outergarment with small tasselled hood worn by women from 1867 to 1870s, made of waterproof fabric. Later became an ankle-length semi-fitted coat with princess lines buttoned down the front. Also see ESMERALDA CLOAK.

**water resistant/repellent** Describing clothing of fabric or leather treated to shed water easily and dry quickly—not entirely *waterproof.*

**water wave** See FINGERWAVE under HAIRSTYLES.

**water wig** See WIGS.

**Watteau back** (wat-toe) Term used in latter half of 19th c. to describe back of a dress, jacket, coat, or dressing gown with box pleats called *Watteau pleats.* Pleats started at the neck-

**WATERPROOF
CLOAK, 1870**

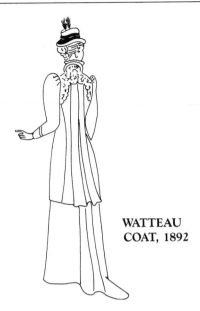

**WATTEAU
COAT, 1892**

line and were stitched down usually to the shoulders. Skirt of dress fell full in the back. *Der.* Named for the artist Watteau. Previously called *sack back*. See POLONAISE #1.

**Watteau body** (wat-toe) Daytime dress bodice worn in early 1850s to mid-1860s having a low square neckline trimmed with ruffles and elbow-length sleeves. Bodice did not meet in front and was fastened with a ribbon lacing exposing a *chemisette* worn underneath. *Der.* Named for the artist Watteau.

**Watteau cape** (wat-toe) Knee-length cape of the 1890s worn by women. Styled with collar fitted on neck then turned over. Made with single box pleat in back, and gathered to neckline in front. Made with separate pieces gathered over the shoulders to form capes over the arms. *Der.* Named for the artist Watteau.

**Watteau coat** (wat-toe) Lady's princess-style coat of the 1890s made in fitted unbuttoned style with waistcoat showing in front. Usually had a standing collar, wide lapels and turned-back cuffs with characteristic single or double box pleat in center back. *Der.* Named for the artist Watteau.

**Watteau dress** (wat-toe) In 1870s adaptation of 18th c. *sack* dress similar to those painted by Watteau. Bodice worn in late 1860s was

styled with a *fichu* in front and *Watteau box pleats* in back. Overskirt was looped up at the sides revealing the underskirt. *Der.* Named for the artist Watteau.

**Watteau hat** (wat-toe) Small hat for the seashore shaped like an upside down saucer worn by women in 1866. Trimmed with ribbons radiating from crown to edge of brim. Sometimes had a rosette with attached streamers on right side. *Der.* Named for the artist Watteau.

**WATTEAU
HAT, 1866**

**Watteau, Jean Antoine** (wat-toe) (1684–1721) French painter who painted many charming pictures of ladies in early 18th-c. dresses. So many pictures showed the *sack dress*, with box pleats set in at the neckline or yoke that this feature was later called a *Watteau pleat*. Later imitations of the *sack dress*, worn in later half of 19th c., were called *Watteau dresses*.

**Watteau pleat** (wat-toe)  See PLEATS.

**Watteau wrapper** (wat-toe)  Fitted full-length dressing gown worn by women in the 1880s and 1890s. Sometimes did not meet in front and tied together with sash at waistline. Had characteristic double or triple box pleats in back sometimes ending in a train. *Der.* Named for the artist Watteau.

**WATTEAU WRAPPER, 1891**

**wearing sleeves**  Term used in 17th c. for sleeves worn on the arms as compared with *hanging sleeves.*

**weasel**  See FURS.

**weave**  Manner in which the *warp* yarns, placed on the loom first, are interlaced with *filling yarns* to make a fabric. The *warp* yarns are threaded through *heddles*, attached to separate *harnesses*, which are raised and lowered to produce different weaves. The *filling yarn*, wound on a *shuttle*, goes back and forth when the heddles are raised.

**webbed belt**  See BELTS.

**webbing**  Durable fabric woven in narrow widths for use in belts and for stiffening. Sometimes made with elastomeric yarns.

**wedding band**  See EARRINGS and RINGS.

**wedding-band collar**  See RING COLLAR under COLLARS.

**wedding dress**  See DRESSES.

**wedding garter**  Decorative garter, usually blue satin trimmed with lace, worn by brides. Traditionally tossed away at reception to an unmarried man. The custom derived from 16th to 18th c. practice, when young men wore pieces of a bride's garter in their hats. Also called BRIDE'S GARTER.

**wedding ring/wedding trio**  See RINGS.

**wedding veil**  See BRIDAL VEIL under VEILS.

**wede**  See WEED.

**wedge**  See DRESSES and HEELS.

**wedgies**  See SHOES.

**Wedgwood® cameo**  See CAMEO and PINS.

**weed**  Term originally used to refer to clothing of any type from medieval times to 16th c. After that meant *mourning* garments of black plus veils to cover the head. Usually worn by widows and then called *widow's weeds. Der.* Old English, *waed*, "garment or clothing". Also spelled *wede, weyd.*

**weepers**  **1.** Muslin armbands or hatbands worn by mourners in 18th and 19th c. Usually black but sometimes white if deceased was a young girl. **2.** Name for ostrich feathers, worn in late 19th c.

**weft**  See FILLING.

**weight belt**  See BELTS.

**weighted silk**  Silk fabric having metallic particles added to it in the finishing process to give the fabric more body so that it drapes better. Must be identified if used. Formerly popular for silk taffetas and tie fabrics. Compare with PURE DYE SILK.

**weighting**  Process of adding metallic salts, particularly to silk, to make the fabric heavier. Cotton can be weighted by additional sizing. Wool fabric can be weighted with a variety of metallic natural salts.

**Weinberg, Chester** See Appendix/Designers.

**Weitz, John** See Appendix/Designers.

**welded seam** See Fused seam under Seams.

**Wellesley wrapper** Above-the-knee double-breasted sack-like coat, worn in 1853 by men and fastened in front with Brandenburgs.

**Wellington hat** Tall beaver hat worn by men in the 1820s and 1830s with a crown at least 8″ high and flared at the top. *Der.* Named for the first Duke of Wellington, British military hero who defeated Napoleon in the Battle of Waterloo in 1815.

**Wellington styles** Men's fashions of early 19th c. Fashions consisted of single-breasted overcoat which buttoned to waist with full skirt to knees and no waistline seam. Also had center back vent, side pleats, and hip buttons. Worn with narrow *pantaloons* with slits from ankle to calf which closed with buttons, boots, a tall flared-top beaver hat, and sometimes a cape. *Der.* Named for the first Duke of Wellington, British military hero who defeated Napoleon in the Battle of Waterloo in 1815. Also see Wellington under Boots.

**welt** **1.** Narrow piece of leather stitched to shoe upper lining and *insole* before being attached to *outsole* with seam concealed. A method of shoe construction which permits shoe to be resoled. **2.** Term used since 16th c. for a border around edge of garment, either for decorative purposes or to reinforce edge. Also see Pockets and Seams.

**weskit** Synonym for Waistcoat and Vests. Also see Dresses.

**western** Styles worn by western United States cowboys. See Western under Looks. Also see Tooled leather under Belts; Cowboy and Dip-top under Boots; Cowboy, Ten-gallon, and Western under Hats; Chaps, Dude jeans, and Western under Pants; Neckerchief under Scarfs; Cowboy, and Western dress under Shirts; Buckskin, Denim, and Western under Sport jackets and Pockets, Shorts, and Suits.

**wet look** A shiny glossy effect with a high degree of reflection. See Looks.

**wet suit** See Sport suits.

**weyd** See Weed.

**whalebone** **1.** Pliable hornlike strips called baleen, obtained from upper jaw of certain whales, and used for stiffening garments since Middle Ages, *e.g.*, whalebone used in waist of woman's dress in 16th and 17th c. **2.** Under bodice stiffened with whalebone, called *stays*, forerunner of Corset.

**wheel farthingale** Drum-shaped *farthingale* worn from 1580 to 1620s. Produced by wheel-shaped piece of whalebone extending skirt outward at waist, permitting it to fall in a drum-like shape. Also called *Catherine-wheel farthingale* and *Italian farthingale*, sometimes worn with Dutch waist.

**whipcord** Medium- to heavyweight worsted fabric with a diagonal wale caused by the steep twill weave. Yarns are hard-twisted and fabric is given a hard finish to make the weave very distinct. Also made of cotton, wool, man-made fibers, or blends. Used for men's and women's suits, coats, riding habits, and uniforms.

**whip stitch** See Stitches.

**whisk** **1.** Wide flat lace-trimmed or plain collar worn by women in 17th c., like *falling band*. **2.** Standing lace collar called *standing whisk*.

**white belt** See Judo belt under Belts.

**white bucks** See Oxfords.

**white crown** Crown of ancient upper Egypt made in tall cylindrical shape tapered in at top and ending with a knob. When Egypt became united this crown was worn together with the red crown of lower Egypt.

**WHITE CROWN**

**white flannels** Man's cuffed trousers, introduced in 1890s and very fashionable until late 1930s, made of white wool flannel. Worn with tailored tweed jacket and usually a sennit straw hat for tennis, boating, and spectator sports. Also see PANTS.

**white fox** See FURS.

**white mink** See MINK under FURS.

**white slip** Narrow border of white piqué along front edges of man's waistcoat, correctly worn only with *morning coat*. A fashion introduced by Edward, Prince of Wales, in 1888.

**white tie** Term used to designate men's *full evening dress*. Compare with BLACK TIE. Also see TIES, and TAILS under COATS.

**white tie and tails** See FULL-DRESS SUIT under SUITS.

**white vest** See VESTS.

**whittle** Large white shawl, usually made of Welsh flannel, worn by country women from 17th c. on.

**whole falls** See FALLS.

**wide-awake** 19th-c. term for man's broad-brimmed low-crowned hat of felt or other material used for country wear.

**wide wale** Term sometimes used to describe ribbed or corded fabrics with wider than average ribs, *e.g.*, wide wale corduroy, wide wale piqué.

**widow's peak** 1. Term for hairline forming a point in center of forehead. 2. Small cap wired in heart-shaped form with peak in center of forehead. Originally worn by Catherine de Medici as a widow's bonnet and much worn by Mary, Queen of Scots. Also see MARIE STUART BONNET.

**widow's weeds** See WEED.

**wig** 1. Contemporary type of false hair, human or artificial, mounted on an elastic net cap or foundation of bands (called *capless*), worn stretched over head to conceal natural hair and styled in conventional cuts and colors, or in fancy arrangements and colors as fashion fad. Popular since mid-1960s. 2. Historically, false hair worn from early Egyptian times and becoming a status symbol of royalty and upper classes through 18th c. Considered a secret device to conceal baldness in 19th and early 20th c. Worn by both men and women as a fashion in late 1960s and early 1970s. For historical wigs see BAGWIG, BOB-WIG, CAMPAIGN, CATTOGAN, DUVILLIER, PHYSICAL, PIGEON-WINGS, SCRATCH, and TITUS WIGS. Also see WIG HAT under HATS.

## ■■■■■ WIGS ■■■■■

**Afro w.** Kinky short-haired wig which fits over the hair, often back combed so that hair stands on end. Introduced in 1968 along with *Afro clothes*.

**beach w.** Modacrylic wig sometimes attached to a bathing cap or made in humorous shapes. Worn instead of beach hats at the shore or the swimming pool.

**corkscrew w.** Wig in various lengths of hair which falls in "corkscrew" fashion.

**crinière w.** Wig cut in Dutch boy style with

bangs in front and made of red, yellow, blue, etc., in synthetic hair or modacrylic fibers. Introduced in Paris by Courrèges, spring 1969.

**George Washington® w.**  Name of a water wig with bangs in front and the rest of the hair pulled back and braided. See WATER WIG®.

**human hair w.**  Imported genuine hair wigs which react like regular hair, therefore are harder to care for, must be set more often, and are more expensive than synthetic wigs.

**postiche**  See WIGLET.

**reserve w.**  Man's short-haired wig worn to cover long hairstyle in 1969–70 by men enrolled in Army Reserves. *Der.* So called because men wearing the wig were in the U.S. Army Reserves.

**stretch w.**  Comfortable cool wig with synthetic hair attached to elastomeric (or elastic) bands running around and over the head in crisscross fashion.

**toupee** (two-pay)  Small partial wig used as an aid to thinning hair or to cover baldness.

**Water w.®**  Modacrylic wigs usually in colors—blue, yellow, etc.—worn during or after swimming. Also see GEORGE WASHINGTON® wig.

**wiglet**  Small hairpiece worn on the top of the head and usually combed into bangs. Worn as an aid for thinning hair by both men and women. Also a fashion item. Also called *postiche.*

---

**wig hat**  See HATS.

**wiglet**  See WIGS.

**wilderness boot**  See BOOTS.

**wild mink**  See FURS.

**wild silk**  Silk filaments from cocoons fed on uncultivated mulberry, oak, or castor-oil plant leaves which produce silk poorer in color, less even in texture, firmer, and less elastic than *cultivated silk.* See TUSSAH.

**William Penn hat**  See HATS.

**Williamson diamond**  See DIAMONDS.

**wimple**  **1.** Piece of linen or silk draped around woman's throat and pinned to the hair above the ears, worn in late 12th to mid-14th c. and still part of some nuns' habits. Also called *guimp, gwimple.* **2.** Gauze veil of 1809 worn with evening dress. Also see BARBE.

**wind-blown bob**  See HAIRSTYLES.

**wind bonnet**  See BONNETS.

**Windbreaker®**  See SPORT JACKETS.

**windbreaker cloth**  Term applied to tightly woven fabric with little porosity which keeps the wind from penetrating the fabric, *e.g.,* poplin, satin, twill, and nylon tightly woven in plain weave cotton. Used for winter outdoor sportswear. Formerly the term was applied to heavy woolen fabrics, *e.g. mackinaw.*

**windowpane**  See CHECKS, PLAIDS, and HOSE.

**Windsor knot/tie**  See TIES.

**wing collar**  See COLLARS.

**wings**  Term used from mid-16th to mid-17th c. for decorative pieces projecting upward from shoulders of a *doublet* or *dress*, sometimes in shape of padded rolls or crescents sewn into *armseye* seam. Also called *shoulder wings.*

**wing-tip**  Decorative leather cap sewn to toe of shoe. Sometimes curved with center point and perforated in patterns. See OXFORDS.

**winkers**  Man's collars with extremely high points reaching nearly to eyes worn from 1816 to 1820.

**winkle pickers**  British slang for exaggeratedly pointed shoes worn by *Teddy boys* and *Teddy girls* in early 1950s. *Der.* From suggestion that the pointed toes can dig out snails, or periwinkles, from the sand.

**Winnie**  See COTY AMERICAN FASHION CRITICS' AWARD.

**Winterhalter, Franz Xaver** (1806–1873) German society painter who painted many exquisite portraits and also groups of women showing detailed costumes of the hoop skirt era. Portraits are lifelike, and it is possible to see details of lace worn, intricate skirts, bodices, and hairstyles. In 1854 he painted a portrait of Empress Eugénie of France.

**wired bra**   See BRAS.

**wires**   See EARRINGS.

**witchoura mantle**   **1.** Woman's cloak worn from 1808 to 1818 made with long fur-trimmed cape. **2.** In 1830s name for a woman's winter mantle with standing collar, large sleeves, and lined or trimmed with fur.

**woad**   Natural pale-blue color prepared by fermenting leaves of woad plant, *Isatis tinctoria*. This natural dyestuff was used until the introduction of *indigo* from India in the 16th c. Also spelled *wad*.

**wolf**   See FURS.

**wolverine**   See FURS.

**women's sizes**   Women's garments in sizes for heavier figure than *misses* range; even-numbered bust sizes range from 38 to 50.

**Women's Wear Daily**   See WWD.

**wooden button**   See BUTTONS.

**woof**   See FILLING.

**wool**   **1.** Animal fiber from fleece of the sheep or lamb characterized by a structure of small scales which enable it to felt. This sometimes causes yarns and fabrics to shrink. Advantages when woven into fabrics include good absorption, warmth, and good affinity for dyes. Disadvantages include tendency to shrink and no resistance to moths unless treated. May be knitted, woven, or felted. May also be blended with other fibers, *e.g.*, used with polyester to give a fabric which is more crease resistant. For types of wool see MERINO and SHETLAND. **2.** Sometimes includes hair of *angora* or *cash-*

*mere goat*; also fibers from hair of *alpaca*, *camel*, or *vicuña*.

**wool broadcloth**   Lustrous wool fabric with a twill weave not visible on the face because of the napped and polished finish. Made of woolen yarns with a soft hand. A milled finish lays the nap all in one direction. Used for women's coats, suits, and men's formal wear. James Monroe wore a suit of wool broadcloth woven in the U.S. for his presidential inauguration in 1809.

**wool crepe**   Fine soft lightweight fabric made of slightly creped worsted yarns in a plain weave. Finished by dyeing or printing. Has a good draping quality and is used for women's dresses in soft draped styles. Also made in heavier weights and used for suits.

**woolen**   **1.** Wool fibers made into yarn. **2.** Woolen fabrics, either woven or knitted. Made with wool yarns composed of shorter fibers which are not *combed*, but may be *carded* two or three times. Generally, woolens are kinkier and softer than worsted yarns. Finishing processes frequently include napping or brushing as the fabrics have a fuzzy warm hand rather than a smooth hand, *e.g.*, *tweeds*, as contrasted with *worsteds*. Spelled *woollen* in England.

**Wool Labeling Act**   Law passed by Congress in 1939 stating that wool products containing *virgin wool*, *reprocessed wool*, and *reused wool* must be labeled for the consumer. Contents of the various types of wool must be properly stated on a label for the customer by percentage. If content is less than 5%, it need not be labeled. (Law has been amended several times.)

**wool sheer**   Term used for lightweight fabrics, usually made of worsted yarns, used for women's suits and dresses.

**Woolworth® shoe**   See SHOES.

**work apron**   See APRONS.

**work clothes**   Apparel of sturdy fabric used

by factory workers and other workmen, *e.g.,* shirts, pants, overalls, coveralls, and jackets, usually made of denim, drill, chino, or duck.

**worked buttonholes**   See BUTTONHOLES.

**worked in the round**   Method of joining fur skins together horizontally so that skins continue around coat or garment.

**workout suit**   See AEROBIC ENSEMBLE under SPORT SUITS.

**World War I helmet**   See HELMETS.

**World War II helmet**   See HELMETS.

**worry beads**   See BEADS.

**worsted**   **1.** Yarn made from long wool fibers which have been combed and tightly twisted. **2.** Term used to designate either a woven or knitted fabric made with long wool fibers which are *carded* several times; *combed* to eliminate short fibers; and then twisted so tightly that there are few fuzzy fibers. After weaving fabric is sometimes *gassed,* or *singed* with a flame, to remove any short fibers. Given a hard press to make them crisp and smooth, *e.g. gabardine, serge.* May be finished by a slight napping to avoid shininess with wear or left with a smooth hard finish.

**wrangler**   **1.** Term used in the West for a cowhand. **2.** Trademark for a brand of western pants, jackets, and other clothing and accessories. Also see PANTS and SPORT JACKETS.

**wrap**   **1.** Loose outergarment which drapes around the body in various ways. Some Eastern countries wear garments which consist of fabric wound around the body, *e.g.,* the Indian *dhoti.* **2.** An outergarment put on when going out of doors, *e.g.,* a *shawl, scarf, cloak,* or *mantle.* Use of the word in this way is not as popular as it was in former years. **3.** In contemporary usage, a shortened form of the word *wraparound.* Also see BLOUSES, CLOSINGS, COATS, DRESSES, JUMPERS, ROBES, SKIRTS, SWEATERS, and TOPS.

**wraparound**   Term used when apparel and accessories are not closed with fasteners, but lapped over and held with sashes but are knotted or tied in a bow. See CLOSINGS, COATS, COLLARS, DRESSES, GLASSES, and SKIRTS.

**wrap cuff links**   Cuff links made with extra band extending around outside of cuff connecting the two parts.

**wrapper**   **1.** 18th-c. term for a woman's dressing gown worn in the boudoir and in bed. **2.** Man's loose overcoat, worn in 1840s, either single- or double-breasted. Sometimes used to indicate a CHESTERFIELD. **3.** In the 1850s, man's loose thigh-length overcoat with shawl collar which wrapped in front, sometimes worn with evening dress. **4.** Early-20th c. term for woman's housedress. One of the first items made by the garment industry in mass production, the wrapper evolved from a woman's dressing gown. **5.** Synonym for *wraparound robe.* See ROBES.

**wrap-rascal**   Man's loose-fitting overcoat made of heavy fabric worn from about 1738 to 1850. The 19th-c. type usually referred to coats worn when traveling on the outside of a coach. Also worn in the country.

**wraps**   Collectively means all outergarments.

**wrinkle resistance**   Ability of fabric to resist creasing. Most fabrics made from man-made fibers are resistant to wrinkling. Extra processes are used for natural fibers to resist wrinkling. See DURABLE PRESS.

**wristband**   Strip of fabric, usually double, seamed to the lower edge of a sleeve and fastened around the wrist. See CUFFS.

**wrist strap**   See BRACELETS.

**wrist watch**   See WATCHES.

**WWD**   Retailer's fashion newspaper published five days weekly by Fairchild Publications. It gives information about new styles, designers, foreign fashion collections, as well as information about new laws, government regulations, and foreign trade. *Der.* Formerly called *Women's Wear Daily.*

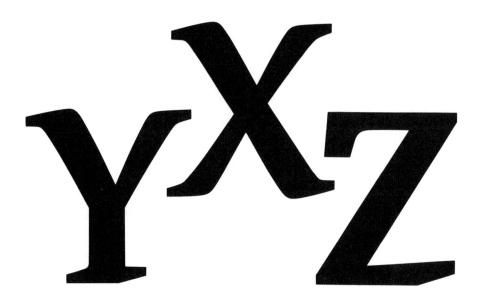

**X** Designation for size *extra large* in men's, women's, and children's clothing. XX and XXX means successively larger.

**x-ray dress** "See-through" dress made of transparent fabric worn with an opaque slip in early 20th c.

**xwa-lin** Peacock feather indicating a minister of rank in Chinese Mandarin Court. Feather was attached to the brim and bent down at an angle from the back of Chinese winter hat which was made of fur and satin.

**yachting cap** See CAPS.

**yachting coat** **1.** Woman's hip-length, square-cut jacket worn from 1860s to 1880s. Made single- or double-breasted with large buttons and loose sleeves. Also called *short paletot.* See PALETOT. **2.** See COATS.

**yachting costume** Ensemble for women popular in 1890s for yachting and other sports, including canoeing and boating. Frequently consisted of a straw sailor hat or commodore hat and full-length two- or three-piece suit with nautical influence or middy blouse.

**Yankee neckcloth** See AMERICAN NECK-CLOTH.

**YACHTING COSTUME, 1896**

**yard** Unit of fabric measure used in the U.S. comprising 36″ or 3′, equivalent to 91.44 centimeters.

**yard goods** Fabric sold by the yard at retail stores for sewing. Also called *piece goods.*

**yarmulka** (ya-mah-ka) **1.** Skullcap worn by Orthodox Jewish men for day wear and especially in the synagogue. May be made of fabric that is embroidered, beaded, or crocheted. Also worn by other Hebrew men for special occasions and religious services. **2.** See CAPS. **3.** See KAPPEL.

**yarn** Textile term for fibers twisted together tightly enough for weaving purposes. The two basic types are *a) staple yarn* made from short fibers, *e.g.,* cotton or wool carded to lay parallel, then twisted; *b) continuous filament man-made yarn* comprised of strands of indefinite length used singly or several filaments twisted together.

**yarn-dyed** Describing fabric that is woven or knitted from yarns already dyed rather than *gray goods* dyed after weaving, *e.g.,* checked *gingham,* striped *chambray,* and any *tartan.*

**yarn number** See COUNT OF YARN.

**yashmak** (yahsh-mahk) Turkish face *veil* worn outdoors by Moslem women that is placed below eyes and hangs to chest. Also spelled *yasmak.*

**yazma** Triangular-shaped large plain or printed headscarf worn by women in Cappadocia, Turkey. It is wrapped around the head, around the face below the nose, and the back corner is brought up and pinned on the crown of the head.

**yelek** Type of long coat worn by Turkish women at home with the *shalwar* (full trousers) and over the *berundjuk* (a silk chemise). Made with buttons to waist and long sleeves open at wrist. Sometimes a second *yelek* of more elaborate fabric, decorated with gold embroidery and pearls, is added for full dress.

**yellow diamond** See FANCY DIAMOND under DIAMONDS.

**yemeni** Headscarf painted with bright flowers and trimmed with fringe worn by married Hebrew women in Turkey in latter part of 19th c.

**yeoman hat** Woman's fabric hat with puffed crown gathered into wide band, sometimes with upturned brim worn with *walking dress* from 1806 to 1812.

**yeri** See HAN-YERI.

**yoke** 1. Portion of garment across shoulders in front or back, usually a separate piece seamed across front and back sometimes lined. In sweaters, yoke is knit in one with body, but may be of different stitch or color pattern. 2. Fitted top of a skirt connected to waistband to which lower part of skirt may be attached by means of shirring, gores, or pleats.

**yoke blouse** Woman's waist or blouse worn from mid-1860s to 1890s with square yoke in front and back outlined with a ruffle. Also has fullness below yoke, elastic at waist, and a ruffle below waist or a waistband. Also called a *yoke waist* or *yoke shirtwaist.*

**yoke collar** Square or V-shaped yoke, extending wide on the shoulders to which two gathered ruffles are attached. Worn by women in mid-1890s with high choker collar at neck.

**YOKE COLLAR
1895**

**York-tan gloves** Gloves of soft fawn-colored suede worn mainly by women from 1780 to 1820s.

**York wrapper** Back-buttoned high-necked woman's morning dress made of muslin worn in 1813. Trimmed with alternate diamond-shaped pieces of needlework in front.

**Youghal lace** See LACES.

**young teens** Size range between *girls* and *juniors;* includes sizes 5/6 to 15/16. Also called *young juniors.*

**Yugoslavian embroidery** See EMBROIDERIES.

**yukata** 1. Japanese unlined *kimono* made of coarse bleached cotton. Used for home wear or for walks on a summer evening. 2. Fabric of blue and white cotton used for *kimonos* in

Japan. Now imitated and used in U.S. and Europe.

**yumoji** (u-mow-gee) Undergarment like short *petticoat* made in rectangular shape of soft cotton. Worn draped around hips by Japanese women.

**zahones** Spanish CHAPS worn for riding.

**zammara** Type of sheepskin coat worn by Spanish shepherds.

**zapato** Shoes or clogs worn in Mexico and Guatemala. *Der.* Spanish, *zapateo*, a "folk dance."

**zarape/zerape** See SERAPE.

**zebra** See FURS.

**zendado** Scarf, usually of black fabric, covering head and falling to waist in front where it is tied. Fashionable in France and Venice in second half of 18th c.

**Zepel®** Trademark of E. I. du Pont for a fluorocarbon chemical compound used to make a fabric stain repellent.

**zephyr** **1.** Term used for lightweight clothing, *e.g.*, a shawl. **2.** Belgian thin dress fabric. See GINGHAM. **3.** Fine soft worsted yarns with a low twist, sometimes silk or man-made fibers are blended with the wool.

**zerape** See SERAPE.

**Zhivago** Clothes inspired by those worn in the film, *Doctor Zhivago*, made in 1965 based on the novel by Boris Pasternak. Styles of Russian Revolution adapted for coats and blouses in late 1960s. Also see BLOUSES, COATS, COLLARS, DRESSES, LOOKS, SHIRTS, and Cossack HAT under HATS.

**zimarra** Italian spelling for SIMAR.

**zigzag stitch** See STITCHES.

**zip-in/zip-out lining** Completely removable lining inserted into the coat by means of a *zipper* around the coat facing. It starts at one side of the hem, runs up side, across back neckline, and down the other side to make a dual-purpose coat. Also called a *shell*.

**zip-off coat** See COATS.

**zipper** Name coined and patented by B. F. Goodrich Co. in 1923 for fastening device consisting of parallel rows of metal or nylon teeth on adjacent edges of an opening, interlocked by sliding tab. Teeth may be covered by fabric tape and almost *invisible*, extra wide and called *industral zipper*, or made in various lengths to use on necklines, skirt plackets, coat and jacket fronts, or handbags and pockets. See CLOSINGS. Invented in early 1890s, and sold by Talon Co. in 1917 for money belts and boots. Used on men's trousers in 1930s and by designer Elsa Schiaparelli in Paris in 1933 for high fashion apparel, and in use for all types of closures by 1960s. Generic name is *slide fastener*, but term *zipper* is in wide use. Also see GIRDLES, PANTS, and POCKETS.

**zircon** See GEMS.

**zirjoumeh** At-home dress of Persian women which consists of a bodice with two or three pleated knee-length skirts with the underskirt starched.

**zodiac** See HANDBAGS and NECKLACES.

**zona** **1.** Maiden's girdle, or belt, worn in ancient Rome. **2.** A money belt.

**zone** (zo-knee) **1.** Woman's fill-in for an open bodice of a dress in 1770s and 1780s with the shape corresponding to the exposed gap. **2.** Belt worn by Greek women, usually the lower one of two, worn around the hips.

**zoot suit** Man's extreme style of the 1940s, including high-waisted, pleated trousers tight at ankle. Worn with extra-long suit coat with wide shoulders and lapels, wide-brimmed hat, and extra-long key chain dangling from watch pocket with attached keys placed in side pocket of pants.

**zori** **1.** Sandals worn by the Japanese made of braided straw, hemp or rawhide—and for special occasions—covered with silk. The two straps come back from between the big and second toe. Most types have low heels. **2.** For American adaptation, see ZORI under SANDALS.

**Zouave** (zoo-ahv)   See ZOUAVE UNIFORM.

**Zouave coat** (zoo-ahv)   Man's cloak of mid-1840s with velvet collar and cuffs and quilted silk lining. Used for riding, walking or worn to the opera. Same as the *oriental wrapper*. *Der.* Arabic, *Zouaova*, a Kabyle tribe, one of the Berbers, living in Algeria or Tunisia.

**Zouave jacket** (zoo-ahv)   **1.** Woman's waist-length, bolero-type jacket fastened at the neck and with curved sides in front. Had three-quarter length sleeves cut rather full. Showed military influence in the trim inspired by Algerian Zouave troops in the Italian war of 1859. Fashionable 1859 to 1870 and revived in the 1890s. **2.** Similar jacket worn by little boys in the 1860s. *Der.* Arabic, *Zouaova*, a Kabyle tribe, one of the Berbers, living in Algeria or Tunisia.

**ZOUAVE JACKET**

**Zouave paletot** (zoo-ahv)   Waterproofed llama wool coat worn by men with or without a suitcoat in 1840s. *Der.* Arabic, *Zouaova*, a Kabyle tribe, one of the Berbers, living in Algeria or Tunisia.

**Zouave pouch** (zoo-ahv)   Small handbag of various shapes—sometimes rectangular, sometimes triangular—finished with tassels and hung by a hook from the waistband placed underneath the zouave jacket. Worn by women in 1860s. *Der.* Arabic, *Zouaova*, a Kabyle tribe, one of the Berbers, living in Algeria or Tunisia.

**ZOUAVE POUCH, 1861**

**Zouave puff** (zoo ahv)   Term for single or double horizontal puffs at the back of the skirt worn from 1870s to 1880s. *Der.* Arabic, *Zouaova*, a Kabyle tribe, one of the Berbers, living in Algeria or Tunisia.

**Zouave shirt** (zoo-ahv)   Back-buttoned shirt with small banded collar with small standing frill and long full puffed sleeves. Decorated down the front with a panel, sometimes made of sheer gathered fabric crossed by bands of lace and trimmed with lace at cuffs and neck. Worn by women under *Zouave jacket* in 1860s. *Der.* Arabic, *Zouaova*, a Kabyle tribe, one of the Berbers, living in Algeria or Tunisia.

**Zouave skirt** (zoo-ahv)   Style of the 1860s made by gathering the full skirt at the hem and attaching it to an inside lining to make it appear like baggy trousers worn by the French Zouaves. *Der.* Arabic, *Zouaova*, a Kabyle tribe, one of the Berbers, living in Algeria or Tunisia.

**Zouave uniform** (zoo-ahv) **1.** Colorful oriental uniform consisting of a waist-length unbuttoned navy-blue jacket worn over a navy-blue blouse (both trimmed in red) combined with below-the-knee red trousers styled like harem pants, short black boots, and *puttees*. A sash of light blue is worn, and a green and red turban with a blue tassel. Worn by French infantry soldiers in Algeria originally composed of Algerians noted for their strength and courage. **2.** Member of a military group who wears a similar uniform which is same style but may vary in color, particularly some volunteer regiments in American Civil War. *Der.* Arabic, *Zouaova*, a Kabyle tribe, one of the Berbers, living in Algeria or Tunisia.

**Z-twist** Yarns twisted during manufacture so that the spirals slope in the direction of the center of a letter Z; from lower left to upper right. Also called *right-hand twist*. Also see S-TWIST.

**zucchetto** Ecclesiastical skullcap worn by Roman Catholic hierarchy: white for the Pope, red for a Cardinal, purple for a Bishop. Same as CALOTTE #3. Also see CAPS.

**zukin** Headscarf consisting of square of challis worn by Japanese women wrapped around head when out of doors.

**Zuni jewelry** Beautiful exotic and unusual bracelets, pins, necklaces, and rings of sterling silver set with genuine turquoise gems. *Der.* Made by Zuni Indians, a North American Indian tribe inhabiting the largest of the Indian pueblos in western New Mexico. See ZUNI SNAKE EYE RING under RINGS.

**zunnar** Belt formerly worn by Jews and Christians to distinguish themselves from Moslems.

# FASHION
# DESIGNERS

## Adolfo (1933– )
*American designer*

Born Adolfo Sardiña in Havana, Cuba. Sent by aunt to study one year on staff of BALENCIAGA in Paris. Came to New York in 1948; designed millinery at Bragaard for several years; joined milliner Emme in 1953. Acknowledged as Adolfo of Emme in 1956. Started his own millinery business in 1962, gradually adding clothing—wrap skirts, capes, sleeveless shifts, and finally switching entirely into apparel. Known for: Panama planter's hat, 1966; shaggy Cossack hat, 1967; lacy white cotton blouses and gingham dirndl skirts worn with big, floppy straw hats, 1968; huge fur berets; fur hoods; snoods; flower-braided pigtails. Introduced a series of knits inspired by Chanel's famous tweed suits; has continued to show variations of this suit in every collection. Introduced perfume, *Adolfo*, in 1978. Design interests include: men's wear, active sportswear, and accessories.

## Adri (Adrienne Steckling-Coen) (c. 1930– )
*American designer*

During her sophomore year at Washington University, St. Louis, was guest editor for college issue of *Mademoiselle* magazine; studied at Parsons School of Design, New York, where CLAIRE MCCARDELL was her critic. Following her studies at Parsons, worked at B. H. Wragge for many years and then for ANNE FOGARTY. Opened a small business for ready-to-wear and leisure wear. Established Adri Clotheslab, Inc. in 1983. Also president and part owner of Adri International. Invited to exhibit clothes at Smithsonian Institution, Washington, D.C., in 1971 honoring two designers under theme, Innovative Contemporary Fashion—the other designer honored was Claire McCardell. Prefers to work in jerseys, knits, challis, crepe de chine, leather. Believes that styles should evolve naturally from one collection to the next so that clients can collect them, add to them, and mix them freely from season to season.

## Adrian, Gilbert (1903–1959)
*American designer*

Born Gilbert Adrian Greenburgh in Naugatuck, Connecticut. Designed for Metro-Goldwyn-Mayer Studios from 1923 to 1939 for such stars as Joan Crawford, Greta Garbo, Norma Shearer, Katharine Hepburn, Rosalind Russell. Opened retail business in Beverly Hills in 1941, for both couture and high-priced ready-to-wear; closed retail business in 1948 but continued in wholesale until 1953. Noted for exaggeratedly wide shoulders on tailored suits; dolman sleeves; tapered waist; pinstripes or set-in patches of color; dramatic animal prints on sinuous black crepe evening gowns; mixed gingham-check cottons; asymmetric lines; diagonal closings; huge ruffle-topped sleeves. Definitely opposed Dior's sloping shoulder of 1947. Influenced by wild animals, zoos, modern and Egyptian art. Retired to Brazil in 1952 with wife, movie star Janet Gaynor, devoting time to painting landscapes. Died in 1959.

## Agnès (*ah*-nyess)
*French millinery designer*

One of top Paris milliners of the 1920s. Talented sculptress, friend of important artists of the time; prolific with avant-garde ideas. Used fabrics designed by painters Léger,

Mondrian, and Delaunay; abstract and zigzag patterns in odd colors; one of first to do turbans inspired by French expedition to Africa ("La Croisiére Noir"). Used novelty materials such as cellophane in 1935.

## Amies, Hardy (1909– )
*British designer*

An original member of the Incorporated Society of London Fashion Designers, 1942. Worked at Lachasse from 1934 to 1941; for House of Worth during World War II. Opened own house in Savile Row in 1948; specialized in tailored suits, coats, cocktail and evening dresses. Dressmaker by appointment to Queen Elizabeth II. Started men's wear designing in 1959; became leading consultant on ties, socks, scarfs, shirts, handkerchiefs, etc. Considered forward-thinking in his contemporary clothes, pantsuits for women; wide yachting pants; casual classics. Published: *Just So Far*, 1954, and *Still Here*, 1984. In 1970 awarded the C.V.O.

## Anthony, John (1938– )
*American designer*

Born Gianantonio Iorio in New York. Studied at N.Y. High School of Art and Design, Fashion Institute of Technology, and Academie de Alta Moda in Rome. Worked at Devonbrook and with Adolph Zelinka before he opened his own business on New York's Seventh Avenue in 1971, backed by Gunther Oppenheim and Sandy Smith of Modelia. Designs in natural fabrics such as wool, crepe, and chiffon and men's wear fabrics; specially noted for cardigan sweaters with pants, mannish shirts and ties, pullovers with skirts, dramatic easy pants and gala dresses in soft satins with sequins and in sheer wool. In late 1980s continues to design couture collections shunning any association with Seventh Avenue ready-to-wear.

## Armani, Giorgio (1934– )
*Italian designer*

Studied medicine and philosophy; worked for seven years as assistant buyer for La Rinascente, a large Italian department store, where he developed his taste and knowledge of men's wear. Designed men's wear for the Cerutti group. Free-lanced with other Italian manufacturers before his first men's wear collection in 1974 in which he attracted attention with his successful unconstructed blazer. Worked on women's wear in 1975 using the fine tailoring techniques and fashion sense he had discovered in men's wear. Shapes are easy and uncontrived; masculine cut with feminine qualities; uses exquisite Italian fabrics in neutral colors such as beige, black, gray, and taupe. Business includes free-standing boutiques in Italy and around the world; accessories and perfumes for men and women. His designs under the Emporio label provides young men and women with his creations in affordable prices.

## Augustabernard (Augusta Bernard)
*French designer*

A Provençal who started as copyist, particularly of Chanel; opened own house in 1919. Great success in late 1920s and 1930s, making custom clothes of unadorned simplicity for private clients and, in New York, for custom departments of Henri Bendel and

Bergdorf Goodman. Specialties include: slim, black, sleeveless crepe dresses with incrusted motifs matched to loose jackets; plain, pastel, bias crepe-satin evening gowns to set off jewels; shirring; cowl or scarf necklines; sunburst pleats for evening. Retired at peak of business in late 1930s.

### Balenciaga, Cristobal (bal-lawn-see-ah-ga) (1895–1972)
*Spanish-French couturier*

Born in Guetaria, Spain, son of a fishing-boat captain and a seamstress; after copying a Paris suit for a rich marquesa at age 14, encouraged to leave home to study clothes design. Eventually supervised three of his own houses called *Eisa*, in Madrid, San Sebastian, and Barcelona. Discouraged by Spanish Civil War, he went to Paris. Opened own business on Ave. Georges V. in 1937 and was immediately successful. Continued until retirement in 1968, creating elegant clothes for cream of international society, royalty, and film stars. Only couturier who could design, cut, sew, and fit a whole garment; revered as the "Master" by his staff and peers. Among his disciples were GIVENCHY, COURRÉGES, and UNGARO. With classic Spanish restraint, created many new silhouettes, always developed slowly from one season to the next, using somber browns and blacks, Goya and Velasquez colors in dramatic gowns. A partial list of his innovations includes: revolutionary semi-fit jacket, 1951; middy dress evolving into chemise, 1955; cocoon coat; balloon skirt; short-front, long-back flamenco evening gown; bathrobe-wrap coat; pillbox hat. With Abraham, a French fabric company, he developed *gazar*, a heavily sized silk. In the late 1950s and early 1960s Balenciaga designed gowns in this fabric inspired by the post-Cubist and abstract-expressionist painters of the period. Came out of retirement to design wedding dress for Carmencita de Martinez Bordiu in 1972. Two weeks later Balenciaga died in Valencia.

### Balmain, Pierre (bal-man, pee-air) (1914–1982)
*French couturier*

Born in Aix-les-Bains; studied architecture at the École des Beaux Arts, designed at MOLYNEUX from 1934 to 1939. Assistant to LUCIEN LELONG, along with Christian Dior, from 1940 to 1945. Opened new house in 1945 in rue François I, which was immediate success. Known for wearable, elegant clothes, which changed little from season to season; safe daytime classics; extravagant evening gowns. Published autobiography, *My Years and Seasons* in 1964. Following his death, house run by Erik Mortenson, his assistant for 30 years.

### Banton, Travis (1894–1958)
*American designer*

Attended Columbia University, the Art Student's League, the School of Fine and Applied Arts. After his return from the Navy in World War I trained as designer with LUCILE and Madame Françis. Went to Hollywood in 1924 at the request of Walter Wanger; head designer at Paramount in the 1930s. Designed all of Marlene Dietrich's costumes, including the famous black dress made of beads and feathers Dietrich wore in *Shanghai Express*. Moved on to 20th Century Fox in 1938; worked on and off for Universal Studios at the same time he ran his own couture business for private clients.

## Beaulard
*French dressmaker*

Rose Bertin's most serious rival as dressmaker to Marie Antoinette in the 18th-c. French court. Credited with the invention of tall headdresses with concealed spring, which allowed them to collapse as ladies entered carriages; also credited with the elaborate headdresses popular in the earlier years of Marie Antoinette's reign.

## Beene, Geoffrey (1927– )
*American designer*

Born in Haynesville, Louisiana; studied medicine in Tulane University for three years; studied design at Traphagen School of Fashion, New York, and sketching and design at Academie Julian, Paris. Returned to New York from 1949 to 1957 designed for Samuel Winston and Harmay; joined Teal Traina in 1958, who put Beene's name on the label. Opened own business in 1962. Characteristics: simplicity, emphasis on cut and line, dressmaking details, and unusual fabrics. In late 1960s extended business to include furs, swimwear, jewelry, scarfs, men's wear, and a boutique collection, *Beene Bag*, in 1970. Licenses include: shoes, gloves, hosiery, eyeglasses, loungewear, bedding, furniture, and perfume, "Grey Flannel." Designed Lynda Bird Johnson's wedding and bridesmaids' gowns in 1967.

## Bertin, Rose (ber-tan) (1744–1813)
*French milliner and dressmaker to Marie Antoinette*

Born Marie-Jeanne Laurent near Abbeville, France. Came to Paris at 16 to work in millinery shop, Pagalle. Sponsored by Princess de Conti; became confidante of Marie Antoinette and court milliner in 1772. Called "Minister of Fashion," she was proud, arrogant, ambitious, and loyal to the Queen until her death. From her shop, "Au Grand Mogol," designed fantastic, humorous headdresses reflecting current events, on which fabulous sums were spent, one of the excesses leading to the French Revolution. First dressmaker to become celebrated and mentioned in contemporary memoirs and encyclopedias; her letters and account books preserved by couturier Jacques Doucet. Fled to England during French Revolution; returned in 1800 and sold trinkets; died in poverty.

## Blanchot, Jane (blahn-show)
*French millinery designer*

Veteran milliner of the 1920s and 1930s. A sculptress from the Auvergne, who catered to elegant, mature women. President in the 1940s of the Chambre Syndicale de la Mode.

## Blass, Bill (1922– )
*American designer*

Born in Fort Wayne, Indiana. In early 1940s, came to New York to study at Parsons School of Design; sketched for sportswear firm David Crystal; enlisted in U.S. Army. After World War II designed for Anna Miller & Co., which merged with Maurice Rentner, Ltd. in 1958; Blass stayed on as head designer, eventually becoming vice president and then owner. Company name changed to Bill Blass Ltd. Noted for women's classic sportswear in men's wear fabrics, elegant mixture of patterns, knits, tweeds and shirtings, coordinated with sweaters, hats, shoes and hose for a total look; glamorous "drop dead" evening wear, laces, ruffles, feathers, completely feminine in contrast to mannish daytime look. Design interests include: rainwear, men's clothing, Vogue patterns, Blassport women's sportswear, loungewear, scarfs, automobiles, uniforms for American Airlines flight attendants, and chocolates. Introduced "Bill Blass" perfume in 1978. Early vice president of the Council of Fashion Designers of America. Enjoys social life with his clients.

## Bohan, Marc (1926– )
*French designer*

Started career working successfully with MOLYNEUX, PIGUET, and MADELEINE DE RAUCH from 1945 to 1953. Opened own business in 1953, but sold it in same year and worked for PATOU for short time. Free-lanced for Originala in New York until 1958. Joined house of DIOR in late 1958, replacing YVES SAINT LAURENT. Continues as chief designer of couture and ready-to-wear for Dior line. Noted for refined and romantic clothes, beautiful workmanship, suited to a wide range of types. His soft prints, details of ruffles, pleats, or embroidery, flattering color sense have made Dior clothes among most commercially successful of all couture.

## Boussac, Marcel (boo-sak, mar-sell)
*French designer*

Born in Chateauroux, son of cloth-factory owner whom he persuaded to add inexpensive brightly colored cotton prints to a drab line and inundated France, becoming millionaire at age 25. During World War I, organized government war production; produced airplane fabric. After war, launched new fashion for surplus lightweight, tan airplane cloth for shirts, dresses, pajamas, etc. Bought more factories; owned successful racing stable. Backed Christian Dior in own house in 1946.

## Brigance, Tom (1913– )
*American designer*

Studied at the Parsons School of Design and the National Academy of Art in New York and at the Sorbonne in Paris. His talent was recognized by Dorothy Shaver, president of Lord & Taylor, and he became the store's designer in 1939. During World Was II was a member of the Air Corps Intelligence returning to Lord & Taylor in 1944. He opened his own business on Seventh Avenue in 1949. Designed coats and suits, dresses for day and evening, blouses and playclothes. Women appreciated the design of his swimwear with their flattering cut and excellent fit. Pioneer in his use of oversized and mixed patterns, geometrics, and florals.

## Brooks, Donald (1928– )
*American designer*

Born in New Haven, Connecticut. Studied Fine Arts at Syracuse University, and at Parsons School of Design in New York. Noted for uncluttered day clothes in clear, unusual colors, carefully detailed; his own designed dramatic prints; romantic evening costumes. Has designed costumes for stage and screen, notably for Diahann Carroll in the musical *No Strings*, Liza Minnelli in the movie *Flora the Red Menace*, and Julie

Andrews in *Star* and *Darling Lili*. Design interests include: furs, swimwear, men's wear, shoes, costume jewelry, wigs, bed linens. After absence of several years, presented fall 1986 collection.

### Bruyère (Mme Marie-Louise)
*French designer*

Mme. Bruyère worked for Jeanne Lanvin before opening her own house in 1929. Became one of the best sources of embroidered, peasant-style dresses, Chinese-inspired over-blouses, practical trouser suits, and wool jumpsuits in earth colors. Also made hats and accessories. In the 1950s, series of other designers ran the house on Place Vendôme.

### Busvine (Richard Busvine)
*British couturier*

Couturier from 1890s to mid-1930s. Best known for tailored suits preferred by Queen Alexandra. Designed all of Queen Mary's clothes. Credited with designing riding habits popular with Edwardian ladies in the 1880s. House closed shortly before outbreak of World War II.

### Callot Soeurs (kal-o sir) (1895–1935)
*French couture house*

One of the great Paris dressmaking houses from 1916 to 1927. Firm founded in 1895 as a lace shop by three sisters, daughters of antique dealer. Eldest and most talented, Mme. Gerber, ran the business; was influence on one of their modellistes, Madeleine Vionnet. Famous for delicate lace blouses; gold and silver lamé; Renaissance patterns; much chiffon, georgette, and organdy; rococo flower embroidery. Closed in 1937.

### Capucci, Roberto (1929– )
*Italian designer*

First showed independently in Rome in 1952 at age 21. Opened in Paris in 1962 and lost some prestige; reopened in Rome 1969. Known for masterful handling of drapery, imaginative cutting, no extra ornamentation, tapered-pants jumpsuits, halter-neck hostess gowns, balloon drapes, huge bubble skirts, kimono and dolman sleeves, sculptured forms. Also designed children's wear, knits, furs, footwear, and millinery.

### Cardin, Pierre (kar-danh, pee-air) (1922– )
*French designer*

Born in Venice and grew up in St. Étienne, France. Studied architecture in Paris, designed costumes for Cocteau's movie *La Belle et la Bête*. Worked at Paquin, then at Schiaparelli and head of workroom at Dior in 1947. Considered one of most creative, intellectual avant-garde couturiers of the 1950s and 1960s. First showing in own house on Faubourg St. Honoré in 1950 at age 25. House consisted of two shops, "Adam" and "Eve," for men and women; sold only ties, vests, and sweaters for men. Success began in 1957 with many innovations for women; coat with draped hemline and loose back panels; envelope, barrel, and bubble skirts; loose chemise; minidress; cartridge-pleated wool; scalloped edges; irregular hem; and first "nude" look in 1966. Called revolutionary for his metal body jewelry, unisex astronaut suits, helmets, batwing jumpsuits, and tunics over tights. Started designing men's wear in 1958 and now considered leader in field of couturiers designing for both sexes. First Paris couturier to sell his own ready-to-wear, designed by André Oliver, to department stores. In 1970, new environment, *L'Éspace Pierre Cardin* in old Théâtre des Ambassadeurs. Owns the famous Paris restaurant, Maxim's; established Maxim's in Beijing. Entered into a trade agreement with the People's Republic of China in 1979, where factories produce Cardin clothes.

## Carnegie, Hattie (1889–1956)
*American designer*

Born in Vienna; worked in New York from 1909 to early 1950s. Adopted her name after Andrew Carnegie "the richest man in the world." Designer of made-to-order and ready-to-wear for society and movie stars, about 20% copies or adaptations of Paris couture. Started in 1909 as Carnegie-Ladies Hatter; became Hattie Carnegie Inc. in 1918; and expanded into multi-million dollar business with resort shops, wholesale business, factories, jewelry, and cosmetics. Tiny, feminine, shrewd, with great taste; influential through the 1930s and 1940s. Noted for "little Carnegie suit," nipped waist and rounded hips; embroidered, beaded evening suits; at-home pajamas; long wool dinner dresses and theater suits. Influential on many designers who worked for her: NORMAN NORELL, JAMES GALANOS, PAULINE TRIGÈRE, and CLAIRE MCCARDELL.

## Carven (Mme. Carmen Mallet)
*French designer*

Daughter of Italian father and French mother; planned to study architecture and archaeology. Opened house in 1944 at Rond Point des Champs Elysée, backed by decorator husband. Specialized in dressing petite young women like herself in imaginative sports and beach clothes, emphasizing tiny waists and rounded hips. Got ideas from travels, *e.g.*, samba dresses from Brazil, beach clothes in African cottons. Successful perfume, "Ma Griffe," packaged in her trademark colors—green and white stripes.

## Cashin, Bonnie (1915– )
*American designer*

Born in California. Considered one of the most innovative of American designers, uninfluenced by Paris. Designed for stage, ballet, and sixty motion pictures, including *Anna and the King of Siam* and *Laura*. Free-lanced since 1953 for sportswear houses Adler and Adler and Philip Sills, bags for Coach Leatherwear. Started The Knittery in 1967, limited editions collections of hand knits; in recent years concentrated on coats and raincoats. Specialized in comfortable country and travel clothes in wool jersey, knits, tweeds, canvas, and leather. Believed in functional layers of clothing, coordinated with her own designs of hoods, bags, boots, and belts, influenced by travels to Japan, Portugal, India, and Italy to collect ethnic fashions and fabrics of proven practicality. Among her specials: the toga cape, shell coat, sleeveless leather jerkin, the poncho, long fringed mohair plaid at-home skirt, kimono coat piped in leather, hooded jersey dress, double-pocket handbag, bag hat, and soft knee-high boots. Established The Innovative Design Fund in early 1980s—a public foundation with the purpose of nurturing uncommon, directional ideas in design, clothing, textiles, home furnishings, and other utilitarian objects.

## Castelbajac, Jean-Charles de (1950– )
*French designer*

Born in Morocco, his family moved to France when he was 5. He worked with his mother in her clothes factory at 18. Has designed for Pierre d'Alby, and after 1974 opened his own retail shop. Best known for: blanket plaids, canvas, quilting, rugged coats.

## Cavanagh, John (1914– )
*British designer*

Born in Ireland, became one of top British designers of the1950s. Worked in Paris, first at Molyneux from 1932 to outbreak of World War II; then at Balmain until 1951; opened own London house in 1952. Known for round-shouldered coats; "scarab" line in dresses; nipped-waist, full-skirt New Look; the sack dress a season before Paris promoted the chemise. In 1957, did wholesale line for Berg of Mayfair. Closed business in 1974.

## Chanel, Gabrielle "Coco" (1883–1971)
*French couturière*

Born in the Auvergne region at Saumur in France. Started with hat shop in 1913; opened own house on rue Cambon 1914; closed in 1954 to triumph again, hardly changing her original concept of simple wearability. Called *La Grande Mademoiselle*. Dynamic nonconformist who interpreted liberated women's desires after World War I. Developed an empire consisting of couture house, textile, and perfume laboratories, and costume-jewelry workshop, spanning years from early 1920s to early 1970s; success based on perfume Chanel No. 5, created in 1922. Early fame associated with casual clothes for working girl in plebeian fabrics, the *garçonne* or little boy look, wool-jersey dresses with white collars and cuffs, pea jackets, bell-bottomed trousers, turtlenecks, bobbed hair, and suntans. By the 1960s her trademarks were the Chanel suit—braid-trimmed, collarless jacket, patch pockets, and knee-length skirt in soft Scottish tweeds; multiple gold chain necklaces with fake jewels; chain-handled quilted handbags; beige and black slingback pumps; flat black hairbows, and a gardenia. She loved to be copied; success was due as much to her personality as to skill and hard work. Personal life and love affairs were as colorful as her professional career; close friend of Duke of Westminster, Stravinsky, Picasso, Cocteau, Diaghilev, and Grand Duke Dimitri of Russia. Her life was basis of musical, *Coco*, starring Katharine Hepburn in 1969. Died in midst of preparing a collection, January 1971. House of Chanel continued directed by a succession of designers: Ready-to-wear added in 1975, with Philippe Guibourgé as designer. Karl Lagerfeld has since taken over design responsibilities for both couture and ready-to-wear.

## Cheruit, Madeleine (share-oo-eet)
*French couturière*

One of first women leaders of haute couture. Took over house of Raudnitz (founded in

1873) in Place Vendôme. First to launch simple, almost severe models in contrast to fussy clothes of the time. Charming, vivacious, and her own best model; not a designer but a critical editor of her house's designs. Louise Boulanger designed for her; PAUL POIRET sold her sketches at beginning of his career. Mme. Cheruit retired in 1923; house continued until 1935 at that point taken over by SCHIAPARELLI.

### Cipullo, Aldo (1936–1984)
*American jewelry designer*

Born in Rome; studied at University of Rome. Came to New York in 1959 and attended School of Visual Arts. Designed for David Webb, Tiffany and Cartier; opened own business in 1974. His jewelry was simple, elegant, functional and very stylish. Jewelry designs included: gold "love" bracelet for men and women that fastened on the wrist with a screw, came with its own small vermeil screwdriver. Designed men's jewelry including wraparound gold nail, lapel pins to replace boutonnieres, pendants. Other design projects: silverware, textiles, china, leather goods, and desk accessories.

### Claiborne, Liz (c. 1929– )
*American designer*

Born in Brussels, Belgium; grew up in New Orleans. Studied painting in Belgium and France. Won a trip to Europe to design and sketch in 1949 in a design contest held by *Harper's Bazaar*. Returned to U.S. and worked as model sketcher; assistant to Tina Leser and others; at Youth Guild from 1960. Established Liz Claiborne, Inc., with her husband Arthur Ortenberg as business manager in 1976. Original interests in sportswear expanded into designs for dresses and children's wear. Business has grown so that her function is largely as editor of the work of other designers. Philosophy: Simple and uncomplicated designs of mix-and-match separates with easy natural look; sensitive use of color; technical knowledge of fabrics; moderate price range.

### Connolly, Sybil (1921– )
*Irish designer*

Born in Wales. Worked for Bradley's, a London dressmaker, in 1938; returned to Ireland at start of World War II and worked as buyer for Richard Alan in Dublin. Discovered in early 1950s by Carmel Snow of *Harper's Bazaar* magazine and The Fashion Group of Philadelphia who were visiting Dublin. Came to U.S. with collection of one-of-a-kind designs and Irish fabrics; formed her own firm with ready-to-wear boutique in 1957. Known for evening gowns with horizontally mushroom-pleated handkerchief linen skirts and ruffled blouses, finely tucked linen shirts, Carrickmacross lace, iridescent Donegal tweeds, Aran Island white homespun, striped linen dish-toweling fabric. Carried by fine specialty stores across the U.S.

### Courrèges, André (koor-ezh, awn-dray) (1923– )
*French designer*

Born in Basque country. Worked first for Jeanne Lafaurie, then with BALENCIAGA from 1952 to 1960. Own house opened in 1961; collection shown on big healthy girls instead of emaciated models; impeccably tailored suits and roomy coats, classical, contemporary balanced in architectural proportion similar to Balenciaga. Aimed to make functional clothes. Labeled *Couturier of the Space Age*, the *Le Corbusier of Paris couture*, "epitome of

Tough Chic," anti-elegance. Remembered for all-white collections, minidresses in crisp squared lines; suspender dresses in checked sequins or wide stripes; tunics over narrow pants with erotic seaming; flat, white baby boots; industrial zippers; slit-eyed tennisball sunglasses. Business sold to L'Oreal perfume company in 1965; retired for year, dressing only private clients. Returned in 1967 with more shockers; see-through dresses, cosmonaut suits, naked look in sheer fabrics and big oval cut-outs, appliquéd flowers on body and knee socks, knit catsuits. By 1972, designs less tough; used feminine ruffles, color pink, softer fabrics in evening gowns and loose pants. Operated boutiques, "Couture Futur" and "Hyperbole," and ready-to-wear in U.S. and other countries. Dressed eccentrically in white shirt, shorts, knee-socks, and baseball cap. Married to Coqueline, his model-assistant. In 1983, Itokin, a Japanese group, purchased 65% of couture firm from L'Oreal.

### Crahay, Jules-François (1917–1988)
*French designer*

Born in Belgium. Started his own fashion house in 1951, closed within a year. Chief designer at NINA RICCI from 1954 to 1964. Went to LANVIN as head designer in 1964; retired in 1984. Known for young uninhibited, civilized, soignee clothes. One of first to glamorize pants as evening wear in organdy or pleated silk; jeweled leather gauchos; Bermuda jumpsuits; updated leg-o-mutton sleeves and *fin de siécle* evening gowns.

### Creed, Charles (1908–1966)
*British designer*

Fifth generation of the oldest name in British fashion. Ancestor opened men's tailoring shop in 1710; his descendant, Charles's grandfather, moved it to Paris in 1750, becoming a Francophile and establishing a reputation for finest tailored riding habits for women in Europe; clients included Rejané, Grand Duchess of Russia, Infanta of Spain, Empress Eugénie of France, England's Queen Victoria, notorious spy Mata Hari, and opera singer Mary Garden. Charles, born in Paris, studied in France and Switzerland, worked in sales in New York at Bergdorf Goodman. Had first showing in London in 1932; reopened after World War II; famous for elegant suits for town and evening as well as country. House closed in 1966 following his death. Married to Patricia Cunningham, fashion editor of British *Vogue*; published his autobiography, *Maid to Measure*, in 1961.

### Cummings, Angela
*American jewelry designer*

Daughter of German diplomat; graduated from art school in Hanau, West Germany; studied at art academy in Perugia, Italy. Joined Tiffany & Co. in 1967; stayed until she opened her own business in 1984. Cummings' boutiques are in Bergdorf Goodman (New York), Macy's (San Francisco), and Bloomingdale's (New York). Works in classical tradition using 18 karat gold, platinum or sterling silver; often combines wood, gold and diamonds. Revived old techniques of goldsmithing such as damascene. Inspired by natural and organic forms, *e.g.*, silver jewelry in the shape of a leaf from a gingko tree.

## Daché, Lilly (c. 1904– )
*American designer*

Leading milliner in U.S. from mid-1930s to early 1950s. Born in Bèigles, France. Apprenticed at Reboux in Paris for four years. Came to New York in 1924; worked as milliner; sold hats at Macy's; opened small shop where she molded hats on customers and established reputation. Opened own building on East 56th St. in 1937, which became showrooms, workrooms, and home. By 1949, she was designing dresses to go with her hats, gloves, hosiery, lingerie, and loungewear, wallets and jewelry; by 1954, added perfume and cosmetics. Remembered for draped turbans, brimmed hats, molded to individual head, half-hats and war-workers' visor caps, colored snoods, romantic massed flower shapes, a wired strapless bra in 1949. Closed business in 1969. Wrote two books on fashion and beauty, *Talking through My Hats* and *Glamour Unlimited.*

## de la Renta, Oscar (1932– )
*American designer*

Born in Dominican Republic. Studied art in Spain. Discovered by Mrs. John Lodge, wife of American ambassador to Spain. Worked for Balenciaga's couture house *Eisa* in Madrid for twelve years, four years with Castillo at Lanvin-Castillo Paris; came to Elizabeth Arden N.Y., in 1963. Partner in Jane Derby in 1965, soon operating under his own label, Oscar de la Renta, Ltd., for luxury ready-to-wear. Noted for his use of opulent fabrics such as taffetas and tulle with sequins for sexy, romantic evening clothes and sophisticated and feminine daywear for his "Ladies Who Lunch" crowd. Design interests include: signature perfume introduced in 1977 and another in 1983; boutique lines, swimwear, wedding gowns, furs, jewelry, bed linens, and loungewear. Married to Françoise de Langlade, a former fashion editor of French *Vogue*, from 1967 until her death in 1983. Supports a rehabilitation center for mentally retarded children in Dominican Republic.

## Dell'Olio, Louis (1948– )
*American designer*

Received Norman Norell Scholarship to Parsons School of Design in 1967. Won Gold Thimble Award for coats and suits at graduation in 1969. Assisted Dominic Rompollo at Teal Traina from 1969 to 1971; designer at Giorgini and Ginori divisions of Originala from 1971 to 1974. Joined DONNA KARAN, a Parsons friend, as co-designer for Anne Klein & Co. in 1974; sole designer for Anne Klein since fall/winter collection 1985. Philosophy modern sophisticated interpretation of classic Anne Klein sportswear; easy shapes in beautiful fabrics. Also designs furs for Michael Forrest.

## de Rauch, Madeleine (de-rok)
*French couturière*

Renowned sportswoman of the 1920s; married to Count de Rauch, a Finn. Wanted proper sports clothes for herself and friends who played tennis and golf, skied, and rode horses. In 1932, started business called "House of Friendship by Mme. de Rauch," aided by two sports-minded sisters. Made beautiful wearable, functional clothes, adaptable to many types of women. Handled checks, plaids, and stripes precisely. Closed in 1973.

### Descat, Rose (?–1954)
*French millinery designer*

One of the big names in French millinery in 1920s and 1930s; house active until early 1950s. Made some of best felt cloches and brimmed hats with manipulated crowns in era when hats were as important as other clothes. Remembered for the Eugénie and mannish fedora; silk turbans; baby sailors tilted forward with face veils; tiny pillboxes or Tyroleans feminized by feather quills and veiling.

### Dessès, Jean (des-say, zhon) (1904–1970)
*French couturier*

Born in Alexandria, Egypt, of Greek ancestry. Studied law in Paris; aimed at diplomatic service but switched to fashion design in 1925, working for Jane, rue de la Paix, for 12 years. Opened own house in 1937 on Ave. Georges V. and in 1948 on Ave. Matignon in mansion of A. G. Eiffel, designer of the Eiffel Tower. Designed directly on the dummy, draping fabric himself; inspired by ethnic garments seen on travels or in museums, especially from Greece or Egypt. Remembered for designing the stole in 1951; draped chiffon evening gowns in beautiful colors; treating fur-like fabric; perfume, *Celui de*. Admired American women; in 1950, designed lower-priced line for them, called "Jean Dessès Diffusion," the beginning of ready-to-wear trend in French couture. Gentle, refined man who loved luxury and Oriental *objets d'art*; customers included Princess Margaret, Duchess of Kent and the Queen of Greece. Gave up couture in 1965 because of ill health and returned to Athens. In semi-retirement ran a boutique until his death.

### Dior, Christian (dee-or, chris-ti-ann) (1905–1957)
*French couturier*

Born in Granville, France (Normandy); son of rich industrialist. Aimed at diplomatic career; operated art gallery from 1930 to 1934; sketched hat designs for Agnès; designed for PIGUET in 1938, and for LUCIEN LELONG in 1941. Backed by textile magnate Marcel Boussac, opened own house on Ave. Montaigne in 1947; launched the revolutionary NEW LOOK, an ultra-feminine silhouette; yards of material in almost ankle-length skirt, with tiny waist, snug bodice, rounded sloping shoulders, and padded hips. In next ten years, devised his own inner construction to shape a dress into the "H," "A," and "Y" lines; each season a greater commercial success, his name standing for fashion to the masses. From 1948 to 1951, added perfumes, scarfs, hosiery, furs, gloves and men's neckties and a young, less-expensive line, "Miss Dior"; became a vast international merchandising operation. House of Dior continued under designing leadership of his assistant, YVES SAINT LAURENT from 1957 to 1960, and since then with MARC BOHAN.

### Doeuillet, Georges (duh-ee-yeh)
*French couturier*

Started as silk merchant. Possessed combination of artistic, business, and social attributes; became business manager for Callot. Opened own house on Place Vendôme in 1900, year of Great Exposition. First to make *robes-de-style*, later called cocktail dresses; specialized in all-over embroidered dresses in pastel crepes in Second Empire style. Still popular in 1920s. Inaugurated live mannequin parade at beginning of each season. In 1928 merged with DOUCET, to become Doeuillet-Doucet; house continued into 1930s.

## Dorothée Bis
*French knitwear house*

A chain of Paris trend-setting boutiques from the 1960s, run by designer-buyer Jacqueline Jacobson and husband, Elie. Credited by some with starting hot pants fad in 1969. Also remembered for long pants tucked into Tibetan boots; see-through knits; mid-calf coats over miniskirts; skinny cardigans and scarfs; knicker pants; sweetheart necklines; shrunken-crochet berets; dolman-sleeved Jacquard knits. Trademark shop display—life-sized rag doll slumped in chair.

## Doucet, Jacques (doo-seh, zhak) (c. 1860–c. 1932)
*French couturier*

One of the first couture houses in Paris in mid-19th c. Grandfather Doucet started in 1815 selling bonnets and fine laces in a sheet stall; by 1844 had own building on rue de la Paix selling gentlemen's haberdashery, laces, and doing laundry for the frills of the dandies, aristocrats, and crowned heads. Grandson, Jacques, started his career as dress designer after the Franco-Prussian war (1870) in competition with Worth; dressed demi-mondaines and actresses, notably the famous Rejané. Favored 18th c. styles and much lace. Apprenticed MADELEINE VIONNET and PAUL POIRET. Flair for collecting 18th c. paintings and furniture; later one of first to collect paintings by Matisse and Picasso. In 1928, firm joined DOEUILLET to become Doeuillet-Doucet.

## Drécoll (dreh-caul)
*French couture house*

One of most prestigious couture houses in Paris from 1900 to 1925. Actual designer was Austrian Mme. de Wagner, who bought the name from Baron Christophe Drécoll, well-known Belgian dressmaker in Vienna. Designs were architectural, of elegant line, often black and white or two colors, reflecting the best of *La Belle Époque*. Drécoll sent a mannequin to the races in the first harem skirt in 1910. Son-in-law took over business in 1925. Daughter, Maggy, formed her own couture house under name Maggy Rouff in 1929.

## Eiseman, Florence (1899–1988)
*American children's wear designer*

Began to sew as a hobby following birth of her second son in 1931; continued to sew for her children and her neighbor's children. Samples of her work shown to Marshall Field, Chicago, by her husband in 1945 instigating a $3,000 order. From that order blossomed a clothing firm selling across the U.S. and abroad. "Children have bellies, not waists," and "You should see the child, and not the dress first," were Eiseman sayings. Simple styles, children not dressed as adults, fine fabrics, excellent workmanship, high prices. Less expensive knits, brother-sister outfits, 1969; a collection of "dress-up" clothes at even higher prices using rich fabrics and hand touches for Neiman-Marcus, Florence Eiseman Couture, 1984. Retrospective of her work at Denver Art Museum in 1984.

### Ellis, Perry (1940–1986)
*American designer*

Born in Portsmouth, Virginia; received B.A. from William and Mary and M.A. in retailing from New York University. Sportswear buyer for Miller & Rhoads in Richmond; buyer at John Meyer of Norwich in 1967; designer for Portfolio Division of Vera in 1975. Perry Ellis Sportswear, Inc. established by Manhattan Industries, parent company of Vera in 1978; Perry Ellis menswear in 1980. Philosophy: Fashion should not be taken seriously or individuals should not be overly concerned with clothing. Young, adventurous, spirited; use of natural fabrics; hand-knitted sweaters in silk, cotton and cashmere. Designed furs, shearling coats for men and women, shoes, legwear, scarfs, Vogue patterns, sheets, towels, blankets for Martex, fragrance. Served two terms as president of Council of Fashion Designers of America and elected to third term at time of his death. Council instituted the "Perry" award in his honor given to new talent having the greatest impact on fashion.

### Fath, Jacques (fat, zhak) (1912–1954)
*French couturier*

Great-grandson of designer for Empress Eugénie, grandson of a painter, son of Alsatian businessman; dabbled in theater and films. Opened his own house in 1937; kept open during war and for next 17 years was immensely successful, designing elegant, flattering, feminine, sexy clothes; had boutique for perfume, stockings, scarfs, and millinery. Remembered for hourglass shapes, swathed hips, plunging necklines, full-pleated skirts, wide cape collars, and stockings with Chantilly-lace tops. Instinctive flair for publicity, sense of showmanship; loved pageantry and elaborate parties at his Corbeille chateau. Married to actress, Genevieve Boucher de la Bruyere. Died of leukemia at age 42 in 1954. Business carried on by wife until 1957.

### Fendi
*Italian fur house*

Founded in 1918 by Adele Fendi specializing in furs, handbags, luggage, and ready-to-wear. In 1954, after she was widowed, Signora Fendi ran business with five daughters: Paola, Anna, Franca, Carla, and Alda. Adele Fendi died in 1978, and her daughters and granddaughters continue to run business. KARL LAGERFELD was hired in 1962 as designer using new, unusual and neglected furs such as squirrel, badger, fox as well as some unpedigreed species. Innovative design techniques: furs woven in strips, unlined, lined with silk, and the double F initials designed by Lagerfeld have become international symbols in design.

### Ferragamo, Salvatore (1898–1960)
*Italian shoe designer*

Italian shoemaker, emigrated to California in 1923, opening cobbler's shop in Hollywood. In 1936, opened business in Florence, Italy, and by the time of his death in 1960 had ten factories in Great Britain and Italy. Said to have originated the wedge heel, platform sole, and transparent Lucite heel. Business carried on after his death by daughters, Fiamma and Giovanna, and his son Ferrucio with an emphasis on elegant, ladylike conservative styling with comfortable fit. Ferragamo name appears on handbags, scarfs, luxury ready-to-wear sold in free-standing boutiques in Europe and U.S. and in major U.S. specialty stores.

## Ferré, Gianfranco (1945– )
*Italian designer*

Studied architecture in Milan, qualifying in 1967. Worked with furniture designer; became known for accessories design by 1970. Designed sportswear and raincoats on a free-lance basis in 1972. Established firm in 1974. His expertise in architecture combined with fine tailoring techniques have made him one of the top European designers.

## Fogarty, Anne (1919–1981)
*American designer*

Designed junior-size dresses between 1948 and 1957 for Youth Guild and Margot, Inc., at Saks Fifth Avenue, from 1957 to 1962; established Anne Fogarty Inc. in 1962. Completed a spring/summer collection of sportswear and dresses at the time of her death. Remembered for "paper-doll" silhouette of 1951, a revival of crinoline petticoats under full-skirted, tiny-waisted shirtwaist dresses; the "camise," a chemise, gathered from a high yoke in 1958; lounging coveralls; and slim Empire dress with tiny puffed sleeves. In early 1970s, showed peasant look with ruffled shirts and long skirts with ruffled hems; hot pants under long quilted skirt. Designs included lingerie, jewelry, shoes, hats, coats, and suits.

## Fontana, Sorelle (Fontana Sisters)
*Italian couture house*

Firm originated in Parma, Italy, in 1907; then to Rome, headed by mother, Amabile, assisted by daughters; Micol and Zoe as designers and Giovanna in sales. Noted for evening gowns, delicate handwork, asymmetric lines, interesting necklines. Showed collection in U.S. in mid-World War II. First in Italy to open doors to American students with awards in 1957. Clients have included Margaret Truman Daniel and Ava Gardner in the movie *The Barefoot Contessa*. One of the leading Italian couture houses in 1950s. Fontana boutiques still exist in Italy and Switzerland.

## Fortuny, Mariano (Mariano Fortuny y Madrazo) (1871–1949)

Born in Venice. He was an innovator, inventor, photographer, stage designer, textile and dress designer. Famous for his long, slender mushroom-pleated silk teagowns, slipped over head, tied at waist by thin silk cord. Most famous design called the DELPHOS GOWN, appearing first in 1907. A two-piece version is called "peplos"—hip-length overblouse or longer, unpleated tunic. The unique pleating technique was first shown in Paris in 1910 and method he used remains a mystery today. Clothes considered a classic all through the 1930s, now rare collector's items. Women who wore his dresses included Lillian Gish, Isadora Duncan, and Martha Graham. Hs work may be seen in Palazzo Orfrie, his former residence in Venice. Fortuny-printed fabrics, used in interior designs are manufactured in Venice.

### Galanos, James (1929– )

*American designer*

Born in Philadelphia of Greek immigrants. Studied fashion in New York; sold sketches; worked at ROBERT PIGUET in Paris from 1947 to 1948, along with MARC BOHAN. Returned to New York and finally settled in Los Angeles, where Jean Louis helped him start his own business in 1951. First show in New York in 1952 launched him on spectacular career; in five years received three Coty Awards and elected into Hall of Fame. Known for luxurious day and evening ensembles: total look for collections; hats, shoes, hosiery, accessories, hair, and makeup. Lives in California but shows only in New York; dresses many wealthy socialites and movie stars. Nancy Reagan chose to wear Galanos originals to both the 1981 and 1985 Presidential Inaugural Balls.

### Galitzine, Princess Irene

*Italian designer*

Born in Tiflis, Russia, she can trace ancestry to Catherine the Great. Family fled to Italy during Russian Revolution. Educated in Italy and England; studied art in Rome. Married to Silvio Medici. Worked for SORELLE FONTANA for three years; started own import business in Rome in 1948. First show of her designs in 1959. Introduced silk PALAZZO PAJAMAS in 1960. Also known for at-home togas, evening suits, tunic-top dresses, lingerie, bare-back or open-sided evening gowns, decorative striped stockings. Closed house in 1968, continuing to design cosmetics, furs, home furnishings. Revived couture collection in 1970 and showed sporadically for several years.

### Gaultier, Jean-Paul (1952– )

*French designer*

At 13 presented a collection of designs to his mother and grandmother, and at 15 invented a coat with bookbag closures. In 1970 sent design portfolio to PIERRE CARDIN, who hired him as design assistant for two years. Also worked for Jacques Esterel and JEAN PATOU, where he worked as assistant to Michel Goma for three years. In 1976 some of his sketches were published by *Mode Internationale*, a French magazine, and received favorable reviews. Presented his first ready-to-wear collection with silhouettes contrary to the current designs. Kashiyama, a Japanese clothing manufacturer, signed Gaultier to an exclusive contract. Inspired by London street dressing, mixes fabrics and shapes that are unusual and controversial, *e.g.*, slinky black jersey dresses with "derriere" cutouts revealing red velvet underpants; crushed velvet gowns and bustiers embellished with foot-long pointed breasts or trenchdresses for both men and women; included shoulder-less jackets in his 1988 collection.

### Gernreich, Rudi (gernrick, roodee) (1922–1985)

*American designer*

Born in Vienna, Austria, emigrated to California in 1938. Specialized in dramatic sport clothes in striking color combinations and cut, bathing suits, underwear and hosiery—usually coordinated for total look. Remembered for maillot swimsuits with no bra and bare suits with deeply cut-out sides in the mid-1950s; the topless swimsuit and see-through blouses in 1964; "no-bra" in skin-color nylon net; knee-high leggings patterned to match tunic tops and tights in 1967; wrap-tied legs and dhoti dresses in 1968.

Announced in 1968 he was taking sabbatical from his fashion career. In 1971 predicted a future trend of bald heads, bare bosoms with pasties, and unisex caftans.

## Givenchy, Hubert de (zhee-von-she, u-bare) (1927– )
*French designer*

Studied at L'École des Beaux Arts. At age 17, started designing at FATH, then at PIGUET and LELONG; spent four years with SCHIAPARELLI, designing separates, cardigan dresses and blouses and became known for the "Bettina" blouse, a peasant shape in shirting material with wide open neck and full ruffled sleeves. Opened own house in 1952 at age 25, near Balenciaga whom he admired above all couturiers. Considered to have been influenced by BALENCIAGA's sober elegance and produced collections in same mood. Noted for clothing of exceptional workmanship, masterly cut, and beautiful fabrics. His ready-to-wear distributed worldwide through his Nouvelle Boutique; perfumes for women and toiletries for men. Licensing agreements include sportswear, men's and women's shirts, leathers, hosiery, furs, eyeglasses, home furnishings. Clientele includes many wealthy conservative women and his favorite movie star, Audrey Hepburn.

## Grès, Alix (gray, ah-leex) (c. 1900– )
*French couturière*

Originally a sculptress, now dedicated to designing women's clothes. Served apprenticeship at PREMET. Started in 1931–1932, making *toiles* under name of Alix Barton; in 1934, showed in house called *Alix* until 1942, closed by Germans; reopened after World War II using her married name, Grès. Noted for superb craftsmanship; molded silhouette over uncorseted body; statuesque Greek-draped evening gowns in cobweb Alix jersey, named for her; bi-color pleated jersey gowns with criss-crossed string belts; cowled black jersey day dresses; asymmetric drapes, bias-cut caftans; loose topcoats with hoods and bat-wing sleeves; at home and beach wear; perfume, *Cabochard*. Approaches design as true artist and is uninfluenced by others, difficult to copy. Served as president of the Chambre Syndicale de la Couture Parisienne in the 1970s.

## Groult, Nicole (188?–1940?)
*French couturière*

Sister of PAUL POIRET worked independent of him. Opened own business in 1920; closed in 1932. Unlike her brother did not die destitute.

## Gucci (goo-chee)
*Italian leather house*

Family business in Italy established in 15th c. by ancestors of the current head Dr. Aldo Gucci. Since 1906, manufacturing and retailing luggage and leather accessories and, since 1969, collections of apparel for men and women. In the 1960s, the walking low-heeled loafer with metal harness-bit ornament across the vamp. The tackroom hardware and red and green canvas stripes used in luggage and accessories are status symbols. The GG signature on bags and apparel is also a status symbol; sold in chain of Gucci shops throughout the world. Members of the Gucci family signed an agreement to keep the business within the family's private domain for at least 100 years.

**Halston** (Roy Halston Frowick) (1932– )
*American designer*

Born in Des Moines, Iowa; studied at Chicago Art Institute; worked for LILLY DACHÉ in N.Y.; and designed hats for Bergdorf Goodman from 1959 to 1968, where he made news with the pillbox hat he designed for Jacqueline Kennedy to wear at the inaugural ceremony in 1961. Started own business on East 68th Street in 1968 for private clients and entertainment world. His formula of casual throwaway chic, using superior fabrics for extremely simple classics made him most talked about designer in early 1970s. Opened ready-to-wear firm, Halston Originals, in fall 1972. Typical ideas: long cashmere dress with sweater tied over shoulders; long, slinky halter-neck jerseys; wraparound skirts and turtlenecks; evening caftans, lots of argyles, angora, and chiffon jersey; ivory jewelry. Pioneered use of Ultrasuede. Worked closely with ELSA PERETTI, using her jewelry with his clothing. Sold his business to Norton Simon Inc., in 1973, which was acquired by Esmark, Inc. in 1983. Created an inexpensive line for J.C. Penney, 1983, at which point many of his accounts dropped his regular line. Attempted to regain the right to design under his name in 1984, but failed and went out of business.

**Hardwick, Cathy** (1933– )
*American designer*

Born in Seoul, Korea; studied music in Korea and Japan. Came to U.S. at 21 and opened boutique in San Francisco. Free-lanced for Alvin Duskin and other firms; moved to New York in 1960s. Opened Cathy Hardwick & Friends in 1972. Philosophy: clean-cut, fluid, sensuous clothing; comfortable and useful as well as fashionable. Has designed tableware for Mikasa and bed linens for Burlington Industries.

**Hartnell, Sir Norman** (1901–1979)
*British designer*

Early experience designing for theatrical productions at Cambridge University; opened dress shop with sister in 1923, his own house in 1930. Became largest couture house in London and famous as dressmaker to the British Court. One of original members of the Incorporated Society of London Fashion Designers in 1942. Known for Coronation gowns for Queen Elizabeth II in 1953, for which he received the Royal Victorian Order; lavishly embroidered ball gowns, fur-trimmed suits, city tweeds. Wrote and illustrated history of his career in *The Silver and The Gold*, 1955, and *Royal Courts of Fashion*, 1971. Knighted in 1977.

**Hechter, Daniel** (esh-tar) (1938– )
*French designer*

Designed for Pierre d'Alby from 1958 to 1962; opened own house in 1962; introduced children's wear in 1965; men's wear in 1968; made paper dresses for Scott Paper Co., U.S., in 1966; collection for Du Pont in 1970; opened own showroom on 7th Avenue in 1972. Licenses include: tennis and ski wear, sunglasses, shoes, and home furnishings.

**Heim, Jacques** (1899–1967)
*French designer*

Paris-born son of Isadore and Jeanne Heim who had founded a fur house in 1898.

Jacques built house into a world-famous couture establishment, starting in 1923 and important for next 40 years. He reflected trends rather than creating them; was conservative editor of clothes. Designer of the first bikini in 1945, which he named *Atome*. Also had success with youthful clothes in boutique, *Heim Jeunes Filles*. Worked with French underground during World War II; president of the Chambre Syndicale de la Couture Parisienne from 1958 to 1962.

## Hermés (air-mes)
*French design house*

Thierry Hermés, saddle- and harness-maker, opened shop in 1837 on Faubourg St. Honoré, adding sporting accessories, toilet articles, boots, scarfs, and jewelry. Couture began in 1920 under Emile Hermés; mainly leather garments but also sweaters, shirts, capes, and shoes. Ready-to-wear called *Hermés-Sport*. Claims to have started boutique trend in 1918. Famous perfume, *Caleche*. In 1980s name continues to flourish.

## Horn, Carol (1936– )
*American designer*

Studied fine arts at Boston and Columbia Universities. Designed junior sportswear for Bryant 9, Benson & Partners, and designer-director of Carol Horn Division of Malcolm Starr International. Opened own company in 1983, Carol Horn Sportswear. Clothing is uncontrived shapes made of natural fabrics and moderately priced.

## James, Charles (1906–1978)
*American couturier*

Born in England and moved to Chicago. Sponsored by Mary Lewis of Best and Co. in N.Y. in 1939. Operated dressmaking salons in London and Paris in 1930s and own custom-order business in 1940s and 1950s. Rated by his peers: "A genius... daring innovator in the shape of clothes... more of an architect or sculptor... independent, stormy, unpredictable, contentious." Acknowledged as an equal by top Paris couture in 1947. Remembered for new technique for dress patterns; new dress forms; elaborate, bouffant ball gowns in odd mixtures of colors and fabrics; batwing oval cape-coat; intricately cut dolman wraps and asymmetric shapes. Now in the costume collections of many museums including the Brooklyn Museum and the Smithsonian Institution in Washington, D.C. Retired from couture design in 1958 to devote himself to sculpture and painting. Conducted seminars in costume design at Rhode Island School of Design and Pratt Institute in 1960 and created a mass-produced line for E.J. Korvette in 1962. In the 1970s worked on organizing his archives and with Antonio, illustrator, who made drawings of all his work to be kept as a permanent record.

## Jenny (Mme. Sacerdote)
*French couturière*

Educated to be professor of literature; switched to fashion and trained at PAQUIN. Opened own house in 1911. Extremely successful with wearable, aristocratic clothes for private clients and theater personalities. Known for slim-skirted dresses with jabot collars, scarfs, or shawls in tan and old rose. Popular with Americans in 1920s. House closed in 1938.

## Mr. John (1906– )
*American millinery designer*

Born John Pico John in Munich, Germany, where his mother was a millinery designer. Studied at the Sorbonne and at the École des Beaux Arts in Paris; came to New York in 1929 and designed millinery for house of Mme. Laurel. Formed John Fredericks with partner Fred Fredericks from 1929 to 1948. Formed own firm, Mr. John, Inc., in 1948. Designed hats worn by Vivien Leigh in *Gone with the Wind*. Most successful in the 1940s and 1950s heyday of hats, putting on spectacular shows and developing his atmosphere in Napoleonic dress and decor. Remembered for forward-tilted doll hats, glorified Stetsons, scarf-attached hats, skullcaps held by tight face veils, wig hats, huge flower or bushy fur toques.

## Johnson, Betsey (1942– )
*American designer*

Graduate of Syracuse University; started as guest editor for *Mademoiselle* magazine where she made sweaters for editors, which were seen by owner of Paraphernalia boutiques, who gave her a job designing. One of the first American designers to design anti-Seventh Avenue fashions in early 1960s. Started, with friends, a boutique, Betsey, Bunky & Nini, in 1969. Known for: the "Basic Betsey," a limp, clinging T-shirt dress in mini, midi, or maxi lengths; a clear vinyl slipdress with kit of paste-on stars, fishes, numbers, etc., "noise" dress with loose grommets at hem; bell trousers; thigh-high boots; loose smock over jeans; quilted flannel coats; thrift-shop accessories. Her body-conscious clothes range from swimwear to bodysuits, tight pants to dance dresses. Designed for Alley Cat, Michael Milea, Butterick Patterns. Established Betsey Johnson, Inc., in 1978, to manufacture sportswear, bodywear, and dresses. In 1980s operates three retail stores called "Betsey Johnson" in New York City.

## Julian, Alexander
*American designer*

Born and raised in Chapel Hill, North Carolina, where his father was in retailing. Julian designed his first shirt at 12; managed his father's store at 18; and owned the shop at 21. Moved to New York in 1975. He designs his own fabrics interpreting traditional themes with wit and imagination. Collections are called *Colours*. Licenses include: men's, women's and children's wear; hosiery; home furnishings and decorative fabrics; small leather goods; pocket accessories. Julian and his wife have established a foundation to improve the quality of children's education in an effort to support their theory that an early exposure to esthetics and art encourages development of tastes and values.

## Kahn, Robin (1947– )
*American jewelry designer*

Born in London, came to U.S. at 5 years old; graduated High School of Art and Design and Parsons School of Design. Trained with goldsmiths at the Haystack Mountain

School of Crafts. Designed accessories for PIERRE CARDIN, OSCAR DE LA RENTA, and KENNETH J. LANE, and one-of-a-kind pieces for Bloomingdale's. Founded Robin Kahn, Inc. in 1978. Forms are bold, clean and elegant; designs directly from metal utilizing brass, copper and bronze; ebony, turquoise, ivory, lapis as well as leather cording and taffeta.

## Kamali, Norma (1945– )
*American designer*

Born Norma Arraez and raised in New York; descendant of Basque and Lebanese parents. Graduated from the Fashion Institute of Technology in 1964 as a student of illustrating. Worked for airlines spending weekends in London. Opened a tiny basement shop selling imports primarily from England and her own designs with her husband, Eddie Kamali, in 1969. Moved to Madison Avenue in 1974 and began designing suits, lace dresses. Divorced in 1977 and in 1978 established a boutique and company called OMO (On My Own). Leased a building on Madison Avenue in 1983 for 99 years. Shows video tape productions of her collections from accessories to couture. Her body-conscious and adventurous designs have become favorites of celebrities such as Donna Summer, Diana Ross, and Barbra Streisand. Noted designs include: swimsuits cut hip-high; draped and shirred "parachute" jumpsuit included in show at Costume Institute of the Metropolitan Museum of Art in 1978; a moderate-priced collection for Jones Apparel Group using cotton sweatshirt fabric; giant removable shoulder pads. Also designed lingerie and children's wear.

## Karan, Donna (1948– )
*American designer*

Attended Parsons School of Design, but after her second year dropped out to work with ANNE KLEIN. Parsons awarded her a degree in 1987. Fired by Klein after nine months; returned in 1968. Became associate designer in 1971; head designer following Klein's illness in 1974. Asked former Parsons classmate, LOUIS DELL'OLIO to co-design Klein collection. Launched a less-expensive line, Anne Klein II, in 1983. Given her own firm by Takihyo Corporation, Japan, Anne Klein's parent company. Design principles include the classic mix-and-match sportswear concept. Her first collection in 1983 included a bodysuit translated into contemporary terms.

## Kawakubo, Rei (1942– )
*Japanese designer*

Born in Tokyo, Japan; graduated from Keio University in Tokyo with major in literature. Worked in advertising department of textile firm; freelance stylist. Established Comme des Garçons Co., Ltd. in 1973; first showing in Tokyo in 1975. Introduced men's wear in 1978 and knitwear in 1981. Also in 1981 showed for first time in Paris, establishing Paris office in 1982. New York company established in 1986. Honored by The Fashion Group, "Night of the Stars Award" in 1986; included in exhibit at the Fashion Institute of Technology, titled "Three Women" Madeleine Vionnet, Claire McCardell, and Rei Kawakubo," in 1987. Originally designed exclusively in black and gray, currently adds some touches of color. Drapes over the model's body in asymmetrical shapes. Uses cotton, linen or canvas and often tears and slashes designs. Has both free-standing and in-store boutiques in Japan, U.S. and Europe.

## Kenzo (Kenzo Takada) (1945– )
*French designer*

Trend-setting French ready-to-wear designer from early 1970s. Came to Paris from Japan in 1965. Prepared 20 collections a year for a style bureau; designed for Mad boutique. Opened own boutique, Jungle Jap, in 1970. Widely distributed in U.S.; Kenzo-Paris boutique opened in New York in 1983; in 1984 Kenzo agreed to produce "Album by Kenzo" for The Limited. Designs based on traditional Japanese clothing; spirited combinations of textures and patterns.

## Khanh, Emmanuelle (kahn, e-man-u-el) (1938– )
*French designer*

French, married to Nyuen Manh (Quasar) Khanh, Vietnamese engineer. Entered fashion world as mannequin for GIVENCHY. Began designing inexpensive ready-to-wear as rebellion against haute couture; sold in Paris and London boutiques. Attracted publicity in 1963; pioneer of the new wave of dress that swept the Paris streets as Mary Quant's did in London. Remembered for: dog's ear collars, droopy revers on long fitted jackets, loose cravat closings on coats and suits; dangling cuff-link fastenings; half-moon money-bag pockets; dresses with lanky 1930s feeling. Labeled "antithesis of hard chic," "sloppy, casual," but reflecting a contemporary approach to individuality symptomatic of the 1960s; continues to design in the 1980s.

## Kieselstein-Cord, Barry (1943– )
*American jewelry designer*

Studied at Parsons School of Design, New York University, and the American Craft League. First jewelry collection for Georg Jensen around 1972. By early 1980s designs sold around the U.S. as well as abroad. In 1984 collection included accessories in precious metals and rare woods. Works with gold and platinum starting from a sketch, then depending on whether piece will be finished by hand or from a mold moves into metal or wax. Finishing by hand. Pieces include: Winchester buckle and palm cuffs.

## Kirk, Alexis (1938– )
*American jewelry designer*

Born in Los Angeles, his grandfather was a jeweler with Lalique in Paris and his father an artist with Walt Disney Studios. Studied jewelry design at the Rhode Island Institute of Design and the Boston Museum of Fine Arts. Studied and taught architecture at the University of Tennessee and while doing research on textiles at Eastman Kodak became interested in fashion. Opened workshop in Newport, Rhode Island, in 1961 to develop jewelry and clothing designs; this followed with the opening of three boutiques. Moved to New York and before establishing his own costume jewelry company in 1969 worked for Designs Research, El Greco Fashions, and Hattie Carnegie Inc.

## Klein, Anne (1923–1974)
*American designer*

Born in Brooklyn, New York, called the all-American designer of classic sportswear for the woman 5'4" and under. Responsible for transforming "junior" clothes from fussy, little-girl type clothes to sleek sophisticated fashion clothing. In 1948 with her first husband, Ben Klein, organized firm Junior Sophisticates; designer from 1951 to 1964. Formed Anne Klein & Co. in 1968 with her second husband; as of 1973 wholly owned by Takihyo Corporation of Japan. Remembered in the 1950s for nipped waist, full skirt; unbelted chemise; "little boy" look; use of white satin with gray flannel. In the 1960s for classic blazers, shirtdresses, long midis, leather gaucho pants, Western and American Indian accessories, Turkish rug coats, hot pants. In the 1970s interested in non-gimmicky, inter-related wardrobe of jackets, sweaters, pants, and skirts, and slinky, hooded jersey dresses for evening. Firm continued after her death, first with DONNA KARAN and LOUIS DELL'OLIO as co-designers; in mid-1980s continued to operate with Dell'Olio as sole designer.

## Klein, Calvin (1942– )
*American designer*

Attended High School of Art and Design and graduated from the Fashion Institute of Technology in 1962. With friend Barry Schwartz he formed Calvin Klein Ltd. in 1968. Designs include: women's and men's ready-to-wear; sportswear; blue jeans, furs, women's undergarments in designs similar to traditional men's undershirts and briefs, bed linens, cosmetics, skin care products, fragrances and pantyhose; a "couture" collection exclusively for Bergdorf-Goodman. Has promoted his products with provocative and controversial TV and print advertising especially ads for jeans and his fragrance, Obsession. His clothing is simple and refined and based on sportswear principles; uses luxurious natural fabrics as well as leather and suede in earth tones and neutrals.

## Lachasse
*British couture house*

Couture house opened in London in 1929, specializing in city and country suits; a branch of Paulette couture opened boutique in 1981. Designers included: Digby Morton (1929–1933), Hardy Amies (1934–1941), Michael (1941–1952), Charles Owen (1953–1974). One of the most successful houses, continues to operate into the 1980s.

## Lacroix, Christian (1951– )
*French designer*

Born in France; studied art history and classic Greek and Latin at Montpellier University; and in 1972 studied at L'École du Louvre in Paris. Worked as museum curator, assistant at Hermés in 1978, and at Guy Paulin. Studied fashion design in Japan. Returned to Paris and designed for JEAN PATOU from 1981 to mid-1987. Opened own couture and ready-to-wear business in mid-1987.

## Lagerfeld, Karl (1939– )
*French designer*

Born in Hamburg, Germany, arrived in Paris in 1953. Worked for BALMAIN from 1954 to

1957, having won an International Wool Secretariat award. Went to work for Chloe, an upscale ready-to-wear house, in 1963, as part of team of four designers. Became sole designer in 1972. From 1982 designed for CHANEL while continuing with Chloe; left Chloe in 1984 for Chanel and to begin collection under his own label. Designed sportswear collection specifically for U.S. in 1985. Designs furs and sportswear for FENDI. Other commitments include shoes for Mario Valentino and Charles Jourdan; sweaters for Ballantyne.

### Lane, Kenneth Jay (1932– )
*American jewelry designer*

Spent two years at the University of Michigan; graduated from the Rhode Island School of Design in 1954. While working on the promotion staff at *Vogue* magazine, he met Roger Vivier, shoe designer, and spent part of each year in Paris working with him. Went to work for Delman shoes as assistant designer; then to Christian Dior Shoes as associate designer. At the same time, in 1963, made some jewelry pieces which were photographed by fashion magazines and bought by some stores. He used his initials K.J.L. and by 1964 designed jewelry full time. Designs are first made in wax or by carving and twisting metal; uses plastic. Likes to see his costume jewelry worn with jewelry made of real gems.

### Lanvin, Jeanne (lahn-van, zhon) (1867–1946)
*French designer*

Born in Brittany, daughter of journalist, eldest of 10 children, apprentice at 13; started as milliner in 1890; designed children's clothes for daughter and friends which led to the establishment of her own business on the Faubourg St. Honoré where she remained for nearly 50 years. Remembered for *robes de style* of 18th and 19th c. flavor, wedding gowns, fantasy evening gowns with metallic embroideries, teagowns, dinner pajamas, dolman wraps and capes. Zouave bloomer skirt in 1936, and perfumes: "My Sin" and "Arpege." Her peak years were between World War I and II when she insisted on her brand of elegance, ignoring the simplicity of the 1920s Chanel school. Branch shops in French resorts added men's accessories, women's sport clothes, furs, children's wear, lingerie, and perfumes. Mme. Lanvin represented France and the couture at numerous international expositions, such as the World's Fair, New York, in 1939; received the Croix de la Légion d'Honneur. Died in 1946 at the age of 79; but house continued under directorship of daughter Contesse de Polignac, who hired Antonio del Castillo (1950–1962) and JULES-FRANÇOIS CRAHAY, (1963–1984). House now run by Bernard Lanvin and as designer, his wife, Maryll.

### Laroche, Guy (c. 1923– )
*French designer*

From cattle-farming family near La Rochelle. Dabbled in hair styling and millinery; worked three years on Seventh Avenue, eight years with JEAN DESSÈS in Paris. First collection in fall of 1957, mostly coats and suits. Greatest fame during the early 1960s; in 1980s maintains his couture atelier but has expanded into ready-to-wear and licensing agreements (intimate apparel, furs, luggage, sportswear, rainwear, dresses, blouses, sunglasses, accessories, fragrances). Remembered for back cowl drapes; short puffed hems for evening; schoolgirl dresses; loose lines in soft coats.

## Lauren, Ralph (1939– )
*American designer*

In 1967 Lauren persuaded a men's wear firm to handle neckties he had designed. They were made by hand in silk. This established the Polo neckwear division. Lauren was contracted to design the Polo line of men's wear for Norman Hilton and as of 1968 a separate company was established producing a total wardrobe for men. Introduced women's ready-to-wear made of Harris tweeds, camel's hair, silk in 1971; followed by Polo boy's wear; Western wear; Ralph Lauren for Girls; a less expensive men's line; Polo University Club for college students and young businessmen; Roughwear, a rugged outdoor collection. Licenses include: men's and women's ready-to-wear including men's robes, swimwear, and furnishings; small leathers, furs, scarfs, fragrances, cosmetics, skin care, luggage, and in 1983 home furnishings. Also designed costumes for men in *The Great Gatsby*, 1973 and for Woody Allen and Diane Keaton in *Annie Hall*, 1977.

## Legroux, House of
*French millinery house*

House of Legroux Soeurs (Heloise and Germaine) began in Roubaix in 1913. Opened in Paris in 1917. Under Mme. Germaine, became important millinery establishment of 1930s and 1940s. Known for off-the-face sport hats, pork pies, padre hats, picture hats with wide brims trimmed with feathers or fur.

## Lelong, Lucien (1889–1958)
*French couturier*

One of the great names in couture of the 1920s and through the 1940s; famed for elegant, feminine clothes of refined taste and lasting wearability. Couture house organized by his parents in 1886. Founded own business in 1919. Not a designer himself but an inspiration to a distinguished atelier of workers, including CHRISTIAN DIOR, PIERRE BALMAIN, HUBERT DE GIVENCHY, and Jean Schlumberger. Launched *Parfums Lucien Lelong* in 1926; started *Editions* department of ready-to-wear, forerunner of boutiques, in 1934; President of the Chambre Syndicale de la Couture from 1937 to 1947. Received Croix de Guerre in World War I; represented couture in World War II during German occupation, (1940–1945), frustrating plan to move couture to Berlin; responsible for revitalizing couture after war. Retired in 1947, because of ill health; died May 1958.

## Leser, Tina (1910–1986)
*American designer*

Born in Philadelphia, member of Wetherill family; traveled extensively in Far East and Europe as child; studied at School of Industrial Art and Academy of Fine Arts, Philadelphia, and at the Sorbonne, Paris. Lived in Hawaii from 1936 to 1942, operating retail store, selling her own hand-blocked floral prints in playclothes. Returned to New York in 1942 and showed her collection of Hawaiian-inspired fun clothes. Associated with Edwin H. Foreman, Inc. from 1943 to 1952; established own company, Tina Leser Inc. in 1952. Retired in 1964; returned to design from 1966 to 1982. Remembered for sarong playclothes; water-boy pants; painted and sequinned cotton blouses; wrapped pareo skirt with bandeau top; costume jewelry in cork, coral, and shells, travel-inspired Mexican, Haitian, Japanese, Indian fabrics, used in original trousers, easy coverup tops, long at-home robes. Credited with making the first dress from cashmere.

### Louiseboulanger
*French designer*

Combination of her name, Louise Boulanger. Started at age 13 as workroom girl; period with Mme. Cheruit. Established own house in 1923 on rue de Berri; flourished until early 1930s. Never influenced by contemporary events or other designers; clothes were advanced in design, more super-chic than pretty. Known for beautiful colors in floral printed taffetas, bias-cut gowns, and evening gowns with billowing massed fullness.

### Lucile (Lady Duff Gordon) (1862(?)–1935)
*British designer*

Born Lucy Kennedy; sister of novelist Elinor Glyn. First woman to enter couture; houses in Paris, London, New York, and Chicago. Contemporary of POIRET, WORTH, and DOUCET in the Edwardian pre-World War I period. Famous for "boudoir lampshade" style of flowing pastel teagowns, chiffon ballroom-dancing dresses laden with beads and lace, coat dresses and jacket costumes that faded from fashion after 1914. Employed CAPT. EDWARD MOLYNEUX at age 17 in first job. Dressed dancers Irene Castle and Florence Walton and actresses; traveled with her celebrated mannequins, Hébé and Dolores, forerunners of couture house models.

### Mackie, Bob (1940– )
*American designer*

Studied art and design in Los Angeles. Worked as sketcher for Jean Louis and Edith Head as well as for Ray Aghayan, his future partner. Mackie and Aghayan have designed costumes for such celebrities as Marlene Dietrich, Carol Burnett, Barbra Streisand, and Cher. Has received Academy Award nominations for costumes designed for *Lady Sings the Blues*, 1972 (with Aghayan and Norma Koch); *Funny Lady*, 1975 (with Aghayan). In mid-1980s successful with a ready-to-wear collection emphasizing glamorous evening clothes.

### Mad Carpentier (mad car-pont-e-ay)
*French couture house*

Partnership of two women, Mad Maltezas, designer, and Suzy Carpentier, organizer and liaison with customers. Both having worked with VIONNET, carried on her tradition of excellence in their own small establishment in 1939; remained open during World War II; regained success after war. House closed in 1957.

### Mainbocher (man-bow-shay) (1890–1976)
*American couturier*

Born Main Rousseau Bocher in Chicago, Illinois; studied art at Chicago Academy of Fine Arts, and then in New York, Paris, and Munich. Went to Paris in 1917 with an

American ambulance unit; stayed after war to study singing. Supported himself as fashion illustrator for *Harper's Bazaar* and *Vogue*. Became a full-time journalist in 1922; first as Paris editor for *Vogue*, then editor of French *Vogue* before resigning to open his own salon in Paris in 1929. Left Paris at outbreak of World War II and opened couture house in New York in 1939. Closed business in June 1971. Noted for Duchess of Windsor's wedding dress in 1936; WAVES' (Women in the Navy) uniform in 1942; Girl Scout uniform in 1948. Ideas widely copied: print-bordered and lined sweaters to match dresses; beaded evening sweaters; dirndl dresses with self-fabric incrustations, often in pastel check gingham; fur-lined coats; rain suits; tweed dinner suits with delicate blouses; embroidered apron evening dresses; and always short white kid gloves, pearl chokers, plain pumps.

## Mandelli, Mariuccia (1933?– )
*Italian designer*

As early as eight years old she wanted to be a designer. First show in 1967 won her excellent reviews and business boomed. With her husband, Aldo Pinto, as partner she formed knitwear company Kriziamaglia in early 1970s. Known for animal sweaters—at each collection a different bird or beast is emphasized. Introduced hot pants in 1960s. Designs include children's wear, a boutique line, and fragrances.

## Maxwell, Vera (1903– )
*American designer*

Worked first with sportswear and coat houses, Adler & Adler and Max Milstein, before opening her own business on Seventh Avenue. Believed in classic approach to go-together separates in finest quality Scottish tweeds, wool jersey, raw silk, Indian embroideries, etc. Inspired by men's Harris tweed jackets and gray flannel Oxford bags. Noteworthy innovations: weekend wardrobe, 1935; Einstein jacket, 1936; fencing suit, 1940; riding-habit suit; war-workers' clothes under L-85 rules; slit-side, braid-edged mandarin coat; wrap-tied blouse; three-piece vest suit; chesterfield coat with slacks; print dress matched to print-lined coat; sleeveless, slit-sided suede "paletot" coats. Honored by retrospective show of designs at Smithsonian Institution in Washington, D.C. in 1970. Party and show given to honor her 75th birthday and her 50th year as a designer at the Museum of the City of New York. Continued to work until early in 1985, when she closed her business. In 1986 designed a collection of dresses, coats, and sportswear for the Peter Lynne Division of Gulf Enterprises.

## McCardell, Claire (1906–1958)
*American designer*

Studied at Parsons School in New York and in Paris. Worked for Robert Turk, Inc., as a model and assistant designer in 1929; in 1931 went with Turk to work at Townley Frocks Inc. After his death, stayed with Townley until 1938; then to Hattie Carnegie for two years. In 1940, returned to Townley, first as designer, then as designer-partner, remaining until her death at the age of 52. Considered top all-American designer of 1940s and 1950s, specializing in practical clothes for average working girl. Credited with originating the "American Look," *i.e.*, the separates concept inspired by travel needs, using sturdy cotton denims, ticking, gingham, and wool jersey. Gathered ideas from basic workclothes of farmers, railroad workers, soldiers and sportsmen, *e.g.*, hook-and-eye fasteners, Levi's topstitching, rivets, side trouser pockets. Many firsts: the monastic dress with natural shoulders and tied waist; harem pajamas; the POPOVER, a surplice-wrapped housedress; kitchen dinner dress; bareback summer dress; long cotton Empire dress, tiny puffed sleeves; diaper-wrap one-piece swimsuit; shoulder bolero over halter dress; balloon bloomer playsuit; signature spaghetti belts; ballet slippers for street.

## McFadden, Mary (1936– )
*American designer*

Attended Traphagen School of Fashion in New York, École Lubec in Paris; studied sociology at Columbia University and at the New School of Social Research. Was director of public relations for Christian Dior-New York from 1962 to 1964. Married a DeBeers' executive and moved to Africa in 1964; became editor of *Vogue* South Africa and when publication ceased went to work on both the French and American *Vogue* staffs. Remarried in 1968 and moved to Rhodesia where she founded "Vokutu," a sculpture workshop for native artists. Returned to New York in 1970 and went to work for *Vogue* as Special Projects Editor. Henri Bendel bought three tunics she had designed from Chinese and African silks she had collected on her trips. The silks were hand painted using resist techniques with oriental colorings. Mary McFadden, Inc. was formed in 1976. Designs are made of unique fabrics using fine pleating and quilting with ropes wrapping the body. She was presented with an award by the American Printed Fabric Council for her approach to fabrics and prints. Designs include: lingerie and at-home wear, Simplicity Patterns, scarfs, eyewear, furs, shoes, bed and bath linens, and upholstery fabrics.

## Missoni, Rosita & Ottavio (Tai)
*Italian designers*

Met in London at the 1948 Olympics where Ottavio (Tai) was member of Italian track team and Rosita a student of languages. Married in 1953 and went into business with four knitting machines. Originally hired free-lance designers such as EMMANUELLE KHANH and Christiane Bailly to style their line. Currently Rosita designs clothing and Tai the knit fabrics. Colors are worked out by Tai always aware of distinctive patterns and stitches. Rosita drapes directly onto a model maintaining simple shapes emphasizing knit designs. A family-run business, their three children are all involved: Vittorio, as administrator; Luca works with his father to develop new patterns, and Angela handles public relations. Styles are so classic that their designs are difficult to date.

## Miyake, Issey (me-ya-key, ee-see) (1938– )
*Japanese designer*

Born in Hiroshima, Japan, he moved to Paris in 1965 to study at La Chambre Syndicale de la Couture Parisienne. Worked as assistant at GUY LAROCHE and GIVENCHY from 1966 to 1968; went New York to work with GEOFFREY BEENE in 1969. Established Miyake Design Studio and Issey Miyake International in Tokyo in 1970; showed in Paris for the first time in 1973; established a company in Europe in 1979 and in the U.S. in 1982. He combines Japanese attitudes of fashion with exotic fabrics of his own designs.

## Molyneux, Edward (1891–1974)
*French couturier*

Born in Ireland; aristocrat, sportsman, officer in Duke of Wellington Regiment, art student. Started at 17 as designer with LUCILE working in London, Chicago, and New York until 1914. Captain in British Army during World War I, where he lost an eye. Opened own house in Paris in 1919, on rue Royale, next to Maxim's. Designed well-bred, elegant, fluid clothes for such celebrities as Gertrude Lawrence, Lynn Fontanne, Princess Marina, and Duchess of Windsor. Remembered for purity of line in printed silk suits with pleated skirts; timeless, softly tailored navy-blue suits, coats, capes; use of zippers to mould figure in 1937; handkerchief-point skirts; ostrich trim; bright Gauguin pink and *bois de rose* as accents with navy blue. Worked for national defense, established international canteen during World War II. Returned to Paris house in 1949, adding furs, lingerie, millinery, and perfumes. One of the original members of the Incorporated Society of London Fashion Designers in 1942. Because of ill health, turned over Paris house to Jacques Griffe in 1950. Returned to Jamaica, West Indies, to devote time to painting, his collection of Impressionist paintings, and travel. Persuaded to reopen in Paris, January 1965, as Studio Molyneux; brought first ready-to-wear collection to U.S. in 1965; venture was not successful. Retired again to Antibes.

## Montana, Claude (1949– )
*French designer*

On a trip to London in 1971 in order to earn money to stay there, he designed papier-mâché jewelry encrusted with rhinestones: stayed for a year. Returned to Paris where he went to work for a leather firm, before establishing himself in his own business. Characteristics: bold, well-defined shapes. His clothes are sold in the better stores in the U.S. as well as in Italy, England, and Germany.

## Mori, Hanae (1925– )
*Japanese designer*

Opened small boutique in Shinjuku section of Tokyo where designs attracted members of the Japanese film industry. Designed costumes for films in 1955. Opened shop on the Ginza and went on to develop multi-million dollar international business. Couture collection shown in Paris in 1977; continues to show there each season. Ready-to-wear sold in fine stores around the world; her boutiques in many countries sell sportswear and accessories. Designed skiwear for the Sapporo Winter Olympic Games in 1972. U.S. business is conducted from a townhouse/showroom on East 79th Street in New York City. She uses unusual and beautiful fabrics, with especially huge flowers, butterflies and classic Japanese feminine motifs. Styles are Western with Oriental details; best known for evening or at-home entertaining wear.

## Mugler, Thierry (1946– )
*French designer*

Made his own clothes as a teenager, his early endeavors include work for the Strasbourg ballet company as well as window dressing for Paris boutiques. Moved to England in 1968 and then on to Amsterdam before returning to Paris two years later. First collection in 1971 under the label Café de Paris and by 1973 designed under his own label. Characteristics include: broad shoulders and well-defined waists.

## Muir, Jean (1933– )
*British designer*

Started as sketcher at Liberty, designed for six years at Jaeger; under her own label for Jane and Jane in 1962; established Jean Muir, Inc. in 1966. Opened the Jean Muir Shop in Henri Bendel, New York, in 1967. Characteristics: soft, classic tailored shapes in leathers or soft fabrics. In 1983 awarded Commander of the British Empire (C.B.E.).

## Norell, Norman (1900–1972)
*American designer*

Born Norman Levinson in Noblesville, Indiana, son of haberdashery store owner in Indianapolis. Came to N.Y. in 1919 to study at Parsons School of Design. Started with theatrical and movie designing for Paramount Pictures and Brooks Costume Co. In 1924 worked for Charles Armour, then for Hattie Carnegie from 1928 to 1940. Partnership in firm Traina-Norell followed in 1941. After death of Traina in 1960, formed own company, Norman Norell, Inc. Rated as top American designer on Seventh Avenue "Dean of the fashion industry," "the American Balenciaga." Known for precision tailoring, dateless purity of line, conservative elegance in the finest imported fabrics; never followed fads. Remembered for trouser-suits for town and travel, widely flared day skirts, at-home "smoking" robe, sweater tops with luxury skirts, straight wool jersey chemises, double-breasted coats over pussy-cat bow blouses and straight skirts, slinky sequinned sheaths, the sailor look. First designer elected to Hall of Fame by Coty Award judges in 1958. Founder and president of the Council of Fashion Designers of America. Suffered stroke on eve of his retrospective show at the Metropolitan Museum of Art, October 15, 1972; died ten days later. Firm continued for a short time after his death under GUSTAVE TASSELL.

## Olive, Frank (1929– )
*American millinery designer*

Studied art and fashion in Milwaukee and Chicago; went to California to try costume design. Worked for a dance company in San Francisco before arriving in New York in early 1950s hoping to design for the theater. NORELL, after reviewing some of his sketches, suggested that Olive design hats. Apprenticed with Chanda, sold fabrics, worked in the Saks Fifth Avenue custom hat department, Tatiana, and Emme. His own firm represents three major hat collections: "Counterfits," mass-market; "Frank's Girl," moderate-priced; "Frank Olive," designer label. Also designs private collections for some clients.

## Oliver, André (1932– )
*French designer*

Born in Toulouse; graduated from École des Beaux Arts in Paris. Joined PIERRE CARDIN in 1955 designing men's wear. Eventually created ready-to-wear for both men and women. Association with Cardin continues as artistic director of Cardin couture with total artistic control, sharing design responsibilities. Cardin gives him full credit for his design contribution.

## Paquin, House of (pak-ann)
*French couture house*

House of Paquin founded in 1891 by Mme. Paquin and banker husband on rue de la Paix. Name is synonymous with elegance in the first decade of 20th c. First woman to achieve importance in haute couture. Remembered for: fur-trimmed tailored suits, furs, lingerie; evening dresses in white, gold lamé, and pale green; blue serge suit trimmed with gold braid and buttons; fine workmanship and no two dresses alike. First to take mannequins to the opera or to the races, as many as ten in same costume. Customers included queens of Belgium, Portugal, and Spain; and the stars of *La Belle Époque*, Liane de Pougy and La Belle Otero, President of the fashion section of the Paris Exposition in 1900; founded first foreign branch of a couture house in London in 1912, and later in Madrid and in Buenos Aires. Mme. Paquin retired in 1920 after selling firm, she died in 1936. House closed in July 1956.

## Parnis, Mollie (1905– )
*American designer*

Born in New York City. One of the most successful women designers on Seventh Avenue. Started in 1939 as designer for Parnis-Livingston with husband, Leon Livingston, specializing in flattering, feminine dresses and ensembles for the well-to-do woman over 30. Boutique collection designed for many years by Morty Sussman until his death in 1979. Mollie Parnis Studio collection aimed at a younger woman was organized in 1979. At end of 1984 dissolved her firm to become a "part-time" consultant at Chevette Lingerie, owned by her nephew. She returned to work full time and produced her first loungewear collection for Chevette, Mollie Parnis At Home, for fall 1985. As a philanthropist, contributed to scholarships in fashion schools and established the Livingston Journalism Awards in memory of her son Robert. Donated funds for creating small parks in underprivileged areas of New York City and Jerusalem. One of the founders of the Council of Fashion Designers of America.

## Patou, Jean (pa-too, zhon) (1887–1936)
*French couturier*

One of the great names in couture of 1920s, 1930s, who brought glamour and showmanship to fashion. He was more of a businessman than designer, specializing in lady-like, elegant and uncluttered country-club clothes. Showed first in 1914; interrupted by World War I in which he served as Captain of Zouaves; reopened in 1919 in shop challed *Parry* and after whole first collection was bought by an American, started new business as Jean Patou on rue St. Florentin, waging war against Chanel's low-waisted garçonne look. Remembered for sensation in 1929 when he lengthened skirts to the ankle, revived natural waistline; made long simple gown to go with important jewels; designed weekend wardrobes; imported six American mannequins to Paris using them alongside French mannequins to show his designs. Also one of first to have gala champagne evening openings; cocktail bar in his shop; exquisite bottles for perfumes—"Amour-Amour" and "Joy." Personally dynamic, charming, fond of fancy-dress balls and devoted to American clientele. Died of stroke, age 49, in 1936. House remains open under Raymond Barbas with series of resident designers: MARC BOHAN (1953–1956), KARL LAGERFELD (1960–1963), Michael Goma (1963–1973), Angelo Tarlazzi (1973–1976), Roy Gonzalez (1977–1982), CHRISTIAN LACROIX (1982–1986).

## Pedlar, Sylvia (1901–1972)
*American lingerie designer*

Born in New York; studied at Cooper Union and Art Students League to be a fashion artist. Founded Iris Lingerie in 1929, and designed there for 40 years. Remembered for reviving the peignoir and matching long-sleeved gown, the Istanbul harem-hem gown, the toga nightdress, short chemise-slip, lace-trimmed silk gowns—sometimes doubling as evening dresses. Retired in 1970. Died in 1972.

## Peretti, Elsa (1940– )
*American jewelry designer*

Born in Florence, Italy. Received a diploma in interior design and worked for an architect. Arrived in London and began modeling; at suggestion of Wilhelmina came to New York. Worked for design firms including HALSTON and OSCAR DE LA RENTA. Designed a few pieces of silver jewelry in 1969 which were used by SANT'ANGELO and Halston. Began working for Tiffany & Co. in 1974—the first time Tiffany carried silver jewelry. Designs include: heart-shaped buckles, silver horseshoe-shaped buckle on a long leather belt (also designed in horn, ebony and ivory); pendants in the form of small vases; small open, slightly lopsided heart pendant that slides on a chain; diamonds-by-the-yard. She has designed a refillable rock crystal bottle for her perfume sold by Tiffany as well as desk and table accessories.

## Piguet, Robert (pee-geh) (1901–1953)
*French couturier*

Born in Yverdon, Switzerland, son of banker. Came to Paris at age 17 to study design with Redfern and POIRET from 1918 to 1928. Opened own house in 1933, using free-lance designers. Great couturiers of the future worked for him: GIVENCHY at age 17 and DIOR in 1937, who said Piguet taught him "the virtues of simplicity...how to suppress." JAMES GALANOS worked for him for three months without pay. Known for refined simplicity of black and white dresses, afternoon clothes, tailored suits with vests, fur-trimmed coats, especially styled for petite women. Closed house in 1951.

## Pipart, Gérard (pee-par, zher-ar) (1933– )
*French couturier*

At age 16, sold sketches to BALMAIN and FATH, and to GIVENCHY three years later; worked with MARC BOHAN; served in army two years. Early star of French ready-to-wear, working with Germaine et Jane, Chloe, and Jean Baillie, Hemcey, gaining experience in youth-oriented fashion. In 1963, at age 30, joined NINA RICCI as chief designer, succeeding JULES-FRANÇOIS CRAHAY; continues at House of Ricci where he is responsible for both couture and boutique collections.

## Poiret, Paul (pwar-ay) (1880–1944)
*French designer*

Labelled King of Fashion from 1904 to 1924. Born in Paris, son of cloth merchant; began by dressing wooden doll; sold sketches to couturiers. First employed by DOUCET in 1896, where he designed for actresses Réjane and Sarah Bernhardt; developed passion for theatrical costuming. Short period at HOUSE OF WORTH. Opened own house in 1904; became fashion tyrant over women, imposed his original ideas and strident colors; banned the corset; shackled legs with the harem and hobble skirts. Remembered for extreme Orientalism, turban with aigrette, minaret skirt, kimono-sleeved tunics, exotic embroidery, barbaric jewels, and eye makeup. Friend of ballet impresario, Diaghilev, and important artists, Bakst, Raoul Dufy, etc., who designed fabrics for him. First couturier to present perfume, called "Rosine." First to travel in 1912 to foreign capitals with entourage of 12 live mannequins; designed new uniform for French soldier in 1914; founded crafts school called Martine. Spent fortunes on costume balls and decorations of his homes. After World War I refused to change his exotic image so faded from the fashion scene. His last display was at the *1925 Èxposition International des Arts Decoratifs et Industriels Modernes* in Paris. Died in Paris in 1944 after years of poverty and illness, leaving his mark on the taste of two decades. Retrospective exhibitions have been held in the Houston Museum of Fine Arts and at the Fashion Institute of Technology in N.Y.

## Porter, Thea (1927– )
*British designer*

Born Dorothea Seal in Damascus; lived in Beirut, Lebanon, and in Turkey from 1950 to 1963. Early environment instilled a fascination with Orientalia. Came to London in 1966 and opened interior design shop in Soho, where her collection of embroidered caftans caught on. Became known for fantasy long clothes with ethnic overtones based on Far Eastern, Japanese, Renaissance, Victorian Gothic designs; all timeless and made in unusual fabrics. In 1968 her clothes sold at Vidal Sassoon's, London, and in Henri Bendel, N.Y. By early 1970s preferred the clothes of the 1940s, used chiffon, mixing several prints in one costume. Opened N.Y. boutique in 1971, closed in 1972. Her career reflects the period of the 1960s and 1970s, anti-couture in mood.

## Potter, Clare
*American designer*

One of the first group of all-American designers honored by Dorothy Shaver at Lord & Taylor in late 1930s. Graduate of Pratt Institute; majored in portrait painting; entered fashion field designing embroidery. Formed own business on Seventh Avenue under name *Clarepotter* during 1940s and 1950s, making classic sport, at-home and dinner clothes. Noted for unusual color combinations, refinement of cut, and no extraneous trimmings. Worked under name Potter Designs Inc. in 1960s; had wholesale firm, Timbertop Inc., in West Nyack, N.Y.

## Premet, House of (prem-eh)
*French couture house*

House of Premet opened around 1911 with Mme. Premet as designer; followed by Mme.

Lefranc. Most successful under Mme. Charlotte from 1918 on through the 1920s. Her biggest commercial success in 1922 was simple black dress called "La Garçonne," which sold in the millions. MME. GRES apprenticed at the House of Premet.

## Pucci, Emilio (poo-chee) (1914– )
*Italian designer*

An aristocrat (Marchese Pucci di Barsento), living in Pucci Palace in Florence; sportsman, Olympic skier, Air Force pilot, member of Italian Parliament. Discovered as designer of own ski clothes by American photograper Toni Frissell in 1947; designed ski wear for Lord & Taylor, New York, following year. Opened workshop in Florence in 1949, and by 1950 had couture house under name *Emilio*, with boutiques in Capri, Rome, Elba, and Montecatini. Known for brilliant heraldic prints on sheer silk jersey, made into clinging chemises, at-home robes, tights; signature scarfs and dresses; resort shirts in designs from Sienese banners, Sicilian or African motifs; the "capsula" (jumpsuit tapered to cover feet with soft boots). The Pucci Look reigned as the status symbol throughout the 1960s and was widely imitated in less expensive jerseys. Design products include: accessories, sportswear, intimate apparel, fragrances for men and women, porcelain, bath linens, and rugs.

## Pulitzer, Lily (1932– )
*American designer*

Socialite daughter of Mrs. Ogden Phipps, living in Palm Beach, Florida, and married to Herbert Pulitzer when in 1960 she designed and sold a printed-cotton shift called a LILLY, which proliferated into nationwide fashion in the 1960s and 1970s. Designed a child's version, called "Minnie," print slacks for men, "sneaky Pete" nightshirts, ruffled hems and short sleeves added to basic Lilly in 1970s. Company was liquidated in mid-1980s.

## Quant, Mary (1934– )
*British designer*

Credited with starting the Chelsea or Mod Look in the mid-1950s, making London the most influential fashion center at that time. Pioneered in body stockings, MOUSERS, hot pants, cosmetics, the layered principle of dressing, etc. At age 23, had two shops called Bazaar, selling her own idea of spirited, unconventional clothes, *e.g.*, tight pants, shaggy sweaters, thick stockings, boyish knickerbockers. By 1967, started the miniskirt revolution, introduced denim, colored flannel, vinyl in "kooky" (her word) clothes, with 1920s flavor. Within ten years had made a less expensive line Ginger, joined huge U.S. department-store chain J.C. Penney Co.; received the O.B.E. on the Queen's Honor List; added furs, lingerie, and cosmetics; designed for Puritan's Youthquake promotion in U.S. Married to Alexander Plunkett-Greene, partner since the beginning. Museum of London organized retrospective exhibit in 1973.

## Rabanne, Paco (1934– )
*French designer*

Born in San Sebastian, Spain, son of Balenciaga's head dressmaker; studied architecture; moved into designing plastic accessories. Opened in Paris in 1966, age 32, causing a sensation with his metal-linked plastic-disk dresses, sun goggles and jewelry made of plastic in primary colors. Continued the linked-disk principle in fur-patched coats, leather-patch dresses, masses of buttons laced with wire, strips of aluminum. Also pioneered in fake-suede dresses in 1970; knit-and-fur coats; dresses of ribbons, feathers, or tassels linked for suppleness. Has two successful fragrances, "Calandre" for women, and "Paco" for men.

## Reboux, Caroline (reh-boo) (1837?–1927)
*French millinery designer*

Founded the most prestigious millinery house in Paris, both during *La Belle Époch* and later in the 1920s and 1930s; daughter of a journalist, who was discovered by same Princess Metternick who sponsored couturier Worth in 1865. Installed in rue de la Paix in 1870, creating hats for leading actresses and aristocracy; barred famous cocottes of the era from her establishment because of her high morals. After her death in 1927, house continued leadership under Mme. Lucienne, making the head-fitting felt cloche the status symbol of fashion for many years. Noted for profile brims, dipping low on one side; forward-tilt tricorns; open-crown lamé turbans; flower bandeaus.

## Redfern, House of
*British couture house*

London house established in 1841 by Englishman John Redfern, dressmaker for Queen Victoria and the aristocacy, who sent his son, Charles Poynter Redfern, to Paris to represent firm in 1881. Responsible for jersey suit made for Lillie Langtry, "Jersey Lil," in 1879. Known for his sober, elegant dark-blue tailored suits. Designed first woman's uniform for the International Red Cross in 1916. To satisfy his imagination, also designed elaborate theater costumes, notably for Mary Garden and Sarah Bernhardt.

## Regny, Jane
*First American sportswear designer*

Pioneer of couture sports clothes in the 1920s. Started in 1922 designing simple clothes for active or spectator sports, the kind of clothes suited to her own life and to that of socialite friends. Remembered for sweaters in geometric patterns, yachting suits with mess jackets and wide pleated pants, three-piece bathing ensembles, three- or four-color wool-jersey dresses with godet or pleated ease.

## Rhodes, Zandra (1942– )
*British designer*

Textile designer graduating from the Royal College of Art in 1966; producing her own designs by 1969. Considered an original and eccentric, wearing fanciful face makeup, rainbow-tinted hair, draperies with ragged ends flying, head swathed in scarfs. Textile innovations include: hand-screened prints on soft fabrics, Art Deco motifs, lipsticks, Teddy bears, zigzags, big splashy patterns. Designed soft, butterfly dresses, slit-sided chiffons, edges cut by pinking shears.

### Ricci, Nina (re-chee, neena) (1883–1970)
*French couturier*

Born Marie Nielli in Turin, Italy; married to Louis Ricci, jeweler. Began by dressing dolls; at age 13 came to Paris to work as seamstress; by 1905 was designing own models on live mannequins. Opened Nina Ricci, on rue des Capucines in 1932; specialized in dresses for mature, elegant women and trousseaux for young women, graceful with superb detailed workmanship, the antithesis of her contemporary Gabrielle Chanel. One of first to show lower-priced models in a boutique. Famous for her perfume, "L'Air du Temps," in a Lalique bottle. Since 1945, house has been managed by son, Robert Ricci, with various designers; JULES-FRANÇOIS CRAHAY (1954–1963) and, since then, GERARD PIPART.

### Rochas, Marcel (ro-shass, mar-sell) (1902–1955)
*French couturier*

Born in Paris. Opened couture house about 1924 in the Faubourg Saint-Honoré, moved to avenue Matignon in 1931. Became popular after eight women appeared at same party wearing identical gowns of his design. Full of fantastic ideas: special bird- and flower-patterned fabric; combinations of as many as ten colors; lots of lace, ribbon, and tulle and a feminine, square-shouldered, hourglass silhouette several years ahead of the New Look. In 1948, invented new corset call GUÉPIERE, which cinched the natural waist. Had boutique for separates and accessories; designed for films; wrote *Twenty-five Years of Parisian Elegance 1925–1950*. Married three times. Packaged famous perfume, "Femme," in black lace.

### Roser, Maud (rose-eh, mode)
*French millinery designer*

Paris milliner, stared in 1926. Opened Maud et Nano in 1942. Known for: red-felt ear-hung beret, called "Danilo," shown with Dior's New Look in 1947; series of small hats called "Les Toits de Paris." Pioneered showing of hat collections before couture, claiming equal importance.

### Rouff, Maggy (roof) (1897–1971)
*French couturière*

Daughter of Austrian, Besancon de Wagner, head of house of Drécoll. Planned to be surgeon but decided on couture in 1918, learning to cut and sew; considered herself an artist. Started own business in 1929 and for 25 years was among the leaders of Paris fashion, standing for refined, feminine elegance as opposed to Chanel's *garçonne* mode. Retired in 1948.

### Roy, Hippolyte (roy, ippo-leet) (1763–1829)
*French couturier*

Known as *Leroy*; Napoleonic couturier in early 19th c., vain, garrulous, arrogant tailor, son of stagehand at Paris opera, encouraged by ROSE BERTIN. Switched to Republican side after French Revolution and designed red, white, and blue patriotic dress. Became dictator of fashion for Empress Josephine, Mme. Tallien, Mme. Récamier, Mme. de Stael, and European royalty. Directed by Napoleon to design luxurious dress to encourage French industry. Created the modified classical lines to be known as Empire, *e.g.*, slim high-waisted gowns in sheer fabrics, heavily embroidered borders, cashmere shawls, brocade and velvet court gowns. Peak of fame at Napoleon's coronation, staged by artist Jacques Louis David. Continued to work for Josephine's successor, his style unchanged through Directorate, Consulate, and Empire—although he never made two dresses alike.

## Rykiel, Sonia (rye-kel)
*French designer*

Started making maternity clothes for herself; designed for husband's firm, Laura. Opened Sonia Rykiel Boutique in 1968, in Paris department store Galeries Lafayette; followed by her own boutique on the Left Bank. Known for tight, long sweaters; sheer gowns over body stockings, long, slit-sided day skirts, layered dresses and sweaters with thick, roll-back cuffs, high-rise wide pants. Her liberated, unconstructed clothes range from folkloric fantasy to basic classics.

## Saint Cyr, Claude (san-seer)
*French millinery designer*

Opened in 1937. Excellent businesswoman who used designers to create her hats. Became one of top-rated houses in 1940s and 1950s. Launched sports and tailored hats in "winter white." Asked to make hats for Queen Elizabeth II of England; had branch in couture house of NORMAN HARTNELL in London.

## Saint Laurent, Yves (sanh la-rahn, eve) (1936– )
*French designer*

Born on Oran, Algeria. Won prize for fashion sketch in design competition judged by Dior; offered position as assistant to Dior. Came to Paris in 1953 at 17 and from 1954 to 1957 worked in the House of Dior. Inherited top designing post at Dior's death in 1957. Time out for army duty and illness from 1960–1962. Opened own house on rue Spontini in 1962 at age 23 with Pierre Bergé; opened a series of prêt-à-porter boutiques called *Rive Gauche* in 1966; designed men's wear in 1974. Licenses using the famous YSL initials include: sweaters, bed and bath linens, eyeglasses, scarfs, children's wear. Created fragrances including "Y," "Rive Gauche," "Opium," and "Paris." Since then has successfully interpreted the contemporary moods of fashion; considered the most influential modern designer for the sophisticated woman. Remembered for the trapeze line, 1958, in the first Dior collection, pea jackets; blazers; chemises divided into Mondrian-blocks of bold color; sportive leather; city pants; military jackets; the nude look in see-through shirts and transparent dresses over nude body stockings in 1966; the fantasy of the rich peasants; smoking jackets; spencer jackets; the tuxedo look. Also designed for theater and ballet especially for Zizi Jeanmaire. By early 1970s, became almost anti-couture, believed in his lower-priced ready-to-wear and designed his couture mainly for private customers. In December 1963 the Metropolitan Museum of Art, New York, mounted a retrospective of 25 years of his work, the first time a living designer has been so honored.

## Sanchez, Fernando (1930?– )
*American lingerie designer*

Born in Spain; studied at École Chambre Syndicale de la Couture in Paris. Won a prize from the International Wool Secretariat (as did Saint Laurent). Both went on to work for CHRISTIAN DIOR—Sanchez handling lingerie. Came to New York to work with the lines represented at Dior European boutiques. Also designed furs for Revillon for approximately 12 years becoming known for such designs as the hide-out mink coat; stopped designing furs until 1984 when he re-signed with Revillon. Opened own lingerie firm in 1973. Known for: lace-trimmed silk gowns, camisole tops, boxer shorts, bikini pants. Developed lingerie based on sportswear principles; mixes color, fabrics, and lengths. Signed with Vanity Fair in 1984 to design a moderate-price line of sleep and loungewear.

## Sant'Angelo, Giorgio (1936– )
*American designer*

Trained as an architect and industrial designer; won scholarship to study art in France with Picasso; came to U.S. in 1962 and created cartoons for Walt Disney. Moved to N.Y. in 1963 and free-lanced as textile designer and stylist; served as design consultant on various environmental projects. Used Lucite for home and fashion accessories n 1964. Founded Sant'Angelo Ready-to-Wear in 1966; di Sant'Angelo, Inc. in 1968. Designs ready-to-wear and separates under the Giorgio Sant'Angelo label. Licenses include: swimwear and active sportswear, furs, tailored suits, outerwear, men's outerwear, neckties and men's wear, fragrances, sheets and domestics, furniture, rugs and carpets. Noted for ethnic themes such as the gypsy look, American Indian, Chinese; body stocking and bodysuit in brilliant bi- and tri-colors to match T-shirts and shorts. Continues to design clothes a bit out of the ordinary and maintains a couture operation for a roster of celebrities.

## Scaasi, Arnold (1931– )
*American designer*

Born Arnold Isaacs in Montreal, Canada; uses his name spelled backwards. Studied at École Chambre Syndicale in Paris; apprenticed with PAQUIN. Arrived in N.Y. and worked as sketcher for CHARLES JAMES; in 1957 opened his own wholesale business. Bought and renovated a Manhattan town house in 1960 for his ready-to-wear collections; switched to couture in 1963. Returned to ready-to-wear with Arnold Scaasi Boutique, in 1983, and showed cocktail and evening dresses in the mid-1980s. Known for spectacular evening wear in luxurious fabrics, often fur- or feather-trimmed, appealing to glamorous actresses and socialites. Has also designed costume jewelry, men's neckties and sweaters, and furs.

## Scherrer, Jean-Louis (1936– )
*French designer*

Designer of soft, refined dresses; popular with wealthy private customers from the 1960s. Began by designing for DIOR about 1959; three years with Louis Feraud; opened own house on avenue Montaigne in 1962. Works in couture and ready-to-wear.

## Schiaparelli, Elsa (skap-a-rell-ee) (1890–1973)
*French couturière*

Born in Rome, daughter of professor of Oriental languages, niece of famous astronomer; has one daughter, Gogo, and granddaughters, Marisa and Berynthia (Berry) Berenson (Mrs. Anthony Perkins). One of the most creative, unconventional couturières of 1930s and 1940s; an innovator whose clothes and accessories were startling conversation pieces, the epitome of hard chic. First designed dressmaker sweaters with designs knit in, *e.g.*, white collar and bow-tie on black. By 1929, had own business, *Pour le Sport*, in rue de la Paix and first boutique at 4 Place Vendôme in 1935. Spectacular success with avant-garde sweaters with tattoo or skeleton motifs; hot-pink color, "Shocking," hourglass-torso bottle of "Shocking" perfume; first evening dress with own jacket; guardsman's coat with square padded shoulders; trouser skirts for all occasions; use of zippers, jewelers' buttons, padlocks and dog-leash fastenings; doll hats, some shaped like lambchops or pink-heeled shoes; printed newsprint and glass fabrics; flying and golf suits, etc. Traveled extensively in India, Portugal, North Africa, Peru, Tyrol, using ideas from native costumes. Only couturière to be in French Industries Fair in Russia. Close friendship with artists Dali, Cocteau, Van Dongen, Schlumberger, and Man Ray, all of whom contributed designs. Stopped designing in 1940 for duration of World War II. Came to the U.S. and returned to Paris after liberation. Reopened in 1945, returning to natural shoulderline, stiff peplums, and timeless black dresses. Great flair for publicity; defied tradition, using aggressive colors and rough materials to shock. Her trademark of "ugly chic" was symptomatic of the snobbism of the prewar society. Published her autobiography, *Shocking Life* in 1954. Remained consultant for companies licensed to produce stockings, perfume, scarfs, etc., under her name after closing her business in February 1954. In retirement lived in Tunisia and in Paris where she died in 1973.

## Schoen, Mila
*Italian designer*

Started in 1959 with her base in Milan, but shows couture and deluxe ready-to-wear in Rome. Famous in the 1960s for use of double-faced fabrics in suits and coats, long beaded evening dresses, bold horizontal stripes, sequin vests and shorts for evening, printed pantyhose. In the 1980s Schoen creates a more fluid, softer line maintaining high standards of design and workmanship. Designs include men's wear, swimsuits, and sunglasses.

## Simpson, Adele (1903– )
*American designer*

Worked with husband, textile designer Wesley Simpson, before becoming designer for Mary Lee in 1942. Established Adele Simpson, Inc. in 1944. Known for pretty feminine clothes in delicate prints and colors—coordinated wardrobe. Donated a notable collection of costumes, dolls, fabrics, and fashion-related books to the Fashion Institute of Technology, New York, in 1978. A younger more fluid look prevails in her 1980s' collections as they are designed by Donald Hopson.

## Smith, Willi (1948–1987)
*American designer*

Born in Philadelphia where he studied painting until 1965 when at 17 he went to New York with two scholarships to Parsons School of Design. As a student, free-lanced as sketcher; left Parsons in 1968 to work in a knitwear firm. Formed WilliWear Ltd. in 1976 as a designer and vice president, and WilliWear Men in 1978. Following his death, WilliWear Ltd. continues to produce the same type of clothing that prompted Smith at one time to say, "People want real clothes, I don't think people want to walk around looking like statements with their shoulders out to there."

## Stavropoulos, George
*American couturier*

Born in Greece, studied dress design in Paris; had well-known custom salon in Athens from 1940 to 1960. Married Greek-American; came to New York in 1961, opening house on New York's 57th Street, slowly building reputation for unusually beautiful, classically simple clothes. Known for draped, tiered, or pleated evening gowns, asymmetric folds, wrapped coats, kimono sleeves, floating panels, capes, bias jerseys.

## Svend
*French millinery designer*

Popular milliner of the 1950s. Known for dinner half-hats in organza, ribbon, feathers, flowers; forward-draped fur berets. Associated with Jacques Heim in 1958.

## Tassell, Gustave (1926– )
*American designer*

Born in Philadelphia; studied painting at Pennsylvania Academy of Fine Arts. Free-lanced designing in New York and had a small couture business in Philadelphia. Planned window displays at Hattie Carnegie; spent two years in Paris selling his sketches. Returned to U.S. in 1956 and with the help of JAMES GALANOS opened his own firm in Los Angeles, California. Known for refined, no-gimmick clothes with stark, clean lines à la Balenciaga; Spanish-shawl embroidered evening gowns. Moved to New York in 1972 to take over design responsibilities at NORELL after designer's death; designed under label, Norman Norell by Tassell. When Norell closed four years later, re-opened his own business.

## Tice, Bill (1946– )
*American lingerie designer*

Arrived in New York in mid-1960s after studying fashion design at the University of Cincinnati. Became designer for Royal Robes in 1968, at Sayour in 1974, and then to Swirl from 1975 to 1984. Introduced many at-home wear concepts such as Jersey float, quilted gypsy look, caftans, fleece robes, sundresses, sarongs, quilted silk coats worn with narrow pants.

## Tilley, Monika (1934– )
*American swimwear designer*

Born in Vienna, Austria; earned a M.A. degree from the Academy of Applied Arts,

Vienna. Came to U.S. in 1957 and worked with JOHN WEITZ; free-lanced designing included skiwear and children's wear. Held design positions at: White Stag, Cole of California, the Anne Klein Studio, Mallory Leathers, and Elon of California. Established Monika Tilley Limited in 1970 for swim and beachwear, children's swimwear, at-home fashions and intimate apparel. Uses bias cuts, madras shirred with elastic, also a technique that angles the weave so that the fabric is molded against the body.

### Tinling, Teddy (1910– )
*British designer*

Famous designer of women's tennis wear since 1927; Master of Ceremonies at tennis tournament at Wimbledon for 22 years until resignation in 1949 after scandal when he departed from classic plainness by putting lace on edge of woman champion Gussie Moran's panties. From then on has pioneered in custom designs for 10 successive Wimbledon winners. Some innovations: A-line minidresses showing scalloped panties, Mao-collared tunics, jumpsuits, princess dresses with appliquéd embroidery, ruffled hems, hot pants, and pastel colors instead of traditional white. Also redesigned men's tennis shorts. Published autobiography, *White Ladies'*, 1963, and another volume in 1983, *Sixty Years in Tennis*.

### Trigère, Pauline (1912– )
*American designer*

Born in Paris; came to New York in 1937. Worked as assistant designer to Travis Banton for Hattie Carnegie in late 1930s. Started New York business 1942 with brother, Robert. Her son Jean-Pierre Radley is president of Trigère Inc. Specializes in coats, capes, suits, dresses and accessories in unusual tweeds and prints, with intricate cut to flatter mature figures. Licenses include: scarfs, jewelry, furs, men's neckties, sunglasses, bedroom fashions, paperworks, servingware, and fragrance. Trademark is the turtle, which turns up in jewelry, scarf, and fabric designs.

### Ungaro, Emanuel (1933– )
*French designer*

Born in France to Italian immigrants. Worked with BALENCIAGA from 1958 to 1963 and then two seasons with COURRÈGES. Showed first collection in 1965. In 1960s known for short, straight, structured dresses in broad stripes or plaids; high-waisted coats; diagonal seaming; little girl A-line dresses; deeply cutout armholes; shorts and blazers. Introduced above-the-knee socks; revived Mary Jane shoes; thigh-high boots; open lace nude dresses; low hipster pants; pinafores over tights and body jewelry. Swiss graphic artist, Sonja Knapp, designs most of his special fabrics and prints and is also his business partner. By early 1970s showed softer lines and fabrics, more long pants and pastel leather coats; drawstring shirtdresses; elasticized shirring on jackets and coats. Designs have become increasingly seductive, evolving into body-conscious, sensuous looks. Has shown a men's wear tailored striped jacket over a slinky flowered evening dress and daytime suits with soft, bias-cut trousers. Ready-to-wear collections sold in Ungaro boutiques in U.S. and Europe; has fragrance, *Diva*. Licenses include: furs, men's wear, sheets, wallcoverings, curtains, knitwear.

**Valentino** (Valentino Garavani) (1932– )
*French couturier*
Born near Milan; went to Paris at 17 to study at Chambre Syndicale de la Couture. Worked for JEAN DESSÈS in 1950 and GUY LAROCHE in 1958. Opened own house, Valentino, in Rome, 1959. First major success in 1962 when designs were bought by I. Magnin. Ready-to-wear collection shown in Paris in 1975; continues to show there each season. Couture shown in Rome. Opened first boutique in 1969 in Milan followed by one in 1972 in Rome, and others around the world including Japan. Noted for refined simplicity, elegantly tailored coats and suits—usually marked with his signature V in seams as well as in gilt V's on belts, shoes, bags and V's woven in hosiery and silk pants; use of brown with off-white; patterned legs; chain prints; dark ruffled chiffons; blazers and wide-brimmed swagger hats; double sleeves and argyle sweaters; entrance-making evening clothes. Design interests include: fragrance, 1978; men's wear; Valentino Piu for gifts and interiors; bed linens, drapery fabrics, table and cookware.

**Valois, Rose** (Mme. Fernand Cleuet)
*French millinery designer*
Opened her own millinery business about 1927 after 10 years training at REBOUX. One of top six millinery designers in the 1920s and 1930s, catering to private clients for 25 years. Known for tailored felts, side-tilted berets, opulent dinner hats.

**Venet, Philippe** (ven-eh, feel-eep) (1929– )
*French designer*
Started at age 14 learning tailoring. Worked two years at SCHIAPARELLI from 1951 to 1953 where he met GIVENCHY; master tailor and cutter at Givenchy from 1953 to 1962. First collection in own house in January 1962. Known for lean suits; rounded shoulders; round-back coats and curved seams; cardigan, caped, or back-wrapped coats in sportive mood; kimono and dolman sleeves. Also designed costumes for Rio de Janeiro Carnival in 1965; furs for Maximilian; men's wear collection in 1970; a ready-to-wear collection.

**Versace, Gianni** (1946– )
*Italian designer*
Born in Calabria to a dressmaker mother. Studied architecture, but became involved in his mother's couture business, eventually becoming her buyer in the late 1960s. Graduated with a degree in architecture and moved to Milan where he continued to study fashion and textile design. He has worked as designer for prêt-à-porter firms such as Genny and Callaghan; presented his first solo men's wear collection in 1979. Since then has designed for women; has established boutiques around the world. Designs include: accessories, leathers, furs, and fragrances for men and women; costumes for La Scala and the ballet.

**Vionnet, Madeleine** (vee-o-neh) (1876–1975)
*French couturière*
One of the three greatest creative fashion designers of the 20th c. ranking with CHANEL and BALENCIAGA in contributions of lasting influence. Called greatest technician of modern couture for her innovation of the bias cut and freeing of the body from corsetry

and whalebone necklines. Born in Aubervilliers, France; began dressmaking at early age; trained in London and in Paris with Mme. Gerber at CALLOT and later at DOUCET, in 1907. Opened own house in 1912. Closed during World War I; reopened in 1922 on the avenue Montaigne, finally closing before World War II in 1940. A Vionnet dress was noted for classical drapery, for wide-open necklines, easy over-the-head entrance, suppression of hooks and eyes, cowl or halter neck, handkerchief-point hem; faggoted seams; Art Deco embroideries; all difficult to copy. Personally draped and cut designs on small wooden mannequin; helpful to protegés PIERRE BALMAIN, Jacques Griffe, MAD MALTEZAS and SUZY CARPENTIER, Marcelle Chaumont. Made Chevalier of Legion d'Honneur in 1929; hated the press and copyists. She died on March 2, 1975 in Paris.

## Von Furstenberg, Diane (1947– )
*American designer*

Born in Brussels, Belgium; obtained a degree in economics from the University of Geneva. Came to U.S. in 1969. In 1971 started her career in fashion with a moderate-priced lightweight jersey wrapdress with surplice top and long sleeves. Left the fashion business in 1977, but returned in 1985 with day and evening wear based on her original wrapdress concept. Business includes: makeup and cosmetics, a fragrance named after her daughter, *Tatiana*, stationery, costume jewelry, furs, loungewear, handbags and small leathers, Vogue Patterns, raincoats, scarfs, shoes, sunglasses, table linens, wallcoverings.

## Vuitton, Louis (vwee-ton, loo-ee)
*Leather designer*

Founder of firm producer of signature luggage with its yellow LV's and *fleuron* patterns on brown ground, first created for Empress Eugénie to transport her hoops and crinolines in mid-19th c. Today, family business is still producing luggage and leathers, making everything from wallets to steamer trunks; still the number-one status symbol luggage and widely copied.

## Weinberg, Chester (1930–1985)
*American designer*

Started career on Seventh Avenue with Harvey Berin; Herbert Sondheim; Patullo-Jo Copeland; at Teal-Traina for 10 years. Opened own house, Chester Weinberg. Ltd. in 1966. From 1977 to 1981, company was a division of Jones Apparel Group. When it closed went to work for Calvin Klein Jeans as design consultant. Known for sophisticated and classic clothes for modern women.

## Weitz, John (1923– )
*American designer*

Born in Berlin. Studied at St. Paul's and Oxford in England. Came to U.S. in 1940. Captain in U.S. Army; now married to actress, Susan Kohner. Won the Sebring World Championship in sports car racing; rides horses, sails, etc. Started with Lord & Taylor, making bulky sweaters and jeans after World War II. One of most versatile pioneers in design of practical clothes for sports and specific lifestyles. Known for women's sports clothes with men's wear look; poplin car coats; hooded, zippered-up cotton jackets; pea jackets with white pants; town pants; strapless dress over bra and shorts, all new ideas in the 1950s. In 1960s, devised "ready-to-wear couture," chosen from sketches and swatches. Added Contour Clothes for men, inspired by Levi-Strauss jeans, cowboy jackets, fatigue coveralls, and jumpsuits. One of first American designers to show both men's and women's wear; one of the first to license his work.

## Worth, Charles Frederick (1826–1895)
*French couturier*

Born in Bourne, Lincolnshire. Famous in 19th c. as dressmaker for Empress Eugénie and the court of France's Second Empire. Considered to be founder of the industry of *haute couture*. Served apprenticeship in London drapery establishments. Came to Paris in 1845, age 20, to Maison Gagelin, dealers in fabrics, shawls, and mantles, soon showing unusual originality. In 1858, opened house on rue de la Paix, called Worth et Bobergh; closed during Franco-Prussian War (1870–1871); opened as Maison Worth in 1874 with assistance of sons, Jean Phillipe and Gaston. For 50 years house was fashion leader without rivals, in the Second Empire and Edwardian eras, dressing ladies of the courts and society all over Europe and America in ceremonial opulence. Famous for the princess-cut dress, the collapsible steel framework for crinolines and later the elimination of crinolines (1867), the court mantle hung from the shoulders, gowns made of interchangeable parts, *i.e.*, various combinations of bodice, sleeve, and skirt with infinite variety of trimmings. Worth was the innovator in the presentation of gowns on live mannequins; first to sell models to be copied in U.S. and England; was inspired by paintings of Van Dyck, Gainsborough, and Velasquez. Opened house in London and introduced Parfums Worth in 1900, continues with "Je Reviens" the best-known fragrance. After death in 1895, house continued under sons and grandsons. House sold in 1954 to Paquin.

DESIGNER
PORTRAITS

*Adolfo*

*John Anthony*

*Giorgio Armani*

*Balenciaga*

*Pierre Balmain*

*Geoffrey Beene*

*Bill Blass*

*Marc Bohan*

*Pierre Cardin*

*Bonnie Cashin*

*Chanel*

André Courrèges

Oscar de la Renta

*Givenchy*

*Christian Dior*

*Perry Ellis*

*James Galanos*

Jean-Paul Gaultier

Rudi Gernreich

Halston

Jacques Heim

Mme. Grès

Betsey Johnson

Norma Kamali

Donna Karan

*Rei Kawakubo*

*Kenzo*

*Anne Klein*

*Calvin Klein*

*Christian Lacroix*

*Karl Lagerfeld*

*Lucien Lelong*

*Ralph Lauren*

*Vera Maxwell*

*Mary McFadden*

*Jeanne Lanvin*

*Mainbocher*

*Tai and Rosita Missoni*

*Issey Miyake*

*Claire McCardell*

Thierry Mugler

Jean Muir

*Edward Molyneux*

*Claude Montana*

*Paul Poiret*

*Thea Porter*

*Norman Norell*

Emilio Pucci

Mary Quant

*Sonia Rykiel*

*Zandra Rhodes*

*Yves Saint Laurent*

*Giorgio Sant'Angelo*

*Elsa Schiaparelli*

*Adele Simpson*

*Willi Smith*

Pauline Trigère

Emanuel Ungaro

*Gianni Versace*

*Valentino*

*Madeleine Vionnet*

*John Weitz*

*Charles Frederick Worth*

DESIGNER
STYLES

*Balenciaga*

*Adolfo, 1984*

*John Anthony, 1987*

1978

Giorgio Armani

1981

*1983*

*Geoffrey Beene*

*1981*

*Bill Blass, 1988*

*Marc Bohan*

1987

1978

Pierre Balmain

Donald Brooks

*Callot Soeurs, 1931*

*Capucci, 1985*

*Pierre Cardin, 1987*

*Bonnie Cashin*

*Chanel*

*Chanel, 1929*

*André Courrèges, 1966*

1988

1979

Oscar de la Renta

*Perry Ellis*

1983

1982

Dior's "New Look"

*Fortuny*

*Rudi Gernreich*

*Jean-Paul Gaultier, 1985*

*Fendi, 1985*

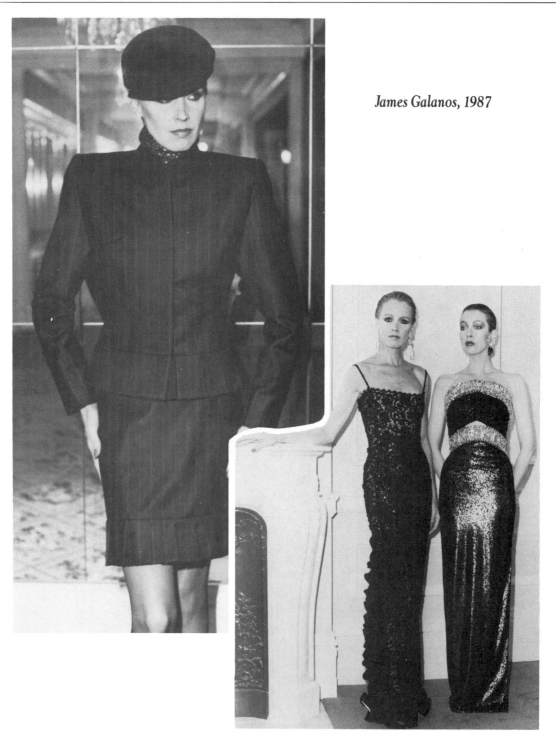

*James Galanos, 1987*

*Givenchy*

1979                                                                        1982

Mme. Grès

*Betsey Johnson, 1986*

*1982*

*1986*

*Kenzo*

*Norma Kamali*

1982

1988

1986

1988

*Donna Karan*

*Anne Klein*

*Louis Dell'Olio, 1987*

*1981*

*Calvin Klein*

*1988*

1987

*Ralph Lauren*

1979

*Karl Lagerfeld, 1988*

*Christian Lacroix, 1987*

*Vera Maxwell*

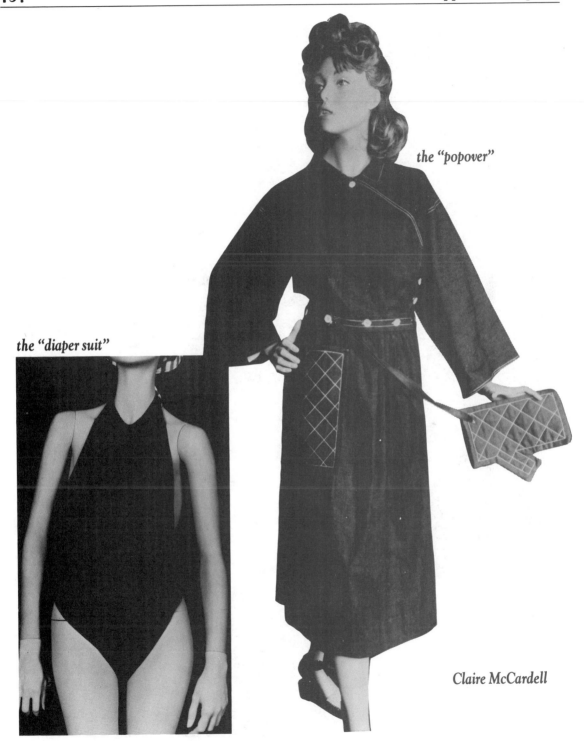

the "popover"

the "diaper suit"

Claire McCardell

*Jean Muir, 1984*

*Mary McFadden, 1976*

*Claude Montana, 1981*

*Thea Porter*

Norman Norell

*Mary Quant*

*Emilio Pucci*

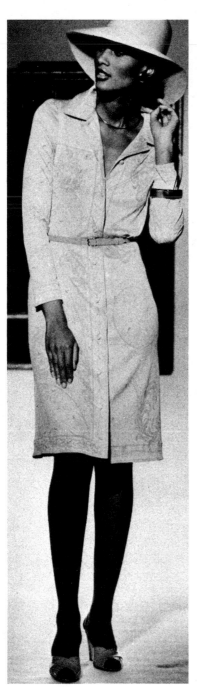

1987

*Yves Saint Laurent*

1979

1978

*Zandra Rhodes*

1975

Pauline Trigère

*Emanuel Ungaro*

1988

1982

Valentino

1988

1978

*Madeleine Vionnet*